SOURCES AND METHODS
LABOUR STATISTICS
VOLUME 4
EMPLOYMENT, UNEMPLOYMENT, WAGES AND HOURS OF WORK
(ADMINISTRATIVE RECORDS AND RELATED SOURCES)

SECOND EDITION

SOURCES ET MÉTHODES
STATISTIQUES DU TRAVAIL
VOLUME 4
EMPLOI, CHÔMAGE, SALAIRES ET DURÉE DU TRAVAIL
(DOCUMENTS ADMINISTRATIFS ET SOURCES ASSIMILÉES)

DEUXIÈME ÉDITION

FUENTES Y METODOS
ESTADISTICAS DEL TRABAJO
VOLUMEN 4
EMPLEO, DESEMPLEO, SALARIOS Y HORAS DE TRABAJO
(REGISTROS ADMINISTRATIVOS Y FUENTES CONEXAS)

SEGUNDA EDICION

SOURCES
AND METHODS
LABOUR STATISTICS
VOLUME 4
EMPLOYMENT, UNEMPLOYMENT, WAGES AND HOURS OF WORK
(ADMINISTRATIVE RECORDS AND RELATED SOURCES)

Companion to the *Yearbook of Labour Statistics*

SECOND EDITION

SOURCES
ET MÉTHODES
STATISTIQUES DU TRAVAIL
VOLUME 4
EMPLOI, CHÔMAGE, SALAIRES ET DURÉE DU TRAVAIL
(DOCUMENTS ADMINISTRATIFS ET SOURCES ASSIMILÉES)

Complément de l'*Annuaire des statistiques du travail*

DEUXIÈME ÉDITION

FUENTES
Y METODOS
ESTADÍSTICAS DEL TRABAJO
VOLUMEN 4
EMPLEO, DESEMPLEO, SALARIOS Y HORAS DE TRABAJO
(REGISTROS ADMINISTRATIVOS Y FUENTES CONEXAS)

Complemento del *Anuario de Estadísticas del Trabajo*

SEGUNDA EDICION

INTERNATIONAL LABOUR OFFICE   GENEVA
BUREAU INTERNATIONAL DU TRAVAIL   GENÈVE
OFICINA INTERNACIONAL DEL TRABAJO   GINEBRA

ISBN 92-2-007358-7
(the set of 2 volumes)
ISSN 0084-3857

ISBN 92-2-007358-7
(le jeu de 2 volumes)
ISSN 0084-3857

ISBN 92-2-007358-7
(el juego de 2 volúmenes)
ISSN 0084-3857

This volume :
ISBN 92-2-015147-2
ISSN 1014-9856

Ce volume :
ISBN 92-2-015147-2
ISSN 1014-9856

Este volumen :
ISBN 92-2-015147-2
ISSN 1014-9856

Second edition 2004

Deuxième édition 2004

Segunda edición 2004

Printed in India

Imprimé en Inde

Impreso en India

AJA

Important

● In order to enhance the usefulness of the *Yearbook of Labour Statistics,* each issue is now accompanied by a methodological volume of the series *Sources and Methods: Labour Statistics* (formerly entitled *Statistical Sources and Methods*).

● This series provides methodological descriptions of the data published in the *Yearbook* and *Bulletin of Labour Statistics.* Each volume covers different subjects according to the source of the data.

● The methodological descriptions include information on the method of data collection, coverage, concepts and definitions, classifications, historical changes, technical references, etc. In each volume the information is presented by country under standard headings.

Important

● Afin de mettre en valeur l'utilité de l'*Annuaire des statistiques du travail,* chaque édition est maintenant accompagnée d'un volume méthodologique de la série *Sources et méthodes: statistiques du travail* (intitulée précédemment *Sources et méthodes statistiques*).

● Cette série fournit des descriptions méthodologiques des données publiées dans l'*Annuaire* et dans le *Bulletin des statistiques du travail.* Chaque volume traite de sujets différents suivant la source des données.

● Les descriptions méthodologiques contiennent des informations sur la méthode de collecte des données, la portée, les concepts et définitions, les classifications, les modifications apportées aux séries, les références techniques, etc. Dans chaque volume, les informations sont présentées par pays sous des rubriques standardisées.

Importante

● Con el fin de mejorar la utilidad del *Anuario de Estadísticas del Trabajo,* ahora cada edición va acompañada de un volumen metodológico de la serie *Fuentes y Métodos: Estadísticas del Trabajo* (titulada anteriormente *Fuentes y Métodos Estadísticos*).

● Esta serie proporciona las descripciones metodológicas de los datos que se publican en el *Anuario* y el *Boletín de Estadísticas del Trabajo.* Cada volumen abarca diferentes temas del *Anuario* de acuerdo con la fuente de los datos.

● Las descripciones metodológicas incluyen informaciones acerca del método de recolección de datos, el alcance, los conceptos y definiciones, las clasificaciones, los cambios históricos, las referencias técnicas, etc. En cada volumen, la información se presenta por país de acuerdo a encabezamientos estándar.

Preface

This is a revised and enlarged version of *Sources and Methods: Labour Statistics* (formerly *Statistical Sources and Methods*), Volume 4: employment, unemployment, wages and hours of work (administrative records and related sources), first published in 1989. The other published volumes of the series are:

Volume 1: Consumer price indices
(third edition, Geneva, 1992)
Volume 2: Employment, wages, hours of work and labour cost (establishment surveys) (second edition, Geneva, 1995)
Volume 3: Economically active population, employment, unemployment and hours of work (household surveys)
(second edition, Geneva, 1990) *
Volume 5: Total and economically active population, employment and unemployment (population censuses)
(second edition, Geneva, 1996) *
Volume 6: Household income and expenditure surveys
(Geneva, 1994) *
Volume 7: Strikes and lockouts
(Geneva, 1993)
Volume 8: Occupational injuries
(Geneva, 1999)
Volume 9: Transition countries
(Geneva, 1999).
Volume 10: Estimates and projections of the economically active population 1950-2010 (Geneva, 2000)

* An updated version of volume 3 will be available in 2003. Revised editions of volumes 5 and 6 are under preparation.
The purpose of this series is to document the national practices used in the collection of various types of labour statistics in order to assist users in assessing their suitability for particular needs, as well as evaluating their quality and comparability. *Sources and Methods: Labour Statistics* can consequently be seen as companion volumes to the various chapters of the ILO *Yearbook of Labour Statistics* and of the *Bulletin of Labour Statistics*; as well as to the corresponding statistics which are available in LABORSTA on line:
http://laborsta.ilo.org/.
This volume consists of two parts. The first part covers unemployment statistics derived from registers of employment services and related institutions. The second part covers statistics on employment, wages, hours of work and related topics derived from social security or insurance records and other related administrative sources. Each part contains structured descriptions which are presented using standard headings in order to facilitate comparisons of the various characteristics.
This volume was prepared by the ILO Bureau of Statistics.

Préface

Cet ouvrage constitue la deuxième édition, actualisée et enrichie, de *Sources et méthodes: statistiques du travail* (précédemment *Sources et méthodes statistiques*), Volume 4: emploi, chômage, salaires et durée du travail (documents administratifs et sources assimilées) dont la première version a été publiée en 1989. Les autres volumes publiés dans cette série sont les suivants :

Volume 1: Indices des prix à la consommation (troisième édition, Genève, 1992)
Volume 2: Emploi, salaires, durée du travail et coût de la main-d'œuvre (enquêtes auprès des établissements)
(deuxième édition, Genève, 1995)
Volume 3: Population active, emploi, chômage et durée du travail (enquête auprès des ménages) (deuxième édition, Genève, 1991, publiée sous forme de Document de travail) *
Volume 5: Population totale et population active, emploi et chômage (recensements de population) (deuxième édition, Genève, 1996) *
Volume 6: Enquêtes sur les revenus et les dépenses des ménages (Genève, 1994). *
Volume 7: Grèves et lock-out
(Genève, 1993)
Volume 8: Lésions professionnelles
(Genève, 1999)
Volume 9: Pays en transition
(Genève, 1999)
Volume 10: Evaluations et projections de la population active 1950-2010 (Genève, 2000)

* Une mise à jour du volume 3 sera disponible en 2003. Des éditions révisées des volumes 5 et 6 sont en préparation. Ces volumes ont pour but de renseigner sur les pratiques nationales appliquées pour établir différentes statistiques du travail, et d'aider ainsi les utilisateurs à en apprécier la qualité, la comparabilité et la valeur pour des besoins différents. On peut donc voir dans les volumes de *Sources et méthodes: statistiques du travail* un complément aux divers chapitres de *l'Annuaire des statistiques du travail* et du *Bulletin des statistiques du travail du BIT*, ainsi qu'aux statistiques correspondantes disponibles dans la base de données LABORSTA en ligne :
http://laborsta.ilo.org/.
Ce volume est divisé en deux parties. La première couvre les statistiques du chômage qui proviennent des registres de bureaux de placement ou d'inscriptions obligatoires au régime de l'assurance chômage. La seconde partie couvre les statistiques de l'emploi, des salaires, de la durée du travail et autres sujets assimilés, fondées sur des registres de sécurité ou d'assurance sociale ou sur des sources analogues. Chaque partie contient des descriptions structurées qui sont établies selon des rubriques normalisées dans le but de faciliter la comparaison des différentes caractéristiques.
Le présent volume a été réalisé par le Bureau de statistique du BIT.

Prefacio

Se presenta aquí una actualización y ampliación del volumen 4 de *Fuentes y Métodos: Estadísticas del Trabajo* (anteriormente *Fuentes y métodos estadísticos*) : Empleo, desempleo, salarios y horas de trabajo (registros administrativos y fuentes conexas), cuya primera versión se publicó en 1989. Los otros volúmenes de esta serie son:

Volumen 1: Indices de los precios del consumo (tercera edición, Ginebra, 1992)
Volumen 2: Empleo, salarios, horas de trabajo y costo de la mano de obra (encuestas de establecimientos) (segunda edición, Ginebra, 1995)
Volumen 3: Población económicamente activa, empleo, desempleo y horas de trabajo (encuestas de hogares) (segunda edición, Ginebra,1992, publicada como Documento de trabajo) *
Volumen 5: Población total y económicamente activa, empleo y desempleo (censos de población) (segunda edición, Ginebra, 1996) *
Volumen 6: Encuestas sobre los ingresos y gastos de los hogares (Ginebra, 1994) *
Volumen 7: Huelgas y cierres patronales (Ginebra, 1993)
Volumen 8: Lesiones profesionales (Ginebra, 1999)
Volumen 9: Países en transición (Ginebra, 1999)
Volumen 10: Evaluaciones y proyecciones de la población económicamente activa, 1950-2010 (Ginebra, 2000)

* Une versión actualizada del volumen 3 se publicará en 2003. Se están preparando revisiones de los volúmenes 5 y 6. El objetivo de estas publicaciones consiste en documentar las prácticas nacionales seguidas para recopilar los diferentes tipos de estadísticas del trabajo y ayudar a los usuarios a evaluar su calidad y comparabilidad, así como su adecuación a las necesidades diferentes. Las *Fuentes y métodos: Estadísticas del Trabajo* se pueden considerar por tanto como volúmenes que acompañan a los diversos capítulos del *Anuario de Estadísticas del Trabajo* y del *Boletín de Estadísticas del Trabajo* de la OIT, así como las estadísticas correspondientes que se encuentran en la base de datos LABORSTA en línea:
http://laborsta.ilo.org/.
Este volumen se ha dividido en dos partes. La primera abarca las estadísticas de desempleo derivadas de los registros de las oficinas de empleo y/o de seguros de paro obligatorios. La segunda parte abarca las estadísticas de empleo, salarios, horas de trabajo y otros temas conexos, extraídas de los archivos de la seguridad social y/o diversos seguros y otras fuentes conexas. Cada parte contiene descripciones estructuradas que se presentan utilizando títulos normalizados para facilitar las comparaciones entre las diversas características.
La producción de este volumen estuvo a cargo de la Oficina de Estadística de la OIT.

CONTENT

Introduction – Part I 1
Algeria 1
Australia 1
Bahrain 2
Barbados 3
Belarus 4
Belgium (1) 5
Belgium (2) 5
Botswana 6
Bulgaria 7
Burkina Faso 8
Cambodia 8
Cameroon 9
Canada 10
Central African Rep. 11
Chad 11
China 12
Colombia 13
Congo 14
Costa Rica 14
Croatia 14
Cyprus 15
Czech Republic 16
Denmark 17
Djibouti 18
Dominican Republic 19
Egypt 19
El Salvador 20
Estonia 21
Ethiopia 22
Finland 22
France 23
French Polynesia 24
Gabon 24
Germany 25
Ghana 26
Greenland 26
Guatemala 27
Guinea 28
Guyana 29
Honduras 29
Hungary 30
Iceland 31
India 32
Iran, Islamic Rep. of 33
Isle of Man 34
Israel 35
Italy 36
Japan (1) 37
Japan (2) 37
Kazakhstan 38
Kenya 39
Latvia 40
Lesotho 41
Lithuania 41
Luxembourg 42
Macedonia, The former Yugoslav Rep. of 43
Madagascar 44
Malaysia 45
Mali 46
Malta 46
Mauritius 47
Moldova, Rep. of 48
Mongolia 49

Morocco 50
Myanmar 51
Netherlands 51
New Caledonia 52
New Zealand 53
Niger 54
Nigeria 54
Norway 55
Panama 56
Papua New Guinea 57
Peru 58
Philippines 58
Poland 59
Portugal 61
Qatar 62
Romania 63
Saint Pierre and Miquelon 63
Serbia and Montenegro 64
Slovenia 65
Spain 66
Suriname 67
Sweden 67
Switzerland 68
Tajikistan 69
Tanzania, United Rep. of 70
Thailand 71
Trinidad and Tobago 71
Tunisia 72
Turkey 73
United States 74
Uruguay 75
Venezuela 75
Zimbabwe 76

Introduction - Part II 78
Austria (1) 79
Austria (2) 79
Costa Rica 80
Cuba 81
France 82
French Polynesia 83
Germany 84
Guatemala 84
Hong Kong, China (1) 85
Hong Kong, China (2) 86
Isle of Man 87
Israel 87
Italy 88
Luxembourg 89
Mexico 90
Netherlands 91
New Caledonia 92
Norway (1) 93
Norway (2) 94
Norway (3) 95
Pakistan 97
Panama 97
Saint Helena 98
Seychelles 99
Singapore 99
Spain 100
Switzerland 101
Turkey 103

TABLE DES MATIERES

Introduction - Partie I 105
Algérie 105
Allemagne 106
Australie 107
Bahreïn 107
Barbade 108
Bélarus 109
Belgique (1) 110
Belgique (2) 111
Botswana 112
Bulgarie 113
Burkina Faso 114
Cambodge 114
Cameroun 115
Canada 116
Rép. centrafricaine 117
Chine 117
Chypre 118
Colombie 119
Congo 121
Costa Rica 121
Croatie 122
Danemark 122
Djibouti 123
République dominicaine 124
Egypte 125
El Salvador 126
Espagne 126
Estonie 127
Etats-Unis 129
Ethiopie 129
Finlande 130
France 131
Gabon 132
Ghana 132
Groenland 133
Guatemala 134
Guinée 135
Guyana 136
Honduras 136
Hongrie 137
Ile de Man 138
Inde 139
Iran, Rép. islamique d' 141
Islande 142
Israël 143
Italie 144
Japon (1) 145
Japon (2) 145
Kazakhstan 146
Kenya 147
Lesotho 148
Lettonie 149
Lituanie 150
Luxembourg 151
Macédoine, Ex-Rép. yougoslave de 152
Madagascar 153
Malaisie 153
Mali 154
Malte 155
Maroc 156
Maurice 157
Moldavie, Rép. de 158

Mongolie 159
Myanmar 160
Niger 161
Nigéria 162
Norvège 163
Nouvelle-Calédonie 164
Nouvelle-Zélande 164
Panama 166
Papouasie-Nouvelle-Guinée 167
Pays-Bas 167
Pérou 168
Philippines 169
Pologne 170
Polynésie française 172
Portugal 172
Qatar 173
Roumanie 174
Saint-Pierre-et-Miquelon 175
Serbie-et-Monténégro 176
Slovénie 177
Suède 178
Suisse 179
Suriname 180
Tadjikistan 181
Tanzanie, Rép.-Unie de 181
Tchad 182
République tchèque 183
Thaïlande 184
Trinité-et-Tobago 185
Tunisie 185
Turquie 186
Uruguay 188
Venezuela 188
Zimbabwe 189

Introduction - Partie II: 191
Allemagne 192
Autriche (1) 192
Autriche (2) 193
Costa Rica 194
Cuba 195
Espagne 196
France 197
Guatemala 198
Hong-kong, Chine (1) 199
Hong-kong, Chine (2) 199
Ile de Man 200
Israël 201
Italie 202
Luxembourg 204
Mexique 204
Norvège (1) 205
Norvège (2) 206
Norvège (3) 208
Nouvelle-Calédonie 209
Pakistan 211
Panama 211
Pays-Bas 212
Polynésie française 213
Sainte-Hélène 214
Seychelles 215
Singapour 215
Suisse 217
Turquie 219

INDICE

Introducción – Parte I 221
Alemania 221
Argelia 222
Australia 222
Bahrein 223
Barbados 224
Belarús 225
Bélgica (1) 226
Bélgica (2) 227
Botswana 228
Bulgaria 228
Burkina Faso 229
Camboya 230
Camerún 231
Canadá 231
Rep. Centroafricana 232
Colombia 233
Congo 234
Costa Rica 234
Croacia 235
Chad 236
República Checa 236
China 237
Chipre 238
Dinamarca 239
Djibouti 240
República Dominicana 241
Egipto 241
El Salvador 242
Eslovenia 243
España 244
Estados Unidos 245
Estonia 245
Etiopía 247
Filipinas 247
Finlandia 248
Francia 249
Gabón 250
Ghana 250
Groenlandia 251
Guatemala 252
Guinea 252
Guyana 253
Honduras 254
Hungría 255
India 256
Irán, Rep. Islámica del 257
Isla de Man 258
Islandia 259
Israel 260
Italia 261
Japón (1) 262
Japón (2) 263
Kazajstán 263
Kenya 264
Lesotho 266
Letonia 266
Lituania 267
Luxemburgo 268
Macedonia, Ex Rep. Yugoslava de 269
Madagascar 270
Malasia 270
Malí 272
Malta 272

Marruecos 273
Mauricio 274
Moldova, Rep. de 275
Mongolia 276
Myanmar 277
Níger 278
Nigeria 278
Noruega 279
Nueva Caledonia 280
Nueva Zelandia 281
Países Bajos 282
Panamá 283
Papua Nueva Guinea 284
Perú 285
Polinesia Francesa 285
Polonia 286
Portugal 288
Qatar 289
Rumania 290
San Pedro y Miquelón 290
Serbia y Montenegro 292
Suecia 292
Suiza 293
Suriname 294
Tailandia 295
Tajikistán 295
Tanzanía, Rep. Unida de 296
Trinidad y Tabago 297
Túnez 298
Turquía 299
Uruguay 300
Venezuela 300
Zimbabwe 301

Introducción - Parte II 303
Alemania 304
Austria (1) 304
Austria (2) 305
Costa Rica 306
Cuba 307
España 308
Francia 308
Guatemala 310
Hong Kong, China (1) 310
Hong Kong, China (2) 311
Isla de Man 312
Israel 313
Italia 314
Luxemburgo 315
México 316
Noruega (1) 317
Noruega (2) 318
Noruega (3) 319
Nueva Caledonia 321
Países Bajos 322
Pakistán 323
Panamá 324
Polinesia Francesa 325
Santa Elena 325
Seychelles 326
Singapur 327
Suiza 328
Turquía 330

Introduction – Part I

The methodological descriptions presented in this Part relate to national unemployment statistics derived from administrative registrations. Many of the corresponding statistical series are published by the ILO in the *Yearbook of Labour Statistics* and/or in the *Bulletin of Labour Statistics*, as well as being made available on its website (http://laborsta.ilo.org).

The 96 descriptions covering 94 countries, areas or territories included in this Part were prepared on the basis of information provided mainly by national employment services in response to a special questionnaire. In order to facilitate comparisons each description follows the same format presenting information under twelve sections with standard headings. However, it should be borne in mind that statistics from administrative records are not strictly comparable between countries, due to differences in relevant legislation and administrative capacities.

Under the different sections information can be found on: the title and starting year of the series; the national institution making the registrations; the specific information which is registered about a person; the criteria used to determine whether or not a person will be registered as unemployed; the definition of unemployed persons used for the statistics; the frequency with which the registers are updated; whether statistics from the registers are used to obtain unemployment rates; the type of statistics of unemployed persons produced and the availability of methodological information on the statistics; whether comparisons have been made with unemployment statistics from other sources, as well as the effect on the statistics of any major changes which may have taken place since their inception.

Classifications referred to in the descriptions:

ISCO-88: International Standard Classification of Occupations, 1988 (International Labour Office, Geneva, 1990);

ISIC, rev. 3: International Standard Industrial Classification of All Economic Activities (United Nations, New York, 1989);

NACE, rev. 1: Statistical Classification of Economic Activities in the European Community (Eurostat, Luxembourg, 1996);

ISCED-97: International Standard Classification of Education (UNESCO, Paris, 1997).

Algeria

1. Series
Title: The *Notes de conjoncture* (circumstantial notes) grouping requests, offers and placements (situation of the employment market).
Starting year: 1994.

2. Agency making the initial registrations of unemployed persons
Name of the agency: Agence nationale de l'Emploi - ANEM (National Employment Agency).
Type of agency: Public service under a national authority.
Name of the national authority: Ministry of Employment and National Solidarity.
Location of the local offices making the registrations: In each district (165 local agencies and 11 regional agencies all over the country).
Type of services provided/administered by the agency:
– Assisting job-seekers to find jobs;
– Assisting employers to find workers;
– Vocational guidance;
– Other: registration of unemployed persons laid off for economic reasons, and registration of higher education graduates seeking employment satisfying the criteria for pre-employment contracts.

3. The following information is registered about a person:
– Name;
– Sex;
– Address of usual residence;
– Date of birth;
– Nationality;
– Educational/vocational attainment, with six categories distinguished. Links to ISCED have not been established;
– Current/past activity status, with two categories distinguished;
– Type of work of past or present job with 20 categories distinguished. Links to ISCO-88 have not been established;
– Type of work of job sought, with 20 categories distinguished;
– Name and address of present or previous employer or work

place;
– Type of business of present or previous employer or workplace, with 22 categories distinguished. Links to ISIC, rev.3 have not been established;
– Previous inscriptions/registrations with the agency;
– Situation as to national military service.

4. Criteria used for inclusion of a person in the registers (R) and/or the statistics of unemployed persons (S):
– Being without work (R) and (S);
– Seeking work (R) and (S);
– Availability for work (R) and (S);
– Age: lower limit: 16 years; upper limit: 60 years (R) and (S);
– Being resident in the country (R) and (S).

5. Criteria used for exclusion of a person from the registers (R) and/or the statistics of unemployed persons (S):
– Death (R) and (S);
– Taking up residency abroad (R) and (S);
– Commencement of a (new) job (R) and (S);
– Commencement of military service (R) and (S);
– Participation in an employment promotion scheme, a public works programme, etc. (R) and (S);
– Eligibility to receive a pension (retirement benefits, etc.) (R) and (S);
– Inability to work (R) and (S).

6. Definition of unemployed persons used for the statistics
The unemployed population includes all persons legally able (16 - 60 years) to work, who have declared that they are unemployed, are looking for a job and registered with a local employment agency. Two categories of registered persons are distinguished: category *STR1* comprising the persons who have already worked, and category *STR2* comprising the persons who have never worked before.

7. Updating of the registers
The registers are updated regularly.

8. Unemployment rates
Statistics from the registers are not used to obtain unemployment rates. The unemployment rates are produced by the national statistics office (ONS) and are based essentially on the household labour force survey and the population census.

9. Type of statistics of unemployed persons produced
Frequency of production: Quarterly.
Descriptive variables used:
– Sex;
– Age;
– Educational level;
– Occupation;
– Industry;
– Previous work experience.
Form of publication: On paper, for limited audience.
Agency responsible for publication: ANEM.
Title and periodicity of the publication: *Note de conjoncture sur la situation du marché de l'emploi* (Circumstantial note on the situation of the labour market), quarterly.

10. Methodological information about the statistics
Form of release:
– Available for internal use;
– On paper, for limited audience.
Agency responsible for the release: ANEM.

11. Comparisons with unemployment statistics from other sources
Comparisons have not been made with unemployment statistics from other sources.

12. Major changes since the start of the statistics
There have been no major changes in legislation, capacity of the agency and/or administrative procedures which had a significant influence on the statistics.

13. Additional remarks
The statistical data of the ANEM only concern persons seeking employment who have registered with this Agency: unemployment statistics fall under the responsibility of the ONS.

Australia

1. Series
Title: Registered unemployment benefit claimants [New Start Allowance (NSA) or Youth Allowance (other) (YA(o)].
Starting year: 1940.

2. Agency making the initial registrations of unemployed persons
– Name of the agency: Centrelink.
Type of agency: Public service under a national authority.
Name of the national authority: Department of Employment and Workplace Relations and the Department of Family and Community Services (FaCS).
Location of the local offices making the registrations: Centrelink have offices in 400 locations throughout Australia.
Type of services provided/administered by the agency:
– Payment of unemployment compensation.
3. The following information is registered about a person:
– Name;
– Sex;
– Address of usual residence;
– Date of birth;
– Citizenship;
– Nationality/ethnic group (non-compulsory information);
– Educational/vocational attainment, with 16 categories distinguished (non-compulsory information);
– Current/past activity status, with six categories distinguished;
– Type of work (occupation) of past or present job;
– Type of work (occupation) of job sought (non-compulsory information);
– Name and address of present or previous employer/ workplace;
– Previous registrations with the agency/service;
– Other: number of dependent children; marital status; housing/ accommodation.
4. Criteria used for inclusion of a person in the registers (R) and/or the statistics of unemployed persons (S):
– Being without work, although registered job-seekers can undertake casual or part-time employment (subject to an income test) and remain qualified to receive payment (R);
– Seeking work (R);
– Availability for work (R);
– Age: lower limit: 15 years; Upper limit: Age Pension age (R);
– Residency in the country (minimum 104 weeks) (R);
– Other: meeting the "Activity Test" requirements showing that he/she is actively looking for work (R).
5. Criteria used for exclusion of a person from the registers (R) and/or the statistics of unemployed persons (S):
– Death (R);
– Taking up residency abroad (R);
– Commencement of a (new) job, excluding part-time or casual work (R);
– Participation in an employment promotion scheme, public works programme, etc., although participation in certain programmes, e.g. "Work for the Dole", does not affect eligibility for unemployment benefits (R);
– Failure to contact agency/service: payment of unemployment benefits are reduced for the first and second breaches and stopped entirely for the third breach (R);
– Refusal of suitable job offers: payment of unemployment benefits are reduced for the first and second breaches and stopped entirely for the third breach (R);
– Refusal of suitable training offers: payment of unemployment benefits are reduced for the first and second breaches and stopped entirely for the third breach (R);
– Receipt of a pension: Age Pension age is 65 for men and 62 for women (R);
– Inability for work (R);
– Other: if income/assets of claimant or spouse/partner exceed fixed limit (R); receipt of a worker's compensation or a work-injury related payment (R).
6. Definition of unemployed persons used for the statistics
The registers are not used to produce statistics on unemployed persons. However, series are available for the count of persons receiving unemployment benefits (through the Newstart Allowance or a Youth Allowance). These include people in receipt of an allowance subject to the inclusions and exclusions detailed in sections 4 and 5 above.
The NSA and YA(o) series generally count people in receipt of allowance between the ages of 15 years and 64 years in the case of men, and 15 to 61 years in the case of women.
7. Updating of the registers
The registers are updated fortnightly (as payments are made fortnightly).

8. Unemployment rates
Statistics from the registers are not used to obtain unemployment rates.
9. Type of statistics of unemployed persons produced
Series: Labour Market and Related Payments.
Reference period: Month.
Frequency of production: Monthly.
Descriptive variables used:
– Sex;
– Age;
– Geographic characteristics;
– Duration of unemployment.
Form of publication: On paper, for general audience.
Agency responsible for publication: FaCS.
Title and periodicity of the publication: *Labour Market and Related Payments* (monthly).
10. Methodological information about the statistics
Form of release: On paper for general audience.
Agency responsible for the release: FaCS.
11. Comparisons with unemployment statistics from other sources
Comparisons have been made with unemployment statistics from the Labour Force Survey.
Frequency of the comparisons: Occasionally (latest year: 2000).
Publication of the methodology/results of the comparisons: For internal use only.
12. Major changes since the start of the statistics
There have been no major changes in legislation, capacity of the agency and/or administrative procedures which had a significant influence on the statistics.

Bahrain

1. Series
Title: Registered unemployment.
Starting year: 1996.
2. Agency making the initial registrations of unemployed persons
Name of the agency: Employment Services Bureau.
Type of agency: Public service under a national authority.
Name of the national authority: Ministry of Labour and Social Affairs.
Location of the local offices making the registrations: Main building of Ministry of Labour and Social Affairs, Isa Town.
Type of services provided/administered by the agency:
– Assisting job-seekers to find jobs;
– Assisting job-seekers to establish their own business;
– Assisting employers to find workers;
– Vocational guidance;
– Job-related training.
3. The following information is registered about a person:
– Name;
– Sex;
– Social security number (or similar identification number also used by other agencies);
– Address of usual residence;
– Date of birth;
– Citizenship;
– Nationality/ethnic group;
– Educational/vocational attainment, with 6 categories distinguished. Links to ISCED have been established;
– Current/past activity status, with 5 categories distinguished;
– Type of work (occupation) of past or present job, with 3 groups distinguished in the classification used for coding "occupation". Links to ISCO-88 have not been established;
– Type of work (occupation) of job sought, with 9 groups distinguished in the classification used for coding "occupation". Links to ISCO-88 have not been established;
– Name and address of present or previous employer or work place;
– Other: languages spoken; training programme(s) undertaken.
4. Criteria used for inclusion of a person in the register (R) and/or the statistics of unemployed persons (S):
– Being without work (R);
– Seeking work (R);
– Availability for work (R);
– Age: lower limit: 17 years; upper limit: 50 years (R);
– Citizenship: must be Bahraini (R);

- Being resident in the country (R);
- Previously employed (R);
- Desired duration of employment and/or number of hours sought (R);
- Previous payment of unemployment insurance contributions (R)

5. Criteria used for exclusion of a person from the registers (R) and/or the statistics of unemployed persons (S):
- Death (S);
- Taking up residency abroad (S);
- Commencement of a (new) job (R);
- Participation in an employment promotion scheme, public works programme, etc. (S);
- Studying or undergoing training (R);
- Failure to contact the agency/service (S);
- Refusal of suitable job offers (S);
- Refusal of suitable training offers (S);
- End of entitlement to receive unemployment
- compensation (R);
- Receipt of a pension (S);
- Inability to work (S).

6. Definition of unemployed persons used for the statistics
Unemployed persons are those included in the General Organisation for Social Insurance (GOSI), Official estimates and registered with the Employment Services Bureau of the Ministry of Labour and Social Affairs as a job seeker or unemployed person.

7. Updating of the registers
The registers are updated both daily and monthly.

8. Unemployment rates
Statistics from the registers are used to obtain unemployment rates.
The source of data on employed persons who are part of the denominator of the unemployment rates is the Social Security register.

9. Type of statistics of unemployed persons produced
Series 1: Daily report of employment conditions.
Reference period: Day.
Frequency of production: Daily, or when needed.
Descriptive variables used:
- Sex;
- Age;
- Educational level;
- Occupation;
- Industry;
- Geographic characteristics:
- Previous work experience;
- Citizenship (nationals/non-nationals);
- Duration of unemployment.

Form of publication: For internal use only.
Series 2: Abbreviated report for all conditions.
Reference period: Month.
Frequency of production: Monthly, or when needed.
Descriptive variables used:
- Sex;
- Age;
- Educational level;
- Occupation;
- Industry;
- Geographic characteristics;
- Previous work experience;
- Citizenship (nationals/non-nationals);
- Duration of unemployment.

Form of publication: For internal use only.
Series 3:
Reference period: Year.
Frequency of production: Yearly, or when needed.
Descriptive variables used:
- Sex;
- Age;
- Educational level;
- Occupation;
- Industry;
- Geographic characteristics:
- Previous work experience;
- Citizenship (nationals/non-nationals);
- Duration of unemployment.

Form of publication: For internal use only.

10. Methodological information about the statistics
Form of release:
- In machine-readable form on request;
- On website www.bah-molsa.com/.

11. Comparisons with unemployment statistics from other sources
Comparisons have been made with unemployment statistics from the Population Census.

12. Major changes since the start of the statistics
No major changes to legislation, capacity of the agency and/or administrative procedures which had a significant influence on the statistics have been reported.

Barbados

1. Series
Title: National Insurance Benefit Statistics.
Starting year: 1881

2. Agency making the initial registrations of unemployed persons
Name of the agency: National Insurance Department.
Type of agency: Public service under a national authority.
Name of the national authority: Ministry of Labour and Social Security.
Location of the local offices making the registrations: In all parts of the country.
Type of services provided/administered by the agency:
- Paying unemployment compensation.

3. The following information is registered about a person:
- Name;
- Social security number (or similar identification number also used by other agencies);
- Address of usual residence;
- Date of birth;
- Current/past activity status;
- Type of work (occupation) of past or present job;
- Type of business (industry) of present/previous employer/workplace;
- Other: any outstanding contributions.

4. Criteria used for inclusion of a person in the registers (R) and/or the statistics of unemployed persons (S):
- Being without work: applicants should be unemployed for at least three weeks (R) and (S);
- Seeking work: a person will not be included if (s)he fails to avail her/himself of an opportunity for suitable employment, or makes no reasonable effort to obtain suitable alternative employment (R) and (S);
- Availability for work (R) and (S);
- Age (lower limit: 18 years; upper limit: 65 years) (R) and (S);
- Being resident in the country (R) and (S);
- Previously employed for at least one year;
- Previous payment of unemployed insurance contributions: The person must have been insured for at least fifty-two weeks, and have at least 20 contributions paid or credited in three consecutive quarters.

5. Criteria used for exclusion of a person from the registers (R) and/or the statistics of unemployed persons (S):
- Taking up residency abroad;
- Commencement of a (new) job;
- Failure to contact the agency/service;
- Refusal of a suitable job offer;
- End of entitlement to receive unemployment compensation (Unemployment benefit is payable for each day of unemployment up to a maximum of 26 weeks).

6. Definition of unemployed persons used for the statistics
Not available.

7. Updating of the registers
The registers are updated twice a week.

8. Unemployment rates
Statistics from the registers are not used to obtain unemployment rates.

9. Type of statistics of unemployed persons produced
Series 1: *National Insurance Annual Report Statistics* (Number of claims received and allowed during the period).
Form of publication: On paper, for general audience;
Agency responsible for publication: National Insurance Department.

4

10. Methodological information about the statistics
Form of release: On paper, for general audience.
Agency responsible for the release: National Insurance Department.
11. Comparisons with unemployment statistics from other sources
Comparisons have not been made with unemployment statistics from other sources.
12. Major changes since the start of the statistics
There have been no major changes in legislation, capacity of the agency and/or administrative procedures which had a significant influence on the statistics.

Belarus

1. Series
Title: Number of registered unemployed placed by the State Employment Service.
Starting year: 1991
2. Agency making the initial registrations of unemployed persons
Name of the agency: State Employment Service.
Type of agency: Public service under a national authority.
Name of the national authority: Employment Services of the Republic of Belarus.
Location of the local offices making the registrations: In all parts of the country, regional, districts and city centres of employment.
Type of services provided/administered by the agency:
- Assisting job-seekers to find jobs;
- Assisting job-seekers to establish their own business;
- Assisting employers to find workers;
- Vocational guidance;
- Job-related training;
- Paying unemployment compensation;
- Other employment-related services;
- Free information on vacancies;
- Possibilities to participate in paid public works;
- Creation of new working places with consequent job placement of unemployed;
- Assistance in temporary job placement of school and university students.
Percentage of job-seekers seeking work through the agency: 30%.
3. The following information is registered about a person:
- Name;
- Sex;
- Address of usual residence;
- Date of birth;
- Citizenship;
- Educational/vocational attainment;
- Current/past activity status, with 30 categories distinguished;
- Type of work (occupation) of past or present job;
- Type of work (occupation) of job sought;
- Name and address of present or previous employer or work place;
- Type of business (industry) of present/previous employer/workplace;
- Previous registrations with the agency/service.
4. Criteria used for inclusion of a person in the registers (R) and/or the statistics of unemployed persons (S):
- Being without work (R) and (S);
- Seeking work (R) and (S);
- Age (lower limit: 16 years; upper limit: 55 years for women and 60 years for men) (R) and (S);
- Previously employed (R) and (S);
5. Criteria used for exclusion of a person from the registers (R) and/or the statistics of unemployed persons (S):
- Death (R) and (S);
- Commencement of a (new) job (R) and (S);
- Commencement of military service (R);
- Participation in an employment promotion scheme, public works programme (R) and (S);
- Failure to contact the agency/service after a period of 12 months (R) and (S);
- Receipt of a pension (R) and (S);
- Inability to work (R).

6. Definition of unemployed persons used for the statistics
Information not available.
7. Updating of the registers
The registers are updated quarterly, and monthly for a short list of indicators.
8. Unemployment rates
Statistics from the registers are used to obtain unemployment rates. The sources of data on employed persons who are part of the denominator of the unemployment rates are establishment surveys, official estimates and population censuses.
Definition of employed persons for this purpose:
Information not available.
9. Type of statistics of unemployed persons produced
Series 1:
Reference period: Month.
Descriptive variables used:
- Geographic characteristics;
- Citizenship (nationals/non nationals);
- Participation of unemployed in paid public works;
- Training and retraining of unemployed.
Form of publication:
- On paper, for general audience;
- On a website.
Series 2:
Reference period: Quarter
Descriptive variables used:
- Sex;
- Geographic characteristics;
- Previous work experience;
- Citizenship (nationals/non nationals);
- Duration of unemployment;
- Participation of unemployed in paid public works;
- Training and retraining of unemployed;
- Creation of new jobs;
- Assistance in the creation of individual businesses.
Form of publication:
- On paper, for general audience;
- On a website.
Series 3:
Reference period: Half-year.
Descriptive variables used:
- Sex;
- Age;
- Educational level;
- Occupation;
- Industry;
- Geographic characteristics;
- Previous work experience;
- Citizenship (nationals/non nationals);
- Duration of unemployment;
- Duration of unemployment benefit receipt.
Form of publication:
- On paper, for general audience;
- On a website.
Agency responsible for publications: Employment Department of the Ministry of Labour and Social Protection, and the Ministry of Statistics and Analysis.
Title of the publications: Official statistical publications in the newspapers: *Labour & Market*.
10. Methodological information about the statistics
Form of release: On paper, for limited audience;
Agency responsible for the release: Employment Department of the Ministry of Labour and Social Protection.
11. Comparisons with unemployment statistics from other sources
Comparisons have been made with unemployment statistics from other types of household surveys and from the population census.
Frequency of the comparisons: Occasionally.
Publication of the methodology/results of the comparisons: These have not been published.
12. Major changes since the start of the statistics
There have been no major changes in legislation, capacity of the agency and/or administrative procedures which had a significant influence on the statistics.

Belgium (1) Brussels Capital

1. Series
Title: *Monthly Report on the Labour Market* and *Annual Statistical Report*.
Starting year: 1989.

2. Agency making the initial registrations of unemployed persons
Name of the agency: Regional Employment Office of Brussels (ORBEM).
Type of agency: Public service under a regional authority.
Location of the local offices making the registrations: Region Brussels-Capital.
Type of services provided/administered by the agency:
- Assisting job-seekers to find jobs;
- Assisting employers to find workers;
- Vocational guidance;
- Other: administration of employment programme, day care centre, language knowledge tests, expert reports on the labour market, etc.

Percentage of job seekers seeking work through the agency: Not available.

3. The following information is registered about a person:
- Name;
- Sex;
- Social security number (or similar identification number also used by other agencies);
- Address of usual residence;
- Date of birth;
- Nationality;
- Educational attainment. Links to ISCED have not been established;
- Type of work of past or present job with 2,216 categories distinguished. Links to ISCO-88 have not been established;
- Type of work of job sought, with 2,216 categories distinguished;
- Type of business of present/previous
- Employer/workplace, with 66 categories distinguished. Links to ISIC have not been established;
- Previous registrations with the agency;
- Other: work permit, duration of unemployment, qualifications, aptitudes, vehicle, driving licence, language knowledge, marital status, number of dependent children.

4. Criteria used for inclusion of a person in the registers (R) and/or the statistics of unemployed persons (S):
- Being without work (S);
- Seeking work (R) and (S);
- Availability for work (S);
- Age (lower limit: 15 years; upper limit: 65 years) (R) and (S);
- Being resident in the country (S).

5. Criteria used for exclusion of a person from the registers (R) and/or the statistics of unemployed persons (S):
- Death (S);
- Taking up residency abroad (S);
- Commencement of a (new) job in the case of placement by the agency or if the agency is informed by the person looking for employment (S);
- Participation in an employment promotion scheme, public works programme, etc (S);
- Studying or undergoing training (S);
- Failure to contact the agency/service following three unanswered letters (S);
- Refusal of suitable job offers (S);
- Refusal of suitable training offers (S);
- End of entitlement to receive unemployment
- Compensation for persons living together: according to article 80, if the duration of unemployment is one and a half times longer than the "regional" average, depending on sex and age category, this will lead to the suspension of compensation for an undetermined period (S);
- Receipt of a pension (retirement benefits, etc) (S);
- Inability to work, in case of inability of more than 66% (S);
- Other: successive absences at communal checking (S).

6. Definition of unemployed persons used for the statistics
Persons over 15 years, without employment, available on the job market and looking for employment. In practical terms, this series includes all non-working job-seekers, i.e.:
- fully unemployed persons receiving compensation;
- young persons (having worked or not previously) receiving a "waiting allowance" while looking for employment;
- unemployed persons looking for employment, registered freely (not entitled to receive compensation);
- other unemployed persons looking for employment with mandatory registration. This category includes:
- certain fully unemployed persons temporarily excluded from receiving compensation, for the duration of their exclusion;
- persons presented by public social assistance centres;
- certain persons depending on community funds for the social and professional integration of handicapped persons who do not satisfy the conditions for unemployment compensation;
- persons having been occupied voluntarily in a part-time job, and who have become fully unemployed;
- unemployed persons who give up voluntarily unemployment compensation;
- young persons with transitional compensation. They are registered as persons looking for part-time employment.

7. Updating of the registers
The registers are updated monthly.

8. Unemployment rates
Statistics from the registers are used to obtain unemployment rates.
The source of data on employed persons who are part of the denominator of the unemployment rates is official estimates.

9. Type of statistics of unemployed persons produced
Reference period: Month.
Frequency of production: Monthly.
Descriptive variables used:
- Sex;
- Age;
- Educational level;
- Occupation;
- Industry;
- Geographic characteristics;
- Nationality;
- Duration of unemployment.

Form of publication:
- On paper, for limited audience;
- Machine-readable form, on request.

Agency responsible for publication: *ORBEM.*
Title and periodicity of the publication: *Rapport mensuel sur l'évolution du marché de l'emploi (*Monthly report on the evolution of the employment market).

10. Methodological information about the statistics
Form of release: On paper, for limited audience.
Agency responsible for the release: *ORBEM.*

11. Comparisons with unemployment statistics from other sources
Comparisons have been made with unemployment statistics from the labour force survey and the population census.
Frequency of the comparisons: Occasional.
Publication of the methodology/results of the comparisons: These have been published.
Title of the publication on the comparisons: Higher Employment Council: *"Comment comptabiliser le nombre de chômeurs? Une grille de lecture des taux de chômage"* (How to post the number of unemployed persons? A reading scale of unemployment rates), published by the Federal Ministry of Employment and Labour.

12. Major changes since the start of the statistics
Major changes in legislation, the capacity of the agency and/or administrative procedures which had a significant influence on the statistics took place in 1994, 1995, 1996 and 2002.

Belgium (2) Flanders

1. Series
Title: Registered job-seekers.
Starting year: 1989.

2. Agency making the initial registrations of unemployed persons
Name of the agency: VDAB (Flemish Service for Employment and Vocational Training).
Type of agency: Public service under regional authorities.
Location of the local offices making the registrations: in Flanders.
Type of services provided/administered by the agency:
- Assisting job-seekers to find jobs;

- Assisting employers to find workers;
- Vocational guidance;
- Job-related training.

3. The following information is registered about a person:
- Name;
- Sex;
- Social security number (or similar identification number also used by other agencies);
- Address of usual residence;
- Date of birth;
- Citizenship;
- Nationality/ethnic group;
- Educational/vocational attainment, with an unspecified number of categories distinguished. Links to ISCED have not been established;
- Current/past activity status, with an unspecified number of categories distinguished;
- Type of work (occupation) of past or present job with an unspecified number of groups distinguished. Links to ISCO-88 have not been established;

- Type of work (occupation) of job sought, with an unspecified number of groups distinguished. Links to ISCO-88 have not been established;
- Type of business (industry) of present/previous employer/workplace, with an unspecified number of groups distinguished. NACE, rev.1 is used at the five-digit level to code this variable. Links to ISIC, rev.3 have been established (tabulation categories level);
- Previous registrations with the agency/service;
- Other: duration of unemployment.

4. Criteria used for inclusion of a person in the registers (R) and/or the statistics of unemployed persons (S):
- Being without work (non-working job-seekers) (R) and (S);
- Seeking work (all job-seekers) (R) and (S);
- Availability for work (R) and (S);
- Age (R) and (S);
- Citizenship (R) and (S);
- Previously employed (R);
- Desired duration of employment and/or number of hours of work sought (minimum duration: one hour) (R).

5. Criteria used for exclusion of a person from the registers (R) and/or the statistics of unemployed persons (S):
- Death (R) and (S);
- Commencement of a (new) job (R) and (S);
- Participation in an employment promotion scheme, public works programme, etc. (R);
- Studying or undergoing training (R) and (S);
- Refusal of a suitable job offer (R);
- Refusal of a suitable training offer (R);
- End of entitlement to receive unemployment compensation (non-working job-seekers with unemployment compensation) (R) and (S);
- Receipt of a pension (R) and (S);
- Inability to work (R) and (S).

6. Definition of unemployed persons used for the statistics
1. Non-working job-seekers:
- Non-working with unemployment compensation;
- Non-working leaving school;
- Non-working, free registration;
- Others.
2. Working job-seekers:
- Part-time workers;
- Full-time workers;
- Others.

7. Updating of the registers
    The registers are updated daily.

8. Unemployment rates
    Statistics from the registers are used to obtain unemployment rates.
    The source of data on employed persons who are part of the denominator of the unemployment rates is the Labour Force Survey.
Definition of employed persons for this purpose: Not specified.

9. Type of statistics of unemployed persons produced
Series 1:
Reference period: Month.
Frequency of production: Monthly.

Descriptive variables used:
- Sex;
- Age;
- Educational level;
- Occupation;
- Industry;
- Geographic characteristics;
- Previous work experience;
- Citizenship (nationals/non nationals);
- Duration of unemployment.
Form of publication:
- On paper, for general audience;
- On a website (www.vdab.be).
Agency responsible for publication: VDAB (Flemish Service for Employment and Vocational Training).
Title and periodicity of the publication: *Maandverlag Arbeidsmarkt Vlaanderen* (monthly).
Series 2:
Reference period: Year.
Frequency of production: Yearly.
Descriptive variables used:
- Sex;
- Age;
- Educational level;
- Occupation;
- Industry;
- Geographic characteristics;
- Previous work experience;
- Citizenship (nationals/non nationals);
- Duration of unemployment.
Form of publication:
- On paper, for general audience;
- On a website (www.vdab.be).
Agency responsible for publication: VDAB (Flemish Service for Employment and Vocational Training).
Title and periodicity of the publication: *Jaarverlag Arbeidsmarkt Vlaanderen* (yearly).
10. Methodological information about the statistics
Form of release:
- On paper, for general audience;
- In machine-readable form, on request;
- On a website (www.vdab.be).
Agency responsible for the release: VDAB (Flemish Service for Employment and Vocational Training).
11. Comparisons with unemployment statistics from other sources
    Comparisons have not been made with unemployment statistics from other sources.
12. Major changes since the start of the statistics
    There have been no major changes in legislation, capacity of the agency and/or administrative procedures which had a significant influence on the statistics.

Botswana

1. Series
Title: Registered unemployment.
Starting year: Not specified.
2. Agency making the initial registrations of unemployed persons
Name of the agency: Department of Labour and Social Security - Employment Services Unit.
Type of agency: Public service under a national authority.
Name of the national authority: Department of Labour and Social Security.
Location of the local offices making the registrations: In all district labour offices.
Type of services provided/administered by the agency:
- Assisting job-seekers to find jobs;
- Assisting employers to find workers.
Percentage of job-seekers seeking work through the agency: 21%.
3. The following information is registered about a person:
- Name;
- Sex;
- Address of usual residence;
- Date of birth;
- Citizenship;

- Nationality/ethnic group;
- Educational/vocational attainment, with 4 categories distinguished. No links to ISCED have been established;
- Current/past activity status;
- Type of work (occupation) of past or present job;
- Type of work (occupation) of job sought. No links to ISCO-88 have been established;
- Name and address of present or previous employer or work place;
- Type of business (industry) of present/previous employer/work place, with 6 groups distinguished. No links to ISIC, rev. 3 have been established;
- Previous registrations with the agency/service;
- Other: registration number; identity card number.

4. Criteria used for inclusion of a person in the registers (R) and/or the statistics of unemployed persons (S):
- Being without work (students are not included) (R) and (S);
- Seeking work (R) and (S);
- Availability for work (R) and (S);
- Age (lower limit: 18 years; no upper limit) (R) and (S);
- Citizenship (non-citizens do not form part of "unemployed persons") (R) and (S);
- Previously employed (R) and (S).

5. Criteria used for exclusion of a person from the registers (R) and/or the statistics of unemployed persons (S):
- Death (R) and (S);
- Commencement of a (new) job (R) and (S);
- Studying or undergoing training (R) and (S);
- Failure to contact the agency/service (registration is renewed at the completion of every year) (R) and (S).

6. Definition of unemployed persons used for the statistics
Labour force remaining without a job or source of income.

7. Updating of the registers
The registers are updated annually.

8. Unemployment rates
Statistics from the registers are used to obtain unemployment rates.
The sources of data on employed persons who are part of the denominator of the unemployment rates are the Labour Force Survey and Official Estimates.
Definition of employed persons for this purpose:
Labour force having a job as a source of income.

9. Type of statistics of unemployed persons produced
Information not available.

10. Methodological information about the statistics
Form of release:
- On paper for general audience;
- On website (www.cso.gov.bw).

Agency responsible for the release: Central Statistics Office.

11. Comparisons with unemployment statistics from other sources
Comparisons have been made with unemployment statistics from unspecified other sources.
Frequency of the comparisons: Regularly, when the statistics are published.
Publication of the methodology/results of the comparisons: These have not been published.

12. Major changes since the start of the statistics
Major changes to legislation, capacity of the agency and/or administrative procedures took place in 1996, 1997, 1998, 1999 and 2000. The resulting changes in the statistics have not been estimated.

Bulgaria

1. Series
Title: Monthly information on the unemployment situation in Bulgaria.
Starting year: 1991.
2. Agency making the initial registrations of unemployed persons
Name of the agency: Employment Agency.
Type of agency: Public service under a national authority.
Name of the national authority: Ministry of Labour and Social Policy.
Location of the local offices making the registrations: There are 122 Labour Offices and 141 Labour Office Branches throughout the country.

Type of services provided/administered by the agency:
- Assisting job-seekers to find jobs;
- Assisting job-seekers to establish their own business;
- Assisting employers to find workers;
- Vocational guidance;
- Job-related training;
- Paying unemployment compensation.

3. The following information is registered about a person:
- Name;
- Sex;
- Social security number (or similar identification number also used by other agencies);
- Address of usual residence;
- Date of birth;
- Citizenship;
- Educational/vocational attainment, with eight categories distinguished. Links to ISCED have not been established;
- Current/past activity status, with four categories distinguished;
- Type of work (occupation) of past or present job with 51 categories distinguished. Links to ISCO-88 have not been established;
- Type of work (occupation of job sought, with 51 categories distinguished. Links to ISCO-88 have not been established;
- Name and address of present or previous employer or work place;
- Type of business (industry) of present/previous employer/workplace, with 280 categories distinguished. Links to NACE, rev.1 (class level) have been established;
- Previous registrations with the agency/service.

4. Criteria used for inclusion of a person in the registers (R) and/or the statistics of unemployed persons (S):
- Being without work (R);
- Seeking work (R);
- Availability for work (R);
- Age: lower limit: 16 years; no upper limit (R);
- Citizenship (R);
- Being resident in the country (R).

5. Criteria used for exclusion of a person from the registers (R) and/or the statistics of unemployed persons (S):
- Death (R);
- Taking up residency abroad (R);
- Commencement of a (new) job (R);
- Commencement of military service (R);
- Participation in an employment promotion scheme, public works programme, etc. (R);
- Studying or undergoing training (R);
- Failure to contact the agency/service (R);
- Refusal of one suitable job offer (R);
- Refusal of one suitable training offer (R);
- Receipt of a pension (R).

6. Definition of unemployed persons used for the statistics
An employed person is one who is out of work, is actively seeking work and is ready to start work within the two weeks of notification by the Employment Agency division.

7. Updating of the registers
The registers are updated regularly.

8. Unemployment rates
Statistics from the registers are used to obtain unemployment rates.
The source of data on employed persons who are part of the denominator of the unemployment rates is the Population Census.

9. Type of statistics of unemployed persons produced
Series 1:
Reference period: Month.
Frequency of production: Monthly.
Descriptive variables used:
- Sex;
- Age;
- Educational level;
- Industry;
- Geographic characteristics;
- Duration of unemployment;
- Other: vocational and educational characteristics.

Form of publication:
- For internal use;
- On paper, for limited audience;
- On a website (www.nsz.government.bg).

Agency responsible for publication: Employment Agency.
Title of the publication: *Monthly information on the unemployment situation in Bulgaria.*
Series 2:
Reference period: Year.
Frequency of production: Yearly.
Descriptive variables used:
- Sex;
- Age;
- Educational level;
- Industry;
- Other: vocational and educational characteristics.

Form of publication: On paper, for general audience.
Agency responsible for publication: National Statistical Institute.
Title of the publication: *Statistics Reference Book.*
Series 3:
Reference period: Year.
Frequency of production: Yearly.
Descriptive variables used:
- Sex;
- Age;
- Educational level;
- Geographic characteristics;
- Other: vocational and educational characteristics.

Form of publication: On paper, for general audience.
Agency responsible for publication: National Statistical Institute.
Title of the publication: *NSI Yearbook.*
10. Methodological information about the statistics
Form of release: Not released, available for internal use only;
Agency responsible: Employment Agency.
11. Comparisons with unemployment statistics from other sources
Comparisons have not been made with unemployment statistics from other sources.
12. Major changes since the start of the statistics
There have been no major changes in legislation, capacity of the agency and/or administrative procedures which had a significant influence on the statistics.

Burkina Faso

1. Series
Title: Annual Activity Reports.
Starting year: 1980.
2. Agency making the initial registrations of unemployed persons
Name of the agency: Office national de la Promotion de l'Emploi - ONPE (National Office for Employment Promotion).
Type of agency: Public service under a national authority.
Name of the national authority: Ministry of Employment, Labour and Social Security.
Location of the local offices making the registrations: Ouagadougou, Bobo-Dioulasso, Banfora, Koudougou and Fada N'Gourma.
Type of services provided/administered by the agency:
- Assisting job-seekers to find jobs;
- Assisting job-seekers to establish their own business;
- Assisting employers to find workers;
- Vocational guidance;
- Job-related training;
- Other: assisting job-seekers to obtain professional experience or training.

3. The following information is registered about a person:
- Name;
- Sex;
- Address of usual residence;
- Date of birth;
- Nationality/ethnic group;
- Educational/vocational attainment, with 10 categories distinguished. Links to ISCED have not been established;
- Current/past activity status, with two categories distinguished;
- Type of work (occupation) of job sought, with six categories distinguished. Links to ISCO-88 have been established (major groups level);
- Previous registrations with the agency/service.

4. Criteria used for inclusion of a person in the registers (R) and/or the statistics of unemployed persons (S):
- Being without work (R) and (S);

- Seeking work (R) and (S);
- Availability for work (R) and (S);
- Age (lower limit: 18 years; upper limit: 55 years) (R) and (S);
- Being resident in the country (R) and (S);
- Previously employed (R) and (S).

5. Criteria used for exclusion of a person from the registers (R) and/or the statistics of unemployed persons (S):
- Death (R) and (S);
- Taking up residency abroad (R) and (S);
- Commencement of a (new) job; The job-seeker is required to inform ONPE within 10 days following the change in his situation (R) and (S);
- Receipt of a pension (R) and (S).

6. Definition of unemployed persons used for the statistics
Economically active persons of working age who are without work, having previously worked or not.
7. Updating of the registers
The registers are updated quarterly.
8. Unemployment rates
Statistics from the registers are not used to obtain unemployment rates.
9. Type of statistics of unemployed persons produced
Reference period: Quarter.
Frequency of production: Quarterly.
Descriptive variables used:
- Sex;
- Age;
- Educational level;
- Occupation;
- Previous work experience.

Form of publication: On paper, for general audience.
Agency responsible for publication: ONPE.
Title and periodicity of the publication(s): *Rapport d'activité trimestriel* (Quarterly Activity Report), *Rapport d'activité semestriel* (Half-yearly Activity Report) and *Rapport d'activité annuel* (Annual Activity Report).
10. Methodological information about the statistics
Form of release: On paper, for general audience.
Agency responsible for the release: ONPE.
11. Comparisons with unemployment statistics from other sources
Comparisons have not been made with unemployment statistics from other sources.
12. Major changes since the start of the statistics
There have been no major changes in legislation, capacity of the agency and/or administrative procedures which had a significant influence on the statistics.

Cambodia

1. Series
Titles:
1. Number of registered job-seekers by level of education, age group and sex.
2. Number of registered job-seekers by skill, age group and sex.
3. Number of registered job-seekers and placement by skill.
Starting year: 2001.
2. Agency making the initial registrations of unemployed persons
Name of the agency: Department of Employment and Manpower.
Type of agency: Public service under national and provincial authorities.
Name of the national authority: Ministry of Social Affairs, Labour, Vocational Training and Youth Rehabilitation.
Location of the local offices making the registrations: Phnom Penh and in four provinces.
Type of services provided/administered by the agency:
- Assisting job-seekers to find jobs;
- Assisting employers to find workers.

3. The following information is registered about a person:
- Name;
- Sex;
- Address of usual residence;
- Date of birth;
- Citizenship;
- Nationality;
- Educational/vocational attainment, with 8 categories distinguished. Links to ISCED have not been established;

- Type of work (occupation) of past or present job. Links to ISCO-88 (minor group level) have been established;
- Type of work (occupation) of job sought. Links to ISCO-88 (minor group level) have been established;
- Name and address of present or previous employer or work place.

4. Criteria used for inclusion of a person in the registers (R) and/or the statistics of unemployed persons (S):
- Being without work (R) and (S);
- Seeking work (R) and (S);
- Availability for work (R) and (S);
- Age (lower limit: 15 years; upper limit: 39 years (R) and (S);
- Citizenship (R);
- Previously employed (R).

5. Criteria used for exclusion of a person from the registers (R) and/or the statistics of unemployed persons (S):
- Death (R) and (S);
- Taking up residency abroad (R) and (S);
- Commencement of a (new) job (R) and (S);
- Commencement of military service (R) and (S);
- Studying or undergoing training (R) and (S);
- Inability to work (R) and (S).

6. Definition of unemployed persons used for the statistics
Persons in the labour force who did not work, had no job, business enterprise or farm of their own from which they were temporarily absent, but were available for work. Persons in this category include: (i) those who had been looking for work and (ii) those who had not been looking for work because of illness or belief that no suitable work was available, were waiting to take up a new job, were waiting for the agricultural season or other reasons.

7. Updating of the registers
The registers are updated annually.

8. Unemployment rates
Statistics from the registers are used to obtain unemployment rates.
The sources of data on employed persons who are part of the denominator of the unemployment rates are the Labour Force Survey, Establishment Survey and Population Census.

Definition of employed persons for this purpose:
Persons in the labour force who worked for at least one hour for wages, profit, dividends or any other kind of payment in kind (who work as employers, employees, own account workers and unpaid family workers).

9. Type of statistics of unemployed persons produced
Series 1: Number of registered job-seekers by level of education, age group and sex.
Reference period: Month; Year.
Frequency of production: Monthly; Annually.
Descriptive variables used:
- Sex;
- Age;
- Educational level.

Form of publication:
- For internal use;
- On paper, for limited audience.

Agency responsible for publication: Department of Employment and Manpower.

Series 2: Number of registered job-seekers by skill, age group and sex.
Reference period: Month; Year.
Frequency of production: Monthly; Annually.
Descriptive variables used:
- Sex;
- Age;
- Occupation;

Series 3: Number of registered job-seekers and placement by skill.
Reference period: Month; Year.
Frequency of production: Monthly; Annually.
Descriptive variables used:
- Sex;
- Occupation.

10. Methodological information about the statistics
Form of release:
- Available for internal use.
- On paper, for limited audience.

Agency responsible for the release: Department of Employment and Manpower.

11. Comparisons with unemployment statistics from other sources
Comparisons have not been made with unemployment statistics from other sources.

12. Major changes since the start of the statistics
There have been no major changes in legislation, capacity of the agency and/or administrative procedures which had a significant influence on the statistics.

Cameroon

1. Series
Title: Databank of job-seekers.
Starting year: 1991.

2. Agency making the initial registrations of unemployed persons
Name of the agency: Fonds national de l'Emploi - FNE (National Fund for Employment).
Type of agency: Parastatal Agency.
Location of the local offices making the registrations: In six out of 10 provinces; however, the geographic coverage is progressively increasing.
Type of services provided/administered by the agency:
- Assisting job-seekers to find jobs;
- Assisting job-seekers to establish their own business;
- Assisting employers to find workers;
- Vocational guidance;
- Job-related training.

Percentage of job-seekers seeking work through the agency: 30%.

3. The following information is registered about a person:
- Name;
- Sex;
- Date of birth;
- Citizenship;
- Nationality;
- Vocational attainment. Links to ISCED have not been established;
- Current/past activity status;
- Type of work (occupation) of past or present job with two categories distinguished. Links to ISCO-88 have not been established;
- Type of work (occupation) of job sought, with two categories distinguished.

4. Criteria used for inclusion of a person in the registers (R) and/or the statistics of unemployed persons (S):
- Being without work (R) and (S);
- Seeking work (R) and (S);
- Availability for work (R) and (S);
- Age (lower limit: 18 years; upper limit: 55 years) (R) and (S).

5. Criteria used for exclusion of a person from the registers (R) and/or the statistics of unemployed persons (S):
- Death (R) and (S);
- Commencement of a (new) job (R) and (S);
- Failure to contact the agency/service (R) and (S).

6. Definition of unemployed persons used for the statistics
Unemployed persons from 18 to 55 years old who are without work, looking for a job and available for work.

7. Updating of the registers
The registers are updated daily.

8. Unemployment rates
Statistics from the registers are not used to obtain unemployment rates.

9. Type of statistics of unemployed persons produced
Frequency of production: Yearly.
Descriptive variables used:
- Sex;
- Age;
- Educational level;
- Occupation;
- Industry;
- Previous work experience;
- Duration of unemployment.

Form of publication: On paper, for general audience.
Agency responsible for publication: FNE.
Title and periodicity of the publication: *Rapport annuel d'activités du FNE* (Annual activities Report of the FNE), available series 1991-2000.

10. Methodological information about the statistics
Form of release: On paper, for general audience.
Agency responsible for the release: FNE.
11. Comparisons with unemployment statistics from other sources
Comparisons have not been made with unemployment statistics from other sources.
12. Major changes since the start of the statistics
There have been no major changes in legislation, capacity of the agency and/or administrative procedures which had a significant influence on the statistics.

Canada

1. Series
Title: Unemployment Benefits Claimants.
Starting year: 1975.
2. Agency making the initial registrations of Unemployment benefits claimants
Name of the agency: Unemployment benefits claimants are registered under the Employment Insurance (EI) Program.
Note: Job-seekers and unemployed persons in Canada are not systematically registered unless they become unemployment benefits claimants under the EI Program. This is an insurance scheme that covers all workers working for an employer under a contract of service; self-employed persons, except in the fishing industry, are not covered.
Type of agency: Public service under national and provincial authorities.
Name of the national authority: Canada Employment Insurance Commission, administered by Human Resources Development Canada (HRDC). Employment benefits and support measures are administered in cooperation with the provinces and territories.
Location of the local offices making the registrations: There are over 300 points of service across the country. Unemployed workers can also apply on-line via the Internet.
Type of services provided/administered by the agency:
– Assisting job-seekers to find jobs;
– Assisting job-seekers to establish their own business;
– Assisting employers to find workers;
– Vocational guidance;
– Paying unemployment compensation;
– Other: electronic Labour Exchange (a free on-line service that connects workers and employers); on-line listing of job postings in the public and private sectors (www.jobs.gc.ca); labour Market Information Website (www.labourmarketinformation.ca); interprovincial Standards "Red Seal" Program (which permits qualified trades people to practise their trade in any province or territory without additional examinations); "Jobs Etc.", a one-stop access point for information on jobs, training, careers and workplace issues; "Job Futures", a long-term occupational outlook for 211 employment groups as classified by the National Occupational Classification (NOC); "Minding your own business", "Catching the wave" and "Venturing out", three programmes designed to help people (including youth) who want to start their own businesses.
3. The following information is registered about a person:
– Name;
– Sex;
– Social security number (or similar identification number also used by other agencies);
– Address of usual residence;
– Date of birth;
– Educational/attainment. No links to ISCED have been established;
– Current/past activity status, with two categories distinguished;
– Type of work (occupation) of past or present job. No links to ISCO-88 have been established;
– Type of work (occupation) of job sought. No links to ISCO-88 have been established;
– Name and address of present or previous employer or work place;
– Type of business (industry) of present/previous employer/workplace. No links to ISIC, rev.3 have been established;
– Previous registrations with the agency/service;
– Other: pension status; preferred language (English or French);

type of income being received; maternity status; whether in jail, in training, able to work, or prevented from working due to a labour dispute.
4. Criteria* used for inclusion (registration) of a person under the Employment Insurance Program (R) and/or the statistics of Unemployment Benefits Claimants (S):
– Being without work (R) and (S);
– Availability for work (R) and (S);
– Previously employed (R) and (S);
– Previous payment of unemployed insurance contributions (between 410 and 910 hours in previous 52 weeks) (R) and (S).
*The above criteria apply only to persons claiming *regular* EI benefits (not to those seeking sickness, maternity and parental benefits).
5. Criteria* used for exclusion (termination of registration) of a person from the Employment Insurance Program (R) and/or the statistics of Unemployment Benefits Claimants (S):
– Death (R) and (S);
– Taking up residency abroad (with the exception of exchange of benefits with the US) (R) and (S);
– Commencement of a (new) full-time job (R) and (S);
– Commencement of full-time military service (R) and (S);
– Participation in a full-time employment promotion scheme, public works programme, etc. (R) and (S);
– Full-time studying or undergoing full-time training (except when sent on training by EI) (R) and (S);
– Failure to contact the agency/service without good cause (R) and (S);
– Refusal of suitable job offers without good cause (R) and (S);
– End of entitlement to receive unemployment compensation (R) and (S);
– Receipt of a pension above a certain amount (R) and (S);
– Inability to work (may be entitled to sickness benefits after four weeks of being unable to work) (R) and (S);
– Other: in jail (R) and (S); not available for work (R) and (S); quitting job or taking a leave of absence without just cause or being fired or suspended for misconduct (R) and (S); temporarily outside Canada (with certain exceptions) (R) and (S); prevented from working due to labour disputes (R) and (S); receipt of earnings from employment or related to employment such as workers' compensation, beyond a certain amount (R) and (S).
*The above criteria apply only to persons claiming *regular* EI benefits (not to those seeking sickness, maternity and parental benefits).
6. Definition of unemployed persons claiming unemployment benefits used for the statistics A person claiming regular benefits (i.e. entitled to receive regular benefits) is a person who is out of work, is able and willing to work, and has sufficient work attachment in the last year to establish a claim.
7. Updating of the registrations
The registrations are updated daily.
8. Unemployment rates
Statistics from the registrations are not used to obtain unemployment rates.
9. Type of statistics of unemployment benefit claimants produced
Series 1: Employment Insurance Claims.
Reference period: Summation for a month.
Frequency of production: Monthly.
Descriptive variables used:
– Sex;
– Age;
– Geographic characteristics;
– Previous work experience (insured hours and weeks);
– Duration of unemployment.
Form of publication:
– For internal use only;
– Machine-readable form, on request (last five years).
Agency responsible for publication: Human Resources Development Canada.
Title of the publication: *SM70 - Initial and renewal claims established*.
Series 2: Employment Insurance Beneficiaries.
Reference period: Point estimate (15th day of a month).
Frequency of production: Monthly.
Descriptive variables used:
– Sex;

- Age;
- Geographic characteristics;
- Previous work experience;
- Duration of unemployment.

Form of publication: Machine-readable form, on request (last five years).
Agency responsible for publication: Human Resources Development Canada and Statistics Canada.
Publication: The information is available (in English and French) in the CANSIM data base.
Series 3: Employment Insurance Benefit Payments.
Reference period: Day.
Frequency of production: Daily.
Form of publication:
- For internal use only;
- Machine-readable form, on request.

Agency responsible for publication: Human Resources Development Canada.
Title of the publication: *Workload Report.*
10. Methodological information about the statistics
Form of release: Not released, available for internal use only.
Agency responsible for the release: Human Resources Development Canada (Financial Research).
11. Comparisons with unemployment statistics from other sources
Comparisons have not been made with unemployment statistics from other sources.
12. Major changes since the start of the statistics
Major changes in legislation (i.e. to the Unemployment Insurance Act and the Employment Insurance Act) which had a significant influence on the statistics took place in 1990, 1993, 1994, 1996, 2000 and 2001 [Bills C-21; C-113; C-17; C-12, EI Reform; C-32 and C-2 respectively].

Central African Rep.

1. Series
The Central African Agency of Vocational Training and Employment is not in charge of the unemployment statistics, but those concerning job-seekers and job offers.
2. Agency making the initial registrations of unemployed persons
Name of the agency: Agence centrafricaine de Formation professionnelle et de l'Emploi - ACFPE (The Central African Agency of Vocational Training and Employment).
Type of agency: Public service under a national authority.
Name of the national authority: Ministry of Civil Service and Social Security.
Location of the local offices making the registrations: In some areas only: Bangui, Berberati, Bouar, Bangassou, Mbaïki, Bambari and others.
Type of services provided/administered by the agency:
- Assisting job-seekers to find jobs;
- Assisting job-seekers to establish their own business;
- Assisting employers to find workers;
- Vocational guidance;
- Job-related training;

3. The following information is registered about a person:
- Name;
- Sex;
- Social security number (or similar identification number also used by other agencies);
- Address of usual residence;
- Date of birth;
- Citizenship;
- Nationality/ethnic group;
- Educational/vocational attainment, with nine categories distinguished. Links to ISCED have not been established;
- Current/past activity status, with two categories distinguished;
- Type of work (occupation) of past or present job. Links to ISCO-88 have been established (class level);
- Type of work (occupation) of job sought, with 11 categories distinguished;
- Name and address of present or previous employer or work place;
- Type of business (industry) of present/previous employer/workplace, with 18 categories distinguished. Links to ISIC have been established;

- Previous registrations with the agency/service;
- Other: duration of previous employment, training desired.

4. Criteria used for inclusion of a person in the registers (R) and/or the statistics of unemployed persons (S):
- Being without work (R) and (S);
- Seeking work (R) and (S);
- Availability for work (R) and (S);
- Age (lower limit: 15 years; upper limit: 54 years) (R) and (S);
- Being resident in the country (R) and (S);
- Previously employed (R) and (S).

5. - 12. No information available.

Chad

1. Series
Title: Yearbook of Labour Market Statistics.
Starting year: 1986.
2. Agency making the initial registrations of unemployed persons
Name of the agency: Office national pour la Promotion de l'Emploi - ONAPE (National Office for Employment Promotion).
Type of agency: Public service under a national authority.
Name of the national authority: Ministry of public Service, Labour, Employment Promotion and Modernisation (MFPTPEM).
Location of the local offices making the registrations: Njamena, Moundou, Sarh, Bougor and Doba.
Type of services provided/administered by the agency:
- Assisting job-seekers to find jobs;
- Assisting job-seekers to establish their own business;
- Assisting employers to find workers;
- Vocational guidance;
- Other: issuing work permits to foreigners.

3. The following information is registered about a person:
- Name;
- Sex;
- Social security number (or similar identification number also used by other agencies);
- Address of usual residence;
- Date of birth;
- Citizenship;
- Nationality/ethnic group;
- Educational/vocational attainment, with eight categories distinguished. Links to ISCED have not been established;
- Current/past activity status;
- Type of work (occupation) of past or present job. Links to ISCO-88 have not been established;
- Type of work (occupation) of job sought;
- Name and address of present or previous employer or work place;
- Type of business (industry) of present/previous employer/workplace, with eight categories distinguished. Links to ISIC, rev.2 have been established.

4. Information not available.
5. Information not available.
6. Information not available.
7. Updating of the registers
The registers are updated daily.
8. Unemployment rates
Statistics from the registers are not used to obtain unemployment rates.
9. Type of statistics of unemployed persons produced
Statistics are produced on various types of services provided or managed by the ONAPE:
- Assisting job-seekers to find jobs;
- Assisting job-seekers to establish their own business;
- Assisting employers to find workers;
- Vocational guidance;
- Other: issuing work permits to foreigners.

Descriptive variables used:
- Sex;
- Age;
- Educational level;
- Occupation;
- Industry;
- Geographic characteristics;
- Previous work experience;
- Citizenship (nationals/non nationals);

– Duration of unemployment.

Form of publication: On paper, for limited audience.

Agency responsible for publication: ONAPE.

10. Methodological information about the statistics

Form of release: On paper, for limited audience.

Agency responsible for the release: ONAPE.

11. Comparisons with unemployment statistics from other sources

Comparisons have not been made with unemployment statistics from other sources.

12. Major changes since the start of the statistics

There have been no major changes in legislation, capacity of the agency and/or administrative procedures which had a significant influence on the statistics.

China

1. Series

Title: Unemployment statistics system.

Starting year: 1980.

2. Agency making the initial registrations of unemployed persons

Name of the agency: Local labour offices in subdistrict office, or employment service centre.

Type of agency: Public service under local authorities.

Location of the local offices making the registrations: In all parts of the country at local level.

Type of services provided/administered by the agency:

– Assisting job-seekers to find jobs;

– Assisting job-seekers to establish their own business;

– Assisting employers to find workers;

– Vocational guidance;

– Job-related training;

– Paying unemployment compensation;

– Other: keeping personal records for the unemployed.

Percentage of job-seekers seeking work through the agency: 25%.

3. The following information is registered about a person:

– Name;

– Sex;

– Social security number (or similar identification number also used by other agencies);

– Address of usual residence;

– Date of birth;

– Citizenship.

– Nationality/ethnic group;

– Educational/vocational attainment, with 8 categories distinguished. No links to ISCED have been established;

– Current/past activity status;

– Type of work (occupation) of past or present job; links to ISCO-88 have been established (sub-major and major groups level);

– Type of work (occupation) of job sought. Links to ISCO-88 have been established (sub-major and major groups level);

– Name and address of present or previous employer or work place;

– Type of business (industry) of present/previous employer/workplace, with 16 groups distinguished. No links to ISIC, rev.3 have been established;

– Previous registrations with the agency/service.

4. Criteria used for inclusion of a person in the registers (R) and/or the statistics of unemployed persons (S):

– Being without work (R) and (S);

– Seeking work (R) and (S);

– Availability for work (R) and (S);

– Age: lower limit: 16 years; upper limit: 60 years for men, 55 years for women; (R) and (S);

– Being resident in the country (R) and (S);

– Previously employed (S).

5. Criteria used for exclusion of a person from the registers (R) and/or the statistics of unemployed persons (S):

– Death (R) and (S);

– Taking up residency abroad (R) and (S);

– Commencement of a (new) job (R) and (S);

– Commencement of military service (R) and (S);

– End of entitlement to receive unemployment compensation (R) and (S);

– Receipt of a pension (R) and (S);

– Inability to work (R) and (S).

6. Definition of unemployed persons used for the statistics

Urban registered unemployment refers to the non-agricultural population, who are of working age (16 years to retirement age), available to work and have registered in the local employment service agencies for seeking a job. The following persons are excluded: (i) students; (ii) those who are above retirement age (60 for men and 55 for women) or who are under retirement age but have already retired/resigned; (iii) disabled with partial work capacity receiving a special settlement.

7. Updating of the registers

No information is available concerning the updating of the registers.

8. Unemployment rates

Statistics from the registers are used to obtain unemployment rates.

The sources of data on employed persons who are part of the denominator of the unemployment rates are Establishment surveys, Social Security register, Employment register and Registration of industrial and commercial enterprises.

Definition of employed persons for this purpose:

Employment refers to the total number of persons engaged in social economic activities that generate income.

9. Type of statistics of unemployed persons produced

Series 1:

Reference period: Quarter.

Frequency of production: Quarterly.

Descriptive variables used:

– Sex;

– Age;

– Educational level;

– Occupation;

– Industry;

– Geographic characteristics.

Form of publication:

– On paper, for general audience;

– Machine-readable form, on request;

– On a website.

Title of the publication: *China Labour Statistical Yearbook.*

Series 2:

Reference period: Year.

Frequency of production: Half-yearly.

Descriptive variables used:

– Sex;

– Age;

– Educational level;

– Occupation;

– Industry;

– Geographic characteristics.

Form of publication:

– On paper, for general audience;

– Machine-readable form, on request;

– On a website.

Title of the publication: *China Labour Statistical Yearbook.*

Series 3

Reference period: Year.

Frequency of production: Yearly.

Descriptive variables used:

– Sex;

– Age;

– Educational level;

– Occupation;

– Industry;

– Geographic characteristics.

Form of publication:

– On paper, for general audience;

– Machine-readable form, on request;

– On a website.

Title of the publication: *China Labour Statistical Yearbook.*

10. Methodological information about the statistics

Form of release:

– On paper, for general audience;

– In machine-readable form, on request;

– On a website.

Agencies responsible for the release: National Bureau of Statistics; Ministry of Labour and Social Security.

11. Comparisons with unemployment statistics from other sources

Comparisons have been made with unemployment statistics from the Population Census and from other sources.

Frequency of the comparisons: Regularly when the statistics are published (latest year: 2001).

Publication of the methodology/results of the comparisons: These have not been published.

12. Major changes since the start of the statistics

Major changes in legislation, capacity of the agency and/or administrative procedures took place in 1986, 1990 and 1995. The resulting changes in the statistics have not been estimated.

Colombia

1. Series
Title: Registered unemployment.
Starting year: 1992.

2. Agency making the initial registrations of unemployed persons
Name of the agency: Servicio Nacional de Aprendizaje - SENA (National Apprenticeship Service).
Type of agency: Public service under a national authority.
Name of the national authority: Ministerio de Trabajo y Seguridad Social (Ministry of Labour and Social Security).
Location of the local offices making the registrations: All over the country.
Type of services provided/administered by the agency:
– Assisting job-seekers to find jobs;
– Assisting job-seekers to establish their own business;
– Assisting employers to find workers;
– Vocational guidance;
– Job-related training;
– Other: providing information on the labour market.
Percentage of job-seekers seeking work through the agency: No record is kept.

3. The following information is registered about a person:
– Name;
– Sex;
– Address of usual residence;
– Date of birth;
– Citizenship;
– Educational/vocational attainment. Links to ISCED have not been established;.
– Current/past activity status, with four categories distinguished;
– Type of work (occupation) of past or present job. Links to ISCO-88 have not been established;
– Type of work (occupation) of job sought. Links to ISCO-88 have not been established;
– Type of business (industry) of present/previous employer/workplace.

4. Criteria used for inclusion of a person in the registers (R) and/or the statistics of unemployed persons (S):
– Being without work (R) and (S);
– Seeking work (R) and (S);
– Availability for work (R) and (S);
– Age (lower limit: 10 years in rural sector and 12 years in urban sector; no upper age limit) (R) and (S);
– Citizenship (only Colombians) (R) and (S);
– Being resident in the country (R) and (S).

5. Criteria used for exclusion of a person from the registers (R) and/or the statistics of unemployed persons (S):
– Death (R) and (S);
– Taking up residency abroad (but if the person is inside the country at the date of the survey, he/she is counted) (R) and (S);
– Commencement of a (new) job (R) and (S);
– Commencement of military service (R) and (S);
– Studying or undergoing training (R) and (S).

6. Definition of unemployed persons used for the statistics
Persons in the following situations during the reference week:
1. Visible unemployment: without employment during the reference week, who had taken steps during the last month, and are available for work.
2. Invisible unemployment: without employment during the reference week, who had not taken steps during the last month, but who had taken them during the last 12 months and who had a good reason to be discouraged, and are available for work.

7. Updating of the registers
The registers are updated regularly.

8. Unemployment rates
Statistics from the registers are not used to obtain unemployment rates.

9. Type of statistics of unemployed persons produced
Series 1:
Reference period: Month.
Frequency of production: Monthly.
Descriptive variables used:
– Sex;
– Age;
– Educational level;
– Occupation;
– Industry;
– Previous work experience;
– Duration of unemployment;
– Other (since 2002): length of time spent looking for employment; means used to look for employment; enterprise.
Form of publication:
– On paper, for general audience;
– On a website: www.sena.gov.co (Since 2002).
Agency responsible for publication: SENA.
Title and periodicity of the publication(s): Various reports (monthly and yearly).
Series 2:
Reference period: Quarter-Half year.
Frequency of production: Monthly.
Descriptive variables used:
– Sex;
– Age;
– Educational level;
– Occupation;
– Industry;
– Previous work experience;
– Duration of unemployment;
– Other (since 2002): length of time spent looking for employment; means used to look for employment; enterprise.
Form of publication:
– On paper, for general audience;
– On a website: www.sena.gov.co (Since 2002).
Agency responsible for publication: SENA.
Title and periodicity of the publication(s): Various reports (monthly and yearly).
Series 3: Year.
Reference period: Year.
Frequency of production: Monthly.
Descriptive variables used:
– Sex;
– Age;
– Educational level;
– Occupation;
– Industry;
– Previous work experience;
– Duration of unemployment;
– Other (since 2002): length of time spent looking for employment; means used to look for employment; enterprise.
Form of publication:
– On paper, for general audience;
– On a website: www.sena.gov.co (Since 2002).
Agency responsible for publication: SENA.
Title and periodicity of the publication(s): Various reports (monthly and yearly).

10. Methodological information about the statistics
Form of release: On paper, for general audience.
Agency responsible for the release: Departamento Administrativo Nacional de Estadísticas -DANE (National Administrative Department of Statistics).

11. Comparisons with unemployment statistics from other sources
Comparisons have been made with unemployment statistics from the labour force survey.
Frequency of the comparisons: from time to time.
Publication of the methodology/results of the comparisons: These have been published in the review *Indicadores de Mercado Laboral* (Indicators of the labour market) and *Informe mensual de gestión del sistema de información para el empleo* (Monthly report

on the administration of the employment information system) SENA, Dirección de Empleo (Employment Department).

12. Major changes since the start of the statistics

There have been no major changes in legislation, capacity of the agency and/or administrative procedures which had a significant influence on the statistics.

However, important modifications will take place in 2002 due to changes in the systematic computerized and virtualized application of the entry mechanism into the labour market.

Congo

1. Series

Title: Statistics on job-seekers. The Public Employment Service in Congo is not in charge of the unemployment statistics, but those concerning job-seekers and job offers.

2. Agency making the initial registrations of unemployed persons

Name of the agency: Office national de l'Emploi et de la Main-d'œuvre - ONEMO (Regional Agencies of the National Employment and Labour Force Office).

Type of agency: Public service under a national authority.

Name of the national authority: Department of Labour, Employment and Social Security.

Location of the local offices making the registrations: Brazzaville, Kouilou, Bouénza, Cuvettes, Sangha, Likouala and Niari.

Type of services provided/administered by the agency:
- Assisting job-seekers to find jobs;
- Assisting job-seekers to establish their own business;
- Assisting employers to find workers;
- Vocational guidance;
- Job-related training.

3. The following information is registered about a person:
- Name;
- Sex;
- Address of usual residence;
- Date of birth;
- Citizenship;
- Nationality;
- Educational/vocational attainment. Links to ISCED have not been established;
- Current/past activity status;
- Type of work (occupation) of past or present job. Links to ISCO-88 have not been established;
- Type of work (occupation) of job sought;
- Name and address of present or previous employer or work place;
- Type of business (industry) of present/previous employer/workplace; Links to ISIC have not been established

4. - 12.: Information not available.

Costa Rica

1. Series

Title: Registered unemployment.

Starting year: Not specified.

2. Agency making the initial registrations of unemployed persons

Name of the agency: Departamento de Prospección de Empleo (Employment Prospecting Department).

Type of agency: Public service under a national authority.

Name of the national authority: Ministerio de Trabajo y Seguridad Social (Ministry of Labour and Social Security).

Location of the local offices making the registrations: Central area of the country.

Type of services provided/administered by the agency:
- Assisting job-seekers to find jobs;
- Assisting employers to find workers;
- Other: surveys on migrant manpower; prospective surveys on employment; surveys to determine the manpower profiles in investment areas; "Programa Construyendo Oportunidades y Creciendo Juntas" (National development programme).

Percentage of job-seekers seeking work through the agency: 10%.

3. The following information is registered about a person:
- Name;
- Sex;

- Social security number (or similar identification number also used by other agencies);
- Address of usual residence;
- Date of birth;
- Citizenship;
- Nationality/ethnic group;
- Educational/vocational attainment, with 11 categories distinguished. Links to ISCED have not been established;
- Current/past activity status, with five categories distinguished;
- Type of work (occupation) of past or present job with three categories distinguished. Links to ISCO-88 have been established;
- Type of work (occupation) of job sought, with three categories distinguished. Links to ISCO-88 have been established;
- Name and address of present or previous employer or work place;
- Type of business (industry) of present/previous employer/workplace, with 64 categories distinguished. Links to ISIC, rev.3 have not been established;
- Previous registrations with the agency/service.

4. Criteria used for inclusion of a person in the registers (R) and/or the statistics of unemployed persons (S):
- Being without work (R) and (S);
- Seeking work (first job; better job or second job) (R) and (S);
- Availability for work (R) and (S);
- Age (lower limit: 15 years; no upper age limit) (R) and (S);
- Citizenship (R);
- Being resident in the country (R) and (S);
- Previously employed (R).

5. Criteria used for exclusion of a person from the registers (R) and/or the statistics of unemployed persons (S):
- Death (R) and (S);
- Commencement of a (new) job (R) and (S);
- Refusal of three suitable job offers (R) and (S).

6. Definition of unemployed persons used for the statistics

Statistics are based on registered offers by occupational groups, sex, work experience, level of education and age.

7. Updating of the registers

The registers are updated daily. They are kept active for six months then they are renewed.

8. Unemployment rates

Statistics from the registers are not used to obtain unemployment rates.

9. Type of statistics of unemployed persons produced

Reference period: Half-year.

Frequency of production: Not specified.

Descriptive variables used:
- Sex;
- Age;
- Educational level;
- Occupation;
- Industry;
- Previous work experience.

Form of publication: For internal use only.

10. Methodological information about the statistics

Form of release: On paper, for general audience.

Agency responsible for the release: Departamento de Prospección de Empleo/Migraciones Laborales (Employment Prospecting Department/Labour Migrations).

11. Comparisons with unemployment statistics from other sources

Comparisons have not been made with unemployment statistics from other sources.

12. Major changes since the start of the statistics

There have been no major changes in legislation, capacity of the agency and/or administrative procedures which had a significant influence on the statistics.

Croatia

1. Series

Title: Unemployed receiving unemployment benefits.

Starting year: 1952

2. Agency making the initial registrations of unemployed persons

Name of the agency: Hrvatski zavod za zapošljavanje (Croatian Employment Service).

Type of agency: Public service under a national authority.

Name of the national authority: Ministry of Labour and Social Affairs.
Location of the local offices making the registrations: 21 regional offices (all counties) and 98 local offices.
Type of services provided/administered by the agency:
- Assisting job-seekers to find jobs;
- Assisting job-seekers to establish their own business;
- Assisting employers to find workers;
- Vocational guidance;
- Job-related training;
- Paying unemployment compensation;
- Other employment-related services.

3. The following information is registered about a person:
- Name;
- Sex;
- Social security number (or similar identification number also used by other agencies);
- Address of usual residence;
- Date of birth;
- Educational/vocational attainment, with 7 categories distinguished; Links to ISCED have not been established;
- Current/past activity status, with 2 categories distinguished;
- Type of work (occupation) of past or present job with 7 categories distinguished. Links to ISCO-88 have been established;
- Type of work (occupation) of job sought, with 3 categories distinguished. Links to ISCO-88 have not been established;
- Type of business (industry) of present/previous employer/workplace, with 17 categories distinguished. Links to ISIC, rev.3 and NACE, rev.1 (class level) have been established;
- Previous registrations with the agency/service.

4. Criteria used for inclusion of a person in the registers (R) and/or the statistics of unemployed persons (S):
- Being without work (R) and (S);
- Seeking work (R) and (S);
- Age (lower limit: 15 years; upper limit: 65 years) (R) and (S);
- Being resident in the country (R) and (S);
- Previously employed (R) and (S).

5. Criteria used for exclusion of a person from the registers (R) and/or the statistics of unemployed persons (S):
- Death (R) and (S);
- Taking up residency abroad (R) and (S);
- Commencement of a (new) job (R) and (S);
- Commencement of military service (R) and (S);
- Participation in an employment promotion scheme, public works programme, etc. (R) and (S);
- Studying or undergoing training (R) and (S);
- Failure to contact the agency/service (R) and (S);
- Refusal of 1 suitable job offer (R) and (S);
- Refusal of 1 suitable training offer (R) and (S);
- Receipt of a pension (R) and (S);
- Inability to work (total disability) (R) and (S);
- Being an unemployment benefit recipient who earned a monthly wage or income from own business performed temporarily in accordance with the income tax regulations (R) and (S);
- Earning a monthly wage or income from business performed temporarily in accordance with the income tax regulations, the amount of which does not exceed the highest amount of unemployment benefit established; (R) and (S);
- Being caught performing illegal work with no job certificate, agreement or work contract (R) and (S);
- Not meeting the requirements of active job search and availability for work (R) and (S);
- Other: serving prison sentence of more than six months (R) and (S).

6. Definition of unemployed persons used for the statistics
Persons aged from 15 to 65 years without a job, but fully or partly able to work, who are active job seekers, who meet the requirements stipulated in the Act on Job Placement (Article 7) and who are on the Croatian Employment Service Register at the end of the reporting month are considered unemployed.

7. Updating of the registers
The registers are updated daily.

8. Unemployment rates
Statistics from the registers are used to obtain unemployment rates.

The sources of data on employed persons who are part of the denominator of the unemployment rates are the Labour Force Survey and the Social Security Register.
Definition of employed persons for this purpose:
Persons employed by an employer for a fixed or unspecified period of time or self-employed.

9. Type of statistics of unemployed persons produced
Reference period: Month; Quarter; Half-year; Year.
Frequency of production: Monthly, Quarterly; Half-yearly; Yearly.
Descriptive variables used:
- Sex;
- Age;
- Educational level;
- Occupation;
- Industry;
- Geographic characteristics;
- Previous work experience;
- Duration of unemployment.

Form of publication:
- On paper, for general audience;
- Machine-readable form, on request;
- On a website (www.hzz.hr).

Agency responsible for publication: Croatian Employment Service.
Title of the publications: *Monthly Statistics Bulletin; Yearbook.*

10. Methodological information about the statistics
Form of release:
- On paper, for general audience;
- In machine-readable form, on request;
- On a website (www.hzz.hr).

Agency responsible for the release: Croatian Employment Service.

11. Comparisons with unemployment statistics from other sources
Comparisons have been made with unemployment statistics from the Labour Force Survey.
Frequency of the comparisons: Regularly, when the statistics are published.
Publication of the methodology and/or results of the comparisons: These are published by the Central Bureau of Statistics in *Monthly Statistical Report.*

12. Major changes since the start of the statistics
There have been no major changes in legislation, capacity of the agency and/or administrative procedures which had a significant influence on the statistics.

Cyprus

1. Series
Title: Statistics on registered unemployed persons.
Starting year: 1960.

2. Agency making the initial registrations of unemployed persons
Name of the agency: Department of Labour through the Employment Service at district level.
Type of agency: Public service under a national authority.
Name of the national authority: Ministry of Labour and Social Insurance.
Location of the local offices making the registrations: In all major cities of the Government controlled area of Cyprus.
Type of services provided/administered by the agency:
- Assisting job-seekers to find jobs;
- Assisting employers to find workers;
- Vocational guidance;
- Other: provision of services for the allocation of port workers.

Percentage of job-seekers seeking work through the agency: about 78%* of unemployed job-seekers seek work through the agency. Another considerable number of employed persons seek better employment through the agency.
* Registered unemployed as a percentage of total LFS unemployed.

3. The following information is registered about a person:
- Name;
- Sex;
- Social security number (or similar identification number also used by other agencies);
- Address of usual residence;
- Date of birth;
- Citizenship;

- Nationality/ethnic group.
- Educational attainment, with 33 categories distinguished. Links to ISCED are in general established with small deviation;
- Current/past activity status, with 6 categories distinguished;
- Type of work (occupation) of past or present job, at the four-digit level. Links to ISCO-88 have been established (unit group level);
- Type of work (occupation) of job sought, at the four-digit level. Links to ISCO-88 have been established (unit group level);
- Name and address of present or previous employer or work place;
- Type of business (industry) of present/previous employer/workplace, at the two-digit level. Links to ISIC, rev.3 have been established (at the two-digit level);
- Previous registrations with the agency/service;
- Other: preferred district for work; type of employer sought (private, public, etc.); transport difficulties; whether current driving licence holder; comments on appearance, speech, manner, etc.; employment history as regards wages; reason for termination of previous employment.

4. Criteria used for inclusion of a person in the registers (R)* and/or the statistics of unemployed persons (S):
- Being totally without paid work (R) and (S);
- Seeking work (R) and (S);
- Availability for work (R) and (S);
- Age (lower limit: 15 years; upper limit: 63-67 years, depending on date of receipt of Social Insurance pension) (R) and (S);
- Citizenship (R) and (S);
- Being resident in the country (R) and (S);
- Desired duration of employment and/or number of hours of work sought (minimum 30 hours per week) (R) and (S).

* Concerns "Unemployed" only; excludes those "Seeking better employment", etc.

5. Criteria used for exclusion of a person from the registers (R) and/or the statistics of unemployed persons (S):
- Death (R) and (S);
- Taking up residency abroad (R) and (S);
- Commencement of a (new) job (R) and (S);
- Commencement of military service (R) and (S);
-
- Participation in an employment promotion scheme, public works programme, etc. (R) and (S);
-
- Studying or undergoing training (R) and (S);
- Failure to contact the agency/service (R) and (S);
- Refusal of 3 suitable job offers (R) and (S);
- Receipt of a pension (R) and (S);
- Inability to work (R) and (S).

6. Definition of unemployed persons used for the statistics

Persons are considered as unemployed if they are registered as totally unemployed and looking for work at the District Labour Offices on the last day of each month. It includes those persons who receive unemployment benefit from the Social Insurance as well as those not entitled to any benefit.

7. Updating of the registers

The registers are updated on a continuous basis.

8. Unemployment rates

Statistics from the registers are used to obtain unemployment rates.

The source of data on employed persons who are part of the denominator of the unemployment rates is Official Estimates.

Definition of employed persons for this purpose:

Persons who worked at least one hour during the reference week or persons who had a job but happened not to work during the reference week.

9. Type of statistics of unemployed persons produced
Series: Number unemployed.
Reference period: Month.
Frequency of production: Monthly; Yearly.
Descriptive variables used:
- Sex;
- Age;
- Educational level;
- Occupation;
- Industry;
- Geographic characteristics;
- Previous work experience;
- Duration of unemployment.

Form of publication:
- On paper, for general audience;
- Machine-readable form, on request.

Agency responsible for publication: Statistical Service, Ministry of Finance.

Title and periodicity of the publications: *Registered Unemployed* (monthly); *Monthly Economic Indicators* (bi-monthly); *Labour Statistics* (yearly).

10. Methodological information about the statistics
Form of release: Press release and internet release.

11. Comparisons with unemployment statistics from other sources

Comparisons have been made with unemployment statistics from the Labour Force Survey.

Frequency of the comparisons: Regularly when the statistics are published.

Publication of the methodology/results of the comparisons: These have not been published.

12. Major changes since the start of the statistics

There have been no major changes in legislation, capacity of the agency and/or administrative procedures which had a significant influence on the statistics. However, systems of classifications of occupations and industries have changed in order to comply with United Nations systems.

Czech Republic

1. Series
Title: Registered job-seekers and vacancies.
Starting year: 1991.

2. Agency making the initial registrations of unemployed persons
Name of the agency: Urad prace (Labour Office).
Type of agency: Public service under a national authority.
Name of the national authority: Ministerstvo prace a socialnich veci (Ministry of Labour and Social Affairs).
Location of the local offices making the registrations: In 77 districts of the country.
Type of services provided/administered by the agency:
- Assisting job-seekers to find jobs;
- Assisting job-seekers to establish their own business;
- Assisting employers to find workers;
- Vocational guidance;
- Job-related training;
- Paying unemployment compensation;
- Other: "Monitoring" of employers; supervisory activities in the area of labour law.

Percentage of job-seekers seeking work through the agency: 95%.

3. The following information is registered about a person:
- Name;
- Sex;
- Social security number (or similar identification number also used by other agencies);
- Address of usual residence;
- Date of birth;
- Citizenship;
- Educational/vocational attainment, with 13 categories distinguished. Links to ISCED-97 have been established;
- Current/past activity status, with 25 categories distinguished;
- Type of work (occupation) of past or present job [optional], with 10 categories distinguished. Links to ISCO-88 have been established;
- Type of work (occupation) of job sought [optional], with 10 categories distinguished]. Links to ISCO-88 have been established;
- Name and address of present or previous employer or work place;
- Type of business (industry) of present/previous employer/workplace [optional], with 17 categories distinguished. Links to ISIC, rev.3 or NACE, rev.1 have been established (class level);
- Previous registrations with the agency/service;
- Other: unemployment duration; repeated unemployment; health status; family status; disadvantaged group (e.g. adolescents, school-leavers and university graduates without experience, pregnant women, persons looking after child under 15 years; job seekers over the age of 50, job-seekers

registered more than six months, persons needing special assistance or who are not socially assimilated).

4. Criteria used for inclusion of a person in the registers (R) and/or the statistics of unemployed persons (S):
– Being without work (R) and (S);
– Seeking work (R) and (S);
– Availability for work (R) and (S);
– Age (lower limit: 15 years; no upper limit) (R) and (S);
– Being resident in the country (R) and (S).

5. Criteria used for exclusion of a person from the registers (R) and/or the statistics of unemployed persons (S):
– Death (R) and (S);
– Taking up residency abroad (R) and (S);
– Commencement of a (new) job (R) and (S);
– Participation in an employment promotion scheme, public works programme, etc. (R) and (S);
– Studying or undergoing training (R) and (S);
– Failure to contact the agency/service (R) and (S);
– Refusal of suitable job offers (R) and (S);
– Other: at own request (R) and (S).

6. Definition of unemployed persons used for the statistics
A citizen who is not in employment or similar relationship, and who does not engage in independent gainful activity, or who is not involved in systematic preparation (studies, training) for a profession or occupation (vocational training) and who personally applies in writing to the Labour Office for assistance in finding suitable employment, shall be registered as a job-seeker [Section 7(1) of the Employment Act].

7. Updating of the registers
The registers are updated on a continuous basis.

8. Unemployment rates
Statistics from the registers are used to obtain unemployment rates.
The source of data on employed persons who are part of the denominator of the unemployment rates is the Labour Force Survey.

Definition of employed persons for this purpose:
The number of employed persons is changed quarterly and calculated as an arithmetical average from the results of the last four Labour Force Surveys (definitions used in the LFS are in full harmony with the definitions of ILO indicators and recommendations).

9. Type of statistics of unemployed persons produced
Series 1: Registered job-seekers and vacancies.
Reference period: Day.
Frequency of production: Monthly.
Descriptive variables used:
– Sex;
– Other: receiving unemployment benefit; undergoing training.
Form of publication:
– On paper, for limited audience;
– Machine-readable form, on request;
– On a website (www.mpsv.cz: Sluzby zamestnanosti (Employment Service)).
Agency responsible for publication: Ministry of Labour and Social Affairs.
Title and periodicity of the publication(s): *Statistical Report,* monthly.
Series 2: Structure of job-seekers and vacancies
Reference period: Day.
Frequency of production: Quarterly.
Descriptive variables used:
– Sex;
– Age group;
– Educational level;
– Occupation;
– Duration of unemployment;
– Other: receiving unemployment benefit.
Form of publication:
– Machine-readable form, on request;
– On a website (http://ssz.mpsv.cz/Statistiky/).
Agency responsible for publication: Ministry of Labour and Social Affairs.

10. Methodological information about the statistics
Form of release: On paper, for limited audience.
Agency responsible for the release: Ministry of Labour and Social Affairs.

11. Comparisons with unemployment statistics from other sources

Comparisons as such have not been made with unemployment statistics from other sources. However, unemployment statistics from the Labour Force Survey are used by the Ministry of Labour and Social Affairs as an additional source of information for labour market analysis.

12. Major changes since the start of the statistics
Major changes to legislation, capacity of the agency and/or administrative procedures resulting in an increase or decrease in the total number of persons registered as unemployed took place in the following years: 1991: -2%; 1992: -5%; 1994: +5%; and 1996: +10%.

Denmark

1. Series
Title: Registered unemployment (compiled from the Central Register of Labour Market Statistics (CRAM)).
Starting year: 1979.

2. Agencies making the initial registrations of unemployed persons
Name of the agencies:
(1) Unemployment Insurance Funds;
(2) Local Authorities;
(3) Job Centres.
Type of agencies: Public services under a national authority.
Name of the national authority:
Arbejdsmarkedsstyrelsen.(Labour Market Authority).
Location of the local offices making the registrations: In all parts of the country.
Type of services provided/administered by the agencies:
(i) Unemployment Insurance Funds:
– Vocational guidance;
– Paying unemployment compensation.
(ii) Local Authorities:
– Assisting job-seekers to find jobs;
– Assisting job-seekers to establish their own business;
– Assisting employers to find workers;
– Vocational guidance;
– Job-related training.
(iii) Job Centres:
– Assisting job-seekers to find jobs;
– Assisting employers to find workers;
– Vocational guidance;
– Job-related training.
Percentage of job-seekers seeking work through these agencies: 22%.

3. The following information is registered about a person:
– Name;
– Sex;
– Social security number (or similar identification number also used by other agencies);
– Address of usual residence;
– Date of birth;
– Citizenship;
– Nationality/ethnic group;
– Other: whether insured or not; name of the agency making the registration.

4. Criteria used for inclusion of a person in the registers (R) and/or the statistics of registered unemployed persons (S):
– Being without work (R) and (S);
– Seeking work (R) and (S);
– Availability for work and (R) and (S);
– Age (lower limit: 16 years; upper limit: 66 years) (R) and (S).

5. Criteria used for exclusion of a person from the registers (R) and/or the statistics of unemployed persons (S):
– Death (R) and (S);
– Commencement of a (new) job (S);
– Commencement of military service (S);
– Participation in an employment promotion scheme, public works programme, etc. (S);
– Studying or undergoing training (S);
– Receipt of a pension (S);
– Inability to work (S).

6. Definition of unemployed persons used for the statistics
Persons who are not employed, are available for work and are actively seeking work.

7. Updating of the registers
The registers are updated monthly.

8. Unemployment rates

Statistics from the registers are used to obtain unemployment rates.

The source of data on employed persons who are part of the denominator of the unemployment rates is the register-based labour force statistics (RAS statistics)).

Definition of employed persons for this purpose:

Employed persons are either employees, self-employed or assisting spouses.

9. Type of statistics of unemployed persons produced

Series 1:

Reference period: Month.

Frequency of production: Monthly.

Descriptive variables used:

- Sex;
- Age;
- Industry by insurance fund;
- Geographic characteristics;
- Insured/not insured.

Form of publication:

- On paper, for general audience;
- On a website (www.statistikbanken.dk).

Agency responsible for publication: Statistics Denmark.

Title of the publications: *Nyt fra Danmarks Statistik* (News from Statistics Denmark); *Arbejdsmarked* (Labour Market) appearing in the series *Statistiske Efterretninger* (Statistical News); *Konjunkturstatistikken* (Main Indicators) (monthly).

Series 2:

Frequency of production: Yearly.

Descriptive variables used:

- Sex;
- Age;
- Industry by insurance fund;
- Insured/not insured;
- Geographic characteristics;
- Previous work experience;
- Citizenship (nationals/non nationals);
- Duration of unemployment.

Form of publication:

- On paper, for general audience;
- On a website (www.statistikbanken.dk).

Agency responsible for publication: Statistics Denmark.

Title of the publications: *Nyt fra Danmarks Statistik* (News from Statistics Denmark); *Arbejdsmarked* (Labour Market) appearing in the series *Statistiske Efterretninger* (Statistical News); *Konjunkturstatistikken* (Main Indicators) (monthly), *Statistisk Årbog* (Statistical Yearbook) and Statistisk Tiårsoversigt (Statistical ten-year review).

10. Methodological information about the statistics

Form of release:

- On paper, for general audience;
- On a website (www.dst.dk/varedeklaration - Arbejdsmarked (Labour market) - Arbejdsløshed (Unemployment)).

Agency responsible for publication: Statistics Denmark.

11. Comparisons with unemployment statistics from other sources

Comparisons are made with unemployment statistics from the Labour Force Survey.

Frequency of the comparisons: Four times a year.

Publication of the methodology/results of the comparisons: These are released on the website of Statistics Denmark (www.dst.dk /varedeklaration - Arbejdsmarked (Labour market) - Arbejdskraftsundersøgelsen (Labour force Survey)).

12. Major changes since the start of the statistics

There have been no major changes in legislation, capacity of the agency and/or administrative procedures which had a significant influence on the statistics.

Djibouti

1. Series

Title: Socio-economic characteristics of job-seekers and hiring by occupation.

Starting year: 1974.

2. Agency making the initial registrations of unemployed persons

Name of the agency: Service national de l'Emploi - SNE (National Employment Office).

Type of agency: Public service under a national authority.

Name of the national authority: Ministry of Employment and National Solidarity, Department of Employment.

Location of the local offices making the registrations: Djibouti City.

Type of services provided/administered by the agency:

- Assisting job-seekers to find jobs;
- Assisting employers to find workers;
- Vocational guidance;
- Other: administration of expatriate workers' files (issue of work permits for expatriate workers).

Percentage of job-seekers seeking work through the agency: 6%.

3. The following information is registered about a person:

- Name;
- Sex;
- Social security number (or similar identification number also used by other agencies);
- Address of usual residence;
- Date of birth;
- Citizenship;
- Educational/vocational attainment, with nine categories distinguished;
- Type of work (occupation) of past or present job with four categories distinguished. Links to ISCO have been established;
- Previous registrations with the service.

4. Criteria used for inclusion of a person in the registers (R) and/or the statistics of unemployed persons (S):

- Being without work and registered at the National Employment Office. The job-seeker is requested to deposit a complete file with his/her address, telephone number or post box number, etc. (R) and (S);
- Seeking work (R) and (S);
- Available for work (R) and (S);
- Age (lower limit: 16 years; upper limit: 55 years) (R) and (S);
- Citizenship: the job-seeker has to present his/her national identity card (R) and (S);
- Being resident in the country. The job-seeker has to report regularly to the National Employment Office;
- Previously employed. The job-seeker has to present his/her work certificates.

5. Criteria used for exclusion of a person from the registers (R) and/or the statistics of unemployed persons (S):

- Death (R) and (S);
- Taking up residency abroad (R) and (S);
- Commencement of a (new) job (R) and (S);
- Failure to contact the agency/service.

6. Definition of unemployed persons used for the statistics

All persons aged 16 to 55 years who are available for work and looking for work.

Statistical data produced by the National Employment Office include only job-seekers who are registered at its offices.

7. Updating of the registers

The registers are updated daily.

8. Unemployment rates

Statistics from the registers are not used to obtain unemployment rates.

9. Type of statistics of unemployed persons produced

Reference period: Month.

Frequency of production: Quarterly.

Descriptive variables used:

- Sex;
- Age;
- Educational level;
- Occupation;
- Previous work experience;
- Citizenship (nationals/non nationals).

Form of publication:

- On paper, for general audience;
- Machine-readable form, on request;
- On a website.

Agency responsible for publication: Direction nationale de la Statistique - DINAS (National Department of Statistics).

10. Methodological information about the statistics

Form of release: For internal use only.

Agency responsible for the release: DINAS.

11. Comparisons with unemployment statistics from other sources

Comparisons have been made with unemployment statistics from the labour force survey.

12. Major changes since the start of the statistics

There have been no major changes in legislation, capacity of the agency and/or administrative procedures which had a significant influence on the statistics.

13. Additional remarks

Although the texts are clear and precise, the employers, both from the public and private sector, as well as the job seekers, do not comply with the texts in force in respect to employment.

Furthermore, Law N°140/AN/97/3rd L of 23.9.97 amending the labour code has liberalized employment; as a result most employers do not apply to the SNE and do not regularize the situation of their staff with the SNE.

Dominican Republic

1. Series
Title: Registered unemployment.
Starting year: Not specified.

2. Agency making the initial registrations of unemployed persons
Name of the agency: Dirección General de Empleo (General Administration of Employment).
Type of agency: Public service under a national authority.
Name of the national authority: Secretaría de Estado de Trabajo (Secretary of State of labour).
Location of the local offices making the registrations: In five provinces; it is planned to cover 10 others before the end of 2002.
Type of services provided/administered by the agency:
– Assisting job-seekers to find jobs;
– Assisting job-seekers to establish their own business;
– Assisting employers to find workers;
– Vocational guidance;
– Other: surveys on the labour market.
Percentage of job-seekers seeking work through the agency: 10%.

3. The following information is registered about a person:
– Name;
– Sex;
– Social security number (or similar identification number also used by other agencies);
– Address of usual residence;
– Date of birth;
– Citizenship;
– Educational/vocational attainment;
– Current/past activity status;
– Type of work (occupation) of past or present job. Links to ISCO-88 have been established (unit groups level);
– Type of work (occupation) of job sought. Links to ISCO-88 have been established (unit groups level);
– Previous registrations with the agency/service.

4. Criteria used for inclusion of a person in the registers (R) and/or the statistics of unemployed persons (S):
– Being without work (R);
– Seeking work (R);
– Availability for work (R);
– Age (lower limit: 16 years; no upper age limit) (R);
– Citizenship (must be Dominican) (R);
– Being resident in the country (R);
– Desired duration of employment and/or number of hours of work sought (R).

5. Criteria used for exclusion of a person from the registers (R) and/or the statistics of unemployed persons (S):
– Death (R);
– Failure to contact the agency/service (R);
– Other: application no longer valid (validity is one year) (R).

6. Definition of unemployed persons used for the statistics

Dominicans aged over 16 years without work, whether they are looking for a job or not.

7. Updating of the registers

The registers are updated yearly.

8. Unemployment rates

Statistics from the registers are not used to obtain unemployment rates.

9. Type of statistics of unemployed persons produced
Reference period: Year.
Frequency of production: Yearly.
Descriptive variables used:
– Sex;
– Age;
– Occupation;
– Industry;
– Geographic characteristics;
– Previous work experience.
Form of publication:
– On paper, for general audience;
– Machine-readable form, on request.

10. Methodological information about the statistics
Form of release:
– On paper, for general audience;
– In machine-readable form, on request;
– On a website: www.bancentral.gov.do/publicaciones
Agency responsible for the release: Banco Central de la República Dominicana (Central Bank of the Dominican Republic).

11. Comparisons with unemployment statistics from other sources Comparisons have been made with unemployment statistics from the labour force survey, other household survey and from the report of the Economic Commission for Latin America and the Caribbean (ECLAC): *Informe de la CEPAL "Comisión Económica para América Latina y el Caribe" (ECLAC Report).*
Frequency of the comparisons: from time to time.
Publication of the methodology/results of the comparisons: These have not been published.

12. Major changes since the start of the statistics

Major changes in legislation, capacity of the agency and/or administrative procedures took place in 2002. The resulting changes in the statistics are being estimated.

Egypt

1. Series
Title: Registered unemployment..
Starting year: 1959.

2. Agency making the initial registrations of unemployed persons
Name of the agency: Ministry of Manpower and Migration (local offices).
Type of agency: Public service under national and local authorities.
Name of the national authority: Ministry of Manpower and Migration.
Location of the local offices making the registrations: In all parts of the country with at least one office in every district; district offices are directed by the main office of the city.
Type of services provided/administered by the agency:
– Assisting job-seekers to find jobs;
– Assisting employers to find workers;
– Vocational guidance;
– Job-related training;
– Paying unemployment compensation;
– Other: Certain offices help applicants to find jobs abroad.
Percentage of job-seekers seeking work through the agency: 8.14%

3. The following information is registered about a person:
– Name;
– Sex;
– Social security number (or similar identification number also used by other agencies);
– Address of usual residence;
– Age;
– Citizenship;
– Nationality/ethnic group;
– Educational/vocational attainment, with 6 categories distinguished. Links to ISCED have been established;
– Current/past activity status, with 3 categories distinguished;
– Type of work (occupation) of past or present job. Links to ISCO-88 have not been established;
– Type of work (occupation of job sought, with 10 categories distinguished. Links to ISCO-88 have not been established;
– Name and address of present or previous employer or work place;
– Previous registrations with the agency/service.

4. Criteria used for inclusion of a person in the registers (R) and/or the statistics of unemployed persons (S):
–   Being without work (R) and (S);
–   Seeking work (R) and (S);
–   Availability for work (R) and (S);
–   Age (lower limit: 12 years; no upper limit) (R) and (S);
–   Citizenship (R) and (S);
–   Being resident in the country (R) and (S);
–   Previously employed (R) and (S).

5. Criteria used for exclusion of a person from the registers (R) and/or the statistics of unemployed persons (S):
–   Death (R) and (S);
–   Commencement of a (new) job (R) and (S);
–   Failure to contact the agency/service (R) and (S);
–   Inability to work (R) and (S).

6. Definition of unemployed persons used for the statistics
(i) Unemployed persons who have worked previously, who have the ability and desire to work and who are seeking work;
(ii) Newcomers to the labour market, who have not worked before, who have the ability and desire to work and who are seeking work;
(iii) Persons already working, but who a looking for a better job, either because their job does not suit them, or does not satisfy them economically or for any other reason.

7. Updating of the registers
The registers are updated monthly.

8. Unemployment rates
Statistics from the registers are used to obtain unemployment rates.
The sources of data on employed persons who are part of the denominator of the unemployment rates are the Labour Force Survey and the Population Census.
Definition of employed persons for this purpose:
Persons who work in an economic activity.

9. Type of statistics of unemployed persons produced
Reference period: Month.
Frequency of production: Quarterly; Yearly.
Descriptive variables used:
–   Sex;
–   Educational level;
–   Occupation;
–   Industry;
–   Geographic characteristics;
–   Previous work experience;
–   Citizenship (nationals/non nationals).
Form of publication:
–   On paper, for limited audience;
–   Machine-readable form, on request;
–   On the website of the Ministry of Manpower and Migration.
Agency responsible for publication: Ministry of Manpower and Migration.
Periodicity of publication: Quarterly; Yearly.

10. Methodological information about the statistics
Form of release:
–   In machine-readable form, on request;
–   On the website of the Ministry of Manpower and Migration.
Agency responsible for the release: Ministry of Manpower and Migration

11. Comparisons with unemployment statistics from other sources
Comparisons have been made with unemployment statistics from the Labour Force Survey and the Population Census.
Frequency of the comparisons: Occasionally.
Publication of the methodology/results of the comparisons: These have not been published.

12. Major changes since the start of the statistics
There have been no major changes in legislation, capacity of the agency and/or administrative procedures which had a significant influence on the statistics.

El Salvador

1. Series
Title: 1. Number of registered persons.
             2. Number of placements.
             3. Number of vacancies.
Starting year: 1998.

2. Agency making the initial registrations of unemployed persons
Name of the agency: Departamento Nacional del Empleo (National Employment Department)
Type of agency: Public service under a national authority.
Name of the national authority: Ministerio de Trabajo y Previsión social (Ministry of Labour and Social Affairs).
Location of the local offices making the registrations: San Salvador; Santa Ana; Sonsonate; Zacatecoluca; San Miguel and La Unión.
Type of services provided/administered by the agency:
–   Assisting job-seekers to find jobs;
–   Assisting employers to find workers;
–   Vocational guidance;
–   Job-related training;
–   Other: specific services for working minors; employment promotion through apprenticeship.
Percentage of job-seekers seeking work through the agency: 15%.

3. The following information is registered about a person:
–   Name;
–   Sex;
–   Social security number (or similar identification number also used by other agencies);
–   Address of usual residence;
–   Date of birth;
–   Nationality/ethnic group;
–   Educational/vocational attainment, with five categories distinguished. Links to ISCED have not been established;
–   Current/past activity status, with three categories distinguished;
–   Type of work (occupation) of past or present job with 10 categories distinguished. Links to ISCO-88 have been established;
–   Type of work (occupation) of job sought, with 10 categories distinguished;
–   Name and address of present or previous employer or work place;
–   Type of business (industry) of present/previous employer/workplace, with 10 categories distinguished. Links to ISIC, rev.3 have not been established.

4. Criteria used for inclusion of a person in the registers (R) and/or the statistics of unemployed persons (S):
–   Being without work (R) and (S);
–   Seeking work (R) and (S);
–   Availability for work (R) and (S);
–   Age (lower limit: 18 years; upper limit: 35 years) (R) and (S);
–   Previously employed (R).

5. Criteria used for exclusion of a person from the registers (R) and/or the statistics of unemployed persons (S):
Not specified.

6. Definition of unemployed persons used for the statistics
Information not available.

7. Updating of the registers
The registers are updated yearly.

8. Unemployment rates
Statistics from the registers are used to obtain unemployment rates.

9. Type of statistics of unemployed persons produced
1. Number of job-seekers registered with the Employment Department.
2. Number of placements.
3. Number of vacancies filled by employers.
Reference period: Month.
Frequency of production: Monthly.
Descriptive variables used:
–   Sex;
–   Age;
–   Educational level;
–   Occupation;
–   Industry.
Form of publication:
–   On paper, for general audience;
–   On a website: www.mtps.gob.sv.
Agency responsible for publication: Ministerio de Trabajo y Previsión social (Ministry of Labour and Social Affairs).
Periodicity of the publication: Monthly.

10. Methodological information about the statistics
Form of release: On paper, for limited audience.

Agency responsible for the release: Ministerio de Trabajo y Previsión social (Ministry of Labour and Social Affairs).

11. Comparisons with unemployment statistics from other sources

Comparisons have not been made with unemployment statistics from other sources.

12. Major changes since the start of the statistics

There have been no major changes in legislation, capacity of the agency and/or administrative procedures which had a significant influence on the statistics.

Estonia

1. Series
Title: Registered unemployment.
Starting year: 1993

2. Agency making the initial registrations of unemployed persons
Name of the agency: Tööhõiveamet (Employment Office).
Type of agency: Public service under a national authority.
Name of the national authority: Labour Market Board (under the Ministry of Social Affairs).
Location of the local offices making the registrations: In all 15 counties, plus one in Tallinn (36 local offices or their representatives throughout the country).
Type of services provided/administered by the agency:
– Giving information on situation in labour market and possibilities of employment training;
– Employment mediation;
– Employment training;
– Employment subsidy to start business;
– Employment subsidy to employers;
– Community placements;
– Vocational guidance;
– Paying unemployment compensation;
– Other: special programmes for disadvantaged groups (disabled, young and long-term unemployed).
Percentage of job-seekers seeking work through the agency: 55%.

3. The following information is registered about a person:
– Name;
– Sex;
– Personal identification code;
– Address of usual residence;
– Date of birth;
– Citizenship;
– Educational/vocational attainment, with 13 categories distinguished. Links to ISCED are planned;
– Activity status, with 9 categories distinguished;
– Occupation of past job, with 9 categories distinguished. Links to ISCO-88 have been established (unit group level);
– Occupation of job sought, with 9 categories distinguished. Links to ISCO-88 have been established (unit group level);
– Type of economic activity of previous employer/ workplace, with 16 categories distinguished. Links to ISIC, rev.3 or NACE, rev.1 have been established (class level);
– Other: estonian-speaking; russian-speaking.

4. Criteria used for inclusion of a person in the registers (R) and/or the statistics of unemployed persons (S):

A person shall be registered as unemployed with an employment office if he or she applies to the employment office and submits all the necessary documents pursuant to the procedure established by the Government of the Republic. Criteria:
– Being without work (S);
– Seeking work (S);
– Availability for work (S);
– Age (lower limit: 16 years; upper limit: pension age) (S);
– Being permanently resident in the country (S).

5. Criteria used for exclusion of a person from the registers (R) and/or the statistics of unemployed persons (S):
– Death (S);
– Taking up residency abroad (S);
– Commencement of a (new) job (S);
– Commencement of military service (S);
– Studying in daytime or full-time study at an educational institution (S);
– Stops seeking work for more than thirty days (S);
– Refusal of 2 suitable job offers (S);

– Refusal of 2 suitable training offers (S);
– Attains the pensionable age or is granted an early-retirement pension (S);
– Inability to work (S);
– Other: termination of employment training without the consent of the Employment Office (S); receipt of employment subsidy (S).

6. Definition of unemployed persons used for the statistics

The registered unemployed person is a person with total or partial capacity for work who has attained at least 16 years of age and is under pensionable age, who is not employed, is ready to commence work immediately and seeks employment. A person seeks employment if he or she reports to an employment office at least once within thirty days, is willing to commence work immediately and is ready to participate in employment training [Source: "Social Protection of the Unemployed Act", ' 3] (http://www.tta.ee/english/law).

7. Updating of the registers

There is no central register for the whole country (one is under preparation). Every county has a database, which is updated regularly.

8. Unemployment rates

Statistics of employment offices are not used to obtain unemployment rates. Unemployment rates are calculated on the basis of Labour Force Survey data, according to the !LO methods. The Labour Market Board calculates the unemployment rate as the share of registered unemployed from working age people (16 - pension age), not from the labour force.**9. Type of statistics of unemployed persons produced**

Series 1:
Reference period: Month
Frequency of production: Monthly.
Descriptive variables used:
– Sex;
– Age group (3);
– Educational level (4);
– Geographic characteristics (county);
– Other: estonian-speaking; russian-speaking; participation in employment services; number of new entrances; number of vacancies; number of placements; share of registered unemployed from working age people; number of unemployed receiving unemployment benefit.
Form of publication:
– On paper;
– For limited audience (by e-mail);
– On a website (http://www.tta.ee).
Agency responsible for publication: Statistical Office of Estonia.
Title and periodicity of the publication: *Estonian Statistics Monthly.*

Series 2:
Reference period: Quarter.
Frequency of production: Quarterly.
Descriptive variables used:
– Sex;
– Age;
– Educational level;
– Occupation;
– Economic activity;
– Geographic characteristics (county and municipality);
– Previous work experience;
– Duration of unemployment;
– Other: estonian-speaking; russian-speaking.
Form of publication:
– On paper (only partly at present, because the register is not yet ready);
– For limited audience (by e-mail).

10. Methodological information about the statistics
Form of release:
– On paper, for general audience;
– On a website (http://www.tta.ee).
Agency responsible for the release: Labour Market Board.

11. Comparisons with unemployment statistics from other sources

Comparisons have been made mainly with unemployment statistics from the Labour Force Survey, but also from a household survey and the Population Census.
Frequency of the comparisons: Regularly when the statistics are published.

Publication of the methodology/results of the comparisons:
These have been published in the following publications:

- *Estonian Labour Market and Labour Market Policy* (Articles, ed. by Raul Eamets), Viljandi-Tartu, 1999;
- Estonian Employment Action Plans for 2000 IVq - 2001, 2002 and 2003;
- *Eesti tööturu areng üleminekuperioodil* (Eamets, R., Philips, K.), Tartu, 1999;
- *Estonian Statistics Monthly* (Estonian Statistical Office).

12. Major changes since the start of the statistics

Major changes to legislation, capacity of the agency and/or administrative procedures which had a significant influence on the statistics took place in: (i) 1995, when the first Social Protection of the Unemployed Act came into force, the resulting effects on the statistics have not been estimated; and (ii) 2000, when the new Social Protection of the Unemployed Act and the Employment Service Act entered into force, which resulted in an increase of 17 percent in the number of persons registered as unemployed.

Ethiopia

1. Series
Title: Employment Exchange Statistics.
Starting year: 1961.
2. Agency making the initial registrations of unemployed persons
Name of the agency: Bureau of Labour and Social Affairs.
Type of agency: Public service under national and regional authorities.
Name of the national authority: Ministry of Labour and Social Affairs.
Location of the local offices making the registrations: In all public employment offices in different regional states and city administrations.
Type of services provided/administered by the agency:
- Assisting job-seekers to find jobs;
- Assisting employers to find workers;
- Vocational guidance (partial responsibility);
- Job-related training (partial responsibility).

3. The following information is registered about a person:
- Name;
- Sex;
- Address of usual residence;
- Date of birth;
- Educational/vocational attainment, with an unspecified number of categories distinguished. Links to ISCED have been established;
- Current/past activity status, with an unspecified number of categories distinguished;
- Type of work (occupation) of past or present job with 5 groups distinguished;
- Previous registrations with the agency/service.

4. Criteria used for inclusion of a person in the registers (R) and/or the statistics of unemployed persons (S):
- Being without work (R) and (S);
- Seeking work (R) and (S);
- Availability for work (R) and (S);
- Age (lower limit: 18 years; upper limit: 55 years) (R) and (S);
- Being resident in the country (R) and (S);
- Previously employed (R) and (S).

5. Criteria used for exclusion of a person from the registers (R) and/or the statistics of unemployed persons (S):
Information not available.

6. Definition of unemployed persons used for the statistics
Information not available.

7. Updating of the registers
The registers are not updated regularly.

8. Unemployment rates
Statistics from the registers are not used to obtain unemployment rates.

9. Type of statistics of unemployed persons produced
Reference period: Year.
Frequency of production: Yearly.
Descriptive variables used:
- Sex;
- Age;
- Educational level;
- Occupation;
- Geographic characteristics;
- Duration of unemployment.

Form of publication: On paper, for general audience.
Agency responsible for publication: Ministry of Labour and Social Affairs.
Title of the publications: *Employment Exchange Information*; *Labour Statistics Bulletin*.
10. Methodological information about the statistics
Form of release: On paper, for general audience.
Agency responsible for the release: Ministry of Labour and Social Affairs.
11. Comparisons with unemployment statistics from other sources
Comparisons have not been made with unemployment statistics from other sources.
12. Major changes since the start of the statistics
Major changes in legislation, capacity of the agency and/or administrative procedures took place in:
1975: The resulting changes in the statistics were not estimated; and
(ii)1993: Resulting in a decrease of 25-30% in the total number of persons registered as unemployed.

Finland

1. Series
Title: Employment Service statistics.
Starting year: 1991.
2. Agency making the initial registrations of unemployed persons
Name of the agency: Employment Offices.
Type of agency: Public service under national, regional and local authorities.
Name of the national authority: Ministry of Labour.
Location of the local offices making the registrations: 175 employment offices cover the whole country.
Type of services provided/administered by the agency:
- Assisting job-seekers to find jobs;
- Assisting job-seekers to establish their own business;
- Assisting employers to find workers;
- Vocational guidance;
- Job-related training;
- Paying unemployment compensation;
- Other: labour market training.

3. The following information is registered about a person:
- Name;
- Sex;
- Social security number (or similar identification number also used by other agencies);
- Date of birth;
- Citizenship;
- Nationality/ethnic group;
- Educational/vocational attainment, with 5 - 6 categories distinguished. Links to ISCED have been established;
- Current/past activity status, with 14 categories distinguished;
- Type of work (occupation) of past or present job with 3300 categories distinguished. Links to ISCO-88 have not been established;
- Type of work (occupation) of job sought, with 3300 categories distinguished. Links to ISCO-88 have not been established;
- Type of business (industry) of present/previous employer/workplace. No links to either ISIC, rev.3 or NACE, rev.1 have been established;
- Previous registrations with the agency/service;
- Other: registration code for employment.

4. Criteria used for inclusion of a person in the registers (R) and/or the statistics of unemployed persons (S):
- Being without work (R) and (S);
- Seeking work (R) and (S);
- Availability for work (R) and (S);
- Age (lower limit: 17 years; upper limit: 65 years) (R) and (S);
- Citizenship (R) and (S);
- Being resident in the country (R) and (S);
- Desired duration of employment and/or number of hours of work sought (R) and (S).

5. Criteria used for exclusion of a person from the registers (R) and/or the statistics of unemployed persons (S):

- Death (R) and (S);
- Taking up residency abroad (R) and (S);
- Commencement of a (new) job (R) and (S);
- Commencement of military service (R) and (S);
- Participation in an employment promotion scheme, public works programme, etc. (R) and (S);
- Studying or undergoing training (R) and (S);
- Failure to contact the agency/service (R) and (S);
- Refusal of one suitable job offer (R) and (S);
- Refusal of one suitable training offer (R) and (S);
- End of entitlement to receive unemployment compensation (R) and (S);
- Receipt of a pension (R) and (S);
- Inability to work (R) and (S).

6. Definition of unemployed persons used for the statistics

All registered job-seekers who are without work and are available for full-time work (defined as work for which the working time is at least half of the normal working time) or have arranged to start a job, but have not yet started it, are unemployed. A job-seeker who can accept a job offered to him/her only after a fixed period or who is seeking only work for which the working time is less than half of the normal working time in the sector is not regarded as an unemployed job-seeker. Full-time students are not recorded as unemployed job-seekers even during holidays.

7. Updating of the registers

The registers are updated monthly.

8. Unemployment rates

Statistics from the registers are used to obtain unemployment rates.

The source of data on employed persons who are part of the denominator of the unemployment rates is the Labour Force Survey.

9. Type of statistics of unemployed persons produced

Series: Employment Service statistics.
Reference period: Month.
Frequency of production: Monthly.
Descriptive variables used:

- Sex;
- Age;
- Educational level;
- Occupation;
- Industry;
- Geographic characteristics;
- Previous work experience;
- Citizenship (nationals/non nationals);
- Duration of unemployment.

Form of publication:

- On paper, for general audience;
- Machine-readable form, on request;
- On a website.

Agency responsible for publication: Ministry of Labour.

10. Methodological information about the statistics

Form of release: On a website (www.mol.fi).
Agency responsible for the release: Ministry of Labour.

11. Comparisons with unemployment statistics from other sources

Comparisons have been made with unemployment statistics from the Labour Force Survey, another type of household survey and the Population Census..

Frequency of the comparisons: Occasionally (latest year: 1997).

Publication of the methodology/results of the comparisons: These have been published in *Unemployment and Employment Statistics*, Statistics Finland, Official Statistics, Labour Market 1997:3.

12. Major changes since the start of the statistics

There have been no major changes in legislation, capacity of the agency and/or administrative procedures which had a significant influence on the statistics.

France

1. Series
Title: Job-seekers.

2. Agency making the initial registrations of unemployed persons

Name of the agency: Agence nationale pour l'Emploi - ANPE (National Employment Agency).
Type of agency: Public service under a national authority.
Name of the national authority: Ministry of Social Affairs, Employment and Solidarity.
Location of the local offices making the registrations: 741 local agencies throughout the country.
Type of services provided/administered by the agency:

- Assisting job-seekers to find jobs;
- Assisting job-seekers to establish their own business;
- Assisting employers to find workers;
- Vocational guidance;
- Assisting employees to find another job.

Percentage of job seekers seeking work through the agency: 100%.

3. The following information is registered about a person:

- Name;
- Sex;
- Address of usual residence;
- Date of birth;
- Nationality;
- Educational/vocational attainment, with 152 categories distinguished. Links to ISCED have not been established;
- Type of business or workplace of present or previous employer, with 75 categories distinguished;
- Previous registrations with the agency;
- Other: category (see point six); qualifications; handicap.

4. Criteria used for inclusion of a person in the registers (R) and/or the statistics of unemployed persons (S):

- Any person, who so wishes, may be registered with the ANPE (including employed persons). Depending on his/her situation in respect to the following criteria (being without work, looking for a job, availability for work, being employed), he/she will be allocated to a particular register (8 categories, see under paragraph 6 below the different definitions). Registration is mandatory for job-seekers receiving indemnities.
- Age: Lower limit: 16 years (R) and (S);
- Being resident in the country (R) and (S);
- Desired duration of employment and/or number of hours of work sought: if the person is seeking part-time employment, he/she will be classified in categories 2 or 7.

5. Criteria used for exclusion of a person from the registers (R) and/or the statistics of unemployed persons (S):

- Death (R) and (S);
- Taking up residency abroad (R) and (S);
- Commencement of a (new) job, depending on the case: if the person is classified in categories 5, 6, 7 or 8, it is possible to combine a reduced activity and registration with the ANPE;
- Commencement of military service (R) and (S);
- Failure to contact the agency/service (R) and (S);
- Refusal of suitable job offers (R) and (S);
- Refusal of suitable training offers (R) and (S);
- False declaration (R) and (S);
- Inability to work (R) and (S).

6. Definition of unemployed persons used for the statistics

Category 1: Unemployed persons, immediately available for work according to Article R.311-3-3, required to actively look for employment, *looking for full-time employment* **of unspecified duration.**
These persons should not have carried out any casual activity or a reduced activity of more than 78 hours during the month in question.

Category 2: Unemployed persons, immediately available for work according to Article R.311-3-3, required to actively look for employment, *looking* **for part-time employment of unspecified duration.**
These persons should not have carried out any casual activity or a reduced activity of more than 78 hours during the month in question.

Category 3: Unemployed persons, immediately available for work according to Article R.311-3-3, required to actively look for employment, *looking* **for temporary or seasonal employment of specified duration,** *including very brief duration.*
These persons should not have carried out any casual activity or a reduced activity of more than 78 hours during the month in question.

Category 4: Unemployed persons, not immediately available for work, looking for employment.

Category 5: Employed persons, looking for another job.

Category 6: Persons not immediately available for work according to Article R.311-3-3 (1), required to actively look for employment, *looking for another job, full-time of unspecified duration.*
These persons will have carried out a casual or reduced activity of more than 78 hours during the month in question.
Category 7: Persons not immediately available for work according to Article R.311-3-3 (1), required to actively look for employment, *looking for another job, part-time of unspecified duration.*
These persons will have carried out a casual or reduced activity of more than 78 hours during the month in question.
Category 8: Persons not immediately available for work according to Article R.311-3-3 (1), required to actively look for employment, *looking for another job, temporary or seasonal of specified duration, including very short duration.*
These persons will have carried out a casual or reduced activity of more than 78 hours during the month in question.

7. Updating of the registers
The registers are updated monthly.

8. Unemployment rates
Unemployment rates are calculated monthly by the INSEE (Institut national de la statistique et des études économiques - National Institute of Statistics and Economical Studies), being the ratio of unemployed persons, according to the definition of the ILO, to the total economically active population.
The number of unemployed persons, according to the ILO definition, is established once a year on the basis of the labour force survey conducted by the INSEE; for the intermediary months, rates are estimated on a parametric model based on the evolution of the number of persons seeking employment registered with the ANPE. in categories 1, 2 and 3.
The economically active population is the sum of: total employment and unemployment.
The population census is the basis of the evaluation of total employment, the labour force survey and other sources allow an annual re-evaluation.

9. Type of statistics of unemployed persons produced
Reference period: Month.
Frequency of production: Monthly.
Descriptive variables used:
- Sex;
- Age;
- Educational level;
- Occupation;
- Geographic characteristics;
- Nationality;
- Duration of unemployment;
- Other: qualifications and handicap.

Form of publication:
- For internal use only (special publication for the ANPE. network);
- On paper, for general audience, on request;
- Machine-readable form, on request;
- On a website:
- http://www.travail.gouv.fr/etudes/etudes_i.html.
Agency responsible for publication: Ministry of Social Affairs, Employment and Solidarity.
Title and periodicity of the publication: *Premières informations* (First information).

10. Methodological information about the statistics
Form of release: In machine-readable form, on request.
Agency responsible: Ministry of Social Affairs, Employment and Solidarity in respect of the number of persons registered with the ANPE; INSEE in respect of the "ILO unemployed".

11. Comparisons with unemployment statistics from other sources
Comparisons have been made with unemployment statistics from the labour force survey and the population census.
Publication of the methodology/Results of the comparisons: These are available on the following website: http://www.insee.fr/fr/indic/indic_conj/donnees/chomrev.pdf.

12. Major changes since the start of the statistics
There have been no major changes in legislation, capacity of the agency and/or administrative procedures which had a significant influence on the statistics; however, there was a reform of the categories in 1995.

French Polynesia

1. Series
Title: Job-seekers.
Starting year: 1990.

2. Agency making the initial registrations of unemployed persons
Name of the agency: Service de l'Emploi, de la Formation et de l'Insertion professionnelle (Employment, Training and Professional Integration Service).
Type of agency: Public service under a local authority: Territorial Public Service, under the authority of the Government of French Polynesia.
Location of the local offices making the registrations: Papeete, chief town, as well as a local office in Uturoa-Raiatea, chief town of the archipelago.
Type of services provided/administered by the agency:
- Assisting job-seekers to find jobs;
- Assisting employers to find workers;
- Vocational guidance;
- Job-related training;
- Other: establishing contacts between job requests and job offers, inciting employers to hire; proposing training and integration possibilities to job seekers.

3. The following information is registered about a person:
- Name;
- Sex;
- Social security number (or similar identification number also used by other agencies);
- Address of usual residence;
- Date of birth;
- Educational/vocational attainment;
- Current/past activity status;
- Type of work (occupation) of past or present job. Links to ISCO have not been established;
- Type of work (occupation) of job sought;
- Previous registrations with the agency/service.

4. Criteria used for inclusion of a person in the registers (R) and/or the statistics of unemployed persons (S):
- Being without work (R) and (S);
- Seeking work (R) and (S);
- Availability for work (R) and (S);
- Age (lower limit: 16 years; no upper age limit) (R) and (S).

5. Criteria used for exclusion of a person from the registers (R) and/or the statistics of unemployed persons (S):
- Commencement of a (new) job (R) and (S);
- Studying or undergoing training (R) and (S);
- Failure to contact the agency/service: date of validity passed (R) and (S).

6. Definition of unemployed persons used for the statistics
Statistics based on the registers are not statistics of the number of unemployed, but statistics on the number of registered job-seekers.

7. Updating of the registers
The registers are updated regularly on a continuous basis.

8. Unemployment rates
Statistics from the registers are not used to obtain unemployment rates.

9. Type of statistics of unemployed persons produced
Information not available.

10. Methodological information about the statistics
Information not available.

11. Comparisons with unemployment statistics from other sources
Comparisons have not been made with unemployment statistics from other sources.

12. Major changes since the start of the statistics
There have been no major changes in legislation, capacity of the agency and/or administrative procedures which had a significant influence on the statistics.

Gabon

1. Series
Title: Activity Report of the National Employment Office.
Starting year: 1994.

2. Agency making the initial registrations of unemployed persons
Name of the agency: Office national de l'Emploi - ONE (National Employment Office).
Type of agency: Public service under a national authority.
Name of the national authority: Ministry of Labour, Employment and Vocational Training.
Location of the local offices making the registrations: Libreville and Port-Gentil.
Type of services provided/administered by the agency:
- Assisting job-seekers to find jobs;
- Assisting job-seekers to establish their own business;
- Assisting employers to find workers;
- Job-related training.

Percentage of job-seekers seeking work through the agency: 34%.

3. The following information is registered about a person:
- Name;
- Sex;
- Address of usual residence;
- Date of birth;
- Citizenship;
- Educational/vocational attainment, with four categories distinguished. Links to ISCED have not been established;
- Current/past activity status, with three categories distinguished;
- Type of work (occupation) of past or present job with four categories distinguished. Links to ISCO have not been established;
- Type of work (occupation) of job sought, with four categories distinguished;
- Name and address of present or previous employer or work place;
- Type of business (industry) of present/previous employer/workplace, with 60 categories distinguished. Links to ISIC have not been established;
- Type of diplomas obtained, type of training.

4. Criteria used for inclusion of a person in the registers (R) and/or the statistics of unemployed persons (S):
- Being without work (R);
- Seeking work (R);
- Availability for work (R);
- Age (lower limit: 16 years; upper limit: 65 years) (R).

5. Criteria used for exclusion of a person from the registers (R) and/or the statistics of unemployed persons (S):
- Death (R);
- Taking up residency abroad (R);
- Commencement of a (new) job (R);
- Commencement of military service (R);
- Participation in an employment promotion scheme, public works programme, etc (R);
- Studying or undergoing training (R);
- Failure to contact the agency/service (R);
- Receipt of a pension (retirement, etc) (R);
- Inability to work (R).

6. Definition of unemployed persons used for the statistics
Not applicable.

7. Updating of the registers
The registers are updated daily.

8. - 12. Not applicable. The ONE is not in charge of producing unemployment statistics. This is the responsibility of other public administrations.

Germany

1. Series
Title: Registered unemployment.
Starting year: Not specified.
2. Agency making the initial registrations of unemployed persons
Name of the agency: Bundesanstalt für Arbeit (Federal Labour Office).
Type of agency: Public service under a national authority.
Name of the national authority: Bundesministerium für Wirtschaft und Arbeit (Ministry of Economy and Labour).
Location of the local offices making the registrations: In all parts of the country.

Type of services provided/administered by the agency:
- Assisting job-seekers to find jobs;
- Assisting job-seekers to establish their own business;
- Assisting employers to find workers;
- Vocational guidance;
- Job-related training;
- Paying unemployment compensation.

Percentage of job-seekers seeking work through the agency: This varies between regions.

3. The following information is registered about a person:
- Name;
- Sex;
- Social security number (or similar identification number also used by other agencies);
- Address of usual residence;
- Date of birth;
- Citizenship;
- Nationality/ethnic group;
- Educational/vocational attainment, with 5 categories distinguished. Links to ISCED have not been established;
- Past activity status, with 5 categories distinguished;
- Type of work (occupation) of past or present job with an unspecified number of groups distinguished. Links to ISCO-88 have been established;
- Type of work (occupation) of job sought, with an unspecified number of groups distinguished. Links to ISCO-88 have been established;
- Type of business (industry) of present/previous employer/workplace, with an unspecified number of groups distinguished. Links to ISIC, rev.3 or NACE, rev.1 have been established (group level).

4. Criteria used for inclusion of a person in the registers (R)* and/or the statistics of unemployed persons (S):
- Being without work (S);
- Seeking work (S);
- Availability for work (S);
- Age (lower limit: 15 years; upper limit: 65 years) (S);
- Citizenship (S);
- Being resident in the country (S);
- Desired duration of employment and/or number of hours of work sought (minimum 15 hours a week) (S).

*Applicants can be listed as unemployed or as non-unemployed job-seekers.

5. Criteria used for exclusion of a person from the registers (R) and/or the statistics of unemployed persons (S):
- Death (R) and (S);
- Commencement of a (new) job (S);
- Commencement of military service (S);
- Participation in an employment promotion scheme, public works programme, etc. (S);
- Studying or undergoing training (S);
- Failure to contact the agency/service (S);
- Refusal of an unspecified number of suitable job offers (S);
- Refusal of an unspecified number of suitable training offers (S);
- Receipt of a pension (S);
- Inability to work (due to illness; maternity leave; cure, etc.) (S).

6. Definition of unemployed persons used for the statistics
Unemployed persons are those who:
- are temporarily not in an employment relationship;
- are seeking a compulsorily insured employment;
- are available for an Employment Office placement;
- are reported as being unemployed at the Employment Office;
- are not more than 65 years old and
- are not unable to work due to sickness.

In order to be counted as unemployed in the statistics all the criteria must be satisfied simultaneously.

7. Updating of the registers
The registers (statistics) are updated monthly.

8. Unemployment rates
Statistics from the registers are used to obtain unemployment rates.

The sources of data on employed persons who are part of the denominator of the unemployment rates are Federal Labour Office employment and unemployment statistics and public service personnel statistics.

Definition of employed persons for this purpose:
- Civilian employees;

– All civilian economically active persons.

9. Type of statistics of unemployed persons produced
Reference period: Month.
Frequency of production: Monthly.
Descriptive variables used:
– Sex;
– Age;
– Educational level;
– Occupation;
– Industry;
– Geographic characteristics;
– Previous work experience;
– Citizenship (nationals/non nationals);
– Duration of unemployment.

Form of publication:
– On paper, for general audience;
– On a website (www.arbeitsamt.de).

Agency responsible for publication: Bundesanstalt für Arbeit (Federal Labour Office).
Title and periodicity of the publication: *Amtliche Nachrichten der Bundesanstalt für Arbeit (ANBA)*, monthly.

10. Methodological information about the statistics
Form of release: On paper, for general audience;
Agency responsible for the release: Bundesanstalt für Arbeit (Federal Labour Office).

11. Comparisons with unemployment statistics from other sources
Comparisons have been made with unemployment statistics from the Labour Force Survey.

12. Major changes since the start of the statistics
There have been no major changes in legislation, capacity of the agency and/or administrative procedures which had a significant influence on the statistics.

Ghana

1. Series
Title: Registered unemployment.
Starting year: 1956.

2. Agency making the initial registrations of unemployed persons
Name of the agency: Public Employment Centres of the Labour Department.
Type of agency: Public service under a national authority.
Name of the national authority: Labour Department, under the Ministry of Manpower, Development and Employment.
Location of the local offices making the registrations: In 66 of the most urbanized centres in the country.
Type of services provided/administered by the agency:
– Assisting job-seekers to find jobs;
– Assisting employers to find workers;
– Vocational guidance;
– Other: administration of workmen's compensation and labour complaints; settlement of industrial disputes.

3. The following information is registered about a person:
– Name;
– Sex;
– Address of usual residence;
– Date of birth;
– Citizenship;
– Nationality/ethnic group;
– Educational/vocational attainment, with three categories distinguished. Links to ISCED have been established;
– Current/past activity status;
– Type of work (occupation) of past or present job with eight groups distinguished. Links to ISCO-88 have been established (major groups level);
– Type of work (occupation) of job sought, with 8 groups distinguished. Links to ISCO-88 have been established (major groups level);
– Name and address of present or previous employer or work place;
– Type of business (industry) of present/previous employer/workplace, with 9 groups distinguished. Links to ISIC, rev.3 have been established (major groups level);
– Previous registrations with the agency/service.

4. Criteria used for inclusion of a person in the registers (R) and/or the statistics of unemployed persons (S):
– Being without work (R) and (S);
– Seeking work (R) and (S);
– Availability for work (R) and (S);
– Age (lower limit: 15 years; upper limit: 55 years) (R) and (S);
– Citizenship (R) and (S);
– Being resident in the country (R) and (S);
– Previously employed (R) and (S);
– Other: physical appearance (R).

5. Criteria used for exclusion of a person from the registers (R) and/or the statistics of unemployed persons (S):
– Death (R) and (S);
– Commencement of a (new) job (R) and (S);
– Failure to contact the agency/service (R) and (S).

6. Definition of unemployed persons used for the statistics
Persons with or without job training/education who fall between the ages of 15 to 55 years, are seeking work and are available for work by reporting regularly to any of the Public Employment Centres in the country.

7. Updating of the registers
The registers are updated quarterly.

8. Unemployment rates
Statistics from the registers are not used to obtain unemployment rates.

9. Type of statistics of unemployed persons produced
Reference period: Quarter.
Frequency of production: Quarterly.
Descriptive variables used:
– Sex;
– Age;
– Educational level;
– Occupation;
– Industry;
– Geographic characteristics;
– Previous work experience;
– Citizenship (nationals/non nationals);
– Duration of unemployment;
– Other: physical characteristics.

Form of publication: On paper, for general audience.
Agency responsible for publication: Labour Department (Employment Information Branch).
Title and periodicity of the publication(s): *Employment Market Report*, quarterly.

10. Methodological information about the statistics
Agency responsible: Labour Department (Employment Information Branch).

11. Comparisons with unemployment statistics from other sources
Comparisons have not been made with unemployment statistics from other sources.

12. Major changes since the start of the statistics
Up to now there have been no major changes in legislation, capacity of the agency and/or administrative procedures which had a significant influence on the statistics; however, a new labour law is in preparation which is expected to influence the statistics.

Greenland

1. Series
Title: Registered unemployment statistics.
Starting year: 1988.

2. Agency making the initial registrations of unemployed persons
Name of the agency: Registrations are made by local authorities (Kommuner) and collected by Statistics Greenland.
Type of agency: Public service under local authorities.
Location of the local offices making the registrations: In all parts of the country (in the regional capitals).
Type of services provided/administered by the agency:
– Assisting job-seekers to find jobs;
– Assisting job-seekers to establish their own business;
– Assisting employers to find workers;
– Vocational guidance;
– Job-related training;
– Paying unemployment compensation.
–

3. **The following information is registered about a person**:
- Name;
- Sex (indirectly through Social security number);
- Social security number;
- Address of usual residence;
- Date of birth;
- Citizenship.
- Educational/vocational attainment. Links to ISCED have been established;
- Previous registrations with the agency/service.

4. **Criteria used for inclusion of a person in the registers (R) and/or the statistics of unemployed persons (S):**
- Being without work (R) and (S);
- Availability for work (R);
- Age (lower limit: 16 years; upper limit: 61 years) (S);
- Citizenship (R) and (S);
- Being resident in the country (R) and (S).

5. **Criteria used for exclusion of a person from the registers (R) and/or the statistics of unemployed persons (S):**
- Failure to contact the agency/service.

6. **Definition of unemployed persons used for the statistics**
Persons who register as unemployed with the local authorities. To be registered as unemployed persons must be between 15 and 62 years and not included in other social categories, such as retirees, must be willing to accept job offers and must not be employed at the time of registration.

7. **Updating of the registers**
The registers are updated monthly.

8. **Unemployment rates**
Statistics from the registers are used to obtain unemployment rates.
The source of data on employed persons who are part of the denominator of the unemployment rates is the Population Census.
Definition of employed persons for this purpose:
All persons between 15 and 62 years, i.e. the potential labour force (at present there is no exact registration of the actual labour force).

9. **Type of statistics of unemployed persons produced**
Series 1:
Reference period: Quarter.
Frequency of production: Quarterly.
Descriptive variables used:
- Sex (indirectly through Social security number);
- Age (indirectly through Social security number);
- Educational level;
- Geographic characteristics.
Form of publication:
- On paper, for general audience;
- On a website (www.statgreen.gl).
Agency responsible for publication: Statistics Greenland.
Title and periodicity of the publication: *Ledigheden* [Period], quarterly.
Series 2:
Reference period: Half-year.
Frequency of production: Half-yearly.
Descriptive variables used:
- Sex (indirectly through Social security number);
- Age (indirectly through Social security number);
- Educational level;
- Geographic characteristics.
Form of publication:
- On paper, for general audience;
- On a website (www.statgreen.gl).
Agency responsible for publication: Statistics Greenland.
Title and periodicity of the publication: *Ledigheden* [Period], quarterly.
Series 3:
Reference period: Year.
Frequency of production: Yearly.
Descriptive variables used:
- Sex (indirectly through Social security number);
- Age (indirectly through Social security number);
- Educational level;
- Geographic characteristics.
Form of publication:
- On paper, for general audience;
- On a website (www.statgreen.gl).

Agency responsible for publication: Statistics Greenland
Title and periodicity of the publication(s): *Ledigheden* [Period], quarterly.

10. **Methodological information about the statistics**
Form of release: On paper, for general audience.
Agency responsible for the release: Statistics Greenland.

11. **Comparisons with unemployment statistics from other sources**
Comparisons have not been made with unemployment statistics from other sources.

12. **Major changes since the start of the statistics**
Major changes in legislation, capacity of the agency and/or administrative procedures took place in 2000, resulting in a decrease of 0.5 percent in the number of persons registered as unemployed.

Guatemala

1. **Series**
Title: Registered persons.
Starting year: 1989.

2. **Agency making the initial registrations of unemployed persons**
Name of the agency: Departamento del Servicio Nacional del Empleo (National Employment Service Department).
Type of agency: Public service under a national authority.
Name of the national authority: Ministerio de Trabajo y Previsión Social (Ministry of Labour and Social Provident).
Location of the local offices making the registrations: In the 22 districts of the country and in three municipal offices (El Carmen, Tecun Umán and Coatepeque).
Type of services provided/administered by the agency:
- Assisting job-seekers to find jobs;
- Assisting job-seekers to establish their own business;
- Assisting employers to find workers;
- Vocational guidance;
- Job-related training.
Percentage of job-seekers seeking work through the agency: 10%.

3. **The following information is registered about a person:**
- Name;
- Sex;
- Age and date of birth;
- Social security number (or similar identification number also used by other agencies);
- Address of usual residence;
- Educational/vocational attainment, with four categories distinguished. Links to ISCED have not been established;
- Current/past activity status, with five categories distinguished;
- Type of work (occupation) of past or present job with three categories distinguished. Links to ISCO-88 have been established (major groups level);
- Type of work (occupation) of job sought, with three categories distinguished. Links to ISCO-88 have been established (major groups level);
- Type of business (industry) of present/previous employer/workplace, with two categories distinguished. Links to ISIC-rev.3 have not been established;
- Maya languages, with categories distinguished such as: spoken, written, translation;
- If the person is a minor, the following is registered: number of the birth certificate; number of the family record book; folio; identity document.

4. **Criteria used for inclusion of a person in the registers (R) and/or the statistics of unemployed persons (S):**
- Being without work (R) and (S);
- Seeking work (R) and (S);
- Availability for work (R);
- Age (lower limit: 14 years; no upper age limit) (R);
- Citizenship (R);
- Being resident in the country (R);
- Desired duration of employment and/or number of hours of work sought (R).

5. **Criteria used for exclusion of a person from the registers (R) and/or the statistics of unemployed persons (S):**
- Death (R);
- Commencement of a (new) job (R);
- Failure to contact the agency/service (the employment search

is kept active for six months, and then becomes inactive; after that, the person has to report to the agency to reactivate the search) (R);
- Other: lack of identity documents (R).

6. Definition of unemployed persons used for the statistics
Persons who have declared that they are without work, who have no income, have completed the request form for a work interview with all the necessary information, have received the appropriate vocational guidance and have presented either an identity card, or a birth certificate, as well as the basic documents requested.

7. Updating of the registers
The registers are updated monthly.

8. Unemployment rates
Statistics from the registers are not used to obtain unemployment rates.

9. Type of statistics of unemployed persons produced
Reference period: Year.
Frequency of production: Monthly.
Descriptive variables used:
- Number of registered persons.

Form of publication: On paper, for general audience.
Agency responsible for publication: Ministerio de Trabajo y Previsión Social (Ministry of Labour and Social Affairs).
Title and periodicity of the publication: *Boletín de Estadísticas del Trabajo* (Bulletin of Labour Statistics), yearly.

10. Methodological information about the statistics
Form of release: On paper, for general audience.
Agency responsible for the release: Departamento de Estadísticas del Trabajo, Ministerio de Trabajo y Previsión Social (Labour Statistics Department, Ministry of Labour and Social Affairs).

11. Comparisons with unemployment statistics from other sources
Comparisons have not been made with unemployment statistics from other sources.

12. Major changes since the start of the statistics
There have been no major changes in legislation, capacity of the agency and/or administrative procedures which had a significant influence on the statistics.

Guinea

1. Series
Title: *Annual Activity Report* and *Information Bulletin*.
Starting year: 1987.

2. Agency making the initial registrations of unemployed persons
Name of the agency: Agence guinéenne pour la Promotion de l'Emploi - AGUIPE (Guinean Agency for Employment Promotion).
Type of agency: Public service under a national authority.
Name of the national authority: Employment and Manpower Services.
Location of the local offices making the registrations: In some areas only: the capital Conakry, and the capital towns of the four natural regions.
Type of services provided/administered by the agency:
- Assisting job-seekers to find jobs;
- Assisting employers to find workers;
- Vocational guidance;
- Other: information and support to training agencies, public services and development partners.

Percentage of job-seekers seeking work through the agency: 45%

3. The following information is registered about a person:
- Name;
- Sex;
- Address of usual residence;
- Date of birth;
- Nationality/ethnic group;
- Educational/vocational attainment; Links to ISCED have been established;.
- Current/past activity status;
- Type of work (occupation) of past or present job. Links to ISCO-88 have been established at the level of the 390 unit groups;
- Type of work (occupation) of job sought;
- Name and address of present or previous employer or work place;

- Other: skills or special abilities.

4. Criteria used for inclusion of a person in the registers (R) and/or the statistics of unemployed persons (S):
- Being without work (S);
- Seeking work (S);
- Availability for work (S);
- Age (lower limit: 18 years; upper limit: 55 years) (S);
- Being resident in the country, and looking for a job within the national territory (S);
- Previously employed (S);
- Desired duration of employment and/or number of hours of work sought (minimum of 20 hours by week).

5. Criteria used for exclusion of a person from the registers (R) and/or the statistics of unemployed persons (S):
- Death (R) and (S);
- Taking up residency abroad (R) and (S);
- Commencement of a (new) job (R) and (S);
- Commencement of military service (R) and (S);
- Participation in an employment promotion scheme, public works programme, etc (R) and (S);
- Studying or undergoing training, if it is a programme of long duration (R) and (S);
- Failure to contact the agency/service by not having replied to several job summonings (R) and (S);
- Refusal of more than three suitable job offers (R) and (S);
- Refusal of more than three suitable training offers (R) and (S);
- Receipt of a pension (R) and (S);
- Inability to work, in the case of permanent disability.

6. Definition of unemployed persons used for the statistics
Any economically active person who is available for work, did not work during the reference period (seven days) for reasons other than sickness, holiday, strike, lay off or bad weather and is looking for a job must be considered as unemployed.

7. Updating of the registers
The registers are updated annually.

8. Unemployment rates
Statistics from the registers are not used to obtain unemployment rates.

9. Type of statistics of unemployed persons produced
Series 1:
Reference period: Year.
Frequency of production: Yearly.
Descriptive variables used:
- Sex;
- Age;
- Educational level;
- Occupation;
- Geographic characteristics;
- Previous work experience;
- Duration of unemployment;
- Other: job requested.

Form of publication: On paper, for general audience.
Agency responsible for publication: AGUIPE.
Title of the publication: *Rapport d'activité annuel* (Annual Activity report).
Series 2:
Reference period: Half-year.
Frequency of production: Half-yearly.
Descriptive variables used:
- Industry;
- Availability;
- Nationality;
- Reorientation.

Form of publication: On paper, for limited audience.
Agency responsible for publication: AGUIPE.
Title of the publication: *Bulletin d'information* (Information Bulletin).

10. Methodological information about the statistics
Form of release: For internal use only.
Agency responsible for the release: AGUIPE Observatory.

11. Comparisons with unemployment statistics from other sources
Comparisons have been made with unemployment statistics from the Labour Force Survey, other Households Surveys, Population Census and other statistical sources.
Frequency of the comparisons: Regularly (latest year: 2001).
Publication of the methodology/results of the comparisons: These have not been published.

12. Major changes since the start of the statistics
Major changes in legislation, capacity of the agency and/or administrative procedures took place in 1992, 1994, 1995, 1997, 1999 and 2000.

Guyana

1. Series
Title: Recruitment and placement statistics.
Starting year: 1993.
2. Agency making the initial registrations of unemployed persons
Name of the agency: Recruitment and Placement Department (Labour Exchange).
Type of agency: Public service under a national authority.
Name of the national authority: Ministry of Labour, Human Services and Social Security.
Location of the local offices making the registrations: In six out of the ten administrative regions of the country (Regions 2, 3, 4, 5, 6 and 10).
Type of services provided/administered by the agency:
– Assisting job-seekers to find jobs;
– Assisting employers to find workers;
– Vocational guidance;
– Job-related training;
Other: publication of a Labour Market Information Service Newsletter and Statistical; bulletin which are circulated widely.
Percentage of job-seekers seeking work through the agency: 20%.
3. The following information is registered about a person:
– Name;
– Sex;
– Social security number (or similar identification number also used by other agencies);
– Address of usual residence;
– Date of birth;
– Citizenship;
– Nationality/ethnic group;
– Educational/vocational attainment, with 5 categories distinguished. Links to ISCED are in the process of being established;
– Current/past activity status, with 3 categories distinguished;
– Type of work (occupation) of past or present job with 9 groups distinguished. Links to ISCO-88 are in the process of being established;
– Type of work (occupation) of job sought, with 9 groups distinguished. Links to ISCO-88 are in the process of being established;
– Name and address of present or previous employer or work place;
– Type of business (industry) of present/previous employer/workplace, with an unspecified number of groups distinguished. Links to ISIC, rev.3 are in the process of being established;
– Previous registrations with the agency/service.
4. Criteria used for inclusion of a person in the registers (R) and/or the statistics of unemployed persons (S):
– Seeking work (R) and (S);
– Availability for work (R) and (S);
– Age (lower limit: 15 years; upper limit: 60 years) (R) and (S);
– Citizenship (must be Guyanese citizen) (R) and (S);
– Being resident in the country (R) and (S).
5. Criteria used for exclusion of a person from the registers (R) and/or the statistics of unemployed persons (S):
Commencement of a (new) job (agency notified by employer) (R) and (S).
6. Definition of unemployed persons used for the statistics
A person who is actively seeking employment, cannot find work and is not presently employed in any capacity.
7. Updating of the registers
As information is received the individual Card is updated. (As the Agency is in the process of being computerized, such information is now being entered in the computer).
8. Unemployment rates
Statistics from the registers are not used to obtain unemployment rates.

9. Type of statistics of unemployed persons produced
Reference period: Year.
Frequency of production: Yearly.
Descriptive variables used:
– Geographic characteristics.
(It is planned to produce more detailed reports as from 2003).
Form of publication: On paper, for limited audience.
Agency responsible for publication: Department of Labour.
Title and periodicity of the publications: *Recruitment and Placement* (annual); *Annual Report.*
10. Methodological information about the statistics
No methodological information about the statistics is available.
11. Comparisons with unemployment statistics from other sources
Comparisons have not been made with unemployment statistics from other sources.
12. Major changes since the start of the statistics
There have been no major changes in legislation, capacity of the agency and/or administrative procedures which had a significant influence on the statistics.
13. Additional remarks
The Recruitment and Placement Department will be fully computerized by 2003.

Honduras

1. Series
Title: Register of job-seekers.
Starting year: The placement services exist since 1980; the statistical series started in 1987.
2. Agency making the initial registrations of unemployed persons
Name of the agency: Servicio de Colocación de la Dirección General de Empleo (Employment Exchange Service of the General Department of Employment).
Type of agency: Public service under a national authority, with local offices.
Name of the national authority: Labour and Social Security Department.
Location of the local offices making the registrations: In the three main cities of the country, covering the central and northern areas.
Type of services provided/administered by the agency:
– Assisting job-seekers to find jobs;
– Assisting job-seekers to establish their own business (applies only to disabled persons);
– Assisting employers to find workers;
– Vocational guidance;
– Job-related training (the employment service sends people to the Institute of Vocational Training, but does not train them directly).
Percentage of job-seekers seeking work through the agency: 3,4% of the number of urban unemployed according to the Multiple Purpose Household Survey.
3. The following information is registered about a person:
– Name;
– Sex;
– Social security number (or similar identification number also used by other agencies);
– Address of usual residence;
– Date of birth;
– Nationality;
– Educational/vocational attainment, with four categories distinguished. Links to ISCED have not been established;
– Current/past activity status, with three categories distinguished;
– Type of work (occupation) of past or present job, with three possible responses. Links to ISCO-88 have been established at the major group level (disaggregation at four digits);
– Type of work (occupation) of job sought, for which the number of possible responses varies according to the job-seeker. The most frequently it is two categories per job-seeker. Links to ISCO-88 have been established at the major group level (disaggregation at four digits);
– Name and address of immediate chief or present or previous work place;
– Previous registrations with the agency/service;

– Other: physical characteristics (size and weight); family status (number of members, children, whether head of family or not); owner of car, or not; type of driving licence; migration (local or external); disability.

4. Criteria used for inclusion of a person in the registers (R) and/or the statistics of unemployed persons (S):
– Being without work (R);
– Seeking work (R);
– Availability for work (R);
– Age (lower limit: 16 years with a minors' work permit; no upper limit) (R);
– Being resident in the country (R).

5. Criteria used for exclusion of a person from the registers (R) and/or the statistics of unemployed persons (S):
– Death (R);
– Taking up residency abroad (R);
– Commencement of a (new) job (R);
– Participation in an employment promotion scheme, public works programme, etc (R);
– Studying or undergoing training incompatible with working hours(R);
– Failure to contact the agency/service during five consecutive years (R);
– Inability to work (indicated by the person concerned) (R).

Note: The information above is registered as marginal notes in the person's file, archived and eliminated only in case of death; in all other cases, the information is kept. The limit for keeping registers is five years.

6. Definition of unemployed persons used for the statistics
This category groups together persons who are affected by so called "open" unemployment, meaning those who have been laid off (i.e. persons who were employed, but had lost their employment for whatever reason, and had actively looked for another job during the reference week, or who had tried to create their own business or agricultural operation) and first job seekers. Job-seekers include unemployed persons who have been laid off, first job seekers, and to a lesser extent employed persons who are looking for a better work opportunity, because they have reached a new skills level or because they desire a higher salary.

7. Updating of the registers
The registers are updated every six months.

8. Unemployment rates
Statistics from the registers are not used to obtain unemployment rates.

9. Type of statistics of unemployed persons produced
Reference period: Year.
Frequency of production: Yearly.
Descriptive variables used:
– Sex;
– Age;
– Educational level;
– Occupation;
– Industry;
– Geographic characteristics;
– Other: occupational status.

Form of publication:
– For internal use only;
– Machine-readable form, on request.

Agency responsible for publication: General Department of Employment.
Title and periodicity of the publication(s): *Boletín Estadístico* (Statistical Bulletin), yearly.

10. Methodological information about the statistics
Form of release:
– Not released, available for internal use only;
– In machine-readable form, on request.

Agency responsible for the release: General Department of Employment.

11. Comparisons with unemployment statistics from other sources
Comparisons have been made with unemployment statistics from the household survey as well as from the population census.
Frequency of the comparisons: From time to time (latest year: 2001); depending on the periodicity of the publication of the household survey, once or twice a year.
Publication of the methodology/results of the comparisons: They are published in the *Statistical Bulletin* and are used as references in analyses on this topic.

12. Major changes since the start of the statistics
There have been no major changes in legislation, capacity of the agency and/or administrative procedures which had a significant influence on the statistics.
However, there has been a change in the method of data entry due to the establishment of an electronic employment exchange, which has contributed to improving mediation services. It is planned to extend this to other cities in the country integrating also employers' organizations through this electronic system.

Hungary

1. Series
Title: Registered unemployment.
Starting year: 1990.

2. Agency making the initial registrations of unemployed persons
Name of the agency: Allami Foglalkoztatási Szolgálat (Public Employment Service).
Type of agency: Public service under a national authority.
Name of the national authority: Ministry of Economic Affairs.
Location of the local offices making the registrations: There are 11 offices in the capital city, Budapest, and 165 offices in the 19 counties of the country (with 20 Labour Centres).
Type of services provided/administered by the agency:
– Assisting job-seekers to find jobs;
– Assisting job-seekers to establish their own business;
– Assisting employers to find workers;
– Vocational guidance;
– Job-related training;
– Paying unemployment compensation;
– Other: administering active labour market programmes; issuing work permits to foreign citizens; providing labour market information at all levels (statistics, analyses, projections).

Percentage of job-seekers seeking work through the agency: 80%.

3. The following information is registered about a person:
– Name;
– Sex;
– Social security number (or similar identification number also used by other agencies);
– Address of usual residence;
– Date of birth;
– Citizenship (only in the case of work permits for foreign citizens);
– Educational/vocational attainment, with 10 categories distinguished. Links to ISCED have been established;
– Current/past activity status, with 4 categories distinguished;
– Type of work (occupation) of past or present job with 632 categories distinguished. Links to ISCO-88 have been established (minor groups level);
– Type of work (occupation) of job sought, with 692 categories distinguished. Links to ISCO-88 have been established (minor groups level);
– Name and address of present or previous employer or work place;
– Type of business (industry) of present/previous employer/workplace, with 503 categories distinguished. Links to NACE, rev.1 have been established (tabulation categories level);
– Previous registrations with the agency/service.

4. Criteria used for inclusion of a person in the registers (R) and/or the statistics of unemployed persons (S):
– Being without work (S);
– Seeking work (S);
– Availability for work (S);
– Age (upper limit: old age pension age) (S);
– Being resident in the country (S).

5. Criteria used for exclusion of a person from the registers (R) and/or the statistics of unemployed persons (S):
– Death (R) and (S);
– Commencement of a (new) job (S);
– Commencement of military service (S);
– Participation in an employment promotion scheme, public works programme, etc. (S);
– Studying or undergoing training (S);
– Failure to contact the agency/service (S);
– Refusal of one suitable job offer (S);

- Refusal of one suitable training offer (S);
- Receipt of a pension (S);
- Inability to work (S);
- Other: at own request (R) and (S).

6. Definition of unemployed persons used for the statistics
Job-seekers who fulfil the following conditions:
- are not employed and do not carry out any other remunerative activity;
- have all the necessary conditions to start a job;
- are not eligible to receive an old age pension;
- are not full-time students of an educational institution;
- cooperate with the local labour office in order to find a job;
- are registered by the local labour office as unemployed.

7. Updating of the registers:
The registers are updated on a continuous basis.

8. Unemployment rates
Statistics from the registers are used to obtain unemployment rates.
The source of data on employed persons who are part of the denominator of the unemployment rates is the annual "*Labour Account of the National Economy*" (reference day: 1 January) published by the Central Statistical Office.

Definition of employed persons for this purpose:
- All employees, individual entrepreneurs and self-employed persons;
- Working owners;
- Helping family members (over a certain amount of time worked).

9. Type of statistics of unemployed persons produced
Series 1:
Reference period: Month.
Frequency of production: Monthly.
Descriptive variables used:
- Sex;
- Age;
- Educational level;
- Geographic characteristics;
- Previous work experience;
- Duration of unemployment.

Form of publication:
- On paper, for general audience;
- Website (under development).
Agency responsible for publication: National Employment Office.
Title of the publication: *Labour Market Situation.*
Series 2:
Reference period: Year.
Frequency of production: Yearly.
Descriptive variables used:
- Sex;
- Age;
- Educational level;
- Geographic characteristics;
- Previous work experience;
- Duration of unemployment.
Form of publication: On paper, for general audience.
Agency responsible for publication: National Employment Office.
Title of the publication: *Time series based on the administrative records of the Public Employment Service.*

10. Methodological information about the statistics
Form of release:
- On paper, for general audience;
- Website (under development).
Agency responsible for the release: National Employment Office.

11. Comparisons with unemployment statistics from other sources
Comparisons have been made with unemployment statistics from the Labour Force Survey and the Population Census.
Frequency of the comparisons: Occasionally (latest year: 1998).
Publication of the methodology/results of the comparisons: They were published for a joint press conference of the Central Statistical Office and the Ministry of Labour in May 1998. The comparison with the results of the 2001 Population Census will be published late 2002.

12. Major changes since the start of the statistics
There have been no major changes in legislation, capacity of the agency and/or administrative procedures which had a significant influence on the statistics.

Iceland

1. Series
Title: Registered unemployment.
Starting year: 1969.

2. Agency making the initial registrations of unemployed persons
Name of the agency: Vinnumálastofnun (Directorate of Labour).
Type of agency: Public service under a national authority.
Name of the national authority: Ministry of Social Affairs.
Location of the local offices making the registrations: In all parts of the country.
Type of services provided/administered by the agency:
- Assisting job-seekers to find jobs;
- Assisting job-seekers to establish their own business;
- Assisting employers to find workers;
- Vocational guidance;
- Job-related training;
- Paying unemployment compensation;
- Other: labour market measures, short courses in different fields.

Percentage of job-seekers seeking work through the agency: Approximately 100%.

3. The following information is registered about a person:
- Name;
- Sex;
- Social security number (or similar identification number also used by other agencies);
- Address of usual residence;
- Date of birth;
- Citizenship.
- Nationality
- Educational/vocational attainment, with 3 categories distinguished. Links to ISCED-76 have been established.
- Current/past activity status, with 31 categories distinguished;
- Type of work (occupation) of past or present job with 374 categories distinguished. Links to ISCO-88 have been established (unit groups level);
- Type of work (occupation) of job sought, with an unlimited number of categories distinguished. Links to ISCO-88 have been established (unit groups level);
- Name and address of present or previous employer or work place;
- Type of business (industry) of present/previous employer/workplace, with 616 categories distinguished. Links to NACE, rev.1 have been established (classes level);
- Previous registrations with the agency/service.

4. Criteria used for inclusion of a person in the registers (R) and/or the statistics of unemployed persons (S):
- Being without work (R) and (S);
- Seeking work (R) and (S);
- Availability for work (R) and (S);
- Age (lower limit: 16 years; upper limit: 70 years) (R) and (S);
- Citizenship (R);
- Being resident in the country (R);
- Previously employed (R);
- Desired duration of employment and/or number of hours of work sought (R) and (S);
- Previous payment of unemployed insurance contributions (R);
- Other: entitlement to unemployment benefits
- accumulated up to 24 months due to sickness, special personal circumstances, imprisonment (R).

5. Criteria used for exclusion of a person from the registers (R) and/or the statistics of unemployed persons (S):
- Death (R) and (S);
- Taking up residency abroad (R) and (S);
- Commencement of a (new) job (R) and (S);
- Participation in an employment promotion scheme, public works programme, etc. (R) and (S);
- Studying or undergoing training (R) and (S);
- Failure to contact the agency/service (R) and (S);
- Refusal of suitable job offers (R) and (S);
- Refusal of suitable training offers (R) and (S);
- End of entitlement to receive unemployment compensation (R) and (S);
- Receipt of a pension (R);
- Inability to work (R).

6. Definition of unemployed persons used for the statistics

Registered unemployed refers to those persons who have no or insufficient work relative to their capacity for it and wishes, based on an eight hour working day or the equivalent (shift work, etc), who register as such at an official employment agency and remain on the register by signing at least once a month.

7. Updating of the registers

The registers are updated weekly, bi-monthly and monthly.

8. Unemployment rates

Statistics from the registers are used to obtain unemployment rates.

The source of data on employed persons who are part of the denominator of the unemployment rates is Official Estimates.

Definition of employed persons for this purpose:

Full-time equivalents.

9. Type of statistics of unemployed persons produced

Series 1:

Reference period: Month.

Frequency of production: Monthly.

Descriptive variables used:

– Sex;
– Age;
– Educational level;
– Occupation;
– Industry;
– Geographic characteristics;
– Duration of unemployment.

Form of publication:

– On paper, for general audience;
– Machine-readable form, on request;
– On a website (www.vinnumalastofnun.is).

Agency responsible for publication: Directorate of Labour.

Title of the publication: *Yfirlit Yfir Atvinnuástand* (Overview of the Employment Situation)

Series 2:

Reference period: Day.

Frequency of production: Quarterly.

Descriptive variables used:

– Sex;
– Age;
– Geographic characteristics;
– Duration of unemployment.

Form of publication: On a website (www.statice.is).

Agency responsible for publication: Statistics Iceland.

Title of the publication: *Skráo atvinnuleysi eftir kyni, aldri og lengd atvinnuleysis.*

10. Methodological information about the statistics

Form of release:

– On paper, for general audience;
– In machine-readable form, on request;
– On a website (Series 1: www.vinnumalastofnun.is);

(Series 2: www.statice.is).

Agency responsible for the release:

– Series 1: Directorate of Labour;
– Series 2: Statistics Iceland.

11. Comparisons with unemployment statistics from other sources

Comparisons have been made with unemployment statistics from the Labour Force Survey.

Frequency of the comparisons: Twice a year (latest year: 2001).

Publication of the methodology/results of the comparisons: These are published by Statistics Iceland in *Labour market surveys on unemployment*, April and November, (www.statice.is /talnaefn/vinna2001/kafli10.pdf).

12. Major changes since the start of the statistics

Major changes in legislation, capacity of the agency and/or administrative procedures took place in 1998. The resulting changes in the statistics have not been estimated.

India

1. Series

Title: Employment Exchange Statistics.

Starting year: 1947.

2. Agency making the initial registrations of unemployed persons

Name of the agency: National Employment Service.

Type of agency: Public service under a national authority, working in close collaboration with State and Union territory administrations.

Name of the national authority: Directorate General of Employment and Training, Ministry of Labour.

Location of the local offices making the registrations: In all parts of the country at district/town level. The network comprises 958 Employment Exchanges.

Type of services provided/administered by the agency:

– Assisting job-seekers to find jobs;
– Assisting job-seekers to establish their own business;
– Assisting employers to find workers;
– Vocational guidance.

3. The following information is registered about a person:

– Name;
– Sex;
– Address of usual residence;
– Date of birth;
– Ethnic group;
– Educational/vocational attainment. Links to ISCED have not been established;
– Name and address of present or previous employer or work place;
– Other: minimum salary; physical fitness and
– characteristics; language knowledge; willingness to join the armed forces or undergo training; willingness to work elsewhere (geographical limitations).

4. Criteria used for inclusion of a person in the registers (R) and/or the statistics of unemployed persons (S):

– Being without work (R) and (S);
– Seeking work (R) and (S);
– Age (lower limit: 14 years; no upper limit) (R) and (S);
– Citizenship (R) and (S);
– Being resident in the country (R) and (S);
– Previously employed (R) and (S).

5. Criteria used for exclusion of a person from the registers (R) and/or the statistics of unemployed persons (S):

– Commencement of a (new) job (R) and (S);
– Failure to renew registration at agency/service (R) and (S).

6. Definition of unemployed persons used for the statistics

All candidates registered at Employment Exchanges are treated as job-seekers.

7. Updating of the registers

The registers are updated monthly.

8. Unemployment rates

Statistics from the registers are not used to obtain unemployment rates.

9. Type of statistics of unemployed persons produced

Series 1: Registrations, placements, submissions made, number on Live Register and vacancies notified.

Reference period: Month.

Frequency of production: Monthly.

Descriptive variables used:

– Sex;
– Geographic characteristics (whether from Rural Areas).

Form of publication: On paper, for general audience.

Agency responsible for publication: Directorate General of Employment and Training.

Title and periodicity of the publication: *Employment Exchanges Statistics*, yearly.

Series 2: Vocational guidance activities by categories of applicants.

Reference period: Quarter.

Frequency of production: Quarterly.

Descriptive variables used:

– Ethnic/social categories (i.e. "Scheduled Castes" (SC); "Scheduled Tribes" (ST); "Other Backward Classes" (OBC);
– Other: physically handicapped (PH);
– Sex (women as total only).

Form of publication: On paper, for general audience.

Agency responsible for publication: Directorate General of Employment and Training.

Title and periodicity of the publication: *Employment Exchanges Statistics*, yearly.

Series 3: Registrations, placements, number on Live Register and submissions made in respect of minority communities.

Reference period: Half-year.

Frequency of production: Half-yearly.

Form of publication: On paper, for general audience.

Agency responsible for publication: Directorate General of Employment and Training.

Title and periodicity of the publication: *Employment Exchanges Statistics*, yearly.

Series 4: Registrations, placements, number on Live Register and submissions made in respect of physically handicapped applicants.

Reference period: Half-year.

Frequency of production: Half-yearly.

Descriptive variables used:
- Type of physical disability;
- Sex (women as total only).

Form of publication: On paper, for general audience.

Agency responsible for publication: Directorate General of Employment and Training.

Title and periodicity of the publication: *Employment Exchanges Statistics*, yearly.

Series 5: Number of educated applicants (10th class and above) registered and placed.

Reference period: Half-year.

Frequency of production: Half-yearly.

Descriptive variables used:
- Educational level (5 levels distinguished; 10 branches distinguished for graduates and post-graduates; 2 branches for diploma holders);
- Ethnic/social categories (i.e. "SC", "ST" and "OBC");
- Sex (women as total only).

Form of publication: On paper, for general audience.

Agency responsible for publication: Directorate General of Employment and Training.

Title and periodicity of the publication: *Employment Exchanges Statistics*, yearly.

Series 6: Registrations, placements, number on Live Register and submissions made in respect of "SC", "ST" and "OBC" applicants.

Reference period: Half-year.

Frequency of production: Half-yearly.

Descriptive variables used:
- Ethnic/social categories.

Form of publication: On paper, for general audience.

Agency responsible for publication: Directorate General of Employment and Training.

Title and periodicity of the publication: *Employment Exchanges Statistics*, yearly.

Series 7: Promotion of self-employment.

Reference period: Half-year.

Frequency of production: Half-yearly.

Descriptive variables used:
- Sex;
- Ethnic/social categories ("SC", "ST", "OBC", "PH" and Minority Communities);
- Geographic characteristics (rural/urban).

Form of publication: On paper, for general audience.

Agency responsible for publication: Directorate General of Employment and Training.

Title and periodicity of the publication: *Employment Exchanges Statistics*, yearly.

Series 8: Vacancies notified, filled, cancelled and outstanding on Live Register by National Classification of Occupations (NCO) in respect of Women, "SC", "ST", "OBC" and "PH" applicants.

Reference period: Year.

Frequency of production: Yearly.

Descriptive variables used:
- Occupation;
- Ethnic/social categories;
- Sex (women as total only);
- Other: "PH".

Form of publication: On paper, for general audience.

Agency responsible for publication: Directorate General of Employment and Training.

Title and periodicity of the publication: *Employment Exchanges Statistics*, yearly.

Series 9: Vacancies notified, filled, cancelled and outstanding by sector.

Reference period: Year.

Frequency of production: Yearly.

Descriptive variables used:
- Sector (Central/State Government, Public/Private Sector, etc.).

Form of publication: On paper, for general audience.

Agency responsible for publication: Directorate General of Employment and Training.

Title and periodicity of the publication: *Employment Exchanges Statistics*, yearly.

Series 10: Number of applicants on Live Register by age group, sex and educational level on 31 December.

Reference period: Year.

Frequency of production: Yearly.

Descriptive variables used:
- Sex;
- Age group;
- Educational level (6 levels distinguished).

Form of publication: On paper, for general audience.

Agency responsible for publication: Directorate General of Employment and Training.

Title and periodicity of the publication: *Employment Exchanges Statistics*, yearly.

Series 11: Number of vacancies reported by establishments as unfilled due to shortage of suitable applicants with reasons for not sponsoring.

Reference period: Year.

Frequency of production: Yearly.

Descriptive variables used:
- Industry (by National Industrial Classification (NIC) code at 3-digit level);
- Occupation (by NCO code);
- Public/Private sector.

Form of publication: On paper, for general audience.

Agency responsible for publication: Directorate General of Employment and Training.

Title and periodicity of the publication: *Employment Exchanges Statistics*, yearly.

Series 12: Registrations, placements effected and number on Live Register by NCO in respect of Full-term Apprentices and Ex-Industrial Training Institute (ITI) Trainees by trades.

Reference period: Year.

Frequency of production: Yearly.

Descriptive variables used:
- Occupation;
- Trade in which trained.

Form of publication: On paper, for general audience.

Agency responsible for publication: Directorate General of Employment and Training.

Title and periodicity of the publication: *Employment Exchanges Statistics*, yearly.

Series 13: Registrations, placements effected and number on Live Register in respect of Displaced Persons.

Reference period: Year.

Frequency of production: Yearly.

Descriptive variables used:
- Geographic characteristics (provenance).

Form of publication: On paper, for general audience.

Agency responsible for publication: Directorate General of Employment and Training.

Title and periodicity of the publication: *Employment Exchanges Statistics*, yearly.

10. Methodological information about the statistics

Form of release: On paper, for general audience.

Agency responsible for the release: Directorate General of Employment and Training.

Iran, Islamic Rep. of

1. Series

Title: Administrative Registers of Employment Centres.

2. Agency making the initial registrations of unemployed persons

Name of the agency:

1. Placement Centres (public);
2. Employment Advisory Centres (public);
3. Placement Centres (private) with the authorization of the Ministry of Labour and Social Affairs.

Type of agency:

1 and 2: Public service under a local authority;

3: Non-profit making private service.

Location of the local offices making the registrations: All over the country. Most of the local offices are located in urban areas. However, some offices have been opened recently in rural areas of the districts.

Type of services provided/administered by the agency:
- Assisting job-seekers to find jobs;
- Assisting job-seekers to establish their own business;
- Assisting employers to find workers;

- Vocational guidance;
- Paying unemployment compensation;
- Other employment-related services.

Percentage of job-seekers seeking work through the agency: 20%.

3. The following information is registered about a person:
- Name;
- Sex;
- Address of usual residence;
- Date of birth;
- Educational level;
- Type of work (occupation) of past or present job;
- Type of business (industry) of present/previous employer/workplace; links to ISIC-rev.3 have not been established;
- Other: school documents, occupational qualification, job outside the country, starting date of unemployment insurance contributions.

4. Criteria used for inclusion of a person in the registers (R) and/or the statistics of unemployed persons (S):
- Being without work (R) and (S);
- Seeking work (R) and (S);
- Availability for work (R) and (S);
- Age (lower limit: 15 years; no upper age limit) (R) and (S);
- Citizenship (R) and (S);
- Being resident in the country (R) and (S);
- Previously employed (R);
- Previous payment of unemployed insurance contributions (R).

5. Criteria used for exclusion of a person from the registers (R) and/or the statistics of unemployed persons (S):
> Information not available.

6. Definition of unemployed persons used for the statistics
> Any person aged 15 years and over, able to work, available for work and registered in a placement centre.

7. Updating of the registers
> The registers are updated regularly.

8. Unemployment rates
> Statistics from the registers are not used to obtain unemployment rates.

9. Type of statistics of unemployed persons produced
Reference period: Year.
Frequency of production: Yearly.
Descriptive variables used:
- Sex;
- Age;
- Educational level;
- Occupational qualification.

Form of publication: On paper, for general audience.
Agency responsible for publication: Ministry of Labour and Social Affairs, Bureau of Statistics.
Title and periodicity of the publication: *Aspects of the labour market* (yearly).

10. Methodological information about the statistics
Form of release: On paper, for limited audience.
Agency responsible for the release: Ministry of Labour and Social Affairs, Bureau of Statistics.

11. Comparisons with unemployment statistics from other sources
> Comparisons have not been made with unemployment statistics from other sources.

12. Major changes since the start of the statistics
> In order to lighten the burden on the public placement centres some placement centres have been privatized with the authorization of the Ministry of Labour and Social Affairs.
> In 2002 a programme of reform was introduced with a view to improving the system of labour market information and also to computerizing it.

11. Comparisons with unemployment statistics from other sources
> Comparisons have not been made with unemployment statistics from other sources.

12. Major changes since the start of the statistics
> There have been no major changes in legislation, capacity of the agency and/or administrative procedures which had a significant influence on the statistics.

Isle of Man

1. Series
Title: Registered unemployment.
Starting year: 1978.

2. Agency making the initial registrations of unemployed persons
Name of the agency: Social Security Division.
Type of agency: Public service under a national authority.
Name of the national authority: Department of Health and Social Security.

Certain functions, including the ongoing registration of unemployed persons, are the responsibility of the Department of Trade and Industry.

Periodic statistics on the unemployed are produced by both Departments, although only some are for general audience.

Location of the local offices making the registrations: In selected areas only, i.e. Douglas (capital city), Ramsey, Peel, Castletown and Port Erin.

Type of services provided/administered by the agency:
- Assisting job-seekers to find jobs;
- Assisting job-seekers to establish their own business*;
- Assisting employers to find workers*;
- Vocational guidance*;
- Job-related training*;
- Paying unemployment compensation.

* Services provided by the Department of Trade and Industry.

Percentage of job-seekers seeking work through the agency: 75%.

3. The following information is registered about a person:
- Name;
- Sex;
- Social security number (or similar identification number also used by other agencies);
- Address of usual residence;
- Date of birth;
- Citizenship;
- Educational/vocational attainment, with 7 categories distinguished. Links to ISCED have not been established;
- Type of work (occupation) of job sought;
- Name and address of present or previous employer or work place;
- Other: driving licence/own transport; construction craft worker status; marital status; health status; indication of criminal record.

4. Criteria used for inclusion of a person in the registers (R) and/or the statistics of unemployed persons (S):
- Being without work (R) and (S);
- Seeking work (R) and (S);
- Availability for work (R) and (S);
- Age (lower limit: 16 years; upper limit: men: 65 years for men; 60 years for women) (R) and (S);
- Being resident in the country (R) and (S);
- Desired duration of employment and/or number of hours of work sought (R) and (S).

5. Criteria used for exclusion of a person from the registers (R) and/or the statistics of unemployed persons (S):
- Death (R) and (S);
- Taking up residency abroad (R) and (S);
- Commencement of a (new) job (R) and (S);
- Commencement of military service (R) and (S);
- Participation in an employment promotion scheme, public works programme, etc. (R) and (S);
- Studying or undergoing training (R) and (S);
- Failure to contact the agency/service (R) and (S);
- Inability to work (R) and (S).

6. Definition of unemployed persons used for the statistics
> Unemployed persons must be:
- (ordinarily) available for employment of at least 40 hours a week;
- taking steps in each week to identify suitable vacancies and to apply for them;
- unemployed, or working less than 16 hours a week;
- capable of working at least 16 hours a week;
- not receiving education, or receiving education involving less than 16 hours guided learning per week;
- over 16 years but under State pensionable age (65 for men; 60 for women);

– resident in the Isle of Man.

7. Updating of the registers
The registers are updated daily.

8. Unemployment rates
Statistics from the registers are used to obtain unemployment rates.

The source of data on employed persons who are part of the denominator of the unemployment rates is the Population Census.

Definition of employed persons for this purpose:
Persons working for an employer (full or part-time) and/or self-employed.

9. Type of statistics of unemployed persons produced
Series 1:
Reference period: Month.
Frequency of production: Monthly.
Descriptive variables used:
– Sex;
– Age*;
– Educational level*;
– Occupation*;
– Industry*;
– Geographic characteristics*;
– Citizenship (nationals/non nationals).
Form of publication:
– For internal use only*;
– On paper, for general audience.
* Refers to statistics produced by the Department of Trade and Industry.
Agency responsible for publication: Economic Affairs Division, Treasury Department.
Title of the publication: *Job Market Statistics.*
Series 2:
Reference period: Quarter.
Frequency of production: Quarterly.
Descriptive variables used:
– Sex;
– Age;
– Educational level*;
– Occupation*;
– Industry*;
– Geographic characteristics;
– Citizenship (nationals/non nationals).
Form of publication:
– For internal use only*;
– On paper, for general audience.
* Refers to statistics produced by the Department of Trade and Industry.
Agency responsible for publication: Department of Health and Social Security.
Title of the publication: *Quarterly Analysis of the Unemployed Register.*

10. Methodological information about the statistics
Form of release: Not released, available for internal use only.

11. Comparisons with unemployment statistics from other sources
Comparisons have been made with unemployment statistics from the Population Census.
Frequency of the comparisons: Regularly, when the statistics are published.

12. Major changes since the start of the statistics
Major changes in legislation, capacity of the agency and/or administrative procedures took place in 1996. The resulting changes in the statistics have not been estimated.

Israel

1. Series
Title: Employment Service data on the labour market.
Starting year: 1960's.

2. Agency making the initial registrations of unemployed persons
Name of the agency: Employment Service.
Type of agency: Corporation under the general supervision of a national authority.
Name of the national authority: Ministry of Labour and Social Affairs.

Location of the local offices making the registrations: Approximately 100 branches dispersed throughout the country in the main population centres.
Type of services provided/administered by the agency:
– Assisting job-seekers to find jobs;
– Assisting job-seekers to establish their own business;
– Assisting employers to find workers;
– Vocational guidance;
– Job-related training (together with the Ministry of Labour and Social affairs);
– Paying unemployment compensation (in cooperation with the National Insurance Institute);
– Other: permits for and allocation of foreign workers; supervision of employment of Palestinian workers and execution of payments to these workers; auditing payments made to foreign workers.
Percentage of job-seekers seeking work through the agency: 7%.

3. The following information is registered about a person:
– Name;
– Sex;
– Social security number (or similar identification number also used by other agencies);
– Address of usual residence;
– Date of birth;
– Educational attainment, with nine categories distinguished. Links to ISCED have been established;
– Current/past activity status, with 16 categories distinguished;
– Type of work (occupation) of past or present job with thousands of occupations distinguished. Links to ISCO-88 have been established (minor groups level);
– Type of work (occupation) of job sought, with thousands of occupations distinguished. Links to ISCO-88 have been established (minor groups level);
– Name and address of present or previous employer or work place;
– Type of business (industry) of present/previous employer/workplace. Links to ISIC, rev.3 have been established (class level);
– Previous registrations with the agency/service;
– Other: referrals to job vacancies; refusals of job offers.

4. Criteria used for inclusion of a person in the registers (R) and/or the statistics of unemployed persons (S):
– Being without work (R) and (S);
– Seeking work (R) and (S);
– Availability for work (R) and (S);
– Age (lower limit: 15 years; upper limit: 65 years) (R) and (S);
– Citizenship (R) and (S);
– Previously employed (R) and (S);
– Desired duration of employment and/or number of hours of work sought (R) and (S);

5. Criteria used for exclusion of a person from the registers (R) and/or the statistics of unemployed persons (S):
– Death (R) and (S);
– Taking up residency abroad (R) and (S).

6. Definition of unemployed persons used for the statistics
A job-seeker who is registered with at least one day of unemployment in the month of the report.

7. Updating of the registers
The registers are updated monthly.

8. Unemployment rates
Statistics from the registers are used to obtain unemployment rates.

The source of data on employed persons who are part of the denominator of the unemployment rates is the Estimates of the total civilian labour force.
Definition of employed persons for this purpose:
According to the definition of the Labour Force Survey: those employed for at least one hour at any job during the determinant week.

9. Type of statistics of unemployed persons produced
Series: Unemployed persons.
Reference period: Month.
Frequency of production: Monthly.
Descriptive variables used:
– Sex;
– Age;
– Educational level;

- Occupation;
- Industry;
- Geographic characteristics;
- Duration of unemployment.

Form of publication: On paper, for general audience;

Agency responsible for publication: Employment Service.

Title and periodicity of the publication: *Employment Service Data on the Labour Market*, monthly.

10. Methodological information about the statistics

Form of release: Not released, available for internal use only.

Agency responsible: The Employment Service.

11. Comparisons with unemployment statistics from other sources

Comparisons have been made with unemployment statistics from the Labour Force Survey.

Frequency of the comparisons: Regularly when the statistics are published.

Publication of the methodology/results of the comparisons: The monthly *Employment Service Data on the Labour Market* shows (national) unemployment rates from the Labour Force Survey and those obtained by the Employment Service (by area for those unemployed 6 days or more and for those unemployed 20 days or more). Comparisons are difficult because of differences in the sources regarding definitions of unemployment and because the Employment Service only counts those unemployed who register at its bureaux. The Employment Service methodology appears in the monthly publication.

12. Major changes since the start of the statistics

Major changes in legislation, capacity of the agency and/or administrative procedures took place in:

1972: The enactment of the Unemployment Insurance Law which required unemployed persons applying for benefits under the law to register for work with the Employment Service caused an increase in unemployed in Employment Service statistics;

1984: The enactment of the Income Maintenance Law under which the Employment Service is responsible for administering the employment test for eligibility for benefits under the law resulted in a rise in the number of unemployed registered with the Service. In 1985 the number of adult job-seekers rose by 12%;

1989-90: The cancellation of compulsory resort to the Employment Service by employers seeking workers reduced by approximately 50% the number of employer applications to the Service for workers.

Italy

1. Series

Title: Employment Office Registrations.

Starting year: 1987.

2. Agency making the initial registrations of unemployed persons

Name of the agency: Employment Agency.

Type of agency: Public service under a local authority.

Location of the local offices making the registrations: In each province.

Type of services provided/administered by the agency:

- Assisting job-seekers to find jobs;
- Assisting employers to find workers;
- Vocational guidance;
- Job-related training;
- Other employment-related services: assistance to handicapped job-seekers; to job-seekers who are nationals of non-European Union countries and to workers temporarily laid off.

3. The following information is registered about a person:

- Name;
- Sex;
- Social security number (or similar identification number also used by other agencies);
- Address of usual residence;
- Date of birth;
- Citizenship;
- Nationality/ethnic group;
- Educational/vocational attainment, with eight categories distinguished. Links to ISCED have not been established;
- Current/past activity status, with four categories distinguished;
- Type of work (occupation) of past or present job. Links to ISCO have not been established;

- Type of work (occupation) of job sought;
- Name and address of present or previous employer or work place;
- Type of business (industry) of present/previous employer/workplace, with four categories distinguished. Links to ISIC have been established;
- Previous registrations with the agency/service;
- Other: early retirement; availability for work; and duration of unemployment.

4. Criteria used for inclusion of a person in the registers (R) and/or the statistics of unemployed persons (S):

- Being without work (R) and (S);
- Seeking work (R) and (S);
- Age (lower limit: 15 years; upper limit: 65 years) (R) and (S);
- Citizenship for nationals of non-European Union countries(R) and (S);
- Being resident in the country (R) and (S);
- Previously employed (R) and (S);
- Previous payment of unemployment insurance contributions, only for workers temporarily laid off (R) and (S).

5. Criteria used for exclusion of a person from the registers (R) and/or the statistics of unemployed persons (S):

- Commencement of a (new) job (R) and (S);
- Failure to contact the agency, if the job-seeker has not come to confirm his/her registration (R) and (S);
- End of entitlement to receive unemployment
- compensation, for workers temporarily laid off (R) and (S).

6. Definition of unemployed persons used for the statistics

Persons without work, immediately available to start work, and who are actively seeking work.

Workers temporarily laid off by a company benefiting from preferential treatment according to "salary integration" and which cannot guarantee the re-employment of the workers. These workers must have at least 12 months of service, six months of which actually worked. They receive for the period which is defined by law an indemnity for being temporarily laid off.

7. Updating of the registers

The registers are updated quarterly.

8. Unemployment rates

Statistics from the registers are not used to obtain unemployment rates.

9. Type of statistics of unemployed persons produced

Reference period: Month.

Frequency of production: Monthly.

Descriptive variables used:

- Sex;
- Age;
- Educational level;
- Occupation;
- Industry;
- Geographic characteristics;
- Previous work experience;
- Citizenship (nationals/non nationals);
- Duration of unemployment.

Form of publication:

- On paper, for limited audience;
- Machine-readable form, on request;
- On a website: www.minwelfare.it

Agency responsible for publication: Ministry of Employment and Social Policy.

Title and periodicity of the publication(s): *Notaflash* (Note Flash), monthly; and *Rapporto di monitoraggio* (Management Report), quarterly.

10. Methodological information about the statistics

Form of release:

- On paper, for limited audience;
- In machine-readable form, on request;
- On a website: www.minwelfare.it

Agency responsible for the release: Ministry of Employment and Social Policy.

11. Comparisons with unemployment statistics from other sources

Comparisons have been made with unemployment statistics from the labour force survey, from the population census and from estimates.

Frequency of the comparisons: Occasionally, latest year: 2001.

Publication of the methodology/results of the comparisons: These have not been published.

12. Major changes since the start of the statistics
Major changes in legislation, capacity of the agency and/or administrative procedures took place in 1999, 2000 and 2001. The resulting changes in the statistics are not known.

Japan (1)

1. Series
Title: Report on Employment Service.
Starting year: 1963.
2. Agency making the initial registrations of unemployed persons
Name of the agency: Koukyo Shokugyo Anteisho (Public Employment Security Office).
Type of agency: Public service under a national authority.
Name of the national authority: Ministry of Health, Labour and Welfare.
Location of the local offices making the registrations: In all 47 prefectures of the country totalling 600 locations.
Type of services provided/administered by the agency:
− Assisting job-seekers to find jobs;
− Assisting job-seekers to establish their own business;
− Assisting employers to find workers;
− Vocational guidance;
− Paying unemployment compensation;
− Other: industrial Employment Information Service: providing specific information on local labour markets and conditions and other useful information for job selection and skill attainment; employment Management Service: providing specific consultation and assistance to employers on employment management-related matters, such as recruitment, assignment, etc. as well as assistance for the adequate employment management of older persons and persons with disabilities); employment Grant Service: providing specific assistance to job-seekers (various benefits to facilitate their re-employment); to employers (in employing job-seekers having trouble finding employment, and various grants to prevent unemployment caused by economic fluctuation).
Percentage of job-seekers seeking work through the agency: 34.3% (February 2001).
3. The following information is registered about a person:
− Name;
− Sex;
− Address of usual residence;
− Date of birth;
− Educational/attainment, with 6 categories distinguished; vocational/attainment, with 650 categories distinguished. Links to ISCED have not been established;
− Current/past activity status, with 2 categories distinguished;
− Type of work (occupation) of past or present job. Direct links to ISCO-88 have not been established;
− Type of work (occupation) of job sought, with 2,167 groups distinguished. Direct links to ISCO-88 have not been established;
− Name of present or previous work place;
− Other: personal family details; desired work conditions; reason for leaving previous or present job.
4. Criteria used for inclusion of a person in the registers (R) and/or the statistics of unemployed persons (S):
− Seeking work (R) and (S);
− Availability for work (R) and (S);
− Age (lower limit: 15 years; no upper limit) (R) and (S).
5. Criteria used for exclusion of a person from the registers (R) and/or the statistics of unemployed persons (S):
− Death (R) and (S);
− Taking up residency abroad (R) and (S);
− Commencement of a new job (R) and (S);
− Failure to contact the agency/service (R) and (S);
− Other: at own request (R) and (S).
6. Definition of unemployed persons used for the statistics
The statistics refer to job-seekers only.
7. Updating of the registers
The registers are not updated regularly.
8. Unemployment rates
Statistics from the registers are not used to obtain unemployment rates.
9. Type of statistics of unemployed persons produced
Series: Report of Employment Service.

Reference period: Month, Quarter, Calender year, Fiscal year (1 April - 31 March).
Frequency of production: Monthly.
Descriptive variables used:
− Sex;
− Age;
− Occupation;
− Industry;
− Geographic characteristics;
− Previous work experience.
Form of publication:
− On paper, for general audience;
− On a website (http://www.mhlw.go.jp) [Japanese only].
Agency responsible for publication: Ministry of Health, Labour and Welfare.
Title and periodicity of the publications: *Monthly Report on Employment Service*; *Annual Report on Employment Service*.
10. Methodological information about the statistics
Form of release:
− On paper, for general audience;
− On a website (http://www.mhlw.go.jp) [Japanese only].
Agency responsible for the release: Ministry of Health, Labour and Welfare.
11. Comparisons with unemployment statistics from other sources
Comparisons have not been made with unemployment statistics from other sources.
12. Major changes since the start of the statistics
There have been no major changes in legislation, capacity of the agency and/or administrative procedures which had a significant influence on the statistics.

Japan (2)

1. Series
Titles: Annual Report on Employment Insurance Service; and Monthly Report on Employment Insurance Service.
Starting year: Annual series: 1975; Monthly series: 1980.
2. Agency making the initial registrations of unemployed persons
Name of the agency: Koukyo Shokugyo Anteisho (Public Employment Security Office).
Type of agency: Public service under a national authority.
Name of the national authority: Ministry of Health, Labour and Welfare.
Location of the local offices making the registrations: In all 47 prefectures of the country totalling 600 locations.
Type of services provided/administered by the agency:
− Assisting job-seekers to find jobs;
− Assisting job-seekers to establish their own business;
− Assisting employers to find workers;
− Vocational guidance;
− Paying unemployment compensation;
− Other: industrial Employment Information Service: providing specific information on local labour markets and conditions and other useful information for job selection and skill attainment; employment Management Service: providing specific consultation and assistance to employers on employment-related matters, such as recruitment, assignment, etc. as well as assistance for the adequate employment management of older persons and persons with disabilities); employment Grant Service: providing specific assistance to job-seekers (various benefits to facilitate their re-employment); to employers (in employing job-seekers having trouble finding employment, and various grants to prevent unemployment caused by economic fluctuation).
Percentage of job-seekers seeking work through the agency: 34.3% (February 2001).
3. The following information is registered about a person:
− Name;
− Sex;
− Address of usual residence;
− Date of birth;
− Current/past activity status, with 2 categories distinguished;
− Type of work (occupation) of past or present job with 9 groups distinguished. Direct links to ISCO-88 have not been established;
− Name and address of present or previous employer or work

place;
– Previous registrations with the agency/service.

4. Criteria used for inclusion of a person in the registers (R) and/or the statistics of unemployed persons (S):
– Being without work (R) and (S);
– Seeking work (R) and (S);
– Availability for work (R) and (S);
– Age (lower limit: 15 years; upper limit: 64 years) (R) and (S);
– Previously employed (R) and (S).

5. Criteria used for exclusion of a person from the registers (R) and/or the statistics of unemployed persons (S):
– Death (R) and (S);
– Commencement of a (new) job (R) and (S);
– Studying or undergoing training (except persons undergoing public vocational training) (R) and (S);
– Failure to contact the agency/service (R) and (S);
– Refusal of a suitable job offer (R) and (S);
– Refusal of a suitable training offer (R) and (S);
– End of entitlement to receive unemployment compensation (normally one year after leaving last job) (R) and (S);
– Inability to work (R) and (S).

6. Definition of unemployed persons used for the statistics
Persons qualifying for benefits: persons who paid an employment insurance contribution for more than six months during a year before leaving their previous job and who are unemployed, and willing and able to work.

7. Updating of the registers
The registers are not updated regularly.

8. Unemployment rates
Statistics from the registers are not used to obtain unemployment rates.

9. Type of statistics of unemployed persons produced
Statistics on the number of persons registered as *beneficiaries*.
Series 1: Annual Report on Employment Insurance Service.
Reference period: Month, year.
Frequency of production: Yearly.
Descriptive variables used:
– Sex;
– Age;
– Occupation;
– Industry;
– Geographic characteristics.
Form of publication: On paper, for general audience.
Agency responsible for publication: Ministry of Health, Labour and Welfare.
Title and periodicity of the publication: *Annual Report on Employment Insurance Service.*
Series 2: Monthly Report on Employment Insurance Service.
Reference period: Month.
Frequency of production: Monthly.
Descriptive variables used:
– Sex;
– Age;
– Occupation;
– Industry;
– Geographic characteristics.
Form of publication: On paper, for general audience.
Agency responsible for publication: Ministry of Health, Labour and Welfare.
Title and periodicity of the publication: *Monthly Report on Employment Insurance Service.*

10. Methodological information about the statistics
Form of release: Not released, available for internal use only.

11. Comparisons with unemployment statistics from other sources
Comparisons have not been made with unemployment statistics from other sources.

12. Major changes since the start of the statistics
There have been no major changes in legislation, capacity of the agency and/or administrative procedures which had a significant influence on the statistics.

Kazakhstan

1. Series
Title: Registered unemployment.
Starting year: 1991.

2. Agency making the initial registrations of unemployed persons
Name of the agency: Authorized bodies on employment (at the regional and urban levels).
Type of agency: Public service under national, regional, provincial and local authorities.
Name of the national authority: Ministry of Labour and Social Protection.
Location of the local offices making the registrations: In all cities and areas of the country, totalling 202 offices.
Type of services provided/administered by the agency:
– Assisting job-seekers to find jobs;
– Assisting job-seekers to establish their own business;
– Assisting employers to find workers;
– Vocational guidance;
– Other: organization of public works by creation of temporary workplaces intended especially for the unemployed.
Percentage of job-seekers seeking work through the agency: 99%.

3. The following information is registered about a person:
– Name;
– Sex;
– Social security number (or similar identification number also used by other agencies);
– Address of usual residence;
– Date of birth;
– Citizenship;
– Educational/vocational attainment, with five categories distinguished. Links to ISCED have been established;
– Current/past activity status, with four categories distinguished;
– Type of work (occupation) of past or present job with nine
– groups distinguished. Links to ISCO-88 have been established (the Kazakhstan Qualifier of Occupations is harmonized with ISCO-88) (unit groups level);
– Type of work (occupation) of job sought, with nine groups distinguished. Links to ISCO-88 have been established (the Kazakhstan Qualifier of Occupations is harmonized with ISCO-88) (unit groups level);
– Name and address of present or previous employer or work place;
– Type of business (industry) of present/previous employer/workplace, with nine groups distinguished. Links to ISIC, rev.3 have been established (tabulation categories level);
– Previous registrations with the agency/service.

4. Criteria used for inclusion of a person in the registers (R) and/or the statistics of unemployed persons (S):
– Being without work (R) and (S);
– Seeking work (R) and (S);
– Availability for work (R) and (S);
– Age (lower limit: 16 years; upper limit: 63 years for men; 58 years for women) (R) and (S);
– Citizenship (R) and (S);
– Being resident in the country (R) and (S).

5. Criteria used for exclusion of a person from the registers (R) and/or the statistics of unemployed persons (S):
– Death (R) and (S);
– Taking up residency abroad (R) and (S);
– Commencement of a (new) job, including temporary work (R) and (S);
– Commencement of military service (R) and (S);
– Failure to contact the agency/service (R);
– Refusal of 2 suitable job offers (R);
– Receipt of a pension (R) and (S);
– Inability to work (R) and (S);
– Other: organization of own business (R) and (S); imprisonment (R) and (S); moving to another district (R) and (S); failure to report to an offered employment or training (R) and (S); unauthorized discontinuation in public works or training (R) and (S).

6. Definition of unemployed persons used for the statistics
Persons of working age who in the reference period fulfilled all three of the following criteria:
(i) Were without work (i.e. had no profitable occupation);
(ii) Were engaged actively in its search;
(iii) Were ready to begin work within a certain period of time.

7. Updating of the registers
The registers are updated monthly.

8. Unemployment rates

Statistics from the registers are used to obtain unemployment rates.

The sources of data on employed persons who are part of the denominator of the unemployment rates are Official Estimates and the economically active population figures presented quarterly by the Republic of Kazakhstan Agency on Statistics.

9. Type of statistics of unemployed persons produced

Series 1:

Descriptive variables used:
- Sex;
- Age;
- Educational level;
- Occupation;
- Industry;
- Geographic characteristics;
- Previous work experience;
- Citizenship (nationals/non nationals);
- Duration of unemployment.

Form of publication: On paper, for limited audience;
Periodicity of the publications: Monthly, quarterly.

Series 2:

Descriptive variables used:
- Sex;
- Age;
- Educational level;
- Occupation;
- Industry;
- Geographic characteristics;
- Previous work experience;
- Citizenship (nationals/non nationals);
- Duration of unemployment.

Form of publication: On paper, for general audience.
Periodicity of the publications: Monthly; Quarterly.

Series 3:

Descriptive variables used:
- Sex;
- Age;
- Educational level;
- Occupation;
- Industry;
- Geographic characteristics;
- Previous work experience;
- Citizenship (nationals/non nationals);
- Duration of unemployment.

Form of publication: On paper, for general audience.
Periodicity of the publications: Monthly; Quarterly.

10. Methodological information about the statistics

Form of release:
- On paper, for general audience;
- On a website (www.enbek.kz).

Agency responsible for the release: Republic of Kazakhstan Agency on Statistics.

11. Comparisons with unemployment statistics from other sources

Comparisons have been made with unemployment statistics from the Labour Force and the Population Census.

Frequency of the comparisons: Regularly when the statistics are published.

Publication of the methodology/results of the comparisons: These are published in the official publications of the Republic of Kazakhstan Agency on Statistics.

12. Major changes since the start of the statistics

Major changes in legislation, capacity of the agency and/or administrative procedures took place in 1990, 1998, 1999 (April and November) and 2001, resulting in a marked tendency towards an annual decrease in the number of registered unemployed after 1996.

Kenya

1. Series

Title: Registered unemployment.
Starting year: 1988.

2. Agency making the initial registrations of unemployed persons

Name of the agency: National Employment Bureau.
Type of agency: Public service under a national authority.

Name of the national authority: Ministry of Labour and Human Resource Development.
Location of the local offices making the registrations: In 41 selected districts.
Type of services provided/administered by the agency:
- Assisting job-seekers to find jobs;
- Assisting job-seekers to establish their own business;
- Assisting employers to find workers;
- Vocational guidance;
- Job-related training;
- Study of the impact of HIV/AIDS at the place of work.

Percentage of job-seekers seeking work through the agency: Not known, but registration is low as many unemployed prefer to seek employment directly at the gates of establishments.

3. The following information is registered about a person:
- Name;
- Sex;
- National identity card number (or similar identification number also used by other agencies);
- Address of usual residence;
- Date of birth;
- Citizenship;
- Nationality/ethnic group;
- Educational/vocational attainment, with four categories distinguished. Links to ISCED have been established;
- Current/past activity status;
- Type of work (occupation) of past or present job with five categories distinguished. Links to ISCO-88 have been established (unit group level);
- Type of work (occupation) of job sought, with nine categories distinguished. Links to ISCO-88 have been established (unit group level);
- Name and address of present or previous employer or work place;
- Type of business (industry) of present/previous employer/workplace, with nine categories distinguished. Links to ISIC, rev.3 have been established (class level);
- Previous registrations with the agency/service.

4. Criteria used for inclusion of a person in the registers (R) and/or the statistics of unemployed persons (S):
- Being without work (R) and (S);
- Seeking work (R) and (S);
- Availability for work (R) and (S);
- Age (lower limit: 18 years; upper limit: 55 years) (R) and (S);
- Citizenship (R) and (S);
- Being resident in the country (R) and (S);
- Previously employed (R) and (S).

5. Criteria used for exclusion of a person from the registers (R) and/or the statistics of unemployed persons (S):
- Death (R) and (S);
- Taking up residency abroad (R) and (S);
- Commencement of a (new) job (R) and (S);
- Commencement of military service (R) and (S);
- Studying or undergoing training (R) and (S);
- Failure to contact the agency/service (R) and (S);
- Receipt of a pension (R) and (S);
- Inability to work (R) and (S).

6. Definition of unemployed persons used for the statistics

Persons who are not engaged in productive economic activities which could serve as a principal source of income, i.e. having zero income as a result of being without work for a certain period of time, and who are willing to work and actively looking for work or waiting to return to work.

7. Updating of the registers

The registers are updated monthly.

8. Unemployment rates

Statistics from the registers are used to obtain unemployment rates.

The sources of data on employed persons who are part of the denominator of the unemployment rates are the Labour Force Survey, Establishment Surveys, Social Security Register, Official Estimates, Population Census.

Definition of employed persons for this purpose:

Persons who are engaged in any productive activity which generates sufficient income to meet basic needs.

9. Type of statistics of unemployed persons produced

Series 1:

Reference period: Month.

Frequency of production: Monthly.
Descriptive variables used:
- Sex;
- Age;
- Educational level;
- Occupation;
- Industry;
- Geographic characteristics;
- Previous work experience;
- Citizenship (nationals/non nationals);
- Duration of unemployment.

Form of publication: On paper, for general audience.
Agency responsible for publication: Department of Human Resource Management, Ministry of Labour and Human Resource Development.
Title and periodicity of the publication: *Departmental Monthly Report.*

Series 2:
Reference period: Quarter.
Frequency of production: Quarterly.
Descriptive variables used:
- Sex;
- Age;
- Educational level;
- Occupation;
- Industry;
- Geographic characteristics;
- Previous work experience;
- Citizenship (nationals/non nationals);
- Duration of unemployment.

Form of publication: On paper, for general audience.
Agency responsible for publication: Department of Human Resource Management, Ministry of Labour and Human Resource Development.
Title and periodicity of the publication: *Departmental Quarterly Report.*

Series 3:
Reference period: Year.
Frequency of production: Yearly.
Descriptive variables used:
- Sex;
- Age;
- Educational level;
- Occupation;
- Industry;
- Geographic characteristics;
- Previous work experience;
- Citizenship (nationals/non nationals);
- Duration of unemployment.

Form of publication: On paper, for general audience.
Agency responsible for publication: Department of Human Resource Management, Ministry of Labour and Human Resource Development.
Title and periodicity of the publication: *Departmental Annual Report.*

10. Methodological information about the statistics
Form of release: On paper, for general audience.
Agency responsible for the release: Department of Human Resource Management, Ministry of Labour and Human Resource Development.

11. Comparisons with unemployment statistics from other sources
Comparisons have been made with unemployment statistics from the Labour Force Survey, other types of household surveys, the Population Census and from private Employment Agencies.
Frequency of the comparisons: Regularly, when the statistics are published (latest year: 2000).
Publication of the methodology/results of the comparisons: These have been published. This information will also be made available in the National Employment and Manpower Information System (NEMIS) which is currently being developed.

12. Major changes since the start of the statistics
There have been no major changes in legislation, capacity of the agency and/or administrative procedures which had a significant influence on the statistics.

13. Additional remarks
It is recognized that the methodology used to obtain the data is rudimentary and that the figures obtained may thus not always be precise.

Latvia

1. Series
Title: Registered unemployment.
Starting year: 1992
2. Agency making the initial registrations of unemployed persons
Name of the agency: Nodarbinatibas Valsts Dienests (State Employment Service).
Type of agency: Public service under a national authority.
Name of the national authority: Ministry of Welfare.
Location of the local offices making the registrations: In all administrative territories of the country.
Type of services provided/administered by the agency:
- Assisting job-seekers to find jobs;
- Assisting employers to find workers;
- Vocational guidance;
- Job-related training;
- Other: organizing paid temporary community works; job Club services.

Percentage of job-seekers seeking work through the agency: 7.6%.
3. The following information is registered about a person:
- Name;
- Sex;
- Social security number (or similar identification number also used by other agencies);
- Address of usual residence;
- Date of birth;
- Citizenship;
- Nationality/ethnic group;
- Educational/vocational attainment, with 6 categories distinguished. Links to ISCED have not been established;
- Type of work (occupation) of past or present job with 10 categories distinguished. Links to ISCO-88 have been established;
- Type of work (occupation) of job sought, with 10 categories distinguished. Links to ISCO-88 have been established;
- Name of present or previous employer or work place;
- Type of business (industry) of present/previous employer/workplace. Links to ISIC, rev.3 or NACE, rev.1 have been established (class level).

4. Criteria used for inclusion of a person in the registers (R) and/or the statistics of unemployed persons (S):
- Being without work (R) and (S);
- Age (lower limit: 15 years; upper limit: 60.5 years for men; 58.5 years for women) (R) and (S);
- Being resident in the country (R) and (S).

5. Criteria used for exclusion of a person from the registers (R) and/or the statistics of unemployed persons (S):
- Death (R) and (S);
- Taking up residency abroad (R) and (S);
- Commencement of a (new) job (R) and (S);
- Commencement of military service (R) and (S);
- Studying (full-time) or undergoing training (R) and (S);
- Failure to contact the agency/service (R) and (S);
- Refusal of 2 suitable job offers (R) and (S);
- Receipt of a pension (retirement age) (R) and (S);
- Inability to work (R) and (S);
- Other: imprisonment (R) and (S).

6. Definition of unemployed persons used for the statistics
Persons able to work, who are citizens or permanent residents of the Republic of Latvia, are of working age, seeking a job, not running a business, are registered with the State Employment Service and who attend the agency at least once a month.

7. Updating of the registers
The registers are updated monthly.

8. Unemployment rates
Statistics from the registers are used to obtain unemployment rates.
The sources of data on employed persons who are part of the denominator of the unemployment rates are the Labour Force Survey, Establishment surveys, Social Security Register, Official Estimates and the Population Census.

Definition of employed persons for this purpose:
Employed persons refer to persons employed in both the public and private sector. The number of employed persons excludes students of working age not gainfully employed. The calculation of the average number of persons employed is based on the results of the Labour Force Survey and regular statistical information.

9. Type of statistics of unemployed persons produced
Series 1:
Reference period: Month.
Frequency of production: Monthly.
Descriptive variables used:
– Sex;
– Geographic characteristics;
– Duration of unemployment.
Form of publication: On a website (www.nvd.gov.lv).
Agency responsible for publication: State Employment Service.
Series 2:
Reference period: Quarter.
Frequency of production: Quarterly.
Descriptive variables used:
– Age;
– Educational level;
– Occupation;
– Geographic characteristics;
– Previous work experience;
– Nationality.
Series 3:
Reference period: Year.
Frequency of production: Yearly.
Form of publication: On paper, for general audience;
Agency responsible for publication: State Employment Service.
Title and periodicity of the publication: *Annual Report*.
10. Methodological information about the statistics
Form of release:
– On paper, for general audience;
– In machine-readable form, on request;
– On a website (www.nvd.gov.lv).
Agencies responsible for the release: State Employment Service; Central Statistics Bureau.
11. Comparisons with unemployment statistics from other sources
Comparisons have not been made with unemployment statistics from other sources.
12. Major changes since the start of the statistics
There have been no major changes in legislation, capacity of the agency and/or administrative procedures which had a significant influence on the statistics.

Lesotho

1. Series
Title: Job-seekers Statistics.
Starting year: 1996.
2. Agency making the initial registrations of unemployed persons
Name of the agency: National Employment Services (NES).
Type of agency: Public service under a national authority.
Name of the national authority: Labour Department.
Location of the local offices making the registrations: District Labour Offices in all districts of the country.
Type of services provided/administered by the agency:
– Assisting job-seekers to find jobs;
– Assisting job-seekers to establish their own business;
– Assisting employers to find workers;
– Vocational guidance;
– Other: dissemination of employment related (labour market) information.
Percentage of job-seekers seeking work through the agency: 30%.
3. The following information is registered about a person:
– Name;
– Sex;
– Social security number (or similar identification number also used by other agencies);
– Address of usual residence;
– Date of birth;
– Citizenship;

– Educational/vocational attainment, with four categories distinguished. Links to ISCED have not been established;
– Type of work (occupation) of past or present job with eight categories distinguished. Links to ISCO-88 have been established (major group level);
– Type of work (occupation) of job sought, with eight categories distinguished. Links to ISCO-88 have been established (major group level);
– Previous registrations with the agency/service.
4. Criteria used for inclusion of a person in the registers (R) and/or the statistics of unemployed persons (S):
– Seeking work (R);
– Age (lower limit: 18 years; upper limit: 55 years) (R);
– Citizenship (must be a Lesotho citizen) (R).
5. Criteria used for exclusion of a person from the registers (R) and/or the statistics of unemployed persons (S):
– Death (R);
– Taking up residency abroad (R);
– Commencement of a (new) job (R).
6. Definition of unemployed persons used for the statistics
Unemployed persons are defined as people who earn zero income.
7. Updating of the registers
The registers are updated daily.
8. Unemployment rates
Statistics from the registers are not used to obtain unemployment rates.
9. Type of statistics of unemployed persons produced
Series: Job-seekers statistics.
Reference period: Quarter.
Frequency of production: Weekly.
Descriptive variables used:
– Sex;
– Age;
– Educational level;
– Occupation.
Form of publication: Machine-readable form, on request;
Title of the publication: *Quarterly Reports*.
10. Methodological information about the statistics
Form of release: In machine-readable form, on request.
Agency responsible for the release: National Employment Services.
11. Comparisons with unemployment statistics from other sources
Comparisons have not been made with unemployment statistics from other sources.
12. Major changes since the start of the statistics
There have been no major changes in legislation, capacity of the agency and/or administrative procedures which had a significant influence on the statistics.

Lithuania

1. Series
Title: Job-seekers and vacancies.
Starting year: 1992
2. Agency making the initial registrations of unemployed persons
Name of the agency: Lietuvos Darbo Birza (Lithuanian Labour Exchange).
Type of agency: Public service under a national authority.
Name of the national authority: Ministry of Social Security and Labour.
Location of the local offices making the registrations: 46 local Labour Exchanges in all parts of the country covering all local labour markets and localities.
Type of services provided/administered by the agency:
– Assisting job-seekers to find jobs;
– Assisting job-seekers to establish their own business;
– Assisting employers to find workers;
– Vocational guidance;
– Job-related training;
– Paying unemployment compensation;
– Other: active labour market measures: public works; supported works; Job Club.
Percentage of job-seekers seeking work through the agency: 67.3%

3. The following information is registered about a person:
- Name;
- Sex;
- Social security number (or similar identification number also used by other agencies);
- Address of usual residence;
- Date of birth;
- Citizenship;
- Educational/attainment, with six categories distinguished. Links to ISCED have been established;
- Current/past activity status, with four categories distinguished;
- Type of work (occupation) of past or present job with 7200 categories distinguished. Links to ISCO-88 have been established (unit group level);
- Type of work (occupation) of job sought, with 7200 categories distinguished. Links to ISCO-88 have been established (unit group level);
- Name and address of present or previous employer or work place;
- Type of business (industry) of present/previous employer/workplace, with 1351 categories distinguished. Links to ISIC, rev.3 or NACE, rev.1 have been established (class level);
- Previous registrations with the agency/service.

4. Criteria used for inclusion of a person in the registers (R) and/or the statistics of unemployed persons (S):
- Being without work (R) and (S);
- Seeking work (R) and (S);
- Availability for work (R) and (S);
- Age (lower limit: 16 years; upper limit: 61.5 years for men; 57.5 years for women) (R) and (S);
- Being resident in the country (R) and (S).

5. Criteria used for exclusion of a person from the registers (R) and/or the statistics of unemployed persons (S):
- Death (R) and (S);
- Taking up residency abroad (R) and (S);
- Commencement of a (new) job (R) and (S);
- Commencement of military service (R) and (S);
- Participation in an employment promotion scheme, public works programme, etc. (R) and (S);
- Studying or undergoing training (R) and (S);
- Failure to contact the agency/service (R) and (S);
- Receipt of a retirement pension (R) and (S);
- Inability to work (R) and (S);
- Other: refusal to make an employment plan (R) and (S).

6. Definition of unemployed persons used for the statistics

Persons able to work, of working age, who are without work shall be considered as unemployed, provided they are not full-time students at an educational institution, and on the condition that they have registered with the national labour exchange of their place of residence as persons looking for a job and ready to go into vocational training.

7. Updating of the registers

The registers are updated whenever there is a change of data.

8. Unemployment rates

Statistics from the registers are used to obtain unemployment rates.

The source of data on employed persons who are part of the denominator of the unemployment rates is Official Estimates.

Definition of employed persons for this purpose:

Employment refers to all persons working in the state sector, cooperatives, private enterprises and the self-employed, including: employees on maternity and child-care leave, military personnel, employees on extended unpaid leave, part-time workers on a full-time equivalent basis, persons outside working age (i.e. 16 - 57.5 for women and 16 - 61.5 for men) who continue to hold paid employment.

9. Type of statistics of unemployed persons produced

Series 1:
Reference period: Month.
Frequency of production: Monthly.
Descriptive variables used:
- Sex;
- Age;
- Geographic characteristics.

Form of publication:
- On paper, for general audience;

- Machine-readable form, on request;
- On a website (www.ldb.lt).

Agency responsible for publication: Statistics Lithuania.
Title and periodicity of the publication: *Economic and social development in Lithuania*, monthly.

Series 2:
Reference period: Quarter.
Frequency of production: Quarterly.
Descriptive variables used:
- Sex;
- Age;
- Educational level;
- Geographic characteristics;
- Previous work experience;
- Duration of unemployment.

Form of publication:
- On paper, for general audience;
- Machine-readable form, on request;
- On a website (www.ldb.lt).

Agency responsible for publication: Statistics Lithuania.
Title of the publication: *Labour market and employment of population (Statistical Bulletin)*.

Series 3:
Reference period: Year.
Frequency of production: Yearly.
Descriptive variables used:
- Sex;
- Age;
- Educational level;
- Industry;
- Geographic characteristics;
- Previous work experience;
- Duration of unemployment.

Form of publication:
- On paper, for general audience;
- Machine-readable form, on request;
- On a website (www.ldb.lt).

Agency responsible for publication: Statistics Lithuania.
Title of the publications: *Labour market and employment of population (Statistical Bulletin and Abstract); Statistical Yearbook of Lithuania.*

10. Methodological information about the statistics
Form of release: On paper, for general audience.
Agency responsible for the release: Ministry of Social Security and Labour.

11. Comparisons with unemployment statistics from other sources

Comparisons have been made with unemployment statistics from the Labour Force Survey.

Frequency of the comparisons: Regularly, when the statistics are published.
Publication of the methodology/results of the comparisons: These are published in *Labour force, employment and unemployment (LFS data, Biannual Bulletin of Statistics Lithuania).*

12. Major changes since the start of the statistics

Major changes in legislation, capacity of the agency and/or administrative procedures took place in 1996, 2000 and 2001. The resulting changes in the statistics have not been estimated.

Luxembourg

1. Series
Title: Employment Situation: monthly data (since 1982).
Luxembourg Employment Bulletin (since 1998).

2. Agency making the initial registrations of unemployed persons
Name of the agency: Employment administration (ADEM).
Type of agency: Public service under a national authority.
Name of the national authority: Ministry of Labour and Employment.
Location of the local offices making the registrations: Luxembourg, Esch/Alzeth, Diekirsch, Wiltz.
Type of services provided/administered by the agency:
- Assisting job-seekers to find jobs;
- Assisting employers to find workers;
- Vocational guidance;
- Job-related training, in collaboration with employers and the

- professional training service of the National Education Ministry;
- Paying unemployment compensation;
- Other employment-related services: payment of the various aids and premiums in favour of job preservation and the integration or reintegration of unemployed persons into economically active life; services to handicapped workers.

3. The following information is registered about a person:
- Name;
- Sex;
- Social security number (or similar identification number also used by other agencies);
- Address of usual residence;
- Date of birth;
- Citizenship;
- Nationality/ethnic group;
- Educational/vocational attainment, with four categories distinguished. Links to ISCED have not been established;
- Type of work (occupation) of job sought with12 categories distinguished. Links to ISCO-68 have been established (close to the Belgian system);
- Name and address of present or previous employer or work place;
- Type of business (industry) of present/previous employer/workplace, with five categories distinguished. Links to NACE, rev.1 have been established;
- Previous registrations with the agency/service;
- Other: information on job and geographic mobility.

4. Criteria used for inclusion of a person in the registers (R) and/or the statistics of unemployed persons (S):
- Being without work (S);
- Seeking work (R) and (S);
- Availability for work (R) and (S);
- Age (lower limit: 16 years; upper limit: 65 years) (R) and (S);
- Citizenship: being native of an European Union member State (R) and (S);
- Being resident in the country: having an official address in Luxembourg (R).

5. Criteria used for exclusion of a person from the registers (R) and/or the statistics of unemployed persons (S):
- Death (R) and (S);
- Taking up residency abroad (R) and (S);
- Commencement of a (new) job (R) and (S);
- Participation in an employment promotion scheme, public works programme, etc (S);
- Studying or undergoing training: participation in a training programme organised in collaboration with the National Education Ministry;
- Failure to contact the agency/service: in principle, job-seekers have to report to the employment service at least once every two weeks (R) and (S);
- Refusal of suitable job offers (after one refusal) (R) and (S);
- Refusal of suitable training offers (after one refusal) (R) and (S);
- Receipt of a pension (R) and (S);
- Inability to work (R) and (S).

6. Definition of unemployed persons used for the statistics

All persons without a job, available on the labour market, looking for an appropriate job, not benefiting from any employment promotion measure, with or without unemployment compensation and who have respected the obligations to be followed as established by the ADEM.

7. Updating of the registers

The registers are updated every month.

8. Unemployment rates

Statistics from the registers are used to obtain unemployment rates.

Calculations are made by STATEC (Central Service of Statistics and Economic Studies), using the following sources: social security registers, official estimates and population censuses.

Definition of employed persons for this purpose:

National employment taken into consideration is domestic employment (Wage earners and non wage-earners); excluded are foreign workers who cross the border every day to work in Luxembourg, Luxembourg nationals who cross the border every day to work abroad and international civil servants.

9. Type of statistics of unemployed persons produced

Series 1:

Reference period: Month.

Frequency of production: Monthly.

Descriptive variables used:
- Sex;
- Age;
- Educational level;
- Occupation;
- Duration of unemployment;
- Unemployed receiving unemployment compensation;
- Job sought.

Form of publication:
- On paper, for general audience;
- On a website: www.etat.lu

Agency responsible for publication: ADEM.

Title of the publication: *Bulletin luxembourgeois de l'emploi* (Luxembourg Employment Bulletin).

Series 2:

Reference period: Month.

Frequency of production: Yearly.

Descriptive variables used:
- Sex;
- Age;
- Educational level;
- Occupation;
- Geographic characteristics;
- Citizenship (nationals/non nationals);
- Duration of unemployment;
- Unemployed receiving unemployment compensation;
- Job sought.

Form of publication: On paper, for limited audience.

Agency responsible for publication: ADEM.

Title of the publication: *Bulletin luxembourgeois de l'emploi* (Luxembourg Employment Bulletin).

10. Methodological information about the statistics

Form of release: Not released, available for internal use only.

Agency responsible for the release: ADEM.

11. Comparisons with unemployment statistics from other sources

Comparisons have not been made with unemployment statistics from other sources.

12. Major changes since the start of the statistics

There were major changes in legislation in 1998. Since 1998, job-seekers benefiting from an employment promotion measure are excluded from the unemployment statistics. "Persons benefiting from an employment promotion measure" represented between 24% (in 1998) and 31% (in 2001) of the total population (job-seekers and persons benefiting from an employment promotion measure) administrated by the ADEM.

Macedonia, The former Yugoslav Rep. of

1. Series

Title: Administrative report on employment, unemployment and unemployment benefit claimants.

2. Agency making the initial registrations of unemployed persons

Name of the agency: Zavon zavrabotuvanje na republika makedonija (Employment Office of the Republic of Macedonia).

Type of agency: Public service under a national authority.

Name of the national authority: Ministry of Labour and Social Policy.

Location of the local offices making the registrations: All over the country (30 regional offices in 30 cities).

Type of services provided/administered by the agency:
- Assisting job-seekers to find jobs;
- Assisting job-seekers to establish their own business;
- Assisting employers to find workers;
- Vocational guidance;
- Job-related training;
- Paying unemployment compensation.

Percentage of job-seekers seeking work through the agency: 32.2%.

3. The following information is registered about a person:
- Name;
- Sex;
- Social security number (or similar identification number also used by other agencies);

- Address of usual residence;
- Date of birth;
- Citizenship;
- Nationality/ethnic group;
- Educational/vocational attainment, with eight categories distinguished. Links to ISCED have not been established;
- Current/past activity status, with 40 categories distinguished;
- Type of work of past or present job with 1,709 categories distinguished. Links to ISCO-88 have not been established;
- Type of work of job sought, with 1,709 categories distinguished;
- Name and address of present or previous employer or work place;
- Type of business (industry) of present/previous employer/workplace, with 602 categories distinguished. Links to ISIC have been established at class groups level;
- Previous registrations with the agency/service.

4. Criteria used for inclusion of a person in the registers (R) and/or the statistics of unemployed persons (S):

- Being without work (R) and (S);
- Seeking work: to come regularly to the office when summoned, to participate in employment promotion programmes (R) and (S);
- Availability for work (R) and (S);
- Age (lower limit: 15 years; upper limit: 65 years) (R) and (S);
- Citizenship (R) and (S);
- Being resident in the country (R) and (S).

5. Criteria used for exclusion of a person from the registers (R) and/or the statistics of unemployed persons (S):

- Death (R) and (S);
- Taking up residency abroad (R) and (S);
- Commencement of a (new) job (R) and (S);
- Commencement of military service (R) and (S);
- Studying or undergoing training (R) and (S);
- Failure to contact the agency/service (R) and (S);
- Refusal of suitable job offers, after two refusals (R) and (S);
- Refusal of suitable training offers, after two refusals (R) and (S);
- Eligibility for a pension (retirement benefits, etc.) (R) and (S);
- Inability to work (R) and (S).

6. Definition of unemployed persons used for the statistics

Unemployed persons are persons registered in the employment register, able to work, willing to work and actively seeking work. A person is considered actively seeking work when he/she is regularly registered with his/her relevant employment office, within the time limits laid down in the labour law.

7. Updating of the registers

The registers are updated regularly, monthly for those receiving unemployment benefits, every three months for those with medical insurance benefits, and every six months for all the others.

8. Unemployment rates

Statistics from the registers are used to obtain unemployment rates.

9. Type of statistics of unemployed persons produced

Reference period: Month, half-year, year.

Frequency of production: Monthly, half-yearly, annually.

Descriptive variables used:

- Sex;
- Age;
- Educational level;
- Occupation;
- Industry;
- Geographic characteristics;
- Previous work experience;
- Citizenship (nationals/non nationals);
- Duration of unemployment.

Form of publication:

- On paper, for general audience;
- Machine-readable form, on request;
- On a website: http://www.zvrm.gov.mk.

Agency responsible for publication: Employment Office of the Republic of Macedonia.

10. Methodological information about the statistics

Form of release:

- On paper, for general audience;
- In machine-readable form, on request;
- On a website: http://www.zvrm.gov.mk.

Agency responsible for the release: Ministry of Labour, Employment Office of the Republic of Macedonia, Statistical Institute.

11. Comparisons with unemployment statistics from other sources

Comparisons have not been made with unemployment statistics from other sources.

12. Major changes since the start of the statistics

There have been no major changes in legislation, capacity of the agency and/or administrative procedures which had a significant influence on the statistics.

Madagascar

1. Series

Title: Labour market statistics.

Starting year: 1979.

2. Agency making the initial registrations of unemployed persons

Name of the agency: Studies, Statistics and Planning Service.

Type of agency: Public service under a national authority.

Name of the national authority: Employment Department.

Location of the local offices making the registrations: In some areas only, nine sub-prefectures out of a total of 111.

Type of services provided/administered by the agency:

- Assisting job-seekers to find jobs;
- Assisting employers to find workers;
- Other: issuing unemployment certificates.

Percentage of job-seekers seeking work through the agency: 5.6%.

3. The following information is registered about a person:

- Name;
- Sex;
- Address of usual residence;
- Date of birth;
- Nationality;
- Educational/vocational attainment, with nine categories distinguished. Links to ISCED have not been established;
- Current/past activity status, with two categories distinguished;
- Type of work (occupation) of past or present job. Links to ISCO-88 have not been established;
- Type of work (occupation) of job sought;
- Name and address of present or previous employer or work place;
- Type of business (industry) of present/previous employer/workplace;
- Previous registrations with the agency/service.

4. Criteria used for inclusion of a person in the registers (R) and/or the statistics of unemployed persons (S):

- Being without work (R);
- Seeking work (R);
- Availability for work (R);
- Age (lower limit: 15 years; upper limit: 40 years, which is the maximum age for entry into the civil service) (R);
- Being resident in the country (R);
- Previously employed (R).

5. Criteria used for exclusion of a person from the registers (R) and/or the statistics of unemployed persons (S):

Information not available.

6. Definition of unemployed persons used for the statistics

On the whole, any person registered with the employment office is considered as "unemployed" if he/she is available for work.

7. Updating of the registers

The registers are updated on a monthly basis.

8. Unemployment rates

Statistics from the registers are not used to obtain unemployment rates.

9. Type of statistics of unemployed persons produced

Reference period: Year.

Frequency of production: Yearly.

Descriptive variables used:

- Sex;
- Educational level;
- Geographic characteristics;
- Previous work experience;
- Citizenship (nationals).

Form of publication: On paper, for limited audience.

10. Methodological information about the statistics
Form of release: On paper, for limited audience.
11. Comparisons with unemployment statistics from other sources
Comparisons have not been made with unemployment statistics from other sources.
12. Major changes since the start of the statistics
There have been no major changes in legislation, capacity of the agency and/or administrative procedures which had a significant influence on the statistics.

Malaysia

1. Series
Title: Registered unemployment.
Starting year: 1969
2. Agency making the initial registrations of unemployed persons
Name of the agency: Jabatan Tenaga Rakyat (Manpower Department).
Type of agency: Public service under a national authority.
Name of the national authority: Ministry of Human Resources (MOHR).
Location of the local offices making the registrations: In all parts of the country totalling 13 state offices and 36 district offices.
Type of services provided/administered by the agency:
- Assisting job-seekers to find jobs;
- Assisting employers to find workers;
- Vocational guidance;
- Job-related training;
- Other: issuing licenses to the private sector employment agencies and monitoring their operation in compliance with the Private Employment Agencies Act, 1981.

Percentage of job-seekers seeking work through the agency: 20%.
3. The following information is registered about a person:
- Name;
- Sex;
- Social security number (or similar identification number also used by other agencies);
- Address of usual residence;
- Date of birth;
- Citizenship;
- Nationality/ethnic group;
- Educational/vocational attainment, with four categories distinguished. Links to ISCED have been established;
- Current/past activity status, with three categories distinguished;
- Type of work (occupation) of past or present job with seven groups distinguished. Links to ISCO-88 have been established (major groups level);
- Type of work (occupation) of job sought, with seven groups distinguished. Links to ISCO-88 have been established (major groups level);
- Name and address of present or previous employer or work place;
- Type of business (industry) of present/previous employer/workplace, with 17 groups distinguished. Links to ISIC, rev.3 have been established (tabulation categories level).

4. Criteria used for inclusion of a person in the registers (R) and/or the statistics of unemployed persons (S):
- Being without work (R) and (S);
- Seeking work (R) and (S);
- Age (lower limit: 15 years; upper limit: 64 years) (R) and (S);
- Citizenship (R) and (S);
- Being resident in the country (R) and (S).

5. Criteria used for exclusion of a person from the registers (R) and/or the statistics of unemployed persons (S):
- Death (S);
- Taking up residency abroad (S);
- Commencement of a (new) job (R) and (S);
- Commencement of military service (R) and (S);
- Participation in an employment promotion scheme, public works programme, etc. (R) and (S);
- Studying or undergoing training (R) and (S);
- Failure to contact the agency/service (registration has to be renewed every 3 months) (R) and (S).

6. Definition of unemployed persons used for the statistics
This includes both actively and inactively unemployed persons. The <u>actively unemployed</u> includes all persons who did not work during the reference week but were available for work and actively looking for work during the reference week. <u>Inactively unemployed</u> persons include the following categories:
(i) persons who did not look for work because they believed no work was available or that they were not qualified;
(ii) persons who would have looked for work if they had not been temporarily ill or had it not been for bad weather;
(iii) persons who were waiting for answers to job applications;
(iv) persons who had looked for work prior to the reference week.
7. Updating of the registers
The registers are updated every week.
8. Unemployment rates
Statistics from the registers are not used to obtain unemployment rates.
9. Type of statistics of unemployed persons produced
Series 1:
Reference period: Week.
Frequency of production: Weekly.
Descriptive variables used:
- Sex;
- Age;
- Educational level;
- Occupation;
- Industry;
- Geographic characteristics;
- Previous work experience;
- Citizenship (nationals/non nationals);
- Duration of unemployment.

Form of publication: On paper, for limited audience;
Agency responsible for publication: MOHR, Manpower Department.
Series 2:
Reference period: Month.
Frequency of production: Monthly.
Descriptive variables used:
- Sex;
- Age;
- Educational level;
- Occupation;
- Industry;
- Geographic characteristics;
- Previous work experience;
- Citizenship (nationals/non nationals);
- Duration of unemployment.

Form of publication:
- On paper, for general audience;
- On a website (www.mohr.gov.my and www.jtr.gov.my).

Agency responsible for publication: MOHR, Manpower Department.
Title of the publication: *Registration of Job Seekers, Job Vacancies and Placements.*
Series 3:
Reference period: Quarter.
Frequency of production: Quarterly.
Descriptive variables used:
- Sex;
- Age;
- Educational level;
- Occupation;
- Industry;
- Geographic characteristics;
- Previous work experience;
- Citizenship (nationals/non nationals);
- Duration of unemployment.

Form of publication:
- On paper, for general audience;
- On a website (www.mohr.gov.my and www.jtr.gov.my).

Agency responsible for publication: MOHR, Manpower Department.
Title of the publication: *Labour Market Trends.*
10. Methodological information about the statistics
Form of release: Not released, available for internal use only.
Agency responsible: MOHR, Manpower Department.

11. Comparisons with unemployment statistics from other sources

Comparisons have been made with unemployment statistics from the Population Census and the Economic Report.

Frequency of the comparisons: Regularly when the statistics are published.

Publication of the methodology/results of the comparisons: These have not been published.

12. Major changes since the start of the statistics

There have been no major changes in legislation, capacity of the agency and/or administrative procedures which had a significant influence on the statistics.

Mali

1. Series

Title: Labour Market Statistical Yearbook.

Starting year: 1995.

2. Agency making the initial registrations of unemployed persons

Name of the agency:

1. Agence nationale pour l'Emploi - ANPE (National Employment Agency).
2. Bureaux privés de placement - BPP (Private Employment offices).

Type of agency:

1. Public service under a national authority;
2. Profit-making private service.

Name of the national authority: Ministry of Employment and Vocational Training.

Location of the local offices making the registrations: All over the country.

Type of services provided/administered by the agency:

– Assisting job-seekers to find jobs;
– Assisting job-seekers to establish their own business;
– Assisting employers to find workers;
– Vocational guidance;
– Job-related training;
– Other: information about the labour market.

Percentage of job-seekers seeking work through the agency: 20%.

3. The following information is registered about a person:

– Name;
– Sex;
– Address of usual residence;
– Date of birth;
– Nationality;
– Educational/vocational attainment, with eight categories distinguished. Links to ISCED have not been established;
– Type of work (occupation) of past or present job with eight categories distinguished. Links to ISCO-88 have been established;
– Type of work (occupation) of job sought, with eight categories distinguished;
– Name and address of present or previous employer or work place;
– Type of business (industry) of present/previous employer/workplace, with nine categories distinguished. Links to ISIC have been established;
– Previous registrations with the agency/service.

4. Criteria used for inclusion of a person in the registers (R) and/or the statistics of unemployed persons (S):

– Being without work (R) and (S);
– Seeking work (R) and (S);
– Availability for work (R) and (S);
– Age (lower limit: 15 years; no upper limit) (R) and (S).

5. Criteria used for exclusion of a person from the registers (R) and/or the statistics of unemployed persons (S):

– Death (R) and (S);
– Taking up residency abroad (R) and (S);
– Commencement of a (new) job (R) and (S);
– Commencement of military service (R) and (S);
– Studying or undergoing training: only for training of long duration (six months and more) (R) and (S);
– Failure to contact the agency/service: after three months without contact (R) and (S);
– Inability to work (R) and (S).

6. Definition of unemployed persons used for the statistics

Any person of legal working age (15 years and over) who, during the reference period (usually one month), was without work, available for work and looking actively for a job.

7. Updating of the registers

The registers are updated monthly.

8. Unemployment rates

Statistics from the registers are not used to obtain unemployment rates.

9. Type of statistics of unemployed persons produced

Reference period: Month.

Frequency of production: Yearly.

Descriptive variables used:

– Sex;
– Age;
– Educational level;
– Occupation;
– Industry;
– Geographic characteristics;
– Previous work experience;
– Citizenship (nationals/non nationals);
– Duration of unemployment.

Form of publication:

– On paper, for general audience;
– Machine-readable form, on request.

Agency responsible for publication: Observatoire de l'Emploi et de la Formation (OEF) (Observatory of Employment and Training).

Title and periodicity of the publication: *Annuaire statistique du marché de l'emploi* (Statistical Yearbook of Labour Market), yearly.

10. Methodological information about the statistics

Form of release:

– On paper, for general audience;
– In machine-readable form, on request.

Agency responsible for the release: OEF.

11. Comparisons with unemployment statistics from other sources

Comparisons have been made with unemployment statistics from the labour force survey, other household surveys and from the population census.

Frequency of the comparisons: Occasionally.

Publication of the methodology/results of the comparisons: These have not been published.

12. Major changes since the start of the statistics

Major changes in legislation and administrative procedures took place in 2000, date of the creation of the ANPE, which replaced the National Office of Manpower and Employment. The resulting changes in the statistics have not been estimated.

Malta

1. Series

Title: Registered unemployment.

Starting year: 1957.

2. Agency making the initial registrations of unemployed persons

Name of the agency: Employment and Training Corporation (ETC).

Type of agency: Public service under local authorities.

Location of the local offices making the registrations: First-time registrations are made at the ETC Head Office in Hal Far; subsequent weekly registrations at one of the 20 local area offices.

Type of services provided/administered by the agency:

– Assisting job-seekers to find jobs;
– Assisting job-seekers to establish their own business;
– Assisting employers to find workers;
– Vocational guidance;
– Job-related training;
– Other: administration of training grants; labour market information; job Centres in 3 areas.

Percentage of job-seekers seeking work through the agency: 73% (according to Labour Force Survey estimates).

3. The following information is registered about a person:

– Name;
– Sex;
– Social security number (or similar identification number also used by other agencies);
– Address of usual residence;
– Date of birth;
– Citizenship;

- Nationality/ethnic group;
- Educational/vocational attainment. Links to ISCED have not been established;
- Current/past activity status, with 3 categories distinguished;
- Type of work (occupation) of past or present job. Links to ISCO-88 have been established (sub-major groups level);
- Type of work (occupation) of job sought, with 476 groups distinguished. Links to ISCO-88 have been established;
- Name and address of present or previous employer or work place;
- Type of business (industry) of present/previous employer/workplace, with 83 groups distinguished. Links to ISIC, rev.3 have been established (group level);
- Previous registrations with the agency/service;
- Other: registration of up to 5 options; type of disability (if any).

4. Criteria used for inclusion of a person in the registers (R) and/or the statistics of unemployed persons (S):
- Being without work (R) and (S);
- Seeking work (R) and (S);
- Availability for work (R) and (S);
- Age (lower limit: 16 years (R), 15 years (S); no upper limit);
- Citizenship (Maltese nationals only) (R);
- Being resident in the country (R);
- Previously employed (R).

5. Criteria used for exclusion of a person from the registers (R) and/or the statistics of unemployed persons (S):
- Death (R) and (S);
- Taking up residency abroad (R) and (S);
- Commencement of a (new) job (R) and (S);
- Participation in certain unemployment promotion schemes and paid public works programmes, etc. (R) and (S);
- Studying or undergoing training (R) and (S);
- Failure to contact the agency/service (R);
- Refusal of a suitable job offer (R);
- Refusal of a suitable training offers (R);
- Receipt of a pension (R);
- Inability to work (R) and (S);
- Other: If found working by inspectorate in the informal sector (R).

6. Definition of unemployed persons used for the statistics
(Criteria to enrol under Part I of the Unemployment Register):
All Maltese citizens who are aged over 16 years and who were:
- made redundant from their earlier job; or
- were school leavers (first time registrants); or
- who were under Part II of the Register, for one of the following reasons, and have passed their six-month penalty period, i.e.: were dismissed from work due to disciplinary action; left work of their own free will; refused work/training opportunities, without giving a valid reason, offered to them by the Placement Officer whilst they were registering under Part I; were struck off the Register after being found working in the informal sector during an inspection by law enforcement personnel; failed to provide all the necessary documents required for registration under Part I (temporary measure).

7. Updating of the registers
The registers are updated daily and weekly.

8. Unemployment rates
Statistics from the registers were used to obtain unemployment rates until August 2001 (since then unemployment rates are obtained through the Labour Force Survey).
The source of data on employed persons forming part of the denominator of the unemployment rates was the Employed Persons Database, based on engagement forms.

9. Type of statistics of unemployed persons produced
Reference period: Month.
Frequency of production: Monthly.
Descriptive variables used:
- Sex;
- Age;
- Educational level;
- Occupation;
- Industry;
- Previous work experience;
- Duration of unemployment.

Form of publication:
- On paper, for general audience;
- On a website (www.nso.gov.mt)

Agency responsible for publication: National Statistical Office.
Title and periodicity of the publication(s): *News Release* (monthly); *Abstract of Statistics*, annual.
10. Methodological information about the statistics
Form of release:
- On paper, for general audience;
- On a website (www.nso.gov.mt).
Agency responsible for the release: ETC.
11. Comparisons with unemployment statistics from other sources
Comparisons have been made with unemployment statistics from the Labour Force Survey and the Population Census.
Frequency of the comparisons: Occasionally (latest: December 2000).
Publication of the methodology/results of the comparisons: These have not been published.
12. Major changes since the start of the statistics
There have been no major changes in legislation, capacity of the agency and/or administrative procedures which had a significant influence on the statistics.

Mauritius

1. Series
Title: Registered unemployment.
Starting year: Circa 1960.
2. Agency making the initial registrations of unemployed persons
Name of the agency: Employment Service.
Type of agency: Public service under a national authority.
Name of the national authority: Ministry of Training, Skills Development and Productivity.
Location of the local offices making the registrations: In all parts of the country.
Type of services provided/administered by the agency:
- Assisting job-seekers to find jobs;
- Assisting employers to find workers;
- Vocational guidance;
- Other: providing information to training/business funding agencies.
Percentage of job-seekers seeking work through the agency: 65%.
3. The following information is registered about a person:
- Name;
- Sex;
- Social security number (or similar identification number also used by other agencies);
- Address of usual residence;
- Date of birth;
- Nationality/ethnic group.
- Educational/vocational attainment. No links to ISCED have been established;
- Current/past activity status;
- Type of work (occupation) of past or present job. Links to ISCO-88 have been established (unit groups level);
- Type of work (occupation) of job sought. Links to ISCO-88 have been established (unit groups level);
- Name and address of present or previous employer or work place;
- Type of business (industry) of present/previous employer/workplace. No links to ISIC, rev.3 have been established;
- Previous registrations with the agency/service;
- Other: dependents; marital status; disabilities.
4. Criteria used for inclusion of a person in the registers (R) and/or the statistics of unemployed persons (S):
- Being without work (R) and (S);
- Seeking work (R) and (S);
- Availability for work (R) and (S);
- Age (lower limit: 15 years; no upper limit) (R) and (S);
- Citizenship (R) and (S);
- Being resident in the country (R) and (S).
5. Criteria used for exclusion of a person from the registers (R) and/or the statistics of unemployed persons (S):
- Death (R) and (S);
- Taking up residency abroad (R) and (S);
- Failure to contact agency/service (R).

6. Definition of unemployed persons used for the statistics

Not only unemployed persons but also persons in employment are eligible for registration, if they are seeking better or alternative jobs.

An Unemployed Person is defined as a person of either sex, aged at least fifteen and declaring him/herself unemployed and willing to accept a job.

7. Updating of the registers

The unemployed register is updated every month and those who have failed to report are removed. Persons in employment report only once a year; this register is updated every four months.

8. Unemployment rates

Statistics from the registers are not used to obtain unemployment rates.

9. Type of statistics of unemployed persons produced

Reference period: January - April; May - August; September - December.

Frequency of production: Every four months.

Descriptive variables used:

– Sex;
– Age;
– Educational level;
– Occupation;
– Industry;
– Geographic characteristics;
– Previous work experience;
– Citizenship (nationals/non nationals);
– Duration of unemployment;
– Other: young persons (15 - 17 years); disabled.

Form of publication: On paper, for general audience.

Agency responsible for publication: Employment Service.

Title and periodicity of the publication: *Statistical Review on Employment*, every four months.

N.B. Some figures on unemployment are available on the website of the Employment Service: http://ncb.intnet.mu/empserv.htm

10. Methodological information about the statistics

Form of release: On paper, for general audience.

Agency responsible for the release: Employment Service.

11. Comparisons with unemployment statistics from other sources

Comparisons have not been made with unemployment statistics from other sources.

12. Major changes since the start of the statistics

There have been no major changes in legislation, capacity of the agency and/or administrative procedures which had a significant influence on the statistics.

Moldova, Rep. of

1. Series

Title: Registered unemployment.

Starting year: 1992

2. Agency making the initial registrations of unemployed persons

Name of the agency: Employment offices, at the regional level.

Type of agency: Public service under national and regional authorities.

Name of the national authority: Labour Force Utilization Department under the Ministry of Labour and Social Protection.

Location of the local offices making the registrations: There are 12 employment offices (one in each county) and 33 employment sections in towns throughout the country that are under the direction of the county employment offices. The employment offices are under the Labour Force Utilization Department.

Type of services provided/administered by the agency:

– Assisting job-seekers to find jobs;
– Assisting job-seekers to establish their own business;
– Assisting employers to find workers;
– Vocational guidance;
– Job-related training;
– Paying unemployment compensation;
– Other: organization and development of Labour Exhibitions, "Labour Club" training and training for remunerated public works.

Percentage of job-seekers seeking work through the agency: 50%.

3. The following information is registered about a person:

– Name;
– Sex;
– Social security number (or similar identification number also used by other agencies);
– Address of usual residence;
– Date of birth;
– Educational/vocational attainment, with five categories distinguished. Links to ISCED have not been established;
– Type of work (occupation) of past or present job. Links to ISCO-88 have been established;
– Type of work (occupation) of job sought. Links to ISCO-88 have been established;
– Name and address of present or previous employer or work place;
– Type of business (industry) of present/previous employer/workplace, with 11 groups distinguished;
– Other: family status; labour card number; details of last job (dates of service, reason for leaving, average salary of the last three months, etc.); category of social protection; category of unemployment benefits; military status; knowledge of foreign languages; special training.

4. Criteria used for inclusion of a person in the registers (R) and/or the statistics of unemployed persons (S):

– Being without work (R) and (S);
– Seeking work (R) and (S);
– Availability for work (R) and (S);
– Age (lower limit: 16 years; upper limit: pension age) (R) and (S);
– Being resident in the country (R) and (S);
– Previously employed (including remunerated public works and temporary work) (R) and (S);
– Previous payment of unemployed insurance contributions (R) and (S).

5. Criteria used for exclusion of a person from the registers (R) and/or the statistics of unemployed persons (S):

– Death (R) and (S);
– Taking up residency abroad (R) and (S);
– Commencement of a (new) job (R) and (S);
– Commencement of military service (R) and (S);
– Participation in an employment promotion scheme, public works programme, etc. (R) and (S);
– Studying or undergoing training (R) and (S);
– Failure to contact the agency/service for over 2 months (R) and (S);
– Refusal of 2 suitable job offers (R) and (S);
– Receipt of a pension (R) and (S);
– Inability to work (R) and (S).

6. Definition of unemployed persons used for the statistics

The Labour Force Utilization State Service follows the definition of the Law on Labour Force Utilization, which reads: "Are considered unemployed the citizens available for work who do not have a suitable job or a legal revenue and who are registered at the employment office of their area of residence as a job-seeker".

7. Updating of the registers

The registers are updated daily.

8. Unemployment rates

Statistics from the registers are used to obtain the "official" unemployment rate for the Republic of Moldova (the "real" unemployment rate is obtained through the Labour Force Survey).

The sources of data on employed persons who are part of the denominator of the unemployment rates are the Labour Force Survey and the Population Census.

Definition of employed persons for this purpose:

Persons of 15 years old and over who have had an economic or social activity, producing goods or providing a service during at least one hour in the given period (a week) for profit, salary or other benefits.

9. Type of statistics of unemployed persons produced

Series 1:

Reference period: Month.

Frequency of production: Monthly

Descriptive variables used:

– Sex.

Form of publication: On paper, for general audience.

Agency responsible for publication: Labour Force Utilization Department.

Title and periodicity of the publication: *Monthly Statistical Report.*

Series 2:

Reference period: Quarter.

Frequency of production: Quarterly.
Descriptive variables used:
- Sex;
- Age;
- Educational level;
- Occupation;
- Industry;
- Geographic characteristics;
- Duration of unemployment.

Form of publication: On paper, for general audience.
Agency responsible for publication: Labour Force Utilization Department.
Title and periodicity of the publication: *Quarterly Statistical Report.*

Series 3:
Reference period: Quarter.
Frequency of production: Quarterly.
Descriptive variables used:
- Sex;
- Age;
- Educational level;
- Occupation;
- Industry.

Form of publication: On paper, for general audience.
Agency responsible for publication: Department of Statistics and Sociology.
Title and periodicity of the publication: *Quarterly Statistical Bulletin.*

Series 4:
Reference period: Year.
Frequency of production: Yearly.
Descriptive variables used:
- Sex;
- Age;
- Educational level;
- Occupation;
- Industry;
- Geographic characteristics;
- Citizenship (nationals/non nationals);
- Duration of unemployment.

Form of publication: On paper, for general audience.
Agency responsible for publication: Department of Statistics and Sociology.
Title and periodicity of the publication: *Statistical Yearbook.*
10. Methodological information about the statistics
Form of release: On paper, for general audience.
Agencies responsible for the release: Labour Force Utilization Department; Department of Statistics and Sociology.
11. Comparisons with unemployment statistics from other sources
    Comparisons are made with unemployment statistics from various other sources; the "official" statistics are compared with the "real" statistics produced by the Department of Statistics and Sociology.
Frequency of the comparisons: Regularly when the statistics are published
Publication of the methodology/results of the comparisons: These are published in the *Quarterly Statistical Bulletin*, *Statistical Yearbook* and other documents.
12. Major changes since the start of the statistics
    There have been no major changes in legislation, capacity of the agency and/or administrative procedures which had a significant influence on the statistics.

Mongolia

1. Series
Title: Unemployed citizens, job-seekers and citizens threatened by unemployment.
Starting year: 1991.
2. Agency making the initial registrations of unemployed persons
Name of the agency: Employment Offices.
Type of agency: Public service under national, regional/provincial and local authorities.
Name of the national authority: Mongolian Government Implementing Agency, Central Employment Office.

Location of the local offices making the registrations: In all provinces and districts throughout the country.
Type of services provided/administered by the agency:
- Assisting job-seekers to find jobs;
- Assisting job-seekers to establish their own business;
- Assisting employers to find workers;
- Vocational guidance;
- Job-related training;
- Paying unemployment compensation;
- Other: support to employers; promotion of self-employment.

Percentage of job-seekers seeking work through the agency: 4.8%.
3. The following information is registered about a person:
- Name;
- Sex;
- Social security number (or similar identification number also used by other agencies);
- Address of usual residence;
- Date of birth;
- Citizenship;
- Educational/vocational attainment, with six categories distinguished. No links to ISCED have been established;
- Current/past activity status, with seven categories distinguished;
- Type of work (occupation) of past or present job with nine groups distinguished. Links to ISCO-88 have been established (major groups level);
- Type of work (occupation) of job sought, with nine groups distinguished. Links to ISCO-88 have been established (major groups level);
- Name and address of present or previous employer or work place;
- Type of business (industry) of present/previous employer/workplace, with 17 groups distinguished. Links to ISIC, rev.3 have been established;
- Previous registrations with the agency/service;
- Other: health status; family status; household income; reason for unemployment; reason for resignation from job; eligibility for unemployment benefit; reason for being threatened by unemployment.

4. Criteria used for inclusion of a person in the registers (R) and/or the statistics of unemployed persons (S):
- Being without work (including self-employed working less than 15 hours a week and earning below the minimum wage) (R) and (S);
- Seeking work (R) and (S);
- Availability for work (R) and (S);
- Age (lower limit: 16 years; upper limit: 60 years) (R) and (S);
- Citizenship (must be a Mongolian citizen) (R) and (S);
- Being resident in the country (R) and (S);
- Other: ability to work (R) and (S).

5. Criteria used for exclusion of a person from the registers (R) and/or the statistics of unemployed persons (S):
- Death (R) and (S);
- Taking up residency abroad (R) and (S);
- Commencement of a (new) job (R) and (S);
- Commencement of military service (R) and (S);
- Participation in an employment promotion scheme, public works programme, etc. (R) and (S);
- Studying or undergoing training (R) and (S);
- Failure to contact the agency/service (R) and (S);
- Refusal of 3 suitable job offers (R) and (S);
- Refusal of 3 suitable training offers (R) and (S);
- Receipt of a retirement pension (R) and (S);
- Inability to work (R) and (S);
- Other: refusal of 3 suitable public works offers (R) and (S).

6. Definition of unemployed persons used for the statistics
    An "unemployed citizen" means an able-bodied citizen of working age ready to accept employment, actively looking for a job and registered at an employment office (Employment Promotion Law of Mongolia, 2001).
7. Updating of the registers
    The registers are updated monthly.
8. Unemployment rates
    Statistics from the registers are used to obtain unemployment rates.
    The sources of data on employed persons who are part of the denominator of the unemployment rates are the Labour Force

Survey, Population Census, Monthly Report on Unemployment (National Statistical Office), Table of Results of the Labour Market Manager Programs (Central Employment Office) and the Annual Employment Survey of the Population (National Statistical Office).

Definition of employed persons for this purpose:

Persons who work in entities or organizations or run a private business with wages or are self-employed are considered as employed persons.

9. Type of statistics of unemployed persons produced

Series 1:

Reference period: Month; year.

Frequency of production: Monthly and yearly.

Descriptive variables used:
- Sex;
- Age;
- Educational level;
- Occupation;
- Industry;
- Geographic characteristics;
- Other: number of vacancies; labour force; job meditation; working age population with inability to work; vocational training; public work; self-employment; unemployment benefit; employment of foreigners; trainers.

Form of publication: On paper, for general audience.

Agency responsible for publication: National Statistical Office.

Title and periodicity of the publication: *The Social Economic Situation of Mongolia*, monthly and yearly.

Series 2:

Reference period: Month; quarter; half-year; year.

Frequency of production: Monthly; quarterly; half-yearly; yearly.

Descriptive variables used:
- Sex;
- Age;
- Educational level;
- Occupation;
- Industry;
- Geographic characteristics;
- Previous work experience;
- Citizenship (nationals/non nationals);
- Duration of unemployment.

Form of publication: On paper, for limited audience.

Agency responsible for publication: Central Employment Office.

Title and periodicity of the publication: *Labour Market Report*, monthly, quarterly, half-yearly and yearly.

Series 3:

Reference period: Year.

Frequency of production: Yearly.

Descriptive variables used:
- Sex;
- Age;
- Educational level;
- Occupation;
- Industry;
- Geographic characteristics;
- Previous work experience;
- Citizenship (nationals/non nationals);
- Duration of unemployment.

Form of publication: On paper, for limited audience.

Agency responsible for publication: National Statistical Office.

Title and periodicity of the publication: *Annual Employment Survey of the Population*, yearly.

10. Methodological information about the statistics

Form of release: On paper, for general audience.

Agencies responsible for the release: National Statistical Office; Ministry of Social Welfare and Labour.

11. Comparisons with unemployment statistics from other sources

Comparisons have been made with unemployment statistics from the Labour Force Survey, another type of household survey and the Population Census.

Frequency of the comparisons: Regularly, when the statistics are published.

Publication of the methodology/results of the comparisons: These have been published.

12. Major changes since the start of the statistics

Major changes in legislation, capacity of the agency and/or administrative procedures took place in (i) 1993; (ii) 1995; (iii) 1997 and (iv) 2001, resulting in an increase of 2.4% in the total number of persons registered as unemployed in 1993; a decrease

of 3.3% in 1995; an increase of 2.2% in 1997 and a decrease of 3.2% in 2001.

1993: Registration of unemployed persons officially;

1995: National Poverty and Unemployment Survey was conducted;

1997: Adoption of Law on Unemployment Benefit, enabling unemployed persons to receive unemployment benefit from the Social Insurance Fund

2001: Employment Promotion Law was adopted.

Morocco

1. Series

Title: Number of registered job-seekers (internal statistics only, calculated for the last three years only).

2. Agency making the initial registrations of unemployed persons

Name of the agency: Agence nationale de Promotion de l'Emploi et des Compétences - ANAPEC (National Agency for Promoting Employment and Skills).

Type of agency: Public service under a national authority.

Name of the national authority: Ministry of Employment, Vocational Training, Social Development and Solidarity.

Location of the local offices making the registrations: 22 local agencies in 19 cities of the Kingdom.

Type of services provided/administered by the agency:
- Assisting job-seekers to find jobs;
- Assisting job-seekers to establish their own business;
- Assisting employers to find workers;
- Vocational guidance;
- Job-related training;
- Other: advice to enterprises concerning the management of jobs and skills; making available to clients information on the labour market; and development of the national index of occupations.

Percentage of job-seekers seeking work through the agency: 20% of skilled job-seekers.

3. The following information is registered about a person:
- Name;
- Sex;
- Social security number (or similar identification number also used by other agencies);
- Address of usual residence;
- Date of birth;
- Educational/vocational attainment;
- Current/past activity status, with three categories distinguished;
- Type of work (occupation) of past or present job with 466 categories distinguished; Links to ISCO-88 have not been established;
- Type of work (occupation) of job sought, with 466 categories distinguished;
- Previous registrations with the agency/service;
- Other: mobility; languages spoken; driving licence; telephone number; e-mail address; family status; length of work experience.

4. Criteria used for inclusion of a person in the registers:
- To have a professional diploma or a specialization acquired in a course of adult training (R);
- To have a diploma of general education (minimum secondary school examination level) (R);
- To have a work experience of at least three years in a qualified job, testified by work certificates (R).

5. Criteria used for exclusion of a person from the registers:
- Death (R);
- Taking up residency abroad (R);
- Commencement of a (new) job: the registration is cancelled when the job-seeker declares that he/she is no longer looking for a job, or when he/she is placed by the ANAPEC in a qualified job (R);
- Studying or undergoing training (R);
- Failure to contact the agency/service: not updating registration during the six months following the last registration (R);
- Refusal of suitable job offers (R).

6. Definition of unemployed persons used for the statistics

Unemployment statistics are established by the Statistics Department, which is under the authority of the Ministry of Planning and Economic Forecasting. Statistics established by the ANAPEC are based on the index of registered job-seekers and are only used internally.

7. Updating of the registers
The registers are updated on a continuous basis.

8. Unemployment rates
Statistics from the registers are not used to obtain unemployment rates.

9. Type of statistics of unemployed persons produced
Reference period: Day.
Frequency of production: Daily.
Descriptive variables used:
– Sex;
– Age;
– Educational level.
Form of publication: For internal use only.

10. Methodological information about the statistics
Form of release: Not released, available for internal use only.

11. Comparisons with unemployment statistics from other sources
Comparisons have not been made with unemployment statistics from other sources.

12. Major changes since the start of the statistics
There have been no major changes in legislation, capacity of the agency and/or administrative procedures which had a significant influence on the statistics.

Myanmar

1. Series
Title: Employment Exchange Statistics.
Starting year: Circa 1950.

2. Agency making the initial registrations of unemployed persons
Name of the agency: Employment and Training Division.
Type of agency: Public service under a national authority.
Name of the national authority: Department of Labour.
Location of the local offices making the registrations: Registrations are made in Employment Exchanges of the Township Labour Offices, of which there are 78 throughout the country.
Type of services provided/administered by the agency:
– Assisting job-seekers to find jobs;
– Assisting employers to find workers;
– Vocational guidance;
– Job-related training;
– Other: overseas employment.

Percentage of job-seekers seeking work through the agency: According to the 1959 Employment Restrictions Act all employers employing five or more workers must recruit their workers through the Employment Exchanges of the Department of Labour.

3. The following information is registered about a person:
– Name;
– Sex;
– Address of usual residence;
– Date of birth;
– Citizenship;
– Educational/vocational attainment. No links to ISCED have been established;
– Current/past activity status;
– Type of work (occupation) of past or present job. Links to ISCO-88 have been established (unit groups level) (the Myanmar Standard Classification of Occupations is based on ISCO-88);
– Type of work (occupation) of job sought. Links to ISCO-88 have been established (unit groups level) (the Myanmar Standard Classification of Occupations is based on ISCO-88);
– Name and address of present or previous employer or work place;
– Type of business (industry) of present/previous employer/workplace, with 10 groups distinguished. No links to ISIC, rev.3 have been established;
– Previous registrations with the agency/service;
– Other: renewal/validation of registration every six months.

4. Criteria used for inclusion of a person in the registers (R) and/or the statistics of unemployed persons (S):
– Being without work (R);
– Seeking work (R);
– Availability for work (R);
– Age (lower limit: 18 years; upper limit: 60 years) (R);
– Citizenship (R);
– Being resident in the country (R);
– Previously employed (R);
– Desired duration of employment and/or number of hours of work sought (R).

5. Criteria used for exclusion of a person from the registers (R) and/or the statistics of unemployed persons (S):
– Death (R);
– Taking up residency abroad (R);
– Commencement of a (new) job (R);
– Commencement of military service (R);
– Participation in an employment promotion scheme, public works programme, etc. (R);
– Studying or undergoing training (R);
– Failure to contact the agency/service for more than six months (R);
– Refusal of 2 suitable job offers (R);
– Refusal of 2 suitable training offers (R);
– Inability to work (R).

6. Definition of unemployed persons used for the statistics
Job-seekers registered at Employment Exchanges.

7. Updating of the registers
The registers are updated monthly.

8. Unemployment rates
Statistics from the registers are not used to obtain unemployment rates.

9. Type of statistics of unemployed persons produced
Series 1:
Reference period: Month.
Frequency of production: Monthly.
Descriptive variables used:
– Sex;
– Age;
– Educational level;
– Occupation;
– Industry;
– Geographic characteristics;
– Previous work experience;
– Citizenship (nationals/non nationals).
– Duration of unemployment.
Form of publication: On paper, for limited audience;
Agency responsible for publication: Central Statistics Organisation.
Periodicity of publication: Annual.
Series 2:
Annual data on the number of Employment Exchanges, fresh registrations, persons placed, lapsed register, persons on register at the end of the year, vacancies notified and vacancies outstanding at the end of the year are published by the Central Statistics Organisation in the *Statistical Yearbook*.

10. Methodological information about the statistics
Form of release: Not released, available for internal use only.

11. Comparisons with unemployment statistics from other sources
Comparisons have not been made with unemployment statistics from other sources.

12. Major changes since the start of the statistics
Major changes in legislation, capacity of the agency and/or administrative procedures took place in 1959. The resulting changes in the statistics have not been estimated.

Netherlands

1. Series
Title: Registered unemployment.

2. Agency making the initial registrations of unemployed persons
Name of the agency: Centre for Work and Income.
Type of agency: public service under a national authority.
Location of the local offices making the registrations: in all parts of the country.
Type of services provided/administered by the agency:
– Assisting job-seekers to find jobs;
– Assisting employers to find workers;
– Supplying labour market information.
Percentage of job-seekers seeking work through the agency: 25%.

3. Information registered about a person:
- Name;
- Sex;
- Social security number (or similar identification number);
- Address of usual residence;
- Date of birth;
- Citizenship;
- Nationality/ethnic group;
- Educational/vocational attainment. Links to ISCED have not been established;
- Current/past activity status;
- Type of work (occupation) of past or present job;
- Type of work (occupation) of job sought. Links to ISCO-88 have not been established;
- Name and address of present or previous employer or work place;
- Type of business (industry) of present/previous employer/work place, with links to ISIC (class level);
- Previous registrations with the agency/service.

4. Criteria used for inclusion of a person in the registers (R) and/or the statistics of unemployed persons (S):
- Being without work (R) and (S);
- Seeking work (R) and (S);
- Availability for work (R) and (S);
- Desired duration of hours of work sought (more than 12 hours per week) (S).

5. Criteria used for exclusion of a person from the registers (R) and/or the statistics of unemployed persons (S):
- Death (R) and (S);
- Failure to contact the agency/service (R) and (S).

6. Definition of unemployed persons used for the statistics
Persons without work, seeking work and available for work. The desired duration of work sought must be more than 12 hours per week.

7. Updating of the registers
The registers are updated regularly.

8. Unemployment rates
Statistics from the registers are used to obtain unemployment rates. The source of data on employed persons who are part of the denominator of the unemployment rates is the Labour Force Survey.

Definition of employed persons for this purpose:
Persons who have worked more than 12 hours during the reference period.

9. Type of statistics of unemployed persons produced
Reference period: Month.
Frequency of production: Monthly.
Descriptive variables used:
- Sex;
- Age;
- Educational level;
- Occupation;
- Industry;
- Geographic characteristics;
- Previous work experience;
- Citizenship;
- Duration of unemployment.

Form of publication:
- On paper, for general audience;
- In machine-readable form, on request.

Agency responsible for publication: Centre for Work and Income.
Title of the publication: *Arbeids-Markt Journaal* (Labour Market Journal).

10. Methodological information about the statistics
Form of release:
- On paper, for general audience;
- In machine-readable form, on request.

11. Comparisons with unemployment statistics from other sources
Comparisons have been made with unemployment statistics from the Social Security.
Frequency of the comparisons: Regularly, when the statistics are published.
Methodology/results of the methodology published: These have not been published.

12. Major changes since the start of the statistics
There have been no major changes in legislation, capacity of the agency and/or administrative procedures which had a significant influence on the statistics.

New Caledonia

1. Series
Title: Statistics on employment demand.
Starting year: 1991.

2. Agency making the initial registrations of unemployed persons
Name of the agency: New Caledonia Employment Agency.
Type of agency: Public service under a local authority.
Location of the local offices making the registrations: A delegation in each of the three provinces, and agencies in several municipalities.
Type of services provided/administered by the agency:
- Assisting job-seekers to find jobs;
- Assisting job-seekers to establish their own business;
- Assisting employers to find workers;
- Vocational guidance;
- Job-related training;
- Other: action plan for assessment of competencies; examination of files with a view to making decisions on unemployment compensation.

Percentage of job-seekers seeking work through the agency: 70%.

3. The following information is registered about a person:
- Name;
- Sex;
- Social security number (or similar identification number also used by other agencies);
- Address of usual residence;
- Date of birth;
- Nationality;
- Educational/vocational attainment, with six categories distinguished. Links to ISCED have been established;
- Current/past activity status;
- Type of work (occupation) of past or present job with 1,178 categories distinguished. Links to ISCO-88 have not been established;
- Type of work (occupation) of job sought, with 1,178 categories distinguished;
- Name and address of present or previous employer or work place;
- Type of business (industry) of present/previous employer/workplace, with 697 categories distinguished. Links to ISIC have not been established;
- Previous registrations with the agency/service.

4. Criteria used for inclusion of a person in the registers (R) and/or the statistics of unemployed persons (S):
- Seeking work (R) and (S);
- Availability for work (R) and (S);
- Age (lower limit: 16 years; no upper limit) (R) and (S);
- Being resident in the country (R) and (S).

5. Criteria used for exclusion of a person from the registers (R) and/or the statistics of unemployed persons (S):
- Death (R) and (S);
- Taking up residency abroad (R) and (S);
- Commencement of a (new) job (R) and (S);
- Commencement of military service (R) and (S);
- Failure to contact the agency/service (R) and (S);
- Inability to work (R) and (S).

6. Definition of unemployed persons used for the statistics
Any person who has come to register at the employment agency claiming to seek employment.

7. Updating of the registers
The registers are updated daily.

8. Unemployment rates
Statistics from the registers are not used to obtain unemployment rates.

9. Type of statistics of unemployed persons produced
Reference period: Month, Quarter, Year.
Frequency of production: Monthly, Quarterly, Yearly.
Descriptive variables used:
- Sex;
- Age;

- Educational level;
- Occupation;
- Geographic characteristics;
- Duration of unemployment.

10. Methodological information about the statistics
Form of release:
- On paper, for limited audience;
- On a website: www.apenc.nc.

11. Comparisons with unemployment statistics from other sources

Comparisons have been made with unemployment statistics from the population census.

12. Major changes since the start of the statistics

There have been no major changes in legislation, capacity of the agency and/or administrative procedures which had a significant influence on the statistics.

New Zealand

1. Series
Title: Number of registered unemployed.
Starting year: 1952.

2. Agency making the initial registrations of unemployed persons
Name of the agency: Work and Income.
Type of agency: Public service under a national authority.
Name of the national authority: Ministry of Social Development.
Location of the local offices making the registrations: Work and Income has around 170 frontline offices throughout the country; 144 of these are full-time offices.
Type of services provided/administered by the agency:
- Assisting job-seekers to find jobs;
- Assisting job-seekers to establish their own business;
- Assisting employers to find workers;
- Vocational guidance;
- Job-related training;
- Income support.

3. The following information is registered about a person:
- Client identification;
- Name (first name, middle name, family name, preferred first name, any alias);
- Gender;
- Residential address (and if applicable postal address);
- Date and place of birth;
- Ethnicity;
- Educational level, with nine categories distinguished;
- Type of work (occupation) of past or present job. Work history is recorded as free text, and occupations are not coded;
- Type of work (occupation) of job sought, with 25 groups distinguished ("NZSCO" classification, five digit level);
- Name of present or previous employer or work place (employment history - length of time employed and type, i.e. full-time or part-time);
- Previous registrations with the agency/service;
- Other: detailed qualifications and skills; disabilities, or other barriers to employment; access to transport; whether driving licence holder; telephone number; partner's name; maximum hours available for work; enrolment date; employment status (unemployed or partially employed).

4. Criteria used for inclusion of a person in the registers (R) and/or the statistics of unemployed persons (S):
- Being without work (can be employed part-time, i.e. less than 30 hours a week, and wish to extend hours or gain full-time employment) (R) and (S);
- Seeking work (as defined in individual action plan developed with case manager) (R) and (S);
- Availability for work (R) and (S);
- Age (lower limit: 16 years; no upper limit) (R) and (S);
- Citizenship (R) and (S);
- Being resident in the country (R) and (S);
- Other: study and training: being in part-time study or training (persons in full-time study or training cannot register as job-seekers) (R) and (S).

5. Criteria used for exclusion of a person from the registers (R) and/or the statistics of unemployed persons (S):
- Death (R) and (S);
- Taking up residency abroad (R) and (S);
- Commencement of a (new) full-time job (R) and (S);

- Participation in certain employment promotion schemes (such as "Task Force Green"), public works programme, etc. (R) and (S);
- Studying full-time or undergoing full-time training (R) and (S);
- Failure to contact the agency/service for 14 weeks (if not recipient of a "work tested benefit") (R) and (S);
- Refusal of suitable job offers (at least four consecutive refusals for recipients of "work tested benefit"; no formal criteria for non recipients of this benefit) (R) and (S);
- Refusal of suitable training offers (at least four consecutive refusals for recipients of "work tested benefit"; no formal criteria for non recipients of this benefit) (R) and (S).

6. Definition of unemployed persons used for the statistics

To be registered as a job seeker, a person must be:
- not working and seeking work, or working less than 30 hours a week and seeking to work more hours; and
- available for work (not already in full-time employment or full-time study or training); and
- aged 16 years or over (or aged 15 with an exemption from the Ministry of Education to leave school early and seek full-time work); and
- resident in New Zealand; and
- legally entitled to work in New Zealand (i.e. a citizen of Australia or New Zealand, a permanent resident of New Zealand, a holder of a New Zealand work permit, or a person born in the Cook Islands, Niue or Tokelau).

7. Updating of the registers

The registers are continually updated.

8. Unemployment rates

Statistics from the registers are not used to obtain unemployment rates.

9. Type of statistics of unemployed persons produced
Series 1: Monthly register
Reference period: Last day of month.
Frequency of production: Monthly.
Descriptive variables used:
- Gender;
- Age;
- Educational level;
- Geographic characteristics;
- Duration of unemployment;
- Income support received;
- Ethnicity;
- Disability;
- Case management group;
- Marital status;
- Age of youngest child.

Form of publication: For internal use only.
Agency responsible for publication: Ministry of Social Development.
Title and periodicity of the publication: *Monthly register.*

Series 2: Quarterly Client Profile.
Reference period: Last day of quarter.
Frequency of production: Quarterly.
Descriptive variables used:
- Gender;
- Age;
- Educational level;
- Geographic characteristics;
- Duration of unemployment;
- Income support received;
- Ethnicity;
- Work test status;
- Participation in employment programmes.

Form of publication:
- On paper, for general audience;
- On a website (www.msd.govt.nz).

Agency responsible for publication: Ministry of Social Development.
Title and periodicity of the publication: *Quarterly Client Profile.*

Series 3: Annual Statistical Profile
Reference period: Last day of financial year.
Frequency of production: Yearly.
Descriptive variables used:
- Gender;
- Age;
- Educational level;
- Geographic characteristics;

- Duration of unemployment;
- Income support received;
- Ethnicity;
- Participation in employment programmes.

Form of publication: On paper, for general audience.

Agency responsible for publication: Ministry of Social Development.

Title and periodicity of the publication: *Annual Statistical Profile*.

10. Methodological information about the statistics

Summary methodological information is included in the above-mentioned publications.

Form of release:
- On paper, for general audience;
- On a website (www.msd.govt.nz).

Agency responsible for the release: Ministry of Social Development.

11. Comparisons with unemployment statistics from other sources

Comparisons are made once a quarter with unemployment statistics from the Household Labour Force Survey (the official measure of unemployment, in accordance with ILO criteria, administered by Statistics New Zealand).

Comparisons were made in 2001 with unemployment statistics from the 1996 Census of Population.

Publication of the methodology/results of the comparisons: These have not been published.

12. Major changes since the start of the statistics

Major changes in legislation, capacity of the agency and/or administrative procedures took place in:

1997: Introduction of work testing of persons receiving selected income support;

1999: Extension of persons receiving work testing of income support to include additional benefits and spouses/partners of persons receiving some income support.

Work testing of persons receiving income support and their spouses required that the persons receiving work tested benefits were also registered as job-seekers, whereas previously they were not required to register as job-seekers.

Niger

1. Series

Title: Job-seekers statistics.

Starting year: 1982.

2. Agency making the initial registrations of unemployed persons

Name of the agency: Agence Nationale pour la Promotion de l'Emploi - ANPE (National Agency for Employment Promotion).

Type of agency: Public service under a national authority.

Location of the local offices making the registrations: Niamey, Tillabery, Dosso, Tahara, Maradi, Zinder, Diffa, Arlit and Agadez.

Type of services provided/administered by the agency:
- Assisting job-seekers to find jobs;
- Assisting job-seekers to establish their own business (only in Niamey);
- Assisting employers to find workers;
- Vocational guidance (only in Niamey);
- Job-related training (only in Niamey);
- Other: insertion programmes for young graduates; production of statistical information on the evolution of the labour market, programme of insertion in the informal sector.

3. The following information is registered about a person:
- Name;
- Sex;
- Date of birth;
- Nationality;
- Educational/vocational attainment, with four categories distinguished. Links to ISCED have not been established;
- Type of work (occupation) of job sought.

4. Criteria used for inclusion of a person in the registers (R) and/or the statistics of unemployed persons (S):
- Being without work (R) and (S);
- Seeking work (R) and (S);
- Availability for work (R) and (S);
- Age (lower limit: 18 years; upper limit: 60 years) (R) and (S);
- Citizenship: the registration card is issued to foreigners only if the conditions required by the rules are fulfilled (R);
- Being resident in the country (R) and (S);

- Previously employed (R) and (S);
- Desired duration of employment and/or number of hours of work sought (R) and (S).

5. Criteria used for exclusion of a person from the registers (R) and/or the statistics of unemployed persons (S):
- Death (R) and (S);
- Taking up residency abroad (R) and (S);
- Commencement of a (new) job (R) and (S);
- Studying or undergoing training (R) and (S);
- Inability to work (R) and (S).

6. Definition of unemployed persons used for the statistics

Unemployment statistics are based on the register in which job-seekers are recorded. Therefore, any person looking for a job and registered with the ANPE during the reference period is considered as unemployed.

7. Updating of the registers

The registers are not updated regularly.

8. Unemployment rates

Statistics from the registers are not used to obtain unemployment rates.

9. Type of statistics of unemployed persons produced

Series 1: Statistics on job-seekers.

Frequency of production: Monthly.

Descriptive variables used:
- Sex;
- Age;
- Occupation.

Form of publication: On paper, for limited audience.

Agency responsible for publication: ANPE.

Title of the publication: *Rapport statistique* (Statistical Report).

Series 2: Statistics on job-seekers and manpower.

Frequency of production: Yearly.

Descriptive variables used:
- Sex;
- Age;
- Level of education;
- Occupation;
- Geographical characteristics.

Form of publication: On paper, for general audience.

Agency responsible for publication: ANPE.

Title of the publication: *Rapport d'activité* (Activity Report).

10. Methodological information about the statistics

Form of release: On paper, for general audience.

Agency responsible for the release: ANPE.

11. Comparisons with unemployment statistics from other sources

Comparisons have not been made with unemployment statistics from other sources.

12. Major changes since the start of the statistics

The National Agency for Employment Promotion was created in 1996. Prior to this, the Manpower Service and the Labour Inspections recorded job-seekers.

Nigeria

1. Series

Title: Employment Exchange Statistics.

2. Agency making the initial registrations of unemployed persons

Name of the agency: Employment Exchange Registries, Professional and Executive Registries.

Type of agency: Public service under a national authority.

Name of the national authority: Federal Ministry of Employment, Labour & Productivity. However, the operation and control of private employment agencies is under consideration.

Location of the local offices making the registrations: In all state capitals of the Federation (37 state networks), in areas where population is dense, where there are industrial establishments that require workers' services and university towns and other tertiary institutions.

Type of services provided/administered by the agency:
- Assisting job-seekers to find jobs;
- Assisting job-seekers to establish their own business;
- Assisting employers to find workers;
- Vocational guidance;
- Job-related training;
- Other: certification of craftsmen for gainful and self-employment.

Percentage of job-seekers seeking work through the agency: 60%.

3. Information registered about a person:
- Name;
- Sex;
- Address of usual residence;
- Date of birth;
- Citizenship;
- Nationality/ethnic group;
- Educational/vocational attainment, with three categories: skilled; semi-skilled and unskilled. Links to ISCED have been established;
- Current/past activity status;
- Type of work (occupation) of past or present job;
- Type of work (occupation) of job sought, with links to ISCO-88 (major group level);
- Name and address of present or previous employer or work place;
- Type of business (industry) of present/previous employer/work place, with links to ISIC (group level);
- Previous registrations with the agency/service.

4. Criteria used for inclusion of a person in the registers (R) and/or the statistics of unemployed persons (S):
- Being without work (R) and (S);
- Seeking work (R) and (S);
- Availability for work (R) and (S);
- Age: lower limit: 18 years; upper limit: 60 years (R) and (S);
- Citizenship: for Nigerians, by birth, by marriage and by naturalisation;
- Being resident in the country.

5. Criteria used for exclusion of a person from the registers (R) and/or the statistics of unemployed persons (S):
- Death (R) and (S);
- Taking up residency abroad (R) and (S);
- Commencement of a (new) job (R) and (S);
- Commencement of military service (R) and (S);
- Participation in an employment promotion scheme, public work programme, etc (R) and (S);
- Studying or undergoing training (R) and (S);
- Failure to contact the agency/service, there is need to renew registration documents periodically (R) and (S)
- Refusal of suitable job offers (R) and (S);
- Refusal of suitable training offers (R) and (S);
- Inability to work (R) and (S).

6. Definition of unemployed persons used for the statistics
Persons who are actively looking for work, willing to work, medically fit, aged between 18 and 60 years, and who are earning below the national minimum wage.

7. Updating of the registers
The registers are updated on a monthly, quarterly and annual basis.

8. Unemployment rates
Statistics from the registers are used to obtain unemployment rates.

The sources of data on employed persons who are part of the denominator of the unemployment rates are the Labour Force Survey, Establishment Survey, Social Security Register and Population Census.

Definition of employed persons for this purpose:
Persons who are actively engaged in work and are not earning below the national minimum wage.

9. Type of statistics of unemployed persons produced
Reference period: Month, quarter, year.
Frequency of production: Quarterly.
Descriptive variables used:
- Sex;
- Age;
- Educational level;
- Occupation;
- Industry;
- Geographic characteristics;
- Previous work experience;
- Citizenship;
- Duration of unemployment..

Form of publication:
- On paper, for general audience;
- In machine-readable form, on request.

Agency responsible for publication: Federal Ministry of Employment, Labour and Productivity.
Title and periodicity of the publication(s): *Employment Exchange & Professional & Executive Registry Statistics*, monthly, quarterly and annual.

10. Methodological information about the statistics
Form of release:
- On paper, for general audience;
- In machine-readable form, on request;
- Planned to be on a website.

11. Comparisons with unemployment statistics from other sources
Comparisons have not been made with unemployment statistics from other sources.

12. Major changes since the start of the statistics
There have been no major changes in legislation, capacity of the agency and/or administrative procedures which had a significant influence on the statistics.

Norway

1. Series
Title: Labour Market Statistics.
Starting year: 1948.

2. Agency making the initial registrations of unemployed persons
Name of the agency: District Employment Service (Aestat).
Type of agency: Public service under a national authority.
Name of the national authority: Directorate of Labour.
Location of the local offices making the registrations: 200 local offices make the main registrations. A national registration centre carries out some updating of registrations and some registrations in connection with vacancy statistics.
Type of services provided/administered by the agency:
- Assisting job-seekers to find jobs;
- Assisting employers to find workers;
- Vocational guidance;
- Job-related training;
- Occupational rehabilitation measures;
- Benefits for unemployed;
- Other employment-related services.

Percentage of job-seekers seeking work through the agency: 75%.

3. The following information is registered about a person:
- Name;
- Sex;
- Social security number (or similar identification number also used by other agencies);
- Address of usual residence;
- Date of birth;
- Citizenship;
- Nationality;
- Educational/vocational attainment, with 8 categories distinguished. Links to ISCED have been established;
- Type of work (occupation) of past job with an unspecified number of groups distinguished. Links to ISCO-88 have been established (unit groups level);
- Type of work (occupation) of job sought, with an unspecified number of groups distinguished. Links to ISCO-88 have been established (unit groups level);
- Previous registrations with the agency/service.

4. Criteria used for inclusion of a person in the registers (R) and/or the statistics of unemployed persons (S):
- Being without work (the last 14 days before the counting day) (S);
- Seeking work (R) and (S);
- Availability for work (R) and (S);
- Being resident in the country (S).

5. Criteria used for exclusion of a person from the registers (R) and/or the statistics of unemployed persons (S):
- Death (R) and (S);
- Taking up residency abroad (R) and (S);
- Commencement of a (new) job (S);
- Commencement of military service (S);
- Participation in an employment promotion scheme, public works programme, etc. (S);
- Studying or undergoing training (students and participants in training schemes are not counted as unemployed, but can still

be job-seekers) (S);
- Failure to send reporting card every 14 days to a national registration centre (R) and (S).

6. Definition of unemployed persons used for the statistics

The main criteria are seeking work, being without paid work and available for work.

Persons are regarded as job-seekers when a reporting card has been received/completed for the preceding two weeks or when they have been to the local employment service for registration. If they report that they had no work in the preceding two weeks they are counted as unemployed. If they had some work in the preceding two weeks they are counted as partly unemployed.

7. Updating of the registers

The registers are updated weekly.

8. Unemployment rates

Statistics from the registers are used to obtain unemployment rates.

The denominator of the unemployment rates is the labour force from the Labour Force Survey.

Definition of employed persons for this purpose:
Aged 16 to 74 years and performed work for pay or profit for at least one hour in the survey week.

9. Type of statistics of unemployed persons produced
Series 1:
Reference period: Month.
Frequency of production: Monthly.
Descriptive variables used:
- Sex;
- Age;
- Educational level;
- Occupation;
- Geographic characteristics;
- Duration of unemployment;
- Other: recipient of unemployment benefit.

Form of publication:
- On paper, for general audience;
- On a website (www.aetat.no).

Agency responsible for publication: Directorate of Labour.
Title and periodicity of the publication: *Månedsstatistikk* (Monthly Statistics).
Series 2:
Reference period: Year.
Frequency of production: Yearly.
Descriptive variables used:
- Sex;
- Age;
- Educational level;
- Occupation;
- Geographic characteristics;
- Duration of unemployment;
- Other: recipient of unemployment benefit.

Form of publication:
- On paper, for general audience;
- On a website (www.aetat.no).

Agency responsible for publication: Directorate of Labour.
Title of the publication: *Historisk Statistikk*, (Historical Statistics).

10. Methodological information about the statistics
Form of release:
- On paper, for general audience;
- On a website (www.aetat.no).

Agency responsible for the release: Directorate of Labour, Planning and Analysis Division.

11. Comparisons with unemployment statistics from other sources

Comparisons have been made with unemployment statistics from the Labour Force Survey.

Frequency of the comparisons: Occasionally.
Publication of the methodology/results of the comparisons: These have been published in *Notater, nr. 99/31* (Statistics Norway): "... Classification of registered unemployment and participants in labour market schemes in the Labour Force Survey" (in Norwegian only).

12. Major changes since the start of the statistics

There have been no major changes in legislation, capacity of the agency and/or administrative procedures which had a significant influence on the statistics.

Panama

1. Series
Title: Registered unemployment.
Starting year: 1990.

2. Agency making the initial registrations of unemployed persons
Name of the agency: Departamento de Mano de Obra, Direccion General de Empleo (Department of Manpower, General Directorate of Employment).
Type of agency: Public service of the General Directorate of Employment, Ministry of Labour and Labour Development (MITRADEL).
Location of the local offices making the registrations: In all the regional departments of the Ministry of Labour and Labour Development.
Type of services provided/administered by the agency:
- Assisting job-seekers to find jobs;
- Assisting job-seekers to establish their own business;
- Assisting employers to find workers;
- Vocational guidance;
- Job-related training;
- Other: cooperation with the employment, training and self-management of companies programme.

Percentage of job seekers seeking work through the agency: 2.3% (in 1999).

3. The following information is registered about a person:
- Name;
- Sex;
- Identity card number;
- Social security number (or similar identification number also used by other agencies);
- Address of usual residence;
- Date of birth;
- Citizenship (according to the province of birth);
- Nationality;
- Educational/vocational attainment, level the person has reached. Links to ISCED have not been established;
- Current/past activity status, with seven categories distinguished taking into consideration all past experience;
- Type of work of past or present job with seven categories distinguished. Links to ISCO-88 have been established. The experience and the title(s) are mentioned in the first, second, third and fourth professions;Type of work of job sought, with seven categories distinguished. Links to ISCO-88 have been established;
- Name and address of present or previous employer or work place;
- Type of business (industry) of present/previous employer/workplace, with five categories distinguished. Links to ISIC have not been established;
- Previous registrations with the agency/service;
- Other: marital status; dependents (ages); driving licence; whether car owner; mobility; preferred working schedule; principal occupation and other occupational options.

4. Criteria used for inclusion of a person in the registers (R) and/or the statistics of unemployed persons (S):
- Being without work (R) et (S);
- Seeking work (R);
- Availability for work (R);
- Age (lower limit: 18 years; no upper limit) (R) and (S);
- Citizenship (province of residence) (R) and (S);
- Previously employed (R);
- Desired duration of employment and/or number of hours of work sought (occasional or permanent) (R) and (S).

5. Criteria used for exclusion of a person from the registers (R) and/or the statistics of unemployed persons (S):
- Death (R);
- Taking up residency abroad (R);
- Commencement of a (new) job (R);
- Participation in an employment promotion scheme, public works programme, etc, (R);
- Studying or undergoing training (R);
- Failure to contact the agency/service (the registration is valid for one year; after this period, the job seeker is required to update his/her file) (R);
- Refusal of two suitable job offers (R);
- Receipt of a pension (in case of sickness) (R);

– Inability to work (R);
– Other: if it has been proved that the beneficiary has committed an offence in the company where he/she has been placed (R).

6. Definition of unemployed persons used for the statistics

Persons aged 18 years and over available for work, who have no occupation or work, but who have previously worked and who have been looking for employment.

Also persons who have not been looking for employment because they had found one and were expecting to start work at a later date, as well as those who have never worked and who are seeking their first employment (first job seekers), and those who have not been looking for employment because they had been looking for one earlier and were waiting for news.

Finally, persons of working age employed or underemployed but looking for employment.

7. Updating of the registers

The registers are updated monthly; however, the publication is annual.

8. Unemployment rates

Statistics from the registers are used to obtain unemployment rates.

9. Type of statistics of unemployed persons produced

Reference period: Year.

Frequency of production: Yearly.

Descriptive variables used:
– Sex;
– Age;
– Educational level;
– Occupation;
– Industry;
– Regions of work;
– Citizenship (nationals/non nationals);
– Duration of unemployment;
– Other: placement in selective jobs only (persons with handicap); worker's status (employed, dismissed or new worker); seamen; auto-management of the company; regional departments of work (employment).

Form of publication: On paper, for public and private institutions, other bodies and for public consultation.

Agency responsible for publication: MITRADEL, General Directorate of Employment.

Title and periodicity of the publication: *Informe Anual de Trabajo de la Dirección General de Empleo* (Annual Report of the General Directorate of Employment).

10. Methodological information about the statistics

Form of release: On paper, for general audience.

Agency responsible for the release: General Directorate of Employment (Department of Research on Employment).

11. Comparisons with unemployment statistics from other sources

Comparisons have not been made with Unemployment statistics from other sources.

The published information is for basic use; it is not used for comparative analyses with other sources.

12. Major changes since the start of the statistics

There have been no major changes in legislation, capacity of the agency and/or administrative procedures, which had a significant influence on the statistics.

Papua New Guinea

1. Series

Title: Annual Labour Statistics Bulletin.

Starting year: 1996.

2. Agency making the initial registrations of unemployed persons

Name of the agency: National Employment Services (NES).

Type of agency: public service under a national authority.

Name of the national authority: Department of Labour and Employment.

Location of the local offices making the registrations: In selected areas only: established in four regional NES offices.

Type of services provided/administered by the agency:
– Assisting job-seekers to find jobs;
– Assisting employers to find workers;
– Vocational guidance;
– Job-related training;
– Providing career information to school leavers.

Percentage of job-seekers seeking work through the agency: 0.8%.

3. Information registered about a person:
– Name;
– Sex;
– Social security number (or similar identification number also used by other agencies);
– Address of usual residence;
– Date of birth;
– Citizenship;
– Nationality/ethnic group;
– Educational/vocational attainment, with six categories distinguished. Links to ISCED have been established;
– Current/past activity status, with three categories distinguished;
– Type of work (occupation) of past or present job, with ten categories distinguished;
– Type of work (occupation) of job sought, with nine categories distinguished. Links to ISCO-88 have been established (major group level);
– Name and address of present or previous employer or work place;
– Type of business (industry) of present/previous employer/work place, with seventeen categories distinguished. Links to ISIC have been established (division level);
– Previous registrations with the agency/service.

4. Criteria used for inclusion of a person in the registers (R) and/or the statistics of unemployed persons (S):
– Being without work (S);
– Seeking work (R);
– Availability for work (R);
– Age (lower limit: 15 years; upper limit: 55 years) (R) and (S);
– Citizenship (R) and (S);
– Being resident in the country (R);
– Previously employed (R);
– Desired duration of employment and/or number of hours of work sought (minimum duration of work sought of eight to ten hours per day) (R).

5. Criteria used for exclusion of a person from the registers (R) and/or the statistics of unemployed persons (S):
– Death (R) and (S);
– Taking up residency abroad (R);
– Commencement of a (new) job (R) and (S);
– Commencement of military service (R) and (S);
– Participation in an employment promotion scheme, public works programme, etc (R) and (S);
– Studying or undergoing training (R);
– Failure to contact the agency/service (R);
– Refusal of suitable job offers (R);
– Refusal of suitable training offers (R);
– End of entitlement to receive unemployment compensation (R);
– Receipt of a pension (R) and (S);
– Inability to work (R).

6. Definition of unemployed persons used for the statistics

Unemployed persons are persons looking for work who have not worked during a specified reference period. It may, in certain circumstances, refer to the extreme cases of underemployment.

7. Updating of the registers

The registers are updated quarterly.

8. Unemployment rates

Statistics from the registers are used to obtain unemployment rates.

The sources of data on employed persons who are part of the denominator of the unemployment rates are the Labour Force Survey, Establishment Survey, Social Security Register and Population Census.

Definition of employed persons for this purpose:

Persons earning money or the equivalent for producing marketable goods and services; including wage and salary earners, employers, self-employed and unpaid family workers.

9. Type of statistics of unemployed persons produced

Reference period: From one to four months.

Frequency of production: Quarterly.

Descriptive variables used:
– Sex;
– Age;

- Educational level;
- Occupation;
- Industry;
- Previous work experience;
- Citizenship;
- Duration of unemployment

Form of publication: On paper, for limited audience.
Agency responsible for publication: NES.
Title and periodicity of the publication: *Annual Statistical Report.*
10. Methodological information about the statistics
Form of release: On paper, for limited audience.
Agency responsible: Department of Labour, Statistical Unit.
11. Comparisons with unemployment statistics from other sources
Comparisons have been made with unemployment statistics from the Labour Force Survey, Population Census and with statistics from other sources.
Frequency of the comparisons: Regularly, when the statistics are published.
Publication of the methodology/results of the comparisons: These have not been published.
12. Major changes since the start of the statistics
Major changes in legislation, capacity of the agency and/or administrative procedures took place in 2000. The resulting changes in the statistics have not been estimated.

Peru

1. Series
Title: Registered job-seekers.
Starting year: Around 1975.
2. Agency making the initial registrations of unemployed persons
Name of the agency: Red de Centros de Colocación e Información Laboral, Red CIL-PROEMPLEO (Placement and Occupational Information Centres Network, Network CIL-PROEMPLO).
Type of agency: Public service under a national authority (There are also private centres integrated in the CIL-PROEMPLEO network, but they are non-profit making).
Name of the national authority: Dirección Nacional de Promoción del Empleo y Formación Profesional (National Employment Promotion and Vocational Training Department).
Location of the local offices making the registrations: 40 offices, in all the main cities of the country.
Type of services provided/administered by the agency:
- Assisting job-seekers to find jobs;
- Assisting employers to find workers;
- Vocational guidance;
- Job-related training;
- Other: guidance for employment search; guidance for own-account workers and SMEs.

Percentage of job-seekers seeking work through the agency: 17.5%.
3. The following information is registered about a person:
- Name;
- Sex;
- Address of usual residence;
- Age;
- Citizenship;
- Educational/vocational attainment, with five categories distinguished. Links to ISCED have been established;
- Current/past activity status, with five categories distinguished;
- Type of work (occupation) of past or present job with10 categories distinguished. Links to ISCO-88 have been established (major groups level);
- Type of work (occupation) of job sought, with 10 categories distinguished. Links to ISCO-88 have been established (major groups level);
- Name and address of present or previous employer or work place;
- Type of business (industry) of present/previous employer/workplace, with 12 categories distinguished. Links to ISIC, rev.3 have been established;
- Previous registrations with the agency/service.

4. Criteria used for inclusion of a person in the registers (R) and/or the statistics of unemployed persons (S):
- Being without work (R) and (S);
- Seeking work (R) and (S);

- Availability for work (R);
- Age (lower limit: 18 years; upper limit: 65 years) (R) and (S);
- Previously employed (S);
- Desired duration of employment and/or number of hours of work sought (S).

5. Criteria used for exclusion of a person from the registers (R) and/or the statistics of unemployed persons (S):
- Commencement of a (new) job (R) and (S);
- Participation in an employment promotion scheme, public works programme, etc (R);
- Failure to contact the agency/service (R) and (S);
- Refusal of suitable job offers (R);
- Inability to work (R) and (S);
- Other: abandon more than once jobs proposed by the service (R).

6. Definition of unemployed persons used for the statistics
Not specified.
7. Updating of the registers
The registers are updated monthly.
8. Unemployment rates
Statistics from the registers are not used to obtain unemployment rates.
9. Type of statistics of unemployed persons produced
Reference period: Quarter.
Frequency of production: Quarterly.
Descriptive variables used:
- Sex;
- Age;
- Educational level;
- Occupation;
- Industry;
- Previous work experience;
- Duration of unemployment;
- Other: training and skills acquisition courses.

Form of publication: On paper, for limited audience.
Agency responsible for publication: National Employment Promotion and Vocational Training Department.
10. Methodological information about the statistics
Form of release: On paper, for limited audience.
Agency responsible for the release: National Employment Promotion and Vocational Training Department.
11. Comparisons with unemployment statistics from other sources
Comparisons have been made with unemployment statistics from the labour force survey and from the population census.
Frequency of the comparisons: From time to time (latest year: 2000).
Publication of the methodology/results of the comparisons: They have been published in *Informe Estadístico Mensual* (Monthly Statistical Report).
12. Major changes since the start of the statistics
There have been no major changes in legislation, capacity of the agency and/or administrative procedures which had a significant influence on the statistics.

Philippines

1. Series
Title: Number of Registered Applicants (by region, by sex and by programme).
2. Agency making the initial registrations of unemployed persons
Name of the agency: Public Employment Service Office (PESO).
Type of agency: public service under a national authority.
Name of the national authority: Department of Labour and Employment.
Location of the local offices making the registrations: In all parts of the country.
Type of services provided/administered by the agency:
- Assisting job-seekers to find jobs;
- Assisting job-seekers to establish their own business;
- Assisting employers to find workers;
- Vocational guidance;
- Job-related training;
- Providing labour market information.

Percentage of job-seekers seeking work through the agency: 20%.

3. Information registered about a person:
- Name;
- Sex;
- Social security number (or similar identification number also used by other agencies);
- Address of usual residence;
- Date of birth;
- Citizenship;
- Nationality/ethnic group;
- Educational/vocational attainment (educational level, course title). Links to ISCED have not been established;
- Current/past activity status (currently employed or previously employed);
- Type of work (occupation) of past or present job, with ten categories distinguished, based on the Philippines Standard Occupational Classification (PSOC);
- Type of work (occupation) of job sought, with ten categories (PSOC); Links to ISCO-88 have been established;
- Name and address of present or previous employer or work place.

4. Criteria used for inclusion of a person in the registers (R) and/or the statistics of unemployed persons (S):
- Being without work (R) and (S);
- Seeking work (R) and (S);
- Availability for work (R);
- Age (lower limit: 15 years; no upper limit) (S);
- Citizenship (R);
- Being resident in the country (R);
- Previously employed (R);
- Desired duration of employment (R).

5. Criteria used for exclusion of a person from the registers (R) and/or the statistics of unemployed persons (S):
- Death (R);
- Taking up residency abroad (R);
- Commencement of a (new) job (R);
- Commencement of military service (R);
- Participation in an employment promotion scheme, public work programme, etc (R);
- Studying or undergoing training (R);
- Failure to contact the agency/service (R);
- Inability to work (R).

6. Definition of unemployed persons used for the statistics
Applicants registered: number of job-seekers who indicate interest in availing themselves of the various employment facilitation services offered by PESO by filling up the registration form.

7. Updating of the registers
The registers are updated regularly.

8. Unemployment rates
Statistics from the registers are not used to obtain unemployment rates.

9. Type of statistics of unemployed persons produced
Series: Number of Registered Applicants.
Reference period: Month.
Frequency of production: Monthly.
Descriptive variables used:
- Sex;
- Age;
- Educational level;
- Occupation;
- Industry;
- Geographic characteristics;
- Previous work experience;
- Citizenship;

Form of publication: On paper, for limited audience.
Agency responsible for publication: Bureau of Local Employment (BLE).

10. Methodological information about the statistics
Form of release: Not released, available for internal use only.

11. Comparisons with unemployment statistics from other sources
Comparisons have been made with unemployment statistics from the Labour Force Survey.
Frequency of the comparisons: Occasionally.
Methodology/results of the methodology published: These have not been published.

12. Major changes since the start of the statistics
Major changes in legislation took place in 1999 (Public Employment Service Office Act (RA 8759)). The resulting changes in the statistics have not been estimated.

Poland

1. Series
Title: Registered unemployment.
Starting year: 1999.

2. Agency making the initial registrations of unemployed persons
Name of the agency: Powiat (district) Labour Offices.
Type of agency: Public service under local authorities.
Location of the local offices making the registrations: In all districts of the country.
Type of services provided/administered by the agency:
- Assisting job-seekers to find jobs;
- Assisting job-seekers to establish their own business;
- Assisting employers to find workers;
- Vocational guidance;
- Job-related training;
- Paying unemployment compensation;
- Other: organization of in-extremis temporary jobs and public work schemes (subsidized employment).

Percentage of job-seekers seeking work through the agency: Not known, as no research has been carried out on this subject.

3. The following information is registered about a person:
- Name;
- Sex;
- Address of usual residence;
- Date of birth;
- Citizenship;
- Educational/vocational attainment, with five categories distinguished. Links to ISCED have not been established;
- Current/past activity status, by employment period (less than one year, 1-5 years, 5-10 years, 10-20 years, 20-30 years, 30 years and over, and never employed);
- Type of work (occupation) of past or present job with an unspecified number of groups distinguished. Links to ISCO-88 have been established (sub-major groups level). (The Polish Classification of Occupations and Specialities is adjusted to ISCO-88);
- Type of work (occupation) of job sought, with an unspecified number of groups distinguished. Links to ISCO-88 have been established (sub-major groups level);
- Name and address of present or previous employer or work place;
- Type of business (industry) of present/previous employer/workplace, with an unspecified number of groups distinguished. Links to NACE, rev. 1 have been established (division level). (The Polish Classification of Activities is based on NACE, rev.1);
- Previous registrations with the agency/service;
- Other: balance of unemployed persons; job offers; unemployed persons taking advantage of active labour market forms (training, vocational guidance, job clubs, etc.).

Note: Statistical reporting does not cover unit data; therefore much of the above information is only recorded in the Registration Card of the unemployed person/job-seeker and is not recorded in the labour market statistics.

4. Criteria used for inclusion of a person in the registers (R) and/or the statistics of unemployed persons (S):
- Being without work (R) and (S);
- Seeking work (R) and (S);
- Availability for work (R);
- Age (lower limit: 18 years (with the exception of juvenile graduates); upper limit: 65 years for men; 60 years for women) (R) and (S);
- Citizenship (R) and (S);
- Being resident in the country (R) and (S);
- Previously employed (R) and (S).

5. Criteria used for exclusion of a person from the registers (R) and/or the statistics of unemployed persons (S):
- Death (R) and (S);
- Taking up residency abroad (R) and (S);
- Commencement of a (new) job (R) and (S);
- Commencement of military service (R) and (S);

– Participation in an employment promotion scheme, public works programme, etc. (R) and (S);
– Studying or undergoing training (R) and (S);
– Failure to contact the agency/service (three months exclusion) (R) and (S);
– Refusal of two suitable job or public works offers (six months exclusion) (R) and (S);
– Receipt of a retirement pension (R) and (S);
– Inability to work (R) and (S);
– Other: voluntary resignation from the status of an unemployed person; receipt of a loan from the Labour Fund or the State Fund for Rehabilitation of the Disabled to start an economic activity; attainment of the age of 65 years for men and 60 years for women; acquisition of the right to a pre-pension allowance or benefit (R) and (S).

6. Definition of unemployed persons used for the statistics

A persons is recognized as unemployed if s/he: is not employed (i.e. does not perform work on the basis of employment or service relationship or outwork); does not perform any other gainful work (i.e. does not perform work on the basis of civil law contracts (agency, commission or for a specific work) or in a period of membership of agricultural production co-operative or rural circles' co-operative (agricultural services); and:

– is able to work and ready to accept employment full-time, according to the rate of hours of work binding for a given occupation or service (with the exception of disabled persons);
– is not attending school in a day system;
– is registered in a powiat labour office, appropriate for place of permanent or temporary residence;
– is aged 18 years or over (with the exception of juvenile graduates);
– is aged less than 65 years for a man and 60 years for a woman;
– has not acquired the right to a retirement pension in respect of incapacity for work, training pension or after termination of employment, other gainful work, after stopping economic activity outside agriculture, does not receive pre-pension benefit or allowance, rehabilitation benefit, sickness allowance, maternity or child-care allowance;
– is not an owner or co-owner of agricultural real estate of an arable area exceeding two hectares taken for the purposes of calculation or is not covered by pension insurance in respect of permanent work as a spouse or member of a household on a farm of an arable area exceeding two hectares taken for the purposes of calculation;
– is not an owner or co-owner of a farm classified under a special section of agricultural production in the meaning of tax regulations, unless the income from a special section of agricultural production, calculated for the purposes of personal income tax is lower than or equal to average income from work in an individual farm of two hectares taken for the purposes of calculation, laid down by the President of the Central Statistical Office, under the regulations concerning rural tax, or is not covered by pension insurance in respect of permanent work as a spouse or member of a household on such a farm;
– has not started economic activity outside agriculture between a day indicated in application to register and a day of de-registering such activity, or is not covered - under separate provisions - by compulsory social insurance, with the exception of social insurance of farmers or pension security;
– is a disabled person, whose health condition allows for taking up employment at least half-time for a given occupation or service;
– is not a temporarily detained person or in a period of imprisonment (deprivation of liberty);
– does not receive monthly income in an amount exceeding half the minimum wage;
– does not receive, under the social assistance legislation, a permanent allowance, permanent compensatory allowance, guaranteed periodic allowance or social pension.

7. Updating of the registers

The registers are updated regularly.

8. Unemployment rates

Statistics from the registers are used to obtain unemployment rates.

The sources of data on employed persons who are part of the denominator of the unemployment rates are the Labour Force Survey, establishment surveys, Official Estimates and the Population Census.

Definition of employed persons for this purpose:

Data concerning employed persons relate to persons performing gainful work (income or earnings generating work). The following are included:

– persons employed on the basis of an employment relationship (employment contract, appointment, nomination or election);
– employers and own-account workers (self-employed persons);
– owners and co-owners of entities engaged in economic activity except for individual farms in agriculture;
– other own-account workers, e.g. self-employed professionals;
– outworkers and others.

9. Type of statistics of unemployed persons produced

Series 1:
Reference period: Unspecified.
Frequency of production: Yearly.
Descriptive variables used:
– Sex;
– Age;
– Educational level;
– Occupation;
– Previous work experience;
– Duration of unemployment;
– Other: inflow - outflow; with right to benefit; unemployment rate; previously not working; graduates; released for reasons concerning enterprise; by place of residence; job offers; taking advantage of active labour market forms.

Form of publication:
– On paper, for general audience;
– On CD-ROM.

Agency responsible for publication: Central Statistical Office.
Title and periodicity of the publication: *Statistical Yearbook of the Republic of Poland.*

Series 2:
Reference period: Unspecified.
Frequency of production: Biennial.
Descriptive variables used:
– Sex;
– Age;
– Educational level;
– Occupation;
– Geographic characteristics;
– Previous work experience;
– Duration of unemployment;
– Other: inflow - outflow; with right to benefit; unemployment rate; previously not working; graduates; released for reasons concerning enterprise; by place of residence; taking advantage of active labour market forms.

Form of publication:
– On paper, for general audience;
– On CD-ROM.

Agency responsible for publication: Central Statistical Office.
Title and periodicity of the publication: *Statistical Yearbook of Labour,* biennial.

Series 3:
Reference period: Unspecified.
Frequency of production: Quarterly.
Descriptive variables used:
– Sex;
– Age;
– Educational level;
– Occupation;
– Industry;
– Geographic characteristics;
– Previous work experience;
– Duration of unemployment;
– Other: inflow - outflow; starting work; with right to benefit; unemployment rate; released for reasons concerning enterprise; previously working or not; graduates; by place of residence; job offers; active labour market forms for registered unemployed persons.

Form of publication: On paper, for general audience.
Agency responsible for publication: Central Statistical Office.
Title and periodicity of the publication: *Registered unemployment,* quarterly.

Other series:
The National Labour Office publishes the following information series:

- Information concerning unemployment state and structure (monthly).
- Unemployed persons for a period exceeding 12 months.
- Labour Market in Poland (yearly).
- Institutional labour market services (yearly).
- Permissions for employment for foreigners (half-yearly; yearly).
- Women's unemployment (half-yearly; yearly).
- Information concerning unemployment state and structure (half-yearly).
- Information concerning registered unemployment state and structure in rural areas (half-yearly; yearly).
- Information concerning youth labour market situation (half-yearly; yearly).
- Unemployed persons and job offers for unemployed persons by occupations and specialities (half-yearly; yearly).
- Unemployed women by occupations and specialities (half-yearly; yearly).
- Unemployed graduates of schools at over-primary level by learnt occupations (half-yearly; yearly).
- Unemployment analysis by the Polish Classification of Activities (half-yearly; yearly).
- Unemployed persons by occupations and specialities (half-yearly; yearly).

10. Methodological information about the statistics
Form of release:
- On paper, for general audience;
- In machine-readable form, on request;
- On a website (http://praca@gov.pl).

Agency responsible for the release: Central Statistical Office; National Labour Office.

11. Comparisons with unemployment statistics from other sources
Comparisons have been made with unemployment statistics from the Labour Force Survey and the Population Census.
Frequency of the comparisons: Regularly, when the statistics are published.
Publication of the methodology/results of the comparisons: These have not been published.

12. Major changes since the start of the statistics
Major changes in legislation, capacity of the agency and/or administrative procedures took place in 1991, 1996, 1997 and 2001. The resulting changes in the statistics have not been estimated.

Portugal

1. Series
Title: *Number of job-seekers* and *Number of unemployed job-seekers.*
Starting year: 1967.
2. Agency making the initial registrations of unemployed persons
Name of the agency: Instituto de Emprego e Formação Profissional - IEPF (Institute of Employment and Vocational Training).
Type of agency: Public service under a national authority.
Name of the national authority: Ministry of Social Security and Labour.
Location of the local offices making the registrations: All over the country. 86 Employment Agencies located in the five regions of the continental part of the country, plus one agency in the autonomous region of Madeira and three agencies in the autonomous region of the Azores (the agencies of the two autonomous regions do not report directly to the IEFP, but to autonomous regional services; however, the statistics are consolidated by the IEFP).

These agencies also establish "employment units", which may or may not be permanent, depending on criteria such as the population density or the number of registered unemployed. Presently, there are almost 150 of such units.
Type of services provided/administered by the agency:
- Assisting job-seekers to find jobs;
- Assisting job-seekers to establish their own business;
- Assisting employers to find workers;
- Vocational guidance;
- Job-related training;
- Paying unemployment compensation: the IEFP is not responsible for these payments, but co-operates with the Social Security in order to monitor the active predisposition of beneficiaries for integration in the labour market.

Percentage of job-seekers seeking work through the agency: 49% (end 2001; source: National Statistical Institute, "Employment Survey").

3. The following information is registered about a person:
- Name;
- Sex;
- Social security number (or similar identification number also used by other agencies);
- Address of usual residence;
- Date of birth;
- Nationality;
- Educational/vocational attainment, with 11 categories distinguished. Links to ISCED have not been established. However, the national classification of educational domains, reviewed in February 2001, has direct links with the ISCED-97;
- Current/past activity status, with seven categories distinguished;
- Type of work (occupation) of past or present job with 355 categories distinguished (unit groups level). Links to ISCO-88 have been established (unit groups level);
- Type of work (occupation) of job sought, with 355 categories distinguished (unit groups level);
- Name and address of present or previous employer or work place;
- Type of business (industry) of present/previous employer/workplace, with 715 categories distinguished. Links to ISIC, rev.3 have been established (divisions level); and to the NACE, rev.1 (classes level);
- Previous registrations with the agency/service;
- Other: Identification of handicapped persons and of the type of handicap, for example.

4. Criteria used for inclusion of a person in the registers (R) and/or the statistics of unemployed persons (S):
- Being without work (R) and (S);
- Seeking dependant work (a request for financial or technical support to create own enterprise is not considered as a request for employment) (R) and (S);
- Availability for work within a maximum of 15 days following the date of registration (R) and (S);
- Age (lower limit: 16 years; no upper limit) (R) and (S);
- Being resident in the country (i.e. obligation to present either an identification document proving that he/she is a resident of Portugal, generally an identity card, or, for non-nationals from non-EEA (European Economic Area) member countries, a residence permit issued by the Department dealing with foreigners and frontiers (R) and (S);
- Applicants have to respect the following obligations: accept any employment offer considered as suitable; comply with the checks made by the Employment Agencies; accept the "personal employment plan" agreed by the agency and the applicant as the most suitable with regard to his/her personal and professional profile, and with the aim of his/her integration into the labour market.
- Unemployed receiving unemployment compensation: also have to accept any job considered of general public utility; accept vocational training offered; actively seek work.

5. Criteria used for exclusion of a person from the registers (R) and/or the statistics of unemployed persons (S):
- Death (R) and (S);
- Taking up residency abroad (R) and (S);
- Commencement of a (new) job (R) and (S);
- Commencement of military service (R) and (S);
- Participation in an employment promotion scheme (R) and (S);
- Participation to a public works programme (R) and (S);
- Studying or undergoing training. This can be a vocational training course or a training-employment programme, and may be promoted by the IEFP (R) and (S);
- Failure to contact the agency: non-attendance without a valid reason following a summoning (either for suitable job offers, vocational training, public utility work, or for a simple presence check) leads to exclusion after the second summoning; equally, not replying to a postal check leads to the exclusion after one month for beneficiaries, and after two months for non-beneficiaries (R) and (S);
- Refusal of a suitable job offer (R) and (S);
- Refusal of a suitable training offer (R) and (S);

– Inability to work: total disability due to sickness (be it temporary or permanent), excludes the possibility of registration as a job-seeker or as unemployed. Disability due to invalidity excludes a person from registration only in case of total invalidity (be it temporary or permanent), applicable to all suitable (or adaptable) occupations, certified by the occupational medicine department of the employment agencies and, in the case of beneficiaries of unemployment compensation, confirmed by the Department of Verification of disabilities (SVI) (R) and (S);

6. Definition of unemployed persons used for the statistics

Is considered as "unemployed" any applicant registered with an employment agency who is without work, looking for work as a dependent worker, immediately available and able to work.

"Immediately available" means that the applicant must commit him/herself to accepting a job within a maximum of 15 days from the day of his/her registration. After this period, acceptance of the job must be immediate.

"Able to work" means that the applicant must prove that he/she has the ability (physical, mental and professional) required to perform a professional activity, and that there is no disability due to sickness.

7. Updating of the registers

The registers are updated regularly, on a continuous basis.

8. Unemployment rates

Statistics from the registers are not used to obtain unemployment rates.

9. Type of statistics of unemployed persons produced
Reference period: Month.
Frequency of production: Monthly.
Descriptive variables used:
– Sex;
– Age;
– Educational level;
– Occupation;
– Industry;
– Geographic characteristics;
– Citizenship (nationals/non nationals);
– Duration of unemployment: duration of registration as job-seeker in an employment agency;
– Other: employment status; looking for a first job/looking for a new job.

Form of publication:
– On paper, for general audience;
– Machine-readable form, on request;
– On a website:
– http://www.iefp.pt/estatisticas/estatmercemp.htm

Agency responsible for publication: IEFP.
Title and periodicity of the publications: *"Monthly information on the labour market"; "The labour market - monthly statistics"; "The employment agencies - monthly statistics"; "Municipalities - registered unemployment statistics and corrected ratios of registered unemployment"* - quarterly statistics; *"Evolution and situation of local labour markets"* - quarterly statistics; *"The labour market"* - annual report.

10. Methodological information about the statistics
Form of publication:
– On paper, for general audience;
– Machine-readable form, on request;
– On a website:
– http://www.iefp.pt/estatisticas/estatmercemp.htm

Agency responsible for publication: IEFP.
11. Comparisons with unemployment statistics from other sources

Comparisons have been made with unemployment statistics from the labour force survey, from other household surveys and from the population census.
Frequency of the comparisons: Regularly.
Publication of the methodology/results of the comparisons: They have not been published.
12. Major changes since the start of the statistics

There have been no major changes in legislation, capacity of the agency and/or administrative procedures which had a significant influence on the statistics.

Qatar

1. Series
Title: Registered unemployment.

Starting year: 1965.
2. Agency making the initial registrations of unemployed persons
Name of the agency: Labour Department.
Type of agency: Public service under a national authority.
Name of the national authority: Ministry of Civil Service and Housing.
Location of the local offices making the registrations: In the Head Office of the Labour Department.
Type of services provided/administered by the agency:
– Assisting job-seekers to find jobs;
– Assisting employers to find workers;
– Vocational guidance;
– Job-related training.
3. The following information is registered about a person:
– Name;
– Sex;
– Address of usual residence;
– Date of birth;
– Citizenship;
– Nationality/ethnic group;
– Educational/vocational attainment, with an unspecified number of categories distinguished. Links to ISCED have been established;
– Current/past activity status, with four categories distinguished;
– Type of work (occupation) of past or present job with 10 groups distinguished. Links to ISCO-88 have been established;
– Type of work (occupation) of job sought, with an unspecified number of groups distinguished. Links to ISCO-88 have been established;
– Name and address of present or previous employer or work place;
– Type of business (industry) of present/previous employer/workplace, with 136 groups distinguished. Links to ISIC, rev.3 have been established (group level);
– Previous registrations with the agency/service;
– Other: work experience.
4. Criteria used for inclusion of a person in the registers (R) and/or the statistics of unemployed persons (S):
– Being without work (R) and (S);
– Seeking work (R) and (S);
– Age (lower limit: 18 years; no upper limit) (R) and (S);
– Being resident in the country (R) and (S);
– Previously employed (R) and (S).
5. Criteria used for exclusion of a person from the registers (R) and/or the statistics of unemployed persons (S):
– Death (R);
– Taking up residency abroad (R);
– Commencement of a (new) job (R);
– Commencement of military service (R);
– Studying (R).
6. Definition of unemployed persons used for the statistics

Unemployed persons are those who were not employed, were desirous to work, were seeking work and did not find jobs during the period of reference (week of survey).
7. Updating of the registers

The registers are updated annually.
8. Unemployment rates

Statistics from the registers are not used to obtain unemployment rates.
9. Type of statistics of unemployed persons produced
Reference period: Week.
Frequency of production: Yearly.
Descriptive variables used:
– Sex;
– Age;
– Educational level;
– Occupation;
– Industry;
– Geographic characteristics;
– Previous work experience;
– Citizenship (nationals/non nationals).
Form of publication: On paper, for limited audience.
Agency responsible for publication: Ministry of Civil Service and Housing.
10. Methodological information about the statistics
Form of release: Not released, available for internal use only.
Agency responsible: Ministry of Civil Service and Housing.

11. Comparisons with unemployment statistics from other sources

Comparisons have been made with unemployment statistics from the Labour Force Survey, another type of household survey and from the Population Census.

Frequency of the comparisons: Regularly, when the statistics are published.

Publication of the methodology/results of the comparisons: These have not been published.

12. Major changes since the start of the statistics

After the adoption by the Ministerial Council, in 1997, of a resolution which encouraged Qataris to work in the private sector the number of registered unemployed persons increased.

Romania

1. Series

Title: Unemployment Statistical Situation.

Starting year: 1991.

2. Agency making the initial registrations of unemployed persons

Name of the agency: Agentia nationala pentru ocuparea fortei de munca (National Agency for Employment).

Type of agency: Public service under a national authority.

Name of the national authority: Ministry of Labour and Social Solidarity.

Location of the local offices making the registrations: In all counties and in the municipality of Bucharest.

Type of services provided/administered by the agency:
– Assisting job-seekers to find jobs;
– Assisting job-seekers to establish their own business;
– Assisting employers to find workers;
– Vocational guidance;
– Job-related training;
– Paying unemployment compensation.

Percentage of job-seekers seeking work through the agency: 75%.

3. The following information is registered about a person:
– Name;
– Sex;
– Social security number (or similar identification number also used by other agencies);
– Address of usual residence;
– Date of birth;
– Citizenship;
– Nationality/ethnic group;
– Educational/vocational attainment, with six categories distinguished;
– Current/past activity status, with five categories distinguished;
– Type of work (occupation) of past or present job with 415 categories distinguished. Links to ISCO-88 have been established (unit groups level);
– Type of work (occupation) of job sought, with 415 categories distinguished. Links to ISCO-88 have been established (unit groups level);
– Name and address of present or previous employer or work place;
– Type of business (industry) of present/previous employer/workplace;
– Previous registrations with the agency/service.

4. Criteria used for inclusion of a person in the registers (R) and/or the statistics of unemployed persons (S):
– Being without work (R) and (S);
– Seeking work (R) and (S);
– Availability for work (R);
– Being resident in the country (R) and (S);
– Previously employed (R) and (S).

5. Criteria used for exclusion of a person from the registers (R) and/or the statistics of unemployed persons (S):
– Death (R) and (S);
– Taking up residency abroad (R) and (S);
– Commencement of a (new) job (R) and (S);
– Commencement of military service (R) and (S);
– Participation in an employment promotion scheme, public works programme, etc (R) and (S);
– Failure to contact the agency/service (it is obligatory to report every month to the employment service) (R) and (S);
– Refusal of a suitable job offer (R) and (S);
– Refusal of a suitable training offer (R) and (S);
– Receipt of a pension (R) and (S).

6. Definition of unemployed persons used for the statistics

According to Law No.76/2002 on the unemployment insurance system and employment promotion, a person is considered as unemployed if (s)he meets all the following requirements:
– is in search of a job and is aged 16 years or over and does not meet the requirements for retirement;
– is in good health, and physically and mentally able to take up employment;
– does not have a job, does not earn any income or the income generated from activities authorised according to the law is lower than the unemployment benefit to which s(he) would be entitled according to this law;
– is ready to start working as soon as a job is found;
– is registered with the National Agency for Employment or with another employment service provider that operates according to the law.

7. Updating of the registers

The registers are updated monthly.

8. Unemployment rates

Statistics from the registers are used to obtain unemployment rates.

The sources of data on employed persons who are part of the denominator of the unemployment rates are the population census and the data from the National Institute for Statistics and Economic Studies.

Definition of employed persons for this purpose: The economically active civilian population.

9. Type of statistics of unemployed persons produced

Reference period: month.

Frequency of production: monthly.

Descriptive variables used:
– Sex;
– Age;
– Educational level;
– Occupation;
– Industry;
– Geographic characteristics;
– Previous work experience;
– Citizenship (nationals/non nationals);
– Duration of unemployment;
– Other: forms of indemnity.

Form of publication:
– On paper, for general audience;
– Machine-readable form, on request.

Title and periodicity of the publication: *Unemployment statistical situation,* monthly.

10. Methodological information about the statistics

Form of release:
– Not released, available for internal use only;
– In machine-readable form, on request.

11. Comparisons with unemployment statistics from other sources

Comparisons have been made with unemployment statistics from other sources by the National Institute for Statistics and Economic Studies.

Frequency of the comparisons: regularly.

12. Major changes since the start of the statistics

The new law on the unemployment insurance system and employment promotion, which entered into force in March 2002, generated important changes, mainly concerning the level of unemployment benefit, the forms of indemnity, the statistics, etc.

Saint Pierre and Miquelon

1. Series

Title: Monthly employment survey.

Starting year: 1980.

2. Agency making the initial registrations of unemployed persons

Name of the agency: Agence nationale pour l'Emploi - ANPE (National Employment Agency).

Type of agency: Public service under a national authority.

Name of the national authority: Ministry in charge of Labour and Employment.

Location of the local offices making the registrations: There is one permanent operational point on the island of St. Pierre and Miquelon.

Type of services provided/administered by the agency:
- Assisting job-seekers to find jobs;
- Assisting employers to find workers;
- Vocational guidance;
- Job-related training.

Percentage of job-seekers seeking work through the agency: All job-seekers up to 57 years of age are required to respond to requests from the ANPE: interviews, making contacts, proposals of assistance, etc. (persons over 57 years are not required to seek work).

3. The following information is registered about a person:
- Name;
- Sex;
- Social security number (or similar identification number also used by other agencies);
- Address of usual residence;
- Date of birth;
- Citizenship;
- Nationality;
- Vocational attainment, with six categories distinguished. Links to ISCED have not been established;
- Current/past activity status;
- Type of work of past or present job with 61 categories distinguished (operational manual of occupations). Links to ISCO have not been established;
- Qualifications.

4. Criteria used for inclusion of a person in the registers (R) and/or the statistics of unemployed persons (S):
- Being without work (R) and (S);
- Seeking work (R) and (S);
- Availability for work (R) and (S);
- Age (lower limit: 16 years; upper limit: 57 years) (R) and (S);
- Citizenship (R) and (S);
- Being resident in the country or in possession of a residence permit (R) and (S).

Desired duration of employment and/or number of hours of work sought: persons seeking part-time employment (of 16 hours minimum per week) are registered in Category 2 of the definitions given under point 6 below.

5. Criteria used for exclusion of a person from the registers (R) and/or the statistics of unemployed persons (S):
- Death (R) and (S);
- Taking up residency abroad (R) and (S);
- Commencement of a (new) job (R) and (S). However, it is possible to combine part-time activities and registration as a job seeker (transfer to Categories 6, 7 or 8 of point 6);
- Participation in an employment promotion scheme, public works programme, etc.(R) and (S);
- Studying or undergoing training (transfer to Category 4 of point 6);
- Failure to contact the agency, refusal to appear following a summoning (R) and (S);
- Refusal of suitable job offers (R) and (S);
- Refusal of suitable training offers (R) and (S);
- Inability to work, periods of sickness (R) and (S), transfer to Category 5 of point 6.

6. Definition of unemployed persons used for the statistics

Category 1: Unemployed persons, immediately available for work according to Article R.311-3-3, required to actively look for employment, looking for full-time employment of unspecified duration.
These persons should not have carried out any casual activity or a reduced activity of more than 78 hours during the month in question.
Category 2: Unemployed persons, immediately available for work according to Article R.311-3-3, required to actively look for employment, looking for part-time employment of unspecified duration.
These persons should not have carried out any casual activity or a reduced activity of more than 78 hours during the month in question.
Category 3: Unemployed persons, immediately available for work according to Article R.311-3-3, required to actively look for employment, looking for temporary or seasonal employment of specified duration, including very brief duration.
These persons should not have carried out any casual or a reduced activity of more than 78 hours during the month in question.

Category 4: Unemployed persons, not immediately available for work, looking for employment.
Category 5: Employed persons, looking for another job.
Category 6: Persons not immediately available for work according to Article R.311-3-3 (1), required to actively look for employment, looking for another job, full-time of unspecified duration.
These persons will have carried out a casual or reduced activity of more than 78 hours during the month in question.
Category 7: Persons not immediately available for work according to Article R.311-3-3 (1), required to actively look for employment, looking for another job, part-time of unspecified duration.
These persons will have carried out a casual or reduced activity of more than 78 hours during the month in question.
Category 8: Persons not immediately available for work according to Article R.311-3-3 (1), required to actively look for employment, looking for another job, temporary or seasonal of specified duration, including of very short duration.
These persons will have carried out a casual or reduced activity of more than 78 hours during the month in question.

7. Updating of the registers
The registers are updated monthly.

8. Unemployment rates
Statistics from the registers are used to obtain unemployment rates. The source of data on employed persons who are part of the denominator of the unemployment rates is the population census.

9. Type of statistics of unemployed persons produced
Reference period: Month.
Frequency of production: Monthly.
Descriptive variables used:
- Sex;
- Age;
- Educational level;
- Occupation sought;
- Duration of unemployment.

Form of publication: For the use of State services, elected representatives and economic and social organisations. The Aperçu mensuel (Monthly Review) is presented by local radios and partially published in the local written press.

Agency responsible for publication: Department of Labour and Employment and Vocational Training: aggregation of data provided by the ANPE with series related to employment policy, as well as comments.

10. Methodological information about the statistics
Only Category 1 (see point 6) is used as a basis for the statistics. Comments may incorporate data relating to other categories, if they are significant.
Form of release: Through the comments of the Aperçu mensuel.
Agency responsible for the release: Service of Labour and Employment and Vocational Training.

11. Comparisons with unemployment statistics from other sources
Comparisons have been made with unemployment statistics from the general population census.
Frequency of the comparisons: Mainly when the census data are first released.
Publication of the methodology/results of the comparisons: Through the comments in the Aperçu mensuel.

12. Major changes since the start of the statistics
Major changes in legislation, capacity of the agency and/or administrative procedures took place in 1995: end of physical clocking in; computerization of the ANPE; and exploitation of the data on long-term unemployment for the adjustment of the employment policy and insertion tools.

Serbia and Montenegro

1. Series
Title: Registered unemployment.
Starting year: Not specified.

2. Agency making the initial registrations of unemployed persons
Name of the agency: Bureau of Labour of the Republics.
Type of agency: Public service under a national authority.
Name of the national authority: Ministry for Labour and Employment.
Location of the local offices making the registrations: In all districts throughout Serbia and Montenegro.
Type of services provided/administered by the agency:
- Assisting job-seekers to find jobs;

– Assisting job-seekers to establish their own business;
– Assisting employers to find workers;
– Vocational guidance;
– Job-related training;
– Paying unemployment compensation;
– Other: providing labour market information; taking active policy measures concerning specific categories of unemployed persons (invalids, etc.).

Percentage of job-seekers seeking work through the agency: 29%.

3. The following information is registered about a person:
– Name;
– Sex;
– Social security number (or similar identification number also used by other agencies);
– Address of usual residence;
– Date of birth;
– Citizenship;
– Educational/vocational attainment, with nine categories distinguished. Links to ISCED have not been established;
– Current/past activity status, with three categories distinguished;
– Type of work (occupation) of past or present job with 74 groups distinguished (about 3,500 individual professions). Links to ISCO-88 have not been established;
– Type of work (occupation) of job sought, with 74 groups distinguished (about 3,500 individual professions). Links to ISCO-88 have not been established;
– Name and address of present or previous employer or work place;
– Type of business (industry) of present/previous employer/workplace, with 17 groups distinguished. Links to ISIC, rev.3 or NACE, rev.1 have been established;
– Previous registrations with the agency/service;
– Other: professional motivation of unemployed person; special knowledge and skills; rights of unemployed person; dates of mediation.

4. Criteria used for inclusion of a person in the registers (R) and/or the statistics of unemployed persons (S):
– Being without work (R) and (S);
– Seeking work (R) and (S);
– Availability for work (R);
– Age (lower and upper limits not specified) (R) and (S);
– Citizenship (R);
– Being resident in the country (R);
– Previously employed (R) and (S);
– Desired duration of employment and/or number of hours of work sought (R);
– Previous payment of unemployed insurance contributions (R).

5. Criteria used for exclusion of a person from the registers (R) and/or the statistics of unemployed persons (S):
– Death (R) and (S);
– Taking up residency abroad (R) and (S);
– Commencement of a (new) job (R) and (S);
– Participation in an employment promotion scheme, public works programme, etc. (R) and (S);
– Failure to contact the agency/service (R);
– Refusal of 1 suitable job offer per month (R);
– End of entitlement to receive unemployment compensation (R);
– Receipt of a pension (R);
– Inability to work (R);
– Other: if subject to a legal penalty or corrective measures for a period longer than six months (R).

6. Definition of unemployed persons used for the statistics
Persons who are not employed, who are available for work, who are seeking work and who are registered in the regular files of the Bureau for Employment.

7. Updating of the registers
The registers are updated monthly and yearly.

8. Unemployment rates
Statistics from the registers are used to obtain unemployment rates. The source of data on employed persons who are part of the denominator of the unemployment rates are the Labour Force Survey and the regular Monthly Reports on Employed Persons and Wages.
Definition of employed persons for this purpose:

Persons employed in enterprises, organizations or in the private sector.

9. Type of statistics of unemployed persons produced
Series 1:
Reference period: Month; Year.
Frequency of production: Monthly.
Descriptive variables used:
– Sex;
– Educational level;
– Industry;
– Geographic characteristics;
– Other: reason for cessation of employment; trainees.
Form of publication: On paper, for general audience.
Agency responsible for publication: Federal Bureau for Labour Market and Migrations.
Title and periodicity of the publication: Monthly Statistical Survey - Employment.
Series 2:
Reference period: Month; Year.
Frequency of production: Monthly.
Descriptive variables used:
– Sex;
– Age;
– Educational level;
– Occupation;
– Geographic characteristics;
– Previous work experience;
– Citizenship (nationals/non nationals);
– Duration of unemployment;
– Other: recipients of unemployment benefits; total cash payments of unemployment benefits made (per month; per year).
Form of publication: On paper, for limited audience.
Agency responsible for publication: Federal Bureau for Labour Market and Migrations.
Title and periodicity of the publication: Statistical Yearbook - Placement of unemployed persons.

10. Methodological information about the statistics
Form of release: On paper, for limited audience.
Agency responsible for the release: Federal Bureau for Labour Market and Migrations.

11. Comparisons with unemployment statistics from other sources
Comparisons have not been made with unemployment statistics from other sources.

12. Major changes since the start of the statistics
There have been no major changes in legislation, capacity of the agency and/or administrative procedures which had a significant influence on the statistics.

Slovenia

1. Series
Title: Registered unemployed persons.
Starting year: 1947.

2. Agency making the initial registrations of unemployed persons
Name of the agency: Zavod rs za zaposlovanje (Employment Service of Slovenia).
Type of agency: Public service under a national authority.
Name of the national authority: Ministry of Labour, Family and Social Affairs.
Location of the local offices making the registrations: In all parts of the country, all administrative units.
Type of services provided/administered by the agency:
– Assisting job-seekers to find jobs;
– Assisting job-seekers to establish their own business;
– Assisting employers to find workers;
– Vocational guidance;
– Job-related training;
– Paying unemployment compensation;
– Other: work permits, national scholarship programme.

Percentage of job-seekers seeking work through the agency: 90%.

3. The following information is registered about a person:
Name;
Sex;

Social security number (or similar identification number also used by other agencies);
Address of usual residence;
Date of birth;
Citizenship;
Educational/vocational attainment, with eight categories distinguished;
Current/past activity status, with three categories distinguished;
Type of work (occupation) of past or present job;
Type of work (occupation) of job sought, with 371categories distinguished. Links to ISCO-88 have been established (unit groups level);
Name and address of present or previous employer or work place;
Previous registrations with the agency/service.

4. Criteria used for inclusion of a person in the registers (R) and/or the statistics of unemployed persons (S):
- Being without work (R) and (S);
- Actively seeking work, which is followed up by an employment adviser (R) and (S);
- Availability for work (R) and (S);
- Age (lower limit: 15 years; upper limit: 60 years for women, 65 years for men) (R) and (S);
- Citizenship (R) and (S).

5. Criteria used for exclusion of a person from the registers (R) and/or the statistics of unemployed persons (S):
- Death (R) and (S);
- Taking up residency abroad (R) and (S);
- Commencement of a (new) job (R) and (S);
- Commencement of military service (R) and (S);
- Participation in an employment promotion scheme, public works programme, etc (S);
- Studying or undergoing training: Only those in short term training programmes are included in the statistics (S);
- Failure to contact the agency/service (R) and (S);
- Refusal of two suitable job offers (R) and (S);
- Refusal of a suitable training offers (R) and (S);
- Receipt of a pension (R) and (S);
- Inability to work (R) and (S);
- Other: following regular education (R) and (S).

6. Definition of unemployed persons used for the statistics
Registered unemployed persons are persons aged 15 to 60 (women), and 15 to 65 (men), who are registered at the employment service, actively seeking employment and are willing to accept employment which corresponds to their educational attainment. Excluded are retired persons, persons in prison for more than six months, owners of enterprises in which they made an income in the last calendar year and which they could use to support themselves - provided that the income they made did not exceed the minimum earnings, and also owners of agricultural or forest areas, which can provide an income for living.

7. Updating of the registers
The registers are updated daily.

8. Unemployment rates
Statistics from the registers are used to obtain registered unemployment rates.
The sources of data on employed persons who are part of the denominator of the unemployment rates are establishment surveys and social security registers.
Definition of employed persons for this purpose: Persons employed regularly on a full or part-time basis, self-employed and farmers.

9. Type of statistics of unemployed persons produced
Reference period: month, quarter and year.
Frequency of production: monthly, quarterly and yearly.
Descriptive variables used:
- Sex;
- Age;
- Educational level;
- Occupation;
- Geographic characteristics;
- Previous work experience;
- Duration of unemployment.

Form of publication:
- On paper, for general audience;
- Machine-readable form, on request;
- On a website: http://www.ess.gov.si.

Agency responsible for publication: Employment Service, Statistical Office of the Republic of Slovenia.

10. Methodological information about the statistics
Form of release:
- On paper, for general audience;
- In machine-readable form, on request;
- On a website.

Agency responsible for the release: Employment Service, Statistical Office.

11. Comparisons with unemployment statistics from other sources
Comparisons have been made with unemployment statistics from the labour force survey (for the LFS data the responsible institution is the Statistical Office).
Frequency of the comparisons: regularly.
Publication of the methodology/results of the comparisons: These have been published.

12. Major changes since the start of the statistics
There have been no major changes in legislation, capacity of the agency and/or administrative procedures which had a significant influence on the statistics.

Spain

1. Series
Title: Registered unemployment.
Starting year: Not specified.

2. Agency making the initial registrations of unemployed persons
Name of the agency: Instituto Nacional de Empleo y Servicios Públicos de Empleo (National Institute of Employment and Public Employment Services).
Type of agency: Public service under a national authority.
Name of the national authority: Ministerio de Trabajo y Asuntos Sociales (Ministry of Labour and Social Affairs).
Location of the local offices making the registrations: All over the country, located by geographical areas.
Type of services provided/administered by the agency:
- Assisting job-seekers to find jobs;
- Assisting job-seekers to establish their own business;
- Assisting employers to find workers;
- Vocational guidance;
- Job-related training;
- Paying unemployment compensation;
- Other: experimental employment and vocational training programmes.

Percentage of job-seekers seeking work through the agency: Not specified.

3. The following information is registered about a person:
- Name;
- Sex;
- Social security number (or similar identification number also used by other agencies);
- Address of usual residence;
- Date of birth;
- Citizenship;
- Nationality;
- Educational/vocational attainment. Links to ISCED have not been established;
- Current/past activity status, with 40 categories distinguished;
- Type of work (occupation) of past or present job. Links to ISCO-88 have been established (unit groups level);
- Type of work (occupation) of job sought, with 3,537 categories distinguished. Links to ISCO-88 have been established (unit groups level);
- Name and address of present or previous employer or work place;
- Type of business (industry) of present/previous employer/workplace, with 63 categories distinguished;
- Previous registrations with the agency/service.

4. Criteria used for inclusion of a person in the registers (R) and/or the statistics of unemployed persons (S):
- Being without work (S);
- Seeking work (R) and (S);
- Availability for work (S);
- Age (lower limit: 16 years; upper limit: 65 years) (S);
- Citizenship (R) and (S);
- Being resident in the country (R) and (S);
- Desired duration of employment and/or number of hours of work sought (S).

5. Criteria used for exclusion of a person from the registers (R) and/or the statistics of unemployed persons (S):
- Death (R) and (S);
- Taking up residency abroad (R) and (S);
- Commencement of a (new) job (persons who have found a job for more than three months are excluded) (R) and (S);
- Participation in an employment promotion scheme, public works programme, etc (R) and (S);
- Studying or undergoing training (persons under 25 years or who have never worked are excluded from the statistics) (S);
- Refusal of a suitable job offer (R) and (S);
- Refusal of a suitable training offer (R) and (S);
- Inability to work (R) and (S).

6. Definition of unemployed persons used for the statistics
Persons registered as job-seekers who do not belong to the following categories: are employed; participating in a work programme of social interest; receiving a full invalidity pension; are retired; are employed for a period of more than three months; are working less than 80 hours per month; are studying; are undergoing vocational training; are absent for medical reasons; are receiving an agricultural allowance; are aged over 65 years.

7. Updating of the registers
The registers are updated daily.

8. Unemployment rates
Statistics from the registers are used to obtain unemployment rates. The source of data on employed persons who are part of the denominator of the unemployment rates is the household labour force survey.
Definition of employed persons for this purpose:
Survey on the economically active population.

9. Type of statistics of unemployed persons produced
Reference period: Month.
Frequency of production: Monthly.
Descriptive variables used:
- Sex;
- Age;
- Educational level;
- Occupation;
- Industry;
- Geographic characteristics;
- Duration of unemployment;
- Other: reasons for exclusion from registered unemployment.

Form of publication:
- On paper, for limited audience;
- Machine-readable form, on request;
- On a website: www.inem.es.

Agency responsible for publication: Instituto Nacional de Empleo (National Institute of Employment).
Title and periodicity of the publication: Estadística de Empleo (Employment statistics), monthly.

10. Methodological information about the statistics
Form of release:
- On paper, for general audience;
- In machine-readable form, on request;
- On a website: www.inem.es.

Agency responsible for the release: National Institute of Employment.

11. Comparisons with unemployment statistics from other sources
Comparisons have not been made with unemployment statistics from other sources.

12. Major changes since the start of the statistics
Major changes in legislation, capacity of the agency and/or administrative procedures took place in 1985, but the resulting changes in the statistics have not been estimated.

Suriname

1. Series
Title: Statistics of registered job-seekers.
Starting year: 1983.
2. Agency making the initial registrations of unemployed persons
Name of the agency: Dienst der Arbeidsbemiddeling (Labour Exchange Bureau).
Type of agency: Public service under a national authority.
Name of the national authority: Ministry of Labour Technological Development and Environment.

Location of the local offices making the registrations: In the districts of Paramaribo, Saramacca and Nickerie.
Type of services provided/administered by the agency:
- Assisting job-seekers to find jobs;
- Assisting employers to find workers;
- Job-related training;
- Other: access to relevant labour market information.

Number of job-seekers seeking work through the agency: About 80 persons per month.

3. The following information is registered about a person:
- Name;
- Sex;
- Social security number (or similar identification number also used by other agencies);
- Address of usual residence;
- Date of birth;
- Citizenship;
- Nationality/ethnic group;
- Educational/vocational attainment, with an unspecified number of categories distinguished. Links to ISCED have been established;
- Current/past activity status, with three categories distinguished;
- Type of work (occupation) of past or present job with nine groups distinguished. No links to ISCO-88 have been established;
- Type of work (occupation) of job sought, with nine groups distinguished. No links to ISCO-88 have been established;
- Name and address of present or previous employer or work place;
- Type of business (industry) of present/previous employer/work-place, with nine groups distinguished. No links to ISIC, rev.3 have been established;
- Previous registrations with the agency/service.

4. Criteria used for inclusion of a person in the registers (R) and/or the statistics of unemployed persons (S):
- Being without work (S);
- Seeking work (S);
- Age (lower limit: 15 years; upper limit: 65 years) (S);
- Desired duration of employment and/or number of hours of work sought (S).

5. Criteria used for exclusion of a person from the registers (R) and/or the statistics of unemployed persons (S):
- Taking up residency abroad (S);
- Studying or undergoing training (S);
- Inability to work (S).

6. Definition of unemployed persons used for the statistics
Information not available.

7. Updating of the registers
It is not known whether the registers are updated regularly.

8. Unemployment rates
Statistics from the registers are not used to obtain unemployment rates.

9. Type of statistics of registered unemployed persons produced
Information not available.

10. Methodological information about the statistics
Information not available.

11. Comparisons with unemployment statistics from other sources
Comparisons do not appear to have been made with unemployment statistics from other sources.

12. Major changes since the start of the statistics
There do not appear to have been any major changes in legislation, capacity of the agency and/or administrative procedures which had a significant influence on the statistics.

Sweden

1. Series
Title: Arbetsmarknadsdata (Labour market data).
Starting year of present series: 1992 (earlier series had different definitions).
2. Agency making the initial registrations of unemployed persons
Name of the agency: Arbetsförmedlingen (Public Employment Service).
Type of agency: Public service under a national authority.

Name of the national authority: National Labour Market Administration.

Location of the local offices making the registrations: There is generally at least one office in each municipality.

Type of services provided/administered by the agency:
- Assisting job-seekers to find jobs;
- Assisting job-seekers to establish their own business;
- Assisting employers to find workers;
- Vocational guidance;
- Job-related training;
- Paying unemployment compensation.

Percentage of job-seekers seeking work through the agency: 50%.

3. The following information is registered about a person:
- Name;
- Sex;
- Social security number (or similar identification number also used by other agencies);
- Address of usual residence;
- Date of birth;
- Citizenship;
- Educational/vocational attainment;
- Current/past activity status, with 30 categories distinguished;
- Type of work (occupation) of job sought, with 700 groups distinguished. Links to ISCO-88 have been established (unit groups level);
- Previous registrations with the agency/service.

4. Criteria used for inclusion of a person in the registers (R) and/or the statistics of unemployed persons (S):
- Being without work (S);
- Availability for work (must be able to take a job immediately) (S);
- Being resident in the country (S).

5. Criteria used for exclusion of a person from the registers (R) and/or the statistics of unemployed persons (S):
- Death (R) and (S);
- Taking up residency abroad (S);
- Commencement of a (new) job (S);
- Commencement of military service (S);
- Participation in an employment promotion scheme, public works programme, etc. (S);
- Studying or undergoing training (S);
- Failure to contact the agency/service (S);
- Receipt of a pension (S);
- Inability to work (to be counted as unemployed a person must be able to take a job or, possibly, be under investigation).

6. Definition of unemployed persons used for the statistics
Persons without a job (except for a secondary job which it is possible to combine with a full-time regular job) receiving placement services or counselling or waiting to take part in an active labour market programme.

7. Updating of the registers
The registers are updated daily.

8. Unemployment rates
Statistics from the registers are used to obtain unemployment rates. The sources of data on employed persons who are part of the denominator of the unemployment rates are the Labour Force Survey and the Population Census.
Definition of employed persons for this purpose:
The population 18 to 64 years of age is most often used; sometimes from the Labour Force Survey (the employed are those who worked for at least one hour during the reference week and those who were temporarily absent).

9. Type of statistics of unemployed persons produced
Series 1:

Reference period: Week.

Frequency of production: Weekly.

Descriptive variables used:
- Sex;
- Age;
- Geographic characteristics;
- Citizenship (nationals/non nationals);
- Duration of unemployment.

Form of publication: On a website (www.ams.se).

Agency responsible for publication: National Labour Market Board.

Periodicity of publication: Weekly.
Series 2:

Reference period: Month; Quarter; Year.

Frequency of production: Monthly.

Descriptive variables used:
- Sex;
- Age;
- Geographic characteristics;
- Citizenship (nationals/non nationals);
- Duration of unemployment.

Form of publication:
- On paper, for general audience;
- On a website (www.ams.se).

Agency responsible for publication: National Labour Market Board.

Title and periodicity of the publication(s): Arbetsmarknadsdata, monthly.

10. Methodological information about the statistics

Form of release:
- On paper, for general audience;
- On a website (www.ams.se).

Agency responsible for the release: National Labour Market Board.

11. Comparisons with unemployment statistics from other sources
Comparisons are made with unemployment statistics from the Labour Force Survey. The response in the LFS is compared with the status according to the register at an individual level.

Frequency of the comparisons: Regularly, when the statistics are published.
Publication of the methodology/results of the comparisons: These have not been published.

12. Major changes since the start of the statistics
There have been no major changes in legislation, capacity of the agency and/or administrative procedures which had a significant influence on the statistics.

Switzerland

1. Series
Title: Registered unemployed; Job vacancies announced; Registered job-seekers; Unemployment compensation beneficiaries.
Starting year: 1936.

2. Agency making the initial registrations of unemployed persons

Name of the agency: Office régional de Placement - ORP (Regional Placement Office).

Type of agency: Public service under a national authority.

Name of the national authority: The basic rules are defined at the national level and the application is the responsibility of the cantons.

Location of the local offices making the registrations: All over the country, via the regional offices for placement.

Type of services provided/administered by the agency:
- Assisting job-seekers to find jobs;
- Assisting job-seekers to establish their own business;
- Assisting employers to find workers;
- Job-related training.

3. The following information is registered about a person:
- Name;
- Sex;
- Social security number (or similar identification number also used by other agencies);
- Address of usual residence;
- Date of birth;
- Citizenship;
- Nationality/ethnic group;
- Educational/vocational attainment, with three categories distinguished. Links to ISCED have not been established;
- Current/past activity status, with ten categories distinguished;
- Type of work (occupation) of past or present job with 15,000 categories distinguished. Links to ISCO-88 have not been established;
- Type of work (occupation) of job sought, with 15,000 categories distinguished;
- Name and address of present or previous employer or work place;
- Type of business (industry) of present/previous employer/workplace, with 220 categories distinguished. Links

to ISIC-rev.3 have not been established; the classification used is the NOGA, derived from the NACE;
- Previous registrations with the agency/service;
- Language skills.

4. Criteria used for inclusion of a person in the registers (R) and/or the statistics of unemployed persons (S):
- Being without work (S);
- Seeking work (R) and (S);
- Availability for work (S);
- Age (lower limit: 15 years; no upper limit) (R) and (S);
- Being resident in the country (foreigners must have a work permit) (R) and (S);
- Other: the person has to register him/herself with a regional office (ORP) (R) and (S).

5. Criteria used for exclusion of a person from the registers (R) and/or the statistics of unemployed persons (S):
- Death (R) and (S);
- Taking up residency abroad (R) and (S);
- Commencement of a (new) job, therefore no longer available (S);
- Commencement of military service (S);
- Participation in an employment promotion scheme, public works programme, etc (S);
- Studying or undergoing training (S);
- Failure to contact the agency/service: after two months, an inactive file is generally crossed off. In principle, a job-seeker should have at least two interviews per month with an adviser from the ORP (R) and (S);
- Inability to work: sickness, accident, imprisonment, etc. (S).

6. Definition of unemployed persons used for the statistics
Registered unemployed: persons registered with a regional placement office, who are without a job and are immediately available for a placement, receiving unemployment compensation or not.
Those who are looking for a full-time job are called fully unemployed, and those who are looking for a part-time job partially unemployed.

7. Updating of the registers
The registers are regularly updated, on a continuous basis.

8. Unemployment rates
Statistics from the registers are used to obtain unemployment rates. The source of data on employed persons who are part of the denominator of the unemployment rates is the population census.
Definition of employed persons for this purpose: Persons aged 15 years and over who are working six hours or more per week.

9. Type of statistics of unemployed persons produced
Series 1: Number of job-seekers and changes (fluctuations).
Reference period: Month, year.
Frequency of production: Monthly.
Descriptive variables used:
- Sex;
- Age;
- Occupation;
- Industry;
- Geographic characteristics;
- Previous work experience;
- Citizenship (nationals/non nationals);
- Duration of unemployment.
Form of publication:
- On paper, for general audience;
- On a website: www.seco-admin.ch
Agency responsible for publication: Secrétatiat d'Etat à l'Economie - SECO (State Department of Economy).
Title and periodicity of the publication: Situation sur le marché du travail (Situation on the labour market), monthly.
Series 2: Number of unemployed.
Reference period: Month, year.
Frequency of production: Yearly.
Descriptive variables used:
- Sex;
- Age;
- Occupation;
- Industry;
- Geographic characteristics;
- Previous work experience;
- Citizenship (nationals/non nationals);
- Duration of unemployment.
Form of publication: On paper, for general audience.

Agency responsible for publication: Office Fédéral de la Statistique - OFS (Federal Statistical Office) and SECO.
Title and periodicity of the publication(s): Le chômage en Suisse (Unemployment in Switzerland), yearly.

10. Methodological information about the statistics
Form of release:
- On paper, for general audience;
- On a website: www.seco-admin.ch.
Agency responsible for the release: SECO.

11. Comparisons with unemployment statistics from other sources
Comparisons have been made with unemployment statistics from the labour force survey.
Frequency of the comparisons: Occasionally (latest year: 1999).
Publication of the methodology/results of the comparisons: These have been published.
Title of the publication containing the methodology/results of the comparisons: Indicateurs du marché du travail 1998 (Labour market indicators 1998, OFS, Neuchâtel 1999, isbn.3-303-03113-4; (page 42).

12. Major changes since the start of the statistics
Major changes in legislation, capacity of the agency and/or administrative procedures took place in 1982, 1995 and 1997. The resulting changes in the statistics are not known.

Tajikistan

1. Series
Title: Registered unemployment.
Starting year: Not specified.

2. Agency making the initial registrations of unemployed persons
Name of the agency: Employment Centre of Population of the Republic of Tajikistan.
Type of agency: State Employment Service of Population.
Location of the local offices making the registrations: In all regions, cities and districts of the country.
Type of services provided/administered by the agency:
- Assisting job-seekers to find jobs;
- Assisting job-seekers to establish their own business;
- Assisting employers to find workers;
- Vocational guidance;
- Job-related training;
- Paying unemployment compensation.
Percentage of job-seekers seeking work through the agency: 13 - 15%.

3. The following information is registered about a person:
- Name;
- Sex;
- Address of usual residence;
- Date of birth;
- Nationality/ethnic group;
- Educational/vocational attainment;
- Current/past activity status;
- Type of work (occupation) of past or present job;
- Type of work (occupation) of job sought.

4. Criteria used for inclusion of a person in the registers (R) and/or the statistics of unemployed persons (S):
- Being without work (S);
- Seeking work (S);
- Availability for work (S);
- Age (lower limit: 15 years; upper limit: 63 years) (S);
- Being resident in the country (S).

5. Criteria used for exclusion of a person from the registers (R) and/or the statistics of unemployed persons (S):
- Death (S);
- Taking up residency abroad (S);
- Commencement of a (new) job (S);
- Commencement of military service (S);
- Participation in an employment promotion scheme, public works programme, etc. (S);
- Studying or undergoing training (S);
- Failure to contact the agency/service (S);
- Refusal of an unspecified number of suitable job offers (S);
- Refusal of an unspecified number of suitable training offers (S);
- Inability to work (S).

6. Definition of unemployed persons used for the statistics
As outlined in the law of the Republic of Tajikistan "About Employment".

7. Updating of the registers
The registers are not updated regularly.

8. Unemployment rates
Statistics from the registers are used to obtain unemployment rates. The source of data on employed persons who are part of the denominator of the unemployment rates is the Survey of Foreign Labour Migration.

9. Type of statistics of unemployed persons produced
Series 1:
Reference period: Month.
Frequency of production: Monthly.
Descriptive variables used:
–   Sex;
–   Age;
–   Educational level;
–   Occupation;
–   Previous work experience;
–   Citizenship (nationals/non nationals);
–   Duration of unemployment.
Form of publication: For internal use only.
Series 2:
Reference period: Quarter.
Frequency of production: Quarterly.
Descriptive variables used:
–   Sex;
–   Age;
–   Educational level;
–   Occupation;
–   Previous work experience;
–   Citizenship (nationals/non nationals);
–   Duration of unemployment.
Form of publication: For internal use only.

10. Methodological information about the statistics
Form of release: On paper, for limited audience.
Agency responsible for the release: Employment Centre of Population under the Ministry of Labour and Social Welfare of the Republic of Tajikistan.

11. Comparisons with unemployment statistics from other sources
Comparisons have been made with unemployment statistics from the Population Census.
Frequency of the comparisons: Occasionally.
Publication of the methodology/results of the comparisons: These have not been published.

12. Major changes since the start of the statistics
There have been no major changes in legislation, capacity of the agency and/or administrative procedures which had a significant influence on the statistics.

Tanzania, United Rep. of

1. Series
Title: Registered unemployment.
Starting year: 2002

2. Agency making the initial registrations of unemployed persons
Name of the agency: Labour Exchange Centre.
Type of agency: Public service under a national authority.
Name of the national authority: Ministry of Labour, Youth and Sports Development.
Location of the local offices making the registrations: In the city of Dar-es-Salaam.
Type of services provided/administered by the agency:
–   Assisting job-seekers to find jobs;
–   Assisting employers to find workers;
–   Vocational guidance.

3. The following information is registered about a person:
–   Name;
–   Sex;
–   Address of usual residence;
–   Date of birth;
–   Citizenship;
–   Nationality/ethnic group;
–   Educational/vocational attainment, with 6 categories distinguished;

–   Current/past activity status, with 3 categories distinguished;
–   Type of work (occupation) of past or present job with 10 groups distinguished. Links to ISCO-88 have been established;
–   Type of work (occupation) of job sought, with 10 groups distinguished. Links to ISCO-88 have been established;
–   Name and address of present or previous employer or work place;
–   Type of business (industry) of present/previous employer/workplace, with an unspecified number of groups distinguished. Links to ISIC, rev.3 have been established (level not specified);
–   Other: kind of employment positions desired (5 kinds); date of referral to the employer; language skills.

4. Criteria used for inclusion of a person in the registers (R) and/or the statistics of unemployed persons (S):
–   Being without work (R);
–   Seeking work (R);
–   Availability for work (R);
–   Age (lower limit: 18 years; upper limit: 60 years) (R);
–   Being resident in the country (R).

5. Criteria used for exclusion of a person from the registers (R) and/or the statistics of unemployed persons (S):
–   Death (R);
–   Taking up residency abroad (R);
–   Commencement of a (new) job (and satisfied by that job) (R);
–   Commencement of military service (R);
–   Studying or undergoing (long) training (R);
–   Inability to work (due to disability) (R).

6. Definition of unemployed persons used for the statistics
The broad definition "being available for work" is used.
The following categories of the currently unemployed are produced:
Unemployment A: Persons currently unemployed who are not only available for work but have taken active steps to find work in the last four weeks;
Unemployment B: Persons unemployed who have not taken active steps to find work in the last four weeks.

7. Updating of the registers
The frequency with which the registers are updated is not specified.

8. Unemployment rates
Statistics from the registers are not used to obtain unemployment rates.

9. Type of statistics of unemployed persons produced
Series 1:
Reference period: Month.
Frequency of production: Monthly.
Descriptive variables used:
–   Sex;
–   Age;
–   Educational level;
–   Occupation;
–   Industry;
–   Geographic characteristics;
–   Previous work experience;
–   Citizenship (nationals/non nationals);
–   Duration of unemployment.
Form of publication: On paper, for general audience.
Agency responsible for publication: Ministry of Labour, Youth and Sports Development.
Title and periodicity of the publications: Employment Outlook; Unemployment. (The periodicity of the publications depends on the availability of funds to produce the data).
Series 2:
Reference period: Year.
Frequency of production: Yearly.
Descriptive variables used:
–   Sex;
–   Age;
–   Educational level;
–   Occupation;
–   Industry;
–   Geographic characteristics;
–   Previous work experience;
–   Citizenship (nationals/non nationals);
–   Duration of unemployment.
Form of publication: On paper, for general audience.
Agency responsible for publication: Ministry of Labour, Youth and Sports Development.

Title and periodicity of the publications: Employment Outlook; Unemployment. (The periodicity of the publications depends on the availability of funds to produce the data).

10. Methodological information about the statistics

Form of release: On paper, for general audience.

Agency responsible for the release: Ministry of Labour, Youth and Sports Development.

11. Comparisons with unemployment statistics from other sources

Comparisons have not yet been made with unemployment statistics from other sources, although it is expected that this will be done in the future.

12. Major changes since the start of the statistics

There have been no major changes in legislation, capacity of the agency and/or administrative procedures which had a significant influence on the statistics.

13. Additional remarks

The Labour Exchange Centre was established on 1st July 2001 and processing of data only started at the beginning of 2002, thus certain information concerning these statistics is not yet available.

Thailand

1. Series

Title: Registered job-seekers.

Starting year: Not specified.

2. Agency making the initial registrations of unemployed persons

Name of the agency: Department of Employment.

Type of agency: Public service under a national authority.

Name of the national authority: Ministry of Labour and Social Welfare.

Location of the local offices making the registrations: 84 Employment Offices throughout the country - in every province and in Bangkok.

Type of services provided/administered by the agency:

- Assisting job-seekers to find jobs;
- Assisting job-seekers to establish their own business;
- Assisting employers to find workers;
- Vocational guidance;
- Job-related training;
- Other: assisting disabled persons to find jobs.

Percentage of job-seekers seeking work through the agency: 20%.

3. The following information is registered about a person:

- Name;
- Sex;
- Social security number (or similar identification number also used by other agencies);
- Address of usual residence;
- Date of birth;
- Citizenship;
- Educational/vocational attainment, with nine categories distinguished. Links to ISCED have not been established;
- Type of work (occupation) of past or present job with nine groups distinguished. Links to ISCO-88 have been established (major groups level);
- Type of work (occupation) of job sought, with nine groups distinguished. Links to ISCO-88 have been established (major groups level);
- Name of previous work place;
- Other: disability (in the case of a disabled person).

4. Criteria used for inclusion of a person in the registers (R) and/or the statistics of unemployed persons (S):

Information not available.

5. Criteria used for exclusion of a person from the registers (R) and/or the statistics of unemployed persons (S):

Information not available.

6. Definition of unemployed persons used for the statistics

Persons who are willing to work but cannot find a job for any reason (end of work contract, mismatched qualifications, etc.).

7. Updating of the registers

It is not indicated whether or not the registers are updated regularly.

8. Unemployment rates

Statistics from the registers are used to obtain unemployment rates. The sources of data on employed persons who are part of the denominator of the unemployment rates are the Labour Force Survey and the Population Census.

Definition of employed persons for this purpose:

Workers (including employers or entrepreneurs) who have an income in money or in kind.

9. Type of statistics of unemployed persons produced

Information not available.

10. Methodological information about the statistics

Information not available.

11. Comparisons with unemployment statistics from other sources

Comparisons have not been made with unemployment statistics from other sources.

12. Major changes since the start of the statistics

There have been no major changes in legislation, capacity of the agency and/or administrative procedures which had a significant influence on the statistics.

Trinidad and Tobago

1. Series

Title: National Employment Service Statistics.

Starting year: Not specified.

2. Agency making the initial registrations of unemployed persons

Name of the agency: National Employment Service.

Type of agency: Public service under a national authority.

Name of the national authority: Ministry of Labour and Small and Micro Enterprise Development.

Location of the local offices making the registrations: In strategic locations, facilitating service to all parts of the country.

Type of services provided/administered by the agency:

- Assisting job-seekers to find jobs;
- Assisting employers to find workers;
- Vocational guidance;
- Other: preparation of résumés; preparation for job interviews.

3. The following information is registered about a person:

- Name;
- Sex;
- Social security number (or similar identification number also used by other agencies);
- Address of usual residence;
- Date of birth;
- Citizenship;
- Educational/vocational attainment, with two categories distinguished. Links to ISCED have not been established;
- Type of work (occupation) of job sought, with an unspecified number of groups distinguished. Links to ISCO-88 have been established (major groups level);
- Previous registrations with the agency/service.

4. Criteria used for inclusion of a person in the registers (R) and/or the statistics of unemployed persons (S):

- Being without work (R) and (S);
- Seeking work (R) and (S);
- Availability for work (R);
- Age (lower limit: 17 years; no upper limit) (R);
- Citizenship (R);
- Being resident in the country (R);
- Previously employed (R);
- Other: students seeking summer employment (R).

5. Criteria used for exclusion of a person from the registers (R) and/or the statistics of unemployed persons (S):

- Death (R);
- Taking up residency abroad (R);
- Inability to work (R).

6. Definition of unemployed persons used for the statistics

Persons aged 17 years and over who are without work, seeking work and available for work (including students seeking summer employment).

7. Updating of the registers

The registers are updated monthly.

8. Unemployment rates

Statistics from the registers are not used to obtain unemployment rates.

9. Type of statistics of unemployed persons produced

Series 1:

Reference period: Month.

Frequency of production: Monthly.

Descriptive variables used:

- Sex;

- Educational level;
- Occupation;
- Industry.

Form of publication: Machine-readable form, on request.
Agency responsible for publication: Ministry of Labour and Small and Micro Enterprise Development.
Series 2:
Reference period: Not specified.
Frequency of production: Year.
Descriptive variables used:
- Sex;
- Educational level;
- Occupation;
- Industry.

Form of publication: Machine-readable form, on request.
Agency responsible for publication: Ministry of Labour and Small and Micro Enterprise Development.
10. Methodological information about the statistics
Form of release: Not released, available for internal use only.
Agency responsible: Ministry of Labour and Small and Micro Enterprise Development.
11. Comparisons with unemployment statistics from other sources
Comparisons have not been made with unemployment statistics from other sources.
12. Major changes since the start of the statistics
There have been no major changes in legislation, capacity of the agency and/or administrative procedures which had a significant influence on the statistics.

Tunisia

1. Series
Title: Labour Market.
Starting year: Available on paper since 1995 (possibly before). Available in electronic format since 1997.
2. Agency making the initial registrations of unemployed persons
Name of the agency: Agence tunisienne de l'Emploi - ATE (Tunisian Employment Agency).
Type of agency: Public service under a national authority.
Name of the national authority: Ministry of Employment.
Location of the local offices making the registrations: All over the country, 80 offices in the 24 main administrative divisions (gouvernorats).
Type of services provided/administered by the agency:
- Assisting job-seekers to find jobs;
- Assisting job-seekers to establish their own business;
- Assisting employers to find workers;
- Vocational guidance;
- Job-related training;
- Other: services related to the insertion of young people and the reinsertion of workers who have been laid off; organisation and administration of work-experience programmes, professional information, assistance and accompaniment sessions, etc.

Percentage of job-seekers seeking work through the agency: 25% to 30% (more than 80% of those with higher education diplomas).
3. The following information is registered about a person:
- Name;
- Sex;
- Social security number (or similar identification number also used by other agencies);
- Address of usual residence;
- Date of birth;
- Citizenship;
- Nationality;
- Educational/vocational attainment, with eight categories distinguished. Links to ISCED have been established;
- Current/past activity status, with three categories distinguished: employed, previously employed and never worked;
- Type of work (occupation) of past or present job with nine categories distinguished. Links to ISCO-88 have not been established;
- Type of work (occupation) of job sought, with nine categories distinguished;

- Name and address of present or previous employer or work place;
- Type of business (industry) of present/previous employer/workplace, with 10 categories distinguished. Links to ISIC have not been established;
- Previous registrations with the agency/service.

4. Criteria used for inclusion of a person in the registers (R) and/or the statistics of unemployed persons (S):
- Seeking work (R) and (S);
- Age (lower limit: 18 years (15 years for vocational guidance); no upper age limit (R) and (S);
- Citizenship (identity card, or residence permit and work permit for foreigners) (R).

5. Criteria used for exclusion of a person from the registers (R) and/or the statistics of unemployed persons (S):
- Taking up residency abroad (R);
- Commencement of a (new) job or creation of a micro-enterprise for example (R);
- Commencement of military service (R);
- Participation in an employment promotion scheme, public works programme, etc (R);
- Studying or undergoing training (R);
- Failure to contact the agency/service, automatically after two months of absence (R).

6. Definition of unemployed persons used for the statistics
The statistics of the Tunisian Employment Agency are based on persons declaring to be looking for employment and registered in one of the 80 offices. They may be unemployed or employed but seeking a better job.
7. Updating of the registers
The registers are updated regularly (automatically by the system).
8. Unemployment rates
Statistics from the registers are not used to obtain unemployment rates.
9. Type of statistics of unemployed persons produced
Series 1:
Reference period: day.
Frequency of production: daily.
Descriptive variables used:
- Sex;
- Age;
- Educational level, diploma, subject studied;
- Occupation;
- Industry;
- Geographic characteristics;
- Previous work experience;
- Duration of waiting;
- Office of registration;
- Gouvernorat.

Form of publication:
- For internal use only;
- On a website: www.emploi.nat.tn.

Agency responsible for publication: ATE.
Title of the publication: Indicateurs d'activité (Activity indicators), available free of charge.
Series 2:
Reference period: Month.
Frequency of production: Monthly.
Descriptive variables used:
- Sex;
- Age;
- Educational level;
- Occupation;
- Industry;
- Geographic characteristics;
- Previous work experience;
- Duration of waiting;
- Office of registration;
- Gouvernorat.

Form of publication:
- For internal use;
- On paper, for limited audience.

Agency responsible for publication: ATE.
Title and periodicity of the publication: Evolution du marché de l'emploi au cours du mois (Evolution of the labour market during the current month), monthly.
Series 3:
Reference period: Month.

Frequency of production: Quarterly and yearly.
Descriptive variables used:
- Sex;
- Age;
- Educational level;
- Occupation;
- Industry;
- Geographic characteristics;
- Previous work experience;
- Duration of waiting;
- Office of registration;
- Gouvernorat.

Form of publication:
- For internal use;
- On paper, for limited audience.

Agency responsible for publication: ATE.
Title and periodicity of the publications: Rapport trimestriel et rapport annuel sur l'activité de l'ATE (Quarterly report and Yearly report on the activity of the ATE).

10. Methodological information about the statistics
Form of release:
- Not released, for internal use;
- On paper, for limited audience;
- On a website: www.emploi.nat.tn;
- Consultation on the spot - general audience.

Agency responsible for the release: ATE.

11. Comparisons with unemployment statistics from other sources
Comparisons have been made with unemployment statistics from the labour force survey, other household surveys and the population census. These statistics are used, on the one hand, to evaluate the penetration of the employment services in the labour market, and on the other hand, to help the managers of the ATE to target their interventions towards the more vulnerable populations.
Frequency of the comparisons: Yearly in relation to the population-employment survey (INS).

12. Major changes since the start of the statistics
Major changes in legislation, capacity of the agency and/or administrative procedures took place in 1995.
Since the creation of the ATE in 1993, and particularly since the introduction of a computerized system of management of the employment market in 1995, the data on job-seekers have become more and more accurate. The coverage of job-seekers at the management level is becoming greater and more representative.

Turkey

1. Series
Title: Registered unemployment.
Starting year: 1946.
2. Agency making the initial registrations of unemployed persons
Name of the agency: Türkiye Iş Kurumu (Işkur) (Turkish Employment Organisation - TEO).
Type of agency: Public service under a national authority.
Name of the national authority: Ministry of Labour and Social Security.
Location of the local offices making the registrations: In all provinces as well as in some districts.
Type of services provided/administered by the agency:
- Assisting job-seekers to find jobs;
- Assisting job-seekers to establish their own business;
- Assisting employers to find workers;
- Vocational guidance;
- Job-related training;
- Paying unemployment compensation (Unemployment Insurance);
- Other: making labour force surveys in the local market and evaluations; establishing and running a labour market information system; compensating work losses.

Percentage of job-seekers seeking work through the agency: 37% (3rd quarter, 2001).
3. The following information is registered about a person:
- Name;
- Sex;
- Social security number (or similar identification number also used by other agencies);
- Address of usual residence;
- Date and place of birth;
- Citizenship;
- Educational attainment, with four categories distinguished. Links to ISCED have been established;
- Current/past activity status, with nine categories distinguished;
- Type of work (occupation) of past or present job with 72 groups distinguished. Links to ISCO-88 have been established (minor groups level);
- Type of work (occupation) of job sought, with 72 groups distinguished. Links to ISCO-88 have been established (minor groups level);
- Name and address of present or previous employer or work place;
- Type of business (industry) of present/previous employer/ workplace, with three groups distinguished. (ISIC, rev.3 is used, but NACE, rev.1 will be used shortly);
- Previous registrations with the agency/service;
- Other: experience in previous work place; additional occupation; foreign language skills; driving license/ Passport number; social situation (disabled, affected by terrorism, etc.); marital status; unemployment duration, sought wage; sector; type of work (permanent or seasonal, etc.); location (home or abroad).

4. Criteria used for inclusion of a person in the registers (R) and/or the statistics of unemployed persons (S):
- Being without work (R) and (S);
- Seeking work (every applicant is registered regardless of current employment status) (R) and (S);
- Availability for work (availability to commence work on the date specified by an employer) (R) and (S);
- Age (lower limit: 15 years; no upper limit) (R) and (S);
- Citizenship (R) and (S);
- Being resident in the country (R) and (S);
- Previously employed (R);
- Desired duration of employment and/or number of hours of work sought (R) and (S);
- Previous payment of unemployed insurance contributions (R) and (S).

5. Criteria used for exclusion of a person from the registers (R) and/or the statistics of unemployed persons (S):
- Death (R) and (S);
- Taking up residency abroad (R) and (S);
- Commencement of a (new) job (placement through TEO) (R) and (S).
- Commencement of military service (R) and (S);
- Studying or undergoing training (R) and (S);
- Failure to contact the agency/service (registrations expire automatically after one year if not renewed) (R) and (S);
- Refusal of 3 suitable job offers (R) and (S);
- Receipt of a pension (R) and (S).

6. Definition of unemployed persons used for the statistics
Any person of working age (15 years and over) who is able and wishes to work and who, at the time of application to the employment office, is earning less than the minimum wage and who is not yet placed in a job by the employment office.

7. Updating of the registers
The registers are updated monthly.

8. Unemployment rates
Statistics from the registers are used to obtain unemployment rates. The source of data on employed persons who are part of the denominator of the unemployment rates is the Labour Force Survey (conducted by the State Institute of Statistics).
Definition of employed persons for this purpose:
According to Turkish labour law, persons working under a contract of employment in any job for wages.

9. Type of statistics of unemployed persons produced
Series 1:
Reference period: Month.
Frequency of production: Monthly.
Descriptive variables used:
- Sex;
- Age;
- Educational level;
- Occupation;
- Industry;
- Geographic characteristics;
- Duration of unemployment;
- Other: profession groups.

Form of publication:
- On paper, for general audience;
- On a website (www.iskur.gov.tr).

Agency responsible for publication: General Directorate of TEO/Employment Department Labour Force Monitoring and Statistics Section.

Title of the publication: Turkish Employment Organisation Statistical Yearbook.

Series 2:

Reference period: Year.

Frequency of production: Yearly.

Descriptive variables used:
- Sex;
- Age;
- Educational level;
- Occupation;
- Industry;
- Geographic characteristics;
- Duration of unemployment;
- Other: profession groups.

Form of publication:
- On paper, for general audience;
- On a website (www.iskur.gov.tr).

Agency responsible for publication: General Directorate of TEO/Employment Department Labour Force Monitoring and Statistics Section.

Title of the publication: Turkish Employment Organisation Statistical Yearbook.

10. Methodological information about the statistics
Form of release:
- On paper, for general audience;
- On a website (www.iskur.gov.tr).

Agency responsible for the release: TEO.

11. Comparisons with unemployment statistics from other sources

Comparisons are made with unemployment statistics from the Labour Force Survey.

Frequency of the comparisons: Regularly, on a quarterly basis.
Publication of the methodology/results of the comparisons: These have not been published.

12. Major changes since the start of the statistics

There have been no major changes in legislation, capacity of the agency and/or administrative procedures which had a significant influence on the statistics.

United States

1. Series

Title: Registered unemployment.

Starting year: 1933

2. Agency making the initial registrations of unemployed persons

Name of the agency: The official name may vary from state to state, but it is generally known as the State Workforce Development Agency or Employment Service.

Type of agency: Public service under a national authority.

Name of the national authority: Employment and Training Administration (administered through a Federal - State cooperative grant).

Location of the local offices making the registrations: In 3,459 local "One-Stop" centres and service points throughout 50 states and 4 territories.

Type of services provided/administered by the agency:
- Assisting job-seekers to find jobs;
- Assisting job-seekers to establish their own business;
- Assisting employers to find workers;
- Vocational guidance;
- Job-related training;
- Paying unemployment compensation;
- Other: various support services may be offered by local "One-Stop" centres.

Percentage of job-seekers seeking work through the agency: Not known.

3. The following information is registered about a person:
- Name;
- Sex;
- Social security number (or similar identification number also used by other agencies);
- Address of usual residence;
- Date of birth;
- Citizenship;
- Nationality/ethnic group;
- Educational/vocational attainment;
- Current/past activity status;
- Type of work (occupation) of past or present job;
- Type of work (occupation) of job sought;
- Name and address of present or previous employer or work place;
- Type of business (industry) of present/previous employer/work-place, with an unspecified number of groups distinguished;
- Previous registrations with the agency/service;
- Other: local "One-Stop" centres may require other job-related information.

4. Criteria used for inclusion of a person in the registers (R) and/or the statistics of unemployed persons (S):
- Being without work (R) and (S)*;
- Seeking work (R) and (S)*;
- Availability for work (R) and (S)*.

* Unemployment Insurance claimants only.

5. Criteria used for exclusion of a person from the registers (R) and/or the statistics of unemployed persons (S):
- Death (R) and (S);
- Taking up residency abroad (R) and (S);
- Commencement of a (new) job (R) and (S);
- Commencement of military service (R) and (S);
- Participation in an employment promotion scheme, public works programme, etc. (R) and (S);
- Studying or undergoing training (R) and (S)*;
- Failure to contact the agency/service (sanctions vary among states) (R) and (S)*;
- Refusal of suitable job offers (sanctions vary among states) (R) and (S)*;
- Refusal of suitable training offers (sanctions vary among states) (R) and (S)*;
- End of entitlement to receive unemployment compensation (R) and (S)*;
- Inability to work (R) and (S)*.

* Unemployment Insurance claimants only.

6. Definition of unemployed persons used for the statistics

For work registration, there is no Federal definition for unemployed persons.

For receipt of Unemployment Insurance persons who claim benefits must be able to work, be available for work and actively seeking work.

7. Updating of the registers

The registers are updated regularly but the frequency varies among states.

8. Unemployment rates

Statistics from the registers are not used to obtain unemployment rates.

9. Type of statistics of unemployed persons produced

Reference period: Quarter.

Frequency of production: Quarterly.

Descriptive variables used:
- Sex;
- Age;
- Educational level;
- Occupation;
- Industry.

Form of publication: On paper, for general audience.

Agency responsible for publication: Employment and Training Administration.

Title of the publication: Wagner-Peyser Act Annual Program Report Data.

10. Methodological information about the statistics

Methodological information about the statistics is not available.

11. Comparisons with unemployment statistics from other sources

Comparisons have not been made with unemployment statistics from other sources.

12. Major changes since the start of the statistics

Major changes in legislation, capacity of the agency and/or administrative procedures took place in 1933, 1950, 1973, 1978, 1982 and 1998. The resulting changes in the statistics have not been estimated.

13. Additional remarks

Work registration policies vary across the United States. Generally, workers who are seeking staff-assisted referrals to jobs must register for work. In some states, workers may receive job vacancy and other information without registering for work.

The work registration policies for those workers who file and receive Unemployment Insurance benefits also vary across the country. However, Unemployment Insurance claimants who are permanently laid off and who do not receive job vacancy information through a trade union hiring hall, must register for work.

All states provide job listings through a computer network called America's Job Bank.

Uruguay

1. Series

Title: Employment offer and demand in private placement agencies and User Register of the Employment Training Programme.

Starting year: 1993.

2. Agency making the initial registrations of unemployed persons

Name of the agency: Dirección Nacional de Empleo - DINAE (National Employment Agency).

Type of agency: Public service under a national authority.

Name of the national authority: Ministerio de Trabajo y Seguridad Social (Ministry of Labour and Social Security).

Location of the local offices making the registrations: All over the country.

Type of services provided/administered by the agency:
- Vocational guidance;
- Job-related training;
- Other: information on the labour market.

3. The following information is registered about a person*:
- Name;
- Sex;
- Social security number (or similar identification number also used by other agencies);
- Address of usual residence;
- Date of birth;
- Citizenship;
- Educational/vocational attainment, with 14 categories distinguished. Links to ISCED have not been established;
- Past activity status;
- Type of work (occupation) of past or present job with four categories distinguished. The National Standard Classification of Occupations (CNUO-95) (four digits), based on ISCO-88, is used;
- Name and address of present or previous employer or work place;
- Type of business (industry) of present/previous employer/workplace, with four categories distinguished. The National Classification of all Branches of Economic Activities (four digits), based on ISIC, rev.3, is used.

* Information concerning workers registered with the Employment Training Programme.

4. Criteria used for inclusion of a person in the registers (R) and/or the statistics of unemployed persons (S):
- Being without work (R);
- Seeking work (R);
- Availability for work (R);
- Age (lower and upper limits: not specified) (R);
- Previously employed (the Employment Training Programme users are considered as unemployed, i.e. they have worked and have lost their job (R);
- Previous payment of unemployed insurance contributions (in order to be registered with the Employment Training Programme, the person has to be benefiting from unemployment compensation, and therefore must have paid his/her contributions (R);
- Other: not having had higher education (only for Employment Training Programme users).

5. Criteria used for exclusion of a person from the registers (R) and/or the statistics of unemployed persons (S):

Not specified.

6. Definition of unemployed persons used for the statistics

Regarding the Employment Training Programme users, criteria for inclusion are the following:
- Receiving unemployment compensation;

- Having been laid off (without possibility of being reintegrated in the company);
- Not having had higher education.

7. Updating of the registers

Not specified.

8. Unemployment rates

Statistics from the registers are used to obtain unemployment rates. The source of data on employed persons who are part of the denominator of the unemployment rates is the labour force survey.

Definition of employed persons for this purpose:

Persons aged 14 years or more who worked at least for one hour during the week preceding the survey.

9. Type of statistics of unemployed persons produced

Not specified.

10. Methodological information about the statistics

Not specified.

11. Comparisons with unemployment statistics from other sources

Comparisons have not been made with unemployment statistics from other sources.

12. Major changes since the start of the statistics

There have been no major changes in legislation, capacity of the agency and/or administrative procedures which had a significant influence on the statistics.

Venezuela

1. Series

Title: Registered unemployment.

Starting year: 1964.

2. Agency making the initial registrations of unemployed persons

Name of the agency: Servicio Nacional de Empleo - Agencia de Empleo (National Employment Service B Employment Agency).

Type of agency: Public service under a national authority.

Name of the national authority: Ministry of Labour.

Location of the local offices making the registrations: In the 16 states and one office in the capital city (25 placement offices).

Type of services provided/administered by the agency:
- Assisting job-seekers to find jobs;
- Assisting job-seekers to establish their own business;
- Assisting employers to find workers;
- Vocational guidance;
- Job-related training.

Percentage of job-seekers seeking work through the agency: 15%.

3. The following information is registered about a person:
- Name;
- Sex;
- Social security number (or similar identification number also used by other agencies);
- Address of usual residence;
- Date of birth;
- Citizenship;
- Educational/vocational attainment, with two categories distinguished. Links to ISCED-97 have been established;
- Current/past activity status, with three categories distinguished;
- Type of work of past or present job with two categories distinguished. Links to ISCO-88 have been established;
- Type of work of job sought, with two categories distinguished. Links to ISCO-88 have been established;
- Name and address of present or previous employer or work place;
- Type of business of present/previous employer/ workplace, with 10 categories distinguished. Links to ISIC, rev.3 have been established;
- Previous registrations with the service.

4. Criteria used for inclusion of a person in the registers (R) and/or the statistics of unemployed persons (S):
- Being without work (R) and (S);
- Seeking work (dismissed person receiving unemployment benefits, active, active job-seeker) (R) and (S);
- Availability for work (R) and (S);
- Age (lower limit: 14 years; no upper age limit) (R) and (S);
- Citizenship (R) and (S);
- Being resident in the country (R) and (S);

- Previously employed (work experience or vocational training) (R) and (S);
- Desired duration of employment and/or number of hours of work sought (R) and (S);
- Previous payment of unemployed insurance contributions (beneficiary of unemployment benefits) (R) and (S);
- Other: unjustified dismissal (after 18 weeks of continuous employment) (R) and (S).

5. Criteria used for exclusion of a person from the registers (R) and/or the statistics of unemployed persons (S):
- Commencement of a (new) job (R) and (S);
- Participation in an employment promotion scheme, public works programme, etc (R) and (S);
- Failure to contact the agency/service (R) and (S).

6. Definition of unemployed persons used for the statistics
Persons seeking work for the first time are considered unemployed, as well as those who for whatever reason are outside the labour market - for example, because they have been dismissed for justified or unjustified reasons, or because they have resigned from an employment.

7. Updating of the registers
The registers are updated annually; any change during the period is indicated in the part of the register concerning the unemployed person.

8. Unemployment rates
Statistics from the registers are not used to obtain unemployment rates.

9. Type of statistics of unemployed persons produced
Series 1:
Reference period: Day.
Frequency of production: Half-yearly.
Descriptive variables used:
- Sex;
- Age;
- Educational level;
- Occupation;
- Industry;
- Geographic characteristics;
- Previous work experience;
- Citizenship (nationals/non nationals);
- Duration of unemployment;
- Other: dismissed persons beneficiaries of unemployment benefits, marital status.

Form of publication: For internal use only.
Agency responsible for publication: Department of Employment.
Series 2:
Reference period: Month.
Frequency of production: Yearly.
Descriptive variables used:
- Sex;
- Age;
- Educational level;
- Occupation;
- Industry;
- Geographic characteristics;
- Previous work experience;
- Citizenship (nationals/non nationals);
- Duration of unemployment;
- Other: dismissed persons beneficiaries of unemployment benefits, marital status.

Form of publication: For internal use only.
Agency responsible for publication: Department of Employment.
10. Methodological information about the statistics
Form of release: On paper, for limited audience.
Agency responsible for the release: Department of Employment.
11. Comparisons with unemployment statistics from other sources
Comparisons have been made with unemployment statistics from the labour force survey, other household surveys and the population census.
Frequency of the comparisons: Regularly, when the statistics are published (latest year: 2001).
Publication of the methodology/results of the comparisons: These have been published in the Boletin de Segmento de Mercado de Trabajo (Bulletin of Segments of the Labour Market).
12. Major changes since the start of the statistics
Major changes in legislation, capacity of the agency and/or administrative procedures took place in 1. 1996; 2. 1997; 3. 1998; 4. 1999; 5. 2000; and 6. 2001, resulting in the following changes in the

number of registered unemployed persons: 1. 1996-97: + 29.43%; 2. 1997-98: + 19.10%; 3. 1998-99: + 85.76%; 4. 1999-2000: + 9.03%, and 5. 2000-01: + 5.70%. (1. Creation of new agencies; 2. Shut down of enterprises; 3. Change of economic activity; 4. Increase of labour force, and 5. Automatisation of Employment Services).

Zimbabwe

1. Series
Title: Registered unemployment.
Starting year: 1959.
2. Agency making the initial registrations of unemployed persons
Name of the agency: National Employment Services Department.
Type of agency: Public service under a national authority.
Name of the national authority: Ministry of Public Service, Labour and Social Welfare.
Location of the local offices making the registrations: In all provincial capitals of the country and two districts.
Type of services provided/administered by the agency:
- Assisting job-seekers to find jobs;
- Assisting job-seekers to establish their own business;
- Assisting employers to find workers;
- Vocational guidance;
- Other: registration and monitoring of private employment agencies; collection and dissemination of labour market information.

Percentage of job-seekers seeking work through the agency: 10%.
3. The following information is registered about a person:
- Name;
- Sex;
- Address of usual residence;
- Date of birth;
- Citizenship;
- Nationality/ethnic group;
- Educational/vocational attainment, with two categories distinguished. Links to ISCED have not been established;
- Current/past activity status, with three categories distinguished;
- Type of work (occupation) of past or present job with an unspecified number of groups distinguished. Links to ISCO-88 have been established (unit groups level);
- Type of work (occupation) of job sought, with an unspecified number of groups distinguished. Links to ISCO-88 have been established (unit groups level);
- Name and address of present or previous employer or work place;
- Previous registrations with the agency/service.

4. Criteria used for inclusion of a person in the registers (R) and/or the statistics of unemployed persons (S):
- Being without work (R) and (S);
- Seeking work (R) and (S);
- Availability for work (R) and (S);
- Age (lower limit: 16 years; upper limit: 60 years) (R) and (S);
- Citizenship (Zimbabwean citizens only) (R);
- Previously employed (R).

5. Criteria used for exclusion of a person from the registers (R) and/or the statistics of unemployed persons (S):
- Death (R) and (S);
- Commencement of a (new) job (R) and (S);
- Failure to contact the agency/service at least once a month (R) and (S).

6. Definition of unemployed persons used for the statistics
Persons available for work, actively seeking work and making job enquiries at least once per month.

7. Updating of the registers
The registers are updated monthly.

8. Unemployment rates
Statistics from the registers are not used to obtain unemployment rates.

9. Type of statistics of unemployed persons produced
Reference period: Day; Week; Month; Half-year; Year.
Frequency of production: Monthly.
Descriptive variables used:
- Sex;
- Age;

- Educational level;
- Occupation;
- Previous work experience;
- Citizenship (nationals/non nationals);
- Duration of unemployment.

Form of publication: For internal use only.

Agency responsible for publication: National Employment Services Department.

Title and periodicity of the publication: Departmental Monthly Statistics and Reports.

10. Methodological information about the statistics

Form of release: On paper, for limited audience.

Agency responsible for the release: National Employment Services Department.

11. Comparisons with unemployment statistics from other sources

Comparisons have not been made with unemployment statistics from other sources.

12. Major changes since the start of the statistics

Major changes in legislation, capacity of the agency and/or administrative procedures took place in 1998, 1999, 2000 and 2001. The resulting changes in the statistics have not been estimated.

Other:

- Decentralization of public employment offices in all provinces;
- Introduction of computerization programme.

Introduction - Part II

The methodological descriptions presented in this part relate to the statistics of employment, wages, hours of work and related topics (e.g. income from employment, vacancies) which are derived from sources other than surveys of households or establishments, such as social security or insurance records, tax returns, collective agreements, administrative reports, etc.

The corresponding statistical series are generally published by the ILO in the *Yearbook of Labour Statistics*, and where relevant, in the quarterly *Bulletin of Labour Statistics* or its special supplement: *Statistics on occupational wages and hours of work and on food prices – October Inquiry results*. They are also available in the LABORSTA database on-line (Internet: http://laborsta.ilo.org/).

In a few cases, the statistics have not yet been published by the ILO but may be made available in a near future.

The descriptions cover 24 countries, areas or territories. Most of them were prepared on the basis of information provided by national statistical agencies or governments in response to a specially designed questionnaire. If no reply was received from the country concerned, information was drawn from a variety of sources, including national and international publications and reports provided to the ILO, and from Websites. Each description was submitted to the country concerned for comments, which were taken into account if received within the limit of the publication programme.

Each description follows the same format, using standard sections and headings so as to facilitate comparisons. However, it should be borne in mind that statistics from administrative records are not strictly comparable between countries, due to differences in sources and relevant legislations. These sections and headings are explained below:

Source of the series
The administrative source of the series, generally the reporting system of a national social security or insurance body, or of wage-setting commissions or collective agreements.

Title of the series
The title of the statistical series.

Organization responsible
The organization responsible for data collection, statistical processing and publication/ dissemination of the data; where these functions are undertaken by separate agencies, each of them is specified.

Main topics covered
The main labour topics on which data are collected (employment, wages, hours of work, employment-related income, etc.).

Periodicity or frequency of availability of the statistics
The frequency with which the statistics are compiled and reported (e.g. monthly, quarterly, half-yearly, once a year).

Reference period
The time period (e.g. a specific date, a full month) for which data are collected.

Coverage of the statistics
Geographical: whether the series covers the whole country or territory and, in cases where the coverage is limited, the relevant geographical areas or regions excluded.

Industrial: the economic activities covered by the series and, in cases where the coverage is limited, the groups of industries or activities excluded.

Establishments: the type and size of establishments covered which furnish the data for the series, as well as their affiliation or relationship with the national insurance or social security system, where relevant.

Persons: the categories of workers covered by the series, such as employees under the national social insurance system; where appropriate, the population coverage in terms of other relevant criteria such as sex, age group, sector of the economy, etc.

Occupations: whether the data are collected by occupation or occupational group, and where relevant, the occupations or occupational groups covered.

Concepts and definitions
The national definitions used in compiling the series for each concept (employment, earnings, wage rates, hours of work, employment-related income); where appropriate, the specific categories of workers included or excluded from the concept, and the minimum and/or maximum thresholds applied to the wages and income definitions.

Classifications
Branch of economic activity (industry): the name of the national industrial classification used, and whenever possible, the number of groups used for coding the data; whether this classification applies to all the data collected; whether the national classification is linked to the International Standard Industrial Classification of all Economic Activities (ISIC), either Rev.3 (1990) or Rev.2 (1968) and at what level.

Occupation: the name of the national occupational classification used, and whenever possible, the number of groups used for coding the data; whether this classification applies to all the data collected; whether the national classification is linked to the International Standard Classification of Occupations (ISCO-88 or ISCO-1968) and at what level.

Status in employment: the name of the national classification used, and whenever possible, the number of groups used for coding the data; whether this classification applies to all the data collected; whether the national classification is linked to the International Classification of Status in Employment (ICSE-1993) and at what level.

Other classifications: Information on the other classifications used, such as establishments characteristics (size, type of ownership, etc.), region, workers' characteristics (sex, age groups, category of workers, nationality/citizenship, etc.), and whether these classifications apply to all the data collected or to some of them only.

Data collection
The procedure, organization and schedule for data collection from social security records, collective agreement registers and related administrative sources; where relevant, information on sampling methods, weighting of sample results and updating of the administrative system.

Data processing, editing and consistency checks
The method used to process the data and on the types of consistency checks which are made on the recorded data.

Adjustments
Where relevant, information on the types of adjustments made and the methods used for under- or over-coverage, double counting, estimation of payments in kind, etc. - to derive the estimates of employment, wages, hours of work and employment-related income; whether the data are calibrated against benchmark data and adjusted for seasonal variations.

Types of estimates
The types of estimates that are made (e.g. totals, averages, medians, distributions), the time unit to which they refer and the methods of computation.

Construction of indices
Where index numbers are constructed from the data, the type of data they refer to and the procedure used.

Indicators of reliability of the estimates
Both qualitative and quantitative information on the reliability of the statistics: proportion of the target population covered by the administrative system; sampling variance estimates; non-sampling errors; conformity with other sources.

Available series
The main tabulations regularly prepared by the country on the basis of the present administrative source, and which appear in national publications.

History of the statistics
The historical background of the statistics: the date of the start of the series and the date and nature of major changes and revisions that have occurred (e.g. in legislation, operational procedures and/or forms, scope, definitions, periodicity).

Documentation and dissemination
The source and title of major national publications in which the statistics and the relevant methodological information appear; the periodicity of the publications and the normal delay between the reference period of the statistics and their release; whether data are available on Internet; and whether data which do not appear in national publications or on Internet can be made available upon request.

Data supplied to the ILO for dissemination
The types of statistics supplied to the ILO for publication in the *Yearbook* and/or the *Bulletin of Labour Statistics* and/or *Statistics on occupational wages and hours of work and on food prices – October Inquiry results*.

Other administrative sources of data: Other administrative sources which provide labour-related statistics: basic information on the title, coverage and periodicity of these statistics.

Austria (1)

Source of the series
Social Security records.
Title of the series
Beschäftigtenstatistik, Einkommensstatistik.
Organization responsible
Data collection, statistical processing and publication/dissemination of the statistics:
Hauptverband der österreichischen Sozialversicherungsträger (Main Association of the Austrian Social Security Institutes).
Main topics covered
Employment and earnings.
Periodicity or frequency of availability of the statistics
Employment: monthly;
Earnings: yearly.
Reference period
Employment: the last day of the month;
Earnings: monthly average of the whole year.
Coverage of the statistics
Geographical: the whole country. Each Land (State) has its own Institute.
Industrial: all branches of economic activities.
Establishments: all types and sizes in the private and public sectors.
Persons: all employees.
Occupations: data are not collected by occupation or occupational group.
Concepts and definitions
Employment: employees, i.e. wage earners and salaried employees.
Earnings: gross monthly earnings refer to all payments subject to social security contributions.
Classifications
Branch of economic activity (industry):
Title of the classification: ÖNACE.
Number of groups used for coding: not available.
Applied to: employment and earnings.
Link to ISIC: Rev.2 and Rev.3.
Other classifications: by sex, employee category, age group and region.
Data collection
Size and coverage of the administrative system: all employers and employees are covered.
Data collection method: data on employees and their earnings subject to social security contributions are reported by employers to the social security institutes on a continuous basis. Employment data are obtained by the actual counting of the number of insured people by the social security institutes. Monthly averages of annual earnings are computed once a year. The records are updated on a continuous basis.
Data processing, editing and consistency checks
The data are processed by computer. In order to check the aggregated results some plausibility checks are carried out. Comparisons with the previous month and year are also made.
Adjustments
None.
Types of estimates
Totals and averages.
Construction of indices
None.
Indicators of reliability of the estimates
Coverage of the administrative system/sampling frame: exhaustive; it is compulsory for all employees in Austria to be insured with the Social Security.
Available series
Monthly and annual number of employees by employee category, sex, economic activity and region;
Average monthly earnings (annually) by employee category, sex, economic activity and region.
History of the statistics
Starting date of the statistical series: January 1948.
Major changes and revisions: None.
Documentation and dissemination
Documentation:
Hauptverband der österreichischen Sozialversicherungsträger: *Die österreichische Sozialversicherung in Zahlen (Vienna, monthly).*
Dissemination: Website: http://www.sozvers.at
Data supplied to the ILO for dissemination
The following statistics are published in the *Yearbook of Labour Statistics* or available in LABORSTA:
Paid employment by sex, by economic activity and in manufacturing, by industry group and by sex (most recent data: 1995);
Average monthly earnings of employees, by employee category and sex, by economic activity and in manufacturing, by industry group.
Monthly series of paid employment (general level) are published in the *Bulletin of Labour Statistics*.

Austria (2)

Source of the series
Kollektivverträge (Collective agreements including payment schemes for civil servants).
Title of the series
Kollektivverträge.
Organization responsible
Data collection and statistical processing: Federation of Austrian Trade Unions.
Publication/ dissemination of the statistics: Trade Unions and Statistics Austria.
Main topics covered
Wage and salary rates, earnings and hours of work.
Periodicity or frequency of availability of the statistics
Monthly.
Reference period
Wage rates, earnings and hours of work: October.
Coverage of the statistics
Geographical: the whole country.
Industrial: all branches of economic activities of the Austrian Chamber of Commerce.
Establishments: all types and sizes in the private and public sectors.
Persons: all employees covered by collective agreements.
Occupations: all occupations covered by collective agreements.
Concepts and definitions
Employment: refers to wage earners, salaried employees and civil servants.
Earnings: refer to the gross remuneration paid to employees.
Wage rates: refer to hourly, weekly and monthly rates, including basic wages and salaries, as well as guaranteed and regularly paid allowances. They are reported separately for wage earners and salaried employees.
Hours of work: normal hours of work are those fixed by collective agreements.
Hours actually worked include hours worked during normal periods of work, overtime, hours for which payment is made under a guaranteed work contract, etc. according to the international definition.
Hours paid for include hours actually worked (as above) and hours paid for but not worked, such as paid annual leave, public holidays, sick leave, etc.
Classifications
Branch of economic activity (industry):
Title of the classification: Classification of the Austrian Chamber of Commerce.
Number of groups used for coding: corresponds to the number of collective agreements in force.
Applied to: wage and salary rates, earnings and hours of work.
Link to ISIC: Rev.2 and Rev.3.
Occupation: all occupations as defined in the collective agreements.
Status in employment: employees: wage earners, salaried employees and civil servants.
Other classifications: employees: by sex; wage and salary rates, earnings and hours of work: by employee category (manual/non-manual) over 18 years of age and by sex.
Data collection
Size and coverage of the administrative system: all collective agreements.
Data collection method: data gathering from all collective agreements and payment schemes for civil servants.
Updating of the administrative system: normally, every year, but on a continuous basis if and when new collective agreements come into force.
Data processing, editing and consistency checks
Simple compilation of data.
Adjustments
None.

Types of estimates
Total number of employees and average wage/salary rates, earnings, and hours of work.

Construction of indices
Over 1500 indices are computed monthly by Statistics Austria from statistics of agreed minimum wage rates based on the collective agreements (Tariflohnindex).

Indicators of reliability of the estimates
Coverage of the administrative system/sampling frame: exhaustive: all collective agreements and payment schemes are covered.

Available series
Total number of employees, weekly normal hours of work, hours actually worked and paid for, average hourly, weekly and monthly wage and salary rates, average hourly, weekly, monthly and yearly earnings, by economic activity and occupation.

History of the statistics
Starting date of the statistical series: the first series started at the end of the 19th century.
Major changes and revisions: in case of new collective agreements.

Documentation and dissemination
Documentation:
Statistics Austria: *Schnellbericht* (Vienna).
Idem: *Statistische Narchrichten* (ibid., monthly); contains the monthly series of Tariflohnindex.
Methodological information on the index is published in *Tariflohnindex 1986, Aufbau und Gewichtung*, 899. Heft (Vienna, 1988).
Dissemination: on Statistics Austria's website:
http://www.statistik.at

Data supplied to the ILO for dissemination
The following statistics are published in *Statistics on occupational wages and hours of work and on food prices - October Inquiry results*:
Average monthly minimum wage rates and normal hours of work, by occupation and sex;
Average monthly earnings and hours actually worked or paid for, by occupation and sex.
In the *Yearbook of Labour Statistics*:
Average monthly wage rates of wage earners in agriculture.

Costa Rica

Source of the series
Records of the Costa Rican Social Security Fund (Planillas de la Caja Costarricense de Seguro Social - CCSS).

Title of the series
Statistics of employers, workers and wages.

Organization responsible
Data collection: Costa Rican Social Security Fund, Actuarial and Economic Planning Directorate.
Statistical processing: Costa Rican Social Security Fund, Information Technology Department.
Publication/ dissemination of the statistics: Costa Rican Social Security Fund, Executive Presidency, Actuarial and Economic Planning Directorate, Department of Statistics.

Main topics covered
Employment, earnings and income from employment.

Periodicity or frequency of availability of the statistics
Once a year.

Reference period
June each year.

Coverage of the statistics
Geographical: the whole country.
Industrial: all branches of economic activity.
Establishments: all types and sizes.
Persons: employers and workers affiliated to CCSS health and pension schemes (for all institutional sectors) and non-wage workers affiliated to the voluntary insurance scheme (self-employed and special agreements).
Occupations: data are not collected on individual occupations or occupational groups.

Concepts and definitions
Employment: includes the following categories of persons in employment affiliated to the CCSS.
Employer: the natural or legal person, private or public, who uses the services of one or more persons covered by the social security schemes.

Insured worker (wage worker, employee): the person who works for an employer and receives remuneration for her/his work in the form of a wage, salary, day wage or piecework, in cash or in kind.
Self-employed worker (independent worker): a person who works alone or with partner(s), without establishing a dependent relationship with an employer.
Worker under special agreements: groups of independent workers organized in associations, trade unions, cooperatives, professional bodies, rotary clubs, homes, museums, etc., who sign an agreement with the CCSS for their insurance.
Direct insured person (contributor/actively employed): a person who by a contribution (quota) generates for him/herself and others the right to receive certain social security benefits. This contribution is paid directly or through third parties (employers).
Earnings: the total wage base, i.e. the total wages reported by direct insured persons in the monthly list. It does not include voluntary insured persons, the self-employed and workers under special agreements.
The average wage is the remuneration received on average each month by a wage worker.
Income related to self-employment: refers to "contributory income", and corresponds to the total income reported by independent workers on which the contribution is calculated (analogous to the wages of actively employed direct insured workers).
Average income: the monthly average income remuneration reported by an independent worker.
Contribution base: the total wages and income reported by employees and independent workers respectively for a given month.

Classifications
Branch of economic activity (industry):
Title of the classification: Manual of Codes of Economic Activities.
Number of groups used for coding: All groups to 4-digit level.
Applied to: all data.
Link to ISIC and level: Rev.3, 1990, at all levels.
Status in employment:
Title of the classification: CCSS classification.
Number of groups used for coding: four groups: employers, independent workers (self-employed), employees and workers under special agreements (groups).
Applied to: all data.
Link to ICSE and level: partial link at one-digit level.
Other classifications: by institutional sector: 6 institutional sectors are defined: Central Government, autonomous and semi-autonomous institutions, private enterprises, self-employed, special agreements and domestic services.
Data are also classified by territorial administrative division: 7 provinces which are divided into 81 cantons: by age group and sex, and size of enterprise.

Data collection
Size and coverage of the administrative system: in June 2000, the records used covered some 52,040 employers, 1,038,816 workers in all institutional sectors and some 313,000 non-wage workers affiliated to the voluntary insurance scheme (self-employed and special agreements), all affiliated to the health insurance scheme.
Data collection method: statistics on employers, workers and wages are collected from various sources of information: (i) monthly lists submitted by employers affiliated to the CCSS with details of workers, wages and economic activity, for the private enterprise, domestic services, autonomous institutions and special agreement sectors; (ii) the government's office automation department provides information on Central Government workers; and (iii) self-employed workers and some special agreements are obtained from CCSS membership records. The data collected from these sources are processed by the Information Technology Department, which provides the information to the Department of Statistics in the Actuarial and Economic Planning Directorate, in text files which are input to the system designed to generate statistics.
Updating of the administrative system: once a year.

Data processing, editing and consistency checks
The data are processed by computer and the system makes the necessary adjustments.

Adjustments
The process of data collection and processing can give rise to errors inherent in that process, such as "unknown" categories in various classifications of workers (sex, age, branch of activity or income unknown). A similar situation occurs with the contribution base. In adjusting the statistics to apportion the workers of unknown

sex and the contribution base in the appropriate categories, rounding differences may occur. However, these differences are kept below 1 per cent.

Types of estimates

All persons insured under the various schemes (health and pensions), by category and various classifications;

Total and average monthly wages and incomes, by category of insured person and by various classifications;

Distributions of insured persons by level of monthly wages and sector.

Construction of indices

None.

Indicators of reliability of the estimates

Not available.

Available series

Employers, insured workers and contribution base by sex, institutional sector, province and canton, by sector, branch of activity and size of enterprise.

Insured workers by branch of economic activity, age group, sector, level of monthly salary, etc.;

Average wages and incomes.

History of the statistics

Starting date of the statistical series: January 1973.

Major changes and revisions: not available.

Documentation and dissemination

Documentation:

Caja Costarricense de Seguro Social: *Anuario Estadístico* (San Jose, annual); each publication gives the data for June of the previous year.

Dissemination: on the CCSS website: http://www.ccss.sa.cr/actuarial/publicaciones.html.

Data supplied to the ILO for dissemination

Statistics of average earnings of employees were published in the *Yearbook of Labour Statistics* until 1986 and can be found in the LABORSTA database.

Cuba

Source of the series

National Statistical Information System (Sistema de Información Estadística Nacional - SIE-N) and human resources records.

Title of the series

Employment and wages.

Organization responsible

Data collection, statistical processing and publication/ dissemination of the statistics: National Statistical Office (Oficina Nacional de Estadísticas – ONE).

Main topics covered

Employment and wages.

Periodicity or frequency of availability of the statistics

Monthly and annual.

Reference period

Employment and wages: every month and the full year.

Coverage of the statistics

Geographical: the whole country.

Industrial: all branches of economic activity.

Establishments: all types and sizes in the private and public sectors.

Persons: all persons in employment.

Occupations: the data are collected by occupational category: manual, technical, administrative, service and managerial workers.

Concepts and definitions

Employment: means all persons engaged in the various activities of the national economy, whether or not of working age (17 years and over), in both State entities and the non-State sector. Any person who on the data reference day was in a formal employment relationship as an employee, for payment in cash or in kind, or self-employed, is considered to be employed.

Employees in State entities are workers whose employment relationship, irrespective of the kind of remuneration applied to them, is based on a contract of employment with a state-owned entity with legal personality and subject to the control of State institutions. It includes workers in Cuban commercial companies and political and mass organizations and those working in State entities which may be organized in the form of unions, enterprises, economic associations, State economic organizations, farms, financial institutions, state-financed health, sports and cultural and institutions and scientific centres, etc.

Employees in the non-State sector include those belonging to the cooperative sector, mixed-ownership enterprises and the private sector (branches of foreign firms, associations and foundations). Self-employed persons in the private sector include:

– own account workers: these persons may or may not own their own tools and equipment, are not subject to a contract of employment with a legal entity, they do not receive wages, they engage in production or provide their services individually or collectively, through appropriate employment as family helper and are responsible for marketing their production or services directly or through another person or entity that represents them legally for that purposes;

– individual tenants: these are persons who do not have another employment and known as tenant farmers (*aparceleros*), to whom the State has leased land for the cultivation of certain crops of State interest, including coffee, tobacco;

– independent farmers: these are small farmers who own the land they cultivate to grow agricultural produce and/or livestock for sale or own consumption;

– workers in credit and service cooperatives: these include small farmers who form groups to benefit from the technical and financial assistance provided by the State for production by the farmers who belong to them;

– members of cooperatives (UBPC and CPA);

– family helpers.

Self-employed persons are considered to be employed even if they have not worked because of the following situations: those present at work on the data reference day who were unable to undertake work for any reasons; and those not present at work for any reason, provided that the employment relationship is continuing.

Earnings: the wage paid is the remuneration in cash received by the worker for the quantity and quality of work performed. It includes, *inter alia*, payment of basic wages, bonuses, allowances for exceptional working conditions, compliance with labour standards, wage supplements, overtime, additional long-service payments or management responsibilities, paid holidays, absence permitted under current legislation.

Classifications

Branch of economic activity (industry):

Title of the classification: not available.

Number of groups used for coding: 9 main groups.

Applied to: employment and earnings.

Link to ISIC and level: Rev.2, 1968.

Occupation:

Title of the classification: Standard Classification of Occupations.

Number of groups used for coding: five occupational groups: managers; technical workers; service workers; administrative workers; manual workers.

Applied to: only employment.

Link to ISCO and level: none.

Status in employment: see under "Concepts and definitions": Employment.

Other classifications: labour force by sex, form of ownership, province and age group.

Data collection

Size and coverage of the administrative system: the National Statistical Information System (SIE-N) and human resources records cover the entire labour force.

Data collection method: not available.

Data processing, editing and consistency checks

The average total number of workers is calculated by subtracting from the number of workers in the register those who are not directly or indirectly paid wages by the entity because they work in other entities from which they receive wages, even though included in the register concerned, and adding those who, while not included in the entity's register work for it and are paid directly or indirectly by that entity. This average is the result of totalling workers on a daily basis, with the above additions and subtractions, including rest days and holidays, and dividing the result by the number of calendar days in the reporting period.

The average monthly wage is calculated by dividing the wages paid by the average total number of workers.

Adjustments

Not available.

Types of estimates

Total number of persons employed; total wages paid and average monthly wage.

Construction of indices

None.

Indicators of reliability of the estimates
Coverage of the administrative system: it covers the entire labour force.
Available series
- Persons employed in the national economy by form of ownership and type of economic activity;
- Persons employed (employees), (total) wages paid and average monthly wage by state and mixed-ownership entities by type of economic activity and province;
- Distribution of the labour force by level of education, age group, occupational category and sex.

History of the statistics
Not available.
Documentation and dissemination
Documentation:
Oficina Nacional de Estadísticas: *Anuario Estadístico de Cuba* (Havana City, annual); contains methodological notes.
Idem: *Cuba en Cifras* (ibid., annual).
Data supplied to the ILO for dissemination
Statistics of average monthly earnings in state and mixed-ownership entities, by branch of economic activity, are published in the *Yearbook of Labour Statistics*.

France

Source of the series
Annual Statement of Social Data (Déclaration annuelle de Données Sociales-DADS).
Title of the series
Wages in industry, commerce and services.
Organization responsible
Data collection: National Old-Age Pensions Fund (Caisse Nationale d'Assurance Vieillesse - CNAV) and Directorate-General of Taxes (DGI).
Statistical processing and publication/ dissemination of the statistics: National Institute of Statistics and Economic Research (Institut National de la Statistique et des Etudes Economiques (INSEE).
Main topics covered
Employment, earnings and hours of work.
Periodicity or frequency of availability of the statistics
Annual.
Reference period
The whole year.
Coverage of the statistics
Geographical: the whole country.
Industrial: all branches of economic activity apart from the State civil service, farming and forestry, domestic services and extra-territorial activities.
Establishments: establishments of all types and sizes. The annual statement of social data (DADS) normally relates to the establishment, but it may exceptionally cover several establishments belonging to the same company.
Persons: all employees.
Occupations: data are collected by socio-occupational group. Home workers, apprentices and trainees are identified separately.
Concepts and definitions
Employment: employees are classified into four groups:
- full-time employees, including employees working 80%;
- intermittent (indefinite-term contracts for permanent jobs which are alternating by their nature), including temps;
- part-time employees;
- home workers (these are excluded from the statistical tables).
Earnings: annual earnings gross and net after deduction of employees social security contributions (social security and unemployment insurance, pension contributions, general social contribution (CSG) and contribution to reimbursement of the national debt (CRDS)). All taxable components of remuneration are included, in particular: direct wages, paid holidays, bonuses of all kinds and the taxable value of benefits in kind declared by the employer (accommodation, meals, fuel for heating, etc.).
Hours of work: paid hours, including paid holidays and sick leave for one year. The data on hours of work exclude travelling representatives and salesmen, as well as home workers, for whom work are hours of w not available. Data are also collected on start and end dates of payment of each employee, from which the length of time present in the establishment can be calculated.

Classifications
Branch of economic activity (industry):
Title of the classification: Nomenclature of French Activities (Nomenclature d'Activités Française (NAF). As from January 2003, it will be replaced by NAF, Rev.1, 2003.
 Number of groups used for coding: 700 groups.
Applied to: all data.
Link to ISIC and level: Rev.3.
Occupation:
Title of the classification: Nomenclature of Occupations and Socio-Occupational Groups.
Number of groups used for coding: 34.
Applied to: all data.
Link to ISCO and level: none.
Other classifications: sex, age, size of enterprise and establishment (based on number of posts at 31 December), location of enterprise headquarters and establishment, and employee's municipality of residence.
Data collection
Size and coverage of the administrative system: Exhaustive collection from employers.
Data collection method: the Annual Statement of Social Data (DADS) is a formal declaration which must be completed by every enterprise (natural or legal person) resident or established in France which pay wages or other remuneration, except for the majority of employers of domestic personnel. It is document common to the social and tax administrations in which employers state total wage remuneration for each establishment and each employee. The statements are submitted in magnetic or printed form to the Regional Health Insurance Funds, then amalgamated by the CNAV for employees covered by the general social security system. For employees covered by special social security schemes, the tax declarations (No.2460) are used by the DGI. They are transmitted to INSEE in each February of the year following the reference year and published the following year in March.
The DADS contains information on the establishment (employer's name or company name, address and branch of activity, identification number, number of personnel at 31 December and gross payroll) and on each employee (identification, nature of employment and qualification, address, start and end dates of payment period, number of paid hours, conditions of work (full-time, part-time, intermittent and home workers), amount of remuneration in cash before and after deductions of social security contributions, estimated value of benefits in kind and amount of expense allowances and reimbursement of expenses.
Updating of the administrative system: annual.
Data processing, editing and consistency checks
The data are processed by computer. Checks are made on identities of establishments and employees (reconciliation of lists of enterprises and individuals) and cross-checks are made between wages, hours of work and conditions of work.
Adjustments
None.
Types of estimates
Distributions, averages and median, for various time units (hour, year).
Employment: total personnel at 31 December of the reference year, and number of paid employees during the reference year; distribution for different variables;
Average net hourly wage: total net payroll divided by number of hours worked;
Average net annual wage: for full-time workers, total net "full-time" payroll divided by number of work-years;
Average annual hours per post: number of paid hours for one year divided by the number of paid posts in the year;
Construction of indices
None.
Indicators of reliability of the estimates
Coverage of the administrative system: over 99% of employees.
Conformity with other sources: comparisons are possible at the level of:
- personnel and payroll, with national accounts;
- trends in wage rates, with the results of the Ministry of Labour ACEMO survey (quarterly survey of establishments by the Ministry of Employment and Social Security (DARES);
- personnel, with other administrative sources.
Available series
"Employers" tables: number of establishments, personnel as number of paid posts in the year, personnel as number of paid posts

at 31 December, gross payroll, by economic activity of the establishment, size, department where located;

"Full-time posts" tables: hourly wage series: personnel as number of posts, as number of work-years, annual hours, total net wages paid, average annual hours of posts and average net hourly wage of posts, by economic activity and size of establishment, by sex, socio-occupational group, age-group, net hourly wage group, etc.;

"Full-time posts" tables: annual wage series: personnel as number of posts, as number of work-years, annual hours, total net wages paid, average annual net wage by work-year, number of permanent employees, average net annual wage by work-year of permanent employees, by different variables and by sex;

"Non full-time posts" tables and "All posts" tables: hourly wage series by the same variables and classifications.

History of the statistics
Starting date of the statistical series: 1967, based on a 1/25 sample; 1993, exhaustive.

Major changes and revisions: up to 1992, farm and forestry workers were not included in the DADS. Since 1997, the exhaustive DADS statements also show wages paid to themselves by directors of public limited companies (SA) and minority directors of private limited companies (SARL), but not majority directors of SARL. It is intended to include farming and forestry in the statistical coverage starting in 2002.

Documentation and dissemination
Documentation:

INSEE: *INSEE Résultats: Les Salaires dans l'Industrie, le Commerce et les Services en...* (Paris, annual); published about 15 months after the data reference period. Contains statistics and methodological information.

Dissemination: on the Website: http://www.alisse.insee.fr
Statistics which do not appear in national publications or on the Internet may be obtained on request.

Data supplied to the ILO for dissemination
None at present.

Other administrative sources of data: statistics on non-wage earnings and income are derived from several administrative sources.

Data on doctors' liberal profession earnings are drawn from two administrative sources: statistics on the national inter-scheme system prepared by the National Employee Health Insurance Fund (Caisse Nationale d'Assurance Maladie des travailleurs salariés - CNAMTS), the Agricultural Mutual Fund (MSA - Mutualité Sociale Agricole) and the National Health Insurance Fund for the Independent Professions (CANAM - Caisse Nationale d'Assurance Maladie des Professions Indépendantes), for fees and number of practitioners; and tax statistics of the Directorate-General of Taxes (DGI). These statistics are prepared annually and cover doctors in normal practice (excluding locums) who have submitted a "controlled tax declaration", regulated or otherwise, including full-time hospital doctors. Based on the assessments of income and expenditure respectively, the average annual income per practitioner from liberal professional activities before income tax can be estimated for each year.

Statistics on income from small entrepreneurs engaged in crafts, commerce and services are prepared on the basis of company activities and tax returns for industrial and commercial profits and non-commercial profits. The records taken from the returns are transmitted to INSEE and, in conjunction with annual company surveys, constitute the unified company statistical system.
The results are published in:
INSEE: *Synthèses: Les revenus d'activité non salariée en...* (Paris, annual); published about 3 years after the data reference period. Contains statistics and information on methodology.

Statistics on State employees' earnings are prepared each year on the basis of a complete set of records: records of civil ministries and public enterprises; additional survey of all State services by questionnaire, records of the Ministry of Defence, records of public establishments, etc.
The results are published in:
INSEE: *INSEE Résultats: Le Salaire des Agents de l'Etat en...* (Paris, annual); published about 3 years after the data reference period. Contains statistics and information on methodology.

French Polynesia

Source of the series
Social Security, Tax administration, and French Representation.
Title of the series
Employment and wages.

Organization responsible
Data collection: Social Provident Fund (Caisse de Prévoyance Sociale (CPS)), High Commissioner (Haut commissariat).
Statistical processing and publication/ dissemination of the statistics: Statistical Institute of French Polynesia (Institut de la Statistique de Polynésie Française (ISPF)).
Main topics covered
Employment, earnings, income and hours of work.
Periodicity or frequency of availability of the statistics
Monthly.
Reference period
The full month.
Coverage of the statistics
Geographical: the whole territory (all archipelagos and districts).
Industrial: all divisions of economic activity.
Establishments: all types and sizes of establishments.
Persons: since 2000, all employed persons (employees and self-employed persons), who are obliged to be covered by the territorial social security insurance scheme, except French civil servants working in French Polynesia.
Prior to 2000, the self-employed who chose a private social insurance were excluded from the scheme and the statistics, together with French civil servants working in French Polynesia.
Occupations: data are not collected by occupation or occupational group.
Concepts and definitions
Employment: for the purpose of the statistics, persons employed include employees and the self-employed (own-account workers) covered by the compulsory territorial social security insurance scheme, whose earnings are above the minimum wage.
Full-time workers are those who work the full legal working time (169 hours per month). Part-time workers are those who work less than the full legal working time.
Young workers in the age group 16-18 years can be separately identified.
Earnings: gross cash monthly earnings above the minimum wage, including overtime payments which can be separately identified on the basis of data on hours of work. The amount of reported earnings is limited to the ceiling fixed for social security contributions.
Hours of work: hours paid for, including overtime, as declared by the employer.
Income related to paid employment: not applicable. As there is no income tax in French Polynesia, not all the components of income are declared.
Income related to self-employment: in principle, net income after deduction of fixed capital consumption. In practice, employment-related income of own-account workers relates to the total value of sales after deduction of all charges related to the economic activity. Reported income is limited to income above the minimum wage and to the income ceiling fixed for social security contributions.
Classifications
Branch of economic activity (industry):
Title of the classification: Nomenclature des activités françaises (NAF).
Number of groups used for coding: 4 groups, 17 sections, 31 sub-sections, 60 divisions, and 697 posts.
Applied to: all data collected.
Link to ISIC: yes.
Status in employment: employees and own-account workers.
Other classifications: employment and earnings/income are classified according to sex, age group, hours of work and localization of the employer (archipelago or district). Employment data are also distributed according to levels of earnings/income.
Data collection
Size and coverage of administrative system: not available.
Data collection method: data on employment and earnings of insured persons are reported monthly by employers to the territorial social security insurance. They are transmitted each quarter to the Statistical Institute, within three months after the reporting quarter.
Updating of the administrative system: continuous.
Data processing, editing and consistency checks
Data are processed by computer and consistency checks are made on wage levels, hours of work, age groups, etc.
Adjustments
None.
Types of estimates
Employment: totals and distributions;
Earnings/income: totals, averages and distributions.
Construction of indices
None.

Indicators of reliability of the estimates
Coverage of the administrative system: some 99 percent of all persons employed since the new legislation was introduced at the end of 2001, retroactively to 2000.
Non-sampling errors: Not available.
Conformity with other sources: some comparisons are made with the results of the population census, and some will be made with the results of the latest survey on family budget (2001).
Available series
Number of employees classified by: sex, age group, level of income, economic activity, sector of activity, archipelago or district of the employer, legal status of the employer, number of hours worked;
Average monthly earnings classified by: sex, age group, economic activity, sector of activity, archipelago or district of the employer, legal status of the employer and number of hours worked;
Average hourly earnings classified by: sex, age group, economic activity, sector of activity, archipelago or district of the employer and legal status of the employer.
All series are available monthly and annually, subject to confidentiality rules.
History of the statistics
Starting date of the statistical series: 1987 for the major part of the series, and 1995 for all available series.
Major changes and revisions: prior to 1995, employment and earnings data were collected by the social security insurance and reported globally. Since 1995, monthly details are available for each insured person.
Documentation and dissemination
Documentation: not available before 2003.
Dissemination: on the following website: http://www.ispf.pf
Results which do not appear on the website can be made available upon request.
Data supplied to the ILO for dissemination
The following statistics are published in the *Yearbook of Labour Statistics*:
Annual average of employees.

Germany

Source of the series: Collective Agreements.
Title of the series
Tariflöhne, Tarifgehälter.
Organization responsible
Data collection, statistical processing and publication/dissemination of the statistics: Statistisches Bundesamt (DESTATIS), Division VI B (Federal Statistical Office of Germany).
Main topics covered
Wage and salary amounts for selected groups of workers and employees and normal hours of work.
Periodicity or frequency of availability of the statistics
Half-yearly.
Reference period
The months up to the reporting month (April and October).
Coverage of the statistics
Geographical: the whole country.
Industrial: all branches of economic activities except: division 71 (renting of machinery and equipment without operator and of personal and household goods), division 72 (computer and related activities), division 73 (research and development), division 74 (other business activities) and division 80 (education).
Establishments: not relevant.
Persons: employees concerned by collective agreements.
Occupations: data are not collected by occupation or occupational group, but in some collective agreements a number of occupational groups are separately identified and are partially available and presented in the publication.
Concepts and definitions
Employment: Salaried employees are those employed persons subject to contributions to the social insurance system for *Angestellte*; wage earners are receivers of wages and fall under the social insurance system for *Arbeiter*.
Wage/salary rates: refer to collectively agreed basic time rates of wages applicable to highest seniority levels.
Hours of work: refer to normal weekly hours of work, as fixed by collective agreements.
Classifications
Branch of economic activity (industry):
Title of the classification: Classification of all Economic Activities (WZ 93), edition 1993.

Number of groups used for coding: two-digit numeric codes except 71-74 and 80.
Applied to: wage/salary rates and hours of work.
Link to ISIC: the WZ 93 is derived from NACE, Rev.1 and can be linked to ISIC, Rev.3.
Other classifications: manual and non-manual workers (i.e. wage earners and salaried employees). Both wage earners and salaried employees are classified into "performance groups" "Leistungsgruppen" (or employment categories), which are established for each collective agreement by the Federal Statistical Office in consultation with the social partners concerned on the basis of the various wage and salary categories. Performance groups are based on the level of training, experience and responsibility required for performing the tasks covered by the various earnings categories.
- Wage earners are classified according to the three performance groups (skilled, semi-skilled and unskilled).
- Salaried employees are classified according to four performance groups (II to V) and two occupational categories: commercial employees, and technical employees and masters.
Data collection
Size and coverage of the administrative system: the data cover about 650 collective agreements.
Data collection method: the data are extracted from the records of collective agreements.
Updating of the administrative system: half-yearly.
Data processing, editing and consistency checks
All collected data are checked for correctness.
Adjustments
None.
Types of estimates
Average minimum/negotiated wage and salary rates per hour, day or month, per occupation.
Construction of indices
Indices of negotiated standard weekly hours of work and wage and salary rates are computed, by economic activity and region.
Indicators of reliability of the estimates
None.
Available series
- Agreed wage rates of wage earners
- Agreed salary rates of salaried employees
- Normal hours of work
- Number of days of vacation per year
- Paid leave
- Payment during sick leave
- Special extra pay.
History of the statistics
Starting date of the statistical series: 1949/50.
Major changes and revisions: Presentation in Euro from 2002 onwards (before in DM).
Documentation and dissemination
Documentation:
Statistisches Bundesamt (DESTATIS): *Fachserie 16, Reihe 4.1Tariflöhne* and *Reihe 4.2, Tarifgehälter* (Wiesbaden, half-yearly); published some four months after the reference periods (April and October); contains both the statistics and methodological information.
Idem: *Fachserie 16, Reihe 4.3, Index der Tariflöhne und -gehälter* (ibd, quarterly).
Dissemination: data are expected to be available on Internet in 2003.
Data supplied to the ILO for dissemination
The following statistics are published in *Statistics on occupational wages and hours of work and on food prices - October Inquiry results*:
Average hourly, daily and monthly wage and salary rates by occupation in specific industries, covering the largest German Länder (i.e. North-Rhine-Westphalia).
Statistics of average hourly wage rates of skilled day workers in agriculture (up to 1994) in the territory of the Federal Republic of Germany before 3.10.1990, are available in LABORSTA.

Guatemala

Source of the series
Records of the Guatemalan Social Security Institute (Instituto Guatemalteco de Seguridad Social - IGSS).
Title of the series

Employment and income from employment (earnings) of workers registered with the IGSS.

Organization responsible
Data collection: Guatemalan Social Security Institute (IGSS).

Main topics covered
Employment and earnings.

Periodicity or frequency of availability of the statistics
Monthly and annually.

Reference period
Employment and earnings: each month and the full year.

Coverage of the statistics
Geographical: the whole country.
Industrial: all branches of economic activity.
Establishments: all types and sizes of establishments in the private and public sector.
Persons: active employers and workers (employees) contributing to the social security system.
Occupations: no data are collected on individual occupations or occupational groups.

Concepts and definitions
Employment: any person who provides material or intellectual services or a combination thereof, under an individual employment contract or relationship, to an employer formally registered or required to register formally under the social security system is a member of the social security system. Also members are State workers, members and employees of legally constituted cooperatives.
Earnings: these refer to the total payroll reported by contributing enterprises.

Classifications
Branch of economic activity (industry):
Title of the classification: not available.
Number of groups used for coding: not available.
Applied to: employers, employees and earnings.
Link to ISIC and level: based on ISIC, Rev.2, 1968.
Other classifications: by region and category of employer/sector (private employers, State budget and State accounts).

Data collection
Size and coverage of the administrative system: IGSS records. At 31 December 2000, the records used covered 908,000 workers enrolled, and a total of some 1,950,000 persons protected.
Data collection method: the data on the number of active employers, contributing employees and earnings are based solely on employers' compulsory reports to the IGSS, which are kept in a central registry.
Updating of the administrative system: every month.

Data processing, editing and consistency checks
Not available.

Adjustments
Under-coverage: annual estimates of employees and wages are adjusted to take account of incomes received as contributions to all social security schemes and to take account of employers' arrears. The State budget data are also corrected to eliminate multiple employment and wage figures are adjusted on the basis of actual budget performance for the year.

Types of estimates
Total active employers, contributing workers and total monthly and annual wages.
Average monthly earnings.

Construction of indices
None.

Indicators of reliability of the estimates
Coverage of the administrative system: at 31 December 2000, members represented some 25 per cent of the economically active population aged 10 years and over, and the total protected population (members and beneficiaries) some 17 per cent of the total population.

Available series
Estimate of active employers at 31 December each year;
Estimate of contributing worker members in June and 31 December, by economic activity, region and category of employer;
Estimate of total annual wages, by economic activity, region and category of employer;
Monthly estimate of contributing workers and earnings by economic activity.

History of the statistics
Starting date of the statistical series: not available.
Major changes and revisions: the IGSS revised the wages and employment estimates for the period 1974-1987.

Documentation and dissemination
Documentation:
Instituto Guatemalteco de Seguridad Social: *Boletín Estadístico* (Guatemala City, annual).
Idem: *Informe Anual de Labores* (ibid., annual).
Banco de Guatemala: *Boletín Estadístico* (ibid., quarterly).
Dissemination: Bank of Guatemala Website:
http://www.banguat.gob.gt
Data supplied to the ILO for dissemination
Statistics of paid employment and average monthly earnings of contributing workers, by economic activity, are published in the *yearbook of Labour Statistics*.

Hong Kong, China (1)

Source of the series
Government Administrative Records.

Title of the series
Civil Service Personnel Statistics - Establishment and Strength of the Civil Service.

Organization responsible
Data collection: Civil Service Bureau, Hong Kong Special Administrative Region (SAR), People's Republic of China.
Statistical processing and publication/ dissemination of the statistics: Census and Statistics Department, Hong Kong SAR.

Main topics covered
Employment and vacancies.

Periodicity or frequency of availability of the statistics
Quarterly.

Reference period
The last full working day in a quarter.

Coverage of the statistics
Geographical: Hong Kong SAR.
Industrial: all divisions of economic activity.
Establishments: all policy bureaux and government departments in the Government of Hong Kong SAR.
Persons: civil servants.
Occupations: all occupations of civil servants in the Government of Hong Kong SAR.

Concepts and definitions
Employment: civil servants are persons who are employed on civil service terms of appointment on the survey reference date. Excluded are Independent Commission Against Corruption Officers, judges and judicial officers in the Judiciary, and locally-engaged staff working in overseas Hong Kong Economic and Trade Offices.
Vacancies: unfilled job openings which are immediately available and for which active recruitment steps are being taken on the survey reference date.

Classifications
Branch of economic activity (industry):
Title of the classification: Hong Kong Standard Industrial Classification Version 1.1 (HSIC V1.1);
Number of groups used for coding: 83 (up to the three-digit level).
Applied to: employment and vacancies.
Link to ISIC and level: HSIC V1.1 is modelled on ISIC, Rev.2 at all levels, with adaptation for the industrial structure in Hong Kong SAR.
Other classifications: employment by sex.

Data collection
Size and coverage of the administrative system: about 100 reporting units, in terms of government departments and bureaux.
Data collection method: departmental returns are submitted quarterly by government departments and bureaux to the Civil Service Bureau. The time lapse between the reference period of the data and data collection/processing is about 12 weeks.
Updating of the administrative system: quarterly.

Data processing, editing and consistency checks
Data are processed by computer. The sum of the components is verified against the total for each reporting unit, and range checks are made with the corresponding figures for the previous quarter.

Adjustments
None.

Types of estimates
Totals.

Construction of indices
None.

Indicators of reliability of the estimates
Coverage of the administrative system: exhaustive in terms of civil servants.

Available series
Quarterly number of civil servants and vacancies.
History of the statistics
Starting date of the statistical series: March 1980.
Major changes and revisions: in June 1999, a minor revision was made to the statistical definition of civil servants: since that month, judges and judicial officers in the Judiciary are excluded from the coverage of civil servants. The definition of civil service vacancies was also revised in June 1999, so that vacancies arising from posts pending deletion and posts held by temporary staff or reserved for other staff are excluded.
Prior to December 2001, figures on the number of civil servants and vacancies referred to the position at the beginning of January, April, July and October. They now refer to the last full working day of the same quarters.
Documentation and dissemination
Documentation:
Census and Statistics Department: *Hong Kong Monthly Digest of Statistics* (Hong Kong SAR);
Idem: *Quarterly Report of Employment and Vacancies Statistics* (ibid.);
Idem: *Hong Kong Annual Digest of Statistics* (ibid.).
These publications contain employment and vacancy statistics, and methodological information. The time lapse between the reference date and the release of statistics is 12 weeks.
Dissemination: on Internet: http://www.info.gov.hk/censtatd
Data supplied to the ILO for dissemination
The following data are supplied to the ILO for publication in the *Yearbook of Labour Statistics*:
Number of employees in the civil service, as part of the statistics on paid employment by economic activity.

Hong Kong, China (2)

Source of the series
Administrative Records: Government Form 527.
Title of the series
Monthly Returns of Wage Rates in the Building Industry.
Organization responsible
Data collection: Works Bureau, Hong Kong Special Administrative Region (SAR), People's Republic of China.
Statistical processing and publication/ dissemination of the statistics: Census and Statistics Department, Hong Kong SAR.
Main topics covered
Employment and wage rates.
Periodicity or frequency of availability of the statistics
Employment: quarterly;
Wage rates: monthly.
Reference period
Employment: the last full working day in a quarter;
Wage rates: the full month.
Coverage of the statistics
Geographical: Hong Kong SAR.
Industrial: construction only.
Establishments: all construction sites under the purview of the Works Bureau, Government of Hong Kong SAR. A construction site is defined as a demarcated locality where one or more stages of construction work are being carried on.
Persons: manual workers.
Occupations: twenty-nine pre-selected occupations.
Concepts and definitions
Employment: manual workers at construction sites refer to craftsmen, semi-skilled and unskilled workers working at those sites on the survey reference date. Manual workers may be either directly employed by the main contractors or being called upon by sub-contractors or gang leaders to work on a casual basis.
Wage rates: daily wage rates include (i) basic wage rate; (ii) cost-of-living allowance; and (iii) guaranteed and regularly paid allowances including meal and transportation allowances. Wage rates in kind are excluded.
Classifications
Branch of economic activity (industry):
Title of the classification: Hong Kong Standard Industrial Classification Version 1.1 (HSIC V1.1);
Number of groups used for coding: Division 5 (construction sites only).
Applied to: employment and wage rates.
Link to ISIC and level: ISIC, Rev.2, at all levels.
Occupation: 29 selected occupations: unskilled labourer, excavator, concretor's labourer, bricklayer's labourer, plasterer's

labourer, concretor, bricklayer, drainlayer, rubble mason, splitting mason, ashlar mason, steelbender, blacksmith, carpenter and joiner, plumber, fitter, plasterer, terrazzo and granolithic worker, glazier, painter, electrician (wireman), plant operator, truck driver, heavy load coolie, pneumatic driller, bamboo worker and scaffolder, structural steel erector, diver and diver's linesman.
Data collection
Size and coverage of the administrative system: about 230 construction sites.
Data collection method: main contractors of all construction sites under the purview of the Works Bureau, Hong Kong SAR, are required by contract to submit Government Form 527 (GF 527) to the Census and Statistics Department through the relevant Works departments on a monthly basis. They provide the number of work-days and the average daily wage rates corresponding to the occupations specified in GF 527, for the workers employed by them or their sub-contractors in the reference month, by the middle of the following month. The Census and Statistics Department carries out some consistency checks and compiles average daily wage rates in the selected occupations within two months after receipt of the data. As regards the number of manual workers, the time lapse between the reference period of the data and the data collection/processing period is 12 weeks.
Updating of the administrative system: continuous.
Data processing, editing and consistency checks
In addition to consistency checks, further verification of the data provided in GF 527 returns is made when:
– the number of work-days of an occupation in a given month is 50 percent higher or lower than that of the previous month;
– the average daily wage rate for an occupation in a given month is 10 percent higher or lower than that of the previous month;
– the average daily wage rate for an occupation in a given month is different from the overall average of that occupation across all contracts, if the site did not employ any employees in that occupation in the previous month.
Adjustments
None.
Types of estimates
Total number of manual workers at construction sites.
Average daily wage rates of selected occupations in construction sites.
Average daily wage rate of an occupation *i*:

$$\frac{\sum_j (\text{work-days worked in the } jth \text{ site} \times \text{average daily wage rate in the } jth \text{ site})}{\sum_j \text{work-days worked in } jth \text{ site}}$$

Average daily wage rates of all occupations covered by the GF 527:

$$\frac{\sum_{ij} (\text{work-days worked in } jth \text{ site} \times \text{average daily wages in } jth \text{ site})}{\sum_{ij} \text{work-days worked in } jth \text{ site}}$$

Construction of indices
A monthly index of the cost of labour is compiled, based on the weighted average wage rates of selected occupations. The weights for each occupation are derived on the basis of the total number of work-days for the respective occupation for a fixed period of time.
Indicators of reliability of the estimates
Coverage of the administrative system: 100 percent of the construction sites under the purview of the Works Bureau.
Available series
Number of manual workers and average daily wage rates.
History of the statistics
Starting date of the statistical series: number of manual workers: March 1976; average daily wage rates: January 1970; index series: December 1975 (base period: November 1975).
Major changes and revisions: revisions in the index series:
June 1989: change in base period (July 1982=100) and weightings;
July 1995: change in base period (June 1995=100) and weightings.
Documentation and dissemination
Documentation:
Census and Statistics Department: *Average Daily Wages of Workers engaged in Government Building and Construction Projects* (Hong Kong SAR, monthly); contains wages statistics only);
Idem: *Hong Kong Monthly Digest of Statistics* (ibid.); contains both wages and employment statistics, and methodological information;
Idem: *Quarterly Report of Employment and Vacancies Statistics* (ibid.); contains employment statistics only, and methodological information;

Idem: *Quarterly Report of Employment and Vacancies at Construction Sites* (ibid.); contains employment statistics only, and methodological information;

Idem: *Hong Kong Annual Digest of Statistics* (ibid.); contains both wages and employment statistics, and methodological information.

Average daily wages of selected occupations are published two months after the reference month. Numbers of manual workers at construction sites are published within 12 weeks after the reference date.

Dissemination: on Internet: http://www.info.gov.hk/censtatd

Data supplied to the ILO for dissemination

The following data are supplied to the ILO for publication in the *Yearbook of Labour Statistics:* number of construction workers and average daily wage rates of construction site workers in "all selected occupations";

In *Statistics on occupational wages and hours of work and on food prices - October Inquiry results:* average daily wage rates of selected occupations: electrician (wireman), plumber, structural steel erector, painter, bricklayer, concretor, carpenter and joiner, plasterer and unskilled labourer.

Isle of Man

Source of the series
Income tax returns.

Title of the series
Isle of Man Employment.

Organization responsible
Data collection: Isle of Man Treasury, Income Tax Division.
Statistical processing and publication/ dissemination of the statistics: Isle of Man Treasury, Economic Affairs Division.

Main topics covered
Employment.

Periodicity or frequency of availability of the statistics
Occasional, as required.

Reference period
A specific date.

Coverage of the statistics
Geographical: the whole Island.
Industrial: all branches of economic activities.
Establishments: all types and sizes.
Persons: all employed persons.
Occupations: data are not collected by occupation or occupational group.

Concepts and definitions
Employment: all employed persons (i.e. employees and self-employed persons) with a taxable source of income from paid and self-employment.

Classifications
Branch of economic activity (industry):
Title of the classification: Isle of Man Trade Classification.
Number of groups used for coding: 31; may be compressed for publication purposes as some groups are very small.
Applied to: employment data.
Link to ISIC: none.
Status in employment: employees and self-employed persons.
Other classifications: employment by size of establishments.

Data collection
The data source is the 40,000 plus income tax records held centrally for the whole Island by the Income Tax Division of the Isle of Man Treasury. The records are required to be kept up to date under the legislation.

Data processing, editing and consistency checks
The data are processed by computer.
Consistency checks are made through comparisons with past data and data from the Population Census benchmark.
The Economic Affairs Division checks the coding of the industrial classification carried out by the Income Tax Division and makes amendments where required.

Adjustments
None.

Types of estimates
Totals at a reference date.

Construction of indices
None.

Indicators of reliability of the estimates
Coverage of the administrative system: it is assumed to cover the total number of persons employed, except the black economy which is considered small because of the relatively small size of the Isle of Man.

Non-sampling errors: potentially, miscoding of the industrial classification, but checks are carried out (see above).
Conformity with other sources: as above.

Available series
Total employment at a specific reference date in 1988.

History of the statistics
Starting date of the statistical series: 1988 (published in 1995).
Major changes and revisions: none, except that new trade classifications have recently been added to cover Information and Communications Technology (ICT).

Documentation and dissemination
Documentation:
Isle of Man Treasury, Economic Affairs Division: *Isle of Man Labour Statistics,* 1995.
The data are produced on request by the Economic Affairs Division to the Income Tax Division. This is an ad-hoc data source, mainly used internally by Government, but available on request to the public.
A methodological note is appended to all tables released.

Data supplied to the ILO for dissemination
None at present.

Israel

Source of the series
Reports to the National Insurance Institute (NII) and other administrative sources.

Title of the series
Employee Posts and Wages.

Organization responsible
Data collection: National Insurance Institute (NII).
Statistical processing and publication/ dissemination of the statistics: Central Bureau of Statistics (CBS).

Main topics covered
Employment and earnings.

Periodicity or frequency of availability of the statistics
Monthly.

Reference period
The whole month.

Coverage of the statistics
Geographical: the whole country.
Industrial: all economic activities, except households employing domestic services.
Establishments: all types and sizes of establishments with one or more employees.
Persons: all employees who worked at least one day in the surveyed month in the establishments concerned, including members of co-operatives, civil workers of the defence forces, and employees from Judea and Samaria and the Gaza Area and from South Lebanon (only those who received their wages through the payment administration of the Employment Service) who work in Israel. Also included are workers from other countries on whom reports are submitted to the National Insurance Institute.
Domestic help workers, kibbutz members working in the kibbutz or in establishments owned by the kibbutz, pupils in vocational and agricultural schools and pupils in institutions for vocational training are excluded.
Occupations: data are not collected by occupation or occupational group.

Concepts and definitions
Employment: refers to the number of employees (permanent and temporary) on the pay-list of establishments or institutions, who worked, or were on paid absence due to illness, vacation, army reserve duty, etc. in the surveyed month at least one day.
Employees appearing on the pay-list of more than one establishment or institution in that month are counted as many times as they appeared in the pay-lists, so that the data refer to the number of employee posts for which wages were paid in that month.
Earnings: refer to gross monthly earnings. They include basic wages, cost of living allowance, seniority allowance, back-pay for previous periods, advance payments, overtime pay, premiums, bonuses and various allowances (current or non-recurrent), such as stand-by, turn-on duty, 13th month salary, fare, recreation allowance, education allowance, recompense for supplementary occupational studies and vehicle maintenance.
Excluded are other labour expenses and sums paid by the employer to funds such as pension funds or employees' insurance, parallel tax and employers' tax.

Classifications

Branch of economic activity (industry):

Title of the classification: Standard Industrial Classification of All Economic Activities, 1993.

Number of groups used for coding: not available.

Applied to: employment and earnings.

Link to ISIC and level: Rev.3.

Other classifications: employment and earnings data are classified by citizenship (Israeli and foreigners).

Data collection

Size and coverage of the administrative system: not available.

Data collection method: data on employment and wages are based mainly on the monthly processing of employers' reports (according to the law) on forms 102 (for Israelis) and 612 (for workers from abroad) to the National Insurance Institute (NII), and partly, on other administrative sources, such as the payment administration of the Employment Service, Malam, the Israel Local Authorities Data Processing Center and the defence forces.

Data on wages and employment in local authorities (municipalities, local councils and regional councils) are based on files of the Israel Local Authorities Data Processing Center and other sources.

Employers' reports are maintained in a central employer card file at the NII. The sample frame is mainly based on this file, and other establishments from samples kept in the CBS and from other sources are added to the frame. The universe is stratified by major economic branch and size of establishment. In each size group of economic branch, a sample of active establishments is drawn, with different sampling fractions.

The sample is updated by exclusion of establishments which cease operating and inclusion of a sample of newly opened establishments. No consideration is given to changes in size of establishments during the updating time. The sample is renewed every few years. The present data are based on the January 1995 sample.

As regards employee posts of foreign workers: in 1994, the data were based on a census of all employers who reported on foreign workers (excluding paid attendants employed by households and reported by their employers as domestic help workers). As of 1995, data are based on a sample of establishments that was drawn from all establishments which report on foreign workers (form 612). The frame was created for 1995 and is updated by adding new establishments that began to employ foreign workers. A sample of additions is drawn and added regularly to the main sample. Establishments which cease to employ foreign workers are not included in the calculations.

Data processing, editing and consistency checks

Monthly estimates for the current year are revised based on additional or corrected employers' reports which arrive later from the National Insurance Institute.

Adjustments

Seasonal variations: the X-11-ARIMA/2000 Seasonal Adjustment Method developed by Statistics Canada is used. The prior adjustment factors were calculated using the special method developed by the Central Bureau of Statistics for estimating the effects of the changing Jewish festival dates and the trading days in Israel.

Types of estimates

Totals of employee posts;

Average monthly wages per employee post: total monthly wages divided by the number of employee posts in a given month; at current and constant prices. It follows from the definition of employee posts that the average monthly wage per employee post is lower than the average monthly wage per employee.

Average net wages in local authorities: gross monthly wages minus deductions to the NII (including health insurance as of January 1995) and to Income Tax.

Separate estimates are produced, including and excluding workers from Judea and Samaria and the Gaza Area.

Construction of indices

Indices of employee posts and wages are computed monthly.

The index of total wages at constant prices is calculated by dividing the index of total wages at current prices by the consumer price index of the respective month on the base 1994=100. Annual, quarterly, etc. estimates are the average of monthly indices at constant prices.

The index of average wage per employee post at constant prices is calculated by dividing the index of total wages at constant prices by the index of employee posts.

The trend is calculated using the Henderson moving averages method.

Indicators of reliability of the estimates

Not available.

Available series

Employee posts, total wages and average monthly wage per employee post, at current and constant prices;

Seasonally-adjusted series;

Trend and monthly percent change of trend.

History of the statistics

Starting date of the statistical series: 1961.

Major changes and revisions: as of January 1995, the statistics are based on a new sample of establishments. Previous data were based on the 1979 sample which was updated in 1983 and in 1986. During the period April 1995 - beginning of 1997, the reports on wages on form 612 were partial: some amounts, reaching nearly NIS 900 per month, were not included. During 1997, some employers began reporting on the whole amounts.

Prior to 1993, data were classified according to the Standard Industrial Classification of All Economic Activities, 1970.

Documentation and dissemination

Documentation:

Central Bureau of Statistics: *Monthly Bulletin of Statistics* (Jerusalem);

Idem: *Supplement to the Monthly Bulletin of Statistics* (ibid.)

Idem: *Statistical Abstract of Israel* (ibid. Annual);

Detailed methodological information on definitions, sources of data, methods of data collection and processing, and limitations of the data, can be found in the *Statistical Abstract of Israel*, No. 51, 2000.

Dissemination: on the CBS web-site: http://www.cbs.gov.il (shows both data and methodological notes).

Data which do not appear in national publications or on the website can be obtained upon request.

Data supplied to the ILO for dissemination

The following data are supplied to the ILO for publication in the *Yearbook of Labour Statistics*:

Paid employment by economic activity and in manufacturing, by industry group;

Average monthly earnings by economic activity and in manufacturing, by industry group.

The corresponding monthly data are published in the *Bulletin of Labour Statistics*.

Italy

Source of the series

Collective Labour Agreements (Contratti Collettivi di lavoro).

Title of the series

Numeri indici delle retribuzioni contrattuali (Indices of Contractual Earnings).

Organization responsible

Data collection, statistical processing and publication/ dissemination of the statistics:

National Statistical Institute (Instituto Nazionale di Statistica - ISTAT).

Main topics covered

Contractual wages.

Periodicity or frequency of availability of the statistics

Monthly.

Reference period

The end of each month.

Coverage of the statistics

Geographical: the whole country.

Industrial: almost all branches of economic activity, including the Public Service, except fishing (Tabulation category B of ISIC, Rev.3), community, social and personal service activities, domestic services and extra-territorial organizations and bodies (Tabulation categories O-Q of ISIC, Rev.3).

Establishments: all types and sizes of establishments taking part in, or covered by, collective agreements.

Persons: full-time employees, excluding managerial staff in the private sector and apprentices.

Occupations: all occupations represented in collective bargaining agreements are covered.

Concepts and definitions

Employment: refers to employees with a regular full-time contract, excluding apprentices and executives in the private sector. In the credit sector, they may include civil servants, while in public administration, they include contractual and non-contractual managerial staff. Wage earners and salaried employees are identified separately. Employment data are used to determine the structure of the wage index in the base year.

Wage rates: contractual wages are those fixed by collective agreements. They represent, each month, the amounts due to employees under the hypothesis that they are always at work during the hours fixed by the relevant labour agreements. They include general and regular pay items such as basic pay, special compensation payments (Indennità di contingenza), length of service premiums, premium pay for shift work and other regular, monthly payments specified in national agreements and payable to all workers, as well as those paid periodically (e.g. the 13th month payment and other seasonal and regular payments). Excluded are bonuses related to individual performance and individual working conditions, supplementary payment agreed at the company level, occasional and ad-hoc payments, amounts awarded through decentralized bargaining, back pay and retroactive Una tantum payments. However, these special payments are taken into account in the computation of annual contractual earnings (Retribuzione contrattuale annua di competenza).

Contractual wage rates are computed separately for manual and non-manual workers and by occupation.

Hours of work: refer to normal hours of work for full-time work on an annual basis, after deduction of hours paid for but not worked, for public and annual holidays, other time off granted with pay (for reduction of annual hours of work, compensation for work done on public and other holidays, meetings and study leave, etc.).

Statistics of contractual hours of work are not published, but are used in the computation of the index of contractual hourly earnings.

Classifications

Branch of economic activity (industry):

Title of the classification: Classification of Economic Activities ATECO 91.

Number of groups used for coding: not available.

Applied to: all data.

Link to ISIC and level: ATECO corresponds to the EU economic activity classification (NACE, Rev.1) at the four-digit level (only index per capita); the latter is directly linked to ISIC, Rev.3, at the two-digit level.

Occupation: Collective agreements are not classified by occupation, but by employee category (manual workers, non-manual workers, executives). The classification by occupation is done by ISTAT once a year, for the purposes of the ILO October Inquiry, by linking a set of variables and codes contained in collective agreements (employee category, level of qualification, tasks and duties, examples of occupations, etc.) to the ILO descriptions of occupations.

Other classifications: according to bargaining sector.

Data collection

Size and coverage of the administrative system: The wage indices are derived from a large selection of the most relevant collective bargaining agreements on wages negotiated between labour unions and employers' associations. The current series uses 2,300 salary points laid down in 80 collective agreements out of a total of over 300 agreements.

Data collection method: the basic data are derived from official records (laws, regulations) and collective agreements; for the agricultural and construction sectors, they are taken from the relevant provincial labour agreements. The statistical units represent a contractual pay level for a given group of functions, often combined with indications for seniority, age or skill in collective agreements. Their characteristics, as well as the number of employees, are decided at the time of constructing the base and remain fixed until a new base is constructed. A special survey is conducted to determine the structure in the base year with the help of employers' and workers' unions. The survey determines the collective agreements used and their distribution over the workforce groups. Several sources are used to calculate the number of employees by collective agreement and according to ATECO: the national accounts, the labour force survey and the Social Security records.

Each contract is updated when it is renewed. The weights are updated every five years.

Data processing, editing and consistency checks

In each unit which computes indices of contractual earnings, each official is responsible for 6 to 13 agreements (according to the level of difficulty). A code is assigned to each component of the remuneration (basic pay, compensation payments, length of service premium, other premiums, hours of work, public and other holidays, etc.). Three-hundred and eleven codes are used, which are recorded on computer. The results are checked against total of all categories of agreements. The data are processed by computer, using COBOL. ISTAT is working on the updating of the base period

of the indices (December 2000=100) and the data will then be processed with ORACLE and viewed in PL/SQL language.

Adjustments

Seasonal variations: none; the published index does not show any seasonality because the monthly gross rates for each group of qualifications in the collective agreement comprises all pay items, as listed under "Concepts and definitions", divided by 12, each month.

Types of estimates

Wage indices;

Percent variations with respect to the previous period (conjunctural variations) and the corresponding period of the previous year (trends).

Annual absolute figures of wage rates.

Construction of indices

The index of wage rates per worker measures the change in the contractually agreed annual rates. The index of collectively agreed hours of work measures the change in the hours of work that employees have to work during the year (excluding the holiday periods). The index of hourly rates is calculated as the ratio of the two indices. Each month, the gross rates for each group of qualifications in the collective agreement are divided by 12. The indices for each group of qualification (elementary cells) are obtained by dividing the absolute value of the current rates and the average rates by the base period figures (December 1995). More aggregated indices are calculated applying a Laspeyres formula to the elementary indices. The weights are the products of the average number of workers in the base year and the corresponding wage value in the base period.

Indicators of reliability of the estimates

Coverage of the administrative system: all collective labour agreements are represented and the indices encompass some 90% of employees.

Available series

Monthly and hourly contractual wage indices, by economic activity and classification groups;

Rates of change over the preceding reporting period and the corresponding reporting period of the previous year;

Annual absolute figures on the composition of pay and labour cost for certain industries and jobs, as well as for working hours.

History of the statistics

Starting date of the statistical series: 1938.

Major changes and revisions: the weights are updated every five years, so as to take account of economic developments.

Documentation and dissemination

Documentation:

Instituto Centrale di Statistica (ISTAT): *Comunicato Stampa*; press release provided to the media at a press conference held 30 minutes prior to the general release of the data, and subsequently distributed by fax and e-mail and posted on ISTAT Internet website; The data are usually released within one month and no later than one quarter after the end of the reference month, except for the January data which are available two months after the end of the reference month.

Idem: *Bolletino Mensile di Statistica*; contains monthly data for the period since 1992 on the total index and indices of sections and classification groups;

Idem: *Collana d'informazione "Lavoro e retribuzioni"* (Rome, monthly); contains, once a year, an overview of the methodology.

Methodological modifications or revisions are communicated through press releases. Detailed information on the methodological changes implemented is disseminated in *Informazioni-Retribuzioni contrattuali*, copies of which can be obtained from ISTAT.

Dissemination: on ISTAT web-site: http://www.istat.it

Methodological notes are also available on this site.

Data supplied to the ILO for dissemination

The following statistics are supplied to the ILO for publication in the *Yearbook of Labour Statistics*:

Indices of contractual hourly wage rates, for wage earners and salaried employees, by economic activity.

Data on contractual wage rates by occupation are published in *Statistics on occupational wages and hours of work and on food prices - October Inquiry results*.

Luxembourg

Source of the series

Records of the Inspectorate General of Social Security (IGSS).

Title of the series

Home paid employment.

Organization responsible
Data collection: Inspectorate General of Social Security.
Statistical processing and publication/ dissemination of the statistics: Central Statistics and Economic Studies Service (Service central de la Statistique et des Etudes économiques - STATEC).
Main topics covered
Employment.
Periodicity or frequency of availability of the statistics
Monthly.
Reference period
A full month.
Coverage of the statistics
Geographical: the whole country.
Industrial: all branches of economic activity.
Establishments: all establishments employing one person and more.
Persons: all persons covered by the concept of home paid employment (see below).
Occupations: data are not collected by occupation or occupational group.
Concepts and definitions
Employment: home paid employment covers all employees with a contract of employment with a resident institutional entity, whether or not they are resident in the territory of the Grand Duchy, and subject to the general Social Security regime. They include foreign cross-border workers, homeworkers, interim, temporary or seasonal workers who fit the definition, apprentices and career members of the armed forces. Luxembourg citizens working in a neighbouring country and officials of international organizations considered to be extra-territorial are excluded.
Classifications
Branch of economic activity (industry):
Title of the classification: Statistical Classification of Economic Activities in the European Community. NACE, Rev. 1.
Number of groups used for coding: publication to 2-digit level, subject to statistical secrecy.
Applied to: home paid employment.
Link to ISIC and level: compatibility between NACE, Rev.1 and ISIC, Rev.3 (1990) at section level (two-digit).
Status in employment: within the concept of home employment, a distinction is made between paid employment (the subject of this series) and non-wage employment (self-employed workers).
Other classifications: by sex.
Data collection
Size and coverage of the administrative system: the administrative records of the social security system cover all employees, in all establishments employing at least one employee.
Data collection method: as regards workers and employees in the private sector, the IGSS and the Social Security Information Technology Centre use the integrated files of the social security agencies (health and pension funds). As regards civil servants and the like (officials of the State, municipalities, railways), the responsible authorities process the files electronically.
The IGSS is responsible for checking the data and every month transmits the global data to STATEC, and annually by branch of activity. STATEC makes the necessary statistical adjustments (see below) and is responsible for disseminating the data.
Data processing, editing and consistency checks
The data are processed manually and electronically.
Adjustments
STATEC makes the following adjustments:
(a) at global level, taking account of volunteers in the army (not included in social security records); (b) at branch level, adjustment of employment figures for large enterprises operating in several branches of activity, as social security records are based on the employer and not the economic activity.
Part-time workers and persons with more than one job each count as one person under the European System of Integrated Economic Accounts (ESA-95).
Types of estimates
Monthly totals and yearly averages.
Construction of indices
None.
Indicators of reliability of the estimates
Coverage of the administrative system: considered to be exhaustive for employees covered by the above definition.
Conformity with other sources: the employment estimates taken from the IGSS records are compared with the results of the labour force sample survey, STATEC surveys of enterprises and administrative data supplied by certain sectors such as the

Luxembourg Metal Industries Group, the Luxembourg Monetary Institute, the Association of Luxembourg Insurance Companies, etc.
Available series
Paid employment, monthly and annual average, by branch of economic activity and sex.
History of the statistics
Starting date of the statistical series: 1970.
Major changes and revisions: there was a break in 1983, when the social security records for manual workers and employees were merged and checked for double counting. STATEC re-estimated total paid employment for years prior to 1983.
Documentation and dissemination
Documentation:
STATEC: *Note trimestrielle de Conjoncture, la Situation économique au Grand-Duché* (Luxembourg);
Idem: *Annuaire Statistique du Luxembourg* (ibid.); published about five months after the statistical reference year. Also contains methodological notes.
Dissemination: on Internet: http://www.statec.lu
Data supplied to the ILO for dissemination
The following statistics are published in the ILO *Yearbook of Labour Statistics:*
Estimates of total employment by economic activity, partly based on this administrative source.
Paid employment by economic activity.
Other administrative sources of data: Since April 1988, the administrative records of the social security system have been the main source of data for the harmonized statistics on earnings, in conjunction with a half-yearly survey of enterprises. Methodological information on the use of this source for the purposes of the *Harmonized Statistics on Average Gross Earnings* (October) are available in:
ILO: *Sources and Methods - Labour Statistics*, Volume 2,: Employment, wages, hours of work and labour cost (establishments surveys) (second edition, Geneva, 1995).

Mexico

Source of the series
Mexican Institute of Social Security (IMSS), Monthly report on the eligible population.
Title of the series
Permanent and temporary insured workers registered with the IMSS; average contributory wage of the permanent and temporary urban contributing population.
Organization responsible
Data collection and statistical processing: Mexican Institute of Social Security (IMSS).
Publication/ dissemination of the statistics: National Institute of Statistics, Geography and Information Technology (INEGI) and Secretariat of Labour and Social Security.
Main topics covered
Employment and wages.
Periodicity or frequency of availability of the statistics
Monthly.
Reference period
The month.
Coverage of the statistics
Geographical: the whole country.
Industrial: all branches of economic activity.
Establishments: all types and sizes in the private and public sectors.
Persons: permanent and temporary urban employees registered with the IMSS. Groups for whom insurance is optional, students, voluntary continuation and family health insurance are excluded.
Occupations: data are not collected for individual occupations.
Concepts and definitions
Employment: covers insured persons who are permanent and temporary urban employees. Permanent insured persons are those who work in a factory, commercial undertaking or any type of company. They are entitled to insurance because they are workers (employees) of the establishment. Urban insured are persons who work in businesses or enterprises established in an urban context whose economic activity may be comprised in the following groups: farming, industrial, commercial or services.
Temporary urban insured are mainly persons working in the construction industry and other industries and not in establishments. Temporary or rural workers are persons who work seasonally in agricultural.
The series published by the ILO only cover permanent workers.

Earnings: they refer to average wages of the permanent contributing population. The basic contributory wage consists of actual payment in cash of daily wages, gratuities, allowances, food, housing, bonuses, commissions, benefits in kind and any other amount of benefit provided to the worker in return for his/her services.

Daily wages that are lower than the general minimum wage of the relevant region or higher than the equivalent of 25 times the general minimum wage of the Federal District are not taken into consideration.

Hours of work: not collected.

Classifications

Branch of economic activity (industry):

Title of the classification: List of Activities for the Classification of Enterprises in Occupational Risks Insurance.

Number of groups used for coding: nine main divisions, 55 groups and 276 categories of economic activity.

Applied to: all data.

Link to ISIC and level: Rev.2, 1968.

Occupation: permanent and temporary urban workers.

Other classifications: by sector of economic activity, geographical area (urban and rural) and federal entity.

Data collection

Data collection method: the information is obtained from data files based on IMSS documents, such as membership applications and employers' and employees' pay documents provided by IMSS collection agencies.

The numbers of insured persons are compiled from membership applications, adding old members and re-entrants, and subtracting leavers, from the monthly balance of the file called "Insured persons master file".

Updating of the administrative system: monthly.

Data processing, editing and consistency checks

Not available.

Adjustments

Not available.

Types of estimates

Totals of insured workers by category, total and average remuneration.

Construction of indices

None.

Indicators of reliability of the estimates

Coverage of the administrative system: the employment series covers the total population of workers registered with the IMSS.

The average contributory wage is that reported by employers to determine health and maternity insurance contributions.

Available series

Monthly series of:

Insured workers by category (permanent, urban and rural) and annual rates of change;

Insured workers in the construction industry by category and annual rates of change.

Permanent insured workers by branch of economic activity and region.

History of the statistics

Starting date of the statistical series: January 1977.

Major changes and revisions: not available.

Documentation and dissemination

Documentation:

INEGI: Mexican Bulletin of Statistical Information (Mexico, quarterly); the data are published two months after the month to which they refer.

Dissemination: on the Website of the Secretariat of Labour and Social Security (Secretaria del Trabajo y Previsión Social): http://www.stps.gob.mx and the INEGI Website: http://www.inegi.gob.mx

Data supplied to the ILO for dissemination

The following series are published in the *Yearbook of Labour Statistics*.

- paid employment by economic activity;
- employees' average daily earnings by economic activity.

Netherlands

Source of the series

Collective Agreements and other wage laws and regulations.

Title of the series

Index Numbers of Wage Rates (Indexcijfers van cao-lonen).

Organization responsible

Data collection, statistical processing and publication/dissemination of the statistics:

Statistics Netherlands (Centraal Bureau voor Statistiek, CBS).

Main topics covered

Indices of contractual wages, working hours and labour costs.

Periodicity or frequency of availability of the statistics

Monthly and yearly.

Reference period

The last day of each month.

Coverage of the statistics

Geographical: the whole country.

Industrial: all branches of economic activity, except private households with employed persons (SBI95) and extra-territorial organizations and bodies (SBI99).

Establishments: all types and sizes of establishments taking part in collective agreements.

Persons: full-time employees.

Occupations: all occupations are covered.

Concepts and definitions

Employment: refers to full-time employees, i.e. persons working for a wage or a salary. Adults and youths are identified separately.

Wage rates: refer to gross wage rates for hours normally worked, before any deductions are made for taxes, social security contributions, pension schemes, etc. They include: wages for normal working hours; all fixed, guaranteed and regular additional payments; and all fixed special payments (not regularly paid), e.g. holiday allowances or end-of-year bonuses. Excluded are additional payments that are conditionally agreed in the collective labour agreement, such as supplements for age or shift work.

Hours of work: refer to the normal annual working hours per year for adult full-time employees as laid down in the collective labour agreement, i.e. the maximum number of working hours, excluding overtime, minus guaranteed paid public holidays (fixed at six days per year), annual leave and reduction of working hours as fixed by or in pursuance of laws, regulations or collective agreement. Conditional reduction of working hours due to age or shift work is not taken into account.

Labour cost rates: include the wages and special payments as agreed in the collective labour agreement, as well as compulsory employer's contributions to social insurance.

Classifications

Branch of economic activity (industry):

Title of the classification: Standard Industrial Classification (SIC, SBI in Dutch, 1993).

Number of groups used for coding: four sectors, 16 branches and a couple of classes.

Applied to: all data.

Link to ISIC and level: based on the EU economic activity classification (NACE, Rev.1) at the four-digit level, which is directly linked to ISIC, Rev.3, at the two-digit level.

Other classifications: collective labour agreement sectors: i.e. a classification of enterprises in the private sector, the government sector and the subsidized sector; and employee category (youths and adults).

Data collection

Size and coverage of the administrative system: covers all collective agreements (at present, over 900 agreements).

Data collection method: the data are extracted from the records of collective agreements and other collective wage regulations. The statistical units are formed by a large number of well-defined points in collective labour agreements. These points represent a contractual pay level for a certain function group, often combined with indications for seniority, age or skill. A special establishment survey is conducted to determine the structure in the base year. It determines the collective agreements used and their distribution over the workforce groups. From this information estimates are made for every relevant collective agreement showing the distribution of workers for the salary structure and points of highest density are selected to develop a partial wage index. The current series uses 8100 salary points laid down in 354 collective agreements, out of a total of over 900 agreements. The current base year is 1990 and in principle, the sample of pay levels is revised every ten years.

Data processing, editing and consistency checks

Data which have been published in collective agreements are entered into a computerized system. For each collective agreement the evolution from the previous period is calculated. Figures which are out of range (much higher or lower than average) are checked again. Results are also compared with all other available information, for instance data published in newspapers.

Adjustments

Under-coverage: monthly indices of contractual wages, labour costs and working hours are subject to change if new collective labour agreements or collective wage regulations come into effect. An adjusted index is published one month at the latest after a new collective labour agreement has become effective. Final figures for year *t* are published not later than in May of the year *t+1*.

Seasonal variations: the data are not seasonally adjusted.

Types of estimates

Monthly and hourly indices of contractual wage rates, working hours and hourly labour costs.

Construction of indices

The 8100 salary points are allocated a base weight in the base year (1990). These base weights are allocated on the basis of their mutual importance within a collective agreement or regulation. They are held constant through the years until the sample is updated.

A second kind of weighting involves the yearly weighting of the industries, made up of collective agreements and regulations. This "external weighting", based on data originating from the System of National Accounts, takes account of the changes in the number of employees and wage bills per industry every year.

The partial indices computed at the level of the statistical units are weighted together to obtain Laspeyres wage indices for aggregates of economic activity. The present series are based on 1990=100.

Indicators of reliability of the estimates

Coverage of the administrative system: the selection of collective labour agreements covers about 350 of them (40% of total), covering about 75% of all employees in 1990).

Available series

– Monthly and hourly contractual wage rate indices including bonuses;
– Monthly indices of contractual working hours;
– Monthly indices of hourly labour costs;
– by employee category, sector and branch of economic activity.

History of the statistics

Starting date of the statistical series: the publication of these statistics started in 1926; the series of gross monthly and hourly wage rate indices, and the indices of contractual annual working hours, have been published monthly since 1980. Publication of some figures regarding hourly labour costs started in 1990.

Major changes and revisions: the series of wage rate indices has been revised and improved upon regularly. There have been no methodological changes in the current time series.

A complete revision of these statistics is planned for 2003.

Documentation and dissemination

Documentation:

Statistics Netherlands: *Statistisch Bulletin* (Voorburg, weekly); the last issue of each month shows provisional wage rate and labour cost indices for the previous month. Final data are published no later than five months after the end of the reference year.

Idem: *Sociaal-economische Maandstatistiek* (Voorburg/Heerlen, monthly). Major changes in methodology are announced in advance in this publication.

A methodological description is also published in *Supplement to the Monthly Bulletin of Socio-economic Statistics*, 1993-3 4.

Dissemination: on CBS web-site: http://www.cbs.nl
Methodological notes are also available on this site.

Data supplied to the ILO for dissemination

The following statistics are supplied to the ILO for publication in the *Yearbook of Labour Statistic:*

Indices of hourly wage rates by economic activity.

The corresponding monthly series are published in the *Bulletin of Labour Statistics*.

Other administrative sources of data: a large number of administrative registers (population register, administration of employee insurance schemes, employment agency files, address and housing registers, etc.) are used in combination with business and household sample surveys, with a view to producing Statistics Netherlands' integrated statistical information system on socio-demographic, socio-economic and socio-cultural characteristics of the population.

New Caledonia

Source of the series

Records of the Compensation Fund for Family Allowances, Occupational Accidents and Pensions for Workers in New Caledonia and Dependencies (Caisse de Compensation des Prestations Familiales, des Accidents du Travail et Prévoyance des Travailleurs - CAFAT).

Title of the series

Employment and wages in New Caledonia.

Organization responsible

Data collection: Compensation Fund for Family Allowances, Occupational Accidents and Pensions for Workers in New Caledonia and Dependencies (CAFAT) and Fiscal Services Department (Direction des Services Fiscaux - DSF).

Statistical processing and publication/ dissemination of the statistics: Institute of Statistics and Economic Studies (Institut de la Statistique et des Etudes Economiques - ISEE), New Caledonia.

Main topics covered

Paid employment, wages and duration of employment.

Periodicity or frequency of availability of the statistics

Paid employment: quarterly;
Wages: annual;
Duration of employment: annual.

Reference period

Wage employees: the quarter;
Wages and duration of employment: the year.

Coverage of the statistics

Geographical: the whole territory.

Industrial: all branches of economic activity, including domestic services.

Establishments: all types and sizes of establishment.

Persons: all employees, and all employers, registered with CAFAT.

Occupations: in wages statistics, data are collected by socio-professional category.

Concepts and definitions

Employment: paid employment refers to all employees in New Caledonia apart from apprentices and trainees.

In the statistics on wages, the annual number of employees, or number of jobs, includes employees who have worked for more than one employer during the year. They are counted as many times as the number of jobs. The average annual number of employees, or permanent full-time equivalent, is the theoretical number of full-time employees throughout the year.

Earnings: means the total gross annual payroll, i.e. all net wages, including emoluments, paid holidays, benefits in kind or in cash and bonuses, increased by employees' social contributions from wages. The average monthly wage corresponds to the payroll for the year for one full-time employee for one month.

Hours of work: corresponds to an employee's duration of employment (in months) during a year.

Classifications

Branch of economic activity (industry):

Title of the classification: ISEE nomenclature of activities (Nomenclature d'Activité ISEE).

Number of groups used for coding: 39 groups, after change from CAFAT nomenclature of activities to the ISEE nomenclature of sectors and activities.

Applied to: all data.

Link to ISIC and level: none.

Occupation: in the statistics on wages, two classifications are used:

Title of the classification: ISEE nomenclature of vocational qualifications (Nomenclature de Qualification Professionnelle ISEE).

Number of groups used for coding: 10 groups, after change from CAFAT nomenclature of socio-professional categories to the ISEE nomenclature of vocational qualifications.

Applied to: all data.

Link to ISCO and level: none.

Status in employment:

Title of the classification: Nomenclature of socio-professional categories and qualification in the civil service (Nomenclature des Catégories Socio-Professionnelles et des Qualifications dans la fonction publique).

Number of groups used for coding: 80 at the most detailed level.

Applied to: all data.

Link to ICSE and level: none.

Other classifications: quarterly paid employment; region (Nouméa, Interior and Combined Islands) and province.

Statistics on wages: sex, age, duration of employment, sector of activity, geographical area, size of establishment and cross-classifications.

Data collection

Size and coverage of the administrative system: exhaustive collection from employers.

Data collection method: two main sources are used. The file of nominal declarations supplied quarterly by employers to CAFAT, which contains information on employment, duration of employment and wages in the private sector; and the file of nominal declarations of wages of the Fiscal Services Department, which contains, among others, the number and wages of civil servants.

For the statistics on wages, ISEE adjusts the files to construct a standard file for all wages. The wages data in the CAFAT file are gross values, in some cases truncated due to ceilings, while the DSF files are not capped, but are net wage values. The wages in CAFAT files below the ceiling are extracted without adjustments, and those which are capped are recalculated. The first step involves comparing these wages with wages in the DSF file, using an identifier made up of sex, date of birth and employer for each employee concerned. The second step is a calculation to determine the gross wages from the DSF files, by calculating the social charges for each wage. Since the employer is known, the values for social security contributions are either taken directly from the files of the various social security agencies mentioned above, or calculated by applying rules which define them (exceptional solidarity contribution) or are estimated (supplementary pensions). The global values for social security contributions determined in this way are then compared, for validation purposes, with figures published in company reports, profit and loss accounts and other administrative documents of the organizations concerned (various mutual organizations, Expatriate Pension Fund (CRE).

Updating of the administrative system: quarterly.

Data processing, editing and consistency checks

The data are processed electronically.

For the statistics on wages, the assistance of the Administrative and Information Technology Methods Service (SMAI) was obtained to enhance the job classifications of public sector workers in 1995, and this served as a base for 1999. Consistency checks are carried out on wages and length of employment from different files.

Double counting: the non nominal CAFAT and DSF files held by ISEE do not allow a determination of how many employees there are for different wage levels (the same employee may have worked for different employers during the year, successively or simultaneously). While the 1996 Population Census of New Caledonia counted 53,944 employees, the CAFAT and DSF files gave 79,893. In order to minimize errors in duration of employment and to gain a better appreciation of wage levels, statistics are also prepared on the basis of employees paid by the same employer for the 12 months of the year (not including domestic services).

Adjustments

Not available.

Types of estimates

Statistics on paid employment: number of employees registered each quarter, and separately, number of employers registered.

Statistics on wages:

Duration of employment (in months) of an employee: number of hours of employment divided by 169, the legal working time of a full-time month;

Average duration of employment (in months): total duration of employment of all employees in the year, divided by the number of jobs. The sum of duration of employment of all employees is equal to the product of the annual number of employees divided by the average duration of employment, or the product of the annual average number of employees divided by 12.

Average annual employees or full-time equivalent: sum of duration of employment (in months) of all employees in the year divided by 12.

Average monthly wage: total payroll divided by the annual average number of employees, divided by 12.

Distribution and breakdown of jobs, wages and duration of employment according to different variables.

Construction of indices

None.

Indicators of reliability of the estimates

Coverage of the administrative system: over 99% of employees.

Non-sampling errors: in the statistics on wages, errors can occur in the duration of employment of employees. The DSF file does not always give the duration of employment. Neither of the CAFAT nor the DSF files provide full information on hours of work (number of hours, part-time, half-time, full time). The monthly wage is therefore estimated by dividing the wage by the number of employment months. This estimate has the disadvantage of under-estimating the actual level of part-time employees' monthly wages. The duration of employment of employees declared to the DSF is sometimes prone to errors. To reduce as far as possible the error in estimating the duration of employment and thus make the value for the monthly wage more reliable, a scrupulous comparison of the different files for 1999 was undertaken, and rectifications were made to duration of employment in 8,685 cases.

Conformity with other sources: comparisons of numbers of employees were made with the results of the New Caledonia population census of 16 April 1996.

Available series

Quarterly statistics of paid employment: number of employees and number of employers by branch of economic activity and region;

Statistics on wages:

Number of jobs by geographical area, sector of activity and activity, wage level and age, and cross-classifications;

Wages by sector of activity and activity, age, sex and age, geographical area and cross-classifications;

Distribution of jobs by duration of employment, wage level, professional qualification.

History of the statistics

Starting date of the statistical series: not available.

Major changes and revisions: not available.

Documentation and dissemination

Documentation:

ISEE: *Informations statistiques* (Nouméa, quarterly); presents statistics on paid employment for the previous quarter;

Idem: *ISEE: Les Salaires - Situation en 1999* (Nouméa, October 2001); contains statistics and methodological information.

Data supplied to the ILO for dissemination

Statistics on paid employment (all economic activities) are published in the *Yearbook of Labour Statistics*. The corresponding quarterly statistics (separately for employees and for all persons engaged) are published in the *Bulletin of Labour Statistics*.

Norway (1)

Source of the series

Norwegian Association of Local and Regional Authorities.

Title of the series

Personal Administrativt Informasjonssystem (PAI) (Staff Administration Information System).

Organization responsible

Data collection: Norwegian Association of Local and Regional Authorities.

Statistical processing and publication/ dissemination of the statistics: Norwegian Association of Local and Regional Authorities and Statistics Norway.

Main topics covered

Employment, earnings, wage rates and hours of work.

Periodicity or frequency of availability of the statistics

Yearly.

Reference period

Employment and wage rates: 1st October

Earnings and hours of work: the pay period which includes 1st October.

Coverage of the statistics

Geographical: the whole country, excluding the municipality of Oslo.

Industrial: public (municipal and county municipal) administration and municipal and county municipal enterprises, including social and health services. Excluded are employees in teaching occupations (see NORWAY (2)), but other staff in municipal education activity are included.

Establishments: all types and sizes in the public sectors covered.

Persons: employees in municipal and county municipal administration, as defined above.

Occupations: data are collected according to the following occupational groups:

- administrative employees;
- technical employees;
- manual workers;
- employees attending to clients at hospitals, etc.
- employees in other service occupations.

Concepts and definitions

Employment: refers to all employees in municipal and county municipal administration and those in municipal and county-owned enterprises that are members of the Norwegian Association of Local and Regional Authorities and follow the Association's collective agreements as of the 1st October of the reference year. Excluded are employees in the municipality of Oslo.

Employees with a minimum of 33 hours worked per week are considered as full-time employees; those with fewer hours are considered to be part-time employees.

Earnings: gross monthly earnings refer to total cash salaries according to salary scales as of 1st October of the census year, plus fixed and variable allowances. They exclude the value of payments in kind and any overtime payments.

Wage rates: refer to basic wage and salary rates actually paid per month, excluding guaranteed and regularly paid allowances and payments in kind.

Hours of work: normal hours of work which are fixed in collective agreements, laws and regulations.

Classifications

Branch of economic activity (industry):

Title of the classification: Standard Industrial Classification (SIC94), Division 75 (public municipal and county municipal administration).

Number of groups used for coding: not applied.

Applied to: all data.

Link to ISIC: none.

Occupation:

Title of the classification: the classification is in accordance with the classification used by the Norwegian Association of Local and Regional Authorities, as designed to serve collective agreements and reflect salary scales.

Number of groups used for coding: 5.

Applied to: all data.

Link to ISCO: it is not necessarily in accordance with the Standard Classification of Occupations (C521) nor with ISCO.

Other classifications: employment, earnings, wage rates and hours of work: by sex and employee category, such as full-time/part-time and adults/youths.

The statistics are also classified by education level. Information about the education of individuals is obtained from Statistics Norway's register on the Population's Highest Level of Education (BHU). Education is classified according to length of education as follows: lower secondary education; upper secondary education; third level education (4 years or less); third level education (more than 4 years); unknown or not completed education.

There is a one-year time lag in education data.

Data collection

Size and coverage of the administrative system: in 2000 the register included 347 544 employees in municipal and county municipal administration (excluding Oslo).

Data collection method: the Norwegian Association of Local and Regional Authorities receives individual records from municipalities and county municipalities in electronic form (diskettes) or on paper and sends the information in electronic form to Statistics Norway, in accordance with the Statistics Act, Section 3-2.

Updating of the administrative system: the Central Register is updated once a year by the Norwegian Association of Local and Regional Authorities.

Data processing, editing and consistency checks

Data are processed both manually and by computer.

Adjustments

None.

Types of estimates

Totals and averages.

Construction of indices

None.

Indicators of reliability of the estimates

Coverage of the administrative system: exhaustive, based on an annual census of all employees in administrations and enterprises that are members of the Norwegian Association of Local and Regional Authorities, except employees in the municipality of Oslo, as of 1 October of each year.

Non-sampling errors: incorrect reporting by the respondents to the Norwegian Association of Local and Regional Authorities and/or processing errors by both the Association and Statistics Norway are possible. In addition, the register of the Population's Highest Education may contain errors in coding of level of education.

Conformity with other sources: these statistics are comparable with other wages statistics since 1997.

Available series

Total employment and average monthly earnings, wage rates and weekly hours of work.

History of the statistics

Starting date of the statistical series: 1958.

Major changes and revisions: Since 1990 employees in the health and social services are included in the statistics.

Since 1993, the statistics exclude employees in the municipality of Oslo.

Since 1997, enterprises in electricity supply are excluded, despite their membership in the Norwegian Association of Local and Regional Authorities. They are included in the statistics for employees in electricity supply (http://www.ssb.no/lonnkraft_en)

The statistics are comparable back to 1997.

Documentation and dissemination

Documentation:

Statistics Norway: *NOS Wage Statistics* (Oslo, annual); also contains methodological information;

Idem: *Statistical Yearbook* (ibid., annual), issued within 6 months after the statistics reference year.

Statistics Norway has published statistics for the years 1958, 1959, 1960 and for about every other year from 1962 to 1976, then annually from 1978 onwards.

Dissemination: through Statistics Norway's website:

Wage statistics. Municipal and county municipal employees: http://www.ssb.no/lonnkomm_en/ (Norwegian and English)

Subject group: 06.05. Wages and labour costs;

http://www.ssb.no/english/subjects/06/05

Data which do not appear in national publications or on the website can be made available upon request.

Wages statistics for employees in Section L of the Standard Industrial Classification, central government employees, are released on: http://www.ssb.no/lonnstat_en (Available in Norwegian and English).

Data supplied to the ILO for dissemination

The following statistics are published in the ILO *Statistics on occupational wages and hours of work and on food prices – October Inquiry results,* and disseminated through the LABORSTA database:

Normal hours of work and average monthly earnings for the following occupations:

- No. 139 - Government executive official b) local authority
- No. 151 - Kindergarten teacher
- No. 154 - Professional nurse (general)
- No. 155 - Auxiliary nurse.

Other administrative sources of data: see description No. 3 for Norway.

Norway (2)

Source of the series

Sentralt Tjenestemannsregister for Skoleverket (STS) (Central Register of Government Employees in the School System).

Title of the series

Statistics of employment and wages in the school system (publicly-maintained schools).

Organization responsible

Data collection, statistical processing and publication/ dissemination of the statistics: since 2002: Statistics Norway; prior to 2002: Ministry of Labour and Government Administration (AAD).

Main topics covered

Employment, earnings, wage rates and hours of work.

Periodicity or frequency of availability of the statistics

Yearly.

Reference period

Employment and wage rates: 1st October of each year;

Earnings and hours of work: the pay period which includes 1st October.

Coverage of the statistics

Geographical: the whole country.

Industrial: publicly-maintained schools, i.e. all municipal and central government primary schools, county municipal and central government upper secondary schools (including Labour Market Training), central government centers for special education expertise and folk high schools (boarding schools for upper-secondary and college level students), both county municipal and private.

Establishments: all types and sizes as described under "Industrial coverage".

Persons: all employees in teaching occupations.

Occupations: for each type of schools (see under Classifications), the following occupations are identified:

- Head masters
- Educational school principals
- School principals
- Lecturers (in secondary and higher level schools)
- Teachers with university degree with advancement
- Teachers with university degree
- Teachers

- Teachers without required training (in primary and lower secondary schools)
- Other occupations.

Concepts and definitions

Employment: refers to all employees in teaching occupations in the institutions described under "Industrial coverage", who at 1st October of the reference year were employed in accordance with agreements made between the central government and the civil servants' organisations, regardless of the type of contract (permanent positions, positions subject to dismissal, temporary and fixed-term positions).

Employees in private education (Section M of the Standard Industrial Classification) are not included in the statistics, but covered by a separate statistical series (Lonnprivund).

Employees with a minimum of 33 hours worked per week are considered as full-time employees; those with fewer hours are considered to be part-time employees.

Earnings: gross monthly earnings refer to total cash salaries according to salary scales as of 1st October of the census year, plus additional fixed and variable allowances and stand-by payments earned in September and paid in October. They exclude the value of payments in kind and any overtime payments.

Wage rates: refer to wage and salary rates actually paid per month, excluding guaranteed and regularly paid allowances and payments in kind.

Hours of work: normal hours of work which are fixed in collective agreements, laws and regulations.

Classifications

Branch of economic activity (industry):

Title of the classification: Standard Industrial Classification (SIC94), Section M: publicly-maintained schools.

Number of groups used for coding: seven: primary schools; combined primary and lower secondary schools; lower secondary schools; schools for handicapped children (primary schools); upper secondary schools; folk high schools; and other type of schools.

Applied to: all data.

Link to ISIC: none.

Occupation:

Title of the classification: the classification is in accordance with the central government salary scales as at 1st October of each year. It is not necessarily in accordance with the Standard Classification of Occupations (C521).

Number of groups used for coding: see the above list of occupations.

Applied to: all data.

Link to ISCO: none.

Other classifications: employment, earnings, wage rates and hours of work: by sex and employee category, such as full-time/part-time and adults/youths.

The statistics are also classified by education level. Information about the education of individuals is obtained from Statistics Norway's register on the Population's Highest Level of Education (BHU). Education is classified according to length of education as follows: lower secondary education; upper secondary education; third level education (4 years or less); third level education (more than 4 years); unknown or not completed education.

There is a one-year time lag in education data.

Data collection

Size and coverage of the administrative system: In 2001 the register included 99 074 employees in publicly-maintained schools.

Data collection method: The Ministry of Labour and Government Administration (AAD) receives individual records from schools in electronic form (diskettes) or on paper and sends the information in electronic form to Statistics Norway, in accordance with the Statistics Act, Section 3-2.

Updating of the administrative system: The Central Register of Government Employees in the School System (STS) is updated once a year by the Ministry of Labour and Government Administration.

Data processing, editing and consistency checks

Data are processed both manually and by computer. Wage data are checked manually and by computer at both the AAD and Statistics Norway.

Adjustments

None.

Types of estimates

Totals and averages.

Construction of indices

None.

Indicators of reliability of the estimates

Coverage of the administrative system: exhaustive, based on an annual census of all employees in the relevant groups as of 1st October of each year.

Non-sampling errors: incorrect reporting by the respondents to the AAD and/or processing errors by both the AAD and Statistics Norway are possible. In addition, the register of the Population's Highest Education may contain errors in coding of level of education.

Conformity with other sources: these statistics are comparable with other wages statistics since 1997.

Available series

Total employment and average monthly earnings, wage rates and weekly hours of work.

History of the statistics

Starting date of the statistical series: 1973.

Major changes and revisions: none. The statistics are comparable back to 1973.

Documentation and dissemination

Documentation:

Statistics Norway: *NOS Wage Statistics* (Oslo, annual); also contains methodological information;

Idem: *Statistical Yearbook* (ibid., annual), issued within 6 months after the statistics reference year.

The statistics were published by Statistics Norway for 1959, 1963, 1967 and annually since 1973.

Dissemination: on Statistics Norway's website:

http://www.ssb.no/lonnkomm_en/

(Available in English and Norwegian).

Data which do not appear in national publications or on the website can be made available upon request.

Wages statistics for employees in private education (based on a sample of enterprises) are released on:

http://www.ssb.no/lonnprivund_en.

Data supplied to the ILO for dissemination

The following statistics are published in *Statistics on occupational wages and hours of work and on food prices – October Inquiry results,* and disseminated through the LABORSTA database.

Average monthly earnings for the following occupations:

- No.147 - Teacher in language and literature (second level)
- No.148 - Mathematical teacher (second level)
- No.150 - First level education teacher.

Data for occupation No.151 - *Kindergarten teacher,* is derived from the Norwegian Association of Local and Regional Authorities, and for occupation No. 149 - *Technical education teacher (second level),* from the State Central Register of Government employees (universities and equivalent institutions).

Other administrative sources of data: see description No. 3 for Norway.

Norway (3)

Source of the series

Statens Sentrale Tjenestemannsregister (SST) (State Central Register of Government Employees).

Title of the series

Statistics on employment and wages of Government employees.

Organization responsible

Data collection, statistical processing and publication/dissemination of the statistics: since 2002: Statistics Norway; prior to 2002: Ministry of Labour and Government Administration (AAD).

Main topics covered

Employment, earnings, wage rates and hours of work.

Periodicity or frequency of availability of the statistics

Yearly.

Reference period

Employment and wage rates: 1st October

Earnings and hours of work: the pay period which includes 1st October.

Coverage of the statistics

Geographical: the whole country.

Industrial: central government public administration and defence, government enterprises, health services as well as universities and equivalent institutions.

Establishments: all types and sizes in the public sectors covered.

Persons: government employees.

Occupations: the occupational groups are fixed in accordance with the central government salary plans:

Published occupations, Central government

Ministries: Deputy directors general; Assistant directors general; Head of divisions; Advisors; Senior executive officers; Executive officers; Junior executive officers; Office secretaries.

Other central administration departments: Deputy director general; Assistant directors general; Head of divisions; Advisors; Head engineers; Senior executive officers; Executive officers; Junior executive officers; Office secretaries; Senior clerks.

Universities and equivalent institutions: Professors; Assistant professors, first grade; Assistant professors; Research officers; Teachers with final university degree; Scholarship holders; Other teaching occupations; Administrative occupations; Executive officers; Office staff.

Health services: Chief physicians; Ward physicians; Bioengineers; Executive officers; Office staff; Specialized nurses; Professional nurses; Assistant nurses.

Other civil services: The clergy; Deans; Vicars; Curates; Catechists.

The judiciary: Presiding judge; City court judges, county court judges, circuit judges; Registrars; Executive officers; Office staff.

Prison administration: Security services; Prison officers; Executive officers; Office staff.

Police force and rural police service: District police superintendents; Assistant commissioners; Inspectors; Sergeants; Sergeants; District police superintendents, special grade; Assistant district policemen; Executive officers; Office staff.

Labour market administration: Head of employment offices; Executive officers; Office staff.

Social insurance administration: Head of insurance divisions; Executive officers; Office staff.

General commissions of taxes, population registers: Tax officers; Secretaries; Executive officers.

Customs service, local administration: Inspectors of customs; Examining customs officers, lower grade; Executive officers; Office staff.

Government enterprises: Road administration; Engineers; Executive officers; Clerks; Inspectors; Foremen; Skilled workers; Specialized workers.

Civil aviation administration: Air traffic control officers; Airport officers; Air traffic control assistants; Engineers.

Defence: Civil personnel; Military personnel.

Concepts and definitions

Employment: refers to all central government employees employed in government occupations at 1st October of the census year.

Employees with a minimum of 33 hours worked per week are considered as full-time employees; those with fewer hours are considered as part-time employees.

Earnings: total gross monthly earnings refer to total cash salaries according to salary scales as of 1st October of the census year, plus fixed and variable allowances earned in September and paid out in October. They exclude the value of payments in kind and any overtime payments.

Wage rates: refer to wage and salary rates actually paid per month, excluding guaranteed and regular paid allowances and payments in kind.

Hours of work: normal hours of work which are fixed in collective agreements, laws and regulations.

Classifications

Branch of economic activity (industry):

Title of the classification: Standard Industrial Classification (SIC94).

Number of groups used for coding: seven: ministries (incl. Office of the Prime Minister and Office of the general auditor); other central administration departments; other civil services; universities and equivalent institutions; government enterprises; defence; and health services.

Applied to: all data.

Link to ISIC: none.

Updating of the administrative system: the Central Register is updated once a year.

Data processing, editing and consistency checks

Data are processed both manually and by computer. Wage data are checked manually and by computer at both the AAD and Statistics Norway.

Adjustments

None.

Types of estimates

Totals and averages.

Construction of indices

None.

Indicators of reliability of the estimates

Coverage of the administrative system: exhaustive, based on an annual census of all employees in the public sectors covered as of 1st October of each year.

Link to ISIC and level: Rev.2, at the two- and three-digit levels.

Occupation:

Title of the classification: Pakistan Standard Classification of Occupations (PSCO-68).

Number of groups used for coding: 76.

Applied to: wage rates and earnings.

Link to ISCO and level: ISCO-1968, at the two- and three-digit levels.

Other classifications: by sex, level of education and employee category.

Data collection

Size and coverage of the administrative system: These administrative reports are restricted to the collection of statistical information on the pre-selected occupations within the pre-selected industry groups.

Non-sampling errors: incorrect reporting by the respondents to the AAD and/or processing errors by both the AAD and Statistics Norway are possible. In addition, the register of the Population's Highest Education may contain errors in coding of level of education.

Conformity with other sources: these statistics are comparable with other wages statistics since 1997.

Available series

Total employment and average monthly earnings, wage rates and weekly hours of work.

History of the statistics

Starting date of the statistical series: 1973.

Major changes and revisions: none. These statistics are comparable back to 1973.

Documentation and dissemination

Documentation:

Statistics Norway: *NOS Wage Statistics* (Oslo, annual); contains methodological information;

Idem: *Statistical Yearbook* (ibid., annual), issued within 6 months after the reference year.

Statistics Norway has published statistics for the years 1959, 1963 and 1967, then annually since 1973.

Dissemination: on Statistics Norway's website:

http://www.ssb.no/lonnkomm_en/ and http://www.ssb.no/lonnstat

Data which do not appear in national publications or on the website can be made available upon request.

Data supplied to the ILO for dissemination

The following statistics are published in *Statistics on occupational wages and hours of work and on food prices – October Inquiry results*:

Normal hours of work and average monthly earnings for the following occupations:

- No. 139 - *Government executive official a) central government*
- No. 149 - *Technical education teacher (second level)*.

Other administrative sources of data: a number of social and economic statistics are computed on the basis of various registers held by different ministries, administrations and institutions, among which:

(1) The *End of year certificate register,* held by the Tax Administration: it provides statistics on total and average gross earnings of all employed persons (*Lonnssummer fra lonns-og trekkopp-gaveregisteret*). Total gross earnings include all wages and salaries for time worked, work done and off-duty periods, vacation pay, bonuses and other remunerations paid out during the income year. The data are classified by branch of economic activity, sex, age group, size of establishment and region.

The data are derived from the end-of-year certificates that employers have to fill in for each of their employees at the beginning of each year with reference to the previous full year, and to transmit to the Tax Administration. The income data are verified by the Tax Administration and a copy of the cleaned files is provided to Statistics Norway for further consistency checks and statistical processing. The statistical series started in 1990 and is annual. The data are available on Statistics Norway's website:

http://www.ssb.no/english/subjects/06/05/lonnltreg_en

(2) Income statistics for persons and families are compiled annually on the basis of various *administrative registers and statistical data sources* (e.g. tax returns, the Tax Register, the End-of-year Certificate Register, the National Insurance Administration, the Ministry of Social Affairs, the State Educational Loan Fund, education statistics, etc.) for the whole population as of 31st

December of the fiscal year. They provide detailed information on incomes from various sources (e.g. employment income, pensions, capital), including income that is not taxable but is found on the registers, such as housing allowance, social assistance, scholarships and cash benefits for parents of small children. The current statistical units are the person and the family and statistics are compiled on the distribution of income and levels for various population groups and geographic areas. The database is also used to obtain income information for other statistical surveys, such as the Surveys of Living Conditions and the Population and Housing Census 2001.

Statistics and methodological information are available on Statistics Norway's website: http://www.ssb.no/english/subjects/05/01. They are published in: *NOS C649 Income Statistics for Persons and Families 1993-1998*.

(3) The *Register of employers and employees* provides annual data on the number of employees and their expected weekly working hours. Included are all employees whose expected duration of employment is more than six days and expected working hours per week is more than three hours. Employment data are classified by branch of economic activity according to the New Standard Industrial Classification since 1995 (prior to 1995, according to the Standard Industrial Classification), sex, age group, education level, region, country of birth and the number of years of residence in Norway; hours of work are classified by region and sex.

This register is held by the National Insurance Institution, which transmits a copy to Statistics Norway once a year and weekly updates throughout the year. Consistency checks are made against the Central Population Register and adjustments are made for double-counting of multiple-job workers. Statistical series are available since 1983. Starting in1992, seamen were included; in 1994, the reference period changed from the 2nd to the 4th quarter of each year and in 1995 the New Standard Industrial Classification was introduced. The statistics are published in:

Statistics Norway: *Labour Market Statistics* (Oslo, annual),

and available on the website:

http://www.ssb.no/english/subjects/06/01

Methodological information is available on Statistics Norway's website, under "About the statistics".

Pakistan

Source of the series
Government Administrative Reports.
Title of the series
Average occupational wages.
Organization responsible
Data collection and statistical processing: Directorates of Labour Welfare, through the Governments of each Province in Pakistan: Balochistan, Punjab, Sindh, North West Frontier Province (NWFP), and Islamabad.
Main topics covered
Employment, wage rates, earnings and hours of work.
Periodicity or frequency of availability of the statistics
Annual.
Reference period
Occupational wages: a month.
Coverage of the statistics
Geographical: each Province of Pakistan separately. This description is limited to the North West Frontier Province (NWFP).
Industrial: NWFP: 29 selected industry groups.
Establishments: establishments and factories covered by the Factories Act, 1934 and the Wages Act, 1936.
Persons: employees covered by the Factories Act, 1934, and the Wages Act, 1936.
Occupations: NWFP: 76 selected occupations within the 29 industry groups.
Concepts and definitions
Employment: employees are persons employed for wages in any manufacturing process or for a business or establishment.
Full-time workers are those employed for the number of working hours specified by laws.
Earnings: refer to net daily and monthly earnings, after deduction of employees' social security contributions - provided these earnings are above the threshold of Rs. 2500.00 per month. They include direct wages in cash for time worked or work done, and cost-of-living, housing and transport allowances. Payments in kind are excluded.
Earnings data are collected separately for wage earners, salaried employees and full-time employees.

Wage rates: refer to basic daily and monthly wage/salary rates, including cost-of-living allowance and other guaranteed and regularly paid allowances - provided these rates are above the threshold of Rs. 2500.00 per month. Wage rates in kind are excluded.
Wage/salary rates are collected separately for wage earners, salaried employees and full-time employees.
Hours of work: refer to normal hours of work as fixed by laws or regulations. Normal hours of work are fixed at 48 hours per week and 9 hours per day, as defined under Sections 34 and 36 of the Factory Act, 1934, and under Section 7 of the West Pakistan shops and establishments Ordinance, 1969.
Classifications
Branch of economic activity (industry):
Title of the classification: Pakistan Standard Industrial Classification of all economic activities (PSIC-70).
Number of groups used for coding: 29.
Applied to: wage rates and earnings.
Data collection method: data on occupational wages are collected from the factories and establishments concerned by labour inspectors from the Directorates of Labour Welfare field offices.
Data processing, editing and consistency checks
Data are processed manually.
Adjustments
None.
Types of estimates
Employment totals and average wage rates, earnings and hours.
Construction of indices
None.
Indicators of reliability of the estimates
Not available.
Available series
Average wage rates, earnings and normal hours of work by occupation.
History of the statistics
Starting date of the statistical series: 1980.
Major changes and revisions: None.
Documentation and dissemination
Documentation: these statistics are not published in national publications
Data supplied to the ILO for dissemination
Statistics of average wage rates and normal hours of work are supplied to the ILO for publication in *Statistics on occupational wages and hours of work and on food prices - October Inquiry results.*
Statistics of average monthly earnings in manufacturing and transport are published in the *Yearbook of Labour Statistics.*

Panama

Source of the series
Lists of contributions of Social Security Institutions.
Title of the series
Employment Series.
Organization responsible
Data collection, statistical processing and publication/ dissemination of the statistics: Dirección de Estadística y Censo, Contraloría General de la República (Directorate of Statistics and Census, Comptroller General of the Republic).
Main topics covered
Employment and earnings.
Periodicity or frequency of availability of the statistics
Once a year.
Reference period
The month of August.
Coverage of the statistics
Geographical: the whole country.
Industrial: all branches of economic activity.
Establishments: establishments of all types and sizes.
Persons: employees paying social security contributions and employees of State institutions.
Occupations: data are not collected on individual occupations or occupational group.
Concepts and definitions
Employment: all employees who pay social security contributions, i.e. all persons who work for another person or entity and are remunerated in money, provided that they have worked on any day in the reference month.
Earnings: gross cash monthly wages and salaries. This means the remuneration received by employees for their work in the reference

period, including paid overtime, payment for time not worked and commissions.

Classifications

Branch of economic activity (industry):

Title of the classification: Standard National Industrial Classification for all Economic Activities.

Number of groups used for coding: 18 categories.

Applied to: employment and earnings in private companies.

Link to ISIC and level: Rev.3 (1990) at all levels.

Occupation:

Title of the classification: National Classification of Occupations.

Number of groups used for coding: 10 groups.

Applied to: employment in autonomous institutions and banana zones.

Link to ISCO and level: ISCO-1988 at all levels.

Other classifications: by sex, type of enterprise/institution and sector.

Data collection

Data collection methods vary depending on the type of employer:

Private enterprises: the data are obtained from lists of contribution payments submitted by employers the to the Social Security Fund. The information relates to the month of August and its scope is at central level. The collection and processing of data takes approximately four months.

Banana Zones: the source of information is the payroll lists of employees in the Banana Producing Estates of Chiriquí and Bocas del Toro. The data collection and processing takes about two months.

Autonomous, semi-autonomous and municipal institutions: the information is obtained from a special list which is requested each month from every institution and which includes occupation, sex, wages of personnel working in them. The data collection and processing takes about four months.

Central Government: the data is contained in the employee payroll list prepared by the National Computer Directorate in the Comptroller-General's Office. Processing takes about one month.

Data processing, editing and consistency checks

The data are processed by computer and wage and salary ranges are checked manually.

Adjustments

None.

Types of estimates

Total paid employment and earnings, and distributions.

Construction of indices

None.

Indicators of reliability of the estimate

Not available.

Available series

Distributions:

- Private companies: number of employees by sex and amount of earnings, by province, branch of activity and monthly wages;
- Banana Zones: number of employees and amount of earnings, by monthly wages, sex, zone and occupation;
- Autonomous, semi-autonomous and municipal institutions: employees by monthly wages, by sex, occupation and institution;
- Central Government: employees by amount of wages and sex, by ministry and institution.

History of the statistics

Starting date of the statistical series: 1958.

Major changes and revisions: in the private enterprise sector, from 1980, the Social Insurance Fund introduced changes in the system of payment of contributions, from quarterly to monthly, using a pre-prepared list. The system produces changes in the figures, since employers submit this list to the Institution even though they do not make the corresponding payments. Prior to that, only the list of actual payments made was accepted.

In the Banana Zones: up to 1976, to calculate the average monthly wage, all employees who worked during the reference month were included irrespective of days worked. From 1977, employees who worked less than 22 days in the month were excluded, so as to obtain an average monthly wage more representative of the activity.

In the Canal area: the transfer of the administration of the Panama Canal on 31 December 1999 to Panamanian hands resulted in a significant increase in the number of employees and the amount of wages and salaries in the public sector.

Documentation and dissemination

Documentation:

Contraloría General de la República, Dirección de Estadística y Censo: *Situación Social – Estadísticas del Trabajo, Volumen II:*

Empleo: Sector público y privado (Panama, annual); published approximately eight months after the data reference period.

Data supplied to the ILO for dissemination

None; distributions are not published in the *Yearbook of Labour Statistics.*

Saint Helena

Source of the series

Tax returns and administrative records.

Title of the series

Employment, wage rates, earnings and hours of work.

Organization responsible

Data collection, statistical processing and publication/ dissemination of the statistics:

Statistics Office, Development and Economic Planning Department.

Main topics covered

Employment, wage and salary rates, earnings, hours of work and income from self-employment.

Periodicity or frequency of availability of the statistics

Yearly.

Reference period

The whole year (from April to March).

Coverage of the statistics

Geographical: the whole island.

Industrial: all economic activities.

Establishments: all types and sizes.

Persons: all employed persons.

Occupations: data are collected on wage rates and hours of work by occupation.

Concepts and definitions

Employment: refers to all persons receiving an income from full-time or part-time paid employment and from self-employment. Adult workers are persons aged 15 years and over.

Full-time workers are persons who work an average of 36.25 hours per week.

Earnings: refer to total annual cash remuneration as reported to the Tax authorities, i.e. gross cash earnings including direct wages and all bonuses, allowances and compensation in cash.

Wage rates: refer to basic wage and salary rates.

Hours of work: refer to normal weekly hours of work, as fixed by laws or regulations: 35 hours for monthly paid workers, and 37.5 hours per week for weekly paid workers.

Income related to paid employment: see under Earnings.

Income related to self-employment: refers to gross cash profit generated by the self-employment activity, after deduction of consumption of fixed capital.

Classifications

Branch of economic activity (industry):

Title of the classification: not available.

Number of groups used for coding: 17 tabulation categories.

Applied to: all data.

Link to ISIC and level: Rev.3 (1990).

Occupation:

Title of the classification: not available.

Number of groups used for coding: nine major groups.

Applied to: all data.

Link to ISCO and level: ISCO-88.

Status in employment: employees and self-employed.

Other classifications: by sex. Wage rates of Government workers are also classified by level of skill.

Data collection

Size and coverage of the administrative system: covers all tax records filled in by the employed population and government records.

Data collection method: collation of data from these tax and other administrative records. The data on wage rates and earnings are obtained from the Department of Finance.

Updating of the administrative system: yearly.

Data processing, editing and consistency checks

Data are processed by computer; different variables are cross-tabulated and various checks are made within the computer database.

Adjustments

None.

Types of estimates

Total number of persons employed, average weekly and monthly wage and salary rates, average monthly earnings and average weekly normal hours of work.

Construction of indices
None.
Indicators of reliability of the estimates
Coverage of the administrative system: exhaustive.
Available series
Number of employed persons by sector and category (employees and the self-employed);
Average monthly earnings;
Average wage rates by level of skill and occupation;
Normal hours of work.
History of the statistics
Starting date of the statistical series: not available.
Major changes and revisions: none.
Documentation and dissemination
Documentation:
Statistics Office: *Statistical Yearbook* (Jamestown, annual); published about one year after the reference period of the statistics.
Dissemination: data which do not appear in national publications can be made available upon request.
Data supplied to the ILO for dissemination
Statistics of average monthly earnings by economic activity and sex are published in the *Yearbook of Labour Statistics*.
Statistics of normal hours of work and average wage rates by occupation are published in *Statistics on occupational wages and hours of work and on food prices - October Inquiry results*.

Seychelles

Source of the series
Social Security records and returns from Government and Parastatal Offices.
Title of the series
Formal Employment and Average Monthly Earnings of Formal Employees.
Organization responsible
Data collection, statistical processing and publication/ dissemination of the statistics: Ministry of Information Technology & Communication, Management & Information Systems Division, Statistics and Database Administration Section.
Main topics covered
Employment and earnings.
Periodicity or frequency of availability of the statistics
Half-yearly.
Reference period
Employment: the last working day of each month of the periods January to June and January to December;
Earnings: the whole month.
Coverage of the statistics
Geographical: the whole country.
Industrial: all divisions of economic activity. Separate data are available for the public, parastatal and private sectors, and for all three sectors together.
Establishments: all types and sizes of formal establishments affiliated to the social security system.
Persons: employees formally employed and affiliated to the social security system. Excluded are domestic workers in private households, family workers and the self-employed.
Occupations: data are not collected by occupation or occupational group.
Concepts and definitions
Employment: employees are all those who are engaged in formal employment and pay social security contributions.
Earnings: refer to average gross monthly earnings, including overtime payments, bonuses and allowances, annual leave and redundancy payments.
Classifications
Branch of economic activity (industry):
Title of the classification: not available.
Number of groups used for coding: 13.
Applied to: employment and earnings.
Link to ISIC and level: not fully compatible either with Rev.2 or with Rev.3.
Other classifications: by sector (private, parastatal and public).
Data collection
Size and coverage of the administrative system: covers all formal employees.
Data collection method: the data are obtained from social security returns covering the private sector and from parastatal and Government returns collected by the Statistics and Database Administration Section of the Management & Information Systems

Division.
Updating of the administrative system: on a continuous basis.
Data processing, editing and consistency checks
The data are recorded and processed by computer in EXCEL spreadsheets.
Adjustments
None.
Types of estimates
Total and average number of employees and average gross monthly earnings.
Construction of indices
None.
Indicators of reliability of the estimates
Coverage of the administrative system: assumed to be exhaustive in terms of formal employees.
Conformity with other sources: the data for the public and parastatal sectors are checked against the records held by Government establishments.
Available series
Monthly and annual series of formal employment and average monthly earnings by industry and sector.
History of the statistics
Starting date of the statistical series: 1975.
Major changes and revisions: since 1988, all employees in formal employment are exempted from Income Tax. As a result, earnings for 1988 onwards cannot be compared to previous years' data.
Documentation and dissemination
Documentation:
Ministry of Information Technology & Communication, Management & Information Systems Division: *Statistical Bulletin* (Mahe, half-yearly);
Idem: *Statistical Abstract* (annual).
No methodological publication has been released.
Dissemination: employment data are available on the Management and Information Systems Division's web-site:
http://www.seychelles.net/misdstat
Data supplied to the ILO for dissemination
The following data are supplied to the ILO for publication in the *Yearbook of Labour Statistics*:
Paid employment by branch of economic activity;
Average monthly earnings of employees, by branch of economic activity.
The corresponding monthly statistics are published in the *Bulletin of Labour Statistics*.

Singapore

Source of the series
Reports on contributions to the Central Provident Fund.
Title of the series
Average monthly earnings.
Organization responsible
Data collection and statistical processing: Central Provident Fund Board.
Publication/ dissemination of the statistics: Manpower Research and Statistics Department, Ministry of Manpower, and Department of Statistics, Ministry of Trade and Industry.
Main topics covered
Earnings and employees.
Periodicity or frequency of availability of the statistics
Quarterly.
Reference period
Each month of the quarter.
Coverage of the statistics
Geographical: the whole country.
Industrial: all branches of economic activities.
Establishments: all types and sizes in the private and public sectors.
Persons: all resident employees, i.e. Singapore citizens and permanent residents, who are Central Provident Fund (CPF) contributors.
Occupations: data are not collected by occupation or occupational group.
Concepts and definitions
Employment: an employee is any person who is employed in Singapore and any Singaporean seaman who is employed by an employer under a contract of service or other agreement entered into in Singapore. Included are:
– salaried company directors,

- part-time and casual employees whose wages exceed $50 a month,
- all school-leavers or students working on a part-time or temporary basis (except tertiary students on full-time industrial attachment, students employed under a training programme approved by their institution and students working during their school holidays),
- national servicemen on reservist service,
- foreigners who have become Singapore permanent residents.

Excluded are foreigners on Employment or Professional Visit Pass, partners, sole proprietors, the self-employed and employees working overseas.

Earnings: average gross monthly earnings refer to total cash remuneration due or granted to employees in respect of their employment, before deduction of employees' CPF contributions and personal income tax. They include basic wage, overtime payments, commissions, allowances (e.g. attendance, cost of living, dirt, education, holiday, housing, maternity, meal, productivity, service, stand-by allowances), leave pay and other monetary payments, annual wage supplements and variable bonuses. They exclude the value of payments in kind and employers' CPF contributions.

Classifications

Branch of economic activity (industry):

Title of the classification: Singapore Standard Industrial Classification (SSIC) 2000.

Number of groups used for coding: 54.

Applied to: earnings and distribution of employees.

Link to ISIC: Rev.3 (1990) at the 3-digit level.

Status in employment: employees only.

Other classifications: earnings: by sex; distribution of employees: by sex and age group.

Data collection

Size and coverage of the administrative system: in 2001, over 80 000 employers contributed to the CPF on behalf of over 1.2 million employees.

Data collection method: statistics of average monthly earnings are based on the returns on social security and savings contributions that every employer is required by law to send to the Central Provident Fund (CPF). Each month, employers must declare the earnings of each employees and send their contributions within 14 days after the end of the month for which such contributions are due and payable. Manual and electronic payment forms are available. The earnings data are then compiled by the CPF monthly and processed two months after the reference period. Quarterly statistics of average monthly earnings are based on the average of the three months.

Updating of the administrative system: continuous; the CPF Board's computerized system detects defaulting employers and lists them out each month for follow-up action by Employer Services Officers. Industry spot-checks on employers' wage records are also conducted to determine the level of compliance of employers to CPF rules and regulations.

Data processing, editing and consistency checks

The data are processed by computer.

Information on consistency checks is not available.

Adjustments

None.

Types of estimates

Average monthly earnings are computed by dividing the sum of the monthly earnings of all active CPF contributors (employees) by the number of active CPF contributors (employees). Quarterly statistics are based on the average of the three months.

Average real monthly earnings correspond to nominal earnings deflated by the corresponding year's Consumer Price Index (at present, on base November 1997-October 1998=100).

Construction of indices

None.

Indicators of reliability of the estimates

Coverage of the administrative system: it is assumed to cover all resident employees.

Available series

Quarterly and annual series of average monthly earnings by economic activity and sex.

Annual series of average real monthly earnings by economic activity and sex.

Annual distribution of CPF contributors by monthly wage level (at year-end), age group and economic activity.

History of the statistics

Starting date of the statistical series: 1981.

Major changes and revisions: prior to 1992, the statistics of average earnings included self-employed persons who had made voluntary CPF contributions. Since 1992, the data exclude all identifiable self-employed persons.

Since 1998, the earnings data from the CPF Board by economic activity are compiled using 5-digit fields, instead of 4-digits. From that date onwards, the statistics are therefore not strictly comparable with the previous years.

Prior to 1998, the statistics were classified according to the Singapore Standard Industrial Classification (SSIC) 1990; between 1998 and 2000, according to SSIC 1996; and since 2001, according to SSIC 2000.

Documentation and dissemination

Documentation:

Ministry of Manpower, Manpower Research and Statistics Department: *Singapore Yearbook of Manpower Statistics* (annual, Singapore); published five months after the statistics' reference year;

Idem: *Report on Wages in Singapore* (annual), published within six months after the statistics' reference year.

Ministry of Trade and Industry, Department of Statistics (Statistics Singapore):

Monthly Digest of Statistics (Singapore) (monthly, ibid.); published three months after the reference quarter;

Idem: *Yearbook of Statistics Singapore* (annual, ibid.); published five months after the statistics' reference year.

Methodological information is not published.

Dissemination: on Internet:

Ministry of Manpower, Manpower Research and Statistics Department: http://www.gov.sg/mom/manpower/manrs/manrs.htm

Ministry of Trade and Industry, Statistics Singapore: http://www.singstat.gov.sg

Information on the definitions of employees covered and wages, and on the CPF procedures, is available on the CPF web-site: http://www.cpf.gov.sg

Data supplied to the ILO for dissemination

The following statistics are published in the *Yearbook* and *Bulletin of Labour Statistics*:

Average monthly earnings by economic activity and (annually) by sex.

Other administrative sources of data: employment statistics are compiled monthly from administrative records of various government agencies.

Spain

Source of the series

Administrative Records of membership of the Social Security System.

Title of the series

Workers' membership of the Social Security System (Afiliación de trabajadores al Sistema de la Seguridad Social).

Organization responsible

Data collection, statistical processing, publication/ dissemination of the statistics: Ministry of Labour and Social Affairs.

Main topics covered

Employment.

Periodicity or frequency of availability of the statistics

Monthly and annual.

Reference period

Each month of the year and the whole calendar year.

Coverage of the statistics

Geographical: the whole country.

Industrial: all branches of activity.

Establishments: all types and sizes.

Persons: workers belonging to the various schemes under the social security system actively employed or equivalent, such as temporary incapacity, suspension under employment regulations, partial unemployment, etc. Unemployed workers, those with special agreements, belonging to enterprises involved in restructuring plans and early retirement schemes are excluded.

Occupations: data are not collected on individual occupations but by contribution group.

Concepts and definitions

Employment: refers to persons engaged in work activity and registered in the Administrative Records of membership of the Social Security System.

Classifications

Branch of economic activity (industry): all branches of economic activity.

Title of the classification: National Classification of Economic Activities (CNAE-93).

Number of groups used for coding: 30 groups, two-digit codes.

Applied to: employment.

Link to ISIC and level: Rev.3, at the 2-digit level.

Occupation:

Title of the classification: contribution groups under the Social Security System.

Number of groups used for coding: 10 occupational categories for workers aged over 18 years.

Applied to: employment.

Link to ISCO and level: none.

Status in employment:

Title of the classification: Employment Status.

Number of groups used for coding: 2 groups: employed, self-employed.

Applied to: employment.

Link to ICSE and level: none.

Other classifications: by size of enterprise; social security scheme; by sex, age group and nationality; by autonomous community and province; by type of mobility of companies.

Data collection

Size and coverage of the administrative system: Administrative Records of membership of the Social Security System.

Data collection method: data are collected at central, regional or local level. Enterprise and employee data are entered in the Records when they commence employment. The information is processed by the Social Security Computer Division and the Sub-Directorate for Data Processing, according to instructions given by the Sub-Directorate of Social and Labour Statistics.

Updating of the administrative system: monthly.

Data processing, editing and consistency checks

The employer for employees and the worker himself if self-employed are required to provide a membership form to the Social Security, the data of which is checked against the national identity card or passport. The data is supplied to the General Treasury of the Social Security Department, processed electronically with certain compulsory fields.

Adjustments

No information available.

Types of estimates

All workers in the Social Security System, by scheme; absolute and relative variations over the previous year.

Construction of indices

None.

Indicators of reliability of the estimates

Coverage of the administrative system: about 99% of the legally employed population.

Conformity with other sources: comparisons are made with data on employment in the Survey of the Economically Active Population carried out by the National Institute of Statistics.

Available series

Monthly and annual series of:

- workers in active employment, by insurance scheme
- workers in active employment, by sex and age
- workers in active employment, by branch of activity
- workers in active employment, by sector of activity and employment status
- workers in active employment, by autonomous community and province.

History of the statistics

Starting date of the statistical series: January 1982.

Major changes and revisions: introduction of distribution by sex and age, and contribution group on 01.01.1995 and classification of economic activities CNAE-93 on 01.01.1998.

Documentation and dissemination

Documentation: Ministry of Labour and Social Affairs: *Boletín de Estadísticas Laborales* (Madrid, quarterly)

idem: *Anuario de Estadísticas Laborales y de Asuntos Sociales* (ibid., annual).

Dissemination: http://www.mtas.es

Data supplied to the ILO for dissemination

None at present.

Switzerland

Source of the series

Accident declarations registered by the Accident Insurance Central Statistical Service (Service de centralisation des statistiques de l'assurance-accidents - SSAA).

Title of the series

Swiss Wages Index.

Normal hours of work in enterprises.

Organization responsible

Data collection: Accident Insurance Central Statistical Service.

Statistical processing, publication/ dissemination of the statistics: Federal Office of Statistics (Office fédéral de la statistique - OFS).

Main topics covered

Wage rates and normal hours of work.

Periodicity or frequency of availability of the statistics

Annual.

Reference period

The calendar year.

Coverage of the statistics

Geographical: the whole country.

Industrial: all branches of economic activity, including horticulture and forestry, but not including agriculture, hunting and related services, and fishing.

Establishments: establishments and enterprises of all types and sizes.

Persons: full-time employees, excluding middle and senior management.

The reference population corresponds to the "interior concept" of the labour market: persons exercising an activity in a unit of production established in the territory of Switzerland, whether domiciled in Switzerland or abroad (e.g. cross-border workers).

Occupations: data are not collected on individual occupations or groups of occupations, but on levels of qualifications (see under "classifications").

Concepts and definitions

Employment: the statistics cover full-time employees, accident victims, and come from the Swiss National Accident Insurance Fund (Caisse nationale suisse d'assurance-accidents -Suva, ex-CNA), or private insurers.

Part-time employees, those affected by reductions in hours of work and middle and senior management are not in principle covered by the statistics.

Wage rates: refer to rates actually paid. The definition used to calculate the index includes the following elements: gross basic wage, inflation increases and the thirteenth month allowance. Bonuses and commissions, family allowances, special bonuses and benefits in kind are recorded but left out of the calculation. When the wages exceed the maximum insured amount (CHF 8,900 per month at 1 January 2000) only the maximum is taken into account (see also under "Adjustments").

Data are collected separately for full-time and part-time workers, apprentices and by sex.

Hours of work: normal weekly hours of work in enterprises, valid for a period of several months or years. In principle, it is the individual hours of work of full-time employees, ignoring overtime, short-time and other absences. They may be fixed by law or regulations, collective agreements or the internal rules of enterprises/establishments, as set out in the employees' contract of employment.

Data are collected separately for full-time and part-time workers, apprentices and by sex.

Classifications

Branch of economic activity (industry):

Title of the classification: General Nomenclature of Economic Activities, 1995 (Nomenclature générale des activités économiques - NOGA), since 1991.

Number of groups used for coding: at Swiss national level, the statistics are broken down by economic class (two digits) and division (one digit); at cantonal level, by economic division.

Applied to: normal hours of work and wage indices.

Link to ISIC and level: NOGA is based on NACE, Rev. 1 and is compatible with ISIC, Rev.3.

Other classifications: wages: level of qualifications (skilled, semi-skilled and unskilled workers); sex; area of activity (production, office and technical (together) and sales); sector (primary: horticulture and forestry; secondary and tertiary); and classifications broken down by canton and region.

Hours of work: by canton and region, and classifications broken down by canton/economic section.

Data collection

Size and coverage of the administrative system: the Accident Insurance Central Statistical Service (SSAA) receives over 300,000 accident statements per year.

Data collection method: the accident statements are forms completed by the victims or their employer which, among the some twenty variables (economic branch, sex, qualifications, area of activity, method of remuneration, working days, age, home address and place of work of the accident victim, type of accident, etc.) include information on the wages of the accident victim and the normal hours of work in the employing company. These forms are sent to the OFS via the SSAA in electronic form and anonymously.

In the statistics on wage trends, the main variables for the selection of data are: level of qualifications, hours of work (full-time employees), age (men: 19-65 years; women: 19-63 years) and the area of activity.

Updating of the administrative system: continuous.

Data processing, editing and consistency checks

The SSAA inputs the computerized data and carries out consistency checks of information gathered based on accident statements.

The OFS extrapolates the results.

Normal hours of work, at section level, economic sector or overall, are calculated using a weighted model, based on the Federal census of enterprises of 1995 and 1998. Each economic division in each canton receives a weighting coefficient. This process allows aggregate values to be calculated in the light of the employment patterns peculiar to each canton and region.

The following data are used to calculate the current weightings for wage statistics: full-time jobs derived from the 1991 census of enterprises; the number of active full-time employees taken from the 1990 population census; production personnel from the October 1991 survey of wages and earnings; and SSAA data for 1991 on employees broken down by type of accident.

Accident statements from certain groups of employees are not proportional in number to the size of these groups on the survey population (e.g. construction and civil engineering). Groups of workers are therefore weighted to avoid distortions in the presentation of the macro-economic trends in wages.

Adjustments

Under-coverage: statistics on wage trends: for certain groups of employees, e.g. skilled men in the economic categories "chemicals", "banking" and "public administration", the unknown amounts of wages which exceed the maximum insured always constitute a considerable proportion, ranging from 5% to 15% of the total wages indicated for these groups. In this case, the declared wages are corrected or extrapolated. The method of correction or extrapolation relies on the assumption that in reality wages are broken down according to a normal log distribution.

Types of estimates

Average annual normal weekly hours of work, weighted by the number of jobs;

Annual nominal and real indices of wage trends.

The average hours of work are the average of all weeks in a calendar year.

The annual wage indices are calculated from accident statements which cover the whole year.

In order to solve the problem of the influence of variations in hours of work on hourly wages, the hourly wage is linked to the individual weekly hours of work of each insured employee and converted to monthly earnings.

Construction of indices

The trend in normal wages is calculated using a Laspeyres index on a constant base (number of employees in homogeneous groups in the base year) which measures variations in wages for a constant type of work (pure wage trend). No account is taken of wage variations resulting from an increase in the proportion of skilled persons or relocation of workers to economic sectors which, on average, pay higher wages. The index is currently constructed on base year 1993 = 100.

The trend in real wages is measured by deflating the nominal wages index by the consumer price index.

Indicators of reliability of the estimates

Coverage of the administrative system: exhaustive. All employees must be covered by accident insurance.

Non-sampling errors: normal time and wages: the weighting system must always be adjusted for the results of the most recent censuses of enterprises, so that it is not possible to analyse very long term trends.

Wages trends: a weakness of the statistics is that they exclude part-time employees, and middle and senior management (who are covered in the accident statements, but not included in the statistical calculations).

Conformity with other sources: normal hours of work: the results of the statistics are compared with other indicators of hours of work, such as the volume of work statistics: the comparison gives practically identical results for full-time employees.

Comparisons are also made with other surveys which provide information on actual hours of work, such as the Federal population census, the Swiss Survey on the economically active population (ESPA), the Survey of wage structure and statistics on collective agreements.

Available series

For years prior to the current year: official indices and wage trends for the overall economy and by economic branch, sex, level of qualifications and/or area of activity.

Index of nominal and real wages, by sex and total, by economic division and sector, area of activity and level of qualifications, and variation compared with the previous year;

Index of nominal wages, total, by economic classification and variation compared with the previous year;

Index of nominal and real wages and variations as a percentage, by category of workers (blue-collar and white-collar workers, sex, categories).

For the current year: wages trends at the most aggregate level.

Normal weekly hours of work in enterprises and variations compared with the previous year in absolute figures and percentages, by economic classification;

Normal weekly hours of work and variations by canton, region and economic division.

History of the statistics

Starting date of the statistical series: statistics on normal hours of work in enterprises and wages trends: 1918, in the secondary sector only. Since 1985, with the entry into force in 1984 of the new Accident Insurance Act, which makes insurance compulsory for all workers, the statistics cover all sectors, apart from agriculture, hunting and fishing.

Major changes and revisions: statistics on wages trends: up to 1993, the official figures came from the October survey of wages and earnings. Since 1994, the present statistics are the official source of data.

Since 1991, the 1995 edition of the General Nomenclature of Economic Activities (NOGA) has replaced the 1985 edition.

Before 1995, the Federal Office of Industry, Arts and Trades and Labour (OFIAMT) (now the Federal Office of Economic Development and Employment - OFDE) was responsible for processing the data collected on normal hours of work and wages, and publishing the results. Since then, it has been the OFS.

The statistics on wages trends are currently being revised. The aim in particular is to achieve the following objectives: (i) to take account of part-time employees; and (ii) to introduce a quarterly indicator of the economic situation.

Documentation and dissemination

Documentation:

OFS: *Durée normale du travail dans les entreprises. Résultats commentés et tableaux* (Berne, annual);

Idem: *Communiqué de presse: statistique du volume du travail* (ibid.); occasional publication;

Idem: *Communiqué de presse: Heures de travail en 2000* (Neuchâtel, February 2002);

Idem: *La statistique du volume du travail. Bases méthodologiques et définitions* (Berne, 1997);

Idem: *Indicateurs du marché du travail* (annual).

Federal Department of Public Economy: *La Vie économique* (Berne, monthly);

OFS: *La nouvelle statistique de l'évolution des salaires. Conception et résultats 1994* (Berne, 1995);

Idem: *Evolution des salaires. Résultats commentés et tableaux* (Neuchâtel, annual).

Idem: *Communiqué de presse: Indice suisse des salaires 2001* (Neuchâtel, April 2002).

Dissemination: OFS Website: http://www.statistique.admin.ch

Statistics not included in national publications or the Website may be obtained on request.

Data supplied to the ILO for dissemination

The following statistics have been supplied to the ILO for publication in the *Yearbook of Labour Statistics* and are available in LABORSTA:

Normal weekly hours of work for employees, by branch of economic activity (up to 1993); and in manufacturing industry; Worker's earnings (up to 1983) by branch of economic activity (secondary sector).

Other administrative sources of data: statistics on collective agreements in Switzerland (*statistique des conventions collectives de travail en Suisse* -ECS) have been produced every two years on 1 May since 1992. Its purpose is to draw up an exhaustive and detailed list of collective agreements and model employment contracts in Switzerland. The survey is carried out directly among the contracting parties to a collective agreement, i.e. employers' associations of enterprises and associations of employees signatories to an agreement. The main structural characteristics recorded are the economic branch, the type of collective agreement, geographical scope, signatories, date of entry into force, the issue of industrial peace and the number of persons covered (employers and employees) by sex.

The annual survey of wage agreements (*Enquête annuelle sur les accords salariaux* - EAS) in areas covered by a collective agreement reports on bargaining between the social partners on changes in effective and minimum wages under collective agreements.

The central register of foreigners (*Registre central des étrangers* - RCE) provides monthly indicators of the number of active foreigners working in the various branches of activity, by sex and type of permit.

The statistics on teachers and health occupations (*statistique des enseignants et celle des emplois dans le domaine de la santé*) provides information on staff numbers and trends in personnel in the two branches.

The statistics on labour disputes (*statistique des conflits collectifs du travail*), carried out by the OFDE, lists strikes for economic reasons lasting at least one day. It is based on basic information drawn from the daily press, which leads to the employers and economic associations concerned. The latter must then complete a questionnaire providing information on the following characteristics: type of dispute (strike or lock-out), reason for dispute, number of employees concerned, length of action, working hours lost, economic branch, number of enterprises concerned and how the dispute was settled.

Synthesis statistics (*statistiques de synthèse*), which combine the primary data (surveys) and secondary data (administrative sources) are also produced, among them:

Statistics on the volume of labour (*statistique du volume du travail*), prepared by the OFS since 1991. The volume of labour of the permanent resident population is calculated on the basis of empirical data provided by the Swiss Survey on the economically active population, in which normal hours of work, overtime and absences are determined and aggregated by job. The volume of labour of other population groups working in Switzerland is calculated from the results of the employed population statistics (number of employed persons) and the population census (average working hours).

Definition of the volume of labour: actual working hours (= normal time + paid or unpaid overtime – absences). The volume of labour is obtained by adding actual annual working hours for all jobs (self-employed and employees who have worked at least one hour for remuneration during the reference year, and persons who, while not being paid, have worked in the family business during the reference year).

Reference period: the calendar year;

Periodicity: annual;

Criteria for breakdown of data on normal hours of work, overtime, absences and volume of labour: sex, origin/type of residence permit, economic section, rate of occupation and activity status.

Publications:

OFS: *Communiqué de presse: statistique du volume du travail* (Berne, annual);

Idem: *La statistique du volume du travail. Bases méthodologiques et définitions* (ibid., 1997);

Idem: *Indicateurs du marché du travail* (Neuchâtel, annual).

Monthly statistics on reductions in hours of work, produced by the Federal Office of Economic Development and Employment (OFDE) provides information on employees (by sex) and enterprises concerned, economic branches, cantons and hours laid-off.

Number of members of the Swiss Trade Union Federation (Union syndicale suisse - USS) and other employees organizations: this is a survey by the USS at 31 December each year of the number of members (persons) of trade unions and employer's associations affiliated to it. The USS publication also gives the membership of other major employees' organizations (Swiss Confederation of Christian Trade Unions (Confédération des syndicats chrétiens de Suisse), Federation of Swiss Employees' Societies (Fédération des sociétés suisses d'employés), Federal Union of Government and State Enterprise Employees (Union fédérative du personnel des administrations et des entreprises publiques) etc.), but excludes small organizations not affiliated to the USS.

Turkey

Source of the series
Social Insurance Institution reports.
Title of the series
Sosyal Sigortalar Kurumu (SSK) Yillik Istatistikler (Social Insurance Institution Annual Statistics).
Organization responsible
Data collection, statistical processing and publication/dissemination of the statistics:
The General Directorate, Social Insurance Institution, attached to the Ministry of Labour and Social Security.
Main topics covered
Employment and earnings.
Periodicity or frequency of availability of the statistics
Annual.
Reference period
The beginning of the month of September.
Coverage of the statistics
Geographical: the whole country.
Industrial: all economic activities.
Establishments: all types and sizes.
Persons: all insured employees employed under a service contract in private and state enterprises.
Occupations: all occupations of those employed under a contract of employment who fall within the scope of the Social Insurance Law No. 506.
Concepts and definitions
Employment: refers to the total number of employees, including apprentices and temporary workers, working in workplaces subject to the Social Insurance Law No. 506. All persons who are registered with the insurance scheme are defined as employed upon entry into service and are thus covered by the statistics.
Earnings: refer to average gross daily earnings, including pay for normal time worked, overtime payments, severance pay and seniority and production premiums. The minimum and maximum limits for daily and monthly earnings used for determining social security contributions and benefits are fixed by law.
Hours of work: refer to normal hours of work. Daily normal hours are 7.5 hours (weekly 45 hours) according to Law No. 1475.
Classifications
Branch of economic activity (industry):
Title of the classification: Branches of Work Covered by the Social Insurance Act.
Number of groups used for coding: 10 (0-9) major groups.
Applied to: employment and earnings.
Link to ISIC and level: Rev.2 (1968).
Other classifications: employment and earnings data are classified by sex and sector (public and private).
Data collection
Data collection method: the data are obtained from information contained in the contribution certificates furnished by employers as monthly insurance reports to the Social Insurance Institution.
Updating of the administrative system: monthly.
Data processing, editing and consistency checks
Information not available.
Adjustments
Not available.
Types of estimates
Total number of employees;
Average daily earnings.
Daily earnings represent the ratio between total earnings taken as the basis for contributions and the number of days for which contributions have been paid.
Construction of indices
None.
Indicators of reliability of the estimates
Not available.
Available series
Number of employees as of September of each year;
Average earnings of employees.
History of the statistics

Starting date of the statistical series: 1950.

Major changes and revisions: The Social Insurance Law No. 506, which is presently in force, entered into effect on 1 March 1965. Its coverage was extended, by comparison with the previous social insurance laws.

Documentation and dissemination

Documentation:

Social Insurance Institution, General Directorate: *Annual Statistics of Social Insurance Institution* (Ankara, annual);

Prime Ministry, State Institute of Statistics: *Statistical Yearbook of Turkey* (ibid., annual); contains employment data for the previous year *(t-1)* and wages data for the year before *(t-2)*, as well as some methodological information on the source of data.

Data supplied to the ILO for dissemination

The following statistics are supplied to the ILO for publication in the *Yearbook of Labour Statistics*:

Paid employment by economic activity and sex;

Average daily earnings of employees, by economic activity and in manufacturing by industry group, and by sex.

Other administrative sources of data: the social security system in Turkey is composed of three major organizations: the Social Insurance Institution (see above); the Government Employees Retirement Fund; and "Bag-Kur", i.e. the Social Security Organization for the self-employed outside the coverage of the Social Insurance Law, such as agricultural workers, craftsmen, artisans and small businessmen, technical and professional people who are registered to a chamber or professional association and shareholders of companies other than cooperatives and joint stock companies. Statistics on the number of persons covered and amounts of benefits provided are derived from The Government Employees Retirement Fund and the General Directorate of Bag-Kur.

Introduction - Partie I

Les descriptions méthodologiques présentées dans cette partie se rapportent aux statistiques nationales sur le chômage dérivées de registres administratifs. Un grand nombre des séries statistiques correspondantes sont publiées par le BIT dans l'*Annuaire des statistiques du travail* et/ou dans le *Bulletin des statistiques du travail*, et sont donc disponibles sur le site Internet du Bureau de statistique du BIT (http://laborsta.ilo.org).

Les 96 descriptions - qui couvrent 94 pays, zones ou territoires - inclues dans cette partie ont été préparées sur la base des informations fournies essentiellement par les agences pour l'emploi nationales en réponse à un questionnaire spécifique. Afin de faciliter les comparaisons, toutes les descriptions suivent le même format, composé de douze sections dont l'intitulé est identique. Cependant, il convient de garder présent à l'esprit que les statistiques provenant de registres administratifs ne sont pas réellement comparables entre les pays, en raison des législations et doc capacités administratives de chaque pays.

Sous les différentes sections, on trouvera les informations suivantes: le titre et la première année disponible de la série; l'organisme national en charge des enregistrements; les informations personnelles spécifiques qui sont enregistrées; les critères utilisés pour déterminer si une personne doit être enregistrée comme étant au chômage; la définition du chômage utilisée pour ces statistiques; la fréquence avec laquelle ces registres sont mis à jour; si les statistiques tirées des registres sont utilisées pour obtenir des taux de chômage; le type de statistiques de chômage produites et la disponibilité de l'information méthodologique sur ces statistiques; si des comparaisons ont été faites avec des statistiques de chômage tirées d'autres sources, ainsi que l'impact sur ces statistiques de tout changement important qui serait advenu depuis leur commencement.

Classifications auxquelles il est fait référence dans les descriptions:

CITP-88: Classification internationale type des professions, 1988 (Bureau international du Travail, Genève, 1990);

CITI-Rév. 3: Classification internationale type, par industrie, de toutes les branches d'activité économique (Nations Unies, New York, 1989);

NACE- Rév. 1: Nomenclature statistique des activités économiques dans la Communauté européenne (Eurostat, Luxembourg, 1996);

CITE-97: Classification internationale type de l'éducation (UNESCO, Paris, 1997).

Algérie

1. Séries statistiques

Titre: Les *Notes de conjoncture* regroupant la demande, l'offre et le placement (situation du marché de l'emploi).

Première année disponible: 1994

2. Organisme responsable de l'enregistrement des chômeurs ou demandeurs d'emploi

Nom de l'organisme: Agence nationale de l'Emploi (ANEM).

Type d'organisme: Organisme public relevant d'une autorité nationale.

Nom de l'autorité nationale: Ministère de l'Emploi et de la Solidarité nationale.

Situation des bureaux chargés de l'enregistrement: Dans chaque préfecture (165 agences locales et 11 agences régionales implantées sur l'ensemble du territoire).

Types de services fournis et/ou gérés par cet organisme:
– Assistance aux demandeurs d'emploi pour trouver du travail;
– Assistance aux employeurs pour trouver de la main-d'œuvre;
– Orientation professionnelle;
– Autres: enregistrement des demandeurs d'emploi licenciés pour raison économique, et enregistrement des demandeurs d'emploi diplômés de l'enseignement supérieur remplissant les conditions pour bénéficier des contrats de pré-emploi.

3. Les informations personnelles suivantes sont enregistrées:
– Nom;
– Sexe;
– Adresse du domicile habituel;
– Date de naissance;
– Nationalité;
– Niveau d'instruction/de formation, en distinguant six catégories. Aucun lien n'a été établi avec la CITE;
– Situation de travail présente et passée, en distinguant deux catégories;
– Type de profession de l'emploi antérieur ou actuel, en distinguant 20 catégories. Aucun lien n'a été établi avec la CITP.;
– Type de profession de l'emploi recherché, avec 20 catégories;
– Nom et adresse de l'employeur ou du lieu de travail actuel ou passé;
– Branche d'activité de l'employeur ou du lieu de travail actuel ou passé, en distinguant 22 catégories. Aucun lien n'a été établi avec la CITI;
– Inscriptions/enregistrements antérieurs auprès de l'organisme;
– Situation vis-à-vis du service militaire national.

4. Critères utilisés pour déterminer si une personne doit être incluse dans le registre (R) et/ou dans les statistiques de chômeurs (S):
– Etre sans travail (R) et (S);
– Etre à la recherche d'un travail (R) et (S);
– Etre disponible pour travailler (R) et (S);
– Age: Minimum: 16 ans; Maximum: 60 ans (R) et (S);
– Etre résident dans le pays (R) et (S).

5. Critères utilisés pour déterminer si une personne doit être exclue du registre (R) et/ou des statistiques de chômeurs (S):
– Avis de décès (R) et (S);
– Etablissement de la personne à l'étranger (R) et (S);
– Commencement d'un (nouveau) travail (R) et (S);
– Commencement du service militaire (R) et (S);
– Participation à un programme de promotion de l'emploi, à un programme de travaux publics, etc. (R) et (S);
– Admission à toucher une pension (retraite, etc.) (R) et (S);
– Incapacité à travailler (R) et (S).

6. Définition des personnes au chômage sur laquelle les statistiques sont établies

La population au chômage comprend l'ensemble des personnes, aptes légalement (16 à 60 ans) à travailler, ayant déclaré être sans emploi, être à la recherche d'un emploi et inscrites auprès des Agences locales de l'emploi. Parmi les personnes inscrites, on distingue deux catégories: les STR1 qui sont les personnes ayant déjà travaillé, et les STR2 qui sont les personnes n'ayant jamais travaillé.

7. Mise à jour des registres
Les registres sont mis à jour régulièrement.

8. Taux de chômage
Les statistiques basées sur les registres ne sont pas utilisées pour obtenir des taux de chômage. Les taux de chômage sont produits par l'Office National des Statistiques (ONS) dons les sources essentielles sont l'enquête auprès des ménages sur la main-d'œuvre et le recensement de population.

9. Type de statistiques produites sur le nombre de chômeurs enregistrés

Fréquence de production: Trimestrielle.

Variables utilisées:
– Sexe;
– Age;
– Niveau d'instruction;
– Profession;
– Branche d'activité;
– Expérience professionnelle antérieure.

Publication: Sur papier, à diffusion restreinte.

Agence responsable de la publication: ANEM.

Titre et périodicité de la publication: *Note de conjoncture sur la situation du marché de l'emploi*, trimestrielle.

10. Information méthodologique au sujet de ces statistiques

Publication:
– A usage interne;
– Sur papier, à diffusion restreinte.

Agence responsable: ANEM.

11. Comparaisons avec des statistiques provenant d'autres sources
Il n'y a pas eu de comparaisons faites avec des statistiques provenant d'autres sources.

12. Principaux changements intervenus depuis le début de ces séries statistiques
Il n'y a pas eu de changement important dans la législation, dans la capacité de l'agence et/ou dans les procédures

administratives susceptibles d'avoir influencé de manière significative les statistiques.

13. Remarques supplémentaires

Les données statistiques de L'ANEM ne concernent que les demandeurs d'emploi inscrits auprès de ses structures, par contre celles relatives au chômage relèvent de la compétence de l'ONS.

Allemagne

1. Séries statistiques

Titre: Chômage enregistré.

Première année disponible: Non spécifiée.

2. Organisme responsable de l'enregistrement des chômeurs ou demandeurs d'emploi

Nom de l'organisme: Bundesanstalt für Arbeit (Agence nationale du Travail).

Type d'organisme: Organisme public relevant d'une autorité nationale.

Nom de l'autorité nationale: Bunderministerium für Wirtschaft und Arbeit (Ministère de l'Economie et du Travail).

Situation des bureaux chargés de l'enregistrement: Dans toutes les régions du pays.

Types de services fournis et/ou gérés par cet organisme:

– Assistance aux demandeurs d'emploi pour trouver du travail;
– Assistance aux demandeurs d'emploi pour créer leur propre entreprise;
– Assistance aux employeurs pour trouver de la main-d'œuvre;
– Orientation professionnelle;
– Formation liée à l'emploi;
– Paiement des indemnités de chômage.

Pourcentage des demandeurs d'emploi qui cherchent un emploi au travers de cet organisme: Variable selon les régions.

3. Les informations personnelles suivantes sont enregistrées:

– Nom;
– Sexe;
– Numéro de sécurité sociale (ou numéro d'identification également utilisé par d'autres organismes);
– Adresse du domicile habituel;
– Date de naissance;
– Citoyenneté;
– Nationalité/groupe ethnique;
– Niveau d'instruction/ de formation, en distinguant cinq catégories. Aucun lien n'a été établi avec la CITE;
– Situation de travail passée, en distinguant cinq catégories;
– Type de travail (profession) de l'emploi antérieur ou actuel, en distinguant un nombre non spécifié de groupes. Des liens ont été établis avec la CITP;
– Type de travail (profession) de l'emploi recherché, avec un nombre non spécifié de groupes. Des liens ont été établis avec la CITP;
– Branche d'activité (industrie) de l'employeur ou du lieu de travail actuel ou passé, en distinguant un nombre non spécifié de groupes. Des liens ont été établis avec la CITI, rév.3 ou NACE, rév.1 au niveau des groupes.

4. Critères utilisés pour déterminer si une personne doit être incluse dans le registre (R)* et/ou dans les statistiques de chômeurs (S):

– Etre sans travail (S);
– Etre à la recherche d'un travail (S);
– Etre disponible pour travailler (S);
– Age: Minimum: 15 ans; Maximum: 65 ans (S);
– Citoyenneté (S);
– Etre résident dans le pays (S);
– Durée souhaitée de l'emploi recherché et/ou du nombre d'heures de travail recherché (minimum 15 heures par semaine) (S).

* Les requérants peuvent être enregistrés comme personnes au chômage ou comme personnes employées à la recherche d'un travail.

5. Critères utilisés pour déterminer si une personne doit être exclue du registre (R) et/ou des statistiques de chômeurs (S):

– Décès (R) et (S);
– Commencement d'un (nouveau) travail (S);
– Commencement du service militaire (S);
– Participation à un programme de promotion de l'emploi, à un programme de travaux publics, etc. (S);
– Défaut de contact avec l'organisme/agence (S);
– Refus d'un nombre non spécifié d'offres d'emploi adaptées (S);
– Refus d'un nombre non spécifié d'offres de formation adaptées (S);
– Admission à toucher une pension (S);
– Incapacité à travailler (due à une maladie; congé de maternité; cure, etc.) (S).

6. Définition des personnes au chômage sur laquelle les statistiques sont établies

Les personnes au chômage sont celles qui:

– Temporairement n'ont pas de lien avec l'emploi;
– Sont à la recherche d'un emploi avec assurance obligatoire;
– Sont disponibles pour un placement par l'agence d'emploi;
– Sont enregistrées comme chômeurs auprès de l'agence pour l'emploi;
– N'ont pas plus que 65 ans et ne sont pas dans l'incapacité de travailler pour cause de maladie.
– Pour être compté comme chômeur dans les statistiques, **tous** les critères doivent être remplis simultanément.

7. Mise à jour des registres

Les registres (statistiques) sont mis à jour mensuellement.

8. Taux de chômage

Les statistiques basées sur les registres sont utilisées pour obtenir des taux de chômage.

Les sources des données d'emploi qui sont partie du dénominateur des taux de chômage sont les statistiques de l'emploi et du chômage du bureau fédéral du travail et les statistiques du personnel de la fonction publique.

Définition des personnes pourvues d'un emploi à cette fin:

– Employé(e)s civil(e)s
– Toutes les personnes actives civiles.

9. Type de statistiques sur le nombre de chômeurs enregistrés produites

Période de référence: Mois.

Fréquence de production: Mensuellement.

Variables utilisées:

– Sexe;
– Age;
– Niveau d'instruction;
– Profession;
– Branche d'activité;
– Caractéristiques géographiques;
– Expérience professionnelle antérieure;
– Citoyenneté (nationaux/non nationaux);
– Durée de chômage.

Publication:

– Sur papier, à diffusion grand public;
– Sur un site Internet (www.arbeitsamt.de).

Agence responsable de la publication: Bundesanstalt für Arbeit (Agence nationale du travail).

Titre et périodicité de la publication: *Amtliche Nachrichten der Bundesanstalt für Arbeit (ANBA)* (nouvelles officielles de l'agence nationale du travail), publication mensuelle.

10. Information méthodologique au sujet de ces statistiques

Publication:

Sur papier, à diffusion grand public.

Agence responsable pour la diffusion de l'information méthodologique: Bundesanstalt für Arbeit (Agence nationale du travail).

11. Comparaisons avec des statistiques provenant d'autres sources

Des comparaisons ont été faites avec des statistiques provenant de l'enquête sur la main d'œuvre.

12. Principaux changements intervenus depuis le début de ces séries statistiques

Il n'y a pas eu de changement important dans la législation, dans la capacité de l'agence et/ou dans les procédures administratives susceptibles d'avoir influencé de manière significative les statistiques.

Australie

1. Séries statistiques
Titre: Registered unemployment benefit claimants [New Start Allowance (NSA) or Youth Allowance (other) (YA (o)] (Demandeurs d'allocations de chômage enregistré [allocation de nouveau départ (*NSA*) ou allocation jeunes (autre) (*YA(o)*].
Première année disponible: 1940.
2. Organisme responsable de l'enregistrement des chômeurs
Nom de l'organisme: Centrelink .
Type d'organisme: Organisme public relevant d'une autorité nationale.
Nom de l'autorité nationale: Department of Employment and Workplace Relations and the Department of Family and Community Services (FaCS) (Département de l'Emploi et des Relations sur le lieu de travail et Département des Services de Communauté).
Situation des bureaux chargés de l'enregistrement: Centrelink a des bureaux dans 400 localités situées dans toute l'Australie.
Types de services fournis ou gérés par cet organisme:
- Paiement des indemnités de chômage.
3. Les informations personnelles suivantes sont enregistrées:
- Nom;
- Sexe;
- Adresse du domicile habituel;
- Date de naissance;
- Citoyenneté;
- Nationalité/groupe ethnique (information non obligatoire);
- Niveau d'instruction/de formation, en distinguant 16 catégories (information facultative);
- Situation de travail présente et passée, en distinguant 6 catégories;
- Type de profession de l'emploi antérieur ou actuel;
- Type de profession de l'emploi recherché (information facultative);
- Nom et adresse de l'employeur ou du lieu de travail actuel ou passé;
- Enregistrements antérieurs auprès de l'organisme;
- Autres: nombre d'enfants à charge; situation de famille; logement/appartement.
4. Critères utilisés pour déterminer si une personne doit être incluse dans le registre (R) et/ou dans les statistiques de chômeurs (S):
- Etre sans travail; les demandeurs d'emploi enregistrés peuvent cependant avoir un emploi occasionnel ou à temps partiel (faisant l'objet d'un examen de revenu) sans perdre leur droit au paiement des indemnités (R);
- Etre à la recherche d'un travail (R);
- Etre disponible pour travailler (R);
- Age: Minimum: 15 ans: Maximum: âge de la retraite (R);
- Etre résident dans le pays (minimum 104 semaines) (R);
- Autre: satisfaire aux critères du "test d'activité" démontrant qu'il/elle est activement à la recherche d'un travail (R).
5. Critères utilisés pour déterminer si une personne doit être exclue du registre (R) et/ou des statistiques de chômeurs (S):
- Avis de décès (R);
- Etablissement de la personne à l'étranger (R);
- Commencement d'un (nouveau) travail, à l'exclusion d'un travail occasionnel ou à temps partiel (R);
- Participation à un programme de promotion de l'emploi, à un programme de travaux publics, etc.; la participation à certains programmes, par exemple: "*Work for the Dole*", n'affecte cependant pas l'éligibilité au paiement des indemnités (R);
- Défaut de contact avec l'organisme/agence: pour la première et la deuxième infraction le paiement des indemnités de chômage est réduit; il est supprimé lors de la troisième infraction (R);
- Refus d'offres d'emploi adaptées; pour la première et la deuxième infraction le paiement des indemnités de chômage est réduit; il est supprimé lors de la troisième infraction (R);
- Refus d'offres de formation adaptées; pour la première et la deuxième infraction le paiement des indemnités de chômage est réduit; il est supprimé lors de la troisième infraction (R);
- Admission à toucher une pension (retraite, etc.): L'âge de la retraite est de 65 ans pour les hommes et de 62 pour

les femmes (R);
- Incapacité à travailler (R);
- Autre: si le revenu/biens du demandeur ou de son conjoint/partenaire dépasse une limite fixée (R); paiement d'une indemnité de compensation ou d'une indemnité pour blessure en relation avec le travail (R).
6. Définition des personnes au chômage sur laquelle les statistiques sont établies
Les registres ne servent pas à produire des statistiques sur le nombre des chômeurs. Cependant, les registres sont utilisés pour compter le nombre des personnes qui reçoivent des indemnités de chômage (*NSA ou YA*). Sont inclues les personnes qui reçoivent une indemnité de chômage en tenant compte des inclusions et exclusions énumérées dans les sections 4 et 5 ci-dessus.

Les séries *NSA* et le *YA(o)* incluent en général les personnes âgées de 15 à 64 ans pour les hommes, et de 15 à 61 ans pour les femmes, qui reçoivent des allocations.
7. Mise à jour des registres
Les registres sont mis à jour tous les 14 jours (le paiement des indemnités est fait tous les 14 jours).
8. Taux de chômage
Les statistiques basées sur les registres ne sont pas utilisées pour obtenir des taux de chômage.
9. Type de statistiques produites sur le nombre de chômeurs
Séries: *Labour Market and Related Payments* (Marché du Travail et Paiements y afférents).
Période de référence: Mois.
Fréquence de production: Mensuelle.
Variables utilisées:
- Sexe;
- Age;
- Caractéristiques géographiques;
- Durée du chômage.
Publication: Sur papier, à diffusion grand public.
Organisme/Agence responsable de la publication: FaCS.
Titre et périodicité de la publication: *Labour Market and Related Payments (*Marché du Travail et Paiements y afférents), publication mensuelle.
10. Information méthodologique au sujet de ces statistiques
Publication: Sur papier, à diffusion grand public.
Agence responsable pour la diffusion de l'information méthodologique: *FaCS.*
11. Comparaisons avec des statistiques provenant d'autres sources
Des comparaisons ont été faites avec les statistiques de chômage provenant de l'enquête de main-d'œuvre.
Fréquence des comparaisons: Occasionnellement (dernière année: 2000).
Publication de la méthodologie et/ou des résultats de la comparaison: A usage interne uniquement.
12. Principaux changements intervenus depuis le début de ces séries statistiques
Il n'y a pas eu de changement important dans la législation, dans la capacité de l'agence et/ou dans les procédures administratives susceptibles d'avoir influencé de manière significative les statistiques.

Bahreïn

1. Séries statistiques
Titre: Chômage enregistré.
Première année disponible: 1996.
2. Organisme responsable de l'enregistrement des chômeurs ou demandeurs d'emploi
Nom de l'organisme: Employment Services Bureau (Bureau des services de l'emploi).
Type d'organisme: Organisme public relevant d'une autorité nationale.
Nom de l'autorité nationale: Ministry of Labour and Social Affairs (Ministère du Travail et des Affaires Sociales).
Situation des bureaux chargés de l'enregistrement: Bâtiment principal du Ministère du Travail et des Affaires Sociales, Isa Town.
Types de services fournis et/ou gérés par cet organisme:
- Assistance aux demandeurs d'emploi pour trouver du travail;
- Assistance aux demandeurs d'emploi pour créer leur propre entreprise;
- Assistance aux employeurs pour trouver de la main-

d'œuvre;
- Orientation professionnelle;
- Formation liée à l'emploi.

3. Les informations personnelles suivantes sont enregistrées:
- Nom;
- Sexe;
- Numéro de sécurité sociale (ou numéro d'identification également utilisé par d'autres organismes);
- Adresse du domicile habituel;
- Date de naissance;
- Citoyenneté;
- Nationalité/groupe ethnique;
- Niveau d'instruction/ de formation, en distinguant six catégories. Des liens ont été établis avec la CITE;
- Situation de travail présente et passée, en distinguant cinq catégories;
- Type de profession de l'emploi antérieur ou actuel, en distinguant trois catégories dans la classification utilisée pour codifier l'emploi. Aucun lien n'a été établi avec la CITP;
- Type de profession de l'emploi recherché, avec neuf catégories distinguées dans la classification utilisée pour codifier l'emploi. Aucun lien n'a été établi avec la CITP;
- Nom et adresse de l'employeur ou du lieu de travail actuel ou passé;
- Autre: langues parlées; programme(s) de formation suivi(s).

4. Critères utilisés pour déterminer si une personne doit être incluse dans le registre (R) et/ou dans les statistiques de chômeurs (S):
- Etre sans travail (R);
- Etre à la recherche d'un travail (R);
- Etre disponible pour travailler (R);
- Age: Minimum: 17 ans; Maximum: 50 ans (R);
- Citoyenneté: obligatoirement Bahraini;
- Etre résident dans le pays (R);
- Avoir précédemment travaillé (R);
- Durée souhaitée de l'emploi recherché et/ou du nombre d'heures de travail recherché (R);
- Acquittement de cotisations d'assurance chômage (R).

5. Critères utilisés pour déterminer si une personne doit être exclue du registre (R) et/ou des statistiques de chômeurs (S):
- Avis de décès (S);
- Etablissement de la personne à l'étranger (S);
- Commencement d'un (nouveau) travail (R);
- Participation à un programme de promotion de l'emploi, à un programme de travaux publics, etc. (S);
- Entreprise d'une formation ou d'études (R);
- Défaut de contact avec l'organisme/agence (S);
- Refus d'offres d'emploi adaptées (S);
- Refus d'offres de formation adaptées (S);
- Fin de droit à l'allocation chômage (R);
- Admission à toucher une pension (retraite, etc.) (S);
- Incapacité à travailler (S).

6. Définition des personnes au chômage sur laquelle les statistiques sont établies
Sont considérées au chômage les personnes incluses dans la "General Organisation for Social Insurance (GOSI)" (l'Organisation générale de Sécurité sociale), et enregistrées auprès du "Employment Services Bureau" (Bureau de l'Emploi) du Ministère du Travail et des Affaires Sociales comme personnes à la recherche de travail ou comme personnes sans emploi.

7. Mise à jour des registres
Les registres sont mis à jour quotidiennement et mensuellement.

8. Taux de chômage
Les statistiques basées sur les registres sont utilisées pour obtenir des taux de chômage.
La source des données d'emploi qui sont partie du dénominateur est le registre de sécurité sociale.

9. Type de statistiques produites sur le nombre de chômeurs enregistrés
Série 1: Rapport journalier sur les conditions d'emploi.
Période de référence: Jour.
Fréquence de production: Quotidienne, ou en cas de besoin.
Variables utilisées:
- Sexe;

- Age;
- Niveau d'instruction;
- Profession;
- Branche d'activité;
- Caractéristiques géographiques;
- Expérience professionnelle antérieure;
- Citoyenneté (nationaux/non nationaux);
- Durée de chômage.

Publication: A usage interne uniquement.
- Série 2: Rapport abrégé pour toutes les conditions.
- Période de référence: Mois.
- Fréquence de production: Mensuelle, ou en cas de besoin.
- Variables utilisées:
- Sexe;
- Age;
- Niveau d'instruction;
- Profession;
- Branche d'activité;
- Caractéristiques géographiques;
- Expérience professionnelle antérieure;
- Citoyenneté (nationaux/non nationaux);
- Durée de chômage.

Publication: A usage interne uniquement.
Série 3:
Période de référence: Année.
- Fréquence de production: Annuellement, ou en cas de besoin.
- Variables utilisées:
- Sexe;
- Age;
- Niveau d'instruction;
- Profession;
- Branche d'activité;
- Caractéristiques géographiques;
- Expérience professionnelle antérieure;
- Citoyenneté (nationaux/non nationaux);
- Durée de chômage.

Forme de publication: A usage interne uniquement.
10. Information méthodologique au sujet de ces statistiques
Publication:
- En format électronique sur demande;
- Sur un site Internet: www.bah-Molsa.com/

11. Comparaisons avec des statistiques provenant d'autres sources
Des comparaisons ont été faites avec des statistiques de chômage provenant de recensements de la population.

12. Principaux changements intervenus depuis le début de ces séries statistiques
Il n'y a pas eu de changement important dans la législation, dans la capacité de l'agence et/ou dans les procédures administratives susceptibles d'avoir influencé de manière significative les statistiques.

Barbade

1. Séries statistiques
Titre: National Insurance Benefit Statistics (Statistiques des Allocations de l'Assurance nationale).
Première année disponible: 1881.

2. Organisme responsable de l'enregistrement des chômeurs ou demandeurs d'emploi
Nom de l'organisme: National Insurance Department (Département national d'Assurance).
Type d'organisme: Organisme public relevant d'une autorité nationale.
Nom de l'autorité nationale: Ministère du Travail et de la Sécurité sociale.
Situation des bureaux chargés de l'enregistrement: Dans toutes les régions du pays.

3. Les informations personnelles suivantes sont enregistrées:
- Nom;
- Numéro de sécurité sociale (ou numéro d'identification également utilisé par d'autres organismes);
- Adresse du domicile habituel;
- Date de naissance;
- Situation de travail présente et passée;

– Type de profession de l'emploi antérieur ou actuel;
– Branche d'activité de l'employeur ou du lieu de travail actuel ou passé;
– Autre: toute contribution remarquable.

4. Critères utilisés pour déterminer si une personne doit être incluse dans le registre (R) et/ou dans les statistiques de chômeurs (S):

– Etre sans travail: les demandeurs devraient être sans travail depuis au moins trois semaines (R) et (S);
– Etre à la recherche d'un travail: ne sera pas incluse toute personne qui néglige de saisir une opportunité d'emploi adapté, ou qui ne fait pas d'effort raisonnable pour trouver un emploi alternatif adapté (R) et (S);
– Etre disponible pour travailler (R) et (S);
– Age: Minimum: 18 ans; Maximum: 65 ans (R) et (S);
– Etre résident dans le pays (R) et (S);
– Avoir précédemment travaillé pendant au moins une année;
– Acquittement de cotisations d'assurance chômage: la personne doit avoir été assurée pendant 52 semaines au moins, et 20 contributions au moins devront avoir été acquittées ou créditées pendant trois trimestres consécutifs.

5. Critères utilisés pour déterminer si une personne doit être exclue du registre (R) et/ou des statistiques de chômeurs (S):

– Etablissement de la personne à l'étranger;
– Commencement d'un (nouveau) travail;
– Défaut de contact avec l'organisme/agence;
– Refus d'offres d'emploi adaptées (une offre);
– Fin de droit à l'allocation chômage (l'allocation-chômage est payable pour chaque jour de chômage pendant un maximum de 26 semaines).

6. Définition des personnes au chômage sur laquelle les statistiques sont établies

Information non disponible

7. Mise à jour des registres

Les registres sont mis à jour deux fois par semaine.

8. Taux de chômage

Les statistiques basées sur les registres ne sont pas utilisées pour obtenir des taux de chômage.

9. Type de statistiques sur le nombre de chômeurs enregistrés produites

Série 1: *National Insurance Annual Report Statistics* (Statistiques du rapport annuel de l'assurance nationale), nombre de demandes enregistrées et acceptées durant l'année.

Publication: Sur papier, à diffusion grand public.

Organisme/Agence responsable de la publication: Département national d'Assurance.

10. Information méthodologique au sujet de ces statistiques

Publication: Sur papier, à diffusion grand public.

Organisme responsable: Département national d'Assurance.

11. Comparaisons avec des statistiques provenant d'autres sources

Il n'y a pas eu de comparaisons faites avec des statistiques provenant d'autres sources.

12. Principaux changements intervenus depuis le début de ces séries statistiques

Il n'y a pas eu de changement important dans la législation, dans la capacité de l'agence et/ou dans les procédures administratives susceptibles d'avoir influencé de manière significative les statistiques.

Bélarus

1. Séries statistiques

Titre: Nombre de chômeurs enregistrés placés par l'Agence national de l'Emploi.

Première année disponible: 1991.

2. Organisme responsable de l'enregistrement des chômeurs ou demandeurs d'emploi

Nom de l'organisme: Agence Nationale de l'Emploi.

Type d'organisme: Organisme public relevant d'une autorité nationale.

Nom de l'organisme national: Employment Services of the Republic of Belarus (Agence de l'Emploi de la République de Belarus).

Situation des bureaux chargés de l'enregistrement: Dans toutes les régions du pays, il y a des centres d'emploi régionaux, de districts et de villes.

Types de services fournis ou gérés par cet organisme:

– Assistance aux demandeurs d'emploi pour trouver du travail;
– Assistance aux demandeurs d'emploi pour créer leur propre entreprise;
– Assistance aux employeurs pour trouver de la main-d'œuvre;
– Orientation professionnelle;
– Formation liée à l'emploi;
– Paiement des indemnités de chômage;
– Autres services liés à l'emploi: information gratuite sur les vacances de postes; possibilités de participer à des travaux publics rémunérés; création de nouvelles places de travail puis placement des demandeurs d'emploi; assistance avec placement temporaire d'écoliers et d'étudiants.

Pourcentage des demandeurs d'emploi qui cherchent un emploi au travers de cet organisme: 30%.

3. Les informations personnelles suivantes sont enregistrées:

– Nom;
– Sexe;
– Adresse du domicile habituel;
– Date de naissance;
– Citoyenneté;
– Niveau d'instruction/de formation;
– Situation de travail présente et passée, en distinguant 30 catégories;
– Type de profession de l'emploi antérieur ou actuel;
– Type de profession de l'emploi recherché;
– Nom et adresse de l'employeur ou du lieu de travail actuel ou passé;
– Branche d'activité de l'employeur ou du lieu de travail actuel ou passé;
– Inscriptions/enregistrements antérieurs auprès de l'organisme.

4. Critères utilisés pour déterminer si une personne doit être incluse dans le registre (R) et/ou dans les statistiques de chômeurs (S):

– Etre sans travail (R) et (S);
– Etre à la recherche d'un travail (R) et (S);
– Age: Minimum: 16 ans; Maximum: 55 ans pour les femmes et 60 ans pour les hommes (R) et (S);
– Avoir précédemment travaillé (R) et (S).

5. Critères utilisés pour déterminer si une personne doit être exclue du registre (R) et/ou des statistiques de chômeurs (S):

– Avis de décès (R) et (S);
– Commencement d'un (nouveau) travail (R) et (S);
– Commencement du service militaire (R);
– Participation à un programme de promotion de l'emploi, à un programme de travaux publics (R) et (S);
– Défaut de contact avec l'organisme/agence (R) et (S) après une période de 12 mois;
– Admission à toucher une pension (retraite, etc.) (R) et (S);
– Incapacité à travailler (R).

6. Définition des personnes au chômage sur laquelle les statistiques sont établies

Information non disponible.

7. Mise à jour des registres

Les registres sont mis à jour trimestriellement, et mensuellement pour une liste sélectionnée d'indicateurs.

8. Taux de chômage

Les statistiques basées sur les registres sont utilisées pour obtenir des taux de chômage.

Les sources des données d'emploi qui sont partie du dénominateur sont les suivantes:

– Enquête auprès des établissements;
– Estimations officielles;
– Recensements de population.

Définition des personnes pourvues d'un emploi à cette fin: Information non disponible.

9. Type de statistiques sur le nombre de chômeurs enregistrés produites

Série 1:

Période de référence: Mois

Variables utilisées:

– Caractéristiques géographiques;
– Citoyenneté (nationaux/non nationaux);

–   Participation de demandeurs d'emploi à des travaux publics rémunérés;
–   Formation et formation continue de demandeurs d'emploi.

Publication:
–   Sur papier, à diffusion grand public;
–   Sur un site Internet

Série 2:
–   Période de référence: Trimestrielle.

Variables utilisées:
–   Sexe;
–   Caractéristiques géographiques;
–   Expérience professionnelle antérieure;
–   Citoyenneté (nationaux/non nationaux);
–   Durée du chômage;
–   Participation de demandeurs d'emploi à des travaux publics rémunérés;
–   Formation et nouvelle formation de demandeurs d'emploi;
–   Création de nouveaux emplois;
–   Assistance à la création d'entreprises individuelles.

Publication:
–   Sur papier, à diffusion grand public;
–   Sur un site Internet

Série 3:
Période de référence: Semestrielle.

Variables utilisées:
–   Sexe;
–   Age;
–   Niveau d'éducation;
–   Profession;
–   Branche d'activité;
–   Caractéristiques géographiques;
–   Expérience professionnelle antérieure;
–   Citoyenneté (nationaux/non nationaux);
–   Durée du chômage;
–   Durée de réception de l'allocation chômage.

Publication:
–   Sur papier, à diffusion grand public;
–   Sur un site Internet

Agence responsable de la publication: Département de l'Emploi du Ministère du Travail et de la Protection sociale, et le Ministère des Statistiques et de l'Analyse.
Titre des publications: Publications statistiques officielles dans les journaux: *Emploi & Marché du travail*.
10. Information méthodologique au sujet de ces statistiques
Publication: Sur papier, à diffusion restreinte.
Agence responsable: Département de l'Emploi du Ministère du Travail et de la Protection sociale.
11. Comparaisons avec des statistiques provenant d'autres sources
Des comparaisons ont été faites avec des statistiques de chômage provenant d'autres types d'enquêtes auprès des ménages et de recensements de population.
Fréquence des comparaisons: Occasionnelle.
Publication de la méthodologie et/ou des résultats de la comparaison: Ils n'ont pas été publiés.
12. Principaux changements intervenus depuis le début de ces séries statistiques
Il n'y a pas eu de changement important dans la législation, dans la capacité de l'agence et/ou dans les procédures administratives susceptibles d'avoir influencé de manière significative les statistiques.

Belgique (1) / Région de Bruxelles - Capitale

1. Séries statistiques
Titre: *Rapport mensuel sur le marché de l'emploi* et *Rapport annuel statistique*.
Première année disponible: 1989
2. Organisme responsable de l'enregistrement des chômeurs ou demandeurs d'emploi
Nom de l'organisme: Office Régional Bruxellois de l'Emploi (ORBEM).
Type d'organisme: Organisme public relevant d'une autorité régionale.
Situation des bureaux chargés de l'enregistrement: Région de Bruxelles-Capitale.

Types de services fournis et/ou gérés par cet organisme:
–   Assistance aux demandeurs d'emploi pour trouver du travail;
–   Assistance aux employeurs pour trouver de la main-d'œuvre;
–   Orientation professionnelle;
–   Autres services liés à l'emploi: gestion de programmes d'emploi, halte-garderie, test des connaissances en langues, expertise sur le marché du travail, etc.
Pourcentage des demandeurs d'emploi qui cherchent un emploi au travers de cet organisme: non disponible.
3. Les informations personnelles suivantes sont enregistrées:
–   Nom;
–   Sexe;
–   Numéro de sécurité sociale (ou numéro d'identification également utilisé par d'autres organismes);
–   Adresse du domicile habituel;
–   Date de naissance;
–   Nationalité;
–   Niveau de formation. Aucun lien n'a été établi avec le CITE;
–   Type de profession de l'emploi antérieur et/ou actuel, en distinguant 2216 catégories. Aucun lien n'a été établi avec la CITP;
–   Type de profession de l'emploi recherché, avec 2216 catégories;
–   Branche d'activité de l'employeur ou du lieu de travail actuel ou passé, en distinguant 66 catégories. Aucun lien n'a été établi avec la CITI;
–   Inscriptions/enregistrements antérieurs auprès de l'organisme;
–   Autre: permis de travail, durée d'inoccupation, qualifications, aptitudes, véhicule, permis de conduire, connaissances linguistiques, état-civil, nombre d'enfants à charge.
4. Critères utilisés pour déterminer si une personne doit être incluse dans le registre (R) et/ou dans les statistiques de chômeurs (S):
–   Etre sans travail (S);
–   Etre à la recherche d'un travail (R) et (S);
–   Etre disponible pour travailler (S);
–   Age: Minimum: 15 ans; Maximum: 65 ans (R) et (S);
–   Etre résident dans le pays (S).
5. Critères utilisés pour déterminer si une personne doit être exclue du registre (R) et/ou des statistiques de chômeurs (S):
–   Avis de décès (S);
–   Etablissement de la personne à l'étranger (S);
–   Commencement d'un (nouveau) travail (S) en cas de placement par l'Office ou de communication à l'Office par le demandeur d'emploi;
–   Participation à un programme de promotion de l'emploi, à un programme de travaux publics, etc. (S);
–   Entreprise d'une formation ou d'études (S);
–   Défaut de contact avec l'organisme/agence au bout de trois lettres restées sans réponse (S);
–   Refus d'offres d'emploi adaptées (S);
–   Refus d'offres de formation adaptées (S);
–   Fin de droit à l'allocation-chômage pour les cohabitants: Selon l'article 80, si la durée du chômage est une fois et demi la durée moyenne «régionale» du chômage, selon le sexe et la catégorie d'âge, cela entraîne la suspension des allocations pour une période indéterminée (S);
–   Admission à toucher une pension (retraite, etc.) (S);
–   Incapacité à travailler, en cas d'incapacité de plus de 66% (S);
–   Autre: absences successives au pointage communal (S).
6. Définition des personnes au chômage sur laquelle les statistiques sont établies
Personnes âgées de plus de 15 ans, sans emploi, disponibles sur le marché du travail et à la recherche d'un travail. En pratique, cette série comprend l'ensemble des demandeurs d'emploi inoccupés, c'est-à-dire:
–   les chômeurs complets indemnisés;
–   les jeunes travailleurs et les jeunes qui perçoivent des allocations d'attente;
–   les demandeurs d'emploi inoccupés, librement inscrits (non indemnisés parce qu'ils n'ont pas droit aux allocations);

les autres demandeurs d'emploi inoccupés et obligatoirement inscrits. Cette catégorie comprend:

- certains chômeurs complets exclus temporairement du bénéfice des allocations de chômage, durant la durée de leur exclusion;
- les personnes présentées par les Centres publics d'aide sociale;
- certaines personnes relevant du Fonds communautaire pour l'intégration sociale et professionnelle des personnes handicapées qui ne répondent pas aux conditions d'octroi des allocations de chômage;
- les travailleurs ayant été occupés dans un emploi à temps partiel devenu volontaire, devenus chômeurs complets;
- les chômeurs qui renoncent volontairement au bénéfice des allocations de chômage;
- les jeunes bénéficiant d'allocations de transition. Ils sont inscrits comme demandeurs d'un emploi à temps partiel.

7. Mise à jour des registres
Les registres sont mis à jour tous les mois.

8. Taux de chômage
Les statistiques basées sur les registres sont utilisées pour obtenir des taux de chômage.

La source des données d'emploi qui sont partie du dénominateur provient d'estimations officielles.

9. Type de statistiques produites sur le nombre de chômeurs enregistrés produites
Période de référence: Mois.
Fréquence de production: Mensuelle.
Variables utilisées:

- Sexe;
- Age;
- Niveau d'instruction;
- Profession;
- Branche d'activité;
- Caractéristiques géographiques;
- Nationalité;
- Durée de chômage.

Publication:

- Sur papier, à diffusion restreinte;
- En format électronique, sur demande.

Organisme responsable de la publication: ORBEM.
Titre et périodicité de la publication / des publications: *Rapport mensuel sur l'évolution du marché de l'emploi.*

10. Information méthodologique au sujet de ces statistiques
Publication: Sur papier, à diffusion restreinte.
Organisme responsable: ORBEM.

11. Comparaisons avec des statistiques provenant d'autres sources
Des comparaisons ont été faites avec des statistiques provenant de l'enquête de main-d'œuvre et du recensement de population.
Fréquence des comparaisons: Occasionnelles.
Publication de la méthodologie et des résultats de la comparaison: Ils ont été publiés.
Titre de la publication contenant la description de la méthodologie et/ou les résultats de cette comparaison: Conseil supérieur de l'emploi: *Comment comptabiliser le nombre de chômeurs ? Une grille de lecture des taux de chômage*, publié par le Ministère Fédéral de l'Emploi et du Travail.

12. Principaux changements intervenus depuis le début de ces séries statistiques
Des changements importants dans la législation, dans la capacité de l'agence et/ou dans les procédures administratives susceptibles d'avoir influencé de manière significative les statistiques sont intervenus en 1994, 1995. 1996 et 2002.

Belgique (2) / Flandres

1. Séries statistiques
Titre: Demandeurs d'emploi enregistrés.
Première année disponible: 1989.

2. Organisme responsable de l'enregistrement des chômeurs ou demandeurs d'emploi
Nom de l'organisme: VDAB (Service flamand de l'Emploi et de la Formation professionnelle).
Type d'organisme: Organisme public relevant d'autorités régionales.
Situation des bureaux chargés de l'enregistrement: En Flandres.

Types de services fournis/gérés par cet organisme:

- Assistance aux demandeurs d'emploi pour trouver du travail;
- Assistance aux employeurs pour trouver de la main-d'œuvre;
- Orientation professionnelle;
- Formation liée à l'emploi.

3. Les informations personnelles suivantes sont enregistrées:

- Nom;
- Sexe;
- Numéro de sécurité sociale (ou numéro d'identification également utilisé par d'autres organismes);
- Adresse du domicile habituel;
- Date de naissance;
- Citoyenneté;
- Nationalité/groupe ethnique;
- Niveau d'instruction/de formation, en distinguant un nombre non spécifié de catégories. Aucun lien n'a été établi avec la CITE ;
- Situation de travail présente/passée, en distinguant un nombre non spécifié de catégories,
- Type de travail (profession) de l'emploi antérieur ou actuel, en distinguant un nombre non spécifié de groupes. Aucun lien n'a été établi avec la CITP-88;
- Type de profession de l'emploi recherché, en distinguant un nombre non spécifié de groupes. Aucun lien n'a été établi avec la CITP-88;
- Branche d'activité (industrie) de l'employeur ou du lieu de travail actuel ou passé, en distinguant un nombre non spécifié de groupes. C'est la NACE-rév.1 qui est utilisée au niveau de cinq chiffres pour coder cette variable. Des liens ont été établis avec la CITI-rév.3 au niveau des catégories de classement;
- Enregistrements antérieurs auprès de l'organisme;
- Autre: durée du chômage.

4. Critères utilisés pour déterminer si une personne doit être incluse dans le registre (R) et/ou dans les statistiques de chômeurs (S):

- Etre sans travail (demandeurs d'emploi sans travail) (R) et (S);
- Etre à la recherche d'un travail (tous les demandeurs d'emploi) (R) et (S);
- Etre disponible pour travailler (R) et (S);
- Age (R) et (S);
- Citoyenneté (R) et (S);
- Avoir précédemment travaillé (R);
- Durée souhaitée de l'emploi recherché et/ou du nombre d'heures de travail recherché (durée minimum: une heure) (R).

5. Critères utilisés pour déterminer si une personne doit être exclue du registre (R) et/ou des statistiques de chômeurs (S):

- Décès (R) et (S);
- Commencement d'un (nouveau) travail (R) et (S);
- Participation à un programme de promotion de l'emploi, à un programme de travaux publics, etc. (R);
- Entreprise d'une formation ou d'études (R) et (S);
- Refus d'une offre d'emploi adaptée (R);
- Refus d'une offre de formation adaptée (R);
- Fin de droit à l'allocation chômage (demandeurs d'emploi sans travail avec allocation chômage) (R) et (S);
- Admission à toucher une pension (R) et (S);
- Incapacité à travailler (R) et (S).

6. Définition des personnes au chômage sur laquelle les statistiques sont établies
1. Demandeurs d'emploi inoccupés:

- Inoccupés touchant des indemnités de chômage;
- Inoccupés à la sortie de l'école;
- Inoccupés, enregistrement volontaire;
- Autres.

2. Demandeurs d'emploi occupés:

- Occupés à temps partiel;
- Occupés à plein temps;
- Autres.

7. Mise à jour des registres
Les registres sont mis à jour quotidiennement.

8. Taux de chômage
Les statistiques basées sur les registres sont utilisées pour obtenir des taux de chômage.

La source des données d'emploi qui sont partie du dénominateur des taux de chômage est l'enquête sur la main-d'œuvre.

Définition des personnes pourvues d'un emploi à cette fin: Non spécifiée.

9. Type de statistiques produites sur le nombre de chômeurs enregistrés

Série 1:

Période de référence: Mois.

Fréquence de production: Mensuelle.

Variables utilisées:
– Sexe;
– Age;
– Niveau d'instruction;
– Occupation;
– Branche d'activité;
– Caractéristiques géographiques;
– Expérience professionnelle antérieure;
– Citoyenneté (nationaux/non nationaux);
– Durée de chômage.

Publication:
– Sur papier, à diffusion grand public;
– Sur un site Internet (www.vdab.be).

Agence responsable de la publication: VDAB

Titre et périodicité de la publication: *Maandverlag Arbeidsmarkt Vlaanderen* (mensuelle).

Série 2:

Période de référence: Année.

Fréquence de production: Annuelle.

Variables utilisées:
– Sexe;
– Age;
– Niveau d'instruction;
– Occupation;
– Branche d'activité;
– Caractéristiques géographiques;
– Expérience professionnelle antérieure;
– Citoyenneté (nationaux/non nationaux);
– Durée de chômage.

Publication:
– Sur papier, à diffusion grand public;
– Sur un site Internet (www.vdab.be).

Agence responsable de la publication: VDAB

Titre et périodicité de la publication: *Jaarverlag Arbeidsmarkt Vlaanderen* (annuelle).

10. Information méthodologique au sujet de ces statistiques

Publication:
– Sur papier, à diffusion grand public;
– En format électronique, sur demande;
– Sur un site Internet (www.vdab.be).

Agence responsable pour la diffusion de l'information méthodologique: VDAB

11. Comparaisons avec des statistiques provenant d'autres sources

Il n'y a pas eu de comparaisons faites avec des statistiques provenant d'autres sources.

12. Principaux changements intervenus depuis le début de ces séries statistiques

Il n'y a pas eu de changement important dans la législation, dans la capacité de l'agence et/ou dans les procédures administratives susceptibles d'avoir influencé de manière significative les statistiques.

Botswana

1. Séries statistiques

Titre: Chômage enregistré.

Première année disponible: Non spécifié.

2. Organisme responsable de l'enregistrement des chômeurs ou demandeurs d'emploi

Nom de l'organisme: Ministère du Travail et de la Sécurité sociale - Services de l'emploi.

Type d'organisme: Organisme public relevant d'une autorité nationale.

Nom de l'autorité nationale: Ministère du Travail et de la Sécurité sociale.

Situation des bureaux chargés de l'enregistrement: Dans tous les bureaux d'emploi des municipalités.

Types de services fournis/gérés par cet organisme:
– Assistance aux demandeurs d'emploi pour trouver du travail;
– Assistance aux employeurs pour trouver de la main-d'œuvre.

Pourcentage des demandeurs d'emploi qui cherchent un emploi au travers de cet organisme: 21%.

3. Les informations personnelles suivantes sont enregistrées:
– Nom;
– Sexe;
– Adresse du domicile habituel;
– Date de naissance;
– Citoyenneté;
– Nationalité/groupe ethnique;
– Niveau d'instruction/de formation, en distinguant quatre catégories. Aucun lien n'a été établi avec la CITE ;
– Situation de travail présente/passée;
– Type de travail (profession) de l'emploi antérieur ou actuel;
– Type de travail (profession) de l'emploi recherché. Aucun lien n'a été établi avec la CITP;
– Nom et adresse de l'employeur ou du lieu de travail actuel ou passé;
– Branche d'activité (industrie) de l'employeur ou du lieu de travail actuel ou passé, en distinguant six groupes. Aucun lien n'a été établi avec la CITI;
– Enregistrements antérieurs auprès de l'organisme;
– Autre: numéro d'enregistrement; numéro de carte d'identité.

4. Critères utilisés pour déterminer si une personne doit être incluse dans le registre (R) et/ou dans les statistiques de chômeurs (S):
– Etre sans travail (les étudiants ne sont pas inclus) (R) et (S);
– Etre à la recherche d'un travail (R) et (S);
– Etre disponible pour travailler (R) et (S);
– Age: Minimum: 18 ans; Pas de limite supérieure (R) et (S);
– Citoyenneté (les non-citoyens ne font pas partie des «chômeurs») (R) et (S);
– Avoir précédemment travaillé.

5. Critères utilisés pour déterminer si une personne doit être exclue du registre (R) et/ou des statistiques de chômeurs (S):
– Décès (R) et (S);
– Commencement d'un nouveau travail (R) et (S);
– Entreprise d'une formation ou d'études (R) et (S);
– Défaut de contact avec l'organisme/agence (l'enregistrement est renouvelé à la fin de chaque année) (R) et (S).

6. Définition des personnes au chômage sur laquelle les statistiques sont établies

La main d'œuvre sans travail ou source de revenu.

7. Mise à jour des registres

Les registres sont mis à jour tous les ans.

8. Taux de chômage

Les statistiques basées sur les registres sont utilisées pour obtenir des taux de chômage.

Les sources des données d'emploi qui sont partie du dénominateur des taux de chômage sont l'enquête sur la main-d'œuvre et les estimations officielles.

Définition des personnes pourvues d'un emploi à cette fin:

La main d'œuvre ayant un travail comme source de revenu.

9. Type de statistiques produites sur le nombre de chômeurs enregistrés

Information non disponible.

10. Information méthodologique au sujet de ces statistiques

Publication:
– Sur papier, à diffusion grand public;
– Sur un site Internet (www.cso.gov.bw).

Agence responsable pour la diffusion de l'information méthodologique: Bureau central des statistiques.

11. Comparaisons avec des statistiques provenant d'autres sources

Des comparaisons ont été faites avec des statistiques provenant de sources non spécifiées.

Fréquence des comparaisons: Régulièrement lors de la publication des statistiques.

Publication de la méthodologie et/ou des résultats de la comparaison: Ils n'ont pas été publiés.

12. Principaux changements intervenus depuis le début de ces séries statistiques

Des changements importants dans la législation, dans la capacité de l'agence et/ou dans les procédures administratives sont intervenus en 1996, 1997, 1998, 1999 et 2000. Les changements concernant les statistiques qui en résultaient n'on pas été évalués.

Bulgarie

1. Séries statistiques
Titre: Information mensuelle sur la situation du chômage en Bulgarie.
Première année disponible: 1991.
2. Organisme responsable de l'enregistrement des chômeurs ou demandeurs d'emploi
Nom de l'organisme: Agence pour l'Emploi.
Type d'organisme: Organisme public relevant d'une autorité nationale.
Nom de l'autorité nationale: Ministère du Travail et de la Politique sociale.
Situation des bureaux chargés de l'enregistrement:
Il y a 122 bureaux de placement et 141 annexes de ces bureaux dans tout le pays.
Types de services fournis et/ou gérés par cet organisme:
- Assistance aux demandeurs d'emploi pour trouver du travail;
- Assistance aux demandeurs d'emploi pour créer leur propre entreprise;
- Assistance aux employeurs pour trouver de la main-d'œuvre;
- Orientation professionnelle;
- Formation liée à l'emploi;
- Paiement des indemnités de chômage.
3. Les informations personnelles suivantes sont enregistrées:
- Nom;
- Sexe;
- Numéro de sécurité sociale (ou numéro d'identification également utilisé par d'autres organismes);
- Adresse du domicile habituel;
- Date de naissance;
- Citoyenneté;
- Niveau d'instruction/ de formation, en distinguant huit catégories. Aucun lien n'a été établi avec la CITE;
- Situation de travail présente et passée, en distinguant quatre catégories;
- Type de profession de l'emploi antérieur ou actuel, en distinguant 51 catégories. Aucun lien n'a été établi avec la CITP;
- Type de profession de l'emploi recherché, avec 51 catégories. Aucun lien n'a été établi avec la CITP;
- Nom et adresse de l'employeur ou du lieu de travail actuel ou passé;
- Branche d'activité de l'employeur ou du lieu de travail actuel ou passé, en distinguant 280 catégories. Des liens ont été établis avec la NACE, rév.1 au niveau des classes;
- Inscriptions/enregistrements antérieurs auprès de l'organisme.
4. Critères utilisés pour déterminer si une personne doit être incluse dans le registre (R) et/ou dans les statistiques de chômeurs (S):
- Etre sans travail (R);
- Etre à la recherche d'un travail (R);
- Etre disponible pour travailler (R);
- Age: Minimum: 16 ans; pas de limite supérieure (R);
- Citoyenneté (R);
- Etre résident dans le pays (R).
5. Critères utilisés pour déterminer si une personne doit être exclue du registre (R) et/ou des statistiques de chômeurs (S):
- Avis de décès (R);
- Etablissement de la personne à l'étranger (R);
- Commencement d'un (nouveau) travail (R);
- Commencement du service militaire (R);
- Participation à un programme de promotion de l'emploi, à un programme de travaux publics, etc. (R);
- Entreprise d'une formation ou d'études (R);

- Défaut de contact avec l'organisme/agence (R);
- Refus d'offres d'emploi adaptées (R);
- Refus d'offres de formation adaptées (R);
- Admission à toucher une pension (R).
6. Définition des personnes au chômage sur laquelle les statistiques sont établies
Est considérée au chômage une personne sans travail, qui cherche activement du travail et qui est prête à commencer à travailler dans les deux semaines suivant la notification du bureau de travail.
7. Mise à jour des registres
Les registres sont mis à jour régulièrement.
8. Taux de chômage
Les statistiques basées sur les registres sont utilisées pour obtenir des taux de chômage.
La source des données d'emploi qui sont partie du dénominateur est le recensement de population.
9. Type de statistiques produites sur le nombre de chômeurs enregistrés
Série 1:
Période de référence: Mois.
Fréquence de production: Mensuelle.
Variables utilisées:
- Sexe;
- Age;
- Niveau d'instruction;
- Profession;
- Branche d'activité;
- Caractéristiques géographiques;
- Durée de chômage;
- Autre: caractéristiques du niveau de formation et d'instruction.
Publication:
- A usage interne uniquement;
- Sur papier, à diffusion restreinte;
- Sur un site Internet (www.nsz.government.bg).
Agence responsable de la publication: Agence pour l'Emploi.
Titre de la publication: *Information mensuelle sur la situation du chômage en Bulgarie.*
Série 2:
Période de référence: Année.
Fréquence de production: Annuelle.
Variables utilisées:
- Sexe;
- Age;
- Niveau d'instruction;
- Profession;
- Autre: caractéristiques de formation et d'instruction.
Publication: Sur papier, à diffusion grand public.
Agence responsable de la publication: Institut National Statistique.
Titre de la publication: *Statistics Reference Book* (livre de référence statistique).
Série 3:
Période de référence: Année.
Fréquence de production: Annuelle.
Variables utilisées:
- Sexe;
- Age;
- Niveau d'instruction;
- Caractéristiques géographiques;
- Autre: caractéristiques du niveau de formation et d'instruction.
Publication: Sur papier, à diffusion grand public.
Agence responsable de la publication: Institut National Statistique.
Titre de la publication: *NSI Yearbook* (Annuaire NSI).
10. Information méthodologique au sujet de ces statistiques
Publication: Pas publiée, disponible à usage interne uniquement.
Agence responsable: Agence pour l'Emploi.
11. Comparaisons avec des statistiques provenant d'autres sources
Il n'y a pas eu de comparaisons faites avec des statistiques provenant d'autres sources.
12. Principaux changements intervenus depuis le début de ces séries statistiques
Il n'y a pas eu de changement important dans la législation, dans la capacité de l'agence et/ou dans les procédures

administratives susceptibles d'avoir influencé de manière significative les statistiques.

Burkina Faso

1. Séries statistiques
Titre: Rapports d'activité annuels.

Première année disponible: 1980
2. Organisme responsable de l'enregistrement des chômeurs ou demandeurs d'emploi
Nom de l'organisme: Office national de la Promotion de l'Emploi (ONPE).
Type d'organisme: Organisme public relevant d'une autorité nationale.
Nom de l'autorité nationale: Ministère de l'Emploi, du Travail et de la Sécurité sociale.
Situation des bureaux chargés de l'enregistrement: Ouagadougou, Bobo-Dioulasso, Banfora, Koudougou et Fada N'Gourma.
Types de services fournis et/ou gérés par cet organisme:
–   Assistance aux demandeurs d'emploi pour trouver du travail;
–   Assistance aux demandeurs d'emploi pour créer leur propre entreprise;
–   Assistance aux employeurs pour trouver de la main-d'œuvre;
–   Orientation professionnelle;
–   Formation liée à l'emploi;
–   Autres: assistance aux demandeurs d'emploi pour acquérir une expérience professionnelle, ou un stage.
3. Les informations personnelles suivantes sont enregistrées:
–   Nom;
–   Sexe;
–   Adresse du domicile habituel;
–   Date de naissance;
–   Nationalité/groupe ethnique;
–   Niveau d'instruction/ de formation, en distinguant 10 catégories. Aucun lien n'a été établi avec le CITE;
–   Situation de travail présente et passée, en distinguant deux catégories;
–   Type de profession de l'emploi recherché, avec six catégories; Des liens ont été établis avec la CITP-88 au niveau des grands groupes;
–   Inscriptions/enregistrements antérieurs auprès de l'organisme.
4. Critères utilisés pour déterminer si une personne doit être incluse dans le registre (R) et/ou dans les statistiques de chômeurs (S):
–   Etre sans travail (R) et (S);
–   Etre à la recherche d'un travail (R) et (S);
–   Etre disponible pour travailler (R) et (S);
–   Age: Minimum: 18 ans; Maximum: 55 ans (R) et (S);
–   Etre résident dans le pays (R) et (S);
–   Avoir précédemment travaillé (R) et (S).
5. Critères utilisés pour déterminer si une personne doit être exclue du registre (R) et/ou des statistiques de chômeurs (S):
–   Avis de décès (R) et (S);
–   Etablissement de la personne à l'étranger (R) et (S);
–   Commencement d'un (nouveau) travail. Le demandeur d'emploi est tenu de signaler à l'ONPE dans les 10 jours qui suivent les changements intervenus dans sa situation (R) et (S);
–   Admission à toucher une pension (retraite, etc.) (R) et (S).
6. Définition des personnes au chômage sur laquelle les statistiques sont établies
     Sont considérées comme chômeurs les personnes actives en âge de travailler et qui sont sans travail, qu'elles aient ou non travaillé auparavant.
7. Mise à jour des registres
     Les registres sont mis à jour trimestriellement.
8. Taux de chômage
     Les statistiques basées sur les registres ne sont pas utilisées pour obtenir des taux de chômage.
9. Type de statistiques produites sur le nombre de chômeurs enregistrés
Période de référence: trimestre.
Fréquence de production: trimestrielle.

Variables utilisées:
–   Sexe;
–   Age;
–   Niveau d'instruction;
–   Profession;
–   Expérience professionnelle antérieure.
Publication: Sur papier, à diffusion grand public.
Agence responsable de la publication: ONPE.
Titre et périodicité des publications: *Rapport d'activité trimestriel*, *Rapport d'activité semestriel* et *Rapport d'activité annuel*.
10. Information méthodologique au sujet de ces statistiques
Publication: Sur papier, à diffusion grand public.
Agence responsable: ONPE.
11. Comparaisons avec des statistiques provenant d'autres sources
     Il n'y a pas eu de comparaisons faites avec des statistiques provenant d'autres sources.
12. Principaux changements intervenus depuis le début de ces séries statistiques
     Il n'y a pas eu de changement important dans la législation, dans la capacité de l'agence et/ou dans les procédures administratives susceptibles d'avoir influencé de manière significative les statistiques.

Cambodge

1. Séries statistiques
Titre:
1. Nombre de chômeurs enregistrés par niveau d'instruction, groupe d'âge et sexe.
2. Nombre de chômeurs enregistrés par niveau de compétence, groupe d'âge et sexe.
3. Nombre de chômeurs enregistrés et placés par niveau de compétence.
Première année disponible: 2001.
2. Organisme responsable de l'enregistrement des chômeurs ou demandeurs d'emploi
Nom de l'organisme: Département de l'emploi et de la main d'œuvre.
Type d'organisme: Organisme public relevant d'une autorité nationale et régionale.
Nom de l'autorité nationale: Ministry of Social Affairs, Labour, Vocational Training and Youth Rehabilitation (Ministère des Affaires sociales, du Travail, de la Formation et de la Réinsertion des jeunes).
Situation des bureaux chargés de l'enregistrement: Phnom Penh et dans quatre provinces.
Types de services fournis et/ou gérés par cet organisme:
–   Assistance aux demandeurs d'emploi pour trouver du travail;
–   Assistance aux employeurs pour trouver de la main-d'œuvre.
3. Les informations personnelles suivantes sont enregistrées
–   Nom;
–   Sexe;
–   Adresse du domicile habituel;
–   Date de naissance;
–   Citoyenneté;
–   Nationalité;
–   Niveau d'instruction/ de formation, en distinguant huit catégories. Aucun lien n'a été établi avec la CITE;
–   Type de profession de l'emploi antérieur ou actuel; des liens ont été établis avec la CITP au niveau des groupes de base;
–   Type de profession de l'emploi recherché; des liens ont été établis avec la CITP au niveau des groupes de base;
–   Nom et adresse de l'employeur ou du lieu de travail actuel ou passé;
4. Critères utilisés pour déterminer si une personne doit être incluse dans le registre (R) et/ou dans les statistiques de chômeurs (S)
–   Etre sans travail (R) et (S);
–   Etre à la recherche d'un travail (R) et (S);
–   Etre disponible pour travailler (R) et (S);
–   Age: Minimum: 15 ans; Maximum: 39 ans (R) et (S);
–   Citoyenneté (R);
–   Avoir précédemment travaillé (R).

5. Critères utilisés pour déterminer si une personne doit être exclue du registre (R) et/ou des statistiques de chômeurs (S):
– Avis de décès (R) et (S);
– Etablissement de la personne à l'étranger (R) et (S);
– Commencement d'un (nouveau) travail (R) et (S);
– Commencement du service militaire (R) et (S);
– Entreprise d'une formation ou d'études`(R) et (S);
– Incapacité à travailler (R) et (S).

6. Définition des personnes au chômage sur laquelle les statistiques sont établies
Sont considérées comme chômeurs les personnes, parmi la population active, qui ne travaillent pas; n'ont pas d'emploi, de commerce ou de ferme leur appartenant d'où elles sont temporairement absentes; mais qui sont disponibles pour travailler. Les personnes dans cette catégorie comprennent: (i) celles qui sont à la recherche d'un travail et (ii) celles qui n'ont pas été à la recherche d'un travail pour cause de maladie ou parce qu'elles pensaient qu'un travail adapté n'était pas disponible, étaient en attente de reprendre un nouveau travail, attendaient la saison agricole ou pour d'autres raisons.

7. Mise à jour des registres
Les registres sont mis à jour annuellement.

8. Taux de chômage
Les statistiques basées sur les registres sont utilisées pour obtenir des taux de chômage.
Les sources des données d'emploi qui sont partie du dénominateur sont les suivantes:
– Enquête auprès des ménages sur la main-d'œuvre;
– Enquête auprès des établissements;
– Recensement de population.

Définition des personnes pourvues d'un emploi à cette fin:
Les personnes parmi la population active qui ont travaillé au moins une heure contre paiement d'un salaire, d'un bénéfice, de dividendes ou autre moyen de rémunération (qui travaillent en tant qu'employeurs, employés, à leur compte, ou travailleurs familiaux non rémunérés).

9. Type de statistiques sur le nombre de chômeurs enregistrés produites
Série 1: Nombre de personnes à la recherche d'un emploi par niveau d'éducation, groupe d'âge et sexe.
Période de référence: Mois; Année.
Fréquence de production: Mensuelle; Annuelle.
Variables utilisées:
– Sexe;
– Age;
– Niveau d'instruction.
Publication:
– A usage interne;
– Sur papier, à diffusion restreinte.
Organisme responsable de la publication: Département de l'Emploi et de la Main-d'œuvre.
Série 2: Nombre de personnes à la recherche d'un emploi par qualifications, groupe d'âge et sexe.
Période de référence: Mois; Année.
Fréquence de production: Mensuelle; Annuelle.
Variables utilisées:
– Sexe;
– Age;
– Profession.
Série 3: Nombre de personnes à la recherche d'un emploi et placement par qualifications.
Période de référence: Mois; Année.
Fréquence de production: Mensuelle; Annuelle.
Variables utilisées:
– Sexe;
– Profession.

10. Information méthodologique au sujet de ces statistiques
Publication:
– A usage interne;
– Sur papier, à diffusion restreinte.
Organisme responsable: Département de l'Emploi et de la Main-d'œuvre.

11. Comparaisons avec des statistiques provenant d'autres sources
Il n'y a pas eu de comparaisons faites avec des statistiques provenant d'autres sources.

12. Principaux changements intervenus depuis le début de ces séries statistiques

Il n'y a pas eu de changement important dans la législation, dans la capacité de l'agence et/ou dans les procédures administratives susceptibles d'avoir influencé de manière significative les statistiques.

Cameroun

1. Séries statistiques
Titre: Banque de données des chercheurs d'emploi.
Première année disponible: 1991
2. Organisme responsable de l'enregistrement des chômeurs ou demandeurs d'emploi
Nom de l'organisme: Fonds national de l'Emploi (FNE).
Type d'organisme: Organisme parapublic.
Situation des bureaux chargés de l'enregistrement: Dans six provinces sur 10 actuellement, mais la couverture géographique s'étend progressivement.
Types de services fournis et/ou gérés par cet organisme:
– Assistance aux demandeurs d'emploi pour trouver du travail;
– Assistance aux demandeurs d'emploi pour créer leur propre entreprise;
– Assistance aux employeurs pour trouver de la main-d'œuvre;
– Orientation professionnelle;
– Formation liée à l'emploi.
Pourcentage des demandeurs d'emploi qui cherchent un emploi au travers de cet organisme: 30%
3. Les informations personnelles suivantes sont enregistrées:
– Nom;
– Sexe;
– Date de naissance;
– Nationalité;
– Niveau de formation. Aucun lien n'a été établi avec la CITE;
– Situation de travail présente et passée;
– Type de profession de l'emploi antérieur ou actuel, en distinguant deux catégories. Aucun lien n'a été établi avec la CITP;
– Type de profession de l'emploi recherché, en distinguant deux catégories.
4. Critères utilisés pour déterminer si une personne doit être incluse dans le registre (R) et/ou dans les statistiques de chômeurs (S):
– Etre sans travail (R) et (S);
– Etre à la recherche d'un travail (R) et (S);
– Etre disponible pour travailler (R) et (S);
– Age: Minimum: 18 ans; Maximum: 55 ans (R) et (S).
5. Critères utilisés pour déterminer si une personne doit être exclue du registre (R) et/ou des statistiques de chômeurs (S):
– Avis de décès (R) et (S);
– Commencement d'un (nouveau) travail (R) et (S);
– Défaut de contact avec l'organisme/agence (R) et (S).
6. Définition des personnes au chômage sur laquelle les statistiques sont établies
Sont considérées au chômage les personnes âgées de 18 à 55 ans qui sont sans travail, à la recherche d'un travail et disponibles pour travailler.
7. Mise à jour des registres
Les registres sont mis à jour quotidiennement.
8. Taux de chômage
Les statistiques basées sur les registres ne sont pas utilisées pour obtenir des taux de chômage.
9. Type de statistiques produites sur le nombre de chômeurs enregistrés
Fréquence de production: Annuelle.
Variables utilisées:
– Sexe;
– Age;
– Niveau d'instruction;
– Profession;
– Branche d'activité;
– Expérience professionnelle antérieure;
– Durée de chômage.
Publication: Sur papier, à diffusion grand public.
Organisme responsable de la publication: FNE.
Titre et périodicité de la publication / des publications: *Rapport annuel d'activités du FNE*, série disponible de 1991 à 2000.

10. Information méthodologique au sujet de ces statistiques
Publication:
–   Sur papier, à diffusion grand public.
Organisme responsable: FNE.
11. Comparaisons avec des statistiques provenant d'autres sources
Il n'y a pas eu de comparaisons faites avec des statistiques provenant d'autres sources.
12. Principaux changements intervenus depuis le début de ces séries statistiques
Il n'y a pas eu de changement important dans la législation, dans la capacité de l'agence et/ou dans les procédures administratives susceptibles d'avoir influencé de manière significative les statistiques.

Canada

1. Séries statistiques
Titre: Bénéficiaires d'allocations de chômage.
Première année disponible: 1975.
2. Organisme responsable de l'enregistrement des bénéficiaires d'allocations de chômage
Nom de l'organisme: Les bénéficiaires d'allocations de chômage sont enregistrés auprès du Programme d'Assurance pour l'Emploi (Programme EI: *Employment Insurance Program*).
Note: Les demandeurs d'emploi et les chômeurs au Canada ne sont pas systématiquement enregistrés, à moins qu'ils ne deviennent bénéficiaires d'allocations de chômage du Programme EI. C'est un régime d'assurance qui couvre tous les travailleurs ayant un contrat de travail auprès d'un employeur; les travailleurs à leur propre compte ne sont pas couverts, sauf dans l'industrie de la pêche.
Type d'organisme: Organisme public relevant d'autorités nationales et régionales.
Nom de l'autorité nationale: Commission d'assurance pour l'emploi du Canada, administrée par le Développement des Ressources humaines du Canada (HRDC). Les mesures d'aide à l'emploi et d'allocations de chômage sont gérées en coopération avec la région et les territoires.
Situation des bureaux chargés de l'enregistrement: Il y a plus de 300 bureaux dans tout les pays. Les chômeurs peuvent aussi s'inscrire par l'Internet
Types de services fournis et/ou gérés par cet organisme:
–   Assistance aux demandeurs d'emploi pour trouver du travail;
–   Assistance aux demandeurs d'emploi pour créer leur propre entreprise;
–   Assistance aux employeurs pour trouver de la main-d'œuvre;
–   Orientation professionnelle;
–   Paiement des indemnités de chômage;
–   Autres services liés à l'emploi:
–   Bourse du travail électronique (un service gratuit en ligne qui connecte les travailleurs et les employeurs);
–   Liste en ligne des vacances de postes dans les secteurs publics et privés (www.jobs.gc.ca);
–   Site Internet d'information sur le marché du travail (www.labourmarketinformation.ca);
–   Programme standard inter-provinces *Red Seal* (qui autorise les commerçants qualifiés à exercer leur métier dans toutes les provinces ou territoires sans examen supplémentaire);
–   "*Jobs Etc.*", un point d'accès centralisant les informations relatives aux offres d'emploi, aux formations, aux carrières et aux questions relatives aux emplois;
–   "*Job Futures*", une prévision à long terme relative aux 211 groupes de professions selon la Classification Nationale des Professions (*NOC - National Occupational Classification*);
–   "*Minding your own business*" (Occupes-toi de ton travail), "*Catching the wave*" (Sautes sur l'occasion) et "*Venturing out*" (Prends des risques), trois programmes destinés à aider les personnes (y compris les jeunes) qui veulent créer leur propre entreprise.
3. Les informations personnelles suivantes sont enregistrées:
–   Nom;
–   Sexe;
–   Numéro de sécurité sociale (ou numéro d'identification également utilisé par d'autres organismes);
–   Adresse du domicile habituel;

–   Date de naissance;
–   Niveau d'instruction/de formation. Aucun lien n'a été établi avec la CITE;
–   Situation de travail présente et passée, en distinguant deux catégories;
–   Type de profession de l'emploi antérieur et/ou actuel. Aucun lien n'a été établi avec la CITP-88;
–   Type de profession de l'emploi recherché. Aucun lien n'a été établi avec la CITP-88;
–   Nom et adresse de l'employeur ou du lieu de travail actuel ou passé;
–   Branche d'activité de l'employeur ou du lieu de travail actuel ou passé. Aucun lien n'a été établi avec la CITI-rév.3;
–   Inscriptions/enregistrements antérieurs auprès de l'organisme;
–   Autres: situation vis-à-vis de la retraite; langue préférée (anglais ou français); type de revenus perçus; état de grossesse; en prison, en formation professionnelle, capable de travailler, ou dans l'incapacité de travailler en raison d'un conflit du travail.
4. Critères* utilisés pour déterminer si une personne doit être incluse dans le Programme d'assurance pour l'emploi (R) et/ou dans les statistiques des bénéficiaires d'allocations de chômage (S):
–   Etre sans travail (R) et (S);
–   Etre disponible pour travailler (R) et (S);
–   Avoir précédemment travaillé (R) et (S);
–   Acquittement de cotisations d'assurance chômage (entre 410 et 910 heures au cours des 52 semaines précédentes), (R) et (S).
* Les critères ci-dessus ne s'appliquent qu'aux personnes réclamant des allocations *régulières* du Programme EI (pas à celles demandant des allocations de maladie, de maternité ou parentales).
5. Critères utilisés pour déterminer si une personne doit être exclue du registre (R) du Programme d'assurance pour l'emploi et/ou des statistiques des bénéficiaires d'allocations de chômage (S):
–   Avis de décès (R) et (S);
–   Etablissement de la personne à l'étranger (à l'exception d'un échange d'allocations avec les Etats-Unis), (R) et (S);
–   Commencement d'un (nouveau) travail à plein temps (R) et (S);
–   Participation à un programme de promotion de l'emploi, à un programme de travaux publics, etc. (R) et (S);
–   Entreprise d'une formation ou d'études à plein temps (sauf si la personne est envoyée à un programme de formation de l'EI), (R) et (S);
–   Défaut de contact avec l'organisme/agence sans un motif sérieux (R) et (S);
–   Refus d'offres d'emploi adaptées à défaut d'un motif sérieux (R) et (S);
–   Refus d'offres de formation adaptées à défaut d'un motif sérieux (R) et (S);
–   Fin de droit à l'allocation-chômage (R) et (S);
–   Admission à toucher une pension (retraite, etc.) supérieure à un certain montant (R) et (S);
–   Incapacité à travailler (la personne peut avoir droit à une indemnité maladie après quatre semaines de maladie), (R) et (S);
–   Autres: en prison (R) et (S); non disponible pour travailler (R) et (S); ayant quitté son emploi ou s'étant absenté sans une raison valable, ou ayant été renvoyé ou suspendu pour mauvaise conduite (R) et (S); absence temporaire du Canada (avec certaines exceptions), (R) et (S); impossibilité de travailler en raison d'un conflit du travail (R) et (S); perception de revenus d'un emploi ou liés à un emploi tels que des indemnités de travail, au delà d'un certain montant (R) et (S).
* Les critères ci-dessus ne s'appliquent qu'aux personnes réclamant des allocations *régulières* du Programme EI (pas à celles demandant des allocations de maladie, de maternité ou parentales).
6. Définition des personnes bénéficiaires d'allocations de chômage sur lesquelles les statistiques sont établies
Une personne peut prétendre à une indemnité régulière (c'est-à-dire a droit à recevoir une indemnité régulière) quand elle est sans travail, capable et désireuse de travailler, et si elle

bénéficiait d'un lien formel avec l'emploi (attachement) au cours de l'année précédente.

7. Mise à jour des registres

Les registres sont mis à jour quotidiennement.

8. Taux de chômage

Les statistiques basées sur les registres ne sont pas utilisées pour obtenir des taux de chômage.

9. Type de statistiques produites sur le nombre de bénéficiaires d'allocations de chômage

Série 1: Requêtes déposées auprès de l'assurance chômage.

Période de référence: Cumul pour un mois donné.

Fréquence de production: Mensuelle.

Variables utilisées:

– Sexe;
– Age;
– Caractéristiques géographiques;
– Expérience professionnelle antérieure (nombre de semaines et d'heures assurées);
– Durée de chômage.

Publication:

– A usage interne uniquement;
– En format électronique, sur demande (cinq dernières années).

Organisme responsable de la publication: Développement des Ressources humaines du Canada.

Titre de la publication: *SM70 - Requêtes déposées et renouvelées.*

Série 2: Bénéficiaires des allocations de chômage.

Période de référence: Estimation ponctuelle (le 15 du mois).

Fréquence de production: Mensuelle.

Variables utilisées:

– Sexe;
– Age;
– Caractéristiques géographiques;
– Expérience professionnelle antérieure;
– Durée de chômage.

Publication:

– En format électronique, sur demande (cinq dernières années).

Organisme responsable de la publication: Développement des Ressources humaines du Canada et Statistiques du Canada.

Publication: L'information est disponible (en anglais et en français) dans la base de données «CANSIM».

Série 3: Paiement des allocations de chômage.

Période de référence: Jour.

Fréquence de production: Quotidienne.

Publication:

– A usage interne uniquement;
– En format électronique, sur demande.

Organisme/Agence responsable de la publication: Développement des Ressources humaines du Canada.

Titre de la publication: *Rapport d'activité.*

10. Information méthodologique au sujet de ces statistiques

Publication:

– Non diffusée, à usage interne uniquement.

Organisme responsable: Développement des Ressources humaines du Canada (Service Financier).

11. Comparaisons avec des statistiques provenant d'autres sources

Il n'y a pas eu de comparaisons faites avec des statistiques provenant d'autres sources.

12. Principaux changements intervenus depuis le début de ces séries statistiques

Des changements importants dans la législation (à savoir la Loi d'assurance Emploi et la Loi d'assurance Chômage) susceptibles d'avoir influencé de manière significative les statistiques sont intervenus en 1990, 1993, 1994, 2000 et 2001 (Projets C-21; C-113; C-17; C-12, Réforme EI; C-32 et C-2 respectivement).

Rép. centrafricaine

1. Séries statistiques

L'Agence centrafricaine de Formation professionnelle et de l'emploi n'a pas en charge la tenue des statistiques de chômage, mais celles relatives à la demande et à l'offre d'emploi.

2. Organisme responsable de l'enregistrement des demandeurs d'emploi

Nom de l'organisme: Agence centrafricaine de Formation professionnelle et de l'Emploi (ACFPE).

Type d'organisme: Organisme public relevant d'une autorité nationale.

Nom de l'autorité nationale: Ministère de la Fonction Publique et de la Prévoyance Sociale.

Situation des bureaux chargés de l'enregistrement: Dans certaines régions uniquement: Bangui, Berberati, Bouar, Bangassou, Mbaïki, Bambari et autres.

Types de services fournis et/ou gérés par cet organisme:

– Assistance aux demandeurs d'emploi pour trouver du travail;
– Assistance aux demandeurs d'emploi pour créer leur propre entreprise;
– Assistance aux employeurs pour trouver de la main-d'œuvre;
– Orientation professionnelle;
– Formation liée à l'emploi.

3. Les informations personnelles suivantes sont enregistrées:

– Nom;
– Sexe;
– Numéro de sécurité sociale (ou numéro d'identification également utilisé par d'autres organismes);
– Adresse du domicile habituel;
– Date de naissance;
– Citoyenneté;
– Nationalité/groupe ethnique;
– Niveau d'instruction/ de formation, en distinguant neuf catégories. Aucun lien n'a été établi avec la CITE;
– Situation de travail présente et passée, en distinguant deux catégories;
– Type de profession de l'emploi antérieur ou actuel. Des liens ont été établis avec la CITP, au niveau des groupes de base;
– Type de profession de l'emploi recherché, avec 11catégories;
– Nom et adresse de l'employeur ou du lieu de travail actuel ou passé;
– Branche d'activité de l'employeur ou du lieu de travail actuel ou passé, en distinguant 18 catégories. Des liens ont été établis avec la CITI;
– Inscriptions/enregistrements antérieurs auprès de l'organisme.
– Autre: durée de l'emploi antérieur, formation souhaitée.

4. Critères utilisés pour déterminer si une personne doit être incluse dans le registre (R) et/ou dans les statistiques de demandeurs d'emploi (S):

– Etre sans travail (R) et (S);
– Etre à la recherche d'un travail (R) et (S);
– Etre disponible pour travailler (R) et (S);
– Age: Minimum: 15; Maximum: 54 (R) et (S);
– Etre résident dans le pays (R) et (S);
– Avoir précédemment travaillé (R) et (S).

5.-12. Information non disponible.

Chine

1. Séries statistiques

Titre: Système statistique du chômage.

Première année disponible: 1980

2. Organisme responsable de l'enregistrement des chômeurs ou demandeurs d'emploi

Nom de l'organisme: Bureau de travail local dans les bureaux des sous-districts, ou centre des services de l'emploi.

Type d'organisme: Organisme public relevant d'une autorité locale.

Situation des bureaux chargés de l'enregistrement: Dans toutes les parties du pays au niveau local.

Types de services fournis et/ou gérés par cet organisme:

– Assistance aux demandeurs d'emploi pour trouver du travail;
– Assistance aux demandeurs d'emploi pour créer leur propre entreprise;
– Assistance aux employeurs pour trouver de la main-d'œuvre;
– Orientation professionnelle;
– Formation liée à l'emploi;
– Paiement des indemnités de chômage;

– Autres: tenue de rapports personnels des chômeurs.

Pourcentage des demandeurs d'emploi qui cherchent un emploi au travers de cet organisme: 25%

3. Les informations personnelles suivantes sont enregistrées:
– Nom;
– Sexe;
– Numéro de sécurité sociale (ou numéro d'identification également utilisé par d'autres organismes);
– Adresse du domicile habituel;
– Date de naissance;
– Citoyenneté;
– Nationalité/groupe ethnique;
– Niveau d'instruction/ de formation, en distinguant huit catégories. Aucun lien n'a été établi avec la CITE;
– Situation de travail présente et passée;
– Type de profession de l'emploi antérieur ou actuel. Des liens ont été établis avec la CITP, au niveau des sous-grands groupes et grands groupes;
– Type de profession de l'emploi recherché. Des liens ont été établis avec la CITP, au niveau des sous-grands groupes et grands groupes;
– Nom et adresse de l'employeur ou du lieu de travail actuel ou passé;
– Branche d'activité de l'employeur ou du lieu de travail actuel ou passé, en distinguant 16 catégories. Aucun lien n'a été établi avec la CITI;
– Inscriptions/enregistrements antérieurs auprès de l'organisme.

4. Critères utilisés pour déterminer si une personne doit être incluse dans le registre (R) et/ou dans les statistiques de chômeurs (S)
– Etre sans travail (R) et (S);
– Etre à la recherche d'un travail (R) et (S);
– Etre disponible pour travailler (R) et (S);
– Age: Minimum: 16 ans; Maximum: 60 ans pour les hommes, 55 ans pour les femmes (R) et (S);
– Etre résident dans le pays (R) et (S);
– Avoir précédemment travaillé (S).

5. Critères utilisés pour déterminer si une personne doit être exclue du registre (R) et/ou des statistiques de chômeurs (S):
– Avis de décès (R) et (S);
– Etablissement de la personne à l'étranger (R) et (S);
– Commencement d'un (nouveau) travail (R) et (S);
– Commencement du service militaire (R) et (S);
– Fin de droit à l'allocation chômage (R) et (S);
– Admission à toucher une pension (R) et (S);
– Incapacité à travailler (R) et (S).

6. Définition des personnes au chômage sur laquelle les statistiques sont établies

Le chômage enregistré urbain s'applique à la population non agricole en âge de travailler (de16 ans à l'âge de la retraite), disponible pour travailler et enregistrée auprès des agences d'emploi locales, à la recherche d'un travail. Les personnes suivantes sont exclues: (i) étudiants; (ii) les personnes qui ont dépassé l'âge de la retraite (60 pour les hommes et 55 pour les femmes) ou qui n'ont pas encore atteint l'âge de la retraite mais ont déjà pris leur retraite/démissionné; (iii) handicapés bénéficiant d'une capacité de travail partielle au bénéfice d'une rente spéciale.

7. Mise à jour des registres

Pas d'information disponible.

8. Taux de chômage

Les statistiques basées sur les registres sont utilisées pour obtenir des taux de chômage.

Les sources des données d'emploi qui sont partie du dénominateur sont les suivantes:
– Enquête auprès des établissements;
– Registres de sécurité sociale;
– Registres de l'emploi;
– Registres d'entreprises industrielles et commerciales.

Définition des personnes pourvues d'un emploi à cette fin:

Toutes les personnes engagées dans des activités socio-économiques génératrices de revenu.

9. Type de statistiques sur le nombre de chômeurs enregistrés produites

Série 1:

Période de référence: Trimestrielle

Fréquence de production: Trimestrielle

Variables utilisées:

– Sexe;
– Age;
– Niveau d'instruction;
– Profession;
– Branche d'activité;
– Caractéristiques géographiques.

Publication:
– Sur papier, à diffusion grand public;
– En format électronique, sur demande;
– Sur un site Internet

Titre de la publication: *China Labour Statistical Yearbook* (Annuaire Chinois des Statistiques du Travail).

Série 2:

Période de référence: Année.

Fréquence de production: Semestrielle.

Variables utilisées:
– Sexe;
– Age;
– Niveau d'instruction;
– Profession;
– Branche d'activité;
– Caractéristiques géographiques.

Publication:
– Sur papier, à diffusion grand public;
– En format électronique, sur demande;
– Sur un site Internet

Titre de la publication: *China Labour Statistical Yearbook* (Annuaire Chinois des Statistiques du Travail).

Série 3:

Période de référence: Année.

Fréquence de production: Annuelle.

Variables utilisées:
– Sexe;
– Age;
– Niveau d'instruction;
– Profession;
– Branche d'activité;
– Caractéristiques géographiques.

Publication:
– Sur papier, à diffusion grand public;
– En format électronique, sur demande;
– Sur un site Internet

Titre de la publication: *China Labour Statistical Yearbook* (Annuaire Chinois Statistique du Travail).

10. Information méthodologique au sujet de ces statistiques Publication:
– Sur papier, à diffusion grand public;
– En format électronique, sur demande;
– Sur un site Internet

Organisme responsable: Bureau National de Statistique; Ministère du Travail et de la Sécurité Sociale.

11. Comparaisons avec des statistiques provenant d'autres sources

Des comparaisons ont été faites avec des statistiques provenant du recensement de la population et d'autres sources.

Fréquence des comparaisons: Régulièrement lors de la publication des statistiques (dernière année: 2001).

Publication de la méthodologie et/ou des résultats de la comparaison: Ils n'ont pas été publiés.

12. Principaux changements intervenus depuis le début de ces séries statistiques

Des changements importants dans la législation, dans la capacité de l'agence et/ou dans les procédures administratives sont intervenus en 1986, 1990 et 1995. Les modifications dans les statistiques qui en ont résulté n'ont pas été évaluées.

Chypre

1. Séries statistiques

Titre: Statistiques sur les chômeurs enregistrés.

Première année disponible: 1960.

2. Organisme responsable de l'enregistrement des chômeurs ou demandeurs d'emploi

Nom de l'organisme: Département du Travail par l'intermédiaire des agences pour l'emploi au niveau des districts.

Type d'organisme: Organisme public relevant d'une autorité nationale.

Nom de l'autorité nationale: Ministère du Travail et de l'Assurance sociale.

Situation des bureaux chargés de l'enregistrement: Dans toutes les principales villes de la zone contrôlée par le gouvernement de Chypre.

Types de services fournis et/ou gérés par cet organisme:

– Assistance aux demandeurs d'emploi pour trouver du travail;
– Assistance aux employeurs pour trouver de la main-d'œuvre;
– Orientation professionnelle;
– Autres: services pour la mise à disposition de travailleurs portuaires.

Pourcentage des demandeurs d'emploi qui cherchent un emploi au travers de cet organisme: Environ 78%* des demandeurs d'emploi au chômage recherchent du travail via l'agence. Un grand nombre de personnes employées recherchent un meilleur emploi via l'agence.

* 78% des chômeurs selon l'enquête de main-d'œuvre sont enregistrés auprès de l'agence.

3. Les informations personnelles suivantes sont enregistrées:

– Nom;
– Sexe;
– Numéro de sécurité sociale (ou numéro d'identification également utilisé par d'autres organismes);
– Adresse du domicile habituel;
– Date de naissance;
– Citoyenneté;
– Nationalité/groupe ethnique;
– Niveau d'instruction, en distinguant 33 catégories. En général, des liens ont été établis avec la CITE avec de petites déviations;
– Situation de travail présente et passée, en distinguant six catégories;
– Type de profession de l'emploi antérieur ou actuel, au niveau de quatre chiffres. Des liens ont été établis avec la CITP au niveau des groupes de base;
– Type de profession de l'emploi recherché, au niveau de quatre chiffres. Des liens ont été établis avec la CITP au niveau des groupes de base;
– Nom et adresse de l'employeur ou du lieu de travail actuel ou passé;
– Branche d'activité de l'employeur ou du lieu de travail actuel ou passé, au niveau de deux chiffres. Des liens ont été établis avec la CITI, au niveau de deux chiffres;
– Enregistrements antérieurs auprès de l'organisme;
– Autre: district préféré pour le travail; type d'employeur recherché (privé, publique, etc.); difficultés de transport; détention d'un permis de conduire; commentaires sur la présentation, l'élocution, le comportement, etc.; historique de l'emploi en ce qui concerne le salaire; raison pour laquelle le dernier emploi a pris fin.

4. Critères utilisés pour déterminer si une personne doit être incluse dans le registre (R)* et/ou dans les statistiques de chômeurs (S):

– Etre totalement sans travail (R) et (S);
– Etre à la recherche d'un travail (R) et (S);
– Etre disponible pour travailler (R) et (S);
– Age: Minimum: 15 ans; Maximum: 63 ou 67 ans selon la date d'octroi de la pension de l'assurance sociale (R) et (S);
– Citoyenneté (R) et (S);
– Etre résident dans le pays (R) et (S);
– Durée souhaitée de l'emploi recherché et/ou du nombre d'heures de travail recherché (minimum 30 heures par semaine) (R) et (S).

* Ne concerne que les chômeurs; sont exclues les personnes «à la recherche d'un meilleur emploi», etc.

5. Critères utilisés pour déterminer si une personne doit être exclue du registre (R) et/ou des statistiques de chômeurs (S):

– Décès (R) et (S);
– Etablissement de la personne à l'étranger (R) et (S);
– Commencement d'un (nouveau) travail (R) et (S);
– Commencement du service militaire (R) et (S);
– Participation à un programme de promotion de l'emploi, à un programme de travaux publics, etc. (R) et (S);
– Entreprise d'une formation ou d'études (R) et (S);
– Défaut de contact avec l'organisme/agence (R) et (S);

– Refus de trois offres d'emploi adaptées (R) et (S);
– Admission à toucher une pension (R) et (S);
– Incapacité à travailler (R) et (S).

6. Définition des personnes au chômage sur laquelle les statistiques sont établies

Sont considérées comme chômeurs les personnes enregistrées sans aucun travail et à la recherche d'un travail dans les agences d'emploi des districts le dernier jour de chaque mois. Sont inclues les personnes qui reçoivent des indemnités de chômage de la sécurité sociale de même que les personnes qui n'ont droit à aucune indemnité.

7. Mise à jour des registres

Les registres sont mis à jour régulièrement.

8. Taux de chômage

Les statistiques basées sur les registres sont utilisées pour obtenir des taux de chômage.

Les sources des données d'emploi qui sont partie du dénominateur sont les estimations officielles.

Définition des personnes pourvues d'un emploi à cette fin:

Les personnes qui ont travaillé au moins une heure durant la semaine de référence ou les personnes qui ont un emploi mais ne travaillaient pas durant la semaine de référence.

9. Type de statistiques sur le nombre de chômeurs enregistrés produites

Séries: Nombre de chômeurs.

Période de référence: Mois.

Fréquence de production: Mensuelle; Annuelle.

Variables utilisées:

– Sexe;
– Age;
– Niveau d'instruction;
– Profession;
– Branche d'activité;
– Caractéristiques géographiques;
– Expérience professionnelle antérieure;
– Durée de chômage.

Publication:

– Sur papier, à diffusion grand public;
– En format électronique, sur demande.

Organisme/Agence responsable de la publication: Service Statistique, Ministère des Finances.

Titre et périodicité des publications: *Registered Unemployed* (chômeurs enregistrés), (mensuelle); *Monthly Economic Indicators* (indicateurs économiques mensuels), (deux fois par mois); *Labour Statistics* (statistiques du travail), (annuelle).

10. Information méthodologique au sujet de ces statistiques

Publiée dans la presse et par Internet

11. Comparaisons avec des statistiques provenant d'autres sources

Des comparaisons ont été faites avec des statistiques de chômage provenant de l'enquête sur la main-d'œuvre.

Fréquence des comparaisons: Régulièrement lors de la publication des statistiques.

Publication de la méthodologie et/ou des résultats de la comparaison: Ils n'ont pas été publiés.

12. Principaux changements intervenus depuis le début de ces séries statistiques

Il n'y a pas eu de changement important dans la législation, dans la capacité de l'agence et/ou dans les procédures administratives susceptibles d'avoir influencé de manière significative les statistiques.

Colombie

1. Séries statistiques

Titre: Chômage enregistré.

Première année disponible: 1992.

2. Organisme responsable de l'enregistrement des chômeurs ou demandeurs d'emploi

Nom de l'organisme: Servicio Nacional de Aprendizaje (SENA) (Service national d'Apprentissage).

Type d'organisme: Organisme public relevant d'une autorité nationale.

Nom de l'autorité nationale: Ministerio de Trabajo y Seguridad Social (Ministère du Travail et de la Sécurité sociale).

Situation des bureaux chargés de l'enregistrement: Dans l'ensemble du pays.

Types de services fournis et/ou gérés par cet organisme

- Assistance aux demandeurs d'emploi pour trouver du travail;
- Assistance aux demandeurs d'emploi pour créer leur propre entreprise;
- Assistance aux employeurs pour trouver de la main-d'œuvre;
- Orientation professionnelle;
- Formation liée à l'emploi;
- Autres services liés à l'emploi: information sur le marché du travail.

Pourcentage des demandeurs d'emploi qui cherchent un emploi au travers de cet organisme: Pas d'indicateur élaboré.

3. Les informations personnelles suivantes sont enregistrées

- Nom;
- Sexe;
- Adresse du domicile habituel;
- Date de naissance;
- Citoyenneté;
- Nationalité;
- Niveau d'instruction/de formation. Aucun lien n'a été établi avec la CITE;
- Situation de travail présente et passée, en distinguant quatre catégories;
- Type de profession de l'emploi antérieur et/ou actuel. Aucun lien n'a été établi avec la CITP;
- Type de profession de l'emploi recherché. Aucun lien n'a été établi avec la CITP;
- Branche d'activité de l'employeur ou du lieu de travail actuel ou passé.

4. Critères utilisés pour déterminer si une personne doit être incluse dans le registre (R) et/ou dans les statistiques de chômeurs (S)

- Etre sans travail (R) et (S);
- Etre à la recherche d'un travail (R) et (S);
- Etre disponible pour travailler (R) et (S);
- Age: Minimum: 10 ans dans le secteur rural et 12 ans dans le secteur urbain; Maximum: il n'y a pas d'âge maximum, (R) et (S);
- Citoyenneté (uniquement des colombiens) (R) et (S);
- Etre résident dans le pays (R) et (S).

5. Critères utilisés pour déterminer si une personne doit être exclue du registre (R) et/ou des statistiques de chômeurs (S)

- Avis de décès (R) et (S);
- Etablissement de la personne à l'étranger (Mais si la personne se trouve dans le pays à la date de l'enquête, elle est comptée) (R) et (S);
- Commencement d'un (nouveau) travail (R) et (S);
- Commencement du service militaire (R) et (S);
- Entreprise d'une formation ou d'études (R) et (S).

6. Définition des personnes au chômage sur laquelle les statistiques sont établies

Personnes qui se trouvaient dans l'une des situations suivantes lors de la semaine de référence:

1. Chômage visible: Sans emploi lors de la semaine de référence, qui avaient entamé des démarches au cours du dernier mois et qui étaient disponibles pour travailler.
2. Chômage occulte: Sans emploi lors de la semaine de référence, qui n'avaient pas entamé de démarches lors du dernier mois mais l'avaient fait au cours des 12 derniers mois et qui avaient une raison valable d'être découragées et qui étaient disponibles pour travailler.

7. Mise à jour des registres

Les registres sont mis à jour régulièrement.

8. Taux de chômage

Les statistiques basées sur les registres ne sont pas utilisées pour obtenir des taux de chômage.

9. Type de statistiques sur le nombre de chômeurs enregistrés produites

Série: 1

Période de référence: Mois

Fréquence de production: Mensuelle

Variables utilisées

- Sexe;
- Age;
- Niveau d'instruction;
- Profession;
- Branche d'activité;
- Expérience professionnelle antérieure;
- Durée de chômage;
- Autres (depuis 2002): date à laquelle la personne a commencé à rechercher un emploi; moyens utilisés pour la recherche d'un emploi; entreprise.

Publication

- Sur papier, à diffusion grand public;
- Sur le site Internet www.sena.gov.co (depuis 2002)

Organisme/Agence responsable de la publication: SENA.

Titre et périodicité des publications: Rapports divers (mensuels et annuels).

Série: 2

Période de référence: Trimestre-semestre.

Fréquence de production: Mensuelle

Variables utilisées

- Sexe;
- Age;
- Niveau d'instruction;
- Profession;
- Branche d'activité;
- Expérience professionnelle antérieure;
- Durée de chômage;
- Autres (depuis 2002): date à laquelle la personne a commencé à rechercher un emploi; moyens utilisés pour la recherche d'un emploi; entreprise.

Publication

- Sur papier, à diffusion grand public;
- Sur le site Internet www.sena.gov.co (depuis 2002).

Organisme/Agence responsable de la publication: SENA.

Titre et périodicité des publications: Rapports divers (mensuels et annuels).

Série: 3

Période de référence: Année

Fréquence de production: Mensuelle

Variables utilisées

- Sexe;
- Age;
- Niveau d'instruction;
- Profession;
- Branche d'activité;
- Expérience professionnelle antérieure;
- Durée de chômage;
- Autres (depuis 2002): date à laquelle la personne a commencé à rechercher un emploi; moyens utilisés pour la recherche d'un emploi; entreprise.

Publication

- Sur papier, à diffusion grand public;
- Sur le site Internet www.sena.gov.co (depuis 2002).

Organisme/Agence responsable de la publication: SENA.

Titre et périodicité des publications: Rapports divers (mensuels et annuels).

10. Information méthodologique au sujet de ces statistiques

Publication

- Sur papier, à diffusion grand public.

Organisme responsable: Departamento Administrativo Nacional de Estadísticas (DANE) (Département administratif national des Statistiques).

11. Comparaisons avec des statistiques provenant d'autres sources

Des comparaisons ont été faites avec des statistiques provenant de l'Enquête sur la main-d'œuvre.

Fréquence des comparaisons: De temps en temps.

Publication de la méthodologie et/ou des résultats de la comparaison: Publiés dans le magazine *Indicadores de Mercado Laboral* et *Informe mensual de gestión del sistema de información para el empleo* (Indicateurs du marché du travail et dans le Rapport mensuel sur la gestion du système d'information pour l'emploi) SENA, Dirección de Empleo (SENA, Direction de l'Emploi).

12. Principaux changements intervenus depuis le début de ces séries statistiques

Il n'y a pas eu de changement important dans la législation, dans la capacité de l'agence et/ou dans les procédures administratives susceptibles d'avoir influencé de manière significative les statistiques.

Par contre, des modifications importantes auront lieu dès l'an 2002 en raison du changement du à l'application systématique de l'informatisation du mécanisme d'entrée sur le marché du travail.

Congo

1. Séries statistiques

Titre: Statistiques sur les demandeurs d'emploi. Le Service public de l'Emploi au Congo n'a pas en charge la tenue des statistiques de chômage, mais celles relatives à la demande et à l'offre d'emploi.

2. Organisme responsable de l'enregistrement des chômeurs ou demandeurs d'emploi

Nom de l'organisme: Les Agences régionales de l'Office national de l'Emploi et de la Main-d'œuvre (ONEMO).

Type d'organisme: Organisme public relevant d'une autorité nationale.

Nom de l'autorité nationale: Ministère du Travail, de l'Emploi et de la Sécurité sociale.

Situation des bureaux chargés de l'enregistrement: Brazzaville, Kouilou, Bouénza, Cuvettes, Sangha, Likouala et Niari.

Types de services fournis et/ou gérés par cet organisme:
–   Assistance aux demandeurs d'emploi pour trouver du travail;
–   Assistance aux demandeurs d'emploi pour créer leur propre entreprise;
–   Assistance aux employeurs pour trouver de la main-d'œuvre;
–   Orientation professionnelle;
–   Formation liée à l'emploi.

3. Les informations personnelles suivantes sont enregistrées:
–   Nom;
–   Sexe;
–   Adresse du domicile habituel;
–   Date de naissance;
–   Citoyenneté;
–   Nationalité;
–   Niveau d'instruction/de formation. Aucun lien n'a été établi avec la CITE;
–   Situation de travail présente et passée;
–   Type de profession de l'emploi antérieur et/ou actuel. Aucun lien n'a été établi avec la CITP;
–   Type de profession de l'emploi recherché;
–   Nom et adresse de l'employeur ou du lieu de travail actuel ou passé;
–   Branche d'activité de l'employeur ou du lieu de travail actuel ou passé. Aucun lien n'a été établi avec la CITI.

Points suivants: information non disponible.

Costa Rica

1. Séries statistiques

Titre: Chômage enregistré.

Première année disponible: Non-spécifiée.

2. Organisme responsable de l'enregistrement des chômeurs ou demandeurs d'emploi

Nom de l'organisme: Departamento de Prospección de Empleo (Département de Prospection de l'Emploi).

Type d'organisme: Organisme public relevant d'une autorité nationale.

Nom de l'autorité nationale: Ministerio de Trabajo y Seguridad Social (Ministère du Travail et de la Sécurité sociale).

Situation des bureaux chargés de l'enregistrement: Région centrale du pays.

Types de services fournis et/ou gérés par cet organisme
–   Assistance aux demandeurs d'emploi pour trouver du travail;
–   Assistance aux employeurs pour trouver de la main-d'œuvre;
–   Autres services liés à l'emploi: enquêtes sur les migrations de main-d'œuvre; enquêtes prospectives sur l'emploi; enquêtes pour déterminer les profils des main-d'œuvre des zones d'investissement; «Programa Construyendo Oportunidades y Creciendo Juntas» (Programme de développement national).

Pourcentage des demandeurs d'emploi qui cherchent un emploi au travers de cet organisme: 10%

3. Les informations personnelles suivantes sont enregistrées
–   Nom;
–   Sexe;
–   Numéro de sécurité sociale (ou numéro d'identification également utilisé par d'autres organismes);
–   Adresse du domicile habituel;
–   Date de naissance;
–   Citoyenneté;
–   Nationalité/groupe ethnique;
–   Niveau d'instruction/de formation, en distinguant 11 catégories. Aucun lien n'a été établi avec la CITE;
–   Situation de travail présente et passée, en distinguant cinq catégories;
–   Type de profession de l'emploi antérieur et/ou actuel, en distinguant trois catégories. Des liens ont été établis avec la CITP-88;
–   Type de profession de l'emploi recherché, avec trois catégories. Des liens ont été établis avec la CITP-88 ;
–   Nom et adresse de l'employeur ou du lieu de travail actuel ou passé;
–   Branche d'activité de l'employeur ou du lieu de travail actuel ou passé, en distinguant 64 catégories. Aucun lien n'a été établi avec la CITI-rév.3;
–   Inscriptions/enregistrements antérieurs auprès de l'organisme.

4. Critères utilisés pour déterminer si une personne doit être incluse dans le registre (R) et/ou dans les statistiques de chômeurs (S)
–   Etre sans travail (R) et (S);
–   Etre à la recherche d'un travail (premier emploi; meilleur emploi ou deuxième emploi) (R) et (S);
–   Etre disponible pour travailler (R) et (S);
–   Age: Minimum: 15 ans; il n'y a pas d'âge maximum (R) et (S);
–   Citoyenneté (R);
–   Etre résident dans le pays (R) et (S);
–   Avoir précédemment travaillé (R).

5. Critères utilisés pour déterminer si une personne doit être exclue du registre (R) et/ou des statistiques de chômeurs (S)
–   Avis de décès (R) et (S);
–   Commencement d'un (nouveau) travail (R) et (S);
–   Refus de trois offres d'emploi adaptées (R) et (S).

6. Définition des personnes au chômage sur laquelle les statistiques sont établies

Les statistiques se basent sur l'Offre Enregistrée par groupes de profession, sexe, niveau d'expérience, niveau d'instruction et par groupe d'âge.

7. Mise à jour des registres

Les registres sont mis à jour quotidiennement. Ils sont maintenus actifs durant six mois puis sont renouvelés.

8. Taux de chômage

Les statistiques basées sur les registres ne sont pas utilisées pour obtenir des taux de chômage.

9. Type de statistiques produites sur le nombre de chômeurs enregistrés

Période de référence: Semestre.

Fréquence de production: Non-spécifiée.

Variables utilisées
–   Sexe;
–   Age;
–   Niveau d'instruction;
–   Profession;
–   Branche d'activité;
–   Expérience professionnelle antérieure.

Publication
–   A usage interne uniquement.

10. Information méthodologique au sujet de ces statistiques

Publication
–   Sur papier, à diffusion grand public.

Organisme responsable: Departamento de Prospección de Empleo/Migraciones Laborales (Département de Prospection de l'Emploi/Migrations de la Main-d'œuvre).

11. Comparaisons avec des statistiques provenant d'autres sources

Aucune comparaison n'a été faite avec des statistiques provenant d'autres sources.

12. Principaux changements intervenus depuis le début de ces séries statistiques

Il n'y a pas eu de changement important dans la législation, dans la capacité de l'agence et/ou dans les procédures administratives susceptibles d'avoir influencé de manière significative les statistiques.

Croatie

1. Séries statistiques
Titre: Chômeurs percevant des indemnités de chômage.
Première année disponible: 1952
2. Organisme responsable de l'enregistrement des chômeurs ou demandeurs d'emploi
Nom de l'organisme: Hrvatski zavod za zaposljavanje (service d'emploi croate).
Type d'organisme: Organisme public relevant d'une autorité nationale.
Nom de l'autorité nationale: Ministère du Travail et des Affaires Sociales.
Situation des bureaux chargés de l'enregistrement: 21 bureaux régionaux (tous les départements) et 98 bureaux locaux.
Types de services fournis et/ou gérés par cet organisme:
– Assistance aux demandeurs d'emploi pour trouver du travail;
– Assistance aux demandeurs d'emploi pour créer leur propre entreprise;
– Assistance aux employeurs pour trouver de la main-d'œuvre;
– Orientation professionnelle;
– Formation liée à l'emploi;
– Paiement des indemnités de chômage;
– Autres services liés à l'emploi.
3. Les informations personnelles suivantes sont enregistrées:
– Nom;
– Sexe;
– Numéro de sécurité sociale (ou numéro d'identification également utilisé par d'autres organismes);
– Adresse du domicile habituel;
– Date de naissance;
– Niveau d'instruction/de formation, en distinguant sept catégories. Aucun lien n'a été établi avec la CITE;
– Situation de travail présente et passée, en distinguant deux catégories;
– Type de profession de l'emploi antérieur ou actuel, en distinguant sept catégories. Des liens ont été établis avec la CITP;
– Type de profession de l'emploi recherché, avec trois catégories. Aucun lien n'a été établi avec la CITP;
– Branche d'activité de l'employeur ou du lieu de travail actuel ou passé, en distinguant 17 catégories. Des liens ont été établis avec la CITI, rév.3, et la NACE, au niveau des classes;
– Inscriptions/enregistrements antérieurs auprès de l'organisme.
4. Critères utilisés pour déterminer si une personne doit être incluse dans le registre (R) et/ou dans les statistiques de chômeurs (S):
– Etre sans travail (R) et (S);
– Etre à la recherche d'un travail (R) et (S);
– Age: Minimum: 15 ans; Maximum: 65 ans (R) et (S);
– Etre résident dans le pays (R) et (S);
– Avoir précédemment travaillé (R) et (S).
5. Critères utilisés pour déterminer si une personne doit être exclue du registre (R) et/ou des statistiques de chômeurs (S):
– Décès (R) et (S);
– Etablissement de la personne à l'étranger (R) et (S);
– Commencement d'un (nouveau) travail (R) et (S);
– Commencement du service militaire (R) et (S);
– Participation à un programme de promotion de l'emploi, à un programme de travaux publics, etc. (R) et (S);
– Entreprise d'une formation ou d'études (R) et (S);
– Défaut de contact avec l'organisme/agence (R) et (S);
– Refus d'une offre d'emploi adaptée (R) et (S);
– Refus d'une offre de formation adaptée (R) et (S);
– Admission à toucher une pension (R) et (S);
– Incapacité totale à travailler (R) et (S);
– Personne au chômage au bénéfice d'une indemnité de chômage ayant perçue un salaire ou un revenu mensuel d'un travail indépendant temporaire en accord avec les lois sur les impôts sur le revenu (R) et (S);
– Percevant un salaire ou un revenu d'un travail indépendant temporaire en accord avec les lois sur les impôts sur le revenu, dont le montant n'excède pas le montant maximal des indemnités de chômage (R) et (S);

– Personne surprise en flagrant délit de travail illégal sans permis de travail, accord de travail ou contrat de travail (R) et (S);
– Personne ne satisfaisant pas les exigences de recherche active d'un travail et de disponibilité pour travailler;
– Autre: emprisonnement pour une durée supérieure à six mois (R) et (S).
6. Définition des personnes au chômage sur laquelle les statistiques sont établies
Sont considérées comme chômeurs les personnes âgées entre 15 et 65 ans, sans travail mais capable de travailler à plein temps ou à temps partiel, activement à la recherche d'un travail, satisfaisant les exigences de la loi sur le placement (article 7) et qui sont inscrites dans le registre du service de l'emploi croate à la fin du mois concerné.
7. Mise à jour des registres
Les registres sont mis à jour quotidiennement.
8. Taux de chômage
Les statistiques basées sur les registres sont utilisées pour obtenir des taux de chômage.
Les sources des données d'emploi qui sont partie du dénominateur sont l'enquête sur la main-d'œuvre et les registres de sécurité sociale.
Définition des personnes pourvues d'un emploi à cette fin:
Les personnes employées par un employeur pour une période fixe ou indéterminée ou celles travaillant à leur compte.
9. Type de statistiques sur le nombre de chômeurs enregistrés produites
Période de référence: Mois; Trimestre; Semestre; Année.
Fréquence de production: Mensuelle; Trimestrielle; Semestrielle; Annuelle.
Variables utilisées:
– Sexe;
– Age;
– Niveau d'instruction;
– Profession;
– Branche d'activité;
– Caractéristiques géographiques;
– Expérience professionnelle antérieure;
– Durée de chômage.
Publication:
– Sur papier, à diffusion grand public;
– En format électronique, sur demande;
– Sur un site Internet (www.hzz.hr).
Agence responsable de la publication: Service de l'emploi croate.
Titre des publications: *Monthly Statistics Bulletin*; *Yearbook* (Bulletin statistique mensuel; Annuaire).
10. Information méthodologique au sujet de ces statistiques
Publication:
– Sur papier, à diffusion grand public;
– En format électronique, sur demande;
– Sur un site Internet (www.hzz.hr).
Agence responsable: Service de l'emploi croate.
11. Comparaisons avec des statistiques provenant d'autres sources
Des comparaisons ont été faites avec des statistiques provenant des enquêtes sur la main-d'œuvre.
Fréquence des comparaisons: Régulièrement lors de la publication des statistiques.
Publication de la méthodologie et/ou des résultats de la comparaison: Ils sont publiés par le bureau central des statistiques dans le rapport mensuel des statistiques.
12. Principaux changements intervenus depuis le début de ces séries statistiques
Il n'y a pas eu de changement important dans la législation, dans la capacité de l'agence et/ou dans les procédures administratives susceptibles d'avoir influencé de manière significative les statistiques.

Danemark

1. Séries statistiques
Titre: Chômage enregistré (compilation depuis le Registre Central des Statistiques de la Main-d'œuvre (CRAM).
Première année disponible: 1979.
2. Agences responsable de l'enregistrement des chômeurs ou demandeurs d'emploi

Nom des agences:
(i)   Fonds d'Assurance Chômage;
(ii)   Autorités locales;
(iii)   Centres de travail.
Type d'agences: Agences publics relevant d'une autorité nationale.
Nom de l'autorité nationale: Arbejdsmarkedsstyrelsen (Autorité de la Main-d'œuvre).
Situation des bureaux chargés de l'enregistrement: Dans toutes les régions du pays.
Types de services fournis ou gérés par ces agences:
(i) Fonds d'Assurance Chômage:
–   Orientation professionnelle;
–   Paiement des indemnités de chômage;
(ii) Autorités Locales:
–   Assistance aux demandeurs d'emploi pour trouver du travail;
–   Assistance aux employeurs pour trouver de la main-d'œuvre;
–   Orientation professionnelle;
–   Formation liée à l'emploi;
        (iii) Centres de travail
–   Assistance aux demandeurs d'emploi pour trouver du travail;
–   Assistance aux employeurs pour trouver de la main-d'œuvre;
–   Orientation professionnelle;
–   Formation liée à l'emploi.
Pourcentage des demandeurs d'emploi qui cherchent un emploi au travers de cet organisme: 22%.
3. Les informations personnelles suivantes sont enregistrées:
–   Nom;
–   Sexe;
–   Numéro de sécurité sociale (ou numéro d'identification également utilisé par d'autres organismes);
–   Adresse du domicile habituel;
–   Date de naissance;
–   Citoyenneté;
–   Nationalité/groupe ethnique;
–   Autre: si la personne est assurée ou ne l'est pas; nom de l'agence qui procède à l'enregistrement.
4. Critères utilisés pour déterminer si une personne doit être incluse dans le registre (R) et/ou dans les statistiques de chômeurs enregistrés (S):
–   Etre sans travail (R) et (S);
–   Etre à la recherche d'un travail (R) et (S);
–   Etre disponible pour travailler (R) et (S);
–   Age: Minimum: 16 ans; Maximum: 66 ans (R) et (S).
5. Critères utilisés pour déterminer si une personne doit être exclue du registre (R) et/ou des statistiques de chômeurs (S):
–   Décès (R) et (S);
–   Commencement d'un (nouveau) travail (S);
–   Commencement du service militaire (S);
–   Participation à un programme de promotion de l'emploi, à un programme de travaux publics, etc. (S);
–   Entreprise d'une formation ou d'études (S);
–   Admission à toucher une pension (S);
–   Incapacité à travailler (S).
6. Définition des personnes au chômage sur laquelle les statistiques sont établies
        Les personnes sans emploi, disponibles pour travailler et activement à la recherche d'un travail.
7. Mise à jour des registres
        Les registres sont mis à jour mensuellement.
8. Taux de chômage
        Les statistiques basées sur les registres sont utilisées pour obtenir des taux de chômage.
        La source des données d'emploi qui est partie du dénominateur des taux de chômage sont les statistiques sur la main-d'œuvre basées sur les registres (statistiques RAS).
Définition des personnes pourvues d'un emploi à cette fin:
        Les personnes pourvues d'un emploi sont soit des employé(e)s, soit des personnes travaillant à leur compte, soit des conjoints assistants.
9. Type de statistiques sur le nombre de chômeurs enregistrés produites
Série 1:
Période de référence: Mois.
Fréquence de production: Mensuelle.

Variables utilisées:
–   Sexe;
–   Age;
–   Profession selon caisse d'assurance;
–   Caractéristiques géographiques;
–   Assuré(e)/non assuré(e).
Publication:
–   Sur papier, à diffusion grand public;
–   Sur un site Internet (www.statistikbanken.dk).
Agence responsable de la publication: Statistiques Danemark.
Titre des publications: *Nyt fra Danmarks Statistik* (Nouvelles des Statistiques Danemark); *Arbejdsmarked* (Marché du Travail) publié dans les séries *Statistike Efterretninger* (Nouvelles Statistiques); *Konjunkturstatistikken* (Indicateurs Principaux) (mensuel) et *Statistik Arborg* (Annuaire Statistique).
Série 2:
Fréquence de production: Annuelle.
Variables utilisées:
–   Sexe;
–   Age;
–   Profession selon caisse d'assurance;
–   Caractéristiques géographiques;
–   Expérience professionnelle antérieure;
–   Citoyenneté (nationaux/non nationaux);
–   Durée de chômage.
Publication:
–   Sur papier, à diffusion grand public;
–   Sur un site Internet (www.statistikbanken.dk).
Agence responsable de la publication: Statistiques Danemark.
Titre des publications: *Nyt fra Danmarks Statistik* (Nouvelles de Statistiques Denmark); *Arbejdsmarked* (Marché du Travail) paraissant dans les séries *Statistike Efterretninger* (Nouvelles Statistiques; *Konjunkturstatistikken* (Indicateurs Principaux) (mensuel) et *Statistik Arborg* (Annuaire Statistique) et *Statistik Tiarsoversigt* (Revue Statistique Décennal).
10. Information méthodologique au sujet de ces statistiques
Publication:
–   Sur papier, à diffusion grand public;
–   Sur un site Internet (www.dst.dk/varedeklaration - Arbejdsmarked - Arbejdsloshed) (Marché du travail – chômage).
Agence responsable: Statistiques Danemark.
11. Comparaisons avec des statistiques provenant d'autres sources
        Des comparaisons sont faites avec des statistiques de chômage provenant des enquêtes sur la main-d'œuvre.

Fréquence des comparaisons: Quatre fois par an.
Publication de la méthodologie et/ou des résultats de la comparaison: Sur le site Internet de Statistiques Danemark (www.dst.dk/varedeklaration-Arbejdsmarked-Arbejdskraftsundersogelsen) (Marché du Travail-Enquête sur la Main-d'œuvre).
12. Principaux changements intervenus depuis le début de ces séries statistiques
        Il n'y a pas eu de changement important dans la législation, dans la capacité de l'agence et/ou dans les procédures administratives susceptibles d'avoir influencé de manière significative les statistiques.

Djibouti

1. Séries statistiques
Titre: Caractéristiques socio-économiques des demandeurs d'emploi et embauches par profession.
Première année disponible: 1974
2. Organisme responsable de l'enregistrement des chômeurs ou demandeurs d'emploi
Nom de l'organisme: Service national de l'Emploi (SNE).
Type d'organisme: Organisme public relevant d'une autorité nationale.
Nom de l'autorité nationale: Ministère de l'Emploi et de la Solidarité nationale, Direction de l'emploi.
Situation des bureaux chargés de l'enregistrement: Djibouti ville.
Types de services fournis ou gérés par cet organisme:
–   Assistance aux demandeurs d'emploi pour trouver du travail;

–   Assistance aux employeurs pour trouver de la main-d'œuvre;
–   Orientation professionnelle;
–   Autres services liés à l'emploi: gestion des dossiers des travailleurs expatriés (délivrance des autorisations de travail pour les travailleurs expatriés).

Pourcentage des demandeurs d'emploi qui cherchent un emploi au travers de cet organisme: 6%

3. Les informations personnelles suivantes sont enregistrées:
–   Nom;
–   Sexe;
–   Numéro de sécurité sociale (ou numéro d'identification également utilisé par d'autres organismes);
–   Adresse du domicile habituel;
–   Date de naissance;
–   Citoyenneté;
–   Niveau d'instruction/ de formation, en distinguant neuf catégories;
–   Type de profession de l'emploi antérieur ou actuel, en distinguant quatre catégories. Des liens ont été établis avec la CITP;
–   Inscriptions/enregistrements antérieurs auprès de l'organisme.

4. Critères utilisés pour déterminer si une personne doit être incluse dans le registre (R) et/ou dans les statistiques de chômeurs (S):
–   Etre sans travail et inscrit au Service national de l'Emploi. Le demandeur d'emploi doit déposer un dossier complet avec ses coordonnées (numéro de téléphone ou boîte postale), (R) et (S);
–   Etre à la recherche d'un travail (R) et (S);
–   Etre disponible pour travailler (R) et (S);
–   Age: Minimum: 16 ans; Maximum: 55 ans (R) et (S);
–   Citoyenneté: le demandeur d'emploi doit se présenter avec une carte d'identité nationale;
–   Etre résident dans le pays. Le demandeur d'emploi doit pointer régulièrement au guichet du SNE;
–   Avoir précédemment travaillé. Le demandeur d'emploi doit présenter ses certificats de travail.

5. Critères utilisés pour déterminer si une personne doit être exclue du registre (R) et/ou des statistiques de chômeurs (S):
–   Avis de décès (R) et (S);
–   Etablissement de la personne à l'étranger (R) et (S);
–   Commencement d'un (nouveau) travail (R) et (S);
–   Défaut de contact avec l'organisme/agence.

6. Définition des personnes au chômage sur laquelle les statistiques sont établies
   Sont considérées comme demandeurs d'emploi toutes les personnes âgées de 16 à 55 ans qui sont disponibles pour travailler et qui recherchent un emploi.
   Les données statistiques produites par le SNE ne représentent que les demandeurs d'emploi qui se déclarent à ses guichets.

7. Mise à jour des registres
   Les registres sont mis à jour quotidiennement.

8. Taux de chômage
   Les statistiques basées sur les registres ne sont pas utilisées pour obtenir des taux de chômage.

9. Type de statistiques sur le nombre de chômeurs enregistrés produites
Période de référence: Mois.
Fréquence de production: Trimestrielle.
Variables utilisées:
–   Sexe;
–   Age;
–   Niveau d'instruction;
–   Profession;
–   Expérience professionnelle antérieure;
–   Citoyenneté (nationaux/non nationaux).
Publication:
–   Sur papier, à diffusion grand public;
–   En format électronique, sur demande;
–   Sur un site Internet

Organisme responsable de la publication: Direction nationale de la Statistique (DINAS)

10. Information méthodologique au sujet de ces statistiques
Publication:
–   A usage interne uniquement.

Organisme responsable: DINAS.

11. Comparaisons avec des statistiques provenant d'autres sources
   Des comparaisons ont été faites avec des statistiques provenant de l'enquête de main-d'œuvre.

12. Principaux changements intervenus depuis le début de ces séries statistiques
   Il n'y a pas eu de changement important dans la législation, dans la capacité de l'agence et/ou dans les procédures administratives susceptibles d'avoir influencé de manière significative les statistiques.

13. Remarques supplémentaires
   Bien que les textes soient clairs et précis, les employeurs, tant du secteur public que du secteur privé, ainsi que les demandeurs d'emploi, ne se conforment pas aux textes en vigueur en matière d'emploi.
   D'autre part, la Loi N°140/AN/97/3ème L du 23.9.97 portant aménagement du Code du travail a libéralisé l'emploi, ce qui fait que la plupart des employeurs ne s'adressent plus au Service national de l'Emploi (SNE) et ne régularisent pas la situation de leur personnel auprès du SNE.

République dominicaine

1. Séries statistiques
Titre: Chômage enregistré
Première année disponible: Non-spécifiée.

2. Organisme responsable de l'enregistrement des chômeurs ou demandeurs d'emploi
Nom de l'organisme: Dirección General de Empleo (Direction Générale de l'Emploi).
Type d'organisme: Organisme public relevant d'une autorité nationale.
Nom de l'autorité nationale: Secretaría de Estado de Trabajo (Secrétariat d'Etat au Travail).
Situation des bureaux chargés de l'enregistrement: Dans cinq provinces; on pense en couvrir 10 autres avant la fin de l'année 2002.
Types de services fournis et/ou gérés par cet organisme
–   Assistance aux demandeurs d'emploi pour trouver du travail;
–   Assistance aux demandeurs d'emploi pour créer leur propre entreprise;
–   Assistance aux employeurs pour trouver de la main-d'œuvre;
–   Orientation professionnelle;
–   Autres services liés à l'emploi: enquêtes sur le marché du travail.

Pourcentage des demandeurs d'emploi qui cherchent un emploi au travers de cet organisme: 10%

3. Les informations personnelles suivantes sont enregistrées
–   Nom;
–   Sexe;
–   Numéro de sécurité sociale (ou numéro d'identification également utilisé par d'autres organismes);
–   Adresse du domicile habituel;
–   Date de naissance;
–   Citoyenneté;
–   Niveau d'instruction/de formation;
–   Situation de travail présente et passée;
–   Type de profession de l'emploi antérieur et/ou actuel. Des liens ont été établis avec la CITP-88, au niveau des groupes de base;
–   Type de profession de l'emploi recherché. Des liens ont été établis avec la CITP-88, au niveau des groupes de base;
–   Inscriptions/enregistrements antérieurs auprès de l'organisme.

4. Critères utilisés pour déterminer si une personne doit être incluse dans le registre (R) et/ou dans les statistiques de chômeurs (S)
–   Etre sans travail (R);
–   Etre à la recherche d'un travail (R);
–   Etre disponible pour travailler (R);
–   Age: Minimum: 16 ans; pas de limite supérieure (R);
–   Citoyenneté (être dominicain) (R);
–   Etre résident dans le pays (R);
–

– Durée souhaitée de l'emploi recherché et/ou du nombre d'heures de travail recherché (R).

5. Critères utilisés pour déterminer si une personne doit être exclue du registre (R) et/ou des statistiques de chômeurs (S)

– Avis de décès (R);
– Défaut de contact avec l'organisme/agence (R);
– Autres: caducité de la demande (le délai est d'une année) (R).

6. Définition des personnes au chômage sur laquelle les statistiques sont établies

Ressortissants dominicains de plus de 16 ans sans travail, qu'ils soient ou non à la recherche d'un emploi.

7. Mise à jour des registres

Les registres sont mis à jour annuellement.

8. Taux de chômage

Les statistiques basées sur les registres ne sont pas utilisées pour obtenir des taux de chômage.

9. Type de statistiques produites sur le nombre de chômeurs enregistrés

Période de référence: Année.
Fréquence de production: Annuelle
Variables utilisées
– Sexe;
– Age;
– Profession;
– Branche d'activité;
– Caractéristiques géographiques;
– Expérience professionnelle antérieure.
Publication
– Sur papier, à diffusion grand public;
– En format électronique, sur demande.

10. Information méthodologique au sujet de ces statistiques

Publication
– Sur papier, à diffusion grand public;
– En format électronique, sur demande;
– Sur le site Internet www.bancentral.gov.do/publicaciones

Organisme responsable: Banco Central de la República Dominicana (Banque Centrale de la République Dominicaine).

11. Comparaisons avec des statistiques provenant d'autres sources

Des comparaisons ont été faites avec des statistiques provenant de l'Enquête sur la main-d'œuvre, d'autres enquêtes auprès des ménages et du rapport de la Commission économique pour l'Amérique latine et les Caraïbes (CEPALC): *Informe de la CEPAL «Comisión Económica para América Latina y el Caribe» (Rapport de la CEPALC)*.

Fréquence des comparaisons: De temps en temps.
Publication de la méthodologie et/ou des résultats de la comparaison: Ils n'ont pas été publiés.

12. Principaux changements intervenus depuis le début de ces séries statistiques

Des changements importants dans la législation, dans la capacité de l'agence et/ou dans les procédures administratives susceptibles d'avoir influencé de manière significative les statistiques sont intervenus en 2002. L'impact résultant sur les statistiques est en cours d'élaboration.

Egypte

1. Séries statistiques

Titre: Chômage enregistré.
Première année disponible: 1959.

2. Agence responsable de l'enregistrement des chômeurs ou demandeurs d'emploi

Nom de l'agence: Ministère de la Main-d'œuvre et de l'Emigration (bureaux locaux).
Type d'organisme: Organisme public relevant d'autorités nationales et locales.
Nom de l'autorité nationale: Ministère de la Main-d'Œuvre et de l'Emigration.
Situation des bureaux chargés de l'enregistrement: Dans toutes les régions du pays avec au moins un bureau dans chaque district; les bureaux de district sont gérés directement par les bureaux principaux de la ville.
Types de services fournis ou gérés par cet organisme:
– Assistance aux demandeurs d'emploi pour trouver du travail;
– Assistance aux employeurs pour trouver de la main-d'œuvre;

– Orientation professionnelle;
– Formation liée à l'emploi;
– Paiement des indemnités de chômage;
– Autre: certains bureaux assistent les demandeurs pour trouver du travail à l'étranger.

Pourcentage des demandeurs d'emploi qui cherchent un emploi au travers de cet organisme: 8.14%

3. Les informations personnelles suivantes sont enregistrées:

– Nom;
– Sexe;
– Numéro de sécurité sociale (ou numéro d'identification également utilisé par d'autres organismes);
– Adresse du domicile habituel;
– Age;
– Citoyenneté;
– Nationalité/groupe ethnique;
– Niveau d'instruction/ de formation, en distinguant six catégories. Des liens ont été établis avec la CITE;
– Situation de travail présente et passée, en distinguant trois catégories;
– Type de profession de l'emploi antérieur ou actuel. Aucun lien n'a été établi avec la CITP;
– Type de travail (profession de l'emploi) recherché, avec 10 catégories. Aucun lien n'a été établi avec la CITP;
– Nom et adresse de l'employeur ou du lieu de travail actuel ou passé;
– Inscriptions/enregistrements antérieurs auprès de l'agence/service.

4. Critères utilisés pour déterminer si une personne doit être incluse dans le registre (R) et/ou dans les statistiques de chômeurs (S):

– Etre sans travail (R) et (S);
– Etre à la recherche d'un travail (R) et (S);
– Etre disponible pour travailler (R) et (S);
– Age: Minimum: 12 ans; pas de limite supérieure (R) et (S);
– Citoyenneté (R) et (S);
– Etre résident dans le pays (R) et (S);
– Avoir précédemment travaillé (R) et (S).

5. Critères utilisés pour déterminer si une personne doit être exclue du registre (R) et/ou des statistiques de chômeurs (S):

– Décès (R) et (S);
– Commencement d'un (nouveau) travail (R) et (S);
– Défaut de contact avec l'agence/service (R) et (S);
– Incapacité à travailler.

6. Définition des personnes au chômage sur laquelle les statistiques sont établies

(i) Les personnes inoccupées ayant déjà travaillé, aptes à travailler, qui désirent travailler et cherchent un emploi;
(ii) Les personnes à la recherche de leur premier emploi, aptes à travailler, qui désirent travailler et cherchent un emploi;
(iii) Les personnes occupées mais qui cherchent un meilleur emploi, soit parce que leur emploi ne leur convient pas, soit parce qu'il ne les satisfait pas d'un point de vue économique ou pour une quelconque autre raison.

7. Mise à jour des registres

Les registres sont mis à jour mensuellement.

8. Taux de chômage

Les statistiques basées sur les registres sont utilisées pour obtenir des taux de chômage.

Les sources des données d'emploi qui sont partie du dénominateur du taux de chômage sont l'enquête sur la main-d'œuvre et le recensement de la population.

Définition des personnes pourvues d'un emploi à cette fin:
Les personnes occupées dans une activité économique.

9. Type de statistiques sur le nombre de chômeurs enregistrés produites

Période de référence: Mois.
Fréquence de production: Trimestrielle; Annuelle.
Variables utilisées:
– Sexe;
– Niveau d'instruction;
– Profession;
– Branche d'activité;
– Caractéristiques géographiques;
– Expérience professionnelle antérieure;
– Citoyenneté (nationaux/non nationaux).

Publication:
–   Sur papier, à diffusion restreinte;
–   En format électronique, sur demande;
–   Sur le site Internet du Ministère de la Main-d'œuvre et de l'Emigration.
Agence responsable de la publication: Ministère de la Main-d'œuvre et de l'Emigration.
Périodicité de la publication: Trimestrielle; Annuelle.
10. Information méthodologique au sujet de ces statistiques
Publication:
–   En format électronique, sur demande;
–   Sur le site Internet du Ministère de la Main-d'œuvre et de l'Emigration.
–   Agence responsable: Ministère de la Main-d'œuvre et de l'Emigration.
11. Comparaisons avec des statistiques provenant d'autres sources
        Des comparaisons ont été faites avec des statistiques de chômage provenant de l'enquête sur la main-d'œuvre et le recensement de la population.
Fréquence des comparaisons: Occasionnelle.
Publication de la méthodologie et/ou des résultats de la comparaison: Ils n'ont pas été publiés.
12. Principaux changements intervenus depuis le début de ces séries statistiques
        Il n'y a pas eu de changement important dans la législation, dans la capacité de l'agence et/ou dans les procédures administratives susceptibles d'avoir influencé de manière significative les statistiques.

El Salvador

1. Séries statistiques
Titres: 1. Nombre de personnes inscrites.
              2. Nombre de personnes placées.
              3. Nombre de postes de travail.
Première année disponible: 1998.
2. Organisme responsable de l'enregistrement des chômeurs ou demandeurs d'emploi
Nom de l'organisme: Departamento Nacional del Empleo (Département national de l'Emploi).
Type d'organisme: Organisme public relevant d'une autorité nationale.
Nom de l'autorité nationale: Ministerio de Trabajo y Previsión Social (Ministère du Travail et de Prévoyance sociale).
Situation des bureaux chargés de l'enregistrement: San Salvador; Santa Ana; Sonsonate; Zacatecoluca; San Miguel et La Unión.
Types de services fournis et/ou gérés par cet organisme
–   Assistance aux demandeurs d'emploi pour trouver du travail;
–   Assistance aux employeurs pour trouver de la main-d'œuvre;
–   Orientation professionnelle;
–   Formation liée à l'emploi;
–   Autres services liés à l'emploi: service spécifique pour des mineurs qui travaillent; promotion de l'emploi à travers l'apprentissage.
Pourcentage des demandeurs d'emploi qui cherchent un emploi au travers de cet organisme: 15%
3. Les informations personnelles suivantes sont enregistrées
–   Nom;
–   Sexe;
–   Numéro de sécurité sociale (ou numéro d'identification également utilisé par d'autres organismes);
–   Adresse du domicile habituel;
–   Date de naissance;
–   Nationalité/groupe ethnique;
–   Niveau d'instruction/de formation, en distinguant cinq catégories. Aucun lien n'a été établi avec la CITE;
–   Situation de travail présente et passée, en distinguant trois catégories;
–   Type de profession de l'emploi antérieur et/ou actuel, en distinguant 10 catégories; Des liens ont été établis avec la CITP-88;
–   Type de profession de l'emploi recherché, avec 10 catégories;
–   Nom et adresse de l'employeur ou du lieu de travail

actuel ou passé;
–   Branche d'activité de l'employeur ou du lieu de travail actuel ou passé, en distinguant 10 catégories. Aucun lien n'a été établi avec la CITI-rév. 3.
4. Critères utilisés pour déterminer si une personne doit être incluse dans le registre (R) et/ou dans les statistiques de chômeurs (S)
–   Etre sans travail (R) et (S);
–   Etre à la recherche d'un travail (R) et (S);
–   Etre disponible pour travailler (R) et (S);
–   Age: Minimum: 18 ans; maximum: 35 ans (R) et (S);
–   Avoir précédemment travaillé (R).
5. Critères utilisés pour déterminer si une personne doit être exclue du registre (R) et/ou des statistiques de chômeurs (S):
        Non-spécifié.
6. Définition des personnes au chômage sur laquelle les statistiques sont établies
        Information non disponible.
7. Mise à jour des registres
        Les registres sont mis à jour annuellement.
8. Taux de chômage
        Les statistiques basées sur les registres sont utilisées pour obtenir des taux de chômage.
9. Type de statistiques produites sur le nombre de chômeurs enregistrés
Séries:
1.   Nombre de personnes à la recherche d'un emploi inscrites au Département de l'Emploi.
2.   Nombre de personnes placées.
3.   Nombre de placements pourvus par les employeurs.
Période de référence: Mois
Fréquence de production: Mensuelle
Variables utilisées
–   Sexe;
–   Age;
–   Niveau d'instruction;
–   Profession;
–   Branche d'activité.
Publication
–   Sur papier, à diffusion grand public;
–   Sur un site Internet: www.mtps.gob.sv
Organisme responsable de la publication: Ministerio de Trabajo y Previsión Social (Ministère du Travail et de Prévoyance sociale).
Périodicité de la publication: Mensuelle.
10. Information méthodologique au sujet de ces statistiques
Publication
–   Sur papier, à diffusion restreinte.
Organisme responsable: Ministerio de Trabajo y Previsión Social (Ministère du Travail et de Prévoyance sociale)
11. Comparaisons avec des statistiques provenant d'autres sources
        Aucune comparaison n'a été faite avec des statistiques provenant d'autres sources.
12. Principaux changements intervenus depuis le début de ces séries statistiques
        Il n'y a pas eu de changement important dans la législation, dans la capacité de l'agence et/ou dans les procédures administratives susceptibles d'avoir influencé de manière significative les statistiques.

Espagne

1. Séries statistiques
Titre: Chômage enregistré.
Première année disponible: Non-spécifiée.
2. Organisme responsable de l'enregistrement des chômeurs ou demandeurs d'emploi
Nom de l'organisme: Instituto Nacional de Empleo y Servicios Públicos de Empleo (Institut national de l'Emploi et Services publiques de l'Emploi).
Type d'organisme: Organisme public relevant d'une autorité nationale.
Nom de l'autorité nationale: Ministerio de Trabajo y Asuntos Sociales (Ministère du Travail et des Affaires sociales).
Situation des bureaux chargés de l'enregistrement: Dans l'ensemble du pays; distribution par zones géographiques.
Types de services fournis et/ou gérés par cet organisme
        Assistance aux demandeurs d'emploi pour trouver du travail;

– Assistance aux demandeurs d'emploi pour créer leur propre entreprise;

– Assistance aux employeurs pour trouver de la main-d'œuvre;

– Orientation professionnelle;

– Formation liée à l'emploi;

– Paiement des indemnités de chômage;

– Autres services liés à l'emploi: programmes expérimentaux d'emploi et de la formation-emploi.

Pourcentage des demandeurs d'emploi qui cherchent un emploi au travers de cet organisme: Non-spécifiée.

3. Les informations personnelles suivantes sont enregistrées

– Nom;

– Sexe;

– Numéro de sécurité sociale (ou numéro d'identification également utilisé par d'autres organismes);

– Adresse du domicile habituel;

– Date de naissance;

– Citoyenneté;

– Nationalité;

– Niveau d'instruction/de formation. Aucun lien n'a été établi avec la CITE;

– Situation de travail présente et passée, en distinguant 40 catégories;

– Type de profession de l'emploi antérieur et/ou actuel. Des liens ont été établis avec la CITP-88, au niveau des groupes de base;

– Type de profession de l'emploi recherché, avec 3.537 catégories. Des liens ont été établis avec la CITP-88, au niveau des groupes de base;

– Nom et adresse de l'employeur ou du lieu de travail actuel ou passé;

– Branche d'activité de l'employeur ou du lieu de travail actuel ou passé, en distinguant 63 catégories;

– Inscriptions/enregistrements antérieurs auprès de l'organisme.

4. Critères utilisés pour déterminer si une personne doit être incluse dans le registre (R) et/ou dans les statistiques de chômeurs (S)

– Etre sans travail (S);

– Etre à la recherche d'un travail (R) et (S);

– Etre disponible pour travailler (S);

– Age: Minimum: 16 ans; Maximum: 65 ans (S);

– Citoyenneté (R) et (S);

– Etre résident dans le pays (R) et (S);

– Durée souhaitée de l'emploi recherché et/ou du nombre d'heures de travail recherché (S).

5. Critères utilisés pour déterminer si une personne doit être exclue du registre (R) et/ou des statistiques de chômeurs (S)

– Avis de décès (R) et (S);

– Etablissement de la personne à l'étranger (R) et (S);

– Commencement d'un (nouveau) travail; (sont exclues du registre les personnes ayant trouvé un emploi pour une durée supérieure à trois mois) (R) et (S);

– Participation à un programme de promotion de l'emploi, à un programme de travaux publics, etc. (S);

– Entreprise d'une formation ou d'études (sont exclues des statistiques les personnes âgées de moins de 25 ans ou qui n'ont jamais travaillé) (S);

– Refus d'une offre d'emploi adaptée (R) et (S);

– Refus d'une offre de formation adaptée (R) et (S);

– Incapacité à travailler (S).

6. Définition des personnes au chômage sur laquelle les statistiques sont établies

Personnes inscrites en tant que demandeurs d'emploi qui n'appartiennent pas aux catégories suivantes: occuper un emploi; participer à des travaux d'intérêt social; titulaire d'une pension d'invalidité totale; retraité; emploi par période de plus de trois mois; travaillant moins de 80 heures par mois; étudiant; étudiant suivant une formation professionnelle; congé maladie; bénéficiaire d'une allocation agricole; âgée de plus de 65 ans.

7. Mise à jour des registres

Les registres sont mis à jour quotidiennement.

8. Taux de chômage

Les statistiques basées sur les registres sont utilisées pour obtenir des taux de chômage.

La source des données d'emploi qui sont partie du dénominateur est l'enquête auprès des ménages sur la main-d'œuvre.

Définition des personnes pourvues d'un emploi à cette fin

Enquête sur la population active.

9. Type de statistiques produites sur le nombre de chômeurs enregistrés

Période de référence: Mois

Fréquence de production: Mensuelle

Variables utilisées

– Sexe;

– Age;

– Niveau d'instruction;

– Profession;

– Branche d'activité;

– Caractéristiques géographiques;

– Durée de chômage;

– Autres: Motif d'exclusion du chômage enregistré.

Publication

– Sur papier, à diffusion restreinte;

– En format électronique, sur demande;

– Sur le site Internet www.inem.es

Organisme responsable de la publication: Instituto Nacional de Empleo (Institut national de l'Emploi).

Titre et périodicité de la publication: *Estadística de Empleo* (Statistiques de l'Emploi) (mensuelle).

10. Information méthodologique au sujet de ces statistiques

Publication

– Sur papier, à diffusion grand public;

– En format électronique, sur demande;

– Sur le site Internet www.inem.es

Organisme responsable: Instituto Nacional de Empleo (Institut national de l'Emploi).

11. Comparaisons avec des statistiques provenant d'autres sources

Aucune comparaison n'a été faite avec des statistiques provenant d'autres sources.

12. Principaux changements intervenus depuis le début de ces séries statistiques

Des changements importants dans la législation, dans la capacité de l'agence et/ou dans les procédures administratives susceptibles d'avoir influencé de manière significative les statistiques sont intervenus en 1985, mais leurs répercussions sur les statistiques n'ont pas été enregistrées.

Estonie

1. Séries statistiques

Titre: Chômage enregistré.

Première année disponible: 1993

2. Organisme responsable de l'enregistrement des chômeurs ou demandeurs d'emploi

Nom de l'organisme: Tööhoiveamet (Bureau de l'Emploi).

Type d'organisme: Organisme public relevant d'une autorité nationale.

Nom de l'autorité nationale: Conseil de la Main-d'Œuvre (sous le Ministère des Affaires Sociales).

Situation des bureaux chargés de l'enregistrement: Dans tous les 15 comtés, plus un à Tallinn (36 bureaux locaux ou leurs représentants à travers le pays).

Types de services fournis et/ou gérés par cet organisme:

– Information sur la situation sur le marché du travail et les possibilités d'emploi et de formation;

– Médiation en ce qui concerne l'emploi;

– Formation en vue d'emploi;

– Subvention d'emploi en vue de création d'entreprise;

– Subvention d'emploi aux employeurs;

– Placements communautaires;

– Orientation professionnelle;

– Paiement d'indemnités de chômage;

– Autre: programmes spéciaux pour des groupes désavantagés (personnes handicapées, jeunes chômeurs et chômeurs de longue durée).

Pourcentage des demandeurs d'emploi qui cherchent un emploi au travers de cet organisme: 55%.

3. Les informations personnelles suivantes sont enregistrées:

– Nom;

– Sexe;

- Code d'identification personnel;
- Adresse du domicile habituel;
- Date de naissance;
- Citoyenneté;
- Niveau d'instruction/ de formation, en distinguant 13 catégories. Il y a un projet d'établir des liens avec la CITE;
- Situation d'activité, en distinguant neuf catégories;
- Type de profession de l'emploi antérieur, en distinguant neuf catégories. Des liens ont été établis avec la CITP, au niveau des groupes de base;
- Type de profession de l'emploi recherché, avec neuf catégories. Des liens ont été établis avec la CITP, au niveau des groupes de base;
- Type d'activité économique de l'employeur ou du lieu de travail précédent, en distinguant 16 catégories. Des liens ont été établis avec la CITI, rév.3 ou NACE au niveau des classes;
- Autre: de langue estonienne; de langue russe.

4. Critères utilisés pour déterminer si une personne doit être incluse dans le registre (R) et/ou dans les statistiques de chômeurs (S):

Une personne est enregistrée comme chômeur auprès d'un bureau chargé de l'enregistrement si elle en fait la demande et produit tous les documents requis selon la procédure établie par le gouvernement de la République. Les critères sont les suivants:
- Etre sans travail (S);
- Etre à la recherche d'un travail (S);
- Etre disponible pour travailler (S);
- Age: Minimum: 16 ans; Maximum: Age de la retraite (S);
- Citoyenneté (S);
- Etre résident de façon permanente dans le pays (S).

5. Critères utilisés pour déterminer si une personne doit être exclue du registre (R) et/ou des statistiques de chômeurs (S):
- Décès (S);
- Etablissement de la personne à l'étranger (S);
- Commencement d'un (nouveau) travail (S);
- Commencement du service militaire (S);
- Poursuit des études pendant la journée ou des études à plein temps dans une institution éducative (S);
- Arrête de chercher du travail pour plus de trente jours (S);
- Refus de deux offres d'emploi adaptées (S);
- Refus de deux offres de formation adaptées (S);
- Fin de droit à l'allocation chômage;
- Atteinte de l'age de la retraite ou bénéficiaire d'une pré-retraite (S);
- Incapacité à travailler (S);
- Autres: fin d'une formation liée à l'emploi sans le consentement du bureau de l'emploi(S); au bénéfice d'un subside d'emploi (S).

6. Définition des personnes au chômage sur laquelle les statistiques sont établies

Est considérée au chômage toute personne avec une capacité de travail totale ou partielle, entre 16 ans et l'âge de la retraite, qui est sans emploi, est prête à commencer un travail immédiatement et est à la recherche d'un emploi. Une personne est considérée à la recherche d'un travail si elle se présente au bureau de travail au moins une fois en trente jours, est prête à commencer un travail immédiatement et à participer à une formation d'emploi (source: "Protection Sociale de la Loi sur le Chômage", par. 3) (http://www.tta.ee/english/law).

7. Mise à jour des registres

Il n'y a pas de registre central pour tout le pays (il y en a un en préparation). Chaque comté a une base de données qui est mise à jour régulièrement.

8. Taux de chômage

Les statistiques basées sur les registres ne sont pas utilisées pour obtenir des taux de chômage. Les taux de chômage sont calculés sur la base de données des enquêtes sur la main-d'œuvre, selon les méthodes du BIT. Le bureau responsable du marché du travail calcule le taux de chômage en prenant en compte le nombre de chômeurs enregistrés par rapport au nombre de personnes en âge de travailler (de 16 ans à l'age de la retraite) et non par rapport à l'ensemble de la main-d'œuvre.

9. Type de statistiques sur le nombre de chômeurs enregistrés produites
Série 1:
Période de référence: Mois.
Fréquence de production: Mensuelle.

Variables utilisées:
- Sexe;
- Groupe d'âge (3);
- Niveau d'instruction (4);
- Caractéristiques géographiques (comtés);
- Autres: de langue estonienne; de langue russe; participation à des services d'emploi; nombre de nouvelles entrées; nombre de vacances de postes; nombre de placements; pourcentage de chômeurs enregistrés par rapport au nombre de personnes en âge de travailler; nombre de chômeurs au bénéfice d'indemnités de chômage.
- Publication:
- Sur papier;
- A diffusion restreinte (par e-mail);
- Sur un site Internet (http://www.tta.ee).

Agence responsable de la publication: Bureau Statistique Estonien.
Titre et périodicité de la publication: Estonian Statistics Monthly (Mensuel des statistiques estoniennes).
Série 2:
Période de référence: Trimestre.
Fréquence de production: Trimestrielle.
Variables utilisées:
- Sexe;
- Age;
- Niveau d'instruction;
- Profession;
- Activité économique;
- Caractéristiques géographiques (comté et municipalité);
- Expérience professionnelle antérieure;
- Durée du chômage;
- Autres: de langue estonienne; de langue russe.
- Publication: Sur papier, à diffusion restreinte (par e-mail).

10. Information méthodologique au sujet de ces statistiques
Publication:
- Sur papier (partiellement seulement, le registre n'étant pas encore tout à fait prêt);
- Sur un site Internet (http://www.tta.ee).

Organisme responsable: Conseil de l'Emploi.

11. Comparaisons avec des statistiques provenant d'autres sources

Des comparaisons ont été faites surtout avec des statistiques de chômage provenant de l'enquête sur la main-d'œuvre, mais aussi d'une enquête auprès des ménages, et le recensement de la population.

Fréquence des comparaisons: Régulièrement lors de la publication des statistiques.
Publication de la méthodologie et/ou des résultats de la comparaison: Ont été publiés dans les publications suivantes:
- *Estonian Labour Market and Labour Market Policy* (Articles, ed. Par Raul Eamets) (Main d'Œuvre Estonienne et Politique de la Main d'Œuvre), Viljandi-Tartu, 1999;
- *Estonian Employment Action Plans for 2000, 2001 and 2002* (Plans d'Action sur l'Emploi Estonien pour 2000, 2001 et 2002);
- *Eesti tööturu areng üllmerenuperiodil* Eamets, R., Philips, K.), Tartu, 1999;
- *Estonian Statistics Monthly* (Mensuel des Statistiques Estoniens) (Bureau de Statistique Estonien).

12. Principaux changements intervenus depuis le début de ces séries statistiques

Des changements importants dans la législation, dans la capacité de l'agence et/ou dans les procédures administratives susceptibles d'avoir influencé de manière significative les statistiques sont intervenus en: (i) 1995, lors de l'entrée en vigueur de la première loi sur la protection sociale des chômeurs, les effets sur les statistiques n'ayant pas été évalués; et (ii) en 2000, lors de l'entrée en vigueur de la nouvelle loi sur la protection sociale des chômeurs et de la loi sur le service de l'emploi avec une augmentation de 17% du nombre des personnes enregistrées comme chômeurs.

Etats-Unis

1. Séries statistiques
Titre: Chômage enregistré.
Première année disponible: 1933.
2. Organisme responsable de l'enregistrement des chômeurs ou demandeurs d'emploi
Nom de l'organisme: Le nom officiel peut varier selon les Etats, mais il est en général connu comme l'Agence Nationale pour le Développement de la Main-d'œuvre ou le Bureau de l'Emploi.
Type d'organisme: Organisme public relevant d'une autorité nationale.
Nom de l'autorité nationale: Administration pour l'Emploi et la Formation (géré par un fonds coopératif d'Etat fédéral).
Situation des bureaux chargés de l'enregistrement: Il y a 3459 points locaux appelés centres «One-Stop» et des services situés dans 50 Etats et 4 Territoires.
Types de services fournis et/ou gérés par cet organisme:
–   Assistance aux demandeurs d'emploi pour trouver du travail;
–   Assistance aux demandeurs d'emploi pour créer leur propre entreprise;
–   Assistance aux employeurs pour trouver de la main-d'œuvre;
–   Orientation professionnelle;
–   Formation liée à l'emploi;
–   Paiement des indemnités de chômage;
–   Autres services liés à l'emploi: un certain nombre de services de soutien sont proposés par les centres locaux «One-Stop».
Pourcentage des demandeurs d'emploi qui cherchent un emploi au travers de cet organisme: Inconnu.
3. Les informations personnelles suivantes sont enregistrées:
–   Nom;
–   Sexe;
–   Numéro de sécurité sociale (ou numéro d'identification également utilisé par d'autres organismes);
–   Adresse du domicile habituel;
–   Date de naissance;
–   Citoyenneté;
–   Nationalité/groupe ethnique;
–   Niveau d'instruction/de formation;
–   Situation de travail présente et passée;
–   Type de profession de l'emploi antérieur et/ou actuel;
–   Type de profession de l'emploi recherché;
–   Nom et adresse de l'employeur ou du lieu de travail actuel ou passé;
–   Branche d'activité de l'employeur ou du lieu de travail actuel ou passé, en distinguant un nombre de groupes non spécifié;
–   Inscriptions/enregistrements antérieurs auprès de l'organisme;
–   Autre: les centres locaux «One-Stop» peuvent demander d'autres informations liées à l'emploi.
4. Critères utilisés pour déterminer si une personne doit être incluse dans le registre (R) et/ou dans les statistiques de chômeurs (S):
–   Etre sans travail (R) et (S);*
–   Etre à la recherche d'un travail (R) et (S);*
–   Etre disponible pour travailler (R) et (S).*
* Ne s'applique qu'aux bénéficiaires d'indemnités de chômage.
5. Critères utilisés pour déterminer si une personne doit être exclue du registre (R) et/ou des statistiques de chômeurs (S):
–   Avis de décès (R) et (S);
–   Etablissement de la personne à l'étranger (R) et (S);
–   Commencement d'un (nouveau) travail (R) et (S);
–   Commencement du service militaire (R) et (S);
–   Participation à un programme de promotion de l'emploi, à un programme de travaux publics, etc. (R) et (S);
–   Entreprise d'une formation ou d'études (R) et (S);*
–   Défaut de contact avec l'organisme/agence (les sanctions varient selon les Etats) (R) et (S);*
–   Refus d'offres d'emploi adaptées (les sanctions varient selon les Etats) (R) et (S);*
–   Refus d'offres de formation adaptées (les sanctions varient selon les Etats) (R) et (S);*
–   Fin de droit à l'allocation-chômage (R) et (S);*
–   Incapacité à travailler (R) et (S).*

* Ne s'applique qu'aux bénéficiaires d'indemnités de chômage.
6. Définition des personnes au chômage sur laquelle les statistiques sont établies
En ce qui concerne l'enregistrement comme demandeur d'emploi, il n'y a pas de définition à l'échelon fédéral.
Pour ce qui est des allocations de chômage, les bénéficiaires doivent être capables de travailler, disponibles pour travailler et rechercher activement un emploi.
7. Mise à jour des registres
Les registres sont mis à jour régulièrement mais la fréquence varie selon les Etats.
8. Taux de chômage
Les statistiques basées sur les registres ne sont pas utilisées pour obtenir des taux de chômage.
9. Type de statistiques produites sur le nombre de chômeurs enregistrés
Période de référence: Trimestre.
Fréquence de production: Trimestrielle.
Variables utilisées:
–   Sexe;
–   Age;
–   Niveau d'instruction;
–   Profession;
–   Branche d'activité.
Publication:
–   Sur papier, à diffusion grand public.
Agence responsable de la publication: Bureau pour l'Emploi et la Formation
Titre de la publication: «*Wagner-Peyser Act Annual program Report Data*»
10. Information méthodologique au sujet de ces statistiques
L'information méthodologique sur ces statistiques n'est pas disponible.
11. Comparaisons avec des statistiques provenant d'autres sources
Il n'y a pas eu de comparaisons faites avec des statistiques provenant d'autres sources.
12. Principaux changements intervenus depuis le début de ces séries statistiques
Des changements importants dans la législation, dans la capacité de l'agence et/ou dans les procédures administratives sont intervenus en 1933, 1950, 1973, 1978, 1982 et 1998. Leur impact sur les statistiques n'a pas été évalué.
13. Remarques supplémentaires
La politique concernant l'enregistrement des demandeurs d'emploi varie au travers des Etats-Unis. Généralement, les travailleurs qui souhaitent bénéficier des services d'aide à la recherche d'offres d'emploi doivent s'inscrire comme demandeurs d'emploi. Dans certains Etats, les travailleurs peuvent recevoir des avis de vacances de postes et autres informations sans être enregistrés.
Les procédures d'enregistrement pour les travailleurs qui demandent et reçoivent des allocations de chômage varient également. Cependant, les demandeurs et bénéficiaires d'allocations de chômage qui sont définitivement mis à pieds et qui ne reçoivent pas d'avis de vacances de postes au travers d'un service d'emploi syndical doivent s'enregistrer comme demandeurs d'emploi.
Tous les Etats fournissent des listes de postes sur un réseau informatique appelé la «Banque du travail de l'Amérique».

Ethiopie

1. Séries statistiques
Titre: Statistiques de la bourse du travail.
Première année disponible: 1961.
2. Organisme responsable de l'enregistrement des chômeurs ou demandeurs d'emploi
Nom de l'organisme: Bureau of Labour and Social Affairs (Bureau du Travail et des Affaires sociales).
Type d'organisme: Organisme public relevant d'autorités nationales et régionales.
Nom de l'autorité nationale: Ministère du Travail et des Affaires sociales.
Situation des bureaux chargés de l'enregistrement: Dans tous les bureaux d'emploi public dans les administrations de différents états régionaux et de villes.

Types de services fournis/gérés par cet organisme:
- Assistance aux demandeurs d'emploi pour trouver du travail;
- Assistance aux employeurs pour trouver de la main-d'œuvre;
- Orientation professionnelle (responsabilité partielle);
- Formation liée à l'emploi (responsabilité partielle).

3. Les informations personnelles suivantes sont enregistrées:
- Nom;
- Sexe;
- Adresse du domicile habituel;
- Date de naissance;
- Niveau d'instruction/de formation, en distinguant un nombre non spécifié de catégories. Des liens ont été établis avec la CITE;
- Situation de travail présente/passée, en distinguant un nombre non spécifié de catégories;
- Type de travail (profession) de l'emploi antérieur ou actuel, en distinguant cinq catégories;
- Enregistrements antérieurs auprès de l'organisme.

4. Critères utilisés pour déterminer si une personne doit être incluse dans le registre (R) et/ou dans les statistiques de chômeurs (S):
- Etre sans travail (R) et (S);
- Etre à la recherche d'un travail (R) et (S);
- Etre disponible pour travailler (R) et (S);
- Age: Minimum: 18 ans; Maximum: 55 ans (R) et (S);
- Etre résident dans le pays (R) et (S);
- Avoir précédemment travaillé (R) et (S).

5. Critères utilisés pour déterminer si une personne doit être exclue du registre (R) et/ou des statistiques de chômeurs (S):
Information non disponible.

6. Définition des personnes au chômage sur laquelle les statistiques sont établies
Information non disponible.

7. Mise à jour des registres
Les registres ne sont pas mis à jour régulièrement.

8. Taux de chômage
Les statistiques basées sur les registres ne sont pas utilisées pour obtenir des taux de chômage.

9. Type de statistiques produites sur le nombre de chômeurs enregistrés
Période de référence: Année.
Fréquence de production: Annuelle.
Variables utilisées:
- Sexe;
- Age;
- Niveau d'instruction;
- Profession;
- Caractéristiques géographiques;
- Durée de chômage.

Publication: Sur papier, à diffusion grand public.
Agence responsable de la publication: Ministère du Travail et des Affaires sociales.
Titre des publications: *Employment Exchange Information* (informations sur la bourse de travail); *Labour Statistics Bulletin* (bulletin statistique du travail).

10. Information méthodologique au sujet de ces statistiques
Publication: Sur papier, à diffusion grand public.
Agence responsable: Ministère du Travail et des Affaires sociales.

11. Comparaisons avec des statistiques provenant d'autres sources
Il n'y a pas eu de comparaisons faites avec des statistiques provenant d'autres sources.

12. Principaux changements intervenus depuis le début de ces séries statistiques
Des changements importants dans la législation, dans la capacité de l'agence et/ou dans les procédures administratives sont intervenus en:
1975: Les changements concernant les statistiques qui en résultaient n'ont pas été estimés; et
1993: Il en résultait une diminution de 25 à 30% du nombre des personnes enregistrées au chômage.

Finlande

1. Séries statistiques
Titre: Statistiques de la Main-d'œuvre.

Première année disponible: 1991.
2. Organisme responsable de l'enregistrement des chômeurs ou demandeurs d'emploi
Nom de l'organisme: Agences pour l'emploi.
Type d'organisme: Organisme public relevant d'une autorité nationale, régionale et locale.
Nom de l'autorité nationale: Ministère du Travail.
Situation des bureaux chargés de l'enregistrement: 175 agences pour l'emploi couvrent tout le territoire.
Types de services fournis et/ou gérés par cet organisme:
- Assistance aux demandeurs d'emploi pour trouver du travail;
- Assistance aux demandeurs d'emploi pour créer leur propre entreprise;
- Assistance aux employeurs pour trouver de la main-d'œuvre;
- Orientation professionnelle;
- Formation liée à l'emploi;
- Paiement des indemnités de chômage;
- Autre: formation liée au marché du travail.

3. Les informations personnelles suivantes sont enregistrées:
- Nom;
- Sexe;
- Numéro de sécurité sociale (ou numéro d'identification également utilisé par d'autres organismes);
- Date de naissance;
- Citoyenneté;
- Nationalité/groupe ethnique;
- Niveau d'instruction/ de formation, en distinguant cinq-six catégories. Des liens ont été établis avec la CITE;
- Situation de travail présente et passée, en distinguant 14 catégories;
- Type de profession de l'emploi antérieur ou actuel, en distinguant 3.300 catégories. Aucun lien n'a été établi avec la CITP;
- Type de profession de l'emploi recherché, avec 3300 catégories. Aucun lien n'a été établi avec la CITP;
- Branche d'activité de l'employeur ou du lieu de travail actuel ou passé. Aucun lien n'a été établi avec la CITI ni avec la NACE;
- Inscriptions/enregistrements antérieurs auprès de l'organisme;
- Autre: code d'enregistrement pour l'emploi.

4. Critères utilisés pour déterminer si une personne doit être incluse dans le registre (R) et/ou dans les statistiques de chômeurs (S):
- Etre sans travail (R) et (S);
- Etre à la recherche d'un travail (R) et (S);
- Etre disponible pour travailler (R) et (S);
- Age: Minimum: 17 ans; Maximum: 65 ans (R) et (S);
- Citoyenneté (R) et (S);
- Etre résident dans le pays (R) et (S);
- Durée souhaitée de l'emploi recherché et/ou du nombre d'heures de travail recherché (R) et (S).

5. Critères utilisés pour déterminer si une personne doit être exclue du registre (R) et/ou des statistiques de chômeurs (S):
- Décès (R) et (S);
- Etablissement de la personne à l'étranger (R) et (S);
- Commencement d'un (nouveau) travail (R) et (S);
- Commencement du service militaire (R) et (S);
- Participation à un programme de promotion de l'emploi, à un programme de travaux publics, etc. (R) et (S);
- Entreprise d'une formation ou d'études (R) et (S);
- Défaut de contact avec l'organisme/agence (R) et (S);
- Refus d'une offre d'emploi adaptée (R) et (S);
- Refus d'une offre de formation adaptée (R) et (S);
- Fin de droit à l'allocation chômage (R) et (S);
- Admission à toucher une pension (R) et (S);
- Incapacité à travailler (R) et (S).

6. Définition des personnes au chômage sur laquelle les statistiques sont établies
Sont considérées comme chômeurs les personnes enregistrées à la recherche d'un travail qui sont sans travail et disponibles pour travailler à plein temps (travail pour lequel le temps de travail est au moins la moitié du temps de travail normal) ou qui se sont arrangées pour commencer un travail mais ne l'ont pas encore commencé. Une personne à la recherche d'un travail qui ne peut accepter une proposition de travail qu'après une période fixe

ou qui cherche du travail pour lequel le temps de travail est inférieur à la moitié du temps de travail normal du secteur n'est pas considérée comme chômeur à la recherche d'un travail. Les étudiants à plein temps ne sont pas enregistrés comme chômeurs à la recherche d'un travail, même en période de vacances.

7. Mise à jour des registres

Les registres sont mis à jour mensuellement.

8. Taux de chômage

Les statistiques basées sur les registres sont utilisées pour obtenir des taux de chômage.

La source des données d'emploi qui est partie du dénominateur des taux de chômage est l'enquête sur la main-d'œuvre.

9. Type de statistiques sur le nombre de chômeurs enregistrés produites

Série 1: Statistiques des Services de l'Emploi.

Période de référence: Mois.

Fréquence de production: Mensuelle.

Variables utilisées:

– Sexe;
– Age,
– Niveau d'instruction;
– Profession;
– Branche d'activité;
– Caractéristiques géographiques;
– Expérience professionnelle antérieure;
– Citoyenneté (nationaux/non nationaux);
– Durée de chômage.

Publication:

– Sur papier, à diffusion grand public;
– En format électronique, sur demande;
– Sur un site Internet

Agence responsable de la publication: Ministère du Travail.

10. Information méthodologique au sujet de ces statistiques

Publication: Sur un site Internet (www.mol.fi).

Agence responsable: Ministère du Travail.

11. Comparaisons avec des statistiques provenant d'autres sources

Des comparaisons ont été faites avec des statistiques provenant de l'enquête sur la main d'œuvre, un autre type d'enquête auprès des ménages et le recensement de la population.

Fréquence des comparaisons: Occasionnellement (dernière année: 1997).

Publication de la méthodologie et/ou des résultats de la comparaison: Ont été publiés dans *Unemployment and Employment Statistics* (Statistiques sur le Chômage et l'Emploi), Statistiques Finlande, Statistiques Officielles, Marché de l'Emploi 1997:3.

12. Principaux changements intervenus depuis le début de ces séries statistiques

Il n'y a pas eu de changement important dans la législation, dans la capacité de l'agence et/ou dans les procédures administratives susceptibles d'avoir influencé de manière significative les statistiques.

France

1. Séries statistiques

Titre: Demandeurs d'emploi.

2. Organisme responsable de l'enregistrement des chômeurs ou demandeurs d'emploi

Nom de l'organisme: Agence Nationale pour l'Emploi (ANPE)

Type d'organisme: Organisme public relevant d'une autorité nationale.

Nom de l'autorité nationale: Ministère des Affaires sociales, du Travail et de la Solidarité.

Situation des bureaux chargés de l'enregistrement: 741 agences locales dans l'ensemble du pays.

Types de services fournis ou gérés par cet organisme:

– Assistance aux demandeurs d'emploi pour trouver du travail;
– Assistance aux demandeurs d'emploi pour créer leur propre entreprise;
– Assistance aux employeurs pour trouver de la main-d'œuvre;
– Orientation professionnelle;
– Assistance aux actifs pour trouver un autre emploi.

Pourcentage des demandeurs d'emploi qui cherchent un emploi au travers de cet organisme: 100%

3. Les informations personnelles suivantes sont enregistrées:

– Nom;
– Sexe;
– Adresse du domicile habituel;
– Date de naissance;
– Nationalité;
– Niveau d'instruction/ de formation, en distinguant 152 catégories. Aucun lien n'a été établi avec la CITE;
– Branche d'activité de l'employeur ou du lieu de travail actuel ou passé, en distinguant 75 catégories;
– Inscriptions antérieures auprès de l'agence;
– Autre: catégorie (voir '6); qualification; handicap.

4. Critères utilisés pour déterminer si une personne doit être incluse dans le registre (R) et/ou dans les statistiques de chômeurs (S):

– Toute personne souhaitant être inscrite à l'ANPE peut s'inscrire (y compris des personnes occupées). En fonction de sa situation au regard des critères suivants (inoccupé, à la recherche d'un travail, disponible pour travailler, occupé), elle sera affectée à un registre particulier (8 catégories, voir plus loin '6 les différentes définitions). L'inscription est obligatoire pour les demandeurs d'emploi indemnisés.
– Age: Minimum: 16 ans (R) et (S);
– Etre résident dans le pays (R) et (S);
– Durée souhaitée de l'emploi recherché et/ou du nombre d'heures de travail recherché: si la personne est à la recherche d'un emploi à temps partiel, elle sera classée dans les catégories 2 ou 7.

5. Critères utilisés pour déterminer si une personne doit être exclue du registre (R) et/ou des statistiques de chômeurs (S):

– Avis de décès (R) et (S);
– Etablissement de la personne à l'étranger (R) et (S);
– Commencement d'un (nouveau) travail, selon les cas: pour les personnes classées dans les catégories 5, 6, 7 ou 8, il est possible de cumuler une activité réduite et une inscription à l'ANPE;
– Commencement du service militaire (R) et (S);
– Défaut de contact avec l'organisme/agence (R) et (S);
– Refus d'offres d'emploi adaptées (R) et (S);
– Refus d'offres de formation adaptées (R) et (S);
– Fausse déclaration (R) et (S);
– Incapacité à travailler (R) et (S).

6. Définition des catégories de demandeurs d'emploi pour lesquelles les statistiques sont établies

Catégorie 1: personnes sans emploi, immédiatement disponibles au sens de l'article R.311-3-3, tenues d'accomplir des actes positifs de recherche d'emploi, *à la recherche d'un emploi à durée indéterminée à plein temps.*
Ces personnes ne doivent pas avoir exercé d'activité occasionnelle ou réduite de plus de 78 heures dans le mois d'actualisation.

Catégorie 2: personnes sans emploi, immédiatement disponibles au sens de l'article R.311-3-3, tenues d'accomplir des actes positifs de recherche d'emploi, *à la recherche d'un emploi à durée indéterminée à temps partiel.*
Ces personnes ne doivent pas avoir exercé d'activité occasionnelle ou réduite de plus de 78 heures dans le mois d'actualisation.

Catégorie 3: personnes sans emploi, immédiatement disponibles au sens de l'article R.311-3-3, tenues d'accomplir des actes positifs de recherche d'emploi, *à la recherche d'un emploi à durée déterminée temporaire ou saisonnier, y compris de très courte durée.*
Ces personnes ne doivent pas avoir exercé d'activité occasionnelle ou réduite de plus de 78 heures dans le mois d'actualisation.

Catégorie 4: personnes sans emploi, non immédiatement disponibles, à la recherche d'un emploi.

Catégorie 5: personnes pourvues d'un emploi, à la recherche d'un autre emploi.

Catégorie 6: personnes non immédiatement disponibles au sens de l'article R.311-3-3 (1à), *à la recherche d'un autre emploi, à durée indéterminée à plein temps,* tenues d'accomplir des actes positifs de recherche d'emploi. Ces personnes ont exercé une activité occasionnelle ou réduite de plus de 78 heures dans le mois d'actualisation.

Catégorie 7: personnes non immédiatement disponibles au sens de l'article R.311-3-3 (1à), *à la recherche d'un autre emploi, à durée indéterminée à temps partiel,* tenues d'accomplir des actes positifs de recherche d'emploi. Ces personnes ont exercé une activité occasionnelle ou réduite de plus de 78 heures dans le mois d'actualisation.

Catégorie 8: personnes non immédiatement disponibles au sens de l'article R.311-3-3 (1à), *à la recherche d'un autre emploi, à durée déterminée, temporaire ou saisonnier, y compris de très courte durée*, tenues d'accomplir des actes positifs de recherche d'emploi. Ces personnes ont exercé une activité occasionnelle ou réduite de plus de 78 heures dans le mois d'actualisation.

7. Mise à jour des registres
Les registres sont mis à jour tous les mois.

8. Taux de chômage
Calculé chaque mois par l'Institut national de la statistique et des études économiques (INSEE), c'est le rapport du nombre de chômeurs au sens du BIT par rapport à la population active totale.

Le nombre de chômeurs au sens du BIT est établi une fois par an à partir de l'enquête annuelle emploi effectuée par l'INSEE, les mois intermédiaires sont estimés par un modèle paramétrique basé sur l'évolution du nombre de demandeurs d'emploi inscrits à l'ANPE en catégories 1, 2 et 3.

La population active est la somme: emploi total et chômage.

Le recensement de la population sert de socle à l'évaluation de l'emploi total, l'enquête emploi et d'autres sources permettent de le ré-évaluer chaque année.

9. Type de statistiques produites sur le nombre de chômeurs enregistrés
Période de référence: Mois.
Fréquence de production: Mensuelle.
Variables utilisées:
– Sexe;
– Age;
– Niveau d'instruction;
– Profession;
– Caractéristiques géographiques;
– Nationalité;
– Durée de chômage;
– Autres: qualifications et handicap.
Publication:
– A usage interne uniquement (publication spéciale pour le réseau ANPE);
– Sur papier, à diffusion grand public, sur demande;
– En format électronique, sur demande;
– Sur un site Internet:
– http://www.travail.gouv.fr/etudes/etudes_i.html
Agence responsable de la publication: Ministère des Affaires sociales, du Travail et de la Solidarité.
Titre et périodicité de la publication: *Premières informations.*
10. Information méthodologique au sujet de ces statistiques
Publication: En format électronique, sur demande.
Organisme responsable: Ministère des Affaires sociales, du Travail et de la Solidarité pour les statistiques du nombre d'inscrits à l'ANPE; INSEE pour le «chômage BIT».
11. Comparaisons avec des statistiques provenant d'autres sources
Des comparaisons ont été faites avec des statistiques provenant de l'enquête emploi et du recensement de population.
Titre de la publication contenant la description de la méthodologie et/ou les résultats de cette comparaison: http://www.insee.fr/fr/indic/indic_conj/donnees/chomrev.pdf
12. Principaux changements intervenus depuis le début de ces séries statistiques
Il n'y a pas eu de changement important dans la législation, dans la capacité de l'agence et/ou dans les procédures administratives susceptibles d'avoir influencé de manière significative les statistiques, mais il y a eu une réforme des catégories en 1995.

Gabon

1. Séries statistiques
Titre: Rapport d'activité de l'ONE (Office national de l'Emploi).
Première année disponible: 1994.
2. Organisme responsable de l'enregistrement des chômeurs ou demandeurs d'emploi
Nom de l'organisme: Office national de l'Emploi (ONE).
Type d'organisme: Organisme public relevant d'une autorité nationale.

Nom de l'autorité nationale: Ministère du Travail, de l'Emploi et de la Formation professionnelle.
Situation des bureaux chargés de l'enregistrement: Libreville et Port-Gentil.
Types de services fournis et/ou gérés par cet organisme:
– Assistance aux demandeurs d'emploi pour trouver du travail;
– Assistance aux demandeurs d'emploi pour créer leur propre entreprise;
– Assistance aux employeurs pour trouver de la main-d'œuvre;
– Formation liée à l'emploi.
Pourcentage des demandeurs d'emploi qui cherchent un emploi au travers de cet organisme: 34%.
3. Les informations personnelles suivantes sont enregistrées:
– Nom;
– Sexe;
– Adresse du domicile habituel;
– Date de naissance;
– Citoyenneté;
– Niveau d'instruction/de formation, en distinguant quatre catégories. Aucun lien n'a été établi avec la CITE;
– Situation de travail présente et passée, en distinguant trois catégories;
– Type de profession de l'emploi antérieur et/ou actuel, en distinguant quatre catégories. Aucun lien n'a été établi avec la CITP;
– Type de profession de l'emploi recherché, avec quatre catégories;
– Nom et adresse de l'employeur ou du lieu de travail actuel ou passé;
– Branche d'activité de l'employeur ou du lieu de travail actuel ou passé, en distinguant 60 catégories. Aucun lien n'a été établi avec la CITI;
– Type de diplômes obtenus, type de formation.
4. Critères utilisés pour déterminer si une personne doit être incluse dans le registre (R):
– Etre sans travail (R);
– Etre à la recherche d'un travail (R);
– Etre disponible pour travailler (R);
– Age: Minimum: 16 ans; Maximum: 65 ans (R).
5. Critères utilisés pour déterminer si une personne doit être exclue du registre (R):
– Avis de décès (R);
– Etablissement de la personne à l'étranger (R);
– Commencement d'un (nouveau) travail (R);
– Commencement du service militaire (R);
– Participation à un programme de promotion de l'emploi, à un programme de travaux publics, etc. (R);
– Entreprise d'une formation ou d'études (R);
– Défaut de contact avec l'organisme/agence (R);
– Admission à toucher une pension (retraite, etc.) (R);
– Incapacité à travailler (R).
6. Définition des personnes au chômage sur laquelle les statistiques sont établies
Ne s'applique pas.
7. Mise à jour des registres
Les registres sont mis à jour quotidiennement.
8. Points suivants:
Ne s'appliquent pas. L'ONE n'a pas pour mission de produire des statistiques sur les chômeurs. Cette mission est dévolue à d'autres administrations publiques.

Ghana

1. Séries statistiques
Titre: Chômage enregistré.
Première année disponible: 1956.
2. Organisme responsable de l'enregistrement des chômeurs ou demandeurs d'emploi
Nom de l'organisme: Centres d'Emploi Publics du Département du Travail.
Type d'organisme: Organisme public relevant d'une autorité nationale.
Nom de l'autorité nationale: Département du Travail, sous le Ministère du Travail, du Développement et de l'Emploi.
Situation des bureaux chargés de l'enregistrement: Dans les 66 centres les plus urbanisés du pays.

Types de services fournis et/ou gérés par cet organisme:

– Assistance aux demandeurs d'emploi pour trouver du travail;
– Assistance aux employeurs pour trouver de la main-d'œuvre;
– Orientation professionnelle;
– Autres: administration de la rémunération des travailleurs et doléances de travail; règlement de disputes industrielles.

3. Les informations personnelles suivantes sont enregistrées:

– Nom;
– Sexe;
– Adresse du domicile habituel;
– Date de naissance;
– Citoyenneté;
– Nationalité/groupe ethnique;
– Niveau d'instruction/ de formation, en distinguant trois catégories. Des liens ont été établis avec la CITE;
– Situation de travail présente et passée;
– Type de profession de l'emploi antérieur ou actuel, en distinguant huit catégories. Des liens ont été établis avec la CITP, au niveau des grands groupes;
– Type de profession de l'emploi recherché, avec huit catégories. Des liens ont été établis avec la CITP, au niveau des grands groupes;
– Nom et adresse de l'employeur ou du lieu de travail actuel ou passé;
– Branche d'activité de l'employeur ou du lieu de travail actuel ou passé, en distinguant neuf catégories. Des liens ont été établis avec la CITI, rév.3 ou NACE au niveau des groupes;
– Inscriptions/enregistrements antérieurs auprès de l'organisme.

4. Critères utilisés pour déterminer si une personne doit être incluse dans le registre (R) et/ou dans les statistiques de chômeurs (S):

– Etre sans travail (R) et (S);
– Etre à la recherche d'un travail (R) et (S);
– Etre disponible pour travailler (R) et (S);
– Age: Minimum: 15 ans; Maximum: 55 ans (R) et (S);
– Citoyenneté (R) et (S);
– Etre résident dans le pays (R) et (S);
– Avoir précédemment travaillé (R) et (S);
– Autre: apparence physique.

5. Critères utilisés pour déterminer si une personne doit être exclue du registre (R) et/ou des statistiques de chômeurs (S):

– Décès (R) et (S);
– Commencement d'un (nouveau) travail (R) et (S);
– Défaut de contact avec l'organisme/agence (R) et (S).

6. Définition des personnes au chômage sur laquelle les statistiques sont établies

Les personnes avec ou sans formation liée à l'emploi/éducation, âgées de 15 à 55 ans, qui cherchent du travail et qui sont disponibles pour travailler en se présentant régulièrement dans l'un des centres publics d'emploi du pays.

7. Mise à jour des registres

Les registres sont mis à jour trimestriellement.

8. Taux de chômage

Les statistiques basées sur les registres ne sont pas utilisées pour obtenir des taux de chômage.

9. Type de statistiques sur le nombre de chômeurs enregistrés produites

Période de référence: Trimestre.
Fréquence de production: Trimestrielle.
Variables utilisées:

– Sexe;
– Age;
– Niveau d'instruction;
– Profession;
– Branche d'activité;
– Expérience professionnelle antérieure;
– Citoyenneté (nationaux/non nationaux);
– Durée de chômage;
– Autre: caractéristiques physiques.

Publication: Sur papier, à diffusion grand public.
Agence responsable de la publication: Département du Travail (Section Information sur la Main-d'Œuvre).

Titre et périodicité de la publication: *Employment Market Report* (Rapport sur le Marché de la Main d'Œuvre), trimestriel.

10. Information méthodologique au sujet de ces statistiques

Agence responsable: Département du Travail (Section Information sur la Main-d'Œuvre).

11. Comparaisons avec des statistiques provenant d'autres sources

Il n'y a pas eu de comparaisons faites avec des statistiques provenant d'autres sources.

12. Principaux changements intervenus depuis le début de ces séries statistiques

Jusqu'à présent il n'y a pas eu de changement important dans la législation, dans la capacité de l'agence et/ou dans les procédures administratives susceptibles d'avoir influencé de manière significative les statistiques; cependant, une nouvelle loi sur le travail est en préparation et l'on peut prévoir qu'elle aura une influence sur les statistiques.

Groenland

1. Séries statistiques
Titre: Statistiques du chômage enregistré.
Première année disponible: 1988.

2. Agence responsable de l'enregistrement des chômeurs ou demandeurs d'emploi

Nom de l'agence: Les enregistrements sont gérés par les autorités locales (Kommuner) et collectés par l'organisme «Statistiques du Groenland».

Type d'agence: Organisme public relevant d'une autorité locale.
Situation des bureaux chargés de l'enregistrement: Dans toutes les régions du pays (dans les capitales régionales).

Types de services fournis et/ou gérés par cette agence:

– Assistance aux demandeurs d'emploi pour trouver du travail;
– Assistance aux demandeurs d'emploi pour créer leur propre entreprise;
– Assistance aux employeurs pour trouver de la main-d'œuvre;
– Orientation professionnelle;
– Formation liée à l'emploi;
– Paiement des indemnités de chômage.

3. Les informations personnelles suivantes sont enregistrées:

– Nom;
– Sexe (indirectement par le numéro de sécurité sociale);
– Numéro de sécurité sociale;
– Adresse du domicile habituel;
– Date de naissance;
– Citoyenneté;
– Niveau d'instruction/ de formation. Des liens ont été établis avec la CITE;
– Enregistrements antérieurs auprès de l'agence/service.

4. Critères utilisés pour déterminer si une personne doit être incluse dans le registre (R) et/ou dans les statistiques de chômeurs (S):

– Etre sans travail (R) et (S);
– Etre disponible pour travailler (R);
– Age: Minimum: 16 ans; Maximum: 61 ans (S);
– Citoyenneté (R) et (S);
– Etre résident dans le pays (R) et (S).

5. Critères utilisés pour déterminer si une personne doit être exclue du registre (R) et/ou des statistiques de chômeurs (S):

– Défaut de contact avec l'agence/service.

6. Définition des personnes au chômage sur laquelle les statistiques sont établies

Les personnes qui demandent leur enregistrement comme chômeurs auprès des autorités locales. Pour être enregistrés comme chômeurs les personnes devront avoir entre 15 et 61 ans et ne pas être incluses dans d'autres catégories telles que retraités, être disposées à accepter des offres de travail et ne pas être employées au moment de l'enregistrement.

7. Mise à jour des registres

Les registres sont mis à jour mensuellement.

8. Taux de chômage

Les statistiques basées sur les registres sont utilisées pour obtenir des taux de chômage.

La source des données d'emploi qui sont partie du dénominateur des taux de chômage est le recensement de population.

Définition des personnes pourvues d'un emploi à cette fin:

Toutes les personnes entre 15 et 61 ans, c'est à dire toute la main-d'œuvre potentielle

(il n'existe pas d'enregistrement exact de la main-d'œuvre actuelle).

9. Type de statistiques sur le nombre de chômeurs enregistrés produites

Série 1:

Période de référence: Trimestre.

Fréquence de production: Trimestrielle.

Variables utilisées:

– Sexe (indirectement par le numéro de sécurité sociale);
– Age (indirectement par le numéro de sécurité sociale);
– Niveau d'instruction;
– Caractéristiques géographiques.

Publication:

– Sur papier, à diffusion grand public;
– Sur un site Internet (www.statgreen.gl).

Agence responsable de la publication: Statistiques Groenland.

Titre et périodicité de la publication: *Ledigheden* (Period), trimestriel.

Série 2:

Période de référence: Semestre.

Fréquence de production: Semestrielle.

Variables utilisées:

– Sexe (indirectement par le numéro de sécurité sociale);
– Age (indirectement par le numéro de sécurité sociale);
– Niveau d'instruction;
– Caractéristiques géographiques.

Publication:

– Sur papier, à diffusion grand public;
– Sur un site Internet (www.statgreen.gl).

Agence responsable de la publication: Statistiques Groenland.

Titre et périodicité de la publication: *Ledigheden* (Period), trimestriel.

Série 3:

Période de référence: Année.

Fréquence de production: Annuelle.

Variables utilisées:

– Sexe (indirectement par le numéro de sécurité sociale);
– Age (indirectement par le numéro de sécurité sociale);
– Niveau d'instruction;
– Caractéristiques géographiques.

Publication:

– Sur papier, à diffusion grand public;
– Sur un site Internet (www.statgreen.gl).

Agence responsable de la publication: Statistiques Groenland.

Titre et périodicité de la publication: *Ledigheden* (Period), trimestriel.

10. Information méthodologique au sujet de ces statistiques

Publication: Sur papier, à diffusion grand public.

Agence responsable: Statistiques Groenland.

11. Comparaisons avec des statistiques provenant d'autres sources

Il n'y a pas eu de comparaisons faites avec des statistiques provenant d'autres sources.

12. Principaux changements intervenus depuis le début de ces séries statistiques

Des changements importants dans la législation, dans la capacité de l'agence et/ou dans les procédures administratives sont intervenus en 2000, résultant en une diminution de 0.5% du nombre des personnes enregistrées comme chômeurs.

Guatemala

1. Séries statistiques

Titre: Personnes inscrites.

Première année disponible: 1989

2. Organisme responsable de l'enregistrement des chômeurs ou demandeurs d'emploi

Nom de l'organisme: Departamento del Servicio Nacional del Empleo (Département du Service national de l'Emploi).

Type d'organisme: Organisme public relevant d'une autorité nationale.

Nom de l'autorité nationale: Ministerio de Trabajo y Previsión Social (Ministère du Travail et de la Prévoyance sociale).

Situation des bureaux chargés de l'enregistrement: Dans les 22 départements du pays, et trois bureaux municipaux (Le Carmen, Tecun Umán et Coatepeque).

Types de services fournis et/ou gérés par cet organisme

– Assistance aux demandeurs d'emploi pour trouver du travail;
– Assistance aux demandeurs d'emploi pour créer leur propre entreprise;
– Assistance aux employeurs pour trouver de la main-d'œuvre;
– Orientation professionnelle;
– Formation liée à l'emploi.

Pourcentage des demandeurs d'emploi qui cherchent un emploi au travers de cet organisme: 10%

3. Les informations personnelles suivantes sont enregistrées

– Nom;
– Sexe;
– Age et date de naissance;
– Numéro de sécurité sociale (ou numéro d'identification également utilisé par d'autres organismes);
– Adresse du domicile habituel;
– Niveau d'instruction/de formation, en distinguant quatre catégories. Aucun lien n'a été établi avec la CITE;
– Situation de travail présente et passée, en distinguant cinq catégories;
– Type de profession de l'emploi antérieur et/ou actuel, en distinguant trois catégories. Des liens ont été établis avec la CITP, au niveau des grands groupes;
– Type de profession de l'emploi recherché, avec trois catégories. Des liens ont été établis avec la CITP, au niveau des grands groupes;
– Branche d'activité de l'employeur ou du lieu de travail actuel ou passé, en distinguant deux catégories. Aucun lien n'a été établi avec la CITI-rév. 3;
– Langues Mayas, en distinguant des catégories telles que: parlée, écrite, traduction.

Lorsque la personne est mineure, on enregistre: le numéro de l'extrait d'acte de naissance; le numéro du livret de naissance; folio; un document d'identité.

4. Critères utilisés pour déterminer si une personne doit être incluse dans le registre (R) et/ou dans les statistiques de chômeurs (S)

– Etre sans travail (R) et (S);
– Etre à la recherche d'un travail (R) et (S);
– Etre disponible pour travailler (R);
– Age: Minimum:14 ans; il n'y a pas d'âge maximum (R);
– Citoyenneté (R);
– Etre résident dans le pays (R);
– Durée souhaitée de l'emploi recherché et/ou du nombre d'heures de travail recherché (S).

5. Critères utilisés pour déterminer si une personne doit être exclue du registre (R) et/ou des statistiques de chômeurs (S)

– Avis de décès (R);
– Commencement d'un (nouveau) travail (R);
– Défaut de contact avec l'organisme/agence (le système maintient active la recherche d'emploi pendant six mois puis elle devient inactive; ensuite, la personne doit se rendre au bureau pour la réactivation de la recherche) (R);
– Autres: sans documents d'identité (R).

6. Définition des personnes au chômage sur laquelle les statistiques sont établies

Personnes qui ont déclaré être sans emploi; qui n'ont pas de revenu(s); qui ont rempli la demande d'entretien professionnel avec l'ensemble des renseignements nécessaires; qui ont reçu l'orientation professionnelle adéquate; qui ont présenté soit une carte d'identité, soit un extrait de naissance, ainsi que les documents de base demandés.

7. Mise à jour des registres

Les registres sont mis à jour mensuellement.

8. Taux de chômage

Les statistiques basées sur les registres ne sont pas utilisées pour obtenir des taux de chômage.

9. Type de statistiques produites sur le nombre de chômeurs enregistrés

Période de référence: Année

Fréquence de production: Mensuelle.

Variables utilisées
- Nombre de personnes inscrites.

Publication: Sur papier, à diffusion grand public.

Organisme responsable de la publication: Ministère du Travail et de la Prévoyance sociale.

Titre et périodicité de la publication: *Boletín de Estadísticas del Trabajo* (Bulletin des statistiques du travail), publication annuelle.

10. Information méthodologique au sujet de ces statistiques

Publication: Sur papier, à diffusion grand public.

Organisme responsable: Département des Statistiques du travail, Ministère du Travail et de la Prévoyance sociale.

11. Comparaisons avec des statistiques provenant d'autres sources

Aucune comparaison n'a été faite avec des statistiques provenant d'autres sources.

12. Principaux changements intervenus depuis le début de ces séries statistiques

Il n'y a pas eu de changement important dans la législation, dans la capacité de l'agence et/ou dans les procédures administratives susceptibles d'avoir influencé de manière significative les statistiques.

Guinée

1. Séries statistiques

Titre: *Rapport d'activité annuel* et *Bulletin d'information.*

Première année disponible: 1987

2. Organisme responsable de l'enregistrement des chômeurs ou demandeurs d'emploi

Nom de l'organisme: Agence guinéenne pour la Promotion de l'Empoi (AGUIPE).

Type d'organisme: Organisme public relevant d'une autorité nationale.

Nom de l'autorité nationale: Services de l'Emploi et de la main-d'œuvre.

Situation des bureaux chargés de l'enregistrement: Dans certaines régions uniquement: la capitale Conakry, et les chef-lieux des quatre régions naturelles.

Types de services fournis et/ou gérés par cet organisme:
- Assistance aux demandeurs d'emploi pour trouver du travail;
- Assistance aux employeurs pour trouver de la main-d'œuvre;
- Orientation professionnelle;
- Autres services liés à l'emploi: information et assistance aux organismes de formation, aux services publics et aux partenaires au développement.

Pourcentage des demandeurs d'emploi qui cherchent un emploi au travers de cet organisme: 45%

3. Les informations personnelles suivantes sont enregistrées:
- Nom;
- Sexe;
- Adresse du domicile habituel;
- Date de naissance;
- Nationalité/groupe ethnique;
- Niveau d'instruction/de formation. Des liens ont été établis avec la CITE;
- Situation de travail présente / passée;
- Type de profession de l'emploi antérieur ou actuel. Des liens ont été établis avec la CITP, au niveau des 390 groupes de base;
- Type de profession de l'emploi recherché;
- Nom et adresse de l'employeur ou du lieu de travail actuel ou passé;
- Autre: compétences ou aptitudes particulières.

4. Critères utilisés pour déterminer si une personne doit être incluse dans le registre (R) et/ou dans les statistiques de chômeurs (S):
- Etre sans travail (S);
- Etre à la recherche d'un travail (S);
- Etre disponible pour travailler (S);
- Age: Minimum: 18 ans; Maximum: 55 ans (S);
- Etre résident dans le pays, et rechercher un travail sur le territoire national;
- Avoir précédemment travaillé (S);
- Durée souhaitée de l'emploi recherché et/ou du nombre d'heures de travail recherché (20 heures par semaine minimum).

5. Critères utilisés pour déterminer si une personne doit être exclue du registre (R) et/ou des statistiques de chômeurs (S):
- Avis de décès (R) et (S);
- Etablissement de la personne à l'étranger (R) et (S);
- Commencement d'un (nouveau) travail (R) et (S);
- Commencement du service militaire (R) et (S);
- Participation à un programme de promotion de l'emploi, à un programme de travaux publics (R) et (S);
- Entreprise d'une formation ou d'études, s'il s'agit d'un programme de formation de longue durée (S);
- Défaut de contact avec l'organisme/agence en n'ayant pas répondu à plusieurs convocations pour un emploi (R) et (S);
- Refus d'offres d'emploi adaptées, après trois refus (R) et (S);
- Refus d'offres de formation adaptées, après trois refus (R) et (S);
- Admission à toucher une pension (retraite, etc.) (R) et (S);
- Incapacité à travailler, dans le cas d'une incapacité permanente.

6. Définition des personnes au chômage sur laquelle les statistiques sont établies

Toute personne active qui est disponible pour travailler, n'a pas travaillé au cours de la période de référence de sept jours pour des raisons autres que la maladie, le congé, la grève, le chômage technique ou les intempéries, et est à la recherche d'un emploi, doit être considérée comme personne au chômage.

7. Mise à jour des registres

Les registres sont mis à jour annuellement.

8. Taux de chômage

Les statistiques basées sur les registres ne sont pas utilisées pour obtenir des taux de chômage.

9. Type de statistiques produites sur le nombre de chômeurs enregistrés

Série 1:

Période de référence: Année.

Fréquence de production: Annuelle

Variables utilisées:
- Sexe;
- Age;
- Niveau d'instruction;
- Profession;
- Caractéristiques géographiques;
- Expérience professionnelle antérieure;
- Durée de chômage;
- Emploi demandé.

Publication:
- Sur papier, à diffusion grand public.

Organisme/Agence responsable de la publication: AGUIPE.

Titre et périodicité de la publication: *Rapport d'activité annuel.*

Série 2:

Période de référence: Semestre.

Fréquence de production: Semestrielle.

Variables utilisées:
- Branche d'activité;
- Disponibilité;
- Nationalité;
- Réorientation.

Publication: Sur papier, à diffusion restreinte.

Organisme/Agence responsable de la publication: AGUIPE.

Titre et périodicité de la publication: *Bulletin d'information.*

10. Information méthodologique au sujet de ces statistiques

Publication: A usage interne uniquement.

Organisme responsable: Observatoire de l'AGUIPE.

11. Comparaisons avec des statistiques provenant d'autres sources

Des comparaisons ont été faites avec des statistiques provenant de l'enquête de main-d'œuvre, d'autres enquêtes auprès des ménages, du recensement de population et d'autres sources statistiques.

Fréquence des comparaisons: Régulièrement (dernière année: 2001).

Publication de la méthodologie et/ou des résultats de la comparaison: Ils n'ont pas été publiés.

12. Principaux changements intervenus depuis le début de ces séries statistiques

Des changements importants dans la législation, dans la capacité de l'agence et/ou dans les procédures administratives susceptibles d'avoir influencé de manière significative les statistiques sont intervenus en 1992, 1994, 1995, 1997, 1999 et 2000.

Guyana

1. Séries statistiques
Titre: Statistiques sur le recrutement et le placement.
Première année disponible: 1993.
2. Organisme responsable de l'enregistrement des chômeurs ou demandeurs d'emploi
Nom de l'organisme: Département du recrutement et du placement.
Type d'organisme: Organisme public relevant d'une autorité nationale.
Nom de l'autorité nationale: Ministère du travail, des Services sociaux et de la Sécurité sociale.
Situation des bureaux chargés de l'enregistrement: Dans six des dix régions administratives du pays (régions 2, 3, 4, 5, 6, et 10).
Types de services fournis ou gérés par cet organisme:
–   Assistance aux demandeurs d'emploi pour trouver du travail;
–   Assistance aux employeurs pour trouver de la main-d'œuvre;
–   Orientation professionnelle;
–   Formation liée à l'emploi;
–   Autre: publication d'un bulletin d'information sur le marché du travail et d'un bulletin de statistiques à grande diffusion.
Pourcentage des demandeurs d'emploi qui cherchent un emploi au travers de cet organisme: 20%.
3. Les informations personnelles suivantes sont enregistrées:
–   Nom;
–   Sexe;
–   Numéro de sécurité sociale (ou numéro d'identification également utilisé par d'autres organismes);
–   Adresse du domicile habituel;
–   Date de naissance;
–   Citoyenneté;
–   Nationalité/groupe ethnique;
–   Niveau d'instruction/ de formation, en distinguant cinq catégories. Des liens sont en cours d'établissement avec la CITE;
–   Situation de travail présente et passée, en distinguant trois catégories;
–   Type de profession de l'emploi antérieur ou actuel, en distinguant neuf catégories. Des liens sont en cours d'établissement avec la CITP;
–   Type de profession de l'emploi recherché, avec neuf catégories. Des liens sont en cours d'établissement avec la CITP;
–   Nom et adresse de l'employeur ou du lieu de travail actuel ou passé;
–   Branche d'activité de l'employeur ou du lieu de travail actuel ou passé, en distinguant un nombre non spécifié de catégories. Des liens sont en cours d'établissement avec la CITI, rév.3 ;
–   Enregistrements antérieurs auprès de l'organisme.
4. Critères utilisés pour déterminer si une personne doit être incluse dans le registre (R) et/ou dans les statistiques de chômeurs (S):
–   Etre à la recherche d'un travail (R) et (S);
–   Etre disponible pour travailler (R) et (S);
–   Age: Minimum: 15 ans; Maximum: 60 ans (R) et (S);
–   Citoyenneté (doit avoir la citoyenneté guyanaise) (R) et (S);
–   Etre résident dans le pays (R) et (S).
5. Critères utilisés pour déterminer si une personne doit être exclue du registre (R) et/ou des statistiques de chômeurs (S):
–   Commencement d'un (nouveau) travail (l'agence est informée par l'employeur) (R) et (S).
6. Définition des personnes au chômage sur laquelle les statistiques sont établies
Une personne qui a pris des dispositions actives pour chercher un emploi, ne trouve pas de travail, et qui n'est pas occupée à ce moment là, dans quelque activité que ce soit.

7. Mise à jour des registres
A fur et à mesure de la réception de l'information, les cartes individuelles sont mises à jour. (L'agence étant actuellement informatisée, les informations sont saisies sur ordinateur).
8. Taux de chômage
Les statistiques basées sur les registres ne sont pas utilisées pour obtenir des taux de chômage.
9. Type de statistiques sur le nombre de chômeurs enregistrés produites
Période de référence: Année.
Fréquence de production: Annuellement.
Variables utilisées: Caractéristiques géographiques.
–   (Il est prévu de produire des rapports plus détaillés dès 2003).
Publication: Sur papier, à diffusion restreinte.
Agence responsable de la publication: Département du travail.
Titre et périodicité des publications: *Recruitment and Placement* (Recrutement et placement), annuelle; *Annual Report* (Rapport annuel).
10. Information méthodologique au sujet de ces statistiques
Il n'y a pas d'information méthodologique disponible.
11. Comparaisons avec des statistiques provenant d'autres sources
Il n'y a pas eu de comparaisons faites avec des statistiques provenant d'autres sources.
12. Principaux changements intervenus depuis le début de ces séries statistiques
Il n'y a pas eu de changement important dans la législation, dans la capacité de l'agence et/ou dans les procédures administratives susceptibles d'avoir influencé de manière significative les statistiques.
13. Remarques supplémentaires
Dès 2003, le service de recrutement et de placement sera entièrement informatisé.

Honduras

1. Séries statistiques
Titre: Registre des personnes à la recherche d'un emploi

Première année disponible: Les services de placement fonctionnent depuis 1980. La série statistique a débuté en 1987.
2. Organisme responsable de l'enregistrement des chômeurs ou demandeurs d'emploi
Nom de l'organisme: Servicio de Colocación de la Dirección General de Empleo (Service de Placement de la Direction générale de l'Emploi).
Type d'organisme: Organisme public relevant d'une autorité nationale, avec des bureaux locaux.
Nom de l'autorité nationale: Secretaría de Trabajo y Seguridad Social (Secrétariat du Travail et de la Sécurité sociale)
Situation des bureaux chargés de l'enregistrement: Dans les trois villes principales du pays, qui couvrent la zone centrale et la zone nord du pays.
Types de services fournis et/ou gérés par cet organisme
–   Assistance aux demandeurs d'emploi pour trouver du travail;
–   Assistance aux demandeurs d'emploi pour créer leur propre entreprise (ne s'applique qu'aux personnes invalides);
–   Assistance aux employeurs pour trouver de la main-d'œuvre;
–   Orientation professionnelle;
–   Formation liée à l'emploi (le service de placement adresse les personnes à l'Institut de formation professionnelle, mais ne les forme pas directement).
Pourcentage des demandeurs d'emploi qui cherchent un emploi au travers de cet organisme: 3,4% par rapport au chiffre des chômeurs urbains selon l'Enquête auprès des ménages à objectifs multiples.
3. Les informations personnelles suivantes sont enregistrées
–   Nom et prénom;
–   Sexe;
–   Numéro de sécurité sociale (ou numéro d'identification également utilisé par d'autres organismes);
–   Adresse du domicile habituel;
–   Date de naissance;
–   Nationalité;

–   Niveau d'instruction/de formation, en distinguant quatre catégories. Aucun lien n'a été établi avec la CITE;
–   Situation de travail présente et passée, en distinguant trois catégories;
–   Type de profession de l'emploi antérieur et/ou actuel, avec trois possibilités de réponse. Des liens ont été établis avec la CITP, au niveau des grands groupes (désagrégation à quatre chiffres);
–   Type de profession de l'emploi recherché, pour lequel le nombre de réponses possibles varie selon le demandeur. Le cas le plus commun est de deux catégories par demandeur. Des liens ont été établis avec la CITP, au niveau des grands groupes (désagrégation à quatre chiffres);
–   Nom et adresse du chef immédiat ou du lieu de travail actuel ou passé;
–   Inscriptions/enregistrements antérieurs auprès de l'organisme;
–   Autres: caractéristiques physiques (taille et poids); données familiales (nombre de membres, enfants, si chef de famille ou pas); possession ou non de voiture; type de permis de conduire; migration (locale et externe); invalidité.

4. Critères utilisés pour déterminer si une personne doit être incluse dans le registre (R) et/ou dans les statistiques de chômeurs (S)
–   Etre sans travail (R);
–   Etre à la recherche d'un travail (R);
–   Etre disponible pour travailler (R);
–   Age: Minimum: 16 ans avec autorisation de travail; il n'y a pas d'âge maximum (R);
–   Etre résident dans le pays (R).

5. Critères utilisés pour déterminer si une personne doit être exclue du registre (R) et/ou des statistiques de chômeurs (S)
–   Avis de décès (R);
–   Etablissement de la personne à l'étranger (R);
–   Commencement d'un (nouveau) travail (R);
–   Participation à un programme de promotion de l'emploi, à un programme de travaux publics, etc. (R);
–   Entreprise d'une formation ou d'études incompatible avec l'horaire de travail (R);
–   Défaut de contact avec l'organisme/agence pendant cinq ans consécutifs (R);
–   Incapacité à travailler (rapporté par la personne concernée) (R).

Note: Les renseignements ci-dessus s'enregistrent en tant que notes marginales dans le dossier de la personne concernée, s'archivent et s'éliminent uniquement en cas de décès; dans les autres cas, l'information est conservée. La limite de la sauvegarde des registres est de cinq ans.

6. Définition des personnes au chômage sur laquelle les statistiques sont établies
Dans cette catégorie, sont regroupées les personnes affectées par le chômage dit «ouvert», à savoir celles qui ont été licenciées (c'est-à-dire, les personnes qui avaient un emploi, qui l'ont perdu pour une raison ou une autre et qui pendant la semaine de référence ont activement cherché une autre place, ou ont essayé de créer leur propre entreprise ou exploitation agricole) ainsi que les nouveaux travailleurs qui cherchent un premier emploi.

Personnes à la recherche d'un emploi: sont inclus dans cette catégorie les chômeurs licenciés, les personnes qui recherchent un emploi pour la première fois, et en moindre proportion les personnes occupées qui cherchent une meilleure opportunité de travail, parce qu'elles ont atteint un nouveau niveau de formation ou qu'elles aspirent à un meilleur salaire.

7. Mise à jour des registres
Les registres sont mis à jour tous les six mois.

8. Taux de chômage
Les statistiques basées sur les registres ne sont pas utilisées pour obtenir des taux de chômage.

9. Type de statistiques produites sur le nombre de chômeurs enregistrés
Période de référence: Année
Fréquence de production: Annuelle
Variables utilisées
–   Sexe;
–   Age;
–   Niveau d'instruction;
–   Profession;

–   Branche d'activité;
–   Caractéristiques géographiques;
–   Autres: Situation professionnelle.

Publication
–   A usage interne uniquement;
–   En format électronique, sur demande.

Organisme/Agence responsable de la publication: Dirección General de Empleo (Direction générale de l'Emploi).
Titre et périodicité de la publication: *Boletín Estadístico* (Bulletin Statistique), annuel.

10. Information méthodologique au sujet de ces statistiques
Publication
–   A usage interne uniquement;
–   En format électronique, sur demande.

Organisme responsable: Dirección General de Empleo (Direction générale de l'Emploi).

11. Comparaisons avec des statistiques provenant d'autres sources
Des comparaisons ont été faites avec des statistiques de chômage provenant tant de l'enquête auprès des ménages que du recensement de la population.
Fréquences des comparaisons: De temps en temps (dernière année: 2001); par rapport à la périodicité de la publication de l'enquête auprès des ménages, une à deux fois par an.
Publication de la méthodologie/résultats des comparaisons: Ils sont publiés dans le Bulletin statistique et sont utilisés en tant que références dans des analyses sur ce même thème.

12. Principaux changements intervenus depuis le début de ces séries statistiques
Il n'y a pas eu de changement important dans la législation, dans la capacité de l'agence et/ou dans les procédures administratives susceptibles d'avoir influencé de manière significative les statistiques.

Cependant, il s'est produit un changement dans le système de saisie des données par rapport à l'établissement d'une bourse électronique de l'emploi, laquelle a contribué à améliorer les services de médiation. Il est prévu de l'étendre à d'autres villes du pays en intégrant également les organisations d'employeurs à travers ce système électronique.

Hongrie

1. Séries statistiques
Titre: Chômage enregistré.
Première année disponible: 1990.

2. Agence responsable de l'enregistrement des chômeurs ou demandeurs d'emploi
Nom de l'agence: Allami Foglalkoztatasi Szolgalat (Service d'Emploi Public).
Type d'organisme: Agence public relevant d'une autorité nationale.
Nom de l'autorité nationale: Ministère des Affaires Economiques.
Situation des bureaux chargés de l'enregistrement: Il y a 11 bureaux dans la capitale Budapest, et 165 bureaux dans 19 comtés du pays (avec 20 centres de travail).
Types de services fournis et/ou gérés par cet organisme:
–   Assistance aux demandeurs d'emploi pour trouver du travail;
–   Assistance aux demandeurs d'emploi pour créer leur propre entreprise;
–   Assistance aux employeurs pour trouver de la main-d'œuvre;
–   Orientation professionnelle;
–   Formation liée à l'emploi;
–   Paiement des indemnités de chômage;
–   Autres: administration de programmes actifs concernant le marché du travail; émission de permis de travail aux citoyens étrangers; mise à disposition d'informations concernant le marché du travail, à tous niveaux (statistiques, analyses, projections).

Pourcentage des demandeurs d'emploi qui cherchent un emploi au travers de cet organisme: 80%.

3. Les informations personnelles suivantes sont enregistrées:
–   Nom;
–   Sexe;
–   Numéro de sécurité sociale (ou numéro d'identification également utilisé par d'autres organismes);
–   Adresse du domicile habituel;
–   Date de naissance;

- Citoyenneté (seulement concernant les permis de travail des citoyens étrangers);
- Niveau d'instruction/ de formation, en distinguant 10 catégories. Des liens ont été établis avec la CITE;
- Situation de travail présente et passée, en distinguant 4 catégories;
- Type de profession de l'emploi antérieur ou actuel, en distinguant 632 catégories. Des liens ont été établis avec la CITP-88, au niveau des sous-groupes;
- Type de profession de l'emploi recherché, avec 692 catégories. Des liens ont été établis avec la CITP -88, au niveau des sous-groupes;
- Nom et adresse de l'employeur ou du lieu de travail actuel ou passé;
- Branche d'activité de l'employeur ou du lieu de travail actuel ou passé, en distinguant 503 catégories. Des liens ont été établis avec NACE, rév.1 au niveau des catégories de tabulation;
- Inscriptions/enregistrements antérieurs auprès de l'organisme.

4. Critères utilisés pour déterminer si une personne doit être incluse dans le registre (R) et/ou dans les statistiques de chômeurs (S):
- Etre sans travail (S);
- Etre à la recherche d'un travail (S);
- Etre disponible pour travailler (S);
- Age maximum: âge de la retraite (S);
- Etre résident dans le pays (S).

5. Critères utilisés pour déterminer si une personne doit être exclue du registre (R) et/ou des statistiques de chômeurs (S):
- Décès (R) et (S);
- Commencement d'un (nouveau) travail (S);
- Commencement du service militaire (S);
- Participation à un programme de promotion de l'emploi, à un programme de travaux publics, etc. (S);
- Entreprise d'une formation ou d'études (S);
- Défaut de contact avec l'organisme/agence (S);
- Refus d'une offre d'emploi adaptée (S);
- Refus d'une offre de formation adaptée (S);
- Admission à toucher une pension (S);
- Incapacité à travailler (S);
- Autre: sur demande personnelle (R) et (S).

6. Définition des personnes au chômage sur laquelle les statistiques sont établies

Les demandeurs d'emploi qui remplissent les conditions suivantes:
- ne sont pas employés et ne poursuivent pas une autre activité rémunérée;
- remplissent toutes les conditions requises pour commencer un travail;
- n'ont pas de droit à recevoir une pension;
- ne sont pas étudiants à plein temps dans une institution d'éducation;
- coopèrent avec le bureau de travail local dans le but de trouver un emploi;

sont enregistrés par le bureau de travail local comme chômeurs.

7. Mise à jour des registres

Les registres sont mis à jour sur une base continue.

8. Taux de chômage

Les statistiques basées sur les registres sont utilisées pour obtenir des taux de chômage.

La source des données d'emploi qui sont partie du dénominateur des taux de chômage est le " *Labour Account of the National Economy*" (Situation du Travail de l'Economie Nationale) annuelle (jour de référence: 1er janvier) publiée par le Bureau Central des Statistiques.

Définition des personnes pourvues d'un emploi à cette fin:
- Les personnes employées, les entrepreneurs individuels et les personnes à leur propre compte;
- Les propriétaires qui travaillent;
- Les membres de la famille qui aident (au-delà d'un certain temps travaillé).

9. Type de statistiques sur le nombre de chômeurs enregistrés produites

Série 1:
Période de référence: Mois.
Fréquence de production: Mensuelle.
Variables utilisées:

- Sexe;
- Age;
- Niveau d'instruction;
- Caractéristiques géographiques;
- Expérience professionnelle antérieure;
- Durée de chômage.

Publication:
- Sur papier, à diffusion grand public;
- Sur un site Internet (en développement).

Agence responsable de la publication: Bureau National de l'Emploi.
Titre de la publication: *Labour Market Situation* (Situation du Marché du Travail).

Série 2:
Période de référence: Année.
Fréquence de production: Annuelle.
Variables utilisées:

- Sexe;
- Age;
- Niveau d'instruction;
- Caractéristiques géographiques;
- Expérience professionnelle antérieure;
- Durée de chômage.

Publication: Sur papier, à diffusion grand public.
Agence responsable de la publication: Bureau National de l'Emploi.
Titre de la publication: *Time series based on the administrative records of the Public Employment Service* (séries basées sur les données administratives du Service de l'Emploi Public).

10. Information méthodologique au sujet de ces statistiques
Publication:
- Sur papier, à diffusion grand public;
- Sur un site Internet (en développement).

Agence responsable: Bureau National de l'Emploi.

11. Comparaisons avec des statistiques provenant d'autres sources

Des comparaisons ont été faites avec des statistiques de chômage provenant de l'enquête sur la main-d'œuvre et le recensement de population.

Fréquence des comparaisons: Occasionnellement (dernière année: 1998).
Publication de la méthodologie et/ou des résultats de la comparaison: Ils ont été publiés à l'occasion d'une conférence de presse commune du Bureau Central des Statistiques et du Ministère du Travail en mai 1998. La comparaison avec le recensement de population de 2001 sera publiée en 2002.

12. Principaux changements intervenus depuis le début de ces séries statistiques

Des changements importants dans la législation, dans la capacité de l'agence et/ou dans les procédures administratives susceptibles d'avoir influencé de manière significative les statistiques sont intervenus.

Ile de Man

1. Séries statistiques
Titre: Chômage enregistré.
Première année disponible: 1978.

2. Organisme responsable de l'enregistrement des chômeurs ou demandeurs d'emploi
Nom de l'organisme: Division de la Sécurité Sociale.
Type d'organisme: Organisme public relevant d'une autorité nationale.
Nom de l'autorité nationale: Département de la Santé et de la Sécurité Sociale.

Certaines fonctions, y compris le suivi de l'enregistrement des chômeurs, sont de la responsabilité du Département du Commerce et de l'Industrie.

Des statistiques périodiques sur le chômage sont produites par les deux Départements. Une partie seulement est destinée à une diffusion grand public.

Situation des bureaux chargés de l'enregistrement: Dans certaines régions seulement, à savoir Douglas (Capitale), Ramsey, Peel, Castletown et Port Erin.

Types de services fournis et/ou gérés par cet organisme:
- Assistance aux demandeurs d'emploi pour trouver du travail;
- Assistance aux demandeurs d'emploi pour créer leur propre entreprise*;

– Assistance aux employeurs pour trouver de la main-d'œuvre*;
– Orientation professionnelle*;
– Formation liée à l'emploi*;
– Paiement des indemnités de chômage.
– * Services fournis par le Département du Commerce et de l'Industrie.

Pourcentage des demandeurs d'emploi qui cherchent un emploi au travers de cet organisme: 75%.

3. Les informations personnelles suivantes sont enregistrées:
– Nom;
– Sexe;
– Numéro de sécurité sociale (ou numéro d'identification également utilisé par d'autres organismes);
– Adresse du domicile habituel;
– Date de naissance;
– Citoyenneté;
– Nationalité/groupe ethnique;
– Niveau d'instruction/ de formation, en distinguant sept catégories. Aucun lien n'a été établi avec la CITE;
– Type de profession de l'emploi recherché;
– Nom et adresse de l'employeur ou du lieu de travail actuel ou passé;
– Autres: permis de conduire/propre moyen de transport; statut de travailleur de construction d'embarcations; état civil; état de santé; casier judiciaire.

4. Critères utilisés pour déterminer si une personne doit être incluse dans le registre (R) et/ou dans les statistiques de chômeurs (S):
– Etre sans travail (R) et (S);
– Etre à la recherche d'un travail (R) et (S);
– Etre disponible pour travaille (R) et (S);
– Age: Minimum: 16 ans; Maximum: hommes: 65 ans; femmes: 60 ans (R) et (S);
– Etre résident dans le pays (R) et (S);
– Durée souhaitée de l'emploi recherché et/ou du nombre d'heures de travail recherché (R) et (S).

5. Critères utilisés pour déterminer si une personne doit être exclue du registre (R) et/ou des statistiques de chômeurs (S):
– Décès (R) et (S);
– Etablissement de la personne à l'étranger (R) et (S);
– Commencement d'un (nouveau) travail (R) et (S);
– Commencement du service militaire (R) et (S);
– Participation à un programme de promotion de l'emploi, à un programme de travaux publics, etc. (R) et (S);
– Entreprise d'une formation ou d'études (R) et (S);
– Défaut de contact avec l'organisme/agence (R) et (S);
– Incapacité à travailler (R) et (S).

6. Définition des personnes au chômage sur laquelle les statistiques sont établies
Les personnes au chômage doivent:
– (en principe) être disponibles pour travailler au moins 40 heures par semaine;
– prendre des dispositions chaque semaine pour identifier des vacances de poste adaptées et poser leur candidature;
– être sans travail, ou travailler moins de 16 heures par semaine;
– être aptes à travailler au moins 16 heures par semaine;
– ne pas poursuivre une formation, ou alors poursuivre une formation comprenant moins de 16 heures d'instruction guidée par semaine;
– avoir plus de 16 ans mais moins que l'âge de la retraite officielle (65 ans pour les hommes et 60 et pour les femmes);
– être résidents de l'Ile de Man.

7. Mise à jour des registres
Les registres sont à jour quotidiennement.

8. Taux de chômage
Les statistiques basées sur les registres sont utilisées pour obtenir des taux de chômage.
La source des données d'emploi qui est partie du dénominateur des taux de chômage est le recensement de population.
Définition des personnes pourvues d'un emploi à cette fin: Personnes travaillant pour un employeur (à plein temps ou à temps partiel) et/ou travaillant à leur compte.

9. Type de statistiques sur le nombre de chômeurs enregistrés produites
Série 1:
Période de référence: Mois.
Fréquence de production: Mensuelle.
Variables utilisées:
– Sexe;
– Age*;
– Niveau d'instruction*;
– Profession*;
– Caractéristiques géographiques*;
– Citoyenneté (nationaux/non nationaux).
Publication:
– A usage interne uniquement*;
– Sur papier, à diffusion grand public.
– * S'applique aux statistiques produites par le Département du Commerce et de l'Industrie.
Agence responsable de la publication: Division des Affaires Economiques, Département des Finances.
Titre de la publication: *Job Market Statistics* (Statistiques du Marché du Travail).
Série 2:
Période de référence: Trimestre.
Fréquence de production: Trimestrielle.
Variables utilisées:
– Sexe;
– Age;
– Niveau d'instruction*;
– Profession*;
– Branche d'activité*;
– Caractéristiques géographiques;
– Citoyenneté (nationaux/non nationaux).
Publication:
– A usage interne uniquement*;
– Sur papier, à diffusion grand public.
– * S'applique aux statistiques produites par le Département du Commerce et de l'Industrie.
Agence responsable de la publication: Département de la Santé et de la Sécurité Sociale.
Titre de la publication: *Quarterly Analysis of the Unemployed Register* (Analyse Trimestrielle du Registre du Chômage).

10. Information méthodologique au sujet de ces statistiques
Publication: N'a pas été publiée, disponible pour utilisation interne seulement.

11. Comparaisons avec des statistiques provenant d'autres sources
Des comparaisons ont été faites avec des statistiques de chômage provenant du recensement de population.
Fréquence des comparaisons: Régulièrement, lors de la publication des statistiques.

12. Principaux changements intervenus depuis le début de ces séries statistiques
Des changements importants dans la législation, dans la capacité de l'agence et/ou dans les procédures administratives susceptibles d'avoir influencé de manière significative les statistiques sont intervenus en 1996. Les changements des statistiques qui en résultent n'ont pas été évalués.

Inde

1. Séries statistiques
Titre: Statistiques du Bureau de l'Emploi.
Première année disponible: 1947.

2. Organisme responsable de l'enregistrement des chômeurs ou demandeurs d'emploi
Nom de l'organisme: National Employment Service (Service National de l'emploi).
Type d'organisme: Organisme public relevant d'une autorité nationale collaborant étroitement avec les administrations des départements et des territoires.
Nom de l'autorité nationale: Administration Générale de l'Emploi et de la Formation, Ministère du Travail.
Situation des bureaux chargés de l'enregistrement: Dans toutes les régions du pays au niveau des départements et des villes. Le réseau comprend 958 bureaux de placement.
Types de services fournis ou gérés par cet organisme:
– Assistance aux demandeurs d'emploi pour trouver du travail;

– Assistance aux demandeurs d'emploi pour créer leur propre entreprise;
– Assistance aux employeurs pour trouver de la main-d'œuvre;
– Orientation professionnelle.

3. Les informations personnelles suivantes sont enregistrées:
– Nom;
– Sexe;
– Adresse du domicile habituel;
– Date de naissance;
– Groupe ethnique;
– Niveau d'instruction/ de formation. Aucun lien n'a été établi avec la CITE;
– Nom et adresse de l'employeur ou du lieu de travail actuel ou passé;
– Autres: salaire minimum; état physique et caractéristiques physiques; connaissances linguistiques; disposition à joindre les forces armées ou à suivre une formation; disposition à travailler ailleurs (limitations géographiques).

4. Critères utilisés pour déterminer si une personne doit être incluse dans le registre (R) et/ou dans les statistiques de chômeurs (S):
– Etre sans travail (R) et (S);
– Etre à la recherche d'un travail (R) et (S);
– Age: Minimum: 14 ans; pas de limite supérieure (R) et (S);
– Citoyenneté (R) et (S);
– Etre résident dans le pays (R) et (S);
– Avoir précédemment travaillé (R) et (S).

5. Critères utilisés pour déterminer si une personne doit être exclue du registre (R) et/ou des statistiques de chômeurs (S):
– Commencement d'un (nouveau) travail (R) et (S);
– Défaut de renouvellement de l'enregistrement avec l'organisme/agence (R) et (S).

6. Définition des personnes au chômage sur laquelle les statistiques sont établies
Tous les candidats enregistrés auprès des bureaux de placement.

7. Mise à jour des registres
Les registres sont mis à jour mensuellement.

8. Taux de chômage
Les statistiques basées sur les registres ne sont pas utilisées pour obtenir un taux de chômage.

9. Type de statistiques sur le nombre de chômeurs enregistrés produites
Série 1: Enregistrements, placements, soumissions, nombre de notification sur les registres actifs (Live Register) des vacances de postes.
Période de référence: Mois.
Fréquence de production: Mensuelle.
Variables utilisées:
– Sexe;
– Caractéristiques géographiques (pour les personnes originaires de régions rurales).
Publication: Sur papier, à diffusion grand public.
Agence responsable de la publication: Administration générale de l'Emploi et de la Formation.
Titre et périodicité de la publication: *Statistiques des bureaux de placement*, annuelle.
Série 2: Activités se rapportant à l'orientation professionnelle par catégorie de candidats.
Période de référence: Trimestre.
Fréquence de production: Trimestrielle.
Variables utilisées:
– Catégories ethniques/sociales (c'est-à-dire ¨castes classées¨ (SC); ¨tribus classées¨ (ST); ¨autres classes peu avancées¨ (OBC);
– Autre: Handicapés physiques (PH);
– Sexe (total des femmes seulement).
Publication: Sur papier, à diffusion grand public.
Agence responsable de la publication: Administration générale de l'Emploi et de la Formation.
Titre et périodicité de la publication: *Statistiques des bureaux de placement*, annuelle.
Série 3: Enregistrements, placements, nombre d'inscrits sur le registre actif et soumissions faites concernant des demandeurs appartenant à des communautés minoritaires.
Période de référence: Semestre.
Fréquence de production: Semestrielle.

Publication: Sur papier, à diffusion grand public.
Agence responsable de la publication: Administration générale de l'Emploi et de la Formation.
Titre et périodicité de la publication: *Statistiques des bureaux de placement*, annuelle.
Série 4: Enregistrements, placements, nombre d'inscrits sur le registre actif et soumissions faites concernant des demandeurs handicapés physiques.
Période de référence: Semestre.
Fréquence de production: Semestrielle.
Variables utilisées:
– Type d'handicap physique;
– Sexe (total des femmes seulement).
Publication: Sur papier, à diffusion grand public.
Agence responsable de la publication: Administration générale de l'Emploi et de la Formation.
Titre et périodicité de la publication: *Statistiques des bureaux de placement*, annuelle.
Série 5: Nombre de demandeurs d'emploi enregistrés et placés selon leur niveau d'éducation ($10^{\text{ème}}$ classe et au dessus).
Période de référence: Semestre.
Fréquence de production: Semestrielle.
Variables utilisées:
– Niveau d'éducation (cinq niveaux distingués, 10 branches distinguées pour les bacheliers et les étudiants; deux branches distinguées pour les diplômés);
– Catégories ethniques/sociales (¨SC¨, ¨ST¨ et ¨OBC¨);
– Sexe (total des femmes seulement).
Publication: Sur papier, à diffusion grand public.
Agence responsable de la publication: Administration générale de l'Emploi et de la Formation.
Titre et périodicité de la publication: *Statistiques des bureaux de placement*, annuelle.
Série 6: Enregistrements, placements, nombre d'inscrits sur le registre actif et soumissions concernant des demandeurs appartenant aux catégories ¨SC¨, ¨ST¨, et ¨OBC¨.
Période de référence: Semestre.
Fréquence de production: Semestrielle.
Variables utilisées:
– Catégories ethniques/sociales.
Publication: Sur papier, à diffusion grand public.
Agence responsable de la publication: Administration générale de l'Emploi et de la Formation.
Titre et périodicité de la publication: *Statistiques des bureaux de placement*, annuelle.
Série 7: Promotion de travailleurs indépendants.
Période de référence: Semestre.
Fréquence de production: Semestrielle.
Variables utilisées:
– Sexe;
– Catégories ethniques/sociales (¨SC¨, ¨ST¨, ¨OBC¨, "PH " et communautés minoritaires);
– Caractéristiques géographiques (zones rurales/urbaines).
Publication: Sur papier, à diffusion grand public.
Agence responsable de la publication: Administration générale de l'Emploi et de la Formation.
Titre et périodicité de la publication: *Statistiques des bureaux de placement*, annuelle.
Série 8: Vacances de postes signalées, pourvues, annulées et ouvertes sur le registre selon la classification nationale des professions (NCO) concernant les femmes, ¨SC¨, ¨ST¨, ¨OBC¨ et ¨PH¨.
Période de référence: Année.
Fréquence de production: Annuelle.
Variables utilisées:
– Profession;
– Catégories ethniques/sociales;
– Sexe (total des femmes seulement);
– Autre: ¨PH¨.
Publication: Sur papier, à diffusion grand public.
Agence responsable de la publication: Administration générale de l'Emploi et de la Formation.
Titre et périodicité de la publication: *Statistiques des bureaux de placement*, annuelle.
Série 9: Vacances de postes signalées, pourvues, annulées et ouvertes par secteur.
Période de référence: Année.
Fréquence de production: Annuelle.

Variables utilisées:
- Secteur (Central/Gouvernement d'Etat, secteur publique/ privé, etc.).

Publication: Sur papier, à diffusion grand public.

Agence responsable de la publication: Administration générale de l'Emploi et de la Formation.

Titre et périodicité de la publication: *Statistiques des bureaux de placement*, annuelle.

Série 10: Nombre de demandeurs d'emploi inscrits sur le registre par groupe d'âge, sexe et niveau d'instruction au 31 décembre.

Période de référence: Année.

Fréquence de production: Annuelle.

Variables utilisées:
- Sexe;
- Groupe d'âge;
- Niveau d'instruction (six niveaux distingués).

Publication: Sur papier, à diffusion grand public.

Agence responsable de la publication: Administration générale de l'Emploi et de la Formation.

Titre et périodicité de la publication: *Statistiques des bureaux de placement*, annuelle.

- **Série 11:** Nombre de postes vacants signalés par l'établissement en raison du manque de demandeurs d'emploi adéquats, avec les motifs ayant entraîné le refus de leur candidature.

Période de référence: Année.

Fréquence de production: Annuelle.

Variables utilisées:
- Industrie (par code de la Classification nationale industrielle (NIC) au niveau de trois chiffres);
- Profession (par code NCO);
- Secteur public/privé.

Publication: Sur papier, à diffusion grand public.

Agence responsable de la publication: Administration générale de l'Emploi et de la Formation.

Titre et périodicité de la publication: *Statistiques des bureaux de placement*, annuelle.

Série 12: Placements effectués et nombre d'inscrits sur le registre actif par NCO concernant les apprentissages à plein temps et les stagiaires ex-ITI (Institut de formation industrielle), par profession.

Période de référence: Année.

Fréquence de production: Annuelle.

Variables utilisées:
- Profession;
- Métier de formation.

Publication: Sur papier, à diffusion grand public.

Agence responsable de la publication: Administration générale de l'Emploi et de la Formation.

Titre et périodicité de la publication: *Statistiques des bureaux de placement*, annuelle.

Série 13: Enregistrements, placements effectués et nombre d'inscrits sur le registre actif concernant les personnes déplacées.

Période de référence: Année.

Fréquence de production: Annuelle.

Variables utilisées:
- Caractéristiques géographiques (origines).

Publication: Sur papier, à diffusion grand public.

Agence responsable de la publication: Administration générale de l'Emploi et de la Formation.

Titre et périodicité de la publication: *Statistiques des bureaux de placement*, annuelle.

10. Information méthodologique au sujet de ces statistiques

Publication: Sur papier, à diffusion grand public.

Agence responsable: Administration Générale de l'Emploi et de la Formation.

11. Comparaisons avec des statistiques provenant d'autres sources

Il n'y a pas eu de comparaisons faites avec des statistiques provenant d'autres sources.

12. Principaux changements intervenus depuis le début de ces séries statistiques

Il n'y a pas eu de changement important dans la législation, dans la capacité de l'agence et/ou dans les procédures administratives susceptibles d'avoir influencé de manière significative les statistiques.

Iran, Rép. islamique d'

1. Séries statistiques

Titre: Registres administratifs des centres de placement.

2. Organisme responsable de l'enregistrement des chômeurs ou demandeurs d'emploi

Nom de l'organisme:

1. Les centres de placement (publics)
2. Les centres consultatifs d'emploi (publics)
3. Les centres de placement (privés) ayant autorisation du Ministère du Travail et des Affaires sociales.

Type d'organisme:

1 et 2. Organismes publics relevant d'une autorité locale;
3. Organisme privé à but non lucratif.

Situation des bureaux chargés de l'enregistrement: Dans l'ensemble du pays. La plupart des bureaux locaux sont situés dans les régions urbaines, mais récemment des bureaux ont été ouverts dans des zones rurales des cantons.

Types de services fournis et/ou gérés par cet organisme:
- Assistance aux demandeurs d'emploi pour trouver du travail;
- Assistance aux demandeurs d'emploi pour créer leur propre entreprise;
- Assistance aux employeurs pour trouver de la main-d'œuvre;
- Orientation professionnelle;
- Paiement des indemnités de chômage;
- Autres services liés à l'emploi.

Pourcentage des demandeurs d'emploi qui cherchent un emploi au travers de cet organisme: 20%

3. Les informations personnelles suivantes sont enregistrées:
- Nom;
- Sexe;
- Adresse du domicile habituel;
- Date de naissance;
- Niveau d'instruction;
- Type de profession de l'emploi antérieur et/ou actuel;
- Nom et adresse de l'employeur ou du lieu de travail actuel ou passé;
- Branche d'activité de l'employeur ou du lieu de travail actuel ou passé. Aucun lien n'a été établi avec la CITI-rév.3;
- Autre: documents scolaires, qualification professionnelle, emploi à l'extérieur du pays, date de début des cotisations d'assurance chômage.

4. Critères utilisés pour déterminer si une personne doit être incluse dans le registre (R) et/ou dans les statistiques de chômeurs (S):
- Etre sans travail (R) et (S);
- Etre à la recherche d'un travail (R) et (S);
- Etre disponible pour travailler (R) et (S);
- Age: Minimum: 15 ans, pas de limite supérieure (R) et (S);
- Citoyenneté (R) et (S);
- Etre résident dans le pays (R) et (S);
- Avoir précédemment travaillé (R);
- Acquittement de cotisations d'assurance chômage (R).

5. Critères utilisés pour déterminer si une personne doit être exclue du registre (R) et/ou des statistiques de chômeurs (S):
Information non disponible.

6. Définition des personnes au chômage sur laquelle les statistiques sont établies
Toute personne âgée de 15 ans révolus ou plus, apte à travailler, disponible pour travailler et enregistrée auprès d'un centre de placement.

7. Mise à jour des registres
Les registres sont mis à jour régulièrement.

8. Taux de chômage
Les statistiques basées sur les registres ne sont pas utilisées pour obtenir des taux de chômage.

9. Type de statistiques produites sur le nombre de chômeurs enregistrés

Série 1: *Visages du marché du travail.*

Période de référence: Annuelle.

Fréquence de production: Annuelle.

Variables utilisées:
- Sexe;
- Age;

–   Niveau d'instruction;
–   Qualifications professionnelles.

Publication: Sur papier, à diffusion grand public.

Organisme responsable de la publication: Ministère du Travail et des Affaires sociales, bureau de statistique.

Titre et périodicité de la publication: *Visages du marché du travail*, publication annuelle.

10. Information méthodologique au sujet de ces statistiques

Publication: Sur papier, à diffusion restreinte.

Organisme responsable: Ministère du Travail et des Affaires sociales, bureau de statistique.

11. Comparaisons avec des statistiques provenant d'autres sources

Il n'y a pas eu de comparaisons faites avec des statistiques provenant d'autres sources.

12. Principaux changements intervenus depuis le début de ces séries statistiques

Afin de diminuer la responsabilité des centres de placement publics, des centres de placement ont été privatisés et ont reçu l'autorisation du Ministère du travail et des Affaires sociales.

En 2002, on a commencé à appliquer un programme de réforme pour améliorer le système d'information sur le marché du travail, et son informatisation.

Islande

1. Séries statistiques

Titre: Chômage enregistré.

Première année disponible: 1969.

2. Organisme responsable de l'enregistrement des chômeurs ou demandeurs d'emploi

Nom de l'organisme: Vinnumalastofnun (Administration du Travail).

Type d'organisme: Organisme public relevant d'une autorité nationale.

Nom de l'autorité nationale: Ministère des Affaires Sociales.

Situation des bureaux chargés de l'enregistrement: Dans toutes les régions du pays.

Types de services fournis et/ou gérés par cet organisme:

–   Assistance aux demandeurs d'emploi pour trouver du travail;
–   Assistance aux demandeurs d'emploi pour créer leur propre entreprise;
–   Assistance aux employeurs pour trouver de la main-d'œuvre;
–   Orientation professionnelle;
–   Formation liée à l'emploi;
–   Paiement des indemnités de chômage;
–   Autre: mesures concernant le marché du travail, cours abrégés dans des domaines variés.

Pourcentage des demandeurs d'emploi qui cherchent un emploi au travers de cet organisme: Approximativement 100%.

3. Les informations personnelles suivantes sont enregistrées:

–   Nom;
–   Sexe;
–   Numéro de sécurité sociale (ou numéro d'identification également utilisé par d'autres organismes);
–   Adresse du domicile habituel;
–   Date de naissance;
–   Citoyenneté;
–   Nationalité/groupe ethnique;
–   Niveau d'instruction/ de formation, en distinguant trois catégories. Des liens ont été établis avec la CITE-76;
–   Situation de travail présente et passée, en distinguant 31 catégories;
–   Type de profession de l'emploi antérieur ou actuel, en distinguant 374 catégories. Des liens ont été établis avec la CITP-88, au niveau des groupes de base;
–   Type de profession de l'emploi recherché, avec un nombre illimité de catégories. Des liens ont été établis avec la CITP-88, au niveau des groupes de base;
–   Nom et adresse de l'employeur ou du lieu de travail actuel ou passé;
–   Branche d'activité de l'employeur ou du lieu de travail actuel ou passé, en distinguant 616 catégories. Des liens ont été établis avec NACE, rév.1 au niveau des classes;

–   Inscriptions/enregistrements antérieurs auprès de l'organisme.

4. Critères utilisés pour déterminer si une personne doit être incluse dans le registre (R) et/ou dans les statistiques de chômeurs (S):

–   Etre sans travail (R) et (S);
–   Etre à la recherche d'un travail (R) et (S);
–   Etre disponible pour travailler (R) et (S);
–   Age: Minimum: 16 ans; Maximum: 70 ans (R) et (S);
–   Citoyenneté (R);
–   Etre résident dans le pays (R);
–   Avoir précédemment travaillé (R);
–   Durée souhaitée de l'emploi recherché et/ou du nombre d'heures de travail recherché (R) et (S);
–   Autres: droit aux indemnités de chômage accumulées jusqu'à 24 mois suite à une maladie, circonstances personnelles spéciales, emprisonnement (R).

5. Critères utilisés pour déterminer si une personne doit être exclue du registre (R) et/ou des statistiques de chômeurs (S):

–   Décès (R) et (S);
–   Etablissement de la personne à l'étranger (R) et (S);
–   Commencement d'un (nouveau) travail (R) et (S);
–   Participation à un programme de promotion de l'emploi, à un programme de travaux publics, etc. (R) et (S);
–   Entreprise d'une formation ou d'études (R) et (S);
–   Défaut de contact avec l'organisme/agence (R) et (S);
–   Refus d'offres d'emploi adaptées (R) et (S);
–   Refus d'offres de formation adaptées (R) et (S);
–   Fin de droit à l'allocation chômage (R) et (S);
–   Admission à toucher une pension (R);
–   Incapacité à travailler (R).

6. Définition des personnes au chômage sur laquelle les statistiques sont établies

Sont considérées au chômage les personnes qui n'ont pas de travail ou un travail insuffisant par rapport à leur capacité de travail et à leurs désirs, basé sur une journée de travail de huit heures ou l'équivalent (travail par roulement, etc.), qui s'inscrivent auprès d'une agence d'emploi officielle comme chômeur et qui restent enregistrées en se présentant au moins une fois par mois auprès de cette agence

7. Mise à jour des registres

Les registres sont mis à jour chaque semaine, chaque quinzaine et mensuellement.

8. Taux de chômage

Les statistiques basées sur les registres sont utilisées pour obtenir des taux de chômage.

Les sources des données d'emploi qui sont partie du dénominateur des taux de chômage sont les estimations officielles.

Définition des personnes pourvues d'un emploi à cette fin: Équivalents à plein temps.

9. Type de statistiques sur le nombre de chômeurs enregistrés produites

Série 1:

Période de référence: Mois.

Fréquence de production: Mensuelle.

Variables utilisées:

–   Sexe;
–   Age;
–   Niveau d'instruction;
–   Profession;
–   Branche d'activité;
–   Caractéristiques géographiques;
–   Durée de chômage.

Publication:

–   Sur papier, à diffusion grand public;
–   En format électronique, sur demande;
–   Sur un site Internet (www.vinnumalastofnun.is).

Agence responsable de la publication: Administration du Travail.

Titre de la publication: *Yfirlit Yfir Atvinnuàstand* (Vue d'ensemble de la situation de l'emploi).

Série 2:

Période de référence: Jour.

Fréquence de production: Trimestrielle.

Variables utilisées:

–   Sexe;
–   Age;
–   Caractéristiques géographiques;
–   Durée de chômage.

Publication: Sur un site Internet (www.statice is).
Agence responsable de la publication: Statistiques d'Islande.
Titre de la publication: *Skrào atvinnuleysi eftir kyni, aldri og lengd atvinnuleysis.*
10. Information méthodologique au sujet de ces statistiques
Publication:
- Sur papier, à diffusion grand public;
- En format électronique, sur demande;
- Sur un site internet (série 1: www.vinnumalastofnun.is); (série 2: www.statice.is).
Agence responsable pour la diffusion de l'information méthodologique:
Série 1: Administration du Travail;
Série 2: Statistiques d'Islande.
11. Comparaisons avec des statistiques provenant d'autres sources
Des comparaisons ont été faites avec des statistiques provenant de l'enquête sur la main-d'œuvre.
Fréquence des comparaisons: Deux fois par an (dernière année: 2001).
Publication de la methodologie et/ou des résultats de la comparaison: Publiés par le Bureau de Statistique d'Islande dans *Labour market surveys on unemployment* (Enquête sur le chômage), avril et novembre, (www.statice.is/talnaefn/vinna2001/kafli10.pdf).
12. Principaux changements intervenus depuis le début de ces séries statistiques
Des changements importants dans la législation, dans la capacité de l'agence et/ou dans les procédures administratives susceptibles d'avoir influencé de manière significative les statistiques sont intervenus en 1998. Les changements dans les statistiques qui en résultaient n'ont pas été évalués.

Israël

1. Séries statistiques
Titre: Données du Service de l'Emploi concernant le marché du travail.
Première année disponible: 1960's.
2. Organisme responsable de l'enregistrement des chômeurs ou demandeurs d'emploi
Nom de l'organisme: Service de l'Emploi.
Type d'organisme: Service sous la supervision générale d'une autorité nationale.
Nom de l'autorité nationale: Ministère du Travail et des Affaires Sociales.
Situation des bureaux chargés de l'enregistrement: Approximativement 100 succursales dispersées dans tout le pays, dans les centres les plus peuplés.
Types de services fournis et/ou gérés par cet organisme:
- Assistance aux demandeurs d'emploi pour trouver du travail;
- Assistance aux demandeurs d'emploi pour créer leur propre entreprise;
- Assistance aux employeurs pour trouver de la main-d'œuvre;
- Orientation professionnelle;
- Formation liée à l'emploi (en collaboration avec le Ministère du Travail et des Affaires Sociales);
- Paiement des indemnités de chômage (en collaboration avec l'Institut National d'Assurance);
- Autres: permis pour et allocation de travailleurs étrangers; supervision de l'emploi de travailleurs palestiniens et exécution des paiements à ces travailleurs; vérifications de paiements aux travailleurs étrangers.
Pourcentage des demandeurs d'emploi qui cherchent un emploi au travers de cet organisme: 7%.
3. Les informations personnelles suivantes sont enregistrées:
- Nom;
- Sexe;
- Numéro de sécurité sociale (ou numéro d'identification également utilisé par d'autres organismes);
- Adresse du domicile habituel;
- Date de naissance;
- Niveau d'instruction/ de formation, en distinguant neuf catégories. Des liens ont été établis avec la CITE;
- Situation de travail présente et passée, en distinguant 16 catégories;
- Type de profession de l'emploi antérieur ou actuel, en distinguant des milliers de catégories. Des liens ont été établis avec la CITP-88, au niveau des groupes de base;
- Type de profession de l'emploi recherché, en distinguant des milliers de catégories. Des liens ont été établis avec la CITP-88, au niveau des groupes de base;
- Nom et adresse de l'employeur ou du lieu de travail actuel ou passé;
- Branche d'activité de l'employeur ou du lieu de travail actuel ou passé. Des liens ont été établis avec la CITI, rév.3 au niveau des classes;
- Inscriptions/enregistrements antérieurs auprès de l'organisme;
- Autres: renvoi à des offres de travail; refus d'offres de travail.
4. Critères utilisés pour déterminer si une personne doit être incluse dans le registre (R) et/ou dans les statistiques de chômeurs (S):
- Etre sans travail (R) et (S);
- Etre à la recherche d'un travail (R) et (S);
- Etre disponible pour travailler (R) et (S);
- Age: Minimum: 15 an; Maximum: 65 ans (R) et (S);
- Citoyenneté (R) et (S);
- Avoir précédemment travaillé (R) et (S);
- Durée souhaitée de l'emploi recherché et/ou du nombre d'heures de travail recherché (R) et (S).
5. Critères utilisés pour déterminer si une personne doit être exclue du registre (R) et/ou des statistiques de chômeurs (S):
- Décès (R) et (S);
- Etablissement de la personne à l'étranger (R) et (S).
6. Définition des personnes au chômage sur laquelle les statistiques sont établies
Une personne à la recherche d'un travail qui est enregistrée avec au moins un jour de chômage au cours du mois en question.
7. Mise à jour des registres
Les registres sont mis à jour mensuellement.
8. Taux de chômage
Les statistiques basées sur les registres sont utilisées pour obtenir des taux de chômage.
La source des données d'emploi qui est partie du dénominateur des taux de chômage est l'estimation du total de la main-d'œuvre civile.
Définition des personnes pourvues d'un emploi à cette fin:
Selon la définition de l'enquête sur la main-d'œuvre: les personnes employées au moins pendant une heure à n'importe quel travail durant la semaine déterminante.
9. Type de statistiques sur le nombre de chômeurs enregistrés produites
Série: Personnes au chômage.
Période de référence: Mois.
Fréquence de production: Mensuelle.
Variables utilisées:
- Sexe;
- Age;
- Niveau d'instruction;
- Profession;
- Branche d'activité;
- Caractéristiques géographiques;
- Durée de chômage.
Publication: Sur papier, à diffusion grand public.
Agence responsable de la publication: Service de l'Emploi.
Titre et périodicité de la publication: *Employment Service Data on the Labour Market* (données sur la main-d'œuvre sur le marché du travail), mensuel.
10. Information méthodologique au sujet de ces statistiques
Publication: Pas de publication, disponible sur demande.
Agence responsable: Service de l'Emploi.
11. Comparaisons avec des statistiques provenant d'autres sources
Des comparaisons ont été faites avec des statistiques provenant de l'enquête sur la main-d'œuvre.
Fréquence des comparaisons: Régulièrement lors de la publication des statistiques.
Publication de la méthodologie et/ou des résultats de la comparaison: Le mensuel *Employment Service Data on the Labour Market* publie les taux de chômage (nationaux) de l'enquête sur la main-d'œuvre et ceux obtenus par le Service de l'Emploi (par région pour les personnes sans travail pendant six jours ou plus et ceux sans travail pendant 20 jours ou plus). Des comparaisons sont

difficiles à cause des définitions du chômage différentes selon les sources et parce que le Service de l'Emploi ne tient compte que des chômeurs qui sont enregistrés dans ses bureaux. La méthodologie du Service de l'Emploi est publiée dans la publication mensuelle.

12. Principaux changements intervenus depuis le début de ces séries statistiques

Des changements importants dans la législation, dans la capacité de l'agence et/ou dans les procédures administratives susceptibles d'avoir influencé de manière significative les statistiques sont intervenus en:

1972: La mise en vigueur de la loi sur l'assurance chômage obligeant les personnes désirant toucher des indemnités sur la base de cette loi à s'inscrire auprès du Service de l'Emploi eut pour résultat une augmentation de chômeurs dans les statistiques du Service de l'Emploi;

1984: La mise en vigueur de la loi sur le maintien des revenus obligeant le Service de l'Emploi à faire passer un test d'emploi, base de l'éligibilité pour recevoir des allocations selon cette loi, eut pour résultat une augmentation des chômeurs enregistrés auprès du Service de l'Emploi. En 1985 le nombre de demandeurs d'emploi adultes avait augmenté de 12%.

1989-1990: L'annulation de l'obligation pour les employeurs à la recherche de main-d'œuvre de faire appel au Service de l'Emploi avait réduit d'approximativement 50% le nombre d'employeurs faisant appel au Service de l'Emploi.

Italie

1. Séries statistiques
Titre: Inscriptions auprès des bureaux de placement.
Première année disponible: 1987.
2. Organisme responsable de l'enregistrement des chômeurs ou demandeurs d'emploi
Nom de l'organisme: Agence pour l'Emploi.
Type d'organisme: Organisme public relevant d'une autorité locale.
Situation des bureaux chargés de l'enregistrement: Dans chaque province.
Types de services fournis et/ou gérés par cet organisme:
– Assistance aux demandeurs d'emploi pour trouver du travail;
– Assistance aux employeurs pour trouver de la main-d'œuvre;
– Orientation professionnelle;
– Formation liée à l'emploi;
– Autres services liés à l'emploi: aide aux demandeurs d'emploi handicapés, aux demandeurs d'emploi ressortissants de pays extérieurs à la Communauté Européenne, et aux travailleurs mis en disponibilité.
3. Les informations personnelles suivantes sont enregistrées:
– Nom;
– Sexe;
– Numéro de sécurité sociale (ou numéro d'identification également utilisé par d'autres organismes);
– Adresse du domicile habituel;
– Date de naissance;
– Citoyenneté;
– Nationalité/groupe ethnique;
– Niveau d'instruction/de formation, en distinguant huit catégories. Aucun lien n'a été établi avec la CITE;
– Situation de travail présente et passée, en distinguant quatre catégories;
– Type de profession de l'emploi antérieur et/ou actuel; Aucun lien n'a été établi avec la CITP;
– Type de profession de l'emploi recherché;
– Nom et adresse de l'employeur ou du lieu de travail actuel ou passé;
– Branche d'activité de l'employeur ou du lieu de travail actuel ou passé, en distinguant 4 catégories. Des liens ont été établis avec la CITI;
– Inscriptions/enregistrements antérieurs auprès de l'organisme;
– Autres: mise à la retraite anticipée, disponibilité pour travailler, et durée de chômage.
4. Critères utilisés pour déterminer si une personne doit être incluse dans le registre (R) et/ou dans les statistiques de chômeurs (S):
– Etre sans travail (R) et (S);

– Etre à la recherche d'un travail (R) et (S);
– Age: Minimum: 15 ans; Maximum: 65 ans (R) et (S);
– Citoyenneté pour les ressortissants de pays extérieurs à la Communauté Européenne (R) et (S);
– Etre résident dans le pays (R) et (S);
– Avoir précédemment travaillé (R) et (S);
– Acquittement de cotisations d'assurance chômage, seulement pour les travailleurs mis en disponibilité (R) et (S).
5. Critères utilisés pour déterminer si une personne doit être exclue du registre (R) et/ou des statistiques de chômeurs (S):
– Commencement d'un (nouveau) travail (R) et (S);
– Défaut de contact avec l'agence, si le demandeur d'emploi n'est pas venu confirmer son inscription (R) et (S);
– Fin de droit à l'allocation-chômage, pour les travailleurs mis en disponibilité (R) et (S).
6. Définition des personnes au chômage sur laquelle les statistiques sont établies
Sont considérées en chômage les personnes sans emploi, qui sont immédiatement disponibles pour commencer à travailler, et qui sont activement à la recherche d'un emploi.
Les travailleurs mis en disponibilité le sont par une entreprise qui a été admise au titre du traitement extraordinaire de l'intégration salariale et qui ne peut garantir le réemploi des dits travailleurs. Ces travailleurs doivent avoir une ancienneté dans le travail d'au moins 12 mois, dont au moins six mois de travail réellement effectué. Ils perçoivent pour la période définie par la loi une indemnité de disponibilité.
7. Mise à jour des registres
Les registres sont mis à jour tous les trois mois.
8. Taux de chômage
Les statistiques basées sur les registres ne sont pas utilisées pour obtenir des taux de chômage.
9. Type de statistiques produites sur le nombre de chômeurs enregistrés
Période de référence: Mois.
Fréquence de production: Mensuelle.
Variables utilisées:
– Sexe;
– Age;
– Niveau d'instruction;
– Profession;
– Branche d'activité;
– Caractéristiques géographiques;
– Expérience professionnelle antérieure;
– Citoyenneté (nationaux/non nationaux);
– Durée de chômage.
Publication:
– Sur papier, à diffusion restreinte;
– En format électronique, sur demande;
– Sur un site Internet: www.minwelfare.it
Organisme responsable de la publication: Ministère de l'Emploi et de la Politique sociale.
Titre et périodicité de la publication: *Notaflash* (Note Flash), publication mensuelle; et *Rapporto di monitoraggio* (Rapport de gestion), publication semestrielle.
10. Information méthodologique au sujet de ces statistiques
Publication:
– Sur papier, à diffusion restreinte;
– En format électronique, sur demande;
– Sur un site Internet: www.minwelfare.it
Organisme responsable: Ministère de l'Emploi et de la Politique sociale.
11. Comparaisons avec des statistiques provenant d'autres sources
Des comparaisons ont été faites avec des statistiques provenant de l'enquête de main-d'œuvre, avec des statistiques du recensement de population et avec des estimations.
Fréquence des comparaisons: Occasionnellement, dernière année en 2001.
Publication de la méthodologie et/ou des résultats de la comparaison: Ils n'ont pas été publiés.
12. Principaux changements intervenus depuis le début de ces séries statistiques
Des changements importants dans la législation, dans la capacité de l'agence et/ou dans les procédures administratives susceptibles d'avoir influencé de manière significative les

statistiques sont intervenus en 1999, 2000 et 2001. L'ampleur des changements induits par ces modifications n'est pas connue.

Japon (1)

1. Séries statistiques
Titre: Rapport sur le service de l'emploi.
Première année disponible: 1963.
2. Organisme responsable de l'enregistrement des chômeurs ou demandeurs d'emploi
Nom de l'organisme: Koukyo Shokugyo Anteisho (Agence de sécurité de l'emploi public).
Type d'organisme: Organisme public relevant d'une autorité nationale.
Nom de l'autorité nationale: Ministère de la Santé, du Travail et de l'Assistance Sociale.
Situation des bureaux chargés de l'enregistrement: Dans toutes les 47 préfectures du pays, au total 600 bureaux.
Types de services fournis et/ou gérés par cet organisme:
- Assistance aux demandeurs d'emploi pour trouver du travail;
- Assistance aux demandeurs d'emploi pour créer leur propre entreprise;
- Assistance aux employeurs pour trouver de la main-d'œuvre;
- Orientation professionnelle;
- Formation liée à l'emploi;
- Paiement des indemnités de chômage;
- Autres: service d'information sur l'emploi industriel: mise à disposition d'informations spécifiques sur les marchés de travail locaux, les conditions de travail et autres informations utiles concernant la sélection de postes et l'acquisition de compétences; service d'administration de l'emploi: consultations spécifiques et assistance aux employeurs concernant des questions en relation avec l'administration de l'emploi telles que le recrutement, l'affectation, etc., de même que l'assistance pour un emploi adéquat de personnes plus âgées et de personnes handicapées; service concernant les allocations liées à l'emploi: assistance spécifique aux demandeurs d'emploi (allocations diverses pour faciliter un nouvel emploi); assistance aux employeurs (à engager des demandeurs d'emploi ayant des problèmes à trouver un emploi, et procurant des allocations diverses permettant d'éviter le chômage dû à des fluctuations économiques).
Pourcentage des demandeurs d'emploi qui cherchent un emploi au travers de cet organisme: 34.3% (février 2001).
3. Les informations personnelles suivantes sont enregistrées:
- Nom;
- Sexe;
- Adresse du domicile habituel;
- Date de naissance;
- Niveau d'instruction/ de formation, en distinguant six catégories; professionnel/ de formation, en distinguant 650 catégories. Des liens n'ont pas été établis avec la CITE;
- Situation de travail présente et passée, en distinguant deux catégories;
- Type de profession de l'emploi antérieur ou actuel. Aucun lien n'a été établi avec la CITP;
- Type de profession de l'emploi recherché, avec 2 167 catégories. Aucun lien n'a été établi avec la CITP;
- Nom et adresse de l'employeur ou du lieu de travail actuel ou passé;
- Autres: détails personnels familiaux; conditions de travail désirées; raisons pour avoir quitté l'emploi actuel ou antérieur.
4. Critères utilisés pour déterminer si une personne doit être incluse dans le registre (R) et/ou dans les statistiques de chômeurs (S):
- Etre à la recherche d'un travail (R) et (S);
- Etre disponible pour travailler (R) et (S);
- Age: Minimum: 15 an; pas de limite supérieure (R) et (S).
5. Critères utilisés pour déterminer si une personne doit être exclue du registre (R) et/ou des statistiques de chômeurs (S):
- Décès (R) et (S);
- Etablissement de la personne à l'étranger (R) et (S);
- Commencement d'un (nouveau) travail (R) et (S);
- Défaut de contact avec l'organisme/agence (R) et (S);
- Autre: sur demande personnelle.
6. Définition des personnes au chômage sur laquelle les statistiques sont établies
Les statistiques s'appliquent aux personnes à la recherche d'un travail seulement.
7. Mise à jour des registres
Les registres sont mis à jour régulièrement.
8. Taux de chômage
Les statistiques basées sur les registres ne sont pas utilisées pour obtenir des taux de chômage.
9. Type de statistiques sur le nombre de chômeurs enregistrés produites
Série 1: Rapport du Service de l'Emploi.
Période de référence: Mois, trimestre, année calendrier, année fiscale (1er avril – 31 mars).
Fréquence de production: Mensuelle.
Variables utilisées:
- Sexe;
- Age;
- Profession;
- Branche d'activité;
- Caractéristiques géographiques;
- Expérience professionnelle antérieure.
Publication:
- Sur papier, à diffusion grand public;
- Sur un site Internet (http://www.mhlw.go.jp) (en japonais seulement).
Agence responsable de la publication: Ministère de la Santé, du Travail et des Affaires Sociales.
Titre et périodicité des publications: *Rapport Mensuel sur le Service de l'Emploi; Rapport Annuel sur le Service de l'Emploi.*
10. Information méthodologique au sujet de ces statistiques
Publication:
- Sur papier, à diffusion grand public;
- Sur un site Internet (http://www.mhlw.go.jp) (en japonais seulement).
Organisme responsable: Ministère de la Santé, du Travail et des Affaires Sociales.
11. Comparaisons avec des statistiques provenant d'autres sources
Il n'y a pas eu de comparaisons faites avec des statistiques provenant d'autres sources.
12. Principaux changements intervenus depuis le début de ces séries statistiques
Il n'y a pas eu de changement important dans la législation, dans la capacité de l'agence et/ou dans les procédures administratives susceptibles d'avoir influencé de manière significative les statistiques.

Japon (2)

1. Séries statistiques
Titre: Rapport annuel sur le service d'indemnisation de l'emploi; et Rapport mensuel sur le service d'indemnisation de l'emploi.
Première année disponible: Séries annuelles: 1975; Séries mensuelles: 1980.
2. Organisme responsable de l'enregistrement des chômeurs ou demandeurs d'emploi
Nom de l'organisme: Koukyo Shokugyo Anteisho (Agence de sécurité de l'emploi public).
Type d'organisme: Organisme public relevant d'une autorité nationale.
Nom de l'autorité nationale: Ministère de la Santé, du Travail et de l'Assistance sociale.
Situation des bureaux chargés de l'enregistrement: Dans toutes les 47 préfectures du pays, au total 600 bureaux.
Types de services fournis et/ou gérés par cet organisme:
- Assistance aux demandeurs d'emploi pour trouver du travail;
- Assistance aux demandeurs d'emploi pour créer leur propre entreprise;
- Assistance aux employeurs pour trouver de la main-d'œuvre;
- Orientation professionnelle;
- Paiement des indemnités de chômage;
- Autres: service d'information sur l'emploi industriel: mise

à disposition d'informations spécifiques sur les marchés de travail locaux, les conditions de travail et autres informations utiles concernant la sélection de postes et l'acquisition de compétences; service d'administration de l'emploi: consultations spécifiques et assistance aux employeurs concernant des questions en relation avec l'administration de l'emploi telles que le recrutement, l'affectation, etc., de même que l'assistance pour un emploi adéquat de personnes plus âgées et de personnes handicapées; service concernant les allocations liées à l'emploi: assistance spécifique aux demandeurs d'emploi (allocations diverses pour faciliter un nouvel emploi); assistance aux employeurs (à engager des demandeurs d'emploi ayant des problèmes à trouver un emploi, et procurant des allocations diverses permettant d'éviter le chômage dû à des fluctuations économiques).

Pourcentage des demandeurs d'emploi qui cherchent un emploi au travers de cet organisme: 34.3% (février 2001).

3. Les informations personnelles suivantes sont enregistrées:
– Nom;
– Sexe;
– Adresse du domicile habituel;
– Date de naissance;
– Situation de travail présente et passée, en distinguant deux catégories;
– Type de profession de l'emploi antérieur ou actuel, en distinguant neuf catégories. Aucun lien n'a été établi avec la CITP;
– Nom et adresse de l'employeur ou du lieu de travail actuel ou passé;
– Inscriptions/enregistrements antérieurs auprès de l'organisme/agence.

4. Critères utilisés pour déterminer si une personne doit être incluse dans le registre (R) et/ou dans les statistiques de chômeurs (S):
– Etre sans travail (R) et (S);
– Etre à la recherche d'un travail (R) et (S);
– Etre disponible pour travailler (R) et (S);
– Age: Minimum: 15 an; Maximum: 64 ans (R) et (S);
– Avoir précédemment travaillé (R) et (S).

5. Critères utilisés pour déterminer si une personne doit être exclue du registre (R) et/ou des statistiques de chômeurs (S):
– Décès (R) et (S);
– Commencement d'un (nouveau) travail (R) et (S);
– Entreprise d'une formation ou d'études (sauf pour les personnes entreprenant une formation professionnelle publique) (R) et (S);
– Défaut de contact avec l'organisme/agence (R) et (S);
– Refus d'offres d'emploi adaptées (R) et (S);
– Refus d'offres de formation adaptées (R) et (S);
– Fin de droit à l'allocation-chômage (normalement une année après avoir quitté son dernier emploi) (R) et (S);
– Incapacité à travailler (R) et (S).

6. Définition des personnes au chômage sur laquelle les statistiques sont établies
Personnes ayant droit à toucher des indemnités: personnes qui ont cotisé auprès du service d'indemnisation de l'emploi pendant plus de six mois au cours de l'année précédant la date à laquelle elles ont quitté leur dernier emploi, et qui se trouvent au chômage, capables et désireuses de travailler.

7. Mise à jour des registres
Les registres ne sont pas mis à jour régulièrement.

8. Taux de chômage
Les statistiques basées sur les registres ne sont pas utilisées pour obtenir des taux de chômage.

9. Type de statistiques sur le nombre de chômeurs enregistrés produites
Statistiques sur le nombre de personnes enregistrées comme *bénéficiaires*.

Série 1: Rapport annuel du Service d'indemnisation de l'Emploi.
Période de référence: Mois, année.
Fréquence de production: Annuelle.
Variables utilisées:
– Sexe;
– Age;
– Profession;
– Branche d'activité;
– Caractéristiques géographiques.

Publication: Sur papier, à diffusion grand public.
Agence responsable de la publication: Ministère de la Santé, du Travail et des Affaires Sociales.
Titre et périodicité des publications: *Rapport annuel sur le Service d'indemnisation de l'Emploi.*
Série 2: Rapport mensuel du Service d'indemnisation de l'Emploi.
Période de référence: Mois.
Fréquence de production: Mensuelle.
Variables utilisées:
– Sexe;
– Age;
– Profession;
– Branche d'activité;
– Caractéristiques géographiques.

Publication: Sur papier, à diffusion grand public.
Agence responsable de la publication: Ministère de la Santé, du Travail et des Affaires Sociales.
Titre et périodicité des publications: *Rapport mensuel sur le Service d'indemnisation de l'Emploi.*

10. Information méthodologique au sujet de ces statistiques
Publication: Non diffusée, à usage interne uniquement.

11. Comparaisons avec des statistiques provenant d'autres sources
Il n'y a pas eu de comparaisons faites avec des statistiques provenant d'autres sources.

12. Principaux changements intervenus depuis le début de ces séries statistiques
Il n'y a pas eu de changement important dans la législation, dans la capacité de l'agence et/ou dans les procédures administratives susceptibles d'avoir influencé de manière significative les statistiques.

Kazakhstan

1. Séries statistiques
Titre: Chômage enregistré.
Première année disponible: 1991.

2. Organisme responsable de l'enregistrement des chômeurs ou demandeurs d'emploi
Nom de l'organisme: Services agréés de l'emploi (au niveau régional et urbain).
Type d'organisme: Organisme public relevant d'autorités nationales, régionales et locales.
Nom de l'autorité nationale: Ministère du Travail et de la Protection sociale.
Situation des bureaux chargés de l'enregistrement: Dans toutes les villes et régions du pays, un total de 202 bureaux.
Types de services fournis et/ou gérés par cet organisme:
– Assistance aux demandeurs d'emploi pour trouver du travail;
– Assistance aux demandeurs d'emploi pour créer leur propre entreprise;
– Assistance aux employeurs pour trouver de la main-d'œuvre;
– Orientation professionnelle;
– Formation liée à l'emploi;
– Autre: organisation de travaux publics en créant des places de travail temporaires destinées particulièrement aux chômeurs.

Pourcentage des demandeurs d'emploi qui cherchent un emploi au travers de cet organisme: 99%.

3. Les informations personnelles suivantes sont enregistrées:
– Nom;
– Sexe;
– Numéro de sécurité sociale (ou numéro d'identification également utilisé par d'autres organismes);
– Adresse du domicile habituel;
– Date de naissance;
– Citoyenneté;
– Niveau d'instruction/ de formation, en distinguant cinq catégories. Des liens ont été établis avec la CITE;
– Situation de travail présente et passée, en distinguant quatre catégories;
– Type de profession de l'emploi antérieur ou actuel, en distinguant neuf catégories. Des liens ont été établis avec la CITP-88 (le registre des professions du Kazakhstan est harmonisé avec la CITP-88), au niveau des groupes de base;

–   Type de profession de l'emploi recherché, avec neuf catégories. Des liens ont été établis avec la CITP-88 (le registre des professions du Kazakhstan est harmonisé avec la CITP-88), au niveau des groupes de base;
–   Nom et adresse de l'employeur ou du lieu de travail actuel ou passé;
–   Branche d'activité de l'employeur ou du lieu de travail actuel ou passé, en distinguant neuf catégories. Des liens ont été établis avec la CITI, rév.3 au niveau des catégories de tabulation;
–   Inscriptions/enregistrements antérieurs auprès de l'organisme.

4. Critères utilisés pour déterminer si une personne doit être incluse dans le registre (R) et/ou dans les statistiques de chômeurs (S):

–   Etre sans travail (R) et (S);
–   Etre à la recherche d'un travail (R) et (S);
–   Etre disponible pour travailler (R) et (S);
–   Age: Minimum: 16 ans; Maximum: 63 ans pour les hommes, 58 ans pour les femmes (R) et (S);
–   Citoyenneté (R) et (S);
–   Etre résident dans le pays (R) et (S).

5. Critères utilisés pour déterminer si une personne doit être exclue du registre (R) et/ou des statistiques de chômeurs (S):

–   Décès (R) et (S);
–   Etablissement de la personne à l'étranger (R) et (S);
–   Commencement d'un (nouveau) travail, y inclus du travail temporaire (R) et (S);
–   Commencement du service militaire (R) et (S);
–   Défaut de contact avec l'organisme/agence (R);
–   Refus de deux offres d'emploi adaptées (R);
–   Admission à toucher une pension (R) et (S);
–   Incapacité à travailler (R) et (S);
–   Autres: organisation d'un travail indépendant (R) et (S); emprisonnement (R) et (S); déménagement dans un autre district; défaut de commencer un travail ou une formation proposés (R) et (S); discontinuation, sans autorisation, de travaux ou de formation publics (R) et (S).

6. Définition des personnes au chômage sur laquelle les statistiques sont établies

Les personnes en âge de travailler qui remplissaient durant la période de référence les trois critères suivants:
(i) Etaient inoccupées (qui n'avaient pas d'occupation lucrative);
(ii) Etaient activement à la recherche de travail;
(iii) Etaient disposées à commencer un travail dans un certain laps de temps.

7. Mise à jour des registres

Les registres sont mis à jour mensuellement.

8. Taux de chômage

Les statistiques basées sur les registres sont utilisées pour obtenir des taux de chômage.

Les sources des données d'emploi qui sont partie du dénominateur des taux de chômage sont les estimations officielles et les chiffres de la population active présentés trimestriellement par l'agence des statistiques de la République du Kazakhstan.

9. Type de statistiques sur le nombre de chômeurs enregistrés produites

Série 1:
Variables utilisées:
–   Sexe;
–   Age;
–   Niveau d'instruction;
–   Profession;
–   Branche d'activité;
–   Caractéristiques géographiques;
–   Expérience professionnelle antérieure;
–   Citoyenneté (nationaux/non nationaux);
–   Durée de chômage.

Publication: Sur papier, à diffusion restreinte.
Périodicité de la publication: Mensuelle, trimestrielle.

Série 2:
Variables utilisées:
–   Sexe;
–   Age;
–   Niveau d'instruction;
–   Profession;
–   Branche d'activité;
–   Caractéristiques géographiques;

–   Expérience professionnelle antérieure;
–   Citoyenneté (nationaux/non nationaux);
–   Durée de chômage.

Publication: Sur papier, à diffusion grand public.
Périodicité de la publication: Mensuelle, trimestrielle.

10. Information méthodologique au sujet de ces statistiques
Publication:
–   Sur papier, à diffusion grand public;
–   Sur un site Internet (www.enbek.kz).

Agence responsable: Agence de Statistique de la République du Kazakhstan.

11. Comparaisons avec des statistiques provenant d'autres sources

Des comparaisons ont été faites avec des statistiques provenant des enquêtes sur la main-d'œuvre et le recensement de population.
Fréquence des comparaisons: Régulièrement lors de la publication des statistiques.
Publication de la méthodologie et/ou des résultats de la comparaison: Publiés dans les publications officielles de l'Agence des Statistiques de la République du Kazakhstan.

12. Principaux changements intervenus depuis le début de ces séries statistiques

Des changements importants dans la législation, dans la capacité de l'agence et/ou dans les procédures administratives susceptibles d'avoir influencé de manière significative les statistiques sont intervenus en 1990, 1998, 1999 (avril et novembre) et 2001; il en résulte une tendance sensible vers une diminution du nombre de chômeurs enregistrés après 1996.

Kenya

1. Séries statistiques
Titre: Chômage enregistré.
Première année disponible: 1988.

2. Organisme responsable de l'enregistrement des chômeurs ou demandeurs d'emploi
Nom de l'organisme: Bureau national de l'Emploi.
Type d'organisme: Organisme public relevant d'une autorité nationale.
Nom de l'autorité nationale: Ministère du Travail et du Développement des Ressources humaines.
Situation des bureaux chargés de l'enregistrement: Dans 41 districts sélectionnés.
Types de services fournis et/ou gérés par cet organisme:
–   Assistance aux demandeurs d'emploi pour trouver du travail;
–   Assistance aux demandeurs d'emploi pour créer leur propre entreprise;
–   Assistance aux employeurs pour trouver de la main-d'œuvre;
–   Orientation professionnelle;
–   Formation liée à l'emploi;
–   Etude de l'impact du HIV/SIDA sur le lieu de travail.

Pourcentage des demandeurs d'emploi qui cherchent un emploi au travers de cet organisme: Inconnu, mais l'enregistrement est faible puisque beaucoup de chômeurs préfèrent chercher du travail directement aux portes des entreprises.

3. Les informations personnelles suivantes sont enregistrées:
–   Nom;
–   Sexe;
–   Numéro de carte d'identité nationale (ou numéro d'identification similaire utilisé par d'autres organismes);
–   Adresse du domicile habituel;
–   Date de naissance;
–   Citoyenneté;
–   Nationalité/groupe ethnique;
–   Niveau d'instruction/ de formation, en distinguant quatre catégories. Des liens ont été établis avec la CITE;
–   Situation de travail présente et passée;
–   Type de profession de l'emploi antérieur ou actuel, en distinguant cinq catégories. Des liens ont été établis avec la CITP-88, au niveau des groupes de base;
–   Type de profession de l'emploi recherché, avec neuf catégories. Des liens ont été établis avec la CITP-88, au niveau des groupes de base;
–   Nom et adresse de l'employeur ou du lieu de travail actuel ou passé;

– Branche d'activité de l'employeur ou du lieu de travail actuel ou passé, en distinguant neuf catégories. Des liens ont été établis avec la CITI, rév.3 au niveau des classes;
– Inscriptions/enregistrements antérieurs auprès de l'organisme.

4. Critères utilisés pour déterminer si une personne doit être incluse dans le registre (R) et/ou dans les statistiques de chômeurs (S):
– Etre sans travail (R) et (S);
– Etre à la recherche d'un travail (R) et (S);
– Etre disponible pour travailler (R) et (S);
– Age: Minimum: 18 ans; Maximum: 55 ans (R) et (S);
– Citoyenneté (R) et (S);
– Etre résident dans le pays (R) et (S);
– Avoir précédemment travaillé (R) et (S).

5. Critères utilisés pour déterminer si une personne doit être exclue du registre (R) et/ou des statistiques de chômeurs (S):
– Décès (R) et (S);
– Etablissement de la personne à l'étranger (R) et (S);
– Commencement d'un (nouveau) travail (R) et (S);
– Commencement du service militaire (R) et (S);
– Entreprise d'une formation ou d'études (R) et (S);
– Défaut de contact avec l'organisme/agence (R) et (S);
– Admission à toucher une pension (R) et (S);
– Incapacité à travailler (R) et (S).

6. Définition des personnes au chômage sur laquelle les statistiques sont établies
Les personnes qui ne sont pas engagées dans un travail économiquement productif pouvant constituer leur source de revenu principale, c'est-à-dire ne disposant d'aucun revenu du fait d'être sans travail pour un certain laps de temps, et qui sont disposées à travailler et cherchent activement du travail ou attendent de retourner au travail.

7. Mise à jour des registres
Les registres sont mis à jour mensuellement.

8. Taux de chômage
Les statistiques basées sur les registres sont utilisées pour obtenir des taux de chômage.
Les sources des données d'emploi qui sont partie du dénominateur des taux de chômage sont l'enquête sur la main-d'œuvre, l'enquête auprès des établissements, le registre de sécurité sociale, des estimations officielles et le recensement de population.

Définition des personnes pourvues d'un emploi à cette fin:
Les personnes engagées dans une activité productive générant suffisamment de revenus pour faire face à leurs besoins essentiels.

9. Type de statistiques sur le nombre de chômeurs enregistrés produites
Série 1:
Période de référence: Mois.
Fréquence de production: Mensuelle.
Variables utilisées:
– Sexe;
– Age;
– Niveau d'instruction;
– Profession;
– Branche d'activité;
– Caractéristiques géographiques;
– Expérience professionnelle antérieure;
– Citoyenneté (nationaux/non nationaux);
– Durée de chômage.
Publication: Sur papier, à diffusion grand public.
Agence responsable de la publication: Département de l'Administration des Ressources Humaines, Ministère du Travail et du Développement des Ressources Humaines.
Titre et périodicité de la publication: *Rapport mensuel du département.*
Série 2:
Période de référence: Trimestre.
Fréquence de production: Trimestrielle.
Variables utilisées:
– Sexe;
– Age;
– Niveau d'instruction;
– Profession;
– Branche d'activité;
– Caractéristiques géographiques;

– Expérience professionnelle antérieure;
– Citoyenneté (nationaux/non nationaux);
– Durée de chômage.
Publication: Sur papier, à diffusion grand public.
Agence responsable de la publication: Département de l'Administration des Ressources Humaines, Ministère du Travail et du Développement des Ressources Humaines.
Titre et périodicité de la publication: *Rapport trimestriel du département.*
Série 3:
Période de référence: Année.
Fréquence de production: Annuelle.
Variables utilisées:
– Sexe;
– Age;
– Niveau d'instruction;
– Profession;
– Branche d'activité;
– Caractéristiques géographiques;
– Expérience professionnelle antérieure;
– Citoyenneté (nationaux/non nationaux);
– Durée de chômage.
Publication: Sur papier, à diffusion grand public.
Agence responsable de la publication: Département de l'Administration des Ressources Humaines, Ministère du Travail et du Développement des Ressources Humaines.
Titre et périodicité de la publication: *Rapport annuel du département.*

10. Information méthodologique au sujet de ces statistiques
Publication: Sur papier, à diffusion grand public.
Agence responsable: Département de l'Administration des Ressources Humaines, Ministère du Travail et du Développement des Ressources Humaines.

11. Comparaisons avec des statistiques provenant d'autres sources
Des comparaisons ont été faites avec des statistiques provenant de l'enquête sur la main-d'œuvre, d'autres enquêtes auprès des ménages, le recensement de population et d'agences d'emploi privées.
Fréquence des comparaisons: Régulièrement lors de la publication d'enquêtes (dernière année: 2000).
Publication de la méthodologie et/ou des résultats de la comparaison: Ils ont été publiés. Cette information sera également disponible dans le système national d'information sur l'emploi et la main-d'œuvre (NEMIS), actuellement en développement.

12. Principaux changements intervenus depuis le début de ces séries statistiques
Il n'y a pas eu de changement important dans la législation, dans la capacité de l'agence et/ou dans les procédures administratives susceptibles d'avoir influencé de manière significative les statistiques.

13. Remarques supplémentaires
Il est reconnu que la méthodologie utilisée pour obtenir les données est rudimentaire et que les chiffres obtenus pourraient par conséquent ne pas être toujours très précis.

Lesotho

1. Séries statistiques
Titre: Statistiques des demandeurs d'emploi.
Première année disponible: 1996.

2. Organisme responsable de l'enregistrement des chômeurs ou demandeurs d'emploi
Nom de l'organisme: Services nationaux de l'Emploi.
Type d'organisme: Organisme public relevant d'une autorité nationale.
Nom de l'autorité nationale: Ministère du Travail.
Situation des bureaux chargés de l'enregistrement: Bureaux du travail de districts dans tous les districts du pays.
Types de services fournis et/ou gérés par cet organisme:
– Assistance aux demandeurs d'emploi pour trouver du travail;
– Assistance aux demandeurs d'emploi pour créer leur propre entreprise;
– Assistance aux employeurs pour trouver de la main-d'œuvre;
– Orientation professionnelle;
– Autre: dissémination d'information en rapport avec l'emploi (marché du travail).

Pourcentage des demandeurs d'emploi qui cherchent un emploi au travers de cet organisme: 30%.

3. Les informations personnelles suivantes sont enregistrées:
– Nom;
– Sexe;
– Numéro de sécurité sociale (ou numéro d'identification également utilisé par d'autres organismes);
– Adresse du domicile habituel;
– Date de naissance;
– Citoyenneté;
– Niveau d'instruction/de formation, en distinguant quatre catégories. Aucun lien n'a été établi avec la CITE;
– Type de profession de l'emploi antérieur ou actuel, en distinguant huit catégories. Des liens ont été établis avec la CITP, au niveau des grands groupes;
– Type de profession de l'emploi recherché, avec huit catégories. Des liens ont été établis avec la CITP, au niveau des grands groupes;
– Inscriptions/enregistrements antérieurs auprès de l'organisme.

4. Critères utilisés pour déterminer si une personne doit être incluse dans le registre (R) et/ou dans les statistiques de chômeurs (S):
– Etre sans travail (R);
– Age: Minimum: 18 ans; Maximum: 55 ans (R);
– Citoyenneté (doit être citoyen du Lesotho) (R).

5. Critères utilisés pour déterminer si une personne doit être exclue du registre (R) et/ou des statistiques de chômeurs (S):
– Décès (R);
– Etablissement de la personne à l'étranger (R);
– Commencement d'un (nouveau) travail (R).

6. Définition des personnes au chômage sur laquelle les statistiques sont établies
Sont considérées au chômage les personnes qui n'ont aucun revenu.

7. Mise à jour des registres
Les registres sont mis à jour quotidiennement.

8. Taux de chômage
Les statistiques basées sur les registres ne sont pas utilisées pour obtenir des taux de chômage.

9. Type de statistiques sur le nombre de chômeurs enregistrés produites
Série 1: Statistiques des demandeurs d'emploi.
Période de référence: Trimestre.
Fréquence de production: Hebdomadaire.
Variables utilisées:
– Sexe;
– Age;
– Niveau d'instruction;
– Profession.
Publication: En format électronique, sur demande.
Titre et périodicité de la publication: *Rapports Trimestriels*.

10. Information méthodologique au sujet de ces statistiques
Publication: En format électronique, sur demande.
Agence responsable: Service National de l'Emploi.

11. Comparaisons avec des statistiques provenant d'autres sources
Il n'y a pas eu de comparaisons faites avec des statistiques provenant d'autres sources.

12. Principaux changements intervenus depuis le début de ces séries statistiques
Il n'y a pas eu de changement important dans la législation, dans la capacité de l'agence et/ou dans les procédures administratives susceptibles d'avoir influencé de manière significative les statistiques.

Lettonie

1. Séries statistiques
Titre: Chômage enregistré.
Première année disponible: 1992.

2. Organisme responsable de l'enregistrement des chômeurs ou demandeurs d'emploi
Nom de l'organisme: Nodarbinatibas Valsts Dienests (Service National de l'Emploi).
Type d'organisme: Organisme public relevant d'une autorité nationale.
Nom de l'autorité nationale: Ministère de Affaires sociales.

Situation des bureaux chargés de l'enregistrement: Dans toutes les régions administratives du pays.

Types de services fournis et/ou gérés par cet organisme:
– Assistance aux demandeurs d'emploi pour trouver du travail;
– Assistance aux employeurs pour trouver de la main-d'œuvre;
– Orientation professionnelle;
– Formation liée à l'emploi;
– Autres: organisation de travaux publics temporaires rémunérés; services de club d'emploi.

Pourcentage des demandeurs d'emploi qui cherchent un emploi au travers de cet organisme: 7.6%.

3. Les informations personnelles suivantes sont enregistrées:
– Nom;
– Sexe;
– Numéro de sécurité sociale (ou numéro d'identification également utilisé par d'autres organismes);
– Adresse du domicile habituel;
– Date de naissance;
– Citoyenneté;
– Nationalité/groupe ethnique;
– Niveau d'instruction/ de formation, en distinguant six catégories. Aucun lien n'a été établi avec la CITE;
– Type de profession de l'emploi antérieur ou actuel, en distinguant 10 catégories. Des liens ont été établis avec la CITP-88;
– Type de profession de l'emploi recherché, avec 10 catégories. Des liens ont été établis avec la CITP-88;
– Nom et adresse de l'employeur ou du lieu de travail actuel ou passé;
– Branche d'activité de l'employeur ou du lieu de travail actuel ou passé. Des liens ont été établis avec la CITI, rév.3 ou NACE, rév.1 au niveau des classes.

4. Critères utilisés pour déterminer si une personne doit être incluse dans le registre (R) et/ou dans les statistiques de chômeurs (S):
– Etre sans travail (R) et (S);
– Age: Minimum: 15 ans; Maximum: 60.5 ans pour les hommes; 58.5 ans pour les femmes (R) et (S);
– Etre résident dans le pays (R) et (S).

5. Critères utilisés pour déterminer si une personne doit être exclue du registre (R) et/ou des statistiques de chômeurs (S):
– Décès (R) et (S);
– Etablissement de la personne à l'étranger (R) et (S);
– Commencement d'un (nouveau) travail (R) et (S);
– Commencement du service militaire (R) et (S);
– Entreprise d'une formation ou d'études (à plein temps) (R) et (S);
– Défaut de contact avec l'organisme/agence (R) et (S);
– Refus de deux offres d'emploi adaptées (R) et (S);
– Admission à toucher une pension (âge de la retraite) (R) et (S);
– Incapacité à travailler (R) et (S);
– Autre: emprisonnement.

6. Définition des personnes au chômage sur laquelle les statistiques sont établies
Les personnes aptes à travailler, qui sont citoyennes ou résidentes permanentes de la République de Lettonie, sont à la recherche d'un travail, ne dirigent pas un commerce, sont enregistrées auprès du service national de l'emploi et qui s'y rendent au moins une fois par mois.

7. Mise à jour des registres
Les registres sont mis à jour mensuellement.

8. Taux de chômage
Les statistiques basées sur les registres sont utilisées pour obtenir des taux de chômage.
Les sources des données d'emploi qui sont partie du dénominateur des taux de chômage sont les suivantes:
– Enquête sur la main-d'œuvre;
– Enquête auprès des établissements;
– Registres de sécurité sociale;
– Estimations officielles;
– Recensement de population.

Définition des personnes pourvues d'un emploi à cette fin:
S'applique aux personnes employées aussi bien dans le secteur public que le secteur privé. Les étudiants en âge de travailler sans emploi rémunéré sont exclus. Le calcul du nombre

moyen des personnes pourvues d'un emploi est basé sur les résultats de l'enquête sur la main-d'œuvre et des informations statistiques régulières.

9. Type de statistiques sur le nombre de chômeurs enregistrés produites

Série 1:
Période de référence: Mois.
Fréquence de production: Mensuelle.
Variables utilisées:
– Sexe;
– Caractéristiques géographiques;
– Durée de chômage.
Publication: Sur un site Internet (www.nvd.gov.lv).
Agence responsable de la publication: Service de l'Emploi National.

Série 2:
Période de référence: Trimestre.
Fréquence de production: Trimestrielle.
Variables utilisées:
– Age;
– Niveau d'instruction;
– Profession;
– Caractéristiques géographiques;
– Expérience professionnelle antérieure;
– Nationalité.

Série 3:
Période de référence: Année.
Fréquence de production: Annuelle.
Publication: Sur papier, à diffusion grand public.
Agence responsable de la publication: Service National de l'Emploi.
Titre et périodicité de la publication: *Rapport annuel.*

10. Information méthodologique au sujet de ces statistiques
Publication:
– Sur papier, à diffusion grand public;
– En format électronique, sur demande;
– Sur un site Internet (www.nvd.gov.lv).
Agences responsable: Service National de l'Emploi; Bureau Central des Statistiques.

11. Comparaisons avec des statistiques provenant d'autres sources
Il n'y a pas eu de comparaisons faites avec des statistiques provenant d'autres sources.

12. Principaux changements intervenus depuis le début de ces séries statistiques
Il n'y a pas eu de changement important dans la législation, dans la capacité de l'agence et/ou dans les procédures administratives susceptibles d'avoir influencé de manière significative les statistiques.

Lituanie

1. Séries statistiques
Titre: Demandeurs d'emploi et postes vacants.
Première année disponible: 1992.

2. Organisme responsable de l'enregistrement des chômeurs ou demandeurs d'emploi
Nom de l'organisme: Lietuvos Darbo Birza (Bourse du travail lithuanienne).
Type d'organisme: Organisme public relevant d'une autorité nationale.
Nom de l'autorité nationale: Ministère de la Sécurité sociale et du Travail.
Situation des bureaux chargés de l'enregistrement: 46 bourses du travail locales dans toutes les régions du pays couvrant tous les marchés du travail locaux et toutes les localités.
Types de services fournis et/ou gérés par cet organisme:
– Assistance aux demandeurs d'emploi pour trouver du travail;
– Assistance aux demandeurs d'emploi pour créer leur propre entreprise;
– Assistance aux employeurs pour trouver de la main-d'œuvre;
– Orientation professionnelle;
– Formation liée à l'emploi;
– Paiement des indemnités de chômage;
– Autre: mesures actives concernant le marché du travail: travaux publics; travaux subventionnés; clubs d'emploi.

Pourcentage des demandeurs d'emploi qui cherchent un emploi au travers de cet organisme: 67.3%.

3. Les informations personnelles suivantes sont enregistrées:
– Nom;
– Sexe;
– Numéro de sécurité sociale (ou numéro d'identification également utilisé par d'autres organismes);
– Adresse du domicile habituel;
– Date de naissance;
– Citoyenneté;
– Niveau d'instruction/ de formation, en distinguant six catégories. Des liens ont été établis avec la CITE;
– Situation de travail présente et passée, en distinguant quatre catégories;
– Type de profession de l'emploi antérieur ou actuel, en distinguant 7200 catégories. Des liens ont été établis avec la CITP-88 au niveau des groupes de base;
– Type de profession de l'emploi recherché, avec 7200 catégories. Des liens ont été établis avec la CITP-88 au niveau des groupes de base;
– Nom et adresse de l'employeur ou du lieu de travail actuel ou passé;
– Branche d'activité de l'employeur ou du lieu de travail actuel ou passé, en distinguant 1351 catégories. Des liens ont été établis avec la CITI, rév.3 ou la NACE, rév.1 au niveau des classes;
– Inscriptions/enregistrements antérieurs auprès de l'organisme.

4. Critères utilisés pour déterminer si une personne doit être incluse dans le registre (R) et/ou dans les statistiques de chômeurs (S):
– Etre sans travail (R) et (S);
– Etre à la recherche d'un travail (R) et (S);
– Etre disponible pour travailler (R) et (S);
– Age: Minimum: 16 ans; Maximum: 61,5 pour les hommes; 57,5 pour les femmes (R) et (S);
– Etre résident dans le pays (R) et (S).

5. Critères utilisés pour déterminer si une personne doit être exclue du registre (R) et/ou des statistiques de chômeurs (S):
– Décès (R) et (S);
– Etablissement de la personne à l'étranger (R) et (S);
– Commencement d'un (nouveau) travail (R) et (S);
– Commencement du service militaire (R) et (S);
– Participation à un programme de promotion de l'emploi, à un programme de travaux publics, etc. (R) et (S);
– Entreprise d'une formation ou d'études (R) et (S);
– Défaut de contact avec l'organisme/agence (R) et (S);
– Admission à toucher une pension de retraite (R) et (S);
– Incapacité à travailler (R) et (S);
– Autre: refus de faire un plan d'emploi (R) et (S).

6. Définition des personnes au chômage sur laquelle les statistiques sont établies
Sont considérées au chômage les personnes aptes à travailler, en âge de travailler, sans emploi (à l'exception des étudiants à plein temps dans un institut de formation), à condition qu'elles soient enregistrées auprès de la bourse national du travail de leur lieu de résidence comme personnes à la recherche d'un travail et prêtes à entreprendre une formation professionnelle.

7. Mise à jour des registres
Les registres sont mis à jour lors de changements dans les données.

8. Taux de chômage
Les statistiques basées sur les registres sont utilisées pour obtenir des taux de chômage.
La source des données d'emploi qui est partie du dénominateur des taux de chômage provient des estimations officielles.

Définition des personnes pourvues d'un emploi à cette fin:
Sont considérées comme pourvues d'un emploi les personnes travaillant dans le secteur public, les coopératives, le secteur privé et les personnes travaillant à leur compte, y compris: les employés en congé de maternité ou en congé parental, le personnel militaire, les employés en congé non payé prolongé, des travailleurs à temps partiel sur une base d'équivalence plein temps, les personnes ayant dépassé les limites d'âge (de 16 à 57,5 ans pour les femmes et de 16 à 61,5 ans pour les hommes) et qui continuent à tenir un emploi rémunéré.

9. Type de statistiques sur le nombre de chômeurs enregistrés produites

Série 1:
Période de référence: Mois.
Fréquence de production: Mensuelle.
Variables utilisées:
– Sexe;
– Age;
– Caractéristiques géographiques.
Publication:
– Sur papier, à diffusion grand public;
– En format électronique, sur demande;
– Sur un site Internet (www.ldb.lt).
Agence responsable de la publication: Statistiques de Lituanie.
Titre et périodicité de la publication: *Economic and social development in Lithuania* (Développement économique et social en Lituanie), mensuel.
Série 2:
Période de référence: Trimestre.
Fréquence de production: Trimestrielle.
Variables utilisées:
– Sexe;
– Age;
– Caractéristiques géographiques;
– Expérience professionnelle antérieure;
– Durée du chômage.
Publication:
– Sur papier, à diffusion grand public;
– En format électronique, sur demande;
– Sur un site Internet (www.ldb.lt).
Agence responsable de la publication: Statistiques de Lituanie.
Titre et périodicité de la publication: *Labour market and employment of population - Statistical Bulletin* (Marché du travail et emploi de la population - Bulletin statistique).
10. Information méthodologique au sujet de ces statistiques
Publication: Sur papier, à diffusion grand public.
Agence responsable: Ministère de la Sécurité Sociale et du Travail.
11. Comparaisons avec des statistiques provenant d'autres sources
Des comparaisons ont été faites avec des statistiques provenant de l'enquête sur la main-d'œuvre.
Fréquence des comparaisons: Régulièrement lors de la publication des statistiques.
Publication de la méthodologie et/ou des résultats de la comparaison: Publiés dans *Labour force, employment and unemployment (LFS data, Biannual Bulletin of Statistics Lithuania)* (Main-d'œuvre, emploi et chômage (Enquête de main-d'œuvre, données, bulletin bisannuel de Statistiques de Lituanie)).
12. Principaux changements intervenus depuis le début de ces séries statistiques
Des changements importants dans la législation, dans la capacité de l'agence et/ou dans les procédures administratives susceptibles d'avoir influencé de manière significative les statistiques sont intervenus en 1996, 2000 et 2001. Les changements dans les statistiques qui en résultent n'ont pas été évalués.

Luxembourg

1. Séries statistiques
Titre: Situation de l'emploi: données mensuelles (depuis 1982), et Bulletin luxembourgeois de l'emploi (depuis 1998).
2. Organisme responsable de l'enregistrement des chômeurs ou demandeurs d'emploi
Nom de l'organisme: Administration de l'Emploi (ADEM)
Type d'organisme: Organisme public relevant d'une autorité nationale.
Nom de l'autorité nationale: Ministère du Travail et de l'Emploi.
Situation des bureaux chargés de l'enregistrement: Luxembourg, Esch/Alzeth, Diekirsch, Wiltz.
Types de services fournis et/ou gérés par cet organisme:
– Assistance aux demandeurs d'emploi pour trouver du travail;
– Assistance aux employeurs pour trouver de la main-d'œuvre;
– Orientation professionnelle;
– Formation liée à l'emploi en collaboration avec les employeurs et le Service de la formation professionnelle du Ministère de l'Education nationale;

– Paiement des indemnités de chômage;
– Autres services liés à l'emploi: paiement des différentes aides et primes en faveur du maintien de l'emploi et de l'insertion ou de la réinsertion des chômeurs dans la vie active ; service des travailleurs handicapés.
3. Les informations personnelles suivantes sont enregistrées:
– Nom;
– Sexe;
– Numéro de sécurité sociale (ou numéro d'identification également utilisé par d'autres organismes);
– Adresse du domicile habituel;
– Date de naissance;
– Citoyenneté;
– Nationalité/groupe ethnique;
– Niveau d'instruction/de formation, en distinguant quatre catégories. Aucun lien n'a été établi avec la CITE;
– Type de profession de l'emploi recherché, en distinguant 12 catégories. Des liens ont été établis avec la CITP-68 (proche du système belge);
– Nom et adresse de l'employeur ou du lieu de travail actuel ou passé;
– Branche d'activité de l'employeur ou du lieu de travail actuel ou passé, en distinguant cinq catégories. Des liens ont été établis avec la NACE, rév. 1;
– Inscriptions/enregistrements antérieurs auprès de l'organisme;
– Autre: information concernant la mobilité professionnelle et la mobilité géographique.
4. Critères utilisés pour déterminer si une personne doit être incluse dans le registre (R) et/ou dans les statistiques de chômeurs (S):
– Etre sans travail (S);
– Etre à la recherche d'un travail (R) et (S);
– Etre disponible pour travailler (R) et (S);
– Age: Minimum: 16 ans; Maximum: 65 ans (R) et (S);
– Citoyenneté: être originaire d'un Etat membre de l'Union Européenne (R) et (S);
– Etre résident dans le pays: posséder une adresse officielle au Luxembourg (R).
5. Critères utilisés pour déterminer si une personne doit être exclue du registre (R) et/ou des statistiques de chômeurs (S):
– Avis de décès (R) et (S);
– Etablissement de la personne à l'étranger (S);
– Commencement d'un (nouveau) travail (S);
– Participation à un programme de promotion de l'emploi, à un programme de travaux publics, etc. (S);
– Entreprise d'une formation ou d'études: participation à une formation organisée en collaboration avec le Ministère de l'Education Nationale;
– Défaut de contact avec l'organisme/agence: En principe les demandeurs d'emploi doivent se présenter auprès du Service pour l'emploi (SPE) au moins une fois tous les quinze jours (R) et (S);
– Refus d'offres d'emploi adaptées (après un refus) (R) et (S);
– Refus d'offres de formation adaptées (après un refus) (R) et (S);
– Admission à toucher une pension (retraite, etc.) (R) et (S);
– Incapacité à travailler (R) et (S).
6. Définition des personnes au chômage sur laquelle les statistiques sont établies
Est considérée comme chômeur toute personne sans emploi, disponible sur le marché du travail, à la recherche d'un emploi approprié, ne bénéficiant pas d'une mesure pour l'emploi, indemnisée ou non indemnisée et ayant respecté les obligations à suivre prescrites par l'ADEM.
7. Mise à jour des registres
Les registres sont mis à jour tous les mois.
8. Taux de chômage
Les statistiques basées sur les registres sont utilisées pour obtenir des taux de chômage.
Les calculs sont réalisés par le STATEC (Service Central de la Statistique et des Etudes Economiques), sur la base des sources suivantes:
– Registres de sécurité sociale;
– Estimations officielles;
– Recensement de population.
Définition des personnes pourvues d'un emploi à cette fin:

L'emploi national pris en compte est composé de l'emploi intérieur (salariés et non salariés); sont exclus les travailleurs frontaliers étrangers travaillant au Luxembourg, les frontaliers luxembourgeois travaillant à l'étranger et les fonctionnaires internationaux.

9. Type de statistiques sur le nombre de chômeurs enregistrés produites
Série 1:
Période de référence: Mois.
Fréquence de production: Mensuelle.
Variables utilisées:
– Sexe;
– Age;
– Niveau d'instruction;
– Profession;
– Durée de chômage;
– Chômeurs bénéficiant de l'indemnité de chômage;
– Emploi recherché.
Publication:
– Sur papier, à diffusion grand public;
– Sur un site Internet: www.etat.lu
Agence responsable de la publication: ADEM.
Titre de la publication: *Bulletin luxembourgeois de l'Emploi.*
Série 2:
Période de référence: Mois.
Fréquence de production: Annuelle.
Variables utilisées:
– Sexe;
– Age;
– Niveau d'instruction;
– Profession;
– Caractéristiques géographiques;
– Citoyenneté (nationaux/non nationaux);
– Durée de chômage;
– Chômeurs bénéficiant de l'indemnité de chômage;
– Emploi recherché.
Publication: Sur papier, à diffusion restreinte.
Organisme/Agence responsable de la publication: ADEM
Titre de la publication: *Bulletin luxembourgeois de l'Emploi.*
10. Information méthodologique au sujet de ces statistiques
– Non diffusée, disponible à usage interne uniquement.
Agence responsable: ADEM
11. Comparaisons avec des statistiques provenant d'autres sources
Il n'y a pas eu de comparaisons faites avec des statistiques provenant d'autres sources.
12. Principaux changements intervenus depuis le début de ces séries statistiques
Des changements importants dans la législation sont intervenus en 1998. Depuis 1998, les demandeurs d'emploi bénéficiant d'une mesure en faveur de l'emploi ne figurent plus dans les statistiques des chômeurs. Les «personnes bénéficiant d'une mesure pour l'emploi» représentent entre 24% (en 1998) et 31% (en 2001) de la population totale (demandeurs d'emploi plus personnes bénéficiant d'une mesure pour l'emploi) gérée par L'ADEM.

Macédoine, Ex-Rép. yougoslave de

1. Séries statistiques
Titre: Bulletin administratif du travail, du chômage, des bénéficiaires d'allocation chômage.
2. Organisme responsable de l'enregistrement des chômeurs ou demandeurs d'emploi
Nom de l'organisme: Bureau d'Emploi de la République de Macédoine (Zavon zavrabotuvanje na republika makedonija).
Type d'organisme: Organisme public relevant d'une autorité nationale.
Nom de l'autorité nationale: Ministère du Travail et de la Politique sociale.
Situation des bureaux chargés de l'enregistrement: Dans l'ensemble du pays (30 bureaux régionaux du travail dans 30 villes).
Types de services fournis et/ou gérés par cet organisme:
– Assistance aux demandeurs d'emploi pour trouver du travail;
– Assistance aux demandeurs d'emploi pour créer leur propre entreprise;
– Assistance aux employeurs pour trouver de la main-d'œuvre;

– Orientation professionnelle;
– Formation liée à l'emploi;
– Paiement des indemnités de chômage.
Pourcentage des demandeurs d'emploi qui cherchent un emploi au travers de cet organisme: 32,2%
3. Les informations personnelles suivantes sont enregistrées:
– Nom;
– Sexe;
– Numéro de sécurité sociale (ou numéro d'identification également utilisé par d'autres organismes);
– Adresse du domicile habituel;
– Date de naissance;
– Citoyenneté;
– Nationalité/groupe ethnique;
– Niveau d'instruction/de formation, en distinguant huit catégories. Aucun lien n'a été établi avec la CITE;
– Situation de travail présente et passée, en distinguant 40 catégories;
– Type de profession de l'emploi antérieur et/ou actuel, en distinguant 1709 catégories. Aucun lien n'a été établi avec la CITP;
– Type de profession de l'emploi recherché, avec 1709 catégories;
– Nom et adresse de l'employeur ou du lieu de travail actuel ou passé;
– Branche d'activité de l'employeur ou du lieu de travail actuel ou passé, en distinguant 602 catégories. Des liens ont été établis avec la CITI, au niveau des classes;
– Inscriptions/enregistrements antérieurs auprès de l'organisme.
4. Critères utilisés pour déterminer si une personne doit être incluse dans le registre (R) et/ou dans les statistiques de chômeurs (S):
– Etre sans travail (R) et (S);
– Etre à la recherche d'un travail, se présenter régulièrement aux convocations du bureau, participer au programme de promotion de l'emploi (R) et (S);
– Etre disponible pour travailler (R) et (S);
– Age: Minimum: 15 ans; Maximum: 65 ans (R) et (S);
– Citoyenneté (R) et (S);
– Etre résident dans le pays (R) et (S).
5. Critères utilisés pour déterminer si une personne doit être exclue du registre (R) et/ou des statistiques de chômeurs (S):
– Avis de décès (R) et (S);
– Etablissement de la personne à l'étranger (R) et (S);
– Commencement d'un (nouveau) travail (R) et (S);
– Commencement du service militaire (R) et (S);
– Entreprise d'une formation ou d'études (R) et (S);
– Défaut de contact avec l'organisme/agence (R) et (S);
– Refus d'offres d'emploi adaptées, après deux refus (R) et (S);
– Refus d'offres de formation adaptées, après deux refus (R) et (S);
– Admission à toucher une pension (retraite, etc.) (R) et (S);
– Incapacité à travailler (R) et (S).
6. Définition des personnes au chômage sur laquelle les statistiques sont établies
Une personne au chômage est une personne inscrite sur le registre du chômage, qui est capable de travailler, souhaite travailler, et recherche activement du travail. Est considérée comme recherchant activement du travail une personne qui s'est régulièrement inscrite auprès de l'organisme dont elle relève, dans les délais conformes à la Loi du travail.
7. Mise à jour des registres
Les registres sont mis à jour régulièrement, tous les mois pour les bénéficiaires d'allocations chômage, tous les trois mois pour les bénéficiaires d'assurance médicale, et tous les six mois pour les autres.
8. Taux de chômage
Les statistiques basées sur les registres sont utilisées pour obtenir des taux de chômage.
9. Type de statistiques sur le nombre de chômeurs enregistrés produites
Période de référence: Mois, semestre, année.
Fréquence de production: Mensuelle, semestrielle, annuelle.
Variables utilisées:
– Sexe;
– Age;

–   Niveau d'instruction;
–   Profession;
–   Branche d'activité;
–   Caractéristiques géographiques;
–   Expérience professionnelle antérieure;
–   Citoyenneté (nationaux/non nationaux);
–   Durée de chômage.

Publication:

–   Sur papier, à diffusion grand public;
–   En format électronique, sur demande;
–   Sur un site Internet: http://www.zvrm.gov.mk

Organisme responsable de la publication: Bureau d'Emploi de la République de Macédoine.

10. Information méthodologique au sujet de ces statistiques
Publication:

–   Sur papier, à diffusion grand public;
–   En format électronique, sur demande;
–   Sur un site Internet: http://www.zvrm.gov.mk

Organisme responsable: Ministère du Travail, Bureau d'emploi de la République de Macédoine, Institut de statistiques.

11. Comparaisons avec des statistiques provenant d'autres sources

Il n'y a pas eu de comparaisons faites avec des statistiques provenant d'autres sources.

12. Principaux changements intervenus depuis le début de ces séries statistiques

Il n'y a pas eu de changement important dans la législation, dans la capacité de l'agence et/ou dans les procédures administratives susceptibles d'avoir influencé de manière significative les statistiques.

Madagascar

1. Séries statistiques
Titre: Statistiques du marché du travail.
Première année disponible: 1979
2. Organisme responsable de l'enregistrement des chômeurs ou demandeurs d'emploi
Nom de l'organisme: Service des études, de la statistique et de la planification.
Type d'organisme: Organisme public relevant d'une autorité nationale.
Nom de l'autorité nationale: Direction de l'Emploi.
Situation des bureaux chargés de l'enregistrement: Dans certaines régions uniquement, neuf sous-préfectures sur les 111 existantes.
Types de services fournis et/ou gérés par cet organisme:

–   Assistance aux demandeurs d'emploi pour trouver du travail;
–   Assistance aux employeurs pour trouver de la main-d'œuvre;
–   Autres services liés à l'emploi: délivrance d'attestations de chômage.

Pourcentage des demandeurs d'emploi qui cherchent un emploi au travers de cet organisme: 5,6%
3. Les informations personnelles suivantes sont enregistrées:

–   Nom;
–   Sexe;
–   Adresse du domicile habituel;
–   Date de naissance;
–   Nationalité;
–   Niveau d'instruction/de formation, en distinguant neuf catégories. Aucun lien n'a été établi avec la CITE;
–   Situation de travail présente et passée, en distinguant deux catégories;
–   Type de profession de l'emploi antérieur et/ou actuel. Aucun lien n'a été établi avec la CITP-88;
–   Type de profession de l'emploi recherché;
–   Nom et adresse de l'employeur ou du lieu de travail actuel ou passé;
–   Branche d'activité de l'employeur ou du lieu de travail actuel ou passé;
–   Inscriptions/enregistrements antérieurs auprès de l'organisme.

4. Critères utilisés pour déterminer si une personne doit être incluse dans le registre (R) et/ou dans les statistiques de chômeurs (S):

–   Etre sans travail (R);

–   Etre à la recherche d'un travail (R);
–   Etre disponible pour travailler (R);
–   Age: Minimum: 15 ans, Maximum:40 ans, qui est l'âge maximum pour entrer dans la fonction publique (R);
–   Etre résident dans le pays (R);
–   Avoir précédemment travaillé (R).

5. Critères utilisés pour déterminer si une personne doit être exclue du registre (R) et/ou des statistiques de chômeurs (S):
Information non disponible.

6. Définition des personnes au chômage sur laquelle les statistiques sont établies

Globalement, toute personne qui s'inscrit au service de placement est considérée comme «chômeur» si elle est disponible pour travailler.

7. Mise à jour des registres
Les registres sont mis à jour tous les mois.

8. Taux de chômage
Les statistiques basées sur les registres ne sont pas utilisées pour obtenir des taux de chômage.

9. Type de statistiques produites sur le nombre de chômeurs enregistrés
Période de référence: Annuelle.
Fréquence de production: Annuelle
Variables utilisées:

–   Sexe;
–   Niveau d'instruction;
–   Caractéristiques géographiques;
–   Expérience professionnelle antérieure;
–   Citoyenneté (nationaux).

Publication: Sur papier, à diffusion restreinte.
10. Information méthodologique au sujet de ces statistiques
Publication: Sur papier, à diffusion restreinte.
11. Comparaisons avec des statistiques provenant d'autres sources

Il n'y a pas eu de comparaisons faites avec des statistiques provenant d'autres sources.

12. Principaux changements intervenus depuis le début de ces séries statistiques

Il n'y a pas eu de changement important dans la législation, dans la capacité de l'agence et/ou dans les procédures administratives susceptibles d'avoir influencé de manière significative les statistiques.

Malaisie

1. Séries statistiques
Titre: Chômage enregistré.

Première année disponible: 1969.
2. Organisme responsable de l'enregistrement des chômeurs ou demandeurs d'emploi
Nom de l'organisme: JabatanTenaga Rakyat (Département de la Main-d'œuvre)
Type d'organisme: Organisme public relevant d'une autorité nationale.
Nom de l'autorité nationale: Ministère des Ressources Humaines (MOHR).
Situation des bureaux chargés de l'enregistrement: Dans toutes les parties du pays avec un total de 13 bureaux nationaux et 36 bureaux de districts.
Types de services fournis et/ou gérés par cet organisme:

–   Assistance aux demandeurs d'emploi pour trouver du travail;
–   Assistance aux employeurs pour trouver de la main-d'œuvre;
–   Orientation professionnelle;
–   Formation liée à l'emploi;
–   Autre: délivrer des licences aux agences d'emploi privées et superviser leurs opérations en accord avec la loi sur les agences d'emploi privées de 1981.

Pourcentage des demandeurs d'emploi qui cherchent un emploi au travers de cet organisme: 20%.
3. Les informations personnelles suivantes sont enregistrées:

–   Nom;
–   Sexe;
–   Numéro de sécurité sociale (ou numéro d'identification également utilisé par d'autres organismes);
–   Adresse du domicile habituel;

- Date de naissance;
- Citoyenneté;
- Nationalité/groupe ethnique;
- Niveau d'instruction/ de formation, en distinguant quatre catégories. Des liens ont été établis avec la CITE;
- Situation de travail présente et passée, en distinguant trois catégories;
- Type de profession de l'emploi antérieur ou actuel, en distinguant sept catégories. Des liens ont été établis avec la CITP-88 au niveau des grands groupes;
- Type de profession de l'emploi recherché, avec sept catégories. Des liens ont été établis avec la CITP-88 au niveau des grands groupes;
- Nom et adresse de l'employeur ou du lieu de travail actuel ou passé;
- Branche d'activité de l'employeur ou du lieu de travail actuel ou passé, en distinguant 17 catégories. Des liens ont été établis avec la CITI, rév.3 au niveau des catégories de classement.

4. Critères utilisés pour déterminer si une personne doit être incluse dans le registre (R) et/ou dans les statistiques de chômeurs (S):
- Etre sans travail (R) et (S);
- Etre à la recherche d'un travail (R) et (S);
- Age: Minimum: 15 ans; Maximum: 64 ans (R) et (S);
- Citoyenneté (R) et (S);
- Etre résident dans le pays (R) et (S).

5. Critères utilisés pour déterminer si une personne doit être exclue du registre (R) et/ou des statistiques de chômeurs (S):
- Décès (S);
- Etablissement de la personne à l'étranger (S);
- Commencement d'un (nouveau) travail (R) et (S);
- Commencement du service militaire (R) et (S);
- Participation à un programme de promotion de l'emploi, à un programme de travaux publics, etc. (R) et (S);
- Entreprise d'une formation ou d'études (R) et (S);
- Défaut de contact avec l'organisme/agence (l'enregistrement doit être renouvelé tous les trois mois) (R) et (S).

6. Définition des personnes au chômage sur laquelle les statistiques sont établies

Sont inclues les personnes au chômage aussi bien actives qu' inactives. Les <u>personnes au chômage actives</u> comprennent toutes les personnes qui n'avaient pas travaillé durant la semaine de référence, mais qui étaient disponibles pour travailler et avaient activement recherché un travail durant la semaine de référence. Les <u>personnes au chômages inactives</u> comprennent les catégories suivantes:
(i) les personnes qui n'avaient pas recherché du travail parce qu'elles pensaient qu'il n'y avait pas de travail disponible ou qu'elles n'étaient pas qualifiées;
(ii) les personnes qui auraient recherché du travail si elles n'avaient pas été temporairement malades ou à cause du mauvais temps;
(iii) les personnes qui attendaient une réponse suite à une demande d'emploi;
(iv) les personnes qui avaient recherché du travail avant la semaine de référence.

7. Mise à jour des registres
Les registres sont mis à jour chaque semaine.

8. Taux de chômage
Les statistiques basées sur les registres ne sont pas utilisées pour obtenir des taux de chômage.

9. Type de statistiques sur le nombre de chômeurs enregistrés produites
Série 1:
Période de référence: Semaine.
Fréquence de production: Hebdomadaire.
Variables utilisées:
- Sexe;
- Age;
- Niveau d'instruction;
- Profession;
- Branche d'activité;
- Caractéristiques géographiques;
- Expérience professionnelle antérieure;
- Citoyenneté (nationaux/non nationaux);
- Durée de chômage.
Publication: Sur papier, à diffusion restreinte.

Agence responsable de la publication: MOHR, département de la main-d'œuvre.
Série 2:
Période de référence: Mois.
Fréquence de production: Mensuelle.
Variables utilisées:
- Sexe;
- Age;
- Niveau d'instruction;
- Profession;
- Branche d'activité;
- Caractéristiques géographiques;
- Expérience professionnelle antérieure;
- Citoyenneté (nationaux/non nationaux);
- Durée de chômage.
Publication:
- Sur papier, à diffusion grand public;
- Sur un site Internet (www.mohr.gov.my et www.jtr.gov.my).
Agence responsable de la publication: MOHR, département de la main-d'œuvre.
Titre de la publication: *Registration of Job Seekers, Job Vacancies and Placements* (enregistrement des personnes à la recherche d'un emploi, vacances de poste et placements).
Série 3:
Période de référence: Trimestre.
Fréquence de production: Trimestrielle.
Variables utilisées:
- Sexe;
- Age;
- Niveau d'instruction;
- Profession;
- Branche d'activité;
- Caractéristiques géographiques;
- Expérience professionnelle antérieure;
- Citoyenneté (nationaux/non nationaux);
- Durée du chômage.
Publication:
- Sur papier, à diffusion grand public;
- Sur un site Internet (www.mohr.gov.my et www.jtr.gov.my).
Agence responsable de la publication: MOHR, Département de la Main-d'œuvre.
Titre de la publication: *Labour Market Trends* (tendances du marché du travail).

10. Information méthodologique au sujet de ces statistiques
Publication: Pas publiée, disponible pour usage interne seulement.
Agence responsable: MOHR, Département de la Main-d'œuvre.

11. Comparaisons avec des statistiques provenant d'autres sources

Des comparaisons ont été faites avec des statistiques provenant du recensement de population et du rapport économique.
Fréquence des comparaisons: Régulièrement lors de la publication des statistiques.
Publication de la méthodologie et/ou des résultats de la comparaison: Ils n'ont pas été publiés.

12. Principaux changements intervenus depuis le début de ces séries statistiques

Il n'y a pas eu de changement important dans la législation, dans la capacité de l'agence et/ou dans les procédures administratives susceptibles d'avoir influencé de manière significative les statistiques.

Mali

1. Séries statistiques
Titre: Annuaire statistique du marché de l'emploi.
Première année disponible: 1995
2. Organisme responsable de l'enregistrement des chômeurs ou demandeurs d'emploi
Nom de l'organisme:
1. Agence nationale pour l'emploi (ANPE).
2. Bureaux privés de placement (BPP).
Type d'organisme:
1. Organisme public relevant d'une autorité nationale.
2. Organisme privé à but lucratif.
Nom de l'autorité nationale: Ministère de l'Emploi et de la Formation professionnelle.

Situation des bureaux chargés de l'enregistrement: Dans l'ensemble du pays.

Types de services fournis et/ou gérés par cet organisme:

- Assistance aux demandeurs d'emploi pour trouver du travail;
- Assistance aux demandeurs d'emploi pour créer leur propre entreprise;
- Assistance aux employeurs pour trouver de la main-d'œuvre;
- Orientation professionnelle;
- Formation liée à l'emploi;
- Autres services liés à l'emploi: information sur le marché du travail.

Pourcentage des demandeurs d'emploi qui cherchent un emploi au travers de cet organisme: 20%

3. Les informations personnelles suivantes sont enregistrées:

- Nom;
- Sexe;
- Adresse du domicile habituel;
- Date de naissance;
- Nationalité;
- Niveau d'instruction/de formation, en distinguant huit catégories. Aucun lien n'a été établi avec la CITE;
- Type de profession de l'emploi antérieur et/ou actuel, en distinguant huit catégories. Des liens ont été établis avec la CITP;
- Type de profession de l'emploi recherché, avec huit catégories;
- Nom et adresse de l'employeur ou du lieu de travail actuel ou passé;
- Branche d'activité de l'employeur ou du lieu de travail actuel ou passé, en distinguant neuf catégories. Des liens ont été établis avec la CITI;
- Inscriptions/enregistrements antérieurs auprès de l'organisme.

4. Critères utilisés pour déterminer si une personne doit être incluse dans le registre (R) et/ou dans les statistiques de chômeurs (S):

- Etre sans travail (R) et (S);
- Etre à la recherche d'un travail (R) et (S);
- Etre disponible pour travailler (R) et (S);
- Age: Minimum: 15 ans; pas de limite supérieure (R) et (S).

5. Critères utilisés pour déterminer si une personne doit être exclue du registre (R) et/ou des statistiques de chômeurs (S):

- Avis de décès (R) et (S);
- Etablissement de la personne à l'étranger (R) et (S);
- Commencement d'un (nouveau) travail (R) et (S);
- Commencement du service militaire (R) et (S);
- Entreprise d'une formation ou d'études, uniquement pour des formations de longue durée (six mois et plus) (R) et (S);
- Défaut de contact avec l'organisme/agence, après trois mois sans contact (R) et (S);
- Incapacité à travailler (R) et (S).

6. Définition des personnes au chômage sur laquelle les statistiques sont établies

Toute personne ayant l'âge légal pour travailler (15 ans et plus), qui au cours de la période de référence (généralement un mois), était:

- sans travail;
- disponible pour travailler;
- à la recherche active d'un emploi.

7. Mise à jour des registres

Les registres sont mis à jour tous les mois.

8. Taux de chômage

Les statistiques basées sur les registres ne sont pas utilisées pour obtenir des taux de chômage.

9. Type de statistiques produites sur le nombre de chômeurs enregistrés

Période de référence: Mois.

Fréquence de production: Annuelle.

Variables utilisées:

- Sexe;
- Age;
- Niveau d'instruction;
- Profession;
- Branche d'activité;

- Caractéristiques géographiques;
- Expérience professionnelle antérieure;
- Citoyenneté (nationaux/non nationaux);
- Durée de chômage.

Publication:

- Sur papier, à diffusion grand public;
- En format électronique, sur demande.

Organisme responsable de la publication: Observatoire de l'Emploi et de la Formation (OEF).

Titre et périodicité de la publication: *Annuaire statistique du marché de l'emploi*, publication annuelle.

10. Information méthodologique au sujet de ces statistiques

Publication:

- Sur papier, à diffusion grand public;
- En format électronique, sur demande.

Organisme responsable: OEF.

11. Comparaisons avec des statistiques provenant d'autres sources

Des comparaisons ont été faites avec des statistiques provenant de l'enquête de main-d'œuvre, avec des statistiques d'autres enquêtes auprès des ménages, et avec des statistiques du recensement de population.

Fréquence des comparaisons: Occasionnelle.

Publication de la méthodologie et/ou des résultats de la comparaison: Ils n'ont pas été publiés.

12. Principaux changements intervenus depuis le début de ces séries statistiques

Des changements importants dans la législation et dans les procédures administratives sont intervenus en 2000, date de la création de L'ANPE en lieu et place de l'Office National de la Main-d'œuvre et de l'Emploi. Il n'y a pas eu d'évaluation de l'augmentation ou de la diminution du nombre total de chômeurs inscrits induite par ce changement.

Malte

1. Séries statistiques

Titre: Chômage enregistré.

Première année disponible: 1957.

2. Organisme responsable de l'enregistrement des chômeurs ou demandeurs d'emploi

Nom de l'organisme: Employment and Training Corporation - ETC (Conseil de l'emploi et de la formation).

Type d'organisme: Organisme public relevant d'autorités locales.

Situation des bureaux chargés de l'enregistrement: Le premier enregistrement se fait au bureau principal de ETC à Hal Far; les enregistrements hebdomadaires suivants sont effectués dans l'un des 20 bureaux locaux régionaux.

Types de services fournis et/ou gérés par cet organisme:

- Assistance aux demandeurs d'emploi pour trouver du travail;
- Assistance aux demandeurs d'emploi pour créer leur propre entreprise;
- Assistance aux employeurs pour trouver de la main-d'œuvre;
- Orientation professionnelle;
- Formation liée à l'emploi;
- Autres: administration de bourses de formation; information sur le marché du travail;
- centres de vacances de poste dans trois régions.

Pourcentage des demandeurs d'emploi qui cherchent un emploi au travers de cet organisme: 73% (selon les estimations de l'enquête sur la main-d'œuvre).

3. Les informations personnelles suivantes sont enregistrées:

- Nom;
- Sexe;
- Numéro de sécurité sociale (ou numéro d'identification également utilisé par d'autres organismes);
- Adresse du domicile habituel;
- Date de naissance;
- Citoyenneté;
- Nationalité/groupe ethnique;
- Niveau d'instruction/ de formation. Des liens n'ont pas été établis avec la CITE;
- Situation de travail présente et passée, en distinguant trois catégories;
- Type de profession de l'emploi antérieur ou actuel. Des liens ont été établis avec la CITP-88 (sous-grands

groupes);
- Type de profession de l'emploi recherché, avec 476 catégories; Des liens ont été établis avec la CITP-88;
- Nom et adresse de l'employeur ou du lieu de travail actuel ou passé;
- Branche d'activité de l'employeur ou du lieu de travail actuel ou passé, en distinguant 83 catégories. Des liens ont été établis avec la CITI, rév.3 au niveau des groupes;
- Inscriptions/enregistrements antérieurs auprès de l'organisme;
- Autres: enregistrement jusqu'à cinq options; genre d'incapacité (s'il y en a).

4. Critères utilisés pour déterminer si une personne doit être incluse dans le registre (R) et/ou dans les statistiques de chômeurs (S):
- Etre sans travail (R) et (S);
- Etre à la recherche d'un travail (R) et(S);
- Etre disponible pour travailler (R) et (S);
- Age: Minimum: 16 ans (R); 15 ans (S); il n'y a pas d'âge maximum;
- Citoyenneté (nationaux de Malte seulement) (R);
- Etre résident dans le pays (R);
- Avoir précédemment travaillé (R).

5. Critères utilisés pour déterminer si une personne doit être exclue du registre (R) et/ou des statistiques de chômeurs (S):
- Décès (R) et (S);
- Etablissement de la personne à l'étranger (R) et (S);
- Commencement d'un (nouveau) travail (R) et (S);
- Participation à un programme de promotion de l'emploi, à un programme de travaux publics, etc. (R) et (S);
- Entreprise d'une formation ou d'études (R) et (S);
- Défaut de contact avec l'organisme/agence (R);
- Refus d'offres d'emploi adaptées (R);
- Refus d'offres de formation adaptées (R);
- Admission à toucher une pension (R);
- Incapacité à travailler (R) et (S);
- Autre: si cette personne est surprise par les inspecteurs à travailler dans le secteur informel (R).

6. Définition des personnes au chômage sur laquelle les statistiques sont établies
(Critères pour inscription selon la partie 1 du registre de chômage):
Tous les citoyens de Malte âgés de 16 ans ou plus qui:
- ont été licenciés de leurs emplois précédents: ou
- viennent de terminer l'école (enregistrés pour la première fois); ou
- qui tombent sous la partie II du registre, pour une des raisons suivantes, après avoir purgé leur période de pénalité de six mois. Ces raisons peuvent être: qu'ils avaient été licenciés pour des raisons disciplinaires; qu'ils avaient quitté leur emploi de leur propre volonté; qu'ils avaient refusé, sans donner de raison valable, des opportunités de travail/de formation qui leur avaient été proposées par le préposé du bureau de placement alors qu'ils étaient enregistrés sous la partie I; qu'ils avaient été biffés du registre après avoir été surpris à travailler dans le secteur informel lors d'une inspection de personnel chargé de l'application de la loi; qu'ils n'avaient pas été en mesure de présenter les documents nécessaires pour l'enregistrement sous la partie I (mesure temporaire).

7. Mise à jour des registres
Les registres sont mis à jour journellement et toutes les semaines.

8. Taux de chômage
Les statistiques basées sur les registres ont été utilisées pour obtenir des taux de chômage jusqu'en août 2001 (depuis, les taux de chômage sont basés sur l'enquête sur la main-d'œuvre).
La source des données d'emploi qui est partie du dénominateur des taux de chômage et la base de données des personnes pourvues d'un emploi, est basée elle même sur les formulaires d'engagement.

9. Type de statistiques sur le nombre de chômeurs enregistrés produites
Série 1:
Période de référence: Mois.
Fréquence de production: Mensuelle.
Variables utilisées:
- Sexe;
- Age;

- Niveau d'instruction;
- Profession;
- Branche d'activité;
- Caractéristiques géographiques;
- Expérience professionnelle antérieure;
- Durée de chômage.

Publication:
- Sur papier, à diffusion grand public;
- Sur un site Internet (www.nso.gov.mt).
Agence responsable de la publication: Bureau National des Statistiques.
Titre et périodicité des publications: *News Release* (publication d'informations), mensuel; *Abstract of Statistics* (abrégé de statistiques), annuel.

10. Information méthodologique au sujet de ces statistiques Publication:
- Sur papier, à diffusion grand public;
- Sur un site Internet (www.nso.gov.mt).
Organisme responsable: Conseil de l'emploi et de la formation.

11. Comparaisons avec des statistiques provenant d'autres sources
Des comparaisons ont été faites avec des statistiques provenant de l'enquête sur la main-d'œuvre et le recensement de population.
Fréquence des comparaisons: Occasionnellement (dernièrement en décembre 2000).
Publication de la méthodologie et/ou des résultats de la comparaison: Ils n'ont pas été publiés.

12. Principaux changements intervenus depuis le début de ces séries statistiques
Il n'y a pas eu de changement important dans la législation, dans la capacité de l'agence et/ou dans les procédures administratives susceptibles d'avoir influencé de manière significative les statistiques.

Maroc

1. Séries statistiques
Titre: Nombre de demandeurs d'emploi enregistrés (statistiques internes uniquement, calculées depuis trois ans seulement).

2. Organisme responsable de l'enregistrement des chômeurs ou demandeurs d'emploi
Nom de l'organisme: Agence nationale de Promotion de l'Emploi et des Compétences (ANAPEC).
Type d'organisme: Organisme public relevant d'une autorité nationale.
Nom de l'autorité nationale: Ministère de l'Emploi, de la Formation professionnelle, du Développement social et de la Solidarité.
Situation des bureaux chargés de l'enregistrement: 22 agences locales dans 19 villes du Royaume.
Types de services fournis et/ou gérés par cet organisme:
- Assistance aux demandeurs d'emploi pour trouver du travail;
- Assistance aux demandeurs d'emploi pour créer leur propre entreprise;
- Assistance aux employeurs pour trouver de la main-d'œuvre;
- Orientation professionnelle;
- Formation liée à l'emploi;
- Autres: conseil aux entreprises en matière de gestion des emplois et des compétences, mise à disposition des clients d'informations sur le marché du travail, élaboration du répertoire national des métiers.

Pourcentage des demandeurs d'emploi qui cherchent un emploi au travers de cet organisme: 20% des chercheurs d'emploi qualifié.

3. Les informations personnelles suivantes sont enregistrées:
- Nom;
- Sexe;
- Numéro de sécurité sociale (ou numéro d'identification également utilisé par d'autres organismes);
- Adresse du domicile habituel;
- Date de naissance;
- Niveau d'instruction/de formation;
- Situation de travail présente et passée, en distinguant trois catégories;
- Type de profession de l'emploi antérieur et/ou actuel, en distinguant 466 catégories. Aucun lien n'a été établi avec la CITP-88;

– Type de profession de l'emploi recherché, avec 466 catégories;
– Inscriptions/enregistrements antérieurs auprès de l'organisme;
– Autre: mobilité, langues parlées, permis de conduire, numéro de téléphone, adresse e-mail, situation familiale, durée de l'expérience professionnelle.

4. Critères utilisés pour déterminer si une personne doit être incluse dans le registre:
– Avoir un diplôme professionnel ou une spécialisation acquise dans un cours de formation des adultes (R);
– Avoir un diplôme de formation générale (baccalauréat au minimum) (R);
– Avoir une expérience professionnelle de trois ans minimum dans un emploi qualifié, attestée par des certificats de travail (R).

5. Critères utilisés pour déterminer si une personne doit être exclue du registre:
– Avis de décès (R);
– Etablissement de la personne à l'étranger (R);
– Commencement d'un (nouveau) travail: l'inscription est annulée lorsque le chercheur d'emploi déclare qu'il n'est plus à la recherche d'un emploi, ou qu'il est placé sur une offre traitée par l'ANAPEC (R) ;
– Entreprise d'une formation ou d'études (R);
– Défaut de contact avec l'organisme/agence: non actualisation dans les six mois qui suivent la date de la dernière inscription (R);
– Refus d'offres d'emploi adaptées (R).

6. Définition des personnes au chômage sur laquelle les statistiques sont établies
Les statistiques concernant le chômage sont établies par la Direction des statistiques, qui relève du Ministère de la Prévision économique et du Plan. Les statistiques établies par L'ANAPEC sont basées sur le fichier des demandeurs d'emploi inscrits et ne sont utilisées qu'en interne.

7. Mise à jour des registres
Les registres sont mis à jour de façon continue.

8. Taux de chômage
Les statistiques basées sur les registres ne sont pas utilisées pour obtenir des taux de chômage.

9. Type de statistiques sur le nombre de demandeurs d'emploi enregistrés
Période de référence: Jour.
Fréquence de production: Quotidienne.
Variables utilisées:
– Sexe;
– Age;
– Niveau d'instruction.
Publication: A usage interne uniquement.

10. Information méthodologique au sujet de ces statistiques
Publication: Non diffusée, à usage interne uniquement.

11. Comparaisons avec des statistiques provenant d'autres sources
Il n'y a pas eu de comparaisons faites avec des statistiques provenant d'autres sources.

12. Principaux changements intervenus depuis le début de ces séries statistiques
Il n'y a pas eu de changement important dans la législation, dans la capacité de l'agence et/ou dans les procédures administratives susceptibles d'avoir influencé de manière significative les statistiques.

Maurice

1. Séries statistiques
Titre: Chômage enregistré.
Première année disponible: Vers 1960.

2. Organisme responsable de l'enregistrement des chômeurs ou demandeurs d'emploi
Nom de l'organisme: Employment Service (Service de l'Emploi).
Type d'organisme: Organisme public relevant d'une autorité nationale.
Nom de l'autorité nationale: Ministère de la Formation, du Développement des Compétences et de la Productivité.
Situation des bureaux chargés de l'enregistrement: Dans toutes les régions du pays.
Types de services fournis et/ou gérés par cet organisme:
– Assistance aux demandeurs d'emploi pour trouver du travail;
– Assistance aux employeurs pour trouver de la main-d'œuvre;
– Orientation professionnelle;
– Autre: fournir des informations aux agences de formation et de financement d'entreprises.

Pourcentage des demandeurs d'emploi qui cherchent un emploi au travers de cet organisme: 65%.

3. Les informations personnelles suivantes sont enregistrées:
– Nom;
– Sexe;
– Numéro de sécurité sociale (ou numéro d'identification également utilisé par d'autres organismes);
– Adresse du domicile habituel;
– Date de naissance;
– Nationalité/groupe ethnique;
– Niveau d'instruction/ de formation. Des liens n'ont pas été établis avec la CITE;
– Situation de travail présente et passée;
– Type de profession de l'emploi antérieur ou actuel. Des liens ont été établis avec la CITP-88 au niveau des groupes de base
– Type de profession de l'emploi recherché. Des liens ont été établis avec la CITP-88 au niveau des groupes de base;
– Nom et adresse de l'employeur ou du lieu de travail actuel ou passé;
– Branche d'activité de l'employeur ou du lieu de travail actuel ou passé. Aucun lien n'a été établi avec la CITI;
– Inscriptions/enregistrements antérieurs auprès de l'organisme;
– Autre: personnes à charge; situation de famille; handicaps.

4. Critères utilisés pour déterminer si une personne doit être incluse dans le registre (R) et/ou dans les statistiques de chômeurs (S):
– Etre sans travail (R) et (S);
– Etre à la recherche d'un travail (R) et (S);
– Etre disponible pour travailler (R) et (S);
– Age: Minimum: 15 ans; pas de limite supérieure (R) et (S);
– Citoyenneté (R) et (S);
– Etre résident dans le pays (R) et (S).

5. Critères utilisés pour déterminer si une personne doit être exclue du registre (R) et/ou des statistiques de chômeurs (S):
– Décès (R) et (S);
– Etablissement de la personne à l'étranger (R) et (S);
– Défaut de contact avec l'organisme/agence (R).

6. Définition des personnes au chômage sur laquelle les statistiques sont établies
Non seulement les chômeurs, mais aussi les personnes pourvues d'un emploi mais à la recherche d'un meilleur emploi ou d'un autre emploi remplissent les conditions requises pour être enregistrées.
Est considérée au chômage une personne de sexe masculin ou féminin, âgée d'au moins 15 ans, se déclarant au chômage et disponible pour accepter un travail.

7. Mise à jour des registres
Les registres sont mis à jour mensuellement et les personnes qui ont omis de contacter l'agence en sont exclues. Les personnes pourvues d'un emploi n'ont à contacter l'agence qu'une seule fois par année; ce registre là est mis à jour tous les quatre mois.

8. Taux de chômage
Les statistiques basées sur les registres ne sont pas utilisées pour obtenir des taux de chômage.

9. Type de statistiques produites sur le nombre de chômeurs enregistrés
Période de référence: Janvier-avril; mai- août; septembre-décembre.
Fréquence de production: Tous les quatre mois.
Variables utilisées:
– Sexe;
– Age;
– Niveau d'instruction;
– Profession;
– Branche d'activité;
– Caractéristiques géographiques;

– Expérience professionnelle antérieure;
– Citoyenneté (nationaux/non nationaux);
– Durée de chômage;
– Autres: jeunes (de 15 à 17 ans); personnes handicapées.

Publication: Sur papier, à diffusion grand public.

Agence responsable de la publication: Service de l'Emploi.

Titre et périodicité de la publication: *Statistical Review on Employment* (Revue statistique de l'emploi), tous les quatre mois.

N.B. Quelques informations sur le chômage sont disponibles sur le site Internet du Service de l'Emploi: http://ncb.intnet.mu/empserv.htm.

10. Information méthodologique au sujet de ces statistiques

Publication: Sur papier, à diffusion grand public.

Agence responsable: Service de l'Emploi.

11. Comparaisons avec des statistiques provenant d'autres sources

Il n'y a pas eu de comparaisons faites avec des statistiques provenant d'autres sources.

12. Principaux changements intervenus depuis le début de ces séries statistiques

Il n'y a pas eu de changement important dans la législation, dans la capacité de l'agence et/ou dans les procédures administratives susceptibles d'avoir influencé de manière significative les statistiques.

Moldavie, Rép. de

1. Séries statistiques

Titre: Chômage enregistré.

Première année disponible: 1992.

2. Organisme responsable de l'enregistrement des chômeurs ou demandeurs d'emploi

Nom de l'organisme: Agences de l'Emploi, au niveau régional.

Type d'organisme: Organisme public relevant d'autorités nationales et régionales.

Nom de l'autorité nationale: Département de l'utilisation de la main d'œuvre, Ministère du Travail et de la Protection Sociale.

Situation des bureaux chargés de l'enregistrement: Il y a 12 bureaux de l'emploi (un par comté) et 33 sections de l'emploi dans les villes dans tout le pays sous la direction des bureaux de l'emploi des comtés. Les bureaux de l'emploi dépendent du département de l'utilisation de la main d'œuvre.

Types de services fournis et/ou gérés par cet organisme:

– Assistance aux demandeurs d'emploi pour trouver du travail;
– Assistance aux demandeurs d'emploi pour créer leur propre entreprise;
– Assistance aux employeurs pour trouver de la main-d'œuvre;
– Orientation professionnelle;
– Formation liée à l'emploi;
– Paiement des indemnités de chômage;
– Autres: organisation et développement d'expositions sur l'emploi, de formation de "Clubs d'emploi" et de formation en vue de travaux publics rémunérés.

Pourcentage des demandeurs d'emploi qui cherchent un emploi au travers de cet organisme: 50%.

3. Les informations personnelles suivantes sont enregistrées:

– Nom;
– Sexe;
– Numéro de sécurité sociale (ou numéro d'identification également utilisé par d'autres organismes);
– Adresse du domicile habituel;
– Date de naissance;
– Niveau d'instruction/ de formation, en distinguant cinq catégories. Aucun lien n'a été établi avec la CITE;
– Type de profession de l'emploi antérieur ou actuel. Des liens ont été établis avec la CITP-88;
– Type de profession de l'emploi recherché. Des liens ont été établis avec la CITP-88;
– Nom et adresse de l'employeur ou du lieu de travail actuel ou passé;
– Branche d'activité de l'employeur ou du lieu de travail actuel ou passé, en distinguant 11 catégories;
– Autres: situation de famille; numéro de la carte de travail; détails sur le dernier travail (dates de service, raison de départ, salaire moyen des trois derniers mois, etc.); catégorie de protection sociale; catégorie

d'indemnités de chômage; situation militaire; connaissance de langues étrangères; formation spéciale.

4. Critères utilisés pour déterminer si une personne doit être incluse dans le registre (R) et/ou dans les statistiques de chômeurs (S):

– Etre sans travail (R) et (S);
– Etre à la recherche d'un travail (R) et (S);
– Etre disponible pour travailler (R) et (S);
– Age: Minimum: 16 ans; Maximum: âge de la retraite (R) et (S);
– Etre résident dans le pays (R) et (S);
– Avoir précédemment travaillé (incluant des travaux publics rémunérés et du travail temporaire) (R) et (S);
– Acquittement de cotisations d'assurance chômage (R) et (S).

5. Critères utilisés pour déterminer si une personne doit être exclue du registre (R) et/ou des statistiques de chômeurs (S):

– Décès (R) et (S);
– Etablissement de la personne à l'étranger (R) et (S);
– Commencement d'un (nouveau) travail (R) et (S);
– Commencement du service militaire (R) et (S);
– Participation à un programme de promotion de l'emploi, à un programme de travaux publics, etc. (R) et (S);
– Entreprise d'une formation ou d'études (R) et (S);
– Défaut de contact avec l'organisme/agence pendant plus de 2 mois (R) et (S);
– Refus de deux offres d'emploi adaptées (R) et (S);
– Admission à toucher une pension (R) et (S);
– Incapacité à travailler (R) et (S).

6. Définition des personnes au chômage sur laquelle les statistiques sont établies

Le service d'état responsable de l'utilisation de la main d'œuvre suit la définition de la loi sur l'utilisation de la main d'œuvre qui est la suivante:

Sont considérés comme chômeurs les citoyens disponibles pour travailler qui n'ont pas d'emploi approprié ou de revenu légal et qui sont enregistrés auprès du bureau de l'emploi de leur région de résidence comme personnes à la recherche d'un emploi.

7. Mise à jour des registres

Les registres sont mis à jour quotidiennement.

8. Taux de chômage

Les statistiques basées sur les registres sont utilisées pour obtenir le taux de chômage "officiel" pour la République de Moldavie (le taux "réel" est obtenu par l'enquête sur la main-d'œuvre).

Les sources des données d'emploi qui sont partie du dénominateur des taux de chômage sont l'enquête sur la main-d'œuvre et le recensement de population.

Définition des personnes pourvues d'un emploi à cette fin:

Les personnes âgées de 15 ans et plus qui ont eu une activité économique ou sociale, produisant des biens ou fournissant un service, durant au moins une heure pendant la période de référence (une semaine), contre un avantage, un salaire ou autres bénéfices.

9. Type de statistiques sur le nombre de chômeurs enregistrés produites

Série 1:

Période de référence: Mois.

Fréquence de production: Mensuelle.

Variables utilisées:

– Sexe.

Publication: Sur papier, à diffusion grand public.

Agence responsable de la publication: Le service responsable de l'utilisation de la main-d'œuvre.

Titre et périodicité de la publication: *Rapport statistique mensuel.*

Série 2:

Période de référence: Trimestre.

Fréquence de production: Trimestrielle.

Variables utilisées:

– Sexe;
– Age;
– Niveau d'instruction;
– Profession;
– Branche d'activité;
– Caractéristiques géographiques;
– Durée du chômage.

Publication: Sur papier, à diffusion grand public.

Agence responsable de la publication: Le service responsable de l'utilisation de la main- d'œuvre.

Titre et périodicité de la publication: *Rapport statistique trimestriel.*

Série 3:

Période de référence: Trimestre.

Fréquence de production: Trimestrielle.

Variables utilisées:

– Sexe;
– Age;
– Niveau d'instruction;
– Profession;
– Branche d'activité.

Publication: Sur papier, à diffusion grand public.

Agence responsable de la publication: Le service responsable de l'utilisation de la main- d'œuvre.

Titre et périodicité de la publication: *Bulletin statistique trimestriel.*

Série 4:

Période de référence: Année.

Fréquence de production: Annuelle.

Variables utilisées:

– Sexe;
– Age;
– Niveau d'instruction;
– Profession;
– Branche d'activité;
– Caractéristiques géographiques;
– Citoyenneté (nationaux/ non nationaux);
– Durée du chômage.

Publication: Sur papier, à diffusion grand public.

Agence responsable de la publication: Le service responsable de l'utilisation de la main- d'œuvre.

Titre et périodicité de la publication: *Annuaire statistique.*

10. Information méthodologique au sujet de ces statistiques

Publication: Sur papier, à diffusion grand public.

Agence responsable: Le service responsable de l'utilisation de la main-d'œuvre.

11. Comparaisons avec des statistiques provenant d'autres sources

Des comparaisons sont faites avec des statistiques de chômage provenant de sources diverses; les statistiques "officielles" sont comparées aux statistiques "réelles" produites par le Département des Statistiques et de Sociologie.

Fréquence des comparaisons: Régulièrement lors de la publication des statistiques.

Publication de la méthodologie et/ou des résultats de la comparaison: Ils sont publiés dans le bulletin statistique trimestriel, l'annuaire statistique et autres documents.

12. Principaux changements intervenus depuis le début de ces séries statistiques

Il n'y a pas eu de changement important dans la législation, dans la capacité de l'agence et/ou dans les procédures administratives susceptibles d'avoir influencé de manière significative les statistiques.

Mongolie

1. Séries statistiques

Titre: Citoyens au chômage, personnes à la recherche de travail et citoyens menacés de chômage.

Première année disponible: 1991.

2. Organisme responsable de l'enregistrement des chômeurs ou demandeurs d'emploi

Nom de l'organisme: Employment Office (Agence de l'Emploi).

Type d'organisme: Organisme public relevant d'autorités nationales, régionales/ départementales et locales.

Nom de l'autorité nationale: Agence Gouvernementale Mongole d'Exécution, Agence Centrale de l'Emploi.

Situation des bureaux chargés de l'enregistrement: Dans toutes les provinces et municipalités du pays.

Types de services fournis et/ou gérés par cet organisme:

– Assistance aux demandeurs d'emploi pour trouver du travail;
– Assistance aux demandeurs d'emploi pour créer leur propre entreprise;
– Assistance aux employeurs pour trouver de la main-d'œuvre;
– Orientation professionnelle;

– Formation liée à l'emploi;
– Paiement des indemnités de chômage;
– Autres: assistance aux employeurs; promotion du travail indépendant.

Pourcentage des demandeurs d'emploi qui cherchent un emploi au travers de cet organisme: 4.8%.

3. Les informations personnelles suivantes sont enregistrées:

– Nom;
– Sexe;
– Numéro de sécurité sociale (ou numéro d'identification également utilisé par d'autres organismes);
– Adresse du domicile habituel;
– Date de naissance;
– Citoyenneté;
– Niveau d'instruction/ de formation, en distinguant six catégories. Aucun lien n'a été établi avec la CITE;
– Situation de travail présente et passée, en distinguant sept catégories;
– Type de profession de l'emploi antérieur ou actuel, en distinguant neuf catégories. Des liens ont été établis avec la CITP-88 au niveau des grands groupes;
– Type de profession de l'emploi recherché, avec neuf catégories; Des liens ont été établis avec la CITP-88 au niveau des grands groupes;
– Nom et adresse de l'employeur ou du lieu de travail actuel ou passé;
– Branche d'activité de l'employeur ou du lieu de travail actuel ou passé, en distinguant 17 catégories. Des liens ont été établis avec la CITI, rév.3;
– Inscriptions/enregistrements antérieurs auprès de l'organisme;
– Autres: état de santé; situation de famille; revenus du ménage; motif du chômage; motif de démission; éligibilité pour le paiement d'indemnités de chômage; motif de menace de chômage.

4. Critères utilisés pour déterminer si une personne doit être incluse dans le registre (R) et/ou dans les statistiques de chômeurs (S):

– Etre sans travail (sont inclues les personnes travaillant à leur compte moins de 15 heures par semaine et percevant un revenu en dessous du revenu minimum) (R) et (S);
– Etre à la recherche d'un travail (R) et (S);
– Etre disponible pour travailler (R) et (S);
– Age: Minimum: 16 ans; Maximum: 60 ans (R) et (S);
– Citoyenneté (on doit être citoyen mongol) (R) et (S);
– Etre résident dans le pays (R) et (S);
– Autre: apte à travailler.

5. Critères utilisés pour déterminer si une personne doit être exclue du registre (R) et/ou des statistiques de chômeurs (S):

– Décès (R) et (S);
– Etablissement de la personne à l'étranger (R) et (S);
– Commencement d'un (nouveau) travail (R) et (S);
– Commencement du service militaire (R) et (S);
– Participation à un programme de promotion de l'emploi, à un programme de travaux publics, etc. (R) et (S);
– Entreprise d'une formation ou d'études (R) et (S);
– Défaut de contact avec l'organisme/agence (R) et (S);
– Refus de trois offres d'emploi adaptées (R) et (S);
– Refus de trois offres de formation adaptées (R) et (S);
– Admission à toucher une retraite (R) et (S);
– Incapacité à travailler (R) et (S);
– Autre: refus de trois offres de travaux publics adaptées (R) et (S).

6. Définition des personnes au chômage sur laquelle les statistiques sont établies

Un "citoyen au chômage" est un citoyen sans handicap, en âge de travailler, prêt à accepter un emploi, activement à la recherche d'un emploi et enregistré auprès de l'agence de l'emploi (Loi sur la promotion de l'emploi de Mongolie 2001).

7. Mise à jour des registres

Les registres sont mis à jour mensuellement.

8. Taux de chômage

Les statistiques basées sur les registres sont utilisées pour obtenir des taux de chômage.

Les sources des données d'emploi qui sont partie du dénominateur des taux de chômage sont les suivantes:

– Enquête sur la main-d'œuvre;

– Recensement de population;
– Rapport mensuel sur le chômage (Bureau National des Statistiques);
– Table des résultats des programmes "Administrateurs Marché du Travail" (Bureau Central de l'Emploi);
– Enquête annuelle de l'emploi de la population (Bureau National des Statistiques).

Définition des personnes pourvues d'un emploi à cette fin:
Des personnes qui travaillent dans des entreprises ou organisations, ou sont à la tête d'une affaire privée et en perçoivent un salaire, ou qui sont à leur compte.

9. Type de statistiques sur le nombre de chômeurs enregistrés produites
Série 1:
Période de référence: Mois; Année.
Fréquence de production: Mensuelle et annuelle.
Variables utilisées:
– Sexe;
– Age;
– Niveau d'instruction;
– Profession;
– Branche d'activité;
– Caractéristiques géographiques;
– Autres: nombre de vacances; main-d'œuvre; réflexion sur le travail; population de personnes handicapées en âge de travailler; formation professionnelle; travail à caractère public; travail indépendant; indemnité de chômage; emploi d'étrangers; formateurs.
– Publication: Sur papier, à diffusion grand public.
Agence responsable de la publication: Bureau National de Statistique.
Titre et périodicité de la publication: *The Social Economic Situation of Mongolia* (la situation socio-économique de la Mongolie), mensuelle et annuelle.
Série 2:
Période de référence: Mois; trimestre; semestre; année.
Fréquence de production: Mensuelle; trimestrielle; semestrielle; annuelle.
Variables utilisées:
– Sexe;
– Age;
– Niveau d'instruction;
– Profession;
– Branche d'activité;
– Caractéristiques géographiques;
– Expérience professionnelle antérieure;
– Citoyenneté (nationaux/non nationaux);
– Durée du chômage.
– Publication: Sur papier, à diffusion restreinte.
Agence responsable de la publication: Bureau Central de l'Emploi.
Titre et périodicité de la publication: *Labour Market Report* (Rapport sur le marché du travail), mensuel, trimestriel, semestriel et annuel.
Série 3:
Période de référence: Année.
Fréquence de production: Annuelle.
Variables utilisées:
– Sexe;
– Age;
– Niveau d'instruction;
– Profession;
– Branche d'activité;
– Caractéristiques géographiques;
– Expérience professionnelle antérieure;
– Citoyenneté (nationaux/non nationaux);
– Durée du chômage.
– Publication: Sur papier, à diffusion restreinte.
Agence responsable de la publication: Bureau National de Statistique.
Titre et périodicité de la publication: *Annual Employment Survey of the Population* (Enquête annuelle de l'emploi de la population), annuelle.

10. Information méthodologique au sujet de ces statistiques
Publication: Sur papier, à diffusion grand public.
Agences responsable: Bureau national de Statistique; Ministère des Affaires sociales et du Travail.

11. Comparaisons avec des statistiques provenant d'autres sources
Des comparaisons ont été faites avec des statistiques de chômage provenant de l'enquête sur la main d'œuvre, un autre type d'enquête auprès des ménages et le recensement de population.
Fréquence des comparaisons: Régulièrement lors de la publication des statistiques.
Publication de la méthodologie et/ou des résultats de la comparaison: Ils n'ont pas été publiés.

12. Principaux changements intervenus depuis le début de ces séries statistiques
Des changements importants dans la législation, dans la capacité de l'agence et/ou dans les procédures administratives sont intervenus en (i) 1993; (ii) 1995; (iii) 1997 et (iv) 2001 dont le résultat était une augmentation de 2.4% des personnes enregistrées comme chômeurs en 1993; une diminution de 3.3% en 1995; une augmentation de 2.2% en 1997 et une diminution de 3.2% en 2001.
– 1993: Début officiel de l'enregistrement des chômeurs;
– 1995: Enquête nationale sur la pauvreté et le chômage;
– 1997: Adoption de la loi sur les indemnités de chômage, permettant aux chômeurs de recevoir des indemnités de chômage du fonds d'assurance sociale.
– 2001: Adoption de la loi sur la promotion de l'emploi.

Myanmar

1. Séries statistiques
Titre: Statistiques de la bourse de l'emploi.
Première année disponible: Vers 1950.

2. Organisme responsable de l'enregistrement des chômeurs ou demandeurs d'emploi
Nom de l'organisme: Division de l'Emploi et de la Formation.
Type d'organisme: Organisme public relevant d'une autorité nationale.
Nom de l'autorité nationale: Ministère du Travail.
Situation des bureaux chargés de l'enregistrement: Les enregistrements sont pris en charge par les bourses du travail des agences pour l'emploi des villes; il y en a 78 dans toutes les régions du pays.
Types de services fournis et/ou gérés par cet organisme:
– Assistance aux demandeurs d'emploi pour trouver du travail;
– Assistance aux employeurs pour trouver de la main-d'œuvre;
– Orientation professionnelle;
– Formation liée à l'emploi;
– Autre: emploi à l'étranger.
Pourcentage des demandeurs d'emploi qui cherchent un emploi au travers de cet organisme: Sur la base de la loi sur la limitation de l'emploi de 1959, tous les employeurs employant plus de cinq travailleurs sont tenus d'engager leurs travailleurs par l'intermédiaire des bourses du travail du Ministère du Travail.

3. Les informations personnelles suivantes sont enregistrées:
– Nom;
– Sexe;
– Adresse du domicile habituel;
– Date de naissance;
– Citoyenneté;
– Niveau d'instruction/ de formation. Aucun lien n'a été établi avec la CITE;
– Situation de travail présente et passée;
– Type de profession de l'emploi antérieur ou actuel. Des liens ont été établis avec la CITP-88 au niveau des groupes de base (la classification standard des emplois au Myanmar est basée sur CITP-88);
– Type de profession de l'emploi recherché. Des liens ont été établis avec la CITP-88 au niveau des groupes de base (la classification standard des emplois au Myanmar est basée sur CITP-88);
– Nom et adresse de l'employeur ou du lieu de travail actuel ou passé;
– Branche d'activité de l'employeur ou du lieu de travail actuel ou passé, en distinguant 10 catégories. Aucun lien n'a été établi avec la CITI;

–   Inscriptions/enregistrements antérieurs auprès de l'organisme;
–   Autre: renouvellement/validation de l'enregistrement tous les six mois.

4. Critères utilisés pour déterminer si une personne doit être incluse dans le registre (R) et/ou dans les statistiques de chômeurs (S):
–   Etre sans travail (R);
–   Etre à la recherche d'un travail (R);
–   Etre disponible pour travailler (R);
–   Age: Minimum: 18 ans; Maximum: 60 ans (R);
–   Citoyenneté (R);
–   Etre résident dans le pays (R);
–   Avoir précédemment travaillé (R);
–   Durée souhaitée de l'emploi recherché et/ou du nombre d'heures de travail recherché (R).

5. Critères utilisés pour déterminer si une personne doit être exclue du registre (R) et/ou des statistiques de chômeurs (S):
–   Décès (R);
–   Etablissement de la personne à l'étranger (R);
–   Commencement d'un (nouveau) travail (R);
–   Commencement du service militaire (R);
–   Participation à un programme de promotion de l'emploi, à un programme de travaux publics, etc. (R);
–   Entreprise d'une formation ou d'études (R);
–   Défaut de contact avec l'organisme/agence pendant plus de six mois (R);
–   Refus de deux offres d'emploi adaptées (R);
–   Refus de deux offres de formation adaptées (R);
–   Incapacité à travailler (R).

6. Définition des personnes au chômage sur laquelle les statistiques sont établies
Les personnes à la recherche d'un travail qui sont enregistrées auprès des bourses du travail.

7. Mise à jour des registres
Les registres sont mis à jour mensuellement.

8. Taux de chômage
Les statistiques basées sur les registres ne sont pas utilisées pour obtenir des taux de chômage.

9. Type de statistiques sur le nombre de chômeurs enregistrés produites
Série 1:
Période de référence: Mois.
Fréquence de production: Mensuelle.
Variables utilisées:
–   Sexe;
–   Age;
–   Niveau d'instruction;
–   Profession;
–   Branche d'activité;
–   Caractéristiques géographiques;
–   Expérience professionnelle antérieure;
–   Citoyenneté (nationaux/non nationaux);
–   Durée du chômage.
Publication: Sur papier, à diffusion restreinte.
Agence responsable de la publication: Organisation centrale de statistique.
Périodicité de la publication: Annuelle.
Série 2:
Les informations concernant le nombre de demandeurs d'emploi, les nouveaux enregistrements, le nombre de personnes placées, de registres périmés, les personnes enregistrées à la fin de l'année, les vacances signalées et les vacances ouvertes à la fin de l'année sont publiées par l'Organisation centrale de statistique dans le *Statistical Yearbook* (Annuaire statistique).

10. Information méthodologique au sujet de ces statistiques
Publication: Ils ne sont pas publiés; Ils sont disponibles sur demande uniquement.

11. Comparaisons avec des statistiques provenant d'autres sources
Il n'y a pas eu de comparaisons faites avec des statistiques provenant d'autres sources.

12. Principaux changements intervenus depuis le début de ces séries statistiques
Des changements importants dans la législation, dans la capacité de l'agence et/ou dans les procédures administratives sont intervenus en 1959. Les changements dans les statistiques qui en résultaient n'ont pas été évalués.

Niger

1. Séries statistiques
Titre: Statistiques des demandeurs d'emploi.
Première année disponible: 1982
2. Organisme responsable de l'enregistrement des chômeurs ou demandeurs d'emploi
Nom de l'organisme: Agence nationale pour la Promotion de l'Emploi.
Type d'organisme: Organisme public relevant d'une autorité nationale.
Situation des bureaux chargés de l'enregistrement: Niamey, Tillabery, Dosso, Tahara, Maradi, Zinder, Diffa, Arlit et Agadez.
Types de services fournis et/ou gérés par cet organisme:
–   Assistance aux demandeurs d'emploi pour trouver du travail;
–   Assistance aux demandeurs d'emploi pour créer leur propre entreprise (à Niamey uniquement);
–   Assistance aux employeurs pour trouver de la main-d'œuvre;
–   Orientation professionnelle (à Niamey uniquement);
–   Formation liée à l'emploi (à Niamey uniquement);
–   Autres services liés à l'emploi: programmes d'insertion des jeunes diplômés; production des informations statistiques sur le suivi du marché de l'emploi, programme d'insertion dans le secteur informel.

3. Les informations personnelles suivantes sont enregistrées:
–   Nom;
–   Sexe;
–   Date de naissance;
–   Nationalité;
–   Niveau d'instruction/de formation, en distinguant quatre catégories. Aucun lien n'a été établi avec la CITE;
–   Type de profession de l'emploi recherché.

4. Critères utilisés pour déterminer si une personne doit être incluse dans le registre (R) et/ou dans les statistiques de chômeurs (S):
–   Etre sans travail (R) et (S);
–   Etre à la recherche d'un travail (R) et (S);
–   Etre disponible pour travailler (R) et (S);
–   Age: Minimum: 18 ans; Maximum: 60 ans (R) et (S);
–   Citoyenneté (R): la carte d'inscription n'est délivrée aux étrangers que lorsque les conditions exigées par les règlements sont remplies;
–   Etre résident dans le pays (R) et (S);
–   Avoir précédemment travaillé (S);
–   Durée souhaitée de l'emploi recherché et/ou du nombre d'heures de travail recherché (R) et (S).

5. Critères utilisés pour déterminer si une personne doit être exclue du registre (R) et/ou des statistiques de chômeurs (S):
–   Avis de décès (R) et (S);
–   Etablissement de la personne à l'étranger (R) et (S);
–   Commencement d'un (nouveau) travail (R) et (S);
–   Entreprise d'une formation ou d'études (R) et (S);
–   Incapacité à travailler (R) et (S).

6. Définition des personnes au chômage sur laquelle les statistiques sont établies
Les statistiques du chômage sont établies sur la base du registre sur lequel sont inscrits les demandeurs d'emploi. De ce fait, est considérée comme chômeur toute personne à la recherche d'un emploi inscrite sur le registre de L'ANPE pendant la période de référence.

7. Mise à jour des registres
Les registres ne sont pas mis à jour régulièrement.

8. Taux de chômage
Les statistiques basées sur les registres ne sont pas utilisées pour obtenir des taux de chômage.

9. Type de statistiques produites sur le nombre de chômeurs enregistrés
Série 1: Statistiques des demandeurs d'emploi.
Fréquence de production: Mensuelle.
Variables utilisées:
–   Sexe;
–   Age;
–   Profession.
Publication: Sur papier, à diffusion restreinte.
Organisme/Agence responsable de la publication: ANPE
Titre de la publication: *Rapport statistique.*

Série 2: Statistiques des demandeurs d'emploi et de la main-d'œuvre.

Fréquence de production: Annuelle.

Variables utilisées:

– Sexe;
– Age;
– Niveau d'instruction;
– Profession;
– Caractéristiques géographiques.

Publication: Sur papier, à diffusion grand public.

Organisme/Agence responsable de la publication: ANPE.

Titre de la publication: *Rapport d'activité*.

10. Information méthodologique au sujet de ces statistiques

Publication: Sur papier, à diffusion grand public.

Agence responsable: ANPE.

11. Comparaisons avec des statistiques provenant d'autres sources

Il n'y a pas eu de comparaisons faites avec des statistiques provenant d'autres sources.

12. Principaux changements intervenus depuis le début de ces séries statistiques

L'Agence nationale pour la promotion de l'emploi existe depuis 1996. Auparavant, c'était le Service de la main-d'œuvre et les inspections du travail qui répertoriait les demandeurs d'emploi.

Nigéria

1. Séries statistiques

Titre: Statistiques sur le marché du travail.

2. Organisme responsable de l'enregistrement des chômeurs ou demandeurs d'emploi

Nom de l'organisme: Bourse de l'Emploi, Registres, Registres professionnels et de direction.

Type d'organisme: Organisme public relevant d'une autorité nationale.

Nom de l'autorité nationale: Ministère fédéral de l'Emploi, du Travail et de la Productivité. Cependant, la mise en place et la gestion d'agences d'emploi privées est envisagée.

Situation des bureaux chargés de l'enregistrement: Dans toutes les capitales d'Etats de la Fédération (un réseau de 37 Etats), dans les régions dans lesquelles la population est importante, dans lesquelles se trouvent des établissements industriels qui requièrent de la main-d'œuvre et dans les villes universitaires ou dotées d'autres institutions du secteur tertiaire.

Types de services fournis et/ou gérés par cet organisme:

– Assistance aux demandeurs d'emploi pour trouver du travail;
– Assistance aux demandeurs d'emploi pour créer leur propre entreprise;
– Assistance aux employeurs pour trouver de la main-d'œuvre;
– Orientation professionnelle;
– Formation liée à l'emploi;
– Certification des artisans comme travailleurs indépendants à leur propre compte.

Pourcentage des demandeurs d'emploi qui cherchent un emploi au travers de cet organisme: 60%.

3. Les informations personnelles suivantes sont enregistrées:

– Nom;
– Sexe;
– Adresse du domicile habituel;
– Date de naissance;
– Citoyenneté;
– Nationalité/groupe ethnique;
– Niveau d'instruction/de formation, en distinguant trois catégories: qualifié, semi-qualifié et non qualifié. Des liens ont été établis avec la CITE;
– Situation de travail présente et passée;
– Type de profession de l'emploi antérieur et/ou actuel;
– Type de profession de l'emploi recherché; Des liens ont été établis avec la CITP-88 (au niveau des grands groupes);
– Nom et adresse de l'employeur ou du lieu de travail actuel ou passé;
– Branche d'activité de l'employeur ou du lieu de travail actuel ou passé. Des liens ont été établis avec la CITI, au niveau des groupes;
– Inscriptions/enregistrements antérieurs auprès de l'organisme.

4. Critères utilisés pour déterminer si une personne doit être incluse dans le registre (R) et/ou dans les statistiques de chômeurs (S):

– Etre sans travail (R) et (S);
– Etre à la recherche d'un travail (R) et (S);
– Etre disponible pour travailler (R) et (S);
– Age: Minimum: 18 ans; Maximum: 60 ans; (R) et (S);
– Citoyenneté: pour les nigérians de naissance, par mariage ou par naturalisation;
– Etre résident dans le pays (R) et (S).

5. Critères utilisés pour déterminer si une personne doit être exclue du registre (R) et/ou des statistiques de chômeurs (S):

– Avis de décès (R) et (S);
– Etablissement de la personne à l'étranger (R) et (S);
– Commencement d'un (nouveau) travail (R) et (S);
– Commencement du service militaire (R) et (S);
– Participation à un programme de promotion de l'emploi, à un programme de travaux publics, etc. (R) et (S);
– Entreprise d'une formation ou d'études (R) et (S);
– Défaut de contact avec l'organisme/agence, il est nécessaire de renouveler les papiers périodiquement (R) et (S);
– Refus d'offres d'emploi adaptées (R) et (S);
– Refus d'offres de formation adaptées (R) et (S);
– Incapacité à travailler (R) et (S).

6. Définition des personnes au chômage sur laquelle les statistiques sont établies

Les personnes qui cherchent activement du travail, désirent travailler, sont en bonne santé âgées de 18 à 60 ans, et qui ont un revenu inférieur au salaire minimum national.

7. Mise à jour des registres

Les registres sont mis à jour régulièrement.

8. Taux de chômage

Les statistiques basées sur les registres sont utilisées pour obtenir des taux de chômage.

Les sources des données d'emploi qui sont partie du dénominateur sont les suivantes:

– Enquête sur la main-d'œuvre,
– Enquête auprès des établissements,
– Registres de sécurité sociale,
– Recensement de population.

Définition des personnes pourvues d'un emploi à cette fin:

Les personnes qui sont activement engagées dans un travail et dont le revenu n'est pas inférieur au salaire minimum national.

9. Type de statistiques produites sur le nombre de chômeurs enregistrés

Période de référence: Mois.

Fréquence de production: Trimestrielle.

Variables utilisées:

– Sexe;
– Age;
– Niveau d'instruction;
– Profession;
– Branche d'activité;
– Caractéristiques géographiques;
– Expérience professionnelle antérieure;
– Citoyenneté;
– Durée de chômage.

Publication:

– Sur papier, à diffusion grand public;
– En format électronique, sur demande.

Agence responsable de la publication: Ministère fédéral de l'Emploi, du Travail et de la Productivité.

Titre et périodicité des publications: «*Employment Exchange & Professional & Executive Registry Statistics*» (Bourse de l'Emploi, Registres, Registres professionnels et de direction), mensuel, trimestriel et annuel.

10. Information méthodologique au sujet de ces statistiques

Publication:

– Sur papier, à diffusion grand public;
– En format électronique, sur demande;
– Prévue sur un site Internet.

11. Comparaisons avec des statistiques provenant d'autres sources

Il n'y a pas eu de comparaisons faites avec des statistiques provenant d'autres sources.

12. Principaux changements intervenus depuis le début de ces séries statistiques

Il n'y a pas eu de changement important dans la législation, dans la capacité de l'agence et/ou dans les procédures administratives susceptibles d'avoir influencé de manière significative les statistiques.

Norvège

1. Séries statistiques
Titre: Statistiques du marché du travail.
Première année disponible: 1948.
2. Organisme responsable de l'enregistrement des chômeurs ou demandeurs d'emploi
Nom de l'organisme: "Aestat" (Service d'emploi de district).
Type d'organisme: Organisme public relevant d'une autorité nationale.
Nom de l'autorité nationale: Directorat du travail.
Situation des bureaux chargés de l'enregistrement: La plupart des enregistrements est faite par 200 bureaux locaux. Un centre national d'enregistrement procède à certaines mises à jour et à quelques enregistrements en rapport avec les statistiques des vacances de postes.
Types de services fournis et/ou gérés par cet organisme:
– Assistance aux demandeurs d'emploi pour trouver du travail;
– Assistance aux employeurs pour trouver de la main-d'œuvre;
– Orientation professionnelle;
– Formation liée à l'emploi;
– Mesures de réhabilitation en rapport avec l'activité professionnelle;
– Paiement des indemnités de chômage;
– Autres services liés à l'emploi.
Pourcentage des demandeurs d'emploi qui cherchent un emploi au travers de cet organisme: 75%.
3. Les informations personnelles suivantes sont enregistrées:
– Nom;
– Sexe;
– Numéro de sécurité sociale (ou numéro d'identification également utilisé par d'autres organismes);
– Adresse du domicile habituel;
– Date de naissance;
– Citoyenneté;
– Nationalité;
– Niveau d'instruction/ de formation, en distinguant huit catégories. Des liens ont été établis avec la CITE;
– Type de travail (profession) de l'emploi antérieur, en distinguant un nombre non spécifié de groupes. Des liens ont été établis avec la CITP, au niveau des groupes de base;
– Type de travail (profession) de l'emploi recherché, avec un nombre non spécifié de groupes. Des liens ont été établis avec la CITP, au niveau des groupes de base;
– Inscriptions/enregistrements antérieurs auprès de l'organisme.
4. Critères utilisés pour déterminer si une personne doit être incluse dans le registre (R) et/ou dans les statistiques de chômeurs (S):
– Etre sans travail (les 14 derniers jours avant le jour du comptage) (S);
– Etre à la recherche d'un travail (R) et (S);
– Etre disponible pour travailler (R) et (S);
– Etre résident dans le pays (S).
5. Critères utilisés pour déterminer si une personne doit être exclue du registre (R) et/ou des statistiques de chômeurs (S):
– Décès (R) et (S);
– Etablissement de la personne à l'étranger (R) et (S);
– Commencement d'un (nouveau) travail (S);
– Commencement du service militaire (S);
– Participation à un programme de promotion de l'emploi, à un programme de travaux publics, etc. (S);
– Entreprise d'une formation ou d'études (les étudiants et les participants à des programmes de formation ne sont pas comptés comme chômeurs, mais peuvent être à la recherche d'un emploi) (S);
– Défaut de l'envoi de la carte de contrôle tous les 14 jours à un centre d'enregistrement national.

6. Définition des personnes au chômage sur laquelle les statistiques sont établies

Etre à la recherche d'un emploi, être sans travail rémunéré et être disponible pour travailler, sont les critères principaux.

Est considérée au chômage toute personne pour laquelle une carte de contrôle a été reçue/complétée pour les deux semaines précédentes ou qui s'était présentée au service de l'emploi local pour se faire enregistrer. Si elle signale avoir été sans emploi pendant les deux semaines précédentes, elle sera comptée comme chômeur. Si elle avait quelque travail pendant les deux semaines précédentes, elle sera comptée comme chômeur partiel.

7. Mise à jour des registres

Les registres sont mis à jour chaque semaine.

8. Taux de chômage

Les statistiques basées sur les registres sont utilisées pour obtenir des taux de chômage.

– Le dénominateur des taux de chômage est la main-d'œuvre de l'enquête sur la main d'œuvre.

Définition des personnes pourvues d'un emploi à cette fin:

Les personnes âgées de 16 à 74 ans qui avaient travaillé, au moins pendant une heure, contre rémunération ou profit pendant la semaine de l'enquête.

9. Type de statistiques sur le nombre de chômeurs enregistrés produites
Série 1:
Période de référence: Mois.
Fréquence de production: Mensuelle.
Variables utilisées:
– Sexe;
– Age;
– Niveau d'instruction;
– Profession;
– Caractéristiques géographiques;
– Durée de chômage;
– Autre: au bénéfice d'indemnités de chômage.
Publication:
– Sur papier, à diffusion grand public;
– Sur un site Internet (www.aetat.no).
Agence responsable de la publication: Directorat du travail.
Titre et périodicité de la publication: *Manedsstatistikk* (statistiques mensuelles).
Série 2:
Période de référence: Année.
Fréquence de production: Annuelle.
Variables utilisées:
– Sexe;
– Age;
– Niveau d'instruction;
– Profession;
– Caractéristiques géographiques;
– Durée de chômage;
– Autre: bénéficiaires d'indemnités de chômage.
Publication:
– Sur papier, à diffusion grand public;
– Sur un site Internet (www.aetat.no).
Agence responsable de la publication: Directorat du travail.
Titre de la publication: *Historisk Statistikk* (statistiques historiques).
10. Information méthodologique au sujet de ces statistiques
Publication:
– Sur papier, à diffusion grand public;
– Sur un site Internet (www.aetat.no).
Agence responsable pour la diffusion de l'information méthodologique: Directorat du travail, division de la planification et de l'analyse.
11. Comparaisons avec des statistiques provenant d'autres sources

Des comparaisons ont été faites avec des statistiques provenant de l'enquête sur la main- d'œuvre.
Fréquence des comparaisons: Occasionnellement.
Publication de la méthodologie et/ou des résultats de la comparaison: Ont été publiés dans *Notater*, nr. 99/31 (statistiques Norvège): "...Classification du chômage enregistré et participants dans des projets de main-d'œuvre lors de l'enquête sur la main-d'œuvre" (en norvégien seulement).

12. Principaux changements intervenus depuis le début de ces séries statistiques

Il n'y a pas eu de changement important dans la législation, dans la capacité de l'agence et/ou dans les procédures administratives susceptibles d'avoir influencé de manière significative les statistiques.

Nouvelle-Calédonie

1. Séries statistiques
Titre: Statistiques de la demande d'emploi.
Première année disponible: 1991
2. Organisme responsable de l'enregistrement des chômeurs ou demandeurs d'emploi
Nom de l'organisme: Agence pour l'emploi de Nouvelle-Calédonie.
Type d'organisme: Organisme public relevant d'une autorité locale.
Situation des bureaux chargés de l'enregistrement: Une délégation dans chacune des trois provinces, et des antennes dans plusieurs communes.
Types de services fournis et/ou gérés par cet organisme:
–   Assistance aux demandeurs d'emploi pour trouver du travail;
–   Assistance aux demandeurs d'emploi pour créer leur propre entreprise;
–   Assistance aux employeurs pour trouver de la main-d'œuvre;
–   Orientation professionnelle;
–   Formation liée à l'emploi;
–   Autres services liés à l'emploi: dispositif de bilan des compétences, instruction des dossiers aux fins de décisions pour les chômeurs indemnisés.
Pourcentage des demandeurs d'emploi qui cherchent un emploi au travers de cet organisme: 70%
3. Les informations personnelles suivantes sont enregistrées:
–   Nom;
–   Sexe;
–   Numéro de sécurité sociale (ou numéro d'identification également utilisé par d'autres organismes);
–   Adresse du domicile habituel;
–   Date de naissance;
–   Nationalité;
–   Niveau d'instruction/de formation, en distinguant six catégories. Des liens ont été établis avec la CITE;
–   Situation de travail présente et passée;
–   Type de profession de l'emploi antérieur et/ou actuel, en distinguant 1178 catégories. Aucun lien n'a été établi avec la CITP;
–   Type de profession de l'emploi recherché, avec 1178 catégories;
–   Nom et adresse de l'employeur ou du lieu de travail actuel ou passé;
–   Branche d'activité de l'employeur ou du lieu de travail actuel ou passé, en distinguant 697 catégories. Aucun lien n'a été établi avec la CITI;
–   Inscriptions/enregistrements antérieurs auprès de l'organisme.
4. Critères utilisés pour déterminer si une personne doit être incluse dans le registre (R) et/ou dans les statistiques de chômeurs (S):
–   Etre à la recherche d'un travail (R) et (S);
–   Etre disponible pour travailler (R) et (S);
–   Age: Minimum: 16 ans; pas de limite supérieure (R) et (S);
–   Etre résident dans le pays (R) et (S).
5. Critères utilisés pour déterminer si une personne doit être exclue du registre (R) et/ou des statistiques de chômeurs (S):
–   Avis de décès (R) et (S);
–   Etablissement de la personne à l'étranger (R) et (S);
–   Commencement d'un (nouveau) travail (R) et (S);
–   Commencement du service militaire (R) et (S);
–   Défaut de contact avec l'agence (R) et (S);
–   Incapacité à travailler (R) et (S).
6. Définition des personnes au chômage sur laquelle les statistiques sont établies

Toute personne physique s'étant présentée pour inscription à l'Agence pour l'Emploi et se disant à la recherche d'un emploi.

7. Mise à jour des registres

Les registres sont mis à jour quotidiennement.

8. Taux de chômage

Les statistiques basées sur les registres ne sont pas utilisées pour obtenir des taux de chômage.

9. Type de statistiques produites sur le nombre de chômeurs enregistrés
Période de référence: Mois, trimestre, année.
Fréquence de production: Mensuelle, trimestrielle, annuelle.
Variables utilisées:
–   Sexe;
–   Age;
–   Niveau d'instruction;
–   Profession;
–   Caractéristiques géographiques;
–   Durée de chômage.
10. Information méthodologique au sujet de ces statistiques
Publication:
–   Sur papier, à diffusion restreinte;
–   Sur un site Internet: www.apenc.nc
11. Comparaisons avec des statistiques provenant d'autres sources

Des comparaisons ont été faites avec des statistiques provenant du recensement de population.

12. Principaux changements intervenus depuis le début de ces séries statistiques

Il n'y a pas eu de changement important dans la législation, dans la capacité de l'agence et/ou dans les procédures administratives susceptibles d'avoir influencé de manière significative les statistiques.

Nouvelle-Zélande

1. Séries statistiques
Titre: Nombre de chômeurs enregistrés.
Première année disponible: 1952.
2. Organisme responsable de l'enregistrement des chômeurs ou demandeurs d'emploi
Nom de l'organisme: Emploi et revenu.
Type d'organisme: Organisme public relevant d'une autorité nationale.
Nom de l'autorité nationale: Ministère du Développement social.
Situation des bureaux chargés de l'enregistrement: Environ 170 bureaux de front dans tout le pays, dont 144 à plein temps.
Types de services fournis et/ou gérés par cet organisme:
–   Assistance aux demandeurs d'emploi pour trouver du travail;
–   Assistance aux demandeurs d'emploi pour créer leur propre entreprise;
–   Assistance aux employeurs pour trouver de la main-d'œuvre;
–   Orientation professionnelle;
–   Formation liée à l'emploi;
–   Autre: soutien financier.
3. Les informations personnelles suivantes sont enregistrées:
–   Identification du client;
–   Nom (prénom, deuxième prénom, nom de famille, prénom préféré, pseudonyme éventuel);
–   Sexe;
–   Adresse du domicile habituel (et, au cas où, adresse postale);
–   Date et lieu de naissance;
–   Groupe ethnique;
–   Niveau d'instruction, en distinguant neuf catégories;
–   Situation de travail (profession) présente et passée. Le curriculum vitae est enregistré sous forme de texte, les professions ne sont pas codées;
–   Type de travail (profession) de l'emploi recherché, en distinguant 25 catégories (classification «NZSCO», au niveau de cinq chiffres);
–   Nom et adresse de l'employeur ou du lieu de travail actuel ou passé (historique de l'emploi - durée de l'emploi et type de l'emploi, c'est-à-dire à plein temps ou à temps partiel);
–   Enregistrements antérieurs auprès de l'organisme;
–   Autres: détails des qualifications et compétences; incapacités, ou autres obstacles à l'emploi; moyen de transport; titulaire d'un permis de conduire; numéro de

téléphone; nom du partenaire; nombre d'heures maximum disponibles pour travailler; date de l'inscription; situation de l'emploi (sans emploi ou avec un emploi partiel).

4. Critères utilisés pour déterminer si une personne doit être incluse dans le registre (R) et/ou dans les statistiques de chômeurs (S):

– Etre sans travail (emploi partiel possible, c'est-à-dire moins de 30 heures par semaine, et désir de travailler plus d'heures ou de trouver un emploi à plein temps) (R) et (S);

– Etre à la recherche d'un travail (comme défini dans le plan d'action individuel élaboré avec le responsable du cas) (R et (S);

– Etre disponible pour travailler (R) et (S);

– Age: Minimum: 16 ans; pas de limite supérieure (R) et (S);

– Citoyenneté (R) et (S);

– Etre résident dans le pays (R) et (S);

– Autre: études ou formation: poursuivant des études ou une formation à temps partiel (une personne poursuivant des études ou une formation à plein temps ne peut pas être enregistrée comme chômeur) (R) et (S).

5. Critères utilisés pour déterminer si une personne doit être exclue du registre (R) et/ou des statistiques de chômeurs (S):

– Avis de décès (R) et (S);

– Etablissement de la personne à l'étranger (R) et (S);

– Commencement d'un (nouveau) travail à plein temps (R) et (S);

– Participation à certains programme de promotion de l'emploi (comme le «TaskForce Green»), à un programme de travaux publics, etc. (R) et (S);

– Entreprise d'une formation ou d'études à plein temps (R) et (S);

– Défaut de contact avec l'organisme/agence pendant 14 semaines (à moins de recevoir une indemnité Awork tested +, à laquelle on a droit après avoir passé un test de capacités professionnelles) (R) et (S);

– Refus d'offres d'emploi adaptées (au moins quatre refus consécutifs pour les personnes recevant une indemnité "work tested +); pas de critères formels pour les personnes ne recevant pas cette indemnité) (R) et (S);

– Refus d'offres de formation adaptées; (au moins quatre refus consécutifs pour les personnes recevant une indemnité "work tested +); pas de critères formels pour les personnes ne recevant pas cette indemnité) (R) et (S).

6. Définition des personnes au chômage sur laquelle les statistiques sont établies

Pour être enregistrée comme chômeur, une personne doit être:

– sans travail et rechercher du travail, ou travailler moins de 30 heures par semaine et chercher à travailler plus d'heures; et

– disponible pour travailler (ne pas déjà travailler à plein temps ou poursuivre des études ou une formation à plein temps); et

– âgée de 16 ans ou plus (ou âgée de 15 ans avec une autorisation du Ministère de l'Education pour quitter l'école plus tôt et chercher un travail à plein temps); et

– résidente de la Nouvelle Zélande; et

– autorisée légalement à travailler en Nouvelle-Zélande (c'est-à-dire citoyen de l'Australie ou de Nouvelle-Zélande, résident permanent de Nouvelle-Zélande, en possession d'un permis de travail de Nouvelle-Zélande, ou une personne née dans les Iles Cook, à Niue ou Tokelau).

7. Mise à jour des registres

Les registres sont mis à jour continuellement.

8. Taux de chômage

Les statistiques basées sur les registres ne sont pas utilisées pour obtenir des taux de chômage.

9. Type de statistiques sur le nombre de chômeurs enregistrés produites

Série 1: Registre mensuel.

Période de référence: Dernier jour du mois.

Fréquence de production: Mensuelle.

Variables utilisées:

– Sexe;

– Age;

– Niveau d'instruction;

– Caractéristiques géographiques;

– Durée de chômage;

– Indemnité reçue;

– Ethnie;

– Incapacité;

– Groupe de management individuel;

– Situation de famille;

– Age de l'enfant le plus jeune.

Publication: A usage interne uniquement.

Agence responsable de la publication: Ministère du Développement social.

Titre et périodicité de la publication: *Registre mensuel.*

Série 2: *Quarterly Client Profile* (Profil clients trimestriel).

Période de référence: Dernier jour du trimestre.

Fréquence de production: Trimestrielle.

Variables utilisées:

– Sexe;

– Age;

– Niveau d'instruction;

– Caractéristiques géographiques;

– Durée de chômage;

– Indemnité reçue;

– Ethnie;

– Situation du test de travail;

– Participation à des programmes d'emploi.

Publication:

– Sur papier, à diffusion grand public;

– Sur un site Internet (www.msd.govt.nz).

Agence responsable de la publication: Ministère du Développement social.

Titre et périodicité de la publication: *Profil clients trimestriel.*

Série 3: *Annual Statistical Profile* (Profil statistique annuel).

Période de référence: Dernier jour de l'année financière.

Fréquence de production: Annuelle.

Variables utilisées:

– Sexe;

– Age;

– Niveau d'instruction;

– Caractéristiques géographiques;

– Durée de chômage;

– Indemnité reçue;

– Ethnie;

– Participation à des programmes d'emploi.

Publication: Sur papier, à diffusion grand public.

Agence responsable de la publication: Ministère du Développement social.

Titre et périodicité de la publication: *Annual Statistical Profile.*

10. Information méthodologique au sujet de ces statistiques

Une information méthodologique sommaire se trouve dans chacune des publications ci-dessus mentionnées.

Publication:

– Sur papier, à diffusion grand public;

– Sur un site internet: www.msd.govt.nz

11. Comparaisons avec des statistiques provenant d'autres sources

Des comparaisons sont faites tous les trimestres avec des statistiques provenant de l'enquête de main-d'œuvre auprès des ménages (qui produit la mesure officielle du chômage, en accord avec les critères du BIT, et qui est administrée par le Bureau de statistique de Nouvelle-Zélande).

Des comparaisons furent faites en 2001 avec les statistiques de chômage du recensement de population de 1996.

Publication de la méthodologie et/ou des résultats de la comparaison: Ils n'ont pas été publiés.

12. Principaux changements intervenus depuis le début de ces séries statistiques

Des changements importants dans la législation, dans la capacité de l'agence et/ou dans les procédures administratives sont intervenus en:

1997: Introduction d'un test de capacités professionnelles (* work testing +) pour les personnes percevant un certain type d'allocation ;

1999: Extension aux personnes percevant déjà une allocation de revenu d'un droit à percevoir un certain nombre d'allocations supplémentaires, ainsi qu'aux conjoints/partenaires des personnes percevant cette allocation de revenu ;

Le test de capacités professionnelles (* work testing +) des personnes percevant une allocation de revenu et de leurs conjoints requéraient que les allocataires soient également enregistrés comme demandeurs d'emploi, alors qu'auparavant ils n'avaient pas à être inscrits.

L'impact de ces deux changements sur le nombre de demandeurs d'emploi enregistrés n'a pas été mesuré.

Panama

1. Séries statistiques
Titre: Chômage enregistré
Première année disponible: 1990
2. Organisme responsable de l'enregistrement des chômeurs ou demandeurs d'emploi
Nom de l'organisme: Departamento de Mano de Obra, Dirección General de Empleo (Département de la Main-d'œuvre, Direction générale de l'Emploi).
Type d'organisme: Organisme public de la Direction générale de l'Emploi - Ministère du Travail et du Développement du Travail (MITRADEL).
Situation des bureaux chargés de l'enregistrement: Dans toutes les directions régionales du Ministère du Travail et du Développement du Travail.
Types de services fournis et/ou gérés par cet organisme
– Assistance aux Assistance aux demandeurs d'emploi pour trouver du travail;
– Assistance aux demandeurs d'emploi pour créer leur propre entreprise;
– Assistance aux employeurs pour trouver de la main-d'œuvre;
– Orientation professionnelle;
– Formation liée à l'emploi;
– Autres: rapport avec le Programme du marché de l'emploi, la formation et l'autogestion de l'entreprise.
Pourcentage des demandeurs d'emploi qui cherchent un emploi au travers de cet organisme: 2.3% (en 1999).
3. Les informations personnelles suivantes sont enregistrées
– Nom;
– Sexe;
– Numéro de la carte d'identité;
– Numéro de sécurité sociale (ou numéro d'identification également utilisé par d'autres organismes);
– Adresse du domicile habituel;
– Date de naissance;
– Citoyenneté (par province de naissance);
– Nationalité;
– Niveau d'instruction/de formation, celui que la personne a atteint. Aucun lien n'a été établi avec la CITE;
– Situation de travail présente et passée, en distinguant sept catégories, dans lesquelles l'ensemble des expériences sont prises en compte;
– Type de profession de l'emploi antérieur et/ou actuel, en distinguant sept catégories; Des liens ont été établis avec la CITP. L'expérience et le(s) titre(s) sont indiqués dans la 1ère, 2ème, 3ème et 4ème professions;
– Type de profession de l'emploi recherché, avec sept catégories. Des liens ont été établis avec la CITP;
– Nom et adresse de l'employeur ou du lieu de travail actuel ou passé;
– Branche d'activité de l'employeur ou du lieu de travail actuel ou passé, en distinguant cinq catégories. Aucun lien n'a été établi avec la CITI ;
– Inscriptions/enregistrements antérieurs auprès de l'organisme;
– Autres: état civil; personne(s) à charge (âges); permis de conduire; possession ou non d'une voiture; mobilité; horaire de travail préféré; profession principale et autres options professionnelles.
4. Critères utilisés pour déterminer si une personne doit être incluse dans le registre (R) et/ou dans les statistiques de chômeurs (S)
– Etre sans travail (R) et (S);
– Etre à la recherche d'un travail (R);
– Etre disponible pour travailler (R);
– Age: Minimum: 18 ans; pas de limite supérieure (R) et (S);
– Citoyenneté (province de résidence) (R) et (S);

– Avoir précédemment travaillé (R);
– Durée souhaitée de l'emploi recherché et/ou du nombre d'heures de travail recherché (occasionnel ou permanent) (R) et (S).
5. Critères utilisés pour déterminer si une personne doit être exclue du registre (R) et/ou des statistiques de chômeurs (S)
– Avis de décès (R);
– Etablissement de la personne à l'étranger (R);
– Commencement d'un (nouveau) travail (R);
– Participation à un programme de promotion de l'emploi, à un programme de travaux publics, etc. (R);
– Entreprise d'une formation ou d'études (R);
– Défaut de contact avec l'organisme/agence (l'inscription est valable une année; terminée cette période, le demandeur d'emploi doit actualiser le dossier) (R);
– Refuser deux offres d'emploi adaptées (R);
– Toucher une pension (en cas de maladie) (R);
– Incapacité à travailler (R);
– Autres: au cas où il a été démontré que le bénéficiaire avait commis un délit dans l'entreprise où il avait été placé (R).
6. Définition des personnes au chômage sur laquelle les statistiques sont établies
Personnes de 18 ans et plus qui sont disponibles pour travailler, qui n'ont pas d'emploi ou de travail, mais qui ont travaillé précédemment et qui étaient à la recherche d'un emploi.

Ce sont également les personnes qui n'ont pas cherché de travail parce qu'elles en avaient trouvé un et qui devaient commencer à exercer à une date ultérieure, ainsi que celles qui n'ont jamais travaillé et qui sont à la recherche de leur premier emploi (nouveau travailleur), ou encore celles qui ne cherchaient pas de travail parce qu'elles en avaient cherché auparavant et qui étaient en attente de nouvelles. Enfin, ce sont aussi les personnes en âge de travailler, employés ou sous-employés mais à la recherche d'un emploi.
7. Mise à jour des registres
Les registres sont mis à jour mensuellement; cependant, la publication est annuelle.
8. Taux de chômage
Les statistiques basées sur les registres sont utilisées pour obtenir des taux de chômage.
9. Type de statistiques produites sur le nombre de chômeurs enregistrés
Période de référence: Année
Fréquence de production: Annuelle
Variables utilisées
– Sexe;
– Age;
– Niveau d'instruction;
– Profession;
– Branche d'activité;
– Régions de travail;
– Citoyenneté (nationaux/non nationaux);
– Durée de chômage;
– Autres: placement dans certains emplois seulement (personnes handicapées); situation du travailleur (employé, licencié ou nouveau travailleur); marins; autogestion de l'entreprise; directions régionales du travail (emploi).
Publication: Sur papier, pour des institutions publiques, privées, autres organismes et consultation publique.
Organisme/Agence responsable de la publication: Ministère du Travail et de Développement du Travail, Direction générale de l'Emploi.
Titre et périodicité de la publication: *Informe Anual de Trabajo de la Dirección General de Empleo* (Rapport annuel du travail de la Direction générale de l'Emploi).
10. Information méthodologique au sujet de ces statistiques
Publication: Sur papier, à diffusion grand public.
Organisme responsable: Direction générale de l'Emploi du Département de Recherches sur l'Emploi.
11. Comparaisons avec des statistiques provenant d'autres sources
Aucune comparaison n'a été faite avec des statistiques provenant d'autres sources.

L'information publiée est d'utilisation de base; elle ne s'utilise pas pour des analyses comparatives avec d'autres sources.

12. Principaux changements intervenus depuis le début de ces séries statistiques

Il n'y a pas eu de changement important dans la législation, dans la capacité de l'agence et/ou dans les procédures administratives susceptibles d'avoir influencé de manière significative les statistiques.

Papouasie-Nouvelle-Guinée

1. Séries statistiques
Titre: Bulletin annuel des statistiques du travail.
Première année disponible: 1996.
2. Organisme responsable de l'enregistrement des chômeurs ou demandeurs d'emploi
Nom de l'organisme: Service national de l'Emploi (National Employment Service NES).
Type d'organisme: Organisme public relevant d'une autorité nationale.
Nom de l'autorité nationale: Ministère du Travail et de l'Emploi.
Situation des bureaux chargés de l'enregistrement: Dans quelques régions seulement: il y a quatre bureaux régionaux NES.
Types de services fournis et/ou gérés par cet organisme:
– Assistance aux demandeurs d'emploi pour trouver du travail;
– Assistance aux employeurs pour trouver de la main-d'œuvre;
– Orientation professionnelle;
– Formation liée à l'emploi;
– Information sur les carrières professionnelles aux étudiants qui quittent l'école.
Pourcentage des demandeurs d'emploi qui cherchent un emploi au travers de cet organisme: 0,8%
3. Les informations personnelles suivantes sont enregistrées:
– Nom;
– Sexe;
– Numéro de sécurité sociale (ou numéro d'identification également utilisé par d'autres organismes);
– Adresse du domicile habituel;
– Date de naissance;
– Citoyenneté;
– Nationalité/groupe ethnique;
– Niveau d'instruction/de formation, en distinguant six catégories. Des liens ont été établis avec la CITE;
– Situation de travail présente et passée, en distinguant dix catégories;
– Type de profession de l'emploi antérieur et/ou actuel, en distinguant neuf catégories. Des liens ont été établis avec la CITP-88, au niveau des grands groupes;
– Nom et adresse de l'employeur ou du lieu de travail actuel ou passé;
– Branche d'activité de l'employeur ou du lieu de travail actuel ou passé, en distinguant 17 catégories. Des liens ont été établis avec la CITI, au niveau des divisions;
– Inscriptions/enregistrements antérieurs auprès de l'organisme.
4. Critères utilisés pour déterminer si une personne doit être incluse dans le registre (R) et/ou dans les statistiques de chômeurs (S):
– Etre sans travail (S);
– Etre à la recherche d'un travail (R);
– Etre disponible pour travailler (R);
– Age: Minimum: 15 ans; Maximum: 55 ans (R) et (S);
– Citoyenneté (R) et (S);
– Etre résident dans le pays (R);
– Avoir précédemment travaillé (R);
– Durée souhaitée de l'emploi recherché et/ou du nombre d'heures de travail recherché: durée minimum de huit à 10 heures de travail par jour (R).
5. Critères utilisés pour déterminer si une personne doit être exclue du registre (R) et/ou des statistiques de chômeurs (S):
– Avis de décès (R) et (S);
– Etablissement de la personne à l'étranger (R);
– Commencement d'un (nouveau) travail (R) et (S);
– Commencement du service militaire (R) et (S);
– Participation à un programme de promotion de l'emploi, à un programme de travaux publics, etc. (R) et (S);
– Entreprise d'une formation ou d'études (R);
– Défaut de contact avec l'organisme/agence (R);

– Refus d'offres d'emploi adaptées (R);
– Refus d'offres de formation adaptées (R);
– Fin de droit à l'allocation-chômage (R);
– Admission à toucher une pension (retraite, etc.) (R) et (S);
– Incapacité à travailler (R).
6. Définition des personnes au chômage sur laquelle les statistiques sont établies
Les personnes au chômage sont les personnes qui cherchent du travail et qui n'ont pas travaillé pendant une période de référence spécifiée. Dans certaines circonstances, cela peut se référer à des cas extrêmes de sous-emploi.
7. Mise à jour des registres
Les registres sont mis à jour tous les trimestres.
8. Taux de chômage
Les statistiques basées sur les registres sont utilisées pour obtenir des taux de chômage.
Les sources des données d'emploi qui sont partie du dénominateur sont l'enquête sur la main-d'œuvre, l'enquête auprès des établissements, le registre de sécurité sociale et le recensement de population.
Définition des personnes pourvues d'un emploi à cette fin:
Les personnes tirant un revenu (financier ou autre) d'une production de biens ou de services destinés au marché ; sont compris les salariés, les employeurs, les travailleurs à leur propre compte et les travailleurs familiaux non rémunérés.
9. Type de statistiques produites sur le nombre de chômeurs enregistrés
Période de référence: De un à quatre mois.
Fréquence de production: Trimestrielle.
Variables utilisées:
– Sexe;
– Age;
– Niveau d'instruction;
– Profession;
– Branche d'activité;
– Expérience professionnelle antérieure;
– Citoyenneté;
– Durée de chômage.
Publication: Sur papier, à diffusion restreinte.
Agence responsable de la publication: Service national de l'Emploi.
Titre et périodicité de la publication: *Rapport annuel statistique.*
10. Information méthodologique au sujet de ces statistiques
Publication: Sur papier, à diffusion restreinte.
Agence responsable: Ministère du Travail, Département des Statistiques.
11. Comparaisons avec des statistiques provenant d'autres sources
Des comparaisons ont été faites avec des statistiques provenant de l'enquête de main-d'œuvre, du recensement de population et avec des statistiques provenant d'autres sources.
Fréquence des comparaisons: Régulièrement, lorsque les statistiques sont publiées.
Publication de la méthodologie et/ou des résultats de la comparaison: Ils n'ont pas été publiés.
12. Principaux changements intervenus depuis le début de ces séries statistiques
Des changements importants dans la législation, dans la capacité de l'agence et/ou dans les procédures administratives ont eu lieu en 2000.

Pays-Bas

1. Séries statistiques
Titre: Chômage enregistré.
2. Organisme responsable de l'enregistrement des chômeurs ou demandeurs d'emploi
Nom de l'organisme: Centre du Travail et des Revenus.
Type d'organisme: Organisme public relevant d'une autorité nationale.
Situation des bureaux chargés de l'enregistrement: Dans toutes les régions du pays.
Types de services fournis et/ou gérés par cet organisme:
– Assistance aux demandeurs d'emploi pour trouver du travail;
– Assistance aux employeurs pour trouver de la main-d'œuvre;
– Autres services liés à l'emploi: information sur le marché du travail.

Pourcentage des demandeurs d'emploi qui cherchent un emploi au travers de cet organisme: 25%.

3. Les informations personnelles suivantes sont enregistrées:
- Nom;
- Sexe;
- Numéro de sécurité sociale (ou numéro d'identification similaire);
- Adresse du domicile habituel;
- Date de naissance;
- Citoyenneté;
- Nationalité/groupe ethnique;
- Niveau d'instruction/de formation. Aucun lien n'a été établi avec la CITE;
- Situation de travail présente et passée;
- Type de profession de l'emploi antérieur et/ou actuel;
- Type de profession de l'emploi recherché. Aucun lien n'a été établi avec la CITP;
- Nom et adresse de l'employeur ou du lieu de travail actuel ou passé;
- Branche d'activité de l'employeur ou du lieu de travail actuel ou passé. Des liens ont été établis avec la CITI, au niveau des classes;
- Inscriptions/enregistrements antérieurs auprès de l'organisme.

4. Critères utilisés pour déterminer si une personne doit être incluse dans le registre (R) et/ou dans les statistiques de chômeurs (S):
- Etre sans travail (R) et (S);
- Etre à la recherche d'un travail (R) et (S);
- Etre disponible pour travailler (R) et (S);
- Durée souhaitée du nombre d'heures de travail recherché supérieure à 12 heures par semaine(S).

5. Critères utilisés pour déterminer si une personne doit être exclue du registre (R) et/ou des statistiques de chômeurs (S):
- Avis de décès (R) et (S);
- Défaut de contact avec l'organisme/agence (R) et (S).

6. Définition des personnes au chômage sur laquelle les statistiques sont établies

Les personnes sans travail, à la recherche d'un travail et disponibles pour travailler. La durée souhaitée du travail recherché doit être supérieure à 12 heures par semaine.

7. Mise à jour des registres

Les registres sont mis à jour régulièrement.

8. Taux de chômage

Les statistiques basées sur les registres sont utilisées pour obtenir des taux de chômage.

La source des données d'emploi qui sont partie du dénominateur est l'enquête auprès des ménages sur la main-d'œuvre.

Définition des personnes pourvues d'un emploi à cette fin:

Les personnes ayant travaillé plus de 12 heures au cours de la période de référence.

9. Type de statistiques produites sur le nombre de chômeurs enregistrés

Période de référence: Mois.

Fréquence de production: Mensuelle.

Variables utilisées:
- Sexe;
- Age;
- Niveau d'instruction;
- Profession;
- Branche d'activité;
- Caractéristiques géographiques;
- Expérience professionnelle antérieure;
- Citoyenneté (nationaux/non nationaux);
- Durée de chômage.

Publication:
- Sur papier, à diffusion grand public;
- En format électronique, sur demande.

Organisme responsable de la publication: Centre du Travail et des Revenus.

Titre de la publication: *Arbeios Marytjournaal*

10. Information méthodologique au sujet de ces statistiques

Publication:
- Sur papier, à diffusion grand public;
- En format électronique, sur demande.

11. Comparaisons avec des statistiques provenant d'autres sources

Des comparaisons ont été faites avec des statistiques provenant des registres de sécurité sociale.

Fréquence des comparaisons: Régulièrement, lorsque les statistiques sont publiées.

Publication de la méthodologie et/ou des résultats de la comparaison: Ils n'ont pas été publiés.

12. Principaux changements intervenus depuis le début de ces séries statistiques

Il n'y a pas eu de changement important dans la législation, dans la capacité de l'agence et/ou dans les procédures administratives susceptibles d'avoir influencé de manière significative les statistiques.

Pérou

1. Séries statistiques

Titre: Personnes enregistrées à la recherche d'un emploi.

Première année disponible: Aux environs de 1975.

2. Organisme responsable de l'enregistrement des chômeurs ou demandeurs d'emploi

Nom de l'organisme: Red de Centros de Colocación e Información Laboral, Red CIL-PROEMPLEO (Réseau de Centres de Placement et d'Information professionnelle, Réseau CIL-PROEMPLEO).

Type d'organisme: Organisme public relevant d'une autorité nationale (il existe également des centres privés intégrés au réseau CIL-PROEMPLEO mais qui n'ont pas de fins lucratives).

Nom de l'autorité nationale: Dirección Nacional de Promoción del Empleo y Formación Profesional (Direction nationale de Promotion de l'Emploi et de la Formation professionnelle).

Situation des bureaux chargés de l'enregistrement: 40 bureaux dans toutes les villes principales du pays.

Types de services fournis et/ou gérés par cet organisme
- Assistance aux demandeurs d'emploi pour trouver du travail;
- Assistance aux employeurs pour trouver de la main-d'œuvre;
- Orientation professionnelle;
- Formation liée à l'emploi;
- Autres services liés à l'emploi: orientation dans la recherche d'emploi; orientation pour les travailleurs indépendants et les PME.

Pourcentage des demandeurs d'emploi qui cherchent un emploi au travers de cet organisme: 17.5%

3. Les informations personnelles suivantes sont enregistrées
- Nom;
- Sexe;
- Adresse du domicile habituel;
- Age;
- Citoyenneté;
- Niveau d'instruction/de formation, en distinguant cinq catégories. Des liens ont été établis avec la CITE;
- Situation de travail présente et passée, en distinguant cinq catégories;
- Type de profession de l'emploi antérieur et/ou actuel, en distinguant 10 catégories. Des liens ont été établis avec la CITP-88, au niveau des grands groupes;
- Type de profession de l'emploi recherché, avec 10 catégories. Des liens ont été établis avec la CITP-88, au niveau des grands groupes;
- Nom et adresse de l'employeur ou du lieu de travail actuel ou passé;
- Branche d'activité de l'employeur ou du lieu de travail actuel ou passé, en distinguant 12 catégories. Des liens ont été établis avec la CITI, Rév. 3;
- Inscriptions/enregistrements antérieurs auprès de l'organisme.

4. Critères utilisés pour déterminer si une personne doit être incluse dans le registre (R) et/ou dans les statistiques de chômeurs (S)
- Etre sans travail (R) et (S);
- Etre à la recherche d'un travail (R) et (S);
- Etre disponible pour travailler (R);
- Age: Minimum: 18 ans; Maximum: 65 ans (R) et (S);
- Avoir précédemment travaillé (S);
- Durée souhaitée de l'emploi recherché et/ou du nombre d'heures de travail recherché (S).

5. Critères utilisés pour déterminer si une personne doit être exclue du registre (R) et/ou des statistiques de chômeurs (S)
– Commencement d'un (nouveau) travail (R) et (S);
– Participation à un programme de promotion de l'emploi, à un programme de travaux publics, etc. (R);
– Défaut de contact avec l'organisme/agence (R) et (S);
– Refus d'offres d'emploi adaptées (R);
– Incapacité à travailler (R) et (S);
– Autres: Abandonner plus d'une fois des postes de travail proposés par le service (R).

6. Définition des personnes au chômage sur laquelle les statistiques sont établies
Non-spécifiée.

7. Mise à jour des registres
Les registres sont mis à jour mensuellement.

8. Taux de chômage
Les statistiques basées sur les registres ne sont pas utilisées pour obtenir des taux de chômage.

9. Type de statistiques produites sur le nombre de chômeurs enregistrés
Période de référence: Trimestre
Fréquence de production: Trimestrielle
Variables utilisées
– Sexe;
– Age;
– Niveau d'instruction;
– Profession;
– Branche d'activité;
– Expérience professionnelle antérieure;
– Durée de chômage;
– Autres: cours de formation et d'acquisition des compétences.
Publication: Sur papier, à diffusion restreinte.
Organisme responsable de la publication: Direction nationale de Promotion de l'Emploi et de la Formation professionnelle.

10. Information méthodologique au sujet de ces statistiques
Publication: Sur papier, à diffusion restreinte;
Organisme responsable: Direction nationale de l'Emploi et de la Formation professionnelle.

11. Comparaisons avec des statistiques provenant d'autres sources
Des comparaisons ont été faites avec des statistiques provenant de l'enquête auprès des ménages et du recensement de population.
Fréquence des comparaisons: De temps en temps (dernière année: 2000).
Publication de la méthodologie et/ou des résultats de la comparaison: La méthodologie et les résultats des comparaisons ont été publiés dans *Informe Estadístico Mensual* (Rapport statistique mensuel).

12. Principaux changements intervenus depuis le début de ces séries statistiques
Il n'y a pas eu de changement important dans la législation, dans la capacité de l'agence et/ou dans les procédures administratives susceptibles d'avoir influencé de manière significative les statistiques.

Philippines

1. Séries statistiques
Titre: Nombre de demandeurs d'emploi enregistrés (par région, par sexe et par programme).

2. Organisme responsable de l'enregistrement des chômeurs ou demandeurs d'emploi
Nom de l'organisme: Public Employment Service Office - PESO (Agence publique de l'Emploi).
Type d'organisme: Organisme public relevant d'une autorité nationale.
Nom de l'autorité nationale: Ministère du Travail et de l'Emploi.
Situation des bureaux chargés de l'enregistrement: Dans toutes les régions du pays.
Types de services fournis et/ou gérés par cet organisme:
– Assistance aux demandeurs d'emploi pour trouver du travail;
– Assistance aux demandeurs d'emploi pour créer leur propre entreprise;
– Assistance aux employeurs pour trouver de la main-d'œuvre;
– Orientation professionnelle;
– Formation liée à l'emploi;
– Autres services liés à l'emploi: information sur le marché du travail.
Pourcentage des demandeurs d'emploi qui cherchent un emploi au travers de cet organisme: 20%.

3. Les informations personnelles suivantes sont enregistrées:
– Nom;
– Sexe;
– Numéro de sécurité sociale (ou numéro d'identification également utilisé par d'autres organismes);
– Adresse du domicile habituel;
– Date de naissance;
– Citoyenneté;
– Nationalité/groupe ethnique;
– Niveau d'instruction/de formation (niveau d'éducation, intitulé des études). Aucun lien n'a été établi avec la CITE;
– Situation de travail présente et passée: actuellement en emploi ou précédemment en emploi;
– Type de profession de l'emploi antérieur et/ou actuel, en distinguant 10 catégories, basées sur la Classification standard des Professions des Philippines (PSOC);
– Type de profession de l'emploi recherché, avec 10 catégories (PSOC); Des liens ont été établis avec la CITP-88;
– Nom et adresse de l'employeur ou du lieu de travail actuel ou passé.

4. Critères utilisés pour déterminer si une personne doit être incluse dans le registre (R) et/ou dans les statistiques de chômeurs (S):
– Etre sans travail (R) et (S);
– Etre à la recherche d'un travail (R) et (S);
– Etre disponible pour travailler (R);
– Age: Minimum: 15 ans; pas de limite supérieure (S);
– Citoyenneté (R);
– Etre résident dans le pays (R);
– Avoir précédemment travaillé (R);
– Durée souhaitée de l'emploi recherché (R).

5. Critères utilisés pour déterminer si une personne doit être exclue du registre (R) et/ou des statistiques de chômeurs (S):
– Avis de décès (R);
– Etablissement de la personne à l'étranger (R);
– Commencement d'un (nouveau) travail (R);
– Commencement du service militaire (R);
– Participation à un programme de promotion de l'emploi, à un programme de travaux publics, etc. (R);
– Entreprise d'une formation ou d'études (R);
– Défaut de contact avec l'organisme/agence (R);
– Incapacité à travailler (R).

6. Définition des personnes au chômage sur laquelle les statistiques sont établies
Demandeurs d'emploi enregistrés: nombre de demandeurs d'emploi qui prouvent leur intérêt à profiter des différents services de recherche d'emploi mis à leur disposition par l'Agence publique de l'Emploi (PESO) en remplissant le formulaire d'enregistrement.

7. Mise à jour des registres
Les registres sont mis à jour régulièrement.

8. Taux de chômage
Les statistiques basées sur les registres ne sont pas utilisées pour obtenir des taux de chômage.

9. Type de statistiques produites sur le nombre de chômeurs enregistrés
Série: Nombre de demandeurs d'emploi enregistrés.
Période de référence: Mois.
Fréquence de production: Mensuelle.
Variables utilisées:
– Sexe;
– Age;
– Niveau d'instruction;
– Profession;
– Branche d'activité;
– Caractéristiques géographiques;
– Expérience professionnelle antérieure;
– Citoyenneté.
Publication: Sur papier, à diffusion restreinte.
Organisme responsable de la publication: Bureau of Local Employment - BLE (Bureau d'Emploi local).

10. Information méthodologique au sujet de ces statistiques
Publication: Non diffusée, à usage interne uniquement.
11. Comparaisons avec des statistiques provenant d'autres sources
Des comparaisons ont été faites avec des statistiques provenant de l'enquête de main-d>œuvre.
Fréquence des comparaisons: Occasionnelles.
Publication de la méthodologie et/ou des résultats de la comparaison: Ils n'ont pas été publiés.
12. Principaux changements intervenus depuis le début de ces séries statistiques
Les principaux changements sont intervenus en 1999 («Loi sur le Agence publique de l'Emploi (RA8759)»).

Pologne

1. Séries statistiques
Titre: Chômage enregistré.
Première année disponible: 1999.
2. Organisme responsable de l'enregistrement des chômeurs ou demandeurs d'emploi
Nom de l'organisme: Powiat (Agences pour l'emploi régionales).
Type d'organisme: Organisme public relevant d'une autorité locale.
Situation des bureaux chargés de l'enregistrement: Dans tous les départements du pays.
Types de services fournis et/ou gérés par cet organisme:
– Assistance aux demandeurs d'emploi pour trouver du travail;
– Assistance aux demandeurs d'emploi pour créer leur propre entreprise;
– Assistance aux employeurs pour trouver de la main-d'œuvre;
– Orientation professionnelle;
– Formation liée à l'emploi;
– Paiement des indemnités de chômage;
– Autres: organisation d'emplois temporaires in extremis et projets de travaux publics (travail subventionné).
Pourcentage des demandeurs d'emploi qui cherchent un emploi au travers de cet organisme: Pas connu, puisque il n'y a pas eu de recherche à ce sujet.
3. Les informations personnelles suivantes sont enregistrées:
– Nom;
– Sexe;
– Adresse du domicile habituel;
– Date de naissance;
– Citoyenneté;
– Niveau d'instruction/de formation, en distinguant cinq catégories. Aucun lien n'a été établi avec la CITE;
– Situation de travail présente/passée, par durée de l'emploi (moins d'une année, de un à cinq ans, de cinq à 10 ans, de 10 à 20 ans, de 20 à 30 ans, plus de 30 ans, et jamais employé(e));
– Type de travail (profession) de l'emploi antérieur ou actuel, en distinguant un nombre non spécifié de groupes. Dès liens ont été établis avec la CITP-88, au niveau des sous-grands groupes. (La classification polonaise des professions et spécialités est ajustée à la CITP-88);
– Type de profession (occupation) de l'emploi recherché, avec un nombre non spécifié de groupes. Des liens ont été établis avec la CITP-88, au niveau des sous-grands groupes;
– Nom et adresse de l'employeur ou du lieu de travail actuel ou passé;
– Branche d'activité (industrie) de l'employeur ou du lieu de travail actuel ou passé, en distinguant un nombre non spécifié de groupes. Des liens ont été établis avec la NACE, rév.1, au niveau des divisions. (La classification polonaise des activités est basée sur la NACE, rév.1);
– Enregistrements antérieurs auprès de l'organisme;
– Autres: solde du nombre des personnes sans emploi; offres d'emploi; chômeurs bénéficiant de différentes formes d'activités liées au marché du travail (formation, orientation professionnelle, clubs d'emploi, etc.).
– Note: Les rapports statistiques ne couvrent pas les données à l'unité; de ce fait une grande partie de l'information ci-dessus est enregistrée seulement sur la carte d'enregistrement de la personne au chômage/de la

personne à la recherche d'un emploi et ne figure pas dans les statistiques sur le marché de l'emploi.
4. Critères utilisés pour déterminer si une personne doit être incluse dans le registre (R) et/ou dans les statistiques de chômeurs (S):
– Etre sans travail (R) et (S);
– Etre à la recherche d'un travail (R) et (S);
– Etre disponible pour travailler (R);
– Age: Minimum: 18 ans (avec exception des jeunes diplômés); Maximum: 65 ans pour les hommes; 60 ans pour les femmes) (R) et (S);
– Citoyenneté (R) et (S);
– Etre résident dans le pays (R) et (S);
– Avoir précédemment travaillé (R) et (S).
5. Critères utilisés pour déterminer si une personne doit être exclue du registre (R) et/ou des statistiques de chômeurs (S):
– Décès (R) et (S);
– Etablissement de la personne à l'étranger (R) et (S);
– Commencement d'un (nouveau) travail (R) et (S);
– Commencement du service militaire (R) et (S);
– Participation à un programme de promotion de l'emploi, à un programme de travaux publics, etc. (R) et (S);
– Entreprise d'une formation ou d'études (R) et (S);
– Défaut de contact avec l'organisme/agence (exclusion pour trois mois) (R) et (S);
– Refus de deux offres d'emploi adaptées ou d'offres de travaux publics (exclusion pour six mois) (R) et (S);
– Admission à toucher une pension de retraite (R) et (S);
– Incapacité à travailler (R) et (S);
– Autres: renonciation volontaire au statut de personne sans emploi; bénéficiaires d'un prêt du fonds du travail ou du fonds de réhabilitation des handicapés pour commencer une activité économique; atteinte de l'age de 65 ans pour les hommes et de 60 ans pour les femmes; admission au droit à toucher une pré-retraite (R) et (S).
6. Définition des personnes au chômage sur laquelle les statistiques sont établies
Une personne est considérée sans emploi si elle:
N'est pas employée (c'est-à-dire ne travaille pas sur la base d'un contrat de travail ou de service, ou comme travailleur extérieur à l'établissement); n'exerce pas un quelconque autre travail rémunéré (c'est-à-dire n'exerce pas de travail sur la base d'un contrat de droit civil (contrat passé par une agence, une commission, ou pour un travail spécifique) ou pendant une période au cours de laquelle cette personne fait partie d'une coopérative de production agricole ou d'une coopérative de cercles ruraux (services agricoles); et:
– Est apte à travailler et prête à accepter un travail à plein temps, selon le nombre d'heures de travail exigé pour un métier ou un service donné (à l'exception des personnes handicapées);
– Ne fréquente pas une école de jour;
– Est enregistrée dans un bureau d'emploi *"powiat"*, compétent pour son lieu de résidence permanente ou temporaire;
– Est âgée de plus de 18 ans (à l'exception des jeunes diplômés);
– Est âgée de moins de 65 ans pour les hommes et de moins de 60 ans pour les femmes;
– N'est pas en droit de percevoir une retraite suite à une incapacité de travail;
– N'est pas propriétaire ou copropriétaire d'un terrain agricole d'une surface cultivable de plus de deux hectares imposables, ou n'est pas couvert par une assurance retraite provenant du travail permanent d'un conjoint ou d'un membre du ménage d'une ferme ou d'un domaine cultivable de plus de 2 hectares imposables;
– N'est pas propriétaire ou copropriétaire d'une ferme classée dans un secteur spécial de production agricole en termes de fiscalité, à moins que le revenu provenant du secteur spécial de production agricole, calculé pour l'impôt sur le revenu, soit inférieur ou égal au revenu moyen provenant d'un travail sur une ferme individuelle de deux hectares imposables, comme déterminé par le président du bureau central des statistiques, basé sur la fiscalité des zones rurales, ou n'est pas couvert par une assurance retraite couvrant le travail permanent d'un conjoint ou d'un membre du ménage sur une telle ferme;

– N'a pas commencé une activité économique non liée à l'agriculture entre le jour indiqué dans le formulaire d'enregistrement et le jour ou l'enregistrement de cette activité a été annulé, ou n'est pas couvert - sur la base de provisions spéciales - par une assurance sociale obligatoire, à l'exception d'assurances sociales pour agriculteurs ou assurances retraite;

– Est une personne handicapée dont l'état de santé lui permet d'accomplir un travail au moins à mi-temps en fonction de la profession ou du service;

– N'est pas temporairement détenue ou qu cours d'une période d'emprisonnement (privation de liberté);

– Ne reçoit pas de revenu mensuel dont le montant dépasse la moitié du revenu minimum;

– Ne reçoit pas, sur la base de la législation sur l'assistance sociale, d'allocation permanente, d'allocation de compensation permanente, d'allocation périodique garantie ou de pension sociale.

7. Mise à jour des registres

Les registres sont mis à jour régulièrement.

8. Taux de chômage

Les statistiques basées sur les registres sont utilisées pour obtenir des taux de chômage.

Les sources des données d'emploi qui sont partie du dénominateur des taux de chômage sont l'enquête sur la main-d'œuvre, l'enquête auprès des établissements, les estimations officielles et le recensement de population.

Définition des personnes pourvues d'un emploi à cette fin:

Les données concernant les personnes pourvues d'un emploi sont en relation avec les personnes exécutant un travail rémunéré (un travail générant un revenu ou des bénéfices). Les catégories suivantes sont incluses:

– Les personnes employées sur la base d'un lien avec l'emploi (contrat de travail, désignation, nomination ou élection);

– Les employeurs et les personnes travaillant à leur compte (personnes indépendantes);

– Les propriétaires et copropriétaires d'entités impliquées dans une activité économique excepté les fermes individuelles agricoles;

– Les autres personnes indépendantes, à savoir les professionnels à leur compte;

– Les travailleurs extérieurs à l'établissement et autres.

9. Type de statistiques produites sur le nombre de chômeurs enregistrés

Série 1:

Période de référence: Non spécifiée.

Fréquence de production: Annuelle.

Variables utilisées:

– Sexe;
– Age;
– Niveau d'instruction;
– Occupation;
– Expérience professionnelle antérieure;
– Durée de chômage;
– Autres: entrées-sorties; ayant droit à des indemnités; taux de chômage; n'ayant jamais travaillé; diplômé(e)s; licencié(e)s pour des raisons inhérentes à l'entreprise; par lieu de résidence; offres d'emploi; bénéficiaires de mesures actives du marché du travail.

Publication:

– Sur papier, à diffusion grand public;
– Sur CD-ROM.

Agence responsable de la publication: Bureau central des statistiques.

Titre et périodicité de la publication: *Annuaire statistique de la république de Pologne.*

Série 2:

Période de référence: Non spécifiée.

Fréquence de production: Bisannuelle.

Variables utilisées:

– Sexe;
– Age;
– Niveau d'instruction;
– Occupation;
– Expérience professionnelle antérieure;
– Caractéristiques géographiques;
– Expérience professionnelle antérieure;
– Durée de chômage;

– Autres: entrées-sorties; ayant droit à des indemnités; taux de chômage; n'ayant jamais travaillé; diplômé(e)s; licencié(e)s pour des raisons inhérentes à l'entreprise; par lieu de résidence; bénéficiaires de mesures actives du marché du travail.

Publication:

– Sur papier, à diffusion grand public;
– Sur CD-ROM.

Agence responsable de la publication: Bureau central des statistiques.

Titre et périodicité de la publication: *Annuaire statistique du travail*, semestriel.

Série 3:

Période de référence: Non spécifiée.

Fréquence de production: Trimestrielle.

Variables utilisées:

– Sexe;
– Age;
– Niveau d'instruction;
– Occupation;
– Caractéristiques géographiques;
– Expérience professionnelle antérieure;
– Durée de chômage;
– Autres: entrées-sorties; début du travail; ayant droit à des indemnités; taux de chômage; licencié(e)s pour des raisons inhérentes à l'entreprise; ayant travaillé précédemment ou non; diplômé(e)s; par lieu de résidence; offres d'emploi; mesures actives du marché du travail pour personnes enregistrées sans emploi.

Publication: Sur papier, à diffusion grand public.

Agence responsable de la publication: Bureau central des statistiques.

Titre et périodicité de la publication: *Chômage enregistré*, trimestriel.

Autres séries:

Le bureau national des statistiques publie les séries d'information suivantes:

1. *Information sur la situation et la structure du chômage*, mensuel.
2. *Personnes sans emploi pour plus de 12 mois.*
3. *Marché du travail en Pologne*, annuel.
4. *Services institutionnels du marché du travail*, annuel.
5. *Autorisations d'emploi pour étrangers*, semestriel, annuel.
6. *Chômage des femmes*, semestriellement, annuel.
7. *Information sur la situation et la structure du chômage*, semestriel.
8. *Information sur la situation et la structure du chômage enregistré dans les régions rurales*, semestriel, annuel.
9. ***Information sur la situation du marché du travail des jeunes,*** semestriel, annuel.
10. *Personnes sans emploi et offres d'emploi pour personnes sans emploi par profession et spécialités*, semestriel, annuel.

11. ***Femmes sans emploi par professions et spécialités,*** semestriel, annuel.
12. *Diplômé(e)s d'écoles au dessus du niveau du primaire par professions apprises*, semestriel, annuel.
13. *Analyse du chômage sur la base de la classification polonaise des activités*, semestriel, annuel.
14. ***Personnes sans emploi par professions et spécialités,*** semestriel, annuel.

10. Information méthodologique au sujet de ces statistiques

Publication:

– Sur papier, à diffusion grand public;
– En format électronique, sur demande;
– Sur un site Internet (http://praca@gov.pl.

Agence responsable: Bureau central des statistiques; bureau national du travail.

11. Comparaisons avec des statistiques provenant d'autres sources

Des comparaisons ont été faites avec des statistiques provenant de l'enquête sur le marché du travail et le recensement de population.

Fréquence des comparaisons: Régulièrement, lors de la publication des statistiques.

Publication de la méthodologie et/ou des résultats de la comparaison: Ils n'ont pas été publiés.

12. Principaux changements intervenus depuis le début de ces séries statistiques

Des changements importants dans la législation, dans la capacité de l'agence et/ou dans les procédures administratives sont intervenus en 1991, 1996, 1997 et 2001. Les changements dans les statistiques qui en résultaient n'ont pas été évalués.

Polynésie française

1. Séries statistiques
Titre: Demandeurs d'emploi.
Première année disponible: 1990.
2. Organisme responsable de l'enregistrement des chômeurs ou demandeurs d'emploi
Nom de l'organisme: Service de l'Emploi, de la Formation et de l'Insertion professionnelle.
Type d'organisme: Organisme public relevant d'une autorité locale: Service public territorial relevant du gouvernement de la Polynésie française.
Situation des bureaux chargés de l'enregistrement: A Papeete, chef-lieu, ainsi qu'une antenne à Uturoa-Raiatea, chef-lieu d'archipel.
Types de services fournis et/ou gérés par cet organisme:
–   Assistance aux demandeurs d'emploi pour trouver du travail;
–   Assistance aux employeurs pour trouver de la main-d'œuvre;
–   Orientation professionnelle;
–   Formation liée à l'emploi;
–   Autres services liés à l'emploi: mise en relation des demandes d'emploi et des offres d'emploi, incitation à l'embauche auprès des employeurs, solutions de formation et d'insertion offertes aux demandeurs.
3. Les informations personnelles suivantes sont enregistrées:
–   Nom;
–   Sexe;
–   Numéro de sécurité sociale (ou numéro d'identification également utilisé par d'autres organismes);
–   Adresse du domicile habituel;
–   Date de naissance;
–   Formation, expérience professionnelle;
–   Situation de travail présente et passée;
–   Type de profession de l'emploi antérieur et/ou actuel. Aucun lien n'a été établi avec la CITP;
–   Type de profession de l'emploi recherché;
–   Inscriptions/enregistrements antérieurs auprès de l'organisme.
4. Critères utilisés pour déterminer si une personne doit être incluse dans le registre (R) et/ou dans les statistiques de chômeurs (S):
–   Etre sans travail (R) et (S);
–   Etre à la recherche d'un travail (R) et (S);
–   Etre disponible pour travailler (R) et (S);
–   Age: Minimum: 16 ans; pas de limite supérieure (R) et (S).
5. Critères utilisés pour déterminer si une personne doit être exclue du registre (R) et/ou des statistiques de chômeurs (S):
–   Commencement d'un (nouveau) travail (R) et (S);
–   Entreprise d'une formation ou d'études (R) et (S);
–   Date de validité de l'inscription dépassée (défaut de contact avec l'agence) (R) et (S).
6. Définition des personnes au chômage sur laquelle les statistiques sont établies
Les statistiques ne sont pas des statistiques sur le nombre de chômeurs, mais des statistiques sur le nombre de demandeurs d'emploi inscrits.
7. Mise à jour des registres
Les registres sont mis à jour régulièrement, en continu.
8. Taux de chômage
Les statistiques basées sur les registres ne sont pas utilisées pour obtenir des taux de chômage.
9. Type de statistiques produites sur le nombre de chômeurs enregistrés
Information non disponible.
10. Information méthodologique au sujet de ces statistiques
Information non disponible.
11. Comparaisons avec des statistiques provenant d'autres sources

Il n'y a pas eu de comparaisons faites avec des statistiques provenant d'autres sources.
12. Principaux changements intervenus depuis le début de ces séries statistiques
Il n'y a pas eu de changement important dans la législation, dans la capacité de l'agence et/ou dans les procédures administratives susceptibles d'avoir influencé de manière significative les statistiques.

Portugal

1. Séries statistiques
Titre: *Nombre de demandeurs d'emploi* et *Nombre de chômeurs demandeurs d'emploi.*
Première année disponible: 1967.
2. Organisme responsable de l'enregistrement des chômeurs ou demandeurs d'emploi
Nom de l'organisme: Instituto de Emprego e Formação Professional (IEPF) (Institut de l'Emploi et de la Formation Professionnelle).
Type d'organisme: Organisme public relevant d'une autorité nationale.
Nom de l'autorité nationale: Ministère de la Sécurité sociale et du Travail.
Situation des bureaux chargés de l'enregistrement: Dans l'ensemble du pays. 86 agences pour l'emploi distribuées dans les cinq régions de la partie continentale du pays, plus une agence dans la région autonome de Madère et trois agences dans la région autonome des Açores (les agences des deux régions autonomes ne dépendent pas directement de l'IEFP, mais des services régionaux autonomes; néanmoins, les statistiques sont consolidées par l'IEFP).
Ces agences créent également des "antennes pour l'emploi", à caractère permanent ou non, en fonction de critères tels que la densité de la population ou les chiffres de chômage enregistré. Actuellement il y a près de 150 de ces antennes.
Types de services fournis et/ou gérés par cet organisme:
–   Assistance aux demandeurs d'emploi pour trouver du travail;
–   Assistance aux demandeurs d'emploi pour créer leur propre emploi ou entreprise;
–   Assistance aux employeurs pour trouver de la main-d'œuvre;
–   Orientation professionnelle;
–   Formation liée à l'emploi;
–   Paiement des indemnités de chômage: l'IEFP n'est pas responsable pour ce paiement mais il coopère avec la Sécurité Sociale pour contrôler les allocataires en ce qui concerne leur prédisposition active pour l'intégration dans le marché du travail.
Pourcentage des demandeurs d'emploi qui cherchent un emploi au travers de cet organisme: 49% (fin 2001; source: Institut National de Statistique, «Enquête sur l'emploi»)
3. Les informations personnelles suivantes sont enregistrées:
–   Nom;
–   Sexe;
–   Numéro de sécurité sociale (ou numéro d'identification également utilisé par d'autres organismes);
–   Adresse du domicile habituel;
–   Date de naissance;
–   Nationalité;
–   Niveau d'instruction/de formation, en distinguant 11 catégories. Aucun lien n'a été établi avec la CITE, néanmoins la classification nationale des domaines de formation, revue en avril 2001, a des liens directs avec la CITE-97;
–   Situation de travail présente et passée, en distinguant sept catégories;
–   Type de profession de l'emploi antérieur et/ou actuel, en distinguant 355 catégories (groupes de base). Des liens ont été établis avec la CITP-88 au niveau des groupes de base;
–   Type de profession de l'emploi recherché, avec 355 catégories (groupes de base);
–   Nom et adresse de l'employeur ou du lieu de travail actuel ou passé;
–   Branche d'activité de l'employeur ou du lieu de travail actuel ou passé, en distinguant 715 catégories. Des liens ont été établis avec la CITI, au niveau des divisions; avec

- la NACE, au niveau des classes;
- Inscriptions/enregistrements antérieurs auprès de l'organisme;
- Autre: identification des personnes handicapées et du type de handicap, par exemple.

4. Critères utilisés pour déterminer si une personne doit être incluse dans le registre (R) et/ou dans les statistiques de chômeurs (S):

- Etre sans travail: (R) et (S);
- Etre à la recherche d'un travail dépendant: une demande de support financier ou technique ayant pour but la création de sa propre entreprise n'est pas considérée comme une demande d'emploi (R) et (S);
- Etre disponible pour travailler dans un délai maximum de 15 jours à compter de la date d'inscription (R) et (S);
- Age: Minimum: 16 ans; pas de limite supérieure (R) et (S);
- Etre résident dans le pays, c'est-à- dire soit présenter un document d'identification qui prouve que l'on réside au Portugal, en général la carte d'identité, soit, pour les citoyens non-nationaux, provenant des pays non membres de l'EEE (Espace Économique Européen), présenter un titre de séjour délivré par le Service des Étrangers et des Frontières (R) et (S);
- Le candidat doit par ailleurs respecter les devoirs suivants: Accepter toute offre d'emploi considérée comme adaptée; accepter les contrôles effectués par les Agences pour l'emploi; accepter le "Plan personnel d'emploi" mis au point par l'Agence et le candidat comme le plus adéquat en fonction de son profil personnel et professionnel, et qui a pour but son intégration dans le marché du travail.
- Quant aux chômeurs qui perçoivent des allocations de chômage, ils doivent également: Accepter un travail considéré comme d'utilité publique; accepter la formation professionnelle qui leur est offerte; être activement à la recherche d'un travail.

5. Critères utilisés pour déterminer si une personne doit être exclue du registre (R) et/ou des statistiques de chômeurs (S):

- Avis de décès (R) et (S);
- Etablissement de la personne à l'étranger (R) et (S);
- Commencement d'un (nouveau) travail (R) et (S);
- Commencement du service militaire (R) et (S);
- Participation à un programme de promotion de l'emploi (R) et (S);
- Participation à un programme de travaux publics (S);
- Entreprise d'une formation ou d'études. Il peut s'agir d'un cours de formation professionnelle ou d'un programme de formation-emploi, promu ou non par l'IEFP (R) et (S);
- Défaut de contact avec l'agence: ne pas se présenter sans justification valable à une convocation (que ce soit pour la présentation des offres d'emploi adaptées, d 'une formation professionnelle, pour un travail considéré comme socialement nécessaire, ou pour un simple contrôle de présence) entraîne la radiation après la 2ème convocation; de la même façon, ne pas répondre à un contrôle postal entraîne la radiation après un mois pour les allocataires, et après deux mois pour les non allocataires (R) et (S);
- Refus d'offres d'emploi adaptées (un refus) (R) et (S);
- Refus d'offres de formation adaptées (un refus) (R) et (S);
- Incapacité à travailler: l'incapacité totale par maladie (qu'elle soit temporaire ou permanente) exclut la possibilité d'enregistrement comme demandeur d'emploi ou comme chômeur. L'incapacité par invalidité n'est admissible comme critère pour l'exclusion d'un enregistrement que dans le cas où elle est totale (qu'elle soit temporaire ou permanente), applicable à toutes les professions adaptées (ou adaptables), attestée par le service de médecine du travail des agences pour l'emploi et, au cas des allocataires de prestations de chômage, confirmée par le Service de Vérification des Incapacités (S.V.I.) (R) et (S).

6. Définition des personnes au chômage sur laquelle les statistiques sont établies

On considère comme "chômeur" un candidat enregistré auprès d'une agence pour l'emploi qui est sans emploi, à la recherche d'un emploi comme travailleur dépendant, immédiatement disponible et apte à travailler.

Par "immédiatement disponible" on entend que le candidat doit s'engager à accepter un emploi dans un délai maximum de 15 jours à compter de la date de son inscription. Au delà de cette période, l'acceptation du poste de travail doit être immédiate.

Par "apte à travailler" on entend que le candidat doit démontrer qu'il possède les aptitudes (physiques, mentales et professionnelles) nécessaires pour l'exercice d'une activité professionnelle, et l'inexistence d'incapacité par maladie.

7. Mise à jour des registres
Les registres sont mis à jour régulièrement, en continu.

8. Taux de chômage
Les statistiques basées sur les registres ne sont pas utilisées pour obtenir des taux de chômage.

9. Type de statistiques sur le nombre de chômeurs enregistrés produites
Période de référence: Mois.
Fréquence de production: Mensuelle.
Variables utilisées:
- Sexe;
- Age;
- Niveau d'instruction;
- Profession;
- Branche d'activité;
- Caractéristiques géographiques;
- Citoyenneté (nationaux/non nationaux);
- Durée de chômage: durée d'enregistrement comme demandeur d'emploi dans une Agence pour l'emploi;
- Autres: situation face à l'emploi - en quête d'un premier emploi / en quête d'un nouvel emploi.

Publication:
- Sur papier, à diffusion grand public;
- En format électronique, sur demande;
- Sur un site Internet:
- http://www.iefp.pt/estatisticas/estatmercemp.htm

Organisme responsable de la publication: IEPF.
Titre et périodicité des publications: *Information mensuelle du marché de l'emploi. Le marché de l'emploi* - statistiques mensuelles. *Les agences pour l'emploi* B *statistiques mensuelles. Les municipalités* B *statistiques du chômage enregistré et ratios corrigés du chômage enregistré* B *statistiques trimestrielles. Evolution et situation des marchés locaux de travail* B *statistiques trimestrielles. Le marché de l'emploi* - rapport annuel.

10. Information méthodologique au sujet de ces statistiques
Publication:
- Sur papier, à diffusion grand public;
- En format électronique, sur demande;
- Sur un site Internet:
- http://www.iefp.pt/estatisticas/estatmercemp.htm

Organisme responsable pour la diffusion de l'information méthodologique: IEPF.

11. Comparaisons avec des statistiques provenant d' autres sources
Des comparaisons ont été faites avec des statistiques provenant de l'enquête de main-d'œuvre, d'autres enquêtes auprès des ménages, et du recensement de population.
Fréquence des comparaisons: régulièrement.
Publication de la méthodologie et/ou des résultats de la comparaison: Ils n'ont pas été publiés.

12. Principaux changements intervenus depuis le début de ces séries statistiques
Il n'y a pas eu de changement important dans la législation, dans la capacité de l'agence et/ou dans les procédures administratives susceptibles d'avoir influencé de manière significative les statistiques.

Qatar

1. Séries statistiques
Titre: Chômage enregistré.
Première année disponible: 1965.

2. Organisme responsable de l'enregistrement des chômeurs ou demandeurs d'emploi
Nom de l'organisme: Ministère du Travail
Type d'organisme: Organisme public relevant d'une autorité nationale.
Nom de l'autorité nationale: Ministère de la Fonction publique et de l'Habitat.

Situation des bureaux chargés de l'enregistrement: Au siège du Ministère du Travail.

Types de services fournis et/ou gérés par cet organisme:
- Assistance aux demandeurs d'emploi pour trouver du travail;
- Assistance aux employeurs pour trouver de la main-d'œuvre;
- Orientation professionnelle;
- Formation liée à l'emploi.

3. Les informations personnelles suivantes sont enregistrées:
- Nom;
- Sexe;
- Adresse du domicile habituel;
- Date de naissance;
- Citoyenneté;
- Nationalité/groupe ethnique;
- Niveau d'instruction/de formation, en distinguant un nombre de catégories non spécifié. Des liens ont été établis avec la CITE;
- Situation de travail présente et passée, en distinguant quatre catégories;
- Type de profession de l'emploi antérieur et/ou actuel, en distinguant 10 catégories. Des liens ont été établis avec la CITP;
- Type de profession de l'emploi recherché, avec un nombre de catégories non spécifié; Des liens ont été établis avec la CITP;
- Nom et adresse de l'employeur ou du lieu de travail actuel ou passé;
- Branche d'activité de l'employeur ou du lieu de travail actuel ou passé, en distinguant 136 catégories. Des liens ont été établis avec la CITI-rév.3 au niveau des groupes;
- Inscriptions/enregistrements antérieurs auprès de l'organisme;
- Autre: expérience professionnelle.

4. Critères utilisés pour déterminer si une personne doit être incluse dans le registre (R) et/ou dans les statistiques de chômeurs (S):
- Etre sans travail (R) et (S);
- Etre à la recherche d'un travail (R) et (S);
- Age: Minimum: 18 ans; pas de limite supérieure (R) et (S);
- Etre résident dans le pays (R) et (S);
- Avoir précédemment travaillé (R) et (S).

5. Critères utilisés pour déterminer si une personne doit être exclue du registre (R) et/ou des statistiques de chômeurs (S):
- Avis de décès (R);
- Etablissement de la personne à l'étranger (R);
- Commencement d'un (nouveau) travail (R);
- Commencement du service militaire (R);
- Entreprise d'une formation ou d'études (R).

6. Définition des personnes au chômage sur laquelle les statistiques sont établies

Les personnes au chômage sont celles qui sont sans emploi, qui désirent travailler, qui cherchent un emploi et qui n'avaient pas trouvé de travail pendant la période de référence (semaine de l'enquête).

7. Mise à jour des registres

Les registres sont mis à jour tous les ans.

8. Taux de chômage

Les statistiques basées sur les registres ne sont pas utilisées pour obtenir des taux de chômage.

9. Type de statistiques produites sur le nombre de chômeurs enregistrés

Période de référence: Semaine.

Fréquence de production: Annuelle.

Variables utilisées:
- Sexe;
- Age;
- Niveau d'instruction;
- Profession;
- Branche d'activité;
- Caractéristiques géographiques;
- Expérience professionnelle antérieure;
- Citoyenneté (nationaux/non nationaux).

Publication: Sur papier, à diffusion restreinte.

Organisme responsable de la publication: Ministère de la Fonction publique et de l'Habitat.

10. Information méthodologique au sujet de ces statistiques
Publication: Non diffusée, à usage interne uniquement
Organisme responsable: Ministère de la Fonction publique et de l'Habitat.

11. Comparaisons avec des statistiques provenant d'autres sources

Des comparaisons ont été faites avec des statistiques provenant de l'enquête de main-d'œuvre, un autre type d'enquête auprès des ménages, et du recensement de population.

Fréquence des comparaisons: Régulièrement, lorsque les statistiques sont publiées.

Publication de la méthodologie et/ou des résultats de la comparaison: Ils n'ont pas été publiés.

12. Principaux changements intervenus depuis le début de ces séries statistiques

Après l'adoption par le Conseil des ministres, en 1997, d'une résolution qui encourageait les Qataris à travailler dans le secteur privé, le nombre de chômeurs enregistrés a augmenté.

Roumanie

1. Séries statistiques
Titre: Situation statistique du chômage.
Première année disponible: 1991.

2. Organisme responsable de l'enregistrement des chômeurs ou demandeurs d'emploi
Nom de l'organisme: Agentia nationala pentru ocuparea fortei de munca (Agence Nationale de l'Emploi).
Type d'organisme: Organisme public relevant d'une autorité nationale.
Nom de l'autorité nationale: Ministère du Travail et de la Solidarité sociale.
Situation des bureaux chargés de l'enregistrement: Dans tous les comtés et dans la municipalité de Bucarest.
Types de services fournis et/ou gérés par cet organisme:
- Assistance aux demandeurs d'emploi pour trouver du travail;
- Assistance aux demandeurs d'emploi pour créer leur propre entreprise;
- Assistance aux employeurs pour trouver de la main-d'œuvre;
- Orientation professionnelle;
- Formation liée à l'emploi;
- Paiement des indemnités de chômage.

Pourcentage des demandeurs d'emploi qui cherchent un emploi au travers de cet organisme: 75%.

3. Les informations personnelles suivantes sont enregistrées:
- Nom;
- Sexe;
- Numéro de sécurité sociale (ou numéro d'identification également utilisé par d'autres organismes);
- Adresse du domicile habituel;
- Date de naissance;
- Citoyenneté;
- Nationalité/groupe ethnique;
- Niveau d'instruction/ de formation, en distinguant six catégories;
- Situation de travail présente et passée, en distinguant cinq catégories;
- Type de profession de l'emploi antérieur ou actuel, en distinguant 415 catégories. Des liens ont été établis avec la CITP-88 au niveau des groupes de base;
- Type de profession de l'emploi recherché, avec 415 catégories. Des liens ont été établis avec la CITP-88 au niveau des groupes de base;
- Nom et adresse de l'employeur ou du lieu de travail actuel ou passé;
- Branche d'activité de l'employeur ou du lieu de travail actuel ou passé;
- Inscriptions/enregistrements antérieurs auprès de l'organisme.

4. Critères utilisés pour déterminer si une personne doit être incluse dans le registre (R) et/ou dans les statistiques de chômeurs (S):
- Etre sans travail (R) et (S);
- Etre à la recherche d'un travail (R) et (S);
- Etre disponible pour travailler (R) et (S);
- Etre résident dans le pays (R) et (S);

– Avoir précédemment travaillé (R) et (S).

5. Critères utilisés pour déterminer si une personne doit être exclue du registre (R) et/ou des statistiques de chômeurs (S):

– Décès (R) et (S);
– Etablissement de la personne à l'étranger (R) et (S);
– Commencement d'un (nouveau) travail (R) et (S);
– Commencement du service militaire (R) et (S);
– Participation à un programme de promotion de l'emploi, à un programme de travaux publics, etc. (R) et (S);
– Défaut de contact avec l'organisme/agence (R) et (S). Le chômeur doit se présenter chaque mois au service de l'emploi;
– Refus d'offres d'emploi adaptées (1 offre), (R) et (S);
– Refus d'offres de formation adaptées (1 offre de formation), (R) et (S);
– Admission à toucher une pension (R) et (S).

6. Définition des personnes au chômage sur laquelle les statistiques sont établies

Selon la loi n°.1/1991 sur l'assurance chômage et l'incitation à l'emploi, «le chômeur est une personne qui remplit cumulativement les critères suivants:

– être à la recherche d'un emploi, en étant âgé de 16 ans ou plus et jusqu'à l'âge de la retraite;
– être apte à travailler physiquement et mentalement;
– ne pas avoir d'emploi, ne pas avoir de revenu ou avoir un revenu provenant d'activités légales inférieur au montant des allocations de chômage auxquelles il/elle aurait droit d'après cette Loi;
– être prêt à commencer à travailler dès qu'il/elle aura trouvé un emploi;
– être enregistré auprès de l'Agence nationale pour l'Emploi ou auprès d'un autre bureau de placement dont l'activité est conforme à la loi.»

7. Mise à jour des registres

Les registres sont mis à jour mensuellement.

8. Taux de chômage

Les statistiques basées sur les registres sont utilisées pour obtenir des taux de chômage.

Les sources des données d'emploi qui sont partie du dénominateur des taux de chômage sont le recensement de population et les données de l'Institut national des statistiques et des études économiques.

Définition des personnes pourvues d'un emploi à cette fin: La population active civile.

9. Type de statistiques produites sur le nombre de chômeurs enregistrés

Période de référence: Mois.
Fréquence de production: Mensuelle.
Variables utilisées:

– Sexe;
– Age;
– Niveau d'instruction;
– Profession;
– Branche d'activité;
– Caractéristiques géographiques;
– Expérience professionnelle antérieure;
– Citoyenneté (nationaux/non nationaux);
– Durée du chômage;
– Autre: type d'indemnités.

Publication:

– Sur papier, à diffusion grand public;
– En format électronique, sur demande.

Titre et périodicité de la publication: *Situation statistique du chômage*, mensuelle.

10. Information méthodologique au sujet de ces statistiques
Publication: Elle n'est pas publiée; disponible à usage interne uniquement; et en format électronique sur demande.

11. Comparaisons avec des statistiques provenant d'autres sources

Des comparaisons ont été faites avec des statistiques de chômage provenant d'autres sources par l'institut national des statistiques et des études économiques.
Fréquence des comparaisons: Régulièrement.

12. Principaux changements intervenus depuis le début de ces séries statistiques

La nouvelle loi sur l'assurance chômage et l'incitation à l'emploi, qui est entrée en vigueur en mars 2002, a généré des changements importants, surtout en ce qui concerne le niveau des indemnités de chômage, les formes d'indemnités, les statistiques, etc.

Saint-Pierre-et-Miquelon

1. Séries statistiques
Titre: Aperçu mensuel de l'emploi.
Première année disponible: 1980.
2. Organisme responsable de l'enregistrement des chômeurs ou demandeurs d'emploi
Nom de l'organisme: Agence Nationale Pour l'Emploi (ANPE).
Type d'organisme: Organisme public relevant d'une autorité nationale.
Nom de l'autorité nationale: Ministère chargé du Travail et de l'Emploi.
Situation des bureaux chargés de l'enregistrement: Un point opérationnel permanent sur l'île de Saint-Pierre.
Types de services fournis et/ou gérés par cet organisme:

– Assistance aux demandeurs d'emploi pour trouver du travail;
– Assistance aux employeurs pour trouver de la main-d'œuvre;
– Orientation professionnelle;
– Formation liée à l'emploi.

Pourcentage des demandeurs d'emploi qui cherchent un emploi au travers de cet organisme: Tous les demandeurs d'emploi jusqu'à 57 ans doivent répondre aux sollicitations de l'ANPE: entretiens, mises en relations, propositions d'accompagnement...(les personnes âgées de plus de 57 ans sont dispensées de rechercher du travail).

3. Les informations personnelles suivantes sont enregistrées:

– Nom;
– Sexe;
– Numéro de sécurité sociale (ou numéro d'identification également utilisé par d'autres organismes);
– Adresse du domicile habituel;
– Date de naissance;
– Citoyenneté;
– Nationalité;
– Niveau de formation, en distinguant six catégories. Aucun lien n'a été établi avec la CITE;
– Situation de travail présente et passée;
– Type de profession de l'emploi antérieur et/ou actuel, en distinguant 61 catégories (Répertoire Opérationnel des Métiers). Aucun lien n'a été établi avec la CITP;
– Qualifications.

4. Critères utilisés pour déterminer si une personne doit être incluse dans le registre (R) et/ou dans les statistiques de chômeurs (S):

– Etre sans travail (R) et (S);
– Etre à la recherche d'un travail (R) et (S);
– Etre disponible pour travailler (R) et (S);
– Age: Minimum: 16 ans; Maximum: 57 ans (R) et (S);
– Citoyenneté (R) et (S);
– Etre résident dans le pays, ou posséder une carte de séjour (R) et (S);
– Durée souhaitée de l'emploi recherché et/ou du nombre d'heures de travail recherché: les personnes qui recherchent un temps partiel (de 16 heures minimum par semaine) sont inscrites en catégorie 2 de la définition du point 6 ci-dessous.

5. Critères utilisés pour déterminer si une personne doit être exclue du registre (R) et/ou des statistiques de chômeurs (S):

– Avis de décès (R) et (S);
– Etablissement de la personne à l'étranger (R) et (S);
– Commencement d'un (nouveau) travail (R) et (S). Cependant, il existe une possibilité de cumul d'activité réduite et d'inscription comme demandeur d'emploi (transfert en catégorie 6, 7 ou 8 du point 6).
– Participation à un programme de promotion de l'emploi, à un programme de travaux publics, etc. (R) et (S);
– Entreprise d'une formation ou d'études (transfert en catégorie 4 du point 6);
– Défaut de contact avec l'agence, refus de présentation à une convocation (R) et (S);

- Refus d'offres d'emploi adaptées (R) et (S);
- Refus d'offres de formation adaptées (R) et (S);
- Incapacité à travailler, périodes de maladie (R) et (S), transfert en catégorie 5 du point 6 ci-dessous.

6. Définition des personnes au chômage sur laquelle les statistiques sont établies

Catégorie 1: personnes sans emploi, immédiatement disponibles au sens de l'article R.311-3-3, tenues d'accomplir des actes positifs de recherche d'emploi, *à la recherche d'un emploi* **à durée indéterminée à plein temps.** Ces personnes ne doivent pas avoir exercé d'activité occasionnelle ou réduite de plus de 78 heures dans le mois d'actualisation.

Catégorie 2: personnes sans emploi, immédiatement disponibles au sens de l'article R.311-3-3, tenues d'accomplir des actes positifs de recherche d'emploi, *à la recherche d'un emploi* **à durée indéterminée à temps partiel.** Ces personnes ne doivent pas avoir exercé d'activité occasionnelle ou réduite de plus de 78 heures dans le mois d'actualisation.

Catégorie 3: personnes sans emploi, immédiatement disponibles au sens de l'article R.311-3-3, tenues d'accomplir des actes positifs de recherche d'emploi, *à la recherche d'un emploi* **à durée déterminée temporaire ou saisonnier,** *y compris de très courte durée.* Ces personnes ne doivent pas avoir exercé d'activité occasionnelle ou réduite de plus de 78 heures dans le mois d'actualisation.

Catégorie 4: personnes sans emploi, non immédiatement disponibles, à la recherche d'un emploi.

Catégorie 5: personnes pourvues d'un emploi, à la recherche d'un autre emploi.

Catégorie 6: personnes non immédiatement disponibles au sens de l'article R.311-3-3 (1à), *à la recherche d'un autre emploi, à durée indéterminée à plein temps,* tenues d'accomplir des actes positifs de recherche d'emploi. Ces personnes ont exercé une activité occasionnelle ou réduite de plus de 78 heures dans le mois d'actualisation.

Catégorie 7: personnes non immédiatement disponibles au sens de l'article R.311-3-3 (1à), *à la recherche d'un autre emploi, à durée indéterminée à temps partiel,* tenues d'accomplir des actes positifs de recherche d'emploi. Ces personnes ont exercé une activité occasionnelle ou réduite de plus de 78 heures dans le mois d'actualisation.

Catégorie 8: personnes non immédiatement disponibles au sens de l'article R.311-3-3 (1à), *à la recherche d'un autre emploi, à durée déterminée, temporaire ou saisonnier, y compris de très courte durée,* tenues d'accomplir des actes positifs de recherche d'emploi. Ces personnes ont exercé une activité occasionnelle ou réduite de plus de 78 heures dans le mois d'actualisation.

7. Mise à jour des registres
Les registres sont mis à jour mensuellement.

8. Taux de chômage
Les statistiques basées sur les registres sont utilisées pour obtenir des taux de chômage.

La source des données d'emploi qui sont partie du dénominateur est le recensement de population.

9. Type de statistiques produites sur le nombre de chômeurs enregistrés
Période de référence: Mois.
Fréquence de production: Mensuelle.
Variables utilisées:
- Sexe;
- Age;
- Niveau de formation;
- Profession recherchée ;
- Durée du chômage.

Publication: En direction des services de l'Etat, des élus et des organismes à vocation économique et sociale. L'*Aperçu mensuel* est présenté par les radios locales et publié partiellement par la presse écrite locale.

Agence responsable de la publication: Service du Travail et de l'Emploi et de la Formation Professionnelle: agrégation des données fournies par l'ANPE avec des séries concernant la politique de l'emploi, et commentaires.

10. Information méthodologique au sujet de ces statistiques
Seule la catégorie 1 (cf. point 6) sert de base aux statistiques. Les commentaires peuvent intégrer les données concernant les autres catégories, si elles sont significatives.

Publication: A travers les commentaires de l'*Aperçu mensuel.*

Agence responsable: Service du Travail de l'Emploi et de la Formation professionnelle.

11. Comparaisons avec des statistiques provenant d'autres sources
Des comparaisons sont faites avec des statistiques provenant du recensement général de population.

Fréquence des comparaisons:
Essentiellement lorsque les données du recensement sont récentes.

Publication de la méthodologie et/ou des résultats de la comparaison:
A travers les commentaires de l'*Aperçu mensuel.*

12. Principaux changements intervenus depuis le début de ces séries statistiques
Des changements importants dans la législation, dans la capacité de l'agence et/ou dans les procédures administratives sont intervenus en 1995: fin du pointage physique, informatisation du service de l'ANPE et exploitation des données du chômage de longue durée, pour l'ajustement des outils de la politique d'emploi et d'insertion.

Serbie-et-Monténégro

1. Séries statistiques
Titre: Chômage enregistré.
Première année disponible: Non spécifiée.

2. Organisme responsable de l'enregistrement des chômeurs ou demandeurs d'emploi
Nom de l'organisme: Bureau de la main-d'œuvre des Républiques.
Type d'organisme: Organisme public relevant d'une autorité nationale.
Nom de l'autorité nationale: Ministère du Travail et de l'Emploi.
Situation des bureaux chargés de l'enregistrement: Dans toutes les régions à travers la Serbie et le Monténégro.
Types de services fournis et/ou gérés par cet organisme:
- Assistance aux demandeurs d'emploi pour trouver du travail;
- Assistance aux demandeurs d'emploi pour créer leur propre entreprise;
- Assistance aux employeurs pour trouver de la main-d'œuvre;
- Orientation professionnelle;
- Formation liée à l'emploi;
- Paiement des indemnités de chômage;
- Autres services liés à l'emploi: information sur le marché du travail; politique en faveur de certaines catégories de chômeurs (invalides, etc.).

Pourcentage des demandeurs d'emploi qui cherchent un emploi au travers de cet organisme: 29%.

3. Les informations personnelles suivantes sont enregistrées:
- Nom;
- Sexe;
- Numéro de sécurité sociale (ou numéro d'identification également utilisé par d'autres organismes);
- Adresse du domicile habituel;
- Date de naissance;
- Citoyenneté;
- Nationalité/groupe ethnique;
- Niveau d'instruction/de formation, en distinguant neuf catégories. Aucun lien n'a été établi avec la CITE;
- Situation de travail présente et passée, en distinguant trois catégories;
- Type de profession de l'emploi antérieur et/ou actuel, en distinguant 74 catégories (environ 3500 professions répertoriées). Aucun lien n'a été établi avec la CITP;
- Type de profession de l'emploi recherché, avec 74 catégories (environ 3500 professions répertoriées); Aucun lien n'a été établi avec la CITP;
- Nom et adresse de l'employeur ou du lieu de travail actuel ou passé;
- Branche d'activité de l'employeur ou du lieu de travail actuel ou passé, en distinguant 17 catégories. Des liens ont été établis avec la CITI, rév.3 ou la NACE, rév.1;
- Inscriptions/enregistrements antérieurs auprès de l'organisme;
- Autres: motivations professionnelles de la personne au chômage; connaissances et qualifications particulières; droits de la personne au chômage; date de la médiation.

4. Critères utilisés pour déterminer si une personne doit être incluse dans le registre (R) et/ou dans les statistiques de chômeurs (S):

- Etre sans travail (R) et (S);
- Etre à la recherche d'un travail (R) et (S);
- Etre disponible pour travailler (R);
- Age: limites d'âge non spécifiées (R) et (S);
- Citoyenneté (R);
- Etre résident dans le pays (R);
- Avoir précédemment travaillé (R) et (S);
- Durée souhaitée de l'emploi recherché et/ou du nombre d'heures de travail recherché (R);
- Acquittement de cotisations d'assurance chômage (R).

5. Critères utilisés pour déterminer si une personne doit être exclue du registre (R) et/ou des statistiques de chômeurs (S):

- Avis de décès (R) et (S);
- Etablissement de la personne à l'étranger (R) et (S);
- Commencement d'un (nouveau) travail (R) et (S);
- Participation à un programme de promotion de l'emploi, à un programme de travaux publics, etc. (R) et (S);
- Défaut de contact avec l'organisme/agence (R);
- Refus d'une offre d'emploi adaptée par mois (R);
- Fin de droit à l'allocation-chômage (R);
- Admission à toucher une pension (retraite, etc.) (R);
- Incapacité à travailler (R);
- Autre: si la personne est sous le coup d'une condamnation légale ou d'une mesure de correction pour une durée supérieure à six mois (R).

6. Définition des personnes au chômage sur laquelle les statistiques sont établies

Les personnes qui sont sans emploi, disponibles pour travailler, à la recherche d'un travail et qui sont enregistrées dans les fichiers réguliers du Bureau de Placement.

7. Mise à jour des registres

Les registres sont mis à jour mensuellement et annuellement.

8. Taux de chômage

Les statistiques basées sur les registres sont utilisées pour obtenir des taux de chômage.

Les sources des données d'emploi qui sont partie du dénominateur sont l'enquête auprès des ménages sur la main-d'œuvre et le Rapport mensuel de l'Emploi et des Salaires.

Définition des personnes pourvues d'un emploi à cette fin: Les personnes pourvues d'un emploi dans les entreprises, les organisations ou dans le secteur privé.

9. Type de statistiques produites sur le nombre de chômeurs enregistrés

Série 1:
Période de référence: Mois; Année.
Fréquence de production: Mensuelle.
Variables utilisées:

- Sexe;
- Niveau d'instruction;
- Branche d'activité;
- Caractéristiques géographiques;
- Autre: motif pour lequel la personne a quitté son emploi; Stagiaires.

Publication: Sur papier, à diffusion grand public.
Agence responsable de la publication: Bureau fédéral du Marché du Travail et des Migrations.
Titre et périodicité de la publication: *Monthly Statistical Survey - Employment* (Enquête statistique mensuelle - Emploi).

Série 2:
Période de référence: Mois; Année.
Fréquence de production: Mensuelle.
Variables utilisées:

- Sexe;
- Age;
- Niveau d'instruction;
- Profession;
- Caractéristiques géographiques;
- Expérience professionnelle antérieure;
- Citoyenneté (nationaux/non nationaux);
- Durée de chômage;
- Autre: bénéficiaires d'allocations de chômage; montant total des paiements d'allocations de chômage effectués (par mois; par année).

Publication: Sur papier, à diffusion restreinte.

Agence responsable de la publication: Bureau fédéral du Marché du Travail et des Migrations.
Titre et périodicité de la publication: *Statistical Yearbook - Placement of unemployed persons* (Annuaire statistique - Placement des chômeurs).

10. Information méthodologique au sujet de ces statistiques
Publication: Sur papier, à diffusion restreinte.
Organisme responsable: Bureau fédéral du Marché du Travail et des Migrations.

11. Comparaisons avec des statistiques provenant d'autres sources

Il n'y a pas eu de comparaisons faites avec des statistiques provenant d'autres sources.

12. Principaux changements intervenus depuis le début de ces séries statistiques

Il n'y a pas eu de changement important dans la législation, dans la capacité de l'agence et/ou dans les procédures administratives susceptibles d'avoir influencé de manière significative les statistiques.

Slovénie

1. Séries statistiques
Titre: Chômage enregistré.
Première année disponible: 1947.

2. Organisme responsable de l'enregistrement des chômeurs ou demandeurs d'emploi
Nom de l'organisme: "Zavod rs za zaposlovanje" (Agence pour l'emploi de Slovénie).
Type d'organisme: Organisme public relevant d'une autorité nationale.
Nom de l'autorité nationale: Ministère du Travail, de la Famille et des Affaires sociales.
Situation des bureaux chargés de l'enregistrement: Dans toutes les parties du pays.
Types de services fournis et/ou gérés par cet organisme:

- Assistance aux demandeurs d'emploi pour trouver du travail;
- Assistance aux demandeurs d'emploi pour créer leur propre entreprise;
- Assistance aux employeurs pour trouver de la main-d'œuvre;
- Orientation professionnelle;
- Formation liée à l'emploi;
- Paiement des indemnités de chômage;
- Autres services liés à l'emploi: permis de travail, programme national de bourses.

Pourcentage des demandeurs d'emploi qui cherchent un emploi au travers de cet organisme: 90%.

3. Les informations personnelles suivantes sont enregistrées:

- Nom;
- Sexe;
- Numéro de sécurité sociale (ou numéro d'identification également utilisé par d'autres organismes);
- Adresse du domicile habituel;
- Date de naissance;
- Citoyenneté;
- Niveau d'instruction/ de formation, en distinguant huit catégories;
- Situation de travail présente et passée, en distinguant trois catégories;
- Type de profession de l'emploi antérieur ou actuel;
- Type de profession de l'emploi recherché, en distinguant 317 catégories. Des liens ont été établis avec la CITP-88 au niveau des groupes de base;
- Nom et adresse de l'employeur ou du lieu de travail actuel ou passé;
- Inscriptions/enregistrements antérieurs auprès de l'organisme.

4. Critères utilisés pour déterminer si une personne doit être incluse dans le registre (R) et/ou dans les statistiques de chômeurs (S):

- Etre sans travail (R) et (S);
- Etre activement à la recherche d'un travail, suivi par un conseiller de l'emploi (R) et (S);
- Etre disponible pour travailler (R) et (S);
- Age: Minimum: 15 ans; Maximum: 60 ans pour les femmes, 65 ans pour les hommes (R) et (S);

– Citoyenneté (R) et (S).

5. Critères utilisés pour déterminer si une personne doit être exclue du registre (R) et/ou des statistiques de chômeurs (S):
– Décès (R) et (S);
– Etablissement de la personne à l'étranger (R) et (S);
– Commencement d'un (nouveau) travail (R) et (S);
– Commencement du service militaire (R) et (S);
– Participation à un programme de promotion de l'emploi, à un programme de travaux publics, etc. (S);
– Entreprise d'une formation ou d'études (S); Seulement les personnes dans des programmes de formation de courte durée sont incluses dans les statistiques.
– Défaut de contact avec l'organisme/agence (R) et (S);
– Refus d'offres d'emploi adaptées (2 postes) (R) et (S);
– Refus d'offres de formation adaptées (1 formation) (R) et (S);
– Admission à toucher une pension (R) et (S);
– Incapacité à travailler (R) et (S);
– Fréquentation de l'école (R) et (S).

6. Définition des personnes au chômage sur laquelle les statistiques sont établies
Sont considérées comme chômeurs enregistrés les personnes âgées de 15 à 60 ans pour les femmes, et de 15 à 65 ans pour les hommes, qui sont enregistrées auprès de l'agence pour l'emploi, recherchent activement un emploi, et sont disposées à accepter un emploi correspondant à leur niveau d'instruction. Sont exclues les personnes à la retraite, les personnes emprisonnées depuis déjà plus de six mois, les propriétaires d'entreprises ayant généré suffisamment des revenus au cours de la dernière année civile pour leur permettre de vivre - à la condition que le revenu qu'ils en tirent ne dépasse pas le salaire minimum garanti, et les propriétaires terriens (de terres cultivables ou de forêts) qui peuvent en vivre.

7. Mise à jour des registres
Les registres sont mis à jour quotidiennement.

8. Taux de chômage
Les statistiques basées sur les registres sont utilisées pour obtenir des taux de chômage enregistré.
Les sources des données d'emploi qui sont partie du dénominateur des taux de chômage sont les enquêtes auprès des établissements et les registres de sécurité sociale.
Définition des personnes pourvues d'un emploi à cette fin: Les personnes régulièrement employées à plein temps ou à temps partiel, les personnes à leur compte et les paysans.

9. Type de statistiques produites sur le nombre de chômeurs enregistrés
Période de référence: Mois, trimestre et année.
Fréquence de production: Mensuelle, trimestrielle et annuelle.
Variables utilisées:
– Sexe;
– Age;
– Niveau d'instruction;
– Profession;
– Branche d'activité;
– Caractéristiques géographiques;
– Expérience professionnelle antérieure;
– Durée de chômage.
Publication:
– Sur papier, à diffusion grand public;
– En format électronique, sur demande;
– Sur un site Internet: http://www.ess.gov.si
Agence responsable de la publication: Agence pour l'emploi, bureau de statistique de la République de Slovénie.

10. Information méthodologique au sujet de ces statistiques
Publication:
– Sur papier, à diffusion grand public;
– En format électronique, sur demande;
– Sur un site Internet
Agence responsable: Agence pour l'emploi, bureau des statistiques.

11. Comparaisons avec des statistiques provenant d'autres sources
Des comparaisons ont été faites avec des statistiques de chômage provenant de l'enquête sur la main-d'œuvre (C'est le Bureau de statistique qui est l'institution responsable des données de l'enquête de main-d'œuvre.
Fréquence des comparaisons: Régulièrement.
Publication de la méthodologie et/ou des résultats de la comparaison: Ils ont été publiés.

12. Principaux changements intervenus depuis le début de ces séries statistiques
Il n'y a pas eu de changement important dans la législation, dans la capacité de l'agence et/ou dans les procédures administratives susceptibles d'avoir influencé de manière significative les statistiques.

Suède

1. Séries statistiques
Titre: *"Arbetsmarknadsdata"* (informations sur le marché du travail).

Première année disponible: 1992 (les séries précédentes avaient des définitions différentes).
2. Organisme responsable de l'enregistrement des chômeurs ou demandeurs d'emploi
Nom de l'organisme: "Arbetsförmedlingen" (Service de l'emploi public).
Type d'organisme: Organisme public relevant d'une autorité nationale.
Nom de l'autorité nationale: Administration nationale du Marché du Travail.
Situation des bureaux chargés de l'enregistrement: Il y a au moins, en règle générale, un bureau dans chaque municipalité.
Types de services fournis/gérés par cet organisme:
– Assistance aux demandeurs d'emploi pour trouver du travail;
– Assistance aux demandeurs d'emploi pour créer leur propre entreprise;
– Assistance aux employeurs pour trouver de la main-d'œuvre;
– Orientation professionnelle;
– Formation liée à l'emploi;
– Paiement des indemnités de chômage.
Pourcentage des demandeurs d'emploi qui cherchent un emploi au travers de cet organisme: 50%.
3. Les informations personnelles suivantes sont enregistrées:
– Nom;
– Sexe;
– Numéro de sécurité sociale (ou numéro d'identification également utilisé par d'autres organismes);
– Adresse du domicile habituel;
– Date de naissance;
– Citoyenneté;
– Niveau d'instruction/ de formation;
– Situation de travail présente et passée, en distinguant 30 catégories;
– Type de travail (profession) de l'emploi recherché, en distinguant 700 groupes. Des liens ont été établis avec la CITP-88 au niveau des groupes de base;
– Enregistrements antérieurs auprès de l'organisme.
4. Critères utilisés pour déterminer si une personne doit être incluse dans le registre (R) et/ou dans les statistiques de chômeurs (S):
– Etre sans travail (S);
– Etre disponible pour travailler (être immédiatement disponible pour travailler) (S);
– Etre résident dans le pays (S).
5. Critères utilisés pour déterminer si une personne doit être exclue du registre (R) et/ou des statistiques de chômeurs (S):
– Décès (R) et (S);
– Etablissement de la personne à l'étranger (S);
– Commencement d'un (nouveau) travail (S);
– Commencement du service militaire (S);
– Participation à un programme de promotion de l'emploi, à un programme de travaux publics, etc. (S);
– Entreprise d'une formation ou d'études (S);
– Défaut de contact avec l'organisme/agence (S);
– Admission à toucher une pension (S);
– Incapacité à travailler (pour être comptée comme chômeur une personne doit être apte à travailler ou, éventuellement, être en train de faire l'objet d'une enquête).

6. Définition des personnes au chômage sur laquelle les statistiques sont établies

Les personnes sans emploi (excepté un emploi secondaire qu'il est possible de combiner avec un travail régulier à plein temps) bénéficiant de services de placement ou de conseils, ou en attente pour participer à un programme de recherche de travail active.

7. Mise à jour des registres

Les registres sont mis à jour quotidiennement.

8. Taux de chômage

Les statistiques basées sur les registres sont utilisées pour obtenir des taux de chômage.

Les sources des données d'emploi qui sont partie du dénominateur des taux de chômage sont l'enquête sur la main-d'œuvre et le recensement de population.

Définition des personnes pourvues d'un emploi à cette fin:

La plupart du temps il s'agit de la population âgée de 18 à 64 ans; parfois les chiffres sont tirés de l'enquête sur la main-d'œuvre (les personnes pourvues d'un emploi sont celles qui avaient travaillé au moins pendant une heure pendant la semaine de référence et celles qui étaient temporairement absentes de leur travail).

9. Type de statistiques sur le nombre de chômeurs enregistrés produites

Série 1:

Période de référence: Semaine.

Fréquence de production: Hebdomadaire.

Variables utilisées:

- Sexe;
- Age;
- Caractéristiques géographiques;
- Citoyenneté (nationaux/non nationaux);
- Durée de chômage.

Publication: Sur un site Internet (www.ams.se).

Agence responsable de la publication: Commission nationale du Marché du Travail.

Périodicité de la publication: Hebdomadaire.

Série 2:

Période de référence: Mois; Trimestre; Année.

Fréquence de production: Mensuelle.

Variables utilisées:

- Sexe;
- Age;
- Caractéristiques géographiques;
- Citoyenneté (nationaux/non nationaux);
- Durée de chômage.

Publication:

- Sur papier, à diffusion grand public;
- Sur un site Internet (www.ams.se).

Agence responsable de la publication: Commission nationale du Marché du Travail.

Périodicité de la publication: *Arbetsmarknadsdata*, mensuelle.

10. Information méthodologique au sujet de ces statistiques

Publication:

- Sur papier, à diffusion grand public;
- Sur un site Internet (www.ams.se).

Agence responsable: Commission nationale du Marché du Travail.

11. Comparaisons avec des statistiques provenant d'autres sources

Des comparaisons sont faites avec des statistiques du chômage provenant de l'enquête sur la main-d'œuvre. La réponse donnée à l'enquête est comparée avec le statut attribué à l'individu selon le registre (à l'échelon individuel).

Fréquence des comparaisons: Régulièrement, lors de la publication des statistiques.

Publication de la méthodologie et/ou des résultats de la comparaison: Ils n'ont pas été publiés.

12. Principaux changements intervenus depuis le début de ces séries statistiques

Il n'y a pas eu de changement important dans la législation, dans la capacité de l'agence et/ou dans les procédures administratives susceptibles d'avoir influencé de manière significative les statistiques.

Suisse

1. Séries statistiques

Titre: Chômeurs inscrits; Vacances de postes annoncées; Demandeurs d'emploi inscrits; Bénéficiaires de l'assurance chômage.

Première année disponible: 1936

2. Organisme responsable de l'enregistrement des chômeurs ou demandeurs d'emploi

Nom de l'organisme: Office régional de placement (ORP).

Type d'organisme: Organisme public relevant d'une autorité nationale.

Nom de l'autorité nationale: Les conditions cadres sont définies au niveau national et l'application est du ressort des cantons.

Situation des bureaux chargés de l'enregistrement: Dans l'ensemble du pays, par le biais des Offices régionaux de placement.

Types de services fournis et/ou gérés par cet organisme:

- Assistance aux demandeurs d'emploi pour trouver du travail;
- Assistance aux demandeurs d'emploi pour créer leur propre entreprise;
- Assistance aux employeurs pour trouver de la main-d'œuvre;
- Formation liée à l'emploi.

3. Les informations personnelles suivantes sont enregistrées:

- Nom;
- Sexe;
- Numéro de sécurité sociale (ou numéro d'identification également utilisé par d'autres organismes);
- Adresse du domicile habituel;
- Date de naissance;
- Citoyenneté;
- Nationalité/groupe ethnique;
- Niveau d'instruction/de formation, en distinguant trois catégories. Aucun lien n'a été établi avec la CITE;
- Situation de travail présente et passée, en distinguant 10 catégories;
- Type de profession de l'emploi antérieur et/ou actuel, en distinguant 15.000 catégories. Aucun lien n'a été établi avec la CITP;
- Type de profession de l'emploi recherché, avec 15.000 catégories;
- Nom et adresse de l'employeur ou du lieu de travail actuel ou passé;
- Branche d'activité de l'employeur ou du lieu de travail actuel ou passé, en distinguant 220 catégories. Aucun lien n'a été établi avec la CITI. La classification utilisée est la NOGA, dérivée de la NACE;
- Inscriptions/enregistrements antérieurs auprès de l'organisme;
- Connaissances linguistiques.

4. Critères utilisés pour déterminer si une personne doit être incluse dans le registre (R) et/ou dans les statistiques de chômeurs (S):

- Etre sans travail (S);
- Etre à la recherche d'un travail (R) et (S);
- Etre disponible pour travailler (S);
- Age: Minimum: 15 ans; pas de limite supérieure (R) et (S);
- Etre résident dans le pays: les étrangers doivent être titulaires d'un permis de travail (R) et (S);
- Autre: la personne doit elle-même s'inscrire auprès d'un ORP (R) et (S).

5. Critères utilisés pour déterminer si une personne doit être exclue du registre (R) et/ou des statistiques de chômeurs (S):

- Avis de décès (R) et (S);
- Etablissement de la personne à l'étranger (R) et (S);
- Commencement d'un (nouveau) travail, donc plus disponible (S);
- Commencement du service militaire (S);
- Participation à un programme de promotion de l'emploi, à un programme de travaux publics, etc. (S);
- Entreprise d'une formation ou d'études (S);
- Défaut de contact avec l'office: après deux mois, un dossier inactif est généralement radié. En principe, un demandeur d'emploi devrait avoir au moins deux

entretiens par mois avec un conseiller de l'ORP (R) et (S);

– Incapacité à travailler: maladie, accident, incarcération, etc. (S).

6. Définition des personnes au chômage sur laquelle les statistiques sont établies

Chômeurs inscrits: Personnes inscrites auprès des offices régionaux de placement, qui sont sans emploi et sont immédiatement disponibles en vue d'un placement, qu'elles soient bénéficiaires ou non d'une allocation de chômage.

On appelle chômeurs complets ceux qui cherchent un emploi à plein temps, et chômeurs partiels ceux qui cherchent un emploi à temps partiel.

7. Mise à jour des registres

Les registres sont mis à jour régulièrement, en continu.

8. Taux de chômage

Les statistiques basées sur les registres sont utilisées pour obtenir des taux de chômage.

La source des données d'emploi qui sont partie du dénominateur est le recensement de population.

Définition des personnes pourvues d'un emploi à cette fin: Les personnes âgées de 15 ans et plus qui travaillent six heures ou plus par semaine.

9. Type de statistiques produites sur le nombre de chômeurs enregistrés

Série 1: Nombre de demandeurs d'emploi et flux (entrées et sorties).

Période de référence: Mois, année.

Fréquence de production: Mensuelle.

Variables utilisées:

– Sexe;
– Age;
– Profession;
– Branche d'activité;
– Caractéristiques géographiques;
– Expérience professionnelle antérieure;
– Citoyenneté (nationaux/non nationaux);
– Durée de chômage.

Publication:

– Sur papier, à diffusion grand public;
– Sur un site Internet: www.seco-admin.ch

Organisme responsable de la publication: Secrétariat d'Etat à l'Economie (SECO).

Titre et périodicité de la publication: *Situation sur le marché du travail*, mensuel.

Série 2: Nombre de chômeurs.

Période de référence: Mois, année.

Fréquence de production: Annuelle.

Variables utilisées:

– Sexe;
– Age;
– Profession;
– Branche d'activité;
– Caractéristiques géographiques;
– Expérience professionnelle antérieure;
– Citoyenneté (nationaux/non nationaux);
– Durée de chômage.

Publication: Sur papier, à diffusion grand public.

Organisme responsable de la publication: Office fédéral de la Statistique (OFS) et SECO.

Titre et périodicité de la publication: *Le chômage en Suisse*, annuel.

10. Information méthodologique au sujet de ces statistiques
Publication:

– Sur papier, à diffusion grand public;
– Sur un site Internet: www.seco-admin.ch

Organisme responsable: SECO.

11. Comparaisons avec des statistiques provenant d'autres sources

Des comparaisons ont été faites avec des statistiques provenant de l'enquête de main-d'œuvre.

Fréquence des comparaisons: Occasionnellement (dernière année: 1999).

Publication de la méthodologie et/ou des résultats de la comparaison: Ils ont été publiés.

Titre de la publication contenant la description de la méthodologie et/ou les résultats de cette comparaison: *Indicateurs du marché du travail 1998*, OFS, Neuchâtel 1999, ISBN 3-303-03113-4 ; (page 42).

12. Principaux changements intervenus depuis le début de ces séries statistiques

Des changements importants dans la législation, dans la capacité de l'agence et/ou dans les procédures administratives sont intervenus en 1982, 1995 et 1997. L'ampleur des changements induits par ces modifications n'est pas connue.

Suriname

1. Séries statistiques
Titre: Statistiques sur les demandeurs d'emploi enregistrés.

Première année disponible: 1983.

2. Organisme responsable de l'enregistrement des chômeurs ou demandeurs d'emploi

Nom de l'organisme: Dienst der Arbeidsbemiddeling (Bureau de Placement).

Type d'organisme: Organisme public relevant d'une autorité nationale.

Nom de l'autorité nationale: Ministère du Travail, du Développement technologique et de l'Environnement.

Situation des bureaux chargés de l'enregistrement: Dans les municipalités de Paramaribo, Saramacca et Nickerie.

Types de services fournis et/ou gérés par cet organisme:

– Assistance aux demandeurs d'emploi pour trouver du travail;
– Assistance aux employeurs pour trouver de la main-d'œuvre;
– Formation liée à l'emploi;
– Autres services liés à l'emploi: accès à l'information sur le marché du travail.

Pourcentage des demandeurs d'emploi qui cherchent un emploi au travers de cet organisme: Environ 80 personnes par mois.

3. Les informations personnelles suivantes sont enregistrées:

– Nom;
– Sexe;
– Numéro de sécurité sociale (ou numéro d'identification également utilisé par d'autres organismes);
– Adresse du domicile habituel;
– Date de naissance;
– Citoyenneté;
– Nationalité/groupe ethnique;
– Niveau d'instruction/de formation, en distinguant un nombre non spécifié de catégories. Des liens ont été établis avec la CITE;
– Situation de travail présente et passée, en distinguant trois catégories;
– Type de profession de l'emploi antérieur et/ou actuel, en distinguant neuf catégories. Aucun lien n'a été établi avec la CITP;
– Type de profession de l'emploi recherché, avec neuf catégories; Aucun lien n'a été établi avec la CITP;
– Nom et adresse de l'employeur ou du lieu de travail actuel ou passé;
– Branche d'activité de l'employeur ou du lieu de travail actuel ou passé, en distinguant neuf catégories. Aucun lien n'a été établi avec la CITI-rév.3;
– Inscriptions/enregistrements antérieurs auprès de l'organisme.

4. Critères utilisés pour déterminer si une personne doit être incluse dans le registre (R) et/ou dans les statistiques de chômeurs (S):

– Etre sans travail (S);
– Etre à la recherche d'un travail (S);
– Age: Minimum: 15 ans; Maximum: 65 ans (S);
– Durée souhaitée de l'emploi recherché et/ou du nombre d'heures de travail recherché (S).

5. Critères utilisés pour déterminer si une personne doit être exclue du registre (R) et/ou des statistiques de chômeurs (S):

– Etablissement de la personne à l'étranger (S);
– Entreprise d'une formation ou d'études (S);
– Incapacité à travailler (S).

6. Définition des personnes au chômage sur laquelle les statistiques sont établies

Information non disponible.

7. Mise à jour des registres

Information non disponible.

8. Taux de chômage

Les statistiques basées sur les registres ne sont pas utilisées pour obtenir des taux de chômage.

9. Type de statistiques produites sur le nombre de chômeurs enregistrés

Information non disponible.

10. Information méthodologique au sujet de ces statistiques

Information non disponible.

11. Comparaisons avec des statistiques provenant d'autres sources

Il n'y a pas eu de comparaisons faites avec des statistiques provenant d'autres sources.

12. Principaux changements intervenus depuis le début de ces séries statistiques

Il n'y a pas eu de changement important dans la législation, dans la capacité de l'agence et/ou dans les procédures administratives susceptibles d'avoir influencé de manière significative les statistiques.

Tadjikistan

1. Séries statistiques

Titre: Chômage enregistré.

Première année disponible: Non spécifiée.

2. Organisme responsable de l'enregistrement des chômeurs ou demandeurs d'emploi

Nom de l'organisme: Agence pour l'Emploi de la Population de la République du Tadjikistan.

Type d'organisme: Agence d'Etat pour l'Emploi de la Population.

Situation des bureaux chargés de l'enregistrement: Dans toutes les régions, villes et arrondissements du pays.

Types de services fournis et/ou gérés par cet organisme:

–   Assistance aux demandeurs d'emploi pour trouver du travail;
–   Assistance aux demandeurs d'emploi pour créer leur propre entreprise;
–   Assistance aux employeurs pour trouver de la main-d'œuvre;
–   Orientation professionnelle;
–   Formation liée à l'emploi;
–   Paiement des indemnités de chômage.

Pourcentage des demandeurs d'emploi qui cherchent un emploi au travers de cet organisme: de 13 à 15%.

3. Les informations personnelles suivantes sont enregistrées:

–   Nom;
–   Sexe;
–   Adresse du domicile habituel;
–   Date de naissance;
–   Nationalité/groupe ethnique;
–   Niveau d'instruction/de formation;
–   Situation de travail présente et passée;
–   Type de profession de l'emploi antérieur et/ou actuel;
–   Type de profession de l'emploi recherché.

4. Critères utilisés pour déterminer si une personne doit être incluse dans le registre (R) et/ou dans les statistiques de chômeurs (S):

–   Etre sans travail (S);
–   Etre à la recherche d'un travail (S);
–   Etre disponible pour travailler (S);
–   Age: Minimum: 15 ans; Maximum: 63 ans (S);
–   Etre résident dans le pays (S).

5. Critères utilisés pour déterminer si une personne doit être exclue du registre (R) et/ou des statistiques de chômeurs (S):

–   Avis de décès (S);
–   Etablissement de la personne à l'étranger (S);
–   Commencement d'un (nouveau) travail (S);
–   Commencement du service militaire (S);
–   Participation à un programme de promotion de l'emploi, à un programme de travaux publics, etc. (S);
–   Entreprise d'une formation ou d'études (S);
–   Défaut de contact avec l'organisme/agence (S);
–   Refus d'un nombre non spécifié d'offres d'emploi adaptées (S);
–   Refus d'un nombre non spécifié d'offres de formation adaptées (S);
–   Incapacité à travailler (S).

6. Définition des personnes au chômage sur laquelle les statistiques sont établies

Telle que définie dans le code du travail de la République du Tadjikistan (Loi sur l'emploi).

7. Mise à jour des registres

Les registres ne sont pas mis à jour régulièrement.

8. Taux de chômage

Les statistiques basées sur les registres sont utilisées pour obtenir des taux de chômage.

La source des données d'emploi qui sont partie du dénominateur est l'enquête sur les migrations de main-d'œuvre étrangère.

9. Type de statistiques produites sur le nombre de chômeurs enregistrés

Série 1:

Période de référence: Mois.

Fréquence de production: Mensuelle.

Variables utilisées:

–   Sexe;
–   Age;
–   Niveau d'instruction;
–   Profession;
–   Expérience professionnelle antérieure;
–   Citoyenneté (nationaux/non nationaux);
–   Durée de chômage.

Publication: A usage interne uniquement.

Série 2:

Période de référence: Trimestre.

Fréquence de production: Trimestrielle.

Variables utilisées:

–   Sexe;
–   Age;
–   Niveau d'instruction;
–   Profession;
–   Expérience professionnelle antérieure;
–   Citoyenneté (nationaux/non nationaux);
–   Durée de chômage.

Publication: A usage interne uniquement.

10. Information méthodologique au sujet de ces statistiques

Publication: Sur papier, à diffusion restreinte.

Agence responsable: Agence pour l'Emploi de la Population, sous le Ministère du Travail et du Bien-être social de la République du Tadjikistan.

11. Comparaisons avec des statistiques provenant d'autres sources

Des comparaisons ont été faites avec des statistiques provenant du recensement de population.

Fréquence des comparaisons: Occasionnelles.

Publication de la méthodologie et/ou des résultats de la comparaison: Ils n'ont pas été publiés.

12. Principaux changements intervenus depuis le début de ces séries statistiques

Il n'y a pas eu de changement important dans la législation, dans la capacité de l'agence et/ou dans les procédures administratives susceptibles d'avoir influencé de manière significative les statistiques.

Tanzanie, Rép.-Unie de

1. Séries statistiques

Titre: Chômage enregistré.

Première année disponible: 2002.

2. Organisme responsable de l'enregistrement des chômeurs ou demandeurs d'emploi

Nom de l'organisme: "Labour Exchange Centre" (Bourse de travail).

Type d'organisme: Organisme public relevant d'une autorité nationale.

Nom de l'autorité nationale: Ministère du Travail et du Développement de la Jeunesse et du Sport.

Situation des bureaux chargés de l'enregistrement: Dans la ville de Dar-es-Salam.

Types de services fournis et/ou gérés par cet organisme:

–   Assistance aux demandeurs d'emploi pour trouver du travail;
–   Assistance aux employeurs pour trouver de la main-d'œuvre;
–   Orientation professionnelle.

3. Les informations personnelles suivantes sont enregistrées:
- Nom;
- Sexe;
- Adresse du domicile habituel;
- Date de naissance;
- Citoyenneté;
- Nationalité/groupe ethnique;
- Niveau d'instruction/ de formation, en distinguant six catégories;
- Situation de travail présente et passée, en distinguant trois catégories;
- Type de profession de l'emploi antérieur ou actuel, en distinguant 10 catégories. Des liens ont été établis avec la CITP, au niveau des groupes de base;
- Type de profession de l'emploi recherché, avec 10 catégories. Des liens ont été établis avec la CITP, au niveau des groupes de base;
- Nom et adresse de l'employeur ou du lieu de travail actuel ou passé;
- Branche d'activité de l'employeur ou du lieu de travail actuel ou passé, en distinguant un nombre non spécifié de catégories. Des liens ont été établis avec la CITI, rév.3 (niveau non spécifié);
- Autres: type d'emploi désiré (cinq types); date de présentation à un employeur ; connaissances de langues.

4. Critères utilisés pour déterminer si une personne doit être incluse dans le registre (R) et/ou dans les statistiques de chômeurs (S):
- Etre sans travail (R);
- Etre à la recherche d'un travail (R);
- Etre disponible pour travailler (R);
- Age: Minimum: 18 an; Maximum: 60 ans (R);
- Etre résident dans le pays (R).

5. Critères utilisés pour déterminer si une personne doit être exclue du registre (R) et/ou des statistiques de chômeurs (S):
- Décès (R);
- Etablissement de la personne à l'étranger (R);
- Commencement d'un (nouveau) travail (et satisfait par ce travail) (R);
- Commencement du service militaire (R);
- Entreprise d'une formation (de longue durée) (R);
- Incapacité à travailler (due à un handicap) (R).

6. Définition des personnes au chômage sur laquelle les statistiques sont établies

Une définition large de *être disponible pour travailler + est utilisée.

Les catégories suivantes des personnes au chômage sont produites:

Chômage A: Personnes actuellement inoccupées qui sont non seulement disponibles pour travailler mais ont pris des dispositions actives au cours des quatre dernières semaines pour trouver du travail;

Chômage B: Personnes inoccupées qui n'ont pas pris de dispositions actives au cours des quatre dernières semaines pour trouver du travail.

7. Mise à jour des registres

La fréquence de mise à jour des registres n'est pas spécifiée.

8. Taux de chômage

Les statistiques basées sur les registres ne sont pas utilisées pour obtenir des taux de chômage.

9. Type de statistiques sur le nombre de chômeurs enregistrés produites

Série 1:
Période de référence: Mois.
Fréquence de production: Mensuellement.
Variables utilisées:
- Sexe;
- Age;
- Niveau d'instruction;
- Profession;
- Branche d'activité;
- Caractéristiques géographiques;
- Expérience professionnelle antérieure;
- Citoyenneté (nationaux/non nationaux);
- Durée de chômage.
Publication: Sur papier, à diffusion grand public.

Agence responsable de la publication: Ministère du travail et du Développement de la Jeunesse et du Sport.
Titre et périodicité des publications: *Employment Outlook; Unemployment* (Perspectives de l'emploi, Chômage). La périodicité des publications dépend de la disponibilité de fonds pour la production des données.
Série 2:
Période de référence: Année.
Fréquence de production: Annuellement.
Variables utilisées:
- Sexe;
- Age;
- Niveau d'instruction;
- Profession;
- Branche d'activité;
- Caractéristiques géographiques;
- Expérience professionnelle antérieure;
- Citoyenneté (nationaux/non nationaux);
- Durée de chômage.
Publication: Sur papier, à diffusion grand public.
Agence responsable de la publication: Ministère du travail et du Développement de la Jeunesse et du Sport.
Titre et périodicité des publications: *Employment Outlook; Unemployment* (Perspectives de l'emploi, Chômage). La périodicité des publications dépend de la disponibilité de fonds pour la production des données.

10. Information méthodologique au sujet de ces statistiques
Publication: Sur papier, à diffusion grand public.
Agence responsable: Ministère du Travail et du Développement de la Jeunesse et du Sport.

11. Comparaisons avec des statistiques provenant d'autres sources

Il n'y a pas eu de comparaisons faites avec des statistiques provenant d'autres sources, bien qu'il soit prévu d'en faire à l'avenir.

12. Principaux changements intervenus depuis le début de ces séries statistiques

Il n'y a pas eu de changement important dans la législation, dans la capacité de l'agence et/ou dans les procédures administratives susceptibles d'avoir influencé de manière significative les statistiques.

13. Remarques supplémentaires

La bourse de travail fut établie le 1er juillet 2001 et le traitement des données a commencé au début de 2002. De ce fait certaines informations concernant ces statistiques ne sont pas encore disponibles.

Tchad

1. Séries statistiques
Titre: Annuaire des statistiques du marché du travail
Première année disponible: 1986
2. Organisme responsable de l'enregistrement des chômeurs ou demandeurs d'emploi
Nom de l'organisme: Office national pour la Promotion de l'Empoi (ONAPE)
Type d'organisme: Organisme public relevant d'une autorité nationale.
Nom de l'autorité nationale: Ministère de la Fonction publique, du Travail, de la Promotion de l'Emploi et de la Modernisation (MFPTPEM).
Situation des bureaux chargés de l'enregistrement: Njamena, Moundou, Sarh, Bougor et Doba.
Types de services fournis et/ou gérés par cet organisme:
- Assistance aux demandeurs d'emploi pour trouver du travail;
- Assistance aux demandeurs d'emploi pour créer leur propre entreprise;
- Assistance aux employeurs pour trouver de la main-d'œuvre;
- Orientation professionnelle;
- Autres services liés à l'emploi: délivrance des autorisation de travail aux étrangers.

3. Les informations personnelles suivantes sont enregistrées:
- Nom;
- Sexe;
- Numéro de sécurité sociale (ou numéro d'identification également utilisé par d'autres organismes);
- Adresse du domicile habituel;

– Date de naissance;
– Citoyenneté;
– Nationalité/groupe ethnique;
– Niveau d'instruction/ de formation, en distinguant huit catégories. Aucun lien n'a été établi avec la CITE;
– Situation de travail présente et passée;
– Type de profession de l'emploi antérieur ou actuel. Aucun lien n'a été établi avec la CITP-88;
– Type de profession de l'emploi recherché;
– Nom et adresse de l'employeur ou du lieu de travail actuel ou passé;
– Branche d'activité de l'employeur ou du lieu de travail actuel ou passé, en distinguant huit catégories. Des liens ont été établis avec la CITI-rév. 2.

4. Critères utilisés pour déterminer si une personne doit être incluse dans le registre (R) et/ou dans les statistiques de chômeurs (S):
– Information non disponible.

5. Critères utilisés pour déterminer si une personne doit être exclue du registre (R) et/ou des statistiques de chômeurs (S): Information non disponible.
Information non disponible.

6. Définition des personnes au chômage sur laquelle les statistiques sont établies
Information non disponible.

7. Mise à jour des registres
Les registres sont mis à jour quotidiennement.

8. Taux de chômage
Les statistiques basées sur les registres ne sont pas utilisées pour obtenir des taux de chômage.

9. Type de statistiques produites sur le nombre de chômeurs enregistrés
Les statistiques produites le sont sur les types de services fournis ou gérés par l'ONAPE:
– Assistance aux demandeurs d'emploi pour trouver du travail;
– Assistance aux demandeurs d'emploi pour créer leur propre entreprise;
– Assistance aux employeurs pour trouver de la main-d'œuvre;
– Orientation professionnelle;
– Autres services liés à l'emploi: délivrance des autorisation de travail aux étrangers.

Variables utilisées:
– Sexe;
– Age;
– Niveau d'instruction;
– Profession;
– Branche d'activité;
– Caractéristiques géographiques;
– Expérience professionnelle antérieure;
– Citoyenneté (nationaux/non nationaux);
– Durée de chômage.

Publication: Sur papier, à diffusion restreinte.
Organisme responsable de la publication: ONAPE.

10. Information méthodologique au sujet de ces statistiques
Publication: Sur papier, à diffusion restreinte;
Organisme responsable: ONAPE.

11. Comparaisons avec des statistiques provenant d'autres sources
Il n'y a pas eu de comparaisons faites avec des statistiques provenant d'autres sources.

12. Principaux changements intervenus depuis le début de ces séries statistiques
Il n'y a pas eu de changement important dans la législation, dans la capacité de l'agence et/ou dans les procédures administratives susceptibles d'avoir influencé de manière significative les statistiques.

République tchèque

1. Séries statistiques
Titre: Chômeurs enregistrés et postes vacants.
Première année disponible: 1991
2. Organisme responsable de l'enregistrement des chômeurs ou demandeurs d'emploi
Nom de l'organisme: Urad Prace (Agence pour l'emploi).

Type d'organisme: Organisme public relevant d'une autorité nationale.
Nom de l'autorité nationale: Ministerstvo prace a socialnich veci (Ministère du Travail et des Affaires sociales).
Situation des bureaux chargés de l'enregistrement: Dans 77 districts du pays.
Types de services fournis et/ou gérés par cet organisme:
– Assistance aux demandeurs d'emploi pour trouver du travail;
– Assistance aux demandeurs d'emploi pour créer leur propre entreprise;
– Assistance aux employeurs pour trouver de la main-d'œuvre;
– Orientation professionnelle;
– Formation liée à l'emploi;
– Paiement des indemnités de chômage;
– Autres: «contrôle»' des employeurs; activités de contrôle dans le domaine du droit du travail.

Pourcentage des demandeurs d'emploi qui cherchent un emploi au travers de cet organisme: 95%.
3. Les informations personnelles suivantes sont enregistrées:
– Nom;
– Sexe;
– Numéro de sécurité sociale (ou numéro d'identification également utilisé par d'autres organismes);
– Adresse du domicile habituel;
– Date de naissance;
– Citoyenneté;
– Niveau d'instruction/ de formation, en distinguant 13 catégories. Des liens ont été établis avec la CITE 97;
– Situation de travail présente et passée, en distinguant 25 catégories;
– Type de profession de l'emploi antérieur ou actuel (facultatif), en distinguant 10 catégories. Des liens ont été établis avec la CITP 88;
– Type de profession de l'emploi recherché (facultatif), en distinguant 10 catégories. Des liens ont été établis avec la CITP 88;
– Nom et adresse de l'employeur ou du lieu de travail actuel ou passé;
– Branche d'activité de l'employeur ou du lieu de travail actuel ou passé (facultatif), en distinguant 17 catégories. Des liens ont été établis avec la CITI, rév.3 ou NACE, rév.1;
– Inscriptions/enregistrements antérieurs auprès de l'organisme;
– Autre: durée du chômage; chômage répétitif; état de santé; situation de famille; groupes défavorisées (ex. adolescents, jeunes en fin de scolarité et jeunes diplômés sans expérience professionnelle, femmes enceintes, personnes ayant un enfant de moins de 15 ans à charge; personnes de plus de 50 ans à la recherche d'un emploi, personnes à la recherche d'un emploi depuis plus de six mois, personnes ayant besoin d'assistance spéciale ou qui ne sont pas assimilées socialement).

4. Critères utilisés pour déterminer si une personne doit être incluse dans le registre (R) et/ou dans les statistiques de chômeurs (S):
– Etre sans travail (R) et (S);
– Etre à la recherche d'un travail (R) et (S);
– Etre disponible pour travailler (R) et (S);
– Age: Minimum: 15 ans; pas de limite supérieure (R) et (S);
– Etre résident dans le pays (R) et (S).

5. Critères utilisés pour déterminer si une personne doit être exclue du registre (R) et/ou des statistiques de chômeurs (S):
– Décès (R) et (S);
– Etablissement de la personne à l'étranger (R) et (S);
– Commencement d'un (nouveau) travail (R) et (S);
– Participation à un programme de promotion de l'emploi, à un programme de travaux publics, etc. (R) et (S);
– Entreprise d'une formation ou d'études (R) et (S);
– Défaut de contact avec l'organisme/agence (R) et (S);
– Refus d'offres d'emploi adaptées (R) et (S);
– Autre: sur demande de la personne (R) et (S).

6. Définition des personnes au chômage sur laquelle les statistiques sont établies

Sont enregistrés comme demandeurs d'emploi (section 7(1) de la loi sur le travail) les citoyens sans emploi ou relation similaire, qui ne poursuivent pas d'activité lucrative, ou qui ne sont pas impliqués dans une préparation systématique (études, formation) à une profession ou un métier (formation professionnelle) et qui adressent personnellement une demande écrite au bureau de l'emploi demandant de l'assistance lors de la recherche d'un emploi adapté.

7. Mise à jour des registres

Les registres sont mis à jour régulièrement.

8. Taux de chômage

Les statistiques basées sur les registres sont utilisées pour obtenir des taux de chômage.

Les sources des données d'emploi qui sont partie du dénominateur des taux de chômage sont les enquêtes sur la main-d'œuvre.

Définition des personnes pourvues d'un emploi à cette fin:

Le nombre des personnes pourvues d'un emploi est mis à jour tous les trimestres ; il est calculé sur la base de la moyenne arithmétique des quatre dernières enquêtes sur la main-d'œuvre (les définitions utilisées correspondent absolument à celles des indicateurs et recommandations du BIT).

9. Type de statistiques produites sur le nombre de chômeurs enregistrés

Série 1: Demandeurs d'emploi enregistrés et postes vacants.

Période de référence: Jour.

Fréquence de production: Mensuelle.

Variables utilisées:

– Sexe;
– Autre: au bénéfice d'indemnités de chômage; en formation.

Publication:

– Sur papier, à diffusion restreinte;
– En format électronique, sur demande;
– Sur un site Internet (www.mpsv.cz: Sluzby zamestnanosti (agence pour l'emploi)).

Organisme responsable de la publication: Ministère de du Travail et des Affaires sociales.

Titre et périodicité de la publication(s): *Statistical Report* (Rapport statistique), mensuel.

Série 2: Structure des demandeurs d'emploi et postes vacants.

Période de référence: Jour.

Fréquence de production: Trimestrielle.

Variables utilisées:

– Sexe;
– Groupe d'âge;
– Niveau d'instruction;
– Profession;
– Durée du chômage;
– Autre: au bénéfice d'indemnités de chômage.

Publication:

– En format électronique, sur demande;
– Sur un site Internet (http://ssz.mpsv.cz/Statistiky/).

Organisme responsable de la publication: Ministère de du Travail et des Affaires sociales.

10. Information méthodologique au sujet de ces statistiques

Publication: Sur papier, à diffusion restreinte.

Organisme responsable: Ministère de du Travail et des Affaires sociales.

11. Comparaisons avec des statistiques provenant d'autres sources

Il n'y a pas eu de comparaisons faites avec des statistiques provenant d'autres sources. Cependant, les statistiques du chômage provenant des enquêtes sur la main-d'œuvre sont utilisées par le Ministère du Travail et des Affaires sociales comme source d'information supplémentaire lors d'analyses du marché du travail.

12. Principaux changements intervenus depuis le début de ces séries statistiques

Des changements importants dans la législation, dans la capacité de l'agence et/ou dans les procédures administratives susceptibles d'avoir augmenté ou diminué le nombre de personnes enregistrées comme chômeurs sont intervenus en 1991: -2%; 1992: -5%; 1994: +5%; et 1996: +10%.

Thaïlande

1. Séries statistiques

Titre: Demandeurs d'emploi enregistrés.

Première année disponible: Non spécifié.

2. Organisme responsable de l'enregistrement des chômeurs ou demandeurs d'emploi

Nom de l'organisme: Département de l'Emploi.

Type d'organisme: Organisme public relevant d'une autorité nationale.

Nom de l'autorité nationale: Ministère du Travail et de l'Assistance publique.

Situation des bureaux chargés de l'enregistrement: 84 bureaux pour l'emploi à travers tout le pays - dans chaque province et à Bangkok.

Types de services fournis et/ou gérés par cet organisme:

– Assistance aux demandeurs d'emploi pour trouver du travail;
– Assistance aux demandeurs d'emploi pour créer leur propre entreprise;
– Assistance aux employeurs pour trouver de la main-d'œuvre;
– Orientation professionnelle;
– Formation liée à l'emploi;
– Autres: assistance aux personnes handicapées pour trouver du travail.

Pourcentage des demandeurs d'emploi qui cherchent un emploi au travers de cet organisme: 20%.

3. Les informations personnelles suivantes sont enregistrées:

– B Nom;
– Sexe;
– Numéro de sécurité sociale (ou numéro d'identification également utilisé par d'autres organismes);
– Adresse du domicile habituel;
– Date de naissance;
– Citoyenneté;
– Niveau d'instruction/de formation, en distinguant neuf catégories. Aucun lien n'a été établi avec la CITE;
– Type de profession de l'emploi antérieur et/ou actuel, en distinguant neuf catégories. Des liens ont été établis avec la CITP-88, au niveau des grands groupes;
– Type de profession de l'emploi recherché, avec neuf catégories. Des liens ont été établis avec la CITP-88, au niveau des grands groupes;
– Nom du lieu de travail précédent;
– Autre: type de handicap (pour les personnes handicapées).

4. Critères utilisés pour déterminer si une personne doit être incluse dans le registre (R) et/ou dans les statistiques de chômeurs (S):

Information non disponible.

5. Critères utilisés pour déterminer si une personne doit être exclue du registre (R) et/ou des statistiques de chômeurs (S):

Information non disponible.

6. Définition des personnes au chômage sur laquelle les statistiques sont établies

Personnes désireuses de travailler mais qui ne trouvent pas de travail pour quelque raison que ce soit (fin de contrat de travail, qualifications inadéquates, etc.).

7. Mise à jour des registres

Il n'y a pas d'information qui indique si les registres sont mis à jour régulièrement.

8. Taux de chômage

Les statistiques basées sur les registres sont utilisées pour obtenir des taux de chômage.

Les sources des données d'emploi qui sont partie du dénominateur sont l'enquête sur la main-d'œuvre et le recensement de population

Définition des personnes pourvues d'un emploi à cette fin:

Les travailleurs (y compris les employeurs ou entrepreneurs) qui perçoivent un revenu, en espèces ou en nature.

9. Type de statistiques produites sur le nombre de chômeurs enregistrés

Information non disponible.

10. Information méthodologique au sujet de ces statistiques

Information non disponible.

11. Comparaisons avec des statistiques provenant d'autres sources

Il n'y a pas eu de comparaisons faites avec des statistiques provenant d'autres sources.

12. Principaux changements intervenus depuis le début de ces séries statistiques

Il n'y a pas eu de changement important dans la législation, dans la capacité de l'agence et/ou dans les procédures administratives susceptibles d'avoir influencé de manière significative les statistiques.

Trinité-et-Tobago

1. Séries statistiques

Titre: Statistiques de l'Agence nationale pour l'Emploi.

Première année disponible: Non spécifiée.

2. Organisme responsable de l'enregistrement des chômeurs ou demandeurs d'emploi

Nom de l'organisme: Agence nationale pour l'Emploi.

Typo d'organisme: Organisme public relevant d'une autorité nationale.

Nom de l'autorité nationale: Ministère du Travail et du Développement de la petite et moyenne Entreprise.

Situation des bureaux chargés de l'enregistrement: En des lieux stratégiques, de façon à faciliter l'accès à ce service à toutes les régions du pays.

Types de services fournis et/ou gérés par cet organisme:
– Assistance aux demandeurs d'emploi pour trouver du travail;
– Assistance aux employeurs pour trouver de la main-d'œuvre;
– Orientation professionnelle;
– Autres: préparation de curriculum vitae; préparation aux interviews d'embauche.

3. Les informations personnelles suivantes sont enregistrées:
B Nom;
– Sexe;
– Numéro de sécurité sociale (ou numéro d'identification également utilisé par d'autres organismes);
– Adresse du domicile habituel;
– Date de naissance;
– Citoyenneté;
– Niveau d'instruction/de formation, en distinguant deux catégories. Aucun lien n'a été établi avec la CITE;
– Type de profession de l'emploi recherché, avec un nombre non spécifié de catégories; des liens ont été établis avec la CITP-88, au niveau des grands groupes;
– Inscriptions/enregistrements antérieurs auprès de l'agence.

4. Critères utilisés pour déterminer si une personne doit être incluse dans le registre (R) et/ou dans les statistiques de chômeurs (S):
– Etre sans travail (R) et (S);
– Etre à la recherche d'un travail (R) et (S);
– Etre disponible pour travailler (R);
– Age: Minimum: 17 ans; pas de limite supérieure (R);
– Citoyenneté (R) ;
– Etre résident dans le pays (R);
– Avoir précédemment travaillé (R);
– Autre: étudiants à la recherche d'un emploi pour l'été (R).

5. Critères utilisés pour déterminer si une personne doit être exclue du registre (R) et/ou des statistiques de chômeurs (S):
– Avis de décès (R);
– Etablissement de la personne à l'étranger (R);
– Incapacité à travailler (R).

6. Définition des personnes au chômage sur laquelle les statistiques sont établies

Personnes âgées de 17 ans et plus qui sont sans emploi, à la recherche d'un emploi et disponibles pour travailler (y compris les étudiants à la recherche d'un emploi pour l'été).

7. Mise à jour des registres

Les registres sont mis à jour mensuellement.

8. Taux de chômage

Les statistiques basées sur les registres ne sont pas utilisées pour obtenir des taux de chômage.

9. Type de statistiques produites sur le nombre de chômeurs enregistrés

Série 1:

Période de référence: Mois.

Fréquence de production: Mensuelle.

Variables utilisées:
– Sexe;
– Niveau d'instruction;
– Profession;
– Branche d'activité.

Publication: En format électronique, sur demande.

Organisme responsable de la publication: Ministère du Travail et du Développement de la petite et moyenne Entreprise.

Série 2:

Période de référence: Non spécifiée.

Fréquence de production: Année.

Variables utilisées:
– Sexe;
– Niveau d'instruction;
– Profession;
– Branche d'activité.

Publication: En format électronique, sur demande.

Organisme responsable de la publication: Ministère du Travail et du Développement de la petite et moyenne Entreprise.

10. Information méthodologique au sujet de ces statistiques

Publication: Non publiée, à usage interne uniquement.

Organisme responsable: Ministère du Travail et du Développement de la petite et moyenne Entreprise.

11. Comparaisons avec des statistiques provenant d'autres sources

Il n'y a pas eu de comparaisons faites avec des statistiques provenant d'autres sources.

12. Principaux changements intervenus depuis le début de ces séries statistiques

Il n'y a pas eu de changement important dans la législation, dans la capacité de l'agence et/ou dans les procédures administratives susceptibles d'avoir influencé de manière significative les statistiques.

Tunisie

1. Séries statistiques

Titre: Marché de l'Emploi

Première année disponible: Disponible sur papier à partir de 1995 (possible avant). Disponible sur système informatisé à partir de 1997.

2. Organisme responsable de l'enregistrement des chômeurs ou demandeurs d'emploi

Nom de l'organisme: Agence Tunisienne pour l'Emploi (ATE).

Type d'organisme: Organisme public relevant d'une autorité nationale.

Nom de l'autorité nationale: Ministère de l'emploi.

Situation des bureaux chargés de l'enregistrement: Dans l'ensemble du pays, 80 bureaux répartis dans les 24 départements (gouvernorats).

Types de services fournis et/ou gérés par cet organisme:
– Assistance aux demandeurs d'emploi pour trouver du travail.
– Assistance aux demandeurs d'emploi pour créer leur propre entreprise.
– Assistance aux employeurs pour trouver de la main-d'œuvre.
– Orientation professionnelle.
– Formation liée à l'emploi.
– Autres services liés à l'emploi, à l'insertion des jeunes et à la réinsertion des licenciés: organisation et gestion de stages d'initiation à la vie professionnelle: information professionnelle, sessions d'assistance et d'accompagnement, etc.

Pourcentage des demandeurs d'emploi qui cherchent un emploi au travers de cet organisme: 25 à 30% (+ de 80% chez les diplômés de l'enseignement supérieur).

3. Les informations personnelles suivantes sont enregistrées:
– Nom
– Sexe
– Numéro de sécurité sociale (ou numéro d'identification également utilisé par d'autres organismes)
– Adresse du domicile habituel

- Date de naissance
- Citoyenneté
- Nationalité
- Niveau d'instruction/de formation, en distinguant huit catégories. Des liens ont été établis avec la CITE
- Situation de travail présente et passée, en distinguant trois catégories (occupé, antérieurement occupé, n'ayant jamais travaillé)
- Type de profession de l'emploi antérieur et/ou actuel, en distinguant neuf catégories. Aucun lien n'a été établi avec la CITP
- Type de profession de l'emploi recherché, avec neuf catégories
- Nom et adresse de l'employeur ou du lieu de travail actuel ou passé
- Branche d'activité de l'employeur ou du lieu de travail actuel ou passé, en distinguant 10 catégories. Aucun lien n'a été établi avec la CITI,
- Inscriptions/enregistrements antérieurs auprès de l'organisme.

4. Critères utilisés pour déterminer si une personne doit être incluse dans le registre (R) et/ou dans les statistiques de chômeurs (S):
- Etre à la recherche d'un travail (R) et (S)
- Age: Minimum: 18 ans (15 ans pour l'orientation professionnelle) ; pas de limite supérieure (R) et (S)
- Citoyenneté (carte d'identité, ou carte de séjour et autorisation de travail pour les étrangers (R).

5. Critères utilisés pour déterminer si une personne doit être exclue du registre (R) et/ou des statistiques de chômeurs (S):
- Etablissement de la personne à l'étranger (R)
- Commencement d'un (nouveau) travail ou création d'une micro-entreprise par exemple (R)
- Commencement du service militaire (R)
- Participation à un programme de promotion de l'emploi, à un programme de travaux publics, etc. (R)
- Entreprise d'une formation ou d'études (R)
- Défaut de contact avec l'organisme/agence, automatiquement après deux mois d'absence (R).

6. Définition des personnes sur laquelle les statistiques sont établies

Les statistiques de l'Agence tunisienne pour l'Emploi sont établies sur les personnes se déclarant à la recherche d'un emploi et enregistrées dans l'un des 80 bureaux pour l'emploi. Ces personnes peuvent être des chômeurs comme elles peuvent être pourvues d'un emploi mais à la recherche d'un meilleur emploi.

7. Mise à jour des registres

Les registres sont mis à jour régulièrement (de façon automatique par le système).

8. Taux de chômage

Les statistiques basées sur les registres ne sont pas utilisées pour obtenir des taux de chômage.

9. Type de statistiques sur le nombre de demandeurs enregistrés produites
Série 1:
Période de référence: jour.
Fréquence de production: quotidienne.
Variables utilisées:
- Sexe
- Age
- Niveau d'instruction, diplôme, spécialité étudiée
- Profession
- Branche d'activité
- Caractéristiques géographiques
- Expérience professionnelle antérieure
- Durée d'attente
- Le bureau d'enregistrement
- Le gouvernorat.

Publication:
- A usage interne uniquement
- Sur un site intranet: www.emploi.nat.tn

Agence responsable de la publication: ATE.
Titre de la publication: *Indicateurs d'activité*, en libre service.
Série 2:
Période de référence: mois.
Fréquence de production: mensuelle.
Variables utilisées:
- Sexe

- Age
- Niveau d'instruction
- Profession
- Branche d'activité
- Caractéristiques géographiques
- Expérience professionnelle antérieure
- Durée d'attente
- Le bureau d'enregistrement
- Le gouvernorat.

Publication:
- A usage interne
- Sur papier, à diffusion restreinte.

Agence responsable de la publication: ATE.
Titre et périodicité de la publication: *Evolution du marché de l'emploi au cours du mois,* périodicité mensuelle.
Série 3:
Période de référence: mois.
Fréquence de production: trimestrielle et annuelle.
Variables utilisées:
- Sexe
- Age
- Niveau d'instruction
- Profession
- Branche d'activité
- Caractéristiques géographiques
- Expérience professionnelle antérieure
- Durée d'attente
- Le bureau d'enregistrement
- Le gouvernorat.

Publication:
- A usage interne
- Sur papier, à diffusion restreinte.

Agence responsable de la publication: ATE.
Titre et périodicité des publications: *Rapport trimestriel et rapport annuel sur l'activité de L'ATE.*

10. Information méthodologique au sujet de ces statistiques
Publication:
- Non diffusée, à usage interne
- Sur papier, à diffusion restreinte
- Sur un site Internet: www.emploi.nat.tn
- Consultation sur place – grand public.

Agence responsable: ATE.

11. Comparaisons avec des statistiques provenant d'autres sources

Des comparaisons ont été faites avec des statistiques provenant de l'enquête de main-d'œuvre, d'autres enquêtes auprès des ménages et avec des statistiques du recensement de la population. Ces statistiques sont utilisées pour d'une part apprécier le niveau de pénétration des services de l'emploi dans le marché du travail, et d'autre part aider les cadres de L'ATE à cibler leurs interventions en direction des populations vulnérables.

Fréquence des comparaisons: Annuellement avec l'enquête population-emploi (INS).

12. Principaux changements intervenus depuis le début de ces séries statistiques

Des changements importants dans la législation, dans la capacité de l'agence et/ou dans les procédures administratives susceptibles d'avoir influencé de manière significative les statistiques sont intervenus en 1995.

Depuis la création de L'ATE en 1993, et particulièrement depuis la mise en œuvre du système d'informatisation et de gestion du marché de l'emploi (informatisé) en 1995, les données sur les demandeurs d'emploi sont devenues de plus en plus fiables. La couverture des demandeurs cadres est de plus en plus élevée et plus représentative.

Turquie

1. Séries statistiques
Titre: Chômage enregistré.
Première année disponible: 1946.
2. Organisme responsable de l'enregistrement des chômeurs ou demandeurs d'emploi
Nom de l'organisme: Türkiye Iş Kurumu (Işkur) (Organisation Turque pour l'Emploi - OET)
Type d'organisme: Organisme public relevant d'une autorité nationale.

Nom de l'autorité nationale: Ministère du Travail et de la Sécurité Sociale.

Situation des bureaux chargés de l'enregistrement: Dans toutes les provinces ainsi que dans quelques municipalités.

Types de services fournis et/ou gérés par cet organisme:

– Assistance aux demandeurs d'emploi pour trouver du travail;

– Assistance aux demandeurs d'emploi pour créer leur propre entreprise;

– Assistance aux employeurs pour trouver de la main-d'œuvre;

– Orientation professionnelle;

– Formation liée à l'emploi;

– Paiement des indemnités de chômage (assurance chômage);

– Autres: conduite d'enquêtes de main-d'œuvre sur le marché du travail local et évaluation des résultats; mise en place et gestion d'un système d'information sur le marché du travail; compensation en cas de perte d'emploi.

Pourcentage des demandeurs d'emploi qui cherchent un emploi au travers de cet organisme: 37% (3ème trimestre, 2001).

3. Les informations personnelles suivantes sont enregistrées:

– Nom;

– Sexe;

– Numéro de sécurité sociale (ou numéro d'identification également utilisé par d'autres organismes);

– Adresse du domicile habituel;

– Date et lieu de naissance;

– Citoyenneté;

– Niveau d'instruction/de formation, en distinguant quatre catégories. Des liens ont été établis avec la CITE;

– Situation de travail présente et passée, en distinguant neuf catégories;

– Type de profession de l'emploi antérieur et/ou actuel, en distinguant 72 catégories. Des liens ont été établis avec la CITP-88, au niveau des sous-groupes;

– Type de profession de l'emploi recherché, avec 72 catégories; Des liens ont été établis avec la CITP-88, au niveau des sous-groupes;

– Nom et adresse de l'employeur ou du lieu de travail actuel ou passé;

– Branche d'activité de l'employeur ou du lieu de travail actuel ou passé, en distinguant trois catégories. La CITI-rév.3 est utilisée, mais on utilisera bientôt la NACE-rév.1);

– Inscriptions/enregistrements antérieurs auprès de l'organisme;

– Autre: expérience dans le poste précédent; profession supplémentaire; connaissance de langues étrangères; permis de conduire/numéro de passeport; situation sociale (handicapé, touché par le terrorisme, etc.); statut matrimonial; durée de chômage; salaire souhaité; secteur; type de travail (permanent ou saisonnier, etc.); localisation (à la maison ou à l'extérieur).

4. Critères utilisés pour déterminer si une personne doit être incluse dans le registre (R) et/ou dans les statistiques de chômeurs (S):

– Etre sans travail (R) et (S);

– Etre à la recherche d'un travail (chaque candidat est enregistré quelque soit sa situation dans l'emploi à ce moment là) (R) et (S);

– Etre disponible pour travailler (disponibilité pour commencer à travailler à la date spécifiée par un employeur) (R) et (S);

– Age: Minimum: 15 ans; pas de limite supérieure (R) et (S);

– Citoyenneté (R) et (S);

– Etre résident dans le pays (R) et (S);

– Avoir précédemment travaillé (R) et (S);

– Durée souhaitée de l'emploi recherché et/ou du nombre d'heures de travail recherché (R) et (S);

– Acquittement de cotisations d'assurance chômage (R) et (S).

5. Critères utilisés pour déterminer si une personne doit être exclue du registre (R) et/ou des statistiques de chômeurs (S):

– Avis de décès (R) et (S);

– Etablissement de la personne à l'étranger (R) et (S);

– Commencement d'un (nouveau) travail (placement par

l'Organisation Turque pour l'Emploi) (R) et (S);

– Commencement du service militaire (R) et (S);

– Entreprise d'une formation ou d'études (R) et (S);

– Défaut de contact avec l'organisme/agence (l'enregistrement est automatiquement supprimé au bout d'une année s'il n'a pas été renouvelé) (R) et (S);

– Refus de trois offres d'emploi adaptées (R) et (S);

– Admission à toucher une pension (retraite, etc.) (R) et (S).

6. Définition des personnes au chômage sur laquelle les statistiques sont établies

Toute personne en âge de travailler (15 ans et plus) qui est capable et désireuse de travailler et qui, au moment du dépôt de sa candidature auprès du Bureau pour l'emploi, gagne moins que le salaire minimum et n'a pas été placée par le Bureau pour l'emploi sur un poste.

7. Mise à jour des registres

Les registres sont mis à jour mensuellement.

8. Taux de chômage

Les statistiques basées sur les registres sont utilisées pour obtenir des taux de chômage.

La source des données d'emploi qui sont partie du dénominateur est l'enquête auprès des ménages sur la main-d'œuvre (conduite par l'Institut National des Statistiques).

Définition des personnes pourvues d'un emploi à cette fin: Conformément à la législation du travail turque, ce sont toutes les personnes pourvues d'un emploi contre rémunération, avec un contrat de travail.

9. Type de statistiques produites sur le nombre de chômeurs enregistrés

Série 1:

Période de référence: Mois.

Fréquence de production: Mensuelle.

Variables utilisées:

– Sexe;

– Age;

– Niveau d'instruction;

– Profession;

– Branche d'activité;

– Caractéristiques géographiques;

– Durée de chômage;

– Autre: groupe de profession.

Publication:

– Sur papier, à diffusion grand public;

– Sur un site Internet: (www.iskur.gov.tr).

Agence responsable de la publication: Directorat général de l'OET/Section du Département de l'emploi contrôlant la main-d'œuvre et les statistiques.

Titre de la publication: *Annuaire Statistique de l'Organisation Turque pour l'Emploi.*

Série 2:

Période de référence: Année.

Fréquence de production: Annuelle.

Variables utilisées:

– Sexe;

– Age;

– Niveau d'instruction;

– Profession;

– Branche d'activité;

– Caractéristiques géographiques;

– Durée de chômage;

– Autre: groupe de profession.

Publication:

– Sur papier, à diffusion grand public;

– Sur un site Internet: (www.iskur.gov.tr).

Agence responsable de la publication: Directorat général de l'OET/Section du Département de l'emploi contrôlant la main-d'œuvre et les statistiques.

Titre de la publication: *Annuaire Statistique de l'Organisation Turque pour l'Emploi.*

10. Information méthodologique au sujet de ces statistiques

Publication:

– Sur papier, à diffusion grand public;

– Sur un site Internet: (www.iskur.gov.tr).

Organisme responsable: OET.

11. Comparaisons avec des statistiques provenant d'autres sources

Des comparaisons ont été faites avec des statistiques provenant de l'enquête de main-d'œuvre.

Fréquence des comparaisons: Régulièrement, sur une base trimestrielle.

Publication de la méthodologie et/ou des résultats de la comparaison: Ils n'ont pas été publiés.

12. Principaux changements intervenus depuis le début de ces séries statistiques

Il n'y a pas eu de changement important dans la législation, dans la capacité de l'agence et/ou dans les procédures administratives susceptibles d'avoir influencé de manière significative les statistiques.

Uruguay

1. Séries statistiques

Titre: Offre et demande d'emploi dans les agences de placement privées et Registre des utilisateurs du Programme de formation pour l'emploi.

Première année disponible: 1993.

2. Organisme responsable de l'enregistrement des chômeurs ou demandeurs d'emploi

Nom de l'organisme: Dirección Nacional de Empleo - DINAE (Direction nationale de l'Emploi).

Type d'organisme: Organisme public relevant d'une autorité nationale.

Nom de l'autorité nationale: Ministerio de Trabajo y Seguridad Social (Ministère du Travail et de la Sécurité sociale).

Situation des bureaux chargés de l'enregistrement: Dans l'ensemble du pays.

Types de services fournis et/ou gérés par cet organisme

– Orientation professionnelle;

– Formation liée à l'emploi;

– Autres: information sur le marché du travail.

3. Les informations personnelles suivantes sont enregistrées*:

– Nom;

– Sexe;

– Numéro de sécurité sociale (ou numéro d'identification également utilisé par d'autres organismes);

– Adresse du domicile habituel;

– Date de naissance;

– Citoyenneté;

– Niveau d'instruction/de formation, en distinguant 14 catégories. Aucun lien n'a été établi avec la CITE;

– Situation de travail passée;

– Type de profession de l'emploi antérieur et/ou actuel, en distinguant quatre catégories C'est la Classification Nationale Type des Professions (CNUO-95) (à quatre chiffres), qui est basée sur la CITP-88, qui a été utilisée;

– Nom et adresse de l'employeur ou du lieu de travail actuel ou passé;

– Branche d'activité de l'employeur ou du lieu de travail actuel ou passé, en distinguant quatre catégories. C'est la classification nationale de toutes les branches d'activité (à quatre chiffres) qui est basée sur la CITI Rév. 3, qui a été utilisée.

* Informations concernant les travailleurs inscrits au Programme de formation pour l'emploi.

4. Critères utilisés pour déterminer si une personne doit être incluse dans le registre (R) et/ou dans les statistiques de chômeurs (S)

– Etre sans travail (R);

– Etre à la recherche d'un travail (R);

– Etre disponible pour travailler (R);

– Age (minimum: non-spécifié; maximum: non-spécifié) (R);

– Avoir précédemment travaillé (les utilisateurs du Programme de formation pour l'emploi sont des chômeurs à part entière, c'est-à-dire qu'ils ont travaillé et qu'ils ont perdu leur emploi) (R);

– Acquittement de cotisations d'assurance chômage (pour pouvoir être inscrite au Programme de formation pour l'emploi, la personne doit bénéficier des prestations de chômage et, par conséquent, avoir payé ses cotisations);

– Autres: ne pas avoir suivi de cours de l'enseignement supérieur (uniquement pour les utilisateurs du Programme de formation pour l'emploi).

5. Critères utilisés pour déterminer si une personne doit être exclue du registre (R) et/ou des statistiques de chômeurs (S)

Non-spécifiée.

6. Définition des personnes au chômage sur laquelle les statistiques sont établies

En ce qui concerne les utilisateurs du Programme de formation pour l'emploi, les critères pour être inclus sont les suivants:

– recevoir des prestations de chômage;

– avoir être licencié (sans possibilité d'être réintégré dans l'entreprise);

– ne pas avoir suivi de cours de l'enseignement supérieur.

7. Mise à jour des registres

Non-spécifiée.

8. Taux de chômage

Les statistiques basées sur les registres sont utilisées pour obtenir des taux de chômage.

La source des données d'emploi qui sont partie du dénominateur est l'enquête auprès des ménages sur la main-d'œuvre.

Définition des personnes pourvues d'un emploi à cette fin:

Toutes les personnes âgées de 14 ans ou plus qui avaient travaillé au moins une heure pendant la semaine précédant l'enquête.

9. Type de statistiques produites sur le nombre de chômeurs enregistrés

Non-spécifié.

10. Information méthodologique au sujet de ces statistiques

Non-spécifiée.

11. Comparaisons avec des statistiques provenant d'autres sources

Aucune comparaison n'a été faite avec des statistiques provenant d'autres sources.

12. Principaux changements intervenus depuis le début de ces séries statistiques

Il n'y a pas eu de changement important dans la législation, dans la capacité de l'agence et/ou dans les procédures administratives susceptibles d'avoir influencé de manière significative les statistiques.

Venezuela

1. Séries statistiques

Titre: Chômage enregistré

Première année disponible: 1964

2. Organisme responsable de l'enregistrement des chômeurs ou demandeurs d'emploi

Nom de l'organisme: Servicio Nacional de Empleo -Agencia de Empleo (Service National de l'Emploi - Agence de l'Emploi).

Type d'organisme: Organisme public relevant d'une autorité nationale.

Nom de l'autorité nationale: Ministerio de Trabajo (Ministère du Travail).

Situation des bureaux chargés de l'enregistrement: Dans les 16 états et un bureau dans l'arrondissement de la capitale (25 Bureaux de placement).

Types de services fournis et/ou gérés par cet organisme

– Assistance aux demandeurs d'emploi pour trouver du travail;

– Assistance aux demandeurs d'emploi pour créer leur propre entreprise;

– Assistance aux employeurs pour trouver de la main-d'œuvre;

– Orientation professionnelle;

– Formation liée à l'emploi.

Pourcentage des demandeurs d'emploi qui cherchent un emploi au travers de cet organisme: 15%

3. Les informations personnelles suivantes sont enregistrées

– Nom;

– Sexe;

– Numéro de sécurité sociale (ou numéro d'identification également utilisé par d'autres organismes);

– Adresse du domicile habituel;

– Date de naissance;

– Citoyenneté;

– Niveau d'instruction/de formation, en distinguant deux catégories. Des liens ont été établis avec la CITE-97;

– Situation de travail présente et passée, en distinguant trois catégories;

– Type de profession de l'emploi antérieur et/ou actuel, avec deux catégories. Des liens ont été établis avec la CITP;

– Type de profession de l'emploi recherché, avec deux catégories. Des liens ont été établis avec la CITP;
– Nom et adresse de l'employeur ou du lieu de travail actuel ou passé;
– Branche d'activité de l'employeur ou du lieu de travail actuel ou passé, en distinguant 10 catégories. Des liens ont été établis avec la CITI Rév. 3 au niveau des classes;
– Inscriptions/enregistrements antérieurs auprès de l'organisme.

4. Critères utilisés pour déterminer si une personne doit être incluse dans le registre (R) et/ou dans les statistiques de chômeurs (S)

– Etre sans travail (R) et (S);
– Etre à la recherche d'un travail (licencié bénéficiaire d'allocations de chômage, demandeur d'emploi en activité) (R) et (S);
– Etre disponible pour travailler (R) et (S);
– Age: Minimum: 14 ans; maximum: il n'y a pas d'âge maximum (R) et (S);
– Citoyenneté (R) et (S);
– Etre résident dans le pays (R) et (S);
– Avoir précédemment travaillé (expérience ou formation professionnelles) (R) et (S);
– Durée souhaitée de l'emploi recherché et/ou du nombre d'heures de travail recherché (S);
– Acquittement de cotisations d'assurance chômage (licenciés bénéficiaires d'allocations de chômage) (R) et (S);
– Autres: licenciement injustifié (après 18 semaines consécutives de travail) (R) et (S).

5. Critères utilisés pour déterminer si une personne doit être exclue du registre (R) et/ou des statistiques de chômeurs (S)

– Commencement d'un (nouveau) travail (R) et (S);
– Participation à un programme de promotion de l'emploi, à un programme de travaux publics, etc. (R) et (S);
– Défaut de contact avec l'organisme/agence (R) et (S).

6. Définition des personnes au chômage sur laquelle les statistiques sont établies

Sont considérées au chômage les personnes qui cherchent du travail pour la première fois ou qui pour une raison quelconque se trouvent en-dehors du marché du travail, soit, par exemple, pour cause de licenciement justifié et injustifié ou parce qu'elles ont démissionné d'un emploi.

7. Mise à jour des registres

Les registres sont mis à jour annuellement; tout changement intervenu pendant la période est indiqué dans le format du registre concernant l'information sur la personne sans emploi.

8. Taux de chômage

Les statistiques basées sur les registres ne sont pas utilisées pour obtenir des taux de chômage.

9. Type de statistiques produites sur le nombre de chômeurs enregistrés

Série: 1
Période de référence: Jour
Fréquence de production: Semestrielle
Variables utilisées
– Sexe;
– Age;
– Niveau d'instruction;
– Profession;
– Branche d'activité;
– Caractéristiques géographiques;
– Expérience professionnelle antérieure;
– Citoyenneté (nationaux/non nationaux);
– Durée de chômage;
– Autres: personnes licenciées bénéficiaires d'allocations de chômage, état civil.

Publication: A usage interne uniquement.
Organisme responsable de la publication: Direction Générale de l'Emploi.
Série: 2
Période de référence: Mois
Fréquence de production: Annuelle
Variables utilisées
– Sexe;
– Age;
– Niveau d'instruction;
– Profession;

– Branche d'activité;
– Caractéristiques géographiques;
– Expérience professionnelle antérieure;
– Citoyenneté (nationaux/non nationaux);
– Durée de chômage;
– Autres: personnes licenciées bénéficiaires d'allocations de chômage, état civil.

Publication: A usage interne uniquement.
Organisme responsable de la publication: Direction Générale de l'Emploi.

10. Information méthodologique au sujet de ces statistiques

Publication: Sur papier, à diffusion restreinte.
Organisme responsable: Direction Générale de l'Emploi.

11. Comparaisons avec des statistiques provenant d'autres sources

Des comparaisons ont été faites avec des statistiques provenant de l'enquête sur la main-d'œuvre, d'autres enquêtes auprès des ménages et du recensement de population

Fréquence des comparaisons: Régulièrement, quand les statistiques sont publiées (dernière année: 2001).
Publication de la méthodologie et/ou des résultats de la comparaison: Publiés dans *Boletín de Segmento de Mercado de Trabajo* (Bulletin de Segment du Marché du Travail).

12. Principaux changements intervenus depuis le début de ces séries statistiques

Des changements importants dans la législation, dans la capacité de l'agence et/ou dans les procédures administratives susceptibles d'avoir influencé de manière significative les statistiques sont intervenus en 1. 1996; 2. 1997; 3. 1998; 4. 1999; 5. 2000 et 6. 2001, donnant les résultats suivants par rapport au nombre total de chômeurs enregistrés: 1. 1996-97: +29.43%; 2. 1997-98: +19.10%; 3. 1998-99: +85.76%; 4. 1999-2000: + 9.03%, y 5. 2000-01: + 5.70%.
(1. Création de nouvelles agences; 2. fermeture d'entreprises; 3. Changement de la branche d'activité économique; 4. Accroissement de la main-d'œuvre, et 5. Automatisation des services de l'emploi).

Zimbabwe

1. Séries statistiques

Titre: Chômage enregistré.
Première année disponible: 1959.

2. Organisme responsable de l'enregistrement des chômeurs ou demandeurs d'emploi

Nom de l'organisme: Département national des Services de l'Emploi.
Type d'organisme: Organisme public relevant d'une autorité nationale.
Nom de l'autorité nationale: Ministère de la Fonction publique, du Travail et des Affaires sociales.
Situation des bureaux chargés de l'enregistrement: Dans toutes les capitales de provinces du pays et dans deux municipalités.
Types de services fournis et/ou gérés par cet organisme:
– Assistance aux demandeurs d'emploi pour trouver du travail;
– Assistance aux demandeurs d'emploi pour créer leur propre entreprise;
– Assistance aux employeurs pour trouver de la main-d'œuvre;
– Orientation professionnelle;
– Autres services liés à l'emploi: enregistrement et contrôle des agences d'emploi privées; collection et dissémination de l'information sur le marché du travail.

Pourcentage des demandeurs d'emploi qui cherchent un emploi au travers de cet organisme: 10%.

3. Les informations personnelles suivantes sont enregistrées:

– Nom;
– Sexe;
– Adresse du domicile habituel;
– Date de naissance;
– Citoyenneté;
– Nationalité/groupe ethnique;
– Niveau d'instruction/de formation, en distinguant deux catégories. Aucun lien n'a été établi avec la CITE;
– Situation de travail présente et passée, en distinguant trois catégories;

–   Type de profession de l'emploi antérieur et/ou actuel, en distinguant un nombre non spécifié de catégories. Des liens ont été établis avec la CITP, au niveau des groupes de base;
–   Type de profession de l'emploi recherché, en distinguant un nombre non spécifié de catégories. Des liens ont été établis avec la CITP, au niveau des groupes de base;
–   Nom et adresse de l'employeur ou du lieu de travail actuel ou passé;
–   Inscriptions/enregistrements antérieurs auprès de l'organisme.

4. Critères utilisés pour déterminer si une personne doit être incluse dans le registre (R) et/ou dans les statistiques de chômeurs (S):
–   Etre sans travail (R) et (S);
–   Etre à la recherche d'un travail (R) et (S);
–   Etre disponible pour travailler (R) et (S);
–   Age: Minimum: 16 ans; Maximum: 60 ans; (R) et (S);
–   Citoyenneté: citoyens du Zimbabwe uniquement (R) et (S);
–   Etre résident dans le pays (R);
–   Avoir précédemment travaillé (R).

5. Critères utilisés pour déterminer si une personne doit être exclue du registre (R) et/ou des statistiques de chômeurs (S):
–   Avis de décès (R) et (S);
–   Commencement d'un (nouveau) travail (R) et (S);
–   Défaut de contact avec l'organisme/agence (R) et (S).

6. Définition des personnes au chômage sur laquelle les statistiques sont établies
Personnes disponibles pour travailler, cherchant activement du travail et faisant des recherches d'emploi au moins une fois par mois.

7. Mise à jour des registres
Les registres sont mis à jour mensuellement.

8. Taux de chômage
Les statistiques basées sur les registres ne sont pas utilisées pour obtenir des taux de chômage.

9. Type de statistiques produites sur le nombre de chômeurs enregistrés
Période de référence: Jour; semaine; mois; semestre; année.
Fréquence de production: Mensuelle.
Variables utilisées:
–   Sexe;
–   Age;
–   Niveau d'instruction;
–   Profession;
–   Expérience professionnelle antérieure;
–   Citoyenneté (nationaux/non nationaux);
–   Durée de chômage.
Publication: A usage interne uniquement.
Organisme responsable de la publication: Département national des Services de l'Emploi.
Titre et périodicité de la publication: *Rapport et statistiques départementales mensuelles.*

10. Information méthodologique au sujet de ces statistiques
Publication: Sur papier, à diffusion restreinte.
Organisme responsable: Département national des Services de l'Emploi.

11. Comparaisons avec des statistiques provenant d'autres sources
Il n'y a pas eu de comparaisons faites avec des statistiques provenant d'autres sources.

12. Principaux changements intervenus depuis le début de ces séries statistiques
Des changements importants dans la législation, dans la capacité de l'agence et/ou dans les procédures administratives susceptibles d'avoir influencé de manière significative les statistiques sont intervenus en 1998, 1999, 2000 et 2001. Les changements induits par ces modifications n'ont pas été évalués.
Autres:
–   Décentralisation des bureaux d'emploi publics dans toutes les provinces;
–   Introduction d'un programme d'informatisation.

Introduction – Partie II

Les descriptions méthodologiques présentées dans cette partie concernent les statistiques de l'emploi, des salaires, de la durée du travail et autres sujets connexes (par ex. revenu de l'emploi, vacances de postes) qui sont obtenues à partir de sources autres que les enquêtes auprès des ménages ou auprès des établissements, telles que registres de sécurité ou d'assurance sociale, registres des impôts, conventions collectives, rapports administratifs, etc.

Les séries statistiques correspondantes sont généralement publiées par le BIT dans l'Annuaire des statistiques du Travail, le cas échéant dans le Bulletin des statistiques du Travail trimestriel ou dans son supplément spécial, Statistiques des salaires et de la durée du travail par profession et des prix de produits alimentaires – Résultats de l'Enquête d'octobre. Elles sont également disponibles dans la base de données en ligne, LABORSTA:

http://laborsta.ilo.org/

Dans quelques rares cas, les statistiques n'ont pas encore été publiées par le BIT, mais devraient l'être à l'avenir.

Les descriptions concernent 24 pays, zones ou territoires. La plupart d'entre elles ont été préparées sur la base des informations communiquées par les organismes statistiques nationaux ou les gouvernements en réponse à un questionnaire spécialement conçu à cet effet. En l'absence de réponse, les informations ont été extraites de différentes sources, incluant les publications et les rapports nationaux et internationaux disponibles au BIT, et des sites Internet. Chaque description a été soumise au pays concerné pour qu'il puisse faire des observations qui ont été prises en compte lorsqu'elles sont parvenues au BIT dans les délais fixés pour la publication.

Chaque description adopte le même format composé de paragraphes et de titres standards afin de faciliter les comparaisons. Cependant il convient de noter que les statistiques provenant de registres administratifs ne sont pas réellement comparables entre les pays, en raison des sources et des législations en vigueur. Ce format est détaillé ci-après:

Source de la série

Source administrative dont est tirée la série, généralement le système de notification d'un organisme national de sécurité sociale ou d'assurance sociale, ou celui d'une commission de fixation des salaires ou de négociation collective.

Titre de la série

Titre de la série statistique.

Organisme responsable

Organisme responsable de la collecte des données, de leur traitement statistique et de leur publication ou diffusion; lorsque ces fonctions sont confiées à plusieurs organismes différents, ceux-ci sont mentionnés.

Principaux sujets couverts

Principaux sujets relatifs au travail pour lesquels des données sont rassemblées (emploi, salaires, durée du travail, revenu lié à l'emploi, etc.).

Périodicité ou fréquence de disponibilité des statistiques

Fréquence avec laquelle sont rassemblées ou établies les statistiques (par exemple, mensuelle, trimestrielle, semestrielle, une fois par an, etc.).

Période de référence

Période de référence (telle qu'une date précise, un mois entier, etc.) à laquelle se rapportent les données.

Portée des statistiques

Géographique: si la série couvre l'ensemble du pays ou du territoire et dans le cas contraire, les zones ou régions exclues.

Branches d'activité: si toutes les branches d'activité économique sont couvertes par la série et dans le cas contraire, les groupes d'activité qui sont exclus.

Etablissements: type et taille des établissements couverts qui fournissent les données relatives à la série, de même que, le cas échéant, leur affiliation ou leur relation avec le système national d'assurance ou de sécurité sociale.

Personnes: catégories de travailleurs couverts par la série, comme, par exemple, les salariés assujettis au régime d'assurance sociale national ; le cas échéant, autres critères utiles relatifs à la population couverte, tels que sexe, groupe d'âge, secteur de l'économie, etc.

Professions: si les données sont recueillies sur les professions individuelles ou des groupes de professions et le cas échéant, les professions ou les groupes couverts.

Concepts et définitions

Définitions nationales utilisées pour l'établissement de la série, pour chaque concept (emploi, gains, taux de salaire ou de traitement, durée du travail, revenu lié à l'emploi) ; le cas échéant, les groupes de travailleurs compris dans le concept ou qui en sont exclus, ainsi que les seuils minima et/ou maxima qui s'appliquent aux définitions de salaires ou de revenu.

Classifications

Branches d'activité économique: nom de la classification nationale par branche d'activité économique, et si possible, nombre de groupes utilisés pour le codage des données; si cette classification s'applique à toutes les données rassemblées; si une corrélation est établie entre la classification nationale et la Classification internationale type, par industrie, de toutes les branches d'activité économique (CITI), Rév.3 (1990) ou Rév.2 (1968), et à quel niveau.

Professions: nom de la classification nationale des professions, et si possible, nombre de groupes utilisés pour le codage des données; si cette classification s'applique à toutes les données rassemblées; si une corrélation est établie entre la classification nationale et la Classification internationale type des professions (CITP-88 ou CITP-1968), et à quel niveau.

Situation dans la profession: nom de la classification nationale d'après la situation dans la profession, et si possible, nombre de groupes utilisés pour le codage des données; si cette classification s'applique à toutes les données rassemblées; si une corrélation est établie entre la classification nationale et la Classification internationale d'après la situation dans la profession (CISP-1993), et à quel niveau.

Autres classifications: autres classifications utilisées, telles que caractéristiques des établissements (taille, type de propriété, etc.), région, caractéristiques des travailleurs (sexe, groupes d'âge, catégorie de travailleurs, nationalité/citoyenneté, etc.), et si les classifications s'appliquent à toutes les données recueillies ou à certaines d'entre elles seulement.

Rassemblement des données

Méthodes, organisation et calendrier de collecte des données d'après les registres de la sécurité sociale, les recueils des conventions collectives et autres sources administratives ; le cas échéant, méthodes d'échantillonnage, pondération de l'échantillon et mise à jour du système administratif.

Traitement et contrôle des données

Méthodes de traitement et procédures de vérification et de contrôles de cohérence appliquées aux données enregistrées.

Ajustements

Le cas échéant, des renseignements sur les types d'ajustements opérés et les méthodes utilisées pour remédier aux distorsions dues aux erreurs de couverture, doubles comptages, aux estimations des paiements en nature, etc., avant de procéder aux estimations de l'emploi, des salaires, de la durée du travail et du revenu lié à l'emploi ; et si les données sont calibrées sur la base de données de référence ou corrigées des variations saisonnières.

Types d'estimations

Types d'estimations établies à partir des données (totaux, moyennes, médianes, distributions), unités de temps auxquelles elles se rapportent et méthodes de calcul.

Calcul d'indices

Lorsque les données servent à établir des indices, type de données auxquelles se réfèrent les indices et méthode utilisée pour leur calcul.

Indicateurs de fiabilité des estimations

Informations tant qualitatives que quantitatives sur la fiabilité des statistiques: proportion de la population cible couverte par le système administratif; estimation de la variance d'échantillonnage ; erreurs non dues à l'échantillonnage; conformité avec d'autres sources.

Séries disponibles

Liste des principaux tableaux régulièrement établis par le pays sur la base de la source administrative décrite, et qui figurent dans les publications nationales.

Historique des statistiques

Historique des statistiques: la date de début de la ou des séries, dates et nature des principales modifications ou révisions intervenues (par exemple, dans la législation, les procédures ou formulaires utilisés, la couverture, les définitions, la périodicité).

Documentation et diffusion

Source et titre des principales publications dans lesquelles paraissent les données et les informations méthodologiques correspondantes; fréquence de parution des publications et délai s'écoulant normalement entre la période de référence des statistiques et leur publication ; si les données sont disponibles sur un site Internet et si les données qui ne figurent pas dans les publications nationales ou sur un site Internet peuvent être obtenues sur demande.

Données communiquées au BIT aux fins de diffusion

Liste des données communiquées au BIT pour publication dans *l'Annuaire des statistiques du Travail* et/ou le *Bulletin des statistiques du Travail* et/ou les *Statistiques des salaires et de la durée du travail par profession et des prix de produits alimentaires – Résultats de l'Enquête d'octobre*.

Autres sources administratives de données: autres sources administratives qui fournissent des statistiques relatives au travail ; brève description du titre, de la couverture et de la périodicité de ces statistiques.

Allemagne

Source de la série
Conventions collectives.
Titre de la série: Tariflöhne, Tarifgehälter.
Organisme responsable
Collecte des données, traitement statistique et publication/diffusion des statistiques:
Statistisches Bundesamt (DESTATIS), Division VI B (Office fédéral des statistiques d'Allemagne).
Principaux sujets couverts
Montants des traitements et salaires pour des groupes sélectionnés d'ouvriers et d'employés ainsi que durée normale du travail.
Périodicité ou fréquence de disponibilité des statistiques
Biannuelle.
Période de référence
Les mois précédant le mois du rapport (avril et octobre).
Portée des statistiques
Géographique: l'ensemble du pays.
Branches d'activité: toutes les branches d'activité économique à l'exception de: division 71 (location de machines et d'équipement sans opérateur ainsi que de biens personnels et ménagers), division 72 (ordinateurs et activités apparentées), division 73 (recherche et développement), division 74 (autres activités commerciales) et division 80 (éducation).
Etablissements: ne s'applique pas.
Personnes: salariés couverts par les conventions collectives.
Professions: les données ne sont pas rassemblées par profession ou groupe professionnel. Toutefois, dans certaines conventions collectives certains groupes professionnels sont identifiés séparément et les données relatives sont partiellement disponibles et présentées dans la publication.
Concepts et définitions
Emploi: les employés sont les personnes qui sont affiliées au système des assurances sociales en tant que *Angestellte*; les ouvriers touchent un traitement et figurent sous le régime des assurances sociales en tant que *Arbeiter*.
Taux de salaire ou de traitement: se réfèrent aux taux de base au temps convenus collectivement et qui s'appliquent aux niveaux d'ancienneté les plus élevés.
Durée du travail: se réfère à la durée hebdomadaire normale du travail, telle que définie dans les conventions collectives.
Classifications
Branches d'activité économique:
Titre de la classification: Classification de toutes les activités économiques (WZ 93), édition 1993.
Nombre de groupes utilisés pour le codage: codes numériques au niveau de l'indicatif à deux chiffres, exceptés 71-74 et 80.
S'applique à: taux de salaire ou de traitement et durée du travail.
Lien avec la CITI: le WZ 93 provient de la NACE, Rév.1 et peut être lié à la CITI, Rév.3.
Autres classifications: travailleurs manuels et non manuels (c.a.d. ouvriers et employés). Les ouvriers tout comme les employés sont classés par groupes de performance "Leistungsgruppen" (ou catégories de salariés), qui sont définis dans chaque convention collective par l'Office fédéral des statistiques en consultation avec les partenaires sociaux concernés, en se basant sur les différentes catégories de traitement et de salaire. Les groupes de performance sont basés sur les niveaux d'expérience, de formation et de responsabilité exigés pour exécuter les tâches couvertes par les différentes catégories de traitement.

– Les ouvriers sont classés en trois groupes de performance (qualifiés, semi-qualifiés et non qualifiés).
– Les employés sont classés en quatre groupes de performance (II à V) et deux groupes professionnels: les employés de commerce, les techniciens et les maîtres.
Rassemblement des données
Type et couverture du système administratif: les données couvrent environ 650 conventions collectives.
Méthode de collecte des données: les données sont tirées des registres des conventions collectives.
Mise à jour du système administratif: biannuelle
Traitement et contrôle des données
Toutes les données rassemblées subissent un contrôle portant sur leur conformité.
Ajustements
Aucun.
Types d'estimations
Taux de salaire ou de traitement moyens minimaux/négociés horaires, journaliers ou mensuels, pour une profession donnée.
Calcul d'indices
Les indices relatifs à la durée standard du travail ainsi qu'aux taux de salaire ou de traitement négociés sont calculés par activité économique et par région.
Indicateurs de fiabilité des estimations
Aucun.
Séries disponibles
– taux de traitement convenus des ouvriers
– taux de salaire convenus des employés
– durée normale du travail
– nombre de jours de congé annuel
– congés payés
– paiement au titre de congés maladie
– paiements spéciaux supplémentaires.
Historique des statistiques
Date de début de la série statistique: 1949/50.
Modifications et révisions principales: présentation en Euros à compter de 2002 (auparavant, en DM).
Documentation et diffusion
Documentation:
Statistisches Bundesamt (DESTATIS): *Fachserie 16, Reihe 4.1Tariflöhne* et *Reihe 4.2, Tarifgehälter* (Wiesbaden, biannuel); publié quatre mois environ après la période de référence (avril et octobre); contient à la fois des statistiques et des informations méthodologiques.
Idem: *Fachserie 16, Reihe 4.3, Index der Tariflöhne und -gehälter* (ibid, trimestriel).
Diffusion: les données devraient être disponibles sur Internet en 2003.
Données communiquées au BIT aux fins de diffusion
Les statistiques suivantes sont publiées dans *Statistiques des salaires et de la durée du travail par profession et des prix de produits alimentaires – Résultats de l'Enquête d'octobre:*
Taux de salaire ou de traitement moyens horaires, journaliers et mensuels par professions dans des industries spécifiées, portant sur les plus grands Etats fédéraux (Westphalie-Rhénanie du Nord).
Les statistiques portant sur les taux horaires moyens des journaliers qualifiés en agriculture (avant 1994) sur le territoire de la République fédérale d'Allemagne avant le 3 octobre 1990 sont disponibles dans LABORSTA.

Autriche (1)

Source de la série
Fichiers de la sécurité sociale.
Titre de la série
Beschäftigtenstatistik, Einkommensstatistik.
Organisme responsable
Collecte des données, traitement statistique et publication/diffusion des statistiques:
Hauptverband der österreichischen Sozialversicherungsträger (principale association des organismes de la sécurité sociale autrichienne).
Principaux sujets couverts
Emploi et gains.
Périodicité ou fréquence de disponibilité des statistiques
Emploi: mensuelle;
Gains: annuelle.
Période de référence
Emploi: le dernier jour du mois;
Gains: moyenne mensuelle pour toute l'année.
Portée des statistiques
Géographique: tout le pays. Chaque Land (province) dispose de son propre organisme.

Branches d'activité: toutes les branches d'activité économique.
Etablissements: de tous types et toutes tailles dans les secteurs public et privé.
Personnes: tous les salariés.
Professions: les données ne sont pas rassemblées par profession ou groupe professionnel.

Concepts et définitions
Emploi: salariés, c'est-à-dire ouvriers et employés.
Gains: les gains mensuels bruts se réfèrent à tous paiements soumis à cotisation à la sécurité sociale.

Classifications
Branches d'activité économique:
Titre de la classification: ÖNACE.
Nombre de groupes utilisés pour le codage: non disponible.
S'applique à: emploi et gains.
Lien avec la CITI et niveau: Rév.2 et Rév.3.
Autres classifications: par sexe, catégorie de salarié, groupe d'âge et région.

Rassemblement des données
Type et couverture du système administratif: tous les employeurs et tous les salariés sont couverts.
Méthode de collecte des données: les données concernant les salariés et leurs gains soumis à cotisation à la sécurité sociale sont communiquées par les employeurs aux organismes de la sécurité sociale de manière continue. Les données concernant l'emploi sont obtenues par le comptage du nombre des personnes assurées auprès des organismes de la sécurité sociale. Les moyennes mensuelles des gains annuels sont calculées une fois par année. Les dossiers sont mis à jour de manière continue.

Traitement et contrôle des données
Les données sont traitées par informatique. On procède à un certain nombre de contrôles pour vérifier la plausibilité des résultats agrégés. On effectue aussi des comparaisons par rapport au mois et à l'année écoulés.

Ajustements
Aucun.

Types d'estimations
Totaux et moyennes.

Calcul d'indices
Aucun.

Indicateurs de fiabilité des estimations
Couverture du système administratif: exhaustive; tous les salariés en Autriche sont obligatoirement affiliés à la sécurité sociale.

Séries disponibles
Nombre mensuel et annuel des salariés par catégorie de salarié, sexe, activité économique et région ;
Gains mensuels moyens (annuellement) par catégorie de salarié, sexe, activité économique et région.

Historique des statistiques
Date de début de la série statistique: janvier 1948.
Modifications et révisions principales: Aucun.
Modifications et révisions principales
Documentation:
Hauptverband der österreichischen Sozialversicherungsträger: *Die österreichische Sozialversicherung in Zahlen (Vienne, mensuel)*.
Diffusion: site Internet: http://www.sozvers.at

Données communiquées au BIT aux fins de diffusion
Les statistiques suivantes sont publiées dans *l'Annuaire des statistiques du travail* ou disponibles dans LABORSTA:
Emploi rémunéré par sexe et par activité économique et, dans les industries manufacturières, par groupe d'industrie et par sexe (données les plus récentes: 1995) ;
Gains mensuels moyens des salariés, par catégorie et sexe, par activité économique et, dans les industries manufacturières, par groupe d'industrie.
Une série mensuelle concernant l'emploi rémunéré (niveau général) paraît dans le *Bulletin des statistiques du travail*.

Autriche (2)

Source de la série
Kollektivverträge (conventions collectives y compris systèmes de paiement destinés aux fonctionnaires).
Titre de la série
Kollektivverträge.
Organisme responsable
Collecte des données, traitement statistique: la Fédération des Syndicats Autrichiens.

Publication/diffusion des statistiques: Syndicats Autrichiens et Statistics Austria.
Principaux sujets couverts
Taux de salaire, gains et durée du travail.
Périodicité ou fréquence de disponibilité des statistiques
Mensuelle.
Période de référence
Taux de salaire, gains et durée du travail: octobre.
Portée des statistiques
Géographique: tout le pays.
Branches d'activité: toutes les branches d'activité économique de la Chambre de Commerce Autrichienne.
Etablissements: de tous types et tailles des secteurs privé et public.
Personnes: tous les salariés couverts par les conventions collectives.
Professions: toutes les professions couvertes par les conventions collectives.

Concepts et définitions
Emploi: se réfère aux ouvriers, aux employés et aux fonctionnaires.
Gains: se réfèrent à la rémunération brute versée aux salariés.
Taux de salaire ou de traitement: se réfèrent aux taux horaires, hebdomadaires et mensuels, y compris traitements et salaires de base, de même que les allocations garanties et régulièrement versées. Ces taux sont rassemblés séparément pour les ouvriers et les employés.
Durée du travail: les heures normales de travail sont celles fixées par les conventions collectives.
Les heures réellement effectuées comprennent les heures travaillées au cours des périodes normales de travail, les heures supplémentaires les heures qui sont rémunérées selon un contrat de travail garanti, etc., conformément à la définition internationale.
Les heures rémunérées comprennent les heures réellement effectuées (comme ci-dessus) et les heures rémunérées mais non travaillées, telles que congé annuel payé, jours fériés publics, congé de maladie, etc.

Classifications
Branches d'activité économique:
Titre de la classification: Classification de la Chambre de Commerce Autrichienne.
Nombre de groupes utilisés pour le codage: correspond au nombre de conventions collectives en vigueur.
S'applique à: taux de salaire ou de traitement, gains et durée du travail.
Lien avec la CITI et niveau: Rév. 2 et Rév. 3.
Professions: toutes les professions telles que définies dans les conventions collectives.
Situation dans la profession: ouvriers, employés et fonctionnaires.
Autres classifications: salariés: par sexe ; taux de traitement et de salaire, gains et durée du travail: par catégorie de salariés (manuel/non-manuel) âgés de plus de 18 ans et par sexe.

Rassemblement des données
Type et couverture du système administratif: l'ensemble des conventions collectives.
Méthode de collecte des données: données rassemblées à partir des conventions collectives et systèmes de paiement destinés aux fonctionnaires.
Mise à jour du système administratif: habituellement annuelle, mais sur une base continue dans le cas où de nouvelles conventions collectives entreraient en vigueur.

Traitement et contrôle des données
Simple compilation des données.
Ajustements
Aucun.
Types d'estimations
Nombre total des salariés et des moyennes des taux de traitement ou de salaire, des gains et de la durée du travail.
Calcul d'indices
Plus de 1500 indices sont calculés par mois par Statistics Austria à partir de statistiques des taux de traitement minimaux garantis sur la base des conventions collectives (Tariflohnindex).
Indicateurs de fiabilité des estimations
Couverture du système administratif: exhaustive: toutes les conventions collectives et les systèmes de paiement sont couverts.
Séries disponibles
Nombre total des salariés, durée normale hebdomadaire du travail, heures réellement effectuées et rémunérées, taux moyens de traitement et de traitement horaires, hebdomadaires et mensuels,

gains moyens horaires, hebdomadaires, mensuels et annuels, par activité économique et par profession.

Historique des statistiques

Date de début de la série statistique: la 1ère série a été produite à la fin du 19e siècle.

Modifications et révisions principales: en cas de nouvelles conventions collectives.

Documentation et diffusion

Documentation:

Statistics Austria: *Schnellbericht* (Vienne)

Idem: *Statistische Narchrichten* (ibid., mensuel); contient les séries mensuelles du Tariflohnindex.

Des informations méthodologiques concernant l'indice sont publiées dans *Tariflohnindex 1986, Aufbau und Gewichtung,* 899. Heft (Vienne, 1988).

Dissémination: sur le site Internet de Statistics Austria: http://www.statistik.at

Données communiquées au BIT aux fins de diffusion

Les statistiques suivantes sont publiées dans *Statistiques des salaires et de la durée du travail par profession et des prix de produits alimentaires – Résultats de l'Enquête d'octobre*:

Taux minimaux de traitements moyens mensuels et durées normales du travail, par profession et par sexe ;

Gains moyens mensuels et heures de travail réellement effectuées, par profession et par sexe.

Dans *l'Annuaire des statistiques du Travail*:

Taux de salaire mensuels moyens des ouvriers occupés dans l'agriculture.

Costa Rica

Source de la série

Registres de la Caisse de Sécurité sociale du Costa Rica (Planillas de la Caja Costarricense de Seguro Social, CCSS).

Titre de la série

Statistiques sur les employeurs, les travailleurs et les salaires.

Organisme responsable

Collecte des données: Caisse de Sécurité sociale du Costa Rica, direction de l'Actuariat et de la Planification économique.

Traitement statistique: Caisse de Sécurité sociale du Costa Rica, direction de l'Informatique.

Publication/diffusion des statistiques: Caisse de Sécurité sociale du Costa Rica, présidence exécutive, direction de l'Actuariat et de la Planification économique, département de la Statistique.

Principaux sujets couverts

Emploi, salaires et revenus liés à l'emploi.

Périodicité ou fréquence de disponibilité des statistiques

Annuelle.

Période de référence

Mois de juin.

Portée des statistiques

Géographique: l'ensemble du pays.

Branches d'activité: toutes les branches d'activité économique.

Etablissements: de tous types et tailles.

Personnes: employeurs et travailleurs affiliés aux régimes Santé et Retraite de la CCSS (issus de tous les secteurs institutionnels) et travailleurs non salariés affiliés au régime d'assurance volontaire (travailleurs indépendants et travailleurs régis par des conventions spéciales).

Professions: les données ne sont recueillies ni par profession individuelle ni par catégories professionnelles.

Concepts et définitions

Emploi: toutes les catégories de travailleurs actifs affiliés à la CCSS énumérées ci-après:

Employeur: personne physique ou morale, du secteur public ou du secteur privé, faisant appel aux services d'une ou plusieurs personnes régies par les divers régimes de la Sécurité sociale.

Travailleur assuré (salarié, employé): personne travaillant pour le compte d'un employeur et percevant une rémunération pour le travail fourni sous forme de salaire payable à la journée, au mois ou à la pièce, que ce soit en argent ou en nature.

Travailleur indépendant: personne travaillant seule ou avec un/des associé(s), non régie par une relation de dépendance à l'égard d'un employeur.

Travailleur régi par des conventions spéciales: personne appartenant à un groupe de travailleurs indépendants organisés en associations, syndicats, coopératives, groupements professionnels, rotary clubs, foyers, musées, etc., ayant signé une convention avec la CCSS aux fins d'être assurés.

Assuré direct (cotisant/actif): personne qui, grâce à une cotisation (quota) versée directement ou par l'intermédiaire d'un tiers (employeur), peut bénéficier – pour elle-même comme pour d'autres – de certaines prestations offertes par la Sécurité sociale.

Gains: l'ensemble de la masse salariale; autrement dit, la totalité des salaires déclarés par les assurés directs dans le registre mensuel. Ne sont pas comptabilisés les revenus des travailleurs affiliés au régime d'assurance volontaire, c'est-à-dire les travailleurs indépendants et les travailleurs régis par des conventions spéciales. Le salaire moyen correspond à la rémunération moyenne perçue chaque mois par un travailleur salarié.

Revenu lié à l'emploi indépendant: il s'agit des "revenus soumis à cotisations", qui correspondent à l'ensemble des revenus déclarés par tous les travailleurs indépendants servant de base au calcul des contributions (l'équivalent du salaire des assurés directs actifs).

Revenu moyen: rémunération mensuelle moyenne déclarée par un travailleur indépendant.

Base de cotisation: l'ensemble des salaires et revenus déclarés respectivement par les travailleurs salariés et par les travailleurs indépendants pour un mois donné.

Classifications

Branches d'activité économique:

Titre de la classification: Manuel des Codes des activités économiques (Manual de Códigos de Actividades Económicas).

Nombre de groupes utilisés pour le codage: tous les groupes, au niveau à 4 chiffres.

S'applique à: toutes les données.

Lien avec la CITI et niveau: rév. 3, 1990, à tous les niveaux.

Situation dans la profession:

Titre de la classification: Classification de la CCSS.

Nombre de groupes utilisés pour le codage: quatre groupes: employeurs, travailleurs indépendants (à leur propre compte), travailleurs salariés et travailleurs régis par des conventions spéciales.

S'applique à: toutes les données.

Lien avec la CISP et niveau: lien partiel, au niveau à un chiffre.

Autres classifications: par secteur institutionnel: 6 secteurs institutionnels ont été définis, à savoir le gouvernement central, les institutions autonomes et semi-autonomes, les entreprises privées, les travailleurs indépendants, les travailleurs régis par des conventions spéciales, et le personnel domestique.

Les données sont également répertoriées par division territoriale administrative: 7 provinces divisées en 81 cantons; par groupe d'âge et par sexe, et selon la taille de l'entreprise.

Rassemblement des données

Type et couverture du système administratif: en juin 2000, les registres utilisés portaient sur 52'040 employeurs et 1'038'816 travailleurs issus de tous les secteurs institutionnels, ainsi que sur 313'000 travailleurs non salariés affiliés au régime d'assurance volontaire (travailleurs indépendants et travailleurs régis par des conventions spéciales), tous étant affiliés au régime d'assurance santé.

Méthode de collecte des données: les Statistiques sur les employeurs, les travailleurs et les salariés sont établies à partir de diverses sources d'information, à savoir: i) les registres mensuels transmis par les employeurs affiliés à la CCSS, qui comportent des données relatives aux travailleurs, aux salaires et à l'activité économique pour les secteurs suivants: entreprises privées, le personnel domestique, institutions autonomes et travailleurs régis par des conventions spéciales; ii) le département gouvernemental de l'Automation, qui transmet des informations sur les fonctionnaires du gouvernement central; et iii) les registres d'affiliation de la CCSS pour les travailleurs indépendants et certains travailleurs régis par des conventions spéciales. Les données collectées à partir de ces sources sont traitées par la direction de l'Informatique, qui les transmet ensuite au département de la Statistique de la direction de l'Actuariat et de la Planification économique, sous forme de fichiers textes servant à alimenter le système élaboré pour établir les statistiques.

Mise à jour du système administratif: une fois par an.

Traitement et contrôle des données

Les données sont traitées informatiquement, et le système procède aux ajustements nécessaires.

Ajustements

Le processus de collecte et de traitement des données peut donner lieu à des erreurs inhérentes au dit processus, par exemple lorsque, dans diverses classifications de travailleurs, certaines catégories sont "inconnues" (sexe, âge, branche d'activité ou revenu). Les mêmes erreurs peuvent se produire avec la base de cotisation. En effet, en ajustant les statistiques de façon à répartir les travailleurs pour lesquels la catégorie "sexe" n'est pas précisée, et la base de cotisation dans les catégories correspondantes, des différences d'arrondissement (des chiffres) peuvent apparaître, différences qui restent toutefois inférieures à 1 pour cent.

Types d'estimations
Ensemble des personnes affiliées aux divers régimes d'assurance (santé et retraite), par catégorie et selon diverses classifications;
Totaux et moyennes des salaires et revenus mensuels, par catégorie de personnes assurées et selon diverses classifications;
Répartition des personnes assurées selon l'échelle des salaires mensuels et par secteur.

Calcul d'indices
Aucun.

Indicateurs de fiabilité des estimations
Non disponibles.

Séries disponibles
Employeurs, travailleurs assurés et base de cotisation en fonction du sexe, du secteur institutionnel, de la province et du canton, du secteur, de la branche d'activité et de la taille de l'entreprise;
Travailleurs assurés selon la branche d'activité économique, le groupe d'âge, le secteur, l'échelle des salaires mensuels, etc.;
Salaires et revenus moyens.

Historique des statistiques
Date de début de la série statistique: janvier 1973.
Modifications et révisions principales: non disponibles.

Documentation et diffusion
Documentation:
Caja Costarricense de Seguro Social: *Anuario Estadístico* (San Jose, annuel); chaque publication présente les données du mois de juin de l'année précédente.
Diffusion: sur le site Internet de la CCSS:
http://www.ccss.sa.cr/actuarial/publicaciones.html
Données communiquées au BIT aux fins de diffusion
Les statistiques sur les gains moyens des salariés ont été publiées dans l'*Annuaire des statistiques du Travail* jusqu'en 1986 et sont disponibles dans la base de données LABORSTA.

Cuba

Source de la série
Système national d'information statistique (Sistema de Información Estadística Nacional, SIEN) et registres du personnel.

Titre de la série
Emploi et salaires.

Organisme responsable
Collecte des données, traitement statistique et publication/ diffusion des statistiques: Bureau national des statistiques (Oficina Nacional de Estadísticas – ONE).

Principaux sujets couverts
Emploi et salaires.

Périodicité ou fréquence de disponibilité des statistiques
Mensuelle et annuelle.

Période de référence
Emploi et salaires: chaque mois de l'année ainsi que l'année civile toute entière.

Portée des statistiques
Géographique: l'ensemble du pays.
Branches d'activité: toutes les branches d'activité économique.
Etablissements: de tous types et tailles, dans le secteur public et dans le secteur privé.
Personnes: toutes les personnes ayant un emploi.
Professions: les données recueillies concernent les catégories professionnelles suivantes: ouvriers, techniciens, personnel administratif, personnel des services, et personnel dirigeant.

Concepts et définitions
Emploi: s'applique à l'ensemble des personnes ayant un emploi dans les diverses activités de l'économie nationale, tant dans le secteur public que dans le secteur privé, qu'elles aient ou non l'âge minimum légal requis pour travailler (au moins 17 ans). Toute personne qui, à la date de référence, était liée en tant que salariée par une relation d'emploi formelle et percevait une rémunération en argent ou en nature, ou qui occupait un emploi indépendant, est considérée comme ayant un emploi.
Les travailleurs salariés des organismes publics sont des travailleurs dont la relation d'emploi, quel que soit le type de rémunération perçue, se fonde sur un contrat de travail établi avec un organisme d'Etat jouissant du statut de personne morale et soumis au contrôle des institutions publiques. Cette catégorie comprend les travailleurs des entreprises commerciales cubaines et des organisations politiques et collectives, ainsi que ceux qui

travaillent dans des organismes publics pouvant prendre la forme de syndicats, d'entreprises, d'associations économiques, d'organisations économiques d'Etat, d'exploitations agricoles, d'institutions financières, d'institutions publiques de santé, sportives et culturelles, de centres scientifiques, etc.
Les travailleurs salariés du secteur privé englobent ceux qui relèvent du secteur coopératif, des entreprises mixtes et du secteur privé (succursales de sociétés étrangères, associations et fondations).
Parmi les travailleurs indépendants du secteur privé figurent:
–   les personnes travaillant pour leur propre compte, c'est-à-dire ceux qui, qu'ils soient propriétaires ou non des outils et équipements de travail, ne sont pas régis par un contrat de travail établi avec une entité juridique, ne perçoivent pas un salaire, exercent des activités de production ou fournissent des services de façon individuelle ou collective, dans le cadre d'un emploi approprié ou de l'aide familiale, et se chargent de la commercialisation de leurs produits ou services soit directement, soit par l'intermédiaire d'une autre personne ou entité qui les représente légalement à cette fin;
–   les fermiers, c'est-à-dire les personnes qui ne sont liées par aucune autre activité professionnelle et qualifiées d'*aparceleros* (fermiers), auxquelles l'Etat loue des terres à bail en vue de la culture de produits d'intérêt national tels que le café ou le tabac;
–   les agriculteurs indépendants, c'est-à-dire les petits agriculteurs qui sont propriétaires des terres qu'ils exploitent et qui se consacrent à la production agricole et/ou à l'élevage, que ce soit pour la vente ou pour leur propre consommation;
–   les travailleurs des coopératives de crédit et de services, c'est-à-dire les petits agriculteurs qui se regroupent aux fins de bénéficier d'une assistance technique et financière fournie par l'Etat en vue de faciliter les conditions de production;
–   les membres des coopératives (UBPC et CPA);
–   et les aides familiales.
Les travailleurs indépendants sont considérés comme ayant un emploi même s'ils ne travaillaient pas, pour une des raisons suivantes: ils étaient présents au travail mais n'ont pu mener à bien leur travail pour quelque raison que ce soit; ils n'étaient pas présents pour une raison donnée, pour autant que la relation d'emploi n'ait pas été interrompue.
Gains: le salaire versé correspond à la rémunération en argent perçue par le travailleur pour la quantité et la qualité du travail effectué. Il comprend entre autres le paiement du salaire de base, des primes pour conditions de travail exceptionnelles ou conformité avec les normes du travail, des compléments de salaire, des heures supplémentaires, des indemnités d'ancienneté et de responsabilité, des congés payés, des absences autorisées par la législation en vigueur.

Classifications
Branches d'activité économique:
Titre de la classification: non disponible.
Nombre de groupes utilisés pour le codage: 9 grands groupes.
S'applique à: l'emploi et aux gains.
Lien avec la CITI et niveau: rév. 2, 1968.
Professions:
Titre de la classification: Classification type des professions.
Nombre de groupes utilisés pour le codage: cinq catégories professionnelles: personnel dirigeant; techniciens; personnel des services; personnel administratif; ouvriers.
S'applique à: l'emploi uniquement.
Lien avec la CITP et niveau: aucun.
Situation dans la profession: voir la rubrique "Emploi" sous "Concepts et définitions".
Autres classifications: par sexe, selon le type de propriété, par province et par groupe d'âge.

Rassemblement des données
Type et couverture du système administratif: le Système national d'information statistique (SIEN) et les registres du personnel couvrent l'ensemble de la main-d'œuvre.
Méthode de collecte des données: non disponible.

Traitement et contrôle des données
On calcule le nombre total de travailleurs, d'une part, en soustrayant du nombre de travailleurs recensés dans le registre du personnel ceux auxquels l'organisme ne verse pas de salaire, que ce soit directement ou indirectement, étant donné qu'ils travaillent dans d'autres organismes qui leur versent un salaire et ce, bien

qu'ils soient répertoriés dans le registre concerné et, d'autre part, en ajoutant ceux qui, bien que ne figurant pas dans le registre du personnel de l'organisme, travaillent pour le compte de ce dernier, dont ils perçoivent directement ou indirectement un salaire. La moyenne est obtenue en totalisant jour par jour le nombre de travailleurs et en procédant aux additions et soustractions indiquées ci-dessus, compte tenu des jours de repos et des congés, et en divisant le résultat ainsi obtenu par le nombre de jours calendaires que compte la période considérée.

Le salaire moyen mensuel se calcule en divisant l'ensemble des salaires versés par le nombre total de travailleurs.

Ajustements
Non disponible.

Types d'estimations
Total des personnes ayant un emploi; total des salaires versés et salaire mensuel moyen.

Calcul d'indices
Aucun.

Indicateurs de fiabilité des estimations
Couverture du système administratif: l'ensemble des personnes occupées.

Séries disponibles
Personnes occupées dans l'ensemble de l'économie nationale, selon le type de propriété et par branche d'activité économique;
Personnes occupées (salariés), total des salaires et salaire mensuel moyen versés par les entreprises publiques et mixtes, par branche d'activité économique et par province;
Répartition de la population active, selon le niveau d'éducation, par groupe d'âge, par catégorie professionnelle et par sexe.

Historique des statistiques
Non disponible.

Documentation et diffusion
Documentation:
Oficina Nacional de Estadísticas: *Anuario Estadístico de Cuba* (La Havane, annuel); contient des notes méthodologiques.
Idem: *Cuba en Cifras* (ibid., annuel).

Données communiquées au BIT aux fins de diffusion
Les statistiques sur les gains mensuels moyens versés par les entreprises publiques et mixtes selon la branche d'activité économique sont publiées dans *l'Annuaire des statistiques du Travail*.

Espagne

Source de la série
Registre administratif d'immatriculation à la Sécurité sociale.

Titre de la série
Immatriculation des travailleurs à la Sécurité sociale (Afiliación de trabajadores al Sistema de la Seguridad Social).

Organisme responsable
Collecte des données, traitement statistique et publication/ diffusion des statistiques: Ministère du Travail et des Affaires sociales.

Principaux sujets couverts
Emploi.

Périodicité ou fréquence de disponibilité des statistiques
Mensuelle et annuelle.

Période de référence
Chaque mois de l'année ainsi que l'année civile toute entière.

Portée des statistiques
Géographique: l'ensemble du pays.
Branches d'activité: toutes les branches d'activité économique.
Etablissements: de tous types et tailles.
Personnes: travailleurs actifs ou assimilés, y compris ceux qui sont en incapacité temporaire de travail, suspendus en vertu des dispositions relatives à l'emploi, au chômage partiel, etc., affiliés aux divers régimes de la Sécurité sociale. Sont exclues les personnes inscrites au chômage, régies par des conventions spéciales, employées par des entreprises en restructuration et celles relevant de régimes de retraite anticipée.
Professions: les données ne sont pas recueillies par profession individuelle mais par catégories professionnelles cotisantes.

Concepts et définitions
Emploi: s'applique aux personnes exerçant une activité professionnelle et inscrites au Registre administratif d'immatriculation à la Sécurité sociale.

Classifications
Branches d'activité économique:
Titre de la classification: Classification nationale des activités économiques (CNAE-93).

Nombre de groupes utilisés pour le codage: 30 groupes, code à 2 chiffres.
S'applique à: Emploi.
Lien avec la CITI et niveau: rév.3, 1988; au niveau à 2 chiffres.
Professions
Titre de la classification: "Groupes cotisants régis par la Sécurité sociale".
Nombre de groupes utilisés pour le codage: travailleurs âgés de plus de 18 ans issus de 10 catégories professionnelles.
S'applique à: Emploi.
Lien avec la CITP et niveau: aucun.
Situation dans la profession:
Titre de la classification: Statut dans la profession.
Nombre de groupes utilisés pour le codage: 2 groupes: salariés, travailleurs indépendants.
S'applique à: Emploi.
Autres classifications: selon la taille de l'entreprise; en fonction du régime de la Sécurité sociale; par sexe, groupe d'âge et nationalité; par communauté autonome et province; selon le degré de mobilité des entreprises.

Rassemblement des données
Type et couverture du système administratif: Registre administratif d'immatriculation à la Sécurité sociale.
Méthode de collecte des données: les données sont recueillies aux niveaux national, régional ou local. Les données relatives aux entreprises et aux travailleurs actifs sont consignées dans le Registre dès lors que débute l'activité professionnelle. Le traitement des informations est assuré par le Service informatique de la Sécurité sociale et par la Direction générale du traitement des données, conformément aux instructions fournies par la Direction générale des statistiques sociales et du travail.
Mise à jour du système administratif: mensuelle.

Traitement et contrôle de données
L'employeur – lorsque les travailleurs sont salariés – et le travailleur lui-même – lorsque ce dernier est indépendant – sont tenus de fournir un document d'immatriculation à la Sécurité sociale, dont les données sont vérifiées au vu de la carte nationale d'identité ou du passeport. Les données sont transmises à la Trésorerie générale de la Sécurité sociale et traitées électroniquement, étant entendu que certains champs doivent obligatoirement être remplis.

Ajustements
Pas d'information disponible.

Types d'estimations
Tous les travailleurs immatriculés à la Sécurité sociale, selon le type de régime; variations absolues et relatives – comparaison avec l'année précédente.

Calcul d'indices
Non.

Indicateurs de fiabilité des estimations
Couverture du système administratif: Environ 99% des travailleurs salariés officiellement.
Conformité avec d'autres sources: Comparaisons effectuées avec les données relatives à l'emploi recueillies lors de l'Enquête sur la population active réalisée par l'Institut national de statistique.

Séries disponibles
Séries mensuelles et annuelles:
- Travailleurs actifs, par régime d'affiliation;
- Travailleurs actifs, par sexe et âge;
- Travailleurs actifs, par branche d'activité;
- Travailleurs actifs, par secteur d'activité et statut (salarié, indépendant);
- Travailleurs actifs, par communauté autonome et province.

Historique des statistiques
Date de début de la série statistique: janvier 1982.
Modifications et révisions principales: adoption, au 1er janvier 1995, de la répartition par sexe, âge et groupe cotisant et, au 1er janvier 1998, de la Classification nationale des activités économiques CNAE-93.

Documentation et diffusion
Documentation:
Ministère du Travail et des Affaires sociales: *Boletín de Estadísticas Laborales* (Madrid, trimestriel).
idem: *Anuario de Estadísticas Laborales y de Asuntos Sociales* (ibid., annuel).
Diffusion: http://www.mtas.es

Données communiquées au BIT aux fins de diffusion
Aucune à présent.

France

Source de la série
Déclaration annuelle de Données Sociales (DADS).

Titre de la série
Les salaires dans l'industrie, le commerce et les services.

Organisme responsable
Collecte des données: Caisse Nationale d'Assurance Vieillesse (CNAV) et Direction Générale des Impôts (DGI).
Traitement et publication/diffusion des statistiques: Institut National de la Statistique et des Etudes Economiques (INSEE).

Principaux sujets couverts
Emploi, gains et durée du travail.

Périodicité ou fréquence de disponibilité des statistiques
Annuelle.

Période de référence
L'année.

Portée des statistiques
Géographique: l'ensemble du pays.
Branches d'activité: toutes les branches d'activité économique à l'exclusion de la fonction publique d'Etat, de l'agriculture et de la sylviculture, des services domestiques et des activités extra-territoriales.
Etablissements: établissements de tous types et de toutes tailles. Une déclaration DADS est en principe relative à l'établissement, mais il arrive exceptionnellement qu'elle porte sur plusieurs établissements d'une même entreprise.
Personnes: l'ensemble des salariés.
Professions: les données sont recueillies par catégories socioprofessionnelles. Les travailleurs à domicile, les apprentis et les stagiaires sont identifiés séparément.

Concepts et définitions
Emploi: salariés. Ils sont classés en quatre groupes:

- salariés à temps complet, y compris les salariés travaillant à 80%;
- intermittents (contrats à durée indéterminée pour des emplois permanents qui comportent par nature une alternance), y compris les intérimaires;
- salariés à temps partiel;
- travailleurs à domicile (ces derniers étant exclus des tableaux statistiques).

Gains: gains annuels bruts et nets après déduction des cotisations sociales des salariés (cotisations aux assurances sociales et à l'assurance-chômage, retenues pour la retraite, contribution sociale généralisée (CSG) et contribution au remboursement de la dette sociale (CRDS). Toutes les composantes imposables de la rémunération sont incluses, et notamment: les salaires directs, les congés payés, les primes de toutes sortes, et la valeur fiscale déclarée par l'employeur des avantages en nature (logement, repas, combustibles pour le chauffage, etc.).
Durée du travail: heures rémunérées, y compris les congés payés et les arrêts de maladie pour une année. Les données sur la durée du travail excluent les VRP (voyageurs-représentants-placiers) et les travailleurs à domicile, dont les heures ne sont pas disponibles. Des données sont également rassemblées sur les dates de début et de fin de période de paie de chaque salarié, ce qui permet de calculer la durée de présence dans l'établissement.

Classifications
Branches d'activité économique:
Titre de la classification: Nomenclature d'Activités Française (NAF). A partir de janvier 2003, elle sera remplacée par la NAF, Rév.1, 2003.
Nombre de groupes utilisés pour le codage: 700 groupes.
S'applique à: l'ensemble des données.
Lien avec la CITI et niveau: rév.3.
Professions:
Titre de la classification: Nomenclature des Professions et Catégories socioprofessionnelles.
Nombre de groupes utilisés pour le codage: 34.
S'applique à: l'ensemble des données.
Lien avec la CITP et niveau: aucun.
Autres classifications: sexe, âge, taille de l'entreprise et de l'établissement (selon le nombre de postes au 31 décembre), localisation du siège de l'entreprise et de l'établissement, et commune de résidence du salarié.

Rassemblement des données
Type et couverture du système administratif: collecte exhaustive auprès des employeurs.
Méthode de collecte des données: la DADS est une formalité déclarative que doit accomplir toute entreprise (personne physique ou morale) domiciliée ou établie en France qui verse des traitements ou des salaires, à l'exclusion de la majorité des employeurs de personnel domestique. Il s'agit d'un document commun aux administrations sociales et fiscales dans lequel les employeurs déclarent pour chaque établissement et chaque salarié l'ensemble des rémunérations salariales. Les déclarations sont transmises, sur supports magnétiques ou imprimés, aux Caisses régionales d'Assurance Maladie, puis centralisées par la CNAV pour ce qui est des salariés relevant du régime général de la sécurité sociale. Pour les salariés qui dépendent de régimes particuliers de sécurité sociale, les déclarations fiscales (no. 2460) sont exploitées par la DGI. Elles sont transmises à l'INSEE chaque année au mois de février de l'année qui suit l'année de référence et publiées l'année suivante en mars.

La DADS contient des renseignements sur l'établissement (nom ou raison sociale de l'employeur, adresse et secteur d'activité, numéro d'identification, effectifs inscrits au 31 décembre de l'année et masse des salaires bruts) et sur chaque salarié (identification, nature de l'emploi et qualification, adresse, dates de début et de fin de période de paie, nombre d'heures salariées, condition d'emploi (à temps complet, à temps partiel, intermittent et travailleurs à domicile), montant des rémunérations en espèces avant et après déduction des retenues pour cotisations sociales, valeur estimée des avantages en nature et montant des indemnités pour frais d'emploi ou de service et de remboursements de frais.
Mise à jour du système administratif: annuelle.

Traitement et contrôle des données
Les données sont traitées par ordinateur. Des vérifications sont effectuées au niveau des identifiants des établissements et des salariés (rapprochement des répertoires entreprises et individus) et des contrôles de cohérence sont effectués entre salaire, durée du travail et conditions d'emploi.

Ajustements
Aucun.

Types d'estimations
Distributions, moyennes et médianes, selon différentes unités de temps (heure, année).
Emploi: effectif total au 31 décembre de l'année de référence, et nombre de salariés rémunérés au cours de l'année de référence; distributions selon diverses variables;
Salaire net horaire moyen: quotient de la masse des salaires nets par le volume d'heures effectué;
Salaire net annuel moyen: pour les salariés à temps complet, quotient de la masse des salaires nets des "temps complet" par le nombre d'années-travail;
Volume d'heures annuel moyen des postes: volume d'heures rémunérées pour une année divisé par le nombre de postes rémunérés dans l'année.

Calcul d'indices
Aucun.

Indicateurs de fiabilité des estimations
Couverture du système administratif: supérieure à 99% en termes de salariés.
Conformité avec d'autres sources: des comparaisons sont possibles au niveau:

- des effectifs et de la masse salariale, avec les comptes nationaux,
- de l'évolution des taux de salaire, avec les résultats de l'Enquête ACEMO du Ministère du Travail (enquête trimestrielle auprès des établissements réalisée par le Ministère de l'Emploi et de la Solidarité (DARES);
- des effectifs, avec d'autres sources administratives.

Séries disponibles
Tableaux "Employeurs": nombre d'établissements, effectif en nombre de postes rémunérés dans l'année, effectif en nombre de postes rémunérés au 31 décembre, masse des salaires bruts, par activité économique de l'établissement, taille, département d'implantation;
Tableaux "Postes à temps complet", série salaire horaire: effectifs en nombre de postes, en nombre d'années-travail, volume d'heures annuel, masse des salaires nets versés, volume d'heures annuel moyen des postes et salaire net horaire moyen des postes, selon l'activité économique et la taille de l'établissement, par sexe, catégorie socioprofessionnelle, tranche d'âge, tranche de salaire net horaire, etc.;
Tableaux "Postes à temps complet", série salaire annuel: effectifs en nombre de postes, en nombre d'années-travail, masse des salaires nets versés, salaire net annuel moyen par année-travail, nombre de permanents, salaire net annuel moyen par année-travail

des permanents, selon diverses variables de classification et par sexe;

Tableaux "Postes à temps non complet" et "Ensemble des postes": séries salaire horaire selon des variables et classifications semblables.

Historique des statistiques

Date de début de la série statistique: 1967, sur la base d'un échantillon au 1/25ème; 1993 de façon exhaustive.

Modifications et révisions principales: jusqu'en 1992, les salariés de l'agriculture et de la sylviculture étaient exclus du champ d'exploitation des DADS. Depuis 1997, les fichiers exhaustifs des DADS permettent, en outre, de connaître les salaires que se versent les dirigeants de sociétés anonymes et les gérants minoritaires de sociétés à responsabilité limitée, mais non les salaires des gérants majoritaires de SARL. Il est prévu d'inclure l'agriculture et la sylviculture dans le champ statistique à partir de 2002.

Documentation et diffusion

Documentation:

INSEE: *INSEE Résultats: Les Salaires dans l'Industrie, le Commerce et les Services en ...* (Paris, annuel); publié environ 15 mois après la période de référence des données. Contient les statistiques et des informations méthodologiques.

Diffusion: sur le site Internet: http://www.alisse.insee.fr

Les statistiques ne paraissant pas dans les publications nationales ou sur Internet peuvent être obtenues sur demande.

Données communiquées au BIT aux fins de diffusion

Aucune à présent.

Autres sources administratives de données: des statistiques sur les revenus d'activité non-salariée sont tirées de plusieurs sources administratives:

Les données sur le revenu libéral des médecins sont établies à partir de deux sources administratives: les statistiques du système national inter-régimes élaborées par la Caisse Nationale d'Assurance Maladie des travailleurs salariés (CNAMTS), la MSA (Mutualité Sociale Agricole) et la CANAM (Caisse Nationale d'Assurance Maladie des Professions Indépendantes), pour les honoraires et les effectifs; et les statistiques fiscales de la Direction Générale des Impôts (DGI) pour les charges professionnelles. Ces statistiques sont établies annuellement et concernent les médecins à activité normale (remplaçants exclus) ayant rempli une déclaration contrôlée, conventionnés ou non, hospitaliers à temps plein compris. Les évaluations respectives des recettes et des charges permettent d'estimer pour chaque année le revenu moyen par praticien provenant de l'activité libérale avant impôt sur le revenu.

Des statistiques sur les revenus d'activité des petits entrepreneurs de l'artisanat, du commerce et des services sont établies sur la base de l'exploitation et du redressement des déclarations fiscales des entreprises sur les bénéfices industriels et commerciaux (BIC) et les bénéfices non commerciaux (BNC). Les fichiers issus des déclarations sont transmis à l'INSEE et constituent, avec les enquêtes annuelles d'entreprises, le système unifié de statistiques d'entreprises.

Les résultats sont publiés dans:

INSEE: *Synthèses: Les revenus d'activité non salariée en ...* (Paris, annuel); publié environ 3 ans après la période de référence des données. Contient les statistiques et des informations méthodologiques.

Des statistiques sur les salaires des agents de l'Etat sont établies chaque année sur la base d'un ensemble de fichiers: fichiers des ministères civils et des exploitants publics; enquête complémentaire par questionnaires auprès de l'ensemble des services de l'Etat, fichiers du ministère de la Défense, fichiers des établissements publics, etc.

Les résultats sont publiés dans:

INSEE: *INSEE Résultats: Le Salaire des Agents de l'Etat en ...* (Paris, annuel); publié environ 3 ans après la période de référence des données. Contient les statistiques et des informations méthodologiques.

Guatemala

Source de la série

Registres de l'Institut de Sécurité sociale du Guatemala (Instituto Guatemalteco de Seguridad Social, IGSS).

Titre de la série

Emploi et revenu du travail (gains) des travailleurs affiliés à l'IGSS.

Organisme responsable

Collecte des données: Institut de Sécurité sociale du Guatemala (IGSS).

Principaux sujets couverts

Emploi et gains.

Périodicité ou fréquence de disponibilité des statistiques

Mensuelle et annuelle.

Période de référence

Chaque mois de l'année ainsi que l'année civile tout entière.

Portée des statistiques

Géographique: l'ensemble du pays.

Branches d'activité: toutes les branches d'activité économique.

Etablissements: de tous types et tailles, dans le secteur public et le secteur privé.

Personnes: employeurs actifs et travailleurs (salariés) cotisant au régime de la Sécurité sociale.

Professions: les données ne sont recueillies ni par profession individuelle ni par catégories professionnelles.

Concepts et définitions

Emploi: est affiliée au régime de la Sécurité sociale toute personne offrant ses services, que ce soit au plan matériel ou intellectuel, ou les deux, et régie par un contrat de travail ou une relation d'emploi la liant à un employeur officiellement inscrit ou tenu de s'inscrire au régime de la Sécurité sociale. Sont également affiliés les fonctionnaires d'Etat, ainsi que les membres et les employés des coopératives légalement constituées.

Gains: il s'agit de la masse salariale, autrement dit de l'ensemble des salaires déclarés par les entreprises cotisantes.

Classifications

Branches d'activité économique:

Titre de la classification: non disponible.

Nombre de groupes utilisés pour le codage:

S'applique à: employeurs, salariés et gains.

Lien avec la CITI et niveau: basée sur la CITI-1968.

Autres classifications: par région et par catégorie d'employeur/secteur (employeurs privés, budget et comptes de l'Etat).

Rassemblement des données

Type et couverture du système administratif: registres de l'IGSS. Au 31 décembre 2000, les registres utilisés couvraient quelques 908'000 travailleurs affiliés, avec un total de 1'950'000 personnes couvertes.

Méthode de collecte des données: les données portant sur le nombre d'employeurs actifs, de salariés cotisants et les salaires sont fondées uniquement sur les rapports mensuels obligatoires remis par les employeurs à l'IGSS et archivés dans un registre centralisé.

Mise à jour du système administratif: mensuelle.

Traitement et contrôle des données

Non disponible.

Ajustements

Couverture insuffisante: les estimations annuelles portant sur les salariés et les salaires sont ajustées en fonction des revenus perçus au titre des cotisations à l'ensemble des régimes de sécurité sociale et compte tenu des arriérés des employeurs. Les données relatives au budget de l'Etat sont elles aussi corrigées en vue d'éliminer les emplois multiples, et les chiffres des salaires sont ajustés sur la base de l'exercice budgétaire.

Types d'estimations

Nombre total d'employeurs actifs, de travailleurs cotisants et total des salaires mensuels et annuels.

Gains mensuels moyens.

Calcul d'indices

Aucun.

Indicateurs de fiabilité des estimations

Couverture du système administratif: au 31 décembre 2000, le nombre d'affiliés représentaient 25 pour cent de la population économiquement active âgée de 10 ans et plus, tandis que le total des personnes couvertes (affiliés et bénéficiaires) représentait 17 pour cent de l'ensemble de la population.

Séries disponibles

Estimation des employeurs actifs au 31 décembre de chaque année;

Estimation des travailleurs affiliés cotisants au mois de juin et au 31 décembre, par activité économique, par région et par catégorie d'employeurs;

Estimation du total des salaires annuels, par activité économique, par région et par catégorie d'employeurs;

Estimation mensuelle des travailleurs cotisants et des gains, par activité économique.

Historique des statistiques

Date de début de la série statistique: non disponible.

Modifications et révisions principales: l'IGSS a revu les estimations en matière d'emploi et de salaires pour la période 1974-1987.

Documentation et diffusion
Documentation:
Instituto Guatemalteco de Seguridad Social (IGSS): *Boletín Estadístico* (Guatemala-City, annuel).
Idem: *Informe Anual de Labores* (ibid., annuel).
Banco de Guatemala: *Boletín Estadístico* (ibid., trimestriel);
Diffusion: sur le site Internet de la Banco de Guatemala: http://www.banguat.gob.gt
Données communiquées au BIT aux fins de diffusion
Les statistiques sur l'emploi rémunéré et le revenu mensuel moyen des travailleurs affiliés cotisants, par branche d'activité économique, sont publiées dans *l'Annuaire des statistiques du Travail*.

Hong-kong, Chine (1)

Source de la série
Registres officiels de l'administration.
Titre de la série
Civil Service Personnel Statistics - Establishment and Strength of the Civil Service.
(Statistiques du personnel de la fonction publique.).
Organisme responsable
Collecte des données: Office de la fonction publique (Civil Service Bureau), région administrative spéciale de Hong-kong (RAS), République populaire de Chine.
Traitement statistique et publication/diffusion des statistiques: Département des statistiques et du recensement (Census and Statistics Department), Hong-kong RAS.
Principaux sujets couverts
Emploi et postes vacants.
Périodicité ou fréquence de disponibilité des statistiques
Trimestrielle.
Période de référence
Le dernier jour ouvrable du trimestre.
Portée des statistiques
Géographique: Hong-kong RAS.
Branches d'activité: toutes les branches d'activité économique.
Etablissements: tous les bureaux politiques et les départements du gouvernement de l'administration de Hong-kong RAS.
Personnes: les fonctionnaires.
Professions: toutes les catégories professionnelles de fonctionnaires de l'administration de Hong-kong RAS.
Concepts et définitions
Emploi: les fonctionnaires sont les personnes employées selon les conditions de nomination de la fonction publique à la date de référence de l'enquête. Sont exclus les membres de la Commission indépendante contre la corruption, les juges et fonctionnaires des organes judiciaires ainsi que le personnel recruté localement par les représentations économiques et commerciales de Hong-kong à l'étranger.
Postes vacants: postes non pourvus qui sont disponibles immédiatement et pour lesquels des mesures actives de recrutement ont été entreprises à la date de référence de l'enquête.
Classifications
Branches d'activité économique:
Titre de la classification: Hong-kong Standard Industrial Classification Version 1.1 (HSIC V1.1).
Nombre de groupes utilisés pour le codage: 83 (au niveau des sous-groupes à 3 chiffres).
S'applique à: emploi et postes vacants.
Lien avec la CITI et niveau: la HSIC V1.1 est modélisée sur la CITI, Rév. 2 à tous les niveaux, avec adaptation à la structure industrielle existant à Hong-kong RAS.
Autres classifications: emploi par sexe.
Rassemblement des données
Type et couverture du système administratif: près de 100 unités déclarantes, en termes de départements et de bureaux de l'administration.
Méthode de collecte des données: les départements et services de l'administration communiquent leurs déclarations sur une base trimestrielle aux bureaux de l'Office de la fonction publique. Le laps de temps entre la période de référence des données et leur collecte / traitement est de 12 semaines environ.
Mise à jour du système administratif: chaque trimestre.
Traitement et contrôle de la qualité des données
Les données sont traitées par informatique. L'ensemble des composantes est vérifié par rapport au total de chaque unité déclarante, et des contrôles des intervalles de variation sont effectués à l'aide des données correspondantes du trimestre précédent.
Ajustements
Aucun.
Types d'estimations
Totaux.
Calcul d'indices
Aucun.
Indicateurs de fiabilité des estimations
Couverture du système administratif: exhaustive en ce qui concerne les fonctionnaires.
Séries disponibles
Nombre trimestriel de fonctionnaires et de postes vacants.
Historique des statistiques
Date de début de la série statistique: mars 1980.
Modifications et révisions principales: en juin 1999, une révision mineure a été apportée à la définition des fonctionnaires. Depuis lors, les juges et les fonctionnaires des organes judiciaires ne font plus partie de la définition de fonctionnaires. La définition des postes vacants dans la fonction publique a été également revue en juin 1999, de sorte qu'en sont exclus les postes vacants en attente de suppression, les postes occupés par du personnel temporaire ou réservés à d'autres membres du personnel.
Avant décembre 2001, les chiffres concernant le nombre de fonctionnaires et de postes vacants faisaient référence à la situation au début de janvier, avril, juillet et octobre. Ces chiffres se réfèrent actuellement au dernier jour ouvrable des trimestres précités.
Documentation et diffusion
Documentation:
Census and Statistics Department: *Hong-kong Monthly Digest of Statistics* (Hong-kong RAS);
Idem: *Quarterly Report of Employment and Vacancies Statistics* (ibid.);
Idem: *Hong-kong Annual Digest of Statistics* (ibid.).
Ces publications contiennent les statistiques de l'emploi et des postes vacants ainsi que des informations méthodologiques. Le laps de temps entre la date de référence et la publication des statistiques est de 12 semaines.
Diffusion: par Internet: http://www.info.gov.hk/censtatd
Données communiquées au BIT aux fins de diffusion
Les données suivantes sont communiquées au BIT aux fins de publication dans *l'Annuaire des statistiques du Travail*:
Nombre des fonctionnaires inclus dans les statistiques concernant l'emploi rémunéré par activité économique.

Hong-kong, Chine (2)

Source de la série
Registres administratifs: formulaire officiel 527.
Titre de la série
Déclarations mensuelles des taux de salaire dans la Construction (Monthly Returns of Wage Rates in the Building Industry).
Organisme responsable
Collecte des données: Office des chantiers (Works Bureau), région administrative spéciale de Hong-kong (RAS), République populaire de Chine.
Traitement statistique et publication/diffusion des statistiques: Département des statistiques et du recensement (Census and Statistics Department), Hong-kong RAS.
Principaux sujets couverts
Emploi et taux de salaire.
Périodicité ou fréquence de disponibilité des statistiques
Emploi: trimestriel,
Taux de salaire: mensuels.
Période de référence
Emploi: le dernier jour ouvrable du trimestre ;
Taux de salaire: le mois.
Portée des statistiques
Géographique: Hong-kong RAS.
Branches d'activité: la Construction uniquement.
Etablissements: tous les chantiers du ressort de l'Office des chantiers, administration de Hong-kong RAS. Un chantier est défini comme une unité distincte où sont réalisées une ou plusieurs étapes de construction.
Personnes: travailleurs manuels.
Professions: vingt-neuf professions présélectionnées.
Concepts et définitions
Emploi: le terme de travailleurs manuels sur chantiers de construction se réfère aux artisans, ouvriers semi-qualifiés ou non

qualifiés employés sur ces sites au moment de la date de l'enquête. Les travailleurs manuels peuvent être directement employés par les entrepreneurs ou bien sur demande par des sous-traitants ou des contremaîtres pour les travaux ponctuels.

Taux de salaire ou de traitement: le taux horaire journalier comprend (i) le taux du salaire de base ; (ii) l'allocation de coût de la vie ; et (iii) les allocations garanties et régulièrement versées y compris pour les repas et le transport. Les traitements en nature en sont exclus.

Classifications

Branches d'activité économique:

Titre de la classification: Hong-kong Standard Industrial Classification Version 1.1 (HSIC V1.1);

Nombre de groupes utilisés pour le codage: Division 5 (chantiers de construction uniquement).

S'applique à: emploi et taux de salaire.

Lien avec la CITI et niveau: rév. 2, à tous les niveaux.

Professions: 29 métiers choisis: ouvrier non qualifié, excaveur, ouvrier fabriquant de béton, manœuvre maçon, plâtrier manœuvre, manœuvre pour la fabrication du béton, maçon, poseur de tuyauterie PVC, maçon en parpaings, tailleur de pierre, couvreur, forgeron, charpentier et menuisier, plombier, ajusteur en mécanique, plâtrier, zingueur et tailleur de pierre, carreleur, peintre, électricien (poseur de câbles), ouvrier d'usine, chauffeur de camion, coolie, foreur en marteau pneumatique, travailleur sur bambou et poseur d'échafaudages, poseur de charpente métallique, scaphandrier et aide-scaphandrier.

Rassemblement des données

Type et couverture du système administratif: environ 230 chantiers de construction.

Méthode de collecte des données: les principaux entrepreneurs de tous les chantiers de construction du ressort de l'Office des chantiers, Hong-kong RAS, sont tenus de remettre le formulaire officiel 527 (GF 527) au Département des statistiques et du recensement, par l'intermédiaire des Départements des travaux compétents et sur une base mensuelle. Ils y indiquent le nombre de journées de travail ainsi que les taux de salaires moyens correspondant aux métiers spécifiés dans le GF 527, concernant les travailleurs qu'eux-mêmes ou leurs sous-traitants ont employés au cours du mois de référence, ceci au plus tard au milieu du mois suivant. Le Département des statistiques et du recensement effectue des contrôles de qualité et calcule les taux de salaire journaliers moyens dans les professions choisies, dans les deux mois qui suivent la réception des données. En ce qui concerne le nombre de travailleurs manuels, le laps de temps entre la période de référence et la collecte et le traitement des données est de 12 semaines.

Mise à jour du système administratif: continue.

Traitement et contrôle des données

Outre les contrôles de qualité, il est procédé à une vérification des données communiquées dans le formulaire GF527 dans les cas suivants:

–   le nombre de jours de travail pour une profession un mois donné, est supérieur ou inférieur de 50% à celui du mois précédent;

–   le taux journalier moyen pour une profession un mois donné, est supérieur ou inférieur de 10% à celui du mois précédent;

–   le taux journalier moyen pour une profession un mois donné, diffère de la moyenne générale pour cette profession obtenue sur la base de l'ensemble des contrats, alors qu'aucun professionnel du métier en question n'a été engagé sur le chantier donné au cours du mois écoulé.

Ajustements

Aucun.

Types d'estimations

Nombre total de travailleurs manuels sur les chantiers de construction.

Taux de salaire journaliers moyens dans des professions déterminées sur les chantiers de construction.

Taux journalier moyen d'une profession i:

Σ (jours ouvrables travaillés sur le chantier jth x taux de salaire journalier moyen sur le chantier jth) j

___

Σ jours ouvrables travaillés sur le chantier jth
j

taux de salaire journaliers moyens pour toutes les professions couvertes par le GF 527:

$\Sigma\Sigma$ (jours ouvrables travaillés sur le chantier jth x salaires journaliers moyens sur le chantier jth)
ij

___

$\Sigma\Sigma$ jours ouvrables travaillés sur le chantier jth
ij

Calcul d'indices

Un indice mensuel du coût du travail est calculé, basé sur les taux de salaire moyens pondérés des métiers choisis. La pondération se fait pour chaque profession sur la base du total de jours ouvrables pour la profession considérée pour une période de temps donnée.

Indicateurs de fiabilité des estimations

Couverture du système administratif: 100 % des chantiers de construction du ressort de l'Office des chantiers.

Séries disponibles

Nombre de travailleurs manuels et taux de salaire journaliers moyens.

Historique des statistiques

Date de début de la série statistique: nombre de travailleurs manuels: mars 1976; taux de salaire journaliers moyens: janvier 1970; indice de la série: décembre 1975 (période de base: novembre 1975).

Modifications et révisions principales: révisions des séries d'indices:

Juin 1989: modification de la période de base (juillet 1982'100) et pondérations;

Juillet 1995: modification de la période de base (juin 1995'100) et pondérations.

Documentation et diffusion

Documentation:

Census and Statistics Department: *Average Daily Wages of Workers engaged in Government Building and Construction Projects* (Hong-kong RAS, mensuel); contient les statistiques salariales uniquement);

Idem: *Hong-kong Monthly Digest of Statistics* (ibid.); contient les statistiques de salaires et d'emploi, ainsi que des informations méthodologiques;

Idem: *Quarterly Report of Employment and Vacancies Statistics* (ibid.); contient les statistiques de l'emploi uniquement, ainsi que des informations méthodologiques;

Idem: *Quarterly Report of Employment and Vacancies at Construction Sites* (ibid.); contient les statistiques de l'emploi uniquement, ainsi que des informations méthodologiques;

Idem: *Hong-kong Annual Digest of Statistics* (ibid.); contient les statistiques de salaires et d'emploi, ainsi que des informations méthodologiques.

Les salaires journaliers moyens pour les professions sélectionnées sont publiés dans les deux mois suivant le mois de référence. Le nombre de travailleurs manuels sur les chantiers de construction est publié dans les 12 semaines suivant la date de référence.

Diffusion: sur le site Internet: http://www.info.gov.hk/censtatd

Données communiquées au BIT aux fins de diffusion

Les données suivantes sont communiquées au BIT aux fins de publication dans *l'Annuaire des statistiques du travail*: le nombre de travailleurs des chantiers ainsi que les taux de salaire journaliers moyens des travailleurs de chantiers de construction pour l'ensemble des professions sélectionnées.

Dans *Statistiques des salaires et de la durée du travail par professions et des prix de produits alimentaires – Résultats de l'Enquête d'octobre*: taux de salaire journaliers moyens dans certaines professions: électricien (câbleur), plombier, poseur de charpente métallique, peintre, maçon, ouvrier spécialisé pour fabriquer du béton, charpentier et menuisier, plâtrier et ouvrier non qualifié.

Ile de Man

Source de la série

Déclarations d'impôt sur le revenu.

Titre de la série

Emploi sur l'Île de Man.

Organisme responsable

Collecte des données: Isle of Man Treasury, Income Tax Division (Trésor de l'Île de Man, Département de l'impôt sur le revenu).

Traitement statistique et publication/diffusion des statistiques: Isle of Man Treasury, Economic Affairs Division (Trésor de l'île de Man, Département des affaires économiques).

Principaux sujets couverts

Emploi.

Périodicité ou fréquence de disponibilité des statistiques

Occasionnelle, sur demande.

Période de référence
Une date précise.
Portée des statistiques
Géographique: toute l'île.
Branches d'activité: toutes les branches d'activité économique.
Etablissements: de tous types et tailles.
Personnes: toutes les personnes ayant un emploi.
Professions: les données ne sont rassemblées ni par profession ni par groupe de professions.
Concepts et définitions
Emploi: toutes les personnes ayant un emploi (c'est-à-dire les salariés et les indépendant avec un revenu imposable dérivé d'un emploi salarié ou indépendant).
Classifications
Branches d'activité économique:
Titre de la classification: Classification du Commerce de l'Île de Man.
Nombre de groupes utilisés pour le codage: 31; ce nombre peut être réduit aux fins de publication, étant donné que certains groupes sont très petits.
S'applique à: l'emploi.
Lien avec la CITI et niveau: aucun.
Situation dans la profession: salariés et indépendants.
Autres classifications: emploi par taille d'établissements.
Rassemblement des données
Les données proviennent de la base centrale comprenant plus de 40'000 enregistrements pour toute l'île, gérée par le Département de l'impôt sur le revenu du Trésor de l'île. Ces enregistrements sont tenus à jour, conformément aux exigences de la loi.
Traitement et contrôle des données
Les données sont traitées par ordinateur.
On vérifie la cohérence des données en les comparant avec les enregistrements précédents ainsi qu'avec les données obtenues lors du recensement de la population.
Le Département des affaires économiques contrôle le codage de la classification industrielle effectué par le Département de l'impôt sur le revenu et procède aux ajustements, si nécessaire.
Ajustements
Aucun.
Types d'estimations
Totaux à une date de référence.
Calcul d'indices
Aucun.
Indicateurs de fiabilité des estimations
Couverture du système administratif: il est supposé couvrir l'ensemble des personnes ayant un emploi, à l'exception du travail au noir lequel est restreint, étant donné les dimensions relativement petites de l'île.
Erreurs non dues à l'échantillonnage: des erreurs de codage de la classification industrielle sont possibles ; des contrôles sont effectués (voir ci-dessus).
Conformité avec d'autres sources: voir ci-dessus.
Séries disponibles
Emploi total à une date de référence précise en 1988.
Historique des statistiques
Date de début de la série statistique: 1988 (publiée en 1995).
Modifications et révisions principales: aucune, à l'exception de nouveaux groupes qui ont été récemment ajoutés à la Classification du Commerce afin de couvrir les technologies de l'information et de la communication (TIC).
Documentation et diffusion
Documentation:
Isle of Man Treasury, Economic Affairs Division: *Isle of Man Labour Statistics*, 1995.
Les données sont produites à la demande du Département des affaires économiques au Département de l'impôt sur le revenu. Il s'agit d'une source de données *ad hoc*, principalement utilisée par l'administration, mais disponible au public sur demande.
Une note méthodologique accompagne tous les tableaux diffusés.
Données communiquées au BIT aux fins de diffusion
Aucune à présent.

Israël

Source de la série
Rapports à l'Institut national d'Assurance (National Insurance Institute - NII) et autres sources administratives.
Titre de la série
Postes de salariés et salaires et traitements.

Organisme responsable
Collecte des données: Institut national d'Assurance (NII).
Traitement statistique et publication/diffusion des statistiques: Bureau central de Statistiques (Central Bureau of Statistics - CBS).
Principaux sujets couverts
Emploi et gains.
Périodicité ou fréquence de disponibilité des statistiques
Mensuelle.
Période de référence
Le mois entier.
Portée des statistiques
Géographique: l'ensemble du pays.
Branches d'activité: toutes les activités économiques, à l'exception des ménages employant des services domestiques.
Etablissements: établissements de tous genres et de toutes tailles employant un ou plusieurs salariés.
Personnes: tous les salariés ayant travaillé au moins un jour au cours de mois de l'enquête dans un des établissements concernés, y compris les membres de coopératives, les travailleurs civils des forces de défense et les salariés de Judée et Samarie de la Zone de Gaza et du Liban-Sud (uniquement les personnes recevant leur salaire de l'administration des paies du Service de l'emploi) qui travaillent en Israël. Sont également inclus tous les travailleurs venant d'autres pays pour lesquels des rapports sont soumis à l'Institut national d'Assurance.
Les travailleurs d'aide à domicile, les membres travaillant dans des kibboutzs ou des établissements appartenant à des kibboutzs, les élèves des écoles professionnelles, des écoles d'enseignement agricole et les élèves des institutions de formation professionnelle sont exclus.
Professions: les données ne sont pas rassemblées par profession ou groupe professionnel.
Concepts et définitions
Emploi: il s'agit du nombre des salariés (permanents et temporaires) qui figurent sur les bordereaux de salaire des établissements ou institutions, qui ont travaillé ou qui ont été payés durant une absence pour raison de maladie, de vacances, d'obligation de réserviste dans l'armée, etc. pour au moins un jour durant le mois de l'enquête.
Les salariés qui figurent sur les bordereaux de salaire de plus d'un établissement ou institutions au cours de ce mois sont comptés autant de fois qu'ils figurent sur ces listes, de sorte que les données portent sur le nombre de postes de salariés pour lesquels des salaires ont été payés au cours de ce mois.
Gains: il s'agit des gains mensuels bruts. Ils englobent les salaires/traitements de base, les indemnités d'indexation pour coût de la vie, les indemnités d'ancienneté, les paiements d'arriérés de la période précédente, les avances sur salaire, les paiements pour heures supplémentaires, les primes, bonifications et diverses indemnités (ordinaires ou extraordinaires), telles que indemnités de permanence, de travail posté, 13e salaire mensuel, frais de déplacement, indemnités de loisirs, d'éducation, de primes pour études professionnelles supplémentaires et d'entretien de véhicules.
Sont exclues les autres dépenses de travail et les sommes que l'employeur verse à des fonds tels que fonds de pensions ou caisse d'assurance des salariés, taxes parallèles et taxes d'employeurs.
Classifications
Branches d'activité économique:
Titre de la classification: Classification type, par industrie, de toutes les branches d'activité économique, 1993.
Nombre de groupes utilisés pour le codage: non disponible.
S'applique à: emploi et gains.
Lien avec la CITI et niveau: rév.3.
Autres classifications: les données sur l'emploi et les gains sont ventilées par citoyenneté (Israéliens et étrangers).
Rassemblement des données
Type et couverture du système administratif: non disponible.
Méthode de collecte des données: les données relatives à l'emploi et aux salaires/traitements sont essentiellement basées sur le traitement des rapports mensuels que les employeurs remettent (conformément à la loi) en utilisant les formulaires 102 (pour les Israéliens) et 612 (pour les travailleurs venant de l'étranger) à l'Institut national d'Assurance (NII), et en partie sur des informations d'autres sources administratives, telles que l'administration des paiements du Service de l'Emploi, Malam, le Centre de traitement des données des autorités israéliennes locales et des forces de défense.
Les données sur l'emploi et les salaires de l'administration locale (communes, conseils locaux et régionaux, etc.) sont basées sur les

registres du Centre de traitement des données des autorités israéliennes locales.

Les rapports des employeurs sont conservés dans un fichier central de l'employeur à l'Institut national d'Assurance. La base de sondage est essentiellement constituée de ce fichier et, des fichiers d'autres établissements conservés au CBS ainsi que des informations d'autres sources qui sont ajoutées au fichier. La base de sondage est stratifiée selon les principales branches d'activité économique et la taille des établissements. De chaque groupe de taille par branche d'activité économique, on extrait un échantillon d'établissements actifs, avec diverses fractions de sondage.

L'échantillon est mis à jour en excluant les établissements qui cessent d'être opérationnels et en incluant dans l'échantillon les nouveaux établissements. Les changements de taille des établissements ne sont pas pris en compte au moment de la mise à jour. L'échantillon est renouvelé après quelques années. Les données actuelles sont basées sur l'échantillon de janvier 1995.

En ce qui concerne les postes de salariés des travailleurs étrangers: en 1994, les données étaient basées sur un recensement de tous les employeurs qui avaient présenté des rapports sur les travailleurs étrangers (en excluant les personnes rémunérées, employées par des ménages qui sont déclarées par leur employeur comme travailleurs d'aide ménagère). Depuis 1995, les données sont basées sur un échantillon d'établissements qui est extrait de la totalité des établissements qui présentent des rapports sur les travailleurs étrangers (formulaire 612). La base de sondage a été créé pour 1995 et, est mise à jour en ajoutant les nouveaux établissements qui commencent à employer des travailleurs étrangers. Un échantillon d'adjonctions est extrait et ajouté régulièrement à l'échantillon principal. Les établissements qui cessent d'employer des travailleurs étrangers ne sont pas inclus dans les calculs.

Traitement et contrôle des données

Les estimations mensuelles de l'année en cours sont révisées sur la base des rapports complémentaires ou corrigés des employeurs qui parviennent ultérieurement à l'Institut national d'Assurance.

Ajustements

Variations saisonnières: On utilise la méthode X-11-ARIMA/2000 d'ajustements pour variations saisonnières, conçue par Statistics Canada. Les facteurs d'ajustements préalables ont été calculés en utilisant la méthode spéciale mise au point par CBS pour évaluer les effets des dates variables des festivals juifs et des jours de place en Israël.

Types d'estimations

Totaux des postes de salariés;

Salaire/traitement moyen par poste de salarié: total des salaires/traitements mensuels divisé par le nombre de postes de salariés au cours d'un mois donné; aux prix courants et constants. En raison de la définition des postes de salariés, le salaire/traitement mensuel moyen par poste de salarié est plus bas que le salaire/traitement mensuel moyen par salarié.

Salaires/traitements nets moyens dans l'administration locale: salaires/traitements mensuels bruts après déduction des contributions à l'Institut national d'Assurance (y compris assurance maladie depuis janvier 1995) et de l'impôt sur le revenu.

Des estimations incluant ou excluant les travailleurs de Judée et Samarie et de la Zone de Gaza sont faites séparément.

Calcul d'indices

Les indices des postes de salariés et des salaires sont calculés mensuellement.

L'indice du total des salaires/traitements à prix constants est calculé en divisant l'indice du total des salaires/traitements à prix courants par l'indice des prix à la consommation de chaque mois sur la base de 1994'100. Les estimations annuelles, trimestrielles, etc. sont la moyenne des indices mensuels à prix constants.

L'indice du salaire moyen par poste à prix constants est calculé en divisant l'indice du total des salaires à prix constants par l'indice des postes de salariés.

La tendance est calculée en utilisant la méthode des moyennes mobiles de Henderson.

Indicateurs de fiabilité des estimations

Non disponible.

Séries disponibles

Postes de salariés, salaires/traitements totaux et salaire/traitement mensuel moyen par poste de salarié, aux prix courants et constants;

Séries corrigées des variations saisonnières;

Tendance et pourcentage de changement mensuel de la tendance.

Historique des statistiques

Date de début de la série statistique: 1961.

Modifications et révisions principales: depuis janvier 1995, les statistiques sont basées sur un nouvel échantillon d'établissements. Les données antérieures étaient basées sur l'échantillon de 1979 qui a été mis à jour en 1983 et en 1986.

Durant la période allant d'avril 1995 au début de 1997, les rapports sur les salaires présentés dans les formulaires 612 étaient partiels: certains montants, pouvant aller jusqu'à NIS 900 par mois, n'étaient pas inclus. A partir de 1997, certains employeurs ont commencé à remettre des rapports sur les montants totaux.

Avant 1993, les données étaient classées selon la Classification type, par industrie, de toutes les branches d'activité économique, 1970.

Documentation et diffusion

Documentation:

Central Bureau of Statistics: *Monthly Bulletin of Statistics* (Bulletin mensuel des statistiques) (Jérusalem);

Idem: *Supplement to the Monthly Bulletin of Statistics* (Supplément au Bulletin mensuel de statistiques) (ibid).

Idem: *Statistical Absract of Israel* (Aperçu statistique d'Israël) (ibid. annuel);

Des informations méthodologiques détaillées sur les définitions, les sources de données, les méthodes de collecte et de traitement des données, et les limites des données, peuvent être trouvées dans la publication *Statistical Absract of Israel*, n° 51, 2000.

Diffusion: sur le site Internet du CBS: http://www.cbs.gov.il (présente à la fois des données et des notes méthodologiques).

Les données qui ne figurent dans les publications nationales ou sur le site Internet peuvent être obtenues sur demande.

Données communiquées au BIT aux fins de diffusion

Les données suivantes sont communiquées au BIT pour être publiées dans l'*Annuaire des statistiques du Travail:*

Emploi rémunéré par branche d'activité économique, et dans les industries manufacturières, par groupe d'industrie;

Gains mensuels moyens par branche d'activité économique, et dans les industries manufacturières, par groupe d'industrie.

Les données mensuelles correspondantes sont publiées dans le *Bulletin des statistiques du Travail.*

Italie

Source de la série

Conventions collectives de travail (Contratti Collettivi di lavoro).

Titre de la série

Numeri indici delle retribuzioni contrattuali (Indices des salaires conventionnés).

Organisme responsable

Collecte des données, traitement statistique et publication/ diffusion des statistiques:

Institut national de statistique (Instituto Nazionale di Statistica - ISTAT).

Principaux sujets couverts

Salaires conventionnés.

Périodicité ou fréquence de disponibilité des statistiques

Mensuelle.

Période de référence

La fin de chaque mois.

Portée des statistiques

Géographique: l'ensemble du pays.

Branches d'activité: pratiquement toutes les branches de l'activité économique, y compris les services publics, à l'exception de: la pêche (catégorie de classement B de la CITI, rév. 3), les activités de services collectifs, sociaux et personnels, les services domestiques ainsi que les organisations et organismes extra-territoriaux (catégories O à Q de la CITI, rév. 3).

Etablissements: établissements de tous types et tailles qui sont partie prenante de, ou couverts par des conventions collectives.

Personnes: salariés à plein temps, à l'exclusion des cadres dans le secteur privé et des apprentis.

Professions: toutes les professions représentées dans le cadre des négociations des conventions collectives sont couvertes.

Concepts et définitions

Emploi: se réfère aux salariés titulaires d'un contrat régulier à plein temps, à l'exception des apprentis et des cadres dans le secteur privé. Dans le secteur du crédit, cela peut inclure les fonctionnaires, tandis que dans l'administration publique, sont inclus les cadres contractuels ou non. Les ouvriers et les employés sont identifiés séparément. Les données d'emploi sont utilisées pour déterminer la structure de l'indice des salaires l'année de base.

Taux de salaire ou de traitement: les salaires conventionnés sont ceux fixés dans les conventions collectives. Ils représentent, chaque mois, les montants dus aux salariés dans l'hypothèse où ils sont effectivement au travail durant les heures fixées dans les conventions collectives appropriées. Sont incluses les composantes générales et régulières de la rémunération, telles que salaire de base, paiements compensatoires spéciaux (Indennita di contingenza), primes pour ancienneté, primes pour travail posté et autres paiements mensuels réguliers spécifiés dans les conventions nationales et payables à tous les travailleurs, de même que les composantes payées périodiquement (ex.: le paiement du 13e mois et autres paiements saisonniers et réguliers). Sont exclus les bonus liés à la performance individuelle et aux conditions individuelles de travail, les paiements supplémentaires convenus au niveau de l'entreprise, les paiements ad-hoc et occasionnels, les montants octroyés par le biais de négociations décentralisées, les paiements rétroactifs et uniques. Toutefois, ces paiements spéciaux sont pris en considération dans le calcul des revenus annuels conventionnés (Retribuzione contrattuale annua di competenza).

Les taux salariaux conventionnés sont calculés séparément pour les travailleurs manuels et non manuels ainsi que par profession.

Durée du travail: se réfère à la durée normale du travail à plein temps sur une base annuelle, après déduction des heures rémunérées mais non travaillées, au titre de jours fériés officiels et de congés annuels et, autre temps libre offert rémunéré (au titre de réduction des heures annuelles de travail, de compensation pour travail accompli durant les jours fériés officiels et autres congés, de réunions et de congés de formation, etc.).

Les statistiques relatives aux heures contractuelles de travail ne sont pas publiées mais sont utilisées pour le calcul de l'indice des salaires horaires conventionnés.

Classifications
Branches d'activité économique:
Titre de la classification: Classification des activités économiques ATECO 91.

Nombre de groupes utilisés pour le codage: non disponible.

S'applique à: toutes les données.

Lien avec la CITI et niveau: ATECO correspond à la classification de l'activité économique de l'UE (NACE, rév. 1) au niveau de l'indicatif à quatre chiffres (indice per capita uniquement), elle-même directement liée à la CITI, rév. 3, au niveau de l'indicatif à deux chiffres.

Professions: les conventions collectives ne sont pas classées par profession, mais par catégorie de salariés (travailleurs manuels, travailleurs non manuels, cadres). La classification par profession est réalisée une fois par an par l'ISTAT, aux fins de l'Enquête d'octobre du BIT, en liant un certain nombre de variables et de codes contenus dans les conventions collectives (catégorie de salariés, niveau de qualifications, tâches et responsabilités, exemples de professions, etc.) aux descriptions des professions du BIT.

Autres classifications: selon le secteur de négociation collective.

Rassemblement des données
Type et couverture du système administratif: Les indices de salaire/traitement proviennent d'une large sélection des conventions collectives sur les salaires les plus appropriées, passées entre les syndicats et les associations d'employeurs. La série actuelle utilise 2'300 points-salaires fixés dans 80 conventions collectives sur un total de plus de 300 conventions.

Méthode de collecte des données: les données de base proviennent des registres officiels (lois, règlements) et des conventions collectives; pour les secteurs agricole et du bâtiment, elles sont tirées des conventions du travail au niveau des provinces. Les unités statistiques représentent un niveau salarial conventionné pour un groupe donné de fonctions, combiné souvent avec des indications relatives à l'ancienneté, l'âge ou les compétences dans les conventions collectives. Leurs caractéristiques ainsi que le nombre de salariés sont décidés au moment de la création de la base et demeurent inchangés jusqu'à ce qu'une nouvelle base soit élaborée. Une enquête spéciale est menée pour déterminer la structure durant l'année de base avec l'aide des associations d'employeurs et de travailleurs. L'enquête détermine les conventions collectives utilisées et leur distribution parmi des groupes de travailleurs. Plusieurs sources sont utilisées pour calculer le nombre de salariés par convention collective et selon l'ATECO: les comptes nationaux, l'enquête auprès de la main-d'œuvre et les registres de la Sécurité sociale.

Chaque contrat est mis à jour lors de son renouvellement. Les pondérations sont mises à jour tous les cinq ans.

Traitement et contrôle des données

Au sein des services chargés du calcul des indices des salaires conventionnés, chaque fonctionnaire est en charge de 6 à 13 conventions (en fonction du degré de difficulté). Un code est assigné à chaque composante de la rémunération (salaire de base, paiements compensatoires, prime pour ancienneté, autres primes, durée du travail, congés payés et autres congés, etc.). On utilise 311 codes, qui sont entrés sur ordinateur. Les résultats sont contrôlés par rapport au total de toutes les catégories de conventions. Les données sont traitées par informatique, en utilisant COBOL. ISTAT travaille actuellement à la mise à jour de la période de base des indices (décembre 2000'100), les données seront ensuite traitées avec ORACLE puis visualisée avec le langage PL/SQL.

Ajustements
Variations saisonnières: aucune; l'indice publié ne montre pas la saisonnalité, car les taux mensuels bruts pour chaque groupe de qualifications dans les conventions collectives comprennent toutes les composantes des salaires, telles qu'énumérées sous « Concepts et définitions », que l'on divise chaque mois par 12.

Types d'estimations
Indices des salaires/traitements;
Variations en pourcentage par rapport à la période précédente (variations conjoncturelles) et à la période correspondante de l'année précédente (tendances).
Chiffres annuels absolus des taux de salaire.

Calcul d'indices
L'indice des taux de salaire par travailleur mesure la variation des taux contractuels annuels. L'indice de la durée du travail contractuelle mesure la variation de la durée du travail que les salariés doivent effectuer au cours de l'année (vacances exclues). L'indice des taux horaires est calculé comme le ratio des deux indices. Chaque mois, les taux bruts de chaque groupe de qualifications dans les conventions collectives sont divisés par 12. Les indices correspondant à chaque groupe de qualification (cellules élémentaires) sont obtenus en divisant la valeur absolue des taux en vigueur et les taux moyens par les chiffres relatifs à la période de base (décembre 1995). Des indices agrégés sont calculés en appliquant aux indices élémentaires une formule de type Laspeyres. Les pondérations sont le multiple du nombre moyen de travailleurs au cours de l'année de base par le salaire correspondant au cours de la période de base.

Indicateurs de fiabilité des estimations
Couverture du système administratif: toutes les conventions collectives du travail sont représentées et les indices portent sur quelque 90% des employés.

Séries disponibles
Indices de salaire conventionné mensuels et horaires, par activité économique et groupes de classification;
Taux de variation par rapport à la période précédente et à la période correspondante de l'année précédente;
Valeurs absolues annuelles sur la structure des salaires et du coût de la main-d'œuvre dans certaines branches d'activité et emplois, de même que pour la durée du travail.

Historique des statistiques
Date de début de la série statistique: 1938.

Modifications et révisions principales: les pondérations sont mises à jour tous les cinq ans, de sorte à tenir compte des développements économiques.

Documentation et diffusion
Documentation:
Instituto Centrale di Statistica (ISTAT): *Comunicato Stampa*; communiqué de presse remis aux media lors d'une conférence de presse tenue 30 minutes avant la publication des données, distribué ensuite par fax et courrier électronique et placé sur le site Internet de l'ISTAT.

Les données sont généralement publiées dans un délai d'un mois et, au plus tard au cours du trimestre suivant la fin du mois de référence, à l'exception des données de janvier qui sont disponibles deux mois après la fin du mois de référence.

Idem: *Bolletino Mensile di Statistica*; contient les données mensuelles pour la période depuis 1992, relatives à l'indice total et aux indices des sections et des groupes de classification.

Idem: *Collana d'informazione "Lavoro e retribuzioni"* (Rome, mensuel); contient, une fois par année, une description méthodologique.

Les modifications ou révisions méthodologiques sont communiquées au moyen de communiqués de presse. Des informations détaillées concernant les modifications méthodologiques mises en place sont diffusées dans *Informazioni-*

Retribuzioni contrattuali, dont des copies peuvent être obtenues auprès de l'ISTAT.

Diffusion: sur le site Internet de l'ISTAT: http://www.istat.it
Des notes méthodologiques sont également disponibles sur ce site.

Données communiquées au BIT aux fins de diffusion
Les statistiques suivantes sont transmises au BIT pour publication dans l'Annuaire des statistiques du Travail:
Indices des taux de salaire horaires conventionnés, pour ouvriers et salariés, par activité économique.
Les données concernant les taux de salaire par profession sont publiées dans *Statistiques des salaires et de la durée du travail par professions et des prix de produits alimentaires – Résultats de l'Enquête d'octobre.*

Luxembourg

Source de la série
Relevés de l'Inspection générale de la Sécurité sociale (IGSS).

Titre de la série
Emploi intérieur salarié.

Organisme responsable
Collecte des données: Inspection générale de la Sécurité sociale.
Traitement statistique et publication/diffusion des statistiques: Service central de la Statistique et des Etudes économiques (STATEC).

Principaux sujets couverts
Emploi.

Périodicité ou fréquence de disponibilité des statistiques
Mensuelle.

Période de référence
Le mois complet.

Portée des statistiques
Géographique: l'ensemble du pays.
Branches d'activité: toutes les branches d'activité économique.
Etablissements: tous les établissements occupant une personne et plus.
Personnes: l'ensemble des salariés répondant au concept d'emploi intérieur salarié (voir ci-dessous).
Professions: les données ne sont pas recueillies sur les professions individuelles ou des groupes de professions.

Concepts et définitions
Emploi: l'emploi intérieur salarié couvre tous les salariés titulaires d'un contrat de travail auprès d'une unité institutionnelle résidente, qu'ils aient ou non leur résidence sur le territoire du Grand Duché, et assujettis au régime général de la Sécurité sociale. Sont inclus: les frontaliers étrangers, les travailleurs à domicile, les travailleurs intérimaires, temporaires ou saisonniers qui répondent à la définition, les apprentis et les militaires de carrière. Les frontaliers luxembourgeois qui travaillent dans un pays limitrophe ainsi que les fonctionnaires des institutions internationales considérées comme extra-territoriales sont exclus.

Classifications
Branches d'activité économique:
Titre de la classification: Nomenclature statistique des activités économiques dans la Communauté Européenne, NACE, Rév. 1.
Nombre de groupes utilisés pour le codage: publication au niveau à deux chiffres, sous réserve du secret statistique.
S'applique à: l'emploi intérieur salarié.
Lien avec la CITI et niveau: compatibilité entre la NACE, Rév. 1 et la CITI, Rév. 3 (1990) au niveau des sections (niveau à deux chiffres).
Situation dans la profession: au niveau du concept d'emploi intérieur, une distinction est faite entre emploi salarié (objet de la présente série) et emploi non salarié (travailleurs indépendants).
Autres classifications: par sexe.

Rassemblement des données
Type et couverture du système administratif: les fichiers administratifs de la Sécurité sociale couvrent l'ensemble des salariés, dans tous les établissements occupant au moins 1 salarié.
Méthode de collecte des données: en ce qui concerne les ouvriers et les employés du secteur privé, l'IGSS et le Centre informatique de la Sécurité sociale exploitent le fichier intégré des organismes de sécurité sociale (caisses de maladie et de pension). En ce qui concerne les fonctionnaires et assimilés (agents de l'Etat, des communes, des chemins de fer), l'exploitation sur informatique des fichiers est effectuée par les organismes responsables.
L'IGSS est responsable du contrôle des données et transmet mensuellement au STATEC les données globales, et annuellement les données par branche d'activité. Le STATEC procède aux

ajustements statistiques nécessaires (voir ci-dessous) et est responsable de la dissémination des données.

Traitement et contrôle des données
Les données sont traitées manuellement et par ordinateur.

Ajustements
Le STATEC procède aux ajustements suivants:
a) au niveau global, prise en compte des volontaires de l'armée (non compris dans les registres de sécurité sociale); b) au niveau des statistiques par branche, ajustement des chiffres de l'emploi pour les grandes entreprises relevant de plusieurs branches d'activité, étant donné que les registres de sécurité sociale se basent sur l'employeur et non sur l'activité économique.
Les travailleurs à temps partiel et les personnes occupant plus d'un emploi comptent chacun pour une personne, selon le Système européen des Comptes économiques intégrés (SEC-95).

Types d'estimations
Totaux mensuels et moyennes annuelles.

Calcul d'indices
Aucun.

Indicateurs de fiabilité des estimations
Couverture du système administratif: considéré comme exhaustif en ce qui concerne les salariés répondant à la définition ci-dessus.
Conformité avec d'autres sources: les estimations de l'emploi tirées des registres de l'IGSS sont comparées avec les résultats de l'enquête par sondage sur les forces de travail, ceux des enquêtes du STATEC auprès des entreprises, et les données administratives fournies par certains secteurs tels que le Groupement des industries sidérurgiques luxembourgeoises, l'Institut monétaire luxembourgeois, l'Association des compagnies d'assurances agréées, etc.

Séries disponibles
Emploi salarié, mensuel et en moyenne annuelle, par branche d'activité et par sexe.

Historique des statistiques
Date de début de la série statistique: 1970.
Modifications et révisions principales: une rupture a eu lieu en 1983, date à laquelle les répertoires de sécurité sociale concernant les ouvriers et employés ont été fusionnés et épurés des doubles comptages. Le STATEC a procédé à une ré-estimation de l'emploi salarié total pour les années antérieures à 1983.

Documentation et diffusion
Documentation:
STATEC: *Note trimestrielle de Conjoncture, la Situation économique au Grand-Duché* (Luxembourg);
Idem: *Annuaire Statistique du Luxembourg* (ibid.); publié environ cinq mois après l'année de référence des statistiques; contient également des notes méthodologiques.
Diffusion: sur Internet: http://www.statec.lu

Données communiquées au BIT aux fins de diffusion
Les statistiques suivantes sont publiées dans l'Annuaire des statistiques du Travail:
Estimations de l'emploi total par activité économique, partiellement basées sur cette source administrative.
Emploi rémunéré par activité économique.
Autres sources administratives de données:
Depuis avril 1988, les **fichiers administratifs de la Sécurité Sociale** constituent la source principale de données pour la statistique harmonisée des gains, en combinaison avec une enquête semestrielle auprès des entreprises. Des informations méthodologiques sur l'utilisation de cette source aux fins de la *Statistique harmonisée sur les gains bruts moyens* (octobre) sont disponibles dans:
BIT: *Sources et Méthodes - Statistiques du Travail*, Volume 2: Emploi, salaires, durée du travail et coût de la main-d'œuvre (enquêtes auprès des établissements) (deuxième édition, Genève, 1995).

Mexique

Source de la série
Institut de Sécurité sociale du Mexique (Instituto Mexicano del Seguro Social, IMSS), Rapport mensuel concernant les ayants droit (Informe Mensual de Población Derechohabiente).

Titre de la série
Travailleurs permanents et temporaires assurés inscrits auprès de l'IMSS; salaire moyen de base de cotisation de la population cotisante permanente et des travailleurs temporaires urbains.

Organisme responsable
Collecte des données et traitement statistique: Institut de Sécurité sociale du Mexique (IMSS).

Publication/diffusion des statistiques: Institut national de statistique, de géographie et de l'informatique (INEGI), et Secrétariat du Travail et de la Sécurité sociale (Secretaría del Traabajo y Previsión Social).

Principaux sujets couverts

Emploi et salaires.

Périodicité ou fréquence de disponibilité des statistiques

Mensuelle.

Période de référence

Chaque mois de l'année.

Portée des statistiques

Géographique: l'ensemble du pays.

Branches d'activité: toutes les branches d'activité économique.

Etablissements: de tous types et tailles, dans le secteur public et dans le secteur privé.

Personnes: salariés urbains permanents et temporaires inscrits auprès de l'IMSS. Sont exclus les groupes affiliés à un régime d'assurance voluntaire, les étudiants, les affiliés au maintien voluntaire et à l'assurance-santé familiale.

Professions: les données ne sont pas recueillies par profession individuelle.

Concepts et définitions

Emploi: s'applique aux assurés entrant dans la catégorie des salariés urbains permanents et temporaires. Les assurés permanents sont des employés d'usine, de commerce ou de tout autre type d'entreprise qui, en tant que travailleurs (salariés), ont droit à une couverture sociale. Les assurés urbains sont des personnes travaillant dans des entreprises ou des commerces implantés en zone urbaine, dont l'activité économique est orientée vers l'exploitation agricole, l'industrie, le commerce ou les services. Les assurés urbains temporaires sont, pour l'essentiel, des personnes travaillant dans l'industrie de la construction et dans d'autres secteurs industriels, sans pour autant être des travailleurs d'usine. Les travailleurs temporaires ou travailleurs agricoles sont des travailleurs saisonniers employés dans le secteur de l'agriculture.

Les séries publiées par le BIT ne portent que sur les travailleurs permanents.

Gains: salaires moyens de la population permanente cotisante. Le salaire moyen de base de cotisation comprend le paiement en espèces du salaire journalier ainsi que les pourboires, les indemnités, la nourriture, le logement, les primes, les commissions, les prestations en nature et toute autre somme ou prestation versée au travailleur en échange des services fournis.

En aucun cas ne seront pris en considération les salaires journaliers inférieurs au minimum général de la zone géographique concernée ou supérieurs à l'équivalent de 25 fois le salaire minimum général du District fédéral.

Durée du travail: données non recueillies.

Classifications:

Branches d'activité économique:

Titre de la classification: Liste des activités pour la classification des entreprises dans l'assurance contre les risques professionnels.

Nombre de groupes utilisés pour le codage: neuf grandes divisions, 55 groupes et 276 catégories d'activité économique.

S'applique à: toutes les données.

Lien avec la CITI et niveau: rév. 2, 1968.

Situation dans la profession: travailleurs permanents et temporaires urbains.

Autres classifications: par secteur d'activité économique, par zone géographique (urbaine et rurale), et par Etat.

Rassemblement des données

Type et couverture du système administratif:

Méthode de collecte des données: les informations proviennent de fichiers de données constitués à partir de documents émanant de l'IMSS, tels que les formulaires de demande d'affiliation et le détail des cotisations ouvrières-patronales fournis par les agences de recouvrement de l'IMSS.

Le nombre d'assurés est calculé à partir des formulaires de demande d'affiliation, auxquels on ajoute les anciens membres ainsi que les personnes ayant été réintégrées, et déduction faite des personnes qui ne sont plus affiliées, pour obtenir le fichier intitulé "Fichier général des assurés".

Mise à jour du système administratif: mensuelle.

Traitement et contrôle des données:

Non disponible.

Ajustements

Non disponible.

Types d'estimations

Total des travailleurs assurés, par catégorie; total et moyenne des rémunérations.

Calcul d'indices

Aucun.

Indicateurs de fiabilité des estimations

Couverture du système administratif: les séries des travailleurs couvrent l'ensemble des travailleurs recensés auprès de l'IMSS.

Le salaire moyen de cotisation correspond aux chiffres fournis par les employeurs aux fins de déterminer les cotisations à l'assurance-maladie et maternité.

Séries disponibles

Séries mensuelles:

– Travailleurs assurés, par catégorie (permanents, urbains et ruraux), et fluctuations annuelles;

– Travailleurs assurés de l'industrie de la construction, par catégorie, et fluctuations annuelles;

– Travailleurs permanents assurés, par branche d'activité économique et par région.

Historique des statistiques

Date de début de la série statistique: janvier 1977.

Modifications et révisions principales: non disponible.

Documentation et diffusion

Documentation:

INEGI: Mexican Bulletin of Statistical Information (México, trimestrielle); les données sont publiées deux mois après le mois auquel elles se réfèrent.

Diffusion: Sur le site Internet du Secrétariat du Travail et de la Sécurité sociale: http://www.stps.gob.mx et sur le site Internet de l'INEGI: http://www.inegi.gob.mx.

Données communiquées au BIT aux fins de diffusion

Les séries suivantes sont publiées dans l'Annuaire des statistiques du Travail:

– Emploi rémunéré, par branche d'activité économique;

– Gains journaliers moyens des salariés, par branche d'activité économique.

Norvège (1)

Source de la série

Association norvégienne des autorités locales et régionales.

Titre de la série

Personal Administrativt Informasjonssystem (PAI) (système d'information du personnel de l'Administration).

Organisme responsable

Collecte des données: Association norvégienne des autorités locales et régionales.

Traitement statistique et Publication/diffusion des statistiques: Association norvégienne des autorités locales et régionales et le Bureau de Statistiques de Norvège (Statistics Norway).

Principaux sujets couverts

Emploi, gains, taux de salaire et durée du travail.

Périodicité ou fréquence de disponibilité des statistiques

Annuelle.

Période de référence

Emplois et taux de salaire: 1er octobre.

Gains et durée du travail: la période de paie qui inclut le 1er octobre.

Portée des statistiques

Géographique: l'ensemble du pays, à l'exclusion de la municipalité d'Oslo.

Branches d'activité: administration publique (municipale et des comtés), entreprises municipales et de comtés, y compris les services sociaux et ceux de la santé. En sont exclus les enseignants (voir NORVEGE (2)), mais le personnel d'autres activités dans l'éducation municipale est inclus.

Etablissements: de tous types et de toutes tailles dans les secteurs publics couverts.

Personnes: salariés de l'administration municipale et des comtés, comme définis ci-dessus.

Professions: les données sont rassemblées selon les groupes professionnels suivants:

– employés administratifs

– employés techniques

– travailleurs manuels

– employés s'occupant de patients dans les hôpitaux, etc.

– employés dans d'autres professions de services.

Concepts et définitions

Emploi: se réfère à tous les employés de l'administration municipale et des comtés, ainsi qu'à ceux des entreprises municipales et appartenant aux comtés, membres de l'Association des autorités locales et régionales et qui sont affiliées à l'Association des conventions collectives au 1er octobre de l'année de référence. En sont exclus les employés de la municipalité d'Oslo. Les employés travaillant un minimum de 33 heures hebdomadaires sont considérés comme des employés à plein temps ; ceux qui travaillent moins d'heures sont considérés comme des employés à temps partiel.

Gains: les gains bruts mensuels se réfèrent aux salaires totaux en espèces conformément aux échelles de salaires en vigueur au 1er octobre de l'année de recensement, allocations fixes et variables en sus. Ne sont pas compris les paiements en nature ni les paiements au titre d'heures supplémentaires.

Taux de salaire ou de traitement: se réfèrent aux taux de salaire de base réellement payés par mois, non compris les allocations garanties et régulièrement versées et les paiements en nature.

Durée du travail: correspond à la durée normale du travail fixée dans les conventions collectives, les lois et les règlements.

Classifications
Branches d'activité économique:
Titre de la classification: Standard Industrial Classification (SIC94), Division 75 (administration publique municipale et des comtés).
Nombre de groupes utilisés pour le codage: ne s'applique pas.
S'applique à: toutes les données.
Lien avec la CITI et niveau: aucun.
Professions:
Titre de la classification: la classification est conforme à la classification utilisée par l'Association norvégienne des autorités locales et régionales, telle que désignée pour servir les intérêts des conventions collectives et refléter les échelles salariales.
Nombre de groupes utilisés pour le codage: 5.
S'applique à: toutes les données.
Lien avec la CITP et niveau: elle n'est pas nécessairement conforme à la Classification standard des Professions (C521) ni avec la CITP.
Autres classifications: emploi, gains, taux de salaire et durée du travail: par sexe et par catégorie d'employés, telles que plein temps/temps partiel et adultes / jeunes.
Les statistiques sont aussi classées par niveau d'éducation. Les informations sur l'éducation des personnes individuelles s'obtiennent du Registre de Statistics Norway sur le niveau le plus élevé d'éducation de la population (BHU). L'éducation est classée en fonction de la durée de celle-ci comme suit: éducation secondaire inférieure, éducation secondaire supérieure ; troisième niveau d'éducation (4 années ou moins), troisième niveau d'éducation (plus de 4 ans), inconnu ou éducation non achevée.
Les données concernant l'éducation sont disponibles un an plus tard.

Rassemblement des données
Type et couverture du système administratif: en 2000 le registre incluait 347 544 employés de l'administration municipale et de comtés (Oslo exclu).
Méthode de collecte des données: l'Association norvégienne des autorités locales et régionales reçoit des dossiers individuels des municipalités et des comtés sous forme électronique (disquettes) ou sur papier, qu'elle transmet sous forme électronique à Statistics Norway, conformément à la loi relative aux statistiques, section 3-2.
Mise à jour du système administratif: le Registre central est mis à jour une fois l'an par l'Association norvégienne des autorités locales et régionales.

Traitement et contrôle des données
Les données sont traitées aussi bien manuellement que par informatique.

Ajustements
Aucun.

Types d'estimations
Totaux et moyennes.

Calcul d'indices
Aucun.

Indicateurs de fiabilité des estimations
Couverture du système administratif: exhaustive, basée sur le recensement annuel de tous les employés de l'administration et des entreprises membres de l'Association norvégienne des autorités locales et régionales, à l'exception des employés de la municipalité d'Oslo, au 1er octobre de chaque année.
Erreurs non dues à l'échantillonnage: un rapport incorrect des déclarants à l'Association norvégienne des autorités locales et régionales et/ou des erreurs de traitement à la fois de l'Association et de Statistics Norway sont possibles. De plus, le registre

concernant le niveau d'éducation le plus élevé de la population peut comporter des erreurs de codage du niveau de l'éducation.
Conformité avec d'autres sources: ces statistiques sont comparables à d'autres statistiques salariales dressées depuis 1997.

Séries disponibles
Emploi total et gains mensuels moyens, taux de salaires et durée du travail hebdomadaire.

Historique des statistiques
Date de début de la série statistique: 1958.
Modifications et révisions principales: depuis 1990, les employés des services sociaux et de la santé sont inclus dans les statistiques. Depuis 1993, les statistiques excluent les employés de la municipalité d'Oslo.
Depuis 1997, les entreprises de distribution d'électricité sont exclues, en dépit du fait qu'elles soient membres de l'Association norvégienne des autorités locales et régionales. Elles sont incluses dans les statistiques des employés du secteur de l'électricité: (http://www.ssb.no/lonnkraft_en)
Ces statistiques peuvent être comparées rétroactivement jusqu'en 1997.

**Documentation et diffusion*:*
Documentation:
Statistics Norway: *NOS Wage Statistics* (Oslo, annuel); contient aussi des informations méthodologiques;
idem: *Statistical Yearbook* (ibid., annuel), publié dans les 6 mois après l'année de référence des statistiques.
Statistics Norway a publié des statistiques pour les années 1958, 1959, 1960, puis une année sur deux de 1962 à 1976, enfin annuellement depuis 1978.
Diffusion: sur le site Internet de Statistics Norway:
Statistiques salariales. Employés municipaux et des comtés:
http://www.ssb.no/lonnkomm_en/ (en norvégien et en anglais)
Groupe: 06.05. salaires et coûts de la main-d'œuvre;
http://www.ssb.no/english/subjects/06/05.
Les données n'apparaissant pas dans les publications nationales ou sur le site Internet sont disponibles sur demande.
Les statistiques salariales pour les employés de la section L de la classification industrielle standard (employés de l'administration centrale), sont diffusées sur: http://www.ssb.no/lonnstat_en (disponible en norvégien et en anglais).
Données communiquées au BIT aux fins de diffusion
Les statistiques suivantes sont publiées dans la publication *Statistiques des salaires et de la durée du travail par profession et des prix de produits alimentaires - Résultats de l'Enquête d'octobre*:
Durée du travail normale et salaires mensuels moyens pour les professions suivantes:
–   No. 139 – Agent administratif, b) autorité locale
–   No. 151 – Maître de jardin d'enfants
–   No. 154 – Infirmier diplômé (général)
–   No. 155 – Infirmier assistant.
Autres sources administratives de données: voir description No. 3 pour la Norvège.

Norvège (2)

Source de la série
Sentralt Tjenestemannsregister for Skoleverket (STS) (Registre central des employés de l'administration du système scolaire).
Titre de la série
Statistiques de l'emploi et des salaires dans le système scolaire (écoles du secteur public).
Organisme responsable
Collecte des données, traitement statistique et publication/ diffusion des statistiques: depuis 2002: Statistics Norway (Bureau de Statistiques de Norvège); avant 2002, Ministère du Travail et de l'Administration centrale (AAD).
Principaux sujets couverts
Emploi, salaires, taux de traitement et durée du travail.
Périodicité ou fréquence de disponibilité des statistiques
Annuelle.
Périodicité ou fréquence de disponibilité des statistiques
Emploi et taux de traitement: 1er octobre de chaque année;
Salaires et durée du travail: la période de paie incluant le 1er octobre.
Portée des statistiques
Géographique: l'ensemble du pays.

Branches d'activité: écoles publiques, c'est-à-dire toutes les écoles primaires municipales et du gouvernement central, les écoles secondaires supérieures de comtés et du gouvernement central (y compris les formations professionnelles), les centres du gouvernement central pour l'éducation spécialisée ainsi que les écoles secondaires (internats d'éducation secondaire supérieure et universitaire), aussi bien municipales de comté que privées.

Etablissements: de tous types et de toutes tailles, tels que décrits sous "Couverture industrielle".

Personnes: toutes les personnes employées dans les professions de l'éducation.

Professions: pour tout type d'école (voir sous Classifications), les professions suivantes sont identifiées:

- Proviseurs
- Maîtres principaux d'école professionnelle
- Maître principal
- Maîtres de conférences (de niveau secondaire et universitaire)
- Enseignants avec diplôme universitaire promus
- Enseignants avec diplôme universitaire
- Enseignants
- Enseignants sans la formation requise (écoles primaires et du secondaire inférieur)
- Autres professions.

Concepts et définitions

Emploi: se réfère à tous les employés professionnels de l'éducation dans les institutions décrites sous « Couverture industrielle » qui, en date du 1er octobre de l'année de référence, étaient employés conformément aux conventions passées entre le gouvernement central et les organisations des fonctionnaires, quel que soit le contrat (positions permanentes, positions avec risque de licenciement, positions temporaires et à durée déterminée).

Les employés de l'éducation privée (section M de la Classification industrielle standard) ne sont pas inclus dans les statistiques, mais couverts par une série statistique séparée (Lonnprivund).

Les employés qui travaillent au minimum 33 heures dans la semaine sont considérés comme des employés à plein temps ; ceux qui travaillent moins d'heures sont considérés comme des employés à temps partiel.

Gains: les salaires mensuels moyens se réfèrent aux échelles salariales au 1er octobre de l'année du recensement, y compris les allocations fixes et variables supplémentaires ainsi que les paiements en attente dus en septembre et versés en octobre.

Sont exclus les paiements en nature et les paiements au titre d'heures supplémentaires.

Taux de salaire ou de traitement: réfèrent aux taux de traitement effectivement payés dans le mois, excluant les allocations garanties et régulièrement versées et les paiements en nature.

Durée du travail: heures de travail normales, telles que fixées selon les conventions collectives, les lois et les règlements.

Classifications

Branches d'activité économique:

Titre de la classification: Classification industrielle standard (SIC94), Section M: écoles financées par le secteur public.

Nombre de groupes utilisés pour le codage: sept: écoles primaires ; écoles de niveaux primaire et secondaire combinés ; écoles du secondaire inférieur ; écoles pour enfants handicapés (écoles primaires) ; écoles du secondaire supérieur ; écoles secondaires traditionnelles; autres types d'écoles.

S'applique à: toutes les données.

Lien avec la CITI et niveau: aucun.

Occupation:

Titre de la classification: la classification est faite en accord avec les échelles salariales du gouvernement central en vigueur dès le 1er octobre de chaque année. Elle n'est pas nécessairement conforme à la Classification standard des professions (C521).

Nombre de groupes utilisés pour le codage: voir la liste des professions ci-dessus.

S'applique à: toutes les données.

Lien avec la CITP et niveau: aucun.

Autres classifications: emploi, gains, taux de traitement et durée du travail: par sexe et catégorie d'employé, telles que plein temps / temps partiel et adultes / jeunes.

Ces statistiques sont aussi classées en fonction du niveau de l'éducation. L'information sur l'éducation des personnes individuelles est obtenue du registre des statistiques de Norvège relatives au niveau de l'éducation le plus élevé de la population (BHU). L'éducation est classée en fonction de la durée des études comme suit: éducation secondaire inférieure, éducation secondaire supérieure, éducation de 3e degré (4 ans ou moins) ; éducation de 3e degré (plus de 4 ans) ; éducation inconnue ou non achevée.

Les données concernant l'éducation ont un décalage d'une année.

Rassemblement des données

Type et couverture du système administratif: en 2001 le registre incluait 99 074 employés dans les écoles publiques.

Méthode de collecte des données: le Ministère du Travail et de l'Administration centrale (AAD) reçoit des écoles les dossiers individuels sous forme électronique (disquettes) ou sur papier ; il transmet l'information sous forme électronique à Statistics Norway, conformément à la loi sur les statistiques, section 3-2.

Mise à jour du système administratif: le Registre central des employés de l'administration du système scolaire (STS) est mis à jour une fois l'an par le Ministère du Travail et de l'Administration centrale.

Traitement et contrôle des données

Les données sont traitées manuellement et par informatique. Les données concernant les traitements sont vérifiées manuellement et par informatique par AAD et Statistics Norway.

Ajustements

Aucun.

Types d'estimations

Totaux et moyennes.

Calculs d'indices

Aucun.

Indicateurs de fiabilité des estimations

Couverture du système administratif: exhaustive, basé sur le recensement annuel de tous les employés des groupes appropriés dès le 1er octobre de chaque année.

Erreurs non dues à l'échantillonnage: un rapport incorrect des déclarants de l'AAD et/ou des erreurs de traitement par AAD ou par Statistics Norway sont toujours possibles. De même, le registre concernant le niveau d'éducation le plus élevé peut contenir des erreurs de codage du niveau d'éducation.

Conformité avec d'autres sources: ces statistiques sont comparables à d'autres statistiques salariales dressées depuis 1997.

Séries disponibles

Emploi total et salaires mensuels moyens, taux de traitement et durée du travail hebdomadaire.

Historique des statistiques

Date de début de la série statistique: 1973.

Modifications et révisions principales: aucune. Les statistiques peuvent être comparées rétroactivement jusqu'en 1973.

Documentation et diffusion

Documentation:

Statistics Norway: *NOS Wage Statistics* (Oslo, annuel); contient aussi des informations méthodologiques;

Idem: *Statistical Yearbook* (ibid., annuel), publié dans les 6 mois suivant l'année de référence statistique.

Les statistiques ont été publiées par Statistics Norway en 1959, 1963, 1967, et annuellement depuis 1973.

Diffusion: sur le site Internet de Statistics Norway: http://www.ssb.no/lonnkomm_en/ (disponible en anglais et en norvégien).

Les données qui n'apparaissent pas dans les publications nationales ou sur le site Internet sont disponibles sur demande.

Les statistiques salariales des employés dans l'éducation privée (basées sur un échantillonnage d'entreprises) sont disponibles sur: http://www.ssb.no/lonnprivund_en

Données communiquées au BIT aux fins de diffusion

Les statistiques suivantes sont publiées dans *Statistiques des salaires et de la durée du travail par profession et des prix de produits alimentaires – Résultats de l'Enquête d'octobre*:

Salaires mensuels moyens pour les professions suivantes:

- No.147 - Professeur de langues et de littérature (second degré).
- No.148 - Professeur de mathématiques (second degré).
- No.150 - Enseignant du premier degré.

Les données pour la profession No.151 - *maître de jardin d'enfants*, proviennent de l'Association norvégienne des autorités locales et régionales, celles pour la profession No. 149 – *Professeur d'enseignement technique (second degré)*, proviennent du Registre central d'Etat des employés de l'administration (universités et institutions équivalentes).

Autres sources administratives de données: voir description No. 3 pour la Norvège.

Norvège (3)

Source de la série
Statens Sentrale Tjenestemannsregister (SST) (Registre central de l'Etat des employés du gouvernement).

Titre de la série
Statistiques de l'emploi et des salaires des employés du gouvernement.

Organisme responsable
Collecte des données, traitement statistique et publication/diffusion des statistiques: depuis 2002: Statistics Norway (Bureau de Statistiques de Norvège); auparavant, Ministère du Travail et de l'Administration centrale (AAD).

Principaux sujets couverts
Emplois, gains, taux de salaire et durée du travail.

Périodicité ou fréquence de disponibilité des statistiques
Annuelle.

Période de référence
Emploi et taux de salaire: 1er octobre.
Gains et durée du travail: la période de paie qui inclut le 1er octobre.

Portée des statistiques
Géographique: l'ensemble du pays.
Branches d'activité: l'administration publique et la défense, les entreprises gouvernementales, les services de la santé ainsi que les université et institutions équivalentes.
Etablissements: de tous types et toutes tailles du secteur public couvert.
Personnes: employés du gouvernement.
Professions: les groupes professionnels sont définis en conformément aux grilles de salaires gouvernement central:

Professions publiées, Gouvernement central
Ministères: Directeurs généraux adjoints ; Directeurs généraux assistants ; Chefs de départements ; Conseillers ; Cadres supérieurs ; Cadres moyens ; Cadres juniors ; Secrétaires de bureau.

Autres départements de l'administration centrale:
Directeur général adjoint ; Assistant Directeur général ; Chefs de départements ; Conseillers ; Ingénieurs en chef ; Cadres supérieurs ; Cadres : Cadres juniors ; Secrétaires de bureau ; Employés de bureau.

Universités et institutions équivalentes: Professeurs ; Professeurs assistants, premier grade ; Professeurs assistants ; Chargés de recherche ; Enseignants titulaires d'un diplôme de fin d'études universitaires ; Boursiers ; Autres professions de l'éducation ; Emplois administratifs ; Cadres supérieurs ; Personnel de bureau.

Services de la santé: Médecins chefs ; Chefs de cliniques ; Biologistes ; Cadres ; Personnel de bureau ; Infirmiers spécialisés ; Infirmiers professionnels ; Infirmiers assistants.

Autres fonctionnaires:
Le clergé: Doyens ; Pasteurs ; Vicaires ; Catéchistes.
Le judiciaire: Juge principal ; Juges municipaux, juges de district, juge de circonscription ; Officiers d'état civil ; Cadres ; Personnel de bureau.
Administration des prisons: Services de la sécurité ; Fonctionnaires de prison ; Cadres ; Personnel de bureau.
Forces de la police et services de police rurale: Commissaires de police de quartier ; Commissaires assistants ; Inspecteurs ; Brigadiers ; Sergents ; Commissaires de police de quartier, avec grade spécial ; Assistants policiers de quartier ; Cadres supérieurs ; Personnel de bureau.
Administration du marché du travail: Chefs des offices de l'emploi ; Cadres ; Personnel de bureau.
Administration des assurances sociales: Chef des départements des assurances ; Cadres ; Personnel de bureau.
Prélèvement de l'impôt, registres de la population: Fonctionnaires des impôts ; Secrétaires ; Cadres.
Services des douanes, administration locale administration: Inspecteurs des douanes ; Fonctionnaires d'inspection des douanes, grade inférieur ; Cadres ; Personnel de bureau.

Entreprises d'Etat:
Administration du réseau routier: Ingénieurs ; Cadres ; Employés de bureau ; Inspecteurs ; Contremaîtres ; Ouvriers qualifiés ; Ouvriers spécialisés.
Administration de l'aviation civile: Officiers du contrôle de trafic ; Officiers d'aéroport ; Assistants du contrôle de trafic aérien ; Ingénieurs.
Défense: Personnel civil ; Personnel militaire.
Concepts et définitions

Emploi: se réfère à tous les employés du gouvernement central employés dans des positions gouvernementales au 1er octobre de l'année de recensement.
Les employés travaillant un minimum de 33 heures hebdomadaires sont considérés comme des employés à plein temps; ceux qui travaillent moins d'heures sont considérés comme des employés à temps partiel.
Gains: réfèrent aux salaires mensuels bruts totaux conformément aux échelles salariales en date du 1er octobre de l'année de recensement, y compris les allocations fixes et variables dues en septembre et versées en octobre. En sont exclus tous les paiements en nature et les paiements au titre d'heures supplémentaires.
Taux de salaire ou de traitement: se réfèrent aux taux salariaux effectivement payés par mois, excluant les allocations garanties et les paiements en nature.
Durée du travail: durée normale du travail fixée dans les conventions collectives, les lois et les règlements.

Classifications
Branches d'activité économique:
Titre de la classification: Classification industrielle standard (SIC94).
Nombre de groupes utilisés pour le codage: sept: ministères: (y compris le Bureau du Premier ministre et le Bureau de l'auditeur général); les autres départements de l'administration centrale, les autres services civils, les universités et institutions équivalentes, les entreprises gouvernementales; la défense ainsi que les services de la santé.
S'applique à: toutes les données.
Lien avec la CITI et niveau: aucun.
Professions:
Titre de la classification: la classification est conforme aux grilles de salaires du gouvernemental central au 1er octobre de chaque année. Elle n'est pas nécessairement conforme à la Classification standard des Professions (C521).
Nombre de groupes utilisés pour le codage: voir liste des professions ci-dessus.
S'applique à: toutes les données.
Lien avec la CITP et niveau: aucun.
Autres classifications: emplois, gains, taux de salaire et durée du travail: par sexe et par catégorie d'employé, telles que plein temps / temps partiel et adultes / jeunes.
Les statistiques sont également classées selon le niveau de l'éducation. L'information sur l'éducation des personnes provient du Registre de Statistics Norway concernant le degré le plus élevé de l'éducation (BHU). L'éducation est classée selon la durée de l'éducation de la manière suivante: éducation secondaire inférieure ; éducation secondaire supérieure, troisième niveau (4 ans voire moins) ; troisième niveau (plus de 4 ans) ; éducation inconnue ou inachevée.
Les données concernant l'éducation sont communiqués avec une année de retard.

Rassemblement des données
Type et couverture du système administratif: en 2001, le registre comprenait 136 152 personnes employées par l'administration publique centrale.
Méthode de collecte des données: le Ministère du Travail et de l'Administration centrale (AAD) reçoit des dossiers individuels des services /institutions sous forme électronique (disquettes) ou sur papier ; il transmet ces informations sous forme électronique à Statistics Norway, conformément à la loi sur les statistiques, section 3-2.
Mise à jour du système administratif: Le Registre central est mis à jour une fois par an.
Traitement et contrôle des données
Les données sont traitées manuellement et par informatique. Les données concernant les salaires sont vérifiées manuellement par AAD et par Statistics Norway.

Ajustements
Aucun.

Types d'estimations
Totaux et moyennes.

Calcul d'indices
Aucun.

Indicateurs de fiabilité des estimations
Couverture du système administratif: exhaustive, basée sur le recensement annuel de tous les employés des secteurs publics couverts au 1er octobre de chaque année.
Erreurs non dues à l'échantillonnage: un rapport incorrect des déclarants à l'ADD et/ou des erreurs de traitement de la part de

AAD et de Statistics Norway sont toujours possibles. De plus, le Registre concernant le niveau d'éducation le plus élevé peut contenir des erreurs de codage du niveau d'éducation.

Conformité avec d'autres sources: ces statistiques sont comparables à d'autres statistiques salariales depuis 1997.

Séries disponibles

Emploi total et gains mensuels moyens, taux de salaire et durée du travail hebdomadaire.

Historique des statistiques

Date de début de la série statistique: 1973.

Modifications et révisions principales: aucun. Ces statistiques sont comparables rétroactivement jusqu'en 1973.

Documentation et diffusion

Documentation:

Statistics Norway: *NOS Wage Statistics* (Oslo, annuel); contient des informations méthodologiques;

Idem: *Statistical Yearbook* (ibid., annuel), publié dans les 6 mois après l'année de référence.

Statistics Norway a publié des statistiques pour les années 1959, 1963 et 1967, puis annuellement à partir de 1973.

Diffusion: sur le site Internet de Statistics Norway:

http://www.ssb.no/lonnkomm_en/ et **http://www.ssb.no/lonnstat**

Les données n'apparaissent ni dans les publications nationales ni sur le site Internet sont disponibles sur demande.

Données communiquées au BIT aux fins de diffusion

Les données suivantes sont publiées dans la publication *Statistiques des salaires et de la durée du travail par profession et des prix de produits alimentaires – Résultats de l'Enquête d'octobre*: Durée normale du travail et salaires mensuels moyens pour les professions suivantes:

No. 139 – Agent administratif a) Gouvernement central.

No. 149 – Professeur d'enseignement (second degré).

Autres sources administratives de données: un certain nombre de statistiques économiques et sociales sont établies sur la base de divers registres détenus par différents ministères, administrations et institutions, et notamment:

(1)Le *Registre des Certificats de fin d'année,* maintenu par l'Administration fiscale: il fournit les statistiques des revenus bruts totaux et moyens de toutes les personnes ayant un emploi (*Lonnssummer fra lonns-og trekkoppgaveregisteret*). Les revenus moyens bruts comprennent tous les traitements et les salaires dus au titre du travail du temps travaillé, du travail fourni et des périodes de congé, des congés payés, primes et autres rémunérations payées au cours de l'exercice. Les données sont classées par branche d'activité économique, sexe, groupe d'âge, tailles d'établissements et région.

Les données proviennent des certificats de fin d'année que les employeurs sont tenus de remplir pour tout employé au début de chaque année, faisant référence à l'année précédente, et de transmettre à l'administration fiscale. Les données relatives aux revenus sont vérifiées par l'administration fiscale, et une copie des dossiers contrôlés est communiquée à Statistics Norway pour d'autres contrôles de qualité et un traitement statistique. Les séries statistiques ont commencé en 1990 et sont annuelles. Les données sont disponibles sur le site Internet de Statistics Norway:

http://www.ssb.no/english/subjects/06/05/lonnltreg_en

(2) Des statistiques relatives aux revenus des personnes physiques et des familles sont compilées annuellement sur la base de différents registres administratifs et de sources de données statistiques (ex.: les déclarations d'impôts, le Registre des impôts, le Registre des certificats de fin d'année, l'Administration nationale des Assurances, le ministère des Affaires sociales, le fonds d'Etat de prêts à l'éducation, les statistiques de l'éducation, etc.) couvrant l'ensemble de la population au 31 décembre de l'année fiscale. Elles fournissent des informations détaillées sur les revenus provenant de différentes sources (ex.: revenu au titre de l'emploi, pensions, capital), y compris le revenu non imposable qui figure dans les registres, tel que allocations de logement, assistance sociale, bourses et allocations en espèces pour les parents d'enfants en bas âge. Les unités statistiques courantes sont la personne physique et la famille, et des statistiques sont compilées sur la distribution des revenus et leurs niveaux pour différents groupes de la population et régions. La base de données permet également de fournir des renseignements relatifs au revenu pour d'autres enquêtes statistiques, telles que l'Enquête sur les conditions de vie ainsi que le Recensement de la population et du logement de 2001.

Les statistiques et des informations méthodologiques sont disponibles sur le site de Statistics Norway:

http://www.ssb.no/english/subjects/05/01.

Elles sont publiées dans:

NOS C649- Income Statistics for Persons and Families 1993-1998.

(3) le *Registre des employeurs et des salariés* fournit des données annuelles relatives au nombre de salariés et à leur durée de travail hebdomadaire attendue. Sont inclus tous les salariés pour lesquels la durée attendue du travail est supérieure à six jours et les heures hebdomadaires supérieures à trois. Les données de l'emploi sont classées par branche d'activité économique conformément à la nouvelle classification industrielle standard (New Standard Industrial Classification) depuis 1995 (avant 1995, conformément à la Classification industrielle standard), par sexe, groupe d'âge, niveau d'éducation, région, pays de naissance et nombre d'années de résidence en Norvège; les heures de travail sont classées par région et par sexe.

Ce registre est tenu par l'Institution nationale des assurances, qui en transmet copie à Statistics Norway une fois l'an, et procède à des mises à jour hebdomadaires tout au long de l'année. Des contrôles de qualité sont effectués par rapport au Registre central de la population, et des ajustements faits pour tenir compte des doubles comptages des travailleurs occupant plusieurs emplois. Les séries statistiques sont disponibles depuis 1983. Depuis 1992, les professions liées à la mer sont incluses; en 1994, la période de référence est passée du 2e au 4e trimestre de chaque année; en 1995 une nouvelle Classification industrielle standard était introduite.

Les statistiques sont publiées dans: Statistics Norway: *Labour Market Statistics* (Oslo, annuel), et disponibles sur le site Internet:

http://www.ssb.no/english/subjects/06/01

Des informations méthodologiques sont disponibles sur le site Internet de Statistics Norway, sous la rubrique « About the statistics ».

Nouvelle-Calédonie

Source de la série

Fichiers de la Caisse de Compensation des Prestations Familiales, des Accidents du Travail et Prévoyance des Travailleurs de Nouvelle-Calédonie et Dépendances (CAFAT).

Titre de la série

L'emploi et les salaires en Nouvelle-Calédonie.

Organisme responsable

Collecte des données: Caisse de Compensation des Prestations Familiales, des Accidents du Travail et Prévoyance des Travailleurs de Nouvelle-Calédonie et Dépendances (CAFAT) et Direction des Services Fiscaux (DSF).

Traitement et publication/diffusion des statistiques: Institut de la Statistique et des Etudes Economiques (ISEE), Nouvelle-Calédonie.

Principaux sujets couverts

Emploi salarié, salaires et durée d'emploi.

Périodicité ou fréquence de disponibilité des statistiques

Emploi salarié: trimestrielle;

Salaires: annuelle ;

Durée d'emploi: annuelle.

Période de référence

Emploi salarié: le trimestre;

Salaires et durée d'emploi: l'année.

Portée des statistiques

Géographique: l'ensemble du territoire.

Branches d'activité: toutes les branches d'activité économique, y compris les services domestiques.

Etablissements: établissements de tous types et de toutes tailles.

Personnes: l'ensemble des salariés, et l'ensemble des employeurs, immatriculés à la CAFAT.

Professions: dans la statistique des salaires, les données sont recueillies par catégories socioprofessionnelles.

Concepts et définitions

Emploi: emploi salarié: se réfère à l'ensemble des salariés de Nouvelle-Calédonie, hors apprentis et stagiaires.

Dans les statistiques des salaires: les effectifs salariés annuels, ou nombre d'emplois, incluent les salariés ayant travaillé pour plus d'un employeur dans l'année; ils sont comptés autant de fois que de nombre d'emplois. L'effectif moyen annuel, ou équivalent permanent à temps plein, correspond à l'effectif théorique de salariés à temps plein pendant toute l'année.

Gains: se réfèrent à la masse salariale brute annuelle, c'est à dire l'ensemble des salaires nets, y compris émoluments, congés payés, avantages en nature ou en espèces et primes, augmenté des cotisations salariales des salariés.

Le salaire moyen mensuel correspond à la masse salariale de l'année ramenée à un salarié à temps plein pendant un mois.

Durée du travail: correspond à la durée d'emploi (en mois) d'un salarié sur une année.

Classifications

Branches d'activité économique:

Titre de la classification: Nomenclature d'Activité ISEE.

Nombre de groupes utilisés pour le codage: 39 postes, après passage de la nomenclature des activités CAFAT aux secteurs d'activité et activités ISEE.

S'applique à: l'ensemble des données.

Lien avec la CITI et niveau: aucun.

Professions: dans la statistique sur les salaires, deux nomenclatures sont utilisées:

Titre de la classification: Nomenclature de Qualification Professionnelle ISEE.

Nombre de groupes utilisés pour le codage: 10, après passage de la nomenclature des catégories socioprofessionnelles aux qualifi-cations professionnelles ISEE.

S'applique à: l'ensemble des données.

Lien avec la CITP et niveau: aucun.

Situation dans la profession:

Titre de la classification: Nomenclature des Catégories Socio-professionnelles et des Qualifications dans la fonction publique.

Nombre de groupes utilités pour le codage: 80 au niveau le plus détaillé.

S'applique à: l'ensemble des données.

Lien avec la CISP et niveau: aucun.

Autres classifications:

emploi salarié trimestriel: région (Nouméa, et Intérieur et Iles ensemble), et province;

Statistique des salaires: sexe, âge, durée d'emploi, secteur d'activité, zone géographique, taille d'établissements, et classifications croisées.

Rassemblement des données

Type et couverture du système administratif: collecte exhaustive auprès des employeurs.

Méthode de collecte des données: deux sources principales sont utilisées. Le Fichier des déclarations nominatives fournies trimestriellement par les employeurs à la CAFAT, qui contient des informations sur l'emploi, la durée d'emploi et les salaires du secteur privé; et le fichier des déclarations nominatives des salaires de la Direction des Services Fiscaux, qui contient notamment les effectifs et salaires des fonctionnaires.

Pour la statistique des salaires, l'ISEE procède à des ajustement de ces fichiers pour construire un fichier uniforme sur l'ensemble des salaires. En effet, les données de salaires du fichier CAFAT correspondent à des valeurs brutes, éventuellement tronquées car limitées à la valeur du plafond, tandis que celles du fichier de la DSF ne sont pas plafonnées mais représentent des valeurs de salaires nets. Les salaires des fichiers CAFAT inférieurs au plafond sont extraits sans modification et ceux qui apparaissent plafonnés sont recalculés: dans une première phase, le calcul consiste à apparier ces salaires avec les salaires déclarés dans le fichier DSF, en utilisant un identifiant constitué du sexe, de la date de naissance et de l'employeur de chaque salarié concerné. Dans une seconde phase, un calcul de détermination des salaires bruts est opéré sur les fichiers de la DSF, en calculant les charges sociales afférentes à chaque salaire. L'employeur étant connu, les valeurs de ces cotisations sociales sont soit directement extraites des fichiers des différents organismes sociaux précités, soit calculées par application des règles de calcul qui les définissent (contribution exceptionnelle de solidarité), soit enfin estimées (retraites complémentaires). Les valeurs globales des cotisations sociales ainsi déterminées sont ensuite confrontées, pour être validées, aux chiffres publiés dans les rapports d'activité, comptes d'exploitation et autres documents administratifs des organismes concernés (diverses mutuelles, Caisse de Retraite des Expatriés (CRE).

Mise à jour du système administratif: trimestrielle.

Traitement et contrôle des données

Les données sont traitées par ordinateur.

Pour la statistique des salaires, la collaboration du Service des Méthodes administratives et de l'Informatique (SMAI) a été obtenue pour enrichir les classifications d'emploi des salariés du secteur public de l'année 1995 et a servi de base pour l'année 1999. Des contrôles de cohérence sont effectués entre salaires et durées d'emploi provenant des différents fichiers.

Ajustements

Non disponible.

Doubles comptages: les fichiers CAFAT et DSF non nominatifs dont dispose l'ISEE ne permettent pas de déterminer à combien de salariés correspondent les différents salaires (un même salarié peut

avoir travaillé dans l'année chez différents employeurs, successivement ou simultanément). Alors que le Recensement de Population de Nouvelle-Calédonie de 1996 répertoriait 53,944 salariés, les fichiers CAFAT et DSF en dénombrent 79,893. Afin de minimiser les erreurs sur les durées d'emploi et de mieux appréhender les niveaux de salaire, des statistiques sont également établies sur la base des salariés rémunérés par un même employeur pendant les 12 mois de l'année (non compris les services domestiques).

Types d'estimations

Statistique de l'emploi salarié: nombre de salariés inscrits chaque trimestre, et séparément, nombre d'employeurs inscrits.

Statistique des salaires:

Durée d'emploi (en mois) d'un salarié: nombre d'heures d'emploi divisé par 169, durée légale d'un mois à temps plein;

Durée moyenne d'emploi (en mois): somme des durées d'emploi de tous les salariés de l'année, divisée par le nombre d'emploi. La somme des durées d'emploi de l'ensemble des salariés est égale au produit de l'effectif salarié annuel par la durée moyenne d'emploi, ou encore au produit de l'effectif moyen annuel par 12.

Effectif moyen annuel ou équivalent permanents à temps plein: somme des durées d'emploi (en mois) de tous les salariés de l'année divisée par 12.

Salaire moyen mensuel: masse salariale divisée par l'effectif moyen annuel, divisé par 12.

Distributions et répartitions des emplois, des salaires et de la durée d'emploi selon diverses variables.

Calcul d'indices

Aucun.

Indicateurs de fiabilité des estimations

Couverture du système administratif: supérieure à 99% en termes de salariés.

Erreurs non dues à l'échantillonnage: dans la statistique des salaires, des erreurs peuvent se produire au niveau de la durée d'emploi des salariés: le fichier de la DSF ne fournit pas toujours la durée d'emploi; aucun des deux fichiers, CAFAT et DSF, ne fournit toute l'information sur la durée de travail (nombre d'heures, temps partiel, mi-temps, plein temps). Le salaire mensuel est donc estimé en divisant le salaire par le nombre de mois d'emploi. Cette estimation présente l'inconvénient de sous-estimer le niveau réel du salaire mensuel des salariés travaillant à temps partiel. La durée d'emploi des salariés déclarés à la DSF est parfois entachée d'erreur. Pour réduire au maximum l'erreur d'évaluation de la durée d'emploi et donner plus de fiabilité à la valeur du salaire mensuel, une minutieuse mise en correspondance des différents fichiers de l'année 1999 a été effectuée, et 8,685 durées d'emploi ont pu être rectifiées.

Conformité avec d'autres sources: des comparaisons des effectifs salariés ont été établies avec les résultats du Recensement de Population de Nouvelle-Calédonie du 16 avril 1996.

Séries disponibles

Statistique trimestrielle de l'emploi salarié: nombre de salariés et nombre d'employeurs, par branche d'activité économique et région;

Statistique des salaires:

Nombre d'emplois par zone géographique, secteur d'activité et activité, par niveau de salaire et âge, et classifications croisées;

Salaires par secteur d'activité et activité, par âge, par sexe et âge, par zone géographique et classifications croisées;

Distributions des emplois par durée d'emploi, niveau de salaire, qualification professionnelle,

Historique des statistiques

Date de début de la série statistique: non disponible.

Modifications et révisions principales: non disponible.

Documentation et diffusion

Documentation:

ISEE: *Informations statistiques* (Nouméa, trimestriel); présente les statistiques de l'emploi salarié pour le trimestre précédent;

Idem: *ISEE: Les Salaires - Situation en 1999* (Nouméa, octobre 2001); contient les statistiques et des informations méthodologiques.

Données communiquées au BIT aux fins de diffusion

Des statistiques sur l'emploi rémunéré (ensemble des activités économiques) sont publiées dans *l'Annuaire des statistiques du travail*; les données trimestrielles correspondantes (séparément pour les salariés et l'ensemble de l'effectif occupé) sont publiées dans le *Bulletin des statistiques du Travail*.

Pakistan

Source de la série
Rapports administratifs du Gouvernement.
Titre de la série
Salaires moyens par profession.
Organisme responsable
Collecte des données et traitement statistique: Directions des services de la Protection du Travail (Directorates of Labour Welfare), par l'intermédiaire des gouvernements de chaque province du Pakistan: Baloutchistan, Pendjab, Sind, Province frontière du Nord-Ouest, et Islamabad.
Principaux sujets couverts
Emploi, taux de salaire ou de traitement, gains et durée du travail.
Périodicité ou fréquence de disponibilité des statistiques
Annuelle.
Période de référence
Salaires ou traitements par profession: un mois.
Portée des statistiques
Géographique: chaque province du Pakistan prise séparément. La présente description ne couvre que la Province frontière du Nord-Ouest (NWFP).
Branches d'activité: NWFP: 29 groupes de branches d'activité sélectionnées.
Etablissements: établissements et usines visés par la loi sur les usines (Factories Act), 1934, et la loi sur les salaires (Wages Act), 1936.
Personnes: salariés visés par la loi sur les usines, 1934 et la loi sur les salaires, 1936.
Professions: NWFP: 76 professions sélectionnées dans les 29 groupes de branches de d'activité.
Concepts et définitions
Emploi: les salariés sont les personnes employées en contrepartie d'un salaire dans toute industrie manufacturière, entreprise commerciale ou tout autre établissement.
Les travailleurs à plein temps sont ceux qui sont employés pour la durée du travail spécifiée par les lois.
Gains: il s'agit des gains journaliers et mensuels nets, après déduction des cotisations de sécurité sociale versées par les salariés – pour autant que ces gains soient supérieurs à 2500,00 roupies par mois. Ils englobent les salaires directs payés en espèces pour la durée du travail effective ou pour le travail effectué, et les indemnités d'indexation sur l'évolution du coût de la vie, de logement et de transport. Les paiements en nature sont exclus.
Les données relatives aux gains sont collectées séparément pour les ouvriers, les employés et les travailleurs à plein temps.
Taux de salaire ou de traitement: il s'agit des taux de salaire/traitement journaliers de base, y compris les indemnités d'indexation sur le coût de la vie et autres indemnités garanties et payées régulièrement - pour autant que ces taux soient supérieurs à 2500,00 roupies par mois. Les taux de salaire en nature sont exclus.
Les données relatives aux taux de salaire/traitement sont collectées séparément pour les ouvriers, les employés et les travailleurs à plein temps.
Durée du travail: il s'agit de la durée de travail normale fixée par les lois ou dispositions réglementaires. La durée du travail normale est de 48 heures par semaine et de 9 heures par jour, comme le précisent les sections 34 et 36 de la loi sur les usines de 1934, et la section 7 de l'ordonnance sur les magasins, ateliers, bureaux et établissements du Pakistan occidental de 1969 (West Pakistan shops and establishments Ordinance, 1969).
Classifications
Branches d'activité économique:
Titre de la classification: Pakistan Standard Industrial Classification of all economic activities (CCISP-70) (Classification industrielle type de toutes les branches d'activité du Pakistan).
Nombre de groupes utilisés pour le codage: 29.
S'applique à: taux de salaire ou de traitement et gains.
Lien avec la CITI et niveau: rév. 2, aux niveaux à deux ou trois chiffres.
Profession:
Titre de la classification: Pakistan Standard Classification of Occupations (PSCO-68) (Classification type des professions du Pakistan).
Nombre de groupes utilisés pour le codage: 76.
S'applique à: taux de salaire/traitement et gains.
Lien avec la CITP et niveau: CITP-1968, aux niveaux à deux et trois chiffres.

Autres classifications: par sexe, niveau d'éducation et catégorie de salariés.
Rassemblement des données:
Type et couverture du système administratif: Ces rapports administratifs sont limités à la collecte d'informations statistiques sur des professions présélectionnées dans des groupes de branches d'activité présélectionnés.
Méthode de collecte des données: les inspecteurs du travail des bureaux extérieurs des Directions de la Protection du Travail collectent les données sur les salaires par profession dans les usines et établissements pertinents.
Traitement et contrôle des données
Les données sont traitées manuellement.
Ajustements
Aucun.
Types d'estimations
Emploi total, taux de salaire et gains moyens et durée du travail.
Calcul d'indices
Aucun.
Indicateurs de fiabilité des estimations
Non disponible.
Séries disponibles
Moyennes des taux de salaire/traitement et gains et de la durée du travail par profession.
Historique des statistiques
Date de début de la série statistique: 1980.
Modifications et révisions principales: aucune.
Documentation et diffusion:
Documentation: ces statistiques ne sont pas diffusées dans des publications nationales.
Données communiquées au BIT aux fins de diffusion
Des statistiques sur les taux de salaire/traitement moyens et la durée du travail normale sont communiquées au BIT aux fins de publication dans *Statistiques des salaires et de la durée du travail par profession et des prix de produits alimentaires - Résultats de l'Enquête d'octobre:*
Des statistiques sur les gains mensuels moyens dans l'industrie manufacturière et les transports sont publiées dans l'*Annuaire des statistiques du Travail*.

Panama

Source de la série
Bordereaux de cotisations des Institutions de Sécurité sociale.
Titre de la série
Séries sur l'emploi.
Organisme responsable
Collecte des données, traitement statistique et publication/ diffusion des statistiques: Dirección de Estadística y Censo, Contraloría General de la República (Direction de la Statistique et du Recensement, Contrôleur général de la République).
Principaux sujets couverts
Emploi et gains.
Périodicité ou fréquence de disponibilité des statistiques
Annuelle.
Période de référence
Le mois d'août.
Portée des statistiques
Géographique: l'ensemble du pays.
Branches d'activité: toutes les branches d'activité économique.
Etablissements: de tous types et tailles.
Personnes: salariés cotisant à la Sécurité sociale et employés des institutions de l'Etat.
Professions: les données ne sont recueillies ni par profession individuelle ni par catégories professionnelles.
Concepts et définitions
Emploi: tout salarié cotisant à la Sécurité sociale, c'est-à-dire toute personne travaillant pour une autre personne ou entité et percevant une rémunération en espèces, pour autant qu'elle ait travaillé un jour, quel qu'il soit, au cours du mois de référence.
Gains: salaires et traitements bruts mensuels en espèces; autrement dit, rémunérations perçues par le salarié pour son travail au cours de la période de référence, y compris le paiement des heures supplémentaires, du temps non travaillé et des commissions.
Classifications
Branches d'activité économique:
Titre de la classification: Classification nationale type par industrie pour toutes les activités économiques.
Nombre de groupes utilisés pour le codage: 18 catégories.

S'applique à: emploi et rémunération dans les entreprises privées.
Lien avec la CITI et niveau rév.3 (1990) à tous les niveaux.
Professions:
Titre de la classification: Classification nationale des professions.
Nombre de groupes utilisés pour le codage: 10 groupes.
S'applique à: Emploi dans les institutions autonomes et les zones bananières.
Lien avec la CITP et niveau: CITP-1988 à tous les niveaux.
Autres classifications: Selon le sexe, le type d'entreprise/d'institution, et le secteur d'activité.

Rassemblement des données
Méthode de collecte des données:
Les méthodes de collecte des données varient selon le type d'employeur:
Entreprises privées: données recueillies sur la base des bordereaux de cotisations versées à la Sécurité sociale, transmises par les employeurs à la Caisse de Sécurité sociale. Les informations concernent le mois d'août et sont collectées au niveau central. La collecte et le traitement de ces données durent environ quatre mois.
Zones bananières: données provenant du registre des bordereaux de salaires des salariés des sociétés de production bananière de Chiriquí et de Bocas del Toro. La collecte et le traitement de ces données durent environ deux mois.
Institutions autonomes, semi-autonomes et municipales: données recueillies sur la base d'une liste spéciale que chacune de ces institutions est tenue de fournir et qui recense la profession, le sexe et le salaire du personnel travaillant dans lesdites institutions. La collecte et le traitement de ces données durent environ quatre mois.
Gouvernement central: données provenant du registre des bordereaux de salaires des salariés préparé par la Direction nationale de l'informatique du Contrôleur général. Le traitement de ces données dure environ un mois.

Traitement et contrôle des données
Les données sont traitées par ordinateur et les intervalles de variation des salaires sont contrôlés manuellement.
Ajustements
Aucun.
Types d'estimations
Totaux de l'emploi salarié et des gains, et leur répartition.
Calcul d'indices
Aucun.
Indicateurs de fiabilité des estimations
Non disponible.
Séries disponibles
Distributions:
Entreprises privées: nombre de salariés par sexe et niveau de gains, par province, branche d'activité et salaire mensuel;
Zones bananières: salariés selon le salaire mensuel, le sexe, la zone et la profession;
Institutions autonomes, semi-autonomes et municipales: salariés selon le salaire mensuel, le sexe, la profession et l'institution;
Gouvernement central: salariés selon le niveau des gains et le sexe, en fonction du ministère et de l'institution.

Historique des statistiques
Date de début de la série statistique: 1958.
Modifications et révisions principales: A partir de 1980, la Caisse de Sécurité sociale a introduit dans le secteur des entreprises privées des changements concernant le système de versement des cotisations, sur la base d'une liste préétablie: auparavant trimestriel, le versement des cotisations s'est mensualisé. Ce nouveau système implique des variations de chiffres étant donné que les employeurs présentent désormais cette liste à la Caisse de Sécurité sociale sans avoir pour autant effectué les versements correspondants, alors qu'auparavant n'étaient acceptées que les listes assorties des versements effectifs.
Zones bananières: Jusqu'en 1976, pour effectuer le calcul du salaire mensuel moyen, tous les salariés qui avaient travaillé au cours du mois de référence étaient comptabilisés, quels que soient les jours effectivement travaillés. Depuis 1977, ne sont plus comptabilisés les salariés ayant travaillé moins de 22 jours au cours du mois de référence, de façon à ce que le salaire mensuel moyen ainsi calculé soit davantage représentatif de l'activité.
Dans la zone du Canal: Le transfert de l'administration du Canal de Panama aux mains du gouvernement panaméen, qui a eu lieu le 31 décembre 1999, s'est traduit par une augmentation sensible du nombre de salariés ainsi que du niveau de salaire et de rémunération dans le secteur public.

Documentation et diffusion
Documentation:
Contraloría General de la República, Dirección de Estadística y Censo: *Situación Social – Estadísticas del Trabajo, Volumen II: Empleo: Sector público y privado* (Panamá, annuel); publié environ huit mois après la période de référence utilisée pour la collecte des données.
Données communiquées au BIT aux fins de diffusion
Aucune; le BIT ne publie pas de données sur les distributions dans l'*Annuaire des statistiques du Travail*.

Pays-Bas

Source de la série
Conventions collectives et autres lois et règlements concernant les salaires.
Titre de la série
Indices des taux de salaire (Indexcijfers van cao-lonen).
Organisme responsable
Collecte des données, traitement statistique et publication/diffusion des statistiques:
Statistiques des Pays-Bas (Centraal Bureau voor Statistiek, CBS).
Principaux sujets couverts
Indices des taux de salaire contractuels, durée du travail et coût de la main-d'œuvre.
Périodicité ou fréquence de disponibilité des statistiques
Mensuelle et annuelle.
Période de référence
Le dernier jour de chaque mois.
Portée des statistiques
Géographique: l'ensemble du pays.
Branches d'activité: toutes les branches d'activité économique, à l'exception des ménages privés employant du personnel domestique (SBI95) et des organisations et organismes extra-territoriaux (SBI99).
Etablissements: établissements de tous types et tailles soumis aux conventions collectives.
Personnes: salariés à plein temps.
Professions: toutes les professions sont représentées.
Concepts et définitions
Emploi: se réfère aux salariés à plein temps, c'est-à-dire aux personnes touchant un salaire ou un traitement. Les adultes et les jeunes sont identifiés séparément.
Taux de salaire ou de traitement: se réfèrent aux taux de salaire bruts pour les heures de travail normales, avant toute déduction au titre de l'impôt sur les salaires, de contributions à la sécurité sociale, aux fonds de retraite, etc. Ces taux comprennent les salaires correspondant à la durée de travail normale, tous les paiements additionnels fixes, garantis et réguliers ainsi que tout autre paiement fixe spécial (périodique ou non) tels que congés payés et primes de fin d'année. En sont exclus tout autre paiement supplémentaire convenu dans la convention collective de travail, par exemple les primes en raison de l'âge ou du travail posté.
Durée du travail: il s'agit de la durée normale annuelle du travail des salariés adultes à plein temps telle qu'établie dans les conventions collectives, à savoir le nombre maximal d'heures de travail, à l'exclusion des heures supplémentaires, des jours fériés rémunérés (fixés à 6 jours par an), du congé payé et des heures non effectuées telles que fixées par la loi, les règlements ou les conventions collectives. Il n'est pas tenu compte de la réduction du temps de travail subordonnée à l'âge ou au travail posté.
Taux de coût de la main-d'œuvre: comprend les salaires et paiements spéciaux tels que convenus dans la convention collective de travail, de même que les contributions obligatoires de l'employeur aux régimes des assurances sociales.
Classifications
Branches d'activité économique:
Titre de la classification: Classification type, par industrie (SIC, SBI en néerlandais, 1993).
Nombre de groupes utilisés pour le codage: quatre secteurs, 16 branches et quelques classes.
S'applique à: toutes les données.
Lien avec la CITI et niveau: basé sur la classification de l'activité économique de l'UE (NACE, Rev.1) au niveau de l'indicatif à quatre chiffres, qui est compatible avec la CITI, Rev.3, au niveau de l'indicatif à deux chiffres.
Autres classifications: par secteur soumis aux conventions collectives de travail, c'est-à-dire classification des entreprises par secteur (privé, public et subventionné) et par catégorie de salariés (jeunes et adultes).

Rassemblement des données
Type et couverture du système administratif: couvre toutes les conventions collectives (à présent, plus de 900 conventions).
Méthode de collecte des données: les données sont extraites des registres des conventions collectives et autres règlements salariaux. Les unités statistiques comprennent un nombre important de points bien définis par les conventions collectives de travail. Ces points représentent un niveau contractuel de salaires par groupe professionnel, qui se combine souvent avec des indications au titre de l'ancienneté, de l'âge ou du niveau de qualification. Une enquête spéciale est menée afin de déterminer la structure pour l'année de base. Elle permet de déterminer quelles sont les conventions collectives utilisées et leur répartition selon les groupes de la main-d'œuvre. A partir de ces données, des estimations sont faites pour chaque convention collective pertinente montrant la répartition des travailleurs en fonction de la structure salariale et un indice salarial partiel est développé à partir des points présentant les plus grandes fréquences. La série actuelle utilise 8100 points relatifs aux salaires figurant dans 354 conventions collectives, sur un total de plus de 900 conventions. L'année de base est actuellement l'année 1990 et, en principe, l'échantillon des niveaux de salaires est revu tous les dix ans.

Traitement et contrôle des données
Les données qui ont été publiées dans des conventions collectives sont introduites dans un système informatisé. L'évolution par rapport à la période précédente est calculée pour chaque convention collective. Les chiffres dépassant la norme (sensiblement plus élevés ou plus bas que la moyenne) font l'objet d'une seconde vérification. Les résultats sont également comparés à toute autre information disponible, par exemple les données publiées dans la presse.

Ajustements
Couverture insuffisante: les indices mensuels des salaires contractuels, du coût de la main-d'œuvre et de la durée du travail sont susceptibles de changer si de nouvelles conventions collectives ou règlements collectifs relatifs aux salaires entrent en vigueur. Un indice corrigé est publié un mois au plus tard après l'entrée en vigueur des règlements collectifs salariaux. Les résultats finaux pour l'année *t* sont publiés au plus tard au mois de mai de l'année *t +1*.
Variations saisonnières: les données ne font pas l'objet d'une correction saisonnière.

Types d'estimations
Indices mensuels et horaires des taux de salaire contractuels, durée du travail et coût horaire de la main-d'œuvre.

Calcul d'indices
Les 8100 points-salaires se voient allouer une pondération de base pour l'année de base (1990). Ces pondérations de base sont allouées en fonction de leur importance mutuelle au sein de la convention ou du règlement collectif. Elles sont maintenues constantes tout au long des années jusqu'à la mise à jour de l'échantillon.
Un autre type de pondération est effectué à partir de la pondération annuelle de l'industrie, dérivant de conventions et règlements collectifs. Cette « pondération externe », basée sur des données provenant du système de la comptabilité nationale, prend en compte les variations annuelles du nombre de salariés et de la masse salariale par branche d'activité économique.
Les indices partiels aux niveaux des unités statistiques servent de base de calcul aux indices de salaire de type Laspeyres pour chaque activité économique aux niveaux des agrégats. L'année de base des séries actuelles est de 1990'100.

Indicateurs de fiabilité des estimations
Couverture du système administratif:
La sélection des conventions collectives de travail en couvre près de 350 (40% du total), ce qui représentait 75% de tous les salariés en 1990.

Séries disponibles
Indices de salaires contractuels mensuels et horaires y compris les primes ;
Indices mensuels de la durée contractuelle du travail ;
Indices mensuels du coût horaire de la main-d'œuvre ;
Par catégorie de salarié, secteur et branche d'activité économique.

Historique des statistiques
Date de début de la série statistique: la publication des présentes statistiques a commencé en 1926; les séries des indices salariaux mensuels et horaires ainsi que les indices de la durée annuelle contractuelle du travail ont fait l'objet d'une publication mensuelle

depuis 1980. La publication de certains résultats concernant le coût horaire de la main-d'œuvre a commencé en 1990.
Modifications et révisions principales: les séries des indices de salaire ont été régulièrement revues et améliorées. Il n'y a pas eu de changement méthodologique majeur dans les séries chronologiques présentées actuellement.
Une révision complète des présentes statistiques est prévue pour 2003.

Documentation et diffusion
Documentation:
Statistics Netherlands (CBS): *Statistisch Bulletin* (Voorburg, hebdomadaire); la dernière édition du mois contient les indices salariaux provisoires ainsi que les indices du coût de la main-d'œuvre relatifs au mois précédent. Les données définitives sont publiées au plus tard cinq mois après la fin de l'année de référence.
Idem: *Sociaal-economische Maandstatistiek* (Voorburg/Heerlen, mensuel). Des changements méthodologiques majeurs sont annoncés à l'avance dans cette publication.
Une description méthodologique est également publiée dans le *Supplement to the Monthly Bulletin of Socio-economic Statistics*, 1993-3 4
Diffusion: sur le site Internet de CBS: http://www.cbs.nl
Les notes méthodologiques figurent également sur le site Internet.
Données communiquées au BIT aux fins de diffusion
Les statistiques suivantes sont communiquées au BIT aux fins de leur publication dans l'*Annuaire des statistiques du Travail:*
Indices des taux de salaires horaires par activité économique.
Les séries mensuelles correspondantes sont publiées dans le *Bulletin des statistiques du Travail*.
Autres sources administratives de données:
Un grand nombre de registres de l'administration (registre de la population, d'administration des régimes d'assurances des salariés, dossiers des agences d'emploi, registre des adresses et de l'habitat, etc.) sont utilisés conjointement avec des enquêtes par sondage auprès des entreprises et des ménages aux fins d'élaboration d'un système d'information statistique intégré sur les caractéristiques socio-démographiques, socio-économiques et socio-culturelles de la population.

Polynésie française

Source de la série
Sécurité sociale, Administration fiscale et Représentation de la France.
Titre de la série
Emplois et salaires.

Organisme responsable
Collecte des données: Caisse de Prévoyance Sociale (CPS), Haut commissariat.
Traitement statistique et publication/diffusion des statistiques:
Institut de la Statistique de la Polynésie française (ISPF).
Principaux sujets couverts
Emplois, gains, revenus et durée du travail.
Périodicité ou fréquence de disponibilité des statistiques
Mensuelle.
Période de référence
Le mois complet.
Portée des statistiques
Géographique: l'ensemble du territoire (tous les archipels et départements).
Branches d'activité: toutes les branches d'activité économique.
Etablissements: de tous types et tailles.
Personnes: depuis 2000, toutes les personnes ayant un emploi (salariés et indépendants) ont l'obligation d'être affiliées à la sécurité sociale, à l'exception des fonctionnaires français travaillant en Polynésie française.
Avant l'année 2000, les indépendants qui avaient choisi une assurance sociale privée étaient exclus du système comme ils l'étaient des statistiques, de même que les fonctionnaires français travaillant en Polynésie française.
Professions: les données ne sont pas rassemblées par profession ou groupes de professions.
Concepts et définitions
Emploi: aux fins de la statistique, on inclut dans les personnes ayant un emploi les salariés et les indépendants (travailleurs à propre compte) couverts par l'assurance de sécurité sociale territoriale obligatoire, dont les revenus se situent au-dessus du salaire minimum.

Les travailleurs à plein temps sont ceux qui travaillent selon la durée légale (169 heures par mois). Les travailleurs à temps partiel sont ceux dont l'horaire de travail est inférieur à cette durée. Il est possible d'identifier séparément les jeunes travailleurs dans le groupe d'âge de 16 à 18 ans.

Gains: gains mensuels bruts supérieurs au salaire minimum, y compris les paiements au titre d'heures supplémentaires, qui peuvent être identifiés sur la base des données relatives aux heures de travail. Le montant des gains déclarés est limité au plafond fixé pour les contributions de la sécurité sociale.

Durée du travail: heures rémunérées, y compris les heures supplémentaires, telles que déclarées par l'employeur.

Revenu lié à l'emploi salarié: ne s'applique pas. Comme il n'existe pas d'impôt sur le revenu en Polynésie française, toutes les composantes du revenu ne sont pas déclarées.

Revenu lié à l'emploi indépendant: en principe, revenu net après déduction de la consommation du capital fixe. De fait, le revenu lié à l'emploi des travailleurs indépendants reflète la valeur totale des ventes après déduction des charges relatives à l'activité économique. Le revenu déclaré se limite au revenu supérieur au salaire minimum et au plafond fixé pour les cotisations au titre de la sécurité sociale.

Classifications
Branches d'activité économique:
Titre de la classification: Nomenclature des activités françaises (NAF).
Nombre de groupes utilisés pour le codage: 4 groupes, 17 sections, 31 sous-sections, 60 divisions, et 697 postes.
S'applique à: toutes les données collectées.
Lien avec la CITI et niveau: oui.
Professions: employés et indépendants.
Autres classifications: l'emploi et les gains/le revenu sont classés par sexe, groupe d'âge, durée du travail et localisation de l'employeur (archipel ou département). Les données concernant l'emploi sont également distribuées selon les niveaux de gains/revenu.

Rassemblement des données
Type et couverture du système administratif: non disponible.
Méthode de collecte des données: les données concernant l'emploi et les revenus des personnes assurées font objet d'une déclaration mensuelle par les employeurs faite à la sécurité sociale territoriale. Elles sont transmises trimestriellement à l'Institut de la statistique, dans les trois mois suivant le trimestre de la déclaration.
Mise à jour du système administratif: continue.

Traitement et contrôle des données
Les données sont traitées par informatique et les contrôles de qualité portent sur le niveau des salaires, la durée du travail, les groupes d'âge, etc.

Ajustements
Aucun.

Types d'estimations
Emploi: totaux et distributions;
Gains/revenus: totaux, moyennes et distributions.

Calcul d'indices
Aucune.

Indicateurs de fiabilité des estimations
Couverture du système administratif: environ 99 % des personnes ayant un emploi depuis l'introduction de la nouvelle législation à la fin de 2001, rétroactivement à 2000.
Erreurs non dues à l'échantillonnage: non disponibles.
Conformité avec d'autres sources: on procède à certaines comparaisons avec les résultats du recensement de la population ; d'autres comparaisons seront faites avec les résultats de la dernière enquête relative au budget des familles (2001).

Séries disponibles
Nombre de salariés classés par sexe, groupe d'âge, niveau de revenu, activité économique, secteur d'activité, archipel ou district de l'employeur, statut juridique de l'employeur et nombre d'heures travaillées ;
Gains mensuels moyens classés par sexe, groupe d'âge, activité économique, secteur d'activité, archipel ou district de l'employeur, statut juridique de l'employeur et nombre d'heures travaillées
Gains horaires moyens classés par sexe, groupe d'âge, activité économique, secteur d'activité, archipel ou district de l'employeur et statut juridique de l'employeur.
Toutes les séries sont disponibles sur une base mensuelle et annuelle, sous réserve des règles de confidentialité.

Historique des statistiques
Date de début de la série statistique: 1987 pour la plupart des séries, 1995 pour l'ensemble des séries disponibles.

Modifications et révisions principales: jusqu'en 1995, les données concernant l'emploi et les revenus étaient réunies par les assurances sociales et communiquées globalement. Depuis 1995, les données mensuelles sont disponibles pour chaque personne assurée.

Documentation et diffusion
Documentation: non disponible avant 2003.
Diffusion: sur le site Internet suivant: http://www.ispf.pf
Les résultats n'apparaissant pas sur le site Internet peuvent être obtenus sur demande.

Données communiquées au BIT aux fins de diffusion
Les statistiques suivantes sont publiées dans *l'Annuaire des statistiques du Travail*: Moyenne annuelle des salariés.

Sainte-Hélène

Source de la série
Déclarations d'impôts et registres administratifs.
Titre de la série
Emploi, taux de salaire, gains et durée du travail.
Organisme responsable
Collecte des données, traitement et publication/diffusion des statistiques:
Statistics Office, Development and Economic Planning Department (Bureau de statistique, Département du Développement et de la Planification économique).
Principaux sujets couverts
Emploi, taux de salaire et traitement, gains, durée du travail et revenu provenant d'une activité indépendante.
Périodicité ou fréquence de disponibilité des statistiques
Annuelle.
Période de référence
L'année (d'avril à mars).
Portée des statistiques
Géographique: toute l'île.
Branches d'activité: toutes les branches d'activité économique.
Etablissements: de tous genres et de toutes tailles.
Personnes: toutes les personnes occupées.
Professions: des données sont collectées sur les taux de salaire et de traitement et sur la durée du travail par profession.
Concepts et définitions
Emploi: il s'agit de toutes les personnes ayant un revenu provenant d'un emploi salarié à plein temps ou à temps partiel ou d'une activité professionnelle indépendante.
Les travailleurs adultes ont au moins 15 ans.
Les travailleurs à plein temps travaillent en moyenne 36,25 heures par semaine.
Gains: il s'agit de la rémunération annuelle totale en espèces déclarée aux autorités fiscales, c'est-à-dire les gains bruts en espèces y compris les salaires directs et toutes les primes, bonifications, prestations et indemnités versées en espèces.
Taux de salaire ou de traitement: il s'agit des taux de salaire et traitement de base.
Durée du travail: il s'agit de la semaine normale de travail, telle qu'elle est fixée par les lois et dispositions réglementaires: 35 heures par semaine pour les travailleurs rémunérés au mois, et 37,5 heures par semaine pour les travailleurs rémunérés à la semaine.
Revenu lié à l'emploi salarié: voir sous Gains.
Revenu lié à l'emploi indépendant: il s'agit du bénéfice brut en espèces provenant d'une activité indépendante, après déduction de la consommation de capital fixe.
Classifications
Branches d'activité économique:
Titre de la classification: non disponible.
Nombre de groupes utilisés pour le codage: 17 catégories de classement.
S'applique à: toutes les données.
Lien avec la CITI et niveau: rév. 3 (1990)
Professions:
Titre de la classification: non disponible.
Nombre de groupes utilisés pour le codage: neuf groupes principaux.
S'applique à: toutes les données.
Lien avec la CITP et niveau: CITP-88.
Situation dans la profession: employés et indépendants.
Autres classifications: par sexe. Les taux de salaire et traitement des employés gouvernementaux sont également ventilés par niveau de qualifications.

Rassemblement des données

Type et couverture du système administratif: le système est basé sur la totalité des déclarations d'impôts remplies par la population occupée et sur des dossiers administratifs.

Méthode de collecte des données: collation des données provenant de ces déclarations d'impôts et d'autres dossiers administratifs. Les données sur les taux de salaire/traitement sont obtenues du département des Finances.

Mise à jour du système administratif: annuelle.

Traitement et contrôle des données

Les données sont traitées électroniquement; diverses variables sont mises en tableaux à entrées multiples et des contrôles sont effectués dans la base de données électronique.

Ajustements

Aucun.

Types d'estimations

Nombre total de personnes occupées, taux de salaire/traitement hebdomadaire et mensuel moyens, gains mensuels moyens et durée moyenne du travail par semaine.

Calcul d'indices

Aucun.

Indicateurs de fiabilité des estimations

Couverture du système administratif: exhaustive.

Séries disponibles

Nombres de personnes occupées par secteur et par catégorie (employés et indépendants);
Gains mensuels moyens;
Taux de salaire/traitement par niveau de qualifications et niveau professionnel.
Durée normale du travail.

Historique des statistiques

Date de début de la série statistique: non disponible.

Modifications et révisions principales: aucune.

Documentation et diffusion

Documentation:

Statistics Office: *Statistical Yearbook* (Jamestown, publication annuelle); l'annuaire paraît environ une année après la fin de la période de référence des statistiques.

Diffusion: les données qui ne figurent pas dans des publications nationales peuvent être obtenues sur demande.

Données communiquées au BIT aux fins de diffusion

Les statistiques sur les gains mensuels moyens par activité économique et par sexe sont publiées dans *l'Annuaire des statistiques du Travail*.

Des statistiques sur la durée normale du travail et les taux de salaire/traitement par profession sont publiés dans *Statistiques des salaires et de la durée du travail par profession et des prix de produits alimentaires – Résultats de l'Enquête d'octobre*.

Seychelles

Source de la série

Fichiers de la sécurité sociale et données communiquées par l'administration et les organismes para-étatiques.

Titre de la série

Emploi formel et gains mensuels moyens des salariés ayant un emploi dans le secteur formel.

Organisme responsable

Collecte des données, traitement statistique et publication/ diffusion des statistiques: Ministry of Information Technology & Communication, Management & Information Systems Division, Statistics and Database Administration Section (Ministère des technologies de l'information et de la communication, Département des systèmes de gestion et de l'information, section des statistiques et de l'administration des bases de données.

Principaux sujets couverts

Emploi et gains.

Périodicité ou fréquence de disponibilité des statistiques

Tous les six mois.

Période de référence

Emploi: le dernier jour ouvrable de chaque mois pour les périodes de janvier à juin et de janvier à décembre;
Gains: le mois entier.

Portée des statistiques

Géographique: l'ensemble du pays.

Branches d'activité: toutes les branches d'activité économique. Des données séparées sont disponibles pour les secteurs public, para-étatique et privé, ainsi que pour les trois secteurs réunis.

Etablissements: établissements du secteur formel de tous types et tailles, affiliés au système de sécurité sociale.

Personnes: salariés du secteur formel, affiliés au système de sécurité sociale. Sont exclus les travailleurs domestiques employés dans les ménages privés, les travailleurs familiaux et les indépendants.

Professions: les données ne sont pas rassemblées par profession ou groupe professionnel.

Concepts et définitions

Emploi: les salariés sont toutes les personnes ayant un emploi « formel » qui versent des cotisations à la sécurité sociale.

Gains: se réfèrent aux gains mensuels bruts, y compris le paiement des heures supplémentaires, bonus et allocations, congés payés et paiements en cas de licenciement.

Classifications

Branches d'activité économique:

Titre de la classification: non disponible.

Nombre de groupes utilisés pour le codage: 13.

S'applique à: emploi et gains.

Lien avec la CITI et niveau: non totalement compatible avec la rév. 2 ni avec la rév.3.

Autres classifications: par secteur (privé, para-étatique et public).

Rassemblement des données

Type et couverture du système administratif: couvre tous les salariés ayant un emploi dans le secteur formel.

Méthode de collecte des données: les données sont rassemblées à partir de fichiers la sécurité sociale couvrant le secteur privé ainsi que des données des organismes para-étatiques et de l'administration rassemblées par la Section des statistiques et de l'administration des bases de données du Département des systèmes de gestion et de l'information.

Mise à jour du système administratif: de manière continue.

Traitement et contrôle des données

Les données sont enregistrées et traitées par informatique en Excel.

Ajustements

Aucun.

Types d'estimations

Total et nombre moyen de salariés et gains mensuels bruts moyens.

Calcul d'indices

Aucun.

Indicateurs de fiabilité des estimations

Couverture du système administratif: il est supposé exhaustif en termes de salariés du secteur formel.

Conformité avec d'autres sources: les données des secteurs public et para-étatique sont contrôlées en les comparant avec les données détenues par les organismes de l'Etat.

Séries disponibles

Séries mensuelles et annuelles de l'emploi formel ainsi que des gains mensuels moyens par branche d'activité et par secteur.

Historique des statistiques

Date de début de la série statistique: 1975.

Modifications et révisions principales: depuis le 1er janvier 1988, tous les salaries ayant un emploi dans le secteur formel sont exemptés d'impôt sur le revenu. En conséquence, les gains moyens depuis 1988 ne sont pas comparables avec les données des années précédentes.

Documentation et diffusion

Documentation:

Ministry of Information Technology & Communication, Management & Information Systems Division, Statistics and Database Administration Section: *Statistical Bulletin* (Mahe, bi-annuel);

Idem: *Statistical Abstract* (annuel).

Aucune publication méthodologique n'a été publiée.

Diffusion: les données concernant l'emploi sont disponibles sur le site Internet du Département de la gestion des systèmes d'information: **http://www.seychelles.net/misdstat**

Données communiquées au BIT aux fins de diffusion

Les données suivantes ont été communiquées au BIT aux fins de publication dans *l'Annuaire des statistiques du Travail*:

Emploi rémunéré par branche d'activité économique ;

Gains mensuels moyens des salariés du secteur formel par branche d'activité économique.

Les statistiques mensuelles correspondantes sont publiées dans le *Bulletin des statistiques du Travail*.

Singapour

Source de la série

Rapports sur les contributions à la Caisse Centrale de Prévoyance (Central Provident Fund - CPF).

Titre de la série
Gains mensuels moyens.
Organisme responsable
Collecte des données et traitement statistique Commission de la Caisse Centrale de Prévoyance (Central Provident Fund Board).
Publication/ diffusion des statistiques: Manpower Research and Statistics Department, Ministry of Manpower (Département de la recherche et des statistiques de la main d'œuvre du Ministère du Travail) et Department of Statistics, Ministry of Trade and Industry (Département des statistiques du Ministère du commerce et de l'industrie).
Principaux sujets couverts
Gains et salariés.
Périodicité ou fréquence de disponibilité des statistiques
Trimestrielle.
Période de référence
Chaque mois du trimestre.
Portée des statistiques
Géographique: l'ensemble du pays.
Branches d'activité: toutes les branches d'activité économique.
Etablissements: de tous types et de toutes tailles dans les secteurs privé et public.
Personnes: tous les salariés résidents, c'est-à-dire les citoyens de Singapour et les résidents permanents, qui contribuent au CPF.
Professions: les données ne sont pas rassemblées par profession ou groupe professionnel.
Concepts et définitions
Emploi: un salarié est une personne employée à Singapour, ainsi que tout marin engagé par un employeur sous contrat de services ou autre convention conclue à Singapour. En font partie:
–   les directeurs salariés de sociétés,
–   les salariés à temps partiel ou occasionnels dont les gains dépassent $50 par mois,
–   les jeunes ayant quitté l'école ou les étudiants travaillant à temps partiel ou sur une base temporaire (à l'exception des étudiants du tertiaire ayant un lien à plein temps avec une activité économique, les étudiants employés sur la base d'un programme de formation approuvé par leur institution ainsi que les étudiants travaillant au cours de leurs vacances scolaires)
–   les militaires réservistes,
–   les étrangers devenus résidents permanents à Singapour.
Sont exclus les étrangers titulaires de permis d'emploi ou de visite professionnelle, les associés et les propriétaires d'entreprises individuelles, les indépendants et les salariés travaillant outremer.
Gains: les gains mensuels moyens bruts se réfèrent à la rémunération totale due ou octroyée aux salariés du fait de leur emploi, avant déductions des contributions des salariés au CPF et des impôts sur le revenu. Ils comprennent le salaire de base, le paiement des heures supplémentaires, les commissions, les allocations (p.ex. de présence, coût de la vie, travail salissant, éducation, vacances, logement, maternité, repas, productivité, service, heures d'astreinte), les congés payés et autres paiements en espèces, les primes salariales annuelles et les bonus variables. En sont exclus les paiements en nature ainsi que les contributions des employeurs au CPF.
Classifications
Branches d'activité économique:
Titre de la classification: Singapore Standard Industrial Classification (SSIC) 2000.
Nombre de groupes utilisés pour le codage: 54.
S'applique à: gains et distribution des salariés.
Lien avec la CITI et niveau: rév.3 (1990) au niveau des codes à 3 chiffres.
Situation dans la profession: les salariés uniquement.
Autres classifications: gains: par sexe; distribution des salariés: par sexe et groupe d'âge.
Rassemblement des données
Type et couverture du système administratif: en 2001, plus de 80 000 employeurs ont contribué au CPF pour le compte de plus de 1,2 million de salariés.
Méthode de collecte des données: les statistiques des gains mensuels moyens sont tirées des déclarations de contributions de sécurité sociale et d'épargne que tout employeur est tenu légalement d'adresser au CPF. Les employeurs sont tenus de déclarer chaque mois les gains de chaque salarié et de verser leurs contributions dans les 14 jours suivant le mois pour lequel ces contributions sont dues et exigibles. Il existe des formulaires de paiement manuels et électroniques. Les données relatives aux salaires sont ensuite compilées chaque mois par le CPF et traitées

dans les deux mois suivant la période de référence. Les statistiques trimestrielles de gains moyens mensuels correspondent à la moyenne des trois mois.
Mise à jour du système administratif: continue; les systèmes informatiques de la Commission du CPF détectent les employeurs pris en défaut, pour lesquels un suivi est assuré chaque mois par les fonctionnaires du Service des Employeurs (Employer Services Officers). Des contrôles ponctuels, par activité économique, des bordereaux de salaires des employeurs sont également effectués pour déterminer le niveau de conformité des employeurs aux statuts et règlements du CPF.
Traitement et contrôle des données
Les données sont traitées par informatique.
Aucune information n'est disponible sur les contrôles de cohérence effectués sur les données.
Ajustements
Aucun.
Types d'estimations
Les gains mensuels moyens sont calculés en divisant le total des gains mensuels de tous les cotisants actifs du CPF (les salariés) par le nombre des cotisants actifs du CPF (salariés). Les statistiques trimestrielles correspondent à la moyenne des trois mois.
Les gains mensuels moyens réels correspondent aux gains nominaux corrigés de la variation des prix par l'indice des prix à la consommation de l'année correspondante (à présent, sur la base de novembre 1997-octobre 1998'100).
Calcul d'indices
Aucun.
Indicateurs de fiabilité des estimations
Couverture du système administratif: il est supposé couvrir tous les salariés résidents.
Séries disponibles
Séries trimestrielles et annuelles des gains mensuels moyens par activité économique et par sexe.
Séries annuelles des gains mensuels moyens réels par activité économique et par sexe.
Distribution annuelle des cotisants au CPF par niveau de salaire mensuel (à la fin de l'année), groupe d'âge et activité économique.
Historique des statistiques
Date de début de la série statistique: 1981.
Modifications et révisions principales: jusqu'en 1992, les statistiques des gains moyens incluaient des indépendants qui avaient cotisé à titre volontaire au CPF. Depuis 1992, les données excluent tous les travailleurs indépendants qui ont pu être identifiés. Depuis 1998, les données sur les gains de la Commission du CPF, par branche d'activité économique sont compilées au niveau des groupes à 5 chiffres, au lieu des groupes à 4 chiffres. A compter de cette date, les statistiques ne sont par conséquent pas strictement comparables avec celles des années précédentes.
Avant 1998, les statistiques étaient classées selon la Classification standard industrielle de Singapour (SSIC) de 1990; de 1998 à 2000, selon la SSIC de 1996 ; depuis 2001, selon la SSIC 2000.
Documentation et diffusion
Documentation:
Ministry of Manpower, Manpower Research and Statistics Department: *Singapore Yearbook of Manpower Statistics* (annuel, Singapour); publié cinq mois après l'année de référence des statistiques;
Idem: *Report on Wages in Singapore* (annuel), publié dans les six mois après l'année de référence.
Ministry of Trade and Industry, Department of Statistics (Statistics Singapore): *Monthly Digest of Statistics* (Singapour) (mensuel, ibid.); publié trois mois après le trimestre de référence;
Idem: *Yearbook of Statistics Singapore* (annuel, ibid.); publié cinq mois après l'année de référence.
Les informations méthodologiques ne sont pas publiées.
Diffusion: sur Internet:
Ministry of Manpower, Manpower Research and Statistics Department:
http//www.gov.sg/mom/manpower/manrs/manrs.htm
Ministry of Trade and Industry, Statistics Singapore:
http://www.singstat.gov.sg
Des informations sur les définitions des salariés couverts et des salaires, et sur les procédures du CPF sont disponibles sur le site Internet du CPF:
http://www.cpf.gov.sg.
Données communiquées au BIT aux fins de diffusion
Les statistiques suivantes sont publiées dans l'*Annuaire* et *le Bulletin des statistiques du Travail*:

Gains mensuels moyens par activité économique et (sur une base annuelle) par sexe.

Autres sources administratives de données: Des statistiques d'emploi sont calculées chaque mois sur la base de registres administratifs de diverses agences gouvernementales.

Suisse

Source de la série
Déclarations d'accidents enregistrées par le Service de centralisation des statistiques de l'assurance-accidents (SSAA).

Titre de la série
Indice suisse des salaires;
Durée normale du travail dans les entreprises (DNT).

Organisme responsable
Collecte des données: Service de centralisation des statistiques de l'assurance-accidents (SSAA).
Traitement statistique et publication/diffusion des statistiques: Office fédéral de la statistique (OFS).

Principaux sujets couverts
Taux de salaires et durée normale du travail.

Périodicité ou fréquence de disponibilité des statistiques
Annuelle.

Période de référence
L'année civile.

Portée des statistiques
Géographique: l'ensemble du pays.
Branches d'activité: toutes les branches d'activité économique, y compris l'horticulture et la sylviculture, mais à l'exclusion de l'agriculture, de la chasse et des services annexes, et de la pêche.
Etablissements: établissements et entreprises de tous types et de toutes tailles.
Personnes: salariés à plein temps, sans les cadres moyens et supérieurs.
La population de référence correspond au "concept intérieur" du marché du travail: personnes qui exercent une activité dans une unité de production implantée sur le territoire suisse, qu'elles soient domiciliées en Suisse ou à l'étranger (par ex. travailleurs frontaliers).
Professions: les données ne sont pas recueillies sur les professions individuelles ou des groupes de professions, mais sur les niveaux de qualification (voir sous « Classifications »).

Concepts et définitions
Emploi: la statistique porte sur les salariés occupés à temps complet, accidentés, et relevant de la Caisse nationale suisse d'assurance-accidents (Suva, ex-CNA), ou des assureurs privés.
Les salariés occupés à temps partiel, ceux touchés par une réduction de l'horaire de travail et les cadres moyens et supérieurs ne sont en principe pas couverts par la statistique.
Taux de salaire ou de traitement: se réfèrent aux taux réellement payés. La définition retenue pour le calcul de l'indice recouvre les composantes suivantes: salaire brut de base, allocation de renchérissement, et treizième salaire. Les primes et les commissions, les allocations familiales, les gratifications, et les paiements en nature sont relevés, mais exclus du calcul. Lorsque le salaire dépasse le montant maximum assuré (soit CHF 8,900 par mois au 1er janvier 2000), seul le maximum est pris en compte (voir également sous "Ajustements").
Les données sont recueillies séparément pour les travailleurs à temps complet et à temps partiel, les apprentis et par sexe.
Durée du travail: durée hebdomadaire normale du travail pratiquée dans les entreprises et valable sur un intervalle de plusieurs mois ou années. Elle correspond en principe à la durée individuelle du travail des salariés engagés à temps complet, sans tenir compte des heures supplémentaires, des réductions d'horaires et d'autres absences. Elle peut être fixée par les lois et règlements, les conventions collectives ou les règlements propres aux entreprises/établissements, telle que stipulée dans le contrat de travail des salariés.
Les données sont recueillies séparément pour les travailleurs à temps complet et à temps partiel, les apprentis et par sexe.

Classifications
Branches d'activité économique:
Titre de la classification: Nomenclature générale des activités économiques 1995 (NOGA), depuis 1991.
Nombre de groupes utilisés pour le codage: au niveau suisse, les statistiques sont désagrégées par classe (niveau à deux chiffres) et division économique (niveau à un chiffre) ; au niveau

cantonal: par division économique.
S'applique à: durée normale du travail et indices des salaires.
Lien avec la CITI et niveau: la NOGA se fonde sur la NACE, Rév.1, et est compatible avec la CITI, Rév.3.
Autres classifications: salaires: niveau de qualification (travailleurs qualifiés, semi-qualifiés et non qualifiés) ; sexe; domaine d'activité (exploitation, bureau et technique (ensemble) et vente); secteur (primaire: horticulture et sylviculture ; secondaire et tertiaire) ; ainsi que classifications croisées par canton et région.
Durée du travail: par canton et région, et classifications croisées canton/section économique.

Rassemblement des données
Type et couverture du système administratif: le Service de centralisation des statistiques de l'assurance-accidents (SSAA) reçoit plus de 300 000 déclarations d'accidents par année.
Méthode de collecte des données: les déclarations d'accidents sont des formulaires remplis par les accidentés ou leur employeur, qui comportent, parmi une vingtaine de variables (branche économique, sexe, qualification, domaine d'activité, mode de rémunération, jours de travail, âge, lieu de domicile et de travail du salarié accidenté, genre d'accident, etc.), des informations sur le salaire de la personne accidentée et la durée normale du travail dans l'entreprise qui l'emploie. Ces formulaires sont transmis à l'OFS, via le SSAA, par voie informatique et sous forme anonymisée.
Dans la statistique sur l'évolution des salaires, les principales variables de la sélection des données sont: le niveau de qualification, la durée du travail (salariés à plein temps), l'âge (hommes: 19-65 ans; femmes: 19-63 ans) et le domaine d'activité.
Mise à jour du système administratif: sur une base continue.

Traitement et contrôle des données
La saisie informatique et les contrôles de plausibilité des informations recueillies sur la base des déclarations d'accidents sont effectués par le SSAA.
L'OFS procède à l'extrapolation des résultats:
La durée normale du travail, au niveau d'une section, d'un secteur économique ou du total, se calcule à l'aide d'un schéma de pondération, dont la base est le recensement fédéral des entreprises de 1995 et de 1998. Chaque division économique de chaque canton reçoit un coefficient de pondération. Ce procédé permet de calculer les valeurs agrégées en fonction des structures de l'emploi propres à chaque canton et à chaque région.
Les données suivantes ont été utilisées pour le calcul des pondérations actuelles de la statistique des salaires: les emplois à temps complet tirés du recensement des entreprises (RFE) de 1991; le nombre de personnes actives occupées à plein temps tiré du recensement de la population (RFP) de 1990; le personnel d'exploitation de l'enquête d'octobre (LOK) de 1991 sur les salaires et traitements; et les données du SSAA de 1991 sur les effectifs de salariés au niveau du genre d'accident.
Les déclarations d'accidents provenant de certains groupes de salariés ne sont pas, en nombre, proportionnelles à l'importance de ces groupes dans l'univers observé (par ex. dans le bâtiment et le génie civil). Les groupes de travailleurs sont donc pondérés en fonction de leur importance relative au sein de cet univers, ce qui permet d'éviter des distorsions dans la présentation de l'évolution macro-économique des salaires.

Ajustements
Couverture insuffisante: statistique sur l'évolution des salaires: pour certains groupes de salariés - par exemple, les hommes qualifiés des classes économiques "chimie", "banques" et "administrations publiques", les salaires inconnus, qui dépassent le montant du gain maximum assuré, représentent en permanence une part relativement importante, située entre 5 et 15% du nombre total d'indications de salaires de ces groupes. Dans ces cas, les salaires déclarés sont corrigés ou extrapolés. La méthode de correction ou d'extrapolation repose sur l'hypothèse qu'en réalité les salaires sont ventilés selon une distribution log-normale.

Types d'estimations
Moyenne annuelle de la durée hebdomadaire normale de travail, pondérée par le nombre d'emplois;
Indices annuels, nominaux et réels, de l'évolution des salaires.
La durée moyenne du travail correspond à la moyenne de toutes les semaines d'une année civile.
Les indices annuels des salaires sont calculés à partir des déclarations d'accidents qui couvrent toute l'année.
Afin de résoudre le problème de l'influence des variations de la durée du travail sur l'évolution des salaires horaires, le salaire horaire est raccordé à la durée hebdomadaire individuelle du travail de chaque assuré et converti en gain mensuel.

Calcul d'indices

L'évolution des salaires nominaux est calculée au moyen d'un indice de Laspeyres à structure constante (effectifs des salariés de groupes homogènes à l'année de base), qui mesure les variations de salaires se rapportant à un travail de nature constante (évolution pure des salaires). Il n'est pas tenu compte des variations salariales résultant de l'augmentation de la proportion des personnes qualifiées ou du déplacement des travailleurs vers des branches économiques qui versent, en moyenne, des salaires plus élevés. L'indice est actuellement calculé sur l'année de base 1993'100.

L'évolution des salaires réels est mesurée en corrigeant l'indice des salaires nominaux de la variation des prix par l'indice des prix à la consommation.

Indicateurs de fiabilité des estimations

Couverture du système administratif: exhaustive. Tous les salariés ont l'obligation d'être assurés contre les accidents.

Erreurs non dues à l'échantillonnage: durée normale et salaires: le schéma de pondération doit toujours être adapté aux résultats des derniers recensements des entreprises, de sorte qu'il n'est pas possible d'analyser l'évolution à très long'terme.

Evolution des salaires: la statistique a le défaut d'exclure les salariés à temps partiel ainsi que les cadres moyens et supérieurs (qui sont couverts dans les déclarations d'accidents, mais non repris dans les calculs statistiques).

Conformité avec d'autres sources: durée normale du travail: les résultats de la statistique sont comparés à d'autres indicateurs sur la durée du travail, tels que la Statistique du volume du travail (SVOLTA): la comparaison donne des résultats pratiquement identiques en ce qui concerne les salariés occupés à plein temps.

Des comparaisons sont également effectuées avec d'autres enquêtes qui fournissent des informations sur la durée du travail effectué, telles que le recensement fédéral de la population, l'enquête suisse sur la population active (ESPA), l'enquête sur la structure des salaires et la statistique des conventions collectives du travail.

Séries disponibles

Pour les années antérieures à l'année courante: indices officiels et évolution des salaires au niveau de l'ensemble de l'économie ainsi que par branche économique, sexe, niveau de qualification et/ou domaine d'activité:

Indice des salaires nominaux et réels, par sexe et total, par division et secteur économique, domaine d'activité et niveau de qualification, et variation par rapport à l'année précédente;

Indice des salaires nominaux, total,, par classe économique et variation par rapport à l'année précédente;

Indice des salaires nominaux et réels et variations en %, par catégories de travailleurs (ouvriers, employés, sexe, catégories).

Pour l'année courante: évolution des salaires au niveau le plus agrégé.

Durée hebdomadaire normale du travail dans les entreprises et variations par rapport à l'année précédente en chiffres absolus et en pourcentages, par classe économique;

Durée hebdomadaire normale du travail et variations, par canton, région et division économique.

Historique des statistiques

Date de début de la série statistique: statistique de la durée normale du travail dans les entreprises et de l'évolution des salaires: 1918, dans le secteur secondaire seulement. Depuis 1985, avec l'entrée en vigueur en 1984 de la nouvelle loi sur l'assurance-accidents (LAA) qui soumet tous les travailleurs à l'obligation de s'assurer, cette statistique couvre tous les secteurs, à l'exception de l'agriculture, de la chasse et de la pêche.

Modifications et révisions principales: statistique sur l'évolution des salaires: jusqu'en 1993, les chiffres officiels provenaient de l'Enquête d'octobre sur les salaires et traitements. Depuis 1994, la présente statistique constitue la source de données officielle.

A partir de 1991, l'édition de 1995 (NOGA) de la Nomenclature générale des activités économiques a remplacé l'édition de 1985.

Avant 1995, l'exploitation des données recueillies sur la durée normale du travail et les salaires, ainsi que la publication des résultats, incombaient à l'Office Fédéral de l'industrie, des arts et métiers et du travail (OFIAMT) (aujourd'hui l'Office Fédéral du développement économique et de l'emploi - OFDE). Depuis, elles relèvent de la compétence de l'OFS.

Une révision de la statistique de l'évolution des salaires est actuellement en cours. Elle vise notamment à atteindre les objectifs suivants: (i) la prise en compte des salariés travaillant à temps partiel; et (ii) l'introduction d'un indicateur conjoncturel trimestriel.

Documentation et diffusion

Documentation:

OFS: *Durée normale du travail dans les entreprises. Résultats commentés et tableaux* (Berne, annuel);

Idem: *Communiqué de presse: statistique du volume du travail* (ibid.); publication occasionnelle;

Idem: *Communiqué de presse: Heures de travail en 2000* (Neuchâtel, février 2002);

Idem: *La statistique du volume du travail. Bases méthodologiques et définitions* (Berne, 1997);

Idem: *Indicateurs du marché du travail* (annuel).

Département fédéral de l'économie publique: *La Vie économique* (Berne, mensuel);

OFS: *La nouvelle statistique de l'évolution des salaires. Conception et résultats 1994* (Berne, 1995);

Idem: *Evolution des salaires. Résultats commentés et tableaux* (Neuchâtel, annuel).

Idem: Communiqué de presse: Indice suisse des salaires 2001 (Neuchâtel, avril 2002).

Diffusion: sur le site Internet de l'OFS:

http://www.statistique.admin.ch

Les statistiques ne paraissant pas dans les publications nationales ou sur Internet peuvent être obtenues sur demande.

Données communiquées au BIT aux fins de diffusion

Les statistiques suivantes ont été communiquées au BIT pour publication dans *l'Annuaire des statistiques du Travail* et sont disponibles dans LABORSTA.

Durée hebdomadaire normale des salariés, par branche d'activité économique (jusqu'en 1993); et dans les industries manufacturières;

Gains des ouvriers (jusqu'en 1983) par branche d'activité économique (secteur secondaire).

Autres sources administratives de données:

La statistique des conventions collectives de travail en Suisse (ECS) est réalisée tous les deux ans le 1er mai depuis 1992. Elle a pour but de dresser un répertoire exhaustif et détaillé des conventions collectives de travail (CCT) et des contrats-types de travail (CTT) en Suisse. Elle s'effectue directement auprès des parties contractantes d'une CCT, à savoir les associations patronales ou entreprises et les associations de salariés signataires d'une convention. Les principales caractéristiques structurelles relevées sont la branche économique, le genre de convention collective, le champ d'application territorial, les signataires, la date d'entrée en vigueur, la question de la paix du travail et le nombre d'assujettis (employeurs et salariés) par sexe.

L'Enquête annuelle sur les accords salariaux (EAS) dans les domaines couverts par une convention collective de travail rend compte des résultats des négociations menées entre les partenaires sociaux sur les adaptations des salaires effectifs et minimaux dans le domaine des conventions collectives de travail.

Le Registre central des étrangers (RCE) fournit des indicateurs mensuels sur le nombre d'étrangers actifs occupés dans les différentes branches d'activité, selon le sexe et le type de permis.

La statistique des enseignants et celle des emplois dans le domaine de la santé renseignent sur les effectifs et l'évolution du personnel dans ces deux branches.

La statistique des conflits collectifs du travail, réalisée par l'OFDE, recense les grèves de caractère économique qui durent au moins un jour. Elle se base sur des informations de base tirées de la presse quotidienne, qui mènent aux employeurs et associations économiques concernés. Ces derniers doivent ensuite compléter un questionnaire fournissant des informations sur les caractéristiques suivantes: type de conflit (grève ou lock-out), raison du conflit, nombre de salariés concernés, durée de l'action, heures de travail non accomplies, branche économique, nombre d'entreprises concernées et manière dont le conflit est résolu.

Des *statistiques de synthèse*, qui combinent des données primaires (enquêtes) et des données secondaires (sources administratives) sont également produites, parmi lesquelles:

La statistique du volume du travail établie par l'OFS depuis 1991. Le volume du travail de la population résidente permanente est calculé sur la base de données empiriques fournies par l'enquête suisse sur la population active (ESPA), dans laquelle la durée normale du travail, les heures supplémentaires et les absences sont déterminées et agrégées par emploi. Le volume du travail des autres groupes de population travaillant en Suisse se calcule sur la base des résultats de la statistique de la population active occupée (SPAO) (nombre de personnes actives occupées) et du recensement de'la population (moyenne des heures de travail).

Définition du volume du travail: heures de travail réellement effectuées (' durée normale, + heures supplémentaires payées ou non, - absences). Le volume du travail s'obtient en additionnant les durées annuelles effectives du travail pour l'ensemble des emplois (indépendants et salariés, qui ont travaillé une heure au moins contre rémunération durant l'année de référence, et personnes qui, sans être rémunérées, ont collaboré dans l'entreprise familiale pendant l'année de référence).

Période de référence: l'année civile

Périodicité: annuelle;

Critères de ventilation des données sur la durée normale du travail, les heures supplémentaires, les absences et le volume du travail: sexe, origine/type de permis de séjour, section économique, taux d'occupation et statut d'activité.

Publications:

OFS: *Communiqué de presse: statistique du volume du travail* (Berne, annuel);

Idem: *La statistique du volume du travail. Bases méthodologiques et définitions* (ibid., 1997);

Idem: *Indicateurs du marché du travail* (Neuchâtel, annuel).

La statistique mensuelle sur la réduction du temps de travail, réalisée par l'Office fédéral du développement économique et de l'emploi (OFDE): elle fournit des informations sur les salariés (par sexe) et les entreprises concernés, les branches économiques, les cantons et les heures chômées.

Les effectifs des membres de l'Union syndicale suisse (USS) et d'autres organisations de salariés: il s'agit d'un relevé établi par l'USS au 31 décembre de chaque année, du nombre de membres (person-nes) des syndicats et des associations patronales qui lui sont affiliés. La publication de l'USS présente, en outre, les effectifs des autres grandes organisations de salariés (Confédération des syndicats chrétiens de Suisse, Fédération des sociétés suisses d'employés, Union fédérative du personnel des administrations et des entreprises publiques, etc.), mais exclut les petites organisations non affiliées à l'USS.

Turquie

Source de la série
Rapports de l'Institution d'assurance sociale.

Titre de la série
Sosyal Sigortalar Kurumu (SSK) Yillik Istatistikler (Statistiques annuelles de l'Institution d'assurance sociale).

Organisme responsable
Collecte des données, traitement statistique et publication/diffusion des statistiques: Direction générale, Institution d'assurance sociale, rattachée au ministère du Travail et de la Sécurité sociale.

Principaux sujets couverts
Emploi et gains

Périodicité ou fréquence de disponibilité des statistiques
Annuelle.

Période de référence
Début septembre.

Portée des statistiques
Géographique: tout le pays.

Branches d'activité: toutes les branches d'activité économique.

Etablissements: de tous types et de toutes tailles.

Personnes: tous les salariés assurés employés en vertu d'un contrat de service dans des entreprises privées et publiques.

Professions: toutes les professions des personnes ayant un contrat d'emploi conforme à ceux prévus par la loi n° 506 sur l'assurance sociale.

Concepts et définitions
Emploi: il s'agit du nombre total de salariés, y compris les apprentis et les travailleurs temporaires, travaillant dans des lieux de travail visés par la loi n° 506 de l'assurance sociale. Toutes les personnes qui sont enregistrées auprès du système d'assurance sont considérées comme des personnes salariées au moment de leur entrée en service et sont par conséquent couvertes par les statistiques.

Gains: il s'agit des gains journaliers bruts moyens, y compris les gains versés pour la durée de travail normale effective, le paiement des heures supplémentaires, les indemnités de licenciement, les primes d'ancienneté et de rendement. Les limites minimales et maximales des gains journaliers et mensuels utilisées pour la détermination des cotisations et des prestations de sécurité sociale sont fixées par la loi.

Durée du travail: il s'agit de la durée du travail normale. Aux termes de la loi n° 1475, la durée du travail journalière est de 7,5 heures (45 heures par semaine).

Classifications
Branches d'activité économique:

Titre de la classification: Branches d'activité couvertes par la loi sur l'assurance sociale.

Nombre de groupes utilisés pour le codage: 10 (0-9) groupes principaux.

S'applique à: emploi et gains.

Lien avec la CITI et niveau: lien avec la CITI, Rev. 2 (1968).

Autres classifications: les données relatives à l'emploi et aux gains sont ventilées par sexe et par secteur (public et privé).

Rassemblement des données
Méthode de collecte des données: les données sont basées sur les informations figurant sur les certificats de cotisations délivrés par les employeurs qui servent de rapports d'assurance mensuels à l'Institution d'assurance sociale.

Mise à jour du système administratif: mensuelle.

Traitement et contrôle des données
Pas d'informations disponibles.

Ajustements
Pas d'informations disponibles.

Types d'estimations
Nombre total de salariés;

Gains journaliers moyens.

Les gains journaliers moyens correspondent au rapport entre le total des gains pris comme base pour le calcul des cotisations et le nombre de jours pour lesquels des cotisations ont été payées.

Calcul d'indices
Aucun.

Indicateurs de fiabilité des estimations
Pas d'informations disponibles.

Séries disponibles
Nombre de salariés au début septembre de chaque année;

Gains moyens des salariés.

Historique des statistiques
Date de début de la série statistique: 1950.

Modifications et révisions principales: La loi n° 506 sur l'assurance sociale, actuellement en vigueur, a pris effet le 1er mars 1965. Comparée aux lois sur l'assurance sociale précédentes, elle a une portée accrue.

Documentation et diffusion
Documentation:

Institution de l'assurance sociale, Direction générale: *Statistiques annuelles de l'Institution d'assurance sociale* (Ankara, publiées chaque année);

Services du Premier Ministre, Institut des statistiques de l'Etat: *Annuaire des statistiques de la Turquie* (ibid., publication annuelle); contient des données sur l'emploi durant l'année précédente *(t-1)* et des données sur les salaires versées durant l'avant-dernière année *(t-2)*, ainsi que certaines informations méthodologiques sur la source des données.

Données communiquées au BIT aux fins de diffusion
Les statistiques suivantes sont communiquées au BIT en vue d'être publiées dans l'*Annuaire des statistiques du Travail:*

Emploi rémunéré, données ventilées par branche d'activité économique et par sexe;

Gains journaliers moyens des salariés par branche d'activité économique, dans les industries manufacturières, par grand groupe ou branche d'industrie, et par sexe.

Autres sources administratives de données: le système de sécurité sociale de la Turquie est constitué par trois organisations principales: l'Institution d'assurance sociale (voir ci-dessus); la Caisse de retraite des employés gouvernementaux, et "Bag-Kur", c'est-à-dire l'organisation de sécurité sociale des personnes travaillant à leur compte qui ne sont pas couvertes pas la loi sur l'assurance sociale, telles que travailleurs agricoles, hommes de métier, artisans, chefs de petites entreprises, techniciens et personnes exerçant une profession scientifique ou libérale qui sont enregistrées auprès d'une chambre ou d'une association professionnelle et actionnaires de sociétés autres que les coopératives et les sociétés par actions. Les statistiques relatives au nombre de personnes couvertes et aux montants des prestations versées sont basées sur les données de la Caisse de retraite des employés gouvernementaux et de la Direction générale de Bag-Kur.

Introducción – Parte I

En esta parte se presentan las descripciones metodológicas que se refieren a las estadísticas de desempleo nacionales derivadas de Inscripciones Administrativas. Muchas de las series estadísticas correspondientes se publican por la OIT en el *Anuario de Estadísticas del Trabajo* y/o en el *Boletín de Estadísticas del Trabajo*, y se encuentran también en su sitio internet (http://laborsta.ilo.org).

Las 96 descripciones - que abarcan 94 países, áreas o territorios - incluidas en esta parte se han preparado tomando como base las informaciones proporcionadas principalmente por las oficinas de colocación nacionales en respuesta a un cuestionario específico. A fin de facilitar comparaciones todas las descripciones tienen el mismo formato y presentan las informaciones bajo doce secciones con subtítulos uniformes. Sin embargo, habría que tener en cuenta que las estadísticas derivadas de inscripciones administrativas ne son estrictamente comparables entre países debido a ciertas diferencias en las legislaciones en cuestión y las capacidades administrativas.

Bajo las diferentes secciones se hallan las informaciones siguientes: el título y el año de inicio de la serie; el organismo nacional responsable de las inscripciones; los datos específicos que se registran de una persona; los criterios utilizados para determinar si una persona será o no inscrita como desempleada; la definición de persona desempleada en la que se basan las estadísticas; la frecuencia de actualización de los registros; si se utilizan las estadísticas derivadas de los registros para obtener tasas de desempleo; el tipo de estadísticas de desempleo que se producen, así como la disponibilidad de información metodológica sobre estas estadísticas; si se han hecho comparaciones con estadísticas de desempleo derivadas de otras fuentes, y las modificaciones importantes que hayan influido significativamente las estadísticas desde su comienzo.

En las descripciones se refiere a las siguientes clasificaciones:

CIUO-88: Clasificación Internacional Uniforme de Ocupaciones, 1988 (Oficina internacional del Trabajo, Ginebra, 1991);

CIIU, Rev. 3: Clasificación Industrial Internacional Uniforme de Todas las Actividades Económicas (Naciones Unidas, Nueva York, 1990);

NACE, Rev. 1: Nomenclatura Estadística de Actividades Económicas de la Comunidad Europea (Eurostat, Luxemburgo, 1996);

CITE-97 Clasificación Internacional Normalizada de la Educación (UNESCO, París, 1997).

Alemania

1. Serie
Título: Desempleo registrado.
Año de inicio: No indicado.
2. Organismo responsable de la inscripción inicial de desempleados
Nombre del organismo: Bundesanstalt für Arbeit (Oficina Federal de Trabajo).
Tipo de organismo: Organismo público subordinado a una autoridad nacional.
Nombre de la autoridad nacional: Bundesministerium für Wirtschaft und Arbeit (Ministerio de Economía y Trabajo).
Ubicación de las oficinas locales donde se hacen las inscripciones: En todo el país.
Tipo de servicios proporcionados/administrados por el organismo:
– Ayuda a personas en busca de empleo a encontrarlo;
– Ayuda a personas en busca de empleo a crear su propia empresa;
– Ayuda a los empleadores a encontrar trabajadores;
– Orientación profesional;
– Formación relacionada con el trabajo;
– Pago de prestaciones de desempleo.
Porcentaje de personas en busca de empleo que buscan trabajo por intermedio de ese organismo: Varía de una región a otra.
3. Se registran los siguientes datos de la persona:
– Nombre y apellido;
– Sexo;
– Número de seguridad social (o número de identificación semejante también utilizado por otros organismos);
– Dirección del domicilio habitual;
– Fecha de nacimiento;
– Ciudadanía;

– Nacionalidad/grupo étnico;
– Nivel de educación/formación: se identifican cinco categorías. No se han establecido vínculos con la CINE;
– Situación laboral anterior: se identifican cinco categorías;
– Tipo de ocupación del empleo actual o anterior: se identifica un número indeterminado de grupos. Se han establecido vínculos con la CIUO-88;
– Tipo de ocupación del empleo que se busca: se identifica un número indeterminado de grupos. Se han establecido vínculos con la CIUO-88;
– Rama de actividad del empleador o del lugar de trabajo actual o anterior: se identifica un número indeterminado de grupos. Se han establecido vínculos con la CIIU Rev. 3 y la NACE Rev. 1, a nivel de grupos.

4. Criterios utilizados para determinar si una persona habrá de incluirse en el registro (R)* y/o en las estadísticas de personas desempleadas (S):
– Estar sin empleo (S);
– Estar en busca de empleo (S);
– Estar disponible para trabajar (S);
– Edad (mínima: 15 años; máxima: 65 años) (S);
– Ciudadanía (S);
– Residir en el país (S);
– Duración y/o número de horas de trabajo del empleo que se busca (mínimo 15 horas por semana) (S).

* Los solicitantes pueden ser inscritos como personas desempleadas en busca de empleo o personas no desempleadas en busca de empleo.

5. Criterios utilizados para determinar si se ha de excluir a una persona del registro (R) y/o de las estadísticas de personas desempleadas (S):
– Certificado de defunción (R) y (S);
– Incorporarse a un (nuevo) empleo (S);
– Comenzar el servicio militar (S);
– Participar en algún programa de promoción del empleo, de obras públicas, etc. (S);
– Estar estudiando o siguiendo una formación (S);
– Incumplir el requisito de tomar contacto con el organismo (S);
– Rechazar un número indeterminado de ofertas de empleo adecuadas (S);
– Rechazar un número indeterminado de ofertas de formación adecuadas (S);
– Cobrar alguna pensión (S);
– Incapacidad para trabajar (debido a enfermedad; licencia de maternidad; cura, etc.) (S).

6. Definición de persona desempleada en la que se basan las estadísticas
Personas desempleadas son aquellas que:
– temporalmente no tienen una relación de empleo;
– están en busca de un empleo con seguro obligatorio;
– están disponibles para aceptar una colocación de la Oficina de Empleo;
– están inscritas como desempleadas en la Oficina de Empleo;
– no tienen más de 65 años, y
– no están incapacitadas para trabajar por motivo de enfermedad.
Para contabilizarlas en las estadísticas como personas desempleadas deben responder a todos estos criterios simultáneamente.

7. Actualización de los registros
Los registros (estadísticas) se actualizan mensualmente.

8. Tasas de desempleo
Se utilizan estadísticas de estos registros para obtener tasas de desempleo.
Fuentes de los datos de empleo incluidos en el denominador de las tasas de desempleo: estadísticas de empleo y desempleo de la Oficina Federal de Trabajo, y estadísticas del personal del servicio público.
Definición de persona empleada que se utiliza a tales efectos:
– Trabajadores civiles;
– Todas las personas civiles económicamente activas.

9. Tipo de estadísticas que se producen sobre desempleados registrados
Período de referencia: Mes.
Frecuencia de producción: Mensual.
Variables utilizadas:
– Sexo;
– Edad;
– Nivel de educación;

- Ocupación;
- Rama de actividad;
- Características geográficas;
- Experiencia laboral previa;
- Ciudadanía (nacionales o no);
- Duración del desempleo.

Publicación:
- En papel, para el público en general;
- En el sitio web www.arbeitsamt.de.

Organismo responsable de la publicación: Oficina Federal de Trabajo.

Título y periodicidad de la publicación: *Amtliche Nachrichten der Bundesanstalt für Arbeit (ANBA)* (mensual).

10. Información metodológica sobre las estadísticas
Divulgación: En papel, para el público en general.
Organismo responsable de la divulgación: Oficina Federal de Trabajo.

11. Comparaciones con estadísticas derivadas de otras fuentes
Se han hecho comparaciones con estadísticas de desempleo derivadas de la Encuesta sobre la fuerza de trabajo.

12. Modificaciones importantes desde el comienzo de las estadísticas
En la legislación, la competencia del organismo y/o los procedimientos administrativos no ha habido modificaciones importantes que hayan influido significativamente en las estadísticas.

Argelia

1. Serie
Título: Las *Notas de coyuntura* reagrupan la demanda, la oferta y la colocación (situación del mercado de trabajo).
Año de inicio: 1994.

2. Organismo responsable de la inscripción inicial de desempleados
Nombre del organismo: Agence nationale de l'Emploi - ANEM (Agencia Nacional de Empleo).
Tipo de organismo: Organismo público subordinado a una autoridad nacional.
Nombre de la autoridad nacional: Ministerio de Empleo y Solidaridad Nacional.
Ubicación de las oficinas locales donde se hacen las inscripciones: En cada prefectura (165 agencias locales y 11 regionales en todo el territorio del país).
Tipo de servicios proporcionados/administrados por el organismo
- Ayuda a personas en busca de empleo a encontrarlo;
- Ayuda a los empleadores a encontrar trabajadores;
- Orientación profesional;
- Otros servicios relacionados con el empleo: Registro de personas en busca de empleo que fueron despedidas por motivos económicos y solicitantes de empleo diplomados de enseñanza superior que reúnen las condiciones para beneficiar de contratos de preempleo.

3. Se registran los siguientes datos de la persona
- Nombre y apellido;
- Sexo;
- Dirección del domicilio habitual;
- Fecha de nacimiento;
- Nacionalidad;
- Nivel de educación/formación: se identifican seis categorías. No se han establecido vínculos con la CINE;
- Situación laboral actual o anterior: se identifican dos categorías;
- Tipo de ocupación del empleo actual o anterior: se identifican 20 categorías. No se han establecido vínculos con la CIUO-88;
- Tipo de ocupación del empleo que se busca: se identifican 20 categorías;
- Nombre y dirección del empleador o del lugar de trabajo actual o anterior;
- Rama de actividad del empleador o del lugar de trabajo actual o anterior: se identifican 22 categorías. No se han establecido vínculos con la CIIU;
- Inscripciones previas en el organismo;
- Situación respecto al servicio militar nacional.

4. Criterios utilizados para determinar si una persona habrá de incluirse en el registro (R) y/o en las estadísticas de personas desempleadas (S)
- Estar sin empleo (R) y (S);
- Estar en busca de empleo (R) y (S);

- Estar disponible para trabajar (R) y (S);
- Edad (mínima: 16 años; máxima: 60 años) (R) y (S);
- Residir en el país (R) y (S).

5. Criterios utilizados para determinar si se ha de excluir a una persona del registro (R) y/o de las estadísticas de personas desempleadas (S)
- Certificado de defunción (R) y (S);
- Establecerse en otro país (R) y (S);
- Incorporarse a un (nuevo) empleo (R) y (S);
- Comenzar el servicio militar (R) y (S);
- Participar en algún programa de promoción del empleo, de obras públicas, etc. (R) y (S);
- Cobrar alguna pensión (jubilación u otras) (R) y (S);
- Incapacidad para trabajar (R) y (S).

6. Definición de persona desempleada en la que se basan las estadísticas
Se entiende por población desempleada, la totalidad de personas, jurídicamente aptas para trabajar (de edades comprendidas entre 16 y 60 años), que han declarado estar sin empleo y estar en busca de empleo, y que se han inscrito en alguna agencia local de empleo. Las personas inscritas se clasifican en dos categorías: STRI, personas que han trabajado y STR2, personas que nunca han trabajado.

7. Actualización de los registros
Los registros se actualizan periódicamente.

8. Tasas de desempleo
No se utilizan estadísticas de estos registros para obtener tasas de desempleo. Dichas tasas son producidas por la Oficina Nacional de Estadística (ONS) cuyas fuentes principales son:
- la Encuesta sobre la fuerza de trabajo, y
- el Censo de población.

9. Tipo de estadísticas que se producen sobre desempleados registrados
Serie 1
Frecuencia de producción: Trimestral.
Variables utilizadas
- Sexo;
- Edad;
- Nivel de educación;
- Ocupación;
- Rama de actividad;
- Experiencia laboral previa.

Publicación: En papel, para un público limitado.
Organismo responsable de la publicación: ANEM.
Título y periodicidad de la publicación: *Note de conjoncture sur la situation du marché de l'emploi.* (Nota de coyuntura sobre la situación del mercado de trabajo), trimestral.

10. Información metodológica sobre las estadísticas
Divulgación:
- Sólo para uso interno;
- En papel, para un público limitado.
Organismo responsable: ANEM.

11. Comparaciones con estadísticas derivadas de otras fuentes
No se han hecho comparaciones con estadísticas de desempleo derivadas de otras fuentes.

12. Modificaciones importantes desde el comienzo de las estadísticas
En la legislación, la competencia del organismo y/o los procedimientos administrativos no ha habido modificaciones importantes que hayan influido significativamente en las estadísticas.

13. Otros comentarios
Los datos estadísticos de la ANEM abarcan únicamente a las personas en busca de empleo inscritas en sus estructuras; los datos relativos al desempleo son competencia de la Oficina Nacional de Estadística (ONS).

Australia

1. Serie
Título: *Registered unemployment benefit claimants - [New Start Allowance (NSA) or Youth Allowance (other) (YA(o)]* Solicitantes de prestaciones de desempleo registrados (Prestaciones de desempleo y prestaciones para jóvenes (otros) YA(o)).
Año de inicio: 1940.

2. Organismo responsable de la inscripción inicial de desempleados
Nombre del organismo: Centrelink.
Tipo de organismo: Organismo público subordinado a una autoridad nacional.

Nombre de la autoridad nacional: *Department of Employment and Workplace Relations and the Department of Family and Community Services* (FaCS) (Departamento de Empleo y Relaciones Laborales, y Departamento de la Familia y Servicios Comunitarios).

Ubicación de las oficinas locales donde se hacen las inscripciones: Centrelink tiene oficinas en 400 localidades de toda Australia.

Tipo de servicios proporcionados/administrados por el organismo:
- Pago de prestaciones de desempleo.

3. Se registran los siguientes datos de la persona:
- Nombre y apellido;
- Sexo;
- Dirección del domicilio habitual;
- Fecha de nacimiento;
- Ciudadanía;
- Nacionalidad /grupo étnico (indicación facultativa);
- Nivel de educación/formación profesional: se identifican 16 categorías (indicación facultativa);
- Situación laboral actual o anterior: se identifican seis categorías;
- Tipo de ocupación en el empleo actual o anterior;
- Tipo de ocupación del empleo que se busca (indicación facultativa);
- Nombre y dirección del empleador/lugar de trabajo actual o anterior;
- Inscripciones previas en el organismo;
- Otros: Número de hijos a cargo; estado civil; vivienda/alojamiento.

4. Criterios utilizados para determinar si una persona habrá de incluirse en el registro (R) y/o en las estadísticas de personas desempleadas (S):
- Estar sin empleo. Ahora bien, las personas en busca de empleo pueden aceptar trabajo ocasional o a tiempo parcial (sujeto a comprobación de ingresos) y seguir teniendo derecho al pago de prestaciones (R);
- Estar en busca de empleo (R);
- Estar disponible para trabajar (R);
- Edad (mínima: 15 años; máxima: edad de jubilación) (R);
- Residir en el país (mínimo 104 semanas) (R);
- Otros: reunir los requisitos de la prueba de búsqueda activa que demuestran que la persona busca empleo activamente (R).

5. Criterios utilizados para determinar si se ha de excluir a una persona del registro (R) y/o de las estadísticas de personas desempleadas (S):
- Certificado de defunción (R);
- Establecerse en otro país (R);
- Incorporarse a un (nuevo) empleo; salvo trabajo a tiempo parcial y trabajo ocasional (R);
- Participar en algún programa de promoción del empleo, de obras públicas, etc. La participación en determinados programas, por ejemplo, *Work for the Dole* (trabajo por ayuda de desempleo) no incide en los derechos de recibir prestaciones de desempleo (R);
- Incumplir el requisito de tomar contacto con el organismo: las dos primeras veces se reduce el pago de las prestaciones de desempleo y la tercera, se suspende (R);
- Rechazar ofertas de empleo adecuadas: las dos primeras veces se reduce el pago de las prestaciones de desempleo y la tercera, se suspende (R);
- Rechazar ofertas de formación adecuadas: las dos primeras veces se reduce el pago de las prestaciones de desempleo y la tercera, se suspende (R);
- Edad de jubilación: 65 años para los hombres y 62 para las mujeres (R);
- Incapacidad para trabajar (R);
- Otros: si los ingresos o bienes de la persona solicitante o su cónyuge superan el máximo previsto (R); cobrar alguna indemnización de trabajadores o alguna otra prestación relacionada con accidentes de trabajo (R).

6. Definición de persona desempleada en la que se basan las estadísticas

Las personas inscritas no se utilizan para obtener estadísticas de personas desempleadas. No obstante, se dispone de series que contabilizan los beneficiarios de prestaciones de desempleo (por conducto de las prestaciones *New Start* y las prestaciones para jóvenes). Estas series abarcan a quienes reciben prestaciones conforme a las inclusiones y exclusiones indicadas en las secciones 4 y 5.

Por lo general, en las series de NSA y YA(o) se contabiliza a los beneficiarios como sigue: hombres de edades comprendidas entre 15 y 64 años, y mujeres de edades comprendidas entre 15 y 61 años.

7. Actualización de los registros

Los registros se actualizan cada 15 días (porque el pago de prestaciones es quincenal).

8. Tasas de desempleo

No se utilizan estadísticas de estos registros para obtener tasas de desempleo.

9. Tipo de estadísticas que se producen sobre desempleados registrados

Serie: *Mercado del trabajo y pagos relacionados.*
Período de referencia: Mes.
Frecuencia de producción: Mensual.
Vriables utilizadas:
- Sexo;
- Edad;
- Características geográficas;
- Duración del desempleo.

Publicación: En papel, para el público en general.
Organismo responsable de la publicación: FaCS.
Título y periodicidad de la publicación: *Labour Market and Related Payments* (Mercado de trabajo y pagos relacionados), mensual.

10. Información metodológica sobre las estadísticas
Divulgación: En papel, para el público en general.
Organismo responsable : FaCS.

11. Comparaciones con estadísticas derivadas de otras fuentes

Se hacen comparaciones con las estadísticas de desempleo de la Encuesta sobre la fuerza de trabajo.
Frecuencia de las comparaciones: De vez en cuando (último año: 2000).
Publicación de la metodología/resultados de las comparaciones: Sólo para uso interno.

12. Modificaciones importantes desde el comienzo de las estadísticas

En la legislación, la competencia del organismo y/o los procedimientos administrativos no ha habido modificaciones importantes que hayan influido significativamente en las estadísticas.

Bahrein

1. Serie
Título: Desempleo registrado.
Año de inicio: 1996.

2. Organismo responsable de la inscripción inicial de desempleados
Nombre del organismo: Oficina de Servicios del Empleo.
Tipo de organismo: Organismo público subordinado a una autoridad nacional.
Nombre de la autoridad nacional: Ministerio de Trabajo y Asuntos Sociales.
Ubicación de las oficinas locales donde se hacen las inscripciones: Edificio principal del Ministerio de Trabajo y Asuntos Sociales, Ciudad de Isá.
Tipo de servicios proporcionados/administrados por el organismo
- Ayuda a personas en busca de empleo a encontrarlo;
- Ayuda a personas en busca de empleo a crear su propia empresa;
- Ayuda a los empleadores a encontrar trabajadores;
- Orientación profesional;
- Formación relacionada con el trabajo.

3. Se registran los siguientes datos de la persona
- Nombre y apellido;
- Sexo;
- Número de seguridad social (o número de identificación semejante también utilizado por otros organismos);
- Dirección del domicilio habitual;
- Fecha de nacimiento;
- Ciudadanía;
- Nacionalidad/grupo étnico;
- Nivel de educación/formación: se identifican seis categorías. Se han establecido vínculos con la CINE;
- Situación laboral actual o anterior: se identifican cinco categorías;
- Tipo de ocupación del empleo actual o anterior: se identifican tres grupos en la clasificación utilizada para codificar la ocupación. No se han establecido vínculos con la CIUO-88;

– Tipo de ocupación del empleo que se busca: se identifican nueve grupos en la clasificación utilizada para codificar la ocupación No se han establecido vínculos con la CIUO-88;

– Nombre y dirección del empleador o del lugar de trabajo actual o anterior;

– Otros: idiomas que se hablan; curso(s) de formación.

4. Criterios utilizados para determinar si una persona habrá de incluirse en el registro (R) y/o en las estadísticas de personas desempleadas (S)

– Estar sin empleo   (R);

– Estar en busca de empleo   (R);

– Estar disponible para trabajar   (R);

– Edad (mínima: 17 años; máxima: 50 años)   (R);

– Ciudadanía (sólo ciudadanos de Bahrain)   (R);

– Residir en el país   (R);

– Haber trabajado   (R);

– Duración y/o número de horas de trabajo del empleo que se busca   (R);

– Pago previo de aportes al seguro de desempleo   (R).

5. Criterios utilizados para determinar si se ha de excluir a una persona del registro (R) y/o de las estadísticas de personas desempleadas (S)

– Certificado de defunción   (S);

– Establecerse en otro país   (S);

– Incorporarse a un (nuevo) empleo   (R);

– Participar en algún programa de promoción del empleo, de obras públicas, etc.   (S);

– Estar estudiando o siguiendo una formación   (R);

– Incumplir el requisito de tomar contacto con el organismo (S);

– Rechazar ofertas de empleo adecuadas   (S);

– Rechazar ofertas de formación adecuadas   (S);

– Fin del período de prestaciones de desempleo   (R);

– Cobrar alguna pensión   (S);

– Incapacidad para trabajar   (S).

6. Definición de persona desempleada en la que se basan las estadísticas

Persona desempleada es aquella que se incluye en las estimaciones de la Organización General de Seguro Social y está inscrita en la Oficina de Servicios del Empleo, del Ministerio de Trabajo y Asuntos Sociales como persona en busca de empleo o persona desempleada.

7. Actualización de los registros

Los registros se actualizan diaria y mensualmente.

8. Tasas de desempleo

Se utilizan estadísticas de estos registros para obtener tasas de desempleo.

Fuente de los datos sobre empleo incluidos en el denominador de las tasas de desempleo: Registro de la Seguridad Social.

9. Tipo de estadísticas que se producen sobre desempleados registrados

Serie 1: Informe diario de las condiciones de empleo.

Período de referencia: Día.

Frecuencia de producción: Diaria, si procede.

Variables utilizadas

– Sexo;

– Edad;

– Nivel de educación;

– Ocupación;

– Rama de actividad;

– Características geográficas;

– Experiencia laboral previa;

– Ciudadanía (ciudadanos/extranjeros);

– Duración del desempleo.

Publicación: Sólo para uso interno.

Serie 2: Informe abreviado de todas las condiciones.

Período de referencia: Mes.

Frecuencia de producción: Mensual, si procede.

Variables utilizadas:

– Sexo;

– Edad;

– Nivel de educación;

– Ocupación;

– Rama de actividad;

– Características geográficas;

– Experiencia laboral previa;

– Ciudadanía (ciudadanos/extranjeros);

– Duración del desempleo.

Publicación: Sólo para uso interno.

Serie 3:

Período de referencia: Año.

Frecuencia de producción: Anual, si procede.

Variables utilizadas:

– Sexo;

– Edad;

– Nivel de educación;

– Ocupación;

– Rama de actividad;

– Características geográficas;

– Experiencia laboral previa;

– Ciudadanía (ciudadanos/extranjeros);

– Duración del desempleo.

Publicación: Sólo para uso interno.

10. Información metodológica sobre las estadísticas Divulgación:

– En un archivo electrónico, previa solicitud;

– En el sitio web: www.bah-Molsa.com/.

11. Comparaciones con estadísticas derivadas de otras fuentes

Se han hecho comparaciones con las estadísticas de desempleo del Censo de población.

12. Modificaciones importantes desde el comienzo de las estadísticas

En la legislación, la competencia del organismo y/o los procedimientos administrativos no ha habido modificaciones importantes que hayan influido significativamente en las estadísticas.

Barbados

1. Serie

Título: Estadísticas nacionales de prestaciones des seguro.

Año de inicio: 1881.

2. Organismo responsable de la inscripción inicial de desempleados

Nombre del organismo: Departamento Nacional de Seguro.

Tipo de organismo: Organismo público subordinado a una autoridad nacional.

Nombre de la autoridad nacional: Ministerio de Trabajo y Seguridad social.

Ubicación de las oficinas locales donde se hacen las inscripciones: Todo el país.

Tipo de servicios proporcionados/administrados por el organismo

– Pago de prestaciones de desempleo.

3. Se registran los siguientes datos de la persona

– Nombre y apellido;

– Número de seguridad social (o número de identificación semejante también utilizado por otros organismos);

– Dirección del domicilio habitual;

– Fecha de nacimiento;

– Situación laboral actual o anterior;

– Tipo de ocupación del empleo actual o anterior;

– Rama de actividad del empleador o del lugar de trabajo actual o anterior;

– Otros: cualquier aporte pendiente.

4. Criterios utilizados para determinar si una persona habrá de incluirse en el registro (R) y/o en las estadísticas de personas desempleadas (S)

– Estar sin empleo (Los solicitantes deben haber estado sin empleo tres semanas como mínimo) (R) y (S);

– Estar en busca de empleo: no se incluirá a aquella persona que no aprovecha la oportunidad de postular a una empleo adecuado o que no haga un esfuerzo razonable para conseguir un empleo alternativo adecuado (R) y (S);

– Estar disponible para trabajar (R) y (S);

– Edad (mínima: 18 años; máxima: 65 años) (R) y (S);

– Residir en el país (R) y (S);

– Haber trabajado un año como mínimo;

– Pago de cotizaciones del seguro de desempleo: la persona tiene que haber estado asegurada por 52 semanas como mínimo y haber pagado o acretidtado 20 cotizaciones como mínimo en los tres trimestres consecutivos.

5. Criterios utilizados para determinar si se ha de excluir a una persona del registro (R) y/o de las estadísticas de personas desempleadas (S)

– Establecerse en otro país;

– Incorporarse a un (nuevo) empleo;

– Incumplir el requisito de tomar contacto con el organismo;

– Rechazar ofertas de trabajo adecuadas (un puesto de trabajo);

– Fin del período de prestaciones de desempleo (Las

prestaciones de desempleo se pagan por cada día de desempleo y hasta 26 semanas como máximo).

6. Definición de persona desempleada en la que se basan las estadísticas
No se dispone de información.

7. Actualización de los registros
Los registros se actualizan dos veces por semana.

8. Tasas de desempleo
No se utilizan estadísticas de estos registros para obtener tasas de desempleo.

9. Tipo de estadísticas que se producen sobre desempleados registrados
Serie 1 *National Insurance Annual Report Statistics* (Estadísticas nacionales del informe anual de seguro (número de solicitudes recibidas y aprobadas durante el período).
Publicación: En papel, para el público en general.
Organismo responsable de la publicación: Departamento Nacional de Seguro.

10. Información metodológica sobre las estadísticas
Divulgación: En papel, para el público en general.
Organismo responsable de la divulgación: Departamento Nacional de Seguro.

11. Comparaciones con estadísticas derivadas de otras fuentes
No se han hecho comparaciones con estadísticas de desempleo derivadas de otras fuentes.

12. Modificaciones importantes desde el comienzo de las estadísticas
En la legislación, la competencia del organismo y/o los procedimientos administrativos no ha habido modificaciones importantes que hayan influido significativamente en las estadísticas.

Belarús

1. Serie
Título: Número de desempleados registrados, colocados por el Servicio Estatal de Empleo.
Año de inicio: 1991.

2. Organismo responsable de la inscripción inicial de desempleados
Nombre del organismo: Servicio Estatal de Empleo.
Tipo de organismo: Organismo público subordinado a autoridades nacionales.
Nombre de la autoridad nacional: Servicio de Empleo de la República de Belarús.
Ubicación de las oficinas locales donde se hacen las inscripciones: Centros de empleo regionales, de distrito y de ciudades de todo el país.
Tipo de servicios proporcionados/administrados por el organismo
–	Ayuda a personas en busca de empleo a encontrarlo;
–	Ayuda a personas en busca de empleo a crear su propia empresa;
–	Ayuda a los empleadores a encontrar trabajadores;
–	Orientación profesional;
–	Formación relacionada con el trabajo;
–	Pago de prestaciones de desempleo;
–	Otros servicios relacionados con el empleo;
–	Información gratuita sobre vacantes;
–	Posibilidad de participar en obras públicas recibiendo remuneración;
–	Creación de nuevos lugares de trabajo con la consiguiente colocación de desempleados;
–	Asistencia de colocación de estudiantes y universitarios en puestos temporarios.
Porcentaje de personas en busca de empleo que buscan trabajo por intermedio de ese organismo: 30%.

3. Se registran los siguientes datos de la persona
–	Nombre y apellido;
–	Sexo;
–	Dirección del domicilio habitual;
–	Fecha de nacimiento;
–	Ciudadanía;
–	Nivel de educación/formación;
–	Situación laboral actual o anterior: se identifican 30 categorías;
–	Tipo de ocupación del empleo actual o anterior;
–	Tipo de ocupación del empleo que se busca;
–	Nombre y dirección del empleador o del lugar de trabajo actual o anterior;
–	Rama de actividad del empleador o del lugar de trabajo

actual o anterior;
–	Inscripciones previas en el organismo.

4. Criterios utilizados para determinar si una persona habrá de incluirse en el registro (R) y/o en las estadísticas de personas desempleadas (S)
–	Estar sin empleo (R) y (S);
–	Estar en busca de empleo (R) y (S);
–	Edad (mínima: 16 años; máxima: 55 años para las mujeres y 60 años para los hombres) (R) y (S);
–	Haber trabajado (R) y (S).

5. Criterios utilizados para determinar si se ha de excluir a una persona del registro (R) y/o de las estadísticas de personas desempleadas (S)
–	Certificado de defunción (R) y (S);
–	Incorporarse a un (nuevo) empleo (R) y (S);
–	Comenzar el servicio militar (R);
–	Participar en algún programa de promoción del empleo, de obras públicas, etc. (R) y (S);
–	Incumplir el requisito de tomar contacto con el organismo tras un período de 12 meses (R) y (S);
–	Cobrar alguna pensión (R) y (S);
–	Incapacidad para trabajar (R).

6. Definición de persona desempleada en la que se basan las estadísticas
No se dispone de información.

7. Actualización de los registros
Los registros se actualizan trimestralmente, y mensualmente en lo que respecta a una corta lista de indicadores.

8. Tasas de desempleo
Se utilizan estadísticas de estos registros para obtener tasas de desempleo.
Fuentes de los datos de empleo incluidos en el denominador de las tasas de desempleo: encuestas de establecimientos; estimaciones oficiales y censos de población.
Definición de persona empleada que se utiliza a tales efectos
No se dispone de información.

9. Tipo de estadísticas que se producen sobre desempleados registrados
Serie 1
Período de referencia: Mes.
Variables utilizadas
–	Características geográficas;
–	Ciudadanía (nacionales o no);
–	Participación remunerada de desempleados en obras públicas;
–	Formación y reconversión profesional de desempleados.
Publicación
–	En papel, para el público en general;
–	En un sitio web.
Serie 2
Período de referencia: Trimestre.
Variables utilizadas
–	Sexo;
–	Características geográficas;
–	Experiencia laboral previa;
–	Ciudadanía (nacionales o no);
–	Duración del desempleo;
–	Participación remunerada de desempleados en obras públicas;
–	Formación y reconversión profesional de desempleados;
–	Creación de nuevos puestos de trabajo;
–	Asistencia para crear empresas individuales.
Publicación
–	En papel, para el público en general;
–	En un sitio web.
Serie 3
Período de referencia: Semestre.
Variables utilizadas
–	Sexo;
–	Edad;
–	Nivel de educación;
–	Ocupación;
–	Rama de actividad;
–	Características geográficas;
–	Experiencia laboral previa;
–	Ciudadanía (nacionales o no);
–	Duración del desempleo;
–	Tiempo que lleva cobrando prestaciones de desempleo.
Publicación
–	En papel, para el público en general;
–	En un sitio web.

Organismo responsable de la publicación: Departamento de Empleo del Ministerio de Trabajo y Protección Social, y Ministerio de Estadística y Análisis.
Título de las publicaciones: Publicación de estadísticas oficiales en el periódico *Trabajo y mercado*.
10. Información metodológica sobre las estadísticas
Divulgación: En papel, para el público en general.
Organismo responsable: Departamento de Empleo del Ministerio de Trabajo y Protección Social.
11. Comparaciones con estadísticas derivadas de otras fuentes
Se han hecho comparaciones con estadísticas de desempleo derivadas de otros tipos de encuestas de hogares y el Censo de población.
Frecuencia de las comparaciones: De vez en cuando.
Publicación de la metodología/resultados de las comparaciones: No se publican.
12. Modificaciones importantes desde el comienzo de las estadísticas
En la legislación, la competencia del organismo y/o los procedimientos administrativos no ha habido modificaciones importantes que hayan influido significativamente en las estadísticas.

Bélgica (1) - Región De Bruselas - Capital

1. Serie
Títulos: Informe mensual sobre el mercado de trabajo y Informe estadístico anual.
Año de inicio: 1989.
2. Organismo responsable de la inscripción inicial de desempleados
Nombre del organismo: Office régional bruxellois de l'Emploi - ORBEM (Oficina Regional de Empleo de Bruselas).
Tipo de organismo: Organismo público subordinado a una autoridad regional.
Ubicación de las oficinas locales donde se hacen las inscripciones: Región de Bruselas-Capital.
Tipo de servicios proporcionados/administrados por el organismo:
– Ayuda a personas en busca de empleo a encontrarlo;
– Ayuda a los empleadores a encontrar trabajadores;
– Orientación profesional;
– Otros: gestión de programas de empleo; guardería infantil de utilización variable; test de conocimiento de idiomas; pericia sobre el mercado de trabajo, etc.
Porcentaje de personas en busca de empleo que buscan trabajo por intermedio de ese organismo: No se dispone de información.
3. Se registran los siguientes datos de la persona:
– Nombre y apellido;
– Sexo;
– Número de seguridad social (o número de identificación semejante también utilizado por otros organismos);
– Dirección del domicilio habitual;
– Fecha de nacimiento;
– Nacionalidad;
– Nivel de formación. No se han establecido vínculos con la CINE;
– Tipo de ocupación del empleo actual o anterior: se identifican 2.216 categorías. No se han establecido vínculos con la CIUO-88;
– Tipo de ocupación del empleo que se busca: se identifican 2.216 categorías;
– Rama de actividad del empleador o del lugar de trabajo actual o anterior: se identifican 66 categorías. No se han establecido vínculos con la CIIU;
– Inscripciones previas en el organismo;
– Otros: Permiso de trabajo; duración del desempleo; calificaciones; competencias; vehículo; licencia de conducir; conocimiento de idiomas; estado civil y número de hijos a cargo.
4. Criterios utilizados para determinar si una persona habrá de incluirse en el registro (R) y/o en las estadísticas de personas desempleadas (S):
– Estar sin empleo (S);
– Estar en busca de empleo (R) y (S);
– Estar disponible para trabajar (S);
– Edad (mínima: 15 años; máxima: 65 años) (R) y (S);
– Residir en el país (S).

5. Criterios utilizados para determinar si se ha de excluir a una persona del registro (R) y/o de las estadísticas de personas desempleadas (S):
– Certificado de defunción (S);
– Establecerse en otro país (S);
– Incorporarse a un (nuevo) empleo, en caso de colocación por conducto de la Oficina o de comunicación a la Oficina por parte de la persona en busca de empleo;
– Participar en algún programa de promoción del empleo, de obras públicas, etc. (S);
– Estar estudiando o siguiendo una formación (S);
– Incumplir el requisito de tomar contacto con el organismo, después de no haber respondido a tres cartas (S);
– Rechazar ofertas de trabajo adecuadas (S);
– Rechazar ofertas de formación adecuadas (S);
– Fin del período de prestaciones de desempleo para quienes viven juntos. Según el Artículo 80, la duración del desempleo equivalente a una vez y media la duración "regional" media del desempleo, por sexo y grupo de edad, conlleva la suspensión de las prestaciones por tiempo indeterminado (S);
– Cobrar alguna pensión (jubilación u otras) (S);
– Incapacidad para trabajar, en caso de que sea superior a 66% (S);
– Otros: no presentarse varias veces sucesivas al control de la oficina comunal.
6. Definición de persona desempleada en la que se basan las estadísticas
Personas mayores de 15 años, sin empleo, disponibles en el mercado de trabajo y que buscan empleo. En práctica, esta serie abarca a todos las personas en busca de empleo que no tienen trabajo, es decir:
– desempleadas totales que reciben prestaciones de desempleo;
– jóvenes (que han trabajado previamente o no) que reciben una prestación de "espera" mientras que buscan trabajo;
– personas en busca de empleo que no tienen trabajo, inscritas por decisión propia (que no tienen derecho a prestaciones);
– demás personas en busca de empleo que están sin trabajo y tienen el deber de inscribirse. Esta categoría engloba a:
  determinadas personas desempleadas totales a quienes se ha excluido temporalmente de las prestaciones de desempleo, durante todo el período de exclusión;
  personas presentadas por los centros públicos de asistencia social;
  determinadas personas cuya situación es competencia del fondo comunitario de integración social y profesional de personas discapacitadas y que no reúnen los requisitos para beneficiar de prestaciones de desempleo;
– trabajadores que por decisión propia ocupaban un empleo a tiempo parcial y pasaron a ser desempleados totales;
– desempleados que por decisión propia renuncian a recibir prestaciones de desempleo, y
– jóvenes que benefician de prestaciones de transición a quienes se registra como personas en busca de empleo a tiempo parcial.
7. Actualización de los registros
Los registros se actualizan mensualmente.
8. Tasas de desempleo
Se utilizan estadísticas de estos registros para obtener tasas de desempleo.
Fuente de los datos de empleo incluidos en el denominador de las tasas de desempleo: Estimaciones oficiales.
9. Tipo de estadísticas que se producen sobre desempleados registrados
Período de referencia: Mes.
Frecuencia de producción: Mensual.
Variables utilizadas:
– Sexo;
– Edad;
– Nivel de educación;
– Ocupación;
– Rama de actividad;
– Características geográficas;
– Nacionalidad;
– Duración del desempleo.
Publicación:

– En papel, para un público limitado;
– En archivo electrónico, previa solicitud.

Organismo responsable de la publicación: ORBEM.

Título y periodicidad de la publicación: *Rapport mensuel sur l'évolution du marché de l'emploi* (Informe mensual sobre la evolución del mercado de trabajo).

10. Información metodológica sobre las estadísticas

Divulgación: En papel, para un público limitado.

Organismo responsable: ORBEM.

11. Comparaciones con estadísticas derivadas de otras fuentes

Se han hecho comparaciones con estadísticas de desempleo derivadas de la Encuesta sobre la fuerza de trabajo y el Censo de población.

Frecuencia de las comparaciones: De vez en cuando.

Publicación de la metodología/resultados de las comparaciones: *Conseil supérieur de l'emploi: Comment comptabiliser le nombre de chômeurs? Une grille de lecture des taux de chômage* (Consejo Superior de Empleo: ¿Cómo contabilizar el número de desempleados? Guía de lectura de las tasas de desempleo), publicado por el Ministerio Federal de Empleo y Trabajo.

12. Modificaciones importantes desde el comienzo de las estadísticas

En la legislación, la competencia del organismo y/o los procedimientos administrativos hubo modificaciones importantes en 1994, 1995, 1996 y 2002 que influyeron significativamente en las estadísticas.

Bélgica (2) - Flandes

1. Serie

Título: Personas en busca de empleo registradas.

Año de inicio: 1989.

2. Organismo responsable de la inscripción inicial de desempleados

Nombre del organismo: VDAB (Servicio de Empleo y Formación Profesional de Flandes).

Tipo de organismo: Organismo público subordinado a autoridades regionales.

Ubicación de las oficinas locales donde se hacen las inscripciones: Flandes.

Tipo de servicios proporcionados/administrados por el organismo:
– Ayuda a personas en busca de empleo a encontrarlo;
– Ayuda a los empleadores a encontrar trabajadores;
– Orientación profesional;
– Formación relacionada con el trabajo.

3. Se registran los siguientes datos de la persona:
– Nombre y apellido;
– Sexo;
– Número de seguridad social (o número de identificación semejante también utilizado por otros organismos);
– Dirección del domicilio habitual;
– Fecha de nacimiento;
– Ciudadanía;
– Nacionalidad/grupo étnico;
– Nivel de educación/formación: se identifica un número indeterminado de categorías. No se han establecido vínculos con la CINE;
– Situación laboral actual o anterior: se identifica un número indeterminado de categorías;
– Tipo de ocupación del empleo actual o anterior: se identifica un número indeterminado de grupos. No se han establecido vínculos con la CIUO-88;
– Tipo de ocupación del empleo que se busca: se identifica un número indeterminado de grupos. No se han establecido vínculos con la CIUO-88;
– Rama de actividad del empleador o del lugar de trabajo actual o anterior: se identifica un número indeterminado de grupos. Se utiliza la NACE Rev. 1, a nivel de cinco cifras, para codificar esta variable. Se han establecido vínculos con la CIIU Rev. 3, a nivel de categorías de tabulación;
– Inscripciones previas en el organismo;
– Otros: duración del desempleo.

4. Criterios utilizados para determinar si una persona habrá de incluirse en el registro (R) y/o en las estadísticas de personas desempleadas (S):
– Estar sin empleo (personas en busca de empleo que no trabajan) (R) y (S);
– Estar en busca de empleo (todas las personas en busca de empleo) (R) y (S);

– Estar disponible para trabajar (R) y (S);
– Edad (R) y (S);
– Ciudadanía (R) y (S);
– Haber trabajado (R);
– Duración y/o número de horas de trabajo del empleo que se busca (duración mínima: una hora) (R).

5. Criterios utilizados para determinar si se ha de excluir a una persona del registro (R) y/o de las estadísticas de personas desempleadas (S):
– Certificado de defunción (R) y (S);
– Incorporarse a un (nuevo) empleo (R) y (S);
– Participar en algún programa de promoción del empleo, de obras públicas, etc. (R);
– Estar estudiando o siguiendo una formación (R) y (S);
– Rechazar una oferta de empleo adecuada (R);
– Rechazar una oferta de formación adecuada (R);
– Fin del período de prestaciones de desempleo (personas en busca de empleo que no trabajan y reciben prestaciones de desempleo) (R) y (S);
– Cobrar alguna pensión (R) y (S);
– Incapacidad para trabajar (R) y (S).

6. Definición de persona desempleada en la que se basan las estadísticas

1. Personas en busca de empleo que no trabajan:
– Sin trabajo y beneficiaria de prestaciones de desempleo;
– Egresados escolares sin trabajo;
– Sin trabajo, registro libre;
– Otras.

2. Personas en busca de empleo que trabajan:
– Trabajadores a tiempo parcial;
– Trabajadores a tiempo completo;
– Otras.

7. Actualización de los registros

Los registros se actualizan a diario.

8. Tasas de desempleo

Se utilizan estadísticas de estos registros para obtener tasas de desempleo.

Fuente de los datos de empleo incluidos en el denominador de las tasas de desempleo: Encuesta sobre la fuerza de trabajo.

Definición de persona empleada que se utiliza a tales efectos: No indicada.

9. Tipo de estadísticas que se producen sobre desempleados registrados

Serie 1:

Período de referencia: Mes.

Frecuencia de producción: Mensual.

Variables utilizadas:
– Sexo;
– Edad;
– Nivel de educación;
– Ocupación;
– Rama de actividad;
– Características geográficas;
– Experiencia laboral previa;
– Ciudadanía (nacionales o no);
– Duración del desempleo.

Publicación:
– En papel, para el público en general;
– En el sitio web www.vdab.be

Organismo responsable de la publicación: VDAB (Servicio de Empleo y Formación Profesional de Flandes).

Título y periodicidad de la publicación: *Maandverlag Arbeidsmarkt Vlaanderen* (mensual).

Serie 2:

Período de referencia: Año.

Frecuencia de producción: Anual.

Variables utilizadas:
– Sexo;
– Edad;
– Nivel de educación;
– Ocupación;
– Rama de actividad;
– Características geográficas;
– Experiencia laboral previa;
– Ciudadanía (nacionales o no);
– Duración del desempleo.

Publicación:
– En papel, para el público en general;
– En el sitio web www.vdab.be.

Organismo responsable de la publicación: VDAB (Servicio de Empleo y Formación Profesional de Flandes).

Título y periodicidad de la publicación: *Jaarverlag Arbeidsmarkt Vlaanderen* (anual).

10. Información metodológica sobre las estadísticas
Divulgación:
–   En papel, para el público en general;
–   En archivo electrónico, previa solicitud;
–   En el sitio web www.vdab.be.
Organismo responsable de la divulgación: VDAB (Servicio de Empleo y Formación Profesional de Flandes).

11. Comparaciones con estadísticas derivadas de otras fuentes
No se han hecho comparaciones con estadísticas de desempleo derivadas de otras fuentes.
12. Modificaciones importantes desde el comienzo de las estadísticas
En la legislación, la competencia del organismo y/o los procedimientos administrativos no ha habido modificaciones importantes que hayan influido significativamente en las estadísticas.

Botswana

1. Serie
Título: Desempleo registrado.
Año de inicio: No indicado.
2. Organismo responsable de la inscripción inicial de desempleados
Nombre del organismo: Departamento de Trabajo y Seguridad Social – Unidad de Servicios de Empleo.
Tipo de organismo: Organismo público subordinado a una autoridad nacional.
Nombre de la autoridad nacional: Departamento de Trabajo y Seguridad Social.
Ubicación de las oficinas locales donde se hacen las inscripciones: Oficinas de trabajo de todos los distritos.
Tipo de servicios proporcionados/administrados por el organismo:
–   Ayuda a personas en busca de empleo a encontrarlo;
–   Ayuda a los empleadores a encontrar trabajadores.
Porcentaje de personas en busca de empleo que buscan trabajo por intermedio de ese organismo: 21%.
3. Se registran los siguientes datos de la persona:
–   Nombre y apellido;
–   Sexo;
–   Dirección del domicilio habitual;
–   Fecha de nacimiento;
–   Cjudadanía;
–   Nacionalidad/grupo étnico;
–   Nivel de educación/formación: se identifican cuatro categorías. No se han establecido vínculos con la CINE;
–   Situación laboral actual o anterior;
–   Tipo de ocupación del empleo actual o anterior;
–   Tipo de ocupación del empleo que se busca. No se han establecido vínculos con la CIUO-88;
–   Nombre y dirección del empleador o del lugar de trabajo actual o anterior;
–   Rama de actividad del empleador o del lugar de trabajo actual o anterior: se identifican seis grupos. No se han establecido vínculos con la CIIU Rev. 3;
–   Inscripciones previas en el organismo;
–   Otros: número del registro; número de la cédula de identidad.
4. Criterios utilizados para determinar si una persona habrá de incluirse en el registro (R) y/o en las estadísticas de personas desempleadas (S):
–   Estar sin empleo (excluye estudiantes) (R) y (S);
–   Estar en busca de empleo   (R) y (S);
–   Estar disponible para trabajar   (R) y (S);
–   Edad (mínima: 18 años; no hay edad máxima:) (R) y (S);
–   Ciudadanía (quienes no son ciudadanos tampoco forman parte de las "personas desempleadas") (R) y (S);
–   Haber trabajado   (R) y (S).
5. Criterios utilizados para determinar si se ha de excluir a una persona del registro (R) y/o de las estadísticas de personas desempleadas (S):
–   Certificado de defunción   (R) y (S);
–   Incorporarse a un (nuevo) empleo   (R) y (S);
–   Estar estudiando o siguiendo una formación   (R) y (S);
–   Incumplir el requisito de tomar contacto con el organismo (el registro se renueva al final de cada año) (R) y (S).

6. Definición de persona desempleada en la que se basan las estadísticas
Persona de la fuerza de trabajo que se quedó sin empleo o fuente de ingresos.
7. Actualización de los registros
Los registros se actualizan anualmente.
8. Tasas de desempleo
Se utilizan estadísticas de estos registros para obtener tasas de desempleo.
Fuentes de los datos de empleo incluidos en el denominador de las tasas de desempleo: Encuesta sobre la fuerza de trabajo y Estimaciones oficiales.
Definición de persona empleada que se utiliza a tales efectos:
Persona de la fuerza de trabajo cuya fuente de ingresos es un empleo.
9. Tipo de estadísticas que se producen sobre desempleados registrados
No se dispone de información.
10. Información metodológica sobre las estadísticas
Divulgación:
–   En papel, para el público en general;
–   En el sitio web www.cso.gov.bw
Organismo responsable: Oficina Central de Estadística.
11. Comparaciones con estadísticas derivadas de otras fuentes
Se han hecho comparaciones con estadísticas de desempleo derivadas de otras fuentes que no se indican.
Frecuencia de las comparaciones: Periódica, cuando se publican las estadísticas.
Publicación de la metodología/resultados de las comparaciones: No se publican.
12. Modificaciones importantes desde el comienzo de las estadísticas
En la legislación, la competencia del organismo y/o los procedimientos administrativos hubo modificaciones importantes en 1996, 1997, 1998, 1999 y 2000. Los cambios consiguientes en las estadísticas no se han estimado.

Bulgaria

1. Serie
Título: Información mensual sobre la situación de desempleo en Bulgaria.
Año de inicio: 1991.
2. Organismo responsable de la inscripción inicial de desempleados
Nombre del organismo: Agencia de Empleo.
Tipo de organismo: Organismo público subordinado a una autoridad nacional.
Nombre de la autoridad nacional: Ministerio de Trabajo y Política Social.
Ubicación de las oficinas locales donde se hacen las inscripciones: Hay 122 oficinas del trabajo y 141 secciones de oficinas del trabajo en todo el país.
Tipo de servicios proporcionados/administrados por el organismo
–   Ayuda a personas en busca de empleo a encontrarlo;
–   Ayuda a personas en busca de empleo a crear su propia empresa;
–   Ayuda a los empleadores a encontrar trabajadores;
–   Orientación profesional;
–   Formación relacionada con el trabajo;
–   Paga prestaciones de desempleo.
3. Se registran los siguientes datos de la persona
–   Nombre y apellido;
–   Sexo;
–   Número de seguridad social (o número de identificación semejante también utilizado por otros organismos);
–   Dirección del domicilio habitual;
–   Fecha de nacimiento;
–   Ciudadanía;
–   Nivel de educación/formación: se identifican 8 categorías. No se han establecido vínculos con la CINE;
–   Situación laboral actual o anterior: se identifican cuatro categorías;
–   Tipo de ocupación del empleo actual o anterior: se identifican 51 categorías. No se han establecido vínculos con la CIUO-88;
–   Tipo de ocupación del empleo buscado: se identifican 51 categorías. No se han establecido vínculos con la CIUO-88;

–   Nombre y dirección del empleador o del lugar de trabajo actual o anterior;
–   Rama de actividad del empleador o del lugar de trabajo actual o anterior: se identifican 280 categorías. Se han establecido vínculos con la NACE, Rev.1 a nivel de clase;
–   Inscripciones previas en el organismo.

4. Criterios utilizados para determinar si una persona habrá de incluirse en el registro (R) y/o en las estadísticas de personas desempleadas (S)
–   Estar sin empleo   (R);
–   Estar en busca de empleo   (R);
–   Estar disponible para trabajar   (R);
–   Edad (mínima: 16 años; no hay edad máxima)   (R);
–   Ciudadanía   (R);
–   Residir en el país   (R).

5. Criterios utilizados para determinar si se ha de excluir a una persona del registro (R) y/o de las estadísticas de personas desempleadas (S)
–   Certificado de defunción   (R);
–   Establecerse en otro país   (R);
–   Incorporarse a un (nuevo) empleo   (R);
–   Comenzar el servicio militar   (R);
–   Participar en algún programa de promoción del empleo, de obras públicas, etc.   (R);
–   Estar estudiando o siguiendo una formación   (R);
–   Incumplir el requisito de tomar contacto con el organismo (R);
–   Rechazar una oferta de empleo adecuada   (R);
–   Rechazar una oferta de formación adecuada   (R);
–   Cobrar alguna pensión   (R).

6. Definición de persona desempleada en la que se basan las estadísticas
Persona desempleada es aquella que no tiene trabajo, está buscando empleo activamente y está dispuesta a trabajar en las dos semanas siguientes a la notificación de la división de la Agencia de Empleo.

7. Actualización de los registros
Los registros se actualizan regularmente.

8. Tasas de desempleo
Se utilizan estadísticas de estos registros para obtener tasas de desempleo.
Fuente de los datos de empleo incluidos en el denominador de las tasas de desempleo: Censo de población.

9. Tipo de estadísticas que se producen sobre desempleados registrados
Serie 1
Período de referencia: Mes.
Frecuencia de producción: Mensual.
Variables utilizadas:
–   Sexo;
–   Edad;
–   Nivel de educación;
–   Rama de actividad;
–   Características geográficas;
–   Duración del desempleo;
–   Otras: características profesionales y de educación.
Publicación:
–   Para uso interno;
–   En papel, para un público limitado;
–   En el sitio web www.nsz.government.bg.
Organismo responsable de la publicación: Agencia de Empleo.
Título de la publicación: *Monthly Information on the unemployment situation in Bulgaria* (Información mensual sobre la situación del desempleo en Bulgaria).
Serie 2
Período de referencia: Año.
Frecuencia de producción: Anual.
Variables utilizadas
–   Sexo;
–   Edad;
–   Nivel de educación;
–   Rama de actividad;
–   Otras: características profesionales y de educación.
Publicación: En papel, para el público en general.
Organismo responsable de la publicación: Instituto Nacional de Estadísticas.
Título de la publicación: *Statistics Reference Book* (Libro de referencia estadística).

Serie 3:
Período de referencia: Año.
Frecuencia de producción: Anual.
Variables utilizadas:
–   Sexo;
–   Edad;
–   Nivel de educación;
–   Características geográficas;
–   Otras: características profesionales y de educación.
Publicación: En papel, para el público en general.
Organismo responsable de la publicación: Instituto Nacional de Estadísticas.
Título de la publicación: *NSI Yearbook* (Anuario INE).

10. Información metodológica sobre las estadísticas
Divulgación: No se divulga; sólo para uso interno.
Organismo responsable: Agencia de Empleo.

11. Comparaciones con estadísticas derivadas de otras fuentes
No se han hecho comparaciones con estadísticas de desempleo derivadas de otras fuentes.

12. Modificaciones importantes desde el comienzo de las estadísticas
En la legislación, la competencia del organismo y/o los procedimientos administrativos no ha habido modificaciones importantes que hayan influido significativamente en las estadísticas.

Burkina Faso

1. Serie
Título: Informes anuales de actividad.
Año de inicio: 1980.

2. Organismo responsable de la inscripción inicial de desempleados
Nombre del organismo: Oficina Nacional de Promoción del Empleo (ONPE).
Tipo de organismo: Organismo público subordinado a una autoridad nacional.
Nombre de la autoridad nacional: Ministerio de Empleo, Trabajo y Seguridad Social.
Ubicación de las oficinas locales donde se hacen las inscripciones: Uagadugú, Bobo-Diulasso, Banfora, Kudugu y Fada N'Gurma.
Tipo de servicios proporcionados/administrados por el organismo
–   Ayuda a personas en busca de empleo a encontrarlo;
–   Ayuda a personas en busca de empleo a crear su propia empresa;
–   Ayuda a los empleadores a encontrar trabajadores;
–   Orientación profesional;
–   Formación relacionada con el trabajo;
–   Otros servicios relacionados con el empleo: Ayuda a las personas en busca de empleo a adquirir experiencia profesional o a encontrar una formación apropiada.

3. Se registran los siguientes datos de la persona
–   Nombre y apellido;
–   Sexo;
–   Dirección del domicilio habitual;
–   Fecha de nacimiento;
–   Nacionalidad/grupo étnico;
–   Nivel de educación/formación: se identifican 10 categorías. No se han establecido vínculos con la CINE;
–   Situación laboral actual o anterior: se identifican dos categorías;
–   Tipo de ocupación del empleo que se busca: se identifican seis categorías. Se han establecido vínculos con la CIUO-88 a nivel de grandes grupos;
–   Inscripciones previas en el organismo.

4. Criterios utilizados para determinar si una persona habrá de incluirse en el registro (R) y/o en las estadísticas de personas desempleadas (S)
–   Estar sin empleo (R) y (S);
–   Estar en busca de empleo (R) y (S);
–   Estar disponible para trabajar (R) y (S);
–   Edad (mínima: 15 años; máxima: 55 años) (R) y (S);
–   Residir en el país (R) y (S);
–   Haber trabajado (R) y (S).

5. Criterios utilizados para determinar si se ha de excluir a una persona del registro (R) y/o de las estadísticas de personas desempleadas (S)
–   Certificado de defunción (R) y (S);
–   Establecerse en otro país (R) y (S);

– Incorporarse a un (nuevo) empleo. La persona en busca de empleo debe comunicar a la ONPE cualquier cambio de su situación en un plazo de 10 días;

– Cobrar alguna pensión (jubilación u otras) (R) y (S).

6. Definición de persona desempleada en la que se basan las estadísticas

Se considera desempleada toda persona activa en edad de trabajar que está sin empleo, haya o no haya trabajado anteriormente.

7. Actualización de los registros

Los registros se actualizan trimestralmente.

8. Tasas de desempleo

No se utilizan estadísticas de estos registros para obtener tasas de desempleo.

9. Tipo de estadísticas que se producen sobre desempleados registrados

Serie 1: Informe trimestral de actividad.

Período de referencia: Trimestre.

Frecuencia de producción: Trimestral.

Variables utilizadas

– Sexo;
– Edad;
– Nivel de educación;
– Ocupación;
– Experiencia laboral previa.

Publicación: En papel, para el público en general.

Organismo responsable de la publicación: ONPE.

Título y periodicidad de las publicaciones: *Rapport d'activité trimestriel* (Informe trimestral de actividad), *Rapport d'activité semestriel* (Informe semestral de actividad) y *Rapport d'activité annuel* (Informe anual de actividad).

10. Información metodológica sobre las estadísticas

Divulgación: En papel, para el público en general.

Organismo responsable: ONPE.

11. Comparaciones con estadísticas derivadas de otras fuentes

No se han hecho comparaciones con estadísticas de desempleo derivadas de otras fuentes.

12. Modificaciones importantes desde el comienzo de las estadísticas

En la legislación, la competencia del organismo y/o los procedimientos administrativos no ha habido modificaciones importantes que hayan influido significativamente en las estadísticas.

Camboya

1. Series

Títulos:

1. Número de personas en busca de empleo registradas, desglosado por sexo, grupo de edad y nivel de educación.

2. Número de personas en busca de empleo registradas, desglosado por sexo, grupo de edad y nivel de competencia.

3. Número de personas en busca de empleo registradas según colocación por nivel de competencia.

Año de inicio: 2001.

2. Organismo responsable de la inscripción inicial de desempleados

Nombre del organismo: Departamento de Empleo y Recursos Humanos.

Tipo de organismo: Organismo público subordinado a autoridad provincial y autoridad nacional.

Nombre de la autoridad nacional: Ministerio de Asuntos Sociales, Trabajo, Formación Profesional y Rehabilitación de la Juventud.

Ubicación de las oficinas locales donde se hacen las inscripciones: Phnom Penh y cuatro provincias.

Tipo de servicios proporcionados/administrados por el organismo

– Ayuda a personas en busca de empleo a encontrarlo;
– Ayuda a los empleadores a encontrar trabajadores.

3. Se registran los siguientes datos de la persona

– Nombre y apellido;
– Sexo;
– Dirección del domicilio habitual
– Fecha de nacimiento;
– Ciudadanía;
– Nacionalidad;
– Nivel de educación/formación: se identifican 8 categorías. No se han establecido vínculos con la CINE;
– Tipo de ocupación del empleo actual o anterior. Se han establecido vínculos con la CIUO-88 a nivel de grupos primarios;

– Tipo de ocupación del empleo que se busca. Se han establecido vínculos con la CIUO-88 a nivel de grupos primarios;

– Nombre y dirección del empleador o del lugar de trabajo actual o anterior.

4. Criterios utilizados para determinar si una persona habrá de incluirse en el registro (R) y/o en las estadísticas de personas desempleadas (S)

– Estar sin empleo (R) y (S);
– Estar en busca de empleo (R) y (S);
– Estar disponible para trabajar (R) y (S);
– Edad (mínima: 15 años; máxima: 39 años) (R) y (S);
– Ciudadanía (R);
– Haber trabajado (R).

5. Criterios utilizados para determinar si se ha de excluir a una persona del registro (R) y/o de las estadísticas de personas desempleadas (S)

– Certificado de defunción (R) y (S);
– Establecerse en otro país (R) y (S);
– Incorporarse a un (nuevo) empleo (R) y (S);
– Comenzar el servicio militar (R) y (S);
– Estar estudiando o siguiendo una formación (R) y (S);
– Incapacidad para trabajar (R) y (S).

6. Definición de persona desempleada en la que se basan las estadísticas

Personas de la fuerza de trabajo que no trabajan, que no tienen empleo, ni tienen una empresa o explotación agrícola propias de la que estuvieron ausentes temporalmente, aun cuando estaban disponibles para trabajar. Esta categoría abarca a quienes i) habían estado buscando trabajo, y ii) quienes no habían buscado trabajo porque estaban enfermos o porque consideraban que no había ningún puesto adecuado para ellos, y a quienes estaban a la espera de incorporarse a un nuevo puesto de trabajo o de la estación agrícola o bien, que no lo habían buscado por otros motivos.

7. Actualización de los registros

Los registros se actualizan anualmente.

8. Tasas de desempleo

Se utilizan estadísticas de estos registros para obtener tasas de desempleo.

Fuentes de los datos de empleo incluidos en el denominador de las tasas de desempleo: Encuesta sobre la fuerza de trabajo, Encuesta de establecimientos, y Censo de población.

Definición de persona empleada que se utiliza a tales efectos

Personas de la fuerza de trabajo que trabajaron una hora como mínimo mediando remuneración, ganancia, dividendos o cualquier otro tipo de pago en especie (ya se trate de empleadores, asalariados, trabajadores por cuenta propia o trabajadores familiares no remunerados).

9. Tipo de estadísticas que se producen sobre desempleados registrados

Serie 1: Número de personas en busca de empleo registradas, desglosado por sexo, grupo de edad y nivel de educación.

Período de referencia: Mes; año.

Frecuencia de producción: Mensual; anual.

Variables utilizadas:

– Sexo;
– Edad;
– Nivel de educación.

Publicación:

– Para uso interno;
– En papel, para un público limitado.

Organismo responsable de la publicación: Departamento de Empleo y Recursos Humanos.

Serie 2: Número de personas en busca de empleo registradas, desglosado por sexo, grupo de edad y nivel de competencia.

Período de referencia: Mes; año.

Frecuencia de producción: Mensual; anual.

Variables utilizadas:

– Sexo;
– Edad;
– Ocupación.

Serie 3: Número de personas en busca de empleo registradas según colocación por nivel de competencia.

Período de referencia: Mes; año.

Frecuencia de producción: Mensual; anual.

Variables utilizadas:

– Sexo;
– Ocupación.

10. Información metodológica sobre las estadísticas

Divulgación

– Para uso interno;
– En papel, para un público limitado.
Organismo responsable: Departamento de Empleo y Recursos Humanos.

11. Comparaciones con estadísticas derivadas de otras fuentes
No se han hecho comparaciones con estadísticas de desempleo derivadas de otras fuentes.

12. Modificaciones importantes desde el comienzo de las estadísticas
En la legislación, la competencia del organismo y/o los procedimientos administrativos no ha habido modificaciones importantes que hayan influido significativamente en las estadísticas.

Camerún

1. Serie
Título: Banco de datos de personas en busca de empleo.
Año de inicio: 1991.
2. Organismo responsable de la inscripción inicial de desempleados
Nombre del organismo: Fondo Nacional de Empleo (FNE).
Tipo de organismo: Organismo parapúblico.
Ubicación de las oficinas locales donde se hacen las inscripciones: Actualmente, en seis de las 10 provincias del país, pero la cobertura geográfica se va extendiendo progresivamente.
Tipo de servicios proporcionados/administrados por el organismo
– Ayuda a personas en busca de empleo a encontrarlo;
– Ayuda a personas en busca de empleo a crear su propia empresa;
– Ayuda a los empleadores a encontrar trabajadores;
– Orientación profesional;
– Formación relacionada con el trabajo.
Porcentaje de personas en busca de empleo que buscan trabajo por intermedio de ese organismo: 30%.
3. Se registran los siguientes datos de la persona
– Nombre y apellido;
– Sexo;
– Fecha de nacimiento;
– Nacionalidad;
– Nivel de formación. No se han establecido vínculos con la CINE;
– Situación laboral actual o anterior;
– Tipo de ocupación del empleo actual o anterior: se identifican dos categorías. No se han establecido vínculos con la CIUO-88;
– Tipo de ocupación del empleo que se busca: se identifican dos categorías.
4. Criterios utilizados para determinar si una persona habrá de incluirse en el registro (R) y/o en las estadísticas de personas desempleadas (S)
– Estar sin empleo (R) y (S);
– Estar en busca de empleo (R) y (S);
– Estar disponible para trabajar (R) y (S);
– Edad (mínima: 18 años; máxima: 55 años) (R) y (S).
5. Criterios utilizados para determinar si se ha de excluir a una persona del registro (R) y/o de las estadísticas de personas desempleadas (S)
– Certificado de defunción (R) y (S);
– Incorporarse a un (nuevo) empleo (R) y (S);
– Incumplir el requisito de tomar contacto con el organismo (R) y (S).
6. Definición de persona desempleada en la que se basan las estadísticas
Se considera desempleada a toda persona de edades comprendidas entre 18 y 55 años que está sin empleo, en busca de empleo y disponible para trabajar.
7. Actualización de los registros
Los registros se actualizan a diario.
8. Tasas de desempleo
No se utilizan estadísticas de estos registros para obtener tasas de desempleo.
9. Tipo de estadísticas que se producen sobre desempleados registrados
Frecuencia de producción: Anual.
Variables utilizadas
– Sexo;

– Edad;
– Nivel de educación;
– Ocupación;
– Rama de actividad;
– Experiencia laboral previa;
– Duración del desempleo.
Publicación: En papel, para el público en general.
Organismo responsable de la publicación: FNE.
Título y periodicidad de la publicación: *Rapport annuel d'activités du FNE* (Informe anual de actividad del FNE), serie disponible de 1991 a 2000.
10. Información metodológica sobre las estadísticas
Divulgación: En papel, para el público en general.
Organismo responsable: FNE.
11. Comparaciones con estadísticas derivadas de otras fuentes
No se han hecho comparaciones con estadísticas de desempleo derivadas de otras fuentes.
12. Modificaciones importantes desde el comienzo de las estadísticas
En la legislación, la competencia del organismo y/o los procedimientos administrativos no ha habido modificaciones importantes que hayan influido significativamente en las estadísticas.

Canadá

1. Serie
Título: Solicitantes de prestaciones de desempleo.
Año de inicio: 1975.
2. Organismo responsable de la inscripción inicial de solicitantes de prestaciones de desempleo
Nombre del organismo: Los solicitantes de prestaciones de desempleo se registran en el marco del Programa de Seguro de Empleo (EI).
Nota: En Canadá, el registro de personas en busca de empleo y personas desempleadas no es sistemático y sólo se registra a aquellas que solicitan prestaciones de desempleo en el marco del Programa EI. Este último es un régimen de seguro que abarca a todos los trabajadores con contrato de servicio que trabajan para un empleador y excluye a los trabajadores por cuenta propia, salvo los de la industria pesquera.
Tipo de organismo: Organismo público subordinado a autoridades nacionales y provinciales.
Nombre de la autoridad nacional: Comisión de Seguro de Empleo de Canadá, administrada por Desarrollo de los Recursos Humanos de Canadá. Las prestaciones de empleo y las medidas de apoyo se administran en cooperación con las provincias y los territorios.
Ubicación de las oficinas locales donde se hacen las inscripciones: Hay 300 puestos de servicio en todo el país. Los trabajadores desempleados también pueden presentar solicitudes en línea, vía Internet.
Tipo de servicios proporcionados/administrados por el organismo:
– Ayuda a personas en busca de empleo a encontrarlo;
– Ayuda a personas en busca de empleo a crear su propia empresa;
– Ayuda a los empleadores a encontrar trabajadores;
– Orientación profesional;
– Pago de prestaciones de desempleo;
– Otros:
– Bolsa de trabajo electrónica (servicio gratuito en línea que permite establecer contactos entre trabajadores y empleadores);
– Publicación en línea de la lista de anuncios de empleo en los sectores público y privado (www.jobs.gc.ca);
– Información sobre el mercado de trabajo (www.labourmarketinformation.ca);
– "Sello rojo", programa interprovincial de calificaciones (permite que los trabajadores calificados puedan ejercer su oficio en cualquier provincia o territorio sin tener que pasar otro examen);
– "Jobs Etc", acceso a un centro de servicios múltiples de información sobre puestos de trabajo, formación, carreras y cuestiones relacionadas con lugares de trabajo;
– "Job Futures", perspectivas de empleo a largo plazo de 211 grupos de empleo según la Clasificación Nacional de Ocupaciones (CNO);
– "Minding your own business", "Catching the wave", y "Venturing out": tres programas destinados a ayudar a personas que quieren crear su propia empresa, jóvenes incluidos.

3. Se registran los siguientes datos de la persona:
- Nombre y apellido;
- Sexo;
- Número de seguridad social (o número de identificación semejante también utilizado por otros organismos);
- Dirección del domicilio habitual;
- Fecha de nacimiento;
- Nivel de educación/formación. No se han establecido vínculos con la CINE;
- Situación laboral actual o anterior: se identifican dos categorías;
-
- Tipo de ocupación del empleo actual o anterior. No se han establecido vínculos con la CIUO-88;
- Tipo de ocupación del empleo que se busca. No se han establecido vínculos con la CIUO-88;
- Nombre y dirección del empleador o del lugar de trabajo actual o anterior;
- Rama de actividad del empleador o del lugar de trabajo actual o anterior. No se han establecido vínculos con la CIIU Rev. 3;
- Inscripciones previas en el organismo;
- Otros: situación respecto a las pensiones; idioma de preferencia (francés o inglés); tipo de ingresos que se reciben; situación respecto a la maternidad; si está en la cárcel, sigue alguna formación, está disponible para trabajar o se encuentra impedida de hacerlo debido a un conflicto laboral.

4. Criterios* utilizados para determinar si una persona habrá de incluirse en el Programa de Seguro de Empleo (R) y/o en las estadísticas de solicitantes de prestaciones de desempleo (S):
- Estar sin empleo (R) y (S);
- Estar disponible para trabajar (R) y (S);
- Haber trabajado (R) y (S)
- Pago de cotizaciones de seguro de desempleo (entre 410 y 910 horas en las 52 semanas anteriores) (R) y (S).

* Estos criterios se aplican únicamente a quienes solicitan prestaciones "habituales" del seguro de empleo (no a quienes solicitan prestaciones de enfermedad, maternidad o parentales).

5. Criterios* utilizados para determinar si se ha de excluir a una persona del Programa de Seguro de Empleo (R) y/o de las estadísticas de solicitantes de prestaciones de desempleo (S):
- Certificado de defunción (R) y (S);
- Establecerse en otro país (salvo acuerdo de prestaciones con EE.UU.) (R) y (S);
- Incorporarse a un (nuevo) empleo a tiempo completo (R) y (S);
- Comenzar el servicio militar a tiempo completo (R) y (S);
- Participar a tiempo completo en algún programa de promoción del empleo, de obras públicas, etc. (R) y (S);
- Estar estudiando o siguiendo una formación a tiempo completo (salvo si esa formación se sigue por recomendación del EI) (R) y (S);
- Incumplir el requisito de tomar contacto con el organismo sin motivo justificado (R) y (S);
- Rechazar ofertas de trabajo adecuadas sin motivo justificado (R) y (S);
- Fin del período de prestaciones de desempleo (R) y (S);
- Cobrar alguna pensión que supere un monto determinado (R) y (S);
- Incapacidad para trabajar (puede tener derecho a prestaciones de enfermedad después de cuatro semanas de incapacidad para trabajar) (R) y (S);
- Otros: estar en prisión (R) y (S); no estar disponible para trabajar (R) y (S); dejar un empleo o tomarse una licencia de ausencia sin motivo justificado o ser despedida o suspendida por mala conducta (R) y (S); estar fuera de Canadá temporalmente (salvo determinadas excepciones) (R) y (S); verse impedida de trabajar debido a conflictos laborales (R) y (S); recibir ingresos procedentes del empleo o relacionados con el empleo tales como indemnización de los trabajadores que superen un monto determinado (R) y (S).

* Estos criterios se aplican únicamente a quienes solicitan prestaciones "habituales" del seguro de empleo (no a quienes solicitan prestaciones de enfermedad, maternidad o parentales).

6. Definición de solicitante de prestaciones de desempleo en la que se basan las estadísticas
La persona que solicita prestaciones habituales (es decir, que tiene derecho a recibirlas) ha de estar sin trabajo, disponible para trabajar y querer hacerlo y haber tenido, en el último año, un vínculo suficiente de empleo como para presentar esa solicitud.

7. Actualización de los registros
Los registros se actualizan a diario.

8. Tasas de desempleo
No se utilizan estadísticas de estos registros para obtener tasas de desempleo.

9. Tipo de estadísticas que se producen sobre solicitantes de prestaciones de desempleo
Serie 1: Solicitudes de seguro de empleo.
Período de referencia: Recapitulación mensual.
Frecuencia de producción: Mensual.
Variables utilizadas:
- Sexo;
- Edad;
- Características geográficas;
- Experiencia laboral previa (horas y semanas aseguradas);
- Duración del desempleo.

Publicación:
- Sólo para uso interno;
- En archivo electrónico, previa solicitud (últimos cinco años).
Organismo responsable de la publicación: Desarrollo de los Recursos Humanos de Canadá.
Título de la publicación: SM70 - *Initial and renewal claims established* (Solicitudes iniciales y renovadas establecidas).
Serie 2: Beneficiarios del seguro de empleo.
Período de referencia: Punto de estimación (15.° día del mes).
Frecuencia de producción: Mensual.
Variables utilizadas:
- Sexo;
- Edad;
- Características geográficas;
- Experiencia laboral previa;
- Duración del desempleo.
Publicación: En archivo electrónico, previa solicitud (últimos cinco años).
Organismo responsable de la publicación: Desarrollo de los Recursos Humanos de Canadá y Estadísticas de Canadá.
Publicación: La información (en francés e inglés) figura en la base de datos CANSIM.
Serie 3: Pago de prestaciones del seguro de empleo.
Período de referencia: Día.
Frecuencia de producción: Diaria.
Publicación:
- Sólo para uso interno;
- En archivo electrónico, previa solicitud.
Organismo responsable de la publicación: Desarrollo de los Recursos Humanos de Canadá.
Título de la publicación: *Workload Report* (Informe sobre el volumen de trabajo).

10. Información metodológica sobre las estadísticas
Divulgación: No se divulga, sólo para uso interno.
Organismo responsable: Desarrollo de los Recursos Humanos de Canadá (Investigación financiera).

11. Comparaciones con estadísticas derivadas de otras fuentes
No se han hecho comparaciones con estadísticas de desempleo derivadas de otras fuentes.

12. Modificaciones importantes desde el comienzo de las estadísticas
En la legislación (es decir, la Ley de seguro de desempleo y la Ley de seguro de empleo) hubo modificaciones importantes en 1990, 1993, 1994, 1996, 2000 y 2001 (leyes C-21; C-113; C-17; C-12, Reforma del seguro de empleo; C-32 y C-2 respectivamente) que influyeron significativamente en las estadísticas.

Rep. Centroafricana

1. Serie
La Agencia Centroafricana de Formación Profesional y Empleo no se ocupa de llevar estadísticas de desempleo sino de las relativas a la oferta y la demanda de empleo.

2. Organismo responsable de la inscripción inicial de desempleados
Nombre del organismo: Agence centrafricaine de Formation professionnelle et de l'Emploi - ACFPE (Agencia Centroafricana de Formación Profesional y Empleo).
Tipo de organismo: Organismo público subordinado a una autoridad nacional.
Nombre de la autoridad nacional: Ministerio de Función Pública y Previsión Social.

Ubicación de las oficinas locales donde se hacen las inscripciones: Sólo en determinadas regiones: Bangui, Berberati, Buar, Bangassu, Mbaïki, Bambari y otras.

Tipo de servicios proporcionados/administrados por el organismo
- Ayuda a personas en busca de empleo a encontrarlo;
- Ayuda a personas en busca de empleo a crear su propia empresa;
- Ayuda a los empleadores a encontrar trabajadores;
- Orientación profesional;
- Formación relacionada con el trabajo.

3. Se registran los siguientes datos de la persona
- Nombre y apellido;
- Sexo;
- Número de seguridad social (o número de identificación semejante también utilizado por otros organismos);
- Dirección del domicilio habitual;
- Fecha de nacimiento;
- Ciudadanía;
- Nacionalidad/grupo étnico;
- Nivel de educación/formación: se identifican nueve categorías. No se han establecido vínculos con la CINE;
- Situación laboral actual o anterior: se identifican dos categorías;
- Tipo de ocupación del empleo actual o anterior. Se han establecido vínculos con la CIUO-88 a nivel de grupos primarios;
- Tipo de ocupación del empleo que se busca: se identifican 11 categorías;
- Nombre y dirección del empleador o del lugar de trabajo actual o anterior;
- Rama de actividad del empleador o del lugar de trabajo actual o anterior: se identifican 18 categorías. Se han establecido vínculos con la CIIU a nivel de clases;
- Inscripciones previas en el organismo;
- Otros: duración del empleo anterior; formación que quiere seguir.

4. Criterios utilizados para determinar si una persona habrá de incluirse en el registro (R) y/o en las estadísticas de personas desempleadas (S)
- Estar sin empleo (R) y (S);
- Estar en busca de empleo (R) y (S);
- Estar disponible para trabajar (R) y (S);
- Edad (mínima: 15 años; máxima: 54 años) (R) y (S);
- Residir en el país (R) y (S);
- Haber trabajo (R) y (S).

5. - 12. No se dispone de información.

Colombia

1. Serie
Título: Desempleo registrado.
Año de inicio: 1992.
2. Organismo responsable de la inscripción inicial de desempleados
Nombre del organismo: Servicio Nacional de Aprendizaje (SENA).
Tipo de organismo: Organismo público adscrito a una autoridad nacional.
Nombre de la autoridad nacional: Ministerio de Trabajo y Seguridad Social.
Ubicación de las oficinas locales donde se hacen las inscripciones: En todo el país.
Tipo de servicios proporcionados/administrados por el organismo:
- Ayuda a personas en busca de empleo a encontrarlo;
- Ayuda a personas en busca de empleo a crear su propia empresa;
- Ayuda a los empleadores a encontrar trabajadores;
- Orientación profesional;
- Formación relacionada con el trabajo;
- Otros: proporciona información sobre el mercado laboral.

Porcentaje de personas en busca de empleo que buscan trabajo por intermedio de ese organismo: No se tiene un indicador elaborado.

3. Se registran los siguientes datos de la persona
- Nombre y apellido;
- Sexo;
- Dirección del domicilio habitual;
- Fecha de nacimiento;
- Ciudadanía;
- Nivel de educación/formación. No se han establecido

vínculos con la CINE;
- Situación laboral actual o anterior: se identifican cuatro categorías;
- Tipo de ocupación del empleo actual o anterior. No se han establecido vínculos con la CIUO-88;
- Tipo de ocupación del empleo que se busca. No se han establecido vínculos con la CIUO-88;
- Rama de actividad del empleador o del lugar de trabajo actual o anterior.

4. Criterios utilizados para determinar si una persona habrá de incluirse en el registro (R) y/o en las estadísticas de personas desempleadas (S)
- Estar sin empleo (R) y (S);
- Estar en busca de empleo (R) y (S);
- Estar disponible para trabajar (R) y (S);
- Edad (mínima: 10 años en el sector rural y 12 años en el urbano. No hay edad máxima) (R) y (S);
- Ciudadanía (solo cobija colombianos) (R) y (S);
- Residir en el país (R) y (S).

5. Criterios utilizados para determinar si se ha de excluir a una persona del registro (R) y/o de las estadísticas de personas desempleadas (S)
- Certificado de defunción (R) y (S);
- Establecerse en otro país (Si la persona se encuentra en el país en el momento de la encuesta se contabiliza, de lo contrario no) (R) y (S);
- Incorporarse a un (nuevo) empleo (R) y (S);
- Comenzar el servicio militar (R) y (S);
- Estar estudiando o siguiendo una formación (R) y (S).

6. Definición de persona desempleada en la que se basan las estadísticas
Personas que en la semana de referencia se encontraban en una de las situaciones siguientes:
- Desempleo abierto: sin empleo en la semana de referencia, hicieron diligencias en el último mes, y disponibilidad.
- Desempleo oculto: sin empleo en la semana de referencia, no hicieron diligencias en último mes, pero sí en los últimos 12 meses y tienen una razón válida de desaliento, y disponibilidad.

7. Actualización de los registros
Los registros se actualizan regularmente.

8. Tasas de desempleo
No se utilizan estadísticas de estos registros para obtener tasas de desempleo.

9. Tipo de estadísticas que se producen sobre desempleados registrados
Serie 1:
Período de referencia: Mes.
Frecuencia de producción: Mensual.
Variables utilizadas:
- Sexo;
- Edad;
- Nivel de educación;
- Ocupación;
- Rama de actividad;
- Experiencia laboral previa;
- Duración del desempleo;
- Otras (a partir del año 2002): tiempo de búsqueda de empleo; medios de búsqueda de empleo; empresa.

Publicación:
- En papel, para el público en general;
- En el sitio web www.sena.gov.co (a partir del año 2002).
Organismo responsable de la publicación: SENA.
Título y periodicidad de las publicaciones: Informes varios (mensual, anual).
Serie 2:
Período de referencia: Trimestre - semestre.
Frecuencia de producción: Mensual.
Variables utilizadas:
- Sexo;
- Edad;
- Nivel de educación;
- Ocupación;
- Rama de actividad;
- Experiencia laboral previa;
- Duración del desempleo;
- Otras (a partir del año 2002): tiempo de búsqueda de empleo; medios de búsqueda de empleo; empresa.

Publicación:
- En papel, para el público en general;
- En el sitio www.sena.gov.co (a partir del año 2002)

Organismo responsable de la publicación: SENA.
Título y periodicidad de las publicaciones: Informes varios (mensual, anual).
Serie 3:
Período de referencia: Año.
Frecuencia de producción: Mensual.
Variables utilizadas:
- Sexo;
- Edad;
- Nivel de educación;
- Ocupación;
- Rama de actividad;
- Experiencia laboral previa;
- Duración del desempleo;
- Otras (a partir del año 2002): tiempo de búsqueda de empleo; medios de búsqueda de empleo; empresa.

Publicación:
- En papel, para el público en general;
- En el sitio web www.sena.gov.co (a partir del año 2002).

Organismo responsable de la publicación: SENA.
Título y periodicidad de las publicaciones: Informes varios (mensual. anual).
10. Información metodológica sobre las estadísticas
Divulgación: En papel, para el público en general.
Organismo responsable de la divulgación: Departamento Administrativo Nacional de Estadística (DANE).
11. Comparaciones con estadísticas derivadas de otras fuentes
Se han hecho comparaciones con estadísticas de desempleo derivadas de la encuesta sobre la fuerza de trabajo.
Frecuencia de las comparaciones: De vez en cuando.
Publicación de la metodología/resultados de las comparaciones: Se publican en *Revista Indicadores de Mercado Laboral* y en *Informe mensual de gestión del sistema de información para el empleo* (SENA, Dirección de Empleo).
12. Modificaciones importantes desde el comienzo de las estadísticas
En la legislación, la competencia del organismo y/o los procedimientos administrativos no ha habido modificaciones importantes que hayan influido significativamente en las estadísticas.
Sin embargo, habrá modificaciones importantes a partir del año 2002 con el cambio en la aplicación sistematizada y la virtualización del sistema de incorporación para el empleo.

Congo

1. Serie
Título: Estadísticas sobre las personas en busca de empleo. En el Congo, el Servicio Público de Empleo no se ocupa de llevar estadísticas de desempleo sino de las relativas a la oferta y la demanda de empleo.
2. Organismo responsable de la inscripción inicial de desempleados
Nombre del organismo: Agences régionales de l'Office national de l'Emploi et de la Main-d'oeuvre - ONEMO (Agencias regionales de la Oficina Nacional de Empleo y Mano de Obra.
Tipo de organismo: Organismo público subordinado a una autoridad nacional.
Nombre de la autoridad nacional: Ministerio de Trabajo, Empleo y Seguridad Social.
Ubicación de las oficinas locales donde se hacen las inscripciones: Brazzaville, Kuilu, Buénza, Cuvettes, Sangha, Likuala y Niari.
Tipo de servicios proporcionados/administrados por el organismo
- Ayuda a personas en busca de empleo a encontrarlo;
- Ayuda a personas en busca de empleo a crear su propia empresa;
- Ayuda a los empleadores a encontrar trabajadores;
- Orientación profesional;
- Formación relacionada con el trabajo.

3. Se registran los siguientes datos de la persona
- Nombre y apellido;
- Sexo;
- Dirección del domicilio habitual;
- Fecha de nacimiento;
- Ciudadanía;
- Nacionalidad;
- Nivel de educación/formación. No se han establecido vínculos con la CINE;
- Situación laboral actual o anterior;

- Tipo de ocupación del empleo actual o anterior. No se han establecido vínculos con la CIUO-88;
- Tipo de ocupación del empleo que se busca;
- Nombre y dirección del empleador o del lugar de trabajo actual o anterior;
- Rama de actividad del empleador o del lugar de trabajo actual o anterior. No se han establecido vínculos con la CIIU.

4. - 12. No se dispone de información sobre los puntos restantes.

Costa Rica

1. Serie
Título: Desempleo registrado.
Año de inicio: No se especifica.
2. Organismo responsable de la inscripción inicial de desempleados
Nombre del organismo: Departamento de Prospección de Empleo.
Tipo de organismo: Organismo público subordinado a una autoridad nacional.
Nombre de la autoridad nacional: Ministerio de Trabajo y Seguridad Social.
Ubicación de las oficinas locales donde se hacen las inscripciones: Región central del país.
Tipo de servicios proporcionados/administrados por el organismo:
- Ayuda a personas en busca de empleo a encontrarlo;
- Ayuda a los empleadores a encontrar trabajadores;
- Otros: estudios de mano de obra migrante; estudios prospectivos de empleo; estudios para medir los perfiles de mano de obra en zonas de inversión; programa Construyendo Oportunidades y Creciendo Juntas.

Porcentaje de personas en busca de empleo que buscan trabajo por intermedio de ese organismo: 10%.
3. Se registran los siguientes datos de la persona:
- Nombre y apellido;
- Sexo;
- Número de seguridad social (o número de identificación semejante también utilizado por otros organismos);
- Dirección del domicilio habitual;
- Fecha de nacimiento;
- Ciudadanía;
- Nacionalidad/grupo étnico;
- Nivel de educación/formación: se identifican 11 categorías. No se han establecido vínculos con la CINE;
- Situación laboral actual o anterior: se identifican cinco categorías;
- Tipo de ocupación del empleo actual o anterior: se identifican tres categorías. Se han establecido vínculos con la CIUO-88;
- Tipo de ocupación del empleo que se busca: se identifican tres categorías. Se han establecido vínculos con la CIUO-88;
- Nombre y dirección del empleador o del lugar de trabajo actual o anterior;
- Rama de actividad del empleador o del lugar del trabajo actual o anterior: se identifican 64 categorías. No se han establecido vínculos con la CIIU Rev. 3;
- Inscripciones previas en el organismo.

4. Criterios utilizados para determinar si una persona habrá de incluirse en el registro (R) y/o en las estadísticas de personas desempleadas (S):
- Estar sin empleo (R) y (S);
- Estar en busca de empleo (por primera vez; mejor empleo o segundo empleo) (R) y (S);
- Estar disponible para trabajar (R) y (S);
- Edad (mínima: 15 años; no hay edad máxima) (R) y (S);
- Ciudadanía (R);
- Residir en el país (R) y (S);
- Haber trabajado (R).

5. Criterios utilizados para determinar si se ha de excluir a una persona del registro (R) y/o de las estadísticas de personas desempleadas (S):
- Certificado de defunción (R) y (S);
- Incorporarse a un (nuevo) empleo (R) y (S);
- Rechazar tres ofertas de empleo adecuadas (R) y (S).

6. Definición de persona desempleada en la que se basan las estadísticas

Las estadísticas se basan en la Oferta Registrada según grupo ocupacional, sexo, nivel de experiencia, nivel de instrucción y edad.

7. Actualización de los registros

Los registros se actualizan diariamente, se mantienen activos durante seis meses y se renuevan.

8. Tasas de desempleo

No se utilizan estadísticas de estos registros para obtener tasas de desempleo.

9. Tipo de estadísticas que se producen sobre desempleados registrados

Período de referencia: Semestre.
Frecuencia de producción: No se especifica.
Variables utilizadas:
- Sexo;
- Edad;
- Nivel de educación;
- Ocupación;
- Rama de actividad;
- Experiencia laboral previa.

Publicación: Sólo para uso interno.

10. Información metodológica sobre las estadísticas
Divulgación: En papel, para un público limitado.
Organismo responsable: Departamento de Prospección de Empleo/Migraciones Laborales.**11. Comparaciones con estadísticas derivadas de otras fuentes**

No se han hecho comparaciones con estadísticas de desempleo derivadas de otras fuentes.

12. Modificaciones importantes desde el comienzo de las estadísticas

En la legislación, la competencia del organismo y/o los procedimientos administrativos no ha habido modificaciones importantes que hayan influido significativamente en las estadísticas.

Croacia

1. Serie
Título: Desempleados que reciben prestaciones de desempleo.
Año de inicio: 1952.
2. Organismo responsable de la inscripción inicial de desempleados
Nombre del organismo: *Hrvatski zavod za zaposljavanje* (Agencia Nacional de Empleo).
Tipo de organismo: Organismo público subordinado a una autoridad nacional.
Nombre de la autoridad nacional: Ministerio de Trabajo y Asuntos Sociales.
Ubicación de las oficinas locales donde se hacen las inscripciones: 21 oficinas regionales (todos los condados) y 98 oficinas locales.
Tipo de servicios proporcionados/administrados por el organismo:
- Ayuda a personas en busca de empleo a encontrarlo;
- Ayuda a personas en busca de empleo a crear su propia empresa;
- Ayuda a los empleadores a encontrar trabajadores;
- Orientación profesional;
- Formación relacionada con el trabajo;
- Pago de prestaciones de desempleo;
- Otros: servicios relacionados con el empleo.

3. Se registran los siguientes datos de la persona:
- Nombre y apellido;
- Sexo;
- Número de seguridad social (o número de identificación semejante también utilizado por otros organismos);
- Dirección del domicilio habitual;
- Fecha de nacimiento;
- Nivel de educación/formación: se identifican siete categorías. No se han establecido vínculos con la CINE;
- Situación laboral actual o anterior: se identifican dos categorías;
- Tipo de ocupación del empleo actual o anterior: se identifican siete categorías. Se han establecido vínculos con la CIUO-88;
- Tipo de ocupación del empleo que se busca: se identifican tres categorías. No se han establecido vínculos con la CIUO-88;
- Rama de actividad del empleador o del lugar de trabajo actual o anterior: se identifican 17 categorías. Se han establecido vínculos con la CIIU Rev. 3 y la NACE Rev.1 a nivel de clase;
- Inscripciones previas en el organismo;

4. Criterios utilizados para determinar si una persona habrá de incluirse en el registro (R) y/o en las estadísticas de personas desempleadas (S):
- Estar sin empleo (R) y (S);
- Estar en busca de empleo (R) y (S);
- Edad (mínima: 15 años; máxima 65 años) (R) y (S);
- Residir en el país (R) y (S);
- Haber trabajado (R) y (S).

5. Criterios utilizados para determinar si se ha de excluir a una persona del registro (R) y/o de las estadísticas de personas desempleadas (S):
- Certificado de defunción (R) y (S);
- Establecerse en otro país (R) y (S);
- Incorporarse a un (nuevo) empleo (R) y (S);
- Comenzar el servicio militar (R) y (S);
- Participar en algún programa de promoción del empleo, de obras públicas, etc. (R) y (S);
- Estar estudiando o siguiendo una formación (R) y (S);
- Incumplir el requisito de tomar contacto con el organismo (R) y (S);
- Rechazar una oferta de empleo adecuada (R) y (S);
- Rechazar una oferta de formación adecuada (R) y (S);
- Cobrar alguna pensión (R) y (S);
- Incapacidad total para trabajar (R) y (S);
- Ser beneficiario de prestaciones de desempleo y haber ganado un salario o ingresos mensuales ejerciendo temporalmente una actividad por cuenta propia según la reglamentación del impuesto sobre la renta (R) y (S);
- Ganar un salario o ingresos mensuales, ejerciendo temporalmente una actividad por cuenta propia según la reglamentación del impuesto sobre la renta, cuyo monto no supere la suma más alta de prestación de desempleo, fijada por ley (R) y (S);
- Haber descubierto que la persona en cuestión trabajaba en el negro sin certificado de empleo ni acuerdo o contrato de trabajo (R) y (S);
- Incumplir los requisitos de búsqueda activa de trabajo y disponibilidad para trabajar (R) y (S);
- Otros: cumplir una condena de más de seis meses (R) y (S).

6. Definición de persona desempleada en la que se basan las estadísticas

Se considera desempleadas a aquellas personas de edades comprendidas entre 15 y 65 años que no tienen trabajo pero están disponibles para trabajar a tiempo completo o tiempo parcial, buscan trabajo activamente, reúnen los requisitos estipulados en el Artículo 7 de la Ley de colocación de empleo y están inscritas en el Registro de la Agencia Nacional de Empleo al final del mes de referencia.

7. Actualización de los registros

Los registros se actualizan a diario.

8. Tasas de desempleo

Se utilizan estadísticas de estos registros para obtener tasas de desempleo.

Fuentes de los datos de empleo incluidos en el denominador de las tasas de desempleo: Encuesta sobre la fuerza de trabajo y Registro de la Seguridad Social.

Definición de persona empleada que se utiliza a tales efectos

Persona empleada por un empleador por un período fijo o indeterminado y persona que trabaja por cuenta propia.

9. Tipo de estadísticas que se producen sobre desempleados registrados
Período de referencia: Mes, trimestre, semestre y año.
Frecuencia de producción: Mensual, trimestral, semestral y anual.
Variables utilizadas:
- Sexo;
- Edad;
- Nivel de educación;
- Ocupación;
- Rama de actividad;
- Características geográficas;
- Experiencia laboral previa;
- Duración del desempleo.

Publicación:
- En papel, para el público en general;
- En archivo electrónico, previa solicitud;
- En el sitio web www.hzz.hr.

Organismo responsable de la publicación: Agencia Nacional de Empleo.
Título de las publicaciones: *Monthly Statistics Bulletin* (Boletín mensual de estadísticas) y *Yearbook* (Anuario).
10. Información metodológica sobre las estadísticas
Divulgación:
- En papel, para el público en general;
- En archivo electrónico, previa solicitud;
- En el sitio web www.hzz.hr.

Organismo responsable: Agencia Nacional de Empleo.
11. Comparaciones con estadísticas derivadas de otras fuentes
Se han hecho comparaciones con estadísticas de desempleo derivadas de la Encuesta sobre la fuerza de trabajo.
Frecuencia de las comparaciones: Periódica, cuando se publican las estadísticas.
Publicación de la metodología/resultados de las comparaciones: *Monthly Statistical Report* (Informe mensual de estadísticas), publicado por la Oficina Central de Estadísticas.
12. Modificaciones importantes desde el comienzo de las estadísticas
En la legislación, la competencia del organismo y/o los procedimientos administrativos no ha habido modificaciones importantes que hayan influido significativamente en las estadísticas.

Chad

1. Serie
Título: Anuario de estadísticas del mercado de trabajo.
Año de inicio: 1986.
2. Organismo responsable de la inscripción inicial de desempleados
Nombre del organismo: Office national pour la Promotion de l'Emploi - ONAPE (Oficina Nacional de Promoción del Empleo).
Tipo de organismo: Organismo público subordinado a una autoridad nacional.
Nombre de la autoridad nacional: Ministerio de Función Pública, Trabajo, Promoción del Empleo y Modernización (MFPTPEM).
Ubicación de las oficinas locales donde se hacen las inscripciones: Ndjamena, Mundu, Sarh, Bugor y Doba.
Tipo de servicios proporcionados/administrados por el organismo
- Ayuda a personas en busca de empleo a encontrarlo;
- Ayuda a personas en busca de empleo a crear su propia empresa;
- Ayuda a los empleadores a encontrar trabajadores;
- Orientación profesional;
- Otros: expide el permiso de trabajo para trabajadores extranjeros.

3. Se registran los siguientes datos de la persona
- Nombre y apellido;
- Sexo;
- Número de seguridad social (o número de identificación semejante también utilizado por otros organismos);
- Dirección del domicilio habitual;
- Fecha de nacimiento;
- Ciudadanía;
- Nacionalidad/grupo étnico;
- Nivel de educación/formación: se identifican ocho categorías. No se han establecido vínculos con la CINE;
- Situación laboral actual o anterior;
- Tipo de ocupación del empleo actual o anterior. No se han establecido vínculos con la CIUO-88;
- Tipo de ocupación del empleo que se busca;
- Nombre y dirección del empleador o del lugar de trabajo actual o anterior;
- Rama de actividad del empleador o del lugar de trabajo actual o anterior: se identifican ocho categorías. Se han establecido vínculos con la CIIU Rev. 2.

4. Criterios utilizados para determinar si una persona habrá de incluirse en el registro (R) y/o en las estadísticas de personas desempleadas (S)
No se dispone de información.
5. Criterios utilizados para determinar si se ha de excluir a una persona del registro (R) y/o de las estadísticas de personas desempleadas (S)
No se dispone de información.
6. Definición de persona desempleada en la que se basan las estadísticas
No se dispone de información.
7. Actualización de los registros

Los registros se actualizan a diario.
8. Tasas de desempleo
No se utilizan estadísticas de estos registros para obtener tasas de desempleo.
9. Tipo de estadísticas que se producen sobre desempleados registrados
Se producen estadísticas sobre los tipos de servicio que ofrece o administra la ONAPE:
- Ayuda a personas en busca de empleo a encontrarlo;
- Ayuda a personas en busca de empleo a crear su propia empresa;
- Ayuda a los empleadores a encontrar trabajadores;
- Orientación profesional;
- Otros: expide el permiso de trabajo para trabajadores extranjeros.

Variables utilizadas
- Sexo;
- Edad;
- Nivel de educación;
- Ocupación;
- Rama de actividad;
- Características geográficas;
- Experiencia laboral previa;
- Ciudadanía (nacionales o no);
- Duración del desempleo.

Publicación: En papel, para un público limitado.
Organismo responsable de la publicación: ONAPE.
10. Información metodológica sobre las estadísticas
Divulgación: En papel, para un público limitado.
Organismo responsable: ONAPE.
11. Comparaciones con estadísticas derivadas de otras fuentes
No se han hecho comparaciones con estadísticas de desempleo derivadas de otras fuentes.
12. Modificaciones importantes desde el comienzo de las estadísticas
En la legislación, la competencia del organismo y/o los procedimientos administrativos no ha habido modificaciones importantes que hayan influido significativamente en las estadísticas.

República Checa

1. Serie
Título: Personas desempleadas registradas y puestos vacantes.
Año de inicio: 1991.
2. Organismo responsable de la inscripción inicial de desempleados
Nombre del organismo: *Urad prace* (Oficina del Trabajo).
Tipo de organismo: Organismo público subordinado a una autoridad nacional.
Nombre de la autoridad nacional: *Ministrestvo prace a socialnich veci* (Ministerio de Trabajo y Asuntos Sociales).
Ubicación de las oficinas locales donde se hacen las inscripciones: En 77 distritos del país.
Tipo de servicios proporcionados/administrados por el organismo:
- Ayuda a personas en busca de empleo a encontrarlo;
- Ayuda a personas en busca de empleo a crear su propia empresa;
- Ayuda a los empleadores a encontrar trabajadores;
- Orientación profesional;
- Formación relacionada con el trabajo;
- Pago de prestaciones de desempleo;
- Otros: "control" de los empleadores; actividades de supervisión en la esfera de la legislación laboral.

Porcentaje de personas en busca de empleo que buscan trabajo por intermedio de ese organismo: 95%.
3. Se registran los siguientes datos de la persona
- Nombre y apellido;
- Sexo;
- Número de seguridad social (o número de identificación semejante también utilizado por otros organismos);
- Dirección del domicilio habitual;
- Fecha de nacimiento;
- Ciudadanía;
- Nivel de educación/formación: se identifican 13 categorías. Se han establecido vínculos con la CINE-97;
- Situación laboral actual o anterior: se identifican 25 categorías;
- Tipo de ocupación del empleo actual o anterior (indicación facultativa): se identifican 10 categorías. Se han

establecido vínculos con la CIUO-88;
- Tipo de ocupación del empleo que se busca (indicación facultativa): se identifican 10 categorías. Se han establecido vínculos con la CIUO-88;
- Nombre y dirección del empleador o del lugar de trabajo actual o anterior;
- Rama de actividad del empleador o del lugar de trabajo actual o anterior (indicación facultativa): se identifican 17 categorías. Se han establecido vínculos con la CIIU Rev. 3 o la NACE Rev.1;
- Inscripciones previas en el organismo;
- Otros: duración del desempleo; desempleo repetido; estado de salud; estado civil; grupos desfavorecidos (por ejemplo adolescentes; egresados escolares y universitarios sin experiencia; mujeres embarazadas; personas con hijos menores de 15 años; personas mayores de 50 años en busca de empleo; personas en busca de empleo inscritas desde hace más de seis meses; personas que necesitan una asistencia particular o personas marginadas socialmente).

4. Criterios utilizados para determinar si una persona habrá de incluirse en el registro (R) y/o en las estadísticas de personas desempleadas (S)
- Estar sin empleo (R) y (S);
- Estar en busca de empleo (R) y (S);
- Estar disponible para trabajar (R) y (S);
- Edad (mínima: 15 años; no hay edad máxima) (R) y (S);
- Residir en el país (R) y (S).

5. Criterios utilizados para determinar si se ha de excluir a una persona del registro (R) y/o de las estadísticas de personas desempleadas (S)
- Certificado de defunción (R) y (S);
- Establecerse en otro país (R) y (S);
- Incorporarse a un (nuevo) empleo (R) y (S);
- Participar en algún programa de promoción del empleo, de obras públicas, etc. (R) y (S);
- Estar estudiando o siguiendo una formación (R) y (S);
- Incumplir el requisito de tomar contacto con el organismo (R) y (S);
- Rechazar ofertas de empleo adecuadas (R) y (S);
- Otros: por iniciativa propia (R) y (S).

6. Definición de persona desempleada en la que se basan las estadísticas
Todo ciudadano que no tenga empleo ni ninguna relación de trabajo, que no ejerza alguna actividad independiente que le genere ingresos o que no siga una preparación sistemática (estudios, formación) para ejercer una profesión u ocupación (formación profesional) y solicite ayuda por escrito a la Oficina del trabajo para encontrar un empleo adecuado será inscrito como persona en busca de empleo (Sección 7, 1) de la Ley de empleo).

7. Actualización de los registros
Los registros se actualizan constantemente.

8. Tasas de desempleo
Se utilizan estadísticas de estos registros para obtener tasas de desempleo.
Fuente de los datos de empleo incluidos en el denominador de las tasas de desempleo: Encuesta sobre la fuerza de trabajo.
Definición de persona empleada utilizada a tales efectos
El número de personas empleadas se actualiza cada trimestre y se calcula la media aritmética a partir de las últimas cuatro encuestas sobre la fuerza de trabajo (las definiciones utilizadas en dichas encuestas se ajustan plenamente a las definiciones de indicadores y a las recomendaciones de la OIT).

9. Tipo de estadísticas que se producen sobre desempleados registrados
Serie 1: Personas desempleadas registradas y puestos vacantes.
Período de referencia: Día.
Frecuencia de producción: Mensual.
Variables utilizadas:
- Sexo;
- Otras: cobrar prestaciones de desempleo; seguir algún curso de formación.
Publicación:
- En papel, para el público en general;
- En archivo electrónico, previa solicitud;
- En el sitio web www.mpsv.cz Sluzby zamestnanosti (Organismo de empleo).
Organismo responsable de la publicación: Ministerio de Trabajo y Asuntos Sociales.
Título y periodicidad de las publicaciones: Statistical Report (Informe estadístico), mensual.

Serie 2: Estructura de las personas en busca de empleo y los puestos vacantes.
Período de referencia: Día.
Frecuencia de producción: Trimestral.
Variables utilizadas:
- Sexo,
- Grupo de edad;
- Nivel de educación;
- Ocupación;
- Duración del desempleo;
- Otras: cobra prestaciones de desempleo.
Publicación:
- En archivo electrónico, previa solicitud;
- En el sitio web http://ssz.mpsv.cz/Statistiky/.
Organismo responsable de la publicación: Ministerio de Trabajo y Asuntos Sociales.
10. Información metodológica sobre las estadísticas
Divulgación: En papel, para un público limitado.
Organismo responsable: Ministerio de Trabajo y Asuntos Sociales.
11. Comparaciones con estadísticas derivadas de otras fuentes
No se han hecho comparaciones con estadísticas de desempleo derivadas de otras fuentes. Ahora bien, el Ministerio de Trabajo y Asuntos Sociales utiliza las estadísticas de desempleo derivadas de la Encuesta sobre la fuerza de trabajo como fuente suplementaria de información para analizar el mercado del trabajo.
12. Modificaciones importantes desde el comienzo de las estadísticas
Las modificaciones importantes en la legislación, la competencia del organismo y/o los procedimientos administrativos han dado lugar a un aumento o una disminución del número de personas desempleadas registradas, a saber: -2% en 1991; -5%, en 1992; +5% en 1994, y +10% en 1996.

China

1. Serie
Título: Desempleo registrado.
Año de inicio: 1980.
2. Organismo responsable de la inscripción inicial de desempleados
Nombre del organismo: Oficinas locales del trabajo en la oficina de cada subdistrito o centro del servicio de empleo.
Tipo de organismo: Organismo público subordinado a la autoridad local.
Ubicación de las oficinas locales donde se hacen las inscripciones: En todo el país.
Tipo de servicios proporcionados/administrados por el organismo
- Ayuda a personas en busca de empleo a encontrarlo;
- Ayuda a personas en busca de empleo a crear su propia empresa;
- Ayuda a los empleadores a encontrar trabajadores;
- Orientación profesional;
- Formación relacionada con el trabajo;
- Pago de prestaciones de desempleo;
- Otros: lleva el archivo personal de los desempleados.
Porcentaje de personas en busca de empleo que buscan trabajo por intermedio de ese organismo: 25%.
3. Se registran los siguientes datos de la persona
- Nombre y apellido;
- Sexo;
- Número de seguridad social (o número de identificación semejante también utilizado por otros organismos);
- Dirección del domicilio habitual;
- Fecha de nacimiento;
- Ciudadanía;
- Nacionalidad/grupo étnico;
- Nivel de educación/formación: se identifican 8 categorías. No se han establecido vínculos con la CINE;
- Situación laboral actual o anterior;
- Tipo de ocupación del empleo actual o anterior. Se han establecido vínculos con la CIUO-88 a nivel de grandes grupos y subgrupos principales;
- Tipo de ocupación del empleo que se busca. Se han establecido vínculos con la CIUO-88 a nivel de grandes grupos y subgrupos principales;
- Nombre y dirección del empleador o del lugar de trabajo actual o anterior;
- Rama de actividad del empleador o del lugar de trabajo actual o anterior: se identifican 16 categorías. No se han

establecido vínculos con clases de la CIIU Rev. 3;
- Inscripciones previas en el organismo.

4. Criterios utilizados para determinar si una persona habrá de incluirse en el registro (R) y/o en las estadísticas de personas desempleadas (S)
- Estar sin empleo (R) y (S);
- Estar en busca de empleo (R) y (S);
- Estar disponible para trabajar (R) y (S);
- Edad (mínima: 16 años; máxima: 60 años para los hombres y 55 años para las mujeres) (R) y (S);
- Residir en el país (R) y (S);
- Haber trabajado (S).

5. Criterios utilizados para determinar si se ha de excluir a una persona del registro (R) y/o de las estadísticas de personas desempleadas (S)
- Certificado de defunción (R) y (S);
- Establecerse en otro país (R) y (S);
- Incorporarse a un (nuevo) empleo (R) y (S);
- Comenzar el servicio militar (R) y (S);
- Fin del período de prestaciones de desempleo (R) y (S);
- Cobrar alguna pensión (R) y (S);
- Incapacidad para trabajar (R) y (S).

6. Definición de persona desempleada en la que se basan las estadísticas
El empleo urbano registrado abarca a las personas económicamente activas que no se dedican a la agricultura, están en edad de trabajar (mayores de 16 años hasta la edad de jubilación), están disponibles para trabajar y se han inscrito en las oficinas de empleo para buscar trabajo. Excluye a: (i) estudiantes; (ii) personas mayores de la edad de jubilación (60 años para los hombres y 55 años para las mujeres) o personas que aún no tienen edad para jubilarse pero ya lo han hecho o han dejado de trabajar; y (iii) personas con discapacidades e incapacidad parcial para trabajar que reciben pago especial.

7. Actualización de los registros
No se dispone de información.

8. Tasas de desempleo
Se utilizan estadísticas de estos registros para obtener tasas de desempleo.
Fuentes de los datos de empleo incluidos en el denominador de las tasas de desempleo: Encuestas de establecimiento, Registro de la Seguridad Social, Registro del empleo y Registro de empresas industriales y comerciales.
Definición de persona empleada que se utiliza a tales efectos
Se entiende por empleo el número total de personas que ejercen actividades socioeconómicas que generan ingresos.

9. Tipo de estadísticas que se producen sobre desempleados registrados
Serie 1
Período de referencia: Trimestre.
Frecuencia de producción: Trimestral.
Variables utilizadas
- Sexo;
- Edad;
- Nivel de educación;
- Ocupación;
- Rama de actividad;
- Características geográficas.
Publicación:
- En papel, para el público en general;
- En archivo electrónico, previa solicitud;
- En un sitio web.
Título de la publicación: *China Labour Statistical Yearbook* (Anuario de estadísticas del trabajo de China).
Serie 2
Período de referencia: Año.
Frecuencia de producción: Semestral.
Variables utilizadas
- Sexo;
- Edad;
- Nivel de educación;
- Ocupación;
- Rama de actividad;
- Características geográficas.
Publicación:
- En papel, para el público en general;
- En archivo electrónico, previa solicitud;
- En un sitio web.

Título de la publicación: *China Labour Statistical Yearbook* (Anuario de estadísticas del trabajo de China).
Serie 3
Período de referencia: Año.
Frecuencia de producción: Anual.
Variables utilizadas
- Sexo;
- Edad;
- Nivel de educación;
- Ocupación;
- Rama de actividad;
- Características geográficas.
Publicación:
- En papel, para el público en general;
- En archivo electrónico, previa solicitud;
- En un sitio web.
Título de la publicación: *China Labour Statistical Yearbook* (Anuario de estadísticas del trabajo de China).
10. Información metodológica sobre las estadísticas
Divulgación:
- En papel, para el público en general;
- En archivo electrónico, previa solicitud;
- En un sitio web.
Organismos responsables: Oficina Nacional de Estadísticas; Ministerio de Trabajo y Seguridad Social.
11. Comparaciones con estadísticas derivadas de otras fuentes
Se han hecho comparaciones con estadísticas de desempleo derivadas del Censo de población y otras fuentes.
Frecuencia de las comparaciones: Periódica cuando se publican las estadísticas (último año: 2001).
Publicación de la metodología/resultados de las comparaciones: No se publican.
12. Modificaciones importantes desde el comienzo de las estadísticas
En la legislación, la competencia del organismo y/o los procedimientos administrativos ha habido modificaciones importantes en 1986, 1990 y 1995. No se ha estimado la repercusión de estas modificaciones en las estadísticas.

Chipre

1. Serie
Título: Estadísticas de personas desempleadas registradas.
Año de inicio: 1960.
2. Organismo responsable de la inscripción inicial de desempleados
Nombre del organismo: Departamento de Trabajo por conducto de la Agencia de Empleo a nivel de distrito.
Tipo de organismo: Organismo público subordinado a una autoridad nacional.
Nombre de la autoridad nacional: Ministerio de Trabajo y Seguro Social.
Ubicación de las oficinas locales donde se hacen las inscripciones: Las principales ciudades de la zona de Chipre controlada por el gobierno.
Tipo de servicios proporcionados/administrados por el organismo
- Ayuda a personas en busca de empleo a encontrarlo;
- Ayuda a los empleadores a encontrar trabajadores;
- Orientación profesional;
- Otros: prestación de servicios de colocación de trabajadores portuarios.
Porcentaje de personas en busca de empleo que buscan trabajo por intermedio de ese organismo: Aproximadamente 78%* de personas desempleadas en busca de trabajo. Otro número importante de personas empleadas también buscan un empleo mejor por intermedio de este organismo.
*Desempleo registrado como porcentaje del total de desempleados de la Encuesta sobre la fuerza de trabajo.
3. Se registran los siguientes datos de la persona
- Nombre y apellido;
- Sexo;
- Número de seguridad social (o número de identificación semejante también utilizado por otros organismos);
- Dirección del domicilio habitual;
- Fecha de nacimiento;
- Ciudadanía;
- Nacionalidad/grupo étnico;
- Nivel de educación/formación: se identifican 33 categorías. Por lo general, se establecen vínculos con la CINE con

- pequeñas desviaciones;
- Situación laboral actual o anterior: se identifican seis categorías;
- Tipo de ocupación del empleo actual o anterior (cuatro dígitos). Se han establecido vínculos con la CIUO-88 a nivel de grupos primarios;
- Tipo de ocupación del empleo que se busca (cuatro dígitos). Se han establecido vínculos con la CIUO-88 a nivel de grupos primarios;
- Nombre y dirección del empleador o del lugar de trabajo actual o anterior;
- Rama de actividad del empleador o del lugar de trabajo actual o anterior (dos dígitos). Se han establecido vínculos con clases de la CIIU Rev. 3 a nivel de división (dos dígitos);
- Inscripciones previas en el organismo;
- Otros: distrito preferido para trabajar; tipo de empleador buscado (privado, público, etc.); dificultades de transporte; licencia de conducir; comentarios sobre aspecto, conversación, modales, etc.; trayectoria en el empleo por lo que atañe a salarios; motivo de finalización del empleo anterior.

4. Criterios utilizados para determinar si una persona habrá de incluirse en el registro (R)* y/o en las estadísticas de personas desempleadas (S):

- Estar sin empleo remunerado (R) y (S);
- Estar en busca de empleo (R) y (S);
- Estar disponible para trabajar (R) y (S);
- Edad (mínima: 15 años; máxima: de 63 a 67 años según la edad de pensión del Seguro Social) (R) y (S);
- Ciudadanía (R) y (S);
- Residir en el país (R) y (S);
- Duración y/o número de horas de trabajo del empleo que se busca (mínimo 30 horas por semana (R) y (S).

*Sólo desempleados, excluye a quienes buscan un empleo mejor u otros.

5. Criterios utilizados para determinar si se ha de excluir a una persona del registro (R) y/o de las estadísticas de personas desempleadas (S):

- Certificado de defunción (R) y (S);
- Establecerse en otro país (R) y (S);
- Incorporarse a un (nuevo) empleo (R) y (S);
- Comenzar el servicio militar (R) y (S);
- Participar en algún programa de promoción del empleo, de obras públicas, etc. (R) y (S);
- Estar estudiando o siguiendo una formación (R) y (S);
- Incumplir el requisito de tomar contacto con el organismo (R) y (S);
- Rechazar tres ofertas de empleo adecuadas (R) y (S);
- Cobrar alguna pensión (R) y (S);
- Incapacidad para trabajar (R) y (S).

6. Definición de persona desempleada en la que se basan las estadísticas

Se considera desempleadas a aquellas personas registradas como personas sin trabajo alguno y que buscan empleo en las oficinas de trabajo del distrito respectivo el último día de cada mes. Incluye a aquellas personas que reciben prestaciones de desempleo del Seguro Social y a aquellas que no tienen derecho a ninguna prestación.

7. Actualización de los registros

Los registros se actualizan constantemente.

8. Tasas de desempleo

Se utilizan estadísticas de estos registros para obtener tasas de desempleo.

Fuente de los datos de empleo incluidos en el denominador de las tasas de desempleo: estimaciones oficiales.

Definición de persona empleada que se utiliza a tales efectos

Persona que trabajó al menos una hora durante la semana de referencia o persona que tenía empleo, pero que por algún motivo no trabajó durante dicha semana.

9. Tipo de estadísticas que se producen sobre desempleados registrados

Serie: Número de desempleados.

Período de referencia: Mes.

Frecuencia de producción: Mensual; anual.

Variables utilizadas:

- Sexo;
- Edad;
- Nivel de educación;
- Ocupación;
- Rama de actividad;

- Características geográficas;
- Experiencia laboral previa;
- Duración del desempleo.

Publicación:

- En papel, para el público en general;
- En archivo electrónico, previa solicitud.

Organismo responsable de la publicación: Servicio de Estadísticas, Ministerio de Finanzas.

Título y periodicidad de las publicaciones: *Registered Unemployed* (Desempleo registrado), mensual; *Monthly Economic Indicators* (Indicadores económicos mensuales), bi-mensual, y *Labour Statistics* (Estadísticas del Trabajo), anual.

10. Información metodológica sobre las estadísticas

Divulgación: Comunicados de prensa e Internet.

11. Comparaciones con estadísticas derivadas de otras fuentes

Se han hecho comparaciones con estadísticas de desempleo derivadas de la Encuesta sobre la fuerza de trabajo.

Frecuencia de las comparaciones: Periódica, cuando se publican las estadísticas.

Publicación de la metodología/resultados de las comparaciones: No se publican.

12. Modificaciones importantes desde el comienzo de las estadísticas

En la legislación, la competencia del organismo y/o los procedimientos administrativos no ha habido modificaciones importantes que hayan influido significativamente en las estadísticas. No obstante, se modificaron los sistemas de clasificación de ocupaciones y ramas de actividad económica para que se ajustaran a los sistemas de las Naciones Unidas.

Dinamarca

1. Serie

Título: Desempleo registrado (Compilado del Registro Central de Estadísticas del Trabajo)

Año de inicio: 1979.

2. Organismo responsable de la inscripción Inicial de desempleados

Nombre de los organismos:

(i) Fondos de seguro de desempleo;

(ii) Autoridades locales;

(iii) Centros de empleo.

Tipo de organismo: Organismos públicos subordinados a una autoridad nacional.

Nombre de la autoridad nacional: *Arbejdsmarkedsstyrelsen* (Dirección del Trabajo).

Ubicación de las oficinas locales donde se hacen las inscripciones: En todo el país.

Tipo de servicios proporcionados/administrados por el organismo:

(i) Fondos de seguro de desempleo:

– Orientación profesional;

– Pago de prestaciones de desempleo.

(ii) Autoridades locales:

– Ayuda a personas en busca de empleo a encontrarlo;

– Ayuda a personas en busca de empleo a crear su propia empresa;

– Ayuda a los empleadores a encontrar trabajadores;

– Orientación profesional;

– Formación relacionada con el trabajo.

(iii) Centros de empleo:

– Ayuda a personas en busca de empleo a encontrarlo;

– Ayuda a los empleadores a encontrar trabajadores;

– Orientación profesional;

– Formación relacionada con el trabajo.

Porcentaje de personas en busca de empleo que buscan trabajo por intermedio de ese organismo: 22%.

3. Se registran los siguientes datos de la persona:

- Nombre y apellido;
- Sexo;
- Número de seguridad social (o número de identificación semejante también utilizado por otros organismos);
- Dirección del domicilio habitual;
- Fecha de nacimiento;
- Ciudadanía;
- Nacionalidad/grupo étnico;
- Otros: si se está asegurado o no; nombre del organismo donde se hizo la inscripción.

4. Criterios utilizados para determinar si una persona habrá de incluirse en el registro (R) y/o en las estadísticas de personas desempleadas (S):

– Estar sin empleo (R) y (S);
– Estar en busca de empleo (R) y (S);
– Estar disponible para trabajar (R) y (S);
– Edad (mínima: 16 años; máxima: 66 años) (R) y (S).

5. Criterios utilizados para determinar si se ha de excluir a una persona del registro (R) y/o de las estadísticas de personas desempleadas (S):
– Certificado de defunción (R) y (S);
– Incorporarse a un (nuevo) empleo (S);
– Comenzar el servicio militar (S);
– Participar en algún programa de promoción del empleo, de obras públicas, etc. (S);
– Estar estudiando o siguiendo una formación (S);
– Cobrar alguna pensión (S);
– Incapacidad para trabajar (S).

6. Definición de persona desempleada en la que se basan las estadísticas
Personas sin empleo que están disponibles para trabajar y buscan empleo activamente.

7. Actualización de los registros
Los registros se actualizan mensualmente.

8. Tasas de desempleo
Se utilizan estadísticas de estos registros para obtener tasas de desempleo.
Fuentes de los datos de empleo incluidos en el denominador de las tasas de desempleo: estadísticas basadas en el registro de la fuerza de trabajo (estadísticas RAS).
Definición de persona empleada que se utiliza a tales efectos
Se entiende por personas empleadas a aquellas que tienen empleo asalariado, trabajan por cuenta propia o ayudan a su cónyuge.

9. Tipo de estadísticas que se producen sobre desempleados registrados
Serie 1:
Período de referencia: Mes.
Frecuencia de producción: Mensual.
Variables utilizadas;
– Sexo;
– Edad;
– Rama de actividad por fondo de seguro;
– Características geográficas;
– Asegurado o no.
Publicación:
– En papel, para el público en general;
– En el sitio web www.statistikbanken.dk.
Organismo responsable de la publicación: Statistics Denmark (Estadísticas de Dinamarca).
Título y periodicidad de las publicaciones: *Nyt fra Danmarks Statistik* (Boletín de Estádisticas de Dinamarca); *Arbejdsmarkd* (Mercado de trabajo) publicado en la serie *Statistiske Efterretninger* (Boletín estadístico), y *Konjunkturstatistikken* (Indicadores principales), mensual.
Serie 2:
Frecuencia de producción: Anual.
Variables utilizadas:
– Sexo;
– Edad;
– Rama de actividad por fondo de seguro;
– Asegurado o no;
– Características geográficas;
– Experiencia laboral previa;
– Ciudadanía (nacional o no);
– Duración del desempleo.
Publicación:
– En papel, para el público en general;
– En el sitio web www.statistikbanken.dk.
Organismo responsable de la publicación: Statistics Denmark (Estadísticas de Dinamarca).
Título y periodicidad de las publicaciones: *Nyt fra Danmarks Statistik* (Boletín de Estádisticas de Dinamarca); *Arbejdsmarkd* (Mercado de trabajo) publicado en la serie *Statistiske Efterretninger* (Boletín de estadísticas); *Konjunkturstatistikken* (Indicadores principales) (mensual); *Statistisk Årbog* (Anuario de estadísticas), y *Statistisk Tiårsoversigt* (Examen estadístico del decenio).

10. Información metodológica sobre las estadísticas
Divulgación:
– En papel, para el público en general;
– En el sitio web www.dst.dk/varedeklaration - *Arbejdsmarked* (Mercado del trabajo) - *Arbejdsløshed* (Desempleo).

Organismo responsable: Statistics Denmark (Estadísticas de Dinamarca).

11. Comparaciones con estadísticas derivadas de otras fuentes
Se han hecho comparaciones con estadísticas de desempleo derivadas de la Encuesta sobre la fuerza de trabajo.
Frecuencia de las comparaciones: Cuatro veces por año.
Publicación de la metodología/resultados de las comparaciones: Se publican en el sitio web de Estadísticas de Dinamarca: www.dst.dk/varedeklaration - *Arbejdsmarked* (Mercado del trabajo) - *Arbejdskraftsundersøgelsen* (Encuesta sobre la fuerza de trabajo).

12. Modificaciones importantes desde el comienzo de las estadísticas
En la legislación, la competencia del organismo y/o los procedimientos administrativos no ha habido modificaciones importantes que hayan influido significativamente en las estadísticas.

Djibouti

1. Serie
Título: Características socioeconómicas de personas en busca de empleo y contratadas por ocupación.
Año de inicio: 1974.

2. Organismo responsable de la inscripción inicial de desempleados
Nombre del organismo: Servicio Nacional de Empleo.
Tipo de organismo: Organismo público subordinado a una autoridad nacional.
Nombre de la autoridad nacional: Dirección de Empleo del Ministerio de Empleo y Solidaridad Social.
Ubicación de las oficinas locales donde se hacen las inscripciones: Ciudad de Djibouti.
Tipo de servicios proporcionados/administrados por el organismo
– Ayuda a personas en busca de empleo a encontrarlo;
– Ayuda a los empleadores a encontrar trabajadores;
– Orientación profesional;
– Otros servicios relacionados con el empleo: Gestión de expedientes de trabajadores extranjeros (expide el permiso de trabajo para dichos trabajadores).
Porcentaje de personas en busca de empleo que buscan trabajo por intermedio de ese organismo: 6%.

3. Se registran los siguientes datos de la persona
– Nombre y apellido;
– Sexo;
– Número de seguridad social (o número de identificación semejante también utilizado por otros organismos);
– Dirección del domicilio habitual;
– Fecha de nacimiento;
– Ciudadanía;
– Nivel de educación/formación: se identifican nueve categorías;
– Tipo de ocupación del empleo actual o anterior: se identifican cuatro categorías. Se han establecido vínculos con la CIUO;
– Inscripciones previas en el organismo.

4. Criterios utilizados para determinar si una persona habrá de incluirse en el registro (R) y/o en las estadísticas de personas desempleadas (S)
– Estar sin empleo e inscrita en el Servicio Nacional de Empleo. La persona en busca de empleo debe presentar un expediente completo con todas sus señas (número de teléfono y apartado postal) (R) y (S);
– Estar en busca de empleo (R) y (S);
– Estar disponible para trabajar (R) y (S);
– Edad (mínima: 16 años; máxima: 55 años) (R) y (S);
– Ciudadanía, la persona en busca de empleo debe presentar la cédula nacional de identidad;
– Residir en el país. La persona en busca de empleo debe presentarse regularmente al control del Servicio Nacional de Empleo;
– Haber trabajado. La persona en busca de empleo debe presentar sus certificados de trabajo.

5. Criterios utilizados para determinar si se ha de excluir a una persona del registro (R) y/o de las estadísticas de personas desempleadas (S)
– Certificado de defunción (R) y (S);
– Establecerse en otro país (R) y (S);
– Incorporarse a un (nuevo) empleo (R) y (S);
– Incumplir el requisito de tomar contacto con el organismo.

6. Definición de persona desempleada en la que se basan las estadísticas

Se considera en busca de empleo a toda persona de edades comprendidas entre 16 y 55 años que está disponible para trabajar y que busca empleo.

Los datos estadísticos producidos por el Servicio Nacional de Empleo versan únicamente sobre las personas en busca de empleo registradas en dicho servicio.

7. Actualización de los registros

Los registros se actualizan a diario.

8. Tasas de desempleo

No se utilizan estadísticas de estos registros para obtener tasas de desempleo.

9. Tipo de estadísticas que se producen sobre desempleados registrados

Período de referencia: Mes.

Frecuencia de producción: Trimestral.

Variables utilizadas

- Sexo;
- Edad;
- Nivel de educación;
- Ocupación;
- Experiencia laboral previa;
- Ciudadanía (nacionales o no).

Publicación

- En papel, para el público en general;
- En archivo electrónico, previa solicitud;
- En un sitio web..

Organismo responsable de la publicación: Dirección Nacional de Estadística (DINAS).

10. Información metodológica sobre las estadísticas

Divulgación: Sólo para uso interno.

Organismo responsable: DINAS.

11. Comparaciones con estadísticas derivadas de otras fuentes

Se han hecho comparaciones con estadísticas de desempleo derivadas de la Encuesta sobre la fuerza de trabajo.

12. Modificaciones importantes desde el comienzo de las estadísticas

En la legislación, la competencia del organismo y/o los procedimientos administrativos no ha habido modificaciones importantes que hayan influido significativamente en las estadísticas.

13. Otros comentarios

A pesar de que los textos son claros y precisos, los empleadores, tanto del sector público como del sector privado, y las personas en busca de empleo no se ciñen a los textos vigentes en materia de empleo.

Por otra parte, la Ley núm. 140/AN/97/3ème L, del 23-9-97, enmendó el Código de trabajo, liberalizando el empleo, por lo que la mayor parte de los empleadores ya no se dirige al Servicio Nacional de Empleo (SNE) para regularizar la situación de su personal.

República Dominicana

1. Serie

Título: Desempleo registrado.

Año de inicio: No se especifica.

2. Organismo responsable de la inscripción inicial de desempleados

Nombre del organismo: Dirección General de Empleo.

Tipo de organismo: Organismo público subordinado a una autoridad nacional.

Nombre de la autoridad nacional: Secretaria de Estado de Trabajo.

Ubicación de las oficinas locales donde se hacen las inscripciones: En cinco provincias, con el programa de expandirse a 10 más antes del fin de 2002.

Tipo de servicios proporcionados/administrados por el organismo:

- Ayuda a personas en busca de empleo a encontrarlo;
- Ayuda a personas en busca de empleo a crear su propia empresa;
- Ayuda a los empleadores a encontrar trabajadores;
- Orientación profesional;
- Otros: estudios de mercado laboral.

Porcentaje de personas en busca de empleo que buscan trabajo por intermedio de ese organismo: 10%.

3. Se registran los siguientes datos de la persona:

- Nombre y apellido;
- Sexo;

- Número de seguridad social (o número de identificación semejante también utilizado por otros organismos);
- Dirección del domicilio habitual;
- Fecha de nacimiento;
- Ciudadanía;
- Nivel de educación/formación;
- Situación laboral actual o anterior;
- Tipo de ocupación del empleo actual o anterior. Se han establecido vínculos con grupos primarios de la CIUO-88;
- Tipo de ocupación del empleo que se busca. Se han establecido vínculos con grupos primarios de la CIUO-88;
- Inscripciones previas en el organismo.

4. Criterios utilizados para determinar si una persona habrá de incluirse en el registro (R) y/o en las estadísticas de personas desempleadas (S):

- Estar sin empleo (R);
- Estar en busca de empleo (R);
- Estar disponible para trabajar (R);
- Edad (mínima: 16 años; no hay edad máxima) (R);
- Ciudadanía (ser dominicano) (R);
- Residir en el país (R);
- Duración y/o número de horas de trabajo del empleo que se busca (R).

5. Criterios utilizados para determinar si se ha de excluir a una persona del registro (R) y/o de las estadísticas de personas desempleadas (S):

- Incorporarse a un (nuevo) empleo (R);
- Incumplir el requisito de ponerse en contacto con el organismo (R);
- Otros: caducación de la solicitud (el plazo es de un año) (R).

6. Definición de persona desempleada en la que se basan las estadísticas

Dominicanos mayores de 16 años que no estén ocupados, no importando que estén o no buscando empleo.

7. Actualización de los registros

Los registros se actualizan anualmente.

8. Tasas de desempleo

No se utilizan estadísticas de estos registros para obtener tasas de desempleo.

9. Tipo de estadísticas que se producen sobre desempleados registrados

Período de referencia: Año.

Frecuencia de producción: Anual.

Variables utilizadas:

- Sexo;
- Edad;
- Ocupación;
- Rama de actividad;
- Características geográficas;
- Experiencia laboral previa.

Publicación:

- En papel, para el público en general;
- En archivo electrónico, previa solicitud.

10. Información metodológica sobre las estadísticas

Divulgación:

- En papel, para el público en general;
- En archivo electrónico, previa solicitud;
- En el sitio web www.bancentral.gov.do/publicaciones.

Organismo responsable: Banco Central de la República Dominicana.

11. Comparaciones con estadísticas derivadas de otras fuentes

Se han hecho comparaciones con estadísticas de desempleo derivadas de la Encuesta sobre la fuerza de trabajo, de otro tipo de encuesta de hogares y del Informe de la CEPAL (Comisión Económica para América Latina y el Caribe).

Frecuencia de las comparaciones: De vez en cuando.

Publicación de la metodología/resultados de las comparaciones: No se han publicado la metodología y/o los resultados de estas comparaciones.

12. Modificaciones importantes desde el comienzo de las estadísticas

Ha habido modificaciones importantes en la legislación, competencia del organismo y/o procedimientos administrativos en 2002; el impacto resultante sobre las estadísticas está elaborándose.

Egipto

1. Serie

Título: Desempleo registrado.

Año de inicio: 1959.

2. Organismo responsable de la inscripción inicial de desempleados

Nombre del organismo: Ministerio de Recursos Humanos y Migración (oficinas locales).

Tipo de organismo: Organismo público subordinado a una autoridad nacional y a autoridades locales.

Nombre de la autoridad nacional: Ministerio de Recursos Humanos y Migración.

Ubicación de las oficinas locales donde se hacen las inscripciones: En todo el país; una oficina como mínimo en cada distrito. Las oficinas de distrito son dirigidas por la oficina principal de la ciudad.

Tipo de servicios proporcionados/administrados por el organismo:

– Ayuda a personas en busca de empleo a encontrarlo;
– Ayuda a los empleadores a encontrar trabajadores;
– Orientación profesional;
– Formación relacionada con el trabajo;
– Pago de prestaciones de desempleo;
– Otros: algunas oficinas ayudan a los usuarios a encontrar trabajo en el extranjero.

Porcentaje de personas en busca de empleo que buscan trabajo por intermedio de ese organismo: 8,14%.

3. Se registran los siguientes datos de la persona:

– Nombre y apellido;
– Sexo;
– Número de seguridad social (o número de identificación semejante también utilizado por otros organismos);
– Dirección del domicilio habitual;
– Edad;
– Ciudadanía;
– Nacionalidad/grupo étnico;
– Nivel de educación/formación: se identifican seis categorías. Se han establecido vínculos con la CINE;
– Situación laboral actual o anterior: se identifican tres categorías;
– Tipo de ocupación del empleo actual o anterior. No se han establecido vínculos con la CIUO-88;
– Tipo de ocupación del empleo que se busca: se identifican 10 categorías. No se han establecido vínculos con la CIUO-88;
– Nombre y dirección del empleador o del lugar de trabajo actual o anterior;
– Inscripciones previas en el organismo.

4. Criterios utilizados para determinar si una persona habrá de incluirse en el registro (R) y/o en las estadísticas de personas desempleadas (S):

– Estar sin empleo (R) y (S);
– Estar en busca de empleo (R) y (S);
– Estar disponible para trabajar (R) y (S);
– Edad (mínima: 12 años; no hay edad máxima) (R) y (S);
– Ciudadanía (R) y (S);
– Residir en el país (R) y (S);
– Haber trabajado (R) y (S).

5. Criterios utilizados para determinar si se ha de excluir a una persona del registro (R) y/o de las estadísticas de personas desempleadas (S):

– Certificado de defunción (R) y (S);
– Incorporarse a un (nuevo) empleo (R) y (S);
– Incumplir el requisito de tomar contacto con el organismo (R) y (S);
– Incapacidad para trabajar (R) y (S).

6. Definición de persona desempleada en la que se basan las estadísticas

(i) Persona desempleada que ha trabajado, tienen la capacidad y la voluntad de trabajar y está en busca de empleo.

(ii) Persona que se incorpora al mercado de trabajo, que no ha trabajado anteriormente, tiene la capacidad y la voluntad de trabajar y está en busca de empleo.

(iii) Persona que tienen empleo, pero que está buscando uno mejor ya sea porque no le conviene, no le satisface desde el punto de vista económico o por cualquier otro motivo.

7. Actualización de los registros

Los registros se actualizan mensualmente.

8. Tasas de desempleo

Se utilizan estadísticas de estos registros para obtener tasas de desempleo.

Fuentes de los datos de empleo incluidos en el denominador de las tasas de desempleo: Encuesta sobre la fuerza de trabajo y Censo de población.

Definición de persona empleada que se utiliza a tales efectos

Persona que trabaja en una actividad económica.

9. Tipo de estadísticas que se producen sobre desempleados registrados

Período de referencia: Mes.

Frecuencia de producción: Trimestral; anual.

Variables utilizadas:

– Sexo;
– Nivel de educación;
– Ocupación;
– Rama de actividad;
– Características geográficas;
– Experiencia laboral previa;
– Ciudadanía (nacionales o no).

Publicación:

– En papel, para un público limitado;
– En archivo electrónico, previa solicitud;
– En el sitio web del Ministerio de Recursos Humanos y Migración.

Organismo responsable de la publicación: Ministerio de Recursos Humanos y Migración.

Periodicidad de las publicaciones: Trimestral; anual.

10. Información metodológica sobre las estadísticas

Divulgación:

– En archivo electrónico, previa solicitud;
– En el sitio web del Ministerio de Recursos Humanos y Migración.

Organismo responsable: Ministerio de Recursos Humanos y Migración.

11. Comparaciones con estadísticas derivadas de otras fuentes

Se han hecho comparaciones con estadísticas de desempleo derivadas de la Encuesta sobre la fuerza de trabajo y el Censo de población.

Frecuencia de las comparaciones: De vez en cuando.

Publicación de la metodología/resultados de las comparaciones: No se publican.

12. Modificaciones importantes desde el comienzo de las estadísticas

En la legislación, la competencia del organismo y/o los procedimientos administrativos no ha habido modificaciones importantes que hayan influido significativamente en las estadísticas.

El Salvador

1. Series

Títulos:

1. Número de personas inscritas.
2. Número de personas colocadas.
3. Número de puestos de trabajo.

Año de inicio: 1998.

2. Organismo responsable de la inscripción inicial de desempleados

Nombre del organismo: Departamento Nacional de Empleo.

Tipo de organismo: Organismo público subordinado a una autoridad nacional.

Nombre de la autoridad nacional: Ministerio de Trabajo y Previsión Social.

Ubicación de las oficinas locales donde se hacen las inscripciones: San Salvador; Santa Ana; Sonsonate; Zacatecoluca; San Miguel y La Unión.

Tipo de servicios proporcionados/administrados por el organismo:

– Ayuda a personas en busca de empleo a encontrarlo;
– Ayuda a empleadores a encontrar trabajadores;
– Orientación profesional;
– Formación relacionada con el trabajo;
– Otros: atención de menores trabajadores; promoción del empleo a través del aprendizaje.

Porcentaje de personas en busca de empleo que buscan trabajo por intermedio de ese organismo: 15%.

3. Se registran los siguientes datos de una persona:

– Nombre y apellido;
– Sexo;
– Número de seguridad social (o número de identificación semejante también utilizado por otros organismos);
– Dirección del domicilio habitual;
– Fecha de nacimiento;

– Nacionalidad/grupo étnico;
– Nivel de educación/formación: se identifican cinco categorías. No se han establecido vínculos con la CINE;
– Situación laboral actual o anterior: se identifican tres categorías;
– Tipo de ocupación del empleo actual o anterior: se identifican 10 categorías. Se han establecido vínculos con la CIUO-88;
– Tipo de ocupación del empleo que se busca: se identifican 10 categorías. Se han establecido vínculos con la CIUO-88;
– Nombre y dirección del empleador o del lugar del trabajo actual o anterior;
– Rama de actividad del empleador o del lugar del trabajo actual o anterior: se identifican 10 categorías. No se han establecido vínculos con la CIIU Rev. 3.

4. Criterios utilizados para determinar si una persona habrá de incluirse en el registro (R) y/o en las estadísticas de personas desempleadas (S):
– Estar sin empleo (R) y (S);
– Estar en busca de empleo (R) y (S);
– Estar disponible para trabajar (R) y (S);
– Edad (mínima: 18 años; máxima: 35 años) (R) y (S);
– Haber trabajado (R).

5. Criterios utilizados para determinar si se ha de excluir a una persona del registro (R) y/o de las estadísticas de personas desempleadas (S):
No se indica.

6. Definición de persona desempleada en la que se basan las estadísticas
No se indica.

7. Actualización de los registros
Los registros se actualizan anualmente.

8. Tasas de desempleo
No se utilizan estadísticas de estos registros para obtener tasas de desempleo.

9. Tipo de estadísticas que se producen sobre desempleados registrados
Series:
1. Número de buscadores de empleo inscritos en el Departamento de Empleo.
2. Número de personas colocadas en el puesto de trabajo.
3. Número de puestos de trabajo afectados por los empleadores.
Período de referencia: Mes.
Frecuencia de producción: Mensual.
Variables utilizadas:
– Sexo;
– Edad;
– Nivel de educación;
– Ocupación;
– Rama de actividad.
Publicación:
– En papel, para un público limitado;
– En el sitio web www.mtps.gob.sv.
Organismo responsable de la publicación: Ministerio de Trabajo y Previsión Social.
Periodicidad de la publicación: Mensual.
10. Información metodológica sobre las estadísticas
Divulgación: En papel, para un público limitado.
Organismo responsable: Ministerio de Trabajo y Previsión Social.
11. Comparaciones con estadísticas derivadas de otras fuentes
No se han hecho comparaciones con estadísticas de desempleo derivadas de otras fuentes.
12. Modificaciones importantes desde el comienzo de las estadísticas
En la legislación, la competencia del organismo y/o los procedimientos administrativos no ha habido modificaciones importantes que hayan influido significativamente en las estadísticas.

Eslovenia

1. Serie
Título: Personas desempleadas registradas.
Año de inicio: 1947.
2. Organismo responsable de la inscripción inicial de desempleados
Nombre del organismo: *Zavod rs za zaposlovanje* (Servicio de Empleo de Eslovenia).
Tipo de organismo: Organismo público subordinado a una autoridad nacional.

Nombre de la autoridad nacional: Ministerio de Trabajo, Familia y Asuntos Sociales.
Ubicación de las oficinas locales donde se hacen las inscripciones: Unidades administrativas de todo el país.
Tipo de servicios proporcionados/administrados por el organismo
– Ayuda a personas en busca de empleo a encontrarlo;
– Ayuda a personas en busca de empleo a crear su propia empresa;
– Ayuda a los empleadores a encontrar trabajadores;
– Orientación profesional;
– Formación relacionada con el trabajo;
– Pago de prestaciones de desempleo;
– Otros servicios relacionados con el empleo: permisos de trabajo y programa nacional de becas.
Porcentaje de personas en busca de empleo que buscan trabajo por intermedio de ese organismo: 90%.
3. Se registran los siguientes datos de la persona
– Nombre y apellido;
– Sexo;
– Número de seguridad social (o número de identificación semejante también utilizado por otros organismos);
– Dirección del domicilio habitual;
– Fecha de nacimiento;
– Ciudadanía;
– Nivel de educación/formación: se identifican ocho categorías;
– Situación laboral actual o anterior: se identifican tres categorías;
– Tipo de ocupación del empleo actual o anterior;
– Tipo de ocupación del empleo que se busca: se identifican 371 categorías. Se han establecido vínculos con la CIUO-88 a nivel de grupos unitarios;
– Nombre y dirección del empleador o del lugar de trabajo actual o anterior;
– Inscripciones previas en el organismo.
4. Criterios utilizados para determinar si una persona habrá de incluirse en el registro (R) y/o en las estadísticas de personas desempleadas (S)
– Estar sin empleo (R) y (S);
– Estar buscando empleo activamente, lo que es seguido por un asesor de empleo (R) y (S);
– Estar disponible para trabajar (R) y (S);
– Edad (mínima: 15 años; máxima: 60 años para las mujeres y 65 años para los hombres) (R) y (S);
– Ciudadanía (R) y (S).
5. Criterios utilizados para determinar si se ha de excluir a una persona del registro (R) y/o de las estadísticas de personas desempleadas (S)
– Certificado de defunción (R) y (S);
– Establecerse en otro país (R) y (S);
– Incorporarse a un (nuevo) empleo (R) y (S);
– Comenzar el servicio militar (R) y (S);
– Participar en algún programa de promoción del empleo, de obras públicas, etc. (S);
– Estar estudiando o siguiendo una formación (En las estadísticas se incluye únicamente a aquellos que siguen un programa de formación de corta duración) (S);
– Incumplir el requisito de tomar contacto con el organismo (R) y (S);
– Rechazar dos ofertas de trabajo adecuadas (R) y (S);
– Rechazar una oferta de formación adecuada (R) y (S);
– Cobrar alguna pensión (R) y (S);
– Incapacidad para trabajar (R) y (S);
– Educación regular (R) y (S).
6. Definición de persona desempleada en la que se basan las estadísticas
Personas desempleadas registradas son las mujeres de edades comprendidas entre 15 y 60 años y los hombres de edades comprendidas entre 15 y 65 años, que están registradas en el servicio de empleo, buscan empleo activamente y están dispuestas a aceptar un empleo que corresponda a su nivel de educación. Quedan excluidas de la definición: las personas jubiladas; las personas que cumplen condena de más de seis meses; los propietarios de empresas que generaron ingresos en el último año civil y que pueden utilizar para su sustento, en caso de que los ingresos no excedan las ganancias garantizadas; los propietarios de terrenos agrícolas o forestales que pueden proporcionarles ingresos para vivir.
7. Actualización de los registros
Los registros se actualizan a diario.
8. Tasas de desempleo

Se utilizan estadísticas de estos registros para obtener tasas de desempleo.

Fuentes de los datos de empleo incluidos en el denominador de las tasas de desempleo: encuestas de establecimientos y registros de la seguridad social.

Definición de persona empleada que se utiliza a tales efectos

Asalariados a tiempo completo o tiempo parcial, trabajadores por cuenta propia y agricultores.

9. Tipo de estadísticas que se producen sobre desempleados registrados

Serie 1

Período de referencia: Mes, trimestre y año.

Frecuencia de producción: Mensual, trimestral y anual.

Variables utilizadas
– Sexo;
– Edad;
– Nivel de educación;
– Ocupación;
– Características geográficas;
– Experiencia laboral previa;
– Duración del desempleo.

Publicación
– En papel, para el público en general;
– En archivo electrónico, previa solicitud;
– En el sitio web http://www.ess.gov.si

Organismo responsable de la publicación: Servicio de Empleo, Oficina Estadística de la República de Eslovenia.

10. Información metodológica sobre las estadísticas

Divulgación
– En papel, para el público en general.
– En archivo electrónico, previa solicitud;
– En un sitio web.

Organismo responsable: Oficina de Estadística de la República de Eslovenia.

11. Comparaciones con estadísticas derivadas de otras fuentes

Se han hecho comparaciones con estadísticas de desempleo derivadas de la Encuesta sobre la fuerza de trabajo (esta última está a cargo de la Oficina de Estadística)

Frecuencia de las comparaciones: Periódica.

Publicación de la metodología/resultados de las comparaciones: Se han publicado.

12. Modificaciones importantes desde el comienzo de las estadísticas

En la legislación, la competencia del organismo y/o los procedimientos administrativos no ha habido modificaciones importantes que hayan influido significativamente en las estadísticas.

España

1. Serie

Título: Paro registrado.

Año de inicio: No se especifica.

2. Organismo responsable de la inscripción inicial de desempleados

Nombre del organismo: Instituto Nacional de Empleo y Servicios Públicos de Empleo.

Tipo de organismo: Organismo público subordinado a una autoridad nacional.

Nombre de la autoridad nacional: Ministerio de Trabajo y Asuntos Sociales.

Ubicación de las oficinas locales donde se hacen las inscripciones: En todo el país, distribuciones por zonas geográficas.

Tipo de servicios proporcionados/administrados por el organismo:
– Ayuda a personas en busca de empleo a encontrarlo;
– Ayuda a personas en busca de empleo a crear su propia empresa;
– Ayuda a los empleadores a encontrar trabajadores;
– Orientación profesional;
– Formación relacionada con el trabajo;
– Pago de las prestaciones de desempleo;
– Otros: Programas experimentales de Empleo y de Formación-Empleo.

Porcentaje de personas en busca de empleo que buscan trabajo por intermedio de ese organismo: No se especifica.

3. Se registran los siguientes datos de la persona:
– Nombre y apellido;
– Sexo;
– Número de seguridad social (o número de identificación semejante también utilizado por otros organismos);
– Dirección del domicilio habitual;
– Fecha de nacimiento;
– Ciudadanía;
– Nacionalidad;
– Nivel de educación/formación. No se han establecido vínculos con la CINE;
– Situación laboral actual o anterior: se identifican 40 categorías;
– Tipo de ocupación del empleo actual o anterior. Se han establecido vínculos con grupos primarios de la CIUO-88;
– Tipo de ocupación del empleo que se busca: se identifican 3.537 categorías. Se han establecido vínculos con grupos primarios de la CIUO-88;
– Nombre y dirección del empleador o del lugar del trabajo actual o anterior;
– Rama de actividad del empleador o del lugar del trabajo actual o anterior: se identifican 63 categorías;
– Inscripciones previas en el organismo.

4. Criterios utilizados para determinar si una persona habrá de incluirse en el registro (R) y/o en las estadísticas de personas desempleadas (S):
– Estar sin empleo (S);
– Estar en busca de empleo (R) y (S);
– Estar disponible para trabajar (S);
– Edad (mínima: 16 años; máxima: 65 años) (S);
– Ciudadanía (R) y (S);
– Residir en el país (R) y (S);
– Duración y/o número de horas de trabajo del empleo que se busca (S).

5. Criterios utilizados para determinar si se ha de excluir a una persona del registro (R) y/o de las estadísticas de personas desempleadas (S):
– Certificado de defunción (R) y (S);
– Establecerse en otro país (R) y (S);
– Incorporarse a un (nuevo) empleo (se excluye del registro si el empleo es superior a tres meses) (R) y (S);
– Participar en algún programa de promoción del empleo, de obras públicas, etc. (S);
– Estar estudiando o siguiendo una formación (se excluye de la estadística si es menor de 25 años o mayor y no ha trabajado anteriormente) (S);
– Rechazar una oferta de trabajo adecuada (R) y (S);
– Rechazar una oferta de formación adecuada (R) y (S);
– Incapacidad para trabajar (S).

6. Definición de persona desempleada en la que se basan las estadísticas

Personas inscritas como demandantes de empleo que no pertenezcan a los siguientes colectivos: están ocupadas en un empleo; participantes en trabajos de colaboración social; pensionistas por invalidez absoluta; jubilados; empleo por periodo superior a 3 meses; jornada mensual inferior a 80 horas; estudiantes; estudiantes de formación profesional; baja médica; beneficiarios del subsidio agrario; mayor de 65 años.

7. Actualización de los registros

Los registros se actualizan diariamente.

8. Tasas de desempleo

Se utilizan estadísticas de estos registros para obtener tasas de desempleo.

Fuente de los datos de empleo incluidos en el denominador de las tasas de desempleo: Encuesta de hogares sobre la fuerza de trabajo.

Definición de persona empleada que se utiliza a tales efectos

Encuesta de la población activa.

9. Tipo de estadísticas que se producen sobre desempleados registrados

Período de referencia: Mes.

Frecuencia de producción: Mensual.

Variables utilizadas:
– Sexo;
– Edad;
– Nivel de educación;
– Ocupación;
– Rama de actividad;
– Características geográficas;
– Duración del desempleo;
– Otras: Causas de exclusión paro registrado.

Publicación:
– En papel, para un público limitado;

–   En archivo electrónico, previa solicitud;

–   En el sitio web www.inem.es.

Organismo responsable de la publicación: Instituto Nacional de Empleo.

Título y periodicidad de la publicación: *Estadística de Empleo* (Mensual).

10. Información metodológica sobre las estadísticas

Divulgación:

–   En papel, para el público en general;

–   En archivo electrónico, previa solicitud;

–   En el sitio web www.inem.es.

Organismo responsable: Instituto Nacional de Empleo.

11. Comparaciones con estadísticas derivadas de otras fuentes

No se han hecho comparaciones con estadísticas de desempleo derivadas de otras fuentes.

12. Modificaciones importantes desde el comienzo de las estadísticas

Ha habido modificaciones importantes en la legislación, la competencia del organismo y/o los procedimientos administrativos en 1985. No ha sido registrada su repercusión en las estadísticas.

Estados Unidos

1. Serie

Título: Desempleo registrado.

Año de inicio: 1933.

2. Organismo responsable de la inscripción inicial de desempleados

Nombre del organismo: El nombre oficial varía de un Estado a otro, pero por lo general se llaman Agencia Estatal de Desarrollo de la Fuerza de Trabajo o Servicio de Empleo.

Tipo de organismo: Organismo público subordinado a una autoridad nacional.

Nombre de la autoridad nacional: Administración de Empleo y Formación (administrada mediante un fondo cooperativo federal y estatal)

Ubicación de las oficinas locales donde se hacen las inscripciones: En 3.459 centros locales (llamados *One-Stop*) y puestos de servicio en 50 Estados y cuatro territorios.

Tipo de servicios proporcionados/administrados por el organismo:

–   Ayuda a personas en busca de empleo a encontrarlo;

–   Ayuda a personas en busca de empleo a crear su propia empresa;

–   Ayuda a los empleadores a encontrar trabajadores;

–   Orientación profesional;

–   Formación relacionada con el trabajo;

–   Pago de prestaciones de desempleo;

–   Otros: los centros locales *One-Stop* pueden ofrecer diversos servicios de apoyo.

Porcentaje de personas en busca de empleo que buscan trabajo por intermedio de ese organismo: Se desconoce.

3. Se registran los siguientes datos de la persona:

–   Nombre y apellido;

–   Sexo;

–   Número de seguridad social (o número de identificación semejante también utilizado por otros organismos);

–   Dirección del domicilio habitual;

–   Fecha de nacimiento;

–   Ciudadanía;

–   Nacionalidad/grupo étnico;

–   Nivel de educación/formación;

–   Situación laboral actual o anterior;

–   Tipo de ocupación del empleo actual o anterior;

–   Tipo de ocupación del empleo que se busca;

–   Nombre y dirección del empleador o del lugar de trabajo actual o anterior;

–   Rama de actividad del empleador o del lugar de trabajo actual o anterior:se identifica un número indeterminado de grupos;

–   Inscripciones previas en el organismo;

–   Otros: los centros locales *One-Stop* pueden solicitar otras informaciones relacionadas con el empleo.

4. Criterios utilizados para determinar si una persona habrá de incluirse en el registro (R) y/o en las estadísticas de personas desempleadas (S):

–   Estar sin empleo   (R) y (S)*;

–   Estar en busca de empleo   (R) y (S)*;

–   Estar disponible para trabajar   (R) y (S)*.

* Únicamente solicitantes de prestaciones del seguro de desempleo.

5. Criterios utilizados para determinar si se ha de excluir a una persona del registro (R) y/o de las estadísticas de personas desempleadas (S):

–   Certificado de defunción   (R) y (S);

–   Establecerse en otro país   (R) y (S);

–   Incorporarse a un (nuevo) empleo   (R) y (S);

–   Comenzar el servicio militar   (R) y (S);

–   Participar en algún programa de promoción del empleo, de obras públicas, etc.   (R) y (S);

–   Estar estudiando o siguiendo una formación   (R) y (S)*;

–   Incumplir el requisito de tomar contacto con el organismo (las sanciones varían de un Estado a otro)   (R) y (S)*;

–   Rechazar ofertas de trabajo adecuadas (las sanciones varían de un Estado a otro)   (R) y (S)*;

–   Rechazar ofertas de formación adecuadas (las sanciones varían de un Estado a otro)   (R) y (S)*;

–   Fin del período de prestaciones de desempleo   (R) y (S)*;

–   Incapacidad para trabajar   (R) y (S)*.

* Únicamente solicitantes de prestaciones del seguro de desempleo.

6. Definición de persona desempleada en la que se basan las estadísticas

En lo que se refiere a la inscripción en los registros, no existe una definición federal de persona desempleada.

Para recibir prestaciones de desempleo las personas solicitantes deben estar en condiciones de trabajar, estar disponibles para trabajar y buscar empleo activamente.

7. Actualización de los registros

Los registros se actualizan periódicamente, pero la frecuencia varía de un Estado a otro.

8. Tasas de desempleo

No se utilizan estadísticas de estos registros para obtener tasas de desempleo.

9. Tipo de estadísticas que se producen sobre desempleados registrados

Período de referencia: Trimestre.

Frecuencia de producción: Trimestral.

Variables utilizadas:

–   Sexo;

–   Edad;

–   Nivel de educación;

–   Ocupación;

–   Rama de actividad.

Publicación: En papel, para el público en general.

Organismo responsable de la publicación: Administración de Empleo y Formación.

Título de las publicaciones: *Wagner-Peyser Act Annual Program Report Data* (Informe de datos del programa anual de la Ley Wagner-Peyser).

10. Información metodológica sobre las estadísticas

No se dispone de información.

11. Comparaciones con estadísticas derivadas de otras fuentes

No se han hecho comparaciones con estadísticas de desempleo derivadas de otras fuentes.

12. Modificaciones importantes desde el comienzo de las estadísticas

En la legislación, la competencia del organismo y/o los procedimientos administrativos hubo modificaciones importantes em 1933, 1950, 1973, 1978, 1982 y 1998. Los cambios consiguientes en las estadísticas no se han estimado.

13. Otros comentarios

Las políticas relativas a los registros de trabajo varían en todos los Estados Unidos. Por lo general, los trabajadores que buscan asistencia del personal para recibir propuestas de empleo deben inscribirse en dichos registros. En algunos Estados, los trabajadores pueden recibir información sobre puestos vacantes y demás sin estar registrados.

Las políticas relativas a los trabajadores que solicitan y reciben prestaciones de desempleo también varían en todo el país. Ahora bien, aquellos solicitantes que están en paro permanente y no reciben información sobre puestos vacantes por conducto de algún servicio sindical de empleo, deben registrarse para encontrar trabajo.

Todos los Estados publican listas de empleo a través de la red informática *America's Job Bank*.

Estonia

1. Serie

Título: Desempleo registrado.
Año de inicio: 1993.
2. Organismo responsable de la inscripción inicial de desempleados
Nombre del organismo: Tööhõiveamet (Oficina de Empleo).
Tipo de organismo: Organismo público subordinado a una autoridad nacional.
Nombre de la autoridad nacional: Junta del Mercado de Trabajo, Ministerio de Asuntos Sociales.
Ubicación de las oficinas locales donde se hacen las inscripciones: En 15 condados y una en Tallín (en todo el país hay 36 oficinas locales o representantes de las mismas).
Tipo de servicios proporcionados/administrados por el organismo:
– Informa sobre la situación del mercado laboral y las posibilidades de formación para el empleo;
– Mediación en materia de empleo;
– Formación para el empleo;
– Subsidios de empleo para crear empresas;
– Subsidios de empleo para empleadores;
– Colocación comunitaria;
– Orientación profesional;
– Pago de prestaciones de desempleo;
– Otros: programas especiales para grupos desfavorecidos (discapacitados, jóvenes y desempleados de larga data).
Porcentaje de personas en busca de empleo que buscan trabajo por intermedio de ese organismo: 55%.
3. Se registran los siguientes datos de la persona:
– Nombre y apellido;
– Sexo;
– Código de identificación personal;
– Dirección del domicilio habitual;
– Fecha de nacimiento;
– Ciudadanía;
– Nivel de educación/formación: se identifican 13 categorías. Se prevé establecer vínculos con la CINE;
– Situación laboral: se identifican nueve categorías;
– Tipo de ocupación del empleo anterior: se identifican nueve categorías. Se han establecido vínculos con la CIUO-88 a nivel de grupo primario;
– Tipo de ocupación del empleo que se busca: se identifican nueve categorías. Se han establecido vínculos con la CIUO-88 a nivel de grupo primario;
– Rama de actividad del empleador o del lugar de trabajo anterior: se identifican 16 categorías Se han establecido vínculos con la CIIU Rev. 3 y la NACE Rev. 1, a nivel de clases;
– Otros: de lengua estonia; de lengua rusa.
4. Criterios utilizados para determinar si una persona habrá de incluirse en el registro (R) y/o en las estadísticas de personas desempleadas (S):
Toda persona será registrada como desempleada en una oficina de empleo si se presenta a una de esas oficinas con todos los documentos necesarios y sigue el procedimiento estipulado por el gobierno de la república. Criterios:
– Estar sin empleo (S);
– Estar en busca de empleo (S);
– Estar disponible para trabajar (S);
– Edad (mínima: 16 años; máxima: edad de jubilación) (S);
– Residir en el país (S).
5. Criterios utilizados para determinar si se ha de excluir a una persona del registro (R) y/o de las estadísticas de personas desempleadas (S):
– Certificado de defunción (S);
– Establecerse en otro país (S);
– Incorporarse a un (nuevo) empleo (S);
– Comenzar el servicio militar (S);
– Estudiar de día o a tiempo completo en una institución de enseñanza (S);
– Haber dejado de buscar empleo por más de 30 días (S);
– Rechazar dos ofertas de empleo adecuadas (S);
– Rechazar dos ofertas de formación adecuadas (S);
– Tener la edad de jubilación o beneficiar de una pensión de jubilación anticipada (S);
– Incapacidad para trabajar (S);
– Otros: interrumpir la formación para el empleo sin consentimiento de la Oficina de Empleo (S); cobrar el subsidio de desempleo (S).
6. Definición de persona desempleada en la que se basan las estadísticas

Persona desempleada registrada es toda persona con capacidad total o parcial para trabajar que tiene 16 años como mínimo o menos de la edad de la jubilación, está sin empleo, está dispuesta a comenzar a trabajar inmediatamente y busca un empleo. La persona que busca empleo es aquella que informa a la oficina de empleo, al menos una vez cada 30 días, está dispuesta a empezar a trabajar inmediatamente y a participar en la formación para el empleo. Fuente: Ley de protección social del desempleado, párrafo 3 (http//www.tta.ee/english/law).
7. Actualización de los registros
No hay un registro central para todo el país (se procede a establecerlo). Cada condado dispone de una base de datos que se actualiza periódicamente.
8. Tasas de desempleo
Las estadísticas de las oficinas de empleo no se utilizan para obtener tasas de desempleo. Estas últimas se calculan a partir de los datos de la Encuesta sobre la población económicamente activa y según los métodos de la OIT. La Junta del Mercado de Trabajo calcula las tasas de desempleo como proporción del desempleo registrado respecto al total de personas en edad de trabajar (16 años - edad de jubilación), no de la fuerza de trabajo.
9. Tipo de estadísticas que se producen sobre desempleados registrados
Serie 1:
Período de referencia: Mes.
Frecuencia de producción: Mensual.
Variables utilizadas:
– Sexo;
– Grupo de edad (3);
– Nivel de educación (4);
– Características geográficas (condado);
– Otras: d e lengua estonia; de lengua rusa; participación en servicios de empleo; número de nuevas incorporaciones; número de vacantes; número de colocaciones; proporción de desempleo registrado respecto a la gente en edad de trabajar; número de desempleados que reciben prestaciones de desempleo.
Publicación:
– En papel;
– Para un público limitado (vía correo electrónico);
– En el sitio web http://www.tta.ee
Organismo responsable de la publicación: Oficina de Estadística de Estonia.
Título y periodicidad de las publicaciones: *Estonian Statistics Monthly* (Estadísticas mensuales de Estonia).
Serie 2:
Período de referencia: Trimestre.
Frecuencia de producción: Trimestral.
Variables utilizadas:
– Sexo;
– Edad;
– Nivel de educación;
– Ocupación;
– Rama de actividad;
– Características geográficas (condado y municipio);
– Experiencia laboral previa;
– Duración del desempleo;
– Otras: de lengua estonia; de lengua rusa.
Publicación:
– En papel (por el momento sólo en parte porque aún no se dispone del registro);
– Para un público limitado (vía correo electrónico).
10. Información metodológica sobre las estadísticas
Divulgación:
– En papel, para el público en general;
– En el sitio web http://www.tta.ee
Organismo responsable de la divulgación: Junta del Mercado de Trabajo.
11. Comparaciones con estadísticas derivadas de otras fuentes
Se han hecho comparaciones con estadísticas de desempleo derivadas de la Encuesta sobre la fuerza de trabajo, una encuesta de hogares y el Censo de población.
Frecuencia de las comparaciones: Periódica, cuando se publican las estadísticas.
Publicación de la metodología/resultados de las comparaciones: Se han publicado en:
– *Estonian Labour Market and Labour Market Policy* (Mercado de trabajo y política del mercado de trabajo de Estonia) (Artículos de Raul Eamets);
– *Estonian Employment Action Plans* (Planes de acción de empleo en Estonia - último trimestre de 2000 - 2001; 2002 -

2003);
– Eesti tööturu areng üleminekuperioodil (Eamets R. y Philips K.), Tartu 1999.
– *Estonian Statistics Monthly* (Estadísticas mensuales de Estonia) (Oficina de Estadísticas de Estonia).

12. Modificaciones importantes desde el comienzo de las estadísticas

En la legislación, la competencia del organismo y/o los procedimientos administrativos hubo modificaciones importantes que influyeron significativamente en las estadísticas, a saber: i) 1995, cuando entró en vigor la Ley de protección social del desempleado cuya repercusión en las estadísticas no se ha estimado, y ii) en 2000, cuando entraron en vigor la nueva Ley de protección social del desempleado y la Ley de servicio de empleo que trajeron aparejado un aumento de 17 por ciento del número de personas desempleadas registradas.

Etiopía

1. Sorio
Título: Estadísticas de la bolsa de trabajo.
Año de inicio: 1961.
2. Organismo responsable de la inscripción inicial de desempleados
Nombre del organismo: Oficina de Trabajo y Asuntos Sociales.
Tipo de organismo: Organismo público subordinado a autoridades nacionales y regionales.
Nombre de la autoridad nacional: Ministerio de Trabajo y Asuntos Sociales.
Ubicación de las oficinas locales donde se hacen las inscripciones: Oficinas públicas de empleo de los distintos Estados regionales y administraciones municipales.
Tipo de servicios proporcionados/administrados por el organismo:
– Ayuda a personas en busca de empleo a encontrarlo;
– Ayuda a los empleadores a encontrar trabajadores;
– Orientación profesional (responsabilidad parcial);
– Formación relacionada con el trabajo (responsabilidad parcial).
3. Se registran los siguientes datos de la persona:
– Nombre y apellido;
– Sexo;
– Dirección del domicilio habitual;
– Fecha de nacimiento;
– Nivel de educación/formación: se identifica un número indeterminado de categorías. Se han establecido vínculos con la CINE;
– Situación laboral actual o anterior: se identifica un número indeterminado de categorías;
– Tipo de ocupación del empleo actual o anterior: se identifican cinco grupos;
– Inscripciones previas en el organismo.
4. Criterios utilizados para determinar si una persona habrá de incluirse en el registro (R) y/o en las estadísticas de personas desempleadas (S):
– Estar sin empleo (R) y (S);
– Estar en busca de empleo (R) y (S);
– Estar disponible para trabajar (R) y (S);
– Edad (mínima: 18 años; máxima: 55 años) (R) y (S);
– Residir en el país (R) y (S);
– Haber trabajado (R) y (S).
5. Criterios utilizados para determinar si se ha de excluir a una persona del registro (R) y/o de las estadísticas de personas desempleadas (S)
No se dispone de información.
6. Definición de persona desempleada en la que se basan las estadísticas
No se dispone de información.
7. Actualización de los registros
Los registros se actualizan periódicamente.
8. Tasas de desempleo
No se utilizan estadísticas de estos registros para obtener tasas de desempleo.
9. Tipo de estadísticas que se producen sobre desempleados registrados
Período de referencia: Año.
Frecuencia de producción: Anual.
Variables utilizadas:
– Sexo;
– Edad;

– Nivel de educación;
– Ocupación;
– Características geográficas;
– Duración del desempleo.
Publicación: En papel, para el público en general.
Organismo responsable de la publicación: Ministerio de Trabajo y Asuntos Sociales.
Título de las publicaciones: *Employment Exchange Information* (Información de la bolsa de trabajo); *Labour Statistics Bulletin* (Boletín de estadísticas del trabajo).
10. Información metodológica sobre las estadísticas
Divulgación: En papel, para el público en general.
Organismo responsable: Ministerio de Trabajo y Asuntos Sociales.
11. Comparaciones con estadísticas derivadas de otras fuentes
No se han hecho comparaciones con estadísticas de desempleo derivadas de otras fuentes.
12. Modificaciones importantes desde el comienzo de las estadísticas
En la legislación, la competencia del organismo y/o los procedimientos administrativos hubo modificaciones importantes en:
1975: los cambios consiguientes en las estadísticas no se han estimado, y
1993: que se tradujeron por una disminución de 25-30% del número total de personas desempleadas registradas.

Filipinas

1. Serie
Título: Número de solicitantes registrados (desglosado por región, sexo y programa).
2. Organismo responsable de la inscripción inicial de desempleados
Nombre del organismo: Public Employment Service Office - PESO (Oficina del Servicio Público de Empleo).
Tipo de organismo: Organismo público subordinado a una autoridad nacional.
Nombre de la autoridad nacional: Departamento de Trabajo y Empleo.
Ubicación de las oficinas locales donde se hacen las inscripciones: Todo el país.
Tipo de servicios proporcionados/administrados por el organismo
– Ayuda a personas en busca de empleo a encontrarlo;
– Ayuda a personas en busca de empleo a crear su propia empresa;
– Ayuda a los empleadores a encontrar trabajadores;
– Orientación profesional;
– Formación relacionada con el trabajo;
– Proporciona información sobre el mercado de trabajo.
Porcentaje de personas en busca de empleo que buscan trabajo por intermedio de ese organismo: 20%.
3. Se registran los siguientes datos de la persona
– Nombre y apellido;
– Sexo;
– Número de seguridad social (o número de identificación semejante también utilizado por otros organismos);
– Dirección del domicilio habitual;
– Fecha de nacimiento;
– Ciudadanía;
– Nacionalidad/grupo étnico;
– Nivel de educación/formación (nivel de educación, título del curso). No se han establecido vínculos con la CINE;
– Situación laboral actual o anterior (empleada actualmente o empleada anteriormente);
– Tipo de ocupación del empleo actual o anterior: se identifican 10 categorías, basadas en la Clasificación Uniforme de Ocupaciones de Filipinas (PSOC);
– Tipo de ocupación del empleo que se busca: se identifican 10 categorías (PSOC). Se han establecido vínculos con la CIUO-88;
– Nombre y dirección del empleador o del lugar de trabajo actual o anterior.
4. Criterios utilizados para determinar si una persona habrá de incluirse en el registro (R) y/o en las estadísticas de personas desempleadas (S)
– Estar sin empleo (R) y (S);
– Estar en busca de empleo (R) y (S);
– Estar disponible para trabajar (R);
– Edad (15 años o más) (S);
– Ciudadanía (R);

- Residir en el país (R);
- Haber trabajado (R);
- Duración del empleo que se busca (R).

5. Criterios utilizados para determinar si se ha de excluir a una persona del registro (R) y/o de las estadísticas de personas desempleadas (S)
- Certificado de defunción (R);
- Establecerse en otro país (R);
- Incorporarse a un (nuevo) empleo (R);
- Comenzar el servicio militar (R);
- Participar en algún programa de promoción del empleo, de obras públicas, etc. (R);
- Estar estudiando o siguiendo una formación (R);
- Incumplir el requisito de tomar contacto con el organismo (R);
- Incapacidad para trabajar (R).

6. Definición de persona desempleada en la que se basan las estadísticas
Solicitantes registrados: número de personas en busca de empleo que demuestran interés por aprovechar los diversos servicios de facilitación de empleo que ofrece la PESO, rellenando el formulario de inscripción en el registro.

7. Actualización de los registros
Los registros se actualizan periódicamente.

8. Tasas de desempleo
No se utilizan estadísticas de estos registros para obtener tasas de desempleo.

9. Tipo de estadísticas que se producen sobre desempleados registrados
Serie: Número de solicitantes registrados.
Período de referencia: Mes.
Frecuencia de producción: Mensual.
Variables utilizadas
- Sexo;
- Edad;
- Nivel de educación;
- Ocupación;
- Rama de actividad;
- Características geográficas;
- Experiencia laboral previa;
- Ciudadanía.

Publicación: En papel, para un público limitado.
Organismo responsable de la publicación: Oficina de Empleo Local (BLE).

10. Información metodológica sobre las estadísticas
Divulgación: No se divulga, sólo para uso interno.

11. Comparaciones con estadísticas derivadas de otras fuentes
Se han hecho comparaciones con estadísticas de desempleo derivadas de la Encuesta sobre la fuerza de trabajo.
Frecuencia de las comparaciones: Una vez, o de vez en cuando.
Publicación de la metodología/resultados de las comparaciones: No se publican.

12. Modificaciones importantes desde el comienzo de las estadísticas
En la legislación hubo modificaciones importantes en 1999 (Ley de la Oficina de Servicio de Empleo – RA 8759).

Finlandia

1. Serie
Título: Estadísticas del Servicio de Empleo.
Año de inicio: 1991.

2. Organismo responsable de la inscripción inicial de desempleados
Nombre del organismo: Oficinas de Empleo.
Tipo de organismo: Organismo público subordinado a autoridades nacionales, regionales y locales.
Nombre de la autoridad nacional: Ministerio de Trabajo.
Ubicación de las oficinas locales donde se hacen las inscripciones: 175 oficinas de empleo en todo el país.
Tipo de servicios proporcionados/administrados por el organismo:
- Ayuda a personas en busca de empleo a encontrarlo;
- Ayuda a personas en busca de empleo a crear su propia empresa;
- Ayuda a los empleadores a encontrar trabajadores;
- Orientación profesional;
- Formación relacionada con el trabajo;
- Pago de prestaciones de desempleo;

- Otros: formación para el mercado de trabajo.

3. Se registran los siguientes datos de la persona:
- Nombre y apellido;
- Sexo;
- Número de seguridad social (o número de identificación semejante también utilizado por otros organismos);
- Fecha de nacimiento;
- Ciudadanía;
- Nacionalidad/grupo étnico;
- Nivel de educación/formación: se identifican de cinco a seis categorías. Se han establecido vínculos con la CINE;
- Situación laboral actual o anterior: se identifican 14 categorías;
- Tipo de ocupación del empleo actual o anterior: se distinguen 3.300 categorías. No se han establecido vínculos con la CIUO-88;
- Tipo de ocupación del empleo que se busca: se distinguen 3.300 categorías. No se han establecido vínculos con la CIUO-88;
- Rama de actividad del empleador o del lugar de trabajo actual o anterior. No se han establecido vínculos con la CIIU Rev. 3 ni la NACE Rev. 1;
- Inscripciones previas en el organismo;
- Otros: código del registro de empleo.

4. Criterios utilizados para determinar si una persona habrá de incluirse en el registro (R) y/o en las estadísticas de personas desempleadas (S):
- Estar sin empleo (R) y (S);
- Estar en busca de empleo (R) y (S);
- Estar disponible para trabajar (R) y (S);
- Edad (mínima: 17 años; máxima: 65 años) (R) y (S);
- Ciudadanía (R) y (S);
- Residir en el país (R) y (S);
- Duración y/o número de horas de trabajo del empleo que se busca (R) y (S).

5. Criterios utilizados para determinar si se ha de excluir a una persona del registro (R) y/o de las estadísticas de personas desempleadas (S):
- Certificado de defunción (R) y (S);
- Establecerse en otro país (R) y (S);
- Incorporarse a un (nuevo) empleo (R) y (S);
- Comenzar el servicio militar (R) y (S);
- Participar en algún programa de promoción del empleo, de obras públicas, etc. (R) y (S);
- Estar estudiando o siguiendo una formación (R) y (S);
- Incumplir el requisito de tomar contacto con el organismo (R) y (S);
- Rechazar una oferta de empleo adecuada (R) y (S);
- Rechazar una oferta de formación adecuada (R) y (S);
- Fin del período de prestaciones de desempleo (R) y (S);
- Cobrar alguna pensión (R) y (S);
- Incapacidad para trabajar (R) y (S).

6. Definición de persona desempleada en la que se basan las estadísticas
Se entiende por desempleada a toda persona en busca de empleo registrada que está sin trabajo, disponible para trabajar a tiempo completo (trabajo cuyo horario equivale como mínimo a la mitad del tiempo normal de trabajo) o que ha encontrado un puesto de trabajo pero que aún no se ha incorporado a él. Toda persona en busca de trabajo que puede aceptar una oferta de empleo solamente después de un período fijo o que busca un empleo cuyo horario es inferior a la mitad del tiempo normal de trabajo en el sector, no se considera como persona en busca de empleo. Los estudiantes a tiempo completo tampoco se registran como desempleados en busca de trabajo ni siquiera durante las vacaciones.

7. Actualización de los registros
Los registros se actualizan mensualmente.

8. Tasas de desempleo
Se utilizan estadísticas de estos registros para obtener tasas de desempleo.
Fuente de los datos de empleo incluidos en el denominador de las tasas de desempleo:
Encuesta sobre la población económicamente activa.

9. Tipo de estadísticas que se producen sobre desempleados registrados
Serie: Estadísticas del servicio de empleo.
Período de referencia: Mes.
Frecuencia de producción: Mensual.
Variables utilizadas
- Sexo;
- Edad;

- Nivel de educación;
- Ocupación;
- Rama de actividad;
- Características geográficas;
- Experiencia laboral previa;
- Ciudadanía (nacionales o no);
- Duración del desempleo.

Publicación:
- En papel, para el público en general;
- En archivo electrónico, previa solicitud;
- En un sitio web.

Organismo responsable de la publicación: Ministerio de Trabajo.

10. Información metodológica sobre las estadísticas
Divulgación: En el sitio web www.mol.fi.
Organismo responsable: Ministerio de Trabajo.

11. Comparaciones con estadísticas derivadas de otras fuentes
Se han hecho comparaciones con estadísticas de desempleo derivadas de la Encuesta sobre la fuerza de trabajo, otro tipo de encuestas de hogares y el Censo de población.
Frecuencia de las comparaciones: De vez en cuando (último año: 1997).
Publicación de la metodología/resultados de las comparaciones:
Se publicaron en *Unemployment and Employment Statistics* (Estadísticas de empleo y desempleo), Estadísticas de Finlandia, Estadísticas Oficiales, Mercado de Trabajo 1997:3.

12. Modificaciones importantes desde el comienzo de las estadísticas
En la legislación, la competencia del organismo y/o los procedimientos administrativos no ha habido modificaciones importantes que hayan influido significativamente en las estadísticas.

Francia

1. Serie
Título: Personas en busca de empleo.
2. Organismo responsable de la inscripción inicial de desempleados
Nombre del organismo: Agence nationale pour l'Emploi - ANPE (Agencia Nacional de Empleo).
Tipo de organismo: Organismo público subordinado a una autoridad nacional.
Nombre de la autoridad nacional: Ministerio de Asuntos Sociales, Trabajo y Solidaridad.
Ubicación de las oficinas locales donde se hacen las inscripciones: 741 agencias locales en todo el país.
Tipo de servicios proporcionados/administrados por el organismo
- Ayuda a personas en busca de empleo a encontrarlo;
- Ayuda a personas en busca de empleo a crear su propia empresa;
- Ayuda a los empleadores a encontrar trabajadores;
- Orientación profesional;
- Ayuda a los trabajadores en actividad a encontrar otro empleo.

Porcentaje de personas en busca de empleo que buscan trabajo por intermedio de ese organismo: 100%.
3. Se registran los siguientes datos de la persona
- Nombre y apellido;
- Sexo;
- Dirección del domicilio habitual;
- Fecha de nacimiento;
- Nacionalidad;
- Nivel de educación/formación: se identifican 152 categorías. No se han establecido vínculos con la CINE;
- Rama de actividad del empleador o del lugar de trabajo actual o anterior: se identifican 75 categorías;
- Inscripciones previas en el organismo;
- Otros: categoría (véase puntos 6); calificación; handicap.

4. Criterios utilizados para determinar si una persona habrá de incluirse en el registro (R) y/o en las estadísticas de personas desempleadas (S)
- Toda persona puede inscribirse en la ANPE si lo desea (incluidas aquellas que tienen trabajo). En función de su situación respecto a los criterios siguientes (estar sin empleo; estar en busca de empleo; estar disponible para trabajar; tener trabajo) se inscribirá en un registro determinado (ocho categorías cuyas definiciones figuran en el punto 6). La inscripción es obligatoria para las personas en busca de empleo que tienen derecho a prestaciones.
- Edad (mínima: 16 años) (R) y (S);

- Residir en el país (R) y (S);
- Duración y/o número de horas de trabajo del empleo que se busca: si la persona busca un empleo a tiempo parcial se la incluirá en las categorías 2 o 7.

5. Criterios utilizados para determinar si se ha de excluir a una persona del registro (R) y/o de las estadísticas de personas desempleadas (S)
- Certificado de defunción (R) y (S);
- Establecerse en otro país (R) y (S);
- Incorporarse a un (nuevo) empleo, según el caso, las personas clasificadas en las categorías 5, 6, 7, u 8 pueden ejercer una actividad reducida y, a la vez, estar inscritas en la ANPE;
- Comenzar el servicio militar (R) y (S);
- Incumplir el requisito de tomar contacto con el organismo (R) y (S);
- Rechazar ofertas de trabajo adecuadas (R) y (S);
- Rechazar ofertas de formación adecuadas (R) y (S);
- Declaración falsa (R) y (S);
- Incapacidad para trabajar (R) y (S).

6. Definición de las categorías de personas en busca de empleo en la que se basan las estadísticas
Categoría 1: Persona sin empleo que está disponible para trabajar inmediatamente a tenor del Artículo R.311-3-3, que *busca un empleo a tiempo completo de duración indeterminada* y tiene el deber de cumplir actos positivos de búsqueda de empleo.
Esta persona no debe haber ejercido ninguna actividad ocasional o limitada de más de 78 horas durante el mes de actualización.
Categoría 2: Persona sin empleo que está disponible para trabajar inmediatamente a tenor del Artículo R.311-3-3, que *busca un empleo a tiempo parcial de duración indeterminada* y tiene el deber de cumplir actos positivos de búsqueda de empleo.
Esta persona no debe haber ejercido ninguna actividad ocasional o limitada de más de 78 horas durante el mes de actualización.
Categoría 3: Persona sin empleo que está disponible para trabajar inmediatamente a tenor del Artículo R.311-3-3, que *busca un empleo de duración determinada, temporal o estacional, incluso de cortísima duración,* y tiene el deber de cumplir actos positivos de búsqueda de empleo.
Esta persona no debe haber ejercido ninguna actividad ocasional o limitada de más de 78 horas durante el mes de actualización.
Categoría 4: Persona sin empleo, que busca empleo y no está disponible inmediatamente.
Categoría 5: Persona con empleo que busca otro.
Categoría 6: Persona que no está disponible para trabajar inmediatamente a tenor del Artículo R.311-3-3 (1.°), que *busca otro empleo a tiempo completo de duración indeterminada* y tiene el deber de cumplir actos positivos de búsqueda de empleo.
Esta persona ha ejercido una actividad ocasional o limitada de más de 78 horas durante el mes de actualización.
Categoría 7: Persona que no está disponible para trabajar inmediatamente a tenor del Artículo R.311-3-3 (1.°), que *busca otro empleo a tiempo parcial de duración indeterminada* y tiene el deber de cumplir actos positivos de búsqueda de empleo.
Esta persona ha ejercido una actividad ocasional o limitada de más de 78 horas durante el mes de actualización.
Categoría 8: Persona que no está disponible para trabajar inmediatamente a tenor del Artículo R.311-3-3 (1.°), que *busca otro empleo de duración determinada, temporal o estacional, incluso de cortísima duración,* y tiene el deber de cumplir actos positivos de búsqueda de empleo.
Esta persona ha ejercido una actividad ocasional o limitada de más de 78 horas durante el mes de actualización.

7. Actualización de los registros
Los registros se actualizan mensualmente.

8. Tasas de desempleo
Calculada cada mes por el Instituto Nacional de Estadística y Estudios Económicos (INSEE) es la relación entre el número de desempleados, según la definición de la OIT y el total de la población activa.
El número de desempleados, según la definición de la OIT, se establece una vez por año a partir de la encuesta anual de empleo que hace el INSEE, en los meses intermedios se estima según un modelo paramétrico basado en la evolución del número de personas en busca de empleo inscritas en la ANPE (categorías 1, 2 y 3).
Población activa es la suma del empleo total y el desempleo.
El censo de población sirve de base para evaluar el total de empleo; la encuesta de empleo y otras fuentes permiten revaluarlo cada año.

9. Tipo de estadísticas que se producen sobre desempleados registrados

Período de referencia: Mes.
Frecuencia de producción: Mensual.
Variables utilizadas
– Sexo;
– Edad;
– Nivel de educación;
– Ocupación;
– Características geográficas;
– Nacionalidad;
– Duración del desempleo;
– Otras: calificaciones y handicap.
Publicación
– Sólo para uso internos (publicación especial destinada a la red de la ANPE);
– En papel, para el público en general, previa solicitud;
– En archivo electrónico, previa solicitud;
– En el sitio web:
– http://www.travail.gouv.fr/etudes/etudes_i.html
Organismo responsable de la publicación: Ministerio de Asuntos Sociales, Trabajo y Solidaridad.
Título de la publicación: *Premières informations* (Primeras informaciones).

10. Información metodológica sobre las estadísticas
Divulgación: En archivo electrónico, previa solicitud.
Organismo responsable: Ministerio de Asuntos Sociales, Trabajo y Solidaridad, en el caso de las estadísticas del número de personas inscitas en la ANPE, y el INSEE en lo que se refiere al "desempleo OIT".

11. Comparaciones con estadísticas derivadas de otras fuentes
Se han hecho comparaciones con estadísticas de desempleo derivadas de la Encuesta de empleo y el Censo de población.
Publicación de la metodología/resultados de las comparaciones: http://www.insee.fr/fr/indic/indic_conj/donnees/chomrev.pdf

12. Modificaciones importantes desde el comienzo de las estadísticas
En la legislación, la competencia del organismo y/o los procedimientos administrativos no ha habido modificaciones importantes que hayan influido significativamente en las estadísticas, pero en 1995, hubo una reforma de categorías.

Gabón

1. Serie
Título: Informe de actividad de la Oficina Nacional de Empleo (ONE).
Año de inicio: 1994.
2. Organismo responsable de la inscripción inicial de desempleados
Nombre del organismo: Office national de l'Emploi - ONE (Oficina Nacional de Empleo).
Tipo de organismo: Organismo público subordinado a una autoridad nacional.
Nombre de la autoridad nacional: Ministerio de Trabajo, Empleo y Formación Profesional.
Ubicación de las oficinas locales donde se hacen las inscripciones: Libreville y Port-Gentil.
Tipo de servicios proporcionados/administrados por el organismo
– Ayuda a personas en busca de empleo a encontrarlo;
– Ayuda a personas en busca de empleo a crear su propia empresa;
– Ayuda a los empleadores a encontrar trabajadores;
– Formación relacionada con el trabajo.
Porcentaje de personas en busca de empleo que buscan trabajo por intermedio de ese organismo: 34%.
3. Se registran los siguientes datos de la persona
– Nombre y apellido;
– Sexo;
– Dirección del domicilio habitual;
– Fecha de nacimiento;
– Ciudadanía;
– Nivel de educación/formación: se identifican cuatro categorías. No se han establecido vínculos con la CINE;
– Situación laboral actual o anterior: se identifican tres categorías;
– Tipo de ocupación del empleo actual o anterior: se identifican cuatro categorías. No se han establecido

vínculos con la CIUO-88;
– Tipo de ocupación del empleo que se busca: se identifican cuatro categorías;
– Nombre y dirección del empleador o del lugar de trabajo actual o anterior;
– Rama de actividad del empleador o del lugar de trabajo actual o anterior: se identifican 60 categorías. No se han establecido vínculos con la CIIU;
– Tipo de diplomas y tipo de formación.
4. Criterios utilizados para determinar si una persona habrá de incluirse en el registro (R)
– Estar sin empleo (R);
– Estar en busca de empleo (R);
– Estar disponible para trabajar (R);
– Edad (mínima: 16 años; máxima: 65 años) (R).
5. Criterios utilizados para determinar si se ha de excluir a una persona del registro (R)
– Certificado de defunción (R);
– Establecerse en otro país (R);
– Incorporarse a un (nuevo) empleo (R);
– Comenzar el servicio militar (R);
– Participar en algún programa de promoción del empleo, de obras públicas, etc. (R);
– Estar estudiando o siguiendo una formación (R);
–
– Incumplir el requisito de tomar contacto con el organismo (R);
– Cobrar alguna pensión (jubilación u otras) (R);
– Incapacidad para trabajar (R).
6. Definición de persona desempleada en la que se basan las estadísticas
No se aplica.
7. Actualización de los registros
Los registros se actualizan a diario.
Puntos siguientes: no se aplican. La ONE no se ocupa de producir estadísticas de desempleo. Esa tarea incumbe a otros organismos públicos.

Ghana

1. Serie
Título: Desempleo registrado.
Año de inicio: 1956.
2. Organismo responsable de la inscripción inicial de desempleados
Nombre del organismo: Centros públicos de empleo del Departamento de Trabajo.
Tipo de organismo: Organismo público subordinado a una autoridad nacional.
Nombre de la autoridad nacional: Departamento de Trabajo, Ministerio de Recursos Humanos, Desarrollo y Empleo
Ubicación de las oficinas locales donde se hacen las inscripciones: 66 de los principales centros urbanos del país.
Tipo de servicios proporcionados/administrados por el organismo:
– Ayuda a personas en busca de empleo a encontrarlo;
– Ayuda a los empleadores a encontrar trabajadores;
– Orientación profesional;
– Otros: administración de prestaciones de los trabajadores y de quejas de carácter laboral; solución de conflictos laborales.
3. Se registran los siguientes datos de la persona:
– Nombre y apellido;
– Sexo;
– Dirección del domicilio habitual;
– Fecha de nacimiento;
– Ciudadanía;
– Nacionalidad/grupo étnico;
– Nivel de educación/formación: se identifican tres categorías. Se han establecido vínculos con la CINE;
– Situación laboral actual o anterior;
– Tipo de ocupación del empleo actual o anterior: se identifican ocho grupos. Se han establecido vínculos con la CIUO-88 a nivel de grandes grupos;
– Tipo de ocupación del empleo que se busca: se identifican ocho grupos. Se han establecido vínculos con la CIUO-88 a nivel de grandes grupos;
– Nombre y dirección del empleador o del lugar de trabajo actual o anterior;
– Rama de actividad del empleador o del lugar de trabajo actual o anterior: se identifican nueve grupos. Se han

establecido vínculos con la CIIU Rev. 3, a nivel de grupos;
- Inscripciones previas en el organismo.

4. Criterios utilizados para determinar si una persona habrá de incluirse en el registro (R) y/o en las estadísticas de personas desempleadas (S):
- Estar sin empleo (R) y (S);
- Estar en busca de empleo (R) y (S);
- Estar disponible para trabajar (R) y (S);
- Edad (mínima: 15 años; máxima: 55 años) (R) y (S);
- Ciudadanía (R) y (S);
- Residir en el país (R) y (S);
- Haber trabajado (R) y (S);
- Otros: aspecto físico (R).

5. Criterios utilizados para determinar si se ha de excluir a una persona del registro (R) y/o de las estadísticas de personas desempleadas (S):
- Certificado de defunción (R) y (S);
- Incorporarse a un (nuevo) empleo (R) y (S);
- Incumplir el requisito de tomar contacto con el organismo (R) y (S).

6. Definición de persona desempleada en la que se basan las estadísticas
Personas con o sin formación para el empleo/educación, de edades comprendidas entre 15 y 55 años que están en busca de empleo, disponibles para trabajar y que se presentan periódicamente a alguno de los centros públicos de empleo del país.

7. Actualización de los registros
Los registros se actualizan trimestralmente.

8. Tasas de desempleo
No se utilizan estadísticas de estos registros para obtener tasas de desempleo.

9. Tipo de estadísticas que se producen sobre desempleados registrados
Período de referencia: Trimestre.
Frecuencia de producción: Trimestral.
Variables utilizadas:
- Sexo;
- Edad;
- Nivel de educación;
- Ocupación;
- Rama de actividad;
- Características geográficas;
- Experiencia laboral previa;
- Nacionalidad (nacionales o no);
- Duración del desempleo;
- Otras: características físicas.

Publicación: En papel, para el público en general.
Organismo responsable de la publicación: Departamento de Trabajo (Sección de Información sobre el Empleo).
Título y periodicidad de las publicaciones: *Employment Market Report* (Informe del mercado de trabajo), trimestral.

10. Información metodológica sobre las estadísticas
Organismo responsable: Departamento de Trabajo (Sección de Información sobre el Empleo).

11. Comparaciones con estadísticas derivadas de otras fuentes
No se han hecho comparaciones con estadísticas de desempleo derivadas de otras fuentes.

12. Modificaciones importantes desde el comienzo de las estadísticas
En la legislación, la competencia del organismo y/o los procedimientos administrativos, por el momento, no ha habido modificaciones importantes que hayan influido significativamente en las estadísticas, pero se prepara una nueva ley del trabajo que, sin duda, influirá en ellas.

Groenlandia

1. Serie
Título: Estadísticas de desempleo registrado.
Año de inicio: 1988.

2. Organismo responsable de la inscripción inicial de desempleados
Nombre del organismo: Las inscripciones están a cargo de las autoridades locales (*Kommuner*) y son acopiadas por Estadísticas de Groenlandia.
Tipo de organismo: Organismo público subordinado a autoridades locales.
Ubicación de las oficinas locales donde se hacen las inscripciones: En las capitales regionales de todo el país.

Tipo de servicios proporcionados/administrados por el organismo:
- Ayuda a personas en busca de empleo a encontrarlo;
- Ayuda a personas en busca de empleo a crear su propia empresa;
- Ayuda a los empleadores a encontrar trabajadores;
- Orientación profesional;
- Formación relacionada con el trabajo;
- Pago de prestaciones de desempleo.

3. Se registran los siguientes datos de la persona:
- Nombre y apellido;
- Sexo (indirectamente, a través del número de seguridad social);
- Número de seguridad social;
- Dirección del domicilio habitual;
- Fecha de nacimiento;
- Ciudadanía;
- Nivel de educación/formación. Se han establecido vínculos con la CINE;
- Inscripciones previas en el organismo.

4. Criterios utilizados para determinar si una persona habrá de incluirse en el registro (R) y/o en las estadísticas de personas desempleadas (S):
- Estar sin empleo (R) y (S);
- Estar disponible para trabajar (R);
- Edad (mínima: 16 años; máxima: 61 años) (S);
- Ciudadanía (R) y (S);
- Residir en el país (R) y (S).

5. Criterios utilizados para determinar si se ha de excluir a una persona del registro (R) y/o de las estadísticas de personas desempleadas (S):
- Incumplir el requisito de tomar contacto con el organismo.

6. Definición de persona desempleada en la que se basan las estadísticas
Personas inscritas como desempleadas en el registro de las autoridades locales. Los requisitos para poder inscribirse son: edades comprendidas entre 15 y 62 años; no formar parte de otras categoría sociales tales como la de jubilado; estar dispuesto a aceptar ofertas de empleo y no tener trabajo en el momento de la inscripción.

7. Actualización de los registros
Los registros se actualizan mensualmente.

8. Tasas de desempleo
Se utilizan estadísticas de estos registros para obtener tasas de desempleo.
Fuente de los datos de empleo incluidos en el denominador de las tasas de desempleo:
Censo de población.
Definición de persona empleada que se utiliza a tales efectos:
Personas de edades comprendidas entre 15 y 62 años; es decir, la fuerza de trabajo potencial (por el momento no se dispone de ningún registro exacto de la fuerza de trabajo real).

9. Tipo de estadísticas que se producen sobre desempleados registrados
Serie 1:
Período de referencia: Trimestre.
Frecuencia de producción: Trimestral.
Variables utilizadas:
- Sexo (indirectamente, a través del número de seguridad social);
- Edad (indirectamente, a través del número de seguridad social);
- Nivel de educación;
- Características geográficas.

Publicación:
- En papel, para el público en general;
- En el sitio web www.statgreen.gl.
Organismo responsable de la publicación: Estadísticas de Groenlandia.
Título y periodicidad de la publicación: *Ledigheden* (Período), trimestral.
Serie 2:
Período de referencia: Semestre.
Frecuencia de producción: Semestral.
Variables utilizadas:
- Sexo (indirectamente, a través del número de seguridad social);
- Edad (indirectamente, a través del número de seguridad social);
- Nivel de educación;
- Características geográficas.

Publicación:
– En papel, para el público en general;
– En el sitio web www.statgreen.gl.
Organismo responsable de la publicación: Estadísticas de Groenlandia.
Título y periodicidad de la publicación: *Ledigheden* (Período), trimestral.
Serie 3:
Período de referencia: Año.
Frecuencia de producción: Anual.
Variables utilizadas:
– Sexo (indirectamente, a través del número de seguridad social);
– Edad (indirectamente, a través del número de seguridad social);
– Nivel de educación;
– Características geográficas.
Publicación:
– En papel, para el público en general;
– En el sitio web www.statgreen.gl
Organismo responsable de la publicación: Estadísticas de Groenlandia.
Título y periodicidad de la publicación: *Ledigheden* (Período), trimestral.
10. Información metodológica sobre las estadísticas
Divulgación: En papel, para el público en general.
Organismo responsable: Estadísticas de Groenlandia.
11. Comparaciones con estadísticas derivadas de otras fuentes
No se han hecho comparaciones con estadísticas de desempleo derivadas de otras fuentes.
12. Modificaciones importantes desde el comienzo de las estadísticas
En la legislación, la competencia del organismo y/o los procedimientos administrativos hubo modificaciones importantes en 2002 que trajeron aparejada una disminución de 0,5 por ciento del número de personas desempleadas registradas.

Guatemala

1. Serie
Título: Personas inscritas.
Año de inicio: 1989.
2. Organismo responsable de la inscripción inicial de desempleados
Nombre del organismo: Departamento del Servicio Nacional del Empleo.
Tipo de organismo: Organismo público subordinado a una autoridad nacional.
Nombre de la autoridad nacional: Ministerio de Trabajo y Previsión Social.
Ubicación de las oficinas locales donde se hacen las inscripciones: En los 22 departamentos del país, contando con 3 oficinas municipales (El Carmen, Tecun Umán y Coatepeque).
Tipo de servicios proporcionados/administrados por el organismo:
– Ayuda a personas en busca de empleo a encontrarlo;
– Ayuda a personas en busca de empleo a crear su empresa propia;
– Ayuda a los empleadores a encontrar trabajadores;
– Orientación profesional;
– Formación relacionada con el trabajo.
Porcentaje de personas en busca de empleo que buscan trabajo por intermedio de ese organismo: 10%.
3. Se registran los siguientes datos de la persona:
– Nombre y apellido;
– Sexo;
– Edad y fecha de nacimiento;
– Número de seguridad social (o número de identificación semejante también utilizado por otros organismos);
– Dirección del domicilio habitual;
– Nivel de educación/formación: se identifican cuatro categorías. No se han establecido vínculos con la CINE;
– Situación laboral actual o anterior: se identifican cinco categorías;
– Tipo de ocupación del empleo actual o anterior: se identifican tres categorías. Se han establecido vínculos con grandes grupos de la CIUO-88;
– Tipo de ocupación del empleo que se busca: se identifican tres categorías. Se han establecido vínculos con grandes grupos de la CIUO-88;

– Rama de actividad del empleador o del lugar del trabajo actual o anterior: se identifican dos categorías. No se han establecido vínculos con la CIIU Rev. 3;
– Idiomas mayas en categorías tales como: hablado, escrito y traducción.
Cuando es una persona menor de edad se registra: número de partida de nacimiento; número de libro de nacimientos; folio; documento de identificación.
4. Criterios utilizados para determinar si una persona habrá de incluirse en el registro (R) y/o en las estadísticas de personas desempleadas (S):
– Estar sin empleo (R) y (S);
– Estar en busca de empleo (R) y (S);
– Estar disponible para trabajar (R);
– Edad (mínima: 14 años; no hay edad máxima) (R);
– Ciudadanía (R);
– Residir en el país (R);
– Duración y/o número de horas de trabajo del empleo que se busca (R).
5. Criterios utilizados para determinar si se ha de excluir a una persona del registro (R) y/o de las estadísticas de personas desempleadas (S):
– Certificado de defunción (R);
– Incorporarse a un (nuevo) empleo (R);
– Incumplir el requisito de ponerse en contacto con el organismo (el sistema tiene activo en la búsqueda de empleo por seis meses y posteriormente pasa a inactivo; después debe abocarse a la oficina para activarse nuevamente) (R);
– Otros: por no poseer documentos de identificación (R).
6. Definición de persona desempleada en la que se basan las estadísticas
Personas que han manifestado estar desempleadas, que no tienen ingresos económicos, que han llenado la solicitud de entrevista ocupacional con todos los datos necesarios, que han recibido la orientación laboral correspondiente, que se han identificado con su cédula de vecindad o certificación de nacimiento, asimismo que hayan presentado la documentación básica requerida.
7. Actualización de los registros
Los registros se actualizan cada mes.
8. Tasas de desempleo
No se utilizan estadísticas de estos registros para obtener tasas de desempleo.
9. Tipo de estadísticas que se producen sobre desempleados registrados
Período de referencia: Año.
Frecuencia de producción: Mensual.
Variable utilizada:
– Cantidad de personas inscritas.
Publicación: En papel, para el público en general.
Organismo responsable de la publicación: Ministerio de Trabajo y Previsión Social.
Título y periodicidad de la publicación: *Boletín de Estadísticas del Trabajo* (anual).
10. Información metodológica sobre las estadísticas
Divulgación: En papel, para el público en general.
Organismo responsable: Departamento de Estadísticas del Trabajo, Ministerio de Trabajo y Previsión Social.
11. Comparaciones con estadísticas derivadas de otras fuentes
No se han hecho comparaciones con estadísticas de desempleo derivadas de otras fuentes.
12. Modificaciones importantes desde el comienzo de las estadísticas
En la legislación, la competencia del organismo y/o los procedimientos administrativos no ha habido modificaciones importantes que hayan influido significativamente en las estadísticas.

Guinea

1. Serie
Título: Informe anual de actividad y Boletín de información.
Año de inicio: 1987.
2. Organismo responsable de la inscripción inicial de desempleados
Nombre del organismo: Agencia de Promoción del Empleo de Guinea (AGUIPE).
Tipo de organismo: Organismo público subordinado a una autoridad nacional.
Nombre de la autoridad nacional: Ministerio de Empleo y Mano de Obra.

Ubicación de las oficinas locales donde se hacen las inscripciones: Sólo en algunas regiones: Conakry, capital del país, y capitales de cuatro regiones naturales.

Tipo de servicios proporcionados/administrados por el organismo

- Ayuda a personas en busca de empleo a encontrarlo;
- Ayuda a los empleadores a encontrar trabajadores;
- Orientación profesional;
- Otros servicios relacionados con el empleo: Información y ayuda a organismos de formación, servicios públicos y asociados de desarrollo.
- Pago de prestaciones de desempleo.

Porcentaje de personas en busca de empleo que buscan trabajo por intermedio de ese organismo: 45%.

3. Se registran los siguientes datos de la persona

- Nombre y apellido;
- Sexo;
- Dirección del domicilio habitual;
- Fecha de nacimiento;
- Nacionalidad/grupo étnico;
- Nivel de educación/formación. Se han establecido vínculos con la CINE;
- Situación laboral actual o anterior;
- Tipo de ocupación del empleo actual o anterior. Se han establecido vínculos con la CIUO-88 a nivel de 390 grupos primarios;
- Tipo de ocupación del empleo que se busca;
- Nombre y dirección del empleador o del lugar de trabajo actual o anterior;
- Otros: Competencias o aptitudes particulares.

4. Criterios utilizados para determinar si una persona habrá de incluirse en el registro (R) y/o en las estadísticas de personas desempleadas (S)

- Estar sin empleo (S);
- Estar en busca de empleo(S);
- Estar disponible para trabajar (S);
- Edad (mínima: 18 años; máxima: 55 años)(S);
- Residir en el país y buscar empleo en el territorio nacional;
- Haber trabajado (S);
- Duración y/o número de horas de trabajo del empleo que se busca (20 horas por semana como mínimo).

5. Criterios utilizados para determinar si se ha de excluir a una persona del registro (R) y/o de las estadísticas de personas desempleadas (S)

- Certificado de defunción (R) y (S);
- Establecerse en otro país (R) y (S);
- Incorporarse a un (nuevo) empleo (R) y (S);
- Comenzar el servicio militar (R) y (S);
- Participar en algún programa de promoción del empleo, de obras públicas, etc. (R) y (S);
- Estar estudiando o siguiendo una formación, si se trata de un programa de formación de larga duración (S);
- Incumplir el requisito de tomar contacto con el organismo. No haber respondido a varias convocatorias para un empleo (R) y (S);
- Rechazar ofertas de empleo adecuadas, después de tres rechazos (R) y (S);
- Rechazar ofertas de formación adecuadas, despúes de tres rechazos (R) y (S);
- Cobrar alguna pensión (jubilación u otras) (R) y (S);
- Incapacidad para trabajar, en caso de que sea permanente.

6. Definición de persona desempleada en la que se basan las estadísticas

Toda persona activa que está disponibles para trabajar, no trabajó durante el período de referencia de siete días por otros motivos que enfermedad, vacaciones, desempleo técnico o inclemencias del tiempo, y está en busca de empleo debe considerarse desempleada.

7. Actualización de los registros

Los registros se actualizan anualmente.

8. Tasas de desempleo

No se utilizan estadísticas de estos registros para obtener tasas de desempleo.

9. Tipo de estadísticas que se producen sobre desempleados registrados

Serie 1:

Período de referencia: Año.

Frecuencia de producción: Anual.

Variables utilizadas

- Sexo;

- Edad;
- Nivel de educación;
- Ocupación;
- Características geográficas;
- Experiencia laboral previa;
- Duración del desempleo;
- Empleo solicitado.

Publicación: En papel, para el público en general.

Organismo responsable de la publicación: AGUIPE.

Título y periodicidad de la publicación: *Rapport d'activité annuel* (Informe anual de actividad).

Serie 2:

Período de referencia: Semestre.

Frecuencia de producción: Semestral.

Variables utilizadas

- Rama de actividad;
- Disponibilidad;
- Nacionalidad;
- Reorientación.

Publicación: En papel, para un público limitado.

Organismo responsable de la publicación: AGUIPE.

Título y periodicidad de la publicación: *Bulletin d'information* (Boletín de información)

10. Información metodológica sobre las estadísticas

Divulgación: Sólo para uso interno.

Organismo responsable de la divulgación: Observatorio de la AGUIPE.

11. Comparaciones con estadísticas derivadas de otras fuentes

Se han hecho comparaciones con estadísticas de desempleo derivadas de la Encuesta sobre la fuerza de trabajo, otras encuestas de hogares, el censo de población y otras fuentes estadísticas.

Frecuencia de las comparaciones: Periódica (último año: 2001).

Publicación de la metodología/resultados de las comparaciones: No se publican.

12. Modificaciones importantes desde el comienzo de las estadísticas

En la legislación, la competencia del organismo y/o los procedimientos administrativos hubo modificaciones importantes en 1992, 1994, 1995, 1997, 1999 y 2000 que influyeron significativamente en las estadísticas.

Guyana

1. Serie

Título: Estadísticas de contratación y colocación.

Año de inicio: 1993.

2. Organismo responsable de la inscripción inicial de desempleados

Nombre del organismo: Departamento de Contratación y Colocación (Bolsa de trabajo).

Tipo de organismo: Organismo público subordinado a una autoridad nacional.

Nombre de la autoridad nacional: Ministerio de Trabajo, Servicios Humanos y Seguridad Social.

Ubicación de las oficinas locales donde se hacen las inscripciones: En seis de las 10 regiones administrativas del país (Regiones: 2, 3, 4, 5, 6, y 10).

Tipo de servicios proporcionados/administrados por el organismo:

- Ayuda a personas en busca de empleo a encontrarlo;
- Ayuda a los empleadores a encontrar trabajadores;
- Orientación profesional;
- Formación relacionada con el trabajo;
- Otros: publicación del Boletín del Servicio de Información del Mercado de Trabajo y el Boletín estadístico a los que se da amplia difusión.

Porcentaje de personas en busca de empleo que buscan trabajo por intermedio de ese organismo: 20%.

3. Se registran los siguientes datos de la persona:

- Nombre y apellido;
- Sexo;
- Número de seguridad social (o número de identificación semejante también utilizado por otros organismos);
- Dirección del domicilio habitual;
- Fecha de nacimiento;
- Ciudadanía;
- Nacionalidad/grupo étnico;
- Nivel de educación/formación: se identifican cinco categorías. Se procede a establecer vínculos con la CINE;

– Situación laboral actual o anterior: se identifican tres categorías;

– Tipo de ocupación del empleo actual o anterior: se identifican nueve grupos. Se procede a establecer vínculos con la CIUO-88;

– Tipo de ocupación del empleo que se busca: se identifican nueve grupos. Se procede a establecer vínculos con la CIUO-88;

– Nombre y dirección del empleador o del lugar de trabajo actual o anterior;

– Rama de actividad del empleador o del lugar de trabajo actual o anterior: se identifica un número indeterminado de grupos. Se procede a establecer vínculos con la CIIU Rev. 3;

– Inscripciones previas en el organismo.

4. Criterios utilizados para determinar si una persona habrá de incluirse en el registro (R) y/o en las estadísticas de personas desempleadas (S):

– Estar en busca de empleo   (R) y (S);

– Estar disponible para trabajar   (R) y (S);

– Edad (mínima: 15 años; máxima: 60 años)   (R) y (S);

– Ciudadanía (ser ciudadano de Guyana)   (R) y (S);

– Residir en el país   (R) y (S).

5. Criterios utilizados para determinar si se ha de excluir a una persona del registro (R) y/o de las estadísticas de personas desempleadas (S):

– Incorporarse a un (nuevo) empleo (el empleador notifica al organismo)   (R) y (S).

6. Definición de persona desempleada en la que se basan las estadísticas

Toda persona que busca empleo activamente, que no puede encontrarlo y que en ese momento no está empleada a ningún título.

7. Actualización de los registros

Cuando se recibe la información, se actualiza la ficha personal.   (Se procede a informatizar el organismo y a entrar esa información en la computadora).

8. Tasas de desempleo

No se utilizan estadísticas de estos registros para obtener tasas de desempleo.

9. Tipo de estadísticas que se producen sobre desempleados registrados

Período de referencia: Año.

Frecuencia de producción: Anual.

Variables utilizadas:

– Características geográficas.

(Está previsto producir informes más detallados a partir de 2003).

Publicación: En papel, para un público limitado.

Organismo responsable de la publicación: Departamento de Trabajo.

Título y periodicidad de las publicaciones: *Recruitment and Placement* (Contratación y colocación), anual; *Annual Report* (Informe anual).

10. Información metodológica sobre las estadísticas

No se dispone de información metodológica sobre las estadísticas.

11. Comparaciones con estadísticas derivadas de otras fuentes

No se han hecho comparaciones con estadísticas de desempleo derivadas de otras fuentes.

12. Modificaciones importantes desde el comienzo de las estadísticas

En la legislación, la competencia del organismo y/o los procedimientos administrativos no ha habido modificaciones importantes que hayan influido significativamente en las estadísticas.

13. Otros comentarios

El Departamento de Contratación y Colocación estára completamente informatizado en 2003.

Honduras

1. Serie

Título: Registro de personas en busca de empleo.

Año de inicio: Los servicios de colocación funcionan desde 1980; la serie estadística que se mantiene tiene como primer año 1987.

2. Organismo responsable de la inscripción inicial de desempleados

Nombre del organismo: Servicio de Colocación de la Dirección General de Empleo.

Tipo de organismo: Organismo público subordinado a una autoridad nacional que tiene oficinas locales.

Nombre de la autoridad nacional: Secretaría de Trabajo y Seguridad Social.

Ubicación de las oficinas locales donde se hacen las inscripciones: En tres ciudades principales del país, que atienden la zona central y norte del país.

Tipo de servicios proporcionados/administrados por el organismo:

– Ayuda a personas en busca de empleo a encontrarlo;

– Ayuda a personas en busca de empleo a crear su propia empresa (se aplica solamente a personas discapacitadas);

– Ayuda a los empleadores a encontrar trabajadores;

– Orientación profesional;

– Formación relacionada con el trabajo (el Servicio de Colocación canaliza personas al Instituto de Formación Profesional – no brinda capacitación directa).

Porcentaje de personas en busca de empleo que buscan trabajo por medio de ese organismo: 3.4% en relación al número de desocupados urbanos que reporta la Encuesta de Hogares de Propósitos Múltiples.

3. Se registran los siguientes datos de la persona:

– Nombre y apellido;

– Sexo;

– Número de seguridad social (o número de identificación semejante también utilizado por otros organismos);

– Dirección del domicilio habitual;

– Fecha de nacimiento;

– Nacionalidad;

– Nivel de educación/formación: se identifican cuatro categorías. No se han establecido vínculos con la CINE;

– Situación laboral actual o anterior: se identifican tres categorías;

– Tipo de ocupación del empleo actual o anterior: se identifican tres categorías. Se han establecido vínculos con grandes grupos de la CIUO-88, a cuatro dígitos de desagregación;

– Tipo de ocupación del empleo buscado; el número de categorías difiere dependiendo del solicitante, el caso que más se repite es dos por solicitante. Se han establecido vínculos con grandes grupos de la CIUO-88, a cuatro dígitos de desagregación;

– Nombre y dirección del jefe inmediato o del lugar del trabajo actual o anterior;

– Inscripciones previas en el organismo;

– Otros: características físicas (estatura, peso); datos familiares (número de familiares, hijos, si es jefe de hogar); si tiene automóvil; tipo de licencia; migración – local y externa; discapacidad.

4. Criterios utilizados para determinar si una persona habrá de incluirse en el registro (R) y/o en las estadísticas de personas desempleadas (S):

– Estar sin empleo (R);

– Estar en busca de empleo (R);

– Estar disponible para trabajar (R);

– Edad (mínima: 16 años, con permiso de menor para trabajar; no hay edad máxima) (R);

– Residir en el país (R).

5. Criterios utilizados para determinar si se ha de excluir a una persona del registro (R) y/o de las estadísticas de personas desempleadas (S):

– Certificado de defunción (R);

– Establecerse en otro país (R);

– Incorporarse a un (nuevo) empleo (R);

– Participar en un programa de promoción del empleo, de obras públicas, etc. (R);

– Estar estudiando o siguiendo una formación que no permita armonizar con un horario de trabajo (R);

– Incumplir el requisito de tomar contacto con el organismo durante cinco años consecutivos (R);

– Incapacidad para trabajar (reportado por el interesado) (R).

Nota: Los aspectos anteriores se registran como notas marginales en el expediente del interesado y se archiva y se eliminan únicamente en caso de fallecimiento; en los otros casos se mantiene la información. El límite para mantener los registros es de cinco años.

6. Definición de persona desempleada en la que se basan las estadísticas

En esta categoría están agrupadas las personas afectadas por el desempleo abierto o sea los cesantes (aquellos que tenían una ocupación, la perdieron por una causa cualquiera y durante la semana de referencia estuvieran activos buscando un empleo nuevo o tratando de establecer un negocio o finca propia) y los trabajadores nuevos que buscaran un empleo por primera vez.

Las personas en busca de empleo: incluye desempleados como cesantes, personas que buscan empleo por primera vez y en menor proporción personas ocupadas que buscan una mejor oportunidad de trabajo, por haber obtenido nuevos niveles de formación o aspirar a un salario mayor.

7. Actualización de los registros

Los registros se actualizan cada seis meses.

8. Tasas de desempleo

No se utilizan estadísticas de estos registros para obtener tasas de desempleo.

9. Tipo de estadísticas que se producen sobre desempleados registrados

Período de referencia: Año.

Frecuencia de producción: Anualmente.

Variables utilizadas:
- Sexo;
- Edad;
- Nivel de educación;
- Ocupación;
- Rama de actividad;
- Características geográficas;
- Otras: Situación ocupacional.

Publicación:
- Sólo para uso interno;
- En archivo electrónico, previa solicitud.

Organismo responsable de la publicación: Dirección General de Empleo.

Título y periodicidad de la publicación: *Boletín Estadístico* (anual).

10. Información metodológica sobre las estadísticas

Divulgación:
- No se divulga; sólo para uso interno;
- En archivo electrónico, previa solicitud.

Organismo responsable: Dirección General de Empleo.

11. Comparaciones con estadísticas derivadas de otras fuentes

Se hacen comparaciones con estadísticas de desempleo derivadas de la Encuesta de Hogares así como del Censo de Población.

Frecuencia de las comparaciones: De vez en cuando (último año: 2001); en relación a la periodicidad de publicación de la Encuesta de Hogares, una o dos veces al año.

Publicación de la metodología/resultados de las comparaciones: Se han publicado en el *Boletín Estadístico* y se utilizan como insumos en análisis sobre el tema.

12. Modificaciones importantes desde el comienzo de las estadísticas

En la legislación, la competencia del organismo y/o los procedimientos administrativos no ha habido modificaciones importantes que hayan influido significativamente en las estadísticas.

Lo que ha ocurrido es un cambio en el procesamiento de los datos en base a la implementación de la bolsa electrónica de empleo, la cual ha venido a mejorar los servicios de intermediación, misma que se proyecta ampliar a otras ciudades del país, integrando además a las organizaciones de empleadores a través de este sistema electrónico.

Hungría

1. Serie

Título: Desempleo registrado.

Año de inicio: 1990.

2. Organismo responsable de la inscripción inicial de desempleados

Nombre del organismo: Allami Foglalkoztatási Szolgálat (Servicio Público de Empleo).

Tipo de organismo: Organismo público subordinado a una autoridad nacional.

Nombre de la autoridad nacional: Ministerio de Asuntos Económicos.

Ubicación de las oficinas locales donde se hacen las inscripciones: Hay 11 oficinas en Budapest, la capital, y 165 oficinas en los 19 condados del país (con 20 Centros del Trabajo).

Tipo de servicios proporcionados/administrados por el organismo:
- Ayuda a personas en busca de empleo a encontrarlo;
- Ayuda a personas en busca de empleo a crear su propia empresa;
- Ayuda a los empleadores a encontrar trabajadores;

- Orientación profesional;
- Formación relacionada con el trabajo;
- Pago de prestaciones de desempleo;
- Otros: administra programas activos de mercado de trabajo; expide permisos de trabajo para extranjeros; proporciona información sobre el mercado de trabajo a todo nivel (estadísticas, análisis y proyecciones).

Porcentaje de personas en busca de empleo que buscan trabajo por intermedio de ese organismo: 80%.

3. Se registran los siguientes datos de la persona:
- Nombre y apellido;
- Sexo;
- Número de seguridad social (o número de identificación semejante también utilizado por otros organismos);
- Dirección del domicilio habitual;
- Fecha de nacimiento;
- Ciudadanía (sólo en el caso de extranjeros con permiso de trabajo);
- Nivel de educación/formación: se identifican 10 categorías. Se han establecido vínculos con la CINE;
- Situación laboral actual o anterior: se identifican cuatro categorías;
- Tipo de ocupación del empleo actual o anterior: se identifican 632 categorías. Se han establecido vínculos con la CIUO-88 a nivel de subgrupos;
- Tipo de ocupación del empleo que se busca: se identifican 692 categorías. Se han establecido vínculos con la CIUO-88 a nivel de subgrupos;
- Nombre y dirección del empleador o del lugar de trabajo actual o anterior;
- Rama de actividad del empleador o del lugar de trabajo actual o anterior: se identifican 503 categorías. Se han establecido vínculos con la NACE Rev.1 a nivel de categorías de tabulación;
- Inscripciones previas en el organismo.

4. Criterios utilizados para determinar si una persona habrá de incluirse en el registro (R) y/o en las estadísticas de personas desempleadas (S):
- Estar sin empleo (S);
- Estar en busca de empleo (S);
- Estar disponible para trabajar (S);
- Edad (máxima: edad de pensión de vejez) (S);
- Residir en el país (S).

5. Criterios utilizados para determinar si se ha de excluir a una persona del registro (R) y/o de las estadísticas de personas desempleadas (S):
- Certificado de defunción (R) y (S);
- Incorporarse a un (nuevo) empleo (S);
- Comenzar el servicio militar (S);
- Participar en algún programa de promoción del empleo, de obras públicas, etc. (S);
- Estar estudiando o siguiendo una formación (S);
- Incumplir el requisito de tomar contacto con el organismo (S);
- Rechazar una oferta de empleo adecuada (S);
- Rechazar una oferta de formación adecuada (S);
- Cobrar alguna pensión (S);
- Incapacidad para trabajar (S);
- Otros: por solicitud del interesado (R) y (S).

6. Definición de persona desempleada en la que se basan las estadísticas

Toda persona en busca de empleo que reúne los siguientes requisitos:
- estar desempleada y no ejercer ninguna otra actividad remunerada;
- estar en las condiciones necesarias para empezar a trabajar;
- no beneficiar de pensión de vejez;
- no ser estudiante a tiempo completo en una institución de enseñanza;
- cooperar con la oficina local de empleo para encontrar un trabajo;
- estar registrada como desempleada en la oficina local de empleo.

7. Actualización de los registros

Los registros se actualizan continuamente.

8. Tasas de desempleo

Se utilizan estadísticas de estos registros para obtener tasas de desempleo.

Fuente de los datos de empleo incluidos en el denominador de las tasas de desempleo: *Labour Account of the National Economy*

(Cuentas del trabajo de la economía nacional) (día de referencia: 1 de enero), publicación anual de la Oficina Central de Estadística.

Definición de persona empleada que se utiliza a tales efectos:
– Todos los trabajadores, empresarios particulares y trabajadores por cuenta propia;
– propietarios que trabajan, y
– trabajadores familiares (si superan una determinada cantidad de tiempo de trabajo).

9. Tipo de estadísticas que se producen sobre desempleados registrados
Serie 1:
Período de referencia: Mes.
Frecuencia de producción: Mensual.
Variables utilizadas:
– Sexo;
– Edad;
– Nivel de educación;
– Características geográficas;
– Experiencia laboral previa;
– Duración del desempleo.
Publicación:
– En papel, para el público en general;
– En un sitio web (en preparación).
Organismo responsable de la publicación: Oficina Nacional de Empleo.
Título de la publicación: *Labour Market Situation* (Situación del mercado laboral).
Serie 2:
Período de referencia: Año.
Frecuencia de producción: Anual.
Variables utilizadas:
– Sexo;
– Edad;
– Nivel de educación;
– Características geográficas;
– Experiencia laboral previa;
– Duración del desempleo.
Publicación: En papel, para el público en general.
Organismo responsable de la publicación: Oficina Nacional de Empleo.
Título de la publicación: *Time series based on the administrative records of the Public Employment Service* (Serie cronológica basada en los archivos administrativos del Servicio Público de Empleo).
10. Información metodológica sobre las estadísticas
Divulgación:
– En papel, para el público en general;
– En un sitio web (en preparación).
Organismo responsable de la divulgación: Oficina Nacional de Empleo.
11. Comparaciones con estadísticas derivadas de otras fuentes
Se han hecho comparaciones con estadísticas de desempleo derivadas de la Encuesta sobre la fuerza de trabajo y el Censo de población.
Frecuencia de las comparaciones: De vez en cuando (último año: 1998).
Publicación de la metodología/resultados de las comparaciones: Se publicaron en mayo de 1998, en ocasión de la conferencia de prensa de la Oficinal Central de Estadística y el Ministerio de Trabajo. La comparación con los resultados del Censo de población de 2001, se publicará en 2002.
12. Modificaciones importantes desde el comienzo de las estadísticas
En la legislación, la competencia del organismo y/o los procedimientos administrativos no ha habido modificaciones importantes que hayan influido significativamente en las estadísticas.

India

1. Serie
Título: Estadísticas de la bolsa de trabajo.
Año de inicio: 1947.
2. Organismo responsable de la inscripción inicial de desempleados
Nombre del organismo: Servicio Nacional de Empleo.
Tipo de organismo: Organismo público subordinado a una autoridad nacional que trabaja en estrecha colaboración con el Estado y las administraciones territoriales de la Unión.
Nombre de la autoridad nacional: Dirección General de Empleo y Formación del Ministerio de Trabajo.

Ubicación de las oficinas locales donde se hacen las inscripciones: En todas partes del país a nivel de distrito y ciudad. La red comprende 958 bolsas de trabajo.
Tipo de servicios proporcionados/administrados por el organismo:
– Ayuda a personas en busca de empleo a encontrarlo;
– Ayuda a personas en busca de empleo a crear su propia empresa;
– Ayuda a los empleadores a encontrar trabajadores;
– Orientación profesional.
3. Se registran los siguientes datos de la persona:
– Nombre y apellido;
– Sexo;
– Dirección del domicilio habitual;
– Fecha de nacimiento;
– Grupo étnico;
– Nivel de educación/formación profesional. No se han establecido vínculos con la CINE;
– Nombre y dirección del empleador o del lugar de trabajo actual o anterior;
– Otros: salario mínimo; buenas condiciones y características físicas; conocimiento de idiomas; si está dispuesta a incorporarse a las fuerzas armadas o a iniciar una formación; si está dispuesta a trabajar en cualquier lugar (límites geográficos).
4. Criterios utilizados para determinar si una persona habrá de incluirse en el registro (R) y/o en las estadísticas de personas desempleadas (S):
– Estar sin empleo (R) y (S);
– Estar en busca de empleo (R) y (S);
– Edad (mínima: 14 años; no hay edad máxima) (R) y (S);
– Ciudadanía (R) y (S);
– Residir en el país (R) y (S);
– Haber trabajado (R) y (S).
5. Criterios utilizados para determinar si se ha de excluir a una persona del registro (R) y/o de las estadísticas de personas desempleadas (S):
– Incorporarse a un (nuevo) empleo (R) y (S);
– Incumplir el requisito de renovar la inscripción en el registro del organismo (R) y (S).
6. Definición de persona desempleada en la que se basan las estadísticas
Todas las personas registradas en las bolsas de trabajo se consideran personas en busca de empleo.
7. Actualización de los registros
Los registros se actualizan mensualmente.
8. Tasas de desempleo
No se utilizan estadísticas de estos registros para obtener tasas de desempleo.
9. Tipo de estadísticas que se producen sobre desempleados registrados
Serie 1: Registros, colocaciones, solicitudes hechas, número del Registro activo y vacantes notificadas.
Período de referencia: Mes.
Frecuencia de producción: Mensual.
Variables utilizadas:
– Sexo;
– Características geográficas (si procede de zonas rurales).
Publicación: En papel, para el público en general.
Organismo responsable de la publicación: Dirección General de Empleo y Formación.
Título y periodicidad de la publicación: *Employment Exchanges Statistics* (Estadísticas de las bolsas de trabajo), anual.
Serie 2: Actividades de orientación profesional por categoría de solicitantes.
Período de referencia: Trimestre.
Frecuencia de producción: Trimestral.
Variables utilizadas:
– Categorías étnicas/sociales; es decir: "castas reconocidas" (SC); "tribus reconocidas" (ST); "otras clases atrasadas" (OBC);
– Otras: discapacidad física ("PH");
– Sexo (mujeres como total únicamente).
Publicación: En papel, para el público en general.
Organismo responsable de la publicación: Dirección General de Empleo y Formación.
Título y periodicidad de la publicación: *Employment Exchanges Statistics* (Estadísticas de las bolsas de trabajo), anual.
Serie 3: Registros, colocaciones, número del Registro activo y solicitudes hechas respecto a comunidades minoritarias.
Período de referencia: Semestre.

Frecuencia de producción: Semestral.
Publicación: En papel, para el público en general
Organismo responsable de la publicación: Dirección General de Empleo y Formación.
Título y periodicidad de la publicación: *Employment Exchanges Statistics* (Estadísticas de las bolsas de trabajo), anual.
Serie 4: Registros, colocaciones, número del Registro activo y solicitudes hechas respecto a solicitantes con discapacidades físicas.
Período de referencia: Semestre.
Frecuencia de producción: Semestral.
Variables utilizadas:
– Tipo de discapacidad física;
– Sexo (mujeres sólo como total).
Publicación: En papel, para el público en general.
Organismo responsable de la publicación: Dirección General de Empleo y Formación.
Título y periodicidad de la publicación: *Employment Exchanges Statistics* (Estadísticas de las bolsas de trabajo), anual.
Serie 5: Número de solicitantes con estudios (10.° curso en adelante) registrados y colocados.
Período de referencia: Semestre.
Frecuencia de producción: Semestral.
Variables utilizadas:
– Nivel de educación (se identifican cinco niveles; se identifican 10 ramas de grado y posgrado universitarios; dos ramas de diplomas);
– Categorías étnicas/sociales (es decir, "SC", "ST" y "OBC");
– Sexo (mujeres como total únicamente).
Publicación: En papel, para el público en general.
Organismo responsable de la publicación: Dirección General de Empleo y Formación.
Título y periodicidad de la publicación: *Employment Exchanges Statistics* (Estadísticas de las bolsas de trabajo), anual.
Serie 6: Registros, colocaciones, número del Registro activo y solicitudes hechas respecto a las categorías de solicitante "SC", "ST" y "OBC".
Período de referencia: Semestre.
Frecuencia de producción: Semestral.
Variables utilizadas:
– Categorías étnicas/sociales.
Publicación: En papel, para el público en general.
Organismo responsable de la publicación: Dirección General de Empleo y Formación.
Título y periodicidad de la publicación: *Employment Exchanges Statistics* (Estadísticas de las bolsas de trabajo), anual.
Serie 7: Promoción del autoempleo.
Período de referencia: Semestre.
Frecuencia de producción: Semestral.
Variables utilizadas:
– Sexo;
– Categorías étnicas/sociales ("SC", "ST", "OBC", "PH" y comunidades minoritarias);
– Características geográficas (zona rural o urbana).
Publicación: En papel, para el público en general.
Organismo responsable de la publicación: Dirección General de Empleo y Formación.
Título y periodicidad de la publicación: *Employment Exchanges Statistics* (Estadísticas de las bolsas de trabajo), anual.
Serie 8: Vacantes notificadas, cubiertas, canceladas y pendientes en el Registro activo según la Clasificación nacional de ocupaciones (CNO) con respecto a solicitantes mujeres; "SC", "ST", "OBC" y "PH".
Período de referencia: Año.
Frecuencia de producción: Anual.
Variables utilizadas:
– Ocupación;
– Categorías étnicas/sociales;
– Sexo (mujeres como total únicamente);
– Otras: "PH".
Publicación: En papel, para el público en general.
Organismo responsable de la publicación: Dirección General de Empleo y Formación.
Título y periodicidad de la publicación: *Employment Exchanges Statistics* (Estadísticas de las bolsas de trabajo), anual.
Serie 9: Vacantes notificadas, cubiertas, canceladas y pendientes desglosadas por sector.
Período de referencia: Año.
Frecuencia de producción: Anual.
Variable utilizada:
– Sector (Central/Gobierno estatal; sector público, sector privado, etc.).
Publicación: En papel, para el público en general.

Organismo responsable de la publicación: Dirección General de Empleo y Formación.
Título y periodicidad de la publicación: *Employment Exchanges Statistics* (Estadísticas de las bolsas de trabajo), anual.
Serie 10: Número de solicitantes del Registro activo, al 31 de diciembre, desglosado por grupo de edad, sexo y nivel de educación.
Período de referencia: Año.
Frecuencia de producción: Anual.
Variables utilizadas:
– Sexo;
– Grupo de edad;
– Nivel de educación (se identifican seis niveles).
Publicación: En papel, para el público en general.
Organismo responsable de la publicación: Dirección General de Empleo y Formación.
Título y periodicidad de la publicación: *Employment Exchanges Statistics* (Estadísticas de las bolsas de trabajo), anual.
Serie 11: Número de vacantes comunicado por los establecimientos y que no se han cubierto por falta de candidatos adecuados a quienes no se puede secundar.
Período de referencia: Año.
Frecuencia de producción: Anual.
Variables utilizadas:
– Rama de actividad (código de la Clasificación nacional industrial de todas las actividades económicas a nivel de tres dígitos);
– Ocupación (según el código de la CNO);
– Sector público/privado.
Publicación: En papel, para el público en general.
Organismo responsable de la publicación: Dirección General de Empleo y Formación.
Título y periodicidad de la publicación: *Employment Exchanges Statistics* (Estadísticas de las bolsas de trabajo), anual.
Serie 12: Registros, colocaciones y número del Registro activo, según la CNO, respecto a aprendices a tiempo completo y ex alumnos del Instituto de Formación Industrial (ITI) por oficios.
Período de referencia: Año.
Frecuencia de producción: Anual.
Variables utilizadas:
– Ocupación;
– Oficio para el cual recibió formación.
Publicación: En papel, para el público en general.
Organismo responsable de la publicación: Dirección General de Empleo y Formación.
Título y periodicidad de la publicación: *Employment Exchanges Statistics* (Estadísticas de las bolsas de trabajo), anual.
Serie 13: Registros, colocaciones y número del Registro activo respecto a personas desplazadas.
Período de referencia: Año.
Frecuencia de producción: Anual.
Variable utilizada:
– Características geográficas (lugar de origen).
Publicación: En papel, para el público en general.
Organismo responsable de la publicación: Dirección General de Empleo y Formación.
Título y periodicidad de la publicación: *Employment Exchanges Statistics* (Estadísticas de las bolsas de trabajo), anual.
10. Información metodológica sobre las estadísticas
Divulgación: En papel, para el público en general.
Organismo responsable: Dirección General de Empleo y Formación.
11. Comparaciones con estadísticas derivadas de otras fuentes
No se han hecho comparaciones con estadísticas de desempleo derivadas de otras fuentes.
12. Modificaciones importantes desde el comienzo de las estadísticas
En la legislación, la competencia del organismo y/o los procedimientos administrativos no ha habido modificaciones importantes que hayan influido significativamente en las estadísticas.

Irán, Rep. Islámica del

1. Serie
Título: Registros administrativos de los centros de colocación.
2. Organismo responsable de la inscripción inicial de desempleados
Nombre del organismo:
1. Centros de colocación (públicos);
2. Centros consultivos de empleo (públicos);

3. Centros de colocación (privados) que cuentan con la autorización del Ministerio de Trabajo y Asuntos Sociales.

Tipo de organismo:
1 y 2: organismos públicos subordinados a una autoridad local;
3: organismos privados sin fines de lucro.

Ubicación de las oficinas locales donde se hacen las inscripciones: Todo el país. La mayoría de las oficinas locales se encuentran en zonas urbanas pero, últimamente, se han abierto oficinas en zonas rurales de las provincias.

Tipo de servicios proporcionados/administrados por el organismo
- Ayuda a personas en busca de empleo a encontrarlo;
- Ayuda a personas en busca de empleo a crear su propia empresa;
- Ayuda a los empleadores a encontrar trabajadores;
- Orientación profesional;
- Pago de prestaciones de desempleo;
- Otros servicios relacionados con el empleo.

Porcentaje de personas en busca de empleo que buscan trabajo por intermedio de ese organismo: 20%.

3. Se registran los siguientes datos de la persona
- Nombre y apellido;
- Sexo;
- Dirección del domicilio habitual;
- Fecha de nacimiento;
- Nivel de educación;
- Tipo de ocupación del empleo actual o anterior;

- Nombre y dirección del empleador o del lugar de trabajo actual o anterior;
- Rama de actividad del empleador o del lugar de trabajo actual o anterior. No se han establecido vínculos con la CIIU Rev.3;
- Otros: Documentos escolares; calificación profesional; empleo fuera del país; fecha en que comenzó a cotizar al seguro de desempleo.

4. Criterios utilizados para determinar si una persona habrá de incluirse en el registro (R) y/o en las estadísticas de personas desempleadas (S)
- Estar sin empleo (R) y (S);
- Estar en busca de empleo (R) y (S);
- Estar disponible para trabajar (R) y (S);
- Edad (mínima: 15 años; no hay edad máxima) (R) y (S);
- Ciudadanía (R) y (S);
- Residir en el país (R) y (S);
- Haber trabajado (R);
- Pago de cotizaciones del seguro de desempleo (R).

5. Criterios utilizados para determinar si se ha de excluir a una persona del registro (R) y/o de las estadísticas de personas desempleadas (S)
No se dispone de información.

6. Definición de persona desempleada en la que se basan las estadísticas
Toda persona de 15 años o más, apta para trabajar, disponible para trabajar y registrada en algún centro de colocación.

7. Actualización de los registros
Los registros se actualizan periódicamente.

8. Tasas de desempleo
No se utilizan estadísticas de estos registros para obtener tasas de desempleo.

9. Tipo de estadísticas que se producen sobre desempleados registrados
Serie 1: Perfiles del mercado de trabajo.
Período de referencia: Año.
Frecuencia de producción: Anual.
Variables utilizadas
- Sexo;
- Edad;
- Nivel de educación;
- Calificaciones profesionales.

Publicación: En papel, para el público en general.
Organismo responsable de la publicación: Oficina de Estadística del Ministerio de Trabajo y Asuntos Sociales.
Título y periodicidad de la publicación: *Visages du marché du travail* (Perfiles del mercado de trabajo), anual.

10. Información metodológica sobre las estadísticas
Divulgación: En papel, para un público limitado.
Organismo responsable: Oficina de Estadística del Ministerio de Trabajo y Asuntos Sociales.

11. Comparaciones con estadísticas derivadas de otras fuentes

No se han hecho comparaciones con estadísticas de desempleo derivadas de otras fuentes.

12. Modificaciones importantes desde el comienzo de las estadísticas
A fin de aliviar las responsabilidades de los centros de colocación públicos, se han privatizado unos centros de colocación con la autorización del Ministerio de Trabajo y Asuntos Sociales.

En 2002, se empezó un programa de reforma para mejorar el sistema de informaciones sobre el mercado de trabajo y para informatizarlo.

Isla de Man

1. Serie
Título: Desempleo registrado.
Año de inicio: 1978.

2. Organismo responsable de la inscripción inicial de desempleados
Nombre del organismo: División de la Seguridad Social.
Tipo de organismo: Organismo público subordinado a una autoridad nacional.
Nombre de la autoridad nacional: Departamento de Salud y Seguridad Social.
Algunas funciones, entre ellas, la de llevar el registro de personas desempleadas, están a cargo del Departamento de Industria y Comercio.
Ambos departamentos producen estadísticas periódicamente, pero sólo algunas están destinadas al público en general.

Ubicación de las oficinas locales donde se hacen las inscripciones: Sólo en determinadas zonas, a saber: Douglas (la capital), Ramsey, Peel, Castletown y Port Erin.

Tipo de servicios proporcionados/administrados por el organismo:
- Ayuda a personas en busca de empleo a encontrarlo;
- Ayuda a personas en busca de empleo a crear su propia empresa;*
- Ayuda a los empleadores a encontrar trabajadores;*
- Orientación profesional;*
- Formación relacionada con el trabajo;*
- Pago de prestaciones de desempleo.

* Servicios proporcionados por el Departamento de Industria y Comercio.

Porcentaje de personas en busca de empleo que buscan trabajo por intermedio de ese organismo: 75%.

3. Se registran los siguientes datos de la persona:
- Nombre y apellido;
- Sexo;
- Número de seguridad social (o número de identificación semejante también utilizado por otros organismos);
- Dirección del domicilio habitual;
- Fecha de nacimiento;
- Ciudadanía;
- Nivel de educación/formación: se identifican siete categorías. No se han establecido vínculos con la CINE;
- Tipo de ocupación del empleo que se busca;
- Nombre y dirección del empleador o del lugar de trabajo actual o anterior;
- Otros: licencia de conducir/vehículo propio; estatuto de trabajador de astilleros; estado civil; estado de salud; prontuario.

4. Criterios utilizados para determinar si una persona habrá de incluirse en el registro (R) y/o en las estadísticas de personas desempleadas (S):
- Estar sin empleo (R) y (S);
- Estar en busca de empleo (R) y (S);
- Estar disponible para trabajar (R) y (S);
- Edad (mínima: 16 años; máxima: 65 años para los hombres y 60 años para las mujeres) (R) y (S);
- Residir en el país (R) y (S);
- Duración y/o número de horas de trabajo del empleo que se busca (R) y (S).

5. Criterios utilizados para determinar si se ha de excluir a una persona del registro (R) y/o de las estadísticas de personas desempleadas (S):
- Certificado de defunción (R) y (S);
- Establecerse en otro país (R) y (S);
- Incorporarse a un (nuevo) empleo (R) y (S);
- Comenzar el servicio militar (R) y (S);
- Participar en algún programa de promoción del empleo, de

obras públicas, etc. (R) y (S);
– Estar estudiando o siguiendo una formación (R) y (S);
– Incumplir el requisito de tomar contacto con el organismo (R) y (S);
– Incapacidad para trabajar (R) y (S).

6. Definición de persona desempleada en la que se basan las estadísticas

La persona desempleada debe:
– (por regla general) estar disponible para trabajar 40 horas por semana como mínimo;
– hacer lo necesario cada semana para encontrar puestos vacantes adecuados y postular a ellos;
– estar desempleada o trabajar 16 horas por semana como máximo;
– estar disponible para trabajar 16 horas por semana como mínimo;
– no estar recibiendo educación o estar recibiéndola a razón de menos de 16 horas por semana de enseñanza guiada;
– tener más de 16 años y menos de la edad de jubilación estipulada por el Estado (65 años para los hombres y 60 años para las mujeres), y
– residir en la Isla de Man.

7. Actualización de los registros

Los registros se actualizan a diario.

8. Tasas de desempleo

Se utilizan estadísticas de estos registros para obtener tasas de desempleo.
Fuente de los datos de empleo incluidos en el denominador de las tasas de desempleo:
Censo de población.
Definición de persona empleada que se utiliza a tales efectos:
Toda persona que trabaja para un empleador (a tiempo completo o parcial) y/o que trabaja por cuenta propia.

9. Tipo de estadísticas que se producen sobre desempleados registrados

Serie 1:
Período de referencia: Mes.
Frecuencia de producción: Mensual.
Variables utilizadas:
– Sexo;
– Edad;*
– Nivel de educación;*
– Ocupación;*
– Rama de actividad*
– Características geográficas*
– Ciudadanía (nacionales o no).
Publicación:
– Sólo para uso interno;*
– En papel, para el público en general.
* Estadísticas del Departamento de Industria y Comercio.
Organismo responsable de la publicación: División de Asuntos Económicos, Departamento del Tesoro.
Título de la publicación: *Job Market Statistics* (Estadísticas del Mercado de Trabajo).
Serie 2:
Período de referencia: Trimestre.
Frecuencia de producción: Trimestral.
Variables utilizadas:
– Sexo;
– Edad;
– Nivel de educación;*
– Ocupación;*
– Rama de actividad;*
– Características geográficas;
– Ciudadanía (nacionales o no).
Publicación:
– Sólo para uso interno;*
– En papel, para el público en general.
* Estadísticas del Departamento de Industria y Comercio.
Organismo responsable de la publicación: Departamento de Salud y Seguridad Social.
Título de la publicación: *Quarterly Analysis of the Unemployed Register* (Análisis trimestral del registro de desempleados).

10. Información metodológica sobre las estadísticas

Divulgación: No se divulga; sólo para uso interno.

11. Comparaciones con estadísticas derivadas de otras fuentes

Se han hecho comparaciones con estadísticas de desempleo derivadas del Censo de población.
Frecuencia de las comparaciones: Periódica, cuando se publican las estadísticas.

12. Modificaciones importantes desde el comienzo de las estadísticas

En la legislación, la competencia del organismo y/o los procedimientos administrativos hubo modificaciones importantes en 1996. Las consiguientes modificaciones en las estadísticas no se han estimado.

Islandia

1. Serie

Título: Desempleo registrado.
Año de inicio: 1969.

2. Organismo responsable de la inscripción inicial de desempleados

Nombre del organismo: *Vinnumálastofnun* (Dirección de Trabajo).
Tipo de organismo: Organismo público subordinado a una autoridad nacional.
Nombre de la autoridad nacional: Ministerio de Asuntos Sociales.
Ubicación de las oficinas locales donde se hacen las inscripciones: En todo el país.
Tipo de servicios proporcionados/administrados por el organismo:
– Ayuda a personas en busca de empleo a encontrarlo;
– Ayuda a personas en busca de empleo a crear su propia empresa;
– Ayuda a los empleadores a encontrar trabajadores;
– Orientación profesional;
– Formación relacionada con el trabajo;
– Pago de prestaciones de desempleo;
– Otro: medidas del mercado de trabajo, cursos cortos en distintos campos.
Porcentaje de personas en busca de empleo que buscan trabajo por intermedio de ese organismo: 100% aproximadamente.

3. Se registran los siguientes datos de la persona:

– Nombre y apellido;
– Sexo;
– Número de seguridad social (o número de identificación semejante también utilizado por otros organismos);
– Dirección del domicilio habitual;
– Fecha de nacimiento;
– Ciudadanía;
– Nacionalidad;
– Nivel de educación/formación: se identifican tres categorías. Se han establecido vínculos con la CINE-76;
– Situación laboral actual o anterior: se identifican 31 categorías;
– Tipo de ocupación del empleo actual o anterior: se identifican 374 categorías. Se han establecido vínculos con la CIUO-88 a nivel de grupos primarios;
– Tipo de ocupación del empleo que se busca: se identifica un número ilimitado de categorías. Se han establecido vínculos con la CIUO-88 a nivel de grupos primarios;
– Nombre y dirección del empleador o del lugar de trabajo actual o anterior;
– Rama de actividad del empleador o del lugar de trabajo actual o anterior: se identifican 616 categorías. Se han establecido vínculos con la NACE Rev. 1, a nivel de clases.
– Inscripciones previas en el organismo.

4. Criterios utilizados para determinar si una persona habrá de incluirse en el registro (R) y/o en las estadísticas de personas desempleadas (S):

– Estar sin empleo (R) y (S);
– Estar en busca de empleo (R) y (S);
– Estar disponible para trabajar (R) y (S);
– Edad (mínima: 16 años; máxima: 70 años) (R) y (S);
– Ciudadanía (R);
– Residir en el país (R);
– Haber trabajado (R);
– Duración y/o número de horas de trabajo del empleo que se busca (R) y (S);
– Pago de cotizaciones del seguro de desempleo (R);
– Otros: cúmulo del derecho a prestaciones de desempleo hasta 24 meses por causa de enfermedad, circunstancias personales particulares o encarcelamiento (R).

5. Criterios utilizados para determinar si se ha de excluir a una persona del registro (R) y/o de las estadísticas de personas desempleadas (S):

– Certificado de defunción (R) y (S);
– Establecerse en otro país (R) y (S);
– Incorporarse a un (nuevo) empleo (R) y (S);
– Participar en algún programa de promoción del empleo, de

obras públicas, etc.   (R) y (S);
– Estar estudiando o siguiendo una formación   (R) y (S);
– Incumplir el requisito de tomar contacto con el organismo (R) y (S);
– Rechazar ofertas de empleo adecuadas   (R) y (S);
– Rechazar ofertas de formación adecuadas   (R) y (S);
– Fin del período de prestaciones de desempleo   (R) y (S);
– Cobrar alguna pensión   (R);
– Incapacidad para trabajar   (R).

6. Definición de persona desempleada en la que se basan las estadísticas
El concepto de desempleo registrado engloba a toda persona sin empleo o con empleo insuficiente en función de su capacidad y sus aspiraciones, basándose en una jornada laboral de ocho horas o equivalente (trabajo por turnos u otros), que está inscrita como tal en un organismo oficial de empleo y que sigue figurando en el registro siempre y cuando siga yendo a firmar al menos una vez por mes.

7. Actualización de los registros
Los registros se actualizan semanal, bi-mensual y mensualmente.

8. Tasas de desempleo
Se utilizan estadísticas de estos registros para obtener tasas de desempleo.
Fuente de los datos de empleo incluidos en el denominador de las tasas de desempleo:
Estimaciones oficiales.

Definición de persona empleada que se utiliza a tales efectos:
Equivalentes a tiempo completo.

9. Tipo de estadísticas que se producen sobre desempleados registrados
Serie 1:
Período de referencia: Mes.
Frecuencia de producción: Mensual.
Variables utilizadas:
– Sexo;
– Edad;
– Nivel de educación;
– Ocupación;
– Rama de actividad;
– Características geográficas;
– Duración del desempleo.
Publicación:
– En papel, para el público en general;
– En archivo electrónico, previa solicitud;
– En el sitio web www.vinnumalastofnun.is.
Organismo responsable de la publicación: Dirección de Trabajo.
Título de la publicación: *Yfirlit Yfir Atvinnuástand* (Panorama de la situación del empleo).
Serie 2:
Período de referencia: Día.
Frecuencia de producción: Trimestral.
Variables utilizadas:
– Sexo;
– Edad;
– Características geográficas;
– Duración del desempleo.
Publicación: En el sitio web www.statice.is
Organismo responsable de la publicación: Estadísticas de Islandia.
Título de la publicación: *Skráo atvinnuleysi eftir kyni, aldri og lengd atvinnuleysis*.

10. Información metodológica sobre las estadísticas
Divulgación:
– En papel, para el público en general;
– En archivo electrónico, previa solicitud;
– En los sitios web www.vinnumalastofnun.is (Serie 1) y www.statice.is (Serie 2).
Organismo responsable:
– Serie 1: Dirección de Trabajo.
– Serie 2: Estadísticas de Islandia.

11. Comparaciones con estadísticas derivadas de otras fuentes
Se han hecho comparaciones con estadísticas de desempleo derivadas de la Encuesta sobre la fuerza de trabajo.
Frecuencia de las comparaciones: Dos veces por año (último año: 2001).
Publicación de la metodología/resultados de las comparaciones:
Son publicados por Estadísticas de Islandia en *Labour market surveys on unemployment* (Encuestas del mercado de trabajo sobre desempleo), abril y noviembre

(www.statice.is/talnaefn/vinna2001/kafli10.pdf).
12. Modificaciones importantes desde el comienzo de las estadísticas
En la legislación, la competencia del organismo y/o los procedimientos administrativos   ha   habido   modificaciones importantes en 1998.   No se ha estimado la repercusión en las estadísticas.

Israel

1. Serie
Título: Datos del Servicio de Empleo sobre el mercado de trabajo.
Año de inicio: Decenio de 1960.
2. Organismo responsable de la inscripción inicial de desempleados
Nombre del organismo: Servicio de Empleo.
Tipo de organismo: Ente bajo supervisión general de una autoridad nacional.
Nombre de la autoridad nacional: Ministerio de Trabajo y Asuntos Sociales.
Ubicación de las oficinas locales donde se hacen las inscripciones: Aproximadamente 100 secciones en los centros más poblados de todo el país.
Tipo de servicios proporcionados/administrados por el organismo:
– Ayuda a personas en busca de empleo a encontrarlo;
– Ayuda a personas en busca de empleo a crear su propia empresa;
– Ayuda a los empleadores a encontrar trabajadores;
– Orientación profesional;
– Formación relacionada con el trabajo (junto con el Ministerio de Trabajo y Asuntos Sociales);
– Pago de prestaciones de desempleo (en cooperación con el Instituto Nacional de Seguros);
– Otros: permisos y asignación de trabajadores extranjeros; supervisión del empleo de trabajadores palestinos y ejecución de pagos a estos trabajadores; auditoría de los pagos hechos a trabajadores extranjeros.
Porcentaje de personas en busca de empleo que buscan trabajo por intermedio de ese organismo: 7%.
3. Se registran los siguientes datos de la persona:
– Nombre y apellido;
– Sexo;
– Número de seguridad social (o número de identificación semejante también utilizado por otros organismos);
– Dirección del domicilio habitual;
– Fecha de nacimiento;
– Nivel de educación/formación: se identifican nueve categorías. Se han establecido vínculos con la CINE;
– Situación laboral actual o anterior: se identifican 16 categorías;
– Tipo de ocupación del empleo actual o anterior: se identifican miles de ocupaciones. Se han establecido vínculos con la CIUO-88 a nivel de subgrupos;
– Tipo de ocupación del empleo que se busca: se identifican miles de ocupaciones. Se han establecido vínculos con la CIUO-88 a nivel de subgrupos;
– Nombre y dirección del empleador o del lugar de trabajo actual o anterior;
– Rama de actividad del empleador o del lugar de trabajo actual o anterior. Se han establecido vínculos con la CIIU Rev. 3, a nivel de clases;
– Inscripciones previas en el organismo;
– Otros: puestos que se le propusieron; rechazo de ofertas de empleo.
4. Criterios utilizados para determinar si una persona habrá de incluirse en el registro (R) y/o en las estadísticas de personas desempleadas (S):
– Estar sin empleo   (R) y (S);
– Estar en busca de empleo   (R) y (S);
– Estar disponible para trabajar   (R) y (S);
– Edad (mínima: 15 años; máxima: 65 años)   (R) y (S);
– Ciudadanía   (R) y (S);
– Haber trabajado   (R) y (S);
– Duración y/o número de horas de trabajo del empleo que se busca   (R) y (S).
5. Criterios utilizados para determinar si se ha de excluir a una persona del registro (R) y/o de las estadísticas de personas desempleadas (S):
– Certificado de defunción   (R) y (S);
– Establecerse en otro país   (R) y (S).

6. Definición de persona desempleada en la que se basan las estadísticas

Persona en busca de empleo que figura en el registro por haber estado desempleada un día como mínimo en el mes de referencia.

7. Actualización de los registros

Los registros se actualizan mensualmente.

8. Tasas de desempleo

Se utilizan estadísticas de estos registros para obtener tasas de desempleo.

Fuente de los datos de empleo incluidos en el denominador de las tasas de desempleo:

Estimaciones del total de la fuerza de trabajo civil.

Definición de persona empleada que se utiliza a tales efectos:

Definición de la Encuesta sobre la fuerza de trabajo: toda persona empleada una hora como mínimo en cualquier trabajo durante la semana de referencia.

9. Tipo de estadísticas que se producen sobre desempleados registrados

Serie: Personas desempleadas.

Período de referencia: Mes.

Frecuencia de producción: Mensual.

Variables utilizadas:

– Sexo;
– Edad;
– Nivel de educación;
– Ocupación;
– Rama de actividad;
– Características geográficas;
– Duración del desempleo.

Publicación: En papel, para el público en general.

Organismo responsable de la publicación: Servicio de Empleo.

Título y periodicidad de la publicación: *Employment Service Data on the Labour Market* (Datos del Servicio de Empleo sobre el mercado de trabajo), mensual.

10. Información metodológica sobre las estadísticas

Divulgación: No se divulga; sólo para uso interno.

Organismo responsable: Servicio de Empleo.

11. Comparaciones con estadísticas derivadas de otras fuentes

Se han hecho comparaciones con estadísticas de desempleo derivadas de la Encuesta sobre la fuerza de trabajo.

Frecuencia de las comparaciones: Periódica, cuando se publican las estadísticas.

Publicación de la metodología/resultados de las comparaciones: La publicación mensual *Datos del Servicio de Empleo sobre el mercado de trabajo* contiene las tasas nacionales de desempleo de la Encuesta sobre la fuerza de trabajo y de las tasas obtenidas por dicho servicio (por zona en lo que se refiere a desempleados durante seis días o más y a desempleados durante 20 días o más). Resulta difícil hacer comparaciones porque la definición de desempleo varía de una fuente a otra, y porque el Servicio de Empleo contabiliza únicamente a los desempleados registrados en sus oficinas. En esa publicación también figura la metodología aplicada por el Servicio de Empleo.

12. Modificaciones importantes desde el comienzo de las estadísticas

En la legislación, la competencia del organismo y/o los procedimientos administrativos hubo modificaciones importantes en:

1972 - La entrada en vigor de la Ley de seguro de desempleo, que estipula que las personas desempleadas solicitantes de prestaciones deben inscribirse en el Servicio de Empleo para buscar trabajo, provocó un aumento de las estadísticas de desempleados del Servicio de Empleo;

1984 - La entrada en vigor de la Ley sobre conservación de ingresos, según la cual compete al Servicio de Empleo administrar la prueba de empleo para determinar si se tiene derecho a las prestaciones, causó un aumento en la cifra de desempleados registrados en dicho servicio. En 1985, el número de adultos en busca de empleo aumentó el 12%;

1989-1990 - En virtud de la supresión de la obligación de los empleadores de recurrir al Servicio de Empleo para encontrar trabajadores, el número de solicitudes de empleadores en busca de trabajadores que recibía dicho servicio disminuyó casi 50 por ciento.

Italia

1. Serie

Título: Inscripciones en las oficinas de colocación.

Año de inicio: 1987.

2. Organismo responsable de la inscripción inicial de desempleados

Nombre del organismo: Agencia de Empleo.

Tipo de organismo: Organismo público subordinado a autoridades locales.

Ubicación de las oficinas locales donde se hacen las inscripciones: En cada provincia.

Tipo de servicios proporcionados/administrados por el organismo

– Ayuda a personas en busca de empleo a encontrarlo;
– Ayuda a los empleadores a encontrar trabajadores;
– Orientación profesional;
– Formación relacionada con el trabajo;
– Otros servicios relacionados con el empleo: ayuda a personas con discapacidades que buscan empleo, a ciudadanos oriundos de países que no pertenecen a la Comunidad Europea que buscan empleo y a trabajadores cesantes.

3. Se registran los siguientes datos de la persona

– Nombre y apellido;
– Sexo;
– Número de seguridad social (o número de identificación semejante también utilizado por otros organismos);
– Dirección del domicilio habitual;
– Fecha de nacimiento;
– Ciudadanía;
– Nacionalidad/grupo étnico;
– Nivel de educación/formación: se identifican ocho categorías. No se han establecido vínculos con la CINE;
– Situación laboral actual o anterior: se identifican cuatro categorías;
– Tipo de ocupación del empleo actual o anterior. No se han establecido vínculos con la CIUO-88;
– Tipo de ocupación del empleo que se busca;
– Nombre y dirección del empleador o del lugar de trabajo actual o anterior;
– Rama de actividad del empleador o del lugar de trabajo actual o anterior: se identifican cuatro categorías. Se han establecido vínculos con la CIIU;
– Inscripciones previas en el organismo;
– Otros: jubilación anticipada; disponibilidad para trabajar y duración del desempleo.

4. Criterios utilizados para determinar si una persona habrá de incluirse en el registro (R) y/o en las estadísticas de personas desempleadas (S)

– Estar sin empleo (R) y (S);
– Estar en busca de empleo (R) y (S);
– Edad (mínima: 15 años; máxima: 65 años) (R) y (S);
– Ciudadanía, en el caso de que sea oriunda de un país que no pertenece a la Comunidad Europea (R) y (S);
– Residir en el país (R) y (S);
– Haber trabajado (R) y (S);
– Pago de cotizaciones del seguro de desempleo, sólo en el caso de trabajadores cesantes (R) y (S).

5. Criterios utilizados para determinar si se ha de excluir a una persona del registro (R) y/o de las estadísticas de personas desempleadas (S)

– Incorporarse a un (nuevo) empleo (R) y (S);
– Incumplir el requisito de tomar contacto con el organismo, si la persona en busca de empleo no se presentó a confirmar su inscripción (R) y (S);
– Fin del período de prestaciones de desempleo, sólo en el caso de trabajadores cesantes (R) y (S).

6. Definición de persona desempleada en la que se basan las estadísticas

Se considera desempleada a toda persona sin empleo, inmediatamente disponible para empezar a trabajar y que busca empleo activamente.

Los trabajadores cesantes, lo son por un empresa reconocida a título de trato extraordinario de "integración salarial" que no puede garantizar que volverá a emplearlos. Dichos trabajadores deben haber trabajado al menos 12 meses y tener seis meses como mínimo de trabajo efectivo. Durante el período estipulado por ley reciben una indemnización de cesantía.

7. Actualización de los registros

Los registros se actualizan trimestralmente.

8. Tasas de desempleo

No se utilizan estadísticas de estos registros para obtener tasas de desempleo.

9. Tipo de estadísticas que se producen sobre desempleados registrados

Período de referencia: Mes.
Frecuencia de producción: Mensual.
Variables utilizadas
- Sexo;
- Edad;
- Nivel de educación;
- Ocupación;
- Rama de actividad;
- Características geográficas;
- Experiencia laboral previa;
- Ciudadanía (nacionales o no);
- Duración del desempleo.

Publicación
- En papel, para un público limitado;
- En archivo electrónico, previa solicitud;
- En el sitio web www.minwelfare.it

Organismo responsable de la publicación: Ministerio del Empleo y Política Social.
Título y periodicidad de las publicaciones: *Notaflash*, mensual y *Rapporto di monitoraggio* (Informe de gestión), semestral.

10. Información metodológica sobre las estadísticas
Divulgación
- En papel, para un público limitado;
- En archivo electrónico, previa solicitud;
- En el sitio web www.minwelfare.it

Organismo responsable: Ministerio del Empleo y Política Social.

11. Comparaciones con estadísticas derivadas de otras fuentes

Se han hecho comparaciones con estadísticas de desempleo derivadas de la Encuesta sobre la fuerza de trabajo, estadísticas del censo de población y estimaciones.
Frecuencia de las comparaciones: De vez en cuando (último año: 2001)
Publicación de la metodología/resultados de las comparaciones: No se publican.

12. Modificaciones importantes desde el comienzo de las estadísticas

En la legislación, la competencia del organismo y/o los procedimientos administrativos hubo modificaciones importantes en 1999, 2000 y 2001 que influyeron significativamente en las estadísticas. Los consiguientes cambios en las estadísticas no se conocen.

Japón (1)

1. Serie
Título: Informe sobre el Servicio de Empleo.
Año de inicio: 1963.
2. Organismo responsable de la inscripción inicial de desempleados
Nombre del organismo: Koukyo Shokugyo Anteisho (Oficina Pública de Seguridad del Empleo).
Tipo de organismo: Organismo público subordinado a una autoridad nacional.
Nombre de la autoridad nacional: Ministerio de Salud, Trabajo y Bienestar.
Ubicación de las oficinas locales donde se hacen las inscripciones: En las 47 prefecturas del país, totalizando 600 localidades.
Tipo de servicios proporcionados/administrados por el organismo:
- Ayuda a personas en busca de empleo a encontrarlo;
- Ayuda a personas en busca de empleo a crear su propia empresa;
- Ayuda a los empleadores a encontrar trabajadores;
- Orientación profesional;
- Pago de prestaciones de desempleo;
- Otros: servicio de Información de Empleo Industrial: da información concreta sobre los mercados y condiciones de trabajo locales, así como otras informaciones útiles para elegir un puesto de trabajo y adquirir calificaciones; servicio de Gestión del Empleo: ofrece consulta y asistencia concretas a los empleadores sobre cuestiones relacionadas con la gestión del empleo, tales como contratación, asignación y demás, así como asistencia para una gestión adecuada del empleo de personas mayores y personas con discapacidades; servicio de Subvención del Empleo: presta asistencia concreta a personas en busca

de empleo (diversas prestaciones para facilitar su reingreso al empleo) y empleadores (para que contraten a personas en busca de empleo que tienen problemas para encontrarlo y ofrece varias subvenciones para prevenir el desempleo causado por fluctuaciones económicas).

Porcentaje de personas en busca de empleo que buscan trabajo por intermedio de ese organismo: 34,3% (en febrero de 2001).
3. Se registran los siguientes datos de la persona:
- Nombre y apellido;
- Sexo;
- Dirección del domicilio habitual;
- Fecha de nacimiento;
- Nivel de educación/formación: se identifican seis categorías. Nivel de formación profesional: se identifican 650 categorías. No se han establecido vínculos con la CINE;
- Situación laboral actual o anterior: se identifican dos categorías;
- Tipo de ocupación del empleo actual o anterior. No se han establecido vínculos directos con la CIUO-88;
- Tipo de ocupación del empleo que se busca: se identifican 2.167 grupos. No se han establecido vínculos directos con la CIUO-88;
- Nombre del empleador o del lugar de trabajo actual o anterior;
- Otros: detalles de la situación familiar; condiciones de trabajo pretendidas; motivo de dejar el empleo anterior o actual.

4. Criterios utilizados para determinar si una persona habrá de incluirse en el registro (R) y/o en las estadísticas de personas desempleadas (S):
- Estar en busca de empleo (R) y (S);
- Estar disponible para trabajar (R) y (S);
- Edad (mínima: 15 años; no hay edad máxima) (R) y (S).

5. Criterios utilizados para determinar si se ha de excluir a una persona del registro (R) y/o de las estadísticas de personas desempleadas (S):
- Certificado de defunción (R) y (S);
- Establecerse en otro país (R) y (S);
- Incorporarse a un nuevo empleo (R) y (S);
- Incumplir el requisito de tomar contacto con el organismo (R) y (S);
- Otros: por solicitud propia (R) y (S).

6. Definición de persona desempleada en la que se basan las estadísticas

Las estadísticas abarcan únicamente a las personas en busca de empleo.
7. Actualización de los registros

Los registros no se actualizan periódicamente.
8. Tasas de desempleo

No se utilizan estadísticas de estos registros para obtener tasas de desempleo.
9. Tipo de estadísticas que se producen sobre desempleados registrados
Serie: Informe sobre el Servicio de Empleo.
Período de referencia: Mes, trimestre, año civil, año fiscal (1 de abril - 31 de marzo).
Frecuencia de producción: Mensual.
Variables utilizadas:
- Sexo;
- Edad;
- Ocupación;
- Rama de actividad;
- Características geográficas;
- Experiencia laboral previa.

Publicación:
- En papel, para el público en general;
- En el sitio web http://www.mhlw.go.jp (sólo en japonés).

Organismo responsable de la publicación: Ministerio de Salud, Trabajo y Bienestar.
Título y periodicidad de las publicaciones: *Monthly Report on Employment Service* (Informe mensual sobre el Servicio de Empleo); *Annual Report on Employment Service* (Informe anual sobre el Servicio de Empleo).

10. Información metodológica sobre las estadísticas
Divulgación:
- En papel, para el público en general;
- En el sitio web http://www.mhlw.go.jp (sólo en japonés).

Organismo responsable: Ministerio de Salud, Trabajo y Bienestar.
11. Comparaciones con estadísticas derivadas de otras fuentes

No se han hecho comparaciones con estadísticas de desempleo derivadas de otras fuentes.

12. Modificaciones importantes desde el comienzo de las estadísticas

En la legislación, la competencia del organismo y/o los procedimientos administrativos no ha habido modificaciones importantes que hayan influido significativamente en las estadísticas.

Japón (2)

1. Series

Títulos: Informe anual sobre el Servicio de Seguro de Empleo; y Informe mensual sobre el Servicio de Seguro de Empleo.

Año de inicio: Serie anual:1975; Serie mensual: 1980.

2. Organismo responsable de la inscripción inicial de desempleados

Nombre del organismo: Koukyo Shokugyo Anteisho (Oficina Pública de Seguridad del Empleo).

Tipo de organismo: Organismo público subordinado a una autoridad nacional.

Nombre de la autoridad nacional: Ministerio de Salud, Trabajo y Bienestar.

Ubicación de las oficinas locales donde se hacen las inscripciones: En las 47 prefecturas del país totalizando 600 localidades.

Tipo de servicios proporcionados/administrados por el organismo:
- Ayuda a personas en busca de empleo a encontrarlo;
- Ayuda a personas en busca de empleo a crear su propia empresa;
- Ayuda a los empleadores a encontrar trabajadores;
- Orientación profesional;
- Pago de prestaciones de desempleo;
- Otros: servicio de Información de Empleo Industrial: da información concreta sobre los mercados y condiciones de trabajo locales, así como otras informaciones útiles para elegir un puesto de trabajo y adquirir calificaciones; servicio de Gestión del Empleo: ofrece consulta y asistencia concretas a los empleadores sobre cuestiones relacionadas con la gestión del empleo, tales como contratación, asignación y demás, así como asistencia para una gestión adecuada del empleo de personas mayores y personas con discapacidades; servicio de Subvención del Empleo: presta asistencia concreta a personas en busca de empleo (diversas prestaciones para facilitar su reingreso al empleo) y empleadores (para que contraten a personas en busca de empleo que tienen problemas para encontrarlo y ofrece varias subvenciones para prevenir el desempleo causado por fluctuaciones económicas).

Porcentaje de personas en busca de empleo que buscan trabajo por intermedio de ese organismo: 34,3% (en febrero de 2001).

3. Se registran los siguientes datos de la persona:
- Nombre y apellido;
- Sexo;
- Dirección del domicilio habitual;
- Fecha de nacimiento;
- Situación laboral actual o anterior: se identifican dos categorías;
- Tipo de ocupación del empleo actual o anterior: se identifican nueve grupos. No se han establecido vínculos directos con la CIUO-88;
- Nombre y dirección del empleador o del lugar de trabajo actual o anterior;
- Inscripciones previas en el organismo.

4. Criterios utilizados para determinar si una persona habrá de incluirse en el registro (R) y/o en las estadísticas de personas desempleadas (S):
- Estar sin trabajo (R) y (S);
- Estar en busca de empleo (R) y (S);
- Estar disponible para trabajar (R) y (S);
- Edad (mínima: 15 años; máxima: 64 años) (R) y (S);
- Haber trabajado (R) y (S).

5. Criterios utilizados para determinar si se ha de excluir a una persona del registro (R) y/o de las estadísticas de personas desempleadas (S):
- Certificado de defunción (R) y (S);
- Incorporarse a un (nuevo) empleo (R) y (S);
- Estar estudiando o siguiendo una formación (salvo personas que siguen alguna formación profesional en establecimientos públicos) (R) y (S);
- Incumplir el requisito de tomar contacto con el organismo

- Rechazar una oferta de empleo adecuada (R) y (S);
- Rechazar una oferta de formación adecuada (R) y (S);
- Fin del período de prestaciones de desempleo (normalmente, un año después de haber dejado el último empleo) (R) y (S);
- Incapacidad para trabajar (R) y (S).

6. Definición de persona desempleada en la que se basan las estadísticas

Personas que reúnen los requisitos para recibir prestaciones: personas que cotizaron al seguro de empleo durante más de seis meses por año antes de dejar su empleo anterior, que están sin empleo, que quieren trabajar y están disponibles para hacerlo.

7. Actualización de los registros

Los registros no se actualizan periódicamente.

8. Tasas de desempleo

No se utilizan estadísticas de estos registros para obtener tasas de desempleo.

9. Tipo de estadísticas que se producen sobre desempleados registrados

Estadísticas del número de personas registradas como *beneficiarias*.

Serie 1: Informe anual sobre el Servicio de Seguro de Empleo.

Período de referencia: Mes y año.

Frecuencia de producción: Anual.

Variables utilizadas:
- Sexo;
- Edad;
- Ocupación;
- Rama de actividad;
- Características geográficas.

Publicación: En papel, para el público en general.

Organismo responsable de la publicación: Ministerio de Salud, Trabajo y Bienestar.

Título y periodicidad de la publicación: *Annual Report on Employment Insurance Service* (Informe anual sobre el Servicio de Seguro de Empleo).

Serie 2: Informe mensual sobre el Servicio de Seguro de Empleo.

Período de referencia: Mes.

Frecuencia de producción: Mensual.

Variables utilizadas:
- Sexo;
- Edad;
- Ocupación;
- Rama de actividad;
- Características geográficas.

Publicación: En papel, para el público en general.

Organismo responsable de la publicación: Ministerio de Salud, Trabajo y Bienestar.

Título y periodicidad de la publicación: *Monthly Report on Employment Insurance Service* (Informe mensual sobre el Servicio de Seguro de Empleo).

10. Información metodológica sobre las estadísticas

Divulgación: No se divulgan, sólo para uso interno.

11. Comparaciones con estadísticas derivadas de otras fuentes

No se han hecho comparaciones con estadísticas de desempleo derivadas de otras fuentes.

12. Modificaciones importantes desde el comienzo de las estadísticas

En la legislación, la competencia del organismo y/o los procedimientos administrativos no ha habido modificaciones importantes que hayan influido significativamente en las estadísticas.

Kazajstán

1. Serie

Título: Desempleo registrado.

Año de inicio: 1991.

2. Organismo responsable de la inscripción inicial de desempleados

Nombre del organismo: Organos competentes en materia de empleo (a escala urbana y regional).

Tipo de organismo: Organismo público subordinado a autoridades nacionales, regionales, provinciales y locales.

Nombre de la autoridad nacional: Ministerio de Trabajo y Protección Social.

Ubicación de las oficinas locales donde se hacen las inscripciones: En todas las ciudades y zonas del país; 202 oficinas en total.

Tipo de servicios proporcionados/administrados por el organismo:
– Ayuda a personas en busca de empleo a encontrarlo;
– Ayuda a personas en busca de empleo a crear su propia empresa;
– Ayuda a los empleadores a encontrar trabajadores;
– Orientación profesional;
– Otros: organización de obras públicas mediante la creación de lugares de trabajo temporal destinados especialmente a personas desempleadas.

Porcentaje de personas en busca de empleo que buscan trabajo por intermedio de ese organismo: 99%.

3. Se registran los siguientes datos de la persona:
– Nombre y apellido;
– Sexo;
– Número de seguridad social (o número de identificación semejante también utilizado por otros organismos);
– Dirección del domicilio habitual;
– Fecha de nacimiento;
– Ciudadanía;
– Nivel de educación/formación: se identifican cinco categorías. Se han establecido vínculos con la CINE;
– Situación laboral actual o anterior: se identifican cuatro categorías;
– Tipo de ocupación del empleo actual o anterior: se identifican nueve grupos. Se han establecido vínculos con la CIUO-88 a nivel de grupos primarios (la Clasificación de Ocupaciones de Kazajstán está armonizada con la CIUO-88);
– Tipo de ocupación del empleo que se busca: se identifican nueve grupos. Se han establecido vínculos con la CIUO-88 a nivel de grupos primarios (la Clasificación de Ocupaciones de Kazajstán está armonizada con la CIUO-88);
– Nombre y dirección del empleador o del lugar de trabajo actual o anterior;
– Rama de actividad del empleador o del lugar de trabajo actual o anterior: se identifican nueve grupos. Se han establecido vínculos con la CIIU Rev. 3, a nivel de categorías de tabulación;
– Inscripciones previas en el organismo.

4. Criterios utilizados para determinar si una persona habrá de incluirse en el registro (R) y/o en las estadísticas de personas desempleadas (S):
– Estar sin empleo (R) y (S);
– Estar en busca de empleo (R) y (S);
– Estar disponible para trabajar (R) y (S);
– Edad (mínima: 16 años; máxima: 63 años para los hombres y 58 años para las mujeres) (R) y (S);
– Ciudadanía (R) y (S);
– Residir en el país (R) y (S).

5. Criterios utilizados para determinar si se ha de excluir a una persona del registro (R) y/o de las estadísticas de personas desempleadas (S):
– Certificado de defunción (R) y (S);
– Establecerse en otro país (R) y (S);
– Incorporarse a un (nuevo) empleo, incluido el trabajo temporario (R) y (S);
– Comenzar el servicio militar (R) y (S);
– Incumplir el requisito de tomar contacto con el organismo (R);
– Rechazar dos ofertas de empleo adecuadas (R);
– Cobrar alguna pensión (R) y (S);
– Incapacidad para trabajar (R) y (S);
– Otros: organización de empresa propia (R) y (S); encarcelamiento (R) y (S); mudarse a otro distrito (R) y (S); no presentarse a un puesto o a un curso de formación ofrecidos (R) y (S); dejar un puesto de obras públicas o un curso de formación sin autorización (R) y (S).

6. Definición de persona desempleada en la que se basan las estadísticas
Toda persona en edad de trabajar que en el período de referencia respondía a los tres criterios siguientes:
– estaba sin trabajo (sin ocupación remunerada);
– buscaba trabajo activamente, y
– estaba disponible para empezar a trabajar en un plazo determinado.

7. Actualización de los registros
Los registros se actualizan mensualmente.

8. Tasas de desempleo
Se utilizan estadísticas de estos registros para obtener tasas de desempleo.

Fuente de los datos de empleo incluidos en el denominador de las tasas de desempleo:
Estimaciones oficiales y cifras de la población económicamente activa que presenta cada trimestre la Agencia de Estadística de la República de Kazajstán.

9. Tipo de estadísticas que se producen sobre desempleados registrados
Serie 1:
Variables utilizadas:
– Sexo;
– Edad;
– Nivel de educación;
– Ocupación;
– Rama de actividad;
– Características geográficas;
– Experiencia laboral previa;
– Ciudadanía (nacionales o no);
– Duración del desempleo.
Publicación: En papel, para un público limitado.
Periodicidad de las publicaciones: Mensual y trimestral.
Serie 2:
Variables utilizadas:
– Sexo;
– Edad;
– Nivel de educación;
– Ocupación;
– Rama de actividad;
– Características geográficas
– Experiencia laboral previa;
– Ciudadanía (nacionales o no);
– Duración del desempleo.
Publicación: En papel, para el público en general.
Periodicidad de las publicaciones: Mensual y trimestral.
Serie 3:
Variables utilizadas:
– Sexo;
– Edad
– Nivel de educación;
– Ocupación;
– Rama de actividad;
– Características geográficas;
– Experiencia laboral previa;
– Ciudadanía (nacionales o no);
– Duración del desempleo.
Publicación: En papel, para el público en general.
Periodicidad de las publicaciones: Mensual y trimestral.

10. Información metodológica sobre las estadísticas
Divulgación:
– En papel, para el público en general;
– En el sitio web www.enbk.kz
Organismo responsable: Agencia de Estadística de la República de Kazajstán.

11. Comparaciones con estadísticas derivadas de otras fuentes
Se han hecho comparaciones con estadísticas de desempleo derivadas de la Encuesta sobre la fuerza de trabajo y el Censo de población.
Frecuencia de las comparaciones: Periódica, cuando se publican las estadísticas.
Publicación de la metodología/resultados de las comparaciones: En publicaciones oficiales de la Agencia de Estadística de la República de Kazajstán.

12. Modificaciones importantes desde el comienzo de las estadísticas
En la legislación, la competencia del organismo y/o los procedimientos administrativos hubo modificaciones importantes en 1990, 1998, 1999 (abril y noviembre) y 2001, lo que dio lugar a una marcada tendencia de disminución del número anual de desempleados registrados después de 1996.

Kenya

1. Serie
Título: Desempleo registrado.
Año de inicio: 1988.
2. Organismo responsable de la inscripción inicial de desempleados
Nombre del organismo: Oficina Nacional de Empleo.
Tipo de organismo: Organismo público subordinado a una autoridad nacional.

Nombre de la autoridad nacional: Ministerio de Trabajo y Desarrollo de Recursos Humanos.

Ubicación de las oficinas locales donde se hacen las inscripciones: 41 distritos seleccionados.

Tipo de servicios proporcionados/administrados por el organismo:
- Ayuda a personas en busca de empleo a encontrarlo;
- Ayuda a personas en busca de empleo a crear su propia empresa;
- Ayuda a los empleadores a encontrar trabajadores;
- Orientación profesional;
- Formación relacionada con el trabajo;
- Estudio del impacto del VIH/SIDA en los lugares de trabajo.

Porcentaje de personas en busca de empleo que buscan trabajo por intermedio de ese organismo: Se desconoce, pero el registro es bajo porque mucho trabajadores prefieren buscar empleo directamente en las puertas de los establecimientos.

3. Se registran los siguientes datos de la persona:
- Nombre y apellido;
- Sexo;
- Número de la cédula de identidad (o número de identificación semejante también utilizado por otros organismos);
- Dirección del domicilio habitual;
- Fecha de nacimiento;
- Ciudadanía;
- Nacionalidad/grupo étnico;
- Nivel de educación/formación: se identifican cuatro categorías. Se han establecido vínculos con la CINE;
- Situación laboral actual o anterior;
- Tipo de ocupación del empleo actual o anterior: se identifican cinco categorías. Se han establecido vínculos con la CIUO-88 a nivel de grupo primario;
- Tipo de ocupación del empleo que se busca: se identifican nueve categorías. Se han establecido vínculos con la CIUO-88 a nivel de grupo primario;
- Nombre y dirección del empleador o del lugar de trabajo actual o anterior;
- Rama de actividad del empleador o del lugar de trabajo actual o anterior: se identifican nueve categorías. Se han establecido vínculos con la CIIU Rev. 3, a nivel de clases;
- Inscripciones previas en el organismo.

4. Criterios utilizados para determinar si una persona habrá de incluirse en el registro (R) y/o en las estadísticas de personas desempleadas (S):
- Estar sin empleo   (R) y (S);
- Estar en busca de empleo   (R) y (S);
- Estar disponible para trabajar   (R) y (S);
- Edad (mínima: 18 años; máxima: 55 años)   (R) y (S);
- Ciudadanía   (R) y (S);
- Residir en el país   (R) y (S);
- Haber trabajado   (R) y (S).

5. Criterios utilizados para determinar si se ha de excluir a una persona del registro (R) y/o de las estadísticas de personas desempleadas (S):
- Certificado de defunción   (R) y (S);
- Establecerse en otro país   (R) y (S);
- Incorporarse a un (nuevo) empleo   (R) y (S);
- Comenzar el servicio militar   (R) y (S);
- Estar estudiando o siguiendo una formación   (R) y (S);
- Incumplir el requisito de tomar contacto con el organismo   (R) y (S);
- Cobrar alguna pensión   (R) y (S);
- Incapacidad para trabajar   (R) y (S).

6. Definición de persona desempleada en la que se basan las estadísticas

Persona que no ejerce ninguna actividad económica productiva que podría ser su principal fuente de ingresos, es decir no tener ingreso alguno en la semana de referencia por haber estado sin trabajo durante algún tiempo, y que está disponible para trabajar y busca empleo activamente o está en espera de volver a trabajar.

7. Actualización de los registros

Los registros se actualizan mensualmente.

8. Tasas de desempleo

Se utilizan estadísticas de estos registros para obtener tasas de desempleo.

Fuentes de los datos de empleo incluidos en el denominador de las tasas de desempleo:

Encuesta sobre la fuerza de trabajo, encuestas de establecimientos, Registro de la Seguridad Social, Estimaciones oficiales y Censo de población.

Definición de persona empleada que se utiliza a tales efectos:

Persona que ejerce alguna actividad productiva que genera ingresos suficientes para subvenir a las necesidades básicas.

9. Tipo de estadísticas que se producen sobre desempleados registrados

Serie 1:

Período de referencia: Mes.

Frecuencia de producción: Mensual.

Variables utilizadas:
- Sexo;
- Edad;
- Nivel de educación;
- Ocupación;
- Rama de actividad;
- Características geográficas;
- Experiencia laboral previa;
- Ciudadanía (nacionales o no);
- Duración del desempleo.

Publicación: En papel, para el público en general.

Organismo responsable de la publicación: Departamento de Gestión de Recursos Humanos, Ministerio de Trabajo y Desarrollo de Recursos Humanos.

Título y periodicidad de la publicación: *Departmental Monthly Report* (Informe departamental mensual).

Serie 2:

Período de referencia: Trimestre.

Frecuencia de producción: Trimestral.

Variables utilizadas:
- Sexo;
- Edad;
- Nivel de educación;
- Ocupación;
- Rama de actividad;
- Características geográficas;
- Experiencia laboral previa;
- Ciudadanía (nacionales o no);
- Duración del desempleo.

Publicación: En papel, para el público en general.

Organismo responsable de la publicación: Departamento de Gestión de Recursos Humanos, Ministerio de Trabajo y Desarrollo de Recursos Humanos.

Título y periodicidad de la publicación: *Departmental Quarterly Report* (Informe departamental trimestral).

Serie 3:

Período de referencia: Año.

Frecuencia de producción: Anual.

Variables utilizadas:
- Sexo;
- Edad;
- Nivel de educación;
- Ocupación;
- Rama de actividad;
- Características geográficas;
- Experiencia laboral previa;
- Ciudadanía (nacionales o no);
- Duración del desempleo.

Publicación: En papel, para el público en general.

Organismo responsable de la publicación: Departamento de Gestión de Recursos Humanos, Ministerio de Trabajo y Desarrollo de Recursos Humanos.

Título y periodicidad de la publicación: *Departmental Annual Report* (Informe departamental anual).

10. Información metodológica sobre las estadísticas

Divulgación: En papel, para el público en general.

Organismo responsable de la divulgación: Departamento de Gestión de Recursos Humanos, Ministerio de Trabajo y Desarrollo de Recursos Humanos.

11. Comparaciones con estadísticas derivadas de otras fuentes

Se han hecho comparaciones con estadísticas de desempleo derivadas de la Encuesta sobre la fuerza de trabajo, otros tipos de encuestas de hogares, el Censo de población y las agencias de empleo privadas.

Frecuencia de las comparaciones: Periódica, cuando se publican las estadísticas (último año: 2000).

Publicación de la metodología/resultados de las comparaciones: Se han publicado. Esta información también se podrá proporcionar a través del Sistema Nacional de Información sobre Empleo y Recursos Humanos (NEMIS) que está en preparación.

12. Modificaciones importantes desde el comienzo de las estadísticas

En la legislación, la competencia del organismo y/o los procedimientos administrativos no ha habido modificaciones importantes que hayan influido significativamente en las estadísticas.

13. Otros comentarios

Se reconoce que la metodología utilizada para obtener los datos es rudimentaria y, por lo tanto, puede darse el caso de que las cifras no sean exactas.

Lesotho

1. Serie
Título: Estadísticas de personas en busca de empleo.
Año de inicio: 1996.
2. Organismo responsable de la inscripción inicial de desempleados
Nombre del organismo: Servicios Nacionales de Empleo.
Tipo de organismo: Organismo público subordinado a una autoridad nacional.
Nombre de la autoridad nacional: Departamento de Trabajo.
Ubicación de las oficinas locales donde se hacen las inscripciones: Oficinas de Trabajo en todos los distritos del país.
Tipo de servicios proporcionados/administrados por el organismo:
- Ayuda a personas en busca de empleo a encontrarlo;
- Ayuda a personas en busca de empleo a crear su propia empresa;
- Ayuda a los empleadores a encontrar trabajadores;
- Orientación profesional;
- Otros: divulgación de información relacionada con el empleo (mercado de trabajo).

Porcentaje de personas en busca de empleo que buscan trabajo por intermedio de ese organismo: 30%.
3. Se registran los siguientes datos de la persona:
- Nombre y apellido;
- Sexo;
- Número de seguridad social (o número de identificación semejante también utilizado por otros organismos);
- Dirección del domicilio habitual;
- Fecha de nacimiento;
- Ciudadanía;
- Nivel de educación/formación: se identifican cuatro categorías. No se han establecido vínculos con la CINE;
- Tipo de ocupación del empleo actual o anterior: se identifican ocho categorías. Se han establecido vínculos con la CIUO-88 a nivel de grandes grupos;
- Tipo de ocupación del empleo que se busca: se identifican ocho categorías. Se han establecido vínculos con la CIUO-88 a nivel de grandes grupos;
- Inscripciones previas en el organismo.

4. Criterios utilizados para determinar si una persona habrá de incluirse en el registro (R) y/o en las estadísticas de personas desempleadas (S):
- Estar en busca de empleo (R);
- Edad (mínima: 18 años; máxima: 55 años) (R);
- Ciudadanía (debe ser ciudadana de Lesotho) (R).

5. Criterios utilizados para determinar si se ha de excluir a una persona del registro (R) y/o de las estadísticas de personas desempleadas (S):
- Certificado de defunción (R);
- Establecerse en otro país (R);
- Incorporarse a un (nuevo) empleo (R).

6. Definición de persona desempleada en la que se basan las estadísticas

Se entiende por persona desempleada a toda persona sin ingreso alguno.

7. Actualización de los registros

Los registros se actualizan a diario.

8. Tasas de desempleo

No se utilizan estadísticas de estos registros para obtener tasas de desempleo.

9. Tipo de estadísticas que se producen sobre desempleados registrados
Serie: Estadísticas de personas en busca de empleo.
Período de referencia: Trimestre.
Frecuencia de producción: Semanal.
Variables utilizadas:
- Sexo;
- Edad;
- Nivel de educación;
- Ocupación.

Publicación: En archivo electrónico, previa solicitud.
Título de la publicación: *Quarterly Reports* (Informes trimestrales).
10. Información metodológica sobre las estadísticas
Divulgación: En archivo electrónico, previa solicitud.
Organismo responsable: Servicios Nacionales de Empleo.
11. Comparaciones con estadísticas derivadas de otras fuentes

No se han hecho comparaciones con estadísticas de desempleo derivadas de otras fuentes.
12. Modificaciones importantes desde el comienzo de las estadísticas

En la legislación, la competencia del organismo y/o los procedimientos administrativos no ha habido modificaciones importantes que hayan influido significativamente en las estadísticas.

Letonia

1. Serie
Título: Desempleo registrado.
Año de inicio: 1992.
2. Organismo responsable de la inscripción inicial de desempleados
Nombre del organismo: Nodarbinatibas Valsts Dienests (Servicio Estatal de Empleo).
Tipo de organismo: Organismo público subordinado a una autoridad nacional.
Nombre de la autoridad nacional: Ministerio de Bienestar.
Ubicación de las oficinas locales donde se hacen las inscripciones: En todos los territorios administrativos del país.
Tipo de servicios proporcionados/administrados por el organismo:
- Ayuda a personas en busca de empleo a encontrarlo;
- Ayuda a los empleadores a encontrar trabajadores;
- Orientación profesional;
- Formación relacionada con el trabajo;
- Otros: organización de trabajos comunitarios remunerados y temporarios; servicios de club de trabajo.

Porcentaje de personas en busca de empleo que buscan trabajo por intermedio de ese organismo: 7,6%.
3. Se registran los siguientes datos de la persona:
- Nombre y apellido;
- Sexo;
- Número de seguridad social (o número de identificación semejante también utilizado por otros organismos);
- Dirección del domicilio habitual;
- Fecha de nacimiento;
- Ciudadanía;
- Nacionalidad/grupo étnico;
- Nivel de educación/formación: se identifican seis categorías. No se han establecido vínculos con la CINE;
- Tipo de ocupación del empleo actual o anterior: se identifican 10 categorías. Se han establecido vínculos con la CIUO-88;
- Tipo de ocupación del empleo que se busca: se identifican 10 categorías. Se han establecido vínculos con la CIUO-88;
- Nombre del empleador o del lugar de trabajo actual o anterior;
- Rama de actividad del empleador o del lugar de trabajo actual o anterior. Se han establecido vínculos con la CIIU Rev. 3 o NACE Rev. 1, a nivel de clases.

4. Criterios utilizados para determinar si una persona habrá de incluirse en el registro (R) y/o en las estadísticas de personas desempleadas (S):
- Estar sin empleo (R) y (S);
- Edad (mínima: 15 años; máxima: 60 años y medio para los hombres y 58 años y medio para las mujeres) (R) y (S);
- Residir en el país (R) y (S).

5. Criterios utilizados para determinar si se ha de excluir a una persona del registro (R) y/o de las estadísticas de personas desempleadas (S):
- Certificado de defunción (R) y (S);
- Establecerse en otro país (R) y (S);
- Incorporarse a un (nuevo) empleo (R) y (S);
- Comenzar el servicio militar (R) y (S);
- Estar estudiando (a tiempo completo) o siguiendo una formación (R) y (S);
- Incumplir el requisito de tomar contacto con el organismo (R) y (S);
- Rechazar dos ofertas de empleo adecuadas (R) y (S);
- Cobrar alguna pensión (edad de jubilación) (R) y (S);

–   Incapacidad para trabajar   (R) y (S);
–   Otros: encarcelamiento   (R) y (S).

6. Definición de persona desempleada en la que se basan las estadísticas

Toda persona disponible para trabajar que sea ciudadana o residente permanente de la República de Letonia, que esté en edad de trabajar y en busca de empleo, que no tenga una empresa, que esté registrada en el Servicio Estatal de Empleo y que se presente en el organismo, como mínimo, una vez por mes.

7. Actualización de los registros

Los registros se actualizan mensualmente.

8. Tasas de desempleo

Se utilizan estadísticas de estos registros para obtener tasas de desempleo.

Fuentes de los datos de empleo incluidos en el denominador de las tasas de desempleo: Encuesta sobre la fuerza de trabajo, encuestas de establecimientos, Registro de la Seguridad Social, Estimaciones oficiales y Censo de población.

Definición de persona empleada que se utiliza a tales efectos: Persona empleada en el sector público o el sector privado. El número de personas empleadas excluye a los estudiantes en edad de trabajar sin empleo remunerado. El cálculo del número promedio de personas empleadas se basa en los resultados de la Encuesta sobre la fuerza de trabajo y la información estadística periódica.

9. Tipo de estadísticas que se producen sobre desempleados registrados

Serie 1:
Período de referencia: Mes.
Frecuencia de producción: Mensual.

Variables utilizadas:
–   Sexo;
–   Características geográficas;
–   Duración del desempleo.
Publicación: En el sitio web www.nvd.gob.lv.
Organismo responsable de la publicación: Servicio Estatal de Empleo.
Serie 2:
Período de referencia: Trimestre.
Frecuencia de producción: Trimestral.
Variables utilizadas:
–   Edad;
–   Nivel de educación;
–   Ocupación;
–   Características geográficas;
–   Experiencia laboral previa;
–   Nacionalidad.
Serie 3:
Período de referencia: Año.
Frecuencia de producción: Anual.
Publicación: En papel, para el público en general.
Organismo responsable de la publicación: Servicio Estatal de Empleo.
Título y periodicidad de la publicación: *Annual Report* (Informe anual).

10. Información metodológica sobre las estadísticas
Divulgación:
–   En papel, para el público en general;
–   En archivo electrónico, previa solicitud;
–   En el sitio web www.nvd.gob.lv.
Organismo responsable: Servicio Estatal de Empleo; Oficina Central de Estadística.

11. Comparaciones con estadísticas derivadas de otras fuentes

No se han hecho comparaciones con estadísticas de desempleo derivadas de otras fuentes.

12. Modificaciones importantes desde el comienzo de las estadísticas

En la legislación, la competencia del organismo y/o los procedimientos administrativos no ha habido modificaciones importantes que hayan influido significativamente en las estadísticas.

Lituania

1. Serie
Título: Personas en busca de empleo y vacantes.
Año de inicio: 1992.

2. Organismo responsable de la inscripción inicial de desempleados

Nombre del organismo: Lietuvos Darbo Birza (Bolsa de Trabajo de Lituania).
Tipo de organismo: Organismo público subordinado a una autoridad nacional.
Nombre de la autoridad nacional: Ministerio de Seguridad Social y Trabajo.
Ubicación de las oficinas locales donde se hacen las inscripciones: 46 bolsas de trabajo en todo el país que abarcan todas las localidades y todos los mercados de trabajo locales.
Tipo de servicios proporcionados/administrados por el organismo:
–   Ayuda a personas en busca de empleo a encontrarlo;
–   Ayuda a personas en busca de empleo a crear su propia empresa;
–   Ayuda a los empleadores a encontrar trabajadores;
–   Orientación profesional;
–   Formación relacionada con el trabajo;
–   Pago de prestaciones de desempleo;
–   Otros: medidas activas de mercado de trabajo: obras públicas, trabajos de apoyo, y Club de trabajo.
Porcentaje de personas en busca de empleo que buscan trabajo por intermedio de ese organismo: 67,3%.

3. Se registran los siguientes datos de la persona:
–   Nombre y apellido;
–   Sexo;
–   Número de seguridad social (o número de identificación semejante también utilizado por otros organismos);
–   Dirección del domicilio habitual;
–   Fecha de nacimiento;
–   Ciudadanía;
–   Nivel de educación/formación: se identifican seis categorías. Se han establecido vínculos con la CINE;
–   Situación laboral actual o anterior: se identifican cuatro categorías;
–   Tipo de ocupación del empleo actual o anterior: se identifican 7.200 categorías. Se han establecido vínculos con la CIUO-88 a nivel de grupo primario;
–   Tipo de ocupación del empleo que se busca: se identifican 7.200 categorías. Se han establecido vínculos con la CIUO-88 a nivel de grupo primario;
–   Nombre y dirección del empleador o del lugar de trabajo actual o anterior;
–   Rama de actividad del empleador o del lugar de trabajo actual o anterior: se identifican 1.351 categorías. Se han establecido vínculos con la CIIU Rev. 3 y la NACE Rev. 1, a nivel de clases;
–   Inscripciones previas en el organismo.

4. Criterios utilizados para determinar si una persona habrá de incluirse en el registro (R) y/o en las estadísticas de personas desempleadas (S):
–   Estar sin empleo   (R) y (S);
–   Estar en busca de empleo   (R) y (S);
–   Estar disponible para trabajar   (R) y (S);
–   Edad (mínima: 16 años; máxima: 61 años y medio para los hombres y 57 años y medio para las mujeres) (R) y (S);
–   Residir en el país   (R) y (S).

5. Criterios utilizados para determinar si se ha de excluir a una persona del registro (R) y/o de las estadísticas de personas desempleadas (S):
–   Certificado de defunción   (R) y (S);
–   Establecerse en otro país   (R) y (S);
–   Incorporarse a un (nuevo) empleo   (R) y (S);
–   Comenzar el servicio militar   (R) y (S);
–   Participar en algún programa de promoción del empleo, de obras públicas, etc.   (R) y (S);
–   Estar estudiando o siguiendo una formación   (R) y (S);
–   Incumplir el requisito de tomar contacto con el organismo (R) y (S);
–   Cobrar jubilación   (R) y (S);
–   Incapacidad para trabajar   (R) y (S);
–   Otros: negarse a establecer un plan de empleo   (R) y (S).

6. Definición de persona desempleada en la que se basan las estadísticas

Toda persona apta para trabajar y en edad de trabajar que está sin empleo se considerará desempleada a condición de que no sea estudiante a tiempo completo en una institución de enseñanza, se haya registrado en la bolsa nacional de trabajo de su lugar de residencia como persona en busca de empleo y esté dispuesta a seguir cursos de formación profesional.

7. Actualización de los registros

Los registros se actualizan cada vez que hay un cambio de datos.

8. Tasas de desempleo

Se utilizan estadísticas de estos registros para obtener tasas de desempleo.

Fuente de los datos de empleo incluidos en el denominador de las tasas de desempleo: Estimaciones oficiales.

Definición de persona empleada que se utiliza a tales efectos:

El término empleo engloba a todas las personas que trabajan en el sector público, cooperativas, empresas privadas y trabajadores por cuenta propia, incluyendo: trabajadores con licencia de maternidad y licencia parental; personal militar; trabajadores con licencia larga sin goce de sueldo; trabajadores a tiempo parcial sobre la base de equivalencia a tiempo completo; personas que no están en edad de trabajar (menores de 16 años, mujeres de 57 años y medio y más, y hombres de 61 años y medio y más), titulares de un empleo remunerado.

9. Tipo de estadísticas que se producen sobre desempleados registrados

Serie 1:

Período de referencia: Mes.

Frecuencia de producción: Mensual.

Variables utilizadas:

- Sexo;
- Edad:
- Características geográficas.

Publicación:

- En papel, para el público en general;
- En archivo electrónico, previa solicitud;
- En el sitio web www.ldb.lt.

Organismo responsable de la publicación: Estadísticas de Lituania.

Título y periodicidad de la publicación: *Economic and social development in Lithuania* (Desarrollo económico y social en Lituania), mensual.

Serie 2:

Período de referencia: Trimestre.

Frecuencia de producción: Trimestral.

Variables utilizadas:

- Sexo;
- Edad;
- Nivel de educación;
- Características geográficas;
- Experiencia laboral previa;
- Duración del desempleo.

Publicación:

- En papel, para el público en general;
- En archivo electrónico, previa solicitud;
- En el sitio web www.ldb.lt.

Organismo responsable de la publicación: Estadísticas de Lituania.

Título de la publicación: *Labour market and employment of population (Statistical Bulletin)* (Mercado de trabajo y empleo de la población (Boletín estadístico)).

Serie 3:

Período de referenia: Año.

Frecuencia de producción: Anual.

Variables utilizadas:

- Sexo;
- Edad;
- Nivel de educación;
- Rama de actividad;
- Características geográficas;
- Experiencia laboral previa;
- Duración del desempleo.

Publicación:

- En papel, para el público en general;
- En archivo electrónico, previa solicitud;
- En el sitio web www.ldb.lt.

Organismo responsable de la publicación: Estadísticas de Lituania.

Título de las publicaciones: *Labour market and employment of population (Statistical Bulletin and Abstract)* (Mercado de trabajo y empleo de la población, (Boletín y resumen estadísticos)); *Statistical Yearbook of Lithuania* (Anuario estadístico de Lituania).

10. Información metodológica sobre las estadísticas

Divulgación: En papel, para el público en general.

Organismo responsable: Ministerio de Seguridad Social y Trabajo.

11. Comparaciones con estadísticas derivadas de otras fuentes

Se han hecho comparaciones con estadísticas de desempleo derivadas de la Encuesta sobre la fuerza de trabajo.

Frecuencia de las comparaciones: Periódica, cuando se publican las estadísticas.

Publicación de la metodología/resultados de las comparaciones: Se publican en *Labour force, employment and unemployment (LFS data, Biannual Bulletin of Statistics Lithuania)* (Fuerza de trabajo, empleo y desempleo (Datos de la EFT, Boletín semestral de Estadísticas de Lituania)).

12. Modificaciones importantes desde el comienzo de las estadísticas

En la legislación, la competencia del organismo y/o los procedimientos administrativos hubo modificaciones importantes en 1996, 2000 y 2001. Los cambios consiguientes en las estadísticas no se han estimado.

Luxemburgo

1. Serie

Título: Situación de empleo: datos mensuales (desde 1982) y Boletín del empleo en Luxemburgo (desde 1998).

2. Organismo responsable de la inscripción inicial de desempleados

Nombre del organismo: Administration de l'Emploi - ADEM (Administración de Empleo).

Tipo de organismo: Organismo público subordinado a una autoridad nacional.

Nombre de la autoridad nacional: Ministerio de Trabajo y Empleo.

Ubicación de las oficinas locales donde se hacen las inscripciones: Luxemburgo, Esch-Alzeth, Diekirsch, Wiltz.

Tipo de servicios proporcionados/administrados por el organismo

- Ayuda a personas en busca de empleo a encontrarlo;
- Ayuda a los empleadores a encontrar trabajadores;
- Orientación profesional;
- Formación relacionada con el trabajo en colaboración con los empleadores y el Servicio de Formación Profesional del Ministerio de Educación Nacional;
- Pago de prestaciones de desempleo;
- Otros: pago de distintas ayudas y primas en favor del mantenimiento del empleo y la inserción o reinserción de desempleados en la vida activa; servicio de trabajadores con discapacidades.

3. Se registran los siguientes datos de la persona

- Nombre y apellido;
- Sexo;
- Número de seguridad social (o número de identificación semejante también utilizado por otros organismos);
- Dirección del domicilio habitual;
- Fecha de nacimiento;
- Ciudadanía;
- Nacionalidad/grupo étnico;
- Nivel de educación/formación: se identifican cuatro categorías. No se han establecido vínculos con la CINE;
- Tipo de ocupación del empleo que se busca: se identifican 12 categorías. Se han establecido vínculos con la CIUO-68 (que se asemeja al sistema belga);
- Nombre y dirección del empleador o del lugar de trabajo actual o anterior;
- Rama de actividad del empleador o del lugar de trabajo actual o anterior: se identifican cinco categorías.. Se han establecido vínculos con la NACE Rev. 1;
- Inscripciones previas en el organismo;
- Otros: información sobre la movilidad profesional y geográfica.

4. Criterios utilizados para determinar si una persona habrá de incluirse en el registro (R) y/o en las estadísticas de personas desempleadas (S)

- Estar sin empleo(S);
- Estar en busca de empleo (R) y (S);
- Estar disponible para trabajar (R) y (S);
- Edad (mínima: 16 años; máxima: 65 años) (R) y (S);
- Ciudadanía, ser oriunda de un Estado miembro de la Unión Europea (R) y (S);
- Residir en el país: tener una dirección oficial en Luxemburgo.

5. Criterios utilizados para determinar si se ha de excluir a una persona del registro (R) y/o de las estadísticas de personas desempleadas (S)

- Certificado de defunción (R) y (S);

– Establecerse en otro país (S);
– Incorporarse a un (nuevo) empleo (S);
– Participar en algún programa de promoción del empleo, de obras públicas, etc. (S);
– Estar estudiando o siguiendo una formación: seguir una formación organizada en colaboración con el Ministerio de Educación Nacional;
– Incumplir el requisito de tomar contacto con el organismo: En principio, la persona en busca de empleo debe presentarse en el Servicio de Empleo (SPE) al menos una vez cada 15 días (R) y (S);
– Rechazar ofertas de empleo adecuadas (después de un rechazo) (R) y (S);
– Rechazar ofertas de formación adecuadas (después de un rechazo) (R) y (S);
– Cobrar alguna pensión (jubilación u otras) (R) y (S);
– Incapacidad para trabajar (R) y (S).

6. Definición de persona desempleada en la que se basan las estadísticas

Se considera desempleada a toda persona sin empleo, disponible en el mercado de trabajo, que busca un empleo adecuado, no beneficia de ninguna medida de empleo, reciba o no prestaciones, y que haya cumplido los requisitos previstos por la ADEM.

7. Actualización de los registros

Los registros se actualizan mensualmente.

8. Tasas de desempleo

Se utilizan estadísticas de estos registros para obtener tasas de desempleo.

Los cálculos están a cargo del Servicio Central de Estadística y Estudios Económicos (STATEC), a partir de las fuentes siguientes:

– Registro de la Seguridad Social;
– Estimaciones oficiales, y
– Censo de población.
–

Definición de persona empleada que se utiliza a tales efectos

El empleo nacional que se tiene en cuenta comprende el empleo interno (asalariados y no asalariados); excluye a los trabajadores extranjeros fronterizos que trabajan en Luxemburgo, los luxemburgueses fronterizos que trabajan en el extranjero y los funcionarios internacionales.

9. Tipo de estadísticas que se producen sobre desempleados registrados

Serie 1

Período de referencia: Mes.

Frecuencia de producción: Mensual.

Variables utilizadas

– Sexo;
– Edad;
– Nivel de educación;
– Ocupación;
– Duración del desempleo;
– Desempleados que benefician de prestaciones de desempleo;
– Empleo que se busca.

Publicación

– En papel, para el público en general;
– En el sitio web: www.etat.lu

Organismo responsable de la publicación: ADEM.

Título y periodicidad de la publicación: *Bulletin luxembourgeois de l'Emploi* (Boletín del empleo en Luxemburgo).

Serie 2

Período de referencia: Mes.

Frecuencia de producción: Anual.

Variables utilizadas

– Sexo;
– Edad;
– Nivel de educación;
– Ocupación;
– Características geográficas;
– Ciudadanía (nacionales o no);
– Duración del desempleo;
– Desempleados que benefician de prestaciones de desempleo;
– Empleo que se busca.

Publicación: En papel, para un público limitado.

Organismo responsable de la publicación: ADEM.

Título y periodicidad de la publicación: *Bulletin luxembourgeois de l'Emploi* (Boletín del empleo en Luxemburgo).

10. Información metodológica sobre las estadísticas

Divulgación: No se divulga, sólo para uso interno.

Organismo responsable: ADEM.

11. Comparaciones con estadísticas derivadas de otras fuentes

No se han hecho comparaciones con estadísticas de desempleo derivadas de otras fuentes.

12. Modificaciones importantes desde el comienzo de las estadísticas

En 1998, hubo modificaciones importantes en la legislación. Desde entonces, las personas en busca de empleo que benefician de alguna medida en favor del empleo no figuran en las estadísticas de desempleo. Dichas personas representaban entre 24% (en 1998) y 31% (en 2001) de la población total (personas en busca de empleo + personas que benefician de alguna medida en favor del empleo) de la que se ocupaba la ADEM.

Macedonia, Ex Rep. Yugoslava de

1. Serie

Título: Boletín administratrivo de empleo, desempleo y beneficiarios de prestaciones de desempleo.

2. Organismo responsable de la inscripción inicial de desempleados

Nombre del organismo: *Zavon zavrabotuvanje na republika makedonija* (Oficina de Empleo de la República de Macedonia).

Tipo de organismo: Organismo público subordinado a una autoridad nacional.

Nombre de la autoridad nacional: Ministerio de Trabajo y Política Social.

Ubicación de las oficinas locales donde se hacen las inscripciones: Todo el país (30 oficinas regionales de trabajo en 30 ciudades).

Tipo de servicios proporcionados/administrados por el organismo

– Ayuda a personas en busca de empleo a encontrarlo;

– Ayuda a personas en busca de empleo a crear su propia empresa;
– Ayuda a los empleadores a encontrar trabajadores;
– Orientación profesional;
– Formación relacionada con el trabajo;
– Pago de prestaciones de desempleo.

Porcentaje de personas en busca de empleo que buscan trabajo por intermedio de ese organismo: 32,2%.

3. Se registran los siguientes datos de la persona

– Nombre y apellido;
– Sexo;
– Número de seguridad social (o número de identificación semejante también utilizado por otros organismos);
– Dirección del domicilio habitual;
– Fecha de nacimiento;
– Ciudadanía;
– Nacionalidad/grupo étnico;
– Nivel de educación/formación: se identifican ocho categorías. No se han establecido vínculos con la CINE;
– Situación laboral actual o anterior: se identifican 40 categorías;
– Tipo de ocupación del empleo actual o anterior: se identifican 1.709 categorías. No se han establecido vínculos con la CIUO-88;
– Tipo de ocupación del empleo que se busca: se identifican 1.709 categorías;
– Nombre y dirección del empleador o del lugar de trabajo actual o anterior;
– Rama de actividad del empleador o del lugar de trabajo actual o anterior: se identifican 602 categorías. Se han establecido vínculos con la CIIU a nivel de clases;
– Inscripciones previas en el organismo.

4. Criterios utilizados para determinar si una persona habrá de incluirse en el registro (R) y/o en las estadísticas de personas desempleadas (S)

– Estar sin empleo (R) y (S);
– Estar en busca de empleo, presentarse regularmente a las convocatorias de la oficina, participar en el programa de promoción del empleo (R) y (S);
– Estar disponible para trabajar (R) y (S);
– Edad (mínima: 15 años; máxima: 65 años) (R) y (S);
– Ciudadanía (R) y (S);
– Residir en el país (R) y (S).

5. Criterios utilizados para determinar si se ha de excluir a una persona del registro (R) y/o de las estadísticas de personas desempleadas (S)

- Certificado de defunción (R) y (S);
- Establecerse en otro país (R) y (S);
- Incorporarse a un (nuevo) empleo (R) y (S);
- Comenzar el servicio militar (R) y (S);
- Estar estudiando o siguiendo una formación (R) y (S);
- Incumplir el requisito de tomar contacto con el organismo (R) y (S);
- Rechazar ofertas de trabajo adecuadas, después de dos rechazos (R) y (S);
- Rechazar ofertas de formación adecuadas, después de dos rechazos (R) y (S);
- Cobrar alguna pensión (jubilación u otras) (R) y (S);
- Incapacidad para trabajar (R) y (S).

6. Definición de persona desempleada en la que se basan las estadísticas

Persona desempleada es toda persona inscrita en el registro de desempleo, que está en condiciones de trabajar, quiere hacerlo y busca activamente un empleo. Se considera que la persona busca activamente empleo cuando se ha inscrito como corresponde en el organismo respectivo y en el plazo estipulado en la Ley de trabajo.

7. Actualización de los registros

Los registros se actualizan periódicamente; todos los meses, en el caso de los beneficiarios de prestaciones de desempleo; cada tres meses, en el caso de los beneficiarios de seguro médico, y cada seis meses, en el resto de los casos.

8. Tasas de desempleo

Se utilizan estadísticas de estos registros para obtener tasas de desempleo.

9. Tipo de estadísticas que se producen sobre desempleados registrados

Período de referencia: Mes, semestre y año.

Frecuencia de producción: Mensual, semestral y anual.

Variables utilizadas
- Sexo;
- Edad;
- Nivel de educación;
- Ocupación;
- Rama de actividad;
- Características geográficas;
- Experiencia laboral previa;
- Ciudadanía (nacionales o no);
- Duración del desempleo.

Publicación:
- En papel, para el público en general;
- En archivo electrónico, previa solicitud;
- En el sitio web http://www.zvrm.gov.mk

Organismo responsable de la publicación: Oficina de Empleo de la República de Macedonia.

10. Información metodológica sobre las estadísticas

Divulgación
- En papel, para el público en general.
- En archivo electrónico, previa solicitud;
- En el sitio web http://www.zvrm.gov.mk

Organismos responsables: Ministerio de Trabajo, Oficina de Empleo de la República de Macedonia, Instituto de Estadística.

11. Comparaciones con estadísticas derivadas de otras fuentes

No se han hecho comparaciones con estadísticas de desempleo derivadas de otras fuentes.

12. Modificaciones importantes desde el comienzo de las estadísticas

En la legislación, la competencia del organismo y/o los procedimientos administrativos no ha habido modificaciones importantes que hayan influido significativamente en las estadísticas.

Madagascar

1. Serie

Título: Estadísticas del mercado de trabajo.

Año de inicio: 1979.

2. Organismo responsable de la inscripción inicial de desempleados

Nombre del organismo: Servicio de Estudios, Estadística y Planificación.

Tipo de organismo: Organismo público subordinado a una autoridad nacional.

Nombre de la autoridad nacional: Dirección de Empleo.

Ubicación de las oficinas locales donde se hacen las inscripciones: Sólo en algunas regiones, nueve de las 111 subprefecturas del país.

Tipo de servicios proporcionados/administrados por el organismo
- Ayuda a personas en busca de empleo a encontrarlo;
- Ayuda a los empleadores a encontrar trabajadores;
- Otros servicios relacionados con el empleo: Expedición de atestaciones de desempleo.

Porcentaje de personas en busca de empleo que buscan trabajo por intermedio de ese organismo: 5,6%.

3. Se registran los siguientes datos de la persona
- Nombre y apellido;
- Sexo;
- Dirección del domicilio habitual;
- Fecha de nacimiento;
- Nacionalidad;
- Nivel de educación/formación: se identifican nueve categorías. No se han establecido vínculos con la CINE;
- Situación laboral actual o anterior: se identifican dos categorías;
- Tipo de ocupación del empleo actual o anterior. No se han establecido vínculos con la CIUO-88;
- Tipo de ocupación del empleo que se busca;
- Nombre y dirección del empleador o del lugar de trabajo actual o anterior.
- Rama de actividad del empleador o del lugar de trabajo actual o anterior;
- Inscripciones previas en el organismo.

4. Criterios utilizados para determinar si una persona habrá de incluirse en el registro (R) y/o en las estadísticas de personas desempleadas (S)
- Estar sin empleo (R);
- Estar en busca de empleo (R);
- Estar disponible para trabajar (R);
- Edad (mínima: 15 años; máxima: 40 años, que es la edad máxima para entrar en la función pública) (R);
- Residir en el país (R);
- Haber trabajado (R).

5. Criterios utilizados para determinar si se ha de excluir a una persona del registro (R) y/o de las estadísticas de personas desempleadas (S)

No se dispone de información.

6. Definición de persona desempleada en la que se basan las estadísticas

Globalmente, toda persona inscrita en el servicio de colocación se considera "desempleada", si está disponible para trabajar.

7. Actualización de los registros

Los registros se actualizan mensualmente.

8. Tasas de desempleo

No se utilizan estadísticas de estos registros para obtener tasas de desempleo.

9. Tipo de estadísticas que se producen sobre desempleados registrados

Período de referencia: Año.

Frecuencia de producción: Anual.

Variables utilizadas
- Sexo;
- Nivel de educación;
- Características geográficas;
- Experiencia laboral previa;
- Ciudadanía (nacionales).

Publicación: En papel, para un público limitado.

10. Información metodológica sobre las estadísticas

Divulgación: En papel, para un público limitado.

11. Comparaciones con estadísticas derivadas de otras fuentes

No se han hecho comparaciones con estadísticas de desempleo derivadas de otras fuentes.

12. Modificaciones importantes desde el comienzo de las estadísticas

En la legislación, la competencia del organismo y/o los procedimientos administrativos no ha habido modificaciones importantes que hayan influido significativamente en las estadísticas.

Malasia

1. Serie

Título: Desempleo registrado.

Año de inicio: 1969.

2. Organismo responsable de la inscripción inicial de desempleados

Nombre del organismo: Jabatan Tenaga Rakyat (Departamento de Mano de Obra).

Tipo de organismo: Organismo público subordinado a una autoridad nacional.

Nombre de la autoridad nacional: Ministerio de Recursos Humanos.

Ubicación de las oficinas locales donde se hacen las inscripciones: 13 oficinas estatales y 36 oficinas de distrito en todo el país.

Tipo de servicios proporcionados/administrados por el organismo:

- Ayuda a personas en busca de empleo a encontrarlo;
- Ayuda a los empleadores a encontrar trabajadores;
- Orientación profesional;
- Formación relacionada con el trabajo;
- Otros: otorga las licencias a las agencias de empleo del sector privado y supervisa su funcionamiento, de conformidad con la Ley de agencias de empleo privadas, de 1981.

Porcentaje de personas en busca de empleo que buscan trabajo por intermedio de ese organismo: 20%.

3. Se registran los siguientes datos de la persona:

- Nombre y apellido;
- Sexo;
- Número de seguridad social (o número de identificación semejante también utilizado por otros organismos);
- Dirección del domicilio habitual;
- Fecha de nacimiento;
- Ciudadanía;
- Nacionalidad/grupo étnico;
- Nivel de educación/formación: se identifican cuatro categorías. Se han establecido vínculos con la CINE;
- Situación laboral actual o anterior: se identifican tres categorías;
- Tipo de ocupación del empleo actual o anterior: se identifican siete grupos. Se han establecido vínculos con la CIUO-88 a nivel de grande grupos;
- Tipo de ocupación del empleo que se busca: se identifican siete grupos. se han establecido vínculos con la CIUO-88 a nivel de grande grupos;
- Nombre y dirección del empleador o del lugar de trabajo actual o anterior;
- Rama de actividad del empleador o del lugar de trabajo actual o anterior: se identifican 17 grupos. Se han establecido vínculos con la CIIU Rev. 3, a nivel de categorías de tabulación.

4. Criterios utilizados para determinar si una persona habrá de incluirse en el registro (R) y/o en las estadísticas de personas desempleadas (S):

- Estar sin empleo (R) y (S);
- Estar en busca de empleo (R) y (S);
- Edad (mínima: 15 años; máxima: 65 años) (R) y (S);
- Ciudadanía (R) y (S);
- Residir en el país (R) y (S).

5. Criterios utilizados para determinar si se ha de excluir a una persona del registro (R) y/o de las estadísticas de personas desempleadas (S):

- Certificado de defunción (S);
- Establecerse en otro país (S);
- Incorporarse a un (nuevo) empleo (R) y (S);
- Comenzar el servicio militar (R) y (S);
- Participar en algún programa de promoción del empleo, de obras públicas, etc; (R) y (S);
- Estar estudiando o siguiendo una formación (R) y (S);
- Incumplir el requisito de tomar contacto con el organismo (la inscripción en el registro debe renovarse cada tres meses) (R) y (S).

6. Definiciones de personas desempleadas en la que se basan las estadísticas

Abarca a personas desempleadas activas e inactivas. Se entiende por desempleado activo a todo aquel que no trabajó durante la semana de referencia, pero estaba disponible para trabajar y buscó empleo activamente en dicha semana. Se entiende por desempleada inactiva a toda persona que responde a alguno de los criterios siguientes:

- persona que no había buscado trabajo por creer que no lo había o que no estaba calificada;
- persona que hubiera buscado trabajo si no hubiera estado temporalmente enferma o si no hubiera sido por el mal tiempo;
- persona que estaba En espera de respuestas sobre los

puestos a los cuales había postulado; persona que había buscado trabajo antes de la semana de referencia.

7. Actualización de los registros

Los registros se actualizan cada semana.

8. Tasas de desempleo

No se utilizan estadísticas de estos registros para obtener tasas de desempleo.

9. Tipo de estadísticas que se producen sobre desempleados registrados

Serie 1:

Período de referencia: Semana.

Frecuencia de producción: Semanal.

Variables utilizadas:

- Sexo;
- Edad;
- Nivel de educación;
- Ocupación;
- Rama de actividad;
- Características geográficas;
- Experiencia laboral previa;
- Ciudadanía (nacionales o no);
- Duración del desempleo.

Publicación: En papel, para un público limitado.

Organismo responsable de la publicación: Departamento de Mano de Obra, Ministerio de Recursos Humanos.

Serie 2:

Período de referencia: Mes.

Frecuencia de producción: Mensual.

Variables utilizadas:

- Sexo;
- Edad;
- Nivel de educación;
- Ocupación;
- Rama de actividad;
- Características geográficas;
- Experiencia laboral previa;
- Ciudadanía (nacionales o no);
- Duración del desempleo.

Publicación:

- En papel, para el público en general;
- En los sitios web www.mohr.gov.my y www.jtr.gov.my

Organismo responsable de la publicación: Departamento de Mano de Obra, Ministerio de Recursos Humanos.

Título de la publicación: *Registration of Job Seekers, Job Vacancies and Placements* (Registro de personas en busca de empleo, puestos vacantes y colocaciones).

Serie 3:

Período de referencia: Trimestre.

Frecuencia de producción: Trimestral.

Variables utilizadas:

- Sexo;
- Edad;
- Nivel de educación;
- Ocupación;
- Rama de actividad;
- Características geográficas;
- Experiencia laboral previa;
- Ciudadanía (nacionales o no);
- Duración del desempleo.

Publicación:

- En papel, para el público en general;
- En los sitios web www.mohr.gov.my y www.jtr.gov.my

Organismo responsable de la publicación: Departamento de Mano de Obra, Ministerio de Recursos Humanos.

Título de la publicación: *Labour Market Trends* (Tendencias del mercado de trabajo).

10. Información metodológica sobre las estadísticas

Divulgación: No se divulgan; sólo para uso interno.

Organismo responsable: Departamento de Mano de Obra, Ministerio de Recursos Humanos.

11. Comparaciones con estadísticas derivadas de otras fuentes

Se han hecho comparaciones con estadísticas de desempleo derivadas del Censo de población y el Informe económico.

Frecuencia de las comparaciones: Periódica, cuando se publican las estadísticas.

Publicación de la metodología/resultados de las comparaciones: No se publican.

12. Modificaciones importantes desde el comienzo de las estadísticas

En la legislación, la competencia del organismo y/o los procedimientos administrativos no ha habido modificaciones importantes que hayan influido significativamente en las estadísticas.

Malí

1. Serie
Título: Anuario estadístico del mercado de trabajo.
Año de inicio: 1995.
2. Organismo responsable de la inscripción inicial de desempleados
Nombre del organismo:
1. Agence nationale pour l'Emploi - ANPE (Agencia Nacional de Empleo);
2. Oficinas de colocación privadas (BPP).
Tipo de organismo:
1. Organismo público subordinado a una autoridad nacional;
2. Organismo privado con fines de lucro.
Nombre de la autoridad nacional: Ministerio de Empleo y Formación Profesional.
Ubicación de las oficinas locales donde se hacen las inscripciones: Todo el país.
Tipo de servicios proporcionados/administrados por el organismo
– Ayuda a personas en busca de empleo a encontrarlo;
– Ayuda a personas en busca de empleo a crear su propia empresa;
– Ayuda a los empleadores a encontrar trabajadores;
– Orientación profesional;
– Formación relacionada con el trabajo;
– Otros servicios relacionados con el empleo: Información sobre el mercado de trabajo.
Porcentaje de personas en busca de empleo que buscan trabajo por intermedio de ese organismo: 20%.
3. Se registran los siguientes datos de la persona
– Nombre y apellido;
– Sexo;
– Dirección del domicilio habitual;
– Fecha de nacimiento;
– Nacionalidad;
– Nivel de educación/formación: se identifican ocho categorías. No se han establecido vínculos con la CINE;
– Tipo de ocupación del empleo actual o anterior: se identifican ocho categorías. Se han establecido vínculos con la CIUO;
– Tipo de ocupación del empleo que se busca: se identifican ocho categorías;
– Nombre y dirección del empleador o del lugar de trabajo actual o anterior;
– Rama de actividad del empleador o del lugar de trabajo actual o anterior: se identifican nueve categorías. Se han establecido vínculos con la CIIU;
– Inscripciones previas en el organismo.
4. Criterios utilizados para determinar si una persona habrá de incluirse en el registro (R) y/o en las estadísticas de personas desempleadas (S)
– Estar sin empleo (R) y (S);
– Estar en busca de empleo (R) y (S);
– Estar disponible para trabajar (R) y (S);
– Edad (mínima: 15 años; no hay edad máxima) (R) y (S).
5. Criterios utilizados para determinar si se ha de excluir a una persona del registro (R) y/o de las estadísticas de personas desempleadas (S)
– Certificado de defunción (R) y (S);
– Establecerse en otro país (R) y (S);
– Incorporarse a un (nuevo) empleo (R) y (S);
– Comenzar el servicio militar (R) y (S);
– Estar estudiando o siguiendo una formación, sólo formación de larga duración (seis meses o más) (R) y (S);
– Incumplir el requisito de tomar contacto con el organismo, después de tres meses sin contacto (R) y (S);
– Incapacidad para trabajar (R) y (S).
6. Definición de persona desempleada en la que se basan las estadísticas
Toda persona en edad de trabajar (15 años o más) que durante el período de referencia (generalmente, un mes) estaba:
– sin empleo;
– disponible para trabajar, y
– en busca de empleo.
7. Actualización de los registros

Los registros se actualizan mensualmente.
8. Tasas de desempleo
No se utilizan estadísticas de estos registros para obtener tasas de desempleo.
9. Tipo de estadísticas que se producen sobre desempleados registrados
Período de referencia: Mes.
Frecuencia de producción: Anual.
Variables utilizadas
– Sexo;
– Edad;
– Nivel de educación;
– Ocupación;
– Rama de actividad;
– Características geográficas;
– Experiencia laboral previa;
– Ciudadanía (nacionales o no);
– Duración del desempleo.
Publicación
– En papel, para el público en general;
– En archivo electrónico, previa solicitud.
Organismo responsable de la publicación: Observatorio de Empleo y Formación (OEF).
Título y periodicidad de la publicación: *Annuaire statistique du marché de l'emploi* (Anuario estadístico del mercado de trabajo), anual.
10. Información metodológica sobre las estadísticas
Divulgación
– En papel, para el público en general;
– En archivo electrónico, previa solicitud.
Organismo responsable: OEF.
11. Comparaciones con estadísticas derivadas de otras fuentes
Se han hecho comparaciones con estadísticas de desempleo derivadas de la Encuesta sobre la fuerza de trabajo, otras encuestas de hogares y el censo de población.
Frecuencia de las comparaciones: De vez en cuando.
Publicación de la metodología/resultados de las comparaciones: No se publican.
12. Modificaciones importantes desde el comienzo de las estadísticas
En la legislación y los procedimientos administrativos hubo modificaciones importantes en 2000, año en que se creó la ANPE, que sustituyó la Oficina Nacional de Mano de Obra y Empleo. No se ha estimado si ese cambio trajo aparejado un aumento o una disminución del número total de desempleado registrados.

Malta

1. Serie
Título: Desempleo registrado.
Año de inicio: 1957.
2. Organismo responsable de la inscripción inicial de desempleados
Nombre del organismo: Employment and Training Corporation - ETC (Organismo Estatal de Empleo y Formación).
Tipo de organismo: Organismo público subordinado a autoridades locales.
Ubicación de las oficinas locales donde se hacen las inscripciones: La primera vez se registra en la oficina central de la ETC, en Hal Far, y los siguientes registros semanales en una de las 20 oficinas locales.
Tipo de servicios proporcionados/administrados por el organismo:
– Ayuda a personas en busca de empleo a encontrarlo;
– Ayuda a personas en busca de empleo a crear su propia empresa;
– Ayuda a los empleadores a encontrar trabajadores;
– Orientación profesional;
– Formación relacionada con el trabajo;
– Otros: administración de fondos de formación; información sobre el mercado laboral; centros de trabajo en tres zonas.
Porcentaje de personas en busca de empleo que buscan trabajo por intermedio de ese organismo: 73% (según estimaciones de la Encuesta sobre la fuerza de trabajo).
3. Se registran los siguientes datos de la persona:
– Nombre y apellido;
– Sexo;
– Número de seguridad social (o número de identificación semejante también utilizado por otros organismos);

– Dirección del domicilio habitual;
– Fecha de nacimiento;
– Ciudadanía;
– Nacionalidad/grupo étnico;
– Nivel de educación/formación. No se han establecido vínculos con la CINE;
– Situación laboral actual o anterior: se identifican tres categorías;
– Tipo de ocupación del empleo actual o anterior. Se han establecido vínculos con la CIUO-88 a nivel de subgrupos principales;
– Tipo de ocupación del empleo que se busca: se identifican 476 grupos. Se han establecido vínculos con la CIUO-88;
– Nombre y dirección del empleador o del lugar de trabajo actual o anterior;
– Rama de actividad del empleador o del lugar de trabajo actual o anterior: se identifican 83 grupos. Se han establecido vínculos con la CIIU Rev. 3 a nivel de grupo;
– Inscripciones previas en el organismo;
– Otros: registro de cinco opciones; tipo de discapacidad (si corresponde).

4. Criterios utilizados para determinar si una persona habrá de incluirse en el registro (R) y/o en las estadísticas de personas desempleadas (S):
– Estar sin empleo (R) y (S);
– Estar en busca de empleo (R) y (S);
– Estar disponible para trabajar (R) y (S);
– Edad (mínima: 16 años (R); 15 años (S); no hay edad máxima);
– Ciudadanía (sólo ciudadanos malteses) (R);
– Residir en el país (R);
– Haber trabajado (R).

5. Criterios utilizados para determinar si se ha de excluir a una persona del registro (R) y/o de las estadísticas de personas desempleadas (S):
– Certificado de defunción (R) y (S);
– Establecerse en otro país (R) y (S);
– Incorporarse a un (nuevo) empleo (R) y (S);

– Participar en algún programa de promoción del empleo, de obras públicas, etc; (R) y (S);
– Estar estudiando o siguiendo una formación (R) y (S);
– Incumplir el requisito de tomar contacto con el organismo (R);
– Rechazar una oferta de empleo adecuada (R);
– Rechazar una oferta de formación adecuada (R);
– Cobrar alguna pensión (R);
– Incapacidad para trabajar (R) y (S);
– Otros: si la inspección constató que trabajaba en el sector informal (R).

6. Definición de persona desempleada en la que se basan las estadísticas
(Criterios de inscripción de la Parte I del Registro de desempleo)
Todo ciudadano maltés mayor de 16 años que fue:
– despedido de su empleo anterior, o
– egresado escolar (usuario que se registra por primera vez) o
– inscrito en la Parte II del Registro por alguno de los motivos siguientes y que han cumplido el período de sanción de seis meses: despedido del trabajo por sanción disciplinaria; renunció al trabajo por decisión propia; rechazó sin dar un motivo válido las oportunidades de empleo o formación que le ofreciera el encargado de colocación cuando estaba inscrito en la Parte I; fue borrado del Registro porque durante una inspección del personal encargado de hacer cumplir la ley se comprobó que trabajaba en el sector informal, o no presentó todos los documentos necesarios para ser inscrito en la Parte I del Registro (medida temporal).

7. Actualización de los registros
Los registros se actualizan diaria y semanalmente.

8. Tasas de desempleo
Hasta agosto de 2001, se utilizaron estadísticas de estos registros para obtener tasas de desempleo; desde entonces, las tasas de desempleo se obtienen a través de la Encuesta sobre la fuerza de trabajo.
La fuente de los datos de empleo incluidos en el denominador de las tasas de desempleo era la Base de datos de personas empleadas, basada en los formularios de contratación.

9. Tipo de estadísticas que se producen sobre desempleados registrados

Período de referencia: Mes.
Frecuencia de producción: Mensual.
Variables utilizadas:
– Sexo;
– Edad;
– Nivel de educación;
– Ocupación;
– Rama de actividad;
– Experiencia laboral previa;
– Duración del desempleo.
Publicación:
– En papel, para el público en general;
– En el sitio web www.nso.gov.mt
Organismo responsable de la publicación: Oficina Nacional de Estadística.
Título y periodicidad de las publicaciones: *News Release* (Boletín informativo), mensual;
Abstract of Statistics (Resumen de Estadísticas), anual.

10. Información metodológica sobre las estadísticas
Divulgación:
– En papel, para el público en general;
– En el sitio web www.nso.gov.mt
Organismo responsable: Organismo Estatal de Empleo y Formación.

11. Comparaciones con estadísticas derivadas de otras fuentes
Se han hecho comparaciones con estadísticas de desempleo derivadas de la Encuesta sobre la fuerza de trabajo y el Censo de población.
Frecuencia de las comparaciones: De vez en cuando (última vez: diciembre de 2000).
Publicación de la metodología/resultados de las comparaciones: No se publican.

12. Modificaciones importantes desde el comienzo de las estadísticas
En la legislación, la competencia del organismo y/o los procedimientos administrativos no ha habido modificaciones importantes que hayan influido significativamente en las estadísticas.

Marruecos

1. Serie
Título: Número de personas en busca de empleo registradas (únicamente estadísticas internas, calculadas desde hace tres años).

2. Organismo responsable de la inscripción inicial de desempleados
Nombre del organismo: Agence nationale de Promotion de l'Emploi et des Compétences - ANAPEC (Agencia Nacional de Promoción del Empleo y Competencias).
Tipo de organismo: Organismo público subordinado a una autoridad nacional.
Nombre de la autoridad nacional: Ministerio de Empleo, Formación Profesional, Desarrollo Social y Solidaridad.
Ubicación de las oficinas locales donde se hacen las inscripciones: 22 agencias locales en 19 ciudades del reino.
Tipo de servicios proporcionados/administrados por el organismo
– Ayuda a personas en busca de empleo a encontrarlo;
– Ayuda a personas en busca de empleo a crear su propia empresa;
– Ayuda a los empleadores a encontrar trabajadores;
– Orientación profesional;
– Formación relacionada con el trabajo;
– Otros servicios relacionados con el empleo: Asesora a empresas en materia de gestión de empleo y competencias; informa a los usuarios sobre el mercado de trabajo; prepara el repertorio nacional de oficios.
Porcentaje de personas en busca de empleo que buscan trabajo por intermedio de ese organismo: 20% de las personas en busca de empleo calificado.

3. Se registran los siguientes datos de la persona
– Nombre y apellido;
– Sexo;
– Número de seguridad social (o número de identificación semejante también utilizado por otros organismos);
– Dirección del domicilio habitual;
– Fecha de nacimiento;
– Nivel de educación/formación;
– Situación laboral actual o anterior: se identifican tres categorías;
– Tipo de ocupación del empleo actual o anterior: se

identifican 466 categorías. No se han establecido vínculos con la CIUO-88;
– Tipo de ocupación del empleo que se busca: se identifican 466 categorías;
– Inscripciones previas en el organismo;
– Otros: movilidad; idiomas que habla; licencia de conducir; número de teléfono; dirección electrónica; situación familiar, y años de experiencia profesional.

4. Criterios utilizados para determinar si una persona habrá de incluirse en el registro:
– Tener un diploma profesional o una especialización adquirida en un curso de formación de adultos (R);
– Tener un diploma de formación general (bachillerato como mínimo) (R);
– Tener experiencia profesional de tres años como mínimo en un empleo calificado, atestada por certificados de trabajo (R).

5. Criterios utilizados para determinar si se ha de excluir a una persona del registro:
– Certificado de defunción (R);
– Establecerse en otro país (R);
– Incorporarse a un (nuevo) empleo: la inscripción se anula cuando la persona en busca de empleo declara que ya no está en busca de empleo o que ha sido colocada mediante una oferta de empleo gestionada por la ANAPEC (R);
– Estar estudiando o siguiendo una formación (R);
– Incumplir el requisito de tomar contacto con el organismo: falta de actualización en los seis meses siguientes a la fecha de la última inscripción (R);
– Rechazar ofertas de empleo adecuadas (R).

6. Definición de persona desempleada en la que se basan las estadísticas
Las estadísticas de desempleo son establecidas por la Dirección de Estadística del Ministerio de Previsión Económica y Plan. Las estadísticas establecidas por la ANAPEC se basan en el fichero de personas en busca de empleo inscritas y son sólo para uso interno.

7. Actualización de los registros
Los registros se actualizan constantemente.

8. Tasas de desempleo
No se utilizan estadísticas de estos registros para obtener tasas de desempleo.

9. Tipo de estadísticas que se producen sobre desempleados registrados
Período de referencia: Día.
Frecuencia de producción: Cotidiana.
Variables utilizadas
– Sexo;
– Edad;
– Nivel de educación.
Publicación: Sólo para uso interno.

10. Información metodológica sobre las estadísticas
Divulgación: No se divulga, sólo para uso interno.

11. Comparaciones con estadísticas derivadas de otras fuentes
No se han hecho comparaciones con estadísticas de desempleo derivadas de otras fuentes.

Mauricio

1. Serie
Título: Desempleo registrado.
Año de inicio: Alrededor de 1960.

2. Organismo responsable de la inscripción inicial de desempleados
Nombre del organismo: Servicio de Empleo.
Tipo de organismo: Organismo público subordinado a una autoridad nacional.
Nombre de la autoridad nacional: Ministerio de Formación, Desarrollo de Capacidades y Productividad.
Ubicación de las oficinas locales donde se hacen las inscripciones: En todo el país.
Tipo de servicios proporcionados/administrados por el organismo:
– Ayuda a personas en busca de empleo a encontrarlo;
– Ayuda a los empleadores a encontrar trabajadores;
– Orientación profesional;
– Otros: proporciona información a organismos de formación/financiación de empresas.
Porcentaje de personas en busca de empleo que buscan trabajo por intermedio de ese organismo: 65%.

3. Se registran los siguientes datos de la persona:
– Nombre y apellido;
– Sexo;
– Número de seguridad social (o número de identificación semejante también utilizado por otros organismos);
– Dirección del domicilio habitual;
– Fecha de nacimiento;
– Nacionalidad/grupo étnico;
– Nivel de educación/formación. No se han establecido vínculos con la CINE;
– Situación laboral actual o anterior;
– Tipo de ocupación del empleo actual o anterior. Se han establecido vínculos con la CIUO-88 a nivel de grupos primarios;
– Tipo de ocupación del empleo que se busca. Se han establecido vínculos con la CIUO-88 a nivel de grupos primarios;
– Nombre y dirección del empleador o del lugar de trabajo actual o anterior;
– Rama de actividad del empleador o del lugar de trabajo actual o anterior. No se han establecido vínculos con la CIIU Rev. 3;
– Inscripciones previas en el organismo;
– Otros: personas a cargo; estado civil; discapacidad.

4. Criterios utilizados para determinar si una persona habrá de incluirse en el registro (R) y/o en las estadísticas de personas desempleadas (S):
– Estar sin empleo (R) y (S);
– Estar en busca de empleo (R) y (S);
– Estar disponible para trabajar (R) y (S);
– Edad (mínima: 15 años; no hay edad máxima) (R) y (S);
– Ciudadanía (R) y (S);
– Residir en el país (R) y (S).

5. Criterios utilizados para determinar si se ha de excluir a una persona del registro (R) y/o de las estadísticas de personas desempleadas (S):
– Certificado de defunción (R) y (S);
– Establecerse en otro país (R) y (S);
– Incumplir el requisito de tomar contacto con el organismo (R).

6. Definición de persona desempleada en la que se basan las estadísticas
En el registro no sólo se inscribe a personas desempleadas sino también a personas empleadas en busca de un trabajo mejor o alternativo.
Se entiende por persona desempleada a toda persona de uno u otro sexo, de 15 años como mínimo que declara estar desempleada y dispuesta a aceptar un trabajo.

7. Actualización de los registros
Los registros se actualizan cada mes y se suprime de ellos a quienes no se presentaron. Las personas empleadas deben presentarse una vez por año y este registro se actualiza cada cuatro meses.

8. Tasas de desempleo
No se utilizan estadísticas de estos registros para obtener tasas de desempleo.

9. Tipo de estadísticas que se producen sobre desempleados registrados
Período de referencia: Enero-abril; mayo-agosto, y septiembre-diciembre.
Frecuencia de producción: Cada cuatro meses.
Variables utilizadas:
– Sexo;
– Edad;
– Nivel de educación;
– Ocupación;
– Rama de actividad;
– Características geográficas;
– Experiencia laboral previa;
– Ciudadanía (nacionales o no);
– Duración del desempleo;
– Otras: jóvenes (de 15 a 17 años); discapacidad.
Publicación: En papel, para el público en general.
Organismo responsable de la publicación: Servicio de Empleo.
Título y periodicidad de la publicación: *Statistical Review on Employment* (Examen estadístico del empleo), cada cuatro meses.
N.B. Algunas cifras de desempleo también se publican en el sitio web del Servicio de Empleo: http://ncb.intent.mu/empserv.htm.

10. Información metodológica sobre las estadísticas

Divulgación: En papel, para el público en general.
Organismo responsable de la divulgación: Servicio de Empleo.
11. Comparaciones con estadísticas derivadas de otras fuentes
No se han hecho comparaciones con estadísticas de desempleo derivadas de otras fuentes.
12. Modificaciones importantes desde el comienzo de las estadísticas
En la legislación, la competencia del organismo y/o los procedimientos administrativos no ha habido modificaciones importantes que hayan influido significativamente en las estadísticas.

Moldova, Rep. de

1. Serie
Título: Desempleo registrado.
Año de inicio: 1992.
2. Organismo responsable de la inscripción inicial de desempleados
Nombre del organismo: Oficinas de empleo a nivel regional.
Tipo de organismo: Organismo público subordinado a autoridades nacionales y regionales.
Nombre de la autoridad nacional: Departamento de Utilización de la Fuerza de Trabajo, Ministerio de Trabajo y Protección Social.
Ubicación de las oficinas locales donde se hacen las inscripciones: Hay 12 oficinas de empleo (una en cada condado) y 33 secciones de empleo en las ciudades de todo el país. Estas secciones están bajo la dirección de las oficinas de empleo de los condados que dependen del Departamento de Utilización de la Fuerza de Trabajo.
Tipo de servicios proporcionados/administrados por el organismo:
– Ayuda a personas en busca de empleo a encontrarlo;
– Ayuda a personas en busca de empleo a crear su propia empresa;
– Ayuda a los empleadores a encontrar trabajadores;
– Orientación profesional;
– Formación relacionada con el trabajo;
– Pago de prestaciones de desempleo;
– Otros: organización y presentación de exposiciones de trabajo, formación en centros de trabajo y formación para trabajos públicos remunerados.
Porcentaje de personas en busca de empleo que buscan trabajo por intermedio de ese organismo: 50%.
3. Se registran los siguientes datos de la persona:
– Nombre y apellido;
– Sexo;
– Número de seguridad social (o número de identificación semejante también utilizado por otros organismos);
– Dirección del domicilio habitual;
– Fecha de nacimiento;
– Nivel de educación/formación: se identifican cinco categorías. No se han establecido vínculos con la CINE;
– Tipo de ocupación del empleo actual o anterior. Se han establecido vínculos con la CIUO-88;
– Tipo de ocupación del empleo que se busca. Se han establecido vínculos con la CIUO-88;
– Nombre y dirección del empleador o del lugar de trabajo actual o anterior;
– Rama de actividad del empleador o del lugar de trabajo actual o anterior: se identifican 11 grupos;
– Otros: estado civil; número de la cédula de identidad; detalles del trabajo anterior (fechas de servicio, motivo de haberlo dejado, salario medio de los tres últimos meses, etc.); categoría de protección social; categoría de prestaciones de desempleo; situación militar; conocimiento de idiomas; formación especial.
4. Criterios utilizados para determinar si una persona habrá de incluirse en el registro (R) y/o en las estadísticas de personas desempleadas (S):
– Estar sin empleo (R) y (S);
– Estar en busca de empleo (R) y (S);
– Estar disponible para trabajar (R) y (S);
– Edad (mínima: 16 años; máxima: edad de jubilación) (R) y (S);
– Residir en el país (R) y (S);
– Haber trabajado (incluidos los trabajos públicos remunerados y el trabajo temporal) (R) y (S);
– Pago de cotizaciones del seguro de desempleo (R) y (S).

5. Criterios utilizados para determinar si se ha de excluir a una persona del registro (R) y/o de las estadísticas de personas desempleadas (S):
– Certificado de defunción (R) y (S);
– Establecerse en otro país (R) y (S);
– Incorporarse a un (nuevo) empleo (R) y (S);
– Comenzar el servicio militar (R) y (S);
– Participar en algún programa de promoción del empleo, de obras públicas, etc. (R) y (S);
– Estar estudiando o siguiendo una formación (R) y (S);
– Incumplir el requisito de tomar contacto con el organismo por más de dos meses (R) y (S);
– Rechazar dos ofertas de empleo adecuadas (R) y (S);
– Cobrar alguna pensión (R) y (S);
– Incapacidad para trabajar (R) y (S).
6. Definición de persona desempleada en la que se basan las estadísticas
El Servicio Estatal de Utilización de la Fuerza de Trabajo se rige por la definición de la Ley de utilización de la fuerza de trabajo que dice:
Se considera desempleado a todo ciudadano disponible para trabajar que no tiene un empleo adecuado ni ingresos legales y que está registrado en la oficina de empleo de su zona o lugar de residencia como persona en busca de empleo.
7. Actualización de los registros
Los registros se actualizan a diario.
8. Tasas de desempleo
Se utilizan estadísticas de estos registros para obtener tasas "oficiales" de desempleo de la República de Moldova (la tasa de desempleo "real" se obtiene a través de la Encuesta sobre la fuerza de trabajo).
Fuentes de los datos de empleo incluidos en el denominador de las tasas de desempleo:
Encuesta sobre la fuerza de trabajo y Censo de población.
Definición de persona empleada que se utiliza a tales efectos:
Persona de 15 años o más que ejerció una actividad económica o social en el sector de producción o de servicios durante una hora, como mínimo, en un determinado período (una semana) mediando salario u otros beneficios.

9. Tipo de estadísticas que se producen sobre desempleados registrados
Serie 1:
Período de referencia: Mes.
Frecuencia de producción: Mensual.
Variables utilizadas:
– Sexo.
Publicación: En papel, para el público en general.
Organismo responsable de la publicación: Departamento de Utilización de la Fuerza de Trabajo.
Título y periodicidad de la publicación: *Monthly Statistical Report* (Informe estadístico mensual).
Serie 2:
Período de referencia: Trimestre.
Frecuencia de producción: Trimestral.
Variables utilizadas:
– Sexo;
– Edad;
– Nivel de educación;
– Ocupación;
– Rama de actividad;
– Características geográficas;
– Duración del desempleo.
Publicación: En papel, para el público en general.
Organismo responsable de la publicación: Departamento de Utilización de la Fuerza de Trabajo.
Título y periodicidad de la publicación: *Quarterly Statistical Report* (Informe estadístico trimestral).
Serie 3:
Período de referencia: Trimestre.
Frecuencia de producción: Trimestral.
Variables utilizadas:
– Sexo;
– Edad;
– Nivel de educación;
– Ocupación;
– Rama de actividad;
Publicación: En papel, para el público en general.

Organismo responsable de la publicación: Departamento de Estadística y Sociología.

Título y periodicidad de la publicación: *Quarterly Statistical Bulletin* (Boletín estadístico trimestral).

Serie 4:

Período de referencia: Año.

Frecuencia de producción: Anual.

Variables utilizadas:
- Sexo;
- Edad;
- Nivel de educación;
- Ocupación;
- Rama de actividad;
- Características geográficas;
- Ciudadanía (nacionales o no);
- Duración del desempleo.

Publicación: En papel, para el público en general.

Organismo responsable de la publicación: Departamento de Estadística y Sociología.

Título y periodicidad de la publicación: *Statistical Yearbook* (Anuario estadístico).

10. Información metodológica sobre las estadísticas

Divulgación: En papel, para el público en general.

Organismos responsables: Departamento de Utilización de la Fuerza de Trabajo; Departamento de Estadística y Sociología.

11. Comparaciones con estadísticas derivadas de otras fuentes

Se han hecho comparaciones con estadísticas de desempleo derivadas de varias fuentes; las estadísticas "oficiales" se comparan con las estadísticas "reales" del Departamento de Estadística y Sociología.

Frecuencia de las comparaciones: Periódica, cuando se publican las estadísticas.

Publicación de la metodología/resultados de las comparaciones: Se publican en *Quarterly Statistical Report* (Informe estadístico trimestral), *Statistical Yearbook* (Anuario estadístico) y otros documentos.

12. Modificaciones importantes desde el comienzo de las estadísticas

En la legislación, la competencia del organismo y/o los procedimientos administrativos no ha habido modificaciones importantes que hayan influido significativamente en las estadísticas.

Mongolia

1. Serie

Título: Ciudadanos desempleados en busca de empleo y ciudadanos que corren el riesgo de quedar desempleados.

Año de inicio: 1991.

2. Organismo responsable de la inscripción inicial de desempleados

Nombre del organismo: Oficinas de empleo.

Tipo de organismo: Organismo público subordinado a autoridades nacionales, regionales, provinciales y locales.

Nombre de la autoridad nacional: Organismo de Ejecución del Gobierno de Mongolia, Oficina Central de Empleo.

Ubicación de las oficinas locales donde se hacen las inscripciones: En todos los distritos y provincias del país.

Tipo de servicios proporcionados/administrados por el organismo:
- Ayuda a personas en busca de empleo a encontrarlo;
- Ayuda a personas en busca de empleo a crear su propia empresa;
- Ayuda a los empleadores a encontrar trabajadores;
- Orientación profesional;
- Formación relacionada con el trabajo;
- Pago de prestaciones de desempleo;
- Otros: apoyo a empleadores; promoción del autoempleo.

Porcentaje de personas en busca de empleo que buscan trabajo por intermedio de ese organismo: 4,8%.

3. Se registran los siguientes datos de la persona:
- Nombre y apellido;
- Sexo;
- Número de seguridad social (o número de identificación semejante también utilizado por otros organismos),
- Dirección del domicilio habitual;
- Fecha de nacimiento;
- Ciudadanía;
- Nivel de educación/formación: se identifican seis

categorías. No se han establecido vínculos con la CINE;
- Situación laboral actual o anterior: se identifican siete categorías;
- Tipo de ocupación del empleo actual o anterior: se identifican nueve grupos. Se han establecido vínculos con la CIUO-88 a nivel de grandes grupos;
- Tipo de ocupación del empleo que se busca: se identifican nueve grupos. Se han establecido vínculos con la CIUO-88 a nivel de grandes grupos;
- Nombre y dirección del empleador o del lugar de trabajo actual o anterior;
- Rama de actividad del empleador o del lugar de trabajo actual o anterior: se identifican 17 grupos. Se han establecido vínculos con la CIIU Rev. 3 ;
- Inscripciones previas en el organismo;
- Otros: estado de salud; estado civil; ingresos del hogar; motivo del desempleo; motivo de haber renunciado al puesto de trabajo; derecho a prestaciones de desempleo; motivo del riesgo de quedar desempleado.

4. Criterios utilizados para determinar si una persona habrá de incluirse en el registro (R) y/o en las estadísticas de personas desempleadas (S):
- Estar sin empleo (incluidos trabajadores por cuenta propia que trabajan menos de 15 horas por semana y ganan menos del salario mínimo) (R) y (S);
- Estar en busca de empleo (R) y (S);
- Estar disponible para trabajar (R) y (S);
- Edad (mínima: 16 años; máxima: 60 años) (R) y (S);
- Ciudadanía (sólo ciudadanos de Mongolia) (R) y (S);
- Residir en el país (R) y (S);
- Otros: cpacidad para trabajar (R) y (S).

5. Criterios utilizados para determinar si se ha de excluir a una persona del registro (R) y/o de las estadísticas de personas desempleadas (S):
- Certificado de defunción (R) y (S);
- Establecerse en otro país (R) y (S);
- Incorporarse a un (nuevo) empleo (R) y (S);
- Comenzar el servicio militar (R) y (S);
- Participar en algún programa de promoción del empleo, de obras públicas, etc. (R) y (S);
- Estar estudiando o siguiendo una formación (R) y (S);
- Incumplir el requisito de tomar contacto con el organismo (R) y (S);
- Rechazar tres ofertas de empleo adecuadas (R) y (S);
- Rechazar tres ofertas de formación adecuadas (R) y (S);
- Cobrar jubilación (R) y (S);
- Incapacidad para trabajar (R) y (S);
- Otros: rechazo de tres ofertas de empleo adecuadas en obras públicas (R) y (S).

6. Definición de persona desempleada en la que se basan las estadísticas

Se entiende por "ciudadano desempleado" a todo aquel físicamente apto para trabajar, que está en edad de trabajar y dispuesto a aceptar un empleo, que busca trabajo activamente y está registrado en la oficina de empleo (Ley de promoción del empleo, 2001).

7. Actualización de los registros

Los registros se actualizan mensualmente.

8. Tasas de desempleo

Se utilizan estadísticas de estos registros para obtener tasas de desempleo.

Fuentes de los datos de empleo incluidos en el denominador de las tasas de desempleo:

Encuesta sobre la fuerza de trabajo; Censo de población; Informe mensual de desempleo (Oficina Nacional de Estadística); Cuadro de resultados de los programas de gestión del mercado de trabajo (Oficina Central de Empleo) y Encuesta anual de empleo de la población (Oficina Nacional de Estadística).

Definición de persona empleada que se utiliza a tales efectos:

Se considera empleada a toda persona que trabaja en entidades u organizaciones o que dirige una empresa privada mediando salario, o que trabaja por cuenta propia.

9. Tipo de estadísticas que se producen sobre desempleados registrados

Serie 1:

Período de referencia: Mes y año.

Frecuencia de producción: Mensual y anual.

Variables utilizadas:
- Sexo;
- Edad;
- Nivel de educación;

- Ocupación;
- Rama de actividad;
- Características geográficas;
- Otras: número de vacantes; fuerza da trabajo; mediación laboral; población en edad de trabajar con incapacidad para trabajar; formación profesional; obra pública; autoempleo; prestaciones de desempleo; empleo de extranjeros; instructores.

Publicación: En papel, para el público en general.

Organismo responsable de la publicación: Oficina Nacional de Estadística .

Título y periodicidad de la publicación: *The Social Economic Situation of Mongolia* (La situación socioeconómica de Mongolia), mensual y anual.

Serie 2:

Período de referencia: Mes, trimestre, semestre y año.

Frecuencia de producción: Mensual, trimestral, semestral y anual.

Variables utilizadas:

- Sexo;
- Edad;
- Nivel de educación;
- Ocupación;
- Rama de actividad;
- Características geográficas;
- Experiencia laboral previa;
- Ciudadanía (nacionales o no);
- Duración del desempleo.

Publicación: En papel, para un público limitado.

Organismo responsable de la publicación: Oficina Central de Empleo.

Título y periodicidad de la publicación: *Labour Market Report* (Informe del mercado de trabajo), mensual, trimestral, semestral y anual.

Serie 3:

Período de referencia: Año.

Frecuencia de producción: Anual.

Variables utilizadas:

- Sexo;
- Edad;
- Nivel de educación;
- Ocupación;
- Rama de actividad;
- Características geográficas;
- Experiencia laboral previa;
- Ciudadanía (nacionales o no);
- Duración del desempleo.

Publicación: En papel, para un público limitado.

Organismo responsable de la publicación: Oficina Nacional de Estadística.

Título y periodicidad de la publicación: *Annual Employment Survey of the Population* (Encuesta anual de empleo de la población), anual.

10. Información metodológica sobre las estadísticas

Divulgación: En papel, para el público en general.

Organismos responsables: Oficina Nacional de Estadística; Ministerio de Bienestar Social y Trabajo.

11. Comparaciones con estadísticas derivadas de otras fuentes

Se han hecho comparaciones con estadísticas de desempleo derivadas de la Encuesta sobre la fuerza de trabajo, otro tipo de encuesta de hogares y el Censo de población.

Frecuencia de las comparaciones: Periódica, cuando se publican las estadísticas.

Publicación de la metodología/resultados de las comparaciones: Se han publicado.

12. Modificaciones importantes desde el comienzo de las estadísticas

En la legislación, la competencia del organismo y/o los procedimientos administrativos hubo modificaciones importantes en i) 1993; ii) 1995; iii) 1997, y iv) 2001 que se tradujeron por: un aumento de 2,4% en el número total de personas desempleadas registradas en 1993; una disminución de 3,3% en 1995; un aumento de 2,2% en 1997, y una disminución de 3,2% en 2001.

1993: Se empezó a llevar el registo oficial de personas desempleadas;

1995: Se llevó a cabo la Encuesta nacional sobre pobreza y desempleo;

1997: Promulgación de la Ley de prestaciones de desempleo por la que se estipula el derecho de las personas desempleadas a recibir prestaciones de desempleo del Fondo de Seguro Social;

2001: Promulgación de la Ley de promoción del empleo.

Myanmar

1. Serie

Título: Estadísticas de la bolsa de trabajo.

Año de inicio: Alrededor de 1950.

2. Organismo responsable de la inscripción inicial de desempleados

Nombre del organismo: División de Empleo y Formación.

Tipo de organismo: Organismo público subordinado a una autoridad nacional.

Nombre de la autoridad nacional: Departamento de Trabajo.

Ubicación de las oficinas locales donde se hacen las inscripciones: Las inscripciones se hacen en las bolsas de trabajo de las oficinas de trabajo municipales; hay 78 en todo el país.

Tipo de servicios proporcionados/administrados por el organismo:

- Ayuda a personas en busca de empleo a encontrarlo;
- Ayuda a los empleadores a encontrar trabajadores;
- Orientación profesional;
- Formación relacionada con el trabajo;
- Otros: empleo en el extranjero.

Porcentaje de personas en busca de empleo que buscan trabajo por intermedio de ese organismo: Según la Ley de restricciones del empleo, de 1959, todo empleador que emplea cinco o más trabajadores debe contratarlos por conducto de las bolsas de trabajo del Departamento de Trabajo.

3. Se registran los siguientes datos de la persona:

- Nombre y apellido;
- Sexo;
- Dirección del domicilio habitual;
- Fecha de nacimiento;
- Ciudadanía;
- Nivel de educación/formación. No se han establecido vínculos con la CINE;
- Situación laboral actual o anterior;
- Tipo de ocupación del empleo actual o anterior. Se han establecido vínculos con la CIUO-88 a nivel de grupos primarios. (La Clasificación Uniforme de Ocupaciones de Myanmar se basa en la CIUO-88);
- Tipo de ocupación del empleo que se busca. Se han establecido vínculos con la CIUO-88 a nivel de grupos primarios. (La Clasificación Uniforme de Ocupaciones de Myanmar se basa en la CIUO-88);
- Nombre y dirección del empleador o del lugar de trabajo actual o anterior;
- Rama de actividad del empleador o del lugar de trabajo actual o anterior: se identifican 10 grupos. No se han establecido vínculos con la CIIU Rev. 3;
- Inscripciones previas en el organismo;
- Otros: renovación y validación del registro cada seis meses.

4. Criterios utilizados para determinar si una persona habrá de incluirse en el registro (R) y/o en las estadísticas de personas desempleadas (S):

- Estar sin empleo (R);
- Estar en busca de empleo (R);
- Estar disponible para trabajar (R);
- Edad (mínima: 18 años; máxima: 60 años) (R);
- Ciudadanía (R);
- Residir en el país (R);
- Haber trabajado (R);
- Duración y/o número de horas de trabajo del empleo que se busca (R).

5. Criterios utilizados para determinar si se ha de excluir a una persona del registro (R) y/o de las estadísticas de personas desempleadas (S):

- Certificado de defunción (R);
- Establecerse en otro país (R);
- Incorporarse a un (nuevo) empleo (R);
- Comenzar el servicio militar (R);
- Participar en algún programa de promoción del empleo, de obras públicas, etc. (R);
- Estar estudiando o siguiendo una formación (R);
- Incumplir el requisito de tomar contacto con el organismo por más de seis meses (R);
- Rechazar dos ofertas de empleo adecuadas (R);
- Rechazar dos ofertas de formación adecuadas (R);
- Incapacidad para trabajar (R).

6. Definición de persona desempleada en la que se basan las estadísticas

Personas en busca de empleo registradas en las bolsas de trabajo.

7. Actualización de los registros

Los registros se actualizan mensualmente.

8. Tasas de desempleo

No se utilizan estadísticas de estos registros para obtener tasas de desempleo.

9. Tipo de estadísticas que se producen sobre desempleados registrados

Serie 1:

Período de referencia: Mes.

Frecuencia de producción: Mensual.

Variables utilizadas:
- Sexo;
- Edad;
- Nivel de educación;
- Ocupación;
- Rama de actividad;
- Características geográficas;
- Experiencia laboral previa;
- Ciudadanía (nacionales o no);
- Duración del desempleo;

Publicación: En papel, para un público limitado.

Organismo responsable de la publicación: Organización Central de Estadística.

Periodicidad de la publicación: Anual.

Serie 2:

Los datos anuales sobre bolsas de trabajo, nuevas personas registradas, personas colocadas, registro caducado, personas registradas a finales del año, vacantes notificadas y puestos que siguen vacantes a finales de año se publican en el *Statistical Yearbook* (Anuario Estadístico) de la Organización Central de Estadística.

10. Información metodológica sobre las estadísticas

Divulgación: No se divulgan; sólo para uso interno.

11. Comparaciones con estadísticas derivadas de otras fuentes

No se han hecho comparaciones con estadísticas de desempleo derivadas de otras fuentes.

12. Modificaciones importantes desde el comienzo de las estadísticas

En la legislación, la competencia del organismo y/o los procedimientos administrativos hubo modificaciones importantes en 1959. Los cambios consiguientes en las estadísticas no se han estimado.

Níger

1. Serie

Título: Estadísticas de personas en busca de empleo.

Año de inicio: 1982.

2. Organismo responsable de la inscripción inicial de desempleados

Nombre del organismo: Agence nationale pour la Promotion de l'Emploi - ANPE (Agencia Nacional de Promoción del Empleo).

Tipo de organismo: Organismo público subordinado a una autoridad nacional.

Nombre de la autoridad nacional: Ministerio de Trabajo

Ubicación de las oficinas locales donde se hacen las inscripciones: Niamey, Tillabery, Dosso, Tahara, Maradi, Zinder, Diffa, Arlit y Agadez.

Tipo de servicios proporcionados/administrados por el organismo
- Ayuda a personas en busca de empleo a encontrarlo;
- Ayuda a personas en busca de empleo a crear su propia empresa (sólo en Niamey);
- Ayuda a los empleadores a encontrar trabajadores;
- Orientación profesional (sólo en Niamey);
- Formación relacionada con el trabajo (sólo en Niamey);
- Otros: programas de inserción de diplomados jóvenes; producción de datos estadísticos sobre la evolución del mercado de trabajo; programa de inserción en el sector informal.

3. Se registran los siguientes datos de la persona
- Nombre y apellido;
- Sexo;
- Fecha de nacimiento;
- Nacionalidad;
- Nivel de educación/formación: se identifican cuatro

categorías. No se han establecido vínculos con la CINE;
- Tipo de ocupación del empleo que se busca.

4. Criterios utilizados para determinar si una persona habrá de incluirse en el registro (R) y/o en las estadísticas de personas desempleadas (S)
- Estar sin empleo (R) y (S);
- Estar en busca de empleo (R) y (S);
- Estar disponible para trabajar (R) y (S);
- Edad (mínima: 18 años; máxima: 60 años) (R) y (S);
- Ciudadanía, la tarjeta de inscripción se expide únicamente a los extranjeros que reúnen las condiciones estipuladas por reglamento (R);
- Residir en el país (R) y (S);
- Haber trabajado(S);
- Duración y/o número de horas de trabajo del empleo que se busca (R) y (S).

5. Criterios utilizados para determinar si se ha de excluir a una persona del registro (R) y/o de las estadísticas de personas desempleadas (S)
- Certificado de defunción (R) y (S);
- Establecerse en otro país (R) y (S);
- Incorporarse a un (nuevo) empleo (R) y (S);
- Estar estudiando o siguiendo una formación (R) y (S);
- Incapacidad para trabajar (R) y (S).

6. Definición de persona desempleada en la que se basan las estadísticas

Las estadísticas de desempleo se establecen a partir del registro en el que se inscribe a las personas en busca de empleo. De ahí que se considere desempleada a toda persona en busca de empleo inscrita en el registro de la ANPE durante el período de referencia.

7. Actualización de los registros

Los registros se actualizan periódicamente.

8. Tasas de desempleo

No se utilizan estadísticas de estos registros para obtener tasas de desempleo.

9. Tipo de estadísticas que se producen sobre desempleados registrados

Serie 1: Estadísticas de personas en busca de empleo.

Frecuencia de producción: Mensual.

Variables utilizadas
- Sexo;
- Edad;
- Ocupación.

Publicación: En papel, para un público limitado.

Organismo responsable de la publicación: ANPE.

Título y periodicidad de la publicación: *Rapport statistique* (Informe estadístico).

Serie 2: Estadísticas de solicitantes de empleo y mano de obra.

Frecuencia de producción: Anual.

Variables utilizadas
- Sexo;
- Edad;
- Nivel de educación;
- Ocupación;
- Características geográficas.

Publicación: En papel, para el público en general.

Organismo responsable de la publicación: ANPE.

Título y periodicidad de la publicación: *Rapport statistique* (Informe estadístico).

10. Información metodológica sobre las estadísticas

Divulgación: En papel, para el público en general.

Organismo responsable de la divulgación: ANPE.

11. Comparaciones con estadísticas derivadas de otras fuentes

No se han hecho comparaciones con estadísticas de desempleo derivadas de otras fuentes.

12. Modificaciones importantes desde el comienzo de las estadísticas

La ANPE existe desde 1996. Anteriormente, el repertorio de personas en busca de empleo estaba a cargo del Servicio de Mano de Obra y las inspecciones del trabajo.

Nigeria

1. Serie

Título: Estadísticas de la bolsa de trabajo.

2. Organismo responsable de la inscripción inicial de desempleados

Nombre del organismo: Bolsa de trabajo, registros, registros profesional y ejecutivo.

Tipo de organismo: Organismo público subordinado a una autoridad nacional.

Nombre de la autoridad nacional: Ministerio Federal de Empleo, Trabajo y Productividad.

Pero se está considerando la operación y el control de agencias de empleo privadas.

Ubicación de las oficinas locales donde se hacen las inscripciones: En la capital de todos los Estados de la Federación (37 redes estatales), en zonas donde hay una alta densidad demográfica, donde hay establecimientos industriales que requieren servicios de trabajadores y en ciudades donde hay universidades y otras instituciones de enseñanza superior.

Tipo de servicios proporcionados/administrados por el organismo

– Ayuda a personas en busca de empleo a encontrarlo;
– Ayuda a personas en busca de empleo a crear su propia empresa;
– Ayuda a los empleadores a encontrar trabajadores;
– Orientación profesional;
– Formación relacionada con el trabajo;
– Certificado de artesano para empleo remunerativo y autoempleo.

Porcentaje de personas en busca de empleo que buscan trabajo por intermedio de ese organismo: 60%.

3. Se registran los siguientes datos de la persona

– Nombre y apellido;
– Sexo;
– Dirección del domicilio habitual;
– Fecha de nacimiento;
– Ciudadanía;
– Nacionalidad/grupo étnico;
– Nivel de educación/formación: se identifican tres categorías: calificada, semicalificada y no calificada. Se han establecido vínculos con la CINE;
– Situación laboral actual o anterior;
– Tipo de ocupación del empleo actual o anterior;
– Tipo de ocupación del empleo que se busca. Se han establecido vínculos con la CIUO-88 a nivel de grandes grupos;
– Nombre y dirección del empleador o del lugar de trabajo actual o anterior;
– Rama de actividad del empleador o del lugar de trabajo actual o anterior. Se han establecido vínculos con la CIIU a nivel de grupos;
– Inscripciones previas en el organismo.

4. Criterios utilizados para determinar si una persona habrá de incluirse en el registro (R) y/o en las estadísticas de personas desempleadas (S)

– Estar sin empleo (R) y (S);
– Estar en busca de empleo (R) y (S);
– Estar disponible para trabajar (R) y (S);
– Edad (mínima:18 años; máxima: 60 años) (R) y (S);
– Ciudadanía: nigerianos de nacimiento, por matrimonio o naturalización;
– Residir en el país.

5. Criterios utilizados para determinar si se ha de excluir a una persona del registro (R) y/o de las estadísticas de personas desempleadas (S)

– Certificado de defunción (R) y (S);
– Establecerse en otro país (R) y (S);
– Incorporarse a un (nuevo) empleo (R) y (S);
– Comenzar el servicio militar (R) y (S);
– Participar en algún programa de promoción del empleo, de obras públicas, etc. (R) y (S);
– Estar estudiando o siguiendo una formación (R) y (S);
– Incumplir el requisito de tomar contacto con el organismo, es preciso renovar los documentos del registro periódicamente (R) y (S);
– Rechazar ofertas de trabajo adecuadas (R) y (S);
– Rechazar ofertas de formación adecuadas (R) y (S);
– Incapacidad para trabajar (R) y (S).

6. Definición de persona desempleada en la que se basan las estadísticas

Personas de edades comprendidas entre 18 y 60 años que buscan empleo activamente, quieren trabajar, están físicamente aptas para hacerlo, y ganan menos del salario mínimo nacional.

7. Actualización de los registros

Los registros se actualizan periódicamente.

Frecuencia de actualización: Mensual, trimestral y anual.

8. Tasas de desempleo

Se utilizan estadísticas de estos registros para obtener tasas de desempleo.

Fuentes de los datos de empleo incluidos en el denominador de las tasas de desempleo: Encuesta sobre la fuerza de trabajo, Encuesta de establecimientos, Registro de la Seguridad Social y Censo de población.

Definición de persona empleada que se utiliza a tales efectos

Personas que participan activamente en el empleo y no ganan menos del salario mínimo nacional.

9. Tipo de estadísticas que se producen sobre desempleados registrados

Período de referencia: Mes.

Frecuencia de producción: Trimestral.

Variables utilizadas

– Sexo;
– Edad;
– Nivel de educación;
– Ocupación;
– Rama de actividad;
– Características geográficas;
– Experiencia laboral previa;
– Ciudadanía;
– Duración del desempleo.

Publicación

– En papel, para el público en general;
– En archivo electrónico, previa solicitud.

Organismo responsable de la publicación: Ministerio Federal de Empleo, Trabajo y Productividad.

Título y periodicidad de la publicación: *Employment Exchange & Professional & Executive Registry Statistics* (Estadísticas de la bolsa de trabajo y el registro profesional y ejecutivo), mensual, trimestral y anual.

10. Información metodológica sobre las estadísticas

Divulgación

– En papel, para el público en general;
– En archivo electrónico, previa solicitud;
– Sitio web en preparación.

11. Comparaciones con estadísticas derivadas de otras fuentes

No se han hecho comparaciones con estadísticas de desempleo derivadas de otras fuentes.

12. Modificaciones importantes desde el comienzo de las estadísticas

En la legislación, la competencia del organismo y/o los procedimientos administrativos no ha habido modificaciones importantes que hayan influido significativamente en las estadísticas.

Noruega

1. Serie

Título: Estadísticas del Mercado de Trabajo.

Año de inicio: 1948.

2. Organismo responsable de la inscripción inicial de desempleados

Nombre del organismo: Servicio de Empleo de Distrito (Aestat).

Tipo de organismo: Organismo público subordinado a una autoridad nacional.

Nombre de la autoridad nacional: Dirección de Trabajo.

Ubicación de las oficinas locales donde se hacen las inscripciones: 200 oficinas locales hacen los registros principales. Un centro nacional de registro lleva a cabo parte de la actualización de los registros y algunos registros relacionados con las estadísticas de vacantes.

Tipo de servicios proporcionados/administrados por el organismo:

– Ayuda a personas en busca de empleo a encontrarlo;
– Ayuda a los empleadores a encontrar trabajadores;
– Orientación profesional;
– Formación relacionada con el trabajo;
– Medidas de rehabilitación laboral;
– Prestaciones para desempleados;
– Otros servicios relacionados con el empleo.

Porcentaje de personas en busca de empleo que buscan trabajo por intermedio de ese organismo: 75%.

3. Se registran los siguientes datos de la persona:

– Nombre y apellido;
– Sexo;
– Número de seguridad social (o número de identificación semejante también utilizado por otros organismos);

- Dirección del domicilio habitual;
- Fecha de nacimiento;
- Ciudadanía;
- Nacionalidad;
- Nivel de educación/formación: se identifican ocho categorías. Se han establecido vínculos con la CINE;
- Tipo de ocupación del empleo actual o anterior: se identifica un número indeterminado de grupos. Se han establecido vínculos con la CIUO-88 a nivel de grupos primarios;
- Tipo de ocupación del empleo que se busca: se identifica un número indeterminado de grupos. Se han establecido vínculos con la CIUO-88 a nivel de grupos primarios;
- Inscripciones previas en el organismo.

4. Criterios utilizados para determinar si una persona habrá de incluirse en el registro (R) y/o en las estadísticas de personas desempleadas (S):
- Estar sin empleo (los últimos 14 días antes del día del recuento) (S);
- Estar en busca de empleo (R) y (S);
- Estar disponible para trabajar (R) y (S);
- Residir en el país (S).

5. Criterios utilizados para determinar si se ha de excluir a una persona del registro (R) y/o de las estadísticas de personas desempleadas (S):
- Certificado de defunción (R) y (S);
- Establecerse en otro país (R) y (S);
- Incorporarse a un (nuevo) empleo (S);
- Comenzar el servicio militar (S);
- Participar en algún programa de promoción del empleo, de obras públicas, etc. (S);
- Estar estudiando o siguiendo una formación (los estudiantes y quienes participan en programas de formación no se contabilizan como desempleados aun cuando puedan ser personas en busca de empleo) (S);
- Incumplir el requisito de enviar la tarjeta de desempleado cada 14 días al centro nacional de registro (R) y (S).

6. Definición de persona desempleada en la que se basan las estadísticas

Los criterios principales son: estar en busca de empleo, no tener trabajo remunerado y estar disponible para trabajar.

Se considera persona en busca de empleo cuando se ha sido recibido/rellenado la tarjeta de desempleado para las dos semanas anteriores o cuando fue a registrarse en el servicio local de empleo. Si indica que no ha tenido trabajo en las dos semanas anteriores, se contabiliza como desempleada. Si tuvo algún empleo en esas dos semanas, se contabiliza como desempleada parcial.

7. Actualización de los registros

Los registros se actualizan semanalmente.

8. Tasas de desempleo

Se utilizan estadísticas de estos registros para obtener tasas de desempleo.

Fuente de los datos de empleo incluidos en el denominador de las tasas de desempleo: Encuesta sobre la fuerza de trabajo.

Definición de persona empleada que se utiliza a tales efectos:

Personas de 16 a 74 años que hicieron un trabajo por el cual recibieron remuneración o beneficios, una hora como mínimo, en la semana de la encuesta.

9. Tipo de estadísticas que se producen sobre desempleados registrados
Serie 1:
Período de referencia: Mes.
Frecuencia de producción: Mensual.
Variables utilizadas:
- Sexo;
- Edad;
- Nivel de educación;
- Ocupación;
- Características geográficas;
- Duración del desempleo;
- Otras: Beneficiario de prestaciones de desempleo.

Publicación:
- En papel, para el público en general;
- En el sitio web www.aetat.no

Organismo responsable de la publicación: Dirección de Trabajo.
Título y periodicidad de la publicación: *Månedsstatistikk* (Estadísticas mensuales).
Serie 2:
Período de referencia: Año.
Frecuencia de producción: Anual.

Variables utilizadas:
- Sexo;
- Edad;
- Nivel de educación;
- Ocupación;
- Características geográficas;
- Duración del desempleo;
- Otras: Beneficiario de prestaciones de desempleo.

Publicación :
- En papel, para el público en general;
- En el sitio web www.aetat.no

Organismo responsable de la publicación: Dirección de Trabajo.
Título de la publicación: *Historisk Statistikk* (Estadísticas históricas).

10. Información metodológica sobre las estadísticas
Divulgación:
- En papel, para el público en general,
- En el sitio web www.aetat.no

Organismo responsable: División de Planificación y Análisis de la Dirección de Trabajo.

11. Comparaciones con estadísticas derivadas de otras fuentes

Se han hecho comparaciones con estadísticas de desempleo derivadas de la Encuesta sobre la fuerza de trabajo.
Frecuencia de las comparaciones: De vez en cuando.
Publicación de la metodología/resultados de las comparaciones: Se publicaron en *Notater, nr. 99/31* (Estadísticas de Noruega): "... Clasificación de desempleo registrado y participantes en programas de mercado de trabajo en la Encuesta sobre la fuerza de trabajo" (sólo en noruego).

12. Modificaciones importantes desde el comienzo de las estadísticas

En la legislación, la competencia del organismo y/o los procedimientos administrativos no ha habido modificaciones importantes que hayan influido significativamente en las estadísticas.

Nueva Caledonia

1. Serie
Título: Estadísticas de la demanda de empleo.
Año de inicio: 1991.

2. Organismo responsable de la inscripción inicial de desempleados
Nombre del organismo: Agencia de Empleo de Nueva Caledonia.
Tipo de organismo: Organismo público subordinado a una autoridad local.
Ubicación de las oficinas locales donde se hacen las inscripciones: Una delegación en cada una de las tres provincias y centros en varias comunas.
Tipo de servicios proporcionados/administrados por el organismo
- Ayuda a personas en busca de empleo a encontrarlo;
- Ayuda a personas en busca de empleo a crear su propia empresa;
- Ayuda a los empleadores a encontrar trabajadores;
- Orientación profesional;
- Formación relacionada con el trabajo;
- Otros: dispositivo de balance de competencias; instrucción de expedientes para tomar decisiones relativas a los desempleados que tienen derecho a prestaciones.

Porcentaje de personas en busca de empleo que buscan trabajo por intermedio de ese organismo: 70%.
3. Se registran los siguientes datos de la persona
- Nombre y apellido;
- Sexo;
- Número de seguridad social (o número de identificación semejante también utilizado por otros organismos);
- Dirección del domicilio habitual;
- Fecha de nacimiento;
- Nacionalidad;
- Nivel de educación/formación: se identifican seis categorías. Se han establecido vínculos con la CINE;
- Situación laboral actual o anterior;
- Tipo de ocupación del empleo actual o anterior: se identifican 1.178 categorías. No se han establecido vínculos con la CIUO-88;
- Tipo de ocupación del empleo que se busca: se identifican 1.178 categorías;
- Nombre y dirección del empleador o del lugar de trabajo actual o anterior;
- Rama de actividad del empleador o del lugar de trabajo

actual o anterior: se identifican 697 categorías. No se han establecido vínculos con la CIIU;
– Inscripciones previas en el organismo.

4. Criterios utilizados para determinar si una persona habrá de incluirse en el registro (R) y/o en las estadísticas de personas desempleadas (S)
– Estar sin empleo (R) y (S);
– Estar disponible para trabajar (R) y (S);
– Edad (mínima: 16 años; no hay edad máxima) (R) y (S);
– Residir en el país (R) y (S).

5. Criterios utilizados para determinar si se ha de excluir a una persona del registro (R) y/o de las estadísticas de personas desempleadas (S)
– Certificado de defunción (R) y (S);
– Establecerse en otro país (R) y (S);
– Incorporarse a un (nuevo) empleo (R) y (S);
– Comenzar el servicio militar (R) y (S);
– Incumplir el requisito de tomar contacto con el organismo (R) y (S);
– Incapacidad para trabajar (R) y (S).

6. Definición de persona desempleada en la que se basan las estadísticas
Toda persona física que se presenta a inscribirse en la Agencia de Empleo y declara estar en busca de empleo.

7. Actualización de los registros
Los registros se actualizan a diario.

8. Tasas de desempleo
No se utilizan estadísticas de estos registros para obtener tasas de desempleo.

9. Tipo de estadísticas que se producen sobre desempleados registrados
Período de referencia: Mes, trimestre y año.
Frecuencia de producción: Mensual, trimestral y anual.
Variables utilizadas
– Sexo;
– Edad;
– Nivel de educación;
– Ocupación;
– Características geográficas;
– Duración del desempleo.

10. Información metodológica sobre las estadísticas
Divulgación
– En papel, para un público limitado;
– En el sitio web www.apenc.nc

11. Comparaciones con estadísticas derivadas de otras fuentes
Se han hecho comparaciones con estadísticas de desempleo derivadas del censo de población.

12. Modificaciones importantes desde el comienzo de las estadísticas
En la legislación, la competencia del organismo y/o los procedimientos administrativos no ha habido modificaciones importantes que hayan influido significativamente en las estadísticas.

Nueva Zelandia

1. Serie
Título: Número de desempleados registrados.
Año de inicio: 1952.

2. Organismo responsable de la inscripción inicial de desempleados
Nombre del organismo: Trabajo e Ingresos.
Tipo de organismo: Organismo público subordinado a una autoridad nacional.
Nombre de la autoridad nacional: Ministerio de Desarrollo Social.
Ubicación de las oficinas locales donde se hacen las inscripciones: El organismo tiene unas 170 oficinas de primera línea en todo el país; 144 de ellas a tiempo completo.
Tipo de servicios proporcionados/administrados por el organismo:
– Ayuda a personas en busca de empleo a encontrarlo;
– Ayuda a personas en busca de empleo a crear su propia empresa;
– Ayuda a los empleadores a encontrar trabajadores;
– Orientación profesional;
– Formación relacionada con el trabajo;
– Ayuda de ingresos.

3. Se registran los siguientes datos de la persona:
– Identificación del usuario;
– Nombre y apellido (así como segundo nombre, nombre preferido y apodo, si corresponde);
– Sexo;
– Dirección del domicilio habitual (y dirección postal si corresponde);
– Fecha y lugar de nacimiento;
– Origen étnico;
– Nivel de educación/formación: se identifican nueve categorías.
– Tipo de ocupación del empleo actual o anterior. La trayectoria laboral se redacta como texto libre y las ocupaciones no se codifican.
– Tipo de ocupación del empleo que se busca: se identifican 25 grupos. (Clasificación "NZSCO" a nivel de cinco dígitos);
– Nombre y dirección del empleador o del lugar de trabajo actual o anterior (trayectoria laboral - duración y tipo de empleo; es decir, a tiempo completo o tiempo parcial);
– Inscripciones previas en el organismo;
– Otros: calificaciones y competencias detalladas; discapacidad u otros impedimentos para trabajar; acceso al transporte; titular de licencia de conducir; número de teléfono; nombre y apellido de la pareja; cantidad máxima de horas que está disponible para trabajar; fecha de inscripción; situación en el empleo (desempleada o empleada parcial).

4. Criterios utilizados para determinar si una persona habrá de incluirse en el registro (R) y/o en las estadísticas de personas desempleadas (S):
– Estar sin empleo (puede tener empleo a tiempo parcial, es decir, menos de 30 horas por semana y querer aumentar el número de horas o acceder a un empleo a tiempo completo) (R) y (S);
– Estar en busca de empleo (tal como definido en el plan de acción individual, establecido junto con el funcionario que lleva el caso) (R) y (S);
– Estar disponible para trabajar (R) y (S);
– Edad (mínima: 16 años; no hay edad máxima) (R) y (S);
– Ciudadanía (R) y (S);
– Residir en el país (R) y (S);
– Otros: Estar estudiando o siguiendo una formación a tiempo parcial (quienes estudian o siguen una formación a tiempo completo no pueden registrarse como personas en busca de empleo) (R) y (S).

5. Criterios utilizados para determinar si se ha de excluir a una persona del registro (R) y/o de las estadísticas de personas desempleadas (S):
– Certificado de defunción (R) y (S);
– Establecerse en otro país (R) y (S);
– Incorporarse a un (nuevo) empleo a tiempo completo (R) y (S);
– Participar en algún programa de promoción del empleo (como el denominado *TaskForce Green*), de obras públicas, etc. (R) y (S);
– Estar estudiando o siguiendo una formación a tiempo completo (R) y (S);
– Incumplir el requisito de tomar contacto con el organismo durante 14 semanas (si no recibe prestaciones sujetas al test de idoneidad para el empleo) (R) y (S);
– Rechazar ofertas de trabajo adecuadas (por lo menos cuatro rechazos consecutivos en el caso de quienes reciben prestaciones sujetas al test de idoneidad para el empleo); no existen criterios oficiales respecto a quienes no reciben dichas prestaciones (R) y (S);
– Rechazar ofertas de formación adecuadas (por lo menos cuatro rechazos consecutivos en el caso de quienes reciben prestaciones sujetas al test de idoneidad para el empleo); no existen criterios oficiales respecto a quienes no reciben dichas prestaciones (R) y (S).

6. Definición de persona desempleada en la que se basan las estadísticas
Será registrada como persona en busca de empleo, toda aquella que reúna los requisitos siguientes:
– no tener trabajo y estar buscando empleo o trabajar menos de 30 horas por semana y estar buscando más horas de trabajo; y
– estar disponible para trabajar (no estar trabajando, estudiando o siguiendo una formación a tiempo completo); y
– tener 16 años o más (o 15 años con autorización del Ministerio de Educación para salir temprano del establecimiento de enseñanza y buscar trabajo a tiempo

completo); y

– residir en Nueva Zelandia; y

– estar autorizado a trabajar en Nueva Zelandia (es decir: ser ciudadano de Australia o Nueva Zelandia; tener residencia permanente en Nueva Zelandia; ser titular de un permiso de trabajo de Nueva Zelandia o haber nacido en las Islas Cook, Niue o Tokelau).

7. Actualización de los registros

Los registros se actualizan constantemente.

8. Tasas de desempleo

No se utilizan estadísticas de estos registros para obtener tasas de desempleo.

9. Tipo de estadísticas que se producen sobre desempleados registrados

Serie 1: Registro mensual.

Período de referencia: Último día del mes.

Frecuencia de producción: Mensual.

Variables utilizadas:

– Sexo;
– Edad;
– Nivel de educación;
– Características geográficas;
– Duración del desempleo;
– Ayuda de ingresos recibida;
– Origen étnico;
– Discapacidad;
– Grupo de gestión del caso;
– Estado civil;
– Edad de los hijos menores.

Publicación: Sólo para uso interno.

Organismo responsable de la publicación: inisterio de Desarrollo Social.

Título y periodicidad de la publicación:

Monthly register (Registro mensual).

Serie 2: Perfil trimestral de usuarios.

Período de referencia: Último día del trimestre.

Frecuencia de producción: Trimestral.

Variables utilizadas:

– Sexo;
– Edad;
– Nivel de educación;
– Características geográficas;
– Duración del desempleo;
– Ayuda de ingresos recibida;
– Origen étnico;
– Situación en el test de idoneidad para el empleo;
– Participación en programas de empleo.

Publicación:

– En papel, para el público en general;
– En el sitio web www.msd.govt.nz

Organismo responsable de la publicación: Ministerio de Desarrollo Social.

Título y periodicidad de la publicación: *Quarterly Client Profile* (Perfil trimestral de usuarios).

Serie 3: Perfil estadístico anual.

Período de referencia: Último día del año fiscal.

Frecuencia de producción: Anual.

Variables utilizadas:

– Sexo;
– Edad;
– Nivel de educación;
– Características geográficas;
– Duración del desempleo;
– Ayuda de ingresos recibida;
– Origen étnico;
– Participación en programas de empleo.

Publicación: En papel, para el público en general.

Organismo responsable de la publicación: Ministerio de Desarrollo Social.

Título y periodicidad de la publicación: *Annual Statistical Profile* (Perfil estadístico anual).

10. Información metodológica sobre las estadísticas

Las publicaciones citadas más arriba incluyen resúmenes de información metodológica.

Divulgación.

– En papel, para el público en general;
– En el sitio web www.msd.govt.nz

Organismo responsable: Ministerio de Desarrollo Social.

11. Comparaciones con estadísticas derivadas de otras fuentes

Una vez por trimestre, se hacen comparaciones con estadísticas de desempleo derivadas de la Encuesta de hogares

sobre la fuerza de trabajo (medición oficial del desempleo,de conformidad con los criterios de la OIT, a cargo de Estadísticas de Nueva Zelandia).

En 2001, se hicieron comparaciones con estadísticas de desempleo del Censo de población de 1996.

Publicación de la metodología/resultados de las comparaciones: No se publican.

12. Modificaciones importantes desde el comienzo de las estadísticas

En la legislación, la competencia del organismo y/o los procedimientos administrativos hubo modificaciones importantes en:

1997: Introducción del test de idoneidad para el empleo de quienes reciben ayuda de ingresos selectiva, y en

1999: Ampliación de las prestaciones para personas que reciben ayuda de ingresos sujeta al test de idoneidad para el empleo a efectos de incluir prestaciones suplementarias y al cónyuge o la pareja de las mismas.

El test de idoneidad para el empleo de las personas que reciben ayuda de ingresos y sus cónyuges exige que dichas personas también estén registradas como personas en busca de empleo; anteriormente, este requisito no existía.

La repercusión de estas dos modificaciones en el número de personas en busca de empleo es indeterminada.

Países Bajos

1. Serie

Título: Desempleo registrado.

2. Organismo responsable de la inscripción inicial de desempleados

Nombre del organismo: Centro de Trabajo e Ingresos.

Tipo de organismo: Organismo público subordinado a una autoridad nacional.

Ubicación de las oficinas locales donde se hacen las inscripciones: Todo el país.

Tipo de servicios proporcionados/administrados por el organismo

– Ayuda a personas en busca de empleo a encontrarlo;
– Ayuda a los empleadores a encontrar trabajadores;
– Proporciona información sobre el mercado de trabajo.

Porcentaje de personas en busca de empleo que buscan trabajo por intermedio de ese organismo: 25%.

3. Se registran los siguientes datos de la persona

– Nombre y apellido;
– Sexo;
– Número de seguridad social (o número de identificación semejante);
– Dirección del domicilio habitual;
– Fecha de nacimiento;
– Ciudadanía;
– Nacionalidad/grupo étnico;
– Nivel de educación/formación. No se han establecido vínculos con la CINE;
– Situación laboral actual o anterior;
– Tipo de ocupación del empleo actual o anterior;
– Tipo de ocupación del empleo que se busca. No se han establecido vínculos con la CIUO-88;
– Nombre y dirección del empleador o del lugar de trabajo actual o anterior;
– Rama de actividad del empleador o del lugar de trabajo actual o anterior. Se han establecido vínculos con la CIIU a nivel de clase;
– Inscripciones previas en el organismo.

4. Criterios utilizados para determinar si una persona habrá de incluirse en el registro (R) y/o en las estadísticas de personas desempleadas (S)

– Estar sin empleo (R) y (S);
– Estar en busca de empleo (R) y (S);
– Estar disponible para trabajar (R) y (S);
– Duración y/o número de horas de trabajo del empleo que se busca (más de 12 horas por semana) (S).

5. Criterios utilizados para determinar si se ha de excluir a una persona del registro (R) y/o de las estadísticas de personas desempleadas (S)

– Certificado de defunción (R) y (S);
– Incumplir el requisito de tomar contacto con el organismo (R) y (S).

6. Definición de persona desempleada en la que se basan las estadísticas

Toda persona sin trabajo que busca un empleo y está disponible para trabajar. La duración del empleo que se busca debe ser superior a 12 horas por semana.

7. Actualización de los registros
Los registros se actualizan periódicamente.

8. Tasas de desempleo
Se utilizan estadísticas de estos registros para obtener tasas de desempleo.
Fuente de los datos de empleo incluidos en el denominador de las tasas de desempleo: Encuesta sobre la fuerza de trabajo.
Definición de persona empleada que se utiliza a tales efectos
Haber trabajado más de 12 horas durantes el período de referencia.

9. Tipo de estadísticas que se producen sobre desempleados registrados
Período de referencia: Mes.
Frecuencia de producción: Mensual.
Variables utilizadas
- Sexo;
- Edad;
- Nivel de educación;
- Ocupación;
- Rama de actividad;
- Características geográficas;
- Experiencia laboral previa;
- Ciudadanía;
- Duración del desempleo.

Publicación
- En papel, para el público en general;
- En archivo electrónico, previa solicitud.
Organismo responsable de la publicación: Centro de Trabajo e Ingresos.
Título y periodicidad de la publicación: *Arbeios Marytjournaal.*

10. Información metodológica sobre las estadísticas
Divulgación
- En papel, para el público en general;
- En archivo electrónico, previa solicitud.

11. Comparaciones con estadísticas derivadas de otras fuentes
Se han hecho comparaciones con estadísticas de desempleo derivadas de las Estadísticas de la Seguridad Social.
Frecuencia de las comparaciones: Periódica, cuando se publican las estadísticas.

12. Modificaciones importantes desde el comienzo de las estadísticas
En la legislación, la competencia del organismo y/o los procedimientos administrativos no ha habido modificaciones importantes que hayan influido significativamente en las estadísticas.

Panamá

1. Serie
Título: Desempleo registrado.
Año de inicio: 1990.

2. Organismo responsable de la inscripción inicial de desempleados
Nombre del organismo: Departamento de Mano de Obra (Dirección General de Empleo).
Tipo de organismo: Organismo público de la Dirección General de Empleo - Ministerio de Trabajo y Desarrollo Laboral (MITRADEL).
Ubicación de las oficinas locales donde se hacen las inscripciones: En todas las Direcciones Regionales del Ministerio de Trabajo y Desarrollo Laboral.
Tipo de servicios proporcionados/administrados por el organismo:
- Ayuda a personas en busca de empleo a encontrarlo;
- Ayuda a personas en busca de empleo a crear su propia empresa propia;
- Ayuda a los empleadores a encontrar trabajadores;
- Orientación profesional;
- Formación relacionada con el trabajo;
- Otros: se relaciona con el Programa Feria de Empleo, Capacitación y Autogestión Empresarial.
Porcentaje de personas en busca de empleo que buscan trabajo por intermedio de ese organismo: 2.3% (en 1999).

3. Se registran los siguientes datos de la persona:
- Nombre y apellido;
- Sexo;
- Número de Cédula o identificación personal;
- Número de seguridad social (o número de identificación semejante también utilizado por otros organismos);

- Dirección del domicilio habitual;
- Fecha de nacimiento;
- Ciudadanía (por Provincia donde nació);
- Nacionalidad;
- Nivel de educación/formación; se identifica la que logra la persona. No se han establecido vínculos con la CINE;
- Situación laboral actual o anterior: se identifican siete categorías donde todas las experiencias son tomadas en cuenta;
- Tipo de ocupación del empleo actual o anterior: se identifican siete categorías. Se han establecido vínculos con la CIUO-88. Con experiencia y título se ubican dentro de la 1ra., 2da., 3ra. y 4ta. ocupación;
- Tipo de ocupación del empleo que se busca: se identifican siete categorías. Se han establecido vínculos con la CIUO-88;
- Nombre y dirección del empleador o del lugar del trabajo actual o anterior;
- Rama de actividad del empleador o del lugar del trabajo actual o anterior: se identifican cinco categorías. No se han establecido vínculos con la CIIU;
- Inscripciones previas en el organismo;
- Otros: estado civil; dependientes (edades); licencia de conducir; si tiene auto propio; movilidad; turno deseado; ocupación principal y opciones de ocupación.

4. Criterios utilizados para determinar si una persona habrá de incluirse en el registro (R) y/o en las estadísticas de personas desempleadas (S):
- Estar sin empleo (R) y (S);
- Estar en busca de empleo (R);
- Estar disponible para trabajar (R);
- Edad (mínima: 18 años; no existe edad máxima) (R) y (S);
- Ciudadanía (se refiere a la provincia donde reside) (R) y (S);
- Haber trabajado (R);
- Duración y/o número de horas de trabajo del empleo que se busca (eventual o permanente) (R) y (S).

5. Criterios utilizados para determinar si se ha de excluir a una persona del registro (R) y/o de las estadísticas de personas desempleadas (S):
- Certificado de defunción (R);
- Establecerse en otro país (R);
- Incorporarse a un (nuevo) empleo (R);
- Participar en algún programa de promoción del empleo, de obras públicas, etc. (R);
- Estar estudiando o siguiendo una formación (R);
- Incumplir el requisito de ponerse en contacto con el organismo (el servicio de colocación tiene un año; terminado este período el aspirante debe actualizar nuevamente su expediente) (R);
- Rechazar dos ofertas de trabajo adecuadas (R);
- Cobrar pensión (si es por enfermedad) (R);
- Incapacidad para trabajar (R);
- Otros: el usuario se le ha comprobado delito dentro de la empresa donde se le ubicó (R).

6. Definición de persona desempleada en la que se basan las estadísticas
Corresponde a las personas de 18 años y más de edad con la disponibilidad de trabajar que no tienen ocupación o trabajo, pero que habían trabajado antes y estaban buscando empleo. Las que no buscaron trabajo porque habían conseguido un empleo que empezarían a ejercer en una fecha posterior. Las que nunca habían trabajado y buscan su primer empleo (trabajador nuevo), o en su efecto las que no estaban buscando trabajo, pero han buscado antes y están esperando noticias. Personas empleadas o subempleadas que buscan empleo en edad activa laboral.

7. Actualización de los registros
Los registros físicos se actualizan mensualmente; no obstante, la publicación es anual.

8. Tasas de desempleo
Se utilizan estadísticas de estos registros para obtener tasas de desempleo.

9. Tipo de estadísticas que se producen sobre desempleados registrados
Período de referencia: Año.
Frecuencia de producción: Anual.
Variables utilizadas:
- Sexo;
- Edad;
- Nivel de educación;
- Ocupación;

– Rama de actividad;
– Regionales de trabajo;
– Ciudadanía (ciudadanos/extranjeros);
– Duración del desempleo;
– Otras: colocaciones de empleo selectivo (impedimento); condición del trabajador (ocupado, cesante o trabajador nuevo); trabajadores del mar; autogestión empresarial; direcciones Regionales de Trabajo (empleo).

Publicación: En papel, para instituciones públicas, privadas, otros organismos y consulta pública.

Organismo responsable de la publicación: Ministerio de Trabajo y Desarrollo Laboral, Dirección General de Empleo.

Título y periodicidad de la publicación: *Informe Anual de Trabajo de la Dirección General de Empleo.*

10. Información metodológica sobre las estadísticas

Divulgación: En papel, para el público en general.

Organismo responsable: Dirección General de Empleo del Departamento de Investigaciones de Empleo.

11. Comparaciones con estadísticas derivadas de otras fuentes

No se han hecho comparaciones con estadísticas de desempleo derivadas de otras fuentes. La información publicada es de uso primario; no se emplea para análisis comparativos con otras fuentes.

12. Modificaciones importantes desde el comienzo de las estadísticas

En la legislación, la competencia del organismo y/o los procedimientos administrativos no ha habido modificaciones importantes que hayan influido significativamente en las estadísticas.

Papua Nueva Guinea

1. Serie

Título: Boletín anual de estadísticas del trabajo.

Año de inicio: 1996.

2. Organismo responsable de la inscripción inicial de desempleados

Nombre del organismo: Service national de l'Emploi - NES (Servicio Nacional de Empleo).

Tipo de organismo: Organismo público subordinado a una autoridad nacional.

Nombre de la autoridad nacional: Departamento de Trabajo y Empleo.

Ubicación de las oficinas locales donde se hacen las inscripciones: Sólo en determinadas zonas, establecidas en cuatro oficinas regionales del NES.

Tipo de servicios proporcionados/administrados por el organismo

– Ayuda a personas en busca de empleo a encontrarlo;
– Ayuda a los empleadores a encontrar trabajadores;
– Orientación profesional;
– Formación relacionada con el trabajo;
– Da información sobre carreras a egresados escolares.

Porcentaje de personas en busca de empleo que buscan trabajo por intermedio de ese organismo: 0,8%.

3. Se registran los siguientes datos de la persona

– Nombre y apellido;
– Sexo;
– Número de seguridad social (o número de identificación semejante también utilizado por otros organismos);
– Dirección del domicilio habitual;
– Fecha de nacimiento;
– Ciudadanía;
– Nacionalidad/grupo étnico;
– Nivel de educación/formación: se identifican seis categorías. Se han establecido vínculos con la CINE;
– Situación laboral actual o anterior: se identifican tres categorías;
– Tipo de ocupación del empleo actual o anterior: se identifican 10 categorías.
– Tipo de ocupación del empleo que se busca: se identifican nueve categorías. Se han establecido vínculos con la CIUO-88 a nivel de grandes grupos;
– Nombre y dirección del empleador o del lugar de trabajo actual o anterior;
– Rama de actividad del empleador o del lugar de trabajo actual o anterior: se identifican 17 categorías. Se han establecido vínculos con la CIIU a nivel de división;
– Inscripciones previas en el organismo.

4. Criterios utilizados para determinar si una persona habrá de incluirse en el registro (R) y/o en las estadísticas de personas desempleadas (S)

– Estar sin empleo (S);
– Estar en busca de empleo (R);
– Estar disponible para trabajar (R);
– Edad (mínima: 15 años; máxima: 55 años) (R) y (S);
– Ciudadanía (R) y (S);
– Residir en el país (R);
– Haber trabajado;
– Duración y/o número de horas de trabajo del empleo que se busca (duración mínima: de 8 a 10 horas por día).

5. Criterios utilizados para determinar si se ha de excluir a una persona del registro (R) y/o de las estadísticas de personas desempleadas (S)

– Certificado de defunción (R) y (S);
– Establecerse en otro país (R);
– Incorporarse a un (nuevo) empleo (R) y (S);
– Comenzar el servicio militar (R) y (S);
– Participar en algún programa de promoción del empleo, de obras públicas, etc. (R) y (S);
– Estar estudiando o siguiendo una formación (R);
– Incumplir el requisito de tomar contacto con el organismo (R);
– Rechazar ofertas de trabajo adecuadas (R);
– Rechazar ofertas de formación adecuadas (R);
– Fin del período de prestaciones de desempleo (R);
– Cobrar alguna pensión (R) y (S);
– Incapacidad para trabajar (R).

6. Definición de persona desempleada en la que se basan las estadísticas

Personas desempleadas son aquellas que están en busca de empleo y que no han trabajado durante un período de referencia concreto. En determinadas circunstancias, el término puede aludir a graves casos de subempleo.

7. Actualización de los registros

Los registros se actualizan trimestralmente.

8. Tasas de desempleo

Se utilizan estadísticas de estos registros para obtener tasas de desempleo.

Fuentes de los datos de empleo incluidos en el denominador de las tasas de desempleo: Encuesta sobre la fuerza de trabajo, Encuesta de establecimientos, Registro de la Seguridad Social y Censo de población.

Definición de persona empleada que se utiliza a tales efectos

Personas remuneradas con dinero o equivalente por producir bienes y servicios comercializables; incluidos quienes ganan sueldo, los asalariados, los empleadores, los trabajadores por cuenta propia y los trabajadores familiares no remunerados.

9. Tipo de estadísticas que se producen sobre desempleados registrados

Período de referencia: De uno a cuatro meses.

Frecuencia de producción: Trimestral.

Variables utilizadas

– Sexo;
– Edad;
– Nivel de educación;
– Ocupación;
– Rama de actividad;
– Experiencia laboral previa;
– Ciudadanía;
– Duración del desempleo.

Publicación: En papel, para un público limitado.

Organismo responsable de la publicación: Servicio Nacional de Empleo

Título y periodicidad de las publicaciones: *Annual Estatistical Report* (Informe estadístico anual).

10. Información metodológica sobre las estadísticas

Divulgación: En papel, para un público limitado.

Organismo responsable de la divulgación: Unidad Estadística del Departamento de Trabajo.

11. Comparaciones con estadísticas derivadas de otras fuentes

Se han hecho comparaciones con estadísticas de desempleo derivadas de la Encuesta sobre la fuerza de trabajo, el Censo de población y estadísticas de otras fuentes.

Frecuencia de las comparaciones: Periódica, cuando se publican las estadísticas.

Publicación de la metodología/resultados de las comparaciones: No se publican.

12. Modificaciones importantes desde el comienzo de las estadísticas

En la legislación, la competencia del organismo y/o los procedimientos administrativos hubo modificaciones importantes en 2000 que tuvieron una influencia significativa en el número de personas desempleadas registradas.

Perú

1. Serie
Título: Personas registradas en busca de empleo.
Año de inicio: Alrededor de 1975.
2. Organismo responsable de la inscripción inicial de desempleados
Nombre del organismo: La Red de Centros de Colocación e Información Laboral (Red CIL-PROEMPLEO).
Tipo de organismo: Organismo público subordinado a una autoridad nacional. (Existen también centros privados integrados a la Red CIL-PROEMPLEO pero sin fines de lucro).
Nombre de la autoridad nacional: Dirección Nacional de Promoción del Empleo y Formación Profesional.
Ubicación de las oficinas locales donde se hacen las inscripciones: Existen 40 oficinas localizadas en todas las ciudades principales del país.
Tipo de servicios proporcionados/administrados por el organismo:
- Ayuda a personas en busca de empleo a encontrarlo;
- Ayuda a los empleadores a encontrar trabajadores;
- Orientación profesional y ocupacional;
- Formación relacionada con el trabajo;
- Otros: asesoría para la búsqueda de empleo; orientación para el autoempleo y PYME.
Porcentaje de personas en busca de empleo que buscan trabajo por intermedio de ese organismo: 17.5%.
3. Se registran los siguientes datos de la persona:
- Nombre y apellido;
- Sexo;
- Dirección del domicilio habitual;
- Edad;
- Ciudadanía;
- Nivel de educación/formación: se identifican cinco categorías. Se han establecido vínculos con la CINE;
- Situación laboral actual o anterior: se identifican cinco categorías;
- Tipo de ocupación del empleo actual o anterior: se identifican 10 categorías. Se han establecido vínculos con grandes grupos de la CIUO-88;
- Tipo de ocupación del empleo que se busca: se identifican 10 categorías. Se han establecido vínculos con grandes grupos de la CIUO-88;
- Nombre y dirección del empleador o del lugar del trabajo actual o anterior;
- Rama de actividad del empleador o del lugar del trabajo actual o anterior: se identifican 12 categorías. Se han establecido vínculos con la CIIU, Rev. 3;
- Inscripciones previas en el organismo.
4. Criterios utilizados para determinar si una persona habrá de incluirse en el registro (R) y/o en las estadísticas de personas desempleadas (S):
- Estar sin empleo (R) y (S);
- Estar en busca de empleo (R) y (S);
- Estar disponible para trabajar (R);
- Edad (mínima: 18 años; máxima: 65 años) (R) y (S);
- Haber trabajado (S);
- Duración y/o número de horas de trabajo del empleo que se busca (S).
5. Criterios utilizados para determinar si se ha de excluir a una persona del registro (R) y/o de las estadísticas de personas desempleadas (S):
- Incorporarse a un (nuevo) empleo (R) y (S);
- Participar en algún programa de promoción del empleo, de obras públicas, etc. (R);
- Incumplir el requisito de ponerse en contacto con el organismo (R) y (S);
- Rechazar ofertas de trabajo adecuadas (R);
- Incapacidad para trabajar (R) y (S);
- Otros: abandonar reiteradamente puestos de trabajo ofrecidos por el servicio (R).
6. Definición de persona desempleada en la que se basan las estadísticas
No se indica.

7. Actualización de los registros
Los registros se actualizan mensualmente.
8. Tasas de desempleo
No se utilizan estadísticas de estos registros para obtener tasas de desempleo.
9. Tipo de estadísticas que se producen sobre desempleados registrados
Período de referencia: Trimestre.
Frecuencia de producción: Trimestral.
Variables utilizadas:
- Sexo;
- Edad;
- Nivel de educación;
- Ocupación;
- Rama de actividad;
- Experiencia laboral previa;
- Duración del desempleo;
- Otras: cursos de formación y capacitación.
Publicación: En papel, para un público limitado.
Organismo responsable de la publicación: Dirección Nacional de Promoción del Empleo y Formación Profesional.
10. Información metodológica sobre las estadísticas
Divulgación: En papel, para un público limitado.
Organismo responsable: Dirección Nacional de Promoción del Empleo y Formación Profesional.
11. Comparaciones con estadísticas derivadas de otras fuentes
Se han hecho comparaciones con estadísticas de desempleo derivadas de la Encuesta de hogares y el Censo de Población.
Frecuencia de las comparaciones: De vez en cuando (último año: 2000).
Publicación de la metodología/resultados de las comparaciones: Se ha publicado la metodología y resultados de las comparaciones en *Informe Estadístico Mensual*.
12. Modificaciones importantes desde el comienzo de las estadísticas
En la legislación, la competencia del organismo y/o los procedimientos administrativos no ha habido modificaciones importantes que hayan influido significativamente en las estadísticas.

Polinesia Francesa

1. Serie
Título: Personas en busca de empleo.
Año de inicio: 1990.
2. Organismo responsable de la inscripción inicial de desempleados
Nombre del organismo: Servicio de Empleo, Formación e Inserción Profesional.
Tipo de organismo: Organismo público subordinado a una autoridad local: Servicio público territorial del gobierno de Polinesia Francesa.
Ubicación de las oficinas locales donde se hacen las inscripciones: Papeete, capital, y un centro en Uturoa-Raiatea, capital del archipiélago.
Tipo de servicios proporcionados/administrados por el organismo
- Ayuda a personas en busca de empleo a encontrarlo;
- Ayuda a los empleadores a encontrar trabajadores;
- Orientación profesional;
- Formación relacionada con el trabajo;
- Otros: vincula demandas y ofertas de empleo; alienta a los empleadores para que contraten; ofrece soluciones de formación e inserción a las personas en busca de empleo.
3. Se registran los siguientes datos de la persona
- Nombre y apellido;
- Sexo;
- Número de seguridad social (o número de identificación semejante también utilizado por otros organismos);
- Dirección del domicilio habitual;
- Fecha de nacimiento;
- Formación, experiencia profesional;
- Situación laboral actual o anterior;
- Tipo de ocupación del empleo actual o anterior. No se han establecido vínculos con la CIUO-88;
- Tipo de ocupación del empleo que se busca;
- Inscripciones previas en el organismo.
4. Criterios utilizados para determinar si una persona habrá de incluirse en el registro (R) y/o en las estadísticas de personas desempleadas (S)
- Estar sin empleo (R) y (S);

– Estar en busca de empleo (R) y (S);
– Estar disponible para trabajar (R) y (S);
– Edad (mínima: 16 años; no hay edad máxima) (R) y (S).

5. Criterios utilizados para determinar si se ha de excluir a una persona del registro (R) y/o de las estadísticas de personas desempleadas (S)
– Incorporarse a un (nuevo) empleo (R) y (S);
– Estar estudiando o siguiendo una formación (R) y (S);
– Caducidad de la validez de la inscripción (incumplir el requisito de tomar contacto con el organismo) (R) y (S).

6. Definición de persona desempleada en la que se basan las estadísticas
Las estadísticas no versan sobre el número de desempleados sino sobre el número de personas en busca de empleo registradas.

7. Actualización de los registros
Los registros se actualizan periódica y constantemente.

8. Tasas de desempleo
No se utilizan estadísticas de estos registros para obtener tasas de desempleo.

9. Tipo de estadísticas que se producen sobre desempleados registrados
No se aplica.

10. Información metodológica sobre las estadísticas
No se aplica.

11. Comparaciones con estadísticas derivadas de otras fuentes
No se han hecho comparaciones con estadísticas de desempleo derivadas de otras fuentes.

12. Modificaciones importantes desde el comienzo de las estadísticas
En la legislación, la competencia del organismo y/o los procedimientos administrativos no ha habido modificaciones importantes que hayan influido significativamente en las estadísticas.

Polonia

1. Serie
Título: Desempleo registrado.
Año de inicio: 1999.

2. Organismo responsable de la inscripción inicial de desempleados
Nombre del organismo: Oficinas de trabajo de distrito (*Powiat*).
Tipo de organismo: Organismo público subordinado a autoridades locales.
Ubicación de las oficinas locales donde se hacen las inscripciones: Todos los distritos del país.
Tipo de servicios proporcionados/administrados por el organismo:
– Ayuda a personas en busca de empleo a encontrarlo;
– Ayuda a personas en busca de empleo a crear su propia empresa;
– Ayuda a los empleadores a encontrar trabajadores;
– Orientación profesional;
– Formación relacionada con el trabajo;
– Pago de prestaciones de desempleo;
– Otros: organización de empleos temporarios in extremis y programas de obras públicas (empleo subvencionado).
Porcentaje de personas en busca de empleo que buscan trabajo por intermedio de ese organismo: No se sabe porque no se han hecho investigaciones al respecto.

3. Se registran los siguientes datos de la persona:
– Nombre y apellido;
– Sexo;
– Dirección del domicilio habitual;
– Fecha de nacimiento;
– Ciudadanía;
– Nivel de educación/formación: se identifican cinco categorías. No se han establecido vínculos con la CINE;
– Situación laboral actual o anterior, por período de empleo (menos de un año; de uno a cinco años; de cinco a 10 años; de 10 a 20 años; de 20 a 30 años, 30 años o más, y no haber trabajado nunca);
– Tipo de ocupación del empleo actual o anterior: se identifica un número indeterminado de grupos. Se han establecido vínculos con la CIUO-88 a nivel de subgrupos principales (la Clasificación de Ocupaciones y Especializaciones de Polonia se ajusta a la CIUO-88);
– Tipo de ocupación del empleo que se busca: se identifica un número indeterminado de grupos. Se han establecido vínculos con la CIUO-88 a nivel de subgrupos principales;

– Nombre y dirección del empleador o del lugar de trabajo actual o anterior;
– Rama de actividad del empleador o del lugar de trabajo actual o anterior: se identifica un número indeterminado de grupos. Se han establecido vínculos con la NACE Rev. 1 a nivel de división (la Clasificación de Actividades de Polonia se basa en la NACE Rev.1;
– Inscripciones previas en el organismo;
– Otros: balance de personas desempleadas; ofertas de empleo; personas desempleadas que benefician de medidas activas de mercado de trabajo (formación, orientación profesional, clubes de empleo, etc.).

Nota: El informe estadístico no contiene datos unitarios; por lo tanto, gran parte de la información anterior sólo se incluye en la ficha de registro de la persona desempleada o en busca de trabajo, y no figura en las estadísticas del mercado de trabajo.

4. Criterios utilizados para determinar si una persona habrá de incluirse en el registro (R) y/o en las estadísticas de personas desempleadas (S):
– Estar sin empleo (R) y (S);
– Estar en busca de empleo (R) y (S);
– Estar disponible para trabajar (R);
– Edad (mínima 18 años, salvo diplomados universitarios menores de esa edad; máxima: 65 años para los hombres y 60 para las mujeres) (R) y (S);
– Ciudadanía (R) y (S);
– Residir en el país (R) y (S);
– Haber trabajado (R) y (S).

5. Criterios utilizados para determinar si se ha de excluir a una persona del registro (R) y/o de las estadísticas de personas desempleadas (S):
– Certificado de defunción (R) y (S);
– Establecerse en otro país (R) y (S);
– Incorporarse a un (nuevo) empleo (R) y (S);
– Comenzar el servicio militar (R) y (S);
– Participar en algún programa de promoción del empleo, de obras públicas, etc. (R) y (S);
– Estar estudiando o siguiendo una formación (R) y (S);
– Incumplir el requisito de tomar contacto con el organismo (tres meses de exclusión) (R) y (S);
– Rechazar dos ofertas de trabajo o de obras públicas adecuadas (seis meses de exclusión) (R) y (S);
– Cobrar jubilación (R) y (S);
– Incapacidad para trabajar (R) y (S);
– Otros: renunciar por decisión propia a la condición de persona desempleada; recibir un préstamo del Fondo de Trabajo o del Fondo Estatal de Rehabilitación de Discapacitados para iniciar una actividad económica; tener edad para jubilarse, 65 años para los hombres y 60 años para las mujeres; acogerse al subsidio o las prestaciones de prejubilación (R) y (S).

6. Definición de persona desempleada en la que se basan las estadísticas
Se considera desempleada a toda persona sin empleo (es decir, que no tiene un trabajo basado en una relación de empleo o de servicio, o trabajo a domicilio); no hace ningún otro trabajo remunerativo (es decir, basado en contratos de derecho civil, a saber: agencia, comisión o trabajo específico) o en un período de participación en la producción agrícola cooperativa o círculos rurales cooperativos (servicios agrícolas) y que:
– está en condiciones de trabajar y dispuesta a aceptar un empleo a tiempo completo según la cantidad de horas de trabajo correspondiente a una ocupación o servicio determinados (salvo personas con discapacidades);
– no asiste a un establecimiento de enseñanza durante el día;
– está registrada en la oficina de trabajo del distrito correspondiente a su lugar de residencia permanente o temporal;
– tiene 18 años o más (salvo diplomados universitarios menores de esa edad);
– tiene menos de 65 años si es hombre y menos de 60 si es mujer;
– no tiene derecho a jubilación en relación con la incapacidad para trabajar ni a pensión de formación o, después de terminado un empleo, no tiene otro trabajo remunerativo, tras haber terminado una actividad económica ajena a la agricultura y tampoco recibe subvención ni prestaciones de prejubilación o prestaciones por concepto de rehabilitación, enfermedad, maternidad o cuidado de los hijos;
– no es propietaria ni copropietaria de una explotación agrícola de una superficie cultivable superior a dos

hectáreas, consideradas con fines de cálculo, o no está cubierta por un seguro de pensión relacionado con un empleo permanente por ser cónyuge o miembro del hogar de una explotación agrícola de una superficie cultivable superior a dos hectáreas, consideradas con fines de cálculo;

– no es propietaria ni copropietaria de una explotación agrícola clasificada en una sección especial de la producción agrícola en lo que respecta a la reglamentación fiscal, salvo que los ingresos generados por una sección especial de la producción agrícola, calculados para determinar el impuesto sobre la renta personal, sean inferiores o iguales a los ingresos medios del trabajo en una explotación agrícola de dos hectáreas, consideradas con fines de cálculo, según lo establecido por el presidente de la Oficina Central de Estadística, de conformidad con la reglamentación relativa al impuesto rural, o no esté cubierta por un seguro de pensión relacionado con un empleo permanente por ser cónyuge o miembro del hogar de dicha explotación agrícola;

– no haya iniciado una actividad económica ajena a la agricultura entre la fecha indicada en la solicitud de inscripción en el registro y la fecha en que se le suprime del mismo o no esté cubierta, de conformidad con otras disposiciones, por un seguro social obligatorio, salvo el seguro social de agricultores o la pensión de seguridad;

– sea una persona discapacitada cuyo estado de salud le permita ejercer un empleo a media jornada, como mínimo, en una ocupación o servicio determinados;

– no esté detenida temporalmente o cumpliendo condena de prisión (privación de libertad);

– no reciba ingresos mensuales de un monto superior a la mitad del salario mínimo;

– no beneficie, de conformidad con la legislación de asistencia social, de una subvención permanente, una subvención compensatoria permanente, una subvención periódica garantizada o una pensión social.

7. Actualización de los registros
Los registros se actualizan periódicamente.

8. Tasas de desempleo
Se utilizan estadísticas de estos registros para obtener tasas de desempleo.
Fuentes de los datos de empleo incluidos en el denominador de las tasas de desempleo: Encuesta sobre la fuerza de trabajo; encuestas de establecimientos; estimaciones oficiales, y Censo de población.

Definición de persona empleada que se utiliza a tales efectos:
Los datos sobre personas empleadas se refieren a personas con un trabajo remunerativo (trabajo generador de ingresos o ganancias) e incluyen lo que sigue:

– personas empleadas sobre la base de una relación de empleo (contrato de empleo, nombramiento, designación o elección);

– empleadores y trabajadores por cuenta propia (personas autoempleadas);

– propietarias o copropietarias de entidades que ejercen alguna actividad económica, salvo explotaciones agrícolas individuales;

– otros trabajadores por cuenta propia; por ejemplo, profesionales independientes;

– trabajadores a domicilio y demás.

9. Tipo de estadísticas que se producen sobre desempleados registrados
Serie 1:
Período de referencia: No indicado.
Frecuencia de producción: Anual.
Variables utilizadas:
– Sexo;
– Edad;
– Nivel de educación;
– Ocupación;
– Experiencia laboral previa;
– Duración del desempleo;
– Otras: entradas - salidas; con derecho a prestaciones; tasa de desempleo; no haber trabajado; diplomas universitarios; cese por motivos relacionados con la empresa; por lugar de residencia; ofertas de empleo; aprovechar medidas activas de mercado de trabajo.

Publicación:
– En papel, para el público en general;
– En CD-ROM.

Organismo responsable de la publicación: Oficina Central de Estadística.
Título y periodicidad de la publicación: *Statistical Yearbook of the Republic of Poland* (Anuario estadístico de la República de Polonia).
Serie 2:
Período de referencia: No indicado.
Frecuencia de producción: Bienal.
Variables utilizadas:
– Sexo;
– Edad;
– Nivel de educación;
– Ocupación;
– Características geográficas;
– Experiencia laboral previa;
– Duración del desempleo;
– Otras: entradas - salidas; con derecho a prestaciones; tasa de desempleo; no haber trabajado; diplomas universitarios; cese por motivos relacionados con la empresa; por lugar de residencia; aprovechar medidas activas de mercado de trabajo.

Publicación:
– En papel, para el público en general;
– En CD-ROM.
Organismo responsable de la publicación: Oficina Central de Estadística.
Título y periodicidad de la publicación: *Statistical Yearbook of Labour* (Anuario de Estadísticas del Trabajo) (bienal).
Serie 3:
Período de referencia: No indicado.
Frecuencia de producción: Trimestral.
Variables utilizadas:
– Sexo;
– Edad;
– Nivel de educación;
– Ocupación;
– Rama de actividad;
– Características geográficas;
– Experiencia laboral previa;
– Duración del desempleo
– Otras: entradas - salidas; empezar a trabajar; con derecho a prestaciones; tasa de desempleo; cese por motivos relacionados con la empresa; haber trabajado o no; diplomas universitarios; por lugar de residencia; ofertas de empleo; medidas activas de mercado de trabajo para personas desempleadas registradas.

Publicación: En papel, para el público en general.
Organismo responsable de la publicación: Oficina Central de Estadística.
Título y periodicidad de las publicaciones: *Registered unemployment* (Desempleo registrado) (trimestral).
Otras series:
La Oficina Nacional de Trabajo publica las siguientes series de información:

– Información sobre la situación y la estructura del desempleo (mensual).
– Personas desempleadas por un período superior a 12 meses.
– El mercado de trabajo de Polonia (anual).
– Servicios institucionales de mercado de trabajo (anual).
– Permisos de trabajo para extranjeros (semestral y anual).
– Mujeres desempleadas (semestral y anual).
– Información sobre la situación y la estructura del desempleo (semestral).
– Información sobre la situación y la estructura del desempleo registrado en zonas rurales (semestral y anual).
– Información sobre la situación de la juventud en el mercado de trabajo (semestral y anual).
– Personas desempleadas y ofertas de empleo para personas desempleadas por ocupación y especialización (semestral y anual).
– Mujeres desempleadas por ocupación y especialización (semestral y anual).
– Desempleados diplomados de establecimientos de enseñanza de nivel superior al primario por ocupaciones aprendidas (semestral y anual).
– Análisis del desempleo según la Clasificación de Actividades de Polonia (semestral y anual).
– Personas desempleadas por ocupación y especialización (semestral y anual).

10. Información metodológica sobre las estadísticas
Divulgación:
En papel, para el público en general;

- En archivo electrónico, previa solicitud;
- En el sitio web http://praca@gov.pl.

Organismo responsable: Oficina Central de Estadística; Oficina Nacional de Trabajo.

11. Comparaciones con estadísticas derivadas de otras fuentes

Se han hecho comparaciones con estadísticas de desempleo derivadas de la Encuesta sobre la fuerza de trabajo y el Censo de población.

Frecuencia de las comparaciones: Periódica, cuando se publican las estadísticas.

Publicación de la metodología/resultados de las comparaciones: No se publican.

12. Modificaciones importantes desde el comienzo de las estadísticas

En la legislación, la competencia del organismo y/o los procedimientos administrativos hubo modificaciones importantes en 1991, 1996, 1997 y 2001. Los cambios consiguientes en las estadísticas no se han estimado.

Portugal

1. Serie

Título: Número de solicitantes de empleo y Número de desempleados en busca de empleo.

Año de inicio: 1967.

2. Organismo responsable de la inscripción inicial de desempleados

Nombre del organismo: Instituto de Empleo y Formación Profesional (IEFP).

Tipo de organismo: Organismo público subordinado a una autoridad nacional.

Nombre de la autoridad nacional: Ministerio de Seguridad Social y Trabajo.

Ubicación de las oficinas locales donde se hacen las inscripciones: En todo el país hay 86 agencias de empleo, situadas en las cinco regiones del continente, más una agencia en la región autónoma de Madera y tres agencias en la región autónoma de las Azores (las agencias de las dos regions autónomas no dependen directamente del IEFP sino de servicios regionales autónomas, pero las estadísticas son consolidadas por el IEFP).

Además, estas agencias crean "centros de empleo" de carácter permanente o no, en función de criterios tales como la densidad demográfica o las cifras de desempleo registrado. Actualmente, hay casi 150 centros de este tipo.

Tipo de servicios proporcionados/administrados por el organismo

- Ayuda a personas en busca de empleo a encontrarlo;
- Ayuda a personas en busca de empleo a crear su propia empresa;
- Ayuda a los empleadores a encontrar trabajadores;
- Orientación profesional;
- Formación relacionada con el trabajo;
- Pago de prestaciones de desempleo: el IEFP no se ocupa de estos pagos pero coopera con la Seguridad Social para controlar la predisposición activa de los beneficiarios para incorporarse al mercado de trabajo.

Porcentaje de personas en busca de empleo que buscan trabajo por intermedio de ese organismo: 49% (a fines de 2001. Fuente: Encuesta de empleo del Instituto Nacional de Estadística).

3. Se registran los siguientes datos de la persona

- Nombre y apellido;
- Sexo;
- Número de seguridad social (o número de identificación semejante también utilizado por otros organismos);
- Dirección del domicilio habitual;
- Fecha de nacimiento;
- Nacionalidad;
- Nivel de educación/formación: se identifican 11 categorías. No se han establecido vínculos con la CINE, pero la clasificación nacional de ramas de formación, revisada en abril de 2001, tiene vínculos directos con la CINE-97;
- Situación laboral actual o anterior: se identifican siete categorías;
- Tipo de ocupación del empleo actual o anterior: se identifican 355 categorías (grupos primarios). Se han establecido vínculos con la CIUO-88 a nivel de grupos primarios.
- Tipo de ocupación del empleo que se busca: se identifican 355 categorías (grupos primarios);

- Nombre y dirección del empleador o del lugar de trabajo actual o anterior;
- Rama de actividad del empleador o del lugar de trabajo actual o anterior: se identifican 715 categorías. Se han establecido vínculos con la CIIU a nivel de divisiones y con la NACE, a nivel de clases;
- Inscripciones previas en el organismo;
- Otros: identificación de personas discapacitadas y del tipo de discapacidad, por ejemplo.

4. Criterios utilizados para determinar si una persona habrá de incluirse en el registro (R) y/o en las estadísticas de personas desempleadas (S)

- Estar sin empleo (R) y (S);
- Estar en busca de empleo (cabe señalar que la solicitud de apoyo financiero o técnico a fin de crear su propia empresa no se considera solicitud de empleo) (R) y (S);
- Estar disponible para trabajar en un plazo de 15 días como máximo, contados a partir de la fecha de inscripción (R) y (S);
- Edad (mínima: 16 años; no hay edad máxima) (R) y (S);
- Residir en el país, es decir, presentar un documento de identidad que demuestre que se reside en Portugal (en general, cédula de identidad), o bien, el permiso de estadía emitido por el Servicio de Extranjeros y Fronteras, en el caso de ciudadanos no nacionales oriundos de países que no son miembros del Espacio Económico Europeo (EEE) (R) y (S);
- Además, el solicitante debe cumplir los requisitos siguientes: aceptar toda oferta de trabajo que se considere adecuada; aceptar los controles que llevan a cabo las agencias de empleo; aceptar el "Plan personal de empleo", establecido por la agencia y el propio solicitante, que mejor se ajusta a su bagaje personal y profesional con objeto de incorporarse al mercado de trabajo;
- Asimismo, los desempleados que cobran prestaciones de desempleo deben: aceptar un trabajo considerado de utilidad pública; aceptar la formación profesional que se le ofrezca; buscar empleo activamente.

5. Criterios utilizados para determinar si se ha de excluir a una persona del registro (R) y/o de las estadísticas de personas desempleadas (S)

- Certificado de defunción (R) y (S);
- Establecerse en otro país (R) y (S);
- Incorporarse a un (nuevo) empleo (R) y (S);
- Comenzar el servicio militar (R) y (S);
- Participar en un programa de promoción del empleo (R) y (S);
- Participar en un programa de obras públicas (S);
- Estar estudiando o siguiendo una formación, puede tratarse de un curso de formación profesional o de un programa de formación-empleo promovido o no por el IEFP (R) y (S);
- Incumplir el requisito de tomar contacto con el organismo: no presentarse sin motivo justificado a una convocatoria (ya se trate de ofertas de trabajo adecuadas, formación profesional, un trabajo considerado necesario desde el punto de vista social o de un simple control de presencia) implica ser radiado después de la segunda convocatoria; asimismo, no responder a un control postal implica ser radiado después de un mes, en el caso de quienes cobran prestaciones de desempleo y después de dos meses para quienes no las cobran (R) y (S);
- Rechazar una oferta de trabajo adecuada (R) y (S);
- Rechazar una oferta de formación adecuada (R) y (S);
- Incapacidad para trabajar: la incapacidad total por enfermedad (ya sea temporal o permanente) excluye la posibilidad de registrase como persona en busca de empleo o desempleada. La incapacidad por invalidez sólo se admite como criterio para la exclusión del registro cuando es total (ya sea temporal o permanente), aplicable a todas las profesiones adaptadas (o adaptables), certificada por el servicio de medicina del trabajo de las agencias de empleo y, en el caso de quienes cobran prestaciones de desempleo, confirmada por el Servicio de Verificación de Incapacidades (SVI) (R) y (S).

6. Definición de persona desempleada en la que se basan las estadísticas

Se considera "desempleado" a todo solicitante de empleo, registrado en una agencia de empleo, que está sin trabajo, en busca de empleo como trabajador dependiente, inmediatamente disponible y apto para trabajar.

Se entiende por "inmediatamente disponible" que el solicitante se compromete a aceptar un empleo en el plazo de 15 días como máximo, contados a partir de la fecha de su inscripción. Pasado ese período, la aceptación del puesto de trabajo debe ser inmediata.

Se entiende por "apto para trabajar" que el solicitante debe demostrar que posee las aptitudes (físicas, mentales y profesionales) necesarias para ejercer una actividad profesional y la inexistencia de incapacidad por enfermedad.

7. Actualización de los registros

Los registros se actualizan periódica y constantemente.

8. Tasas de desempleo

No se utilizan estadísticas de estos registros para obtener tasas de desempleo.

9. Tipo de estadísticas que se producen sobre desempleados registrados

Período de referencia: Mes.

Frecuencia de producción: Mensual.

Variables utilizadas
– Sexo;
– Edad;
– Nivel de educación;
– Ocupación;
– Rama de actividad;
– Características geográficas;
– Ciudadanía (nacionales o no);
– Duración del desempleo: tiempo que lleva inscrito como solicitante de empleo en una agencia de empleo;
– Otras: Situación respecto al empleo, es decir, en busca del primer empleo o en busca de otro empleo.

Publicación
– En papel, para el público en general;
– En archivo electrónico, previa solicitud;
– En el sitio web:
– http://www.iefp.pt/estatisticas/estatmercemp.htm

Organismo responsable de la publicación: Instituto de Empleo y Formación Profesional (IEFP).

Título y periodicidad de las publicaciones:
Información mensual del mercado de trabajo.
El mercado de trabajo – estadísticas mensuales.
Agencias de empleo – estadísticas mensuales.
Municipios – estadísticas de desempleo registrado y proporciones corregidas de desempleo registrado, estadísticas trimestrales.
Evolución y situación de los mercados locales de trabajo, estadísticas trimestrales.
El mercado de trabajo, informe anual.

10. Información metodológica sobre las estadísticas

Divulgación
– En papel, para el público en general.
– En archivo electrónico, previa solicitud;
– En el sitio web:
http://www.iefp.pt/estatisticas/estatmercemp.htm

Organismo responsable de la divulgación: IEFP.

11. Comparaciones con estadísticas derivadas de otras fuentes

Se han hecho comparaciones con estadísticas de desempleo derivadas de la Encuesta sobre la fuerza de trabajo, otras encuestas de hogares y el Censo de población.

Frecuencia de las comparaciones: Periódica.

Publicación de la metodología/resultados de las comparaciones: No se publican.

12. Modificaciones importantes desde el comienzo de las estadísticas

En la legislación, la competencia del organismo y/o los procedimientos administrativos no ha habido modificaciones importantes que hayan influido significativamente en las estadísticas.

Qatar

1. Serie

Título: Desempleo registrado.

Año de inicio: 1965.

2. Organismo responsable de la inscripción inicial de desempleados

Nombre del organismo: Departamento de Trabajo.

Tipo de organismo: Organismo público subordinado a una autoridad nacional.

Nombre de la autoridad nacional: Ministerio de Administración Pública y Vivienda.

Ubicación de las oficinas locales donde se hacen las inscripciones: Oficina Central del Departamento de Trabajo.

Tipo de servicios proporcionados/administrados por el organismo:
– Ayuda a personas en busca de empleo a encontrarlo;
– Ayuda a los empleadores a encontrar trabajadores;
– Orientación profesional;
– Formación relacionada con el trabajo.

3. Se registran los siguientes datos de la persona:
– Nombre y apellido;
– Sexo;
– Dirección del domicilio habitual;
– Fecha de nacimiento;
– Ciudadanía;
– Nacionalidad/grupo étnico;
– Nivel de educación/formación: se identifica un número indeterminado de categorías. Se han establecido vínculos con la CINE;
– Situación laboral actual o anterior: se identifican cuatro categorías;
– Tipo de ocupación del empleo actual o anterior: se identifican 10 grupos. Se han establecido vínculos con la CIUO-88;
– Tipo de ocupación del empleo que se busca: se identifica un número indeterminado de grupos. Se han establecido vínculos con la CIUO-88;
– Nombre y dirección del empleador o del lugar de trabajo actual o anterior;
– Rama de actividad del empleador o del lugar de trabajo actual o anterior: se identifican 136 grupos. Se han establecido vínculos con la CIIU Rev. 3, a nivel de grupos;
– Inscripciones previas en el organismo;
– Otros: experiencia laboral.

4. Criterios utilizados para determinar si una persona habrá de incluirse en el registro (R) y/o en las estadísticas de personas desempleadas (S):
– Estar sin empleo (R) y (S);
– Estar en busca de empleo (R) y (S);
– Edad (mínima: 18 años; no hay edad máxima:) (R) y (S);
– Residir en el país (R) y (S);
– Haber trabajado (R) y (S).

5. Criterios utilizados para determinar si se ha de excluir a una persona del registro (R) y/o de las estadísticas de personas desempleadas (S):
– Certificado de defunción (R);
– Establecerse en otro país (R);
– Incorporarse a un (nuevo) empleo (R);
– Comenzar el servicio militar (R);
– Estar estudiando (R).

6. Definición de persona desempleada en la que se basan las estadísticas

Personas desempleadas son aquellas que no estaban empleadas, querían trabajar, estaban buscando empleo y no lo habían encontrado en el período de referencia (semana de la encuesta).

7. Actualización de los registros

Los registros se actualizan anualmente.

8. Tasas de desempleo

No se utilizan estadísticas de estos registros para obtener tasas de desempleo.

9. Tipo de estadísticas que se producen sobre desempleados registrados

Período de referencia: Semana.

Frecuencia de producción: Anual.

Variables utilizadas:
– Sexo;
– Edad;
– Nivel de educación;
– Ocupación;
– Rama de actividad;
– Características geográficas;
– Experiencia laboral previa;
– Ciudadanía (nacionales o no).

Publicación: En papel, para un público limitado.

Organismo responsable de la publicación: Ministerio de Administración Pública y Vivienda.

10. Información metodológica sobre las estadísticas

Divulgación: No se divulgan, sólo para uso interno.

Organismo responsable: Ministerio de Administración Pública y Vivienda.

11. Comparaciones con estadísticas derivadas de otras fuentes

Se han hecho comparaciones con estadísticas de desempleo derivadas de la Encuesta sobre la fuerza de trabajo, otro tipo de encuesta de hogares y el Censo de población.

Frecuencia de las comparaciones: Periódica, cuando se publican las estadísticas.

Publicación de la metodología/resultados de las comparaciones: No se publican.

12. Modificaciones importantes desde el comienzo de las estadísticas

Después de que el Consejo Ministerial adoptara en 1997 una resolución por la que se alienta a los ciudadanos de Qatar a trabajar en el sector privado, el número de personas desempleadas registradas aumentó.

Rumania

1. Serie

Título: Situación estadística del desempleo.

Año de inicio: 1991.

2. Organismo responsable de la inscripción inicial de desempleados

Nombre del organismo: Agentia nationala pentru ocuparea fortei de munca (Agencia Nacional de Empleo).

Tipo de organismo: Organismo público subordinado a una autoridad nacional.

Nombre de la autoridad nacional: Ministerio de Trabajo y Solidaridad Social.

Ubicación de las oficinas locales donde se hacen las inscripciones: En todos los condados y en el municipio de Bucarest.

Tipo de servicios proporcionados/administrados por el organismo

– Ayuda a personas en busca de empleo a encontrarlo;
– Ayuda a personas en busca de empleo a crear su propia empresa;
– Ayuda a los empleadores a encontrar trabajadores;
– Orientación profesional;
– Formación relacionada con el trabajo;
– Pago de prestaciones de desempleo.

Porcentaje de personas en busca de empleo que buscan trabajo por intermedio de ese organismo: 75%.

3. Se registran los siguientes datos de la persona

– Nombre y apellido;
– Sexo;
– Número de seguridad social (o número de identificación semejante también utilizado por otros organismos);
– Dirección del domicilio habitual;
– Fecha de nacimiento;
– Ciudadanía;
– Nacionalidad/grupo étnico;
– Nivel de educación/formación: se identifican seis categorías;
– Situación laboral actual o anterior: se identifican cinco categorías;
– Tipo de ocupación del empleo actual o anterior: se identifican 415 categorías. Se han establecido vínculos con la CIUO-88 a nivel de grupos unitarios;
– Tipo de ocupación del empleo que se busca: se identifican 415 categorías. Se han establecido vínculos con la CIUO-88 a nivel de grupos unitarios;
– Nombre y dirección del empleador o del lugar de trabajo actual o anterior;
– Rama de actividad del empleador o del lugar de trabajo actual o anterior;
– Inscripciones previas en el organismo.

4. Criterios utilizados para determinar si una persona habrá de incluirse en el registro (R) y/o en las estadísticas de personas desempleadas (S)

– Estar sin empleo (R) y (S);
– Estar en busca de empleo (R) y (S);
– Estar disponible para trabajar (R);
– Residir en el país (R) y (S);
– Haber trabajado (R) y (S).

5. Criterios utilizados para determinar si se ha de excluir a una persona del registro (R) y/o de las estadísticas de personas desempleadas (S)

– Certificado de defunción (R) y (S);
– Establecerse en otro país (R) y (S);
– Incorporarse a un (nuevo) empleo (R) y (S);
– Comenzar el servicio militar (R) y (S);

– Participar en algún programa de promoción del empleo, de obras públicas, etc. (R) y (S);
– Incumplir el requisito de tomar contacto con el organismo. La persona desempleada debe presentarse una vez por mes en el servicio de empleo (R) y (S);
– Rechazar una oferta de trabajo adecuada (R) y (S);
– Rechazar una oferta de formación adecuada (R) y (S);
– Cobrar alguna pensión (R) y (S).

6. Definición de persona desempleada en la que se basan las estadísticas

Según la Ley sobre el sistema de seguro de desempleo y estímulo del empleo (núm. 76/2002) "se entiende por desempleada a la persona que reúne los requisitos siguientes:

– estar en busca de empleo, a partir de los 16 años y hasta que reúna los requisitos para jubilarse;
– gozar de buena salud y ser física y mentalmente apta para ocupar un empleo;
– estar sin trabajo, no ganar ingreso alguno o ganar ingresos generados por actividades autorizadas por la ley y que son inferiores a la prestación de desempleo a la que tiene derecho según lo estipulado por la presente ley;
– estar disponible para empezar a trabajar en cuanto encuentre un empleo;
– estar registrada en la Agencia Nacional de Empleo o en algún otro servicio de empleo que opere de conformidad con la ley".

7. Actualización de los registros

Los registros se actualizan mensualmente.

8. Tasas de desempleo

Se utilizan estadísticas de estos registros para obtener tasas de desempleo.

Fuentes de los datos de empleo incluidos en el denominador de las tasas de desempleo: Censo de población y datos del Instituto Nacional de Estadística y Estudios Económicos.

Definición de persona empleada que se utiliza a tales efectos
Población civil económicamente activa.

9. Tipo de estadísticas que se producen sobre desempleados registrados

Período de referencia: Mes.

Frecuencia de producción: Mensual.

Variables utilizadas

– Sexo;
– Edad;
– Nivel de educación;
– Ocupación;
– Rama de actividad;
– Características geográficas;
– Experiencia laboral previa;
– Ciudadanía (nacionales o no);
– Duración del desempleo;
– Otras: modalidad de indemnización.

Publicación

– En papel, para el público en general;
– En archivo electrónico, previa solicitud.

Título y periodicidad de las publicaciones: Situación estadística del desempleo, mensual.

10. Información metodológica sobre las estadísticas Divulgación:

– No se divulga, sólo para uso interno;
– En archivo electrónico, previa solicitud.

11. Comparaciones con estadísticas derivadas de otras fuentes

El Instituto Nacional de Estadística y Estudios Económicos ha hecho comparaciones con estadísticas de desempleo derivadas de otras fuentes.

Frecuencia de las comparaciones: Periódica.

12. Modificaciones importantes desde el comienzo de las estadísticas

La nueva ley sobre el sistema de seguro de desempleo y estímulo del empleo, que entró en vigor en marzo de 2002, generó modificaciones importantes, principalmente, en lo que respecta al nivel de las prestaciones de desempleo, las modalidades de indemnización, las estadísticas, etc.

San Pedro y Miquelón

1. Serie

Título: Panorama mensual del empleo

Año de inicio: 1980.

2. Organismo responsable de la inscripción inicial de desempleados

Nombre del organismo: Agence nationale pour l'Emploi - ANPE (Agencia Nacional de Empleo).

Tipo de organismo: Organismo público subordinado a una autoridad nacional.

Nombre de la autoridad nacional: Ministerio Encargado de Trabajo y Empleo.

Ubicación de las oficinas locales donde se hacen las inscripciones: Un puesto operativo permanente en la isla San Pedro.

Tipo de servicios proporcionados/administrados por el organismo
– Ayuda a personas en busca de empleo a encontrarlo;
– Ayuda a los empleadores a encontrar trabajadores;
– Orientación profesional;
– Formación relacionada con el trabajo.

Porcentaje de personas en busca de empleo que buscan trabajo por intermedio de ese organismo: Hasta los 57 años, toda persona en busca de empleo debe responder a las convocatorias de la ANPE: entrevistas; puesta en contacto; propuestas de seguimiento (las personas mayores de 57 años no tienen obligación de buscar empleo).

3. Se registran los siguientes datos de la persona
– Nombre y apellido;
– Sexo;
– Número de seguridad social (o número de identificación semejante también utilizado por otros organismos);
– Dirección del domicilio habitual;
– Fecha de nacimiento;
– Ciudadanía;
– Nacionalidad;
– Nivel de formación: se identifican seis categorías. No se han establecido vínculos con la CINE;
– Situación laboral actual o anterior;
– Tipo de ocupación del empleo actual o anterior: se identifican 61 categorías (Repertorio operativo de oficios). No se han establecido vínculos con la CIUO.
– Calificaciones.

4. Criterios utilizados para determinar si una persona habrá de incluirse en el registro (R) y/o en las estadísticas de personas desempleadas (S)
– Estar sin empleo (R) y (S);
– Estar en busca de empleo (R) y (S);
– Estar disponible para trabajar (R) y (S);
– Edad (mínima: 15 años; máxima: 57 años) (R) y (S);
– Ciudadanía (R) y (S);
– Residir en el país o ser titular de una tarjeta de estadía (R) y (S);
– Duración y/o número de horas de trabajo del empleo que se busca: las personas que buscan empleo a tiempo parcial (mínimo 16 horas por semana) son inscrita de la Categoría 2 que se define en el punto 6.

5. Criterios utilizados para determinar si se ha de excluir a una persona del registro (R) y/o de las estadísticas de personas desempleadas (S)
– Certificado de defunción (R) y (S);
– Establecerse en otro país (R) y (S);
– Incorporarse a un (nuevo) empleo. Existe la posibilidad de ejercer una actividad reducida y, a la vez, estar inscrita como persona en busca de empleo (transferencia en la categoría 6, 7 u 8 descritas en el punto 6);
– Participar en algún programa de promoción del empleo, de obras públicas, etc. (R) y (S);
– Estar estudiando o siguiendo una formación (transferencia en la Categoría 4 descrita en el punto 6);
– Incumplir el requisito de tomar contacto con el organismo o no presentarse a una convocatoria (R) y (S);
– Rechazar ofertas de trabajo adecuadas (R) y (S);
– Rechazar ofertas de formación adecuadas (R) y (S);
– Incapacidad para trabajar, períodos de enfermedad (transferencia en la Categoría 5 descrita en el punto 6).

6. Definiciones de persona desempleada en las que se basan las estadísticas

Categoría 1: Persona sin empleo que está disponible para trabajar inmediatamente a tenor del Artículo R.311-3-3, que *busca un empleo* **a tiempo completo de duración indeterminada** y tiene el deber de cumplir actos positivos de búsqueda de empleo.
Esta persona no debe haber ejercido ninguna actividad ocasional o limitada de más de 78 horas durante el mes de actualización.

Categoría 2: Persona sin empleo que está disponible para trabajar inmediatamente a tenor del Artículo R.311-3-3, que *busca un empleo* **a tiempo parcial de duración indeterminada** y tiene el deber de cumplir actos positivos de búsqueda de empleo,
Esta persona no debe haber ejercido ninguna actividad ocasional o limitada de más de 78 horas durante el mes de actualización.

Categoría 3: Persona sin empleo que está disponible para trabajar inmediatamente a tenor del Artículo R.311-3-3, que *busca un empleo* **de duración determinada, temporal o estacional,** *incluso de cortísima duración,* y tiene el deber de cumplir actos positivos de búsqueda de empleo.
Esta persona no debe haber ejercido ninguna actividad ocasional o limitada de más de 78 horas durante el mes de actualización.

Categoría 4: Persona sin empleo, que busca empleo y no está disponible inmediatamente.

Categoría 5: Persona con empleo que busca otro.

Categoría 6: Persona que no está disponible para trabajar inmediatamente a tenor del Artículo R.311-3-3 (1.°), que *busca otro empleo a tiempo completo de duración indeterminada* y tiene el deber de cumplir actos positivos de búsqueda de empleo.
Esta persona ha ejercido una actividad ocasional o limitada de más de 78 horas durante el mes de actualización.

Categoría 7: Persona que no está disponible para trabajar inmediatamente a tenor del Artículo R.311-3-3 (1.°), que *busca otro empleo a tiempo parcial de duración indeterminada* y tiene el deber de cumplir actos positivos de búsqueda de empleo.
Esta persona ha ejercido una actividad ocasional o limitada de más de 78 horas durante el mes de actualización.

Categoría 8: Persona que no está disponible para trabajar inmediatamente a tenor del Artículo R.311-3-3 (1.°), que *busca otro empleo de duración determinada, temporal o estacional, incluso de cortísima duración,* y tiene el deber de cumplir actos positivos de búsqueda de empleo.
Esta persona ha ejercido una actividad ocasional o limitada de más de 78 horas durante el mes de actualización.

7. Actualización de los registros
Los registros se actualizan mensualmente.

8. Tasas de desempleo
Se utilizan estadísticas de estos registros para obtener tasas de desempleo.
Fuente de los datos de empleo incluidos en el denominador de las tasas de desempleo: Censo de población.

9. Tipo de estadísticas que se producen sobre desempleados registrados
Período de referencia: Mes.
Frecuencia de producción: Mensual.
Variables utilizadas
– Sexo;
– Edad;
– Nivel de educación;
– Ocupación que se busca;
– Duración del desempleo.

Publicación: Dirigida a servicios estatales, representantes electos y organismos de carácter económico y social. El panorama mensual es presentado por las radios locales y la prensa local publica fragmentos del mismo.

Organismo responsable de la publicación: Servicio de Trabajo, Empleo y Formación Profesional: agregación de los datos proporcionados por la ANPE con series relativas a la política de empleo y comentarios.

10. Información metodológica sobre las estadísticas
Sólo la Categoría 1, descrita en el punto 6, sirve de base para las estadísticas. Los comentarios pueden contener datos relativos a las demás categorías, si son significativos.

Divulgación: A través de los comentarios del panorama mensual.
Organismo responsable de la divulgación: Servicio de Trabajo, Empleo y Formación Profesional.

11. Comparaciones con estadísticas derivadas de otras fuentes
Se han hecho comparaciones con estadísticas de desempleo derivadas del Censo general de población.
Frecuencia de las comparaciones: Principalmente, cuando los datos del censo son recientes.
Publicación de la metodología/resultados de las comparaciones: A través de los comentarios del panorama mensual.

12. Modificaciones importantes desde el comienzo de las estadísticas
En la legislación, la competencia del organismo y/o los procedimientos administrativos hubo modificaciones importantes en 1995, a saber: anulación del requisito de presentarse al control; informatización del servicio de la ANPE; y explotación de los datos

relativos al desempleo de larga duración mediante ajuste de las herramientas de política de empleo e inserción.

Serbia y Montenegro

1. Serie
Título: Desempleo registrado.
Año de inicio: No indicado.
2. Organismo responsable de la inscripción inicial de desempleados
Nombre del organismo: Oficina de Trabajo de las Repúblicas.
Tipo de organismo: Organismo público subordinado a una autoridad nacional.
Nombre de la autoridad nacional: Ministerio de Trabajo y Empleo.
Ubicación de las oficinas locales donde se hacen las inscripciones: En todos los distritos de Serbia y Montenegro.
Tipo de servicios proporcionados/administrados por el organismo:
- Ayuda a personas en busca de empleo a encontrarlo;
- Ayuda a personas en busca de empleo a crear su propia empresa;
- Ayuda a los empleadores a encontrar trabajadores;
- Orientación profesional;
- Formación relacionada con el trabajo;
- Pago de prestaciones de desempleo;
- Otros: da información sobre el mercado de trabajo; toma medidas de política activa respecto a determinadas categorías de personas desempleadas (inválidas y demás).

Porcentaje de personas en busca de empleo que buscan trabajo por intermedio de ese organismo: 29%.
3. Se registran los siguientes datos de la persona:
- Nombre y apellido;
- Sexo;
- Número de seguridad social (o número de identificación semejante también utilizado por otros organismos);
- Dirección del domicilio habitual;
- Fecha de nacimiento;
- Ciudadanía;
- Nivel de educación/formación: se identifican nueve categorías. No se han establecido vínculos con la CINE;
- Situación laboral actual o anterior: se identifican tres categorías;
- Tipo de ocupación del empleo actual o anterior: se identifican 74 grupos (unas 3.500 profesiones individuales). No se han establecido vínculos con la CIUO-88;
- Tipo de ocupación del empleo que se busca: se identifican 74 grupos (unas 3.500 profesiones individuales). No se han establecido vínculos con la CIUO-88;
- Nombre y dirección del empleador o del lugar de trabajo actual o anterior;
- Rama de actividad del empleador o del lugar de trabajo actual o anterior: se identifican 17 grupos. Se han establecido vínculos con la CIIU Rev. 3 y la NACE Rev. 1;
- Inscripciones previas en el organismo;
- Otros: motivación profesional de la persona desempleada; conocimientos y competencias especiales; derechos de la persona desempleada; fechas de mediación.

4. Criterios utilizados para determinar si una persona habrá de incluirse en el registro (R) y/o en las estadísticas de personas desempleadas (S):
- Estar sin empleo (R) y (S);
- Estar en busca de empleo (R) y (S);
- Estar disponible para trabajar (R);
- Edad (mínima: no indicada; máxima: no indicada) (R) y (S);
- Ciudadanía (R);
- Residir en el país (R);
- Haber trabajado (R) y (S);
- Duración y/o número de horas de trabajo del empleo que se busca (R);
- Pago de cotizaciones del seguro de desempleo (R).

5. Criterios utilizados para determinar si se ha de excluir a una persona del registro (R) y/o de las estadísticas de personas desempleadas (S):
- Certificado de defunción (R) y (S);
- Establecerse en otro país (R) y (S);
- Incorporarse a un (nuevo) empleo (R) y (S);
- Participar en algún programa de promoción del empleo, de obras públicas, etc; (R) y (S);
- Incumplir el requisito de tomar contacto con el organismo (R);

- Rechazar una oferta de trabajo por mes (R);
- Fin del período de prestaciones de desempleo (R);
- Cobrar alguna pensión (R);
- Incapacidad para trabajar (R);
- Otros: si está sujeta a alguna condena o pena correccional de más de seis meses (R).

6. Definición de persona desempleada en la que se basan las estadísticas
Persona que no tiene trabajo, que está disponible para trabajar, que busca empleo y que está inscrita en el registro regular de la Oficina de Empleo.
7. Actualización de los registros
Los registros se actualizan mensual y anualmente.
8. Tasas de desempleo
Se utilizan estadísticas de estos registros para obtener tasas de desempleo.
Fuentes de los datos de empleo incluidos en el denominador de las tasas de desempleo: Encuesta sobre la fuerza de trabajo e informes mensuales sobre personas empleadas y salarios.
Definición de persona empleada que se utiliza a tales efectos:
Personas que trabajan en empresas, organizaciones o en el sector privado.
9. Tipo de estadísticas que se producen sobre desempleados registrados
Serie 1:
Período de referencia: Mes y año.
Frecuencia de producción: Mensual.
Variables utilizadas:
- Sexo;
- Nivel de educación;
- Rama de actividad;
- Características geográficas;
- Otras: motivo del cese de empleo; personas que siguen cursos de formación.

Publicación: En papel, para el público en general.
Organismo responsable de la publicación: Oficina Federal de Mercado de Trabajo y Migraciones.
Título y periodicidad de la publicación: *Monthly Statistical Survey - Employment* (Encuesta estadística mensual - Empleo).
Serie 2:
Período de referencia: Mes y año.
Frecuencia de producción: Mensual.
Variables utilizadas:
- Sexo;
- Edad;
- Nivel de educación;
- Ocupación;
- Características geográficas;
- Experiencia laboral previa;
- Ciudadanía (nacionales o no);
- Duración del desempleo;
- Otras: beneficiarios de prestaciones de desempleo; total de pagos en efectivo de prestaciones de desempleo (por mes y por año).

Publicación: En papel, para un público limitado.
Organismo responsable de la publicación: Oficina Federal de Mercado de Trabajo y Migraciones.
Título y periodicidad de la publicación: *Statistical Yearbook - Placement of unemployed persons* (Anuario estadístico - Colocación de personas desempleadas).
10. Información metodológica sobre las estadísticas
Divulgación: En papel, para un público limitado.
Organismo responsable: Oficina Federal de Mercado de Trabajo y Migraciones.
11. Comparaciones con estadísticas derivadas de otras fuentes
No se han hecho comparaciones con estadísticas de desempleo derivadas de otras fuentes.
12. Modificaciones importantes desde el comienzo de las estadísticas
En la legislación, la competencia del organismo y/o los procedimientos administrativos no ha habido modificaciones importantes que hayan influido significativamente en las estadísticas.

Suecia

1. Serie
Título: Arbetsmarknadsdata (Datos del mercado de trabajo).
Año de inicio: 1992 (en las series anteriores había definiciones diferentes).

2. Organismo responsable de la inscripción inicial de desempleados
Nombre del organismo: Arbetsförmedlingen (Servicio Público de Empleo).
Tipo de organismo: Organismo público subordinado a una autoridad nacional.
Nombre de la autoridad nacional: Administración Nacional del Mercado de Trabajo.
Ubicación de las oficinas locales donde se hacen las inscripciones: Por lo general, hay al menos una oficina en cada municipio.
Tipo de servicios proporcionados/administrados por el organismo:
– Ayuda a personas en busca de empleo a encontrarlo;
– Ayuda a personas en busca de empleo a crear su propia empresa;
– Ayuda a los empleadores a encontrar trabajadores;
– Orientación profesional;
– Formación relacionada con el trabajo;
– Pago de prestaciones de desempleo.
Porcentaje de personas en busca de empleo que buscan trabajo por intermedio de ese organismo: 50%.
3. Se registran los siguientes datos de la persona:
– Nombre y apellido;
– Sexo;
– Número de seguridad social (o número de identificación semejante también utilizado por otros organismos);
– Dirección del domicilio habitual;
– Fecha de nacimiento;
– Ciudadanía;
– Nivel de educación/formación;
– Situación laboral actual o anterior: se identifican 30 categorías;
– Tipo de ocupación del empleo que se busca: se identifican 700 grupos. Se han establecido vínculos con la CIUO-88 a nivel de grupos unitarios;
– Inscripciones previas en el organismo.
4. Criterios utilizados para determinar si una persona habrá de incluirse en el registro (R) y/o en las estadísticas de personas desempleadas (S):
– Estar sin empleo (S);
– Estar disponible para trabajar (debe estar disponible para ocupar un puesto de inmediato) (S);
– Residir en el país (S).
5. Criterios utilizados para determinar si se ha de excluir a una persona del registro (R) y/o de las estadísticas de personas desempleadas (S):
– Certificado de defunción (R) y (S);
– Establecerse en otro país (S);
– Incorporarse a un (nuevo) empleo (S);
– Comenzar el servicio militar (S);
– Participar en algún programa de promoción del empleo, de obras públicas, etc. (S);
– Estar estudiando o siguiendo una formación (S);
– Incumplir el requisito de tomar contacto con el organismo (S);
– Cobrar alguna pensión (S);
– Incapacidad para trabajar (para que la persona se contabilice como desempleada debe estar en condiciones de trabajar o bien, su expediente puede estar sujeto a investigación).
6. Definición de persona desempleada en la que se basan las estadísticas
Personas sin empleo (salvo empleo secundario que se pueda combinar con un empleo regular a tiempo completo) que reciben servicios de colocación o asesoramiento, o que están en espera de incorporarse a un programa activo de mercado de trabajo.
7. Actualización de los registros
Los registros se actualizan a diario.
8. Tasas de desempleo
Se utilizan estadísticas de estos registros para obtener tasas de desempleo.
Fuentes de los datos de empleo incluidos en el denominador de las tasas de desempleo: Encuesta sobre la fuerza de trabajo y Censo de población.
Definición de persona empleada que se utiliza a tales efectos:
Población de 18 a 64 años es la más utilizada; a veces, se utiliza la definición de la Encuesta sobre la fuerza de trabajo (se entiende por personas empleadas aquellas que habían trabajado una hora como mínimo durante la semana de referencia y aquellas que estaban temporalmente ausentes).

9. Tipo de estadísticas que se producen sobre desempleados registrados
Serie 1:
Período de referencia: Semana.
Frecuencia de producción: Semanal.
Variables utilizadas:
– Sexo;
– Edad;
– Características geográficas;
– Ciudadanía (nacionales o no);
– Duración del desempleo.
Publicación: En el sitio web www.ams.se.
Organismo responsable de la publicación: Junta Nacional del Mercado de Trabajo.
Periodicidad de la publicación: Semanal.
Serie 2:
Período de referencia: Mes, trimestre y año.
Frecuencia de producción: Mensual.
Variables utilizadas:
– Sexo;
– Edad;
– Características geográficas;
– Ciudadanía (nacionales o no);
– Duración del desempleo.
Publicación:
– En papel, para el público en general;
– En el sitio web www.ams.se.
Organismo responsable de la publicación: Junta Nacional del Mercado de Trabajo.
Título y periodicidad de la publicación: *Arbetsmarknadsdata* (mensual).
10. Información metodológica sobre las estadísticas
Divulgación:
– En papel, para el público en general;
– En el sitio web www.ams.se.
Organismo responsable: Junta Nacional del Mercado de Trabajo.
11. Comparaciones con estadísticas derivadas de otras fuentes
Se hacen comparaciones con las estadísticas de desempleo de la Encuesta sobre la fuerza de trabajo. La respuesta dada en dicha encuesta se compara con la situación según el registro individual.
Frecuencia de las comparaciones: Periódica, cuando se publican las estadísticas.
Publicación de la metodología/resultados de las comparaciones: No se publican.
12. Modificaciones importantes desde el comienzo de las estadísticas
En la legislación, la competencia del organismo y/o los procedimientos administrativos no ha habido modificaciones importantes que hayan influido significativamente en las estadísticas.

Suiza

1. Serie
Título: Desempleados registrados; Anuncios de puestos vacantes; Personas en busca de empleo registradas; Beneficiarios del seguro de desempleo.
Año de inicio: 1936.
2. Organismo responsable de la inscripción inicial de desempleados
Nombre del organismo: Oficina Regional de Colocación.
Tipo de organismo: Organismo público subordinado a una autoridad nacional.
Nombre de la autoridad nacional: Las condiciones marco se definen a escala nacional y la aplicación incumbe a los cantones.
Ubicación de las oficinas locales donde se hacen las inscripciones: Todo el país, a través de las oficinas regionales de colocación.
Tipo de servicios proporcionados/administrados por el organismo
– Ayuda a personas en busca de empleo a encontrarlo;
– Ayuda a personas en busca de empleo a crear su propia empresa;
– Ayuda a los empleadores a encontrar trabajadores;
– Formación relacionada con el trabajo.
3. Se registran los siguientes datos de la persona
– Nombre y apellido;
– Sexo;
– Número de seguridad social (o número de identificación semejante también utilizado por otros organismos);

- Dirección del domicilio habitual;
- Fecha de nacimiento;
- Ciudadanía;
- Nacionalidad/grupo étnico;
- Nivel de educación/formación: se identifican tres categorías. No se han establecido vínculos con la CINE;
- Situación laboral actual o anterior: se identifican 10 categorías;
- Tipo de ocupación del empleo actual o anterior: se identifican 15.000 categorías. No se han establecido vínculos con la CIUO-88;
- Tipo de ocupación del empleo que se busca: se identifican 15.000 categorías;
- Nombre y dirección del empleador o del lugar de trabajo actual o anterior;
- Rama de actividad del empleador o del lugar de trabajo actual o anterior: se identifican 220 categorías. No se han establecido vínculos con la CIIU. Se utiliza la clasificación NOGA, derivada de la NACE;
- Inscripciones previas en el organismo;
- Conocimiento de idiomas.

4. Criterios utilizados para determinar si una persona habrá de incluirse en el registro (R) y/o en las estadísticas de personas desempleadas (S)
- Estar sin empleo (S);
- Estar en busca de empleo (R) y (S);
- Estar disponible para trabajar (S);
- Edad (mínima: 15 años; no hay edad máxima) (R) y (S);
- Residir en el país: estar domiciliado en Suiza y, en el caso de los extranjeros, ser titular de un permiso de trabajo (R) y (S);
- Otros: la persona de inscribirse personalmente en alguna oficina regional de colocación.

5. Criterios utilizados para determinar si se ha de excluir a una persona del registro (R) y/o de las estadísticas de personas desempleadas (S)
- Certificado de defunción (R) y (S);
- Establecerse en otro país (R) y (S);
- Incorporarse a un (nuevo) empleo, y por lo tanto, dejar de estar disponible (S);
- Comenzar el servicio militar (S);
- Participar en algún programa de promoción del empleo, de obras públicas, etc. (S);
- Estar estudiando o siguiendo una formación (S);
- Incumplir el requisito de tomar contacto con el organismo: después de dos meses, por lo general, se suprime el expediente inactivo. En principio, la persona en busca de empleo debe tener, como mínimo, dos entrevistas por mes con un asesor de la oficina regional de empleo (R) y (S);
- Incapacidad para trabajar: enfermedad, accidente, encarcelamiento...(S).

6. Definición de persona desempleada en la que se basan las estadísticas
Desempleado registrado: Toda persona inscrita en alguna oficina regional de colocación, que está sin empleo e inmediatamente disponible con miras a una colocación, beneficie o no de prestaciones de desempleo.
Se entiende por desempleado completo a quien busca un empleo a tiempo completo, y por desempleado parcial a quien busca un empleo a tiempo parcial

7. Actualización de los registros
Los registros se actualizan periódica y constantemente.

8. Tasas de desempleo
Se utilizan estadísticas de estos registros para obtener tasas de desempleo.
Fuente de los datos de empleo incluidos en el denominador de las tasas de desempleo: Censo de población.
Definición de persona empleada utilizada a tales efectos
Toda persona de 15 años o más que trabaja seis horas o más por semana.

9. Tipo de estadísticas que se producen sobre desempleados registrados
Serie 1: Número de personas en busca de empleo y flujo (entradas y salidas).
Período de referencia: Mes y año.
Frecuencia de producción: Mensual.
Variables utilizadas
- Sexo;
- Edad;
- Ocupación;
- Rama de actividad;

- Características geográficas;
- Experiencia laboral previa;
- Ciudadanía (nacionales o no);
- Duración del desempleo.

Publicación
- En papel, para el público en general;
- En el sitio web: www.seco-admin.ch

Organismo responsable de la publicación: Secretaría Estatal de Economía (SECO).
Título y periodicidad de la publicación: *Situation sur le marché du travail* (Situación del mercado de trabajo), mensual.
Serie 2: Número de desempleados.
Período de referencia: Mes y año.
Frecuencia de producción: Anual.
Variables utilizadas
- Sexo;
- Edad;
- Ocupación;
- Rama de actividad;
- Características geográficas;
- Experiencia laboral previa;
- Ciudadanía (nacionales o no);
- Duración del desempleo.

Publicación: En papel, para el público en general.
Organismo responsable de la publicación: Oficina Federal de Estadística (OFS) y SECO.
Título y periodicidad de la publicación: *Le chômage en Suisse* (El desempleo en Suiza), anual.

10. Información metodológica sobre las estadísticas
Divulgación:
- En papel, para el público en general;
- En el sitio web: www.seco-admin.ch

Organismo responsable: SECO.

11. Comparaciones con estadísticas derivadas de otras fuentes
Se han hecho comparaciones con estadísticas de desempleo derivadas de la Encuesta sobre la fuerza de trabajo.
Frecuencia de las comparaciones: De vez en cuando (último año: 1999).
Publicación de la metodología/resultados de las comparaciones: Se publicaron en: *Indicateurs du marché du travail 1998* (Indicadores del mercado de trabajo - 1998), *OFS,* Neuchâtel 1999, ISBN. 3-303-03113-4 (*page 42*).

12. Modificaciones importantes desde el comienzo de las estadísticas
En la legislación, la competencia del organismo y/o los procedimientos administrativos hubo modificaciones importantes en 1982, 1995 y 1997. No se conoce el alcance de los cambios que trajeron aparejados dichas modificaciones.

Suriname

1. Serie
Título: Estadísticas de personas en busca de empleo registradas.
Año de inicio: 1983.

2. Organismo responsable de la inscripción inicial de desempleados
Nombre del organismo: Dienst der Arbeidsbemiddeling (Oficina de la Bolsa de Trabajo).
Tipo de organismo: Organismo público subordinado a una autoridad nacional.
Nombre de la autoridad nacional: Ministerio de Desarrollo Tecnológico del Trabajo y Medio Ambiente.
Ubicación de las oficinas locales donde se hacen las inscripciones: Distritos de Paramaribo, Saramacca y Nickerie.
Tipo de servicios proporcionados/administrados por el organismo:
- Ayuda a personas en busca de empleo a encontrarlo;
- Ayuda a los empleadores a encontrar trabajadores;
- Formación relacionada con el trabajo;
- Otros: acceso a información pertinente sobre el mercado de trabajo.

Número de personas en busca de empleo que buscan trabajo por intermedio de ese organismo: Unas 80 por mes.

3. Se registran los siguientes datos de la persona:
- Nombre y apellido;
- Sexo;
- Número de seguridad social (o número de identificación semejante también utilizado por otros organismos);
- Dirección del domicilio habitual;
- Fecha de nacimiento;

- Ciudadanía;
- Nacionalidad/grupo étnico;
- Nivel de educación/formación: se identifica un número indeterminado de categorías. Se han establecido vínculos con la CINE;
- Situación laboral actual o anterior: se identifican tres categorías;
- Tipo de ocupación del empleo actual o anterior: se identifican nueve grupos. No se han establecido vínculos con la CIUO-88;
- Tipo de ocupación del empleo que se busca: se identifican nueve grupos. No se han establecido vínculos con la CIUO-88;
- Nombre y dirección del empleador o del lugar de trabajo actual o anterior;
- Rama de actividad del empleador o del lugar de trabajo actual o anterior: se identifican nueve grupos. No se han establecido vínculos con la CIIU Rev. 3;
- Inscripciones previas en el organismo.

4. Criterios utilizados para determinar si una persona habrá de incluirse en el registro (R) y/o en las estadísticas de personas desempleadas (S):
- Estar sin empleo (S);
- Estar en busca de empleo (S);
- Edad (mínima: 15 años; máxima: 65 años) (S);
- Duración y/o número de horas de trabajo del empleo que se busca (S).

5. Criterios utilizados para determinar si se ha de excluir a una persona del registro (R) y/o de las estadísticas de personas desempleadas (S):
- Establecerse en otro país (S);
- Estar estudiando o siguiendo una formación (S);
- Incapacidad para trabajar (S).

6. Definición de persona desempleada en la que se basan las estadísticas
No se dispone de información.

7. Actualización de los registros
No se sabe si los registros se actualizan periódicamente.

8. Tasas de desempleo
No se utilizan estadísticas de estos registros para obtener tasas de desempleo.

9. Tipo de estadísticas que se producen sobre desempleados registrados
No se dispone de información.

10. Información metodológica sobre las estadísticas
No se dispone de información.

11. Comparaciones con estadísticas derivadas de otras fuentes
Según resulta, no se han hecho comparaciones con estadísticas de desempleo derivadas de otras fuentes.

12. Modificaciones importantes desde el comienzo de las estadísticas
Según resulta, en la legislación, la competencia del organismo y/o los procedimientos administrativos no ha habido modificaciones importantes que hayan influido significativamente en las estadísticas.

Tailandia

1. Serie
Título: Personas en busca de empleo registradas.
Año de inicio: No se indica.
2. Organismo responsable de la inscripción inicial de desempleados
Nombre del organismo: Departamento de Empleo.
Tipo de organismo: Organismo público subordinado a una autoridad nacional.
Nombre de la autoridad nacional: Ministerio de Empleo y Bienestar Social.
Ubicación de las oficinas locales donde se hacen las inscripciones: 84 Oficinas de Empleo en el país - en cada provincia y en Bangkok.
Tipo de servicios proporcionados/administrados por el organismo
- Ayuda a personas en busca de empleo a encontrarlo;
- Ayuda a personas en busca de empleo a crear su propia empresa;
- Ayuda a los empleadores a encontrar trabajadores;
- Orientación profesional;
- Formación relacionada con el trabajo;

- Otros: ayuda a personas con discapacidades a encontrar trabajo.

Porcentaje de personas en busca de empleo que buscan trabajo por intermedio de ese organismo: 20%.
3. Se registran los siguientes datos de la persona
- Nombre y apellido;
- Sexo;
- Número de seguridad social (o número de identificación semejante también utilizado por otros organismos);
- Dirección del domicilio habitual;
- Fecha de nacimiento;
- Ciudadanía;
- Nivel de educación/formación: se identifican nueve categorías. No se han establecido vínculos con la CINE;
- Tipo de ocupación del empleo actual o anterior: se identifican nueve categorías. Se han establecido vínculos con grandes grupos de la CIUO-88;
- Tipo de ocupación del empleo que se busca: se identifican nueve categorías. Se han establecido vínculos con grandes grupos de la CIUO-88;
- Nombre del lugar de trabajo anterior;
- Otros: incapacidad (en el caso de una persona discapacitada).

4. Criterios utilizados para determinar si una persona habrá de incluirse en el registro (R) y/o en las estadísticas de personas desempleadas (S)
No se dispone de información.

5. Criterios utilizados para determinar si se ha de excluir a una persona del registro (R) y/o de las estadísticas de personas desempleadas (S)
No se dispone de información.

6. Definición de persona desempleada en la que se basan las estadísticas
Personas que están dispuestas a trabajar pero no encuentran empleo por cualquiera razón (fin de contrato de trabajo, calificaciones inadecuadas, etc.).

7. Actualización de los registros
No se indica si los registros se actualizan regularmente.

8. Tasas de desempleo
Se utilizan estadísticas de estos registros para obtener tasas de desempleo.
Fuentes de los datos de empleo incluidos en el denominador de las tasas de desempleo: Encuesta sobre la fuerza de trabajo y el Censo de población.
Definición de persona empleada que se utiliza a tales efectos:
Trabajadores (incluidos empleadores o empresarios) que reciben un ingreso en metálico o en especie.

9. Tipo de estadísticas que se producen sobre desempleados registrados
No se dispone de información.

10. Información metodológica sobre las estadísticas
No se dispone de información.

11. Comparaciones con estadísticas derivadas de otras fuentes
No se han hecho comparaciones con estadísticas de desempleo derivadas de otras fuentes.

12. Modificaciones importantes desde el comienzo de las estadísticas
En la legislación, la competencia del organismo y/o los procedimientos administrativos no ha habido modificaciones importantes que hayan influido significativamente en las estadísticas.

Tajikistán

1. Serie
Título: Desempleo registrado.
Año de inicio: No indicado.
2. Organismo responsable de la inscripción inicial de desempleados
Nombre del organismo: Centro de Empleo de la Población de la República de Tayikistán.
Tipo de organismo: Servicio Estatal de Empleo de la Población.
Ubicación de las oficinas locales donde se hacen las inscripciones: En todas las regiones, ciudades y distritos del país.
Tipo de servicios proporcionados/administrados por el organismo
- Ayuda a personas en busca de empleo a encontrarlo;
- Ayuda a personas en busca de empleo a crear su propia empresa;
- Ayuda a los empleadores a encontrar trabajadores;
- Orientación profesional;

– Formación relacionada con el trabajo;
– Pago de prestaciones de desempleo.

Porcentaje de personas en busca de empleo que buscan trabajo por intermedio de ese organismo: 13 –15%.

3. Se registran los siguientes datos de la persona:
– Nombre y apellido;
– Sexo;
– Dirección del domicilio habitual;
– Fecha de nacimiento;
– Nacionalidad/grupo étnico;
– Nivel de educación/formación;
– Situación laboral actual o anterior;
– Tipo de ocupación del empleo actual o anterior;
– Tipo de ocupación del empleo que se busca.

4. Criterios utilizados para determinar si una persona habrá de incluirse en el registro (R) y/o en las estadísticas de personas desempleadas (S):
– Estar sin empleo (S);
– Estar en busca de empleo (S);
– Estar disponible para trabajar (S);
– Edad (mínima: 15 años; máxima: 63 años) (S);
– Residir en el país (S).

5. Criterios utilizados para determinar si se ha de excluir a una persona del registro (R) y/o de las estadísticas de personas desempleadas (S):
– Certificado de defunción (S);
– Establecerse en otro país (S);
– Incorporarse a un (nuevo) empleo (S);
– Comenzar el servicio militar (S);
– Participar en algún programa de promoción del empleo, de obras públicas, etc. (S);
– Estar estudiando o siguiendo una formación (S);
– Incumplir el requisito de tomar contacto con el organismo (S);
– Rechazar un número indeterminado de ofertas de trabajo adecuadas (S);
– Rechazar un número indeterminado de ofertas de formación adecuadas (S);
– Incapacidad para trabajar (S).

6. Definición de persona desempleada en la que se basan las estadísticas
La que figura en la Ley de empleo de la República de Tayikistán.

7. Actualización de los registros
Los registros no se actualizan periódicamente.

8. Tasas de desempleo
Se utilizan estadísticas de estos registros para obtener tasas de desempleo.
Fuente de los datos de empleo incluidos en el denominador de las tasas de desempleo: Encuesta sobre la migración de mano de obra extranjera.

9. Tipo de estadísticas que se producen sobre desempleados registrados
Serie 1:
Período de referencia: Mes.
Frecuencia de producción: Mensual.
Variables utilizadas:
– Sexo;
– Edad;
– Nivel de educación;
– Ocupación;
– Experiencia laboral previa;
– Ciudadanía (nacionales o no);
– Duración del desempleo.
Publicación: Sólo para uso interno.
Serie 2:
Período de referencia: Trimestre.
Frecuencia de producción: Trimestral.
Variables utilizadas:
– Sexo;
– Edad;
– Nivel de educación;
– Ocupación;
– Experiencia laboral previa;
– Ciudadanía (nacionales o no);
– Duración del desempleo.
Publicación: Sólo para uso interno.

10. Información metodológica sobre las estadísticas
Divulgación: En papel, para un público limitado.

Organismo responsable: Centro de Empleo de la Población, dependencia del Ministerio de Trabajo y Bienestar Social de la República de Tayikistán.

11. Comparaciones con estadísticas derivadas de otras fuentes
Se han hecho comparaciones con estadísticas de desempleo derivadas del Censo de población.
Frecuencia de las comparaciones: De vez en cuando.
Publicación de la metodología/resultados de las comparaciones: No se publican.

12. Modificaciones importantes desde el comienzo de las estadísticas
En la legislación, la competencia del organismo y/o los procedimientos administrativos no ha habido modificaciones importantes que hayan influido significativamente en las estadísticas.

Tanzanía, Rep. Unida de

1. Serie
Título: Desempleo registrado.
Año de inicio: 2002.

2. Organismo responsable de la inscripción inicial de desempleados
Nombre del organismo: Centro de la Bolsa de Trabajo.
Tipo de organismo: Organismo público subordinado a una autoridad nacional.
Nombre de la autoridad nacional: Ministerio de Trabajo, Juventud y Desarrollo del Deporte.
Ubicación de las oficinas locales donde se hacen las inscripciones: Dar-es-Salaam, la capital.
Tipo de servicios proporcionados/administrados por el organismo:
– Ayuda a personas en busca de empleo a encontrarlo;
– Ayuda a los empleadores a encontrar trabajadores;
– Orientación profesional.

3. Se registran los siguientes datos de la persona:
– Nombre y apellido;
– Sexo;
– Dirección del domicilio habitual;
– Fecha de nacimiento;
– Ciudadanía;
– Nacionalidad/grupo étnico;
– Nivel de educación/formación: se identifican seis categorías;
– Situación laboral actual o anterior: se identifican tres categorías;
– Tipo de ocupación del empleo actual o anterior: se identifica 10 grupos. Se han establecido vínculos con la CIUO-88;
– Tipo de ocupación del empleo que se busca: se identifican 10 grupos. Se han establecido vínculos con la CIUO-88;
– Nombre y dirección del empleador o del lugar de trabajo actual o anterior;
– Rama de actividad del empleador o del lugar de trabajo actual o anterior: se identifica un número indeterminado de grupos. Se han establecido vínculos con la CIIU Rev. 3 (no se indica el nivel);
– Otros: tipo del puesto de trabajo que se busca (cinco tipos); fecha en que se remitió al empleador; conocimiento de idiomas.

4. Criterios utilizados para determinar si una persona habrá de incluirse en el registro (R) y/o en las estadísticas de personas desempleadas (S):
– Estar sin empleo (R);
– Estar en busca de empleo (R);
– Estar disponible para trabajar (R);
– Edad (mínima: 18 años; máxima: 60 años) (R);
– Residir en el país (R).

5. Criterios utilizados para determinar si se ha de excluir a una persona del registro (R) y/o de las estadísticas de personas desempleadas (S):
– Certificado de defunción (R);
– Establecerse en otro país (R);
– Incorporarse a un (nuevo) empleo (y estar satisfecho con el mismo) (R);
– Comenzar el servicio militar (R);
– Estar estudiando o siguiendo una formación (larga) (R);
– Incapacidad para trabajar (debido a alguna discapacidad) (R).

6. Definición de persona desempleada en la que se basan las estadísticas

La definición general que se utiliza es: "estar disponible para trabajar".

Las personas desempleadas se dividen en las dos categorías siguientes:

Desempleo A:

Persona que en ese momento está desempleada y no sólo está disponible para trabajar sino que además dio los pasos necesarios para encontrar trabajo en las últimas cuatro semanas;

Desempleo B:

Persona desempleada que no dio los pasos necesarios para encontrar trabajo en las últimas cuatro semanas.

7. Actualización de los registros

No se indica la frecuencia con que se actualizan los registros.

8. Tasas de desempleo

No se utilizan estadísticas de estos registros para obtener tasas de desempleo.

9. Tipo de estadísticas que se producen sobre desempleados registrados

Serie 1:

Período de referencia: Mes.

Frecuencia de producción: Mensual.

Variables utilizadas:

- Sexo;
- Edad;
- Nivel de educación;
- Ocupación;
- Rama de actividad;
- Características geográficas;
- Experiencia laboral previa;
- Ciudadanía (nacionales o no);
- Duración del desempleo.

Publicación: En papel, para el público en general.

Organismo responsable de la publicación: Ministerio de Trabajo, Juventud y Desarrollo del Deporte.

Título y periodicidad de las publicaciones: *Employment Outlook* (Perspectivas del empleo); *Unemployment* (Desempleo). La periodicidad de las publicaciones depende de la disponibilidad de fondos para producir los datos.

Serie 2:

Período de referencia: Año.

Frecuencia de producción: Anual.

Variables utilizadas:

- Sexo;
- Edad;
- Nivel de educación;
- Ocupación;
- Rama de actividad;
- Características geográficas;
- Experiencia laboral previa;
- Ciudadanía (nacionales o no);
- Duración del desempleo.

Publicación: En papel, para el público en general.

Organismo responsable de la publicación: Ministerio de Trabajo, Juventud y Desarrollo del Deporte.

Título y periodicidad de las publicaciones: *Employment Outlook* (Perspectivas del empleo); *Unemployment* (Desempleo). La periodicidad de las publicaciones depende de la disponibilidad de fondos para producir los datos.

10. Información metodológica sobre las estadísticas

Divulgación: En papel, para el público en general.

Organismo responsable de la divulgación: Ministerio de Trabajo, Juventud y Desarrollo del Deporte.

11. Comparaciones con estadísticas derivadas de otras fuentes

Por el momento, no se han hecho comparaciones con estadísticas de desempleo derivadas de otras fuentes, pero se espera poder hacerlas en el futuro.

12. Modificaciones importantes desde el comienzo de las estadísticas

En la legislación, la competencia del organismo y/o los procedimientos administrativos no ha habido modificaciones importantes que hayan influido significativamente en las estadísticas.

13. Otros comentarios

El Centro de la Bolsa de Trabajo fue inaugurado el 1 de julio de 2001 y el procesamiento de datos recién comenzó a principios de 2002; de ahí que aún no se disponga de determinada información sobre estas estadísticas.

Trinidad y Tabago

1. Serie

Título: Estadísticas del Servicio Nacional de Empleo.

Año de inicio: No indicado.

2. Organismo responsable de la inscripción inicial de desempleados

Nombre del organismo: Servicio Nacional de Empleo.

Tipo de organismo: Organismo público subordinado a una autoridad nacional.

Nombre de la autoridad nacional: Ministerio de Trabajo y Creación de Pequeñas Empresas y Microempresas.

Ubicación de las oficinas locales donde se hacen las inscripciones: En localidades estratégicas, lo que facilita el servicio en todas partes del país.

Tipo de servicios proporcionados/administrados por el organismo:

- Ayuda a personas en busca de empleo a encontrarlo;
- Ayuda a los empleadores a encontrar trabajadores;
- Orientación profesional;
- Otros: preparación de curricula vitae; preparación para entrevistas de empleo.

3. Se registran los siguientes datos de la persona:

- Nombre y apellido;
- Sexo;
- Número de seguridad social (o número de identificación semejante también utilizado por otros organismos);
- Dirección del domicilio habitual;
- Fecha de nacimiento;
- Ciudadanía;
- Nivel de educación/formación: se identifican dos categorías. No se han establecido vínculos con la CINE;
- Tipo de ocupación del empleo que se busca: se identifica un número indeterminado de grupos. Se han establecido vínculos con la CIUO-88 a nivel de grandes grupos;
- Inscripciones previas en el organismo.

4. Criterios utilizados para determinar si una persona habrá de incluirse en el registro (R) y/o en las estadísticas de personas desempleadas (S):

- Estar sin empleo (R) y (S);
- Estar en busca de empleo (R) y (S);
- Estar disponible para trabajar (R);
- Edad (mínima: 17 años; no hay edad máxima) (R);
- Ciudadanía (R);
- Residir en el país (R);
- Haber trabajado (R);
- Otros: estudiantes en busca de empleo para el verano (R).

5. Criterios utilizados para determinar si se ha de excluir a una persona del registro (R) y/o de las estadísticas de personas desempleadas (S):

- Certificado de defunción (R);
- Establecerse en otro país (R);
- Incapacidad para trabajar (R).

6. Definición de persona desempleada en la que se basan las estadísticas

Personas de 17 años o más que están sin trabajo, están en busca de empleo y disponibles para trabajar (incluidos los estudiantes en busca de empleo para el verano).

7. Actualización de los registros

Los registros se actualizan mensualmente.

8. Tasas de desempleo

No se utilizan estadísticas de estos registros para obtener tasas de desempleo.

9. Tipo de estadísticas que se producen sobre desempleados registrados

Serie 1:

Período de referencia: Mes.

Frecuencia de producción: Mensual.

Variables utilizadas:

- Sexo;
- Nivel de educación;
- Ocupación;
- Rama de actividad.

Publicación: En archivo electrónico, previa solicitud.

Organismo responsable de la publicación: Ministerio de Trabajo y Creación de Pequeñas Empresas y Microempresas.

Serie 2:

Período de referencia: No indicado.

Frecuencia de producción: Año.
Variables utilizadas:
–   Sexo;
–   Nivel de educación;
–   Ocupación;
–   Rama de actividad.
Publicación: En archivo electrónico, previa solicitud.
Organismo responsable de la publicación: Ministerio de Trabajo y Creación de Pequeñas Empresas y Microempresas.
10. Información metodológica sobre las estadísticas
Divulgación: No se divulgan, sólo para uso interno.
Organismo responsable: Ministerio de Trabajo y Creación de Pequeñas Empresas y Microempresas.
11. Comparaciones con estadísticas derivadas de otras fuentes
          No se han hecho comparaciones con estadísticas de desempleo derivadas de otras fuentes.
12. Modificaciones importantes desde el comienzo de las estadísticas
          En la legislación, la competencia del organismo y/o los procedimientos administrativos no ha habido modificaciones importantes que hayan influido significativamente en las estadísticas.

Túnez

1. Serie
Título: Mercado de trabajo.
Año de inicio: Versión impresa, disponible a partir de 1995 (tal vez, antes); versión electrónica, disponible a partir de 1997.
2. Organismo responsable de la inscripción inicial de desempleados
Nombre del organismo: Agence Tunisienne de l'Emploi - ATE (Agencia de Empleo de Túnez).
Tipo de organismo: Organismo público subordinado a una autoridad nacional.
Nombre de la autoridad nacional: Ministerio de Empleo.
Ubicación de las oficinas locales donde se hacen las inscripciones: Todo el país; 80 oficinas repartidas en los 24 departamentos (gobernaciones).
Tipo de servicios proporcionados/administrados por el organismo
–   Ayuda a personas en busca de empleo a encontrarlo;
–   Ayuda a personas en busca de empleo a crear su propia empresa;
–   Ayuda a los empleadores a encontrar trabajadores;
–   Orientación profesional;
–   Otros: inserción de jóvenes y reinserción de trabajadores despedidos; organización y gestión de cursos de introducción a la vida profesional; información profesional; sesiones de ayuda y acompañamiento, etc.
Porcentaje de personas en busca de empleo que buscan trabajo por intermedio de ese organismo: 25 a 30% (+ de 80%, en el caso de diplomados de enseñanza superior).
3. Se registran los siguientes datos de la persona
–   Nombre y apellido;
–   Sexo;
–   Número de seguridad social (o número de identificación semejante también utilizado por otros organismos);
–   Dirección del domicilio habitual;
–   Fecha de nacimiento;
–   Ciudadanía;
–   Nacionalidad;
–   Nivel de educación/formación: se identifican ocho categorías. Se han establecido vínculos con la CINE;
–   Situación laboral actual o anterior: se identifican tres categorías (ocupado; ocupado anteriormente; nunca trabajó) ;
–   Tipo de ocupación del empleo actual o anterior: se identifican nueve categorías. No se han establecido vínculos con la CIUO-88;
–   Tipo de ocupación del empleo que se busca: se identifican nueve categorías;
–   Nombre y dirección del empleador o del lugar de trabajo actual o anterior;
–   Rama de actividad del empleador o del lugar de trabajo actual o anterior: se identifican 10 categorías. No se han establecido vínculos con la CIIU;
–   Inscripciones previas en el organismo.
4. Criterios utilizados para determinar si una persona habrá de incluirse en el registro (R) y/o en las estadísticas de personas desempleadas (S)

–   Estar sin empleo (R) y (S);
–   Edad (mínima: 18 años –15 años en lo que respecta a la orientación profesional–, no hay edad máxima) (R) y (S);
–   Ciudadanía (cédula de identidad o tarjeta de estadía y permiso de trabajo para extranjeros (R).
5. Criterios utilizados para determinar si se ha de excluir a una persona del registro (R) y/o de las estadísticas de personas desempleadas (S)
–   Establecerse en otro país (R);
–   Incorporarse a un (nuevo) empleo o crear, por ejemplo, una microempresa (R);
–   Comenzar el servicio militar (R);
–   Participar en algún programa de promoción del empleo, de obras públicas, etc. (R);
–   Estar estudiando o siguiendo una formación (R);
–   Incumplir el requisito de tomar contacto con el organismo, automáticamente después de dos meses de ausencia (R).
6. Definición de persona desempleada en la que se basan las estadísticas
          Las estadísticas de la Agencia de Empleo de Túnez versan sobre las personas que declararon estar en busca de empleo y se registraron en una de las 80 oficinas de empleo. Puede tratarse de personas desempleadas o de personas empleadas en busca de un empleo mejor.
7. Actualización de los registros
          Los registros son actualizados periódicamente (en forma automática por el sistema).
8. Tasas de desempleo
          No se utilizan estadísticas de estos registros para obtener tasas de desempleo.
9. Tipo de estadísticas que se producen sobre desempleados registrados
Serie 1
Período de referencia: Día.
Frecuencia de producción: Cotidiana.
Variables utilizadas
–   Sexo;
–   Edad;
–   Nivel de educación, diploma, especialización estudiada;
–   Ocupación;
–   Rama de actividad;
–   Características geográficas;
–   Experiencia laboral previa;
–   Tiempo de espera;
–   Oficina de inscripción en el registro;
–   Gobernación.
Publicación
–   Sólo para uso interno;
–   En el sitio web: www.emploi.nat.tn
Organismo responsable de la publicación: ATE.
Título y periodicidad de la publicación: *Indicateurs d'activité* (Indicadores de actividad), servicio libre.
Serie 2
Período de referencia: Mes.
Frecuencia de producción: Mensual.
Variables utilizadas
–   Sexo;
–   Edad;
–   Nivel de educación;
–   Ocupación;
–   Rama de actividad;
–   Características geográficas;
–   Experiencia laboral previa;
–   Tiempo de espera;
–   Oficina de inscripción en el registro;
–   Gobernación.
Publicación
–   Sólo para uso interno;
–   En papel, para un público limitado.
Organismo responsable de la publicación: ATE.
Título y periodicidad de la publicación: *Evolution du marché de l'emploi au cours du mois* (Evolución del mercado de trabajo en el curso del mes), mensual.
Serie 3
Período de referencia: Mes.
Frecuencia de producción: Trimestral y anual.
Variables utilizadas
–   Sexo;
–   Edad;
–   Nivel de educación;
–   Ocupación;

–   Rama de actividad;
–   Características geográficas;
–   Experiencia laboral previa;
–   Tiempo de espera;
–   Oficina de inscripción en el registro;
–   Gobernación.

Publicación:
–   Sólo para uso interno;
–   En papel, para un público limitado.

Organismo responsable de la publicación: ATE.

Título y periodicidad de la publicación: *Rapport trimestriel et rapport annuel sur l'activité de l'ATE* (Informe trimestral e informe anual de actividad de la ATE).

10. Información metodológica sobre las estadísticas

Divulgación
–   No se divulga, sólo para uso interno;
–   En papel, para un público limitado;
–   En el sitio web: www.emploi.nat.tn
–   Consulta en el organismo, público en general.

Organismo responsable de la divulgación: ATE.

11. Comparaciones con estadísticas derivadas de otras fuentes

Se han hecho comparaciones con estadísticas de desempleo derivadas de la Encuesta sobre la fuerza de trabajo, otras encuestas de hogares y el Censo de población. Estas estadísticas se utilizan, por un lado, para apreciar el nivel de incidencia de los servicios de empleo en el mercado de trabajo y, por el otro, para ayudar a funcionarios de la ATE a orientar sus intervenciones en dirección de las poblaciones vulnerables.

Frecuencia de las comparaciones: Anual con la encuesta de población y empleo (INS).

12. Modificaciones importantes desde el comienzo de las estadísticas

En la legislación, la competencia del organismo y/o los procedimientos administrativos hubo modificaciones importantes en 1995 que influyeron significativamente en las estadísticas.

Desde la creación de la ATE en 1993, y principalmente, después de la puesta en marcha del sistema de informatización y gestión del mercado de trabajo (informatizado), en 1995, los datos sobre personas en busca de empleo son cada vez más fidedignos. La cobertura de personal técnico y ejecutivo en busca de empleo es cada vez más alta y representativa.

Turquía

1. Serie

Título: Desempleo registrado.

Año de inicio: 1946.

2. Organismo responsable de la inscripción inicial de desempleados

Nombre del organismo: Türkiye Iş Kurumu (Işkur) - OET (Organización de Empleo de Turquía).

Tipo de organismo: Organismo público subordinado a una autoridad nacional.

Nombre de la autoridad nacional: Ministerio de Trabajo y Seguridad Social.

Ubicación de las oficinas locales donde se hacen las inscripciones: En todas las provincias y en algunos distritos.

Tipo de servicios proporcionados/administrados por el organismo:
–   Ayuda a personas en busca de empleo a encontrarlo;
–   Ayuda a personas en busca de empleo a crear su propia empresa;
–   Ayuda a los empleadores a encontrar trabajadores;
–   Orientación profesional;
–   Formación relacionada con el trabajo;
–   Pago de prestaciones de desempleo (Seguro de desempleo);
–   Otros: encuestas sobre la fuerza de trabajo en el mercado local y evaluación; establecimiento y manejo del sistema de información sobre el mercado de trabajo; indemnización por pérdidas de trabajo.

Porcentaje de personas en busca de empleo que buscan trabajo por intermedio de ese organismo: 37% (en el tercer trimestre de 2001).

3. Se registran los siguientes datos de la persona:
–   Nombre y apellido;
–   Sexo;
–   Número de seguridad social (o número de identificación semejante también utilizado por otros organismos);
–   Dirección del domicilio habitual;

–   Fecha y lugar de nacimiento;
–   Ciudadanía;
–   Nivel de educación/formación: se identifican cuatro categorías. Se han establecido vínculos con la CINE;
–   Situación laboral actual o anterior: se identifican nueve categorías;
–   Tipo de ocupación del empleo actual o anterior: se identifican 72 grupos. Se han establecido vínculos con la CIUO-88 a nivel de subgrupos;
–   Tipo de ocupación del empleo que se busca: se identifican 72 grupos. Se han establecido vínculos con la CIUO-88 a nivel de subgrupos;
–   Nombre y dirección del empleador o del lugar de trabajo actual o anterior;
–   Rama de actividad del empleador o del lugar de trabajo actual o anterior: se identifican tres grupos. (Se utiliza la CIIU Rev. 3 y la NACE Rev. 1 comenzará a utilizarse en breve);
–   Inscripciones previas en el organismo;
–   Otros: experiencia en el lugar de trabajo anterior; ocupación suplementaria; idiomas extranjeros; licencia de conducir/Número de pasaporte; situación social (discapacitada, afectada por el terrorismo, etc.); estado civil; duración del desempleo; salario pretendido; sector; tipo de trabajo (permanente, estacional, etc.); lugar (en el país o en el extranjero).

4. Criterios utilizados para determinar si una persona habrá de incluirse en el registro (R) y/o en las estadísticas de personas desempleadas (S):
–   Estar sin empleo   (R) y (S);
–   Estar en busca de empleo (se registra a todo solicitante, independientemente de su situación actual en el empleo) (R) y (S);
–   Estar disponible para trabajar (disponible para empezar a trabajar en la fecha indicada por el empleador)   (R) y (S);
–   Edad (mínima: 15 años; no hay edad máxima)   (R) y (S);
–   Ciudadanía   (R) y (S);
–   Residir en el país   (R) y (S);
–   Haber trabajado   (R);
–   Duración y/o número de horas de trabajo del empleo que se busca   (R) y (S);
–   Pago de cotizaciones del seguro de desempleo   (R) y (S).

5. Criterios utilizados para determinar si se ha de excluir a una persona del registro (R) y/o de las estadísticas de personas desempleadas (S):
–   Certificado de defunción   (R) y (S);
–   Establecerse en otro país   (R) y (S);
–   Incorporarse a un (nuevo) empleo (colocación a través de la OET)   (R) y (S);
–   Comenzar el servicio militar   (R) y (S);
–   Estar estudiando o siguiendo una formación   (R) y (S);
–   Incumplir el requisito de tomar contacto con el organismo (si no se renueva, el registro caduca automáticamente un año después)   (R) y (S);
–   Rechazar tres ofertas de trabajo adecuadas   (R) y (S);
–   Cobrar alguna pensión   (R) y (S).

6. Definición de persona desempleada en la que se basan las estadísticas

Toda persona en edad de trabajar (15 años o más) que está en condiciones de trabajar y quiere hacerlo; que en el momento en que se presenta a la oficina de empleo gana menos del salario mínimo, y que aún no ha sido colocada en un puesto de trabajo por la oficina de empleo.

7. Actualización de los registros

Los registros se actualizan mensualmente.

8. Tasas de desempleo

Se utilizan estadísticas de estos registros para obtener tasas de desempleo.

Fuente de los datos de empleo incluidos en el denominador de las tasas de desempleo: Encuesta sobre la fuerza de trabajo que lleva a cabo el Instituto Estatal de Estadística.

Definición de persona empleada que se utiliza a tales efectos:

Según la Ley de trabajo de Turquía, toda persona con contrato de empleo que ocupa cualquier puesto de trabajo por el que recibe salario.

9. Tipo de estadísticas que se producen sobre desempleados registrados

Serie 1:

Período de referencia: Mes.

Frecuencia de producción: Mensual.

Variables utilizadas:
- Sexo;
- Edad;
- Nivel de educación;
- Ocupación;
- Rama de actividad;
- Características geográficas;
- Duración del desempleo;
- Otras: Grupos profesionales.

Publicación:
- En papel, para el público en general;
- En el sitio web www.iskur.gov.tr.

Organismo responsable de la publicación: Dirección General de la Organización de Empleo de Turquía, Departamento de Empleo, Sección de Seguimiento y Estadísticas de la Mano de Obra.

Título de la publicación: *Turkish Employment Organisation Statistical Yearbook* (Anuario estadístico de la Organización de Empleo de Turquía).

Serie 2:

Período de referencia: Año.

Frecuencia de producción: Anual.

Variables utilizadas:
- Sexo;
- Edad;
- Nivel de educación;
- Ocupación;
- Rama de actividad;
- Características geográficas;
- Duración del desempleo;
- Otras: grupos profesionales.

Publicación:
- En papel, para el público en general;
- En el sitio web www.iskur.gov.tr.

Organismo responsable de la publicación: Dirección General de la Organización de Empleo de Turquía, Departamento de Empleo, Sección de Seguimiento y Estadísticas de la Mano de Obra.

Título de la publicación: *Turkish Employment Organisation Statistical Yearbook* (Anuario estadístico de la Organización de Empleo de Turquía).

10. Información metodológica sobre las estadísticas

Divulgación:
- En papel, para el público en general.
- En el sitio web www.iskur.gov.tr.

Organismo responsable: Organización de Empleo de Turquía.

11. Comparaciones con estadísticas derivadas de otras fuentes

Se han hecho comparaciones con estadísticas de desempleo derivadas de la Encuesta sobre la fuerza de trabajo.

Frecuencia de las comparaciones: Periódica, cada tres meses.

Publicación de la metodología/resultados de las comparaciones: No se publican.

12. Modificaciones importantes desde el comienzo de las estadísticas

En la legislación, la competencia del organismo y/o los procedimientos administrativos no ha habido modificaciones importantes que hayan influido significativamente en las estadísticas.

Uruguay

1. Serie

Título: Demanda, oferta de empleo en agencias privadas de colocación y Registro de usuarios del Programa de Capacitación laboral.

Año de inicio: 1993.

2. Organismo responsable de la inscripción inicial de desempleados

Nombre del organismo: Dirección Nacional de Empleo (DINAE).

Tipo de organismo: Organismo público subordinado a una autoridad nacional.

Nombre de la autoridad nacional: Ministerio de Trabajo y Seguridad Social.

Ubicación de las oficinas locales donde se hacen las inscripciones: En todo el país.

Tipo de servicios proporcionados/administrados por el organismo:
- Orientación profesional;
- Formación relacionada con el trabajo;
- Otros: información sobre el Mercado de Trabajo.

3. Se registran los siguientes datos de la persona*:
- Nombre y apellido;
- Sexo;

- Número de seguridad social (o número de identificación semejante también utilizado por otros organismos);
- Dirección del domicilio habitual;
- Fecha de nacimiento;
- Ciudadanía;
- Nivel de enseñanza/formación: se identifican 14 categorías. No se han establecido vínculos con la CINE;
- Situación laboral anterior;
- Tipo de ocupación del empleo actual o anterior: se identifican cuatro categorías. Se usa la Clasificación Nacional Uniforme de Ocupaciones (CNUO-95) (a nivel de cuatro dígitos) que se basa en la CIUO-88;
- Nombre y dirección del empleador o del lugar del trabajo actual o pasado;
- Rama de actividad del empleador o del lugar del trabajo actual o pasado: se identifican cuatro categorías. Se usa la clasificación industrial nacional (a nivel de cuatro dígitos) que se base en la CIIU, rev. 3.

* Informaciones relativas a los trabajadores inscritos en el Programa de Capacitación Laboral.

4. Criterios utilizados para determinar si una persona habrá de incluirse en el registro (R) y/o en las estadísticas de personas desempleadas (S):
- Estar sin empleo (R);
- Estar en busca de empleo (R);
- Estar disponible para trabajar (R);
- Edad (mínima: no se indica; máxima: no se indica) (R);
- Haber trabajado (los usuarios del Programa de Capacitación Laboral lo son en calidad de desocupados propiamente dichos, es decir, haber trabajado y perdido el empleo) (R);
- Pago de las contribuciones de seguro de desempleo (al ser usuario del Programa de Capacitación Laboral es porque está en seguro de desempleo lo que significa que se realizaron aportes) (R);
- Otros: no tener educación terciaria (se aplica a los usuarios del Programa de Capacitación Laboral) (R).

5. Criterios utilizados para determinar si se ha de excluir a una persona del registro (R) y/o de las estadísticas de personas desempleadas (S):

No se indica.

6. Definición de persona desempleada en la que se basan las estadísticas

En lo que concierne los usuarios del Programa de Capacitación Laboral los criterios de inclusión en el mismo son:
- estar en seguro por desempleo;
- ser despedido (no reintegrado a la empresa)
- no tener educación terciaria.

7. Actualización de los registros

No se indica si los registros se actualizan regularmente.

8. Tasas de desempleo

Se utilizan estadísticas de estos registros para obtener tasas de desempleo.

Fuente de los datos de empleo incluidos en el denominador de las tasas de desempleo: Encuesta de hogares sobre la fuerza de trabajo.

Definición de persona empleada que se utiliza a tales efectos:

Persona mayor de 14 años que trabajó al menos una hora en la semana anterior a la encuesta.

9. Tipo de estadísticas que se producen sobre desempleados registrados

No se indica.

10. Información metodológica sobre las estadísticas

No se indica.

11. Comparaciones con estadísticas derivadas de otras fuentes

No se han hecho comparaciones con estadísticas de desempleo derivadas de otras fuentes.

12. Modificaciones importantes desde el comienzo de las estadísticas

En la legislación, competencia del organismo y/o procedimientos administrativos no ha habido modificaciones importantes que hayan influido significativamente en las estadísticas.

Venezuela

1. Serie

Título: Desempleo registrado.

Año de inicio: 1964.

2. Organismo responsable de la inscripción inicial de desempleados

Nombre del organismo: Servicio Nacional de Empleo (Agencia de Empleo).

Tipo de organismo: Organismo público subordinado a una autoridad nacional.

Nombre de la autoridad nacional: Ministerio del Trabajo.

Ubicación de las oficinas locales donde se hacen las inscripciones: En 16 Estados y una en el Distrito Capital (25 Oficinas de Empleo).

Tipo de servicios proporcionados/administrados por el organismo:
– Ayuda a personas en busca de empleo a encontrarlo;
– Ayuda a personas en busca de empleo a crear su propia empresa;
– Ayuda a los empleadores a encontrar trabajadores;
– Orientación profesional;
– Formación relacionada con el trabajo.

Porcentaje de personas en busca de empleo que buscan trabajo por intermedio de ese organismo: 15%.

3. Se registran los siguientes datos de la persona:
– Nombre y apellido;
– Sexo;
– Número de seguridad social (o número de identificación semejante también utilizado por otros organismos);
– Dirección del domicilio habitual;
– Fecha de nacimiento;
– Ciudadanía;
– Nivel de educación/formación: se identifican dos categorías. Se han establecido vínculos con la CINE-97;
– Situación laboral actual o anterior: se identifican tres categorías;
– Tipo de ocupación del empleo actual o anterior: se identifican dos categorías. Se han establecido vínculos con la CIUO-88;
– Tipo de ocupación del empleo que se busca: se identifican dos categorías. Se han establecido vínculos con la CIUO-88;
– Nombre y dirección del empleador o del lugar del trabajo actual o anterior;
– Rama de actividad del empleador o del lugar del trabajo actual o anterior: se identifican 10 categorías. Se han establecido vínculos con la CIIU Rev. 3;
– Inscripciones previas en el organismo.

4. Criterios utilizados para determinar si una persona habrá de incluirse en el registro (R) y/o en las estadísticas de personas desempleadas (S):
– Estar sin empleo (R) y (S);
– Estar en busca de empleo (Cesante, Beneficiario del paro forzoso; Cesante - Activo) (R) y (S);
– Estar disponible para trabajar (R) y (S);
– Edad (mínima: 14 años; no hay edad máxima) (R) y (S);
– Ciudadanía (R) y (S);
– Residir en el país (R) y (S);
– Haber trabajado (experiencia laboral o formación profesional) (R) y (S);
– Duración y/o número de horas de trabajo del empleo que se busca (R) y (S);
– Pago de las contribuciones de seguro de desempleo previamente (Beneficiario del seguro de paro forzoso) (R) y (S);
– Otros: despido injustificado (18 semanas consecutivas laborando) (R) y (S).

5. Criterios utilizados para determinar si se ha de excluir a una persona del registro (R) y/o de las estadísticas de personas desempleadas (S):
– Incorporarse a un (nuevo) empleo (R) y (S);
– Participar en algún programa de promoción del empleo, de obras públicas, etc. (R) y (S);
– Incumplir el requisito de ponerse en contacto con el organismo (R) y (S).

6. Definición de persona desempleada en la que se basan las estadísticas

Sector de la fuerza laboral que busca trabajo por primera vez, que por alguna razón se encuentra fuera del mercado de trabajo, bien sea por despido justificado e injustificado o por haber renunciado a un empleo.

7. Actualización de los registros

Los registros se actualizan anualmente, cualquier cambio surgido durante el período se actualiza en el formato de registro de la información del usuario desocupado.

8. Tasas de desempleo

No se utilizan estadísticas de estos registros para obtener tasas de desempleo.

9. Tipo de estadísticas que se producen sobre desempleados registrados

Serie 1:

Período de referencia: Día.

Frecuencia de producción: Semestral.

Variables utilizadas:
– Sexo;
– Edad;
– Nivel de educación;
– Ocupación;
– Rama de actividad;
– Características geográficas;
– Experiencia laboral previa;
– Ciudadanía (ciudadanos/extranjeros);
– Duración del desempleo;
– Otras: beneficiario de paro forzoso; estado civil.

Publicación: Sólo para uso interno.

Organismo responsable de la publicación: Dirección General de Empleo.

Serie 2:

Período de referencia: Mes.

Frecuencia de producción: Anual

Variables utilizadas:
– Sexo;
– Edad;
– Nivel de educación;
– Ocupación;
– Rama de actividad;
– Características geográficas;
– Experiencia laboral previa;
– Ciudadanía (ciudadanos/extranjeros);
– Duración del desempleo;
– Otras: beneficiario de paro forzoso; estado civil.

Publicación: Sólo para uso interno.

Organismo responsable de la publicación: Dirección General de Empleo.

10. Información metodológica sobre las estadísticas

Divulgación: En papel, para un público limitado.

Organismo responsable de la divulgación: Dirección General de Empleo.

11. Comparaciones con estadísticas derivadas de otras fuentes

Se han hecho comparaciones con estadísticas de desempleo derivadas de la Encuesta sobre la fuerza de trabajo, de otro tipo de encuesta de hogares y del Censo de Población.

Frecuencia de las comparaciones: Regularmente, cuando las estadísticas se publican (último año: 2001).

Publicación de la metodología/resultados de las comparaciones: Se publican en *Boletín de Segmento de Mercado de Trabajo*.

12. Modificaciones importantes desde el comienzo de las estadísticas

En la legislación, competencia del organismo y/o procedimientos administrativos ha habido modificaciones importantes en: 1. 1996; 2. 1997; 3. 1998; 4. 1999; 5. 2000 y 6. 2001, dando los resultados siguientes en el número total de desempleados registrados: 1. 1996-97: +29.43%; 2. 1997-98: +19.10%; 3. 1998-99: +85.76%; 4. 1999-2000: + 9.03%, y 5. 2000-01: + 5.70%. (1. Creación de nuevas Agencias; 2. Cierre de empresas; 3. Cambio de Actividad Económica; 4. Incremento de la fuerza laboral; 5. Automatización de los Servicios de Empleo).

Zimbabwe

1. Serie

Título: Desempleo registrado.

Año de inicio: 1959.

2. Organismo responsable de la inscripción inicial de desempleados

Nombre del organismo: Departamento Nacional de Servicios de Empleo.

Tipo de organismo: Organismo público subordinado a una autoridad nacional.

Nombre de la autoridad nacional: Ministerio de Servicio Público, Trabajo y Bienestar Social.

Ubicación de las oficinas locales donde se hacen las inscripciones: En las capitales provinciales de todo el país y en dos distritos.

Tipo de servicios proporcionados/administrados por el organismo:

- Ayuda a personas en busca de empleo a encontrarlo;
- Ayuda a personas en busca de empleo a crear su propia empresa;
- Ayuda a los empleadores a encontrar trabajadores;
- Orientación profesional;
- Otros: registro y supervisión de agencias de empleo privadas; acopio y divulgación de información sobre el mercado de trabajo.

Porcentaje de personas en busca de empleo que buscan trabajo por intermedio de ese organismo: 10%.

3. Se registran los siguientes datos de la persona:

- Nombre y apellido;
- Sexo;
- Dirección del domicilio habitual;
- Fecha de nacimiento;
- Ciudadanía;
- Nacionalidad/grupo étnico;
- Nivel de educación/formación: se identifican dos categorías. No se han establecido vínculos con la CINE;
- Situación laboral actual o anterior: se identifican tres categorías;
- Tipo de ocupación del empleo actual o anterior: se identifica un número indeterminado de grupos. Se han establecido vínculos con la CIUO-88 a nivel de grupos primarios;
- Tipo de ocupación del empleo que se busca: se identifica un número indeterminado de grupos. Se han establecido vínculos con la CIUO-88 a nivel de grupos primarios;
- Nombre y dirección del empleador o del lugar de trabajo actual o anterior;
- Inscripciones previas en el organismo.

4. Criterios utilizados para determinar si una persona habrá de incluirse en el registro (R) y/o en las estadísticas de personas desempleadas (S):

- Estar sin empleo (R) y (S);
- Estar en busca de empleo (R) y (S);
- Estar disponible para trabajar (R) y (S);
- Edad (mínima: 16 años; máxima: 60 años) (R) y (S);
- Ciudadanía (únicamente ciudadanos de Zimbabwe) (R);
- Haber trabajado (R).

5. Criterios utilizados para determinar si se ha de excluir a una persona del registro (R) y/o de las estadísticas de personas desempleadas (S):

- Certificado de defunción (R) y (S);
- Incorporarse a un (nuevo) empleo (R) y (S);
- Incumplir el requisito de tomar contacto con el organismo, al menos una vez por mes (R) y (S).

6. Definición de persona desempleada en la que se basan las estadísticas

Toda persona que está disponible para trabajar, busca empleo activamente y hace solicitudes de empleo al menos una vez por mes.

7. Actualización de los registros

Los registros se actualizan mensualmente.

8. Tasas de desempleo

No se utilizan estadísticas de estos registros para obtener tasas de desempleo.

9. Tipo de estadísticas que se producen sobre desempleados registrados

Período de referencia: Día, semana, mes, semestre y año.

Frecuencia de producción: Mensual.

Variables utilizadas:

- Sexo;
- Edad;
- Nivel de educación;
- Ocupación;
- Experiencia laboral previa;
- Ciudadanía (nacionales o no);
- Duración del desempleo.

Publicación: Sólo para uso interno.

Organismo responsable de la publicación: Departamento Nacional de Servicios de Empleo.

Título y periodicidad de la publicación: *Departmental Monthly Statistics and Reports* (Estadísticas e informes departamentales mensuales).

10. Información metodológica sobre las estadísticas

Divulgación: En papel, para un público limitado.

Organismo responsable: Departamento Nacional de Servicios de Empleo.

11. Comparaciones con estadísticas derivadas de otras fuentes

No se han hecho comparaciones con estadísticas de desempleo derivadas de otras fuentes.

12. Modificaciones importantes desde el comienzo de las estadísticas

En la legislación, la competencia del organismo y/o los procedimientos administrativos hubo modificaciones importantes en 1998, 1999, 2000 y 2001. Los cambios consiguientes en las estadísticas no se han estimado.

Otros:

- Descentralización de las oficinas públicas de empleo de todas las provincias;
- Introducción del programa de informatización.

Introducción - Parte II

Las descripciones metodológicas presentadas en esta parte se refieren a las estadísticas de empleo, salarios, horas de trabajo y otros temas afines (por ejemplo los ingresos relacionados con el empleo, vacantes), que se obtienen de fuentes distintas de las encuestas de hogares o de establecimientos, tales como los registros de seguro social u otros seguros, de impuestos, de convenios colectivos, informes administrativos, etc.

Las series estadísticas correspondientes por lo general se publican en el *Anuario de Estadísticas del Trabajo* de la OIT, si llega el caso, en el *Boletín de Estadísticas del Trabajo,* o en su suplemento especial *Estadísticas sobre salarios y horas de trabajo por ocupación y precios de artículos alimenticios – Resultados de la Encuesta de octubre.* También se encuentran disponibles en la base de datos en línea, LABORSTA (Sitio Internet : http://laborsta.ilo.org).

En algunos casos, las estadísticas todavía no han sido publicadas por la OIT, pero deberían serlo próximamente.

Las descripciones abarcan a 24 países, áreas y territorios. La mayor parte de las mismas se prepararon a partir de la información proporcionada por los organismos de estadísticas nacionales o por los gobiernos en el cuestionario que se les remitiera a tales efectos. En el caso de los países que no respondieron, la información se sacó de distintas fuentes, en particular, las publicaciones y informes nacionales e internacionales disponibles en la OIT, y de sitios Internet. Cada una de las descripciones fue enviada al país interesado para obtener sus comentarios, que se han tomado en consideración toda vez que hayan sido recibidos dentro de los plazos previstos en el programa de publicaciones.

Todas las descripciones se presentan en un mismo formato dividido en secciones y epígrafes para facilitar las comparaciones. Sin embargo, habría que tener en cuenta que las estadísticas derivadas de archivos administrativos no son estrictamente comparables entre países debido a ciertas diferencias en las fuentes y legislaciones de actualidad. A continuación se resume el contenido de los mismos.

Fuente de la serie
Fuente administrativa de la cual se deriva la serie, en forma general, el sistema de informes de un organismo nacional de seguridad o seguro social o, de comisiones de fijación de salarios o convenios colectivos de trabajo.

Título de la serie
Título de la serie estadística.

Organismo responsable
Organismo responsable de la recolección de datos, su elaboración estadística y publicación o difusión; se indica cuando estas tareas están a cargo de organismos distintos.

Temas laborales principales abarcados
Temas laborales principales para los cuales se compilan datos (empleo, ganancias, horas de trabajo, ingresos relacionados con el empleo, etc.).

Periodicidad o frecuencia de disponibilidad de las estadísticas
Frecuencia con la cual se recogen o compilan las estadísticas (por ejemplo, mensual, trimestral, semestral, una vez por año, etc.).

Período de referencia
Período de referencia al que se refieren los datos (por ejemplo, una fecha determinada, un mes completo, etc.).

Alcance de las estadísticas
Ámbito geográfico: si la serie abarca a todo el país o territorio, y en caso negativo, qué áreas o regiones están excluidas.

Ámbito industrial: si la serie abarca todas las ramas de actividad económica, y en caso negativo, las ramas de industria o actividad que se excluyen.

Establecimientos: los tipos y tamaños de establecimientos abarcados que proporcionan datos para la serie, así como su afiliación o relaciones con el sistema de seguro o seguridad social cuando corresponde.

Personas cubiertas: las categorías de trabajadores abarcados por la serie, tales como los asalariados sujetos al régimen de seguro social nacional; llegado el caso, otras características pertinentes de la población cubierta, como sexo, grupo de edad, sector de la economía, etc.

Ocupaciones: si los datos se recogen sobre ocupaciones individuales o grupos de ocupaciones, y cuando corresponda, las ocupaciones o grupos que están comprendidos.

Conceptos y definiciones
Definiciones nacionales utilizadas para elaborar la serie, correspondientes a cada uno de los conceptos citados (empleo, ganancias, tasas de sueldo o salario, ingresos relacionados con el empleo). Llegado el caso, los grupos de trabajadores que se incluyen o excluyen, así como los límites mínimo y/o máximo que se aplican a las definiciones de salarios o ingresos.

Clasificaciones
Ramas de actividad económica: nombre de la clasificación nacional por rama de actividad económica (industria) y de ser posible, número de grupos que se utilizan para la codificación; si esta clasificación se aplica a todos los datos compilados; si se han establecido vínculos entre la clasificación nacional y la Clasificación Industrial Internacional Uniforme de Todas las Actividades Económicas (CIIU), Rev.3 (1990) o Rev.2 (1968), y a qué nivel.

Ocupaciones: nombre de la clasificación nacional por ocupación y de ser posible, número de grupos que se utilizan para la codificación; si esta clasificación se aplica a todos los datos compilados; si se han establecido vínculos entre la clasificación nacional y la Clasificación Internacional Uniforme de Ocupaciones (CIUO-88 o CIUO-1968), y a qué nivel.

Situación en el empleo: nombre de la clasificación nacional de la situación en el empleo, y de ser posible, número de grupos que se utilizan para la codificación; si esta clasificación se aplica a todos los datos compilados; si se han establecido vínculos entre la clasificación nacional y la Clasificación Internacional de la Situación en el Empleo (CISE-1993), y a qué nivel.

Otras clasificaciones: otras clasificaciones utilizadas, tales como por características de los establecimientos (tamaño, tipo de propiedad, etc.), región, características de los trabajadores (por sexo, grupos de edad, categoría de trabajador, nacionalidad/ciudadanía, etc.), y si las clasificaciones se aplican a todos los datos compilados o sólo a algunos de ellos.

Recolección de datos
Procedimiento, organización, y plan de recolección de datos de los archivos de la seguridad social, los registros de convenios colectivos de trabajo y otras fuentes similares. Cuando corresponda, métodos de muestreo, ponderación de la muestra y actualización del sistema administrativo.

Procesamiento y verificación de datos
Métodos de procesamiento y procedimientos de verificación y pruebas de congruencia que se realizan sobre los datos compilados.

Ajustes
Cuando corresponda, tipos de ajustes que se hacen y métodos utilizados para corregir desviaciones debidas a errores de representatividad, dobles anotaciones, estimación de los pagos en especie, etc., antes de hacer las estimaciones de empleo, salarios, horas de trabajo o ingresos relacionados con el empleo; si se utilizan datos de referencia para ajustar los datos, o si se ajustan las estadísticas para tener en cuenta las variaciones estacionales.

Tipos de estimaciones
Tipos de estimaciones que se hacen a partir de los datos (totales, promedios, medianas, distribuciones), unidades de tiempo a las cuales se refieren y métodos de cálculo.

Construcción de índices
Cuando se construyen números índices utilizando los datos, tipo de datos al que se refieren los índices y procedimiento empleado para construirlos.

Indicadores de fiabilidad de las estimaciones
Informaciones tanto cualitativas como cuantitativas sobre la fiabilidad de las estadísticas: proporción de la población total de referencia abarcada por el sistema administrativo; estimación de la varianza de muestreo; errores no relacionados con el muestreo; conformidad con otras fuentes.

Series disponibles
Lista de las tabulaciones que se preparan periódicamente en el país con base en la fuente que se describe, y que se encuentran en las publicaciones nacionales.

Historia de las estadísticas
Información sobre la historia de las estadísticas: fecha de iniciación de la(s) serie(s), fechas y naturaleza de los cambios importantes y revisiones efectuados (por ejemplo, en la legislación, los procedimientos o formularios utilizados, el alcance, las definiciones, la periodicidad).

Documentación y difusión
Fuente y títulos de las publicaciones principales que contengan los datos y la información metodológica correspondiente; periodicidad de las publicaciones y demora normal entre el período de referencia de las estadísticas y su publicación; cuando haya lugar, si se difunden las estadísticas en un sitio Internet y si se pueden obtener, a pedido, las estadísticas que no figuran en las publicaciones nacionales o en un sitio Internet.

Datos suministrados a la OIT para su difusión
Lista de estadísticas que se han comunicado a la OIT para publicación en el *Anuario de Estadísticas del Trabajo* y/o el *Boletín de*

Estadísticas del Trabajo y/o las *Estadísticas sobre salarios y horas de trabajo por ocupación y precios de artículos alimenticios – Resultados de la Encuesta de octubre.*
Otras fuentes administrativas de datos: otras fuentes administrativas que son las fuentes de estadísticas relacionadas con el trabajo; breve indicación del título, alcance y periodicidad de estas estadísticas.

Alemania

Fuente de la serie
Contratos colectivos.
Título de la serie
Tariflöhne, Tarifgehälter.
Organismo responsable
Recolección de datos, elaboración estadística y publicación de las estadísticas : Statistisches Bundesamt (DESTATIS), División VI B (Oficina Federal de Estadística de Alemania).
Temas laborales principales abarcados
Salarios y sueldos de grupos seleccionados de obreros y empleados y horas normales de trabajo.
Periodicidad o frecuencia de disponibilidad de las estadísticas
Semestral.
Período de referencia
Los meses hasta el mes del informe (abril y octubre).
Alcance de las estadísticas
Ambito geográfico: todo el país.
Ambito industrial: todos los sectores de la actividad económica, excepto: división 71 (alquiler de maquinarias y equipo sin operador y de personal y bienes del hogar), división 72 (actividades informáticas y conexas), división 73 (investigación y desarrollo), división 74 (otras actividades comerciales) y división 80 (educación).
Establecimientos: no procede.
Personas cubiertas: asalariados incluidos en contratos colectivos.
Ocupaciones: los datos no se recopilan por ocupación o grupo ocupacional, pero algunos grupos ocupacionales, en algunos contratos colectivos, se identifican por separado y se incluyen y presentan parcialmente en las publicaciones.
Conceptos y definiciones
Empleo: los empleados son las personas sometidas a las cotizaciones del sistema del seguro social *Angestellte*; los obreros son los receptores de salarios que están incluidos en el sistema del seguro social *Arbeiter*.
Ganancias: se refieren a las tasas básicas por tiempo aprobadas colectivamente que se aplican a los niveles más altos de antigüedad.
Horas de trabajo: se refieren a las horas normales de trabajo semanal, determinadas en los contratos colectivos.
Clasificaciones
Ramas de actividad económica:
Título de la clasificación: Clasificación de todas las actividades económicas (WZ 93), edición de 1993.
Número de grupos utilizados para la codificación: códigos numéricos de dos dígitos, salvo del 71 al 74 y el 80.
Se aplica a: tasas de salarios/sueldos y horas de trabajo.
Vínculos con la CIIU y nivel: la WZ 93 se obtiene de la Rev. 1 de la NACE, Rev.1, y puede estar vinculada a la Rev. 3 de la CIIU.
Otras clasificaciones: trabajadores manuales y no manuales (es decir, obreros y empleados). Tanto los obreros como los empleados se clasifican en "grupos de rendimiento" "Leistungsgruppen" (o categorías de empleo), que establece la Oficina Federal de Estadística para cada uno de los contratos colectivos, en consulta con los interlocutores sociales interesados sobre la base de varias categorías de salarios y sueldos. Los grupos de rendimiento se basan en el nivel de capacitación, experiencia y responsabilidad requerida para realizar las tareas incluidas en las diversas categorías de ingresos.

- Los obreros se clasifican de acuerdo con tres grupos de rendimiento (calificados, semi-calificados y no calificados);
- Los empleados se clasifican de acuerdo a cuatro grupos de rendimiento (II a V) y dos categorías ocupacionales: empleados comerciales, y empleados técnicos y patrones.

Recolección de datos
Tipo y alcance del sistema administrativo: los datos abarcan unos 650 contratos colectivos.
Método de recolección de datos: Los datos se extraen de los registros de los contratos colectivos.
Actualización del sistema administrativo: semestralmente.
Procesamiento y verificación de datos
Todos los datos recopilados se controlan para hacer las correcciones necesarias, si procede.

Ajustes
Ninguno.
Tipos de estimaciones
Tasas del promedio mínimo/negociado de salarios y sueldos por hora, día o mes, por ocupación.
Construcción de índices
Los índices generales de horas negociadas por semana de trabajo y de las tasas de salarios y sueldos se calculan por actividad económica y región.
Series disponibles
- Tasas saláriales aprobadas de obreros
- Tasas de sueldos aprobadas de empleados
- Horas normales de trabajo
- Número de días de vacaciones por año
- Licencias pagadas
- Pagos durante licencia por enfermedad
- Pagos extraordinarios especiales.

Historia de las estadísticas
Fecha de iniciación de la serie estadística: 1949/50.
Cambios y revisiones principales: Presentación en Euros a partir del 2002 (antes en marcos alemanes).
Documentación y difusión
Documentación:
Statistisches Bundesamt (DESTATIS): *Fachserie 16, Reihe 4.1Tariflöhne* and *Reihe 4.2, Tarifgehälter* (Wiesbaden, semestralmente); se publica cuatro meses después del período de referencia (abril y octubre); contiene estadísticas e información metodológica.
Ídem: *Fachserie 16, Reihe 4.3, Index der Tariflöhne und -gehälter* (ibd, trimestralmente).
Difusión: Se espera que los datos estarán disponibles en el Internet en 2003.
Datos suministrados a la OIT para su difusión
Las siguientes estadísticas se publican en las *Estadísticas sobre salarios y horas de trabajo por ocupación y precios de artículos alimenticios – Resultados de la Encuesta de octubre*:
Promedio horario, diario y mensual de las tasas de salarios y sueldos por ocupación en determinadas industrias, que abarcan los principales Länder alemanes (es decir, Rin del norte -Westphalia).
Se pueden obtener en LABORSTA, las estadísticas sobre el promedio de las tasas de salario por hora de los trabajadores diurnos calificados que trabajaban en el sector de la agricultura (hasta 1994) en el territorio de la República Federal de Alemania antes del 3.10.1990.

Austria (1)

Fuente de la serie
Registros de la seguridad social.
Título de la serie
Beschäftigtenstatistik, Einkommensstatistik.
Organismo responsable
Recolección de datos, elaboración estadística y publicación o difusión de las estadísticas:
Hauptverband der österreichischen Sozialversicherungsträger (Principal Asociación de los Institutos de Seguridad Social de Austria).
Temas laborales principales abarcados
Empleo e ganancias.
Periodicidad o frecuencia de disponibilidad de las estadísticas
Empleo: mensualmente;
Ganancias: anualmente.
Período de referencia
Empleo: el último día del mes;
Ganancias: promedio mensual de todo el año.
Alcance de las estadísticas
Ambito geográfico: todo el país. Cada Land (Estado) tiene su propio Instituto.
Ambito industrial: todos los sectores de la actividad económica.
Establecimientos: todos los tipos y tamaños de los sectores privado y público.
Personas cubiertas: todos los asalariados.
Ocupaciones: los datos no se recopilan por ocupación ni grupo ocupacional.
Conceptos y definiciones
Empleo: asalariados, es decir obreros y empleados.
Ganancias: las ganancias brutas mensuales se refieren a todos los pagos sometidos a las cotizaciones a la seguridad social.

Clasificaciones

Ramas de actividad económica:

Título de la clasificación: ÖNACE.

Número de grupos utilizados para la codificación: no se dispone.

Se aplica a: empleo e ganancias.

Vínculos con la CIIU y nivel: Rev.2 y Rev.3.

Otras clasificaciones: por sexo, categoría de asalariado, grupo de edad y región.

Recolección de datos

Tipo y alcance del sistema administrativo: abarca todos los empleadores y asalariados.

Método de recolección de datos: los empleadores comunican de manera continua a los institutos de la seguridad social los datos de los asalariados y sus ganancias sometidas a las cotizaciones de la seguridad social. Los datos sobre el empleo se obtienen mediante el conteo real del número de personas aseguradas por los institutos de la seguridad social. Una vez al año se calculan los promedios mensuales de ganancias. Los registros se actualizan continuamente.

Procesamiento y verificación de datos

Los datos se procesan por computadora. Se realizan algunos controles de credibilidad para verificar los resultados agregados. Se realizan también comparaciones con los datos del mes y el año anteriores.

Ajustes

Ninguno.

Tipos de estimaciones

Totales y promedios.

Construcción de índices

Ninguno.

Indicadores de fiabilidad de las estimaciones

Alcance del sistema administrativo: exhaustiva; todos los asalariados en Austria deben estar asegurados en la seguridad social.

Series disponibles

Número mensual y anual de asalariados, por categoría, sexo, actividad económica y región;

Promedio de ganancias mensuales (anualmente), por categoría, sexo, actividad económica y región.

Historia de las estadísticas

Fecha de iniciación de la serie estadística: enero de 1948.

Cambios y revisiones principales: ninguno.

Documentación y difusión

Documentación:

Hauptverband der österreichischen Sozialversicherungsträger: *Die österreichische Sozialversicherung in Zahlen (Viena, mensualmente)*.

Difusión: En el sitio Internet: http://www.sozvers.at

Datos suministrados a la OIT para su difusión

Las siguientes estadísticas se publican en el *Anuario de Estadísticas del Trabajo*:

Empleo remunerado: por sexo y actividad económica; producción, por grupo de industria y sexo (datos más recientes: 1995) (en LABORSTA);

Promedio de ganancias mensuales de asalariados: por categoría del empleado, sexo y actividad económica; producción, por grupo de industria.

Las series mensuales de empleo remunerado (nivel general) se publican en el *Boletín de Estadísticas del Trabajo*.

Austria (2)

Fuente de la serie

Kollektivverträge (Contratos colectivos, incluidos sistemas de pago para funcionarios públicos).

Título de la serie

Kollektivverträge.

Organismo responsable

Recolección de datos y elaboración estadística: Federación de Sindicatos de Austria.

Publicación o difusión de las estadísticas: Sindicatos y Oficina de Estadística de Austria.

Temas laborales principales abarcados

Tasas de salarios y sueldos, ganancias y horas de trabajo.

Periodicidad o frecuencia de disponibilidad de las estadísticas

Mensual.

Período de referencia

Tasas de salarios, ganancias y horas de trabajo: octubre.

Alcance de las estadísticas

Ambito geográfico: todo el país.

Ambito industrial: todos los sectores de actividad económica de la Cámara de Comercio de Austria.

Establecimientos: todos los tipos y tamaños de los sectores público y privado.

Personas cubiertas: todos los asalariados cubiertos por contratos colectivos.

Ocupaciones: todas las ocupaciones cubiertas por contratos colectivos.

Conceptos y definiciones

Empleo: se refiere a los obreros, empleados y funcionarios públicos.

Ganancias: se refieren a la remuneración bruta que se paga a los asalariados.

Tasas de sueldo o salario: se refieren a las tasas por horas, semanales y mensuales, incluidos salarios y sueldos básicos, así como subsidios garantizados y pagados periódicamente. Estos datos se comunican separadamente para obreros y empleados.

Horas de trabajo: las horas normales de trabajo son las establecidas en los contratos colectivos.

En las horas realmente trabajadas se incluyen las horas trabajadas durante períodos de trabajo normales, horas extraordinarias, horas para las cuales el pago se hace en el marco de un contrato de trabajo garantizado, etc., de acuerdo con la definición internacional.

En las horas pagadas se incluyen las horas realmente trabajadas (como se indica en el párrafo anterior) y las horas pagadas pero no trabajadas, como la licencia anual pagada, las vacaciones públicas, la baja por enfermedad, etc.

Clasificaciones

Ramas de actividad económica:

Título de la clasificación: Clasificación de la Cámara de Comercio de Austria.

Número de grupos utilizados para la codificación: corresponde al número de los contratos colectivos en vigor.

Se aplica a: tasas de salarios y sueldos, ganancias y horas de trabajo.

Vínculos con la CIIU y nivel: Rev.2 y Rev.3.

Ocupaciones: todas las ocupaciones que se definen en los contratos colectivos.

Situación en el empleo: asalariados: obreros, empleados y funcionarios públicos.

Otras clasificaciones: asalariados: por sexo; tasas de salarios y sueldos, ganancias y horas de trabajo: por categoría del asalariado (manual/no manual) mayor de 18 años y por sexo.

Recolección de datos

Tipo y alcance del sistema administrativo: todos los contratos colectivos.

Método de recolección de datos: los datos se recopilan a partir de todos los contratos colectivos y sistemas de pago de los funcionarios públicos.

Actualización del sistema administrativo: normalmente, cada año, pero de manera continua siempre que entra en vigor un nuevo contrato colectivo.

Procesamiento y verificación de datos

Recopilación sencilla de datos.

Ajustes

Ninguno.

Tipos de estimaciones

Número total de asalariados y promedio de salarios y sueldos, ganancias y horas de trabajo.

Construcción de índices

La Oficina de Estadística de Austria calcula mensualmente más de 1500 índices a partir de las estadísticas de salarios mínimos establecidos en los contratos colectivos (Tariflohnindex).

Indicadores de fiabilidad de las estimaciones

Alcance del sistema administrativo: exhaustiva: se abarcan todos los contratos colectivos y sistemas de pago.

Series disponibles

Número total de asalariados, horas de trabajo normal semanales, horas de trabajo realmente trabajadas y pagadas, promedio de sueldos y salarios por horas, semanas y meses, promedio de ganancias por horas, semanas, meses y años, por actividad económica y ocupación.

Historia de las estadísticas

Fecha de iniciación de la serie estadística: las primeras series comenzaron a fines del siglo XIX.

Cambios y revisiones principales: en caso de nuevos contratos colectivos.

Documentación y difusión

Documentación:

Oficina de Estadística de Austria: *Schnellbericht* (Viena).

Idem: *Statistische Narchrichten* (ibid., mensualmente); contiene las series mensuales de Tariflohnindex.

La información metodológica sobre los índices se publicó en *Tariflohnindex 1986, Aufbau und Gewichtung*, 899. Heft (Viena, 1988).

Difusión: en el sitio Internet de la Oficina de Estadística de Austria: http://www.statistik.at

Datos suministrados a la OIT para su difusión

Las siguientes estadísticas se publican en las *Estadísticas sobre salarios y horas de trabajo por ocupación y precios de artículos alimenticios – Resultados de la Encuesta de octubre*:

Promedio mensual de salarios mínimos y horas de trabajo normales, por ocupación y sexo;

Promedio mensual de ganancias y horas realmente trabajadas y pagadas, por ocupación y sexo.

En el *Anuario de Estadísticas del Trabajo*:

Promedio mensual de salarios de los obreros en el sector de la agricultura.

Costa Rica

Fuente de la serie
Planillas de la Caja Costarricense de Seguro Social (CCSS).

Título de la serie
Estadística de Patronos, Trabajadores y Salarios.

Organismo responsable
Recolección de datos: Caja Costarricense de Seguro Social, Dirección actuarial y de Planificación económica.
Elaboración estadística: Caja Costarricense de Seguro Social, Dirección de Informática.
Publicación o difusión de las estadísticas: Caja Costarricense de Seguro Social, Presidencia Ejecutiva, Dirección actuarial y de Planificación económica, Departamento de Estadística.

Temas laborales principales abarcados
Empleo, ganancias e ingresos relacionados con el empleo.

Periodicidad o frecuencia de disponibilidad de las estadísticas
Anual.

Período de referencia
Junio de cada año.

Alcance de las estadísticas
Ambito geográfico: todo el país.
Ambito industrial: todas las ramas de actividad económica.
Establecimientos: de todos tipos y tamaños.
Personas cubiertas: los patronos (empleadores) y trabajadores afiliados a los regímenes de Salud y Pensiones de la CCSS (de todos los sectores institucionales) y los trabajadores no asalariados afiliados al seguro voluntario (Cuenta propia y Convenios especiales).
Ocupaciones: no se recogen datos sobre ocupaciones individuales o grupos de ocupaciones.

Conceptos y definiciones
Empleo: incluye las siguientes categorías de personas con empleo afiliadas a la CCSS:
Patrono: es la persona natural o jurídica, particular o de derecho público, que utiliza los servicios de una o más personas amparadas por los regímenes de Seguridad Social.
Trabajador asegurado (asalariado, empleado): es la persona que trabaja para un patrono y recibe una remuneración por su trabajo en forma de sueldo, salario, jornal o pago a destajo, ya sea en dinero o en especie.
Trabajador por cuenta propia (trabajador independiente): es la persona que trabaja sola o asociada, sin establecer una relación de dependencia con un patrono.
Trabajador por convenios especiales: corresponde a grupos de trabajadores independientes organizados en asociaciones, sindicatos, cooperativas, colegios profesionales, clubes rotarios, hogares, museos, etc. que suscriben convenio con la CCSS para su aseguramiento.
Asegurado directo (cotizante/activo): es la persona que mediante una cotización (cuota) genera para sí mismo y para otros el derecho a recibir ciertos beneficios de la Seguridad Social; esta contribución la hace en forma directa o por intermedio de terceros (patronos).
Ganancias: se refieren a la masa salarial, es decir el total de salarios reportados por los asegurados directos en la planilla mensual. No incluye lo correspondiente a seguro voluntario, cuenta propia y convenios especiales.
El salario promedio es la remuneración que en promedio recibe mensualmente un trabajador asalariado.
Ingresos relacionados con el empleo independiente: se refieren a "ingresos de cotización" y corresponden al total de ingresos reportados por los trabajadores independientes, sobre los cuales se calcula la cuota de contribución (el análogo al salario de los asegurados directos activos).

Ingreso promedio: se refiere a la remuneración que en promedio reporta mensualmente un trabajador independiente.
Masa cotizante: es la suma de los salarios y los ingresos reportados por los trabajadores asalariados y los trabajadores independientes, respectivamente, para un mes determinado.

Clasificaciones
Ramas de actividad económica:
Título de la clasificación: Manual de Códigos de Actividades Económicas.
Número de grupos utilizados para la codificación: todos los grupos a nivel de 4 dígitos.
Se aplica a: todos los datos.
Vínculos con la CIIU y nivel: basado en la CIIU-1990 a todos los niveles.
Situación en el empleo:
Título de la clasificación: Clasificación de la CCSS.
Número de grupos utilizados para la codificación: cuatro (patronos (empleadores), trabajadores independientes (por cuenta propia), trabajadores (asalariados) y trabajadores por convenios especiales (colectivos).
Se aplica a: todos los datos.
Vínculos con la CISE y nivel: parcial vínculo a nivel de un dígito.
Otras clasificaciones: por sector institucional: se identifican 6 sectores institucionales a saber: Gobierno Central, Instituciones Autónomas y Semi-autónomas, Empresas privadas, Cuenta propia, Convenios especiales y Servicio doméstico.
También se clasifican los datos por división territorial administrativa: 7 provincias, las cuales se subdividen en 81 cantones; por grupos de edad y sexo, y tamaño de empresas.

Recolección de datos
Tipo y alcance del sistema administrativo: en junio de 2000, los registros utilizados abarcaban a unos 52,040 patronos, y 1,038,816 trabajadores de todos los sectores institucionales; y a unos 313,000 no asalariados afiliados al seguro voluntario (por cuenta propia y de convenios especiales) - todos afiliados al seguro de salud.
Método de recolección de datos: la Estadística de Patronos, Trabajadores y Salarios se genera a partir de varias fuentes de información: (i) la planillas mensuales que envían los patronos afiliados a la CCSS con el detalle de los trabajadores, salarios y actividad económica, para los sectores Empresa Privada, Servicio doméstico, Instituciones Autónomas y Convenios especiales; (ii) la Oficina Técnica Mecanizada del Gobierno proporciona la información sobre los trabajadores del Gobierno Central; y (iii) los trabajadores independientes y algunos de Convenios especiales se obtienen de los registros de afiliación de la CCSS. Los datos que se captan en estas fuentes son procesados por la Dirección de Informática, la cual suministra dicha información al Departamento de Estadística de la Dirección actuarial y de Planificación económica, en archivos tipo texto que alimenta el sistema diseñado para generar las estadísticas.
Actualización del sistema administrativo: una vez por año.

Procesamiento y verificación de datos
Se procesan los datos por computadora y el sistema hace los ajustes necesarios.

Ajustes
El proceso de captación y procesamiento de datos puede dar origen a errores propios de este proceso, tales como categorías desconocidas en distintas clasificaciones a nivel de trabajadores (sexo, edad, rama de actividad o ingresos desconocidos). Situación similar ocurre con la masa cotizante. Al ajustar las estadísticas para distribuir proporcionalmente los trabajadores de sexo desconocido y la masa cotizante en las categorías que corresponden, se pueden presentar diferencias de redondeo entre los resultados. Sin embargo, estas diferencias se mantienen por debajo del 1 por ciento.

Tipos de estimaciones
Totales de personas aseguradas a los varios seguros (salud y pensiones), por categoría y según varias clasificaciones;
Totales y promedios de salarios e ingresos mensuales, por categoría de personas aseguradas y según varias clasificaciones;
Distribuciones de asegurados por escala de salarios mensuales y sector.

Construcción de índices
Ninguno.

Indicadores de fiabilidad de las estimaciones
No se dispone.

Series disponibles
Patronos, trabajadores asegurados y masa cotizante por sexo, según sector institucional, provincia y cantón, según sector, rama de actividad y tamaño de empresa;
Trabajadores asegurados por rama de actividad económica, grupo de edad, sector, escala de salario mensual, etc.;

Promedios de salarios e ingresos.
Historia de las estadísticas
Fecha de iniciación de la serie estadística: enero de 1973.
Cambios y revisiones principales: no se dispone.
Documentación y difusión
Documentación:
Caja Costarricense de Seguro Social: *Anuario Estadístico* (San Jose, anual); cada publicación presenta los datos del mes de junio del año precedente.
Difusión: en el sitio Internet de la CCSS:
http://www.ccss.sa.cr/actuarial/publicaciones.html
Datos suministrados a la OIT para su difusión
Estadísticas de ganancias medias de los asalariados se publicaron en el *Anuario de Estadísticas del Trabajo* hasta 1986 y se encuentran en la base de datos LABORSTA.

Cuba

Fuente de la serie
Sistema de Información Estadística Nacional (SIE-N) y Balances de Recursos Humanos.
Título de la serie
Trabajo y Salarios.
Organismo responsable
Recolección de datos, elaboración estadística, y publicación o difusión de las estadísticas: Oficina Nacional de Estadísticas (ONE).
Temas laborales principales abarcados
Empleo y salarios.
Periodicidad o frecuencia de disponibilidad de las estadísticas
Mensual y anual.
Período de referencia
Empleo y salarios: cada mes del año y el año completo.
Alcance de las estadísticas
Ambito geográfico: todo el país.
Ambito industrial: todas las ramas de actividad económica.
Establecimientos: de todos tipos y tamaños en los sectores privado y público.
Personas cubiertas: el total de ocupados en la economía.
Ocupaciones: se recogen datos sobre categorías ocupacionales: obreros, técnicos, administrativos, de servicio y dirigentes.
Conceptos y definiciones
Empleo: corresponde al total de personas ocupadas en las distintas actividades de la economía nacional, estén o no comprendidas en la edad laboral (17 años y más), tanto en las entidades estatales como en el sector no estatal. Se considera como ocupada a toda persona que en el día de cierre de la información mantenía vínculo laboral formalizado con un empleo asalariado en metálico o en especie, o un empleo independiente.
Los trabajadores asalariados de entidades estatales son los trabajadores cuya relación laboral, independientemente de la forma de retribución que se les aplica, se establece a través de un contrato de trabajo con una entidad de propiedad estatal que cuenta con personalidad jurídica y está sujeta al control de instituciones estatales. Incluyen a los trabajadores de las Sociedades Mercantiles Cubanas y las Organizaciones Políticas y de Masas y los que laboran en las entidades estatales que organizativamente pueden tener forma de uniones, empresas, asociaciones económicas, organizaciones económicas estatales, granjas, instituciones financieras, instituciones de unidades presupuestadas de salud, deporte, cultura y centros científicos, etc.
Los trabajadores asalariados del sector no estatal incluyen a los que pertenecen al sector cooperativo, a las Empresas Mixtas y al sector privado (sucursales de firmas extranjeras, asociaciones y fundaciones).
Dentro de las personas con empleo independiente en el sector privado, se consideran:
- los trabajadores por cuenta propia: son aquellos que siendo o no propietarios de los medios y objetos de trabajo, no están sujetos a un contrato laboral con una entidad jurídica, no reciben una remuneración salarial, elaboran su producción o prestan sus servicios de una forma individual o colectiva, mediante el empleo según procede, de ayuda familiar y se encargan directamente de la comercialización, o a través de otra persona o entidad que los represente legalmente a estos efectos;
- los usufructuarios individuales: son aquellas personas que no tienen otro vínculo laboral y denominados como "parceleros", a los que el Estado les ha entregado tierras en usufructo con el fin de desarrollar determinados cultivos de interés estatal, entre los que se encuentra el café, tabaco, entre otros;

- los campesinos independientes: se refieren a los agricultores pequeños, propietarios de las tierras que explotan para la obtención de productos agrícolas y/o pecuarios para la venta o autoconsumo;
- los trabajadores de Cooperativas de Créditos y Servicios: comprenden a los agricultores pequeños que se agrupan a los fines de viabilizar la asistencia técnica y financiera que el Estado brinda a la producción de los campesinos integrados en ella.;
- los cooperativistas (UBPC y CPA); y
- los ayudantes familiares.
Se consideran como ocupadas a las personas con empleo independiente aun cuando no hubieran trabajado por algunas de las situaciones siguientes: los que asistieron al trabajo en la fecha de referencia de la información y no pudieron realizar sus laborares por cualquier cause; y los que no asistieron al trabajo por alguna causa, siempre que se mantenga el vínculo laboral con el empleo.
Ganancias: el salario devengado es la remuneración en dinero que recibe el trabajador por la cantidad y calidad del trabajo realizado. Incluye entre otros, los pagos por tarifas salariales, por primas, condiciones laborales anormales, sobre cumplimiento de las normas de trabajo, plus salarial, trabajo extra, asignaciones adicionales por años de servicio o cargo de dirección, descanso retribuido, ausencias autorizadas por la legislación vigente.
Clasificaciones
Ramas de actividad económica:
Título de la clasificación: No se dispone.
Número de grupos utilizados para la codificación: 9 grandes grupos.
Se aplica a: empleo y ganancias.
Vínculos con la CIIU y nivel: con la Rev.2, 1968.
Ocupaciones:
Título de la clasificación: Clasificador Uniforme de Ocupaciones (CUO).
Número de grupos utilizados para la codificación: cinco categorías ocupacionales: dirigentes; técnicos; trabajadores de los servicios; trabajadores administrativos; obreros.
Se aplica a: sólo el empleo.
Vínculos con la CIUO y nivel: ninguno.
Situación en el empleo: Véase bajo "Conceptos y definiciones".
Empleo
Otras clasificaciones: fuerza de trabajo por sexo, formas de propiedad, provincia y grupos de edad.
Recolección de datos
Tipo y alcance del sistema administrativo: el Sistema de Información Estadística Nacional (SIE-N) y los Balances de Recursos Laborales abarcan al conjunto de la fuerza de trabajo.
Método de recolección de datos: no se dispone.
Procesamiento y verificación de datos
El promedio de trabajadores total se calcula, deduciendo del número de trabajadores en el registro, aquellos a los que no se les paga salario directa ni indirectamente por la entidad por encontrarse laborando en otras entidades por las cuales cobran su salario, aún estando incluidos en el citado registro, y adicionando los que sin estar incluidos en el registro de trabajadores de la entidad realizan el trabajo y se les paga salario directa o indirectamente por la misma. Este promedio es el resultado de sumar día a día los trabajadores teniendo presente las adiciones y deducciones antes mencionadas, incluyendo los días de descanso, festivos y feriados, y dividiendo el resultado obtenido entre los días calendarios del período que se informa.
El salario medio mensual se calcula dividiendo el salario devengado por el promedio de trabajadores total.
Ajustes
No se dispone.
Tipos de estimaciones
Totales de ocupados; total de salario devengado y salario medio mensual.
Construcción de índices
Ninguno.
Indicadores de fiabilidad de las estimaciones
Alcance del sistema administrativo: abarca al conjunto de la fuerza de trabajo.
Series disponibles
Ocupados en la economía nacional por forma de propiedad y clase de actividad económica;
Ocupados (asalariados), salario devengado (total) y salario medio mensual en entidades estatales y mixtas por clase de actividad económica y provincia;
Distribución de la fuerza de trabajo por nivel educacional, grupos de edad, categoría ocupacional y sexo.

Historia de las estadísticas
No se dispone.
Documentación y difusión
Documentación:
Oficina Nacional de Estadísticas: *Anuario Estadístico de Cuba* (Ciudad Habana, anual); contiene notas metodológicas.
Idem: *Cuba en Cifras* (ibid., anual).
Datos suministrados a la OIT para su difusión
Estadísticas de promedios de ganancias mensuales en las entidades estatales y mixtas, por rama de actividad económica se publican en el *Anuario de Estadísticas del Trabajo*.

España

Fuente de la serie
Fichero administrativo de afiliación al Sistema de la Seguridad Social.
Título de la serie
Afiliación de trabajadores al Sistema de la Seguridad Social (AFI).
Organismo responsable
Recolección de datos, elaboración estadística y publicación o difusión de las estadísticas: Ministerio de Trabajo y Asuntos Sociales.
Temas laborales principales abarcados
Empleo.
Periodicidad o frecuencia de disponibilidad de las estadísticas
Mensual y anual.
Período de referencia
Cada mes del año y el año civil entero.
Alcance de las estadísticas
Ámbito geográfico: todo el país.
Ámbito industrial: todas las ramas de actividad.
Establecimientos: de todos tipos y tamaños.
Personas cubiertas: trabajadores afiliados a los distintos regímenes del Sistema de la Seguridad Social en situación de alta laboral y situaciones asimiladas al alta, tales como incapacidad temporal, suspensión por regulación de empleo, desempleo parcial, etc. Se excluyen los trabajadores en situación de desempleo, con convenios especiales, pertenecientes a empresas acogidas a planes de reconversión y que reciben ayudas en concepto de jubilación anticipada.
Ocupaciones: no se recogen datos sobre ocupaciones individuales, sino por grupo de cotización.
Conceptos y definiciones
Empleo: Se refiere a las personas que desarrollan una actividad laboral y están inscritas o figuran en el fichero administrativo de afiliación de trabajadores al Sistema de la Seguridad Social.
Clasificaciones
Ramas de actividad económica:
Título de la clasificación: Clasificación Nacional de Actividades Económicas (CNAE-93).
Número de grupos utilizados para la codificación: 30 grupos, codificados a dos dígitos.
Se aplica a: empleo.
Vínculos con la CIIU y nivel: con la Rev.3, 1988 a nivel de 2 dígitos.
Ocupaciones:
Título de la clasificación: "Grupos de cotización por el Sistema de la Seguridad Social".
Número de grupos utilizados para la codificación: 10 categorías de ocupación relativas a los trabajadores más de 18 años.
Se aplica a: empleo.
Vínculos con la CIUO y nivel: ninguno.
Situación en el empleo:
Título de la clasificación: Dependencia Laboral.
Número de grupos utilizados para la codificación: 2 grupos: asalariados, trabajadores por cuenta propia.
Se aplica a: empleo.
Otras clasificaciones: por tamaño de la empresa; por régimen de seguridad; por sexo, grupos de edad y nacionalidad; por comunidad autónoma y provincia; según tipo de movilidad de las empresas.
Recolección de datos
Tipo y alcance del sistema administrativo: Fichero administrativo de Afiliación al Sistema de la Seguridad Social.
Método de recolección de datos: se recogen los datos en nivel central, regional o local. Los datos de empresas y de personas con empleo se incluyen en el Fichero cuando inician una actividad laboral. La explotación de la información es efectuada por la Gerencia de Informática de la Seguridad Social y por la Subdirección General de Proceso de Datos, siguiendo las instrucciones dadas por la Subdirección General de Estadísticas Sociales y Laborales.
Actualización del sistema administrativo: mensual

Procesamiento y verificación de datos
El empresario para los trabajadores asalariados y el propio trabajador si es trabajador por cuenta propia están obligados a presentar un documento de afiliación a la Seguridad Social, cuyos datos se verifican a través del DNI o Pasaporte. Los datos se suministran a la Tesorería General de la Seguridad Social, procesándolos a través de medios electrónicos y con obligación de cumplimiento de diversos campos.
Ajustes
No se dispone de la información.
Tipos de estimaciones
Totales de trabajadores afiliados al Sistema de la Seguridad Social, por régimen; variaciones absolutas y relativas, sobre el año anterior.
Construcción de índices
Ninguno.
Indicadores de fiabilidad de las estimaciones
Alcance del sistema administrativo: Alrededor del 99% de la población legalmente ocupada.
Conformidad con otras fuentes: Se realizan comparaciones con los datos de ocupados de la Encuesta de Población Activa (EPA) que realiza el Instituto Nacional de Estadística.
Series disponibles
Series mensuales y anuales de:
- Trabajadores afiliados en alta laboral, según regímenes;
- Trabajadores afiliados en alta laboral, según sexo y edad;
- Trabajadores afiliados en alta laboral, según rama de actividad;
- Trabajadores afiliados en alta laboral, según sector de actividad y dependencia laboral;
- Trabajadores afiliados en alta laboral, por comunidad autónoma y provincia.

Historia de las estadísticas
Fecha de iniciación de la serie estadística: Enero de 1982.
Cambios y revisiones principales: se introdujeron las distribuciones por sexo y edad así como por grupo de cotización en 01.01.1995 y la clasificación de actividades económicas CNAE-93 en 01.01.1998.
Documentación y difusión
Documentación:
Ministerio de Trabajo y Asuntos Sociales: *Boletín de Estadísticas Laborales* (Madrid, trimestral)
idem: *Anuario de Estadísticas Laborales y de Asuntos Sociales* (ibid., anual).
Difusión: http://www.mtas.es
Datos suministrados a la OIT para su difusión
Ninguno hasta ahora.

Francia

Fuente de la serie
Declaración anual de datos sociales (Déclaration annuelle de Données Sociales-DADS).
Título de la serie
Los salarios en la industria, el comercio y los servicios.
Organismo responsable
Recolección de datos: Caisse Nationale d'Assurance Vieillesse (CNAV) y Direction Générale des Impôts (DGI).
Elaboración estadística y publicación o difusión de las estadísticas: Institut National de la Statistique et des Etudes Economiques (INSEE).
Temas laborales principales abarcados
Empleo, ganancias y duración del trabajo.
Periodicidad o frecuencia de disponibilidad de las estadísticas
Anual.
Período de referencia
El año.
Alcance de las estadísticas
Ámbito geográfico: todo el país.
Ámbito industrial: todos los sectores de la actividad económica, excluida la función pública del Estado, la agricultura y la silvicultura, los servicios domésticos y las actividades extraterritoriales.
Establecimientos: establecimientos de todos los tipos y todos los tamaños. Una declaración DADS se refiere en principio al establecimiento, pero a veces se puede referir a varios establecimientos de una misma empresa.
Personas cubiertas: todos los asalariados.
Ocupaciones: los datos se recopilan por categoría socioprofesional. Los trabajadores a domicilio, aprendices y personas en formación se identifican por separado.

Conceptos y definiciones

Empleo: asalariados. Se dividen en cuatro grupos:

- asalariados a tiempo completo, incluidos los que trabajan al 80%;
- intermitentes (contratos de duración indeterminada para empleos permanentes que por naturaleza implica una alternancia), incluidos los interinos;
- asalariados a tiempo parcial;
- trabajadores a domicilio (se excluyen de los cuadros estadísticos).

Ganancias: ingresos brutos y netos anuales después de deducir las cotizaciones sociales de los asalariados (cotizaciones a los seguros sociales y al seguro de desempleo, deducciones para la jubilación, contribuciones sociales generales (CSG) y contribución al reembolso de la deuda social (CRDS)). Se incluyen todos los componentes impositivos de la remuneración, y sobre todo: los salarios directos, las licencias pagadas, las primas de todo tipo y el valor fiscal declarado por el empleador de los beneficios en especie (vivienda, comidas, combustible para la calefacción, etc.).

Horas de trabajo: horas remuneradas, incluidas las licencias pagadas y baja por enfermedad en un año. En los datos sobre la duración del trabajo se excluyen los VRP (viajeros-representantes-corredores) y los trabajadores a domicilio, cuyas horas de trabajo no se dispone.

También se recopilan datos sobre las fechas de inicio y finalización del período de pago de cada asalariado, lo que permite calcular la duración de presencia en el establecimiento.

Clasificaciones

Ramas de actividad económica:

Título de la clasificación: Nomenclatura de Actividades Francesas (NAF). A partir de enero de 2003 se aplicará la NAF, Rev.1, 2003.

Número de grupos utilizados para la codificación: 700 grupos.

Se aplica a: todos los datos.

Vínculos con la CIIU y nivel: Rev.3, 1990.

Ocupaciones:

Título de la clasificación: Nomenclatura de Profesiones y Categorías socioprofesionales.

Número de grupos utilizados para la codificación: 34.

Se aplica a: todos los datos.

Vínculos con la CIUO y nivel: ninguno.

Otras clasificaciones: sexo, edad, tamaño de la empresa y el establecimiento (de acuerdo con el número de cargos al 31 de diciembre), ubicación de la sede de la empresa y del establecimiento, y comunidad de residencia del asalariado.

Recolección de datos

Tipo y alcance del sistema administrativo: recopilación exhaustiva a partir de los empleadores.

Método de recolección de datos: la DADS es una declaración formal que debe efectuar toda empresa (persona física o moral) domiciliada o establecida en Francia que paga un tratamiento o salario, excluida la mayoría de empleadores de personal doméstico.

Se trata de un documento común de las administraciones sociales y fiscales en el que los empleadores declaran todas las remuneraciones salariales por cada establecimiento y cada asalariado. Las declaraciones se transmiten, en medios informáticos o impresos, a las Cajas Regionales de Seguros de Enfermedad y, luego, la CNAV centraliza los datos de los asalariados que dependen del sistema general de la seguridad social. La DGI utiliza las declaraciones fiscales (no. 2460) de los asalariados que dependen de sistemas particulares de la seguridad social. Esas declaraciones se transmiten al INSEE cada año, en el mes de febrero del año siguiente al año de referencia, y se publican el año siguiente en marzo.

La DADS contiene toda la información sobre los establecimientos (nombre o razón social del empleador, dirección y sector de actividad, número de identificación, trabajadores inscritos al 31 de diciembre de año y masa de salarios brutos) y los asalariados (identificación, tipo de empleo y calificaciones, dirección, datos de inicio y finalización del período de pago, número de horas pagadas, condición de empleo (tiempo completo, parcial, intermitente y trabajadores a domicilio), suma de las remuneraciones en especie antes y después de las deducciones retenidas para las cotizaciones sociales, valor estimado de los beneficios en especie y monto de las indemnizaciones por gastos de empleo o servicio y del reembolso de gastos.

Actualización del sistema administrativo: anual.

Procesamiento y verificación de datos

Los datos se procesan por computadora. Se realizan verificaciones a nivel de identificadores de los establecimientos y los asalariados (comparación de listas de empresas y personas) y se hacen los controles de coherencia entre salario, duración del trabajo y condiciones de empleo.

Ajustes

Ninguno.

Tipos de estimaciones

Distribuciones, promedios y medias, según las diversas unidades de tiempo (hora, año).

Empleo: total de trabajadores al 31 de diciembre del año de referencia, y número de asalariados remunerados durante el año de referencia; distribuciones según las diversas variables;

Salario neto medio por hora: cociente de la masa de salarios netos por el volumen de horas efectuadas;

Salario neto anual medio: para los asalariados a tiempo completo, cociente de la masa de salarios netos de "tiempo completo" por el número de años de trabajo;

Volumen de horas anuales medio de los cargos: volumen de horas remuneradas en un año dividido entre el número de cargos remunerados en el año.

Construcción de índices

Ninguno.

Indicadores de fiabilidad de las estimaciones

Alcance del sistema administrativo: superior al 90% en términos de asalariados.

Conformidad con otras fuentes: se pueden hacer comparaciones a nivel de:

- trabajadores y masa salarial, con las cuentas nacionales,
- evolución del índice de los salarios, con los resultados de la Encuesta de la ACEMO del Ministerio del Trabajo (encuesta trimestral realizada en los establecimientos por el Ministerio del Empleo y la Solidaridad (DARES);
- trabajadores, con otras fuentes administrativas.

Series disponibles

Cuadros de "Empleadores": número de establecimientos, trabajadores en número de cargos remunerados en el año, trabajadores en número de cargos remunerados al 31 de diciembre, masa de salarios brutos, por actividad económica del establecimiento, tamaño, departamento en el que está ubicado el establecimiento;

Cuadros de "Cargos a tiempo completo", serie de salarios horarios: trabajadores en número de cargos, en número de años de trabajo, volumen de horas anuales, masa de salarios netos pagados, promedio del volumen de horas anuales de los cargos y promedio de salarios netos horarios de los cargos, según la actividad económica y el tamaño del establecimiento, por sexo, categoría socioprofesional, grupo de edad, grupo de salario neto horario, etc.;

Cuadros de "Cargos a tiempo completo", serie de salario anual: trabajadores en número de cargos, en número de años de trabajo, masa de salarios netos pagados, promedio de salario neto anual por año de trabajo, número de permanentes, promedio de salario neto anual por año de trabajo de los permanentes, según diversas variables de clasificación y por sexo;

Cuadros de "Cargos a tiempo no completo" y "Conjunto de cargos": series de salarios horarios según variables y clasificaciones parecidas.

Historia de las estadísticas

Fecha de iniciación de la serie estadística: 1967, en base a una muestra de una quinta parte; 1993 de manera exhaustiva.

Cambios y revisiones principales: hasta 1992, los asalariados del sector de la agricultura y la silvicultura estaban excluidos del campo de explotación de las DADS. Desde 1997, los ficheros exhaustivos de la DADS permiten, además, conocer los salarios que se pagan a los dirigentes de las sociedades anónimas y a gerentes minoritarios de sociedades de responsabilidad limitada, pero no los salarios de gerentes mayoritarios de SARL. Está previsto incluir la agricultura y la silvicultura en las estadísticas a partir de 2002.

Documentación y difusión

Documentación:

INSEE: *INSEE Résultats: Les Salaires dans l'Industrie, le Commerce et les Services en ...* (París, anual); se publica unos 15 meses después del período de referencia de los datos. Contiene las estadísticas e información metodológica.

Difusión: en el sitio Internet: http://www.alisse.insee.fr

Se pueden obtener, previa solicitud, las estadísticas que no figuran en las publicaciones nacionales o en la Internet.

Datos suministrados a la OIT para su difusión

Ninguno hasta ahora.

Otras fuentes administrativas de datos: las estadísticas sobre los ingresos de actividades no asalariadas se obtienen de diversas fuentes administrativas:

Los datos sobre el ingreso liberal de los médicos se establecen a partir de dos fuentes administrativas: las estadísticas del sistema nacional interegímenes elaboradas por la Caisse Nationale d'Assurance Maladie des travailleurs salariés (CNAMTS), la MSA (Mutualité Sociale Agricole) y la CANAM (Caisse Nationale d'Assurance Maladie des Professions Indépendantes), para los honorarios y los trabajadores; y las estadísticas fiscales de la Direction Générale des Impôts (DGI) para las cargas profesionales. Esas estadísticas se establecen anualmente y se refieren a los médicos con actividades normales (se excluyen los sustitutos) que hayan completado una declaración controlada, convencional o no, incluido el personal que trabaja en hospitales a tiempo completo. Las evaluaciones respectivas de los ingresos y las cargas permiten hacer estimaciones para cada año sobre el ingreso medio de los médicos con actividad liberal antes de deducir el impuesto sobre la renta.

Las estadísticas sobre los ingresos de actividades de pequeños empresarios de la artesanía, el comercio y los servicios se establecen en base a la explotación y reorganización de las declaraciones fiscales de las empresas de los beneficios industriales y comerciales (BIC) y los beneficios no comerciales (BNC). Los ficheros que se hacen con las declaraciones se transmiten al l'INSEE y constituyen, con las encuestas anuales de las empresas, el sistema unificado de estadísticas de empresas.

Los resultados se publican en:

INSEE: *Synthèses: Les revenus d'activité non salariée en ...* (París, anual); se publican unos 3 años después del período de referencia de los datos. Contiene estadísticas e información metodológica.

Las estadísticas sobre los salarios de los agentes del Estado se establecen cada año en base a un conjunto de ficheros: ficheros de los ministerios civiles y explotadores públicos; encuesta complementaria por cuestionario realizada entre el conjunto de servicios del Estado, ficheros del Ministerio de Defensa, ficheros de establecimientos públicos, etc.

Los resultados se publican en:

INSEE: *INSEE Résultats: Le Salaire des Agents de l'Etat en ...* (París, anual); se publican unos 3 años después del período de referencia de los datos. Contiene estadísticas e información metodológica.

Guatemala

Fuente de la serie
Registros del Instituto Guatemalteco de Seguridad Social (IGSS).
Título de la serie
Empleo e Ingreso del trabajo (ganancias) de los trabajadores afiliados al IGSS.
Organismo responsable
Recolección de datos: Instituto Guatemalteco de Seguridad Social (IGSS).
Temas laborales principales abarcados
Empleo y ganancias.
Periodicidad o frecuencia de disponibilidad de las estadísticas
Mensual y anual.
Período de referencia
Empleo y ganancias: cada mes del año y el año completo.
Alcance de las estadísticas
Ambito geográfico: todo el país.
Ambito industrial: todas las ramas de actividad económica.
Establecimientos: de todos tipos y tamaños en los sectores privado y público.
Personas cubiertas: patronos activos y trabajadores (asalariados) afiliados cotizantes al Régimen de Seguridad Social.
Ocupaciones: no se recogen datos sobre ocupaciones individuales o grupos de ocupaciones.
Conceptos y definiciones
Empleo: es afiliada al Régimen de Seguridad Social toda persona que preste sus servicios materiales, intelectuales o de ambos géneros, en virtud de un contrato o relación individual de trabajo, a un patrono declarado formalmente inscrito u obligado a inscribirse formalmente en el Régimen de SS. También son afiliados al trabajador del Estado, el asociado a las cooperativas legalmente constituidas y los trabajadores asalariados de éstas.
Ganancias: se refieren a la masa salarial, es decir el total de salarios reportados por las empresas cotizantes.
Clasificaciones
Ramas de actividad económica:
Título de la clasificación: no se dispone.
Número de grupos utilizados para la codificación: no se dispone.
Se aplica a: empleadores, asalariados y ganancias.
Vínculos con la CIIU y nivel: basada en la CIIU-1968.
Otras clasificaciones: por región y categoría de empleador/sector

(patronos particulares, Estado-Presupuesto y Estado-Planillas).
Recolección de datos
Tipo y alcance del sistema administrativo: registros del IGSS. Al 31 de diciembre de 2000, los registros utilizados abarcaban a unos 908,000 trabajadores afiliados, con un total de unos 1,950,000 personas protegidas.
Método de recolección de datos: los datos sobre el número de empleadores activos, los asalariados cotizantes y las ganancias se basan únicamente en los informes mensuales obligatorios de los empleadores al IGSS, que se archivan en un registro central.
Actualización del sistema administrativo: cada mes.
Procesamiento y verificación de datos
No se dispone.
Ajustes
Sub-representatividad: las estimaciones anuales de asalariados y salarios se ajustan tomando en consideración los ingresos percibidos por concepto de cuotas de todos los programas de seguro social y para tomar en cuenta la mora patronal. También se corrigen los datos del Estado Presupuesto para eliminar la multiplicidad de plazas y las cifras de salarios se ajustan con base en la Ejecución Presupuestaria del año.
Tipos de estimaciones
Totales de patronos activos (empleadores), trabajadores cotizantes y total de salarios mensuales y anuales.
Ganancias medias mensuales.
Construcción de índices
Ninguno.
Indicadores de fiabilidad de las estimaciones
Alcance del sistema administrativo: al 31 de diciembre de 2000, los afiliados representaban unos 25 por ciento de la población económicamente activa de 10 años y más, y el total de la población protegida (afiliados y beneficiarios), unos 17 por ciento de la población total.
Series disponibles
Estimación de patronos activos al 31 de diciembre de cada año;
Estimación de trabajadores afiliados cotizantes el mes de junio y al 31 de diciembre, por actividad económica, región y categoría de empleador;
Estimación del total de salarios anuales, por actividad económica, región y categoría de empleador;
Estimación mensual de trabajadores cotizantes y ganancias, por actividad económica.
Historia de las estadísticas
Fecha de iniciación de la serie estadística: no disponible.
Cambios y revisiones principales: el IGSS revisó las estimaciones de empleo y salarios para el periodo 1974-1987.
Documentación y difusión
Documentación:
Instituto Guatemalteco de Seguridad Social: *Boletín Estadístico* (Ciudad de Guatemala, anual).
Idem: *Informe Anual de Labores* (ibid., anual).
Banco de Guatemala: *Boletín Estadístico* (ibid., trimestral);
Difusión: en el sitio Internet del Banco de Guatemala: http://www.banguat.gob.gt
Datos suministrados a la OIT para su difusión
Estadísticas de empleo remunerado y promedios de ganancias mensuales de los trabajadores afiliados cotizantes, por actividad económica, se publican en el *Anuario de Estadísticas del Trabajo*.

Hong Kong, China (1)

Fuente de la serie
Registros administrativos gubernamentales.
Título de la serie
Estadísticas del Personal del Servicio Público – Establecimiento·y Fortalecimiento del Servicio Público (Civil Service Personnel Statistics - Establishment and Strength of the Civil Service).
Organismo responsable
Recolección de datos: Oficina del Servicio Público (Civil Service Bureau), Región Administrativa Especial de Hong Kong (RAE), República Popular de China.
Elaboración estadística y publicación o difusión de las estadísticas : Departamento de Censo y Estadística (Census and Statistics Department), RAE de Hong Kong.
Temas laborales principales abarcados
Empleo y puestos vacantes.
Periodicidad o frecuencia de disponibilidad de las estadísticas
Trimestralmente.
Período de referencia
El último día de trabajo completo en un trimestre.

Alcance de las estadísticas

Ambito geográfico: RAE de Hong Kong.
Ambito industrial: todas las ramas de actividad económica.
Establecimientos: todas las oficinas políticas y los departamentos gubernamentales del Gobierno de la RAE de Hong Kong.
Personas cubiertas: funcionarios públicos.
Ocupaciones: todas las ocupaciones de funcionarios públicos en el Gobierno de la RAE de Hong Kong.

Conceptos y definiciones

Empleo: los funcionarios públicos son las personas empleadas según las condiciones de nombramiento del servicio público para la fecha de referencia de la encuesta. Se excluyen los funcionarios de la Comisión Independiente contra la Corrupción, jueces y funcionarios judiciales de la Judicatura, y el personal contratado localmente que trabaja en oficinas comerciales y económicas de Hong Kong en el extranjero.
Puestos vacantes: puestos de trabajo no cubiertos, pero que se pueden ocupar inmediatamente y para los cuales se han tomado las medidas de contratación necesarias para la fecha de referencia de la encuesta.

Clasificaciones

Ramas de actividad económica:
Título de la clasificación: Clasificación Industrial Uniforme de Hong Kong, Versión 1.1 (HSIC V1.1)
Número de grupos utilizados para la codificación: 83 (hasta el nivel de tres dígitos).
Se aplica a: empleo y puestos vacantes.
Vínculos con la CIIU y nivel : la HSIC, V1.1, se basa en el modelo de la CIIU, Rev.2, en todos los niveles, adaptada a la estructura industrial de la RAE de Hong Kong.
Otras clasificaciones: empleo por sexo.

Recolección de datos

Tipo y alcance del sistema administrativo: unas 100 unidades declarantes, en términos de departamentos y oficinas gubernamentales.
Método de recolección de datos: los departamentos y oficinas gubernamentales envían trimestralmente las declaraciones departamentales a la Oficina de Servicios Públicos. El lapso de tiempo transcurrido entre el período de referencia de los datos y la recopilación/proceso de datos es de unas 12 semanas.
Actualización del sistema administrativo: trimestralmente.

Procesamiento y verificación de datos

Los datos se procesan por computadora. El total de los componentes se verifica con el total de cada una de las unidades de información, y la variación se comprueba con las cifras correspondientes del trimestre anterior.

Ajustes

Ninguno.

Tipos de estimaciones

Totales.

Construcción de índices

Ninguno.

Indicadores de fiabilidad de las estimaciones

Alcance del sistema administrativo: exhaustiva por lo que se refiere a funcionarios públicos.

Series disponibles

Número trimestral de funcionarios públicos y puestos vacantes.

Historia de las estadísticas

Fecha de iniciación de la serie estadística: marzo de 1980.
Cambios y revisiones principales: en junio de 1999, se hizo una revisión menor de la definición estadística de funcionario público: desde esa fecha, se excluyen de esta definición los jueces y funcionarios judiciales de la Judicatura. La definición de puestos vacantes del servicio público también fue revisada en junio de 1999; a partir de esa fecha se excluyen los puestos vacantes que están en espera de ser suprimidos y los cargos ocupados por personal temporero o reservados para otros miembros del personal.
Antes de diciembre de 2001, las cifras sobre el número de funcionarios públicos y puestos vacantes se referían a los puestos que había a comienzo de enero, abril, julio y octubre. En la actualidad, se refieren al último día de trabajo completo de estos trimestres.

Documentación y difusión

Documentación:
Census and Statistics Department: *Hong Kong Monthly Digest of Statistics* (RAE de Hong Kong);
Idem: *Quarterly Report of Employment and Vacancies Statistics* (ibid.);
Idem: *Hong Kong Annual Digest of Statistics* (ibid.).

Estas publicaciones contienen estadísticas sobre empleo y puestos vacantes, así como información metodológica. El lapso de tiempo transcurrido entre la fecha de referencia y la publicación de las estadísticas es de 12 semanas.
Difusión: en el sitio Internet: http://www.info.gov.hk/censtatd
Datos suministrados a la OIT para su difusión
Los siguientes datos se suministran en el *Anuario de Estadísticas del Trabajo*:
Número de empleados del servicio público, incluido en las estadísticas sobre empleo remunerado por actividad económica.

Hong Kong, China (2)

Fuente de la serie

Registros administrativos: Formulario gubernamental 527.

Título de la serie

Declaraciones mensuales de tasas de salarios en la industria de la construcción.

Organismo responsable

Recolección de datos: Oficina de Obras (Works Bureau), Región Administrativa Especial de Hong Kong (RAE), República Popular de China.
Elaboración estadística y publicación o difusión de las estadísticas: Departamento de Censo y Estadística (Census and Statistics Department), RAE de Hong Kong.

Temas laborales principales abarcados

Empleo y tasas de salarios.

Periodicidad o frecuencia de disponibilidad de las estadísticas

Empleo: trimestral;
Tasas de salarios: mensual.

Período de referencia

Empleo: el último día de trabajo completo en un trimestre;
Tasas de salarios: todo el mes.

Alcance de las estadísticas

Ambito geográfico: RAE de Hong Kong.
Ambito industrial: construcción únicamente.
Establecimientos: todos los sitios de construcción bajo la égida de la Oficina de Obras del Gobierno de la RAE de Hong Kong. Un sitio de construcción se define como una localidad delimitada donde se encuentran una o más obras de construcción.
Personas cubiertas: trabajadores manuales.
Ocupaciones: veintinueve ocupaciones preseleccionadas.

Conceptos y definiciones

Empleo: los obreros en sitios de construcción se refieren a artesanos, obreros semicalificados y obreros no calificados que trabajan en esos sitios en la fecha de referencia de la encuesta. Los obreros pueden ser contratados directamente por los principales contratistas, o por los subcontratistas o jefes de cuadrillas para trabajar de manera esporádica.
Tasas de sueldo o salario: las tasas de salarios diarios incluyen (i) tasa de salario básico; (ii) subsidios por costo de la vida; y (iii) subsidios pagados garantizados y periódicos, incluidos los subsidios alimenticios y de transporte. Se excluyen las ganancias en especie.

Clasificaciones

Ramas de actividad económica:
Título de la clasificación: Versión 1.1 de la Clasificación Industrial Uniforme de Hong Kong (HSIC V1.1).
Número de grupos utilizados para la codificación: División 5 (sólo sitios de construcción).
Se aplica a: empleo y tasas de salarios.
Vínculos con la CIIU y nivel: Rev.2, en todos los niveles.
Ocupaciones: 29 ocupaciones seleccionadas: obrero no calificado, excavador, mezclador de cemento, enladrillador, cementero, albañil, vaciador, mampostero, fragmentador de piedras, albañil de piedra labrada, herrero de obra, herrero, carpintero y ebanista, plomero, ajustador, yesero, trabajador de terrazzo y granolítico, vidriero, pintor, electricista (electricista de obras), operador de planta, camionero, peón de trabajos pesados, taladrador, trabajador de bambú y de andamiaje, montador de estructuras de acero, buzo y buzo instalador de líneas.

Recolección de datos

Tipo y alcance del sistema administrativo: unos 230 sitios de construcción.
Método de recolección de datos: a los principales contratistas de todos los sitios de construcción bajo la égida de la Oficina de Obras de la RAE de Hong Kong se les pide que mensualmente envíen, por cada contrato, el Formulario Gubernamental 527 (GF 527) al Departamento de Censo y Estadística por intermedio de los diversos Departamentos de Obras. Deben suministrar el número de días de trabajo y el promedio de tasas de salarios diarios correspondientes a

las ocupaciones que figuran en el formulario GF 527, de los obreros que trabajan para ellos o los subcontratistas en el mes de referencia, al más tardar a mediados del mes siguiente. El Departamento de Censo y Estadística realiza algunas verificaciones de congruencia y determina el promedio de tasas de salarios diarios en las ocupaciones seleccionadas dos meses después de recibir los datos. En cuanto al número de obreros, el intervalo de tiempo entre el período de referencia de los datos y el período de recopilación/proceso de datos es de 12 semanas.

Actualización del sistema administrativo: continuamente.

Procesamiento y verificación de datos

Además del control realizado constantemente, se hacen otras verificaciones de los datos que figuran en el formulario GF 527 cuando:

- el número de días de trabajo para una ocupación en un determinado mes es 50 por ciento superior o inferior al del mes anterior;
- el promedio del salario diario para una ocupación en un determinado mes es 10 por ciento superior o inferior al del mes anterior;
- el promedio del salario diario para una ocupación en un determinado mes es diferente del promedio general de esa ocupación en todos los contratos, si en ese sitio no se empleó a nadie en esa ocupación el mes anterior.

Ajustes

Ninguno.

Tipos de estimaciones

Número total de obreros en sitios de construcción.

Promedio de tasas de salarios diarios de ocupaciones seleccionadas en sitios de construcción.

Promedio de tasas de salarios diarios de una ocupación i:

$$\frac{\sum_j (\text{días de trabajo trabajados en el sitio } jth \text{ x promedio de tasas de salarios diarios en el sitio } jth)}{\sum_j \text{días de trabajo trabajados en el sitio } jth}$$

Promedio de tasas de salarios diarios de todas las ocupaciones incluidas en el GF 527:

$$\frac{\sum_i \sum_j (\text{días de trabajo trabajados en el sitio } jth \text{ x promedio de tasas de salarios diarios en el sitio } jth)}{\sum_i \sum_j \text{días de trabajo trabajados en el sitio } jth}$$

Construcción de índices

Se prepara un índice mensual de los costos laborales basado en el promedio ponderado de las tasas de salarios de ocupaciones seleccionadas. Las ponderaciones para cada ocupación se deducen a partir del número total de días de trabajo para la respectiva ocupación por un período de tiempo fijo.

Indicadores de fiabilidad de las estimaciones

Alcance del sistema administrativo: 100 por ciento de los sitios de construcción bajo la égida de la Oficina de Obras.

Series disponibles

Número de obreros y promedio de tasas de salarios diarios.

Historia de las estadísticas

Fecha de iniciación de la serie estadística: número de obreros: marzo de 1976; promedio de tasas de salarios diarios: enero de 1970; series de índices: diciembre de 1975 (período de base: noviembre de 1975).

Cambios y revisiones principales: revisiones de las series de índices:

Junio de 1989: cambio en el período de base (julio 1982=100) y ponderaciones;

Julio de 1995: cambio en el período de base (junio 1995=100) y ponderaciones.

Documentación y difusión

Documentación:

Census and Statistics Department: *Average Daily Wages of Workers engaged in Government Building and Construction Projects* (RAE de Hong Kong, mensual); contiene estadísticas de tasas de salarios únicamente);

Idem: *Hong Kong Monthly Digest of Statistics* (ibid.); contiene estadísticas de tasas de salarios y de empleo, así como información metodológica;

Idem: *Quarterly Report of Employment and Vacancies Statistics* (ibid.); contiene estadísticas de empleo únicamente, así como información metodológica;

Idem: *Quarterly Report of Employment and Vacancies at Construction Sites* (ibid.); contiene estadísticas de empleo únicamente, así como información metodológica;

Idem: *Hong Kong Annual Digest of Statistics* (ibid.); contiene estadísticas de tasas de salarios y de empleo, así como información metodológica.

El promedio de tasas de salarios diarios de ocupaciones seleccionadas se publica dos meses después del mes de referencia. El número de obreros en sitios de construcción se publica 12 semanas después de la fecha de referencia.

Difusión: en el sitio Internet: http://www.info.gov.hk/censtatd

Datos suministrados a la OIT para su difusión

Los siguientes datos se suministran en el *Anuario de Estadísticas del Trabajo*: número de trabajadores de la construcción y promedio de tasas de salarios diarios de los trabajadores de sitios de construcción en todas las ocupaciones seleccionadas;

En las *Estadísticas sobre salarios y horas de trabajo por ocupación y precios de artículos alimenticios – Resultados de la Encuesta de octubre*: promedio de tasas de salarios diarios de ocupaciones seleccionadas: electricista (electricista de obras), plomero, montador de estructuras de acero, pintor, albañil, cementero, carpintero y ebanista, yesero y obrero no calificado.

Isla de Man

Fuente de la serie

Declaraciones de impuestos sobre la renta.

Título de la serie

Empleo de la Isla de Man.

Organismo responsable

Recolección de datos: Isle of Man Treasury, Income Tax Division (Tesoro de la Isla de Man, División de Impuestos sobre la Renta).

Elaboración estadística y publicación o difusión de las estadísticas: Isle of Man Treasury, Economic Affairs Division (Tesoro de la Isla de Man, División de Asuntos Económicos).

Temas laborales principales abarcados

Empleo.

Periodicidad o frecuencia de disponibilidad de las estadísticas

Ocasional, según proceda.

Período de referencia

Una fecha específica.

Alcance de las estadísticas

Ambito geográfico: toda la Isla.

Ambito industrial: todos los sectores de la actividad económica.

Establecimientos: de todos tipos y tamaños.

Personas cubiertas: todas las personas con empleo.

Ocupaciones: los datos no se recopilan por ocupación ni grupo ocupacional.

Conceptos y definiciones

Empleo: todas las personas con empleo (es decir, asalariados y personas que trabajan por cuenta propia) con una fuente de ingresos imponibles provenientes del empleo remunerado o del trabajo realizado por cuenta propia.

Clasificaciones

Ramas de actividad económica:

Título de la clasificación: Clasificación del Comercio de la Isla de Man.

Número de grupos utilizados para la codificación: 31; se puede reducir con fines de publicación porque algunos grupos son muy pequeños.

Se aplica a: datos de empleo.

Vínculos con la CIIU y nivel: ninguno.

Situación en el empleo: asalariados y trabajadores por cuenta propia.

Otras clasificaciones: empleo por tamaño de establecimiento.

Recolección de datos

La fuente de datos cuenta con más de 40 000 registros de impuestos sobre la renta que centraliza para toda la Isla la División de Impuestos sobre la Renta del Tesoro de la Isla de Man. De acuerdo con la legislación los registros deben mantenerse actualizados.

Procesamiento y verificación de datos

Los datos se procesan por computadora.

Se realizan verificaciones de congruencia mediante la comparación con datos anteriores y datos de referencia del censo de la población.

La División de Asuntos Económicos verifica la codificación de la clasificación industrial que efectúa la División de Impuestos sobre la Renta y hace las enmiendas necesarias.

Ajustes
Ninguno.
Tipos de estimaciones
Totales para una fecha de referencia.
Construcción de índices
Ninguno.
Indicadores de fiabilidad de las estimaciones
Alcance del sistema administrativo: se prevé que abarque a todas las personas con empleo, salvo las que intervienen en la economía paralela que se considera insignificante en vista del tamaño relativamente pequeño de la Isla.
Errores no relacionados con el muestreo: es posible que se haga una codificación errónea de la clasificación industrial, pero se hacen verificaciones constantemente (véase más arriba).
Conformidad con otras fuentes: como se indica más arriba.
Series disponibles
Empleo total para una fecha de referencia específica en 1988.
Historia de las estadísticas
Fecha de iniciación de la serie estadística: 1988 (publicada en 1995).
Cambios y revisiones principales: ninguno, salvo que recientemente se añadieron algunos nuevos grupos a la Clasificación del Comercio para incluir la tecnología de la información y las telecomunicaciones (TIC).
Documentación y difusión
Documentación:
Isle of Man Treasury, Economic Affairs Division: *Isle of Man Labour Statistics*, 1995.
Los datos se recopilan tras la solicitud de la División de Asuntos Económicos a la División de Impuestos sobre la Renta. Es una fuente especial de datos, utilizada sobre todo a nivel interno por el Gobierno, pero que el público puede consultar, previa solicitud.
Se incluye una nota metodológica a todos los cuadros difundidos.
Datos suministrados a la OIT para su difusión
Ninguno hasta la actualidad.

Israel

Fuente de la serie
Informes al Instituto Nacional de Seguros (NII) y a otras fuentes administrativas.
Título de la serie
Cargos y Salarios de Asalariados.
Organismo responsable
Recolección de datos: Instituto Nacional de Seguros (NII).
Elaboración estadística y publicación o difusión de las estadísticas: Oficina Central de Estadística (Central Bureau of Statistics - CBS).
Temas laborales principales abarcados
Empleo y ganancias.
Periodicidad o frecuencia de disponibilidad de las estadísticas
Mensual.
Período de referencia
Todo el mes.
Alcance de las estadísticas
Ambito geográfico: todo el país.
Ambito industrial: todas las actividades económicas, salvo los hogares privados con servicio doméstico.
Establecimientos: todos los tipos y tamaños de establecimientos con uno o más asalariados.
Personas cubiertas: todos los asalariados que trabajaron como mínimo un día durante el mes de la encuesta en los establecimiento concernidos, incluidos miembros de cooperativas, funcionarios públicos de las fuerzas de defensa, y asalariados de Judea y Samaria y la Zona de Gaza y del Sur del Líbano (sólo aquellos que perciben un salario a través de la Oficina de Pagos del Servicio del Empleo) que trabajan en Israel. Se incluyen también los trabajadores de otros países sobre los que se entregaron informes al Instituto Nacional de Seguros.
Se excluyen los trabajadores domésticos, los miembros de kibutz que trabajan en los kibutz o en establecimiento que son propiedad de los kibutz, los estudiantes de escuelas profesionales y agrícolas y los estudiantes de instituciones de formación profesional.
Ocupaciones: los datos no se recopilan por ocupación ni grupo ocupacional.
Conceptos y definiciones
Empleo: se refiere al número de asalariados (permanentes y temporeros) de la nómina de establecimientos o instituciones, que trabajaron o que tenían licencia con goce de sueldo por enfermedad, vacaciones, cumplimiento del servicio militar, etc., al menos un día,

durante el mes de la encuesta.
Los asalariados que figuran ese mes en la nómina de más de un establecimiento o institución se tienen en cuenta todas las veces que figuran en las nóminas, de manera que los datos se refieren al número de cargos para los cuales se pagaron salarios en ese mes.
Ganancias: se refiere a las ganancias brutas mensuales. Se incluyen salarios básicos, subsidios por costo de la vida, subsidios por antigüedad, pagos pendientes de períodos anteriores, pagos adelantados, pagos de horas extraordinarias, primas, bonos y diversos subsidios (corrientes y extraordinarios), tales como de reserva, de servicio, 13er mes de salario, subsidio para fines recreativos, subsidio educativo, subsidio para estudios profesionales suplementarios o para mantenimiento de vehículo.
Se excluyen otros gastos y sumas laborales que el empleador paga a fondos tales como el fondo de pensión o el seguro de asalariado, impuestos paralelos e impuesto del empleador.
Clasificaciones
Ramas de actividad económica:
Título de la clasificación: Clasificación Industrial Uniforme de Todas las Actividades Económicas de 1993.
Número de grupos utilizados para la codificación: no se dispone.
Se aplica a: empleo y ganancias.
Vínculos con la CIIU y nivel: Rev.3, 1990.
Otras clasificaciones: los datos de empleo y ganancias se clasifican según la nacionalidad (israelíes y extranjeros).
Recolección de datos
Tipo y alcance del sistema administrativo: no se dispone.
Método de recolección de datos: los datos sobre empleo y salarios se obtienen principalmente del procesamiento mensual de los informes de empleadores (de acuerdo con la ley) presentados en los formularios 102 (para israelíes) y 612 (para trabajadores extranjeros) al Instituto Nacional de Seguros (NII), y parcialmente, de otras fuentes administrativas, tales como la Oficina de Pagos del Servicio de Empleo, Malam, el Centro de Procesamiento de Datos de las Autoridades Locales de Israel y las fuerzas de defensa.
Los datos sobre salarios y empleo de las autoridades locales (municipales, consejos locales y consejos regionales) proceden de los archivos del Centro de Procesamiento de Datos de las Autoridades Locales de Israel y de otras fuentes.
Los informes de los empleadores se mantienen en el archivo central de empleadores del NII. El marco de muestreo se basa principalmente en este archivo, además de las muestras de otros establecimientos que mantiene la CBS y otras fuentes. El universo se estratifica por las principales ramas de actividad económica y el tamaño de establecimientos. De cada tamaño de rama económica se toma una muestra de los establecimientos activos, con diversos fracciones de muestreo.
La muestra se actualiza al excluir los establecimientos que han dejado de funcionar e incluir una muestra de los establecimientos recientemente abiertos. No se toma en cuenta el cambio de tamaño de los establecimientos durante el período de actualización. La muestra se actualiza cada ciertos años. Los datos actuales se basan en el muestreo de enero de 1995.
Con respecto a los cargos de trabajadores extranjeros: en 1994, los datos se basaban en un censo realizado a todos los empleadores que informaron tener trabajadores extranjeros (excluidas personas empleadas en los hogares y declaradas por sus empleadores como ayudantes domésticos). En 1995, los datos se basaban en una muestra de establecimientos tomada de todos los establecimientos que informaron tener trabajadores extranjeros (formulario 612). Se preparó el marco para 1995 y se actualizó al añadir los nuevos establecimientos que comenzaron a emplear trabajadores extranjeros. Se toma una muestra de adiciones y se añade periódicamente a la muestra principal. No se incluyen en los cálculos los establecimientos que dejan de emplear trabajadores extranjeros.
Procesamiento y verificación de datos
Las estimaciones mensuales para el año en curso se revisan en base a los informes adicionales o corregidos de los empleadores que se reciben posteriormente del Instituto Nacional de Seguros.
Ajustes
Variaciones estacionales: Se utiliza el Método de Ajuste Estacional X-11-ARIMA/2000 creado por la Oficina de Estadística de Canadá. Los factores de ajuste anteriores se calculan utilizando el método especial creado por la Oficina Central de Estadística para estimar los efectos de los cambios de las fechas de fiestas judías y los días de comercio en Israel.
Tipos de estimaciones
Totales de cargos;
Salario medio mensual por cargo: el total de salarios mensuales se divide entre el número de cargos en un mes determinado; a precios

actuales y constantes. Según la definición de cargo, el salario medio mensual por cargo es inferior que el salario medio mensual por asalariado.

Salario medio neto de autoridades locales: salarios brutos mensuales menos las deducciones para el NII (incluido el seguro de enfermedad al mes de enero de 1995) y los impuestos sobre la renta.

Se preparan estimaciones separadas en las que se incluyen y excluyen los trabajadores de Judea y Samaria y la Zona de Gaza.

Construcción de índices

Los índices de cargos y salarios se calculan mensualmente.

El índice salarios totales a precios constantes se calcula dividiendo el índice de salarios totales a precios actuales entre el índice de precios al consumidor del mes respectivo según la base de 1994=100. Las estimaciones anuales, trimestrales, etc., constituyen el promedio de los índices mensuales a precios constantes.

El índice del salario medio por cargo a precios constantes se calcula dividiendo el índice de salarios totales a precios constantes entre el índice de cargos.

La tendencia se calcula utilizando el método de medias móviles de Henderson.

Indicadores de fiabilidad de las estimaciones

No se dispone.

Series disponibles

Cargos, salarios totales y salarios medios mensuales por cargo, a precios actuales y constantes;

Series ajustadas estacionalmente;

Tendencia y porcentaje mensual del cambio de la tendencia.

Historia de las estadísticas

Fecha de iniciación de la serie estadística: 1961.

Cambios y revisiones principales: al mes de enero de 1995, las estadísticas se basaron en un nuevo muestreo de establecimientos. Los datos anteriores se basaban en el muestreo de 1979, que se actualizó en 1983 y 1986.

Durante el período de abril de 1995 y comienzos de 1997, los informes sobre salarios incluidos en el formulario 612 eran parciales: no incluían algunas cantidades que llegaban casi a 900 NIS por mes. En 1997, algunos empleadores comenzaron a informar sobre cifras totales.

Antes de 1993, los datos se clasificaban de acuerdo con la Clasificación Industrial Uniforme de Todas las Actividades Económicas de 1970.

Documentación y difusión

Documentación:

Central Bureau of Statistics: *Monthly Bulletin of Statistics* (Jerusalén);

Idem: *Supplement to the Monthly Bulletin of Statistics* (ibid.)

Idem: *Statistical Abstract of Israel* (ibid. Anual);

La publicación *Statistical Abstract of Israel*, No. 51, 2000 contiene información metodológica detallada sobre definiciones, fuentes de datos, métodos de recopilación y procesamiento de datos y limitaciones de los datos.

Difusión: en el sitio Internet de la CBS: http://www.cbs.gov.il (contiene datos y notas metodológicas).

Los datos que no aparecen en las publicaciones nacionales o en el sitio Internet se pueden obtener previa solicitud.

Datos suministrados a la OIT para su difusión

Los siguientes datos se suministran a la OIT para su publicación en el *Anuario de Estadísticas del Trabajo*:

Empleo remunerado por actividad económica y en la industria manufacturera, por grupo de industria;

Ganancias medias mensuales por actividad económica y en la industria manufacturera, por grupo de industria.

Los datos mensuales correspondientes se publican en el *Boletín de Estadísticas del Trabajo*.

Italia

Fuente de la serie

Contratos Laborales Colectivos (Contratti Collettivi di lavoro).

Título de la serie

Numeri indici delle retribuzioni contrattuali (Índices de Salarios Contractuales).

Organismo responsable

Recolección de datos, elaboración estadística y publicación o difusión de las estadísticas:

Instituto Nacional de Estadística (Instituto Nazionale di Statistica - ISTAT).

Temas laborales principales abarcados

Salarios contractuales.

Periodicidad o frecuencia de disponibilidad de las estadísticas

Mensualmente.

Período de referencia

Fin de cada mes.

Alcance de las estadísticas

Ambito geográfico: todo el país.

Ambito industrial: casi todas las ramas de actividad económica, incluido el Servicio Público, salvo la pesca (Categoría B de Tabulación de la Rev. 3 de la CIIU), actividades de servicios comunitario, social y personal, servicios domésticos y organizaciones y órganos extraterritoriales (Categorías O-Q de Tabulación de la Rev. 3 de la CIIU).

Establecimientos: de todos tipos y tamaños, que forman parte o están abarcados por los contratos colectivos.

Personas cubiertas: asalariados a tiempo completo, excluido el personal directivo del sector privado y los aprendices.

Ocupaciones: todas las ocupaciones representadas en las negociaciones de contratos colectivos.

Conceptos y definiciones

Empleo: se refiere a los asalariados con un contrato regular a tiempo completo, excluidos los aprendices y ejecutivos del sector privado. En el sector crediticio, se incluyen los funcionarios públicos, mientras que en la administración pública se incluye el personal directivo contractual y no contractual. Los obreros y empleados se identifican por separado. Los datos de empleo se utilizan para determinar la estructura del índice salarial en el año de base.

Tasas de sueldo o salario: los salarios contractuales son los que se fijan en contratos colectivos. Representan, cada mes, la cantidad debida a los asalariados según la hipótesis de que siempre están trabajando en las horas establecidas por los contratos laborales pertinentes. Se incluyen los pagos generales y periódicos, tales como el pago básico, los pagos por concepto de compensación (Indennità di contingenza), las primas por tiempo de servicio, trabajo por turnos y otros pagos mensuales y periódicos determinados en contratos nacionales y pagables a todos los trabajadores, así como otros pagos periódicos (por ejemplo, el 13er mes y otros pagos estacionales y periódicos). Se excluyen las bonificaciones relativas al rendimiento personal y condiciones individuales de trabajo, pagos suplementarios aprobados a nivel de empresa, pagos ocasionales y especiales, cantidades otorgadas por intermedio de negociaciones descentralizadas, sueldos con efecto retroactivo y pagos que se realizan una sola vez. Con todo, estos pagos especiales se tienen en cuenta en el cálculo de los ingresos contractuales anuales (Retribuzione contrattuale annua di competenza).

Las tasas de salarios contractuales se calculan por separado para los trabajadores manuales y no manuales y por ocupación.

Horas de trabajo: se refieren a las horas normales de trabajo de cargos a tiempo completo en un año, después de deducir las horas pagadas pero no trabajadas, vacaciones públicas y anuales, otro tiempo no trabajado pero remunerado (para la reducción de las horas de trabajo anuales, compensación de trabajo realizado durante vacaciones públicas y de otro tipo, reuniones y licencias de estudio, etc.).

No se publican las estadísticas de las horas contractuales de trabajo, pero se utilizan en el cálculo del índice de los salarios por hora contractuales.

Clasificaciones

Ramas de actividad económica:

Título de la clasificación: Clasificación de Actividades Económicas de ATECO 91.

Número de grupos utilizados para la codificación: no se dispone.

Se aplica a: todos los datos.

Vínculos con la CIIU y nivel: La ATECO corresponde a la clasificación de las actividades económicas de la Unión Europea (NACE, Rev.1) a nivel de cuatro dígitos (sólo el índice per capita), que está directamente vinculada con la Rev. 3 de la CIIU, a nivel de dos dígitos.

Ocupaciones: Los contratos colectivos no se clasifican por ocupación sino por categoría de asalariado (trabajadores manuales, trabajadores no manuales, ejecutivos). El ISTAT realiza, una vez al año, la clasificación por ocupación para los fines de la Encuesta de octubre de la OIT, vinculando una serie de variables y códigos contenidos en los contratos colectivos (categoría de asalariado, nivel de calificaciones, tareas y ocupaciones, ejemplos de ocupaciones, etc.) con las descripciones de ocupaciones de la OIT.

Otras clasificaciones: de acuerdo con el sector de negociación.

Recolección de datos

Tipo y alcance del sistema administrativo: Los índices salariales se obtienen a partir de una amplia selección de los contratos más pertinentes sobre los salarios negociados entre los sindicatos y las asociaciones de empleadores. Las series actuales utilizan 2.300

puntos salariales establecidos en 80 contratos colectivos de un total de más de 300 contratos.

Método de recolección de datos: los datos básicos se obtienen de los registros oficiales (leyes, reglamentos) y contratos colectivos; para los sectores de la agricultura y de la construcción, se toman de los contratos laborales pertinentes de cada provincia. Las unidades estadísticas representan un nivel de salario contractual para un determinado grupo de funciones, a menudo combinado con indicaciones sobre años de servicio, edad o competencias técnicas en los contratos colectivos. Sus características, así como el número de asalariados, se deciden en momentos de establecer la base y se mantienen fijas hasta que se establece una nueva base. Se realiza una encuesta especial para determinar la estructura en el año de base con la ayuda de las asociaciones de empleadores y trabajadores. La encuesta permite determinar los contratos colectivos utilizados y su distribución en los grupos de la fuerza laboral. Se utilizan varias fuentes para calcular el número de trabajadores por contrato colectivo y de acuerdo con la ATECO: las cuentas nacionales, la encuesta sobre la fuerza laboral y los registros de la Seguridad social.

Cada contrato se actualiza cuando se renueva. Las ponderaciones se actualizan cada cinco años.

Procesamiento y verificación de datos

En cada una de las unidades que calcula los índices de salarios contractuales, cada funcionario está encargado de 6 a 13 contratos (según el nivel de dificultad). Se asigna un código a cada componente de la remuneración (salario básico, pagos por concepto de compensación, prima por tiempo de servicio, otras primas, horas de trabajo, vacaciones públicas y otras vacaciones, etc.). Se utilizan 311 códigos, que se registran por computadora. Los resultados se verifican con el total de todas las categorías de contratos. Los datos se procesan por computadora, para lo cual se usa el sistema COBOL. El ISTAT se ocupa actualmente de la actualización del período de base de los índices (diciembre de 2000=100) y los datos se procesarán posteriormente con el sistema ORACLE y se podrán visualizar en lenguaje PL/Sql.

Ajustes

Variaciones estacionales: ninguna; los índices publicados no muestran ninguna variación estacional porque los índices brutos mensuales de cada grupo de clasificaciones en los contratos colectivos incluyen todos los elementos de pago, como se enumeran en el apartado "Conceptos y definiciones", dividido por 12, cada mes.

Tipos de estimaciones

Índices salariales;

Variaciones porcentuales con respecto al período anterior (variaciones coyunturales) y el período correspondiente del año anterior (tendencias).

Cifras anuales absolutas de tasas de salarios.

Construcción de índices

El índice de las tasas de salario por trabajador mide el cambio en las tasas anuales contractuales aprobadas. El índice de horas de trabajo aprobadas colectivamente mide el cambio en las horas de trabajo que los asalariados tienen que trabajar durante el año (excluidos los períodos de vacaciones). El índice de tasas horarias se calcula a partir de la relación que existe entre ambos índices. Cada mes, las tasas brutas de cada grupo de calificaciones en el contrato colectivo se dividen entre 12. Los índices de cada grupo de calificación (células elementales) se obtienen dividiendo el valor absoluto de las tasas vigentes y el promedio de las tasas entre las cifras del período de base (diciembre de 1995). Otros índices agregados se calculan aplicando a los índices elementales una fórmula de tipo Laspeyres. Las ponderaciones resultan del promedio del número de trabajadores en el año de base y el valor del salario correspondiente en el período de base.

Indicadores de fiabilidad de las estimaciones

Alcance del sistema administrativo: todos los contratos laborales colectivos están representados y los índices abarcan un 90% de asalariados.

Series disponibles

Índices salariales contractuales mensuales y horarios, por actividad económica y grupos de clasificación;

Tasas de cambio respecto al período anterior y al período correspondiente del año anterior;

Cifras absolutas anuales sobre la composición del pago y el costo laboral de algunas industrias y trabajos, así como sobre horas de trabajo.

Historia de las estadísticas

Fecha de iniciación de la serie estadística: 1938.

Cambios y revisiones principales: las ponderaciones se actualizan cada cinco años a fin de tener en cuenta la evolución económica.

Documentación y difusión

Documentación:

Instituto Centrale di Statistica (ISTAT): *Comunicato Stampa*; comunicado de prensa que se suministra a los medios de comunicación en conferencias de prensa celebradas 30 minutos antes de la publicación general de los datos, y posteriormente se distribuye por fax y correo electrónico y se publica a través de Internet en el sitio Web del ISTAT;

Los datos generalmente se publican un mes más tarde pero antes de un trimestre después de finalizar el mes de referencia, salvo los datos de enero que se publican dos meses después de finalizar el mes de referencia.

Idem: *Bolletino Mensile di Statistica*; contiene datos mensuales para el período que comienza en 1992 sobre el índice total y los índices de secciones y grupos de clasificación.

Idem: *Collana d'informazione "Lavoro e retribuzioni"* (Roma, mensual); contiene, una vez al año, una descripción de la metodología.

Las modificaciones o revisiones metodológicas se comunican a través de comunicados de prensa. La información detallada sobre los cambios metodológicos aplicados se publica en *Informazioni-Retribuzioni contrattuali*, y se pueden obtener ejemplares de esa información en el ISTAT.

Difusión: en el sitio Internet del ISTAT: http://www.istat.it

Las notas metodológicas también están disponibles en este sitio.

Datos suministrados a la OIT para su difusión

Se suministran las siguientes estadísticas a la OIT para su publicación en el *Anuario de Estadísticas del Trabajo*:

Índices de tasas salariales contractuales por hora, de obreros y empleados, por actividad económica.

Los datos de tasas salariales contractuales por ocupación se publican en *Estadísticas sobre salarios y horas de trabajo por ocupación y precios de artículos alimenticios – Resultados de la Encuesta de octubre.*

Luxemburgo

Fuente de la serie

Informes de la Inspección General del Seguro Social (Inspection générale de la Sécurité sociale - IGSS).

Título de la serie

Empleo interior asalariado.

Organismo responsable

Recolección de datos: Inspección General del Seguro Social.

Elaboración estadística y publicación o difusión de las estadísticas: Servicio Central de Estadística y Estudios Económicos (Service central de la Statistique et des Etudes économiques (STATEC).

Temas laborales principales abarcados

Empleo.

Periodicidad o frecuencia de disponibilidad de las estadísticas

Mensual.

Período de referencia

El mes completo.

Alcance de las estadísticas

Ambito geográfico: todo el país.

Ambito industrial: todas las ramas de actividad económica.

Establecimientos: todos los establecimientos que emplean una persona o más.

Personas cubiertas: el conjunto de asalariados que responden al concepto de empleo interior asalariado (véase más abajo).

Ocupaciones: los datos no se recopilan según las diversas profesiones ni por grupos de profesiones.

Conceptos y definiciones

Empleo: el empleo interior asalariado abarca a todos los asalariados que han concertado un contrato de trabajo con una unidad institucional residente, que tengan o no su residencia en el territorio del Gran Ducado, sujetos al régimen general de la Seguridad Social. Se incluyen los trabajadores fronterizos extranjeros, trabajadores a domicilio, trabajadores interinos, temporeros o estacionales que responden a la definición, aprendices y militares de carrera. Se excluyen los trabajadores fronterizos de Luxemburgo que trabajan en un país limítrofe, así como los funcionarios de instituciones internacionales considerados como extraterritoriales.

Clasificaciones

Ramas de actividad económica:

Título de la clasificación: Nomenclatura Estadística de Actividades Económicas en las Comunidades Europeas (NACE) Rev. 1.

Número de grupos utilizados para la codificación: publicación a nivel de dos cifras, bajo reserva del secreto estadístico.

Se aplica a: el empleo interior asalariado.

Vínculos con la CIIU y nivel: compatibilidad entre la NACE, Rev. 1 y la CITI, Rev. 3 (1990) a nivel de los secciones (nivel de dos cifras).

Situación en el empleo: a nivel del concepto de empleo interior, se hace una diferencia entre el empleo asalariado (tema de esta serie) y empleo no asalariado (trabajadores independientes).

Otras clasificaciones: por sexo.

Recolección de datos

Tipo y alcance del sistema administrativo: los ficheros administrativos de la Seguridad Social abarcan todos los asalariados, de todos los establecimientos que emplean al menos 1 asalariado.

Método de recolección de datos: en cuanto a los obreros y los empleados del sector privado, la IGSS y el Centro Informatizado de la Seguridad Social utilizan el fichero integrado de los organismos de seguridad social (cajas de enfermedad y de pensión). En relación con los funcionarios y asimilados (agentes del Estado, las comunidades, los ferrocarriles), los organismos encargados procesan los ficheros por computadora.

La IGSS está encargada de controlar los datos y transmitir mensualmente los datos globales al STATEC, y anualmente los datos por rama de actividad económica. El STATEC realiza los ajustes estadísticos necesarios (véase más abajo) y está encargado de difundir los datos.

Procesamiento y verificación de datos

Los datos se procesan manualmente y por computadora.

Ajustes

El STATEC realiza los siguientes ajustes:

a) a nivel global, tiene en cuenta los voluntarios del ejército (que no están incluidos en los registros de la seguridad social); b) a nivel de las estadísticas por rama de actividad, ajusta las cifras del empleo para las grandes empresas relacionadas con varios sectores de la actividad económica, dado que los registros de la seguridad social se basan en el empleador y no en la actividad económica.

Los trabajadores a tiempo parcial y las personas que ocupan más de un empleo cuentan por una persona, según el Sistema Europeo de Cuentas Económicas Integradas (Système européen des Comptes économiques intégrés (SEC-95)).

Tipos de estimaciones

Totales mensuales y medias anuales.

Construcción de índices

Ninguno.

Indicadores de fiabilidad de las estimaciones

Alcance del sistema administrativo: considerada exhaustiva en cuanto a los asalariados que responden a la definición que figura más arriba.

Conformidad con otras fuentes: las estimaciones del empleo que se obtienen a partir de los registros de la IGSS se comparan con los resultados de la encuesta por muestra sobre las fuerzas de trabajo, los de las encuestas del STATEC en las empresas, y los datos administrativos que suministran algunos sectores como el Grupo de Industrias Siderúrgicas de Luxemburgo, el Instituto Monetario de Luxemburgo, la Asociación de Compañías de Seguros admitidas, etc.

Series disponibles

Empleo asalariado, mensual y media anual, por rama de actividad económica y por sexo.

Historia de las estadísticas

Fecha de iniciación de la serie estadística: 1970.

Cambios y revisiones principales: se produjo una ruptura en 1983, fecha en la que los repertorios de la seguridad social sobre obreros y empleados se fusionaron y depuraron de un doble conteo. El STATEC llevó a cabo una nueva estimación del empleo asalariado total para los años anteriores a 1983.

Documentación y difusión

Documentación:

STATEC : *Note trimestrielle de Conjoncture, la Situation économique au Grand-Duché* (Luxemburgo);

Idem : *Annuaire Statistique du Luxembourg* (ibid.); se publica unos cinco meses después del año de referencia de las estadísticas; también contiene notas metodológicas.

Difusión: en Internet: http://www.statec.lu

Datos suministrados a la OIT para su difusión

Las estadísticas siguientes se publican en el *Anuario de Estadísticas del Trabajo*:

Estimaciones del empleo total por actividad económica, basadas parcialmente en esta fuente administrativa.

Empleo remunerado por actividad económica.

Otras fuentes administrativas de datos:

Desde abril de 1988, los **ficheros administrativos de la Seguridad Social** constituyen la fuente principal de datos para las estadísticas armonizadas de ganancias, en combinación con una encuesta semestral realizada en las empresas. Se puede obtener información metodológica sobre el uso de esta fuente en relación con las *Estadísticas armonizadas sobre las ganancias brutas medias* (octubre) en:

OIT: *Fuentes y Métodos Estadísticos del Trabajo*, Volumen 2: Empleo, salarios, horas de y costo de la mano de obra (encuestas realizadas a los establecimientos) (segunda edición, Ginebra, 1995).

México

Fuente de la Serie

Instituto Mexicano del Seguro Social (IMSS), Informe Mensual de Población Derechohabiente.

Título de la Serie

Trabajadores asegurados permanentes y eventuales registrados en el IMSS; Salario Promedio de Cotización de la población cotizante y eventuales urbanos.

Organismo Responsable

Recolección de datos y elaboración estadística: Instituto Mexicano del Seguro Social (IMSS).

Publicación o difusión de las estadísticas: Instituto Nacional de Estadística, Geografía e Informática (INEGI) y Secretaría del Trabajo y Previsión Social.

Temas laborales principales abarcados

Empleo y Remuneraciones salariales.

Periodicidad o frecuencia de disponibilidad de las estadísticas

Mensual.

Período de referencia

El mes.

Alcance de las estadísticas

Ambito geográfico: todo el país.

Ambito industrial: todas las ramas de la actividad económica.

Establecimientos: de todos tipos y tamaños en los sectores privado y público.

Personas cubiertas: asalariados permanentes y eventuales urbanos registrados en el IMSS. Se excluyen los grupos de Seguro Facultativo, estudiantes, continuación voluntaria y el seguro de salud para la familia.

Ocupaciones: no se recogen datos sobre ocupaciones individuales.

Conceptos y definiciones

Empleo: abarca a los asegurados con la categoría de asalariados permanentes y eventuales urbanos. Los asegurados permanentes son las personas que por laborar dentro de una factoría, comercio o cualquier tipo de empresa, tienen efectivo el derecho al seguro por ser trabajadores (asalariados) de planta. Los asegurados urbanos son las personas aseguradas que laboran en negocios o empresas establecidas en un ámbito urbano cuya actividad económica a que se dedican puede entrar en los grupos: agropecuario, industrial, comercial o de servicios.

Los asegurados eventuales urbanos son principalmente las personas que laboran en la industria de la construcción y en otras industrias y que no son trabajadores de planta. Los trabajadores eventuales o del campo son las personas que trabajan considerando la estacionalidad de las actividades agrícolas.

Las series que publica la OIT sólo abarcan a los trabajadores permanentes.

Ganancias: se refieren a los salarios medios de la población cotizante permanente. El salario base de cotización se integra con los pagos hechos en efectivo por cuota diaria y las gratificaciones, percepciones, alimentación, habitación, primas, comisiones, prestaciones en especie y cualquier otra cantidad o prestación que se entregue al trabajador por sus servicios.

En ningún caso se consideraran, para este efecto, salarios diarios inferiores al mínimo general de la zona geográfica respectiva o superiores al equivalente a veinticinco veces el salario mínimo general del Distrito Federal.

Horas de Trabajo: no se recopilan.

Clasificaciones:

Ramas de actividad económica:

Título de la clasificación: Catálogo de Actividades para la Clasificación de las Empresas en el Seguro de Riesgos de Trabajo.

Número de grupos utilizados para la codificación: nueve grandes divisiones, 55 grupos y 276 fracciones de actividades económicas.

Se aplica a: todos los datos.

Vínculos con la CIIU y nivel: Rev 2, 1968.

Situación en el empleo: trabajadores permanentes y eventuales urbanos.

Otras clasificaciones: por sector de actividad económica, por ámbito geográfico (urbano y campo) y por entidad federativa.

Recolección de datos

Método de recolección de datos: la información se obtiene de archivos de datos que se forman con base en documentos del IMSS, como los avisos de afiliación y los documentos de pago de las cuotas obrero-patronales que aportan los servicios de cobranza del IMSS.

Las cifras sobre asegurados se dictaminan con bases en los avisos de afiliación, sumando las altas y los reingresos y restando las bajas, al saldo mensual del archivo denominado "Maestra de Asegurados".

Actualización del sistema administrativo: mensual.

Procesamiento y verificación de datos:
No se dispone.

Ajustes
No se dispone.

Tipos de estimaciones
Totales de trabajadores asegurados por categoría, totales y promedio de remuneraciones.

Construcción de índices
Ninguno.

Indicadores de fiabilidad de las estadísticas
Alcance del sistema administrativo: Las series de trabajadores reportan el universo total de trabajadores afiliados al IMSS.

El salario medio de cotización corresponde al reportado por los patrones para determinar las aportaciones por seguro de Enfermedades y Maternidad.

Series disponibles
Series mensuales de:
Trabajadores asegurados por categoría (permanentes, urbanos y campo) y tasas de cambio anual;
Trabajadores asegurados de la industria de la construcción, por categoría y tasas de cambio anual;
Trabajadores asegurados permanentes por rama de actividad económica y por región.

Historia de las estadísticas
Fecha de iniciación de la serie estadística: Enero de 1977.
Cambios y revisiones principales: no se dispone.

Documentación y difusión
Documentación:
INEGI: *Mexican Bulletin of Statistical Information* (México, trimestral); los datos se publican dos meses después del mes al que se refieren.
Difusión: en el sitio Internet de la Secretaria del Trabajo y Previsión Social: http://www.stps.gob.mx
y en el sitio del INEGI: http://www.inegi.gob.mx
Datos suministrados a la OIT para su difusión
Se publican en el *Anuario de Estadísticas del Trabajo* las series siguientes:
- Empleo remunerado por actividad económica
- Ganancias medias por día de los asalariados por actividad económica.

Noruega (1)

Fuente de la serie
Asociación Noruega de Autoridades Locales y Regionales.

Título de la serie
Personal Administrativt Informasjonssystem (PAI) (Sistema de Información del Personal de la Administración Pública).

Organismo responsable
Recolección de datos: Asociación Noruega de Autoridades Locales y Regionales.
Elaboración estadística y publicación o difusión de las estadísticas: Asociación Noruega de Autoridades Locales y Regionales y Oficina de Estadística de Noruega (Statistics Norway).

Temas laborales principales abarcados
Empleo, ganancias, tasas de salarios y horas de trabajo.

Periodicidad o frecuencia de disponibilidad de las estadísticas
Anual.

Período de referencia
Empleo y tasas de salarios: 1° de octubre
Ingresos y horas de trabajo: el período de paga que incluye el 1° de octubre.

Alcance de las estadísticas
Ambito geográfico: todo el país, salvo la municipalidad de Oslo.
Ambito industrial: administración pública (municipal y municipalidad de condados) y empresas municipales y de condados, incluidos servicios sociales y sanitarios. Se excluye el personal docente (véase NORUEGA (2)), pero se incluyen otros miembros del personal trabajando en actividades municipales de educación.
Establecimientos: de todos los tipos y tamaños en los sectores públicos abarcados.

Personas cubiertas: empleados en la administración municipal y municipalidad de condados, como se indica más arriba.
Ocupaciones: los datos se recopilan de acuerdo con los siguientes grupos ocupacionales:
- empleados administrativos;
- empleados técnicos;
- trabajadores manuales;
- empleados de hospitales, etc.;
- empleados en ocupaciones de otros servicios.

Conceptos y definiciones
Empleo: se refiere a todos los empleados de la administración municipal y municipalidad de condados y de empresas municipales y de propiedad de los condados que son miembros de la Asociación Noruega de Autoridades Locales y Regionales y que se acogen a los contratos colectivos de la Asociación, en vigor al 1° de octubre del año de referencia. Se excluyen los empleados de la municipalidad de Oslo.
Se consideran empleados a tiempo completo los que trabajan como mínimo 33 horas por semana; los que tienen menos horas de trabajo se consideran empleados a tiempo parcial.
Ganancias: las ganancias brutas mensuales se refieren al total de sueldos en efectivo de acuerdo con la escala de salarios en vigor al 1° de octubre del año del censo, más los subsidios fijos y variables. Se excluye el valor de los pagos en especie y cualquier pago por horas extraordinarias.
Tasas de sueldo o salario: se refieren a las tasas de salarios y sueldos básicos realmente pagados por mes, excluidos los subsidios garantizados y periódicos y los pagos en especie.
Horas de trabajo: horas de trabajo normales establecidas en contratos colectivos, leyes y reglamentos.

Clasificaciones
Ramas de actividad económica:
Título de la clasificación: Clasificación Industrial Uniforme (SIC94), División 75 (administración pública municipal y municipalidad de condados).
Número de grupos utilizados para la codificación: no se aplica.
Se aplica a: todos los datos.
Vínculos con la CIIU y nivel: ninguno.
Ocupaciones:
Título de la clasificación: la clasificación se hace de acuerdo con la clasificación utilizada por la Asociación Noruega de Autoridades Locales y Regionales, que sirve para establecer los contratos colectivos y refleja la escala de sueldos.
Número de grupos utilizados para la codificación: 5.
Se aplica a: todos los datos.
Vínculos con la CIUO y nivel: no corresponde necesariamente a la Clasificación de Ocupaciones Uniforme (C521), ni a la CIUO.
Otras clasificaciones: empleo, ganancias, tasas de salarios y horas de trabajo: por sexo y categoría del empleado, como tiempo completo/tiempo parcial y adultos/jóvenes.
Las estadísticas se clasifican también según el grado de instrucción. La información sobre la capacitación de los empleados se obtiene del Registro de la Oficina de Estadística de Noruega sobre el Nivel más Alto de Educación de la Población (BHU). La formación se clasifica de acuerdo con los siguientes años de estudio realizados: educación secundaria inferior, educación secundaria superior, tercer nivel de educación (4 años o menos); tercer nivel de educación (más de 4 años); formación desconocida o no completada.
Hay un año de retraso en los datos de educación.

Recolección de datos
Tipo y alcance del sistema administrativo: en 2000, el registro incluyó 347 544 empleados de la administración municipal y municipalidad de condados (excluido Oslo).
Método de recolección de datos: la Asociación Noruega de Autoridades Locales y Regionales recibe información sobre el personal que trabaja en los municipios y las municipalidades de condados en formato electrónico (disquetes) o en papel y envía esa información en formato electrónico a la Oficina de Estadística de Noruega, de conformidad con la Sección 3-2 de la Ley de Estadísticas.
Actualización del sistema administrativo: la Asociación Noruega de Autoridades Locales y Regionales actualiza una vez al año el Registro Central.

Procesamiento y verificación de datos
Los datos se procesan tanto manualmente como por computadora.

Ajustes
Ninguno.

Tipos de estimaciones
Totales y promedios.

Construcción de índices
Ninguno.
Indicadores de fiabilidad de las estimaciones
Alcance del sistema administrativo: exhaustivo, basado en el censo anual de todos los empleados de las administraciones y empresas miembros de la Asociación Noruega de Autoridades Locales y Regionales, salvo los empleados de la municipalidad de Oslo, al 1 de octubre de cada año.
Errores no relacionados con el muestreo: es posible que las personas que rellenan los informes comuniquen información incorrecta a la Asociación Noruega de Autoridades Locales y Regionales y/o que se produzcan errores de procesamiento en la Asociación o la Oficina de Estadística de Noruega. Además, el registro del Nivel más Alto de Educación de la Población puede contener errores en la codificación del nivel de enseñanza.
Conformidad con otras fuentes: estas estadísticas se pueden comparar con otras estadísticas de salarios realizadas desde 1997.
Series disponibles
Total de empleo y promedio de ganancias mensuales, tasas de salarios y horas de trabajo semanales.
Historia de las estadísticas
Fecha de iniciación de la serie estadística: 1958.
Cambios y revisiones principales: Desde 1990, en las estadísticas se incluyen los empleados de los servicios sociales y sanitarios.
Desde 1993, en las estadísticas se excluyen los empleados de la municipalidad de Oslo.
Desde 1997, se excluyen las empresas de suministro eléctrico, pese a que son miembro de la Asociación Noruega de Autoridades Locales y Regionales. Los empleados de estas empresas se incluyen en las estadísticas de empleados del suministro eléctrico. (http://www.ssb.no/lonnkraft_en)
Las estadísticas se pueden comparar a partir de 1997.
Documentación y difusión
Documentación:
Statistics Norway: *NOS Wage Statistics* (Oslo, anual); también contiene información metodológica;
Idem: *Statistical Yearbook* (ibid., anual), se publica 6 meses después del a   ño de referencia de las estadísticas.
La Oficina de Estadística de Noruega publicó las estadísticas de 1958, 1959, 1960; las estadísticas se publicaron cada dos años desde 1962 a 1976, y anualmente a partir de 1978.
Difusión: en el sitio Internet de Statistics Norway:
Estadísticas de salarios. Empleados municipales y municipalidades de condados: http://www.ssb.no/lonnkomm_en/ (disponibles en noruego e inglés);
Tipos de grupos: 06.05. Salarios y costos laborales; http://www.ssb.no/english/subjects/06/05
Se pueden obtener, previa solicitud, los datos que no figuran en las publicaciones nacionales o en el sitio web.
Las estadísticas de salarios para empleados incluidos en la Sección L de la Clasificación Industrial Uniforme de empleados del gobierno central se pueden obtener en: http://www.ssb.no/lonnstat_en (disponibles en noruego e inglés).
Datos suministrados a la OIT para su difusión
Las siguientes estadísticas se publican en las *Estadísticas sobre salarios y horas de trabajo por ocupación y precios de artículos alimenticios – Resultados de la Encuesta de octubre*:
Horas de trabajo normales y promedio mensual de ganancias de las siguientes ocupaciones:
- No. 139 – *Funcionario ejecutivo del Gobierno b) autoridad locas*
- No. 151 – *Maestro de párvulos*
- No. 154 – *Enfermero diplomado (general)*
- No. 155 – *Enfermero auxiliar.*

Otras fuentes administrativas de datos: véase la descripción No. 3 de Noruega.

Noruega (2)

Fuente de la serie
Sentralt Tjenestemannsregister for Skoleverket (STS) (Registro Central de Empleados Gubernamentales del Sistema Escolar).

Título de la serie
Estadísticas de empleo y salarios del sistema escolar (escuelas públicas).
Organismo responsable
Recolección de datos, elaboración estadística y publicación o difusión de las estadísticas: desde 2002: Oficina de Estadística de Noruega (Statistics Norway); antes de 2002: Ministerio del Trabajo y Administración Pública (AAD).

Temas laborales principales abarcados
Empleo, ganancias, tasas de salarios y horas de trabajo.
Periodicidad o frecuencia de disponibilidad de las estadísticas
Anual.
Período de referencia
Empleo y tasas de salarios: 1° de octubre de cada año;
Ganancias y horas de trabajo: el período de pago que incluye el 1° de octubre.
Alcance de las estadísticas
Ambito geográfico: todo el país.
Ambito industrial: escuelas públicas, es decir todas las escuelas primarias del gobierno municipal y central, escuelas secundarias superiores del gobierno municipal de los condados y del gobierno central (incluida la formación para el mercado del trabajo), centros del gobierno central para la formación especializada y escuelas secundarias (internados para estudiantes de secundaria superior y de educación terciaria), tanto de municipios de condados como privados.
Establecimientos: de todos tipos y tamaños como se describe en "Cobertura industrial".
Personas cubiertas: todos los empleados en ocupaciones docentes.
Ocupaciones: para cada tipo de escuela (véase en Clasificaciones) se determinan las siguientes ocupaciones:
- Rector
- Director de escuela secundaria
- Director de escuela primaria
- Profesor (de escuela secundaria y nivel superior)
- Profesor con grado universitario superior
- Profesor con grado universitario
- Maestro
- Maestro sin capacitación requerida (de escuela primaria y escuela secundaria inferior)
- Otras ocupaciones.
Conceptos y definiciones
Empleo: se refiere a todos los empleados en ocupaciones docentes en las instituciones descritas en "Cobertura industrial" que, al 1° de octubre de 2000, estaban empleados de conformidad con acuerdos concertados entre el gobierno central y las organizaciones de funcionarios públicos, independientemente del tipo de contrato (cargos permanentes, cargos sujetos a despido, cargos temporales y fijos).
Los empleados de la educación privada (Sección M de la Clasificación Industrial Uniforme) no están incluidos en las estadísticas, pero se incluyen en otra serie de estadísticas (Lonnprivund).
Se consideran empleados a tiempo completo los que trabajan como mínimo 33 horas por semana; los que tienen menos horas de trabajo se consideran empleados a tiempo parcial.
Ganancias: los ingresos brutos mensuales se refieren al total de sueldos en efectivo de acuerdo con la escala de salarios en vigor al 1° de octubre del año del censo, más los subsidios adicionales fijos y variables y pagos pendientes ganados en septiembre y pagados en octubre. Se excluye el valor de los pagos en especie y cualquier pago por horas extraordinarias.
Tasas de sueldo o salario: se refiere a las tasas de salarios y sueldos realmente pagados por mes, excluidos los subsidios garantizados y periódicos y los pagos en especie.
Horas de trabajo: horas de trabajo normales establecidas en contratos colectivos, leyes y reglamentos.
Clasificaciones
Ramas de actividad económica:
Título de la clasificación: Clasificación Industrial Uniforme (SIC94), Sección M: escuelas públicas.
Número de grupos utilizados para la codificación: siete: escuelas primarias; escuelas combinadas de primaria y secundaria inferior; escuelas de secundaria inferior; escuelas para niños discapacitados (escuelas primarias); escuelas de secundaria superior; escuelas secundarias tradicionales; y otros tipos de escuelas.
Se aplica a: todos los datos.
Vínculos con la CIIU y nivel: ninguno.
Ocupaciones:
Título de la clasificación: la clasificación se hace de acuerdo con la escala de sueldos del gobierno central en vigor al 1° de octubre de cada año. No corresponde necesariamente a la Clasificación de Ocupaciones Uniforme (C521).
Número de grupos utilizados para la codificación: véase la lista de ocupaciones que figura más arriba.
Se aplica a: todos los datos.
Vínculos con la CIUO y nivel: ninguno.

Otras clasificaciones: empleo, ganancias, tasas de salarios y horas de trabajo: por sexo y categoría del empleado, como tiempo completo/tiempo parcial y adultos/jóvenes.

Las estadísticas se clasifican también según el grado de instrucción. La información sobre el nivel de capacitación de los empleados se obtiene de los registros de la Oficina de Estadística de Noruega sobre el Nivel más Alto de Educación de la Población (BHU). La formación se clasifica de acuerdo con los siguientes años de estudios realizados: educación secundaria inferior; educación secundaria superior; tercer nivel de educación (4 años o menos); tercer nivel de educación (más de 4 años); formación desconocida o no completada. Hay un año de retraso en los datos de educación.

Recolección de datos

Tipo y alcance del sistema administrativos: En 2001, el registro incluyó 99 074 empleados de escuelas públicas.

Método de recolección de datos: El Ministerio del Trabajo y la Administración Pública (AAD) reciben información sobre el personal de las escuelas en formato electrónico (disquetes) o en papel y envían esa información en formato electrónico a la Oficina de Estadística de Noruega, de conformidad con la Sección 3-2 de la Ley de Estadísticas.

Actualización del sistema administrativo: El Ministerio del Trabajo y la Administración Pública actualizan una vez al año el Registro Central de Empleados Gubernamentales del Sistema Escolar (STS).

Procesamiento y verificación de datos

Los datos se procesan manualmente y por computadora. Los datos de salarios se verifican manualmente y por computadora en la AAD y la Oficina de Estadística de Noruega.

Ajustes

Ninguno.

Tipos de estimaciones

Totales y promedios.

Construcción de índices

Ninguno.

Indicadores de fiabilidad de las estimaciones

Alcance del sistema administrativo: exhaustiva, basada en el censo anual de todos los empleados en los grupos pertinentes al 1° de octubre de año.

Errores no relacionados con el muestreo: es posible que las personas que rellenan los informes comuniquen información incorrecta a la AAD y/o que se produzcan errores de procesamiento en la AAD o en la Oficina de Estadística de Noruega. Además, el registro de Nivel más Alto de Educación de la Población puede contener errores en la codificación del nivel de enseñanza.

Conformidad con otras fuentes: estas estadísticas se pueden comparar con otras estadísticas de salarios realizadas desde 1997.

Series disponibles

Total de empleo y promedio de ganancias mensuales, tasas de salarios y horas de trabajo semanales.

Historia de las estadísticas

Fecha de iniciación de la serie estadística: 1973.

Cambios y revisiones principales: ninguno. Estas estadísticas se pueden comparar a partir de 1973.

Documentación y difusión

Documentación:

Statistics Norway: *NOS Wage Statistics* (Oslo, anual); también contiene información metodológica;

Idem: *Statistical Yearbook* (ibid., anual), se publica 6 meses después del año de referencia de las estadísticas.

Statistics Norway publicó las estadísticas de 1959, 1963, 1967; las estadísticas se publican anualmente desde 1973.

Difusión: en el sitio Internet de Statistics Norway: http://www.ssb.no/lonnkomm_en/ (disponible en inglés y noruego).

Se pueden obtener, previa solicitud, los datos que no figuran en las publicaciones nacionales o en el sitio web.

Las estadísticas de salarios de los empleados de la educación privada (basadas en muestras de empresas) se publican en: http://www.ssb.no/lonnprivund_en

estadísticas se publican en las *Estadísticas sobre salarios y horas de trabajo por ocupación y precios de artículos alimenticios – Resultados de la Encuesta de octubre:*

-    *y literatura (enseñanza secundaria)*

Los datos para la ocupación No.151 - *Maestro de párvulos,* se obtienen de la Asociación Noruega de Autoridades Locales y

-    No.148 - *Profesor de matemáticas (enseñanza secundaria)*
-    No.150 - *Maestro de enseñanza primaria.*

Promedio de salarios mensuales en las siguientes ocupaciones:

No.147 - *Profesor de lenguas*

Regionales, y para la ocupación No. 149 – *Profesor de enseñanza técnica (enseñanza secundaria)*, **Datos suministrados a la OIT para su difusión**

Las siguientes del Registro Estatal Central de Empleados Gubernamentales (universidades e instituciones equivalentes).

Otras fuentes administrativas de datos: véase la descripción No. 3 de Noruega.

los planes salariales del gobierno central:

Noruega (3)

Fuente de la serie

Statens Sentrale Tjenestemannsregister (SST) (Registro Estatal Central de Empleados Gubernamentales).

Título de la serie

Estadísticas sobre empleo y salarios de empleados gubernamentales.

Organismo responsable

Recolección de datos y publicación o difusión de las estadísticas: desde 2002: Oficina de Estadística de Noruega (Statistics Norway); antes de 2002: Ministerio del Trabajo y Administración Pública (AAD).

Temas laborales principales abarcados

Empleo, ganancias, tasas de salarios y horas de trabajo.

Periodicidad o frecuencia de disponibilidad de las estadísticas

Anualmente.

Período de referencia

Empleo y tasas de salarios: 1° de octubre

Ganancias y horas de trabajo: el período de pago que incluye el 1° de octubre.

Alcance de las estadísticas

Ambito geográfico: todo el país.

Ambito industrial: administración y defensa públicas del gobierno central, empresas gubernamentales, servicios sanitarios, así como universidades e instituciones equivalentes.

Establecimientos: de todos tipos y tamaños del sector público.

Personas cubiertas: empleados gubernamentales.

Ocupaciones: los grupos ocupacionales se determinan de acuerdo con

Ocupaciones publicadas del Gobierno central

Ministerios: Subdirectores generales; Asistente de directores generales; Jefe de Divisiones; Asesores; Funcionarios ejecutivos principales; Funcionarios ejecutivos; Funcionarios ejecutivos subalternos; Secretarias de oficina.

Otros departamentos de la administración central: Subdirector general; Asistentes de directores generales; Jefes de divisiones; Asesores; Ingenieros jefes; Funcionarios ejecutivos principales; Funcionarios ejecutivos; Funcionarios ejecutivos subalternos; Secretarias de oficina; Empleados superiores.

Universidades e instituciones equivalentes: Profesores; Profesores asistentes, primer grado; Profesores asistentes; Funcionarios de investigación; Profesores con grado universitario; Becarios; Otras ocupaciones docentes; Ocupaciones administrativas; Funcionarios ejecutivos; Personal de oficina.

Servicios sanitarios: Médicos jefes; Médicos de sala; Bioingenieros; Funcionarios ejecutivos; Personal de oficina; Enfermeros especializados; Enfermeros profesionales; Enfermeros asistentes.

Otros servicios públicos

El clero: Sacerdotes; Pastores; Curas; Catequistas.

La Judicatura: Presidentes de tribunal; Jueces de tribunales urbanos, jueces de tribunales de condado, jueces territoriales; Secretarios; Funcionarios ejecutivos; Personal de oficina.

Administración de prisiones: Servicios de seguridad; Funcionarios de prisión; Funcionarios ejecutivos; Personal de oficina.

Fuerzas policiales y servicio de policía rural: Comisarios de policía de distrito; Inspectores asistentes; Inspectores; Sargentos; Comisarios de policía de distrito, grado especial; Asistentes de policías de distrito; Funcionarios ejecutivos; Personal de oficina.

Administración del Mercado laboral: Jefe de oficinas de empleo; Funcionarios ejecutivos; Personal de oficina.

Administración de seguros sociales: Jefe de divisiones de seguros; Funcionarios ejecutivos; Personal de oficina.

Comisiones generales fiscales, registros de la población

Recaudadores de impuesto

Secretarias

Funcionarios

Servicios aduaneros, administración local: Inspectores de aduanas; Funcionarios de inspección de aduanas, grado inferior; Funcionarios ejecutivos; Personal de oficina; Empresas gubernamentales.

Administración de caminos: Ingenieros; Funcionarios ejecutivos; Oficinistas; Inspectores; Capataces; Obreros calificados; Obreros especializados.

Administración de la aviación civil: Controladores de tráfico aéreo; Funcionarios de aeropuerto; Asistentes de controladores de tráfico aéreo; Ingenieros.

Defensa: Personal civil; Personal militar.

Conceptos y definiciones

Empleo: se refiere a todos los empleados del gobierno central que ocupan un cargo gubernamental al 1° de octubre del año del censo.

Se consideran empleados a tiempo completo los que trabajan como mínimo 33 horas por semana; los que tienen menos horas se consideran empleados a tiempo parcial.

Ganancias: el total de ganancias brutas mensuales se refiere al total de sueldos en efectivo de acuerdo con la escala de salarios en vigor al 1° de octubre del año del censo, más los subsidios fijos y variables ganados en septiembre y pagados en octubre. Se excluye el valor de los pagos en especie y cualquier pago por horas extraordinarias.

Tasas de sueldo o salario: se refiere a las tasas de salarios y sueldos realmente pagados por mes, excluidos los subsidios garantizados y periódicos y los pagos en especie.

Horas de trabajo: horas de trabajo normales establecidas en contratos colectivos, leyes y reglamentos.

Clasificaciones

Ramas de actividad económica:

Título de la clasificación: Clasificación Industrial Uniforme (SIC94).

Número de grupos utilizados para la codificación: siete: ministerios (incluida la Oficina del Primer Ministro y la Oficina del Auditor General); otros departamentos de la administración central; otros servicios públicos; universidades e instituciones equivalentes; empresas gubernamentales; defensa y servicios sanitarios.

Se aplica a: todos los datos.

Vínculos con la CIIU y nivel: ninguno.

Ocupaciones:

Título de la clasificación: la clasificación se hace de acuerdo con la escala de sueldos del gobierno central en vigor al 1° de octubre de cada año. No corresponde necesariamente a la Clasificación de Ocupaciones Uniforme (C521).

Número de grupos utilizados para la codificación: véase la lista de ocupaciones que figura más arriba.

Se aplica a: todos los datos.

Vínculos con la CIUO y nivel: ninguno.

Otras clasificaciones: empleo, ganancias, tasas de salarios y horas de trabajo: por sexo y categoría del empleado, como tiempo completo/tiempo parcial y adultos/jóvenes.

Las estadísticas también se clasifican según el grado de instrucción. La información sobre la capacitación de los empleados se obtiene de los registros de la Oficina de Estadística de Noruega sobre el Nivel más Alto de Educación de la Población (BHU). La formación se clasifica de acuerdo con los siguientes años de estudio realizados: educación secundaria inferior; educación secundaria superior; tercer nivel de educación (4 años o menos); tercer nivel de educación (más de 4 años); formación desconocida o no completada.

Hay un año de retraso en los datos de educación.

Recolección de datos

Tipo y alcance del sistema administrativo: en 2001, el registro incluyó 136 152 empleados en la administración pública del gobierno central.

Método de recolección de datos: el Ministerio del Trabajo y la Administración Pública (AAD) reciben información sobre el personal de los servicios e instituciones en formato electrónico (disquetes) o en papel y envían esa información en formato electrónico a la Oficina de Estadística de Noruega, de conformidad con la Sección 3-2 de la Ley de Estadísticas.

Actualización del sistema administrativo: el Registro Central se actualiza una vez al año.

Procesamiento y verificación de datos

Los datos se procesan manualmente o por computadora. Los datos de salarios se verifican manualmente y por computadora en la AAD y la Oficina de Estadística de Noruega.

Ajustes

Ninguno.

Tipos de estimaciones

Totales y promedios.

Construcción de índices

Ninguno.

Indicadores de fiabilidad de las estimaciones

Alcance del sistema administrativo: exhaustiva, basada en el censo anual de todos los empleados del sector público, al 1° de octubre de cada año.

Errores no relacionados con el muestreo: es posible que las personas entrevistadas comuniquen información incorrecta a la AAD y/o que se produzcan errores de procesamiento en la AAD o la Oficina de Estadística de Noruega. Además, el registro de Nivel más Alto de Educación de la Población puede contener errores en la codificación del nivel de enseñanza.

Conformidad con otras fuentes: estas estadísticas se pueden comparar con otras estadísticas de salarios realizadas desde 1997.

Series disponibles

Totales de empleo y promedio de ganancias mensuales, tasas de salarios y horas de trabajo semanales.

Historia de las estadísticas

Fecha de iniciación de la serie estadística: 1973.

Cambios y revisiones principales: ninguno. Estas estadísticas se pueden comparar a partir de 1973.

Documentación y difusión

Documentación:

Statistics Norway: *NOS Wage Statistics* (Oslo, anual); contiene información metodológica;

Idem: *Statistical Yearbook* (ibid., anual), se publica 6 meses después del año de referencia.

Statistics Norway publicó las estadísticas de 1959, 1963, 1967; las estadísticas se publican anualmente desde 1973.

Difusión: en el sitio Internet de Statistics Norway: http://www.ssb.no/lonnkomm_en/ y http://www.ssb.no/lonnstat

Se pueden obtener, previa solicitud, los datos que no figuran en las publicaciones nacionales o en el sitio Internet.

Datos suministrados a la OIT para su difusión

Las siguientes estadísticas se publican en *Estadísticas sobre salarios y horas de trabajo por ocupación y precios de artículos alimenticios – Resultados de la Encuesta de octubre*:

Horas de trabajo normales y promedio de ganancias mensuales de las siguientes ocupaciones:-

No.139 – *Agente administrativo a) administración pública central*.

No.149 – *Profesor de enseñanza técnica (enseñanza secundaria)*.

Otras fuentes administrativas de datos: varias estadísticas sociales y económicas se preparan basándose en los diversos registros que mantienen los diferentes ministerios, administraciones e instituciones, entre los cuales figuran:

(1) El *Registro de certificados de fin de año*, que mantiene la Administración Fiscal: suministra estadísticas sobre totales y promedios de las ganancias brutas de todos los asalariados (*Lonnssummer fra lonns-og trekkoppgaveregisteret*). En el total de las ganancias brutas se incluyen todos los salarios y sueldos por tiempo trabajado, trabajo realizado y períodos fuera de servicio, pago de vacaciones, primas u otras remuneraciones pagadas durante el año de ganancias. Los datos se clasifican por rama de actividad económica, sexo, grupo de edad, tamaño del establecimiento y región.

Los datos se derivan de los certificados de fin de año que los empleadores deben llenar para cada uno de sus empleados al comienzo de cada año con respecto a todo el año anterior, y transmitir a la Administración Fiscal, que verifica los datos de ganancias y envía una copia final a la Oficina de Estadística de Noruega para otras verificaciones y el procesamiento estadístico. Las series estadísticas comenzaron en 1990 y son anuales. Se pueden obtener los datos en el sitio Internet de Statistics Norway: http://www.ssb.no/english/subjects/06/05/lonnltreg_en

(2) Las estadísticas de ingresos por persona y familia se compilan anualmente en base a las diversas *fuentes administrativas de registros y datos estadísticos* (por ejemplo, declaraciones de ingresos, Registro Fiscal, Registro de certificados de fin de año, Administración Nacional de Seguros, Ministerio de Asuntos Sociales, Fondo Estatal de Préstamos Educativos, estadísticas de educación, etc.) para toda la población al 31 de diciembre del año fiscal. Esas estadísticas contienen información detallada sobre los ingresos de varias fuentes (por ejemplo, ingresos por empleo, pensiones, capital), incluidos los ingresos que no son gravables pero que se encuentran en los registros, como subsidios a los hogares, asistencia social, becas e ingresos en efectivo para padres de niños de corta edad. Las unidades estadísticas actuales son la persona y la familia y las estadísticas se recopilan sobre la distribución de ingresos y los niveles para varios grupos de la población y zonas geográficas. Se utiliza también este base de datos para obtener información sobre los ingresos en otras encuestas estadísticas, tales como las Estadísticas sobre las condiciones de vida y el Censo de población y hogares de 2001.

Se pueden obtener las estadísticas e información metodológica en el sitio Internet de Statistics Norway:

http://www.ssb.no/english/subjects/05/01. Esas estadísticas se publican en:
NOS C649 Income Statistics for Persons and Families 1993-1998.
(3) El *Registro de empleadores y asalariados* proporciona datos anuales sobre el número de empleados y sus horas de trabajo semanales previstas. Se incluyen todos los empleados cuya duración de tiempo previsto en el empleo es superior a seis días y las horas de trabajo previstas por semana son más de tres horas. Los datos de empleo se clasifican por rama de actividad económica de acuerdo con la Nueva Clasificación Industrial Uniforme de 1995 (antes de 1995, según la Clasificación Industrial Uniforme), sexo, grupo de edad, grado de instrucción, región, país de nacimiento y número de años de residencia en el país; las horas de trabajo se clasifican por región y sexo.
El Instituto Nacional de Seguros está a cargo de este registro, del cual transmite copia a la Oficina de Estadística de Noruega una vez al año y hace actualizaciones semanales durante todo el año. Se hacen verificaciones constantes con los datos del Registro Central de la Población y se hacen los ajustes necesarios en caso de doble conteo de trabajadores con diversos empleos. Desde 1983 se dispone de series estadísticas. A comienzos de 1992 se incluyeron los marineros; en 1994, el período de referencia pasó del segundo al cuarto trimestre de cada año y en 1995, se introdujo la Nueva Clasificación Industrial Uniforme. Las estadísticas se publican en:
Statistics Norway: *Labour Market Statistics* (Oslo, anual),
y están disponibles en el sitio Internet:
http://www.ssb.no/english/subjects/06/01
Se puede obtener información metodológica en el sitio Internet de Statistics Norway, en "About the statistics".

Nueva Caledonia

Fuente de la serie
Archivos de la Caja de Compensación de Prestaciones Familiares, de Accidentes del Trabajo y de Previsión de los Trabajadores de Nueva Caledonia y Dependencias (Caisse De Compensation des Prestations Familiales, des Accidents du Travail et Prévoyance des Travailleurs - CAFAT).
Título de la serie
El empleo y los salarios en Nueva Caledonia.
Organismo responsable
Recolección de datos: Caja de Compensación de Prestaciones Familiares, de Accidentes del Trabajo y de Previsión de los Trabajadores de Nueva Caledonia y Dependencias (CAFAT) y Dirección de los Servicios Fiscales (DSF).
Elaboración estadística y publicación o difusión de las estadísticas : Instituto de Estadística y Estudios Económicos (Institut de la Statistique et des Etudes Economiques - ISEE), Nueva Caledonia.
Temas laborales principales abarcados
Empleo asalariado, salarios y duración del empleo.
Periodicidad o frecuencia de disponibilidad de las estadísticas
Empleo asalariado: trimestral;
Salarios: anual;
Duración del empleo: anual.
Período de referencia
Empleo asalariado: el trimestre;
Salarios y duración del empleo: el año.
Alcance de las estadísticas
Ambito geográfico: todo el territorio.
Ambito industrial: todos los sectores de la actividad económica, incluido el servicio doméstico.
Establecimientos: establecimientos de todos los tipos y tamaños.
Personas cubiertas: el conjunto de asalariados, y el conjunto de empleadores, inscritos en la CAFAT.
Ocupaciones: en las estadísticas sobre los salarios, los datos se recopilan según la categoría socioprofesional.
Conceptos y definiciones
Empleo: el empleo asalariado se refiere al conjunto de asalariados de Nueva Caledonia, excluidos aprendices y pasantes.
Estadísticas de los salarios: en los asalariados anuales, o número de empleos, se incluyen los asalariados que trabajaron para más de un empleador en el año; se cuentan tantas veces como el número de empleos. El número medio anual de asalariados, o equivalente permanente a tiempo completo, corresponde al número teórico de asalariados a tiempo completo durante todo el año.
Ganancias: se refieren a la masa salarial bruta anual, es decir todos los salarios netos, incluidos sueldos, licencias pagadas, beneficios en especie o en efectivo y primas, más las cotizaciones salariales de los asalariados.

El salario medio mensual corresponde a la masa salarial del año convertida en salario de un asalariado a tiempo completo durante un mes.
Horas de trabajo: corresponde a la duración del empleo (en meses) de un asalariado en un año.
Clasificaciones
Ramas de actividad económica:
Título de la clasificación: Nomenclatura de Actividad del ISEE.
Número de grupos utilizados para la codificación: 39 cargos, después de pasar de la nomenclatura de actividades de la CAFAT a los sectores de actividad y actividades del ISEE.
Se aplica a: todos los datos.
Vínculos con la CIIU y nivel: ninguno.
Ocupaciones: en las estadísticas sobre los salarios se utilizan dos nomenclaturas.
Título de la clasificación: Nomenclatura de Calificaciones Profesionales del ISEE.
Número de grupos utilizados para la codificación: 10, después de pasar de la nomenclatura de las categorías socioprofesionales a las calificaciones profesionales del ISEE.
Se aplica a : todos los datos.
Vínculos con la CIUO y nivel: ninguno.
Título de la clasificación: Nomenclatura de las Categorías Socioprofesionales y de las Calificaciones en la función pública.
Número de grupos utilizados para la codificación: 80 al nivel más detallado.
Se aplica a: todos los datos.
Vínculos con la CISE y nivel: ninguno.
Otras clasificaciones: empleo asalariado trimestral: región (Numea, y el Interior y las islas en conjunto), y provincia;
Estadísticas de salarios: sexo, edad, duración del empleo, sector de actividad, zona geográfica, tamaño del establecimiento y clasificaciones cruzadas.
Recolección de datos
Tipo y alcance del sistema administrativo: recopilación exhaustiva de los empleadores
Método de recolección de datos: se utilizan dos fuentes principales. El archivo de las declaraciones nominativas suministradas trimestralmente por los empleadores a la CAFAT, que contienen información sobre el empleo, la duración del empleo y los salarios del sector privado; y el archivo de las declaraciones nominativas de los salarios de la Dirección de los Servicios Fiscales, que contienen información, entre otras cosas, sobre el número y los salarios de los funcionarios.
Para la estadística de los salarios, el ISEE procede a ajustar esos archivos para preparar un archivo uniforme sobre todos los salarios. En efecto, los datos sobre los salarios del archivo de la CAFAT corresponden a los valores brutos, a veces truncados porque están limitados al valor máximo, mientras que los del archivo de la DSF no están limitados, pero representan los valores de los salarios netos. Los salarios de los archivos de la CAFAT que son inferiores al tope se extraen sin modificación y los que aparecen limitados se vuelven a calcular: en una primera fase, el cálculo consiste en equiparar esos salarios con los declarados en el archivo de la DSF, utilizando elementos identificadores como el sexo, la fecha de nacimiento y el empleador de cada asalariado concernido. En una segunda fase, se realiza un cálculo para determinar los salarios brutos de los archivos de la DSF, calculando las cargas sociales correspondientes a cada salario. Al conocerse el empleador, se extraen los valores de esas cotizaciones sociales: directamente de los archivos de los diferentes organismos sociales antes mencionados, calculándolos mediante la aplicación de las reglas de cálculo que las determinan (contribución excepcional de solidaridad), o estimándolos (jubilaciones complementarias). Los valores globales de las cotizaciones sociales determinadas de esa manera se cotejan después, para validarlas, con las cifras publicadas en los informes de actividad, cuentas de explotación y otros documentos administrativos de los organismos concernidos (diversas mutuales, Caja de Jubilación de Expatriados (CRE)).
Actualización del sistema administrativo: trimestral.
Procesamiento y verificación de datos
Los datos se procesan por computadora.
Para la estadística de salarios, se obtuvo la colaboración del Servicio de Métodos Administrativos y de la Informática (SMAI) para mejorar las clasificaciones del empleo de los asalariados del sector público del año 1995, que sirvió de base para el año 1999. Se realizan verificaciones de coherencia entre los datos de salarios y la duración del empleo que proceden de diferentes archivos.
Dobles anotaciones: los archivos de la CAFAT y la DSF no nominativos de los que dispone el ISEE no permiten determinar cual

es el número de asalariados que corresponden a los diferentes salarios (un mismo asalariado puede haber trabajado en el año con diferentes empleadores, sucesiva o simultáneamente). Mientras que el Censo de Población de Nueva Caledonia de 1996 registró 53.944 asalariados, los archivos la CAFAT y la DSF indicaron 79.893. Para reducir al mínimo los errores sobre la duración del empleo y usar mejor los niveles de salario, las estadísticas también se establecen sobre la base de los asalariados remunerados por un mismo empleador durante los 12 meses del año (se excluyen los servicios domésticos).

Tipos de estimaciones

Estadísticas del empleo asalariado: número de asalariados inscritos cada trimestre, y por separado, número de empleadores inscritos.

Estadísticas de los salarios:

Duración del empleo (en meses) de un asalariado: número de horas del empleo dividido entre 169, duración legal de un mes a tiempo completo;

Duración media del empleo (en meses): suma de la duración del empleo de todos los asalariados en el año, dividido entre el número de empleos. La suma de la duración de los empleos del conjunto de asalariados es igual al producto del conjunto asalariado anual por la duración media del empleo, o también al producto del conjunto asalariado medio anual por 12.

Número medio anual de asalariados o equivalente permanente a tiempo completo: suma de la duración de los empleos (en meses) de todos los asalariados del año dividida entre 12.

Salario medio mensual: masa salarial dividida entre el número medio anual de asalariados, dividido entre 12.

Distribuciones y reparticiones de los empleos, salarios y duración del empleo según diversas variables.

Construcción de índices

Ninguno.

Indicadores de fiabilidad de las estimaciones

Alcance del sistema administrativo: superior al 99% en términos de asalariados.

Errores no relacionados con el muestreo: en las estadísticas de salarios se pueden producir errores en cuanto a la duración del empleo de los asalariados: el archivo de la DSF no siempre suministra la duración del empleo; ninguno de los dos archivos, CAFAT y DSF, suministra toda la información sobre la duración del trabajo (número de horas, tiempo parcial, medio tiempo, tiempo completo). Por lo tanto, el salario mensual se calcula dividiendo el salario entre el número de meses de empleo. Esta estimación tiene el inconveniente de que subestima el nivel real del salario mensual de los asalariados que trabajan a tiempo parcial. La duración del empleo de los asalariados declarados a la DSF a veces tiene errores. Para reducir al máximo el error de evaluación de la duración de empleo y dar más fiabilidad al valor del salario mensual, se realizó una minuciosa comparación con los diversos archivos del año1999, lo que permitió rectificar 8.685 datos sobre la duración del empleo.

Conformidad con otras fuentes: se establecieron comparaciones de los asalariados con los resultados del Censo de Población de Nueva Caledonia realizado el 16 de abril de 1996.

Series disponibles

Estadística trimestral del empleo asalariado: número de asalariados y número de empleadores, por sector de actividad económica y región;

Estadísticas de salarios:

Número de empleos por zona geográfica, sector de actividad y actividad, por nivel de salario y edad, y clasificaciones cruzadas;

Salarios por sector de actividad y actividad, por edad, sexo y edad, zona geográfica y clasificaciones cruzadas;

Distribuciones de los empleos por duración del empleo, nivel de salario, calificación profesional.

Historia de las estadísticas

Fecha de iniciación de la serie estadística: no se dispone.

Cambios y revisiones principales: no se dispone.

Documentación y difusión

Documentación:

ISEE: *Informations statistiques* (Numea, trimestral); contiene las estadísticas del empleo asalariado del trimestre anterior;

Idem: *ISEE: Les Salaires - Situation en 1999* (Numea, octubre de 2001); contiene las estadísticas e informaciones metodológicas.

Datos suministrados a la OIT para su difusión

Las estadísticas sobre el empleo remunerado (conjunto de actividades económicas) se publican en el *Anuario de Estadísticas del Trabajo*; los datos trimestrales correspondientes (por separado para los asalariados y el conjunto del efectivo ocupado) se publican en el *Boletín de Estadísticas del Trabajo*.

Países Bajos

Fuente de la serie

Convenios colectivos y otros reglamentos y leyes salariales.

Título de la serie

Números de índices de tasas de salarios (Indexcijfers van cao-lonen).

Organismo responsable

Recolección de datos, elaboración estadística y publicación o difusión de las estadísticas:

Oficina de Estadística de los Países Bajos (Centraal Bureau voor Statistiek, CBS).

Temas laborales principales abarcados

Índices de salarios contractuales, horas de trabajo y costo de la mano de obra.

Periodicidad o frecuencia de disponibilidad de las estadísticas

Mensual y anualmente.

Período de referencia

El último día de cada mes.

Alcance de las estadísticas

Ambito geográfico: todo el país.

Ambito industrial: todos los sectores de la actividad económica, salvo los hogares privados con servicio doméstico (SBI95) y organizaciones y órganos extraterritoriales (SBI 99).

Establecimientos: todos los tipos y tamaños de establecimientos incluidos en los convenios colectivos.

Personas cubiertas: asalariados a tiempo completo.

Ocupaciones: se abarcan todas las ocupaciones.

Conceptos y definiciones

Empleo: se refiere a los asalariados a tiempo completo, es decir las personas que trabajan por un salario o sueldo. Se establece una clasificación separada para jóvenes y adultos.

Tasas de sueldo o salario: se refieren a las tasas de salarios brutos por horas normalmente trabajadas, antes de hacer cualquier deducción para impuestos, cotizaciones a la seguridad social, sistemas de pensiones, etc. Se incluyen los salarios por horas de trabajo normales; todos los pagos adicionales fijos, garantizados y periódicos y todos los pagos especiales fijos (no pagados con regularidad), por ejemplo, prestaciones por vacaciones o primas de fin de año. Se excluyen los pagos adicionales cuya aprobación está supeditada al convenio laboral colectivo, tales como los suplementos por concepto de edad o trabajo en turnos.

Horas de trabajo: se refieren a las horas de trabajo anual normales por año para los asalariados adultos que trabajan a tiempo completo según se establece en los convenios laborales colectivos, es decir el número máximo de horas de trabajo, excluidas las horas extraordinarias, menos los días feriados públicos garantizados (establecidos a seis días por año), licencia anual y reducción de las horas de trabajo de acuerdo con lo establecido por la ley, los reglamentos o los convenios colectivos o de conformidad con ellos. No se tienen en cuenta la reducción condicional de las horas de trabajo debido a la edad o al trabajo en turnos.

Tasas de costo de la mano de obra: incluyen los salarios y pagos especiales según lo convenido en el convenio laboral colectivo, así como las cotizaciones obligatorias del asalariado a la seguridad social.

Clasificaciones

Ramas de actividad económica:

Título de la clasificación: Clasificación Industrial Uniforme (CIU, SBI en holandés, 1993).

Número de grupos utilizados para la codificación: cuatro sectores, 16 divisiones y un par de clases.

Se aplica a: todos los datos.

Vínculos con la CIIU y nivel: basada en la clasificación de la actividad económica de la UE (NACE, Rev.1) a nivel de cuatro dígitos, que está directamente relacionada con la CIIU, Rev.3, a nivel de dos dígitos.

Otras clasificaciones: sectores del convenio laboral colectivo, es decir clasificación de empresas del sector privado, del sector gubernamental y del sector subsidiado, y categoría de asalariado (jóvenes y adultos).

Recolección de datos

Tipo y alcance del sistema administrativo: abarca todos los convenios colectivos (actualmente, más de 900).

Método de recolección de datos: los datos se extraen de los registros de los convenios colectivos y otros reglamentos salariales. Las unidades estadísticas están compuestas por un gran número de puntos bien definidos en los convenios laborales colectivos. Estos puntos representan un nivel de pago contractual para un cierto grupo de funciones, a menudo combinados con indicaciones de antigüedad, edad o capacidades técnicas. Se realiza una encuesta especial para determinar la estructura en el año de base, en la cual se indican los convenios colectivos utilizados y su distribución en los grupos de la población activa. A partir de esta información se hacen estimaciones para cada convenio colectivo pertinente que refleja la distribución de los trabajadores en la estructura salarial y se seleccionan los puntos de mayor densidad para preparar un índice parcial de salarios. En las series actuales se utilizan 8100 puntos de salario establecidos en 354 convenios colectivos, de un total de más de 900. El año de base actual es 1990 y, en principio, la muestra de nivel de pago se revisa cada 10 años.

Procesamiento y verificación de datos

Los datos que se publican en los convenios colectivos se introducen en un sistema informatizado. Para cada convenio colectivo se calcula la evolución a partir del período anterior. Se vuelven a verificar las cifras que están fuera de alcance (muy superior o inferior al promedio). Los resultados también se comparan con toda otra información disponible, por ejemplo datos publicados en periódicos.

Ajustes

Sub-representatividad: los índices mensuales de salarios contractuales, costo de la mano de obra y horas de trabajo pueden cambiar si entran en vigor nuevos convenios laborales colectivos o reglamentos salariales colectivos. Se publica un índice ajustado como mínimo un mes después de que ha entrado en vigor un nuevo convenio laboral colectivo. Las cifras finales para el año *t* se publican a más tardar en mayo del año *t+1*.
Variaciones estacionales: los datos no se ajustan estacionalmente.

Tipos de estimaciones

Índices mensuales y horarios de tasas de salarios contractuales, horas de trabajo y costo de la mano de obra por hora.

Construcción de índices

A los 8100 puntos salariales se atribuye una factor de ponderación para el año de base (1990). Esos factores de ponderación básicos se asignan de acuerdo con la importancia mutua dentro de un convenio o reglamento colectivos. Durante años se mantienen constantes hasta que se actualiza la muestra.

Un segundo tipo de ponderación incluye la ponderación anual de las industrias, preparada a partir de los convenios y reglamentos colectivos. Esta "ponderación externa", basada en datos del Sistema Nacional de Cuentas, tiene en cuenta los cambios ocurridos en el número de asalariados y los costos salariales por actividad económica cada año.

Los índices parciales se calculan al nivel en que las unidades estadísticas se ponderan juntas para obtener índices salariales de Laspeyres para los agregados de la actividad económica. Las series actuales se basan en 1990=100.

Indicadores de fiabilidad de las estimaciones

Alcance del sistema administrativo: la selección de convenios laborales colectivos abarca unos 350 (40% del total), lo que representaba 75% de todos los asalariados en 1990.

Series disponibles

Índices mensuales y horarios de tasas de salarios contractuales, incluidas las primas;
Índices mensuales de horas de trabajo contractuales;
Índices mensuales del costo de la mano de obra horario;
por categoría de asalariado, sector y división de la actividad económica.

Historia de las estadísticas

Fecha de iniciación de la serie estadística: la publicación de esas estadísticas comenzó en 1926; las series de índices de tasas brutas de salarios mensuales y horarios y los índices de horas de trabajo contractuales anuales se han publicado mensualmente desde 1980. La publicación de algunas cifras relativas al costo de la mano de obra horario comenzó en 1990.
Cambios y revisiones principales: las series de índices de tasas de salarios se revisan y mejoran periódicamente. No se han hecho cambios metodológicos en las series cronológicas actuales.
Está prevista una revisión completa de estas estadísticas para 2003.

Documentación y difusión

Documentación:
Oficina de Estadística de los Países Bajos: *Statistisch Bulletin* (Voorburg, semanalmente); en la última publicación de cada mes figuran índices provisionales de tasas de salarios y costo de la mano de obra del mes anterior. Los datos finales se publican a más tardar cinco meses después de finalizado el año de referencia.
Idem: *Sociaal-economische Maandstatistiek* (Voorburg/Heerlen, mensualmente). Los principales cambios metodológicos se anuncian con anterioridad a esta publicación.
Se publica también una descripción metodológica en *Supplement to the Monthly Bulletin of Socio- economic Statistics*, 1993-3 4.
Difusión: en el sitio Internet de CBS: http://www.cbs.nl

Se pueden consultar también notas metodológicas en este sitio.
Datos suministrados a la OIT para su difusión
Se suministran las siguientes estadísticas a la OIT para su publicación en el *Anuario de Estadísticas del Trabajo* :
Índices de tasas de salarios horarios por actividad económica.
Las series mensuales correspondientes se publican en el *Boletín de Estadísticas del Trabajo*.
Otras fuentes administrativas de datos: un gran número de registros administrativos (registro de la población, administración de sistemas de seguros de asalariados, ficheros de agencias de empleo, registros de direcciones y viviendas, etc.) se utiliza en combinación con las encuestas en los establecimientos y las encuestas por muestreo en los hogares para preparar el sistema de información de estadísticas integradas de la Oficina de Estadística de los Países Bajos sobre las características sociodemográficas, socioeconómicas y socioculturales de la población.

Pakistán

Fuente de la serie
Informes administrativos del Gobierno.
Título de la serie
Promedio de salarios por ocupación.
Organismo responsable
Recolección de datos y elaboración estadística: Direcciones de los servicios de Protección del Trabajo (Directorates of Labour Welfare), por intermedio del Gobierno de cada Provincia: Balochistán, Punjab, Sindh, Provincia fronteriza noroccidental (NWFP) e Islamabad.
Temas laborales principales abarcados
Empleo, tasas de salarios, ganancias y horas de trabajo.
Periodicidad o frecuencia de disponibilidad de las estadísticas
Anual.
Período de referencia
Salario por ocupación: un mes.
Alcance de las estadísticas
Ambito geográfico: cada Provincia por separado. Esta descripción sólo se refiere a la Provincia fronteriza noroccidental (NWFP).
Ambito industrial: NWFP: 29 grupos industriales seleccionados.
Establecimientos: establecimientos e industrias abarcadas por la Ley de Industrias (Factories Act) de 1934, y la Ley sobre Salarios (Wages Act), 1936.
Personas cubiertas: empleados abarcados por la Ley de Industrias de 1934, y la Ley sobre Salarios, 1936.
Ocupaciones: NWFP: 76 ocupaciones seleccionadas entre los 29 grupos de industrias.
Conceptos y definiciones
Empleo: los asalariados son personas empleadas por un salario en cualquier proceso manufacturero o por una empresa o establecimiento.
Los trabajadores a tiempo completo son empleados que trabajan el número de horas que establece la ley.
Ganancias: se refieren a las ganancias diarias y mensuales netas, después de deducir las cotizaciones del asalariado a la seguridad social, siempre que esas ganancias sean superiores al límite de 2500.00 Rs. mensuales. En ellas se incluyen los salarios directos en efectivo por tiempo trabajado o trabajo realizado, y los subsidios por costo de la vida, de vivienda y de transporte. Se excluyen los pagos en especie.
Los datos sobre ganancias se recopilan separadamente para los obreros, empleados y trabajadores a tiempo completo.
Tasas de sueldo o salario: se refiere a las tasas de salarios/sueldos diarios y mensuales, incluidos el subsidio por costo de la vida y otros subsidios pagados y garantizados y periódicos, siempre que las tasas sean superiores al límite de 2500.00 Rs mensuales.
Las tasas de salarios/sueldos se recopilan separadamente para los obreros, empleados y trabajadores a tiempo completo.
Horas de trabajo: se refiere a las horas normales de trabajo impuestas por leyes o reglamentos. Se ha establecido que las horas normales de trabajo son 48 horas semanales y 9 horas al día, como se indica en las Secciones 34 y 36 de la Ley de Industrias de 1934, y en la Sección 7 de la Ordenanza para tiendas y establecimientos del Pakistán Occidental de 1969.
Clasificaciones
Ramas de actividad económica:
Título de la clasificación: Clasificación Industrial Uniforme de todas las actividades económicas de Pakistán (PSIC-70).
Número de grupos utilizados para la codificación: 29.
Se aplica a: tasas de salarios y ganancias.
Vínculos con la CIIU y nivel: Rev.2, a nivel de dos y tres dígitos.

Ocupaciones:
Título de la clasificación: Clasificación Uniforme de Ocupaciones de Pakistán (PSCO-68).
Número de grupos utilizados para la codificación: 76.
Se aplica a: tasas de salarios y ganancias.
Vínculos con la CIUO y nivel: CIUO-1968, a nivel de dos y tres dígitos.
Otras clasificaciones: por sexo, nivel de educación y categoría de empleado.
Recolección de datos
Tipo y alcance del sistema administrativo: Estos informes administrativos se limitan a la recopilación de información estadística sobre las ocupaciones preseleccionadas en grupos de industrias preseleccionadas.
Método de recolección de datos: salarios por ocupación: los inspectores de oficinas sobre el terreno de las Direcciones de la Protección del Trabajo recopilan los datos de las fábricas y los establecimientos concernidos.
Procesamiento y verificación de datos
Los datos se procesan manualmente.
Ajustes
Ninguno.
Tipos de estimaciones
Totales de empleo y promedio de tasas de salario, ganancias y horas de trabajo.
Construcción de índices
Ninguno.
Indicadores de fiabilidad de las estimaciones
No se dispone.
Series disponibles
Promedio de tasas de salario, ganancias y horas normales de trabajo por ocupación.
Historia de las estadísticas
Fecha de iniciación de la serie estadística: 1980.
Cambios y revisiones principales: Ninguno.
Documentación y difusión
Documentación: estas estadísticas no se publican en publicaciones nacionales.
Datos suministrados a la OIT para su difusión
Las estadísticas de los promedios de tasas de salarios y horas de trabajo normales se proporcionan a la OIT para su publicación en las *Estadísticas sobre salarios y horas de trabajo por ocupación y precios de artículos alimenticios – Resultados de la Encuesta de octubre.*
Las estadísticas del promedio de ganancias mensuales en el sector manufacturero y los transportes se publican en el *Anuario de Estadísticas del Trabajo.*

Panamá

Fuente de la serie
Planillas de pago de Instituciones de Seguro Social.
Título de la serie
Serie de Empleo.
Organismo responsable
Recolección de datos, elaboración estadística y publicación o difusión de las estadísticas: Dirección de Estadística y Censo, Contraloría General de la República.
Temas laborales principales abarcados
Empleo y ganancias.
Periodicidad o frecuencia de disponibilidad de las estadísticas
Anual.
Período de referencia
El mes de Agosto.
Alcance de las estadísticas
Ambito geográfico: todo el país.
Ambito industrial: todas las ramas de actividad económica.
Establecimientos: establecimientos de todos tipos y tamaños.
Personas cubiertas: asalariados cotizantes del Seguro Social y empleados de Instituciones estatales.
Ocupaciones: no se recogen datos sobre ocupaciones individuales o grupos de ocupaciones.
Conceptos y definiciones
Empleo: todos los asalariados que cotizan en el Seguro Social, es decir todas las personas que trabajan para otra persona o entidad y que reciben remuneración en dinero, siempre y cuando hayan trabajado cualquier día del mes de referencia.
Ganancias: sueldos y salarios brutos mensuales en dinero. Se entiende la retribución que el asalariado recibe por su trabajo en el período de referencia, incluyéndose el pago de horas extras, la remuneración por tiempo no trabajado y las comisiones.
Clasificaciones
Ramas de actividad económica:
Título de la clasificación: Clasificación Industrial Nacional Uniforme de todas las Actividades Económicas.
Número de grupos utilizados para la codificación: 18 categorías.
Se aplica a: empleo y ganancias en las empresas particulares.
Vínculos con la CIIU y nivel: Rev.3 (1990) a todos los niveles.
Ocupaciones:
Título de la clasificación: Clasificación Nacional de Ocupaciones.
Número de grupos utilizados para la codificación: 10 grupos.
Se aplica a: el empleo en las Instituciones Autónomas y las Zonas Bananeras.
Vínculos con la CIUO y nivel: CIUO-1988 a todos los niveles.
Otras clasificaciones: por sexo, tipo de empresas/instituciones y sector.
Recolección de datos
Método de recolección de datos
Los métodos de recolección de datos difieren según el tipo de empleador:
Empresas particulares: los datos se obtienen de las planillas de pagos de cuotas que presentan los patronos a la Caja de Seguro Social. La información se refiere al mes de agosto y su alcance es a nivel central. La recolección y procesamiento de los datos toman aproximadamente cuatro meses.
Zonas Bananeras: la fuente de información la constituyen las planillas de pagos de los asalariados en las Fincas Productoras de Banano en Chiriquí y Bocas del Toro. Su recolección y procesamiento toman aproximadamente dos meses.
Instituciones Autónomas, Semi-autónomas y Municipios: la información se obtiene mediante una planilla especial que se solicita a cada una de las Instituciones y que comprende la ocupación, sexo y salario del personal que labora en las mismas. Su recolección y procesamiento toman aproximadamente cuatro meses.
Gobierno Central: los datos están contenidos en la planilla de pago de los asalariados que prepara la Dirección Nacional de Informática de la Contraloría General. Su procesamiento se realiza aproximadamente en un mes.
Procesamiento y verificación de datos
Los datos se procesan por computadora y se verifican manualmente los rangos de sueldos y salarios.
Ajustes
Ninguno.
Tipos de estimaciones
Totales de empleo asalariado y ganancias, y distribuciones.
Construcción de índices
No se construyen números índices.
Indicadores de fiabilidad de las estimaciones
No se dispone de la información.
Series disponibles
Distribuciones:
Empresas particulares: número de asalariados por sexo y monto de ganancias, según provincia, rama de actividad y sueldo mensual;
Zonas Bananeras: asalariados y monto de ganancias según sueldo mensual, por sexo, según zona y ocupación;
Instituciones autónomas, semi-autónomas y municipios: asalariados por sueldo mensual, según sexo, ocupación e institución;
Gobierno central: asalariados por monto de sueldos y sexo, según ministerio e institución.
Historia de las estadísticas
Fecha de iniciación de la serie estadística: 1958
Cambios y revisiones principales: en el sector de las empresas particulares, a partir del año 1980, la Caja de Seguro Social introdujo cambios en el sistema de pago de las cotizaciones, de trimestral a mensual, en planilla pre-elaborada. Este sistema produce cambios en las cifras, en vista de que los patronos presentan esta planilla a la Institución aunque no hagan el pago correspondiente de la misma. Anteriormente se aceptaba solamente la planilla cancelada.
En las Zonas Bananeras: hasta 1976, para efectos del cálculo del sueldo medio mensual, se incluían todos los asalariados que trabajaron durante el mes de referencia independientemente de los días trabajados. A partir de 1977, se excluyen los asalariados que trabajaron menos de 22 días en el mes, a fin de obtener un sueldo medio mensual más representativo de la actividad.
En el Área del Canal: la transferencia de la administración del Canal de Panamá el 31 de diciembre de 1999 a manos panameñas, trajo como consecuencia un aumento importante en el número de empleados y monto de sueldos y salarios del sector público.

Documentación y difusión

Documentación:

Contraloría General de la República, Dirección de Estadística y Censo: *Situación Social – Estadísticas del Trabajo, Volumen II: Empleo: Sector público y privado* (Panamá, anual); se publica aproximadamente ocho meses después del período de referencia de los datos.

Datos suministrados a la OIT para su difusión: Ninguno; no se publican distribuciones en el Anuario de Estadísticas del Trabajo.

Polinesia Francesa

Fuente de la serie
Seguridad social, Administración fiscal y Representación Francesa.

Título de la serie
Empleo y salarios.

Organismo responsable
Recolección de datos: Fondo de Previsión Social (Caisse de Prévoyance Sociale (CPS)), Alto Comisariado (Haut Commissariat).
Elaboración estadística y publicación o difusión de las estadísticas : Instituto de Estadística de Polinesia Francesa (Institut de la Statistique de Polynésie Française (ISPF).

Temas laborales principales abarcados
Empleo, ganancias, ingresos y horas de trabajo.

Periodicidad o frecuencia de disponibilidad de las estadísticas
Mensual.

Período de referencia
El mes.

Alcance de las estadísticas
Ambito geográfico: todo el territorio (todos los archipiélagos y distritos).
Ambito industrial: todas las ramas de actividad económica.
Establecimientos: de todos tipos y tamaños.
Personas cubiertas: desde 2000, todas las personas con empleo (asalariados y trabajadores por cuenta propia), que deben estar cubiertas por el sistema territorial de la seguridad social, salvo funcionarios públicos franceses que trabajan en la Polinesia Francesa.
Antes de 2000, los trabajadores independientes que habían elegido tener un seguro social privado estaban excluidos del sistema y de las estadísticas, así como los funcionarios públicos franceses que trabajaban en la Polinesia Francesa.
Ocupaciones: los datos no se recopilan por ocupación ni grupo ocupacional.

Conceptos y definiciones
Empleo: para los fines de las estadísticas, en la definición de persona con empleo se incluyen los asalariados y los trabajadores independientes (por cuenta propia) cubiertos por el sistema territorial de seguridad social obligatorio, cuyos ingresos son superiores al salario mínimo.
Los trabajadores a tiempo completo son los que cumplen todo el horario de trabajo legal (169 horas al mes). Los trabajadores a tiempo parcial son los que trabajan menos horas que las establecidas en el horario legal.
Los trabajadores jóvenes, de 16 a 18 años, se pueden identificar por separado.
Ganancias: ganancias brutas mensuales en efectivo superiores al salario mínimo, incluidos pagos por horas extraordinarias que se pueden identificar separadamente en base a los datos sobre las horas de trabajo. El importe de ganancias informadas se limita al máximo fijado para las cotizaciones de seguridad social.
Horas de trabajo: horas pagadas, incluidas horas extraordinarias, según las declaraciones del empleador.
Ingresos relacionados con el empleo remunerado: no se aplica. Como en la Polinesia Francesa no se aplica el impuesto sobre la renta, no se declaran todos los componentes de los ingresos.
Ingresos relacionados con el empleo independiente: en principio, ingresos netos después de deducir el consumo de capital fijo. En la práctica, el ingreso de los trabajadores por cuenta propia se refiere al total del valor de ventas después de deducir todas las cargas relativas a la actividad económica. El ingreso informado se limita al ingreso superior al salario mínimo y al ingreso máximo establecido para las cotizaciones de seguridad social.

Clasificaciones
Ramas de actividad económica:
Título de la clasificación: Nomenclature des activités françaises (NAF).
Número de grupos utilizados para la codificación: 4 grupos, 17 secciones, 31 subsecciones, 60 divisiones, y 697 cargos.
Se aplica a: todos los datos recopilados.

Vínculos con la CIIU y nivel: sí.
Situación en el empleo: asalariados y trabajadores por cuenta propia.
Otras clasificaciones: el empleo y las ganancias/ingresos se clasifican de acuerdo con el sexo, el grupo de edad, las horas de trabajo y la ubicación del empleador (archipiélago o distrito). Los datos de empleo también se distribuyen de acuerdo con los niveles de ingresos.

Recolección de datos
Tipo y alcance del sistema administrativo: no se dispone.
Método de recolección de datos: los empleadores comunican mensualmente a la seguridad soial territorial los datos sobre el empleo y los ingresos de las personas aseguradas. Esos datos se transmiten trimestralmente al Instituto de Estadística, dentro de los tres meses después del trimestre de declaración.
Actualización del sistema administrativo: continuamente.

Procesamiento y verificación de datos
Los datos se procesan por computadora y se hacen verificaciones de congruencia sobre los niveles de salarios, horas de trabajo, grupos de edad, etc.

Ajustes
Ninguno.

Tipos de estimaciones
Empleo: totales y distribuciones;
Ganancias/Ingresos: totales, promedios y distribuciones.

Construcción de índices
Ninguno.

Indicadores de fiabilidad de las estimaciones
Alcance del sistema administrativo: un 99 por ciento de todas las personas con empleo desde que entró en vigor la nueva legislación a fines de 2001, con carácter retroactivo al 2000.
Errores no relacionados con el muestreo: No se dispone.
Conformidad con otras fuentes: se hacen algunas comparaciones con los resultados del censo de la población y otras con los resultados de la última encuesta sobre el presupuesto familiar (2001).

Series disponibles
Número de asalariados clasificado por sexo, grupo de edad, nivel de ganancias, actividad económica, sector de actividad, ubicación del empleador (archipiélago o distrito), situación jurídica del empleador, número de horas trabajadas;
Promedio de ganancias mensuales clasificado por sexo, grupo de edad, actividad económica, sector de actividad, ubicación del empleador (archipiélago o distrito), situación jurídica del empleador y número de horas trabajadas;
Promedio de ganancias por hora clasificado por sexo, grupo de edad, actividad económica, sector de actividad, ubicación del empleador (archipiélago o distrito) y situación jurídica del empleador.
Todas las series están disponibles mensual y anualmente, y están sometidas a las normas de confidencialidad de la información.

Historia de las estadísticas
Fecha de iniciación de la serie estadística: 1987 para la mayor parte de las series, y 1995 para todas las series disponibles.
Cambios y revisiones principales: antes de 1995, la seguridad social recopilaba los datos sobre el empleo y los ingresos y presentaba un informe global sobre esos datos. Desde 1995, se puede obtener información mensual detallada sobre cada persona asegurada.

Documentación y difusión
Documentación: no está disponible antes de 2003.
Difusión: en el sitio Internet: http://www.ispf.pf
Se puede obtener, previa solicitud, la información que no figura en el sitio Internet.

Datos suministrados a la OIT para su difusión
Las siguientes estadísticas se publican en el *Anuario de Estadísticas del Trabajo*: Promedio anual de empleo asalariado.

Santa Elena

Fuente de la serie
Declaraciones fiscales y registros administrativos.

Título de la serie
Empleo, tasas de salarios, ganancias y horas de trabajo.

Organismo responsable
Recolección de datos, elaboración estadística y publicación o difusión de las estadísticas:
Oficina de Estadística, Departamento del Desarrollo y de la Planificación económica (Statistics Office, Development and Economic Planning Department).

Temas laborales principales abarcados
Empleo, tasas de salarios y sueldos, ganancias, horas de trabajo e ingresos del trabajo independiente.
Periodicidad o frecuencia de disponibilidad de las estadísticas
Anual.
Período de referencia
El año (de abril a marzo).
Alcance de las estadísticas
Ambito geográfico: toda la isla.
Ambito industrial: todas las actividades económicas.
Establecimientos: de todos tipos y tamaños.
Personas cubiertas: todas las personas con empleo.
Ocupaciones: se recopilan datos sobre tasas de salarios y horas de trabajo por ocupación.
Conceptos y definiciones
Empleo: se refiere a todas las personas que reciben ingresos por un empleo asalariado a tiempo completo o a tiempo parcial y por un trabajo independiente.
Los trabajadores adultos son personas que tienen 15 años de edad y más.
Los trabajadores a tiempo completo son personas que trabajan un promedio de 36,25 horas por semana.
Ganancias: se refiere al total anual de remuneración en efectivo según se informa a las autoridades fiscales, es decir las ganancias brutas en efectivo, incluidos los salarios directos y todos los bonos, subsidios y compensaciones en efectivo.
Tasas de sueldo o salario: se refiere al sueldo y salario básico.
Horas de trabajo: se refiere a las horas normales de trabajo semanales como establecen las leyes o los reglamentos: 35 horas para los trabajadores pagados mensualmente y 37,5 horas para los trabajadores pagados semanalmente.
Ingresos relacionados con el empleo remunerado: véase en Ganancias.
Ingresos relacionados con el empleo independiente: se refiere al beneficio bruto en efectivo generado por las actividades realizadas por trabajadores independientes, después de hacer las deducciones de consumo de capital fijo.
Clasificaciones
Ramas de actividad económica:
Título de la clasificación: no se dispone.
Número de grupos utilizados para la codificación: 17 categorías de tabulación.
Se aplica a: todos los datos.
Vínculos con la CIIU y nivel: Rev. 3 (1990).
Ocupaciones:
Título de la clasificación: no se dispone.
Número de grupos utilizados para la codificación: nueve grupos principales.
Se aplica a: todos los datos.
Vínculos con la CIUO y nivel: CIUO-88.
Situación en el empleo: asalariados y trabajadores independientes.
Otras clasificaciones: por sexo. Las tasas de salarios de trabajadores gubernamentales también se clasifican según el nivel de calificación.
Recolección de datos
Tipo y alcance del sistema administrativo: abarca todas las declaraciones fiscales de la población ocupada y algunos registros gubernamentales.
Método de recolección de datos: recopilación de datos a partir de los registros fiscales y de otros registros administrativos. Los datos sobre las tasas de salarios e ingresos se obtienen del Departamento de Finanzas.
Actualización del sistema administrativo: anualmente.
Procesamiento y verificación de datos
Los datos se procesan por computadora; se hacen tabulaciones cruzadas de diferentes variables y varias verificaciones de la base de datos informatizada.
Ajustes
Ninguno.
Tipos de estimaciones
Total del número de personas ocupadas, promedio semanal y mensual de tasas de salarios y sueldos, promedio de ganancias mensuales y promedio de horas de trabajo normales semanales.
Construcción de índices
Ninguno.
Indicadores de fiabilidad de las estimaciones
Alcance del sistema administrativo: exhaustiva.
Series disponibles
Número de personas ocupadas por sector y categoría (asalariados y trabajadores independientes);

Promedio de ganancias mensuales;
Promedio de tasas de salarios por nivel de calificación y por ocupación;
Horas de trabajo normales.
Historia de las estadísticas
Fecha de iniciación de la serie estadística: no se dispone.
Cambios y revisiones principales: ninguno.
Documentación y difusión
Documentación:
Statistics Office: *Statistical Yearbook* (Jamestown, anual); se publica casi un año después del período de referencia de las estadísticas.
Difusión: los datos que no figuran en las publicaciones nacionales se pueden obtener previa solicitud.
Datos suministrados a la OIT para su difusión
Las estadísticas del promedio de ganancias mensuales por actividad económica y por sexo se publican en el *Anuario de Estadísticas del Trabajo*.
Las estadísticas de las horas normales de trabajo y el promedio de las tasas de salarios por ocupación se publican en las *Estadísticas sobre salarios y horas de trabajo por ocupación y precios de artículos domésticos – Resultados de la Encuesta de octubre.*

Seychelles

Fuente de la serie
Registros del sistema de seguridad social y declaraciones del Gobierno y de oficinas autónomas.
Título de la serie
Empleo formal y promedio de ganancias mensuales de asalariados en el sector formal.
Organismo responsable
Recolección de datos, elaboración estadística y publicación o difusión de las estadísticas: Ministry of Information Technology & Communication, Management & Information Systems Division, Statistics and Database Administration Section (Sección de Administración de Estadísticas y Bases de Datos de la División de Sistemas de Gestión e Información del Ministerio de Información, Tecnología y Comunicación).
Temas laborales principales abarcados
Empleo y ganancias.
Periodicidad o frecuencia de disponibilidad de las estadísticas
Semestral.
Período de referencia
Empleo: el último día de trabajo de cada mes de los períodos comprendidos entre enero y junio y enero y diciembre;
Ganancias: todo el mes.
Alcance de las estadísticas
Ambito geográfico: todo el país.
Ambito industrial: todas las ramas de actividad económica. Se pueden obtener datos por separado de cada uno de los sectores (público, autónomo y privado) y de los tres sectores juntos.
Establecimientos: todos los tipos y tamaños de establecimientos formales afiliados al sistema de seguridad social.
Personas cubiertas: empleados oficialmente empleados y afiliados al sistema de seguridad social. Se excluyen los trabajadores domésticos en viviendas privadas, trabajadores familiares y personas que trabajan por cuenta propia.
Ocupaciones: los datos no se recopilan por ocupación ni grupo ocupacional.
Conceptos y definiciones
Empleo: se refiere a las personas que ocupan un empleo formal y cotizan al sistema de seguridad social.
Ganancias: se refieren al promedio bruto de ingresos mensuales, incluidos los pagos de horas extraordinarias, bonificaciones y subsidios, pagos de licencia anual e indemnizaciones por despido.
Clasificaciones
Ramas de actividad económica:
Título de la clasificación: no se dispone.
Número de grupos utilizados para la codificación: 13.
Se aplica a: empleo y ganancias.
Vínculos con la CIIU y nivel: no es totalmente compatible con la Rev.2 o la Rev.3.
Otras clasificaciones: por sector (privado, autónomo y público).
Recolección de datos
Tipo y alcance del sistema administrativo: abarca todos los empleados formales.
Método de recolección de datos: los datos se obtienen de las declaraciones a la seguridad social del sector privado y las de oficinas autónomas y gubernamentales recopiladas por la Sección de

Administración de Estadísticas y Bases de Datos de la División de Sistemas de Gestión e Información.
Actualización del sistema administrativo: continuamente.

Procesamiento y verificación de datos
Los datos se registran y procesan por computadora en el sistema EXCEL.

Ajustes
Ninguno.

Tipos de estimaciones
Totales y promedios de empleados y promedio de ganancias brutas mensuales.

Construcción de índices
Ninguno.

Indicadores de fiabilidad de las estimaciones
Alcance del sistema administrativo: se supone que sea exhaustiva en función de los empleados formales.
Conformidad con otras fuentes: los datos de los sectores público y autónomo se verifican en comparación con los registros que mantienen los establecimientos gubernamentales.

Series disponibles
Series mensuales y anuales del empleo formal y promedio de ganancias mensuales por rama de actividad y sector.

Historia de las estadísticas
Fecha de iniciación de la serie estadística: 1975.
Cambios y revisiones principales: desde 1 de enero de 1988, los asalariados del sector formal están libres de impuestos sobre la renta. Por consiguiente los datos de ganancias desde 1988 no se pueden comparar con los de los años anteriores.

Documentación y difusión
Documentación:
Ministry of Information Technology & Communication, Management & Information Systems Division: *Statistical Bulletin* (Mahe, semestral); Idem: *Statistical Abstract* (anual).
No existen publicaciones metodológicas.
Difusión: los datos sobre el empleo se pueden obtener en el sitio Internet de la División de Sistemas de Gestión e Información: http://www.seychelles.net/misdstat

Datos suministrados a la OIT para su difusión
Los siguientes datos se suministran a la OIT para su publicación en el *Anuario de Estadísticas del Trabajo*:
Empleo remunerado por rama de actividad económica;
Promedio mensual de ganancias de empleados formales, por rama de actividad económica.
Las estadísticas mensuales correspondientes se publican en el *Boletín de Estadísticas del Trabajo*.

Singapur

Fuente de la serie
Informes sobre cotizaciones al Fondo Central de Previsión (Central Provident Fund-CPF).

Título de la serie
Promedio de ganancias mensuales.

Organismo responsable
Recolección de datos y elaboración estadística : Junta del Fondo Central de Previsión (Central Provident Fund Board).
Publicación o difusión de las estadísticas: Manpower Research and Statistics Department, Ministry of Manpower (Departamento de Investigaciones y Estadísticas del Trabajo del Ministerio del Trabajo), y Department of Statistics, Ministry of Trade and Industry (Departamento de Estadística del Ministerio de Comercio y la Industria).

Temas laborales principales abarcados
Ganancias y asalariados.

Periodicidad o frecuencia de disponibilidad de las estadísticas
Trimestralmente.

Período de referencia
Cada mes del trimestre.

Alcance de las estadísticas
Ambito geográfico: todo el país.
Ambito industrial: todas las ramas de actividad económica.
Establecimientos: todos los tipos y tamaños de los sectores público y privado.
Personas cubiertas: todos los asalariados residentes, es decir ciudadanos singapurenses y residentes permanentes que contribuyen al CPF.
Ocupaciones: los datos no se recopilan por ocupación ni grupo ocupacional.

Conceptos y definiciones
Empleo: asalariado es toda persona empleada en Singapur o marinero singapurense empleado de conformidad con un contrato de servicio u otro acuerdo concertado en el país. Se incluyen:
- directores asalariados de empresas,
- asalariados a tiempo parcial o temporeros con salarios superiores a $50 mensuales,
- todos los jóvenes que han terminado sus estudios o estudiantes que trabajan a tiempo parcial o temporal (salvo estudiantes de nivel terciario incorporados a una actividad económica a tiempo completo, estudiantes empleados en el marco de un programa de formación aprobado por sus instituciones y estudiantes que trabajan durante las vacaciones escolares),
- personal militar en reserva,
- extranjeros que pasaron a ser residentes permanentes del país.
Se excluyen todos los extranjeros con visa de empleo o de visita profesional, socios, propietarios únicos y personas que trabajan por cuenta propia o que trabajan en el extranjero.
Ganancias: el promedio de ganancias brutas mensuales se refiere al total de remuneración en efectivo debido u otorgado a los asalariados con respecto a su empleo, antes de las deducciones para las cotizaciones al CPF e impuestos sobre la renta personales. Se incluyen salario básico, pago de horas extraordinarias, comisiones, subsidios (por ejemplo, asistencia, costo de vida, trabajos sucios, educación, vacaciones, hogar, maternidad, comidas, productividad, servicios, subsidios en reserva), licencias pagadas y otros pagos monetarios, salarios anuales suplementarios y diversos bonos. Se excluyen el valor de los pagos en especie y las cotizaciones de los empleadores al CPF.

Clasificaciones
Ramas de actividad económica:
Título de la clasificación: Clasificación Industrial Uniforme de Singapur (SSIC) 2000.
Número de grupos utilizados para la codificación: 54.
Se aplica a: ganancias y distribución de asalariados.
Vínculos con la CIIU y nivel: Rev.3 (1990) a nivel de 3 dígitos.
Situación en el empleo: asalariados únicamente.
Otras clasificaciones: ganancias: por sexo; distribución de asalariados: por sexo y grupo de edad.

Recolección de datos
Tipo y alcance del sistema administrativo: en 2001, más de 80 000 empleadores contribuyeron al CPF en nombre de más de 1 200 000 asalariados.
Método de recolección de datos: las estadísticas del promedio de ganancias mensuales se basan en los informes sobre las deducciones para las cotizaciones a la seguridad social y los ahorros que por ley cada empleador debe enviar al CPF. Cada mes, los empleadores deben declarar las ganancias de cada asalariado y enviar sus cotizaciones 14 días después de finalizar el mes para el cual se deben y se pagan las cotizaciones. Se pueden hacer pagos manuales y electrónicos. Los datos de ganancias son recopilados luego por el CPF mensualmente y procesados dos meses después del período de referencia. Las estadísticas trimestrales del promedio de ganancias mensuales se basan en el promedio de los tres meses.
Actualización del sistema administrativo: continua; con el sistema informatizado del CPF se detectan los errores de los empleadores y se hace una lista de ellos cada mes para que los funcionarios de los Servicios de Empleadores (Employer Services Officers) tomen las medidas de seguimiento pertinentes. Se realizan también verificaciones puntuales sobre los registros de salarios de los empleadores, por rama de actividad económica, para determinar el nivel de conformidad de los empleadores a las normas y reglamentos del CPF.

Procesamiento y verificación de datos
Los datos se procesan por computadora.
No se dispone de información sobre las verificaciones de congruencia que se pueden realizar.

Ajustes
Ninguno.

Tipos de estimaciones
Los promedios de ganancias mensuales se calculan dividiendo la suma de las ganancias mensuales de todos los contribuyentes activos del CPF (asalariados) entre el número de contribuyentes activos (asalariados). Las estadísticas trimestrales se basan en el promedio de los tres meses.
El promedio de ganancias mensuales reales corresponde a la división de las ganancias nominales (efectuando una deflación) por el índice de precios al consumidor del año correspondiente (en la actualidad, con base en noviembre de 1997-octubre de 1998=100).

Construcción de índices
Ninguno.
Indicadores de fiabilidad de las estimaciones
Alcance del sistema administrativo: se supone que abarca todos los residentes asalariados.
Series disponibles
Series trimestrales y anuales del promedio de ganancias mensuales por actividad económica y sexo.
Series anuales del promedio de ganancias reales mensuales por actividad económica y sexo.
Distribución anual de los contribuyentes al CPF por nivel de salario mensual (al final del año), grupo de edad y actividad económica.
Historia de las estadísticas
Fecha de iniciación de la serie estadística: 1981.
Cambios y revisiones principales: antes de 1992, las estadísticas del promedio de ganancias incluían las personas que trabajaban por cuenta propia y que contribuían de manera voluntaria con el CPF. Desde 1992, en los datos se excluyen todas las personas que trabajan por cuenta propia.
Desde 1998, los datos de ganancias del CPF por actividad económica se compilan utilizando los niveles de clasificación a dígitos, en lugar de 4 dígitos. A partir de esa fecha, las estadísticas no se comparan de manera rigurosa con las estadísticas de años anteriores.
Antes de 1998, las estadísticas se clasificaban de acuerdo con la Clasificación Industrial Uniforme de Singapur (SSIC) 1990; entre 1998 y 2000, de acuerdo con la SSIC 1996; y desde 2001, de acuerdo con la SSIC 2000.
Documentación y difusión
Documentación:
Ministry of Manpower, Manpower Research and Statistics Department: *Singapore Yearbook of Manpower Statistics* (anual, Singapur); se publica cinco meses después del año de referencia de las estadísticas;
Idem: *Report on Wages in Singapore* (anual), se publica seis meses después del año de referencia de las estadísticas.
Ministry of Trade and Industry, Department of Statistics (Statistics Singapore): *Monthly Digest of Statistics* (Singapur) (mensual, ibid.); se publica tres meses después del trimestre de referencia;
Idem: *Yearbook of Statistics Singapore* (anual, ibid.); se publica cinco meses después del año de referencia de las estadísticas.
No se publica información metodológica.
Difusión: a través de los siguientes sitios Internet:
Ministry of Manpower, Manpower Research and Statistics Department: http://www.gov.sg/mom/manpower/manrs/manrs.htm
Ministry of Trade and Industry, Statistics Singapore:
http://www.singstat.gov.sg
Se puede obtener información sobre las definiciones de asalariados y salarios, así como sobre los procedimientos utilizados por el CPF en el sitio Internet del CPF: http://www.cpf.gov.sg
Datos suministrados a la OIT para su difusión
Las siguientes estadísticas se publican en el *Anuario* y *Boletín de Estadísticas del Trabajo*:
Promedio de ganancias mensuales por actividad económica y (anualmente) sexo.
Otras fuentes administrativas de datos: estadísticas de empleo se compilan mensualmente a partir de registros administrativos de varios organismos gubernamentales.

Suiza

Fuente de la serie
Declaraciones de accidentes registrados por el Service de centralisation des statistiques de l'assurance-accidents (SSAA).
Título de la serie
Índice suizo de salarios;
Duración normal de trabajo en las empresas (DNT).
Organismo responsable
Recolección de datos: Service de centralisation des statistiques de l'assurance-accidents (SSAA).
Elaboración estadística y publicación o difusión de las estadísticas: Oficina Federal de Estadística (OFS).
Temas laborales principales abarcados
Tasas de salarios y duración normal de trabajo.
Periodicidad o frecuencia de disponibilidad de las estadísticas
Anual.
Período de referencia
El año civil.
Alcance de las estadísticas
Ambito geográfico: todo el país.

Ambito industrial: todos los sectores de la actividad económica, incluidas la horticultura y la silvicultura, pero se excluyen la agricultura, la caza y los servicios anexos, y la pesca.
Establecimientos: establecimientos y empresas de todos los tipos y tamaños.
Personas cubiertas: asalariados a tiempo completo, excluidos los cuadros medios y superiores.
La población de referencia corresponde al "concepto interior" del mercado de trabajo: personas que ejercen una actividad en una unidad de producción implantada en el territorio suizo, domiciliadas en Suiza o en el extranjero (por ejemplo, trabajadores fronterizos).
Ocupaciones: los datos no se recopilan por profesión ni grupos de profesiones, sino según el nivel de calificaciones (véase en "Clasificaciones").
Conceptos y definiciones
Empleo: las estadísticas se refieren a los asalariados a tiempo completo, accidentados, asegurados por la Caisse nationale suisse d'assurance-accidents (Suva, antigua CNA), o los seguros privados.
En principio, las estadísticas no abarcan los asalariados a tiempo parcial, los que tienen una reducción del horario de trabajo ni los cuadros medios y superiores.
Tasas de sueldo o salario: se refieren a las tasas realmente pagadas. La definición utilizada para el cálculo del índice abarca los siguientes componentes: salario bruto de base, subsidios por el encarecimiento de la vida y decimotercero mes de salario. Se recopilan datos sobre primas y comisiones, subsidios familiares, gratificaciones y pagos en especie, pero se excluyen de los cálculos. Cuando el salario supera el monto máximo garantizado (es decir CHF 8 900 mensuales al 1° de enero de 2000), sólo se tiene en cuenta el valor máximo (véase también "Ajustes").
Los datos se recopilan separadamente para asalariados a tiempo completo y a tiempo parcial, aprendices y por sexo.
Horas de trabajo: duración semanal normal del trabajo practicada en las empresas y válida en un intervalo de varios meses o años. Corresponde en principio a la duración individual del trabajo de los asalariados a tiempo completo, sin tener en cuenta las horas suplementarias, las reducciones de horarios y otras ausencias. Puede ser establecida por ley o reglamentos, convenios colectivos o reglamentos internos de las empresas o establecimientos, como se estipula en el contrato de trabajo de los asalariados.
Los datos se recopilan separadamente para asalariados a tiempo completo y a tiempo parcial, aprendices y por sexo.
Clasificaciones
Ramas de actividad económica:
Título de la clasificación: Nomenclatura general de las actividades económicas de 1995 (NOGA), desde 1991.
Número de grupos utilizados para la codificación: a nivel nacional, las estadísticas se desagregan por clase (nivel de dos cifras) y división económica (nivel de una cifra); a nivel cantonal: por división económica.
Se aplica a: duración normal del trabajo e índices de salarios.
Vínculos con la CIIU y nivel: la NOGA se basa en la NACE, Rev.1, y es compatible con la CIIU, Rév.3.
Otras clasificaciones: salarios: nivel de calificación (trabajadores calificados, semicalificados y no calificados); sexo; ámbito de actividad (explotación, oficina y técnica (totalidad) y venta); sector (primario: horticultura y silvicultura; secundario y terciario); así como clasificaciones cruzadas por cantón y región.
Duración del trabajo: por cantón y región, y clasificaciones cruzadas por cantón y sector económico.
Recolección de datos
Tipo y alcance del sistema administrativo: el Service de centralisation des statistiques de l'assurance-accidents (SSAA) recibe más de 300 000 declaraciones de accidente al año.
Método de recolección de datos: las declaraciones de accidentes son formularios completados por los accidentados o sus empleadores, en los que figuran unas veinte variables (sector económico, sexo, calificación, ámbito de actividad, modo de remuneración, días de trabajo, edad, lugar de domicilio y de trabajo del empleado accidentado, tipo de accidente, etc.), informaciones sobre el salario de la persona accidentada y duración normal del trabajo en la empresa que lo emplea. Estos formularios se transmiten a la OFS, por intermedio del SSAA, a través de medios informatizados y de manera anónima.
En las estadísticas sobre la evolución de los salarios, las principales variables de la selección de los datos son: nivel de calificación, duración del trabajo (asalariados a tiempo completo), edad (hombres: 19 a 65 años; mujeres: 19 a 63 años) y el ámbito de actividad.
Actualización del sistema administrativo: continuamente.

Procesamiento y verificación de datos

El SSAA se encarga del registro informatizado y los controles de credibilidad de las informaciones recopiladas basadas en las declaraciones de accidentes.

La OFS procede a la extrapolación de los resultados:

La duración normal del trabajo, a nivel de una sección, un sector económico o del total, se calcula con ayuda de un sistema de ponderación, basado en el censo federal de las empresas de 1995 y 1998. Cada división económica de cada cantón recibe un coeficiente de ponderación. Este procedimiento permite calcular los valores agregados en función de las estructuras del empleo propias de cada cantón y cada región.

Los siguientes datos se utilizan para calcular las ponderaciones actuales de las estadísticas de los salarios: empleos a tiempo completo obtenidos en el censo de las empresas (RFE) de 1991; número de personas activas a tiempo completo obtenido del censo de la población (RFP) de 1990; personal de explotación de la encuesta de octubre (LOK) de 1991 sobre los salarios y tratamientos; y datos del SSAA de 1991 sobre los asalariados según el tipo de accidente.

Las declaraciones de accidentes procedentes de algunos grupos de asalariados no son, en cifras, proporcionales a la importancia de esos grupos en el universo observado (por ejemplo, en la construcción y la ingeniería). En consecuencia, los grupos de trabajadores se ponderan en función de su importancia relativa en ese universo, lo que permite evitar distorsiones en la presentación de la evolución macroeconómica de los salarios.

Ajustes

Sub-representatividad: estadísticas sobre la evolución de los salarios: para algunos grupos de asalariados – por ejemplo, personas calificadas de las clases económicas "química", "bancos" y "administraciones públicas", los salarios desconocidos, superiores al monto de ingresos máximos garantizados, representan en permanencia una parte relativamente importante, situada entre el 5 y el 15% del número total de indicaciones de salarios de esos grupos. En ese caso, los salarios declarados se corrigen o extrapolan. El método de corrección o de extrapolación se basa en la hipótesis de que en realidad los salarios se desglosan según una distribución logarítmica normal.

Tipos de estimaciones

Promedio anual de la duración semanal normal del trabajo, ponderado por el número de empleos;

Índices anuales, nominales y reales, de la evolución de los salarios.

La duración media del trabajo corresponde a la media de todas las semanas de un año civil.

Los índices anuales de los salarios se calculan a partir de las declaraciones de accidentes en todo el año.

Para resolver el problema de la influencia de las variaciones de la duración del trabajo en la evolución de los salarios horarios, el salario horario se relaciona con la duración semanal individual del trabajo de cada asegurado y se convierte en ingresos mensuales.

Construcción de índices

La evolución de los salarios nominales se calcula con el índice de Laspeyres de estructura constante (asalariados de grupos homogéneos en el año de base), que mide las variaciones de salarios relativos a un trabajo de tipo constante (evolución pura de los salarios). No se tienen en cuenta las variaciones salariales que se deben al aumento de la proporción de las personas calificadas o al desplazamiento de los trabajadores hacia sectores económicos que pagan, en promedio, salarios más altos. El índice se calcula actualmente para el año de base de 1993=100.

La evolución de los salarios reales se mide efectuando una deflación del índice de salarios nominales por el índice de precios al consumo.

Indicadores de fiabilidad de las estimaciones

Alcance del sistema administrativo: exhaustivo. Todos los asalariados están obligados a tener un seguro de accidentes.

Errores no relacionados con el muestreo: duración normal y salarios: el sistema de ponderación se debe adaptar siempre a los resultados de los últimos censos de las empresas, de manera que no es posible analizar la evolución a largo plazo.

Evolución de los salarios: las estadísticas tienen el defecto de excluir los asalariados a tiempo parcial, así como los cuadros medios y superiores (que están cubiertos en las declaraciones de accidentes, pero que no se incluyen en los cálculos estadísticos).

Conformidad con otras fuentes: duración normal del trabajo: los resultados de las estadísticas se comparan con otros indicadores sobre la duración del trabajo, tales como las Estadísticas del volumen de trabajo (SVOLTA): la comparación da resultados prácticamente idénticos en cuanto se refiere a los asalariados a tiempo completo.

También se hacen comparaciones con otras encuestas que proporcionan información sobre la duración del trabajo efectuado, como el censo federal de la población, la encuesta suiza sobre la población activa (ESPA), la encuesta sobre la estructura de los salarios y las estadísticas de los convenios colectivos de trabajo.

Series disponibles

Para los años anteriores al año actual: índices oficiales y evolución de los salarios a nivel de toda la economía, así como por sector económico, sexo, nivel de calificación y/o ámbito de actividad:

Índice de salarios nominales y reales, por sexo y total, por división y sector económico, ámbito de actividad y nivel de calificación, y variación con respecto al año anterior;

Índice de salarios nominales, total, por clase económica y variación con respecto al año anterior;

Índice de salarios nominales y reales y variaciones en porcentaje, por categorías de trabajadores (obreros, empleados, sexo, categorías).

Para el año en curso: evolución de los salarios al nivel agregado más alto.

Duración semanal normal del trabajo en las empresas y variaciones con respecto al año anterior en cifras absolutas y en porcentajes, por clase económica;

Duración semanal normal del trabajo y variaciones, por cantón, región y división económica.

Historia de las estadísticas

Fecha de iniciación de la serie estadística: estadísticas sobre la duración normal del trabajo en las empresas y la evolución de los salarios: 1918, en el sector secundario únicamente. Desde 1985, con la entrada en vigor en 1984 de la nueva ley sobre seguros de accidentes (LAA) que somete a todos los trabajadores a la obligación de asegurarse, estas estadísticas abarcan todos los sectores, salvo la agricultura, la caza y la pesca.

Cambios y revisiones principales: estadísticas sobre la evolución de los salarios: hasta 1993, la cifras oficiales se obtenían de la Encuesta de octubre sobre los salarios y tratamientos. Desde 1994, las estadísticas actuales constituyen la fuente de datos oficiales.

A partir de 1991, la versión de 1995 (NOGA) de la Nomenclature générale des activités économiques sustituyó la versión de 1985.

Antes de 1995, la explotación de los datos recopilados sobre la duración normal del trabajo y los salarios, así como la publicación de los resultados, era una labor de la Office Fédéral de l'industrie, des arts et métiers et du travail (OFIAMT) (actualmente Office Fédéral du développement économique et de l'emploi - OFDE). A partir de esa fecha, la OFS realiza esa tarea.

Actualmente se realiza una revisión de las estadísticas de la evolución de los salarios, mediante la cual se trata sobre todo de lograr los siguientes objetivos: i) tener en cuenta los asalariados a tiempo parcial; y ii) introducir un indicador coyuntural trimestral.

Documentación y difusión

Documentación:

OFS: *Durée normale du travail dans les entreprises. Résultats commentés et tableaux* (Berna, anual);

Idem: *Communiqué de presse: statistique du volume du travail* (ibid.); publicación ocasional;

Idem: *Communiqué de presse: Heures de travail en 2000* (Neuchâtel, febrero de 2002);

Idem: *La statistique du volume du travail. Bases méthodologiques et définitions* (Berna, 1997);

Idem: *Indicateurs du marché du travail* (anual).

Département fédéral de l'économie publique: *La Vie économique* (Berna, mensual);

OFS: *La nouvelle statistique de l'évolution des salaires. Conception et résultats 1994* (Berna, 1995);

Idem: *Evolution des salaires. Résultats commentés et tableaux* (Neuchâtel, anual).

Idem: *Communiqué de presse: Indice suisse des salaires 2001* (Neuchâtel, abril de 2002).

Difusión: en el sitio Internet de la OFS:

http://www.statistique.admin.ch

Se pueden obtener, previa solicitud, las estadísticas que no figuran en las publicaciones nacionales o en Internet.

Datos suministrados a la OIT para su difusión

Las estadísticas siguientes se publicaron en el *Anuario de Estadísticas del Trabajo* y se encuentran en la base de datos LABORSTA:

Duración semanal normal de asalariados, por sector de la actividad económica (hasta 1993); y en las industrias manufactureras;

Ganancias de los obreros (hasta 1983) por sector de la actividad económica (sector secundario).

Otras fuentes administrativas de datos:
Las *Estadísticas de convenios colectivos de trabajo en Suiza* (ECS) se realizan cada dos años, el 1º de mayo, desde 1992. El objetivo de estas estadísticas es preparar un repertorio exhaustivo y detallado de los convenios colectivos de trabajo (CCT) y de contratos-tipo de trabajo (CTT) en Suiza. La encuesta se realiza directamente ante las partes contratantes de un CCT, es decir los asociados patronales o empresas y las asociaciones de trabajadores signatarios de un convenio. Las principales características estructurales que se desprenden son el sector económico, el tipo de convenio colectivo, el campo de aplicación territorial, los firmantes, la fecha de entrada en vigor, la cuestión de la paz laboral y número de personas incluidas (empleadores y asalariados) por sexo.

La *Encuesta anual sobre los acuerdos salariales* (EAS) en los ámbitos abarcados por un convenio colectivo de trabajo da cuenta de los resultados de las negociaciones entabladas entre las partes sociales sobre las adaptaciones de los salarios efectivos y los mínimos en el ámbito de los convenios colectivos de trabajo.

El *Registro central de extranjeros* (RCE) suministra indicadores mensuales sobre el número de extranjeros activos ocupados en los diversos sectores de la actividad económica, según el sexo y el tipo de permiso.

Las *estadísticas del personal docente y de asalariados del sector de la salud* contienen información sobre los trabajadores y la evolución del personal en ambos sectores.

En las *estadísticas sobre conflictos colectivos laborales*, realizadas por la OFDE, se recopila información sobre las huelgas de carácter económico que duran como mínimo un día. Se basan en la información obtenida de la prensa cotidiana, que conduce a los empleadores y a las asociaciones económicas concernidas. Estas últimas deben completar un cuestionario en el que suministran información sobre los siguientes aspectos: tipo de conflicto (huelga o cierre de la empresa), causa del conflicto, número de asalariados concernidos, duración de la medida, horas de trabajo no realizadas, sector económico, número de empresas concernidas y manera como se resolvió el conflicto.

Se prepararan también *estadísticas de síntesis,* que combinan datos primarios (encuestas) y datos secundarios (fuentes administrativas), entre otras:

Las *estadísticas del volumen de trabajo* realizadas por la OFS desde 1991. El volumen de trabajo de la población residente permanente se calcula en base a datos empíricos obtenidos en la encuesta suiza sobre la población activa (ESPA), en la que se determinan y agregan por empleo la duración normal del trabajo, las horas suplementarias y las ausencias. El volumen de trabajo de otros grupos de la población que trabajan en Suiza se calcula en base a los resultados de las estadísticas de la población activa ocupada (SPAO) (número de personas activas ocupadas) y del censo de la población (promedio de horas de trabajo).

Definición del volumen de trabajo: horas de trabajo realmente efectuadas (= duración normal, + horas suplementarias pagadas o no, - ausencias). El volumen de trabajo se obtiene al sumar las duraciones anuales efectivas del trabajo para el conjunto de empleos (independientes y asalariados, que trabajan una hora como mínimo por una remuneración durante el año de referencia, y personas que, sin ser remuneradas, colaboraron en la empresa familiar durante el año de referencia).

Período de referencia: el año civil;
Periodicidad: anual;
Criterios de desglose de los datos sobre la duración normal del trabajo, las horas suplementarias, las ausencias y el volumen de trabajo: sexo, origen/tipo de permiso de estadía, sección económica, tasa de ocupación y situación jurídica y social de la actividad.

Publicaciones:
OFS: *Communiqué de presse: statistique du volume du travail* (Berna, anual);
Idem: *La statistique du volume du travail. Bases méthodologiques et définitions* (ibid., 1997);
Idem: *Indicateurs du marché du travail* (Neuchâtel, anual).
Las *estadísticas mensuales sobre la reducción de las horas de trabajo*, realizadas por la Office fédéral du développement économique et de l'emploi (OFDE): suministra información sobre los asalariados (por sexo) y las empresas concernidas, los sectores económicos, los cantones y las horas sin trabajar.

El *número de miembros de la Unión sindical Suiza (USS) y otras asociaciones de trabajadores*: se trata de un registro establecido por la USS al 31 de diciembre de cada año, del número de miembros (personas) de los sindicatos y de las asociaciones patronales afiliadas. La publicación de la USS incluye, además, los efectivos de otras grandes organizaciones de empleados (Confederación de

sindicatos cristianos de Suiza, Federación de sociedades suizas, Unión Federal del personal de las administraciones y las empresas públicas, etc.), pero excluye las pequeñas organizaciones no afiliadas a la USS.

Turquía

Fuente de la serie
Informes del Instituto de Seguros Sociales.
Título de la serie
Sosyal Sigortalar Kurumu (SSK) Yillik Istatistikler (Estadísticas Anuales del Instituto de Seguros Sociales).
Organismo responsable
Recolección de datos, elaboración estadística y publicación o difusión de las estadísticas:
La Dirección General, Instituto de Seguros Sociales, adjunto al Ministerio del Trabajo y de la Seguridad Social.
Temas laborales principales abarcados
Empleo y ganancias.
Periodicidad o frecuencia de disponibilidad de las estadísticas
Anual.
Período de referencia
A comienzos del mes de septiembre.
Alcance de las estadísticas
Ambito geográfico: todo el país.
Ambito industrial: todas las actividades económicas.
Establecimientos: todos los tipos y tamaños.
Personas cubiertas: todos los asalariados asegurados empleados de conformidad con un contrato de servicio en empresas privadas o estatales.
Ocupaciones: todas las ocupaciones de asalariados contratados según un contrato de empleo que se acoge a la Ley del Seguro Social No. 506.
Conceptos y definiciones
Empleo: se refiere al número total de asalariados, incluidos aprendices y trabajadores temporeros, que trabajan en lugares de trabajo supeditados a la Ley del Seguro Social No. 506. Todas las personas que están inscritas en el sistema de seguros se consideran como personas empleadas y, por lo tanto, están incluidas en las estadísticas.
Ganancias: se refieren al promedio de ganancias brutas diarias, incluido el pago del tiempo normal trabajado, los pagos de horas extraordinarias, la indemnización por cesantía y primas por antigüedad y producción. La ley determina los límites mínimo y máximo para ganancias diarias y mensuales utilizados para determinar las cotizaciones que se hacen al seguro social y los beneficios que se obtienen de este sistema.
Horas de trabajo: se refieren a las horas normales de trabajo. Las horas normales diarias de trabajo son 7,5 horas (45 horas semanales) de conformidad con la Ley No. 1475.
Clasificaciones
Ramas de actividad económica:
Título de la clasificación: Sectores del Trabajo que abarca la Ley del Seguro Social.
Número de grupos utilizados para la codificación: 10 (0-9) grupos principales.
Se aplica a: empleo y ganancias.
Vínculos con la CIIU y nivel: vinculada a la Rev.2, 1968.
Otras clasificaciones: los datos de empleo y ganancias se clasifican por sexo y sector (público y privado).
Recolección de datos
Método de recolección de datos: los datos se obtienen de la información contenida en los certificados de contribución que presentan los empleadores como informes mensuales de seguro al Instituto de Seguros Sociales.
Actualización del sistema administrativo: mensualmente.
Procesamiento y verificación de datos
No se dispone de información.
Ajustes
No se dispone de información.
Tipos de estimaciones
Número total de asalariados;
Promedio de ganancias diarias.
Las ganancias diarias representan la relación entre el total de ganancias tomadas como base para las cotizaciones y el número de días para los cuales se pagan las cotizaciones.
Construcción de índices
Ninguna.
Indicadores de fiabilidad de las estimaciones
No se dispone de información.

Series disponibles

Número de asalariados al mes de septiembre de cada año;

Promedio de ganancias de los asalariados.

Historia de las estadísticas

Fecha de iniciación de la serie estadística: 1950.

Cambios y revisiones principales: La Ley de Seguro Social No. 506, que actualmente está vigente, entró en vigor el 1 de marzo de 1965. Se amplió su cobertura en comparación con las leyes anteriores del seguro social.

Documentación y difusión

Documentación:

Social Insurance Institution, General Directorate: *Annual Statistics of Social Insurance Institution* (Ankara, anual);

Prime Ministry, State Institute of Statistics: *Statistical Yearbook of Turkey* (ibid., anual); contiene datos de empleo del año anterior *(t-1)* y datos de salarios del año anterior *(t-2)*, así como información metodológica sobre la fuente de los datos.

Datos suministrados a la OIT para su difusión

Las siguientes estadísticas se suministran a la OIT para su publicación en el *Anuario de Estadísticas del Trabajo*:

Empleo remunerado por actividad económica y sexo;

Promedio de ganancias diarias de asalariados, por actividad económica y en las industrias manufactureras, por grupo de industria, y por sexo.

Otras fuentes administrativas de datos: el sistema del seguro social en Turquía está compuesto por tres organismos principales: el Instituto de Seguros Sociales (véase más arriba); el Fondo de Jubilación de Empleados Gubernamentales; y el "Bag-Kur", es decir, el organismo de seguro social para los trabajadores independientes que no están cubiertos por la Ley del Seguro Social, tales como trabajadores agrícolas, artesanos, artesanos y pequeños empresarios, técnicos y profesionales que están inscritos en una cámara o asociación de profesionales y accionistas de otro tipo de empresas que no sean cooperativas y sociedades anónimas. Las estadísticas sobre el número de personas cubiertas y las sumas de beneficios proporcionados se obtienen del Fondo de Jubilación de Empleados Gubernamentales y de la Dirección General de Bag-Kur.